BRITISH INTERNATIONAL LAW CASES
VOL. 8

British Institute Studies in International and Comparative Law No. 1

This volume may be cited as 8 B.I.L.C.

AUSTRALIA
The Law Book Company Ltd.
Sydney : Melbourne : Brisbane

GREAT BRITAIN
Stevens & Sons Ltd.
London

INDIA
N. M. Tripathi Private Ltd.
Bombay

ISRAEL
Steimatzky's Agency Ltd.
Jerusalem : Tel Aviv : Haifa

MALAYSIA : SINGAPORE : BRUNEI
Malayan Law Journal (Pte) Ltd.
Singapore

NEW ZEALAND
Sweet & Maxwell (N.Z.) Ltd.
Wellington

PAKISTAN
Pakistan Law House
Karachi

NORTH AND SOUTH AMERICA
AND THE PHILIPPINES
Oceana Publications Inc.
Dobbs Ferry, New York

British Institute Studies in International
and Comparative Law No. 1

BRITISH INTERNATIONAL LAW CASES

A Collection of Decisions of Courts in the British Isles on Points of International Law, prepared under the Auspices of the International Law Fund and The British Institute of International and Comparative Law

by

CLIVE PARRY, LL.D.

SUPPLEMENTARY VOLUME
8
1960-1965

LONDON · STEVENS & SONS
DOBBS FERRY, N.Y., U.S.A. · OCEANA PUBLICATIONS
1971

Published in 1971 by
Stevens & Sons Limited of
11 New Fetter Lane, London
and
Oceana Publications Inc.
of Dobbs Ferry, New York

Printed in Great Britain by
Northumberland Press Ltd.
Gateshead

Oceana SBN 379 14028 4
Stevens SBN 420 42670 1
Library of Congress Catalogue
Card No. 63-22348

CONTENTS

B. AGENTS ON SPECIAL MISSIONS

C. CONSULAR OFFICERS

6

TREATIES

ADDENDUM

SUPPLEMENT 1951-1960

VOLUME 8

1

STATES AS INTERNATIONAL PERSONS

A. IN GENERAL

3

JURISDICTION

A. TERRITORIAL JURISDICTION

4

THE INDIVIDUAL IN INTERNATIONAL LAW

A. NATIONALITY

C. ALIENS

D. EXTRADITION

PREFACE

In this volume a further supplement, covering the years 1961-65, to the original collection is presented. This contains a Table of Cases cumulative to those of the earlier volumes. But because it is proposed to proceed at once with the preparation of the ninth volume, covering the remainder of the decade, the cumulative Index, which already occupies eighty-one pages in volume 7, has been omitted from this volume. The compiler is again indebted to Mr. J. A. Hopkins, M.A., LL.B., and to Mr. Anthony Parry, B.A. for assistance in collecting the cases, and to Mr. Hopkins for help with the proof-reading.

Downing College, Cambridge.
July 1970

CLIVE PARRY.

CUMULATIVE TABLE OF CASES REPORTED IN VOLUMES 1 TO 8

[*Numbers in* **heavy** *type refer to the volume in which the report appears*]

1

STATES AS INTERNATIONAL PERSONS

A.

IN GENERAL

1

EXISTENCE OF STATE: PROOF: BEGINNING OF STATE'S EXISTENCE

IN RE HARSHAW CHEMICAL COMPANY'S PATENT

([1965] R.P.C. 97)

March 9, 10, 11; May 13, 1964: Patent Office, Mr. Biles

Patent—Extension—War loss—"Hostilities between His Majesty and any foreign state"—Korean war—Extension refused.

Patents Act, 1949, *s.* 24.

An application for extension of the term of a patent relating to a method of electroplating using nickel, was made on the ground of war loss based on the difficulty of developing the invention over the period of nickel scarcity caused by the Korean war.

Held, *that the patentee had failed to show loss under section* 24 *"by reason of hostilities between His Majesty and any foreign state," because the Democratic People's Rupublic of Korea was not a "state" recognized by H.M. Government at any relevant time.*

Obiter. *If North Korea was a "state," then the facts were such as to justify a finding that "hostilities" had existed.*

Courtaulds Ltd.'s Application [1956] R.P.C. 208; *Ransburg's Patent* [1960] R.P.C. 242; *Mangold's Patent** (1951) 68 R.P.C. 1, and *The Arantzazu Mendi** [1939] A.C. 256 H.L., considered.

The applicants, The Harshaw Chemical Company, were the registered proprietors of letters patent No. 622,761, dated 31st March, 1947, relating to a method of bright nickel plating. Their application for an extension in respect of war loss was opposed by W. Canning & Co. Ltd. (Canning), Wilmot-Breeden Ltd., and Albright & Wilson (Mftg.) Ltd. (Albright). The applicants asked for an extension of six years based entirely on the shortage of nickel between 1950 and 1957 which they alleged was caused by the Korean war. The opponents contended that the shortage of nickel was not occasioned "by reason of hostilities between His Majesty and any foreign state" and asked that the Comptroller or one of the opponents should inquire from the Foreign Office as to whether there were any hostilities with a foreign state. The Foreign Office's reply to an inquiry by the Comptroller was in these terms:—

> "The United Kingdom was one of the States which as Members of the United Nations participated in the hostilities against the so-called Democratic People's Republic of Korea. These hostilities lasted from June 25, 1950, to July 27, 1953. The decision to send United Kingdom troops to Korea was taken on July 26, 1950; these troops arrived in Korea on August 29, 1950. **[98]**
>
> The Democratic People's Republic of Korea was not recognised by either His late Majesty's Government or Her Majesty's Government as an independent sovereign State at any time during the above-mentioned period of hostilities, and it has not subsequently been so recognised by Her Majesty's Government."

The remaining facts and the arguments presented by counsel appear from the following decision of Mr. S. H. Biles, dated 13th May, 1964.

Vivian Price instructed by *Mathys & Squire*, appeared for the applicants.

Peter Ford instructed by *Marks & Clark*, appeared for W. Canning & Co. Ltd. and Wilmot-Breedon Ltd. *Dr. A. W. White*, of Albright & Wilson (Mfg.) Ltd., appeared for that company.

MR BILES stated the facts substantially as set out above and continued: Mr. Price argued that the absence of recognition did not alter the fact that the Democratic People's Republic is a "state." A "state" is merely a country with certain sovereignty, as, for example, a member state of the U.S.A. The Foreign Office statement admits the existence of the Democratic People's Republic as an entity, and it is clear from the reference thereto in Whittaker's Almanac that it is just as much a "state" as the Republic of Korea.

Mr. Ford, on the other hand, submitted that the reference in section 24(8) of the Act to "a person who is a subject of such a foreign state is as mentioned in sub-section (1) of this section" necessarily infers that a "state" within the meaning of section 24 must have subjects. This in turn introduces the concept of sovereignty, which the Democratic People's Republic does not possess because it has not been recognised as an "independent sovereign state." Mr. Ford referred to "International Law" by L. Oppenheim, Volume 1, seventh edition, page 145, in support of his contention that recognition is a declaration, on the part of the recognising state, that a foreign community or authority is in possession of the necessary qualifications of statehood, these qualifications being the existence of a people, a country, a government and a sovereign government. It followed that in the absence of recognition there was no evidence that the facts are such that the Democratic People's Republic of Korea comprised a state. Its name implied a claim for authority over the whole state of Korea whereas there existed also a government in South Korea representing the "Republic of Korea." The necessary qualification of sovereignty was therefore not satisfied.

Later, Mr. Ford referred to Halsbury's *Laws of England*, third edition, volume 15, paragraph 612, on page 336, as the authority that the courts take notice of the existence and titles of foreign states which are recognised by the British Government as independent, and, as appears from the footnote (r) that the existence and status of foreign states not so recognised are not noticed by the judges.

Dr. White supported Mr. Ford's arguments and stressed that the applicants had failed to supply any evidence to prove that the hostilities in Korea were between the Crown and a foreign state. He submitted that section 24 must be construed strictly and that it would be wrong for the Comptroller to hold that the Democratic People's Republic was a state under section 24 in the face of the Foreign Office statement. The history of events shows that Korea was a single unitary state divided in itself, and the United Nations intervened in Korea to restore order and unify the country. Crown intervention in a civil war does not qualify for loss under section 24.

In reply, Mr. Price argued that the Democratic People's Republic clearly possessed all the qualifications of statehood, and it was not necessary for sovereignty to be **[99]** complete for a "state" to exist. On recognition, the concern in the present case is with facts and not the niceties of international diplomacy. The acceptance of North Korea is evidenced by the references in the Post Office Guide on the sending of letters to North or South Korea, and the Comptroller can act accordingly under section 24 without prejudicing the position of the Crown.

In deciding on this question I am impressed with the force of Dr. White's argument that section 24(1) must be construed strictly. In developing this he referred to *Courtaulds Ltd.'s Application* [1956] R.P.C. 208 where *Lloyd-Jacob*, J., sitting as the Patents Appeal Tribunal rejected an appeal from a decision of the Superintending Examiner acting for the Comptroller in which it was held that an equitable right to an exclusive licence at all times was not sufficient to enable an applicant to proceed as a licensee under section 25 of the Act. The learned Judge observed that the language of section 25 is consistent only with the execution of an actual licence as a pre-requisite for consideration of any loss or damage. Other cases referred to were *Ransburg and Ors' Patent* (*Extension*) [1960] R.P.C. 242, wherein it was held by the Patents Appeal Tribunal that unless and until the right to be the patentee has been created by the filing of the appropriate application for patent protection in this country, no potential loss or damage for consideration under the Patents Act, 1949, section 24, can arise, and *Mangold's Patent** (1951), 68 R.P.C. 1, wherein it was held by *Lloyd-Jacob, J.*, in an application by originating summons for an extension of the term of a patent that (unless German law, as it was up to the outbreak of hostilities between His Majesty and Germany, otherwise provided) for the purposes of section 24(8), an Austrian national became a German national upon the recognised annexation of Austria by Germany and so became an enemy at the outbreak of hostilities with Germany. Whilst none of the cases mentioned have any direct bearing on the present issue, nevertheless I agree that they point to a strict interpretation of the wording of the relevant sections of the Act. As I see it, therefore, I should regard the word "state" in section 24(1) as meaning a state which exists manifestly with all the qualifications required for statehood in international law, and not just any entity, whatever its status. Indeed, if it was the intention of section 24 to provide relief for loss sustained by reason of any hostilities involving the Crown, then presumably the section would have been worded accordingly. It does not appear to me that such was the intention and I take the view that the reference to "state" in the wording of section 24 is intended to limit the scope of the section. To be effective, therefore, the word "state" must be construed rigidly, and to be consistent it must be defined in accordance with established law as implying independence and sovereignty. This appears to me to follow also from the reference in section 24(8) to a person who is "a subject of such a foreign state," because unless such significance is attached to the word "state" then considerable difficulty may arise in deciding on questions under section 24(8), such as the issue decided in *Mangold's* case.*

Having reached the conclusion that the word "state" must be construed rigidly, then as I see it, on the authority to which Mr. Ford referred, I cannot ignore the dictum that the courts cannot take judicial notice of the existence and status of "states" which are not recognised by the British Government as independent. The footnote (r) to paragraph 612 of Halsbury's *Laws of England*, which I have already mentioned refers to a number of cases in which this dictum has been followed and in which it is established that the proper course on any question of the status of a foreign country is to ascertain the facts from H.M. Government, and that the court is bound to act on the information given to it through the proper department. As Lord Atkin stated in the case of *The Arantzazu Mendi** [1939] A.C. 256, H.L., at **[100]** page 264, "Our state cannot speak with two voices on such a matter, the judiciary saying one thing, the executive another." This being so, then, in the light of the Foreign Office statement, I am bound to decide that the Democratic People's Republic of Korea, or, as it is more commonly referred to, North Korea, cannot be regarded at any relevant time as comprising a "state" within the meaning of section 24 of the Act. It is interesting to note here the significance attached in *Mangold's* case to the recognition by His Majesty's Government of the annexation of Austria in March, 1938, and of the existence of Austria as a state in January, 1946.

However, in view of the submissions made at the hearing on the necessary qualifications of statehood and particularly the submission of Mr. Price that the absence of recognition by the Crown does not alter the fact that the Democratic People's Republic of Korea is a "state," it is perhaps desirable that I should also state my views on the matter in the light of these submissions.

The applicants have not adduced any evidence to show that the Democratic People's Republic of Korea constitutes a "state" despite the fact that they have been aware of the Foreign Office statement since the end of May, 1963. Of course, the facts on Korea as set out in Whittaker's Almanac are within recent memory, and it may be that the applicants feel that these known facts are sufficient to prove the existence of the Democratic People's Republic as a "state," but in my view the contrary is the case. As I see it, since the end of Japanese rule in 1945, the country of Korea has been a focal point of East-West conflict, with the country divided into North and South areas. Prior to the outbreak of hostilities in June, 1950, each area had set up its own government and constitution, with South Korea calling itself the "Republic of Korea," and North Korea "The Democratic People's Republic of Korea." It may fairly be said that the Republic of Korea, which was formally inaugurated in August, 1948 and has been recognised by Her Majesty's Government and by most other countries except the U.S.S.R. and her satellities, came into existence in accordance with a resolution passed by the General Assembly of the United Nations in November, 1947. On the other hand, the Democratic People's Republic was set up in September, 1948 under the auspices of the U.S.S.R. and has been recognised by the U.S.S.R. and her satellites.

The names adopted by the two areas each suggest a claim to represent the whole territory of Korea, and certainly the aim of the United Nations at all times has been to bring about the unification of the country. There is but one Korean people and, for reasons which are of no concern in these proceedings, this people is divided among itself. It is significant in this respect that the government of the Republic of Korea did not accept the armistice agreement, signed by the U.N. Commander-in-Chief and the commanders of the North Korean forces in July, 1953, wherein the line of division between North and South Korea remained in the neighbourhood of the 38th parallel.

It seems to me, therefore, that the hostilities in Korea were more in the nature of a civil war rather than a war between two "states." The United Nations intervened on the side of the government of the Republic of Korea, which had come into being under United Nations sponsorship and which was recognised by the majority of the member states of the United Nations including the United Kingdom. The armistice of 1953 brought about the cessation of hostilities, and in 1954 the Geneva Conference discussed Korea with a view to agreeing measures for reunifying the country. No agreement was reached, but the fact that such discussion took place suggests to me that, up to then at least, the Democratic People's Republic was considered to be no more than a "belligerent power." On the facts available to me nothing has **[101]** happened since to so consolidate the division of Korea as would confer the status of statehood on the so-called Democratic People's Republic. In my view, therefore, the Democratic People's Republic has not at any time been a "state" for the purposes of section 24.

Having reached this conclusion, it is unnecessary for me to decide the second question, namely, whether the hostilities in North Korea were "between His Majesty and any foreign state." I think I should say, however, that if, contrary to this conclusion, I had formed the opinion that the Democratic People's Republic could be regarded as a state for the purposes of section 24, I would have had no hesitation in concluding that the Korean hostilities were hostilities within the meaning of section 24. The participation of the United Kingdom in the hostilities, with the sending of troops to Korea in 1950, was by decision of His late Majesty's Government. The fact that the decision was taken in response to a Security Council recommendation that United Nations members should furnish assistance in Korea does not detract from it as a sovereign act. Likewise the fact that the United Kingdom troops engaged in the hostilities were under a unified command led by the U.S.A. did not mean an abrogation of the overriding authority of His late Majesty's Government to decide on the degree of participation and the number of troops provided. The action in Korea was not undertaken by a United Nations force as such maintained and controlled entirely by the United Nations, and it is only under such conditions, in my view, that the committal of His late Majesty to the action would be open to doubt.

The Hearing Officer went on to consider the facts of the case and found that even if the Korean war fell within the scope of section 24, the applicants had failed to prove that the circumstances justified the grant of any extension.

2
SOVEREIGNTY AND INDEPENDENCE

ii

INDEPENDENCE

GOHOHO v. GUINEA PRESS LTD. AND ANOTHER

([1963] 1 Q.B. 948)

October 9, 15, 1962: Court of Appeal: Lord Denning M.R., Upjohn, Diplock L.JJ.

Practice—Writ—Service out of jurisdiction—Ghana—Whether writ or notice of writ to be served—Whether Ghanaian company in "British dominions"—Preservation of existing provisions of United Kingdom statutes on Ghana becoming a republic—Ghana (Consequential Provision) Act, 1960 (8 & 9 *Eliz.* 2, *c.* 41), *s.* 1 (1)—*R.S.C., Ord.* 11, *r.* 6.

Ghana—Status—Whether "British dominion"—Service of writ out of **[949]** *jurisdiction on Ghanaian company—Ghana having become a republic—R.S.C., Ord.* 11, *r.* 6—*Ghana* (*Consequential Provision*) *Act,* 1960, *s.* 1 (1).

Commonwealth—Republican member—Status—Whether a "British dominion"—R.S.C., Ord. 11, *r.* 6—*Ghana* (*Consequential Provision*) *Act,* 1960, *s.* 1 (1).

By R.S.C., Ord. 11, r. 6: "When the defendant is neither a British subject nor in British dominions, notice of the writ, and not the writ itself, is to be served upon him."

The defendants to an action claiming damages for libel appealed against a refusal to have an interlocutory judgment in default of appearance against them set aside on the ground that the service of the writ on them had been null and void. The defendants, a company registered in Ghana, who had been served there with a copy of the writ, leave having been obtained to serve the writ out of the jurisdiction, relied on R.S.C., Ord. 11, r. 6, and claimed that instead of being served with a copy of the writ in Ghana, they should have been served with notice of the writ because Ghana had become a republic at the material time and, therefore, was not a "British dominion":—

Held, that, by virtue of section 1 (1) of the Ghana (Consequential Provision) Act, 1960,[1] whatever the status of Ghana might be, so far as the English courts were concerned Ghana was still within the Commonwealth, and the laws affecting Ghana in those courts were to be treated until altered as having effect in the same way as before Ghana became a republic; that, accordingly, for the purposes of R.S.C., Ord. 11, r. 6, Ghana was still to be treated as being a "British dominion" and the service of the copy of the writ in Ghana was valid.

Decision of Mocatta J. affirmed.

INTERLOCUTORY APPEAL.

On January 27, 1961, the plaintiff, Moses Fairchild Gohoho issued a writ in the High Court in an action against the Guinea Press Ltd. (hereinafter called

[1] Ghana (Consequential Provision) Act, 1960, s. 1 (1): "On and after the date on which Ghana becomes a republic [July 1, 1960], all existing law, that is to say, all law which, whether being a rule of law or a provision of an Act of Parliament or of any other enactment or instrument whatsoever, is in force on that date . . . shall, until provision to the contrary is made by an authority having power to alter that law . . . have the same operation in relation to Ghana, and to persons and things in any way belonging to or connected with Ghana, as it would have had if Ghana had not become a republic."

the applicants), a company registered in Accra, Ghana, and against the African and Overseas Press Agency Ltd. The writ was endorsed with a claim for damages for libel contained in an issue of a newspaper called the "Evening News" published in Accra, Ghana, and dated March 19, 1959. **[950]**

The plaintiff obtained leave to serve the applicants in Accra, having stated in his affidavit supporting his application for leave to serve the writ out of the jurisdiction, that they were "a corporate body whose registered office is situate at Accra, Ghana, West Africa, a republic within the British Commonwealth of Nations." In December, 1961, he served on the applicants a copy of the writ at their place of business in Accra. They did not enter an appearance and, on February 6, 1962, judgment was signed against them for damages to be assessed. In May, 1962, when the damages were about to be assessed, the applicants applied to the English court to have the proceedings set aside on the ground that the service on them of a copy of the writ was a nullity. They claimed that at the material time Ghana had become a republic within the Commonwealth and was not a "British dominion" and that, therefore, by virtue of R.S.C., Ord. 11, r. 6, the plaintiff had no right to serve a writ or a copy of the writ on them but that he should have served them with notice of the writ. Mocatta J. held that the service of the copy was not a nullity and the applicants appealed. When the matter came before the Court of Appeal it was adjourned to enable notice to be given to the Attorney-General and to the Attorney-General for Ghana because it appeared at that time that the status of Ghana might be an issue in the appeal.

Glynn Blackledge Q.C. and *John Wood* for the applicants, the first defendants in the action. Notice of the writ and not the writ itself or a copy of it should have been served. The service of the writ was invalid and the applicants have not done anything to waive the irregularity. Ghana is not a British dominion and it is contrary to the comity of nations to exercise dominion over or to interfere in the affairs of foreign countries. The Queen's writ does not run in a foreign country though it may run for a British subject. Ghana is completely independent. It is a republic and no rights of sovereignty of the British Crown are exercisable over it.

When the Ghana Independence Act, 1957, came into force on March 6, 1957, Ghana became a dominion and no United Kingdom Act passed on or after that date applied to Ghana, and the United Kingdom Parliament had no responsibility over it. Very wide powers were conferred on Ghana but the legislative powers were subject to certain restrictions: see Schedule I to the Act of 1957. The first constitution of Ghana was imposed from outside. **[951]** By the Ghana (Constitution) Order in Council, 1957 (S.I. No. 277) the executive power of Ghana was vested in the Queen (paragraph 6) and it was plain that between 1957 and 1960 the Queen's writ still ran in Ghana. There followed, however, the Constituent Assembly and Plebiscite Act, 1960 (No. 1 of 1960 of Ghana) which whittled down the power exercisable over Ghana, and the brake contained in paragraph 32 of the Ghana (Constitution) Order in Council, 1957, was taken off. This was done in a constitutional manner acting within the powers of the Ghanaian legislative body, but these new powers were irreconcilable with the first constitution and turned the Ghanaian assembly into a constituent assembly which could dispense with the Queen's assent to legislation. This led to the passing of the Ghana (Consequential Provision) Act, 1960, of the United Kingdom, section 1 of which was similar to section 1 of the India (Consequential Provision) Act, 1949 (12, 13 & 14 Geo. 6, c. 92). In the Act of 1960 the United Kingdom legislature acknowledged that Ghana was about to become a republic, and it did in fact become a republic on July 1, 1960. The Ghanaian constitution of 1960 was enacted on June 29, 1960, and came into operation on July 1, 1960, and in deciding what was the "existing law" of Ghana at midnight of June 30, the Act creating the constitution of Ghana must be included, and that has to be read with section 1 (1) of the Ghanaian (Consequential Provision) Act, 1960, as part of the existing law. It was inherent in that constitution as well as in the Ghana (Consequential Provision) Act, 1960, that the Act creating Ghana a British dominion and all the constitution of 1957 had been impliedly repealed before Ghana should become a republic on July 1, 1960, and those provisions had ceased to be part of the existing law of Ghana before that date.

The "existing law" on June 30, 1960, includes that passed on June 2, 1960, and R.S.C., Ord. 11, r. 6, but the issue is whether Ghana is "a dominion" or not within that rule. The nub is whether because of section 1 (1) of the Ghana (Consequential Provision) Act it must be held artificially that Ghana is not a republic. Section 1 (1) does not, of course, attempt to control events in Ghana. As from June 29, the Queen ceased to control the progress of Ghana to complete constitutional independence; the Ghanaian Act was passed constitutionally, so, immediately before June 30, the "existing law" from the point of view of what was accepted by the English Parliament was that the independence of Ghana had been accepted by the English **[952]** Parliament in their own Act. If so, as from July 1, Ghana became a foreign country in effect, so that if it should be held that the effect of section 1 (1) is that the Queen's writ runs in Ghana, it would be purporting to enact that the Queen's writ should run in respect of a foreign country, and that would be contrary to the ordinary presumption that the legislature does not intend to exceed its territorial jurisdiction: Maxwell, Interpretation of Statutes, 11th ed. (1962), p. 138. But if the British Parliament has enacted in inescapable terms something which is in conflict with a foreign Act, then one must apply the English Act, but the court would seek a reasonable interpretation which would avoid such a result. The reasonable interpretation is that before July 1, 1960, Ghana, with the consent of the Crown, had removed as from June 29, 1960, the powers of the Crown over Ghana.

John Wood following. The writ ran in Ghana prior to Ghana becoming a republic and formed part of the law of Ghana. By section 1 (*a*) of the Act of 1957 the Parliament of the United Kingdom expressly stated that no Act of the United Kingdom should extend to Ghana or be deemed to extend to Ghana, so at the time when the Act of 1960 came into force the constituent assembly in Ghana had power to create itself a republic and the United Kingdom Parliament could do nothing to affect the Parliament of Ghana.

In section 1 (1) of the Act of 1960 the draftsman was careful to avoid wording which would have had the clear effect of providing for persons or things in Ghana. He said "in relation to" Ghana. [Reference was made to *Hewitson* v. *Fabre*.[2]] The wording of section 1 (1) is not so clear as to have the effect of saying that the writ shall run in Ghana despite the terms of the constitution which excludes the sovereignty of the Crown. Section 1 (1) was clearly intended to provide for persons and things related to Ghana which were outside Ghana —for example, to provide (1) for the continued application of the extradition Acts, (2) for the reciprocal enforcement of judgments and (3) that Ghanaian nationals in the United Kingdom should not be treated as foreigners for the purposes of English law. This should be contrasted with the wording of the proviso to section 1 of the Act of 1957 which says "in" and not "in relation to." [Reference was also made to section 2 (1) of the Eire Act, 1949.]

The plaintiff appeared in person but was not called on to argue. **[953]**

Sir John Hobson Q.C., A.-G. and *J. A. Cumming-Bruce* as amici curiae. The question is one of the practice and procedure of this court and, therefore, English law alone applies. The service should be treated as good for two reasons. First, before July 1, 1960, R.S.C., Ord. 11, r. 6, operated so as to provide for service of the writ by virtue of section 1 of the Act of 1957. The effect of section 1 (1) of the Act of 1960, is that R.S.C., Ord. 11, r. 6, shall have operation on and after July 1, 1960, in Ghana in exactly the same way as before.

Secondly, section 1 of the Act of 1957 provides that Ghana should form part of Her Majesty's dominions. For the purposes of these courts and the law of this country the Act of 1957 is still in force and not impliedly repealed, and could not be impliedly repealed by the Act of the Ghanaian Parliament. There-

[2] (1888) 21 Q.B.D. 6; 4 T.L.R. 510, D.C.

fore, by virtue of section 1 (1) of the Act of 1960, Ghana should be regarded as part of the British dominions for the purposes specified in that section, though for other purposes it may be that it is not a dominion. This comes out clearly in a case on the Fugitive Offenders Act, 1881: see *In re Government of India and Mubavak Ali Ahmed.*[3]* That Act could not have operated as still being in force unless for the purposes of that Act India had remained a British dominion. Ghana is still within the Commonwealth and although, by virtue of section 2 (1) of the British Nationality Act, 1958, citizens of Ghana are no longer citizens of the United Kingdom and Colonies, section 2 of the Ghana Independence Act, 1957, has the effect of writing Ghana into the list of territories in section 1 (3) of the British Nationality Act, 1948, so that citizens of Ghana are Commonwealth citizens and consequently British subjects. That provision of the Act of 1957 was part of "the existing law" of Ghana, and, therefore, so far as individuals are concerned, our rules of procedure still apply to allow service of the writ in Ghana. [*Zacharia v. Republic of Cyprus*[4]* was also referred to.]

LORD DENNING M.R. The plaintiff, Moses Fairchild Gohoho, brought an action in the High Court by a writ on January 27, 1961, against the Guinea Press Ltd. and the African and Overseas Press Agency Ltd. On the endorsement of the writ he claimed damages for libel in an issue of a newspaper called the "Evening News" published in Accra, Ghana, and dated March 19, 1959. **[954]** It is quite clear from what we have seen that words were published in that newspaper which were defamatory of the plaintiff.

[His Lordship stated the facts and continued:] This is, as Mr. Blackledge said in opening the case, a highly technical point. This difference between service of the writ itself and service of notice of the writ arose in the middle of the last century when it was thought to be against the dignity of a country that another country should be allowed to serve a writ within it; and, therefore, it was provided, as a matter of courtesy, that one country should not serve a writ within another, but, as a matter of courtesy, it should only serve notice of the writ. This was said by a Divisional Court in 1888 in *Hewitson* v. *Fabre*[5] to be a most fundamental matter. It was held in that case that if a plaintiff served a writ, whereas he should only have served a notice of it, it was a fatal defect and all the proceedings were a nullity. That is the law which the applicants invoke in this case. They acknowledge that they were served with the writ itself or a copy of the writ, but they say that was quite wrong. They ought only to have been given notice of it.

Such is the point, and if it is good we must give effect to it. It all depends on whether Ghana is a "British dominion" or not for the purpose of R.S.C., Ord. 11, r. 6. We have been taken through the statutes relating to the position of Ghana. It is quite plain that in 1957, by the Ghana Independence Act, 1957, Ghana became independent: but still it formed part of Her Majesty's Dominions at that time and its subjects were Commonwealth citizens and British subjects. An Order in Council was made from which it was quite plain that from 1957 onwards until 1960 the Queen was still the Sovereign Queen of Ghana.[6] Then in 1960 the position was altered. Ghana became a republic and the Queen ceased to be Sovereign Queen of Ghana. An Act was passed by the Ghana Parliament[7] providing that the head of the state there was to be the President of Ghana and the executive power of the state was vested and conferred upon the President of Ghana. Just before Ghana became a republic in that way, an Act of Parliament was passed here, in June, 1960, called the Ghana (Consequential Provision) Act, 1960. The question in this case depends on the true interpretation of that Act, because although Ghana became a republic on July 1, 1960, and although **[955]** the Queen ceased to have sovereign authority

[3] [1952] 1 All E.R. 1060, D.C.
[4] [1962] 2 W.L.R. 1163; [1962] 2 All E.R. 438, H.L.(E).
[5] (1888) 21 Q.B.D. 6; 4 T.L.R. 510, D.C.
[6] Ghana (Constitution) Order in Council, 1957 (S.I. No. 277).
[7] The Constituent Assembly and Plebiscite Act, 1960 (No. 1 of 1960, Ghana).

in Ghana, nevertheless Ghana remained a member of the Commonwealth. The Act expressly provided in section 1 (1): "On and after the date on which Ghana becomes a republic, all existing law, that is to say, all law which, whether being a rule of law or a provision of an Act of Parliament or of any other enactment or instrument whatsoever, is in force on that day"—I am missing out immaterial words—"shall have the same operation in relation to Ghana, and to persons and things in any way belonging to or connected with Ghana, as it would have had if Ghana had not become a republic." That section makes it clear, so far as these courts are concerned, that although Ghana becomes a republic, the laws affecting it are to be treated in just the same way and have the same operation as if Ghana had never become a republic.

What does that mean? Although Ghana is a republic, we still turn to the laws as they were before to see how it should be treated in this country. This section is in exactly the same words as a similar section enacted when India became a republic.[8] It was held by the Divisional Court in *In re Government of India and Mubarak Ali Ahmed*[9]* that the Fugitive Offenders Act, 1881 (which again is confined to Her Majesty's Dominions), applied in relation to India and to her people in just the same way after India became a republic as it had done before. Although it was a republic, it was for the purposes of these courts and this country to be treated as if it had not become a republic. So here it seems to me quite plain that, for the purpose of considering what is a "British dominion" within R.S.C., Ord. 11, r. 6, Ghana is to be treated now as if it was a British dominion still; and, therefore, the writ itself can be served there now since July 1, 1960, when Ghana became a republic, in just the same way as it could before that date.

Although allegiance to the Queen may not be present after Ghana becomes a republic, nevertheless Ghana is still within the Commonwealth: and the laws applicable in these courts, such as the Fugitive Offenders Act, 1881, and the rules as to service, remain as operative as if it had not become a republic. In my judgment Mocatta J. was quite right in saying that section 1 of the Act of 1960 enabled the service to be made and that it was perfectly good. **[956]**

I would only add this. The Attorney-General drew our attention to the fact that so far as individuals (not companies) are concerned in Ghana, it is plain, from a series of enactments which he read, that Ghanaians are Commonwealth citizens and British subjects, and as such service of a writ can still be effected there in accordance with our rules on individuals. That bears out what I have said, that so far as the service of writs is concerned, the writ itself can still be served in Ghana. It is not necessary for a notice to be served. *Hewitson* v. *Fabre*[10] (even if it were correctly decided, as to which I say nothing) has no application to Ghana. It only applies to foreign countries, strictly so called, and does not avail the defendants in this case.

I would, therefore, affirm the decision of Mocatta J. and I would dismiss the appeal.

UPJOHN L.J. I agree with the judgment that has just been delivered.

The point really is of the shortest. By the Ghana Independence Act, 1957, the former colony called the Gold Coast became one of Her Majesty's Dominions under the name of Ghana. It was quite clear thereafter that that was a British dominion for the purposes of R.S.C., Ord. 11, r. 6, so that the writ itself, or a copy of it rather than notice of it, could properly be served in Ghana in proceedings against individuals or companies resident there. In due time, however, the citizens of Ghana desired to become a republic. They formed a constituent assembly which passed an Act defining the constitution of the Republic of Ghana on June 29, 1960, and that came into operation on July 1 of the same year. The United Kingdom Parliament, recognising this desire for a transfer of power, passed the Ghana (Consequential Provision) Act, 1960, on June 2 of that year.

[8] Section 1 (1) of the India (Consequential Provision) Act, 1949 12, 13 & 14 Geo. 6, c. 92).

[9] [1952] 1 All E.R. 1060, D.C.

[10] 21 Q.B.D. 6.

It provided in section 1, putting it very shortly, that "On and after the date on which Ghana becomes a republic, all existing law . . . shall have the same operation in relation to Ghana, and to persons and things in any way belonging to or connected with Ghana, as it would have had if Ghana had not become a republic." The relevant existing law is R.S.C., Ord. 11, r. 6, and that is to operate as though Ghana had not become a republic. If Ghana had not become a republic, she would have remained a British dominion. It seems to me quite plain, therefore, that the writ itself or a copy of it was properly ordered to be served upon the **[957]** appellants. It seems to me that the case before us is really quite indistinguishable from *In re Government of India and Mubarak Ali Ahmed*[11]* to which the Master of the Rolls has referred.

I agree that this appeal must be dismissed.

DIPLOCK L.J. I also agree that this appeal should be dismissed. When the matter came before us last Monday, it appeared possible that some serious question might arise as to the constitution of Ghana and its status. Now that the matter has been examined, I think it quite plain that no such question does arise and that this case turns entirely upon the true construction of section 1 of the Ghana (Consequential Provision) Act, 1960. What happened was this, and it has happened in the case of other dominions. In 1957 Ghana became completely independent by virtue of the Ghana Independence Act, 1957, and the Order in Council made under prerogative powers of the Crown in that same year.[12] She became completely independent but she became a constitutional monarchy in which the Queen remained the head of the state, acting, of course, through the Governor-General upon the advice of Her Ministers in Ghana and not upon the advice of Her Ministers anywhere else. This complete independence left remaining the tie of allegiance to the Crown, and there is no question that at that time Ghana remained a British dominion, but only in this technical sense. In 1960 Ghana became a republic. There arose a question of English law as to what was the most convenient way (on the breaking of this bond of allegiance with the retention as a member of the Commonwealth of the links of common interest and convenience) to retain for Ghana such of those advantages and provisions as it was desired to retain. A method was adopted, which had been first adopted in the case of India when India became a republic, to provide, as is provided by section 1 (1) of the Ghana (Consequential Provision) Act, 1960, that all existing law, which includes rules of law as well as statutes and statutory instruments, which existed at the date when Ghana became a republic, should continue to have the same operation as if Ghana had not become a republic until provisions to the contrary were made by an authority having power to alter that law. I pass on to subsection (3), for that is an important subsection that gives to Her Majesty the power by Order in Council to make any consequential amendments which are thought to be expedient or necessary as **[958]** the result of Ghana becoming a republic, and gives her power to do so by Order in Council either before or after Ghana becomes a republic and to make Orders in Council with retrospective effect after Ghana has become a republic. The only possible argument that section 1 (1) does not have the effect which my Lord has declared, and with which I entirely agree, is that there is a rule of comity of nations that one country does not authorise the service of a writ in the other but sends—to use the words of the Divisional Court in 1888—a courteous notice of the writ, to which in fact a copy of the writ is attached. Accordingly, there was a possible argument that one must assume that the wide, general words of section 1 (1) do not cover what would be, it is suggested, a breach of the rule of comity of nations. On the question as to whether there would be any force in that argument if section 1 (1) stood alone, I do not desire to express any view, but in the presence of subsection (3), which expressly provides for consequential amendments to any existing laws, it seems to me that such an argument carries no weight.

[11] [1952] 1 All E.R. 1060.
[12] S.I. 277, 1957.

I merely desire to add this. The view taken by this court makes it unnecessary to decide whether *Hewitson* v. *Fabre*[13] was correct in determining that proceedings were void and not merely irregular if R.S.C., Ord. 11, r. 6, was not strictly complied with. It purports to be based on an assumption as to the comity of nations without any evidence that other countries act in the same sort of way. I doubt very much whether they do, because I doubt very much whether in all, or indeed the majority of other countries, writs are issued in the name of the State at all. I merely say if that matter were to come up for decision, it would deserve serious consideration.

I agree this appeal should be dismissed.

Appeal dismissed with costs.

Solicitors: *Peter Kingshill; Treasury Solicitor.*

BUCK AND OTHERS v. ATTORNEY-GENERAL

([1965] 1 Ch. 745)

April 29, 30, May 5, 1964: Chancery Division: Wilberforce J.
February 10, 11, 12, 1965: Court of Appeal: Harman, Diplock, Russell L.JJ.

Sierra Leone—Constitution—Validity—Colony—Land of "Free Settlers" by grant, subsequently chartered Crown colony and statutory "British settlement"—Protectorate—Act of British Parliament providing for joint independence—Order in Council providing for constitution of new independent state—Joint constitution for former colony and adjoining protectorate—Order made 13 days before day appointed for coming into force of Act of independence—To **[746]** *come into operation on appointed day—Validity—Whether "necessary for the peace, order, and good government of Her Majesty's subjects and others within any British settlement"—Jurisdiction to make orders relating to British settlement and to delegate such powers—Whether power validly executed—Whether jurisdiction to make declaration as to validity—Whether land held on trust for free settlers by Crown as trustee—British Settlements Act,* 1887 (50 & 51 *Vict. c.* 54), *s.* 2—*—Sierra Leone Independence Act,* 1961 (9 & 10 *Eliz.* 2, *c.* 16)*—Sierra Leone (Constitution) Order in Council,* 1961 (*S.I.* 1961, *No.* 741).

Colony—Constitution—Powers of Crown—British Settlements Act, 1887, *s.* 2*—Whether applicable—Protectorate adjacent to colony—Act of Parliament providing for joint independence of colony and protectorate—Order in Council providing for constitution of new independent state—"Whether power to make order"—Order made* 13 *days before day appointed for coming into force of Act of independence—To come into operation on appointed day—Validity—Whether "necessary for peace, order, and good government of Her Majesty's subjects and others within any British settlement"—Sierra Leone.*

Conflict of Laws—Constitution of independent state—Validity—Declaration—Not ancillary to other relief—Independent state not a party to action—No submission by independent state to jurisdiction—Jurisdiction to make.

Practice—Declaratory judgment—Jurisdiction to make—Effectiveness—Validity of constitution of independent state.

In about May, 1787, a group of persons, mainly freed slaves, were settled with the Crown's consent, or authority and encouragement, in an area on the west coast of Africa, which eventually comprised Freetown and its immediate neighbourhood and was to become the colony of Sierra Leone. This area was to be enjoyed by these first settlers, known as the "free community of Settlers," their heirs and successors for ever, under a grant of 1788 from the then chief

[13] 21 Q.B.D. 6.

[King Naimbana] who swore allegiance to H.M. King Geo. III.[1] In **[747]** or about 1824, the free community was enlarged by settlement in the area with Crown authority of others, mostly also freed slaves. The descendants of both groups of settlers were known as "Creoles" and were banded together in the Settlers' Descendants Union. From 1791 to 1807 the area comprising the Sierra Leone colony was held by the Sierra Leone company under charter from the Crown, but in 1807 that charter was annulled, the company's land revested in the Crown, and in 1809, by a fresh charter, Sierra Leone became a Crown colony, the majority of its inhabitants being then, and at all material times thereafter until April 27, 1961, settled freed slaves or their descendants.

[1] Text of grant by King Naimbana: "Know all men by those presents that I, King Naimbaner (sic), Chief of Sierra Leone on the Grain Coast of Africa, by and with the consent of the other Kings, Princes, Chiefs and Potentates subscribing hereto, in consideration of the presents, as by a list annexed, now made me by Captain John Taylor, of His Britannic Majesty's Brig 'Miro' in behalf and for the sole benefit of the free community of settlers, their heirs and successors, lately arrived from England and under the protection of the British Government, have granted, and by these presents do forever quit claim to a certain district of land for the settling of the said free community to be theirs, their heirs and successors for ever, That is to say:—All the land, wood, water, &c., &c., which are now contained from the bay, commonly called Frenchman's Bay, but by these presents changed to that of St. George's Bay, coastwise up the River Sierra Leone to Gambia Island, and southerly or inland from the riverside 20 miles. And further be it known unto all men that I, King Nambaner, do faithfully promise and swear for my Chiefs, gentlemen and people, likewise my heirs and successors, that I will bear true allegiance to His Most Gracious Majesty King George the Third, King of Great Britain, France and Ireland, &c., &c., &c., and protect the said free settlers, his subjects to the utmost of my power against the insurrections and attacks of all nations or people whatever. And I do hereby bind myself, my heirs and successors, to grant the said free settlers a continuance of a quiet and peaceable possession of the land granted, their heirs and successors for ever. In witness whereof I and my Chiefs have set our hands and seals this 22nd day of August, 1788.

"And it is also further agreed by the aforesaid Contracting Parties that the customs payable by vessels anchoring in St. George's Bay shall pay (sic ? 'be') ten bars to the Free Settlers and subjects of His Britannic Majesty, and the customs paid for watering to be paid to King Nambaner, his representatives and successors, that is to say, 15 bars as customary, and if to anchor and not to water, the customs as above to be paid to the free settlers of St. George's Bay as aforesaid.

"In witness whereof to this additional part of these presents and all others contained herein. We have made our marks and signed our names with our seals affirmed this 22nd day of August, 1788.

(signed) John Taylor Richard Weaver Thomas Peall Benjamin Ellett
their King X Nambaner James X Dowder marks
Pabongee Dick Robbin Abram Elliot Griffith Secretary to the King.

"A list of the presents given in consideration for completing the purchase of the land hereunder annexed, viz:

"One embroidered bersode coat, waistcoat, and breeches.
"A crimson satin embroidered waistcoat.
"A lead coloured satin coat, waistcoat and breeches.
"A mock diamond ring.
"Two pairs of pistols.
"One telescope.
"Two pairs of gold earrings with necklaces and drops.
"Eight dozen bottles of wine.
"One puncheon of rum.
"A tierce or three hundredweight of pork.
"One box of smoking pipes.
"Seven muskets.
"20 pounds of tobacco.
"One piece of fine white cotton or calico.
"Ten pounds of beads in lots.
"Two cheeses weighing 28 pounds.
"200 gun flints.
"12 bottles of red port wine."

In 1887, by the British Settlements Act, 1887,[2] the colony admittedly became a British settlement for **[748]** the purposes of that Act. On August 31, 1896, the adjacent territory, the hinterland of the colony, the inhabitants of which were for the most part indigenous, was proclaimed a protectorate ("the Sierra Leone protectorate"),[3] the power of the Crown, under the Foreign Jurisdiction Act, 1890, to legislate therefor by Order in Council being conferred on the governor and legislative council of the colony. From 1924, the executive council of the colony was the executive council of the protectorate, and there was a single legislative council with members from both colony and protectorate. In 1951 the composition of this legislative council was altered so as to give the protectorate a majority of directly elected members, and this majority was increased in 1957, but throughout the colony remained a Crown colony and a British settlement.

On April 27, 1961, by virtue of the Sierra Leone Independence Act, 1961 (passed on March 28, 1961),[4] the former colony and protectorate were combined in the independent state, within the Commonwealth, of Sierra Leone. The constitution of the new state was provided for by the Sierra Leone (Constitution) Order in Council, 1961,[5] made on April 14, 1961, to come into **[749]** operation immediately before the coming into effect of the Independence Act. The plaintiffs, six citizens of Sierra Leone, who were and had been domiciled in the territory of the former colony, and were British subjects, and were, and claimed to represent, the descendants of settled freed slaves, brought an action claiming declarations, first, that the Sierra Leone (Constitution)

[2] British Settlements Act, 1887, s. 2: "It shall be lawful for Her Majesty the Queen in Council from time to time to establish all such laws and institutions, and constitute such courts and officers, and make such provisions and regulations for the proceedings in the said courts and for the administration of justice, as may appear to Her Majesty in Council to be necessary for the peace, order, and good government of Her Majesty's subjects and others within any British settlement."

S. 5: "It shall be lawful for Her Majesty the Queen in Council from time to time to make, and when made to alter and revoke, orders for the purposes of this Act."

S. 6: "For the purposes of this Act . . . the expression 'British settlement' means any British possession which has not been acquired by cession or conquest, and is not for the time being within the jurisdiction of the legislature, constituted otherwise than by virtue of this Act or of any Act repealed by this Act, of any British possession."

[3] Foreign Jurisdiction Act, 1890: "Whereas by treaty, capitulation, grant, usage, sufferance, and other lawful means, Her Majesty the Queen has jurisdiction within divers foreign countries, and it is expedient to consolidate the Acts relating to the exercise of Her Majesty's jurisdiction out of Her dominions: . . .

"1. It is and shall be lawful for Her Majesty the Queen to hold, exercise, and enjoy any jurisdiction which Her Majesty now has or may at any time hereafter have within a foreign country in the same and as ample a manner as if Her Majesty had acquired that jurisdiction by the cession or conquest of territory . . .

"3. Every act and thing done in pursuance of any jurisdiction of Her Majesty in a foreign country shall be as valid as if it had been done according to the local law then in force in that country."

[4] Sierra Leone Independence Act, 1961, s. 1: "(1) On April 27, 1961 (in this Act referred to as 'the appointed day'), the Sierra Leone Colony and the Sierra Leone Protectorate (of which the combined area is that specified in the First Schedule to this Act) shall together constitute part of Her Majesty's dominions under the name of Sierra Leone. (2) No Act of the Parliament of the United Kingdom passed on or after the appointed day shall extend, or be deemed to extend, to Sierra Leone as part of the law thereof, and as from that day—(*a*) Her Majesty's Government in the United Kingdom shall have no responsibility for the government of Sierra Leone; . . ."

[5] Sierra Leone (Constitution) Order in Council, 1961: "Her Majesty, by virtue and in exercise of the powers in that behalf by The Foreign Jurisdiction Act, 1890, or otherwise in Her Majesty vested, is pleased, by and with the advice of Her Privy Council, to order, and it is hereby ordered, as follows: 1. . . . 2. This order shall come into operation immediately before April 27, 1961: . . ."

"3. Subject to the provisions of this order, the constitution of Sierra Leone set out in the second schedule to this order (in this order referred to as 'the constitution') shall come into effect in Sierra Leone at the commencement of this order."

Order in Council, 1961, was, in so far as it applied or purported to apply, to the colony, ultra vires and void, contending, inter alia, that the Order in Council was outside the powers conferred by the British Settlements Act, 1887, and, therefore, invalid because it did not regulate the British settlement known as the colony of Sierra Leone but purported to destroy it, and because it handed over the government of those within the settlement, including British subjects, to the government of the protectorate; second, that the land comprised in the colony was held by the Crown as sovereign in trust for the free community of settlers and their descendants (or under an obligation voluntarily undertaken in the nature of such a trust); third, that both order and constitution were in a breach of that trust or obligation; and, fourth, that the constitution and government allegedly set up by it were unlawful, invalid and ineffectual in so far as they purported to apply to the colony and that the power to set up a constitution and government was vested in the settlers' descendants. Wilberforce J., on May 5, 1964, dismissed the plaintiffs' claim, holding, inter alia, that although the settlement and Crown colony had, as from April 27, 1961, ceased to exist, that was by virtue of the Act of 1961, and not of the Order in Council, and that the government of the settlement had not been transferred to the protectorate, but merely further integrated with that of the protectorate. The plaintiffs appealed, contending that the court had had jurisdiction to make, and, in the circumstances of the case, ought to have made, the declarations sought:—

Held, that the judgment of Wilberforce J., and his reasons therefor, should be affirmed; moreover, the English courts could not, either as a matter of international comity or on the ground of effectiveness, make a declaration impugning the validity of the laws or constitution of a foreign independent sovereign state, at any rate where that was the object of the action, and should not in any event do so.

Per Diplock L.J. Even apart from the comity rule, the court has no jurisdiction to give a declaratory judgment in a suit against a party who has no interest in the subject-matter of the declaration. So far as the punctum temporis between the making of the Order in Council on April 14, 1961, and the coming to independence of Sierra Leone on April 27, 1961, is concerned, (a) in applying the **[750]** rule of comity one looks to the substance of the issue, not to its form, and the Order in Council was, on the face of it, intended to provide the constitution not of the colony but of the new independent sovereign state; thus, the issue as to its validity was in substance, at the date of the writ, an issue as to the validity of the constitution of an independent sovereign state; (*b*) as soon as Sierra Leone had become independent the Order in Council had ceased to have any effect as such; whatever effect it then had was as part of the law of an independent sovereign state, and whether it had been valid during the punctum temporis during which it had been in force as an Order in Council was a subject-matter in which the parties, at the time of suit, had no interest.

Per Diplock and Russell L.JJ. The Order in Council could clearly have been considered by the Crown to be a provision "necessary for the peace, order, and good government of Her Majesty's subjects and others within" the colony, and thus within section 2 of the British Settlements Act, 1887, in the sense that it was clearly desirable in the interests of the inhabitants of the colony that the independent state of which it was shortly to become part should already be provided with a suitable constitution.

Decision of Wilberforce J. affirmed.

ACTION.

The Crown colony of Sierra Leone was established by charter in 1809, the majority of its inhabitants being then, and at all material times thereafter until April 27, 1961, settled freed slaves or their descendants. In 1887, by the British Settlements Act, 1887, the colony became a British settlement for the purposes of that Act. On August 31, 1896, the adjacent territory, the inhabitants of which were for the most part indigenous, was proclaimed a protectorate ("the

Sierra Leone protectorate"). On April 27, 1961, by virtue of the Sierra Leone Independence Act, 1961 (passed on March 28, 1961), the former colony and protectorate were combined in the independent state, within the Commonwealth, of Sierra Leone. The constitution of the new state was provided for by the Sierra Leone (Constitution) Order in Council, 1961, made on April 14, 1961, to come into operation immediately before the coming into effect of the Independence Act.

The plaintiffs, six citizens of Sierra Leone, who were and had been domiciled in the territory of the former colony and were British subjects, and were, and claimed to represent, the descendants of settled freed slaves, brought an action praying for declarations, (1) that the Sierra Leone (Constitution) Order in Council 1961, was, in so far as it applied or purported to apply, to the colony, ultra vires, unlawful, null and void; (2) that the land comprised in the colony had at all material times been and was **[751]** now held by the Crown as Sovereign in trust for the Free Community of Settlers and their descendants, alternatively under an obligation, voluntarily undertaken, in the nature of such trust; (3) that the order, in so far as it and the constitution purported to apply to the colony, were [sic] in breach of the trust, alternatively the obligation; and (4) that the constitution purported to be set up by the order and the alleged government now purporting and claiming to exist under and by virtue of that constitution were, in so far as they purported to apply to the colony, unlawful, invalid, and of no force or effect in law and that the descendants of the settlers were now entitled to set up in and for the colony such constitution and government as they might think fit. By their statement of claim, they contended inter alia, that, notwithstanding the Act of 1961, and subject to the provisions thereof, the colony still subsisted as a British settlement and a Crown colony; that, in so far as the Order in Council purported to apply to the colony, there were no powers vested in the Crown by the Foreign Jurisdiction Act, 1890, by virtue or in exercise of which the order could lawfully have been made; that if, contrary to the plaintiffs' contention, the order was, in so far as it purported to apply to the colony, lawful and valid, it had had the consequences (i) that the colony had thereby ceased to exist as a Crown colony or a British settlement within the meaning of the British Settlements Act, 1887, (ii) that it had thereby become merged in and replaced by a new state in which the population of the protectorate of Sierra Leone, by reason of its considerable numerical superiority, occupied a predominant position in relation to the population of the colony, (iii) that the plaintiffs had thereby lost, or were in danger of losing, such rights, benefits and advantages as the law allowed them by virtue of their allegiance as British subjects to the Crown as sovereign, and (iv) that the purpose for which the first land in the colony had been acquired, *i.e.*, that the same should be enjoyed by the settlers of the colony, their heirs and successors, for ever, had been or was, in danger of being defeated; and that, in the premises, it had been outside the powers of the Crown, whether contained in the British Settlements Act, 1887, or otherwise, to make the order.

Edward Gardner Q.C. and *Ralph Millner* for the plaintiffs. The whole point of the colony of Sierra Leone was to establish freed slaves in Africa. It was founded in 1787 as a sovereign state for the "free community of settlers" and has never been **[752]** conquered, ceded, or made the subject of a treaty. The plaintiffs are British subjects domiciled in Sierra Leone, known as Creoles or "settlers' descendants" and generally accepted as being members of the free community of settlers, in which body the bulk of the settlers' descendants are banded together. Much of the land of the colony was and still is peopled by settlers' descendants, who still are the kind of persons for whom the colony was intended, and it is important that this state of affairs should continue. King Naimbana's grant was to the Crown, which here is in the position of a trustee: *Rustomjee* v. *The Queen*.[6]* The only powers vested in the Crown in relation to a settled colony are those set out in the British Settlements Act, 1887, as having been defined

[6] (1876) 2 Q.B.D. 69, C.A.

and created by statute. [Reference was made to *Attorney-General* v. *De Keyser's Royal Hotel Ltd.*[7]] The argument that the Order in Council is ultra vires and void appears flawless. True it is that the constitutional provisions which it created are part of the law of Sierra Leone: but those provisions originated in English law and an English court can therefore quite properly be asked to decide whether they are valid or not. If it decided that they were invalid, the government of the protectorate of Sierra Leone would be for all practical purposes without power to govern unless and until it took steps to promote the appropriate legislation, which the plaintiffs could support or oppose, as they thought fit. In 1960 the plaintiffs sought to challenge by a High Court action the power to make the order, but it was already made before the action could be brought to trial. They ought therefore to be free to challenge it now. Its effect has been to deliver the government of the people in the settlement to the protectorate. Thus, so far from regulating the settlement, it put an end to it altogether, and so could not be said to have been made under powers conferred by the British Settlements Act, 1887. The trust which the Crown is under an obligation to administer stems from the very nature of the relationship of the Sovereign to the subject, in which each owes a duty to the other. The obligation of each is voluntarily undertaken. Therefore the plaintiffs ask the court to consider their claim and to make the declarations sought.

Sir Peter Rawlinson Q.C., S.-G. and *E. B. Stamp* for the Attorney-General. The declarations ought not to be made. The court has no jurisdiction in the matter. The question whether the constitutional provisions created by the Order in Council are **[753]** part of the law of Sierra Leone could not concern the English courts. The plaintiffs have no right to a declaration by an English court as to the validity of an Order in Council establishing the laws and institutions of a foreign state. [Reference was made to *Rex* v. *Crewe, Ex parte Sekgome.*[8]*] What created the State of Sierra Leone was not the Order in Council challenged, but the Sierra Leone Independence Act, 1961. [Reference was made to *Morice* v. *Durham* (*Bishop*)[9]; *Inland Revenue Commissioners* v. *Broadway Cottages Trust*[10] and *Hoani Te Heuheu Tukino* v. *Aotea District Maori Land Board.*[11]*] Certainly there is nothing in the law to prevent the Crown from becoming a trustee, but it has not done so in this case. Even if the trust had been created, the beneficiaries are wholly incapable of being ascertained. [Reference was made to *Administrator of German Property* v. *Knoop.*[12]*] The basis of the declaration asked for is that the matter is one for the court and for the court's discretion. The court, however, has no jurisdiction; even if it had, the court in its discretion should not grant it. [Reference was made to *Dyson* v. *Attorney-General.*[13]]

Edward Gardner Q.C. and *Ralph Millner* in reply. With regard to jurisdiction, this Order in Council was laid before Parliament in England on April 14, 1961, and the plaintiffs contend that the Crown had no power to make it. It has not been suggested on behalf of the Attorney-General that any court other than an English court could entertain a challenge to the submissions for the plaintiffs. The Crown has power to do what is plainly set out in section 2 of the British Settlements Act, 1887, but only "within any British settlement." These powers are quite unconnected with any provisions for the destruction of a British settlement, which is the purpose of the Order in Council. In all the circumstances, it cannot be said that in fact or in law any declaration affecting this order must be of no consequence.

Cur. adv. vult.

[7] [1920] A.C. 508; 36 T.L.R. 600. H.L.
[8] [1910] 2 K.B. 576; 26 T.L.R. 439, C.A.
[9] (1805) 10 Ves. 522.
[10] [1955]Ch. 20; [1954] 3 W.L.R. 438; [1954] 3 All E.R. 120, C.A.
[11] [1941] A.C. 308; 57 T.L.R. 419; [1941] 2 All E.R. 93, P.C.
[12] [1933] Ch. 439; 49 T.L.R. 109.
[13] [1911] 1 K.B. 410; 27 T.L.R. 143, C.A.

May 5, 1964. WILBERFORCE J. On April 27, 1961, by virtue of an Act of the United Kingdom Parliament called the Sierra Leone Independence Act, 1961, passed on March 28 but not **[754]** effective till April 27, 1961, there came into existence the independent state, within the Commonwealth, of Sierra Leone. Its constitution was established by an Order of Her Majesty in Council, made on April 14, 1961, to come into force on April 27, 1961, immediately before the coming into effect of the Independence Act.

In this action, started in August, 1961, the plaintiffs, who are six citizens of Sierra Leone, domiciled there, ask the court to declare that the Order in Council was ultra vires and is null and void. That is their principal and original claim, but by re-amendment made in July, 1963, they have expanded and added to it. The expansion consists in a prayer for a declaration that the constitution set up by the Order in Council and the government now purporting to exist under it are, as regards the former colony of Sierra Leone, unlawful and invalid and that a group of persons whom the plaintiffs claim to represent is entitled to set up their own constitution and government. The addition consists in a claim that the land comprised in the former colony is held by the Crown upon trust, or subject to an obligation in the nature of a trust, for the benefit, broadly speaking, of the same group.

I deal first with the main claim as to the constitution and government. It is obvious, from the first glance, that the claim is far-reaching. The plaintiffs are asking a court in the United Kingdom to make a declaration respecting the constitution and government of a foreign state; to do so in the absence of that state or of anyone representing it; to make it against H.M.'s Attorney-General representing the Crown through the Government of the United Kingdom which has had, since April 27, 1961, no responsibility for Sierra Leone and which has no power of legislation or executive action in that country.

It is not surprising that the defendant submits that no such declaration can, or at least should, be made. On the plaintiffs' side it is urged that, although the constitutional provisions in the Order in Council have passed into the law of Sierra Leone, their root lies in the law of the United Kingdom; that it is consequently appropriate to ask an English court to examine their validity under that law; that a declaration of invalidity would not be ineffective since by cutting off the powers of the putative government of Sierra Leone at their source it would compel that government, in practice, to take steps by legislation to rectify the position, which legislation could be opposed or influenced, by the plaintiffs and their supporters. Further, the plaintiffs point to the fact that so long ago as July, 1960, well before the Order in **[755]** Council was made, they took steps by action in these courts to challenge the power to make it and that it was no fault of theirs that the action they brought could not be brought to trial before the order was made: consequently they should not be deprived of the right to challenge it ex post facto. I understand the plaintiffs' motives and the hopes which they entertain, but this understanding does not eliminate or greatly reduce the reluctance which I continue to feel against an exercise of the court's discretionary power to grant a declaratory judgment such as the plaintiffs request. The objections to its doing so seem to me most formidable; but, as the plaintiffs' substantive case on the Order in Council has been fully argued and as I have reached a decision on it, adverse to the plaintiffs, I shall rest my judgment on that decision rather than reach a final conclusion on the more elusive questions of jurisdiction and discretion.

In order to understand the Order in Council it is necessary to go back to the origins of the Colony of Sierra Leone. In stating certain relevant facts, I also mention those relevant to the plaintiffs' additional claim regarding the lands.

The United Kingdom's first effective contact with Sierra Leone was in 1787, when, as a new and noble experiment in England's relations with Africa, a group of humanitarians, encouraged and supported by the Government, fixed upon the area round what is now St. George's Bay, near Freetown, for the settlement of liberated slaves, this being of course 20 years before the abolition of the trade itself by Parliament.

The first document we have is a grant of land dated August 22, 1788, made by King Naimbana, Chief of Sierra Leone. (It appears that there was an earlier grant made by King Tom but that it was superseded by the grant in question.) This document expressed to be made in consideration of some rather miscellaneous presents, according to a list, by Captain John Taylor of His Britannic Majesty's brig *Miro* in behalf of and for the sole benefit of the free community of settlers, their heirs and successors, lately arrived from England and under the protection of the British Government, granted an extent of land in what is now the Freetown peninsula, "for the settling of the said free community to be theirs, their heirs and successors for ever." The chief also swore allegiance to H.M. King George the Third.

The first settlers, who included no doubt a number of those former slaves who had gained their liberty on English soil from Lord Mansfield C.J.'s celebrated judgment in *Sommersett's* case,[14] **[756]** were followed at intervals by others, including liberated American slaves brought from Nova Scotia, former slaves from Jamaica (called "Maroons") and after the abolition of slavery in 1807 liberated African slaves. These settlers, or a group of them, and their descendants came to be known as "Creoles," a name which, according to those of the plaintiffs who gave evidence, distinguishes the descendants of free settlers from tribal Africans, the distinction being easily recognisable through their English, Scottish, Welsh, Irish or German names as well as by their physique, occupations, customs, costume, attitudes and other attributes.

Returning to the legal history of the peninsula, in 1791, by the Act 31 Geo. 3, c. 55, the Sierra Leone Company was incorporated, with a number of distinguished proprietors, among whom I may without indiscretion mention Granville Sharp and Henry Thornton. The long title mentions among the purposes of the company that of holding by grant from His Majesty and from the native princes of Africa the peninsula of Sierra Leone now vested in His Majesty or belonging to the said princes. This was followed on July 5, 1799, by a charter by which the Crown granted to the company so much of the peninsula as was vested in the Crown and created the colony of Sierra Leone extending over the whole peninsula, with detailed provisions for the government of the colony. In 1807, by 47 Geo. 3, sess. 2, c. 44, the charter was annulled, and the lands belonging to the company were vested in the Crown, and on August 9, 1809, by a fresh charter, provision was made for the government of the colony as a Crown colony. It remained a Crown colony until 1961.

In 1887 there was passed the British Settlements Act, replacing an earlier Act of 1843. It is clear, and it is admitted by both sides, that the Crown colony of Sierra Leone was a British settlement within the Act, and the Act is of crucial importance. I must read section 2. That says: "It shall be lawful for Her Majesty the Queen in Council from time to time to establish all such laws and institutions, and constitute such courts and officers, and make such provisions and regulations for the proceedings in the said courts and for the administration of justice, as may appear to Her Majesty in Council to be necessary for the peace, order, and good government of her Majesty's subjects and others within any British settlement." Section 3 gave power to delegate the powers of the Crown in a manner which was later extended by the British Settlements Act, 1945. Under the extended powers, delegation could be by **[757]** Order in Council to any specified person or persons or authority without the previous limitation that they must be within the settlement.

In 1896 a protectorate was proclaimed over the much larger and more populous hinterland to the colony, over which, accordingly, the Crown acquired powers of legislation by Order in Council made under the Foreign Jurisdiction Act, 1890. It is an important fact that, from the very first, power to legislate for the protectorate was conferred upon the governor and legislative council of the colony of Sierra Leone and an ordinance, providing for the government of the protectorate, was made by those authorities on September 16, 1896.

Between then and independence a number of similar legislative steps were taken in relation to colony and protectorate as representative institutions deve-

[14] (1772) 20 State Tr. 1.

loped leading to an increasing degree of administrative fusion of the two areas. In 1924 it was again laid down that the executive council of the colony should be the executive council of the protectorate and provision was made for a legislative council for both colony and protectorate, with members taken from both. In 1951, the composition of the legislative council, for colony and protectorate, was altered so that the protectorate acquired 12 directly-elected members as against seven for the colony, and the preponderance of the protectorate was carried further in 1957. However, the status of the colony of Sierra Leone as a Crown colony, and as a British settlement, was throughout preserved.

Then, on April 14, 1961, while the colony was still a colony and a British settlement, the Order in Council was made and laid before Parliament. It is expressed to be made "by virtue and in exercise of the powers in that behalf by the Foreign Jurisdiction Act, 1890, or otherwise in Her Majesty vested," and the plaintiffs say that there was no power to make it. It is clear that there was no power to enact legislation affecting the colony under the Foreign Jurisdiction Act, 1890, so that the order must have been made, as regards the colony, under the words "or otherwise in Her Majesty vested."

The defendant's case is that the Order in Council, as regards the colony, was made under the British Settlements Act, 1887, as amended. The use of that Act is clearly permissible under the words "or otherwise in Her Majesty vested" if in fact power existed under that Act. I have already read section 2, and to my mind it is beyond doubt that the Order in Council was validly made under that section. The section gives power to **[758]** establish laws and institutions for the peace, order and good government of her Majesty's subjects and others within any British settlement. There is nothing in this which requires the laws and institutions so established to be such as relate exclusively to the settlement in question. The laws and institutions provided by the Order in Council of 1961 are none the less for the peace, order and good government of those within the settlement because they are also for the peace, order and good government of the adjoining protectorate, and are none the less so because the institutions of government set up are joint or mixed institutions. This is sufficient to support the order, but I should mention that, if it were necessary so to do, the defendant would also invoke the provisions of section 3, and would justify the order as a delegation of power under that section. I need express no opinion as to this contention.

Counsel for the plaintiffs did not, in his argument against the validity of the Order in Council, attack the contents of it. His objection was the more general one that the Order in Council could not be made under powers conferred by the British Settlements Act because it does not regulate the settlement but destroys it and because it hands over the government of those within the settlement, including British subjects, to the government of a protectorate. I cannot accept this. It is true that the British settlement, and the Crown colony, has, from April 27, 1961, ceased to exist, but that is not by virtue of the Order in Council but of the Act of Independence which is not, and cannot be, the object of challenge here and as regards government, it is not the case that government of the settlement is transferred to the protectorate. Institutions and a government are set up which are joint institutions for colony and protectorate, just as the pre-existing institutions were joint institutions. The process of integration, has no doubt been carried further, but it is still integration, not transfer. I, therefore, reach the conclusion that the main claim cannot succeed.

I must now consider the additional claim raised by the re-amendment. This is a claim which attracts some sympathy. It is based upon the reality that the territory of the former colony was selected and settled for a particular purpose, accepted and encouraged by governments in this country, namely, the establishment in Africa of Africans (and others) who had suffered from the institution of slavery. It is also based on the reality that a great part of the territory of the colony (it is impossible to give quantitative evidence) has been and still is occupied by persons **[759]** descended from the original settlers forming a civilisation group with characteristics derived from the original purposes of the settlement. These are real values, which I can understand that the plaintiffs are anxious to preserve. What is lacking, unhappily for the plaintiffs, is any real legal basis for any claim to any interest in or rights over the land of the former colony. Apart from the general reference in 1788 to the grant of lands for "the settling of the free community to be theirs, their heirs and successors for ever," there is nothing which could even found an argument for the creation of a trust, or any other legal obligation which could be enforced against the Crown. There is no other document which supports this contention and no oral evidence has been called in aid of it. I hope I am not discourteous to the plaintiffs and to their counsel, who argued this point most economically, if I state, without expansion, some of the objections which appear to me to be fatal to this claim.

1. Assuming in the plaintiffs' favour (which in fact appears to me to be far from clear on the evidence available) that the grant of 1788 was a grant to the Crown, there is first the difficulty that it is well established, as a general rule, that the Crown, in concluding arrangements with foreigners, does not do so as agent or as trustee for its subjects, and that the subjects acquire no rights unless the arrangement is incorporated in municipal law. See *Hoani Te Heuheu Tukino* v. *Aotea District Maori Land Board.*[15]*

2. Although, in law, it is possible for the Crown to assume the position of a trustee (see *Rustomjee* v. *The Queen*[16]*), the language of the grant here is, in my judgment, quite insufficient to support the assumption by the Crown of any equitable, contractual or innominate obligation.

3. If the language of the grant were otherwise such as to give rise to a trust or analogous obligation, the beneficiaries of the trust are incapable of ascertainment. It is only too apparent that even if the original members of the free community could be ascertained, that cannot be said of their heirs, their successors, or their descendants. Whichever of these classes now represents the beneficiaries (a matter which is itself one of doubt), it is clear in each case that the persons concerned have by 1961 become so mixed and diluted by intermarriage into and out of the Creole community, as well as by emigration and immigration, as to be **[760]** beyond the possibility of identification and a trust with unascertainable beneficiaries cannot be enforced.

4. Even if a valid trust was created by the grant of 1788, the trust could not, without express provision, have survived the successive Acts of 1791 and 1807, and the charter of 1799 which did not incorporate the terms or purposes of the grant or of the alleged trust in the title of the company or of the Crown to the lands in question.

5. Even if any trust existed as regards the land of the colony, the trustee now, it seems to me, would be Her Majesty, in right of her dominion in Sierra Leone, and no basis would exist for enforcing it in these courts. In fact, I was glad to hear that certain of the plaintiffs are in enjoyment of land in the colony, inherited from their settler ancestors: it was not claimed that anything in the Order in Council or in the Independence Act directly affects their title to this land and I am unable to see how their position, which nobody would wish to see disturbed, would be improved by any declaration that could be made here.

However that may be, I can come to no other conclusion than that the plaintiffs' second claim is, so far as this court is concerned, legally hopeless, and that the action as a whole must be dismissed with costs.

Action dismissed with costs.

The plaintiffs appealed, contending, inter alia, that Wilberforce J. had been wrong in law and fact in rejecting the argument that the order had been outside the powers conferred by the Act of 1887, and, therefore, invalid because it did not regulate the British settlement known as the colony of Sierra Leone but purported to destroy it, and further that the court had had jurisdiction to make, and, in the circumstances of the case, ought to have made, the declaration sought by the plaintiffs. By a respondents' notice, the defendant contended that the order of Wilberforce J. ought to be affirmed on the grounds, additional to

[15] [1941] A.C. 308; 57 T.L.R. 419; [1941] 2 All E.R. 93, P.C.
[16] (1876) 2 Q.B.D. 69, C.A.

those relied upon by Wilberforce J., that by the effect of the Act of 1961 the former colony of Sierra Leone had become part of an independent state for the government of which Her Majesty's Government in the United Kingdom had not, and had not at the date of the issue of the writ in the action, had, any responsibility, and that, accordingly, there was no jurisdiction in the High Court **[761]** of Justice in England in a suit against Her Majesty's Attorney-General to make any such declaration as was sought in the present action on any declaration affecting the constitution of the said independent state, and that no such declaration ought in any event to be made, more particularly in the absence of the said independent state.

At the hearing of the appeal, the first and sixth plaintiffs by leave of the court severed from their co-plaintiffs (post, p. 764), the first plaintiff making submisssions in person on their behalf. They submitted to the court a supplemental notice of appeal relying upon the following additional grounds: (1) that Wilberforce J. had erred in refusing to grant the declaration sought by the plaintiffs in view of paragraph 14 of the statement of claim.[17] Paragraph 14 of the statement of claim alleged contempt of court and prejudice which were neither denied nor refuted in the defence. The plaintiffs had left the court in no doubt that they relied particularly on paragraph 14 for the relief which they sought; (2) that Wilberforce J. had misdirected himself by his failure to be guided by paragraph 7 of the defence[18] which left the court in no doubt that it was not the Order in Council which had brought about the merger of the colony and protectorate. The merger had been brought about by the Act of Independence which simply stated that on April 27, 1961, the colony and **[762]** protectorate of Sierra Leone should together constitute one of Her Majesty's dominions under the name of Sierra Leone. The Act did not specify how they were to be brought together. Section 2 of the Act envisaged or anticipated another constitutional instrument, and even another enactment. Wilberforce J. had erred in not granting the fourth prayer of the plaintiffs;[19] (3) that Wilberforce J. had erred in refusing to grant the declaration sought because of section 5 of the British Settlements Act, 1887, which stated inter alia: "the Crown can assume, revoke or amend these delegatory powers" [sic]; (4) that Wilberforce J. had misdirected himself in failing to be guided by section 30 of the 1947 Amended British Settlement Act [sic], which stated that the Crown could assume, amend and revoke these delegatory powers; (5) that Wilberforce J. had misdirected himself by his failure to be guided by the vital admission of paragraph 1 of the defence which was a reply to the allegations of paragraph 1 of the statement of claim.[20] The

[17] Paragraph 14 of the re-amended statement of claim: "In inviting this honourable court to exercise its discretion to grant the relief hereinafter prayed for, the plaintiffs will further rely upon the fact that prior to the said order in council being made they sought relief, namely, a declaration that such order in council (if made) would, in so far as the same applied to the said colony, be outside the powers of the Crown and ultra vires and unlawful, in an action commenced in this honourable court (Queen's Bench Division), 1960 B. No. 2958, by writ on July 26, 1960, against Her Majesty's Attorney-General and the Rt. Hon. MacLeod, M.P., one of Her Majesty's Secretaries of State, then Her Majesty's Secretary of State responsible for colonial affairs, and that the said order in council was made on April 18 [sic], 1961, notwithstanding that the said action was then pending, and directions had been given on April 11, 1961, for inter alia trial by a judge alone, the action to be set down for hearing within 10 weeks, and a speedy trial. The plaintiffs will refer to the proceedings in the said action."

[18] Paragraph 7 of the re-amended defence read, so far as material: "The defendant admits that the colony of Sierra Leone has ceased to exist as a Crown colony or a British settlement within the meaning of the British Settlements Act, 1887, and has become merged in and replaced by a new state. . . Such cesser and merger were effected by and are consequential on the Sierra Leone Independence Act, 1961 (to which the defendant will refer for its full terms and effect), and not consequential on the Sierra Leone (Constitution) Order in Council, 1961."

[19] See (4), *ante*, p. 751.

[20] Paragraph 1 of the re-amended statement of claim alleged, in effect, the original settlement of 1787, and that the first settlers were, and were commonly known as, the "Free Community of Settlers." Paragraph 1 of the re-amended defence admitted paragraph 1 of the re-amended statement of claim.

treaty of 1788 was the basis of the whole action, and the Crown admitted its responsibilities under this treaty which made the forebears of the appellants British subjects long before the coming into being of the British Settlements Act, 1887. By that admission the Crown recognised its responsibilities under the treaty to safeguard and uphold the integrity of the Free Community of Settlers and the express purposes for which the settlement had been created—i.e., that the settlers and their heirs should be in control of their lands and that they should govern themselves forever; (6) that Wilberforce J. had misdirected himself by his failure to be guided by a vital admission made in paragraph 4 of the defence in reply to allegations made in paragraph 4 of the statement of claim, which was that the appellants were British subjects. That allegation had further been sustained in paragraph 8 of the statement of claim which stated that, by the Liberated Africans Act, 1853, the ancestors of the plaintiffs had been made natural-born British subjects. It had never been, and it was not, within the prerogative of the Crown to put British subjects in a settled territory any more than British subjects in the United Kingdom under a local government representing foreigners or persons other than themselves: see Wade and Phillips, Constitutional Law, **[763]** 6th ed. (1962), p. 390, which stated, inter alia: "the Crown could grant institutions but could not take away rights."

Edward Gardner Q.C. and *Ralph Millner* for the plaintiffs, other than the first and sixth. The Crown colony of Sierra Leone has remained as such since the date of the charter to it in 1809. The freed slaves who formed part of the "first wave" of settlers came there by the authority of the Crown in 1789, on a British warship. The protectorate was not established until 87 years later, in 1896. The boundaries of the colony were fixed, but the plaintiffs do not rely either upon the charter or upon the definition of its limits therein contained. It is sufficient for their purpose to establish that the Crown colony did come into existence in 1809, and remained as such throughout until the Act of Independence, in 1961. The Order in Council purported to be made under the powers provided by the British Settlements Act, 1887. No such powers, however, existed, and the order is therefore ultra vires: see section 5 of the Act of 1887. The Act of 1961 was passed on March 28, 1961, to come into effect on April 27, but it is submitted that the relevant dates are April 27 and April 14, when the constitution purported to be established by Her Majesty in Council—also to take force on April 27. The constitution was therefore created by that Order in Council, not by the Act.

The Order in Council of 1961 is invalid because there is no power contained in the British Settlements Act, 1887, to make an order which has as its purpose the effect which this order has. The inevitable effect of this order is to put an end of the existence of the Crown colony. This is not a question of mere integration, but one which goes to the whole existence of the settlement.

If the order went beyond the powers contained in the Act of 1887, it was invalid when it was made. It was invalid between April 14 and 27, 1961. The whole purpose was invalid. The Act of 1887 presupposes the continuance of the settlement. The "good order," etc., referred to is *for the settlement.* [Reference was made to Sierra Leone Independence Act, 1961, Sch. 2, para. 6[21] and *Attorney-General* v. *De Keyser's Royal Hotel.*[22]] **[764]**

[21] Sierra Leone Independence Act, 1961, Sch. 2, para 6: "Nothing in this Act shall confer on the legislature of Sierra Leone any power to repeal, amend or modify the constitutional provisions otherwise than in such manner as may be provided for in those provisions.

"In this paragraph, the expression 'the constitutional provisions' means this Act, any Order in Council made before the appointed day, which revokes Parts II to VI of the Sierra Leone (Constitution) Order in Council, 1958, and the Sierra Leone Protectorate Orders in Council, 1951 to 1960, and any law, or instrument made under a law, of the legislature of Sierra Leone made on or after that day which amends, modifies, re-enacts with or without amendment or modification, or makes different provision in lieu of, any of the provisions of this Act, that Order in Council or any such law or instrument previously made."

[22] [1920] A.C. 508; 36 T.L.R. 600, H.L.

[RUSSELL L. J. A statute imposing a condition may limit the prerogative, but I expressed doubts in *Sabally and N'Jie* v. *Attorney-General*[23]* as to whether it necessarily does so if no condition is imposed.]

Here, the Act of 1887 gives limited powers, not extending to powers which would put an end to the settlement. Nor would the prerogative have given any wider powers. The most formidable obstacle facing the plaintiffs is to persuade the court that, if they are right in law that the Order in Council of 1961 is ultra vires, there are circumstances of sufficient cogency to persuade it to exercise its discretion and give a declaratory judgment. On the question of discretion, the plaintiffs make the following four points: (1) The importance of this matter as a matter of public interest, not only to the plaintiffs, but to thousands of their followers. (2) If the court took the view that their submission in law was correct, they have a prima facie right to the exercise of the discretion in their favour. (3) The plaintiffs' conduct in pursuit of their claim—their diligence. (4) The fact —it may be one which would raise some sympathy—that at the time when the original action in the Queen's Bench Division was in course of being tried the Act of Independence supervened and the plaintiffs had to begin the present action. There are, therefore, grounds on which the court can and should exercise its discretion if the plaintiffs' submission in law is correct.

Dr. Prince Gustavus Buck, on behalf of himself and the sixth plaintiff, Jonathan Michael Rose, made submissions based upon and supporting the supplemental notice of appeal referred to above (ante, p. 716).

Sir F. Elwyn Jones Q.C., A.-G. and *J. P. Warner* for the Crown. First, a declaration should not be made concerning the validity of the constitution of an independent state where that state does not submit to the jurisdiction, at all events if the declaration would not be ancillary to the enforcement of some legal right cognisable in the English courts. The court has no **[765]** jurisdiction to make such a declaration. Alternatively, it should not exercise its discretion in favour of doing so. The plaintiffs' first prayer in substance constitutes an attack on the constitution of an independent sovereign state. Where proceedings seek that kind of result, the court should refuse to entertain them. Her Majesty's Attorney-General for England is not a proper defendant to such proceedings. The make the declaration sought would offend both against the principle of effectiveness and against the principle of international comity. As to the latter principle, see *Rahimtoola* v. *Nizam of Hyderabad*[24]* and *Duff Development Co.* v. *Kelantan Government.*[25]*

Secondly, it was by the Sierra Leone Independence Act, 1961, not by the Order in Council, that the state of Sierra Leone was created. The colony retained its separate existence until the Act came into force. The Order in Council did not put an end to it. The Order in Council was clearly within the powers conferred by the British Settlements Act, 1887, as regards the colony, and within the powers conferred by the Foreign Jurisdiction Act, 1890, as regards the protectorate. It was clearly competent for the Crown under those powers to provide for the two territories to be governed as one.

Gardner Q.C. in reply. The plaintiffs are not seeking to do anything to offend against the dignity of a foreign state. They ask only for a declaration that the Order was made ultra vires. Sierra Leone may now be an independent Commonwealth state, but the plaintiffs ask for a judgment against the *manner* in which the order was made, not its contents. The powers in the British Settlements Act, 1887, do not extend to making this order.

HARMAN L.J. This is an appeal against an order made by Wilberforce J. on May 5, 1964,[26] dismissing this action in which the plaintiffs sought against the Attorney-General, representing the Crown in this country, a declaratory judgment declaring void an Order in Council made on April 14, 1961, which

[23] [1965] I Q.B. 273; [1964] 3 W.L.R. 732; [1964] 3 All E.R. 377, C.A.
[24] [1958] A.C. 379; [1957] 3 W.L.R. 884; [1957] 3 All E.R. 441, H.L.
[25] [1924] A.C. 797, 820; 40 T.L.R. 566, H.L.
[26] *Ante*, p. 753; [1964] 3 W.L.R. 850; [1964] 2 All E.R. 663.

propounded, or sought to propound a constitution for the new state of Sierra Leone. This state came into existence on April 27, 1961, under an Act of the British Parliament passed on March 28 of that year, called the Sierra Leone Independence Act, 1961. The effect of that Act was to combine in the new state, one of the independent **[766]** dominions of the Crown, both the Crown colony known as Sierra Leone colony and the Sierra Leone protectorate.

The plaintiffs are, and have at all material times, been British subjects and domiciled in the former Crown colony. They are, and claim to represent, the descendants of manumitted slaves who had been attracted from various sources to Freetown, now the capital of Sierra Leone, at the end of the eighteenth or in the early years of the nineteenth century. These people form a community distinct from the indigenous inhabitants of the neighbouring protectorate, and have described themselves as the "Free Community of Settlers." They feel aggrieved by this amalgamation, which, according to them, having regard to the great numerical superiority of the inhabitants of the protectorate, subjects them to the latter, who, until the passing of the Act of 1961, were British protected persons and not British subjects, and deprives them of the position which they had always cherished of free subjects of the Queen.

The plaintiffs recognised that they could not question the Act of Parliament. What they did attack was the Order in Council, which was entitled The Sierra Leone (Constitution) Order in Council, 1961. Their claim was that either the order did not on its true construction apply to the colony at all, or, if it did purport so to do, it was ultra vires the Crown acting as Her Majesty did under the powers conferred upon her by the British Settlements Act, 1887.

Wilberforce J. expressed grave doubts about both the jurisdiction to grant, and the propriety of granting, a declaration such as is claimed in this case. For the purposes, however, of his judgment, he set those considerations aside and decided the case on the construction of the Act of 1887 adversely to the plaintiffs, holding that there was power vested in Her Majesty under the Act to make the Order in Council in question, its object and effect being to supply the colony and the protectorate, when amalgamated by the Act of Parliament, with a constitution.

That was enough to dispose of the relief asked for by the writ. Other claims, however, were added by amendment to the prayer of the statement of claim which depended upon an alleged trust of lands in the colony said to be vested in the Crown in favour of the members of the so-called "Free Community of Settlers" and their descendants. Wilberforce J. found conclusive answers to these latter contentions and rejected them, and nothing has been heard of them in this court. Finally, there was a fourth item added to the prayer which alleged that the free settlers were **[767]** now entitled to set up in the colony such constitution as they thought fit. This contention was not urged by Mr. Gardner, who appeared for all the plaintiffs except the first and the last. These latter at the last moment expressed their wish to sever from their co-plaintiffs, apparently for the purpose of putting forward contentions with which Mr. Gardner declined to be associated, particularly the last-mentioned, and by way of indulgence, and without objection by the Attorney-General, we thought it right to allow this irregular course and heard the first plaintiff on his own behalf and on that of the last plaintiff. He addressed us with considerable eloquence, and without much attention to the point at issue. I reject his submissions so far as I have been able to understand them.

The background and facts of the case have been admirably stated by Wilberforce J.,[27] and I adopt them and do not propose to elaborate on his recital. With the substance of his judgment also I agree, and should be content to add nothing on my own account. In this court, however, it was pressed upon us by the Attorney-General that we ought not to flinch from a decision on the point of jurisdiction, and I am persuaded that it is one with which we ought to deal.

This, then, is an action seeking a declaration that the constitution of Sierra Leone (that is to say, the combined areas of the Crown colony and the

[27] *Ante,* p. 753.

protectorate) propounded by the statutory instrument is, in so far as the plaintiffs and their followers are concerned, void and of no legal validity. This relief is sought in the absence of any representative of the state whose constitution is attacked. In the course of an interlocutory application in this case I suggested to the appellants that they might give notice of this appeal to the authorities in Sierra Leone in case they should wish to intervene in the proceedings. That notice, I understand, was given, but, not unexpectedly, there has been no intervention. If there had been, that might have been a submission by the Government of Sierra Leone to the jurisdiction of this court, but there has been no such submission. The only respondent, then, is the Attorney-General representing the Queen in Great Britain.

The plaintiffs' argument is, I understand, twofold. First, they argue that they attempted, before the promulgation of independence, to raise the question of the validity of the Order in Council by an action in the Queen's Bench Division[28] of the High Court at a time when the colony was a Crown colony, and the question, **[768]** therefore, was justiciable in these courts, and that it was only the exigencies of time which prevented that action from coming to trial before the appointed day when independence became an established fact. That action was then stayed[29] and this fresh action started, and the plaintiffs say that they ought not to be treated differently because they have been overtaken by time in this way. To that I answer that the Act of Parliament which set up the independent state has made all the difference, deplore it as the plaintiffs may, and that they can only be treated on the facts as they are, and were when the writ was issued, namely, as litigants seeking to impeach in these courts the independence of an independent state.

The second argument was that the Order in Council was a statutory instrument laid before the British Parliament, and, therefore, must be cognisable in the British courts, and that section 3 of the order and the second schedule propounding the constitution of Sierra Leone (that is to say, for both the colony and the protectorate immediately before any independence became an established fact under the Act of Parliament) must be a matter into which these courts can inquire.

In my judgment, neither of those arguments ought to prevail. These courts cannot, in my view, make a declaration impugning the validity of the constitution of a foreign or independent state, at any rate where that is the object of the action. This may be put as a matter of international comity, or upon the ground of effectiveness. No relief effective in this country or anywhere else is sought by the action. Any declaration which the court might make may be ignored with impunity by the independent country into whose affairs it pretends to pry, and I am of opinion that it would be not only improper, but contrary to law in those circumstances to make such a declaration as is here sought. Even if, however, I thought that we could, I should still think that we should not make such a declaration which would amount to an unwarrantable interference in the affairs of an independent member of the British Commonwealth.

That is enough, apart from the grounds on which Wilberforce J. decided the case, to condemn this appeal to dismissal. About those grounds I propose to say no more than that I agree with them, and should be prepared to adopt them as part of this judgment. **[769]**

DIPLOCK L.J. In this appeal, the only claims for relief sought are declarations as to the validity of the present constitution of Sierra Leone and of the Order in Council by which that constitution was made. Sierra Leone has, since April 27, 1961, been an independent sovereign state within the Commonwealth. We have no need to inquire of the executive as to its status, which is that of an independent sovereign state. Its status as an independent sovereign state is recognised and conferred by section 1 of the Sierra Leone Independence Act, 1961. The government of this independent sovereign state is not a party to this action. The only defendant is the Attorney-General of England, acting on behalf

[28] Unreported.

[29] Unreported.

of the Queen as sovereign of the United Kingdom, not as sovereign of Sierra Leone. The Attorney-General has nothing to do with Sierra Leone, or with its government.

When the action was before Wilberforce J., there were additional claims which, on the face of them, asserted the existence of an English trust of lands in Sierra Leone of which it was alleged that the Crown, as sovereign of the United Kingdom, was trustee. Furthermore, it was not clear upon the pleadings that it was common ground that Sierra Leone was an independent sovereign state. It was, therefore, necessary for Wilberforce J. to investigate the plaintiffs' case upon its legal merits before reaching a decision as to whether he had jurisdiction to entertain the action. In the course of so doing, he held the claims as to the existence of a trust to be without foundation, and the claims for declarations that the present constitution of Sierra Leone and the Order in Council by which it was made were invalid to be without legal merits, and he so stated in his judgment without expressing any concluded opinion as to whether he would have had jurisdiction to make the declarations claimed.

In this appeal, the claims as to the existence of a trust have been abandoned. The appeal comes before us as an action in which the plaintiffs seek only the two declarations as to the validity of the present constitution of Sierra Leone and the Order in Council which underlies it. In my view, once this court is satisfied that Sierra Leone is an independent sovereign state, it has no jurisdiction to deal further with the claims for those declarations. As was pointed out in *Garthwaite* v. *Garthwaite*[30]: "In its narrow and strict sense, the 'jurisdiction' of a validly constituted court connotes the limits which are imposed upon its **[770]** power to hear and determine issues between persons seeking to avail themselves of its process by reference (1) to the subject-matter of the issue or (2) to the persons between whom the issue is joined or (3) to the kind of relief sought, or to any combination of these factors."

The only subject-matter of this appeal is an issue as to the validity of a law of a foreign independent sovereign state, in fact, the basic law containing its constitution. The validity of this law does not come in question incidentally in proceedings in which the High Court has undoubted jurisdiction, as, for instance, the validity of a foreign law might come in question incidentally in an action upon a contract to be performed abroad. The validity of the foreign law is what this appeal is about: it is about nothing else. This is a subject-matter over which the English courts, in my view, have no jurisdiction.

As a member of the family of nations, the Government of the United Kingdom (of which this court forms part of the judicial branch) observes the rules of comity, videlicet, the accepted rules of mutual conduct as between state and state which each state adopts in relation to other states and expects other states to adopt in relation to itself. One of those rules is that it does not purport to exercise jurisdiction over the internal affairs of any other independent state, or to apply measures of coercion to it or to its property, except in accordance with the rules of public international law. One of the commonest applications of this rule by the judicial branch of the United Kingdom Government is the well-known doctrine of sovereign immunity. A foreign state cannot be impleaded in the English courts without its consent: see *Duff Development Co.* v. *Kelantan Government*.[31]* As was made clear in *Rahimtoola* v. *Nizam of Hyderabad*,[32]* the application of the doctrine of sovereign immunity does not depend upon the persons between whom the issue is joined, but upon the subject-matter of the issue. For the English court to pronounce upon the validity of a law of a foreign sovereign state within its own territory, so that the validity of that law became the res of the res judicata in the suit, would be to assert jurisdiction over the internal affairs of that state. That would be a breach of the rules of comity. In my view, this court has no jurisdiction so to do.

I do not think that this rule, which deprives the court of **[771]** jurisdiction over

[30] [1964] P. 356, 387; [1964] 2 W.L.R. 531, 1108; [1964] 2 All E.R. 233, C.A.
[31] [1924] A.C. 797, 820; 40 T.L.R. 566, H.L.
[32] [1958] A.C. 379; [1957] 3 W.L.R. 884; [1957] 3 All E.R. 441, H.L.

the subject-matter of this appeal because assumption of such jurisdiction would involve an assertion of jurisdiction over the internal affairs of a foreign sovereign state, can be eluded by the device of making the Attorney-General of England a party instead of the Government of Sierra Leone. Mr. Gardner, for the plaintiffs, concedes (as he is bound to) that no declaration made in this action could create res judicata binding upon the Government of Sierra Leone. In so far as a declaration is sought as to the validity of the constitution of Sierra Leone, the Attorney-General of England, representing the United Kingdom Government, has no interest in the subject-matter of the issue. Even apart from the comity rule, the court has no jurisdiction to give a declaratory judgment in a suit against a party who has no interest in the subject-matter of the declaration. In such a case there is no lis between the parties for adjudication. There could be no judgment but only an advisory opinion, and this court has no jurisdiction to give advisory opinions.

Mr. Gardner urges, however, that there was a moment of time when the Order in Council purported to be in force before Sierra Leone became an independent sovereign state, while the Government of the United Kingdom was still the sovereign government of the colony of Sierra Leone. He submits that, during that period, the English court would have had jurisdiction to declare the Order in Council to be ultra vires, and that it does not lose that jurisdiction merely because Sierra Leone has subsequently become a foreign sovereign state.

I should in any event reject this argument. In applying the rule of comity, one looks to the substance of the issue, not to its form. The Order in Council was, on the face of it, intended to provide the constitution not of the colony of Sierra Leone, but of the new independent foreign state. The issue as to the validity of the Order in Council was thus, in substance, at the date of the writ, an issue as to the validity of the constitution of an independent sovereign state. But there is, I think, a technical answer also. As soon as Sierra Leone became independent, the Order in Council ceased to have any effect as an Order in Council, that is, as an exercise of the sovereign power of the United Kingdom Government represented by the Attorney-General of England. Whatever effect it then had was as part of the law of a foreign sovereign state, into the validity of which this court has no jurisdiction to inquire. Whether it was valid during the punctum temporis during which it was in force before Sierra Leone became independent is a subject-matter in which the parties have **[772]** no interest. No legal rights or liabilities can depend upon it, except in so far as, the instant afterwards, it became part of the law of the independent sovereign state of Sierra Leone, into the validity of which we have no jurisdiction to inquire. The claim that the court has jurisdiction to make a declaration limited to the validity of the Order in Council, therefore, also fails on the ground that the parties at the time of suit had no interest in its subject-matter.

I understand and appreciate the plaintiffs' sense of grievance that their attempts to get their contentions litigated while the court would, before Sierra Leone became independent, still have had jurisdiction to consider them, were thwarted by the passing of the Sierra Leone Independence Act, 1961, and, as the legal merits of their submissions were fully argued in this court and before Wilberforce J. without protest by the Attorney-General, I hope that it may mitigate that sense of grievance if I say obiter that, even if the court had jurisdiction, I do not think that their contentions could ever have succeeded on the legal merits. I adopt in full the judgment of Wilberforce J. upon that aspect of the case.

The only argument with which Wilberforce J. does not deal in detail, but which was pressed upon us by Mr. Gardner, is an argument based upon section 2 of the British Settlements Act, 1887, under which the Order in Council was made. He contends that the Order in Council, when one examines it, cannot be said to have been a provision "necessary for the peace, order and good government of Her Majesty's subjects and others within any British settlement" because it is obvious that it was intended to operate when the colony of Sierra Leone had ceased to be a British settlement. On April 14, 1961, it was certain that the colony of Sierra Leone would on April 27, 1961, become part of an independent state, for that was already provided for in the Sierra Leone Independence Act, 1961, which was passed on March 28 of that year. While it is, of course, for Her Majesty in Council to determine as a matter of policy what is necessary for the peace, order and good government of Her Majesty's subjects and others within any British settlement, I think that it is plain that Her Majesty could, as a matter of policy, bona fide take the view that it was necessary for the peace, order and good government of her subjects in this settlement that, at the moment at which they became citizens of an independent state, they should do so already endowed with a constitution which the **[773]** Crown considered to be suitable for their future welfare as citizens of that state. On those grounds, I reject the argument that Mr. Gardner has urged so eloquently before us.

I agree with my Lords that this appeal should be dismissed.

Russell L.J. As a matter of political merits, the plaintiffs and their Creole group consider that they have a serious grievance. They assert that they, and what they describe as their long-established British way of life, will be swamped by the indigenous inhabitants of the former protectorate of Sierra Leone. In this court, however, we have no concern at all with political merits; only the legal merits of the plaintiffs' case are relevant here.

On the legal merits, apart from the question of jurisdiction, the only argument for the plaintiffs which appeared to me, with all respect to Mr. Gardner and Dr. Buck, to be worthy of serious attention was that which Diplock L.J. has mentioned, based on the construction of section 2 of the British Settlements Act, 1887, in the context of the preamble to that Act, which states that "it is expedient to extend the power of Her Majesty to provide for the government of such settlements." It is argued that an Order in Council such as that in the present case, which provided a constitution which could have no practical operation in the territory while it was still a British settlement, could not have been considered by the Crown to be necessary for the peace, order and good government of persons within the British settlement consisting of the colony. It must be appreciated that that argument, if valid, would mean that, under the Act of 1887, provision for a constitution on the occasion of a statute establishing the sovereign independence of such a settlement by itself would have to be contained in the statute and not in an Order in Council, and that would certainly be a situation undesirable in the highest degree. In any event, however, I cannot accept the particular argument. The constitution is provided during a punctum temporis for the inhabitants of a British settlement. The Order in Council was made on April 14, 1961, at a time when the statute was inevitably about to produce an independent sovereign state, including in part the British settlement in question, and it was most certainly necessary that the Crown should produce a constitution which would meet the fact that the settlement and its inhabitants were on the brink of a new status.

For the rest, on the legal merits, I am well content to adopt the reasoning of Wilberforce J.

As to jurisdiction, I agree that the courts in this country have **[774]** no jurisdiction to pronounce by declaration upon the validity of the constitution of an independent sovereign state when that declaration is all that is sought and no ancillary rights justiciable in these courts depend upon such a declaration. The proper and only forum in such circumstances is to be found in the courts of that independent sovereign state.

For these reasons, I agree that the appeal fails.

Appeal dismissed with costs.

Solicitors: *Cree, Godfrey & Wood; Treasury Solicitor.*

BUCK AND OTHERS v. ATTORNEY-GENERAL

([1965] 1 W.L.R. 860)

May 12, 1965: House of Lords: Lords Reid, Hodson, Upjohn.

PETITION for leave to appeal to the House of Lords from a decision of the Court of Appeal.[1]*

The Appeal Committee dismissed the petition.

[1] [1965] 2 W.L.R. 1033; [1965] 1 All E.R. 882, C.A.

iii

Foreign State as Plaintiff

ROYAL NORWEGIAN GOVERNMENT v. CONSTANT & CONSTANT AND CALCUTTA MARINE ENGINEERING COMPANY, LTD.

([1960] 2 Ll. Rep. 431)

December 12, 13, 1960: Queen's Bench Division: Diplock J.

Repairs to ship—Payment—Dispute as to charges—Deposit of moneys by requisitioning Government held jointly by agents of ship-repairers and the Government—Whether Government entitled to release to them of deposit—Whether counterclaim by ship-repairers to release to them of deposit was time-barred.

Steamship *Hallbjorg*, under requisition to plaintiff Norwegian Government, repaired by defendants in 1946—Dispute between Government and ship-repairers as to repair costs—£18,000 paid on account by Government and £9400 deposited by Government in London, in joint names of agents of ship-repairers and Government as security for any further liability—Claim by Government (commenced in 1955) to release to it of moneys held jointly alleging (1) that it was an implied term of the agreement that ship-repairers would institute proceedings within a reasonable time to recover balance due; that ship-repairers had failed to institute proceedings within a reasonable time; and that, therefore, Government was entitled to release of deposit; (2) that any claim by ship-repairers in High Court or Courts of Norway to recover balance was time-barred; that, accordingly, Government was under no legal liability for balance; and that, therefore, the agreement was frustrated; and (3) that, if (as alleged by ship-repairers) a trust was created in contemplation that agreement would be reached respecting the balance or ship-repairers would institute proceedings to establish liability of Government, no such agreement was reached or proceedings instituted; and that, therefore, the trust became inoperative and Government was entitled to release to it of trust fund—Contentions by ship-repairers (1) that deposit should be held until precise extent of Government's liability to ship-repairers had been ascertained; and that such liability had not been ascertained; and (2) that, although it was a term of the agreement that the Government would submit to jurisdiction of Indian Courts, or arbitration, it had refused to do so; that ship-repairers could have exercised their **[432]** lien on vessel and forced Government to pay charges or to institute proceedings in Indian Courts to procure release of vessel; and that, accordingly, ship-repairers were not time-barred from recovering sums due to them from Government—Counterclaim by ship-repairers alleging that they were entitled to a reasonable price; that price was agreed and was a reasonable price; and that, therefore, they were entitled to release of deposit moneys—Preliminary issues: (a) Whether Government entitled to release to them of deposit; (b) If answer to (a) was "No," whether ship-repairers' counterclaim was time-barred; (c) If answer to (b) was "No," determination of amount recoverable by ship-repairers should be stood over—Agreement between parties as to facts relating to Indian and other foreign law.

———*Held*, (1) that it was agreed between agents of parties that £9400 should be held in their joint names until legal liability of Government to ship-repairers had been determined; that, upon such determination, the amount should be paid out to ship-repairers; and that there was no express agreement as to how liability was to be determined; (2) that the Government's liability had not been determined; and that, *prima facie*, Government was not entitled to release of deposit; that legal liability of Government to ship-repairers in respect of the repairs continued although, under English law, the remedy by action was time-barred; that there was no ground for implying term that ship-repairers must institute proceedings, and remedy was in Government's hands, in that it could have started proceedings when it liked; and that, therefore, Government could not recover deposit, and answer to Question (a) was "No"; (3) that the moneys were held in trust; that the amount of the fund to which ship repairers were entitled had not been determined and that, therefore, time had not started to run; that, even if the amount had been determined, there was no limitation period in respect of an action (as here) by a beneficiary to a trust to recover trust property from a trustee; that, therefore, ship-repairers' counterclaim was not time-barred; that determination of the Government's liability was a condition precedent to ship-repairers' recovery from the trust fund; and that when that liability had been determined ship-repairers would be entitled to payment out.

———*In re Hepburn,* (1884) 14 Q.B.D. 394, not followed.

The following cases were referred to:
Curwen v. Milburn, (1889) 42 Ch.D. 424; Hepburn, *In re*, (1884) 14 Q.B.D. 394.

In this action, the plaintiffs, the Royal Norwegian Government, claimed from the second defendants, Calcutta Marine Engineering Company, Ltd., of Calcutta, the release of a deposit of £9400 put up by the Norwegian Shipping and Trade Mission (a department of the plaintiff Government) as security for any liability in excess of £18,000 already paid for repairs carried out by the second defendants to the steamship *Hallbjorg* (which was under requisition by the plaintiffs), at Calcutta, in 1946.

The second defendants counterclaimed for a declaration that the plaintiffs were liable to them for £9356 2s. 9d.

At previous proceedings, the Court had ordered that the present proceedings should determine whether the plaintiffs were entitled to release, and whether the defendants' counterclaim was time-barred. The determination of any amount due under the counterclaim was to stand over.

On Oct. 11, 1956, Mr. Justice Devlin ordered by consent that all further proceedings against Messrs. Constant & Constant be stayed, and that the deposit be transferred from the joint names of the Mission and Messrs. Constant & Constant to the Mission and Messrs. J. A. & H. E. Farnfield, the defendants' present solicitors.

According to the plaintiffs' case, the Norwegian Shipping and Trade Mission (hereinafter called "the Mission") was a department of, and acted on behalf of, the Ministry of Industry, Handicrafts and Shipping of the Royal Norwegian Government.

The first defendants, Messrs. Constant & Constant, acted as solicitors for and on behalf of the second defendants (hereinafter called "the Calcutta company") who carried on business in Calcutta as ship-repairers.

In 1946, sundry repairs were carried out in Calcutta to the steamship *Hallbjorg* by the Calcutta company and by letter to Messrs. Constant & Constant dated Aug. 21, 1946, the Mission accepted liability for the repairs and thereafter paid to Messrs. Constant & Constant, on behalf of the Calcutta company, a total sum of £18,000 in respect of the repairs.

On Sept. 12, 1946, the Mission further established a deposit with Hambros Bank, Ltd., London, in the amount of £9400. That deposit was established in the joint **[433]** names of the Mission and of Messrs. Constant & Constant, pursuant to an oral agreement made on Sept. 12, 1946, between Mr. Musaeus of the Mission and Mr. Barker of Messrs. Constant & Constant on behalf of the Calcutta company, whereby it was agreed that, in consideration of the establishment by the Mission of such deposit by way of security, the Calcutta company would allow the *Hallbjorg* to leave Calcutta on completion of the repairs and would refrain from exercising a lien upon her for the amount claimed by the Calcutta company as the balance of the cost of the repairs.

The plaintiffs said that it was an implied term and/or condition of that agreement that, if the Mission should thereafter dispute its liability to pay to the Calcutta company the amount claimed by the Calcutta company as the balance of the cost of the repairs and if the Calcutta company did not, within a reasonable time thereafter, institute proceedings to recover such balance as was claimed, the plaintiff Government, or, alternatively, the Mission, should be entitled to the release to it of the amount of the deposit together with any interest accrued thereon. Such implication arose as a matter of law and/or from the fact that the deposit was to be established by way of security in favour of the Calcutta company in respect of the legal liability of the plaintiff Government and/or the Mission for the balance of the cost of the repairs as claimed by the Calcutta company or for any part of such balance.

Pursuant to that agreement, the Calcutta company allowed the vessel to leave Calcutta in September, 1946, on completion of the repairs. The material repair accounts were thereupon submitted to the Mission by or on behalf of the Calcutta company, and, after scrutiny of them, the Mission by letter to Messrs. Constant and Constant, dated Dec. 2, 1946, disputed its liability to pay to the Calcutta company any part of the amount claimed by the Calcutta company as the balance of the cost of the repairs.

The plaintiffs alleged that the Calcutta company had failed within a reasonable time, or at all, to institute proceedings to recover such balance as was claimed by it and, accordingly, the plaintiff Government, or, alternatively, the Mission was entitled to release to it of the amount of the deposit (namely £9400) together with interest accrued thereon.

The plaintiffs alleged, further, that the plaintiff Government, or alternatively, the Mission was entitled to release to it of the amount of the deposit (namely £9400) together with interest accrued thereon by reason of the frustration and discharge of the agreement pursuant whereto the deposit was established.

The plaintiffs said that the purpose of the agreement was to provide security in favour of the Calcutta company in respect of the legal liability of the plaintiff Government and/or of the Mission for the balance of the cost of the repairs as claimed by the Calcutta company or for any part of such balance, and, any claim prosecuted in the High Court or in the Courts of Norway by the Calcutta company to recover the balance could and would be met and defeated by a plea that by the law of each such jurisdiction such claim had become and was barred by effluxion of time. Accordingly, the plaintiff Government and/or the Mission were under no legal liability for the balance and the purpose of the agreement had accordingly become frustrated and destroyed.

The plaintiffs alleged, alternatively, that if, by virtue of the agreement, there was (as alleged by the Calcutta company) created a trust in respect of the sum deposited pursuant to the agreement, that trust was constituted in contemplation that agreement would thereafter be reached respecting the further amount (if any) payable to the Calcutta company or that, in default of such agreement, the Calcutta company would institute proceedings to establish liability in the plaintiff Government. No such agreement was ever reached and the Calcutta company had not instituted such proceedings within such time as would have enabled the purpose of the trust to be fulfilled, and, accordingly, the trust had become inoperative and the plaintiff Government, or, alternatively, the Mission, was entitled to release to it of the trust fund.

The plaintiffs claimed (1) against both defendants, a declaration that the plaintiff Government, or, alternatively, the Mission, was entitled to release to it of the amount of the deposit (namely £9400) established pursuant to the agreement on Sept. 12, 1946, with Hambros Bank, Ltd., London, together with interest accrued thereon, and (2) against the second defendants, an order that those defendants do all things and procure the signature of all **[434]** documents necessary to secure the release to the plaintiff Government, or, alternatively, to the Mission, of the amount of the deposit (namely £9400) together with interest accrued thereon.

According to the defendants' case, the steamship *Hallbjorg* (hereinafter called "the vessel") was at all material times owned by A/S P. Klippe, of Venderen, Norway, and was under requisition by the plaintiffs. In February, 1946, those defendants were instructed by the plaintiffs' representatives in Calcutta, the Norwegian Shipping and Trade Mission, to execute, and in fact executed, extensive repairs to the vessel. By a letter dated Apr. 24, 1946, the plaintiffs' representatives asked those defendants for an estimate of the cost of the repairs, including repairs not then completed. By a letter dated May 11, 1946, those defendants informed the plaintiffs' representatives that the repairs were estimated to cost approximately 350,000 rs.

Those repairs were completed in September, 1946, having been supervised by the master of the vessel and by surveyors acting on behalf of the plaintiffs. Those defendants submitted to the plaintiffs bills for the repairs signed as to part by Captain Gulbrandson and as to the remainder by Captain Klippe, both acting on behalf of the plaintiffs. The plaintiffs' Calcutta representatives including Mr. Foss, the superintendent engineer, examined the bills in detail and requested reductions in charges for some of the items. Those defendants reduced their bills accordingly to an amount of 310,514.4.0 rs. Accordingly, it was agreed between the plaintiffs and those defendants that that amount was a proper and reasonable charge for the repairs.

During the course of the repairs, K. Lall & Co. supplied stores to a value of 54,234.4.9 rs. to the vessel at the request of the plaintiffs.

On some date unknown to those defendants, disputes arose between the owners of the vessel and the plaintiffs concerning their respective liabilities to those defendants. Those disputes were resolved, so far as those defendants and K. Lall & Co. were concerned, by letters dated Aug. 21, 1946, and Sept. 6, 1946, from the Mission to the first defendants as solicitors for those defendants, whereby the plaintiffs expressly accepted liability for the repairs and stores, and impliedly agreed to pay approximately 350,000 rs. for the repairs and a reasonable sum (by letter dated Dec. 2, 1946, agreed by the Mission as being 54,234.4.9. rs.) for the stores.

Those defendants said that the plaintiffs paid to the first defendants sums totalling £18,000 on Aug. 23 and Sept. 13, 1946, on account of the plaintiffs' liability to those defendants for the repairs, and to K. Lall & Co. for the stores. Those sums were paid by the first defendants to those defendants for division between those defendants, and K. Lall & Co. 54,234.4.9. rs. of those sums were appropriated and paid to K. Lall & Co., who, accordingly, had been paid in full by the plaintiffs for the stores.

On Sept. 12, 1946, it was orally agreed between the plaintiffs and those defendants, acting by Mr. Barker, that, in consideration of the plaintiffs' depositing the sum of £9400 in the joint names of the first defendants (acting as solicitors and agents for those defendants) and the Mission, to be applied as hereinafter set out, those defendants would refrain from exercising a lien upon the vessel and would allow the vessel to sail from Calcutta. In fulfilment of their obligations under that agreement, those defendants did not exercise a lien on the vessel and allowed her to sail from Calcutta. Those defendants said that it was an express, or, alternatively, an implied, term of that agreement that the Mission and the first defendants would hold that sum of £9400 in trust for the plaintiffs and those defendants until such time as the precise extent of the legal liability of the plaintiffs to those defendants in excess of £18,000 less the sterling equivalent of 54,234.4.9. rs. was agreed or determined, and would thereafter pay the amount of such excess to the plaintiffs or to those defendants, or partly to the plaintiffs and partly to those defendants, in accordance with such agreement or determination. No agreement on, or determination of, such liability had been reached or made.

Those defendants alleged, alternatively, that it was express, or, alternatively, an implied, term of that agreement that, in the event of it becoming necessary for the liability of the plaintiffs to be determined, the plaintiffs would submit to the jurisdiction of the Indian Courts, or, alternatively, to arbitration, but the plaintiffs had refused so to submit. Those defendants said that, in so far as the

[435] term was implied, it was to be implied from the express terms of the agreement and from the facts that the plaintiffs were a sovereign government; that those defendants carried on business exclusively in India; that the relevant evidence was most easily assembled in India; and that those defendants, by exercising a lien on the vessel, could have forced the plaintiffs to pay their charges or to have instituted proceedings against those defendants in the Indian Courts to procure the release of the vessel.

Those defendants, accordingly, said that if a reasonable time for the institution of proceedings by those defendants to recover the sums due to them from the plaintiffs would otherwise have expired, such time had not expired, or, alternatively, that the plaintiffs could not be heard to rely upon the expiry of such a time.

By their counterclaim, those defendants contended that if no price had been agreed between the plaintiffs and those defendants for the repairs those defendants were entitled to be paid a reasonable price.

Those defendants said that 310,514.4.0 rs. was the price accepted by the plaintiffs, or, alternatively, was a reasonable price for the repairs. Accordingly, those defendants contended that the plaintiffs were liable to them in the sum of 364,748.8.9. rs. or £27,356 2s. 9d. at a rate of exchange of 1 rupee = 1s. 6d., less the sum of £18,000 paid by the plaintiffs and received by those defendants on account.

Those defendants counterclaimed (1) a declaration that the plaintiffs were liable to the defendants, Calcutta Marine Engineering Company, Ltd., in the sum of £9356 2s. 9d., and that those defendants were entitled to the release to them of the sum of £9356 2s. 9d. out of the moneys held on joint account by the plaintiffs and Messrs. Constant & Constant; and (2) an order that the plaintiffs do all things and sign all documents necessary to secure the release to Calcutta Marine Engineering Company, Ltd., of the sum of £9356 2s. 9d., together with interest accrued thereon out of the moneys held on joint account by the plaintiffs and Messrs. Constant & Constant.

In their reply, the plaintiffs said that the letter dated Apr. 24, 1946, was written solely for the purpose of obtaining information which had been called for by the London office of the Norwegian Shipping and Trade Mission and for transmission thereto in connection with a dispute which had arisen between the Mission and the owners of the vessel in regard to apportionment of responsibility for the repairs which were then in course of being carried out to the vessel at Calcutta.

The plaintiffs admitted that the Norwegian Shipping and Trade Mission, by letter dated Nov. 17, 1953, to those defendants' Calcutta solicitor, indicated that they were not willing to refer the dispute to arbitration in Calcutta as had been proposed by that solicitor in a letter to the Mission dated July 3, 1953. At the time of the proposal and at the time of that refusal those defendants' claim had already become barred by effluxion of time and, accordingly, those defendants were not entitled to rely upon such refusal as operating to extend the time for prosecution of the claim or as otherwise affecting the legal relations of the parties.

The plaintiffs alleged further, that if (which was denied) those defendants were entitled to any further time in which to prosecute their claim by reason of the plaintiffs' refusal, such reasonable time was at most six months from the dispatch of a letter dated Feb. 18, 1954, from the solicitor to the Mission, wherein the solicitor informed the Mission that his clients had been advised to pursue their legal remedy if they had such remedy and whereby he requested information (*inter alia*) regarding the constitution of the Mission. Alternatively, the plaintiffs alleged that such reasonable time was at most six months from the date of receipt by the solicitor of the Mission's reply to that letter by letter dated Feb. 27, 1954. The plaintiffs said that, in any event, such further reasonable time had expired prior to the date of institution of these proceedings.

In their defence to counterclaim, the plaintiffs denied that it was an express or implied term of the agreement made on Sept. 12, 1946, that the sum of £9400 should be held in trust as alleged in the amended defence.

The plaintiffs alleged, further, that if (which was denied) the sum was held in trust, those defendants' claim to be entitled to release of the sum had been lost by reason of their laches. The plaintiffs relied upon the fact that those defendants were at all material times from about July, 1952, onwards represented by the solicitor referred to in the reply, and **[436]** contended that those defendants' delay in instituting proceedings was wholly unexplained.

The plaintiffs pleaded the Limitation Act, 1939, and alleged that the debt and any cause of action in respect thereof arose in 1946, and, accordingly, the counterclaim had become barred by effluxion of time.

The plaintiffs said that a reasonable price for the repairs (including stores supplied in connection therewith) was at most £18,000.

Mr. Basil Eckersley (instructed by Messrs. Sinclair, Roche & Temperley) represented the plaintiffs; Mr. J. F. Donaldson (instructed by Messrs. J. A. & H. E. Farnfield) appeared for the second defendants.

Mr. *Eckersley*, for the plaintiffs, said that although an oral agreement was pleaded, the parties agreed that there should be no oral evidence and that his Lordship should be invited to reach his decision drawing such inferences from the documents as he thought fit.

The plaintiffs contended that the documents made it quite plain that they had been throughout maintaining that the repair account had been grossly overcharged and not merely were they saying that they were not letting a penny of the deposit go to the repairers but in fact they had been saying that they ought to have some money back.

Counsel said that the vessel was one of many which had been requisitioned by the Norwegian Government during the 1939-45 War, and, early in 1946, was due for derequisition and return to her owners. Substantial repairs were put in hand, but a dispute arose between the Mission and the owners regarding the apportionment of the liability for the repairs. Eventually they agreed that the Mission should pay in the first instance.

By August, 1946, the repairs were nearing their end and the defendants were pressing for payment. In view of the dispute between the Mission and the owners it was necessary for all the repair bills to be vetted by both. It was obvious this could not be done before the vessel was going to be ready for delivery. The solution arrived at was that the Mission should pay £18,000 on account and then the £9400 deposit as security for any further liability.

The deposit was paid into Hambros Bank, Ltd., in London and had remained there ever since, in the joint names now of the Mission and the defendants' present solicitors.

Counsel submitted that the money on deposit was security for whatever liability might be determined either by agreement or by the result of the institution of proceedings by the defendants. Here there was no agreement, he contended, and no proceedings by the defendants. It was a simple contractual deposit in joint names until the legal position was clarified. It was not a case where money was being held by a stakeholder.

Mr. Justice Diplock said that the creditors of Hambros Bank Ltd., would appear to be both the plaintiffs and the defendants who held legal ownership jointly, and this appeared to constitute a trust as to beneficial ownership.

His Lordship said that it was clear from the correspondence that the defendants were threatening to put a lien upon the vessel and it was to avert this threat that the Norwegian Government put up the money. That appeared to be the bargain they had made.

Counsel said that the defendants had been given rope enough in all conscience—nine years before the plaintiffs launched the present proceedings. The purpose for which the money had been put up had long since gone and the money should be returned.

Mr. *Donaldson*, for the defendants, said that the defendants sued not on the original repair contract but on the contract under which this money was paid into joint names in London. It seemed to be agreed that it was implicit that in default of any agreement the money would be paid out in accordance with such liability as might be determined by a Court.

This was a Court of competent jurisdiction and the defendants were asking for determination—though the issue of *quantum* was not for his Lordship at the present hearing.

Counsel said that the plaintiffs contended that a time limit for the defendants' proceedings should be implied from the agreement, but he submitted that there was absolutely no necessity for that. The deposit in this case had all the ingredients of a trust, and there was no period of limitation imposed upon an action by a beneficiary under a trust such as this. **[437]**

JUDGMENT.

Mr. Justice DIPLOCK: This case comes before me for the hearing of certain preliminary issues which have been agreed between the parties. A vessel, the *Hallbjorg,* was in the spring of 1946 under requisition to the Norwegian Government. She was about to come off requisition and revert to her Norwegian owners. She was sent to Calcutta for repairs, and those repairs were undertaken by the second defendants, Calcutta Marine Engineering Company, Ltd. Bills were rendered for the repairs by the second defendants (who I shall call "the defendants" hereafter) to the Norwegian Government through the Norwegian Shipping and Trade Mission. Certain disputes (with which I am not concerned) arose between the Mission and the owners as to the apportionment of liability between them for those repairs. As a result, it became necessary to send the bills to Norway for scrutiny by the owners, and there was delay on the part of the Mission in paying the bills.

As a result, in August, 1946, the defendants were threatening to exercise a lien on the vessel unless their repair bills were paid. On Aug. 21, the Norwegian Government, through the Mission, accepted liability for the whole of the repairs, leaving the matter as to apportionment to be decided between them and the Norwegian owners. On Aug. 22, 1946, the Norwegian Government paid £10,000 on account of the bills, and said that the bills would have to be sent to the owners in Norway for agreement. At the beginning of September, the defendants, being dissatisfied with this, threatened to detain the ship in Calcutta unless the bills were paid in full. It was out of that threat that the circumstances arose which have given rise to this action.

On Sept. 6, 1946, the Norwegian Shipping and Trade Mission was in touch with Messrs. Constant & Constant, who were then the English solicitors for the defendants. By letter of that date, written to Messrs. Constant & Constant, they offered to deposit in joint names the balance of the bills which had been sent in. They said in that letter:

> . . . In order not to risk delay to the vessel we are prepared to go beyond our agreement as confirmed in our letter of the 4th inst. [—that was the agreement to accept liability for the repairs—], and beg to confirm our telephone message this afternoon when we informed your Secretary, in your absence, that we were prepared to deposit in joint names here the balance of your Clients' account. . . .

That deposit in fact took place on Sept. 12, 1946, as a result of discussions between Mr. Barker, of Messrs. Constant & Constant, and Mr. Musaeus, of the Norwegian Shipping and Trade Mission. Mr. Barker has, unfortunately, since died, and the parties have agreed that I shall make a finding of fact as to the agreement between them, which was oral, as to the terms on which this deposit was made. The material available to me is certain contemporaneous correspondence (to which I shall refer) and also, though naturally of less probative value, a letter by Mr. Musaeus written some years afterwards, in which he gives his recollection of what occurred.

On Sept. 12, Mr. Barker wrote to the Norwegian Shipping and Trade Mission confirming what was agreed. I think it is necessary that I should read that letter, or much of it. After some preliminary remarks, he says:

> . . . we were glad to have been able to reach an agreement with you during the course of this morning under which you were to remit to us a further

£8000/- on account and arrange for the deposit of the sum of £9400 in the joint names of yourselves and us with Hambros Bank Ltd.

Immediately following our telephone talk we had a word with Mr. Bowerman [—who was the London agent of the defendants—] and he has despatched a cable at urgent rates to the Calcutta Marine Engineering Co. reading more or less as follows:—

AGREEMENT REACHED NOTRASHIP [—which is the telegraphic name of the MISSION—] PAID FURTHER EIGHT THOUSAND POUNDS ON ACCOUNT STOP BALANCE STERLING NINE THOUSAND FOUR HUNDRED POUNDS DEPOSITED HAMBROS JOINT NAMES NOTRASHIP CONSTANTS PENDING FINAL AGREEMENT ALL BILLS STOP FOREGOING AGAINST CONSTANTS UNDERTAKING HALLBJORG ALLOWED IMMEDIATELY LEAVE CALCUTTA FREED FROM ALL YOUR CLAIMS STOP ARRANGING REMIT FURTHER EIGHT THOUSAND CABLE DATE HOUR DEPARTURE HALLBJORG STOP AIRMAIL DUPLICATES ALL ACCOUNTS REFERRED YOUR ELEVENTH. **[438]**

Then there are some details of the outstanding account, and then the letter goes on:

Whilst we agree as to the difficulty of finding some reasonable formula for settling the accounts and releasing the amount of the deposit within a fixed period, we have assured our client that you may be counted upon to do your utmost to agree figures within the shortest possible time but should a dispute arise which cannot be overcome by negotiation, we desire to reserve our clients right either to litigate or arbitrate here or in Calcutta as they may decide. We more or less agreed about this in the course of our last telephone talk and it follows that if it becomes a question of proceedings in Calcutta we shall rely upon you to make arrangements for accepting the jurisdiction of the Calcutta Courts as promised.

The next letter which I need read is the reply to that, written by Mr. Musaeus on behalf of the Mission on Sept. 13. It reads as follows:

We have received your letter of the 12th inst., and note the contents of the cable sent to Calcutta.

We do not agree to the views expressed in the penultimate paragraph of your letter. We discussed the jurisdiction in connection with a time limit which you would like to have agreed in the interests of your Clients but we decided on a simple deposit, leaving the other questions in abeyance until we see whether we can have the matter settled on a friendly basis. You mentioned that this was a matter of detail which we most probably would be able to agree on later. You will understand that we preferred a deposit here to a bail in Calcutta and in order to achieve this we made another payment on account. . . .

Then he goes on to say that it was clear that there should be no claim against the ship. He adds at the end:

We are not aware of any promise, as you mentioned by you, [*sic*] except that we will try to have the matter settled as quickly as possible.

To that, Mr. Barker replied on Sept. 17, the relevant passage in his letter being this:

As regards the question of jurisdiction, the writer's recollection is that that matter was conceded by you, and on the balance of convenience, assuming, which we hope is not the case, there is to be some dispute about the eventual liability to our clients, it would have been better to have given them the right, if they so wished, to proceed in Calcutta where all the evidence is presumably available.

We did not and still do not think that we were asking you for a concession, although of course we admit that if the vessel had been arrested in Calcutta and bail there had been put up, the Indian Courts would have had jurisdiction assuming any part of the repair or stores accounts become the subject matter of a legal dispute.

We have explained the matter at some length as above lest it be thought that we are seeking to bind you to an arrangement which is in the least unfair. Throughout the whole of the negotiations we have done our best to meet the point of view of both parties . . .

The final letter to which I should refer is a letter written by Mr. Musaeus on Feb. 11, 1952, some 5½ years after, giving his recollection of what occurred. I think I need do no more than read this passage:

. . . I offered deposit in London of the balance of the bills, amounting to £9,400/-. Mr. Barker, on behalf of his clients, demanded deposit in Calcutta, with the proviso that the dispute should be referred to decision by the courts in Calcutta in case we did not reach an amicable agreement. I refused to accept such conditions and renewed the offer of deposit in joint names with Hambros Bank in London, which was reluctantly accepted. In response the Mission procured the deposit, which was made on 12th September, 1946.

On that material and the remainder of the material in the bundle of correspondence I hold that it was agreed between Mr. Barker, on behalf of the defendants, and Mr. Musaeus, on behalf of the Norwegian Government, that the £9400 should be held in joint names—Messrs. Constant & Constant and the Norwegian Shipping and Trade Mission—until the legal liability of the Norwegian Government to the defendants in excess of £18,000 already paid was agreed or determined, and that, upon such agreement or **[439]** determination, the amount of such excess (if any) should be paid out to the defendants, and the balance (if any) should be paid to the Norwegian Government.

I should perhaps add that if interest accumulated upon the sum deposited, the interest would be divided in similar proportions.

I further hold that there was no express agreement between the parties as to the method in which the liability was to be determined in default of agreement.

It is, I think, necessary for me to deal, though I hope briefly, with the subsequent events which have occupied the next 14 years. On Dec. 2, 1946, after examination of the bills, the Norwegian Government expressed its view that it had been grossly overcharged, and indeed demanded a refund of some of the £18,000 already paid. In February, 1947, it sent details of the overcharges, and the matter dragged on throughout 1947, until, at the end of that year, on Dec. 24, Messrs. Constant & Constant suggested that the matter should be referred to arbitration. Nothing came of that suggestion. In the course of 1948, the person who ran the managing agents of the defendants in India died, and there seems, from the correspondence, to have been a great deal of dispute as to the destination of his estate and who was to succeed him as manager of the company.

In the result, nothing happened noteworthy for something over a year, until on Jan. 20, 1949, the Norwegian Government wrote again to Messrs. Constant & Constant and said:

. . . I have to day sent your clients a letter as per enclosed copy and hope that your clients will agree to the amount deposited being released, otherwise I feel that it will be necessary to institute proceedings in order to have this long outstanding matter brought at an end.

That was in January, 1949, but very shortly afterwards, on Jan. 26, Mr. Musaeus had second thoughts, and said that, in his view, it was for the defendants to make the first move, and that the Norwegian Government would then counterclaim for what it thought it had overpaid. In June, 1949, the Norwegian Government, again acting by Mr. Musaeus, expressed its intention of instituting proceedings shortly in London "in case the matter cannot be solved within" a short time. After that, discussions went on intermittently in India and elsewhere with the Norwegian Consul in Calcutta, and in June, 1951, the Consul-General proposed arbitration. It is not quite clear whether the Consul-General was acting as an agent for the Norwegian Government or whether he was merely using his good offices to seek to get this dispute solved.

The defendants, however, at that time, said that they were going to make an attempt to get the matter dealt with on a diplomatic level, and if that failed, they would have to refer the matter to arbitration or the law. Nothing came of any attempt to get the matter dealt with on a diplomatic level, and a further period elapsed, until, in July, 1952, an Indian solicitor, acting on behalf of the defendants, proposed arbitration.

In December, 1952, the matter was again referred to an expert by the Norwegian Government, who reported in May, 1953; and, in July, 1953, the Indian solicitor, on behalf of the defendants, again offered arbitration. That was refused on Nov. 17, 1953, by the Norwegian Government; and time has elapsed again, with some moves of a desultory kind going on in India.

Almost exactly a year later, in November, 1954, the defendants said that they would pursue their legal remedy, but again nothing happened, until Mar. 29, 1955, when the Norwegian Government wrote a letter to Messrs. Constant & Constant, in the following terms. After reference to some discussions, they said:

> . . . we beg to inform you that unless you are able—within the end of April this year—to release to us the deposit which was made on Sept. 12th 1946 in joint names with Hambro's Bank Ltd. we shall be forced to institute an action against you in order to have the account closed.

That action was in due course started by the issue of a writ on Oct. 10, 1955, and has proceeded at a speed which seems typical in this action, and has been brought to trial on certain preliminary issues yesterday, Dec. 12, 1960.

With that brief outline of the facts, I must now turn to the pleadings, because the issues which I have to decide arise out of various matters alleged in the pleadings. The points of claim set out the circumstances in which the deposit was made on Sept. 12, 1946, and the plaintiffs put their case in the first instance in this way, set out in pars. 5 and 7 of the points of claim: **[440]**

> 5. It was an implied term and/or condition of the agreement aforesaid [—that is the agreement under which the £9400 was deposited—] that, if the Mission should thereafter dispute its liability to pay to the Calcutta company the amount claimed by the said company as the balance of the alleged cost of the said repairs and if the Calcutta company did not within a reasonable time thereafter institute proceedings to recover such balance as was claimed, the Plaintiff Government or altenatively the Mission should be entitled to the release to it of the amount of the said deposit together with any interest accrued thereon. Such implication arises as a matter of law and/or from the fact that the said deposit was to be established by way of security in favour of the Calcutta company in respect of any legal liability of the Plaintiff Government and/or of the Mission for the balance of the alleged cost of the said repairs as claimed by the Calcutta company.

Then, in par. 7:

> The Calcutta company has failed within a reasonable time or at all to institute proceedings to recover such balance as was claimed by it and in the premises the Plaintiff Government or alternatively the Mission is entitled to release to it of the amount of the said deposit (namely £9,400) together with interest accrued thereon.

So the claim is first put on an implied term of the contract.

The claim is put in an alternative way on frustration. That appears in par. 8, and is pleaded as follows:

> Further or alternatively the Plaintiff Government or alternatively the Mission is entitled to release to it of the amount of the said deposit (namely £9,400) together with interest accrued thereon by reason of the frustration and discharge of the said agreement pursuant whereto the said deposit was established. The purpose of the said agreement was to provide security in favour of the Calcutta company in respect of the legal liability of the Plaintiff Government and/or of the Mission for the balance of the cost of the said repairs as claimed

by the Calcutta company or for any part of such balance. Any claim now prosecuted in this Honourable Court or in the Courts of Norway by the Calcutta company to recover the balance aforesaid could and would be met and defeated by a plea that by the law of each such jurisdiction such claim has become and is barred by effluxion of time. In the premises the Plaintiff Government and/or the Mission has ceased to be and is under no legal liability for the balance aforesaid or any part thereof and the purpose of the said agreement has accordingly become and is frustrated and destroyed.

The third manner in which it is put in the points of claim in par. 9 is a resulting trust, pleaded as follows:

> Further or alternatively if by virtue of the agreement aforesaid there was (as alleged by the Calcutta company) created a trust in respect of the sum deposited pursuant to the said agreement the said trust was constituted in contemplation that agreement would thereafter be reached respecting the further amount (if any) payable to the Calcutta company or that, in default of such agreement, the Calcutta company would institute proceedings to establish liability in the Plaintiff Government. No such agreement was ever reached and the Calcutta company has not instituted such proceedings as aforesaid within such time as would have enabled the purpose of the trust to be fulfilled. In the premises the trust has become inoperative and the Plaintiff Government or alternatively the Mission is entitled to release to it of the trust fund.

The defence, to which I must now turn, takes two points. In par. 7, after setting out the circumstances of the deposit, it is pleaded as follows:

> . . . It was an express or alternatively an implied term of the said Agreement that the Mission and the first Defendants acting as aforesaid would hold the said sum of £9,400 in trust for the Plaintiffs and these Defendants until such time as the precise extent of the legal liability of the Plaintiffs to these Defendants in excess of £18,000 less the sterling equivalent of Rs.54,234.4.9 was agreed or determined and would thereafter pay the amount of such excess to the Plaintiffs or to these Defendants or partly to the Plaintiffs and partly to these Defendants in accordance with such agreement or determination. No agreement on or determination of such liability has yet been reached or made.

I should perhaps say, in parenthesis, that the reference to 54,234.4.9 rs. is a reference to some out-of-pocket expenses **[441]** in respect of bills which the defendants had paid. In so far as it is suggested that it should be taken into account in the manner suggested in the defence, I disagree. I have already expressed my view that it is in excess of £18,000 and nothing else.

The second way in which it is put in the defence is in par. 8, where the defendants, in turn, rely upon an implied term, where they say:

> . . . Further or alternatively it was express or alternatively an implied term of the said Agreement that in the event of it becoming necessary for the said liability of the Plaintiffs to be determined the Plaintiffs would submit to the jurisdiction of the Indian Courts or alternatively to arbitration, but the Plaintiffs have refused so to submit. In so far as the said term is implied, it is to be implied from the express terms of the said Agreement and from the facts that the Plaintiffs are a sovereign government, that these Defendants carry on business exclusively in India, that the relevant evidence is most easily assembled in India and that these Defendants by exercising a lien on the vessel could have forced the Plaintiffs to pay their charges or to have instituted proceedings against these Defendants in the Indian Courts to procure the release of the vessel. In the premises if (which is denied) a reasonable time for the institution of proceedings by these Defendants to recover the sums due to them from the Plaintiffs would otherwise have expired, such time has not expired. Alternatively, the Plaintiffs cannot in the premises be heard to rely upon the expiry of such a time.

The defendants also pleaded a counterclaim, in which they repeat pars. 1 to 7 of their points of defence, and allege that there was a price agreed, and allege in the alternative that they are entitled to be paid a reasonable price. By par. 14 they say that they are entitled to the sum they allege was agreed, and plead that, alternatively, it was a reasonable price, and they counterclaim for a declaration that the plaintiffs are liable to the defendants in a specified sum, and that the defendants are entitled to release to them of that sum of the moneys held on joint account by the plaintiffs and Messrs. Constant & Constant, and they ask for a consequential order for payment.

An order was made, by agreement between the parties, on Dec. 5, 1960, that the hearing should be limited to three issues:

(a) Whether the Plaintiffs are entitled to release to them of the deposit on the grounds claimed by them;

(b) If the answer to (a) is "No", whether the Defendants' Counterclaim is time-barred;

(c) If the answer to (b) is "No", the determination of the amount (if any) recoverable by the Defendants shall stand over.

Since some of the argument turns upon Indian law, there was an agreement between the parties as to the facts relating to Indian and other foreign law. That agreement was in these terms:

(1) That no proceedings for recovery of the balance claimed by the Calcutta company could at any material time have been instituted by the Calcutta company against the Plaintiff Government or the Mission in the Indian Courts unless the Plaintiff Government had submitted to the jurisdiction of such Courts.

(2) That any proceedings instituted subsequent to the date of issue of the writ herein by the Calcutta company for recovery of the said balance in the Norwegian Courts could be defeated by a plea that the claim has become and is barred under Norwegian law by effluxion of time.

There was also a provision that the parties should be at liberty to refer to certain provisions of the Indian code.

I have already held what the terms of the oral agreement were, namely, that the sum of £9400 should be held in joint names until the legal liability of the Norwegian Government to the defendants in excess of £18,000 already paid was agreed or determined, and that, upon such agreement or determination, the amount of such excess (if any) to be paid out to the defendants and the balance (if any) to be paid to the Norwegian Government.

I find, on the evidence before me, that the Norwegian Government's liability has not been agreed or determined. *Prima facie*, therefore, on the terms of the agreement as I have found it, they are not entitled to the release of the deposit. Mr. Eckersley has argued that the Norwegian Government has ceased to be under any legal liability to the defendants **[442]** because, if proceedings were brought on the original cause of action in respect of work and labour done in these Courts, the claim would be time-barred. I think he also relies upon the fact that it would be time-barred in the Norwegian Courts as well; but he relies, primarily, upon the English rule as to the limitation of action, and his contention is that when the limitation period has expired, the right is extinguished, and that to-day, more than six years having passed since the disputed debt was incurred, there is no longer any liability on the part of the plaintiffs.

It seems to me to be clear law that the expiry of the limitation period bars the remedy by action and does not extinguish the right. As Lord Justice Cotton said in *Curwen* v. *Milburn*, (1889) 42 Ch.D. 424, at p. 434:

> . . . Statute-barred debts are due, though payment of them cannot be enforced by action. . . .

It seems to me, with the greatest respect to Mr. Eckersley, to be elementary law that the expiry of the limitation period in English law bars the remedy, but does not extinguish the right.

Mr. Eckersley has relied upon an old decision of Mr. Justice Cave, sitting at

Nisi Prius, in 1884, the case of *In re Hepburn, Ex parte Snaith*, (1884) 14 Q.B.D. 394. The passage on which he relies is at p. 399, where Mr. Justice Cave says:

> . . . It is said that the statute bars the remedy but not the right, and consequently that the executors still remain indebed to the joint creditors although the latter cannot enforce their right by action. This, although not an uncommon, is in my judgment an incorrect, way of stating the effect of the Statute of Limitations. There is in law no right without a remedy; and, if all remedies for enforcing a right are gone, the right has in point of law ceased to exist. In the case of a debt the ordinary and universal remedy is by action against the debtor. . . .

Then he goes on (*ibid.*, at p. 400):

> . . . When the debt is barred by the statute and the creditor has no lien, the debt is gone for all purposes. . . .

The particular decision in that case was one arising under the bankruptcy law. If and in so far as Mr. Justice Cave was intending his words to be of wider application in saying that the Statute of Limitations extinguishes the debt or the right and not merely the remedy, it seems to me that is contrary to all authority, and, with the greatest respect, I would not follow it.

I hold, therefore, that the legal liability of the plaintiffs to the defendants in respect of the repairs still continues to exist notwithstanding that under English law the remedy by action would be barred by Sect. 2 (1) of the Limitation Act, 1939.

It seems to me, therefore, that, in order to succeed, the plaintiffs have got to rely upon an implied term, and the implied term on which they seek to rely is that if the defendants did not within a reasonable time thereafter institute proceedings to recover such balance, the plaintiff Government would be entitled to release of the deposit.

As I have held, there was no agreement between the parties as to the method in which the liability of the plaintiffs to the defendants was to be ascertained if they failed to agree upon the bill. There are various possible methods of determination in such an event. In the first place, there would be arbitration, which would seem a common-sense way to decide what is entirely a technical quality dispute. But arbitration would require agreement between the parties, and there is no way of one party forcing the other to agree to arbitration. No doubt the Norwegian Government would have preferred arbitration in Norway than in India, and the defendants not unnaturally would have preferred it in India.

The second way of determination would be by litigation in a Court of competent jurisdiction. Either party could initiate litigation without the consent of the other party, but, owing to the fact that the plaintiffs are a sovereign government, the defendants could initiate litigation only in Norway, because, outside Norway, submission to the jurisdiction of the Court on the part of the plaintiffs would be required, and the defendants were not in a position to enforce that. The plaintiffs, on the other hand, could have initiated litigation in England (as they have in fact done), or possibly—the matter has not been discussed before me—in India. *Prima facie*, one would suppose that they could, because the defendants are resident in India. I assume that they could not have initiated litigation in Norway, because presuming **[443]** that Norwegian law is the same as English law, there would not be jurisdiction to serve a writ out of the jurisdiction in this case, the matter of the contract being an English contract and the events having occurred in India.

I can see no grounds for implying a term that the defendants must take the initiative in starting proceedings to determine where the rights in this fund lay, and indeed it is apparent from some of the correspondence which I have read that the legal adviser to the Norwegian Government was proposing at one stage to initiate proceedings on behalf of the Government. Why should there be an implication that it must be the defendants who initiate proceedings to determine who is entitled to the fund? Both the parties were out of their money; both had an equal inducement to get the matter determined; and, accordingly, I can see no reason for implying that the deposit should be paid to the Norwegian Government if the defendants did not take steps to recover such balance as was claimed.

It follows, therefore, that the remedy was at all times in the Norwegian Government's hands. It could have started proceedings when it liked. In those circumstances, Mr. Eckersley fails in persuading me that an implied term such as he pleads is a necessary implication from the agreement and the circumstances in which it was made. Equally, Mr. Donaldson fails to persuade me that the implied term which he has pleaded in par. 8 of the defence is a necessary implication in the agreement, but he does not need it. Liability of the Norwegian Government to the defendants in excess of the £18,000 has not yet been agreed or determined, and therefore, in my view, the Government cannot recover the deposit.

I accordingly answer the first question put to me as "No".

Having answered question (a) "No", it becomes necessary to answer question (b), namely, whether the defendants' counterclaim is time-barred. That really follows from the answer which I have already given to question (a). I have set out what I hold the agreement to have been. The counterclaim is based, in my view, and so pleaded, not upon the original liability of the plaintiffs to the defendants (if any) for the balance of the bills, but upon the terms of the agreement reached on Sept. 12, 1946. By that agreement Messrs. Constant & Constant and the Mission became trustees of the fund, and they held it upon trust for whichever of the parties, the plaintiffs or the defendants, should be entitled to it upon the agreement or determination of the liability of the plaintiffs to the defendants in respect of the bills for the work which had already been done.

Mr. Eckersley seems to get nervous at the idea of such a Chancery notion as a trust being mentioned in the Commercial Court, but, whenever money is paid to a stakeholder, where the legal ownership is in the stakeholder and the beneficial ownership in someone else, the stakeholder holds the money as trustee, and, at the present moment, those who hold the fund—and the parties have agreed that no technical point is being taken about the disappearance of Messrs. Constant & Constant as trustees—hold it upon trust for whichever of the parties may turn out to be entitled to it when the liability has been determined.

The first answer to the plea of the Statute of Limitations in regard to the defendants' counterclaim is that the right to the trust moneys has not yet arisen, because the liability of the plaintiffs to the defendants and, therefore, the amount of the fund to which the defendants are entitled has not yet been ascertained. Time therefore has not started to run. In any event, even if that had been determined, it would have been prevented from running by Sect. 19 (1) (b) of the Limitation Act 1939, which provides:

> (1) No period of limitation prescribed by this Act shall apply to an action by a beneficiary under a trust, being an action—
> (b) to recover from the trustee trust property or the proceeds thereof in the possession of the trustee . . .

The claim in this case is a claim against trustees for the recovery of trust property. It is a necessary condition precedent to the right of the defendants to any moneys out of the trust fund that the liability of the plaintiffs to them should be determined. In this action, they are claiming a determination of that amount. When that has been determined, they will be entitled to payment out of the excess (if any)—and I know not whether there will be any excess or not—of the plaintiffs' liability to them over the £18,000 already **[444]** paid. I hold, therefore, that the defendants' counterclaim, based, as it is, upon the agreement of Sept. 12, 1946, is not time-barred.

Questions of *quantum* and the determination of the amount (if any) recoverable by the defendants must stand over, and, while I have throughout this case talked about the balance owing by the plaintiffs to the defendants, I did that as a matter of convenience, and in every case the words "if any" in brackets should be regarded as being inserted in my judgment. I do not know, and no one has sought to discuss before me, whether there is any balance due to the defendants or not.

iv

Recognition of Act of Foreign State

THE STATE (AT THE PROSECUTION OF THOMAS WILLIAM HULLY) v. SUPERINTENDENT JAMES FRANCIS HYNES, GARDA SIOCHANA AND IN THE MATTER OF THE COURTS OF JUSTICE ACTS, 1924 TO 1936, AND IN THE MATTER OF THE CONSTITUTION.

([1961] 100 I. L.T. 145)

1961: Republic of Ireland: High Court: Davitt P., Haugh, Teevan JJ.

October 30, 31, November 1, 2, 3, 8, 9, 10, December 12, 14, 1961: Republic of Ireland, Supreme Court: Maguire C.J., Lavery, Kingsmill Moore, O'Daly, McLoughlin JJ.

Habeas corpus—*Arrest—English citizen resident in Eire—Charges of offences in England contrary to the Forgery Act,* 1913, *s.* 4, *sub-s.* (1)—*Whether charges of forgery a cloak for charges of revenue offences—English warrant endorsed for execution in Eire by the Deputy Commissioner of the Garda Siochana—Warrant endorsed for execution in the countries of Dublin and Wicklow—Arrest under warrant—Validity of endorsements and backing of warrant—Retirement from the Garda Siochana of Garda who endorsed warrant—Whether warrant bad on its face—Retirement of Garda Officer to whom conditional order of* habeas corpus *directed—Whether prosecutor detained in accordance with law—Petty Sessions* (*Ireland*) *Act,* 1851, *ss.* 11, 25, 26, 27, 28, 29, 30, 31 *and* 32—*Constitution,* 1937, *Articles* 1, 5, 6, 29, 40, 50, 73.

The prosecutor, an English citizen resident in this country since 1956, *was arrested at Shankill, County Dublin, on the* 12*th May,* 1959, *by Detective Sergeant Joseph Kelly on the instructions of his superior officer, Superintendent Hynes, the respondent. The prosecutor was conveyed to Bray Garda Station where he was detained until released on bail under order of the High Court, following a conditional order of* habeas corpus.

The arrest was made on the authority of a warrant dated 10*th April,* 1959, *over the hand of a Justice of the Peace for the City of Lancaster in England, on a charge of forgery.*

The warrant was issued on the information of James Rankin, an Inland Revenue Officer, who alleged that Hully did, between the 1*st July,* 1946, *and the* 7*th November,* 1947, *at* 56 *Penny Street, Lancaster, with intent to defraud certain partners of his, forge an hotel record book, purporting to be a true record of partnership monies paid and received by the partnership, trading as the Lion Hotel, Machynlleth, contrary to section* 4 *sub-section* (1) *of the Forgery Act,* 1913. *The warrant commanded that the prosecutor be brought before the Magistrate's Court sitting at Lancaster forthwith to answer to the said information. Deputy Commissioner Garrett Brennan endorsed the warrant for execution in the Counties of Dublin and Wicklow.*

The prosecutor obtained a conditional order of habeas corpus ad subjiciendum *directed to Superintendent Hynes.*

On the hearing of his application to make absolute notwithstanding cause shown the conditional order of habeas corpus *it was* Held *by the High Court* (*Davitt P., Haugh and Teevan JJ.*), *allowing the cause shown;*

1. *That the prosecutor was in lawful custody on the construction of the relevant*

sections of the Petty Sessions (Ireland) Act, 1851.
2. *That the warrant was validly addressed for execution in the County of Wicklow, and that it could be validly executed in such county.*
3. *That there was sufficient evidence of a valid warrant and that the prosecutor was validly in custody under the provisions of the Petty Sessions (Ireland) Act,* 1851.

On appeal by the prosecutor to the Supreme Court it was
HELD *by the Supreme Court, overruling the High Court and making absolute the conditional order of* habeas corpus:—

1. *That the prosecutor was not being detained in accordance with law.*
2. *That the Courts will not enforce or aid in the enforcement of political or fiscal offences against the law of another State.*
3. *That the conditional order should be made absolute on the grounds that Superintendent Hynes, the person showing cause to justify the detention of the applicant, had now retired from office.*
4. *That the Deputy Commissioner who had backed the warrant had now retired from office and the warrant was bad in its face and in its execution.* **[146]**

HABEAS CORPUS

This was a Motion on Notice to make absolute nothwithstanding cause shown a conditional order dated the 12th day of May, 1959, for the issue of an order of *habeas corpus* directed to Superintendent Hynes.

The conditional order was obtained on the affidavit of the prosecutor, in which having stated that he was then residing at Shankill, Co. Dublin, he set out the facts prior to his arrest. He averred that he had been living in Ireland since 1956, that he had been in partnership in the hotel business in Wales with his sister and brother-in-law, Mr. and Mrs. Moore for some years, which hotel business was subsequently sold at a profit. That the charge of forgery against him on the warrant was unfounded, and that it was only a device to make him amenable to some Revenue charge, on his being returned to England. He admitted to falsifying the books of the hotel business in order to evade income tax but that this was done with the consent of his partners, but denied that he had defrauded his partners in business. He further averred that the affairs of the partnership had been investigated by the Revenue Commissioners, all necessary adjustments made and the proper income tax paid. He admitted to owing the Revenue authorities some £5,000 for income tax, but not connected with the partnership business.

A further affidavit was sworn by Mr. and Mrs. Moore, the prosecutor's former partners, was filed confirming the averments of the prosecutor, that no monies were owed to them on the partnership agreement, and that all outstanding and necessary adjustments had been made with the Revenue authorities.

Cause was shown against making absolute the conditional order.

Richard McGonigal, S.C., Desmond Bell, S.C., and *William Hamill* for the prosecutor.

Brian Walsh, S.C., and *Rchard Cooke* for the respondents.

Cur. adv. vult.

DAVITT P.

The facts of this matter appear to be as follows. The prosecutor, Thomas William Hully, we are informed by his counsel, is by profession a stockbroker and accountant who has been resident in this country since 1956. In 1943 he was resident in England; and, together with a cousin Robert Moore and his wife Gladys Moore, he purchased premises known as the Lion Hotel, Machynlleth, Wales. It was a joint purchase, the necessary money being obtained from a bank on their joint guarantee. Mr. and Mrs. Moore lived in, and managed the hotel and kept the books; sending periodic statements to the prosecutor at his office in Lancaster, where all accounts were paid as they became due. All three proprietors concurred in falsifying the hotel accounts by assigning a reduced value to the stock and inflating creditors' accounts. The hotel was sold in 1947 at a profit of approximately £6,000 which was divided equally.

In 1956 Mr. James Rankin who, it appears, is an officer of the Inland Revenue Inquiry Branch at Manchester, interviewed and interrogated Mr. and Mrs. Moore. He told them that his investigation had revealed discrepancies in the books of the partnership, and that there was a certain amount of tax owing. He suggested that the prosecutor had defrauded them, which they strenuously denied. He demanded payment of a certain sum which included tax and penalties. This, he said, they would have to pay in full, including the prosecutor's share, which they could afterwards recover from him. The full amount was paid in December, 1958; and thereafter they had no further communication from the Inquiry Branch, and regarded the matter as closed.

Questions arose as to the prosecutor's tax liability in respect of income apart from that derived from the partnership; and he executed a power of attorney appointing his wife to deal with the matter. Her solicitors were Messrs. Gorna and Co., of Manchester; and correspondence took place, in November, 1958, and March and April, 1959, between them and Mr. Rankn with a view to having the prosecutor's tax affairs discussed at a meeting to be arranged. Messrs. Gorna suggested April 6th as a suitable date. On April 3rd Mr. Rankin wrote Messrs. Gorna saying that the offices of the Inquiry Branch were in process of being moved, and that April 6th would not be a convenient date. He said he would get in touch with them later.

On April 10th, 1959, Mr. Rankin appears to have sworn an information before Mr. James Pye, one of the Justices of the Peace for the City of Lancaster, alleging that the [**147**] prosecutor Thomas William Hully, with intent to defraud certain partners of his, forged a certain book purporting to be a true record of partnership monies paid and received by the partnership trading as the Lion Hotel, Machynlleth. On the strength of such information, it appears, Mr. Pye issued a warrant for the arrest of Mr. Hully. The warrant was directed to each and all of the Constables of the City of Lancaster. It was transmitted to Deputy Commissioner Garret Brennan of the Garda Siochana together with what appears to be the affidavit of Arthur Thompson Chief Superintendent of the County Police Office, Skerton, Lancashire, verifying the signature on the warrant as being that of "James Pye one of Her Majesty's Justices of the Peace for the City of Lancaster". Deputy Commissioner Brennan endorsed the warrant as follows: —

"Proof upon oath having this day been produced before me that the signature 'James Pye' to this warrant is in the handwriting of the Justice of the Peace within mentioned, I hereby endorse this warrant for execution in the Counties of Dublin and Wicklow.

Garrett Brennan,
Deputy Commissioner of the
Garda Siochana.

"This 8th day of May, 1959.

"To: The Superintendent,
Garda Siochana,
Bray, Co. Wicklow."

The warrant so endorsed, together with the Affidavit was transmitted to Superintendent James Francis Hynes at Bray, to whom it was addressed. He in turn endorsed it: "To Detective Sergeant Kelly and his assistant for legal execution" and signed the endorsement, dating it the 11th May, 1959. The warrant was that same day issued for execution to Detective Sergeant Joseph Kelly who, with three other Gardai, took the prosecutor into custody the same day at his residence at Shankill, Co. Dublin, and brought him to the Garda Station at Bray. On the following day the prosecutor obtained from this Court a conditional Order of Habeas Corpus. On May 14th he was by further Order of this Court admitted to bail. Affidavits shewing cause having been filed on behalf of the respondent,

Superintendent Hynes, Counsel for the prosecutor now move to have the cause shewn disallowed and the conditional Order made absolute.

The practice of backing British Warrants for execution here is a survival from the regime which existed before 1922. As far as this case is concerned it depends for legality upon the relevant sections of the Petty Sessions Act, 1851. The sections dealing with the issue and execution of warrants are sections 11, 25, 26, 27, 28, 29, 30, 31 and 32. In reviewing these sections I shall for convenience deal with them as they read without making the necessary adaptations. Section 11 provides that, where an information has been made in writing and an oath complaining that a person has committed an indictable offence, a Justice may issue a warrant to arrest and bring such person before him to answer the complaint made in the information. The warrant, under the provisions of section 25, must be addressed to the District Inspector or Head Constable of the Constabulary who acts for the place where the petty sessions Court is held for the district in which the warrant issued. Section 26 provides that if the alleged offender is found in such place the warrant can be executed by either of these officers or by any other Head Constable or Constable whom either shall appoint. If the alleged offender is not to be found in such place, but is to be found elsewhere in the same County, the District Inspector or Head Constable can certify on the warrant the place where he believes the offender can be found, and also his belief that the signature on the warrant is genuine. He can then transmit it for execution to the District Inspector or Head Constable of the place where he believes the offender can be found; whereupon those last mentioned officers can execute the warrant, provided they find the offender, in the same way as if it had originally been addressed to them. Where it appears that the accused is not to be found in the County the District Inspector or Head Constable certifies accordingly as before, and transmits the warrant to the Inspector General of the Constabulary. When the Inspector General receives the warrant the following procedure is provided by section 27: (1) Where it appears that the alleged offender is in Ireland in any place outside the Dublin Metropolitan Police District the Inspector General or either of the Deputy Inspectors General, may endorse the warrant according to the form prescribed, and transmit it to the District Inspector for the place where it is believed the offender can be found, and he can then execute it as if it had been addressed to him in the first instance; (2) If it appears that the offender is to be found in the Dublin Metropolitan Police District the warrant can be endorsed and **[148]** transmitted to the Commissioners of the Dublin Metropolitan Police for execution by them; (3) Where it appears that the offender is to be found in England, Scotland, Man, or the Channel Islands the warrant may be endorsed accordingly as prescribed. Thereupon any Justice or officer having power to issue any warrant or process in the nature of a warrant, for the arrest of offenders in any of the said places, upon proof on oath of the handwriting either of the officer endorsing the warrant, or of the Justice who issued it, can himself endorse the same as prescribed authorising its execution within his jurisdiction by the person bringing the same, or by any constable or other peace officer of the County or place where it shall be so endorsed. Section 28 deals with warrants addressed to persons other than members of the Constabulary. Section 28 reads as follows: "Whenever any person against whom any warrant shall be issued by any Justice or such other officer as aforesaid in England or Scotland, or in the Isles of Man, Guernsey, Jersey, Alderney or Sark, for any crime or offence shall reside or be, or be suspected to reside or be, in any place in Ireland, it shall be lawful for the said Inspector General or for either of the said Deputy Inspector General, or for any Justice of the said last mentioned place, to indorse the same in like manner and upon like proof as aforesaid, authorising execution of the same within his jurisdiction." I understand this to mean that when any Justice having power to issue warrants for the apprehension of offenders in any of the places mentioned issues one for the arrest of an alleged offender, it can be transmitted to the Inspector General and can be backed by him or either of his deputies for execution anywhere in Ireland outside the Dublin Metropolitan Police District. Alternatively, it can be transmitted to a Justice of the Peace who can back it for execution in his district. Section 30 deals with Judges' warrants. Section 31 provides:

"Whenever any warrant addressed either to the Constabulary or to any other person, shall be so indorsed by the said Inspector General, or by either of the said Deputy Inspectors General, or by any Justice or other such officer as aforesaid; it shall be a sufficient authority to the person bringing such warrant, and also to all constables or peace officers of the County or place where such warrant shall be so indorsed, to execute the same by arrest, committal or levy, as the case may be, within the jurisdiction of the said Justice or officer, and in case of a warrant to arrest any person to convey him when arrested, before the Justice or officer by whom the same was issued, or before some other Justice or officer, of the same County or place, to be dealt with according to law." Then follows a proviso which I will deal with later.

This is not a particularly clear enactment. Accepting for the moment the submission, made on behalf of the prosecutor, that by "the person bringing the warrant" is meant one of the public officers named in the warrant bringing it here to be backed, a strictly literal interpretation would mean that, except where the warrant is backed here by a Justice, such "foreign" officer is the only person who can execute it. The only other persons named in the section as having power to execute, are "the constables and Peace officers of the County or place where such warrant shall be so endorsed". This provision appears clearly to have reference only to the case where the warrant is backed here by a Justice. If it could be construed as having reference to the case where the warrant is backed only by the Inspector General or one of his deputies, it seems to me that a near absurdity would result. Normally he would endorse the warrant in his office which is in Dublin Castle. But the Castle was always in the Dublin Metropolitan Police District, and he had no authority over the Dublin Metropolitan Police. He had, as is clear from s. 27, no power to direct its execution by them. They would, however, be the only constables or peace officers of the county (i.e. the County of the City of Dublin) or the place where the warrant is endorsed. The result would still be that the only person who could execute the warrant would be the "foreign" officer, who would normally be a complete stranger to the country. The whole idea of backing British warrants is, it seems to me, to enable them to be executed by the police here. I hardly think that the purpose of s. 31 is to provide that the only person who can execute the warrant is the officer who brings it over here.

I take the view that when sections 29 and 31 are read together they show that the Inspector General had power to endorse the warrant for execution anywhere within his jurisdiction, that is, anywhere the Royal Irish Constabulary could act. In the normal course he would endorse it for execution by the County or District Inspector acting for the place where the offender was suspected to be. The "person bringing the warrant" is not, in my opinion, a "foreign" police officer who brings it here to be backed, but the officer of the police here to whom, after backing, it is eventually entrusted for execution. **[149]**

It was submitted, however, that when that officer had arrested the offender in execution of the warrant he must himself convey him before the Justice who had issued it; and that he had no power to hand him over to anyone else. The section does not say that the warrant is to be sufficient authority to the person bringing it, to execute it and bring the offender before the Justice who issued it. This is an enabling provision and cannot be read, in my opinion, so as to take away the power of the constables originally named in the warrant to execute it by receiving custody of the alleged offender from the officers who arrested him here. I think that the clear meaning of the relevant sections is that the officers who make the arrest here can hand over custody of the offender to any of the persons to whom the warrant was originally addressed. The warrant would be handed over at the same time, and the officer receiving it would then become the "person bringing the warrant", i.e. carrying the warrant at the time the person named is taken into custody.

The prosecutor in this case says in his affidavit that on the morning of his arrest one of the Gardai telephoned the Bray Garda Station from his residence, and that he heard him ask someone there to telephone the London Police and ask for an escort to come and collect him. In the same paragraph, however, he says that he had been informed by one of the Gardai that he would be detained at Bray Garda Station to await the arrival of an escort from the Lancaster Police. The matter is not dealt with in any of the affidavits showing cause, and will have to he cleared before the application is finally disposed of. The Guards have no authority to hand him over to the London Police.

The next submission made on behalf of the prosecutor was that a warrant could be validly backed under the provisions of section 29 only when certain conditions had been fulfilled; viz. that the person who issued the warrant was a Justice of the Peace; that he had jurisdiction to issue the warrant; and that the offence mentioned in the warrant is a crime or offence according to English law. It was submitted that the fulfilment of these conditions could not be assumed, but must be proved. The argument was on the following lines. Under the old regime this proof may not have been necessary because England and Ireland were a United Kingdom, one political entity, with one common system of law; and judicial notice could be taken of such law. Now all that has been changed; and it is no longer permissible for the Court to take judicial notice of English law. Justices of the Peace no longer exist here. There is a presumption that the law in England is the same as here; and any party who alleges any difference must establish it in evidence. It should be presumed, therefore, until the contrary is proved, that there are no Justices of the Peace in England.

It is, of course, the fact that this country and England were formerly one political entity; and that there was a common system of law. The several places mentioned in section 29 did not, however, all enjoy the same laws. Scots law is, in many respects, different from ours; and the law of the Channel Islands derives from the customs of Normandy and not from the Common law. I doubt very much, moreover, whether the presumption as to the identity of laws can be relied on to the extent claimed in the argument; but, be that as it may, I think that quite independently of the question as to whether I can take judicial notice of English law, I am entitled to take judicial notice of the fact that in England, Justices of the Peace have not ceased to exist, but continue to flourish as a very lively institution. We stand here in a somewhat special relation to English law. Our law libraries regularly contain text-books, legal periodicals, sets of the various reports, and sets of statutes up to date which are solely related to English law. English authorities are constantly cited to us, and we refer to them in our judgments. Among such authorities are to be found very recent cases in which the decisions of Justices of the Peace in England are the subject of review by the Superior Courts. English text-books are constantly used, and sometimes cited. Amongst them is Stones Justices Manual. We are all well aware, not as a matter of knowledge acquired by private reading, but as a matter of unavoidable information acquired by us in carrying out our judicial functions that Justices of the Peace continue to function in England. It would be the height of judicial affectation for me to pretend that I am not well aware of the fact.

It has been contended, however, that we cannot take judicial notice of the fact that a Justice of the Peace has power to issue a warrant for the apprehension of an alleged offender against whom information has been sworn, or that the offence mentioned in the warrant is a criminal offence. This submission must likewise fail, and for the same reason. Under the Courts of Justice Act, 1924, **[150]** sections 77 and 78 (as interpreted in several cases including the *Dowling* (No. 2) *Case* [1937] I.R. 699) a District Justice has all the powers formerly possessed by a Justice of the Peace. Under section 88 a Peace Commissioner has all the powers formerly vested in a Justice of the Peace in respect of the signing of warrants. I must, therefore, take judicial notice of what those powers were. As far as this case is concerned it is sufficient to say that they included the power to issue a warrant for the apprehension of a person against whom a sworn information has been laid alleging that he has committed a criminal offence. Applying the presumption of the identity of laws I must hold that a Justice of the Peace in England has the same power. The offence in respect of which the warrant in question in this case was issued is an offence against section 4 (1) of the Forgery Act, 1913. That enactment is still in force here and I must take judicial notice of it.

In my opinion there is no need in this case to establish in evidence the fulfilment of any of the conditions mentioned in section 29 of the Petty Sessions Act, for the valid backing of a warrant. This conclusion can be supported on grounds other than those I have mentioned. In the Dowling (No. 1) *Case* [1937] I.R. 483 there was question as to the validity of a warrant issued by the Sheriff Substitute of the Sheriff Court of Lanarkshire, which had been backed here under the provisions of section 29. At page 497 Hanna J. said: "I adhere to the view which I expressed in Kennedy's case* as to the presumption that the warrant is good, and this presumption applies equally to warrants to be backed under section 29 as to those under the Fugitive Offenders Act, 1881. If the warrant comes to the authorities in the Saorstat from an official and proper source, the Court and the officials dealing with the warrant, are entitled to presume that it is in order as a warrant when it arrived in this country and in my opinion there is no duty on the Court to enquire whether according to Scottish law, the warrant discloses an offence." In that case it was held that the warrant had not been validly backed; but it is quite clear that if it had been validly backed it would have been held to be effective without proof of the fulfilment of the conditions mentioned in section 29. When an exactly similar warrant was properly backed it was held effective, in the *Dowling* (No. 2) *Case*, already referred to, and apparently without proof of the fulfilment of these conditions.

It was next submitted that the information leading to the warrant in this case was a mere subterfuge adopted to make the prosecutor amenable to the revenue laws in England. The argument was on the following lines. The Courts here will lend no assistance towards enforcing the revenue laws of another state. Consistent with this principle the Garda Authorities will, as a matter of practice, not back for execution here a warrant for the arrest of a person on a charge of defrauding the British revenue. The real purpose of the warrant in this case is to effect the arrest of the prosecutor so that he may be brought to England and made liable either civilly or criminally, or both, for his evasions of his tax liability. It was realised that a warrant which on its face shewed that the prosecutor was wanted for a revenue offence, would not be backed for execution. In those circumstances a misleading information was sworn making a charge of forgery, which could not be substantiated, in order to secure the issue of a warrant which would be backed for execution here.

This submission depends for acceptance upon the question whether this Court can enquire whether there were sufficient grounds for the issue of the warrant. If we have no such power, we have no right to assume that there were not sufficient grounds. If we cannot assume that we cannot accept that the swearing of the information was a subterfuge. If we cannot accept that, we cannot accept the submission. It may be that the information in this case was sworn with an ulterior motive; and yet the information may be well founded. If a person has committed in England an offence against, what I may call, the ordinary criminal law, I can see nothing wrong in his being brought back from this country to be dealt with for that offence, even though it is sought to make him amenable also to the revenue laws. That, however, is by way. We as a State have seen fit to continue in force these enactments as to the backing of warrants. They provide no safeguards whereby the person concerned can ask the Courts here to enquire whether or not there are sufficient grounds for the issue of the warrant. Provided that they do not conflict with the Constitution they are laws to which effect must be given when they are invoked. As Meredith J. said in the *Dowling* (No. 2) *Case* at p. 756; the Courts have no jurisdiction to set up regulatory principles of their own invention. We have, in my opinion, no right to accept this submission. **[151]**

It was next submitted that these enactments as to the backing of warrants were inconsistent with the sovereignty of this State, were therefore repugnant to the Constitution, and were accordingly not continued in force by Article 50 and were invalid. Interwoven with this submission was the suggestion that if the application before the Court were not granted we would in some way be lending assistance to the enforcement of the English revenue laws contrary to the principle applied in the case of *Buchanan* v. *McVey** [1954] I.R. p. 89 and that enactments which permitted this were on that account repugnant to the Constitution and invalid.

I do not agree that if we refuse this application we will in any way be lending assistance to the enforcement of the English revenue laws. Let me, however, for the sake of the argument assume that we would. This could not affect the constitutional validity of the enactments in question. The principle applied in *Buchanan* v. *McVey* is one of ordinary law. It is not comprised in any article of the Constitution. There is nothing in the Constitution, as far as I am aware, which would prevent the legislature from enacting legislation which would permit the Court to entertain suits brought for the purpose of enforcing the revenue claims of foreign States, and thus nullifying as an authority the decision in Buchanan's case. The question whether or not the enactments in question are repugnant to the Constitution has, in any event, been decided by the Supreme Court in *Dowling* (No. 2) *Case* and in *The State* (*Duggan*) v. *Tapley** [1952] I.R. p. 52; and it is not now open to this Court to hold that they are invalid. The point was argued by counsel for the prosecutor mainly for the purpose of keeping open the right to argue it on an appeal being taken from the decision of this Court.

Closely allied to the argument as to the Constitutional validity of the enactments in question was a submission, which I am not quite sure I fully appreciate. As far as I understand it, it was on the following lines. The machinery provided by the enactments for the backing and execution of British warrants in this country was designed to deal with what were, up to the constitutional change of 1922, internal matters. In the circumstances created by the Constitution of 1922 and 1937 the machinery has become obsolete to the extent of being unworkable. This becomes apparent by a consideration of the proviso to section 31 of the Petty Sessions Act, 1851, and of section 33. The proviso to section 31 is as follows:—

> Provided always, that if the prosecutor, or any of the witnesses for the prosecution, in cases of indictable offences, shall then be in the county or place where any person shall have been arrested under any warrant so backed as aforesaid, the constable or other person who shall have arrested such person shall, if so directed by the justice who shall have indorsed the warrant, bring the person so arrested before him or some other justice of the same county or place who may thereupon take the examinations of such prosecutor or witnesses, and proceed in every respect as hereinbefore directed with respect to persons charged before a justice with an indictable crime or offence alleged to have been committed in any other county or place than that in which such person shall have been arrested.

It was contended that this proviso, and indeed the whole of section 31, had reference only to warrants endorsed under the provisions of section 29; and that for instance, their effect under the old regime was: that if a person committed an indictable offence in London and then came over here; and a warrant for his apprehension was issued by a London justice and backed for execution here by one of the Dublin Metropolitan magistrates that he, in the unlikely event of the complainant and all the witnesses for the prosecution being in Dublin, could proceed to take depositions and return the accused for trial. If this contention is correct, the problem arises as to what Court the return for trial would be made. The proper venue would be London; and I entertain considerable doubt that it was ever intended to give an Irish Justice under the old regime power to return an accused for trial before a Court sitting in England. The terms of the proviso give colour to the view that section 31 was not confined in reference only to warrants endorsed under section 29.

We were then referred to section 33, which provides that whenever the person to whom a warrant is "so addressed, transmitted, or endorsed for execution" is unable to find the person against whom the warrant is issued, he is to return the same to the justice who issued it with a certificate of the reasons why the warrant has not been executed.

It was contended that sections 31 and 33 were essential parts of the machinery in question; that they were inoperable in the changed circumstances created by the con-**[152]**-stitutional changes of 1922 and 1937; and that they and the rest of the machinery were therefore not continued in force by the relevant articles of these constitutions. I think that the answer to this contention is that neither the proviso to section 31, nor section 33 is essential to the machinery. The machinery is quite workable without them, and is not obsolete. Solvitur ambulando, or can we say operando; it has been working without apparent difficulty for a period of 37 years and has survived two attempts to challenge its constitutional validity. Lest it should be thought that the point has been overlooked, I must mention that counsel for the respondent referred us to a passage in the judgment of O'Byrne J. in *The State* (*Kennedy*) v. *Little** 65 I.L.T.R. 91; [1931] I.R. p. 59 where he accepts the contention put forward by Lavery J. then at the Bar, that any statute in force in this country on December 6th, 1922, should be considered as continued by Article 73 of the 1922 Constitution, unless it is in principle, inconsistent with that Constitution; and that the circumstance that it might require adaptations or amendments to give it full force and effect in the changed circumstances of the new State, was no proof of such inconsistency. In my opinion, this last submission made on behalf of the prosecutor fails like the others.

Having regard to the decision in the *Dowling* (No. 1) *Case* it is, perhaps, as well to mention that no question was raised as to the right of Deputy Commissioner Brennan to endorse the warrant in this case. The difficulty which arose in that case was overcome by the Petty Sessions (Ireland) Act, 1851, Adaptation Order, 1938. In my opinion the warrant in this case must be considered to be a valid warrant, properly endorsed by Deputy Commissioner Brennan, properly addressed by him to the respondent Superintendent Hynes, and by him properly entrusted for execution to Detective Sergeant Kelly. It has been properly executed by Sergeant Kelly and the other guards. The prosecutor is notionally in custody. That custody is, I am satisfied perfectly legal.

HAUGH J.:—

I agree with the judgment which has just been delivered by the President.

TEEVAN J.:—

Thomas William Hully, the prosecutor (who is an English citizen, resident in this country since 1956), was arrested at Shankill, County Dublin, on the 12th May, 1959, by Detective Sergeant Joseph Kelly on the instructions of his superior officer, Superintendent James Francis Hynes, the respondent. The prosecutor was conveyed thence to Bray Garda Station, where he was detained until released on bail under Order of this Court following a conditional order of *habeas corpus*.

The arrest was made on the authority of a warrant dated the 10th April, 1959, over the hand of a Justice of the Peace for the City of Lancaster in England, on a charge of forgery. The warrant was addressed to each and all constables of that city.

The warrant is expressed as having been issued on the information of James Rankin of 18 Far Ridings, Romiley, in the County of Chester:

> "that Thomas William Hully late of 290, Heysham Road, Morecambe, in the County of Lancaster (hereinafter called the defendant), between the 1st July, 1946, and 7th November, 1947, at Penny Street, Lancaster, in the County aforesaid, with intent to defraud certain partners of his forged a certain book purporting to be a true record of partnership monies paid and received by the partnership trading as the Lion Hotel, Machynlleth, contrary to section 4, subsection (1) of the Forgery Act, 1913." The addressee was commanded: "to bring the defendant before the Magistrates' Court sitting at the Town Hall, Lancaster, forthwith to answer to the said information."

Deputy Commissioner Garret Brennan endorsed the back of this warrant in the following terms:—

"Proof upon oath having on this day been produced before me that the signature 'James Pye' to this warrant is in the handwriting of the Justice of the Peace within mentioned. I hereby endorse this warrant for execution in the Counties of Dublin and Wicklow.

"To: The Superintendent,
Garda Siochana,
Bray, Co. Wicklow."

The proof referred to was the Affidavit of Arthur Thompson, Chief Superintendent of County Police Office, Skerton, Lancaster, verifying the signature of the Justice of the Peace who signed the warrant, as being that Justice's own handwriting.

On the 12th May, 1959, the prosecutor **[153]** obtained from this Court, a conditional Order of *habeas corpus* and shortly afterwards was released on bail. Cause has been shown and the prosecutor now moves to disallow the cause and to have the order made absolute.

The authority for the backing for execution in this State of English warrants is claimed in virtue of section 29 of the Petty Sessions (Ireland) Act, 1851 (14 & 15 Vict. c. 93) which states: "Whenever any person against whom any warrant shall be issued by any justice or other such officer as aforesaid in England or Scotland, or the Isles of Man, Guernsey, Jersey, Alderney or Sark, for any crime or offence shall reside or be, or be suspected to reside or be, in any place in Ireland, it shall be lawful for the said inspector general (of constabulary) or for either of the said deputy inspectors-general or for any justice of the said last mentioned place, to indorse the same in like manner and upon like proof as aforesaid, authorising the execution of the same within his jurisdiction."

According to an uncontradicted averment in the affidavit of the prosecutor he was told after his arrest that it was intended to convey him to Bray Garda Station, there to await the arrival from England of a police escort that would conduct him to Lancaster. The prosecutor was in fact conveyed to the Garda Station at Bray, County Wicklow, and was detained there when he obtained his conditional order of *habeas corpus*.

I do not think it is of much, if any, importance whether the custody by the Irish Police would have ended at Bray, or in accordance with, what we have been told, is the usual practice in this country, at, or near the place of embarkation for England where the English police custody would commence. For what importance may be thought to attach to such a matter, it has not been proved, nor do I accept, that the transfer would have been effected in Bray, or otherwise than in accordance with the established practice in such cases. (It is notorious that English warrants for arrest have been executed here, and Irish warrants in England, repeatedly before and since political separation of the countries and the re-establishment of a separate state here.)

The prosecutor avers that the charge laid against him is unfounded and contends that it is a device to get him into England for the purpose of making him amenable to some revenue charge or liability. He denies on affidavit that he defrauded his former partners in the enterprise mentioned in the charge. His former partners have filed an affidavit in support of the prosecutor and they likewise deny the charge, and any intention on his part to defraud them.

The prosecutor confesses to deliberate falsifying of the books of the business but says the object was the evasion of income tax by concealing the true trading position, not from his associates, but from the (English) revenue authorities: the forgery, if forgery it was, and fraud, as fraud it undoubtedly was, were, it is contended, for the purpose of defrauding those authorities and no-one else.

The affidavits show that the affairs of the partnership have been investigated by the Revenue Commissioners, the necessary adjustments made and the proper income tax paid by the prosecutor's partners. He, however, says that he still owes the English Revenue Commissioners some £5,000 for income tax but the true inference from the affidavits seems to be that this is not connected with the partnership business concerned in the charge laid. It was conceded by prosecutor's counsel that this liability relates to some other source.

It further appears from the affidavits that the informant of the charge, James Rankin, is the Inland Revenue Officer of the Special Investigations Branch who investigated the tax evasion, which appears to have come to light on the sale of the partnership business. This is not contradicted by the respondent—who, it should be said at once, submits that he is not concerned with such matters, or with the substance, truth or merits of the charge: in justifying the backing of the warrant and its execution he, it is submitted on his behalf, is concerned with the apparent validity of the warrant and the statutory proofs, matters which need not yet be considered in detail.

The grounds and submissions urged by Mr. McGonigal for rejection of the cause shown, may be summarised in the following main classification:—

1. (a) That the power of arrest under an English warrant, backed here in virtue of section 29 of the Petty Sessions (Ireland) Act, is that conferred by section 31 of the same Act; and the latter section is confined to warrants so backed.
(b) The very terms of section 31, he contends, reveal an anomaly which now ren[**154**]ders this machinery unworkable, or impracticable, in the altered political relationship between the two countries since the re-separation of states. The argument here overlaps that addressed to the constitutional objection to both the said sections of the Act.
(c) That, allowing the constitutionality and consequent survival and validity of the Act, the arrest and detention cannot be said to have been for any of the purposes of section 31 and was therefore illegal. Section 31 only permits arrest (after backing) in this country by the officer to whom the warrant was initially directed (without Irish police intervention) and the conveyance of the arrested person by the former to the magistrates of the place of issue; or arrest by the Irish police, who must retain the custody and themselves effect the transfer to the place of issue; or an arrest within and for purposes of the proviso to section 31. There is no justification, or provision in the latter section for, as intended here, an arrest by the Garda Siochana, detention by them until the arrival of English police and surrender to the latter, in Ireland, of the prisoner.
(In fact the arrest was made on the 12th May, 1959, and the prosecutor was told he would be held until the arrival of police from England, who might arrive "to-day or to-morrow". He was two days in custody before being released on bail by order of this Court.)
2. That, particularly since the separation of powers and jurisdictions as between England and this country, proof should be required that the person signing the warrant had authority to do so and that the charge was one legally preferable in England. Here the proof stops short as proving the signature of the Lancaster Justice of the Peace who signed the warrant: there is no proof of his authority; or that the office of Justice of the Peace subsists and continues invested with the power of issuing warrants, which it formerly carried.
3. That the true and only purpose of the warrant was to bring the prosecutor within the jurisdiction in England to answer revenue proceedings; that it is a principle of international recognition (and followed in England and Ireland) that one state will not enforce, or aid the enforcement, of the revenue laws of another—particularly, that the Court having been invoked, should not assist the surrender of a person to answer the revenue demands of the other state and should disregard the ostensible purpose of the warrant in favour of what the prosecutor in his affidavits sets up as the real object.
4. That in so far as the backing of the warrant is discretionary (and its being mandatory, if such be the case, lends force to the argument against its constitutionality):
(a) the discretion cannot be said to have been properly exercised by reason of the dishonest suppression of the true purpose.
(b) The Court having been advised by Counsel for the respondent that the practice of the Executive is to refuse to back warrants for charges of revenue (and political) offences: and such presumably being the standing

instruction of the execution to the Garda Commissioners, the backing here did not follow a proper exercise of discretion by reason of the falsity already mentioned. If the person on whose information the warrant was obtained, cloaks the real offence in such disguise to deceive the Deputy Commissioner, the detention should not be supported by the Court; the Court should assume that if a revenue offence had been apparent, the warrant would not have been backed.

5. That section 29 and 31 of the Petty Sessions (Ireland) Act are inconsistent with the Constitution and hence did not remain in force as law brought over by the Constitution.

6. That even if these sections were brought over as part of the general law, recognition of the principle of international law referred to, should be had in interpreting their provisions. In so far as revenue offences might literally be included, the sections should be treated to that extent as inconsistent with the Constitution; and such offences should be treated as exceptions to and be excluded from the operation of sections 29 and 31.

It is convenient to take the constitutional argument first, it can be readily disposed of, for Mr. McGonigal concedes that this Court being bound by the decision in *The State* (*Duggan*) v. *Tapley** 85 I.L.T.R. 22; [1959] I.R. 62, must uphold the constitutionality of sections 29 and 31 of the Petty Sessions (Ireland) Act, 1855. Nevertheless, Mr. McGonigal desires to submit, for the purpose of keeping open for future debate, if necessary, certain **[155]** contentions which he says were not considered, or given weight to, in *Tapley's Case** and *The State* (*Dowling*) v. *Kingston* (No. 2) [1937] I.R. 699 and 717. These decisions he contends follow and are based on the reasoning in *The State* (*Kennedy*) v. *Little** 65 I.L.T.R. 91; [1931] I.R. 39. There is, however, a vital distinction which likewise can be drawn in the present case, between the Fugitive Offenders Act, 1881, the subject of the latter case and the Petty Sessions (Ireland) Act, the subject of the other cases and the present case.

In the later case the reliance placed in *Kennedy's Case** on the safeguards provided in the Fugitive Offenders Act was lost sight of. The Petty Sessions (Ireland) Act provides no safeguard for the prisoner, comparable with the safeguards contained in the Fugitive Offenders Act; in the later cases this vital distinction was not set up, or given decisive importance.

I would find it difficult to accept this argument or agree that this distinction was not in mind in the *Dowling* (No. 2) *Case*. It seems to have been set up by Mr. Ryan in his argument in the Supreme Court (p. 722) dealt with on the other side by Mr. McCarthy (p. 729) considered in the High Court by Gavan Duffy J. and must have been in mind by Meredith J. in the Supreme Court, when he said (at p. 755): "The Constitution of any state might regulate the terms and conditions and restrictions and safeguards subject to which such international arrangements might be entered into on behalf of the state, and might make the validity of any law implementing such arrangements dependent upon such terms, conditions, restrictions, or safeguards being secured. Our Constitution is silent on the matter of such safeguards. It follows, therefore, that laws implementing such arrangements are either all valid, or all invalid, and that the Courts cannot distinguish between one such law and another." That I take to mean that distinction cannot be made, as affecting constitutional validity, between the Fugitive Offenders Act with its safeguards, and the Petty Sessions (Ireland) Act with its minimal safeguards. And see the direct reference to the topic at p. 758. However, the point does not now call for decision in this court and I may pass from it.

Turning to section 31, I cannot accept Mr. McGonigal's argument that it relates solely to arrests pursuant to section 29. Section 31 provides:—"Whenever any warrant, addressed either to the constabulary, or to any other person, shall be so endorsed by the said inspector-general, or by either of the said deputies inspector-general, or by any justice or other such officers as aforesaid, it shall be a sufficient authority to the person bringing such warrant, and also to all constables or peace officers of the county or place where such warrant shall be so indorsed, to execute the same by arrest, committal, or levy, as the case may be, within the jurisdiction of the said justice or officer, and in the case of a warrant to arrest any person, to convey him, when arrested before the justice or officer by whom the same was issued, or before some other justice or officer of the same county or place to be dealt with according to law; provided always, that if the prosecutor, or any of the witnesses for the prosecution, in cases of indictable offences, shall then be in the county or place where any person shall have been arrested under any warrant so backed as aforesaid the constable or other officer who shall have arrested such person shall, if so directed by the justice who shall have endorsed the warrant, bring the person so arrested before him or some other justice of the same county or place, who may thereupon take the examinations of such prosecutor or witnesses, and proceed in every respect as hereinbefore directed with respect to persons charged before a Justice with an indictable crime or offence alleged to have been committed in any other county or place than that in which such person shall have been arrested."

It seems to me unlikely to have been in contemplation that a person arrested by the constabulary in Ireland on a warrant issued say, in Guernsey, and backed by the Inspector General of the Royal Irish Constabulary, must be conveyed by the latter to Guernsey: or that the police of the latter county must come here with their warrant, have it backed and proceed to arrest themselves in any part of Ireland.

Consideration of the proviso shows, I think, that it could not have been intended for arrests on foreign warrants. The Justice endorsing the warrant may in the circumstances set out in the proviso, direct that the person arrested may be brought before him or such other Justice as is mentioned. The procedure to be followed is as previously in the Act directed with respect to persons charged before a Justice with an indictable crime or offence alleged to have been committed in any other county or place than that in which such person shall have been arrested. This **[156]** latter procedure is found in clause 2 of section 15 and would not at all suit the case of a person arrested in Ireland on a charge of an offence committed in any of the other countries named in section 29. The proviso must have other arrests in contemplation, or be worthless.

Again the concurrence of events provided for in the proviso is so unlikely in relation to offences committed outside Ireland, or certainly outside the then United Kingdom as hardly to have been contemplated by the legislature or to have been considered, if it should happen, as calling for such special treatment.

The section opens with the reference to any warrant "so endorsed by the said inspector general . . ." Why should these words be referred back solely to section 29? Section 26 also authorises backing of warrants by the Inspector General of constabulary. Clause 3 of that section provides that where the person against whom a warrant issues, or his goods, are not to be found in the county to which the sub-inspector, or head constable, to whom a warrant has been addressed shall belong, the warrant is to be backed by the Inspector General of constabulary. The phrase in section 31: ". . . shall be endorsed by the said inspector general . . ." cannot therefore refer exclusively to warrants in virtue of section 29, on literal interpretation. In my opinion, such an interpretation is not displaced by the argument advanced that section 27 contains all the necessary authority for the execution of warrants backed in virtue of clause 5 of section 26, that is to say, of warrants issued in this country which may have to be executed without the local jurisdiction of the addressee, or abroad in any of the places mentioned in Clause 3 of section 27.

It seems to me that the objective of the series of sections 25 to 35 may be summarised as regulating:—

(a) the addressing of warrants (section 25);
(b) The duties and powers of District Inspectors and Head Constables in relation to warrants addressed to them (section 26), including in clause 3 of section 26, the directive for backing.
(c) the manner of backing (sections 27 and 28);
(d) the extension of the power of backing to warrants issued in England,

Scotland, Isles of Man, Guernsey, Jersey, Alderney and Sark (section 29); (e) section 31, which I will have to treat more fully. (Section 30 is of no present moment.)

So far, the statute has laid down the powers and method of endorsement and the validity and force of warrants when so endorsed or backed. For cases where the person to be made amenable is not to be found in the county wherein the addressee enjoys his jurisdiction, the statute has done no more than authorise indorsement and arrest (except to grant the limited outside jurisdiction conferred by the proviso to section 26). Was anything further considered necessary? In my opinion, yes.

Justice's jurisdiction were confined within local limits. "A Justice being out of the county where he is in commission, is but a 'private man' (Dalton 5th Ed. c. 6, p. 24). Therefore, apart from statute three things must occur to ground the Justice's jurisdictions (a) that the matter of enquiry must have arisen within the area of the Justice's jurisdiction; (b) that the Justice in exercising his jurisdiction is within such area; and (c) that the person sought to be made amenable is within such area, for the Justice cannot cause a person to be brought before him out of a foreign area" (O'Connor, Justice of The Peace, 2nd Ed. Vol. 1. p. 50). One statutory delimitation of such jurisdiction may be found in Petty Sessions (Ireland) Act, 1851, section 7. It is apparent, even in that statute, that the powers, jurisdictions and authority of the police were somewhat similarly confined.

With the foregoing in mind it might well be considered that the words, in section 27 ". . . and the same (backed warrant) shall be executed in like manner as any warrant addressed to him (the sub-Inspector of the place where the person is and against whom the warrant is issued) in the first instance", would not give sufficient cover or protection to the person executing such a warrant. Section 31 completes the authority and protection and I think necessarily so, when there is taken into account that the executing constable or officer may be obliged to act without his district in the conveyance of an arrested person to the local jurisdiction of the issuing justice.

It may not be of such importance but at least is worthy of passing notice that the **[157]** draftsman displays in sections 25, 26, 27 and 32 and elsewhere in the Act, his method of categorising in clauses, procedural provisions to meet varying circumstances in relation to the subject matter of the sections. This was not done with sections 29 and 31, if the latter was intended to be linked solely to the former.

I therefore come to the conclusion that the true meaning and purpose of section 31 is to regulate throughout the country the execution of any warrants backed by the former Inspector General (and now as required by the Adaptation Order of 1938) and which have to be executed without the jurisdiction of the issuing authority, whether emanating within this country, or the named other countries. The words "bringing such warrant" can be more easily understood as bringing it for execution, rather than as bringing it for the purpose of having it backed. And this, I believe, accords with the practice over many years.

Construed thus the several provisions of section 31 becomes feasible, both before and since 1922: probable situations can be envisaged which they will suit and a probable necessity envisaged for all of them. On the other hand, confining section 31 to section 29 warrants, we have, at least in the proviso, a machinery hardly to be thought workable; and a combination of circumstances necessary to bring it into operation, too unlikely of concurrence to justify the enactment.

It follows that the contention that the arrest not having been for any of the purposes of section 31 and was therefore illegal, fails.

On the question of proof of the validity of the warrant, I have already summarised the case submitted on behalf of the prosecutor. Mr. Walsh, for the respondent, contends that the latter is concerned with no more than justifying the arrest. He was the recipient of a warrant good on its face, bearing the appearance of a properly issued warrant, and the backing in due form of the Deputy Commissioner invested with the necessary power of backing such warrants. He relies on the statutory direction in section 29 empowering the

Inspector General or Deputy Inspector General (now the Commissioner or Deputy Commissioner) to endorse such warrants, "upon like proof as aforesaid"; that is to say, "upon proof on oath of the handwriting of the justice who shall have signed the Warrant" (section 28 and clause 3 of section 27).

The verification of the signature of the issuing justice in the present case was before the Deputy Commissioner, is exhibited in the present proceedings and has not been questioned by the prosecutor.

Further, the Deputy Commissioner should be satisfied that the document is a warrant disclosing an offence and directing apprehension. Here, Mr. Walsh points out, the warrant was issued for an offence under the Forgery Act—a statute which is actually part of the law of this country (although it is not essential that the offence charged should be likewise an offence here).

We are here concerned simply with a warrant of apprehension (and I have, for simplicity, throughout treated the sections only in their applications to apprehensions) and the point is covered by the authority of *The State* (*Kennedy*) v. *Little** 65 I.L.T.R. 91; [1931] I.R. 39 at pp. 50-51. Johnson J. deals with a somewhat similar warrant under the Fugitive Offenders Act. Just as in that case the warrant here is simply a warrant to apprehend "and its endorsement . . . is the determining authorisation to apprehend." Johnson J. goes on to cite *Ex Parte Teraz** (4 Ex. Div. 63) on the distinction between warrants for apprehension, the latter being directed to the officer for his protection.

The challenge on proof fails. We are considering a statute which is, or has become, part of the statute law of the State. By its very terms it validates warrants issued by Justices in England and recognises the power of the latter to issue such warrants as are within its terms. To accede to the argument that the indorsing authority, or the Courts when invoked, as in this case, should require proof of the law existing at the moment in England relating to the powers of Justices of the Peace to issue warrants, would amount to an attempt to supplement the statutory authorisation with special safeguards. It will be seen that this is a function exclusively for parliament.

Mr. Bell went so far, indeed, as to urge that in the absence of factual proof of the law in a foreign land or state, the Courts should apply its own law on a given subject and assume it to be the law of such foreign state; it should be assumed that the office of Justice of the Peace having been abolished in our state, does not now exist in England. No authority was advanced for applying that principle to the extent of assuming that, until the contrary be proved, Justices of the Peace have been replaced in like manner as in this state. **[158]**

While Mr. Walsh did contend that the Deputy Commissioner was not concerned with the merits of the charge in the warrant, indeed it was one of his main contentions, he informed the Court that in practice an executive discretion is exercised. That he states was a matter of policy and in pursuance of such policy, the executive (and the Commissioner and Deputy Commissioner by instruction) in face do not back warrants for revenue offences. Nevertheless, he contended that as a matter of construction, section 29 is unqualified; it speaks of "any crime or offence". The parliament of any state may permit the surrender of persons in such state to the jurisdiction of other states to meet even revenue charges and *Buchanan* v. *McVey** is inapplicable in the present case.

I assume that it might be expected that the principles evolved and preserved by the Courts would be following in surrenders in virtue of such legislation—as we are assured is in fact the practice. But to provide an express exemption is for the Oireachtas. "What is fundamental is that section 29 implements an arrangement, however originated, which as matters stand, regulated relations of an international character; that the Courts are given no jurisdiction to review or in any way pass judgment on the propriety of such arrangements, that the Constitution leaves such arrangements and the terms and conditions on which they may be entered into or maintained in the unrestricted control of the Oireachtas and that such control is in no way prejudiced by section 2—being continued in force under Article 13, since it may at any time be repealed or amended by the Oireachtas", per Meredith J. in the *State* (*Dowling*) v. *Kingston* (No. 2) supra at p. 737.

This is not affected by *Buchanan & Another* v. *McVey** [1954] I.R. 89, so strongly relied on by the prosecutor. In that action the plaintiffs claimed an account and payment of monies due by the defendant as director, trustee and agent of the plaintiff company. The substantial defence was that the ostensible claim was in reality a process of recovery of foreign income tax. This defence prevailed. Kingsmill Moore J. expresses the principle at p. 102, ". . . that the Courts of our country will not enforce the revenue claims of a foreign country in a suit brought for the purpose by a foreign public authority, or the representative of such an authority: and that even if a judgment for a foreign penalty or debt be obtained in the country in which it occurred, it is not possible successfully to sue in this country on such judgment. (The decisions) do not expressly go further though some of the dicta suggest that there may be a principle that our Courts will not lend themselves indirectly to the collection of a foreign tax and will not entertain a suit which is brought for that object. Such a wide extension is also suggested by the authorities which establish that our Courts will not entertain an action for the enforcement of a penalty imposed by the laws of a foreign state, a principle which seems to have been the parent of the rule as to not enforcing foreign revenue claims."

In his consideration of the history and origin of the principle, Kingsmill Moore J., while showing perhaps a common basis for its application to revenue as to penal laws and a like reasoning for their basis, does not, on my reading of his decision, assimilate them as Mr. Walsh submitted. Mr. Walsh contended that the *ratio decidendi* of that judgment is that foreign revenue claims were deprived the aid of the Court, simply because they were penal in nature. This argument was relevant to his further submissions that section 29 was concerned entirely with extra territorial penal laws; that if the latter be excluded the section collapses and can never be invoked.

In my view the distinction between *Buchanan* v. *McVey** and the present case is that in the former the aid of the Court was invoked; in the present the aid of the executive was invoked. In the present case the Courts are not even lending "themselves indirectly to the collection of a foreign tax"—assuming such an aim in the warrant was established.

When the section was originally enacted the enforcement of extra territorial revenue laws could not be in question certainly as between Great Britain and Ireland, although possibly so as between Ireland and the Channel Islands. Now, the revenue laws of Ireland and Great Britain are distinct. This grounded the alternative argument of Mr. McGonigal; that to the extent the section might be construed as covering warrants in relation to the enforcement of English revenue law, it was unconstitutional. That argument cannot prevail. Here I can again draw upon the authority of Meredith J. in *The State* (*Dowling*) v. *Kingston* (No. 2) at p. 575:—

> "whether the continuance of section 29 is now appropriate or not depends upon political considerations which are not for the Courts. The existing reciprocal provisions for the backing of warrants implies a high **[159]** degree of mutual confidence in respect of what pertains to the administration of justice and a very real and close bond of association on that important plane. It is for the Oireachtas to determine whether, notwithstanding the alteration in our status, that confidence and that bond of association should continue or not. Changes in the laws enforced in the different associated units and the preservation or otherwise of the reciprocity at present existing, will also be for the consideration of the Oireachtas."

In my opinion the Deputy Commissioner in backing the warrant and Superintendent Hynes in causing the arrest of the prosecutor, were carrying out a statutory requirement, which put very generally, requires the handing over of persons for subjection to the criminal laws of England; that they justify the execution of these duties by, in the one case having the authority prescribed by the section established, and in the other the proper backing; and that the entire proceeding was executive, or administrative, involving no judicial process in this country and therefore in no way conflicting with *Buchanan's Case*.*

I do not think that this Court should act on the evidence tendered as to the substance, or lack of substance in the charge laid, or determine the bona fides of the informant, or whether the charge conceals a revenue claim, or offence.

What is in question now is the backing of the warrant by the Deputy Commissioner. Are we to say that he should set enquiries on foot to see if under cover of the charge is hidden a device for getting the subject into England to answer a revenue charge or claim? I think not. It has been argued and I think correctly, that if the power conferred by the section is discretionary the discretion is in the executive and akin to the discretion reviewed by the English Court of Appeal in *In re Galwey** (1896) 1 Q.B. 230, where the Court refused to interfere with the discretion vested in the executive government. It is true that the discretion was there expressly stated in the treaty between Great Britain and Belgium and consequently was to be read into the Extradition Act, but the principle applies, however the discretion be established.

It was further submitted that section 29 by its words "it shall be lawful . . ." is enabling only, and not mandatory, and it is for those alleging the contrary in a particular case, to establish a mandatory intention. We were referred to *Julius* v. *Lord Bishop of Oxford* 5 A.C. 214 and particularly to Lord Cairns L.C. at pp. 222-223. In my view, however, this does not call for decision. Mr. McGonigal does not contend for a mandatory construction but rather that if a discretion existed, it should be reviewed by this Court and if found to have been exercised in a mistaken reliance on the form of charge set up in the warrant, should be held to have been improperly exercised. I accept and follow the judgment in *In re Galwey* supra. If a discretion exists it is reposed in the person designated to back the warrant and/or the executive and a discretion over which the Court has no control.

The cause shown should be allowed.

From this judgment the Prosecutor appealed to the Supreme Court.

The grounds of the appeal were as follows:—

1. That the High Court was wrong in law in discharging the said Conditional Order.
2. That there was no evidence that the Prosecutor was in lawful custody and that the High Court was wrong in law in so holding.
3. That the High Court erred in law in so construing the relevant provisions of the Petty Sessions Act, 1851, as to enable the Court to hold that the prosecutor was in lawful custody.
4. That the warrant having been backed by the Deputy Commissioner of the Garda Siochana in Dublin the High Court was wrong in holding:
   (a) that the warrant was validly addressed for execution in the County of Wicklow, and
   (b) that it could be validly executed in such County by any person other than the person bringing such warrant to be backed.
5. That the arrest conveyance to and detention of the prosecutor in Bray Garda Siochana Station for the purpose of there handing him over to the Lancaster police was illegal.
6. That the High Court was wrong in law in holding:
   (a) that there was sufficient evidence of a valid warrant; **[160]**
   (b) that there was a presumption of the validity of a warrant backed under section 29 of the Petty Sessions Act, 1851, without factual proof of English law, and of the fact that the offence charge constituted a crime thereunder;
   (c) that the warrant was valid without factual proof of English law relating to the existence and powers of Justice of the Peace at the time of the issue of the said warrant.
7. That the High Court was wrong in law in holding that the Prosecutor was validly in custody under the provisions of the Petty Sessions Act, 1851.
8. That the provisions of the said Act relating to the backing of warrants are inconsistent with the sovereignty of this State, repugnant to the Constitution, illegal and invalid.
9. That in the circumstances created by the enactment of the Constitutions of this State in 1922 and 1937, the provisions of the Petty Sessions Act, 1851, in so

far as they relate to the backing and enforcement within the State of warrants issued by a foreign State have been rendered obsolete, inoperable and unenforceable.

10. That the High Court was wrong in law in failing to make absolute the Conditional Order on the ground that the said warrant was backed by the Deputy Commissioner of the Garda Siochana in exercise of a discretion exercised by him on the faith of a misleading sworn information making a charge of forgery which could not be substantiated and which had been sworn for the purpose of making the Prosecutor, when arrested, liable, for offences in respect of which the Deputy Commissioner had he known the true facts would not have backed the said warrant.

At the hearing of the appeal in the Supreme Court counsel on behalf of the prosecutor were given liberty to amend the said notice of appeal in manner following:—

1. By adding the words "issue and" before the word "backing" in ground number 8.
2. By adding a new ground namely ground 11 as follows:—"That the said warrant was not endorsed in the manner and upon the proof required by section 29 of the Petty Sessions Act, 1851, and is therefore bad."
3. By adding a further new ground namely ground 12, as follows:—

"That the prosecutor is not detained in accordance with law on the grounds:—

"(i) That the said Superintendent J. F. Hynes of the Garda Siochana is not and has not been since the 21st day of May, 1961, the Superintendent Garda Siochana, Bray, Co. Wicklow, and is not and has not been since the said date a member of the Garda Siochana and is *functus officii.*

"(ii) That Garrett Brennan Deputy Commissioner of the Garda Siochana who indorsed the warrant for execution is not and has not been since the 6th day of October, 1959, Deputy Commissioner and he is not and has not been since the said date a member of the Garda Siochana and is *functus officii* and if the said endorsement had any validity it ceased to be valid so as to justify the detention of the Prosecutor as and from the said 6th day of October, 1959."

R. McGonigal, S.C., Desmond Bell, S.C., and *William Hamill* for the applicant, referred to the following:—

The King v. *Kynaston* 1 East 117; *Huntington* v. *Attrill** [1893] A.C. 150; *The State* (*Kennedy*) v. *Little** 65 I.L.T.R. 91; [1931] I.R. 39; *The State* (*Dowling*) v. *Kingston* (No.2) [1937] I.R. 699; *The State* (*Duggan*) v. *Tapley** [1952] I.R. 62; *Brennan and Kingston,* 71 I.L.T.R. 90; [1937] I.R. 483; *The State* (*Dowling*) v. 85 I.L.T.R. 22; *Buckley and Others* (*Sinn Fein*) v. *Attorney General and Another* [1950] I.R. 67; *Buchanan Ltd. and Another* v. *McVey** 90 I.L.T.R. 121; [1954] I.R. 89; *Rex* v. *Governor of Brixton Prison Percival ex parte** [1907]; 1 K.B. 696; *Rex* v. *Crossman* (1908) L.T. 760; *Abouloff* v. *Oppenheimer & Co.* [1882] 10 Q.B.D. 295; *In re Amand** [1941] 2 K.B. 239; *Government of India* v. *Taylor** [1955] A.C. 491; Courts of Justice Act, 1924, 77, 78.

Richard Cooke, S.C., and *John Coleman* for Superintendent Hynes referred to the following:

District Court Rules, 1948 Rule 61 (2); *The State* (*Dowling*) v. *Brennan and Kingston* [1937] I.R. 483; (No. 2) [1937] I.R. 699; *The State* (*Kennedy*) v. *Little** [1931] I.R. 39; *Government of India* v. *Taylor** [1955] A.C. 491; *In re Galwey** [1896] 1 Q.B. 230; *In re Delhi Electric Supply and Traction Co. Ltd.** [1953] 3 W.L.R. 1085; *Frederick Guilder Julius* v. *The Right Reverend The Lord* **[161]** *Bishop of Oxford; The Reverend Thomas Thellusoon Carter* (1880) 5 App. Cas. 214; *R.* v. *Metropolitan Police Commissioner ex parte Malia* [1957] 1 W.L.R. 1065; [1957] 3 All E.R. 440; *R.* v. *Cohen* [1951] 1 K.B. 505; [1951] I All E.R. 203; *Princess Paley Olga* v. *Weisz** [1929] 1 K.B. 718; *Attorney General* v. *Blennerhasset and Others* [1933] 67 I.L.T.R. 136; The Courts of Justices Act, 1924 ss. 77, 78; *Buchanan Ltd and Another* v. *McVey** [1954] I.R. 89.

Cur. adv. vult.

On 10th November, 1961, the Supreme Court gave the following judgment:

MAGUIRE C.J.:—

We are all satisfied that because the respondent has retired from the Garda Siochana he cannot in this Court justify his authority to detain the prosecutor. Having reached this conclusion the Court thinks it desirable that this case should be met by allowing the appeal and making the conditional order absolute.

We will give our opinion on other points argued at a later date.

Judgment was delivered on 14th December, 1961, giving the opinion of the Supreme Court on the other points argued.

LAVERY J:—

The Court has already made absolute the Order for the release of the applicant on the short ground that Superintendent Hynes who was the person shewing cause to justify the detention of the applicant had retired from office and had not any authority.

That disposed of the matter but the Court thought proper to consider and express an opinion on the wider issues which were so fully argued—and indeed to rest its decision thereon.

I should first say that, in my opinion, the Order of 1938 (S.R. & O./300 of 1938) is adequate to empower the Commissioner of the Garda Siochana or the Deputy Commissioners to endorse a warrant from a justice in the United Kingdom for execution in any part of the Republic to which it may be endorsed to the appropriate officers having jurisdiction in the area. I recognise the difficulties of applying the provisions of sections 25-31 of the Petty Sessions (Ireland) Act, 1851, to the changed condition of to-day.

It may be, indeed *it is* necessary somewhat to strain the language in order to make it fit. This is not a new problem. I quote O'Byrne J. in *State* (*Kennedy*) v. *Little** 65 I.L.T.R. 91; [1931] I.R. at p. 59:—

> "I accept as good law the contention put forward by Mr. Lavery that any Statute of the British Parliament which was in force in this country on the 6th day of December, 1922, should be considered as being continued by Art. 73, unless it is, *in principle*, inconsistent with the Constitution. The fact that it may require adaptations or amendments in order to give it full force and effect in the changed circumstances of the new State is, in my opinion, no proof of such inconsistency."

In my opinion the warrant was properly endorsed for execution by Superintendent Hynes.

I express no opinion on the formal defects in the warrant which other members of the Court consider important as they certainly are.

It is not necessary for me to do so.

Apart from these issues peculiar to the particular case the fundamental issue is whether the High Court or this Court on appeal can supervise or control the action of the Executive or of a Justice or of a Garda officer when the Court is invoked under Article 40. 4. 2. of the Constitution to grant *habeas corpus* and to declare that the person applying to the Court is illegally detained. This is *the* fundamental right which the Courts must maintain.

It must do so, but according to law.

It is a recognised principle of international law that a state does not enforce or aid in the enforcement of political or fiscal offences against the laws of another state.

A distinction should, I think, be made here.

An offence claimed to be political in character is peculiarly and perhaps exclusively within the province of the Executive Government and not one which the Courts could consider. The present case does not raise this problem so I leave it.

It is claimed that the warrant charging the applicant that he did "between the 1st July, 1946, and the 7th November, 1947, at 56 Penny Street, Lancaster in the City aforesaid **[162]** with intent to defraud certain partners of his, forged a certain book purporting to be a true record of partnership monies paid and received by the Partnership trading as the Lion Hotel, Machynlleth contrary to sec. 4 subsec. (i) of the Forgery Act, 1913," was not obtained bona fide and is intended to secure his arrest in Ireland and to bring him to England, not to answer the charge made which, it is said, cannot be sustained but to make him amenable to tax liabilities and penalties.

This is a very serious matter requiring careful consideration.

The complainant is James Rankin, an officer of Inland Revenue, whose interest in the particular complaint is not apparent but who is concerned as the responsible officer to require Mr. Hully to meet his tax liabilities or to suffer penalties for failing to do so.

Mr. and Mrs. Moore who it is charged have been defrauded by forgery and falsification of accounts have on affidavit testified that what was done by the applicant was done with their full knowledge and consent and that the common purpose was to reduce the tax liability of the partnership of which they were members.

This Court is not required to express an opinion on this course of conduct but, if the evidence is accepted, the information upon which the warrant was obtained colourably charged an offence for an ulterior purpose.

There has been no answer to this allegation. Possibly none was called for and I do not impute blame to anyone.

But the Court has to determine under Article 40. 4. 2. of the Constitution whether it is satisfied that the applicant is being legally detained.

I am not so satisfied: and for the short point upon which the Court made the Order of *habeas corpus* absolute and for the reasons I have stated I consider this should be done.

KINGSMILL MOORE J.:—

Thomas William Hully, a British citizen, came to live in Ireland in 1956. On May 12th, 1959, four police officers came to his house at Shankill and one of them stated he had a warrant for his arrest, which he read out. The prosecutor was then taken to Bray Garda Station and detained. On the same day a conditional order for *habeas corpus* was obtained directed to Superintendent Hynes and the order was directed to be served on Superintendent Hynes and the Attorney General. Bail was granted on May 14th and the prosecutor was released from custody on entering into recognizances with sureties to surrender himself at Bray Garda Station, on a day and hour whereof notice would be given him by Superintendent Hynes, and not to depart the country in the interval without leave.

The time for showing cause having been several times extended, the motion to make absolute, despite cause shown, came on for hearing before the High Court on October 6th: and judgment, allowing the cause shown and discharging the conditional order, was delivered on November 20th. From this judgment and the order consequential thereon the prosecutor now appeals.

Three affidavits were filed in showing cause. Deputy Commissioner Garrett Brennan deposed that he had received from the office of the Commissioner of the Garda Siochana a warrant for the arrest of the prosecutor issued on April 10th by James Pye, a justice of the peace of the city of Lancaster, on the information of one James Rankin; and that attached to the warrant was a sworn statement of Arthur Thompson, Chief Superintendent of Police, Lancaster, identifying the signature to the warrant as that of James Pye, a justice of the peace for Lancaster. The Deputy Commissioner further swore that he then endorsed the warrant, for execution in the counties of Dublin and Wicklow, to the Superintendent, Garda Siochana, in Bray, because he had reason to believe that the person named in the warrant would be found at or near Bray in one of the counties named. Superintendent Hynes deposed in his affidavit that he had received the warrant with the sworn statement of Arthur Thompson attached and that he issued the warrant for execution to Detective Sergeant Joseph Kelly and his assistants. Detective Sergeant Joseph Kelly deposed that he received the warrant, read it over to the prosecutor, arrested him and took him to Bray Garda Station.

Before the High Court and before us the arrest was justified under the provisions of the Petty Sessions Act, 1851. Sec. 29 of that Act provides—"whenever any person against whom any warrant shall be issued by any justice . . . in England for any crime or offence shall reside or be, or be suspected to reside or be in any place in Ireland, it shall be lawful for the said Inspector General, or **[163]** for either of the said deputy inspectors general, or for any justice of the said last mentioned place, to indorse the same in like manner and upon like proof as aforesaid, authorising the execution of the same within his jurisdiction." By adaptation order, Petty Sessions (Ireland) Act, 1851, Adaptation Order, 1938, it has been provided that the Act is to be read as if Commissioner of the Garda Siochana and Deputy Commissioner of the Garda Siochana were substituted for Inspector General and Deputy Inspector General.

Sec. 31 provides that "whenever any warrant, addressed either to the constabulary or to any other person, shall be so indorsed by the said inspector general, or either of the said deputies inspector general, or by any justice or other such officer as aforesaid, it shall be sufficient authority to the person bringing such warrant, and also to all constables or peace officers of the county or place where such warrant shall be so indorsed, to execute the same by arrest, committal, or levy, as the case may be, within the jurisdiction of the said justice or officer, and in case of a warrant to arrest any person, to convey him when arrested, before the justice or officer by whom the same was issued or before some other justice or officer of the same county or place, to be dealt with according to law."

It was submitted for the prosecutor that the provisions of ss. 29 and 31 could not be relied on as justification because the warrant had not been indorsed in the manner and upon the proof required: because, where a warrant was indorsed by an assistant commissioner (as opposed to indorsement by a justice of the peace) it was only an authority to the "person bringing such warrant" to make the arrest and bring the person arrested before the issuing justice, and that the "person bringing such warrant" meant the person bringing the warrant from England for indorsement; and because on the retirement of Assistant Commissioner Brennan in October, 1959, the backing of the warrant ceased to have any validity in the same way as a warrant issued by a justice ceased (at common law) to have any validity on the death of the justice (*Dickinson* v. *Brown* 1 Peak N.P.C. 234), and (semble) on his ceasing to hold office (O'Connor, Justice of Peace Vol. 1. 74).

It transpired in the course of the hearing that Superintendent Hynes who was the Superintendent at Bray to whom the warrant was directed by the endorsement, who had taken the prosecutor into his custody, and to whose custody the prisoner was to be returned by the conditions of the bail bond, had retired from the force since the hearing before the High Court. He alone had shown cause against the conditional order and he was no longer in a position to do so. Nor had he any longer the right—or the ability—to detain the prosecutor in custody. The court were unanimously of opinion that in these circumstances the order for *habeas corpus* must be granted and the cause shown disallowed.

But, as these circumstances did not arise till after the decision of the High Court, it is necessary in order to decide the liability as to costs to consider if, on the facts existing at the date of this order, the prosecutor was entitled to *habeas corpus.* I do not consider it necessary to express any concluded opinion on the objections taken to the validity of the warrant on the grounds that it was not backed in proper form, or was not endorsed to the correct person (i.e. the person bringing such warrant to the commissioner), but I do not wish to be taken as dissenting from the views as to these matters expressed in the judgment of O'Daly J. In my view, however, *habeas corpus* should have been granted by the High Court on a wider issue.

The Constitution requires the court to order the release of a person from detention unless satisfied that he is being detained in accordance with the law. The effect of this wording is to throw on the person showing cause the onus of justifying the detention in all respects to the satisfaction of the court. A very wide field of enquiry is open to the court on an application for *habeas corpus* and, where the detention is by an act of the executive, the court can enquire into all the circumstances. It is concerned not only to see that the documents are correct in form: it can investigate whether the necessary conditions exist to justify the execution of such documents and can enquire whether they have been executed by mistake or whether their execution has been procured by fraud. Moreover the court can enquire if the executive has misused its powers. *Eshugbayi Eleko* v. *Government of Nigeria* (1931) A.C. 662 at pp. 670, 671 and *R.* v. *Governor of Brixton Prison** [1916] 2 K.B. 742 Lord Reading C.J. at p. 749.

In effect the prosecutor charges that the warrant in this case was obtained by a fraudulent information and was endorsed in ignorance of the true facts of the case and that an endorsement so obtained is a nullity. **[164]**

The information on oath on which the warrant issued was sworn by James Rankin, an officer of the British Revenue, and was to the effect that the prosecutor between July 1st, 1946, and November 7th, 1947, with intent to defraud certain partners of his, forged a certain book purporting to be a true record of partnership monies paid and received at the Lion Hotel, Machynlleth, contrary to section 4 sub-section (1) of the Forgery Act, 1913.

The prosecutor in his affidavit denies that he ever forged any books with intent to defraud any partners of his, and says that the warrant was obtained with a view to making him amenable to the jurisdiction of the English Revenue Authorities, and that the charge is merely a cloak for this purpose and an attempt to use indirectly the laws and forces of the state in aid of the Revenue laws of a foreign country. He admits that he owes a sum of £5,000 to the British Revenue for Income Tax, apparently in connection with sources of income other than the hotel.

The evidence afforded by the documents produced and by the facts sworn to in affidavits which are not contradicted by other affidavits, nor sought to be shaken by cross-examination of the deponents, is such that in my opinion no court could come to any conclusion other than that the prosecutor has made out a case which, so long as it remains unanswered, supports his contentions.

The prosecutor says that in 1943 he and two other persons, his cousin Robert Moore and his cousin's wife Gladys Moore, purchased the Lion Hotel with monies obtained from the Bank on their joint guarantee. In 1947 the hotel was sold at a profit and the profits divided equally between the three. In the meantime Robert and Gladys Moore lived in the hotel, keeping the books of account and sending weekly and monthly statements to the prosecutor's office, from which all accounts were paid. The three partners jointly agreed to falsify the accounts by reducing the amounts of stock and inflating the accounts of creditors, the object being to avoid payment of income tax.

A joint affidavit was sworn by Robert and Gladys Moore explaining somewhat more fully the way the partnership was operated. It goes on to aver that in 1956 Mr. Rankin interviewed them stating that his investigations of the books of the partnership showed that there was tax owing. He suggested that the prosecutor had defrauded them, which they denied. The last interview with Mr. Rankin took place in September, 1958, and they paid in December, 1958, all sums demanded from the partnership for tax and penalties, including the prosecutor's share of such demand. They swear that they never made any allegations against the prosecutor and that they believe that Mr. Rankin's allegations in his information are wholly without foundation; that the prosecutor never defrauded them in any way and that they are satisfied he never took any money without their authority.

Mr. Eyre, managing clerk for John Gorna, a firm of solicitors acting for the prosecutor in Manchester, made an affidavit exhibiting correspondence between his firm and Mr. Rankin. From this it appears that Mr. Rankin was pressing Mr. Gorna for an interview in regard to Mr. Hully's affairs at such time and date as would suit Mr. Gorna: that Mr. Gorna wrote on March 20th, 1959, suggesting 12 noon on April 6th, or, if that was not convenient, some alternative date or time which Mr. Rankin could arrange on the telephone: that Mr. Rankin replied on 3rd April saying that he could not see Mr. Gorna on April 6th as his branch was moving to Didsbury next week and the office was in a somewhat chaotic state, but that he would communicate again when he had settled down.

Mr. Rankin never communicated as he had said he would, but neither his move to Didsbury nor the "somewhat chaotic state" of his office prevented him from swearing an information, on or before the 10th day of April, to procure the warrant. On the very same day the signature of the justice issuing the warrant was verified by Mr. Thompson.

I return to consider the warrant. It alleges that an information has been sworn charging the prosecutor with forgery of a partnership book with an intent to defraud the partners. It is not sworn by either partner or by anyone purporting to act on their behalf. It is not sworn by a police authority. It is sworn by Mr. Rankin, a revenue officer, who has already been assured by the partners (as they swore) that there was no fraud. Mr. Rankin was entitled as a common informer to make the information, but it was not an offence for which he could receive portion of a penalty. One is tempted to ask why he sought the issue of a warrant for an offence, which was no concern of his and which, if the evidence of the Moores is to be believed, could never be substantiated. The prosecutor charges that Mr. Rankin's object was to en-**[165]**-sure that he should be brought within the English jurisdiction on a charge never intended to be prosecuted, in order to make him available for arrest and prosecution for a revenue offence. On the uncontradicted evidence I can only come to the conclusion that this is so. Assuming it to be so what result follows?

Mr. McGonigal was coerced by the authority of the decisions to which I shall refer to admit that ss. 29 and 31 of the Petty Sessions Act had been made part of our law by Article 73 of the Saorstat Eireann Constitution and Article 50 of our Constitution. But now, he says, they "wear their rue with a difference" and their operation is conditioned by the change in the political status of Ireland brought about by two Constitutions. Sec. 29, though a piece of domestic legislation, must now be construed as if it were formulated by an independent state to give force to an extradition treaty, and it is almost common form in such treaties to exclude from their provisions political offences and offences against fiscal laws. At the same time as s. 29 was incorporated in our *corpus juris* there were also incorporated all other parts of the existing law which were not inconsistent with the Constitution. It was, he says, part of the existing law that the British State, of which Ireland was a part, should not extradite persons for revenue offences, and he quotes Sir Raymond Evershed in *Re Cohen, a bankrupt,* [1950] 2 All E.R. 36 at p. 39. "As is well known it is not the practice of civilised countries, such as France or England, to enforce the revenue laws of the other of them."

The Petty Sessions Act was passed at a time when England and Ireland were one state, with one legislature, one executive authority, one revenue and one common citizenship. "England" and "Ireland", as used in s. 29 of the Act, are merely words describing geographical areas and the effect of the Act was only to facilitate the transportation of a person accused of crime from one part of the state to another. In 1922 Ireland became a separate state with a separate legislature, executive and revenue. The words "Ireland" and "England" in s. 29 must now be construed as referring not merely to geographical areas but also to separate states. Article 73 of the Saorstat Eireann Constitution provided that, subject to the Constitution, and to the extent that they were not inconsistent therewith, the laws in force in Saorstat Eireann at the date of the coming into operation of the Constitution should continue to be in full force and effect until repealed or amended by enactment of the Oireachtas. Clearly a strong argument could be put forward that the provisions of ss. 29 and 31 of the Petty Sessions Act, framed for operation in a unitary state, were inconsistent with the Constitution. Such an argument was adduced in *Dowling* v. *Kingston* (No. 1) 71 I.L.T.R. 90; [1937] I.R. 483 and in *Dowling* v. *Kingston* (No. 2) [1937] I.R. 699, and found favour in the High Court with Gavan Duffy J. in both cases, but in both cases Maguire P. and Hanna J. rejected it. It was again rejected by all the judges of the Supreme Court before whom *Dowling* v. *Kingston* (No. 2) came on appeal [1937] I.R. 717. Meredith J. after referring to the difference in the position as it was in 1851 and as it was in 1922 said at p. 757: "In my opinion this difference does exist, but I do not think that it constitutes a vital difference as regards essentials. What is fundamental is that s. 29 implements an arrangement, however originated, which, as matters stand, regulates relations of an international character: that the Courts are given no jurisdiction to review or in any way pass judgment on the propriety of such arrangements, but the Constitution leaves such arrangements and the terms and conditions on which they may be entered into or maintained in the unrestricted control of the Oireachtas, and that such control is in no way prejudiced by s. 29 being continued in force under Article 73, since it may at any time be repealed or amended by the Oireachtas."

The matter was reagitated in *State (Duggan)* v. *Tapley** 85 I.L.T.R. 22; [1952] I.R. 62. Since the decisions in *Dowling* v. *Kingston* our present Constitution had come into force. By Article 5 it had declared Ireland to be a sovereign and independent state and Article 29, 3 stated that "Ireland accepts the generally recognised principles of international law as its rule of conduct in its relations with other States". It was held by the High Court and Supreme Court that there had been no change in the law as laid down in the *Dowling Cases*. S. 29 had been taken over by the Constitution as part of the law in force and any modification was a matter for the legislature.

Mr. McGonigal argued that, as it was undoubted law in both England and Ireland that the courts would not enforce directly or indirectly the fiscal laws of another country, s. 29 must be interpreted in such a way as to except from its provisions warrants which charged a fiscal offence or, as in this case, a **[166]** warrant designed to enable a fiscal offence to be prosecuted.

It is undoubted law now, and it also was the law before 1922, that the courts of England and Ireland would not lend their aid to the enforcement of the fiscal laws of another country, either directly or indirectly. *Buchanan* v. *McVey** [1954] I.R. 89; *Government of India* v. *Taylor** [1955] A.C. 491. Mr. McGonigal contends that the executive must follow the practice of the courts in regard to fiscal laws. But, whatever may have been the practice of the courts, I can find no authority for the view that the executive could not, if they so desired, deport a non-citizen (and possibly also a citizen) to stand his trial in another country for a fiscal offence. It is undisputed law that *the courts* will not enforce directly or indirectly the penal laws of a foreign state, but nevertheless the executive can deport a man to stand his trial for a crime committed in another country; that is the effect of s. 29. The action of the courts and of the executive lie in different spheres, though the courts may restrain the executive if it acts illegally. In the realm of law, as opposed to practice, I can see no difference between deporting a man to stand trial for a revenue offence, a political offence, or an ordinary crime. That there may be grave reasons of policy, or even a recognised practice among civilised states, not to extradite persons for political or fiscal offences does not prevent an executive from doing so if they are so authorised by law.

The true view appears to be that a sovereign state may derogate from its sovereignty—or, as it was put by Hanna J. in *Dowling* (No. 2) at p. 710, may exercise its sovereignty—by expelling even a citizen from its territory, and for that purpose may pass laws empowering the executive authorities to take action in such a way as may be prescribed to secure this result. The legislature could have enacted ss. 29 and 31 of the Petty Sessions Act. The effect of the Saorstat Constitution and our Constitution, as interpreted in the *Dowling* and *Tapley Cases,* is that these sections came over into our law as if so enacted. "I cannot see any reason why the laws of this State should not provide that a citizen, who is alleged to have committed an offence while in another country, should be delivered up to the police of that country in order that he may be brought to trial there." Sullivan C.J. *Dowling* (No. 2) at p. 731. "If it would be, as I do not think can be disputed, within the competence of the Dail to enact s. 29 to-day with the adaptations made in 1923 I can see no ground for holding that this could not be done by Dail Eireann sitting as a Constituent Assembly, and, if they could, I think they did it by Article 73." Fitzgibbon J. at p. 747.

I am constrained by the judgments in the *Dowling* and *Tapley Cases** to hold that if a warrant issued in England and openly expressed to be for a revenue offence were presented to the Assistant Commissioner and if he, in his discretion, were to endorse it in due form, the action would be legal and the courts could not interfere with the arrest and deporting of the person named in the warrant.

But I am of opinion that the words "it shall be lawful" in s. 29 are not mandatory but permissive, and that they give a discretion to the Assistant Commissioner, a discretion which it is his duty to exercise. Extradition treaties and the domestic legislation which gives them effect commonly exclude from the offences for which extradition may be used such offences as appear to be of a political or fiscal nature. It would be natural and proper if the discretion given by s. 29 were to be exercised along the same lines, and this, it seems, has been done. Counsel for the Attorney General has told us, on the authority of the Attorney General, that it has been the established practice not to endorse warrants for fiscal offences. If this be so I am forced to assume that if the Assistant Commissioner were informed that a warrant, apparently for an offence not of a fiscal nature, had been issued not for the purpose of prosecuting the offence alleged but only in order to facilitate a prosecution for a fiscal offence, he would exercise his discretion by refusing to endorse it. This is but a logical deduction from what we are told is the authorised practice.

On the facts before the court I am constrained to hold that the warrant in this case was not issued for the purpose of prosecuting the offence alleged therein but that the real purpose was to bring the prosecutor within the English jurisdiction in order to pursue proceedings against him for a fiscal offence and that the warrant took the form it did in order to conceal the real object and so evade the established practice that a warrant is not backed for a fiscal offence. If, as I am forced to conclude, the endorsement was procured by non-disclosure of the true facts, so preventing the Assistant Commissioner from exercising his discretion along established lines, it appears to me that, when the facts are revealed, this Court must treat the endorsement as a nullity, hold that it is not satisfied that the prosecutor is being legally detained, and order his release. **[167]**

O'Daly J.:—

This appeal has already been allowed, and the prosecutor is at liberty.

Supt. Hynes of the Garda Siochana, the person claiming to detain the prosecutor, had, at the date of the hearing of the appeal, retired from the force, and was then a civilian and without authority to detain the prosecutor.

On this ground the court immediately on the conclusion of the argument unanimously allowed the appeal.

The appeal also raised a number of other questions, the chief of which I propose to consider briefly.

The answers to two of these questions turn, in the main, on the construction to be placed on ss. 29 and 31 of the Petty Sessions (Ireland) Act, 1851. It is here I begin my investigation. Ss. 29 and 31 read as follows:—

S. 29:—

"Whenever any person against whom any warrant shall be issued by any justice or such other officer as aforesaid in England or Scotland, or in the Isles of Man, Guernsey, Jersey, Alderney, or Sark, for any crime or offence shall reside or be, or be suspected to reside or be, in any place in Ireland, it shall be lawful for the said inspector-general, or for either of the said deputy inspectors-general, or for any justice of the said last mentioned place, to indorse the same in like manner and upon like proof as aforesaid, authorising the execution of the same within his jurisdiction."

S. 31:—

"Whenever any warrant, addressed either to the constabulary or to any other person, shall be so indorsed by the said inspector-general, or by either of the said deputy inspectors-general, or by any justice or other such officer as aforesaid, it shall be a sufficient authority to the person bringing such warrant, and also to all constables or peace officers of the county or place where such warrant shall be so indorsed, to execute the same by arrest, committal, or levy, as the case may be, within the jurisdiction of the said justice or officer, and in the case of a warrant to arrest any person, to convey him, when arrested, before the justice or officer by whom the same was issued, or before some other justice or officer of the same county or place to be dealt with according to law."

The section concludes with a proviso which need not now concern us.

An enquiry as to the form of endorsement and proof required by s. 29 carries one back to a consideration of ss. 25, 26 and 27.

Section 25 specifies the persons to whom warrants shall be addressed for execution. In the case of offences, punishable either by indictment or upon summary conviction, the requirement is that the warrant is to be addressed to the sub-inspector (later, district inspector: 46/47 Vict. c. 14 s. 12) or head constable who shall act for the petty sessions district where the warrant was issued.

Next, s. 26 deals with the persons by whom such warrants may be executed. Three cases arise: (1) execution within the petty sessions district where the warrant was issued; (2) execution in other petty sessions districts of the same county; and (3) execution outside the said county. In the first case, the sub-inspector, or head constable, or any head or other constable to be named by him, is authorised to execute the warrant. In the second case, the sub-inspector or head constable is required to certify on the warrant, according to the form G.b., the place where he believes the person against whom the warrant shall have been issued or his goods are to be found and also, having first satisfied himself as to the fact, that he believes the signature to the warrant to be genuine; and then, transmitting the warrant so endorsed to the sub-inspector or head constable of the other petty sessions district, the same shall be executed in like manner as any warrant addressed to him in the first instance. In the third case, a G.b. certificate must also be endorsed and the warrant transmitted forthwith to the inspector-general of the constabulary force as provided in s. 27.

The G.b. certificate to be given by a member of the constabulary is in the following form:—

"I (*certify*) that I have reason to believe that the person against whom the within warrant was issued (*is to be found*) at .... in the county of .... and that I believe the signature to the within warrant to be in the hand-writing of the said justice.

"Signed ....

(To whom this warrant was delivered for execution)

This............day of...........185..

"To...........of..........." **[168]**

Section 27 deals with the backing of warrants certified and transmitted under s. 26, cl. 3. The section takes the three cases of backing for execution elsewhere out of the county as follows:—

(1) Petty Sessions Ireland, i.e. Ireland excluding the Dublin Metropolitan Police District.
(2) The Dublin Metropolitan Police District.
(3) England, Scotland, Man and the Channel Isles.

In the first case, it is provided that it shall be lawful for the inspector-general or either of his deputies to endorse the warrant according to the form G.c. and to transmit the same to the sub-inspector who shall act for the place where it appears the person against whom the warrant shall have been issued or his goods are to be found; and the same shall then be executed in like manner as a warrant originally addressed to him. In the second case, the inspector general or a deputy again endorses the warrant according to the form G.c., but it is transmitted to the commissioners of metropolitan police; and the same shall be executed in like manner as any warrant addressed to them in the first instance. In the third case, there is also a G.c. endorsement by the inspector general or deputy. A further G.c. endorsement is, however, required, this time by "any justice or officer having power to issue any warrant . . . for the arrest of offenders in any of the said places (England, Scotland, Man and Channel Isles), upon proof on oath of the handwriting either of the inspector general or deputy by whom the same shall have been indorsed or of the justice by whom the warrant shall have been issued." This second endorsement is to authorise the execution of the warrant "within the jurisdiction of the said justice or officer by the person bringing the same or by any constable or other police officer of the county or place where it shall be so indorsed." The section concludes, as follows:—

"And the said provisions shall also apply to cases in which the sub-inspector shall only certify that the signature to the warrant is genuine but in which the place where the said person or his goods are to be found shall appear by other means than the said certificate."

The G.c. endorsement to be made by inspector-general or his deputy is as follows:—

"It being (*certified*) to me as above, I hereby endorse the within warrant for execution in the said county of...........(or metropolitan district or other place).

"Signed........................

Inspector-General *or* Deputy *or* Justice.

This...........day of...........185..

"To....................."

On the basis of these provisions it was submitted on behalf of the prosecutor, by Mr. McGonigal, that the warrant in question here was bad in two respects:—

(i) because it does not appear, by certificate, or other indorsement on the warrant that the prosecutor was to be found or was suspected to be in Ireland and,

(ii) because the jurisdiction of the inspector general or deputy inspector general (now the deputy Commissioner) was to indorse the warrant for execution by one person only, "the person bringing such warrant", that is to say, the person bringing such warrant from the English jurisdiction here to the deputy Commissioner for indorsement.

Mr. Cooke on the respondent's behalf answered the first point by submitting that it is unnecessary that the warrant should bear a certificate or indorsement that the prosecutor was to be found or suspected to be in Ireland. This, he said, is included in the first limb of form G.b. as a matter of convenience—a convenient mode of informing the indorsing authority of the whereabouts of the person to be arrested and is not, he submitted, a jurisdictional requirement. His answer to the second point was that the words "the person bringing such warrant" meant the bearer of such warrant, that is to say, the person having it in his possession for execution.

In seeking to resolve these questions it will serve some purpose at this stage to look briefly at the several statutes passed between the Act of Union and 1851 making provisions for the execution of warrants throughout the entire of the new United Kingdom.

One of the first fruits of the Union was the passage of 44 Geo. III c. 92 (1804) which is entitled "an act to render more easy the apprehending and bringing to trial offenders escaping from one part of the United Kingdom to the other and also from one county to another." Section 4 dealt with offenders escaping from Great Britain into Ireland. The section provided as follows:—**[169]**

"It shall and may be lawful for any justice of the peace of the county or place in Ireland whither or where such person or persons shall escape, go into, or reside, or be, to indorse his name on such warrant, which warrant so indorsed shall be a sufficient authority to the person or persons bringing such warrant and to all persons to whom such warrant was originally directed and also to all sheriffs, officers, constables and other police officers of the county or place where such warrant shall be so indorsed to execute the said warrant in the county or place in Ireland where it is so indorsed etc. . . ."

So much of 44 Geo. III c. 92 as related to the apprehension of offenders escaping from Ireland into England and from England into Ireland and as to the backing of warrants against such offenders was repealed by the Indictable Offences (Ireland) Act, 1849 (12 & 13 Vict. c. 69), s. 34.

The Act of 1849 at s. 12 in effect re-enacted the provisions of s. 4 of the Act of 1804, limited, however, to indictable offences, and added a form of endorsement, form K. Form K reads "whereas proof upon oath hath this day been made before me one of Her Majesty's Justices of the Peace of the said County of .... etc. that the name J.S. to the warrant subscribed is of the handwriting of the justice of the peace within mentioned I do therefore authorise *W. T. who bringeth to me this warrant* and all other persons to whom this warrant was originally directed and also all constables and other police officers of the said county of .... to execute the same etc. . . ." This form is the same as form K in the Schedule of the English Indictable Offences Act (11 & 12 Vict. c. 42) of the preceding year to which our attention was called by counsel. The Summary Convictions (Ireland) Act, 1849, s. 2 (12 & 13 Vict. c. 70) incorporated in respect of summary offences the provisions of the Indictable Offences Act (c. 69) with regard to the backing of warrants. Both the Indictable Offences Act (c. 69) and the Summary Convictions Act (c. 70) were repealed by the Petty Sessions (Ireland) Act, 1851, s. 43. The provisions of ss. 25 to 31 of the Act of 1851 are substituted.

I turn first to consider whether, as Mr. Cooke submitted, it is unnecessary that a warrant endorsed for execution outside the district of issue should bear a certificate or endorsement that the person against whom the warrant has been issued is to be found (or is suspected to be) in the new district. The terms of the G.c. endorsement which, by virtue of s. 29, the warrant should bear have already been quoted. It begins thus:—

"It being (*certified*) to me as above." The above certificate (form G.b.) is in respect of two matters: (1) as to whereabouts of the person against whom the warrant has issued, stating place and county and (ii) as to belief as to genuineness of the justice's signature.

Under s. 29, in respect of the justice's signature, more is required than a certificate of belief as to the genuineness; there must be proof on oath. The second limb of the G.b. certificate is thus dispensed with. The first limb remains. It has, however, been argued that the concluding words of s. 27 indicate that it is enough that the endorsing authority should be personally aware or made aware of the whereabouts or suspected whereabouts of the wanted person.

I see in the inclusion in form G.c. of the opening recital clause the strongest indication to the contrary. If that clause were absent from form G.c. the argument of respondent's counsel would have some weight. But its presence in my opinion can have had only one purpose: to bring to the notice of the endorsing authority (inspector general or justice) in the clearest possible manner that he should endorse for execution in a new petty sessions area (or its equivalent) only on intimation of belief or suspicion that the wanted person was in such new area.

The concluding words of s. 27 dispensed the sub-inspector form certifying the new whereabouts of the wanted person, but it left intact the requirement that his whereabouts should appear by other means, and it did nothing to relieve the endorsing authority from reciting the whereabouts (believed or suspected) of the wanted person as a preliminary to certifying for execution in the new area.

One may readily acknowledge that the machinery for backing warrants contained in the Petty Sessions Act is elaborate and, for a United Kingdom, perhaps unnecessary. But it cannot be overlooked that Parliament was not prepared even to allow a warrant to be executed outside the petty sessions area of issue but within the same county except on a certificate endorsed on the warrant that the wanted person was to be found elsewhere in the county. The object of this and the subsequent provisions is clear enough: it is to **[170]** confine justices' warrants within the area of jurisdiction of their issue save for specific exceptions. Parliament might well have said "if a wanted man is found anywhere in the United Kingdom let him be arrested on the original warrant without any endorsement and conveyed before the justice who issued the warrant." Instead of this the plainest intention is manifested to allow warrants be authorised for execution outside the area of issue only in clearly defined circumstances which were to be recited on the warrant.

The recital as to whereabouts in my opinion is shown to be a jurisdictional requirement and not an informational device. It follows that the warrant in question here, lacking the recital as to whereabouts, is bad and was no authority for the arrest of the prosecutor.

The indorsement of the warrant under s. 29, whether by the inspector general, his deputy or a justice is an indorsement "authorising the execution of the same within his jurisdiction." The term "jurisdiction" is not appropriate to describe the area of authority of the inspector general or his deputy *qua* police officer. But it is appropriate when it is borne in mind that by the Constabulary (Ireland) Act, 1836 (6 Wm. IV, c. 13), s. 7, it was provided that:

> "every inspector general and deputy inspector general shall on his appointment to such office forthwith take before any two magistrates the oaths by law required to be taken by justices of the peace in Ireland, and also the oath hereinafter contained, and shall thereupon be and become without further qualification or appointment and continue so long as he shall hold the said office, but no longer, a justice of the peace for every county, county of a city, county of a town, and town and liberties in Ireland."

This additional *status* of the inspector general and his deputies is expressly adverted to in the Petty Sessions Act, s. 7. It was provided as follows in clause 3:—

> "The inspector-general, or either of the deputy inspectors-general of constabulary, being a justice of any county, may act in all matters arising within such county, wherever he may happen to be at the time."

In the light of these provisions it is made clear that the function of backing warrants to be exercised by the inspector general or his deputy under s. 29 is a function exercisable *qua* justice and not *qua* police officer; and it is for this reason that the indorsement is to authorise the execution of the warrant "within his jurisdiction".

The marginal heading to the form of endorsement (G.c.), it may be noted, is "Backing by inspector general or *other* justice".

In 1938 by the Petty Sessions (Ireland) Act, 1851, Adaptation Order, 1938 (S.R. & O. No. 300 of 1938), the references to inspector general and deputy inspector general in ss. 29 and 31 of the Petty Sessions Act, 1851, were adapted to read Commissioner of the Garda Siochana and Deputy Commissioner respectively. This adaptation was found necessary consequent upon the decision of the High Court in *State* (*Dowling*) v. *Kingston* (No. 1) 71 I.L.T.R. 90; [1937] I.R. 483.

How effective has the Adaptation Order of 1938 been to revive in the Commissioner and Deputy Commissioner the powers of the Inspector General and his deputy under ss. 29 and 31? It can be accepted that the intention was to revive them to the full. What in fact the Adaptation Order does is simply to substitute in these sections Commissioner for Inspector General and Deputy Commissioner for Deputy Inspector General. (It may be pointed out that since the operation of s. 2 of the Constabulary (Ireland) Act, 1859, the number of Deputy Inspectors General had been reduced to one.) The Order does not effect any further or other adaptation. It is not adverted to that the Inspector General and his deputies were in 1851, and subsequently, justices of the peace and that the meaning and effect of ss. 29 and 31 is not to be understood unless this is borne in mind. It is the explanation of the use of the word "jurisdiction" both in s. 29 and 31. In the case of an endorsement by the Commissioner or Deputy Commissioner, no longer a justice of the peace, it is not appropriate to speak of the officer authorising the execution of the warrant "within his jurisdiction". The word jurisdiction has, therefore, to be read in two senses: in the case of an indorsement by a district justice the word stands, but in the other case it requires to be read as meaning "area of authority". Taking this step one then moves to s. 31. This is the section which specifies by whom and in what area a warrant endorsed by the inspector general and his deputy may be executed (and, of course, also a warrant endorsed by a justice or other warrant-issuing officer). The essential words of the section may be repeated. The warrant, the section says, "shall be a sufficient authority to the person bringing the same and **[171]** also to all constables or police officers of the county or place where such warrant shall be so indorsed *to execute the same by arrest . . . within the jurisdiction of the said justice or officer*." We see that the section in terms does not refer to the county or place where it shall be lawful to execute a warrant indorsed by the inspector general or his deputy. The reason is, these high police officers were justices under the Constabulary Ireland Act, 1838; they were comprehended in the term "justice".

Let me now ask if prior to 1921 the Inspector General or his deputy sitting in his office in Dublin City (in the county of the city of Dublin) could effectively have indorsed a warrant for execution in the county of Dublin or the county of Wicklow. The words of s. 31 taken by themselves give a negative answer to the question. Clause 3 of s. 7 of the Act is perhaps to be construed as modifying the firm words of s. 31 and as rendering effective for execution in any county in Ireland a warrant endorsed in Dublin city. But the powers of s. 7 clause 3 are given expressly to the inspector general and his deputy *qua* justice. It may be doubted if this section is capable of adaptation; in any event, it has not been adapted.

It follows that the limitation imposed by the words of section 31, restricting the execution of warrants to the place or county where indorsed, remains, with such inconvenience as may be attendant thereon. And, accordingly, a Deputy Commissioner's indorsement made in the county of the city of Dublin must be restricted to the county of the city of Dublin. If it is to be indorsed for another county it must be indorsed by the Deputy Commissioner in that county. The section provides an alternative; and that is, to apply for an indorsement to the local justice. It may be pointed out that that is the only mode provided for the backing of Irish warrants in England.

If an English warrant is to be presented for backing to a district justice, by whom is such presentation to be made? The answer seems clear enough: by the person bringing such warrant. Who is this person? Is he (as was submitted on behalf of the respondents) the person having such warrant in his possession for execution?

If the warrant had in fact been brought here in what circumstances would the District Justice for the Shankill area have indorsed it for execution there? On it appearing to him by certificate G.b., or otherwise on the information of the person bringing the warrant, or of some other person, that the accused resided or was or was suspected to reside or be in the area. Without such information the District Justice would clearly have no jurisdiction to indorse the warrant for execution in his area. This, in my opinion, is the significance of the recital in the opening part of the endorsement G.c. which he is required to make—adapted, of course, in the case where a G.b. certificate is absent: it is to show the jurisdiction on the warrant.

Lastly, I turn briefly to the prosecutor's contention that the conditional order of *habeas corpus* should, in any event, be made absolute because, as he says, the charge of forgery of partnership accounts is a mere cloak to get him to England in order that he may there be made amenable for certain revenue offences and the charge of forgery is shown by him and his partners to be wholly groundless.

The information in respect of the alleged forgery was laid by one James Rankin. The prosecutor and his cousin Robert Moore and Moore's wife carried on an hotel business in partnership, and the offence alleged is that the prosecutor forged certain books purporting to be records of money paid and received by the partnership with intent to defraud the Moores. Mr. Rankin is identified as an Inland Revenue enquiry officer. In the course of an investigation into the affairs of the partnership for income tax purposes certain false entries came to Mr. Rankin's notice. He spoke to the Moores about these entries and pointed out that certain further income tax was due. He suggested to them that they had been defrauded by the prosecutor. The Moores in their affidavit say they denied this strenuously to Mr. Rankin. They also say they are satisfied that the prosecutor did not take any of the partnership moneys without authority. Incidentally, they have in fact discharged the additional income tax for which the partnership was assessed.

In his affidavit the prosecutor put this matter further. He says the Moores and he jointly agreed to falsify the accounts for the purpose of avoiding the payment of income tax, and that it is completely untrue that he falsified any books with intent to defraud his partners. The warrant, he says, was obtained with a view to rendering him amenable to the jurisdiction of the English Revenue authorities and is a cloak for this purpose and an attempt to use the forces of this state in aid of the revenue laws of a foreign country. **[172]**

English warrants in respect of revenue offences are not backed for execution by the Irish authorities. This practice is doubtlessly well known to the English Revenue authorities. It is in the context of that practice that the prosecutor makes the case that the charge of forgery of the partnership books is brought—and brought by a Revenue enquiry officer, James Rankin, with the real purpose of getting the prosecutor to England in order that he may be made amenable for revenue offences.

Mr. Rankin has not had formal notice of these proceedings, but Mr. McGonigal has told us that in the High Court he invited the respondents to communicate with him. But it does not appear that this was done.

It cannot be doubted that it would be well within the jurisdiction of the High Court, and of this Court, to grant *habeas corpus* to a person who was about to be sent out of the country to answer a charge not made *bona fide* but with the object of getting the person accused into the foreign jurisdiction for another purpose.

To attempt to use the provisions of the Act of 1851 in this way would clearly be an abuse of the statute, and any detention pursuant to such attempt must be said to be unlawful.

I adopt what Mr. Justice Low said in *Ex parte Sarno** (1916) 2 K.B. at p. 752.

> "I wish before parting with this case, emphatically to protect myself from being supposed to assent to some of the arguments which have been used at the Bar. For instance, I do not agree that if the Executive were to come into this Court and simply say 'A person is in our custody and therefore a writ of *habeas corpus* does not apply because the custody is at the moment technically legal', the Court would have no power to consider the matter and, if necessary, deal with the application for the writ. In my judgment that answer from the Crown in reply to an application for the writ would not be sufficient if this Court were satisfied that what was really in contemplation was the exercise of an abuse of power. The arm of the law in this country would have grown very short, and the power of this Court very feeble if it were subject to such a restriction in the exercise of its power to protect the liberty of the subject as that proposition involves."

Here all the evidence points only one way—that the English forgery proceedings are a cloak to have the prosecutor sent to England in order that he be made amenable for Revenue offences. On an application for *habeas corpus* it is enough that the Court is not satisfied of the lawfulness of the detention. If it were necessary to do so I would be prepared to support an order of *habeas corpus* on this ground also.

McLoughlin J:—

Thomas William Hully, the prosecutor in this case, has invoked the provisions of Article 40. 4. 2° of the Constitution which enacts, in short, that any person who alleges that he is being wrongfully detained may apply to the High Court to inquire into the legality of his detention and the High Court, after inquiry, *shall* order his release unless satisfied that he is being detained in accordance with the law.

The prosecutor has sworn that the warrant on which he was arrested and detained was obtained by one James Rankin, an officer of the Inland Revenue Enquiry Branch of the Chief Inspector of Taxes, Manchester on a fictitious criminal charge and not for the purpose of having this charge investigated by a Justice of the Peace in England but for the ulterior purpose of having him brought to England to enforce payment by him of arrears of income tax. There were affidavits made on behalf of the prosecutor strongly substantiating this allegation.

One of the main arguments made on his behalf was that, if this allegation is correct, and that it should be taken to be correct is not controverted, the issuing of the warrant would be vitiated *ab initio* as having been obtained by fraud, and anything done on foot of the warrant would be therefore illegal.

The only person showing cause against the complaint is Superintendent Hynes and he purports to do so by producing the warrant and showing by his affidavit and by an affidavit of Deputy Commissioner Brennan how the warrant came to be executed by Guards under his direction. It is clear from these affidavits and from the submissions made on his behalf that he does not dispute the allegation raised by the prosecutor but relies solely on the provisions of ss. 29 and 31 of the Petty Sessions Act, 1851, as justification for executing the warrant by arresting and detaining the prosecutor. **[173]**

S. 29 reads as follows:—

"Whenever any person against whom any warrant shall be issued by any justice or such other officer as aforesaid in England . . . for any crime or offence shall reside or be, or be suspected to reside or be, in any place in Ireland, it shall be lawful for the said inspector-general or for either of the said deputy inspectors-general, or for any justice of the said last mentioned place to indorse the same in like manner and upon like proof as aforesaid, authorising the execution of the same within his jurisdiction."

S. 31, which is the section giving authority for the arrest of the person outside the jurisdiction and country of the Justice issuing the warrant, reads:—

"Whenever any warrant, addressed either to the constabulary or to any other person, shall be indorsed by the said inspector-general or by either of the said deputies inspector-general, or by any justice or other such officer as aforesaid, it shall be a sufficient authority *to the person bringing such warrant*, and also to all constables or peace officers of the county or place where such warrant shall be so indorsed, to execute the same by arrest, committal, or levy, as the case may be, within the jurisdiction of the said justice or officer, and in the case of a warrant to arrest any person, to convey him, when arrested, before the Justice or officer by whom the same was issued, or before some other justice or officer of the same county or place to be dealt with according to law" etc.

This section pre-supposes a "person bringing such warrant" and I agree with the conclusion come to by An Breitheamh O'Daly that this does not mean the officer having it in his possession at the time of the arrest but the person bringing the warrant from the place where it issued to the place where it is indorsed.

In this case, maybe to suit the convenience of those responsible for police administration in the two jurisdictions, we have no information as to any such person, nor is there any information as to how this warrant left its jurisdiction of origin and came to be within this jurisdiction. All we are told is that Deputy Commissioner Brennan received it from the Office of the Commissioner and that attached to it was a sworn statement by Chief Supt. Arthur Thompson, County Police, Lancaster, identifying the signature of the issuing Justice of the Peace in Lancaster; whereupon the Deputy Commissioner indorsed it to the Garda Superintendent, Bray, Co. Wicklow, for execution in one of the Counties of Dublin or Wicklow. Before such indorsement the warrant itself carried no certificate or indorsement whatsoever.

When the warrant and sworn statement are examined it appears that the two documents may have been attached together to each other by a pin or staple as they both have numerous pin holes in the top left corner. Apart from this they are not, in my opinion, properly related one to the other for reasons which I now state. The sworn statement says "that the signature to the *document* now produced and shown to me and marked 'A' is in the handwriting of James Pye etc." On the warrant itself there is no reference to the sworn statement but on a piece of paper about 3″ × 2″ in size which is pasted or stuck over the Royal insignia on the front of the warrant there is this text "This is the 'Document' marked 'A' referred to in the annexed declaration of Arthur Thompson taken before me this Tenth day of April, 1959," and it is signed by the same Justice of the Peace before whom the statement was sworn. In my opinion this is a most improper way to identify a document in a sworn statement.

There are three other methods which could have been adopted more properly to identify the signature of the Justice on the warrant. The text "This is the 'Document' marked 'A' " could have been inscribed directly on the warrant, alternatively the sworn statement could have been indorsed on the warrant or, if not so indorsed, the sworn statement could have explicitly identified the warrant by such words as "I hereby swear that the signature to the warrant now produced and shown to me being for the arrest of one Thomas William Hully issued on the information of one James Rankin and dated 10th April, 1959, is the handwriting of James Pye one of Her Majesty's Justices of the Peace for the City of Lancaster". The slipshod method of swearing to the signature on the warrant adopted in this case is open to the suspicion of fraud and, in a case of this kind, where the allegation is that the warrant itself was obtained by a trick, it cannot, in my view, be accepted as sufficient sworn identification of the signature. This is the "Proof upon oath . . . produced before me that the signature James Pye . . . is in the handwriting of the Justice of the Peace within mentioned", quoting from the indorsement of **[174]** Deputy Commissioner Brennan. In my opinion it was not and is not acceptable proof.

Whilst I have considerable doubt about the matter I do not think that the warrant is otherwise bad for want of indorsement or backing.

The only other matter upon which I wish to express a view concerns the issue as to whether the prosecutor's arrest and detention under the warrant was illegal having regard to the allegation of fraud in the obtaining of it and having regard also the admission of counsel for the Attorney-General that, in accordance with judicial decisions that the Courts in this country and likewise in Britain will not act to enforce the revenue laws of another State, it is the practice of An Garda Siochana not to back British warrants for fiscal offences. On this issue I think the position can be shortly stated in this way. Clearly the Deputy Commissioner backed this foreign warrant for execution in this country on the basis that the offence as set out in the warrant was an ordinary criminal offence and not a revenue offence. If the warrant in this form was obtained by James Rankin by a trick then the indorsement by the Deputy Commissioner was obtained by the like trick. Mr. McGonigal submitted on the authority of *the Duchess of Kingston's Case* that fraud will vitiate the most solemn judicial acts and this proposition is not disputed by Mr. Cooke. There is nothing very solemn about the judicial act challenged in this case—the issue of an arrest warrant by a magistrate on the *ex parte* information of a private informer. To declare such an act to be vitiated is not a matter of great consequence. To do so, however, may give rise to this apparent inconsistency that, whereas the Garda Siochana may be justified in executing an English warrant on its face legal, the High Court may declare it to be vitiated and illegal. The answer to that is that there is no duty on the Garda Siochana to look behind the warrant but there is a Constitutional duty imposed on the High Court so to do when relief by way of *habeas corpus* is sought.

I do not know what lines of communication there are between the police authorities in Britain and in this country. From the affidavits it appears that the Bray Gardai had some contact with the police both in Lancaster and in London with the object of handing over the prosecutor to the custody of a British police escort. But that is all. There is nothing to show how this warrant came to be in this country and nothing to indicate if any steps were taken to investigate the allegation of fraud in the obtaining of the warrant, and I do not think that James Rankin and the Constabulary of Lancaster are unaware of the reasons why a warrant issued by a Justice of the Peace of that City on the 10th April, 1959, has not yet been effectively executed.

It may well be that the conditional order made in this case on the 12th May, 1959, or notice of it should have been served upon the Chief Superintendent of the Lancaster Police and upon James Rankin but I doubt if this would have altered the situation and as it now stands I have to ask myself this question: the prosecutor having come to the High Court asking for an enquiry into the legality of his detention, could the Court be satisfied that he was being detained in accordance with law? For the reasons I have given I am satisfied that the answer must be "No", and, therefore, that the cause shown be disallowed and the conditional order made absolute.

Formally I wish to add that I agree with the decision already given that, as the respondent, Supt. Hynes, the only person showing cause, had retired from office since the hearing in the High Court, an order of *habeas corpus* must, for that reason alone, be granted.

Solicitor for the Prosecution:
The Chief State Solicitor.

Solicitor for the appellant:
T. G. McVeagh.

METAL INDUSTRIES (SALVAGE) LIMITED v. OWNERS OF THE S.T. "HARLE".

([1962] S.L.T. 114)

July 12, 1961: Court of Session (Outer House): Lord Cameron, Lord Ordinary.

International law—Maritime lien—Sale of foreign ship—Lex fori—Lex situs—Claims on behalf of foreign government in respect of unpaid arrears of compulsory contributions due by employers to state scheme for health insurance and family benefits—Enforcement of foreign revenue laws—Competency.

A preferential ranking in a multiplepoinding arising out of the sale of a French trawler by order of the Court was claimed on behalf of the French Government in respect of arrears of compulsory employers' contributions to a state health insurance and family benefits scheme for seamen. A salvage company claiming declarator of maritime lien in respect of expenses connected with the **[115]** sale of the ship, and for salvage services, contended that the question of preference to the fund was to be determined by the *lex fori* and that the claim was incompetent in as much as the French Government was endeavouring to enforce a revenue claim, which could not, according to Scots law, be enforced. It was maintained for the French Government that the nature of a claim was to be determined by the law of the country in which the claim arose, and that the action of a foreign government which might affect proprietory rights in a thing might be valid and effectual in Scotland if valid and effectual in the foreign country.

Held that the claims by the French Government for arrears of compulsory contributions to the health insurance and family benefits scheme were incompetent, since they were an attempt to enforce the revenue laws of a foreign state.

In a multiplepoinding arising out of the sale of the French trawler the S.T. "Harle", Metal Industries (Salvage) Limited claimed preferential rankings: (1) in respect of the expenses connected with the sale of the ship; and (2) in respect of salvage services rendered by them. The Consul-General for France, as representing the French Government, claimed *inter alia*, a preferential ranking in respect of arrears of compulsory contributions due to the owners of the trawler, as employers, in respect of state schemes for health insurance and family benefits. Metal Industries (Salvage) Limited opposed this claim.

The respective contentions of the parties appear sufficiently from the Lord Ordinary's opinion.

On 12th July 1961, Lord Cameron *held* that Metal Industries (Salvage) Limited were entitled to a preferential ranking in respect of expenses connected with the sale of the ship; that they were entitled to a preferential ranking in respect of their salvor's lien for such sum as might be found due to them for salvage services rendered; and that the preferential claims made on behalf of the French Government for arrears of contributions to the state scheme for health insurance and family benefits were incompetent as being an attempt to enforce the revenue laws of a foreign state.

LORD CAMERON—This multiplepoinding arises out of the sale of a French trawler which was sold by order of the Court in terms of Rule of Court 159. Deducting dues payable up to the date of adjudication the fund consigned in Court now amounts to £4,938 7s. 7d. Claims on this fund are made by the pursuers and also by the Consul-General for France as representing the French Government and in particular two organisations both of which are under the authority of the Ministry of Public Works and Transport in France.

The pursuers aver that salvage services were rendered by them to this trawler between 28th and 31st December 1958, and that, in the course of the salvage proceedings brought by them against the vessel, she was sold on 16th June 1960, at a price of £5,700, and that by interlocutor of 2nd August 1960, they are entitled preferably to the amount of the expenses of sale and further in respect of their lien for the sum of £50,000 over the vessel for salvage services in terms of an interlocutor dated 15th October, 1959, which declared their lien. In virtue of these interlocutors they claim the whole of the consigned fund. The French Consul-General claims to be ranked and preferred on the fund to the sums of £3,044 17s. 9d., and £1,538 4s. 4d., preferably in virtue of an alleged lien and in addition to an ordinary ranking in respect of a further sum of £14,658 6s. 2d. The first two of the sums in respect of which a preferential claim is made by the French Government represent unpaid arrears of compulsory contributions due by employers, the owners of the trawler, in respect of state schemes for health insurance and family benefits. The third sum is in respect of the balance of a loan secured by a mortgage over the vessel, granted by the Ministry of Public Works and Transport towards the purchase price of the trawler. The mortgage is dated 31st October, 1950. The claims in respect of arrears of compulsory contributions due by the former owners of the trawler are resisted by the pursuers as incompetent on the ground that they are an attempt to enforce French revenue law and they are also attacked as irrelevant. Parties are not in dispute that the pursuers are entitled to payment out of the consigned fund of the amount of the expenses of the action of declarator and sale and of bringing the vessel to sale and selling it, or that in respect of the alleged mortgage the French Government would be entitled to an ordinary ranking on the fund if any remains after satisfaction of preferential claims.

Equally, the French Government did not challenge the declarator of maritime lien in respect of salvage services alleged to have been performed by the pursuers, though the value of these services is not admitted.

The real dispute between the parties arises out of the first two heads of claim for the French Government. At the end of the debate, Counsel for the Government obtained leave to consider whether he could expand his averments as to the nature of the contributions represented by his first two heads of claim, but he has since stated that he has not found himself in a position to do so, and asked me to dispose of the case on the averments as they stand in the closed record. Both parties agreed in asking me to make findings rather than deal positively with their claims at this stage except in so far as they are admitted. I am indebted to counsel on both sides for two excellent arguments on the legal issues raised in the dispute. The pursuers' counsel maintained in the first place that the question of preference to a fund of this kind is one to be decided by the *lex fori*, which in this case would be Scots law. Scots law would determine whether a lien or liens should be recognised and, if so, the order in which they would rank. See *The Union* (1860) 1 Lushington 128, applied in *The Tagus* [1903] P. 44. He maintained further that as there is no averment by the French Government that **[116]** any maritime lien is recognised in Scots law in respect of compulsory contribution to insurance benefits of any kind, therefore there is no relevant basis on which the first two heads of claim can be supported. Dealing then with the substance of the French Government's claim, he argued that the claimants' averments showed that they were doing nothing other than trying to enforce a revenue claim; however French law might regard the matter, and this being the view of the matter which Scots law would take, the first two heads of claim were incompetent and the averments in their support irrelevant. He founded strongly upon the cases of *Huntington* v. *Attrill** [1893] A.C. 150 and *Government of India* v. *Taylor** [1955] A.C. 491. Counsel for the French Government did not challenge the pursuers' general statement of law as to determining the order of creditors in preferential claims, but he maintained that the nature of the claim is to be determined not by the *lex fori* but by the *lex situs*, that is, the law of the country where the claim arises, and in support of this proposition he referred to *Cheshire*, 5th edition, page 665, and *The Colorado* [1923] P. 102, and he maintained that in these circumstances it was proper to look at the foreign law to consider the nature of the right which is claimed. He further argued that the action of a foreign government which may affect proprietory rights in a thing may be valid and effectual here in Scotland if valid and effectual in the foreign country, and in support of this he referred to Dicey, *Conflict of Laws*, 7th edition, Rule 130, and the case of *Luther* v. *Sagor** [1921] 3 K.B. 532. He also referred to *The Jupiter* (*No.* 3)* [1927] P. 122, and the *National Bank of Scotland* v. *The Government of Spain*,* 1939 S.C. 413, per Lord Justice-Clerk Aitchison, at page 427, 1939 S.L.T. 317, at page 324. From this he argued that it is for the pursuers to show, if they can, that a valid and effectual right over the French ship had not been created when the liability to pay the insurance and other contributions arose and was not satisfied by payment, and further to show that any claim based on such right would not be recognised in Scotland. Counsel for the French Government further argued that the averments which he has made as to the compulsory contributions to state insurance schemes are relevant to go to proof because he said that, as there was no suggestion that at the time of accrual of the liability French law could not create a valid and effectual right in the organisations which levied the contributions, therefore French law must be resorted to to ascertain the nature of the right which the French Government have in the ship. But while I do not doubt the validity of the general contention put forward by him, as illustrated by the cases to which he referred, I think it is not of such universal application as to cover the type of claim which counsel for the pursuers contends this is. The latter's short and simple point was that as regards these first two heads of claim, the French Government is seeking to enforce French revenue law, and that if that is so then, in accordance with a well recognised and well established rule, no such claim is enforceable here; and further that in determining whether these are in fact attempts to enforce revenue law, they have to be considered in light of the *lex fori*, and it is irrelevant to consider whether these contributions are regarded by French law as fiscal. (See *Huntington* v. *Attrill** (*supra*)). It is a general rule of law that no state will act as a tax gatherer for another or permit its courts to be used for that purpose, and it is a corollary of that rule that what is a revenue or fiscal claim is to be determined by the Courts of the country where the claim is sought to be enforced and in accordance with the *lex fori*. Now what is fiscal and what would be regarded as enforcement of a revenue claim or an attempt to recover taxes due under foreign law seems to me to depend, not so much upon the form which the imposition takes or the object upon or in respect of which it is levied, but upon the substance of the claim as viewed by a Scottish Court applying Scots law. There is practically nothing in the world which is not or may not be taxed and few, if any, human activities which at one time or another have not been the subject of fiscal imposition. At the same time as the complexity and scope of the activities of the state expand, so too increase the number and variety of its agencies, and the number and variety of those entrusted with the assessment and collection of its revenues. In the case of *Attorney General for Canada* v. *Schulze & Co.* (1901) 9 S.L.T. 4, Lord Stormonth Darling dismissed an action to recover costs awarded by a Canadian Court in proceedings arising out of the seizure by Canadian customs of certain imported tweeds for alleged infringement of Revenue Laws and in so doing his Lordship said:— "It is a well established rule of international law that the Courts of one country will not execute or enforce the penal laws of another; and this rule applies 'not only to prosecutions and sentences for crimes and misdemeanours, but to all suits in favour of the state for recovery of pecuniary penalties for any violation of its statutes for the protection of its revenue or other municipal laws and to all judgments for such penalties.'" In *Sydney Municipal Council* v. *Bull* [1909] 1 K.B. 7, the council sued in England for a municipal improvement rate in respect of land in Australia and in dismissing the action Grantham, J. said:— "Some limit must be placed upon the available means of enforcing the sumptuary laws enacted by foreign states for their own municipal purposes. The action is in the nature of an action for a penalty to recover a tax; it is analogous to an action brought in one country to enforce the revenue laws of another. In such cases it has always been held that an action will not lie outside the confines of the last-mentioned state." In the case of *In re Visser, Queen of Holland* v. *Drukker** [1928] 1 Ch. 877, the Queen sued in England the administrator of a Dutch subject to recover Dutch death duties and the action was dismissed by Tomlin, J. on the authority of *Sydney Municipal Council* v. *Bull*. These authorities were approved in the House of Lords in the case of *Government of India* v. *Taylor** (*supra*). In addition, as Lord Simonds pointed out in the last mentioned case, the Foreign Judgments (Reciprocal Enforcement) Act, 1933, excludes by **[117]** section 1 (2) (b) from its operation and advantages a judgment for "a sum payable in respect of taxes or other charges of a like nature or in respect of a fine or other penalty". The Irish case of *Buchanan* v. *McVey** [1955] A.C. 516, approved by Lord Keith in *Taylor**, illustrates very clearly the point that it is the substance and not the form of the matter that will be regarded in determining whether a claim is really one to enforce a foreign revenue or fiscal liability. In the present case, the claimant is the French Consul-General as representing the Government of France, so that he is claiming money on behalf of that Government and in particular two organisations which are specifically averred to come under the authority of a French Ministry. These are just agencies of the Ministry for particular purposes. The levies which they impose are presumably levied with Government authority because they are to defray and support state schemes for health insurance for seamen and for family benefits. The contributions are compulsory. So far as the averments go it would appear that the schemes are state-administered. If a municipal improvement rate levied by a city corporation in Australia is to be treated as a tax which cannot be recovered in a Scottish Court, I should have thought that a compulsory contribution to a state insurance scheme levied on French citizens by a French Government agency was in no better position and that the sums so levied were properly to be regarded as part of the revenue of the state. "Revenue" in the Shorter Oxford English Dictionary is defined as "6. The annual income of a government or state, from all sources, out of which the public expenses are defrayed." Quite apart from this, it seems to me that compulsory contributions levied by state organisations, both of which come under the authority of a minister, and which are contributions due by employers in respect of state schemes for health, insurance and family benefits for persons employed, are nothing more nor less than taxes or at least charges or impositions of a like nature, and that the sums so levied form part of the revenues of the state. If this view of the matter is correct then it is unnecessary to proceed any further because the first two claims put forward on behalf of the French Government must necessarily fail as being an attempt to enforce a revenue debt of a foreign country.

I have already indicated that parties were agreed in asking me at this stage to make findings and not to proceed to rank and prefer either of the claimants to any part of the fund in medio. I shall therefore find that the pursuers are entitled to a preferential ranking in respect of the expenses connected with the sale of the ship; that they are entitled to a preferential ranking in respect of their salvor's lien for such sum as may be found due to them for such salvage services as were rendered; that the preferential claims made on behalf of the French Government are incompetent as being an attempt to enforce in this country the revenue laws of a foreign state; and that, as regards the sum claimed in respect of the mortgage, the French Government would be entitled to an ordinary ranking as an ordinary creditor on any balance of the fund *in medio* which may remain after satisfying the claims of the preferential claimants. *Quoad ultra* I shall continue the cause for further procedure.

Counsel for Pursuers, First Claimants, Grieve, Q.C., Weir; Solicitors, Dundas & Wilson C.S. (for Maclay, Murray & Spens, Glasgow).—Counsel for Fifth Claimants, Strachan; Solicitors, Scott Moncrieff & Trail, W.S.

[This report has been prepared and published by special request.]—EDITOR.

ROSSANO v. MANUFACTURERS' LIFE INSURANCE CO.

([1963] 2 Q.B. 352)

February 14, 15, 16, 19, 20, 21, March 7, 1962: Queen's Bench Division: McNair J.

Conflict of Laws—Contract—Proper law—Insurance policies entered into in Egypt—Insurance company's head office in Canada—Where moneys payable—Proper law of contract—Situs of debt—Contractual place of performance—Whether Egypt or Ontario—Whether Egyptian garnishee orders enforceable in England.
Conflict of Laws—Chose in action or debt—Situs—Whether foreign law of situs relevant—Insurance policies entered into in Egypt with Ontario company.
Conflict of Laws—Confiscatory or political legislation—Exchange control legislation—Effect on moneys payable under insurance policies—Place of performance.
Conflict of Laws—Revenue laws—Whether enforceable in other State—Garnishee orders in Egypt in favour of Egyptian revenue authorities.

The plaintiff who, in 1940, was an Egyptian national residing and carrying on business as a cotton merchant in Egypt, applied for three 20-year endowment policies of insurance for £3,000, £4,000 and United States $10,000 with the defendant insurance company, who had branches in many parts of the world with their head office in Toronto, Canada. On October 31, 1940, the defendants' Cairo office issued to the plaintiff a single interim policy covering the two applications for sterling policies; and on November 25, 1940, the final policies were executed at Toronto in the plaintiff's favour, each policy being the form used by the defendants for foreign business. The total 20 years' premiums under the dollar policy were paid in advance to the head office in Toronto by means of a draft on a bank in Boston; and the plaintiff likewise paid the full 20 years' premiums in respect of the sterling policies by sterling cheque to the defendants' Cairo office. Under the first two policies, the parties agreed that money was to be made payable in banker's demand drafts on London for pounds sterling. As to the third policy, it was agreed that the money was to be paid in banker's demand draft on New York for U.S. dollars.

The policies all matured on March 15, 1960, and the plaintiff brought an action claiming the money due under them. The defendants relied on two defences: (a) that the proper law of the contracts being Egyptian or the situs of the debt or the contractual place of performance being in Egypt, payment by the defendants would be illegal under the Egyptian exchange control law if effected without the permission of the Egyptian control authorities; (b) that as there were two garnishee orders, served upon the defendants' branch in Egypt by the Egyptian revenue authorities in respect of tax alleged to be due by the plaintiff, payment to the plaintiff would expose them to penalties or to the risk of having to pay the money twice and they were, therefore, not liable to pay the sums claimed:— **[353]**

Held, (1) that applying the test as laid down by Lord Simonds in *Bonython* v. *Commonwealth of Australia* [1951] A.C. 201, 219; 66 T.L.R. (Pt. 2) 969, P.C., and accepted by the House of Lords in *In re United Railways of Havana and Regla Warehouses Ltd.* [1961] A.C. 1007; [1960] 2 W.L.R. 969; [1960] 2 All E.R. 332, H.L., as being "the system of law by reference to which the contract was made and that with which the transaction has its closest and most real connection," the proper law of the contracts was the law of Ontario, and, accordingly the Egyptian control legislation did not apply to the policies as part of the proper law of the contracts (post, p. 371).

Pick v. *Manufacturers' Life Insurance Co.* [1958] 2 Lloyd's Rep. 93 applied.

(2) That Egyptian exchange control legislation did not apply to the policies merely by reason of the situs of the debt being in Egypt (post, p. 371).

Kleinwort, Sons & Co. v. *Ungarische Baumwolle Industrie Akt. & Hungarian General Creditbank* [1939] 2 K.B. 678; 55 T.L.R. 814; [1939] 3 All E.R. 38, C.A. applied.

(3) That in considering what was the place of performance of the contracts, the relevant act of performance was the payment of the policy moneys; and that although Egypt was a permissible place of performance, the defendants had not the right to insist on payment only in Egypt, and accordingly Egypt was not the relevant place of performance and the Egyptian control legislation did not apply (post, p. 372).

Pick v. *Manufacturers' Life Insurance Co.* [1958] 2 Lloyd's Rep. 93, considered.

(4) That the recognition of the garnishee orders served on the defendants would offend against the well-settled principle that English courts will not recognise or enforce directly or indirectly a foreign revenue law or claim (post, p. 376); and that, accordingly, the defendants could not escape liability on the policies by reason of the garnishee orders and the plaintiff's claim succeeded.

Peter Buchanan Ltd. & Macharg v. *McVey** [1955] A.C. 516n. and *Indian and General Transport Trust Ltd.* v. *Borax Consolidated Ltd.* [1920] 1 K.B. 539; 36 T.L.R. 125 applied.

Per curiam. I should not be deterred from holding that the situs of the debt was not in Egypt on evidence that by Egyptian law the situs of the debt was Egypt (post, p. 380).

ACTION.

The following statement of facts is taken from the judgment of McNair J. In 1940 Charles Rossano, the plaintiff, was an Egyptian national by birth residing in Egypt where, with others, he carried on business in Alexandria as a partner in a limited partnership firm by the name of Levi Rossano & Co. At that time the Italian forces were threatening Egypt, and it was clear that Egypt might become the seat of war. In those circumstances discussion took place between the plaintiff and Mr. Harrari, the **[354]** district manager of the defendants' Alexandria office, which ultimately resulted in the issue of the policies sued upon. The policies were three 20-year endowment policies and were issued as follows: (1) On November 25, 1940, for £3,000 sterling, payable on March 15, 1960, such amount being expressly made payable in banker's demand drafts on London for pounds sterling. (2) On November 25, 1940, for £4,000 sterling payable on March 15, 1960, such amount being expressly made payable in banker's demand drafts on London for pounds sterling. (3) On January 21, 1941, for U.S. 10,000 dollars payable on March 15, 1960, such amount being expressly made payable in banker's demand draft on New York for United States dollars.

The defendants were a company incorporated according to the law of Canada, and having branches in many countries outside Canada, including a branch in Egypt, through which the policies in question were negotiated. The policies matured on March 15, 1960, and the amount alleged to be due was a sum of £9,906 9s. 10d.

The plaintiff brought an action to recover this sum and the amount being due was not disputed.

The defendants relied upon two main defences. First, that the proper law of the contracts being Egyptian law, or alternatively the situs of the debt being in Egypt, or in the further alternative the contractual place of performance, that was, payment of the policy moneys, being Egypt, payment by the defendants would be illegal under the Egyptian Exchange Control laws if effected without the permission of the Egyptian Control authorities as it would involve a payment of foreign currency between two persons occupying the status of residents under that law. It was admitted that no permission had been granted by the Exchange Control.

Secondly, the defendants said that by virtue of two garnishee orders, the one dated November 16, 1960, and the second dated January 23, 1962, served upon the defendants' branch in Egypt by the Egyptian revenue authorities in respect of tax alleged to be due by the plaintiff, payment by them of the policy moneys to the plaintiff would expose them to penalties under the law of Egypt, or expose them to the risk of having to pay the money twice, and that they were not liable to pay the sums claimed. The plaintiff denied that he was under any tax liability, but in any event submitted that for a variety of reasons each of the orders was a nullity, and further, seeing that to give effect to **[355]** them or either of them would be at least indirectly to enforce a foreign revenue law, the court would not recognise them.

In view of the fact that the defendants carried on business in many countries outside Canada, it was urged by the defendants that the case was of the greatest importance to them far exceeding the money involved since they might, if the plaintiff's case was well founded, be involved in great difficulties in connection with other policies issued in Egypt or in many of the other countries in which they carried on business.

John F. Donaldson Q.C. and *Adrian Hamilton* for the plaintiff. (1) The defence is based first on provisions of Egyptian exchange control legislation alleged to prohibit the payment of the policy moneys outside Egypt. These provisions will not be recognised in the English courts unless Egyptian law is either the proper law of the contract, or the law of the place where the contract has to be performed: *Kleinwort, Sons & Co. Ltd.* v. *Ungarische Baumwolle Industrie Aktiengesellschaft*[1] and Dicey's Conflict of Laws, 7th ed., p. 919 et seq. Neither of these conditions is fulfilled

(2) The proper law of the contracts is not Egyptian law, but the law of Ontario, or alternatively in the case of the sterling policies, English law, and

[1] [1939] 2 K.B. 678; 55 T.L.R. 814; [1939] 3 All E.R. 38, C.A.

in the case of the U.S. dollar policy, the law of the State of New York. The test laid down by the House of Lords in *In re United Railways of Havana Ltd.*,[2] adopting the test of Lord Simonds delivering the judgment of the Privy Council in *Bonython* v. *Commonwealth of Australia*,[3] is the system of law by reference to which the contract was made or that with which the transaction has its closest and most real connection. In *The Assunzione*[4] the test applied by the Court of Appeal was the test of Lord Wright in *Mount Albert Borough Council* v. *Australasian Temperance and Mutual Life Assurance Society Ltd.*,[5] namely, that the duty of the court is to determine for the parties what is the proper law which, as just and reasonable persons, they ought to have intended if they had thought about the question when they made the contract. In *Pick* v. *Manufacturers' Life Assurance Co.*[6] Diplock J. held **[356]** that a policy issued by the same defendants, and, the plaintiff contends, in distinguishable form, was governed by the law of Ontario.

The following factors in particular point to the proper law being the law of Ontario, and not Egyptian law: (a) The policies are on a standard form and there is a presumption that all policies in that form will be subject to the same law. The defendants cannot have intended their policy to have different meanings in different countries. (b) At the time the contracts were entered into there was a world war in progress and the assured (who was and is of the Jewish faith) wanted to be able to draw money anywhere in the world. The defendants assured him that he could do so in any country in which the defendants operated subject to local regulations. (c) The defendants' Cairo office had no authority to issue policies. Such authority had to be given by the defendants' head office in Toronto. No alteration in the terms of a policy could be agreed unless agreed to in writing by the head office. Notice of any assignment had to be given to the head office. (d) Payment of amounts due under the policy by or to the company were to be made in the case of the sterling policies by bankers' demand drafts on London for pounds sterling, and in the dollar policy by bankers' demand drafts on New York, U.S.A. for United States dollars. (e) The plaintiff asked for the policy to be written in English, rather than French—the commercial language of Egypt. (f) In the case of the dollar policy the premiums were prepaid in Toronto by drafts on Boston, and it was originally agreed that this policy should be delivered in Boston, although ultimately it was in fact delivered in Cairo. (g) In the case of all the policies a claim could be made to the defendants' head office or their nearest authorised representative. (h) The defendants were incorporated and had their head office in Toronto, Ontario, and were subject to Ontario law, including the Insurance Act of Ontario, on which the form of policy was substantially based. The statutory restrictions referred to in the application form incorporated in the policy relate to the Ontario statute. (i) In the case of a 20-year endowment policy there is the possibility of a policy-holder becoming interested in the liquidation of the insurer, which in the present case would have taken place under the law of Ontario.

(3) In any event, if Egyptian law is applicable, the exchange laws, on their true construction, do not prohibit payment by the defendants' London branch. **[357]**

(4) The law of the place of performance is not Egyptian law. There is no term in the policy that the policy moneys are only payable in Egypt. The notice on the policies invites the policyholder who wishes to make a claim to write to the head office or nearest authorised representative of the defendants. The primary place of payment and performance is London, in the case of the sterling policies, and New York in the case of the dollar policy, and Diplock J. was right in so holding in *Pick's* case.[7]

[2] [1961] A.C. 1007; [1960] 2 W.L.R. 969; [1960] 2 All E.R. 332, H.L.
[3] [1951] A.C. 201, 219; 66 T.L.R. (Pt. 2) 969, P.C.
[4] [1954] P. 150; [1954] 2 W.L.R. 234; [1954] 1 All E.R. 278, C.A.
[5] [1938] A.C. 224, P.C.
[6] [1958] 2 Lloyd's Rep. 93.
[7] [1958] 2 Lloyd's Rep. 93.

(5) The second limb of the defence is based on two alleged Egyptian garnishee orders. English law will not recognise these orders since the lex situs of the debts is not Egyptian law. The lex situs of a debt governs its validity and effect: Dicey's Conflict of Laws, 7th ed., p. 556; *Swiss Bank Corporation* v. *Boehmische Bank.*[8] The lex situs of these debts was Canadian, or alternatively English or New York law, and not Egyptian law: *New York Life Insurance Co.* v. *Public Trustee*[9]; *Pick's* case.[10]

(6) English courts will not recognise either of the garnishee orders because they relate to alleged tax liabilities of the plaintiff in Egypt, and their recognition would involve indirect enforcement of foreign revenue law: *Government of India* v. *Taylor*[11]*; *Peter Buchanan Ltd.* v. *McVey*[12]* and *Indian and General Investment Trust Ltd.* v. *Borax Consolidated Ltd.*[13]

(7) These garnishee orders are administrative orders, and not the orders of any court. There is no authority for English courts to give judicial recognition to an administrative garnishee order issued in a foreign country, and no such recognition should be given.

(8) Both garnishee orders are later in date than the maturity dates of the policies. The defendants should have paid the policies on maturity before the garnishee orders were made, and cannot now take advantage of their default in payment by relying on these garnishee orders.

(9) On the facts both garnishee orders were invalid as they were not proved to have been signed by the Minister of Finance or his duly authorised deputy, and were not served within the time required by Egyptian law. [*Brook's Wharf and Bull Wharf Ltd.* v. *Goodman Bros.*[14] was referred to.] **[358]**

Eustace Roskill K.C. and *Anthony Lloyd* for the defendants. This case raises important questions of principle for the defendants, namely, (1) what is the proper law of the contracts of insurance contained in the policies, and (2) are the defendants obliged to pay the policy moneys to the plaintiff in England if to do so would be illegal by Egyptian law or would put the defendants in peril of having to pay twice.

First, the proper law of the contracts is Egyptian law. The correct test is that laid down in *Bonython* v. *Commonwealth of Australia*[15] and applied in *In re United Railways of Havana and Regla Warehouses Ltd.*,[16] namely, the law of the country with which the contract has the closest connection. The following factors point to Egyptian law as the proper law of the contracts. (1) The plaintiff was an Egyptian national resident in Egypt at the time the contracts were made. It was the plaintiff's intention to remain in Egypt indefinitely. (2) The defendants had an office in Cairo which was responsible for all business transacted by the defendants in the Middle East. This office was empowered to issue interim policies and to adjust and settle claims. (3) The preliminary negotiations for the contracts were carried on in Egypt. The contracts were made in Egypt, since by their express terms they did not become binding until delivery of the policies, which in the present case took place in Egypt. The policies were kept in Egypt, and were on the defendants Egyptian register. (4) The policies provided for payment of premiums in Egypt.

Pick v. *Manufacturers' Life Insurance Co.*[17] is distinguishable on all the above grounds. Alternatively, it was wrongly decided.

Assuming Egyptian law to be the proper law of the contracts then Egyptian exchange control legislation will be given full effect by English courts: *In re*

[8] [1923] 1 K.B. 673.
[9] [1924] 2 Ch. 101; 40 T.L.R. 430, C.A.
[10] [1958] 2 Lloyd's Rep. 93.
[11] [1955] A.C. 491, 510, H.L.
[12] [1955] A.C. 516n.
[13] [1920] 1 K.B. 539; 36 T.L.R. 125.
[14] [1937] 1 K.B. 534; 53 T.L.R. 126; (1936) 3 All E.R. 696, C.A.
[15] [1951] A.C. 201.
[16] [1961] A.C. 1007; [1960] 2 W.L.R. 969; [1960] 2 All E.R. 332, H.L.
[17] [1958] 2 Lloyd's Rep. 93.

Helbert Wagg & Co. Ltd.[18]*; *Kahler* v. *Midland Bank*[19]; *Zivnostenska Banka National Corporation* v. *Frankman.*[20] Payment of the policy moneys has at all material times been prohibited by the Egyptian exchange control legislation without the consent of the proper authorities. Accordingly, the defendants have a good defence to this claim.

Alternatively, if Egyptian law is not the proper law of the contracts, Egyptian exchange control legislation applies since **[359]** Egypt is the place of performance. The policies do not expressly provide where the policy moneys are to be paid, but there is an implied term that they are to be paid in Egypt. That is what the parties must have intended when the contracts were made. The argument that the parties must have intended the policy moneys to be payable at the defendants' head office failed in *New York Life Insurance Co.* v. *Public Trustee.*[21] The reference in the policies to payment by banker's demand drafts on London and New York relates to the mode of payment, not to the place of payment.

Secondly, the debts on the policies are situated in Egypt. That is the place where they are primarily payable by virtue of an implied term in the contracts, or where they would have been paid according to the ordinary course of business: *F. & K. Jabbour* v. *Custodian for Israeli Absentee Property.*[22]*

The debts have been validly attached according to Egyptian law by two garnishee orders. English courts will recognise and give effect to that attachment, since it is valid according to the law of the place where the debts are situated: *Swiss Bank Corporation* v. *Boehmische Bank.*[23] Alternatively, English courts will as a matter of comity give effect to the garnishee orders since by Egyptian law, the law of the place of attachment, the debts are situated in Egypt, or alternatively, since both debtor and garnishee are subject to the jurisdiction of the Egyptian courts: *Martin* v. *Nadel*[24]; Cheshire, Private International Law, 4th ed., p. 460; 6th ed., p. 499. By giving effect to the Egyptian garnishee orders the English court would not be enforcing a foreign revenue law. There is a distinction between a foreign government suing to recover tax in these courts, which has never been permitted, and the recognition of a valid attachment by a foreign government. Such recognition would not even be indirect enforcement of the foreign revenue law. The rule against enforcing foreign revenue laws has never been carried so far.

Cur. adv. vult.

1962. March 7. McNair J. read the following judgment, which after stating the facts substantially as set out above, continued:

(1) The first and most important matter which falls for my **[360]** decision is as to the proper law of the policies. None of the policies contain any express provision as to what law is to govern the contract. On behalf of the defendants it is submitted that the proper law is Egyptian law; on behalf of the plaintiff it is submitted that the proper law of all three policies is the law of Ontario, or alternatively as to two of the policies for £3,000 and £4,000 sterling respectively payable in banker's demand drafts on London for pounds sterling, the proper law is the law of England, and in respect of the third policy for 10,000 United States dollars payable in banker's demand draft on New York for United States dollars, the proper law is the law of the state of New York.

The test to be applied in determining the proper law of the contract in the absence of any express provision in the policy or any provision in the policy as to jurisdiction has in my judgment been authoritatively determined in a manner binding upon me by the decision of the House of Lords in *In re United Railways of Havana and Regla Warehouses Ltd.*, sub nom. *Tomlinson and First*

[18] [1956] 1 Ch. 323.
[19] [1950] A.C. 24; 65 T.L.R. 663; [1949] 2 All E.R. 621, H.L.
[20] [1950] A.C. 57; [1949] 2 All E.R. 671, H.L.
[21] [1924] 2 Ch. 101; 40 T.L.R. 430, C.A.
[22] [1954] 1 W.L.R. 139; [1954] 1 All E.R. 145, 146.
[23] [1923] 1 K.B. 673.
[24] [1906] 2 K.B. 26.

Pennsylvanian Banking & Trust Co.,[25] where their Lordships by a majority expressly accepted the test laid down in the judgment of the Privy Council delivered by Lord Simonds in *John Lavington Bonython* v. *Commonwealth of Australia*[26] as being "the system of law by reference to which the contract was made or that with which the transaction has its closest and most real connection." Later Lord Simonds said[27]: "The question then, is, what is the proper law of the contract, or, to relate the general question to the particular problem, within the framework of what monetary or financial system should the instrument be construed. On the assumption that express reference is made to none, the question becomes a matter of implication to be derived from all the circumstances of the transaction." In the *United Railways* case[28] (a case of immense complexity) one of the issues was as to the proper law of a lease executed in New York of certain rolling stock used on a railway undertaking in Cuba, the lease forming the security for repayment of a loan raised in the United States of America for the purchase of the rolling stock. Lord Denning said[29]: "the test is simply with what country has the transaction **[361]** the closest and most real connection: see *Bonython* v. *Commonwealth of Australia.*[30] Applying this test, I think the proper law of the transaction, including the lease, is the law of one of the United States." It may be observed that Lord Denning probably per incuriam has substituted the word "country" for "system of law" in Lord Simonds' test, but it is clear that no change was intended. Lord Morris said[31]: "If, then, the question is posed as to what is the law 'by reference to which the contract was made or that with which the transaction has its closest and most real connection' . . . I would answer—the law of Pennsylvania." Lord Simonds[32] stated that he was wholly in agreement with Lord Morris's conclusion of law upon the question of the law to be applied. Lord Reid[33] expressed his agreement with the reasons given by Lord Denning and Lord Morris for adopting the law of Pennsylvania. Lord Radcliffe took a rather different view when he said[34]: "I do not think that the tests for determining the proper law of a contract can ever be comprehended under a single phrase, so various are the situations and considerations that have to be taken account of; but this is a case in which, in my opinion, the law of the place of performance ought to be regarded as of preponderating importance, and of those two possible places Pennsylvania, which is both the home of the trustee and the place where the capital is to be repaid, seems to me clearly the natural choice."

In the course of the argument I was referred to the test formulated in rather different terms in the Court of Appeal in *The Assunzione,*[35] adopting a passage from the judgment of Lord Wright in *Mount Albert Borough Council* v. *Australasian Temperance and General Mutual Life Assurance Society,*[36] that the duty of the court is "to determine for the parties what is the proper law which, as just and reasonable persons, they ought . . . [to] have intended if they had thought about the question when they made the contract" (*per* Singleton L.J.[37] and *per* Birkett L.J.[38]). It does not appear from the reports that the *Bonythan* case[39] was cited in the argument in the Court of Appeal in the *Assunzione* case[40] or that

25 [1961] A.C. 1007; [1960] 2 W.L.R. 969; [1960] 2 All E.R. 332, H.L.
26 [1951] A.C. 201, 219; 66 T.L.R. (Pt. 2) 969.
27 Ibid. 221.
28 [1961] A.C. 1007.
29 Ibid. 1068.
30 [1951] A.C. 201; 66 T.L.R. (Pt. 2) 969.
31 [1961] A.C. 1007, 1081.
32 [1961] A.C. 1007, 1035.
33 Ibid. 1050.
34 Ibid. 1058.
35 [1954] P. 150; [1954] 2 W.L.R. 234; [1954] 1 All E.R. 278, C.A.
36 [1938] A.C. 224.
37 [1954] P. 150, 175.
38 Ibid. 186.
39 [1951] A.C. 201; 66 T.L.R. (Pt. 2) 969.
40 [1954] P. 150; [1954] 2 W.L.R. 234; [1954] 1 All E.R. 278, C.A.

the latter was cited in the argument in the *United* **[362]** *Railways of Havana* case.[41] In these circumstances I propose to apply the test as laid down by Lord Simonds in the *Bonython* case[42] and accepted by the House of Lords in the *United Railways of Havana* case.[43]

One further preliminary point. The proper law must be determined as at the making of the contract, though the court will, of course, give effect to changes in that proper law which arise after the making of the contract. See *Kahler* v. *Midland Bank*[44] and *Zivnostenska Banka National Corpn.* v. *Frankman*,[45] both cases in which the proper law of the contract being a foreign law including its exchange control law, the English courts gave effect to subsequent changes in that law.

(2) I now turn to the facts. At all material times the defendants had an office in Cairo which was responsible for all business transacted by the defendants over a wide area in the Middle East including Egypt, the Sudan, Palestine, Cyprus, Lebanon, Syria and Iraq. This office was under the control of Baird, who held a direct power of attorney from the defendants. By this power Baird was empowered (inter alia): "(1) To establish and manage agencies of the company; (2) to canvass for and solicit applications for insurance with the company on the lives of individuals; (3) to countersign and issue interim policies of insurance and official receipts under the conditions sanctioned by the company and on forms having the signatures of the proper officers of the company; . . . (7) to receive and collect all vouchers proofs and documents of what kind so ever which shall concern any loss; and to institute all necessary inquiries and examinations touching every such loss and to adjust and settle the same with the respective claimants."

From the evidence of McNab, now the vice-president and chief agency officer of the defendants, and at the material time the agency superintendent for the defendants covering the Middle East Area, it appears that in practice the authority of the Cairo office in the person of Baird to issue interim policies was probably restricted as to amount and some degree of control from head office; that in the case of final policies, the decision whether to issue them or not was taken in Toronto where the policy was sealed, and that it was merely transmitted to the branch for handing over; that claims, whether under an interim policy or a **[363]** final policy presented by the insured in Egypt, would be dealt with by the Cairo office subject to corroboration or authorisation from Toronto, though Cairo may have had authority to pay claims of a certain amount by themselves. Furthermore, apart from exchange control regulations, an assured, to obtain payment, could in practice go to the head office or any branch for payment wherever the policy was issued. Indeed for the plaintiff one of the attractions in dealing with the defendant company was that they were a foreign insurance company abroad, and that if Egypt was invaded, and he was not in occupied territory, he would be able to draw his policy moneys anywhere in the world. Confirmation that Harrari so understood the position is to be found in two letters which he wrote to the plaintiff under date June 11, 1960, in which he stated that payments due in connection with the policies would be made by drafts on London for sterling policies or draft on New York for United States dollar policies, and such payments would be made through any of the company's branch offices in any country in which the company operated provided that the company was not prevented from doing so by legal restrictions or exchange regulations of the Governments concerned. This evidence of the attitude of the plaintiff and Harrari I regard as significant and admissible not for the purpose of importing into the contract any contractual terms to the effect stated, but as part of the surrounding circumstances in which the policies were negotiated.

(3) As the result of these negotiations the plaintiff on June 11, 1940, signed

[41] [1961] A.C. 1007.
[42] [1951] A.C. 201; 66 T.L.R. (Pt. 2) 969.
[43] [1961] A.C. 1007.
[44] [1950] A.C. 24; 65 T.L.R. 663; [1949] 2 All E.R. 621, H.L.
[45] [1950] A.C. 57; [1949] 2 All E.R. 671, H.L.

three application forms addressed to the defendants by which he applied for three 20-year endowment policies for £3,000, £4,000 and United States dollars 10,000 respectively. These application forms, which were ultimately incorporated into the final policies, contained the following provisions: (a) The necessity for mise en demeure by huissier is expressly waived; (b) policy to be written in English; (c) a declaration by the plaintiff that in the event of his death the insurance was to be paid to his wife; and (d) a declaration that he reserved the right to change the beneficiary subject to statutory restrictions. The significance, if any, of these provisions I shall refer to later.

(4) Payment of premiums. The total 20 years' premiums under the dollar policy were paid in advance by the plaintiff with the application direct to the defendants' head office in Toronto by means of a draft on the First National Bank of Boston where the plaintiff had dollar funds since before the war. These dollars had been duly declared by the plaintiff to the Egyptian exchange **[364]** control authorities. As regards the sterling policies, the plaintiff likewise in the first instance paid the full 20-year premium with the application amounting to just under £5,000 by sterling cheque to the defendants' Cairo office, but subsequently £2,700 of this sum was repaid to the plaintiff.

(5) Issue of Interim Policies. On October 26 Baird of the defendants' Cairo office cabled to the defendants in Toronto for permission to issue interim policies covering the plaintiff's application for the sterling policies. On October 28 the defendants in Toronto instructed their Cairo office to discuss with the exchange control authorities the question of the prepaid premiums, and to secure their written permission to the issue of each of the policies, including the dollar policy, showing the amount of the policy and the amount of the prepaid premium, and for permission for the delivery of the policies in the United States as had been requested by the plaintiff on June 19. No evidence was tendered as to what was done on these instructions except that on December 10, 1940, the plaintiff made a formal declaration that the dollars paid for the premiums of the dollar policy formed part of a pre-war balance to his credit at New York; but I infer that no objection was taken by the exchange control authorities as to the issue of any of these policies provided they were delivered in Egypt. On October 31, 1940, the defendants' Cairo office issued to the plaintiff a single interim policy for a period of five months for £7,000 covering the two applications for the sterling policies under the counter-signature of Baird. These policies provided (so far as is material) as follows: "This interim policy shall cease to be effective when a policy is issued to supersede the insurance hereunder. This interim policy may be cancelled at any time during the said period of five months." No interim policy for the dollar insurance appears to have been issued.

(6) Issue of final policies sued upon. On November 25, 1940, three policies for £3,000, £4,000 and United States $10,000 were executed at Toronto in favour of the plaintiff bearing the signatures of the general manager and of the president, and under the seal of the defendant company. The dollar policy was apparently lost in transit, and a new policy so signed and sealed was executed on January 21, 1941. Subject to variations necessary in the dollar policy to take account of the dollar obligations as to the payment of the premiums and of the amount insured, each of the policies was in identical form, this being the form used by the company for foreign business. **[365]**

The policy for £3,000 recited that "the Manufacturers' Life Insurance Company Limited head office Toronto Canada hereby insure the life of Charles Rossano . . . under this policy of insurance, the particulars of which are as follows: (1) Plan of insurance—twenty year endowment. (2) Sum insured—three thousand pounds sterling. (3) When payable: (a) on March 15, 1960, if the life insured is living and this policy is in force; (b) on receipt and approval of the prior death of the life insured while this policy is in force. (4) Beneficiary. If the policy becomes payable as provided in (a) above, the insured. If the policy becomes payable as provided in (b) above, Mary Rossano, subject to the provisions on the succeeding pages hereof. . . . (8) Surplus. Apportioned annually in accordance with the annual dividend options on the succeeding pages of this policy. The provisions and options printed and written by the company on the succeeding pages hereof form part of this contract form as fully as if stated over the seal and signatures hereto affixed." Overleaf there are set out a number of printed conditions and two added rubber stamp clauses to which reference will be made.

It is only necessary to set out in this judgment certain of these clauses as follows: "Condition (1) The Contract. This policy and the application therefor a copy of which is attached constitute the entire contract. This policy shall not take effect until it has been delivered and the first premium paid to the company in exchange for the official receipt, no change having taken place in the insurability of the life insured subsequent to the completion of the application. No provision or condition of this policy may be waived or modified except by endorsement hereon signed by the president, vice-president or general manager. (2) Incontestability. . . . (3) Payment of Premiums. . . . A grace of one month (of not less than 30 days) from the actual due date of the premium stated herein will be allowed for payment of renewal premiums" (the first sentence of this clause dealing with payment of the first premium had been struck out in view of the payments of the premiums in advance above referred to). "(4) Currency. All amounts payable under the terms of this policy either to or by the company are payable in bankers demand drafts on London, England, for pounds sterling." (In the case of the dollar policy the final words read "bankers demand draft on New York U.S.A. for United States Dollars.") "(5) Automatic premium loan. . . . (6) Loan values. . . . (7) Cash and paid up insurance values. . . . (8) Extended insurance. . . . (9) Reinstatement. . . . (10) **[366]** Payment of claims. When this policy becomes a claim it must be delivered to the company with a valid discharge thereto. The amount of any lien or indebtedness on the policy will be deducted from the amount payable. (11) Suicide. . . . (12) Proof of age." There then follow provisions dealing with annual dividend options which are not material.

Next follows a printed clause dealing with appointment of beneficiary, and finally (so far as is material) a printed clause dealing with assignment in the following terms: "Any assignment of this policy shall be in duplicate and both copies sent to the head office, Toronto, Canada."

Of the added clauses appearing by rubber stamp two are or may be relevant: "(1) War Risks. Notwithstanding anything herein contained to the contrary, this policy is issued on the condition that the total sum payable hereunder shall not be greater than the net amount of premium paid . . . with interest, (a) if the life insured serves in any military, naval or air force and the death of the life insured results directly from war . . . (b) if the life insured travels beyond the geographical boundaries of Egypt and Palestine and the death of the life insured results directly or indirectly from war. . . . (2) Payment of any sum to keep this policy in force must be made at the company's offices at Cairo or Alexandria—or to persons empowered to receive them—in exchange for the company's official receipt signed by the general manager and countersigned by an agent or cashier of the company."

On the back of the policy the following notice is printed: "Important. When it is desired to obtain payment of any benefit under this contract write direct to the Manufacturers' Life Insurance Company, Toronto, Canada, or communicate with the nearest authorised representative of the company. By so doing time and expense may be saved as the company will furnish free of charge the required forms for completion together with any necessary advice and instructions." The policies having been executed in Canada were sent to the company's branch in Egypt and there delivered to the plaintiff. They remained in Egypt until January or February, 1961, when they reached this country.

(7) Canadian Insurance Law. (a) The Manufacturers' Life Insurance Company as an insurance company is subject to the Canadian and British Insurance Companies Act, a Dominion Statute broadly similar to the English Assurance Companies Acts containing provisions designed to secure their financial stability, **[367]** their deposits and the rights of different classes of policy holders in winding up.

(b) In Part V of the Insurance Act of Ontario (chapter 183 in the Revised

Statutes of Ontario, 1950) there are some 60 sections (sections 131–191) containing detailed provisions relating to the rights and obligations arising under contracts of life insurance. Section 132 provides as follows: "(1) Notwithstanding any agreement, condition or stipulation to the contrary, this Part shall apply to every contract of life insurance made in the Province after January 1, 1925, and any term in any such contract inconsistent with this Part shall be null and void. . . . (3) This Part shall apply to every other contract of life insurance made after January 1, 1925, where the contract provides that this Part shall apply or that the contract shall be construed or governed by the law of the Province."

Mr. McVitty, a member of the Ontario Bar, and a partner in the firm of J. K. Henry and Associates of Toronto, who act for the defendants in this case, was called on behalf of the defendants to speak as to the effect of this Act, and I am indebted to him for his careful and informed evidence as to the effect of this law, and as to forms of contract in practice used by the defendants. It appears that the defendants use five types of policy forms: The Canadian form, the United States form, the United Kingdom form, the Foreign General form and the Foreign British Commonwealth form. The policies issued to the plaintiff were on the Foreign General form. Accordingly, unless the policies were on the facts stated above made in Ontario, and unless on their true construction they provided that Part V shall apply, or that the contract shall be construed or governed by the law of the Province, Part V would not as a matter of law apply to them. Mr. McVitty, however, agreed that the agreement of the parties that Part V should apply, or that it should be governed and construed by the law of the Province, might be express or implied. A comparison between the terms of the Home or Canadian Policy and the terms of the Foreign General Policy showed that they were almost identical, and admittedly the terms of the Home or Canadian policy are founded upon the compulsory requirements of Part V. The only points of difference at all between the plaintiff's policy and the Home or Canadian policy which were relied upon were (1) the war risk clause; (2) the second of the rubber stamp clauses dealing with payments of sums required to keep the policy alive, and (3) the clause entitled "Appointment of Beneficiary."

Very considerable discussion arose on the terms of this last **[368]** clause which, according to Mr. McVitty, would be void under the Ontario Statute in so far as it would or might permit the plaintiff to substitute another beneficiary for his wife. Under the Ontario Statute the wife is within the class of preferred beneficiaries whose rights are safeguarded by this statute. Inasmuch, however, as in the application form which formed part of the policy the plaintiff "reserved the right to change the beneficiary subject to statutory restrictions," the effect of reading these two provisions together is, in my judgment, that the proviso to the printed beneficiary clause to which objection was taken would not operate if the change of beneficiary was not permitted by the statutory restrictions, which I think can refer only to the statutory restrictions contained in the Ontario Act. I did not understand Mr. McVitty to say anything to the contrary, though he did say that the proviso offended against the law of Ontario, and that the reservation of the right to change the application form would not be of any particular value to the plaintiff. I think it is quite plain that the Foreign Form is in all essentials based upon the terms of the Ontario Statute even though that statute may not as a matter of law apply to all insurances effected on the Foreign Form. Before leaving this branch of the case I should just note that, according to Mr. McVitty, a policy issued in Toronto providing for payment in sterling or dollars would normally or not unusually provide in the currency clause for payment by bankers' draft on London or New York as the case may be.

(8) Egyptian Insurance Law. By law No. 156 of 1950, which re-enacted with amendments law No. 92 of 1939 which applies to Egyptian undertakings and foreign undertakings which transact in Egypt life insurance, it is provided by article 16 that every undertaking shall maintain a register of policies transacted by the undertaking, and by article 20 that they shall maintain in Egypt assets of value at least equal to the mathematical liability in respect of operations transacted or fulfilled in Egypt. These assets by article 24 are (subject to certain conditions) made available to holders of such policies. The plaintiff's policies

were in accordance with this law registered on the company's register in Egypt, and the necessary deposits maintained in Egypt, but there was no evidence that the plaintiff had any knowledge of any of the matters referred to in this paragraph.

(9) I have now set out at some length the material evidence in this case bearing upon the issue of the proper law of the contract. If the test had been with what country had the transaction the **[369]** closest and most real connection, following the language used by Lord Denning, as I think per incuriam, in the *United Railways of Havana* case,[46] it may well be that there was much to be said for the view that the transaction had its closest and most real connection with Egypt, seeing that the policies were negotiated between two parties in Egypt and were delivered in Egypt. But if the real question is what intention as to the proper law is to be imputed to the parties, and if the answer to this question is to be tested by consideration of what is the system of law by reference to which the contract was made or that with which the transaction has its closest connection, I think the answer must quite clearly be not the law of Egypt but rather the law of Ontario. The policy form is clearly based on the law of Ontario. The defendant corporation had its head office in Ontario. The negotiations for the insurance conducted in Egypt could never have led to a policy unless the terms of the application had been accepted by the superior officers of the company in Toronto. No alteration or modification of the printed conditions of the policy could be effected unless expressly agreed to in writing by the officers of the company in Toronto. No assignment could be effective unless notice was given to the company in Toronto. There is no provision in the policy requiring the policies to be presented to the company for payment in Egypt. Both the policy moneys and the premiums are expressed in a currency other than Egyptian. The notice on the back of the policy advises the policy-holder who wishes to obtain payment to write direct to the head office in Canada or communicate with the nearest authorised representative of the company. Further, it seems to me that where a resident in a territory seeks life insurance from a foreign insurance company through its local agent in that territory, it is manifest that normally he chooses the foreign company because he has faith not only in that company, but in the system of law under which it operates. One further observation may be added. It seems clear that under the *Bonython*[47] test the question is still what intention is to be imputed to the parties: see the speech of Lord Simonds.[48]

(10) Earlier in my judgment I reserved for later consideration the relevance (if any) of two special provisions in the application form as follows: (a) "The necessity for mise en demeure by huissier is expressly waived," and (b) "Policy to be written in English." As to (a) the evidence was that mise en demeure **[370]** relates and relates only to a procedural provision of the mixed courts in Egypt (abolished in 1947) which required that before proceedings could be instituted a formal claim (similar to a solicitor's letter before action) should be served upon the alleged debtor by an official process server. It was submitted that this indicated that the parties had in mind that, in the event of dispute, resort would be made to the mixed court. Even if this be so, I had evidence that the mixed court applied a wide variety of laws by no means confined to the law of Egypt. I am unable to infer anything relevant from this provision. (b) "Policy to be written in English." There was evidence that in 1940 the normal commercial language in Egypt was French. From this it was argued that but for the plaintiff's election to have the policies in English, the policies would have been in French, the commercial language of Egypt. It could be equally argued that the plaintiff's choice of English indicated that he wanted to secure that the language used should not be the commercial language of Egypt but should be the language of Ontario.

(11) I am fortified in the conclusion which I have reached by the decision of Diplock J. in *Pick* v. *Manufacturers' Life Insurance Co.*,[49] and by the reasoning

[46] [1961] A.C. 1007.
[47] [1951] A.C. 201.
[48] Ibid. 219-222.
[49] [1958] 2 Lloyd's Rep. 93.

expressed by that judge for his conclusion that the policy in question in that case was not governed by the law of Palestine (now Israel) but by the law of Ontario.

It was submitted by Mr. Roskill that that case was distinguishable from this case, as I understand it, on three grounds. First, that in *Pick's* case[49] the assured, a German refugee in Palestine, 'had in the back of his mind that he might return to Germany if circumstances made that country again a congenial place of residence," whereas the plaintiff was an Egyptian born and bred, permanently residing there, with no intention in 1940 of leaving Egypt; but it is clear from the plaintiff's evidence (which I accept) that at the time when the policies were negotiated there was war on the Egyptian border, and being of Jewish faith he feared that he might have to leave the country, and wished accordingly to have policies payable anywhere in the world. Secondly, that in *Pick's* case[49] there was no evidence that anyone had power to issue interim policies in Palestine. This appears to be true, but in my view is irrelevant. Thirdly, that in *Pick's* case[49] the first sentence of the clause relating to payment of premiums had not been struck out. As I have already stated, **[371]** in the present case the plaintiff paid the whole 20 years' premiums on the dollar policy direct to the defendants in Toronto, and the premiums on the sterling policies by a sterling cheque to the defendants' Cairo office. Such payments made the first sentence of the clause unnecessary and inappropriate in the present case. I cannot appreciate that this factor provided any valid ground of distinction. In my judgment, accordingly, the Egyptian control legislation does not apply to these policies as part of the proper law of the contracts.

(12) I next have to consider whether it applies (a) by reason of the situs of the debt being in Egypt or (b) by reason of the fact that Egypt is the contractual place of performance. Though it is pleaded in paragraph 6 of the re-amended defence that the Egyptian control legislation would apply as part of the law of the situs of the debt under the policy, that situs being Egypt, I did not understand from the argument addressed to me that the lex situs was advanced as a ground for applying the Egyptian control legislation independent of the law of the place of performance. So far as I recall no authority was cited to me on this branch of the case supporting such distinction, and I knew of none. It may be observed that the lex situs is not stated to be such a ground in rule 178 of the 7th edition of Dicey which provides as follows: "(1) A contractual obligation may be invalidated or discharged by exchange control legislation if—(a) such legislation is part of the law of the contract; or (b) it is part of the law of the place of performance; or (c) it is part of English law and the relevant statute or statutory instrument is applicable to the contract." In a note on page 921 the editors observe: "The mere fact that exchange control legislation is in force at the place at which a party to the contract resides or carries on business or in the State of which he is a national and that the performance of the contract is excused or made illegal by such legislation, is no defence to an action on the contract, unless either the law to which this legislation belongs is the proper law of the contract, or the contract was to be performed at the place where the legislation is in force." The passage is in my judgment abundantly supported by the decision in the Court of Appeal in *Kleinwort, Sons & Co.* v. *Ungarische, etc.*[50]

Accordingly I have next to consider what was the place of performance of these contracts, and for this purpose the relevant act of performance is the payment of the policy moneys; for a **[372]** contract may contain obligations which have to be performed in different countries so that the law of the place of performance of one obligation may be different from the law of the place of performance of another. The policies do not expressly provide for the place of performance; the mode of performance of the material obligation is stated in condition 4 of the policy to be, in the case of the sterling policies, "in bankers demand drafts on London England for pounds sterling," or in the case of the dollar policy in bankers demand drafts on New York U.S.A. for United States

[50] [1939] 2 K.B. 678; 55 T.L.R. 814; [1939] 3 All E.R. 38, C.A.

dollars." Both these modes of payment are normal or not unusual modes of payment in Ontario of sterling or dollar obligations. They may be (though there was no direct evidence on this point) also normal modes of payment in Egypt.

Reliance was placed upon the fact that the policies were physically in Egypt at maturity date. I attach no significance to this. Perhaps rather more weight should be given to the fact that the policies were on the defendants' Egyptian register and backed by deposits in Egypt, albeit they were also backed by deposits in Canada. But I can find no express or implied term in the policies which justifies the defendants in saying that the policy moneys are payable only in Egypt. Indeed there is no express term in the policy or any term necessarily to be implied to require the defendants to maintain a branch in Egypt authorised to pay. Furthermore, the notice on the back of the policies clearly invites the policy-holder who desires to obtain payment to write direct to the head office or the nearest authorised representative of the company. Though Egypt was a permissible place of performance, the defendants had no right to insist upon payment only in Egypt, and accordingly Egypt was not the relevant place of performance.

In *Pick's* case[51] Diplock J. said[52]: "I apprehend that the principal obligation of the defendants is to pay sterling, the currency in which the policy is expressed, and that banker's drafts when delivered amount to conditional payment only, and, if dishonoured on payment" (query "presentation") "in London do not discharge the contract. The contract is finally discharged only when the draft is honoured in London, which is, in my view, the primary place of payment in the strict sense of that word." This may well be so.

(13) Though as stated above I have reached the conclusion that the Egyptian control legislation does not apply either as **[373]** part of the proper law or as part of the law of the place of performance, it is probably desirable that I should state shortly my understanding as to the Egyptian control legislation on the assumption that it does apply to the facts of this case in view of the evidence which was called by the defendants on this point.

For this purpose it is necessary to state certain further facts. As stated above, in 1940 Rossano was an Egyptian national residing and carrying on business as a cotton merchant with others as a partner in a limited partnership firm by the name of Levi Rossano & Co. He is a member of the Jewish community. In the course of his business he had occasion to make many visits abroad. In 1948, whilst Rossano was out of Egypt for health reasons, his property in Egypt was sequestrated for a short time until July 3, 1949. He returned to Egypt in March, 1950, and remained there (apart from short business trips abroad) until August 4, 1956, when he left Egypt again on a business trip, having obtained a tax clearance from the Egyptian revenue authorities before leaving. In November, 1956, the Suez crisis arose. Fearing that he would be subject to further discrimination on the grounds of his faith, Rossano abandoned any intentions of returning to Egypt. His Egyptian passport was withdrawn, and he assumed Italian nationality by tracing descent from his grandfather (a registered Italian national) and thereafter severed his connections wholly from Egypt so far as to do so was within his power.

No evidence as to Egyptian law was called on behalf of the plaintiff, but on behalf of the defendants there was called Mr. Theodore Page, a member of the Inner Temple, who practised before the mixed courts and British consular courts in Egypt until they ceased to function as such in 1949. Since that date Mr. Page had no right of audience before any Egyptian courts, but has continued to advise clients both in London and Egypt on matters of Egyptian law and has done his best to keep his knowledge of Egyptian law up to date. No objection was taken as to the qualification of Mr. Page to give evidence on Egyptian law as it exists today.

On the basis of Mr. Page's evidence it is I think clear that (a) the plaintiff, notwithstanding his attempt to sever his connections with Egypt, would be regarded as a "resident" for the purpose of the Egyptian control law; and (b) that

[51] [1958] 2 Lloyd's Rep. 93.
[52] Ibid. 99.

a payment by the defendants' branch in Egypt to the plaintiff of sterling or dollar currency would be illegal without the permission of **[374]** the exchange control authorities. (See the statutory provisions relied upon by the defendants by way of amendment in paragraph 6 of the re-amended defence which were in force at the material date of the policies, namely, March 15, 1960, when they were replaced by decree No. 893 of 1960 which came into force on October 22, 1960.) Mr. Page further stated that a payment of sterling or dollars by the defendants in Toronto would also be illegal by the same laws, and would expose the defendants' Cairo branch and its personnel to penalties under Egyptian law.

It seems clear that under article 24 of chapter I, section 3 of the Exchange Control Regulations of 1960, the defendant company itself would rank as a "non-resident"; but their Egyptian branch being "a branch or office of a foreign institution carrying out any activity in the Egyptian Province" would rank as a resident. The basis of Mr. Page's theory that payment by the defendant company abroad would involve the branch in Egypt in illegality was that, from the Egyptian point of view, the liability of the company is the liability of the branch and the branch is a resident, and that the only place in the Egyptian view where the policies could be paid being Egypt, a payment by the head office outside Egypt would be a payment by the head office as agent for the Cairo office. I confess that I find the greatest possible difficulty in following this theory, and had it been necessary for my decision I should have held that I was left in doubt whether as a strict matter of Egyptian law, as distinct from the practice of the exchange control authorities, a payment by the defendants' head office outside Egypt would be illegal. In so stating my view I am not unmindful of the limitation on the power of the court to draw conclusions as to foreign law where the evidence of an expert on foreign law has been given. (See Dicey, 7th edition, page 1112, "Use of foreign sources" and the cases there cited.)

(14) I now turn to the defence based upon the alleged garnishee orders. The facts as to the garnishee orders are pleaded in paragraph 10 of the re-amended defence as follows: "On November 16, 1960, the defendants were served with a garnishee order," (the first garnishee order), "in respect of an amount of £E5,677 alleged to be due from the plaintiff to the Egyptian tax department for the years 1950/51 to 1955/56 plus interest at 6 per cent. from November 27, 1960. Further or alternatively on or about January 23, 1962, the defendants were served with a second garnishee order in respect of an amount of £E12,291 alleged to be due from the plaintiff to the Egyptian **[375]** tax department for the years 1951 and 1952 exclusive of interest. The said orders purported to attach all securities belonging to the plaintiff in the hands of the defendants and all sums of money falling due hereunder and to require the defendants to remit the same to the said department or so much thereof as might be necessary to cover the said amounts."

In support of this plea the defendants put in (without objection as to their formal proof) two documents in Arabic purporting to be the garnishee orders relied upon, together with English translations. I accept that orders in this form were served on the defendants in Cairo. The English translation of the first garnishee order so far as is material provides as follows: "In accordance with the authority empowered legally to us: We hereby have levied an executory attachment against the taxpayer Charles Rossano in the hands of the Manufacturers' Life Insurance Company, of 20, Sharia Adj Pacha, Cairo, on all what it would have in its custody such as money, securities, deeds or otherwise. We have notified the company not to effect payment of what it would have in its hands or to hand over same to the taxpayer. We have asked the said company to file a declaration within fifteen days from the date hereof regarding what it would have in its custody and to show therein an accurate and detailed description thereof as well as its number and measure or its weight or amount; and remit same within forty days from the date hereof or remit what would cover the said taxes plus interest re late payment or deposit same with the Treasury of the inspectorate in case the date of settlement has fallen due, otherwise it should be withheld in its hands until such date falls due when the company should remit same or deposit it with the Treasury of the inspectorate." The document bears the signatures of a tax inspector and of a controller. Pursuant to this notice the defendants' Cairo office on November 29, 1960, wrote to the controller setting out particulars of the three policies sued upon showing the maturity date to be March 15, 1960, and stating with regard to remitting the amounts as requested by the inspectorate: "We wish to draw your attention firstly that the above mentioned policies are expressed in foreign currencies and payable to a non-resident person and that the matter necessitates the obtainment of approval from the Exchange Control before we effect any payment in accordance with the prevailing laws and regulations." In spite of further requests for payment by the tax authorities no payments have been made. For completeness I should add that the tax in **[376]** question is alleged to be a liability of Charles Rossano in his capacity as partner of Levi Rossano & Company.

On behalf of the defendants it was submitted (1) that whatever be the proper law of the contract, the debt is and was situated in Cairo and that debt has been validly attached in the country where it was situated; (2) that an English court will as a matter of private international law recognise and give effect to the validity of that attachment and not put the garnishee in peril of having to pay twice, and that it does not matter whether the attachment proceedings are in respect of a revenue claim; (3) that if the debt is not situated in Egypt, the English court will as a matter of comity give effect to the proceedings and will not put the garnishee in peril of having to pay twice if the court is satisfied (a) that by the law of the place of attachment the situs of the debt is in that place, that is, Egypt; or (b) that by the law of the place of attachment there is jurisdiction over the debtor, the garnishee and the garnishor.

The plaintiff, on the other hand, by his counsel submitted (1) that the situs of the debt was not Egypt; (2) that the garnishee orders were invalid (a) because not signed by the Minister of Finance or his duly authorised deputy, and (b) because not served on the debtor within six days as required by article 28 of the relevant law; (3) that the garnishee orders provide no defence since (a) no payment has been made under either or (b) neither of them was made until after the maturity date on which the defendants should have paid; (4) that this court should not recognise the garnishee as to do so would be indirectly at least to enforce a foreign revenue law; and (5) that the orders being in the nature of administrative orders and not orders of any court, an English court will not enforce them.

Many of the points raised in these submissions raise difficult questions of private international law upon which English authority is scanty. But as I have reached the conclusion that the fundamental objection to the recognition of these orders is that their recognition would offend against the well-settled principle that the English court will not recognise or enforce directly or indirectly a foreign revenue law or claim, it is not necessary for me as a matter of decision to deal with many of the other points raised. The basic principle underlying the proposition stated above is to be found stated with characteristic trenchancy by Lord Mansfield C.J. in *Planche* v. *Fletcher*,[53] *Holman* v. **[377]** *Johnson*[54] and *Lever* v. *Fletcher*[55] that "no country ever takes notice of the revenue laws of another." (See the speech of Lord Simonds in *Government of India* v. *Taylor*,[56]* which is a direct authority, if authority be needed, that the English courts will not entertain a suit by a foreign State to recover a tax.) But in the speech of Lord Keith[57] reference is made with approval to the judgment of Kingsmill Moore J. in the High Court of Eire in *Peter Buchanan Ltd. & Macharg* v. *McVey*[58]* as illustrating the position which is relevant to the present case "that in no circumstances will the courts directly or indirectly enforce the revenue laws of another country."

In the course of the judgment above referred to, Kingsmill Moore J.[59] says this: "If I am right in attributing such importance to the principle, then it is clear that its enforcement must not depend merely on the form in which the claim is

[53] (1779) 1 Doug.K.B. 251.
[54] (1775) I Cowp. 341.
[55] (1780) unreported.
[56] [1955] A.C. 491; [1955] 2 W.L.R. 303; [1955] 1 All E.R. 292, H.L.
[57] [1955] A.C. 491, 510.
[58] [1955] A.C. 516n.
[59] Ibid. 529.

made. It is not a question whether the plaintiff is a foreign State or the representative of a foreign State or its revenue authority. In every case the substance of the claim must be scrutinised, and if it then appears that it is really a suit brought for the purpose of collecting the debts of a foreign revenue it must be rejected." In my judgment for this court to allow the defendants to set up in diminution or extinction of the plaintiff's claim a foreign garnishee order or attachment served upon them by the Egyptian tax authorities would clearly be contrary to the principles above stated.

Another application of the same principle is to be found in *Indian and General Investment Trust Ltd.* v. *Borax Consolidated Ltd.*,[60] where the defendant guarantors of certain gold bonds issued by a railway company in the United States, who undertook to pay the principal money and interest in London, sought to deduct from the annual payment under the bonds an income tax of 2 per cent. imposed under the United States Government tax legislation which required the railway company to deduct this tax on payment of interest. Sankey J., in rejecting the defence, said[61]: "There is no Act of Parliament which allows payment of income tax to another country to be reckoned as a discharge." If in the present case the defendants had **[378]** actually remitted the amount of the tax to the Egyptian authorities, this would not, on the basis of Sankey J.'s judgment, have been reckoned a discharge. Still less, if no payment has been made, can a mere attachment of a debt by a foreign revenue authority amount to a defence.

It is perhaps not without significance to observe that if this court by its judgment decreed that the defendants were not liable on the policies by reason of these orders, theoretically at least there would be nothing to prevent the Egyptian revenue authorities from recovering their alleged debt from some other property of the plaintiff's in Egypt and not persisting in their claim against the defendants under these orders. I am, of course, not suggesting for a moment that the defendants, if released from the claim under the garnishee, would not pay the plaintiff in spite of the discharge of their policy debt by the judgment.

Though I have preferred to rest my rejection of the defendants' defence based upon the garnishee orders upon the ground stated above, it is probably convenient that I should deal with at least some of the other points debated before me on this branch of the case.

(15) Situs of debt. In *New York Life Insurance Co.* v. *Public Trustee*[62] the question arose whether moneys due under life policies of a New York insurance company signed by the president and secretary of the company and countersigned by the general manager for Europe, which had been issued in London to German nationals before the First World War, were caught by the charge imposed pursuant to the Treaty of Versailles. The policy money was expressed to be paid in London. The Court of Appeal, basing themselves primarily upon the provision in the policies as to payment in London, held that the debt was situated here and so subject to the charge. There is no such express provision in the policies here in suit. There being no express provision in these policies as to the place of payment, the defendants accordingly relied upon the statement of principle by Pearson J. in *F. & K. Jabbour* v. *Custodian of Israeli Absentee Property*[63]* in the following terms: "Where a corporation has residence in two or more countries, the debt or chose in action is properly recoverable, and therefore situated in that one of those countries where the sum payable is primarily payable, and that is where it is required to be paid **[379]** by an express or implied provision of the contract or, if there is no such provision, where it would be paid according to the ordinary course of business."

In the policies here sued upon there is no express provision as to the place of payment. The mode of payment is prescribed as "in banker's demand draft on London," or in the case of the dollar policy "on New York." In *Pick's* case[64] above referred to Diplock J. expressed the view that the primary place for the

[60] [1920] 1 K.B. 539; 36 T.L.R. 125.
[61] [1920] 1 K.B. 539, 549.
[62] [1924] 2 Ch. 101; 40 T.L.R. 430, C.A.
[63] [1954] 1 W.L.R. 139; [1954] 1 All E.R. 145, 146.
[64] [1958] 2 Lloyd's Rep. 93.

delivery of the banker's draft on London was the head office in Toronto, but that until the draft was honoured in London the delivery of the draft was conditional payment only, and the primary place of payment was London. The plaintiff, if all had gone well, would have collected his money by presenting his banker's draft in London and New York though he might of course have discounted the draft elsewhere. But in the ordinary course of business he would not, I think, have collected sterling or dollars from the defendants in Egypt. I should accordingly hold that the situs of the debt was not in Egypt.

It was argued, however, that even if this is so by English law, the debt for the policy moneys was by Egyptian law situated in Egypt. According to the uncontradicted evidence of Mr. Page, this is so. But I am by no means certain that by English law or by English principles of private international law this is in any way relevant. In *New York Life Insurance Co.* v. *Public Trustee* (supra)[65] Warrington L.J. says: "according to the law of one country it may be that these debts which we are prepared to hold are localised in England might be held to be localised elsewhere, but what we have to do is to give our decision upon the municipal law of this country and upon the facts and circumstances of this particular case."

It is true that the court there were considering the application of an English statute, but I am not sure that this is the critical point. Furthermore, there is some authority that an English court would not be debarred from determining on its own principles that the proper law of a contract is the law of A. by the fact that the courts of B. have held or would hold that the proper law of the contract was the law of B. or some law other than the law of A. (See *In re United Railways* (supra),[66] *per* Jenkins L.J.[67] and *per* Willmer L.J.[68]) By parity of reasoning **[380]** it would seem to me that I should not be deterred from holding that the situs of the debt was not in Egypt on the evidence of Mr. Page that by Egyptian law the situs of the debt was Egypt.

(16) Validity of the garnishee order. This question was debated at great length in the evidence of Mr. Page. In summary the effect of his evidence was as follows: In the case of an ordinary non-governmental debt it is open to the creditor A. to go to the judge in chambers, and on production to him of prima facie evidence of a debt due from B. to apply for an order against C. attaching by way of "precautionary execution" or cautionary sequestration any debt due by C. to B. By the practice of the Egyptian courts such attachment will be valid unless and until the debtor B. satisfies the judge in chambers that no debt is due by him to A. In the case of governmental debts the department concerned may proceed by "the administrative way"; that is to say, without any application to the judge in chambers they may by an order signed by the minister or his duly authorised deputy, or, in the case of a tax liability, on the basis of a tax assessment signed by the minister or his duly authorised deputy, issue a similar attachment signed by the minister or his duly authorised deputy, issue a similar attachment order on a third party who holds funds belonging to the debtor (for example, in the case of a banker and customer) or who owes money either in praesenti, or subject to a condition requiring the person upon whom the order is served to declare to the department what funds of the debtor he holds or what moneys he owes the debtor either in praesenti or subject to a condition, and further requiring him to pay the money over to the department within 40 days of the service of the notice in the case of a present debt, or on the fulfilment of the condition in the case of a conditional debt.

Two major points were taken on this topic by the plaintiff (i) that neither the tax assessment referred to in the attachments relied upon nor the attachment orders were proved to have been signed by the minister or his duly authorised deputy; and (ii) that it was not proved that article 29 of the law 308 of 1955 requiring notice to the debtor within eight days had been complied with. As to (i) Mr. Page's evidence was to the effect that, by a general directive issued by the Minister of Finance soon after the law was made, tax inspectors and con-

[65] [1924] 2 Ch. 101, 117.
[66] [1961] A.C. 1007.
[67] [1960] Ch. 52, 97.
[68] Ibid. 114.

trollers of the relevant tax departments were authorised to sign the relevant tax assessments and to issue and sign such orders; but no such general directive was produced or otherwise proved before me. **[381]**

As to (ii) the material part of article 29 in the certified true translation put before the court provided as follows: "A copy of the attachment notice must be notified to the debtor within eight days following the date of the notice served on the third party whereby it should be mentioned the date on which the notice was served on the third party otherwise the attachment will be void." Though Mr. Page at first accepted this translation as accurate, subsequently he said that the true translation or meaning of the concluding words was that "it was voidable at the instance of the alleged debtor" or "under sanction of the garnishee or seizure being voidable at the instance of the debtor," this being Mr. Page's translation of the French words "sous peine de nullite de la saisie-arret."

I find some difficulty in accepting either of these expressions as being true translations of the French text. Mr. Page was, however, quite definite in his view that the garnishee himself has no right to challenge the validity of the order and that it was binding upon him unless the alleged debtor applies to the court to set it aside. No provision of the statute or any decision of the court was produced in support of this view, but it was said to be based upon the practice of the court. According to Mr. Page, this result would follow even if the debtor being abroad had in fact received no notice of the alleged tax assessment or of the garnishee order. There being no evidence to the contrary I feel constrained to accept this as the true view, however unreasonable it may be, though I confess I have reached this conclusion with considerable reluctance and hesitation, especially as I formed the view that Mr. Page (under the pressure of cross-examination) perhaps unconsciously was at times inclined to depart from the position of a dispassionate expounder of the law and assumed the role of an advocate.

But on the assumption that the garnishee orders or either of them are valid by Egyptian law, and by that law binding upon the defendants, two further points remain for consideration. First, being garnishee or sequestration orders imposed by the act of the executive, and not the result of any judicial proceedings, must or should an English court afford them recognition? I have been referred to no authority of our courts in which the effect of administrative garnishee has been discussed. The editors of Dicey when stating in rule 92 that the validity and effect of an attachment or garnishment of a debt is governed by the lex situs of the debt are clearly referring to garnishee orders made by a **[382]** competent court. I should not be disposed on general principles to extend the recognition further.

Secondly, it is submitted on behalf of the plaintiff that on the facts of this case the defendants should not be held entitled to rely upon them since both of them are later in date than the maturity dates of the policies upon which date, upon my previous findings, the policy moneys should have been paid. If allowed now to rely upon them, they would, it is said, in effect be taking advantage of their own wrong or default. In my judgment this plea is well-founded, and should be accepted.

(17) I now turn to the third submission advanced on behalf of the defendants. This may be stated as follows: That the English courts will as a matter of comity give effect to foreign garnishee proceedings if the court is satisfied (a) that by the law of the place of attachment the situs of the debt is in the country of attachment, namely, Egypt, or (b) that by the law of the place of attachment there is jurisdiction over the garnishee, the debtor and his garnishor.

As to the first limb of this proposition I have already stated my views as to the situs of the debt and need not develop this point further since so far as I know no separate authority was relied upon under this branch of the argument.

As to the second limb of this submission based upon the jurisdiction of the foreign court over the debtor the garnishee and the garnishor, as at present advised I should not be prepared to accept that on the facts proved the Egyptian court had jurisdiction over Rossano. At the time in question Rossano, though according to Egyptian law still an Egyptian national (albeit also an Italian national by Italian law) and "resident" for the purpose of Egyptian exchange control regulations, was not physically in Egypt, had no intention of returning to Egypt, and so far as lay in his power had severed his connections with Egypt. He personally had no knowledge of the orders. The limited partnership firm of Levi Rossano & Co. had ceased to be registered on the Egyptian Commercial Register and had ceased to be a legal entity, and it was not proved to my satisfaction that anyone in Egypt had any authority from him to accept service of any proceedings or documents in relation to any personal liability of his. Even if the attachment order had been an order of the Egyptian court upon Rossano personally so as to have the status of a judgment of a foreign court, as at present advised I should not have concluded that the Egyptian courts had such **[383]** jurisdiction over Rossano as to justify enforcement of that judgment at common law in the English courts.

Though the Foreign Judgments (Reciprocal Enforcement) Act, 1933, has no application even to a judgment of an Egyptian court seeing that the Act has not been applied to Egypt, the provisions of section 2 of that Act, which set out the grounds upon which a foreign court is to be deemed to have jurisdiction, were designed to reproduce the common law rules appropriate to the enforcement of a foreign judgment at common law, and according to the editors of Dicey, at p. 109, may be relied upon as stating the rules of the common law. If this is so, it is to be observed that in this section neither nationality nor allegiance is stated as founding jurisdiction, nor would submission merely for the purpose of protecting or otherwise obtaining the release of property seized, or threatened with seizure, have founded jurisdiction. I should not be disposed to accept the third submission as well founded.

I am much indebted to counsel for the help they have given to me in this case by their wide-ranging arguments. In case this case should go further, it is right that I should state that there were a number of points taken in the arguments before me with which I have not thought it necessary to deal specifically.

There will be judgment for the plaintiff for the sum of £9,906 9s. 10d. together with interest thereon at the rate of 5 per cent. per annum from March, 1960.

Judgment for the plaintiff with costs.

Solicitors: *Parker, Garrett & Co.; Fladgate & Co.*

IN RE RUSSIAN COMMERCIAL AND INDUSTRIAL BANK

((1963) 107 Sol. Jo. 415)

May 7, 1963: Chancery Division: Buckley J.

Company Law—Dissolution of Foreign Company under Foreign Law—Winding up in England—Proof of Debts.

Adjourned summons.

A French bank, incorporated in France, carried on its business in London through its branch here. A Russian bank was founded in 1889 under the laws of Imperial Russia; it had a large number of branches within the country and two branches outside it, one in Paris and the other in London. In the course of business the French bank from time to time provided banking facilities to the Russian bank. The Russian bank had to satisfy its obligations arising under those facilities in sterling in London. In the political conditions obtaining in 1914 the Russian bank found itself unable to cover the debt arising out of the transactions in respect of those facilities. To meet the exceptional circumstances the two banks entered into arrangements postponing payment of the debt thus arising until after the 1914–18 war and securing its ultimate payment by a collateral security in the meantime. In December, 1917, and January, 1918, the Russian Government passed decrees dissolving all private banks in the country, confiscating their share capital and merging them with the State bank. In

February, 1922, an application was **[416]** made in England to wind up the Russian bank's branch here, and a winding-up order was made on 24th October, 1922. On 18th September, 1925, the French bank lodged a proof in the winding up treating the debt as having arisen in August, 1919, when the last of the series under the arrangement matured. In 1961 the liquidator rejected the proof and the French bank appealed.

BUCKLEY, J., said that the debt arising from the transactions between the banks was situated in London and accrued in 1914. In contemplation of Russian law the Russian bank had no longer any corporate existence, at any rate after January, 1918, when the decree was passed confiscating the bank's share capital. But under English law the dissolution of a foreign company under foreign law was to be ignored for the purposes of winding up or was to be deemed not to have occurred. A creditor whose debt had accrued before the dissolution of a foreign company under the law of its incorporation could prove in respect of that debt in a winding up in this country. Accordingly, the dissolution of the Russian bank in 1918 was no bar to the French bank's proof of the debt which accrued before that date. But the proof was based on a debt shown to have arisen after the Russian bank was dissolved. Accordingly, the liquidator was entitled to reject the proof. The French bank was, however, entitled to prove in the winding up for the debt as having accrued in 1914. Appeal dismissed.

APPEARANCES: *Andrew Bateson (Tamplin, Joseph & Flux); Raymond Walton, Q.C. (Stafford Clark & Co.).*

U.G.S. FINANCE, LTD. v. NATIONAL MORTGAGE BANK OF GREECE AND NATIONAL BANK OF GREECE, S.A.

([1964] 1 Lloyds Rep. 446)

1, 2, 3, 6, 7, 8, 9 May 2, July 1963: Court of Appeal: Lord Denning M.R., Harman, Pearson L.JJ.

Contract—Bonds—Interest on overdue coupons—Limitation of action—Condition as to payment—Whether applicable—Alleged fundamental breach precluding reliance on condition—Alleged waiver of condition by evincing intent not to pay.

Issue of bonds to be redeemed on or before Dec. 1, 1957, by first defendants, N.M. Bank of Greece, guaranteed by second defendants, N. Bank of Greece —Payment of principal and interest to be made in London—Condition 13 of bonds providing:

> 13. PAYMENT of interest in respect of drawn Bonds will cease on the date upon which the Bonds become payable out of the amortisation moneys in the hands of the Bankers. Drawn Bonds when presented for payment must be accompanied by all unmatured coupons. The equivalent of any missing unmatured coupons will be deducted from the amount of the Bond. Coupons not presented for payment within 6 years of their due date and Bonds not presented within 20 years of the date of redemption are proscribed and void.

Half-yearly interest coupons on bonds stating:

> Coupon payable on [relevant due date] This Coupon is payable in Sterling in London . . . This coupon will be forfeited if not presented within six years from due date.

Bonds not honoured after 1940. Acquisition by plaintiffs in October and

November, 1960, of some unpaid bonds with coupons attached and some detached coupons for period 1941 to 1950—Payment of principal and interest from (1954 to 1960) recovered by plaintiffs—Claim by plaintiffs for payment on attached coupons for period from 1941 to 1954 and on detached coupons for period from 1941 to 1950, those coupons having been presented, but not paid—Allegation by defendants that coupons were void under Condition 13—Contentions by plaintiffs, (1) that Condition 13 applied to missing unmatured coupons only; (2) that defendants were in fundamental breach of contract (in that defendants were unable to pay) and were disentitled from relying on Condition 13; and (3) that, by evincing an intention not to pay the coupons, defendants had waived condition—Plaintiffs' claim dismissed by McNair, J.

——Appeal by plaintiffs.

————*Held*, by C.A. (Lord Denning, M.R. Harman and Pearson, L.JJ.), (1) that last sentence of Condition 13 applied to all coupons; (2) (a) that inability to pay after 1941 would only have been a breach if bondholders had treated inability as equivalent to repudiation and had elected to treat contract as at an end, which no bondholder had done; (b) that Condition 13 was not an exemption clause (it left bondholder free to sue if he chose, but, if he did, he would have been met, not by Condition 13, but by Limitation Act); and that, therefore, doctrine of fundamental breach had no application to this case; (3) that the conduct of defendants amounted to a waiver of the six-year clause, but that waiver only operated in favour of couponholders who were actually influenced by it (and there was no evidence that holders of coupons within six-year period were misled by defendants' failure to provide funds for payment of coupons); and that, in this case, when plaintiffs purchased coupons, they could have seen that coupons had not been presented within 6 years; (4) that, as claim on attached coupons failed, there was no point in considering extra defences raised on detached coupons; and that, therefore, appeal should be dismissed.

The following cases were referred to:

Adams and Others v. National Bank of Greece S.A.* [1961] A.C. 255;
Adel Bosholi v. Allied Commercial Exporters, Ltd., (unreported);
Akerib v. Booth and Others, Ltd., [1961] 1 W.L.R. 367;
Alexander v. Railway Executive, [1951] 2 K.B. 882;
Atlantic Shipping and Trading Company, Ltd. v. Louis Dreyfus & Co., [1922] 2 A.C. 250; (1922) 10 Ll.L.Rep. 703;
Bontex Knitting Works, Ltd. v. St. John's Garage, (1943) 60 T.L.R. 44; (C.A.) (1944) 60 T.L.R. 253;
Bowes and Others v. Howe, (1813) 5 Taunt. 30;
Cap Palos, [1921] P. 458;
Charterhouse Credit Company, Ltd. v. Tolly, [1963] 2 W.L.R. 1168;
Gibaud v. Great Eastern Railway Company, [1921] 2 K.B. 426; [**447**]
Joachimson v. Swiss Bank Corporation, [1921] 3 K.B. 110; (1921) 6 Ll.L.Rep. 435;
Jones and Another v. Barkley (1781) 2 Doug. 684;
Karsales (Harrow), Ltd. v. Wallis [1956] 1 W.L.R. 936;
Kingston-upon-Hull Corporation v. Harding and Another, [1892] 2 Q.B. 494;
Lilley v. Doubleday, (1881) 7 Q.B.D. 510;
London and North Western Railway Company v. Neilson, [1922] 2 A.C. 263;
National Bank of Greece and Athens S.A. v. Metliss,* [1957] 2 Q.B. 33; [1958] A.C. 509;
Puckett and Smith's Contract, *In re*, [1902] 2 Ch. 258;
Rothschild & Sons v. Commissioners of Inland Revenue, [1894] 2 Q.B. 142;
Sir Anthony Main's Case (1596) 5 Co. Rep. 20b;
Smeaton, Hanscomb & Co., Ltd. v. Sassoon I. Setty, Son & Co., [1953] 2 Lloyd's Rep. 580; [1953] 1 W.L.R. 1468;
Spurling Ltd. v. Bradshaw, [1956] 1 Lloyd's Rep. 392; [1956] 1 W.L.R. 461;
Sze Hai Tong Bank, Ltd. v. Rambler Cycle Company, Ltd., [1959] A.C. 576; [1959] 2 Lloyd's Rep. 114;

Szymonowski & Co. v. Beck & Co., [1923] 1 K.B. 457;
Tate & Lyle, Ltd. v. Hain Steamship Company, Ltd., (1936) 55 Ll.L. Rep. 159; (1936) 41 Com. Cas. 350;
Tulk v. Moxhay, (1848) 2 Ph. 774;
Turnbull & Co. Proprietary, Ltd. v. Mundas Trading Company (Australasia) Proprietary, Ltd., [1954] 2 Lloyd's Rep. 198;
Universal Cargo Carriers Corporation v. Citati, [1957] 2 Q.B. 401; [1957] 1 Lloyd's Rep. 174.

This was an appeal by the plaintiffs, U.G.S. Finance, Ltd., from a decision of Mr. Justice McNair in the Queen's Bench Division (Commercial Court) in favour of the defendants, National Mortgage Bank of Greece and National Bank of Greece, S.A. The plaintiffs had acquired bonds with coupons attached and some detached coupons, and they sought to recover payment on the coupons more than six years old. The defendants contended that the bonds were subject to a special condition that coupons would be forfeited if not presented within six years of their due date.

The plaintiffs alleged (1) that the special condition applied only to certain other coupons; (2) that the defendants were guilty of a fundamental breach of contract in that they were not willing or able to pay the coupons after 1941; and (3) that the defendants had waived the condition by their having evinced an intent not to pay the coupons, even if they had been presented.

The further facts and arguments are sufficiently stated in their Lordships' judgments.

Mr. John Foster, Q.C., Mr. Mark Littman, Q.C., and Mr. P. Lewis (instructed by Messrs. Herbert Smith & Co.) appeared for the appellant plaintiffs; Mr. T. G. Roche, Q.C., and Mr. H. Lever (instructed by Messrs. Stibbard, Gibson & Co.) represented the respondent defendants.

Judgment was reserved.

Tuesday, July 2, 1963

JUDGMENT

Lord DENNING, M.R. (read by Lord Justice HARMAN): We are here concerned with yet another case about the Greek bonds. I need not recite again the history of them. It will be found in the reports of *National Bank of Greece and Athens S.A.* v. *Metliss** [1958] A.C. 509, and *Adams and Others* v. *National Bank of Greece S.A.*,* [1961] A.C. 255. As a result of those cases, many of the bondholders have obtained judgments against the guarantors and have succeeded in getting paid the principal on the bonds and also the interest for the last six years. Since those cases an enterprising company called U.G.S. Finance, Ltd., in October and November, 1960, bought up a number of the unpaid bonds with coupons attached. They have recovered payment of the principal on the bonds and interest on the coupons for the last six years (from Dec. 1, 1954, to Dec. 1, 1960) just as the other bondholders have. But they now seek in this action to recover interest on the coupons more than six years old, that is, those from June 1, 1941, to June 1, 1954. The company have also bought up a lot of old coupons which were detached from the bonds when the previous holders were paid off. They bought these loose for a song, 1s. apiece. And they now seek to recover interest on those old detached coupons. These fell due from June 1, 1941, to June 1, 1950.

The simple answer made by the defendants to these claims is that the bonds were subject to a special condition that coupons would be forfeited if not presented within six years of their due date. I will refer to **[448]** the conditions, but before doing so I must say that it is common ground that the bonds, with the coupons attached, are negotiable instruments and are governed by the law of England. Each series of the bonds was in the same form. I will set out the material terms of the first series and underline[1] the most important parts of them:

The Mortgage Bank for value received hereby unconditionally promises *to pay in Sterling to the Bearer of this Bond* on the 1st day of December 1957 or on such earlier day as the principal moneys hereby secured shall become payable in *accordance with the conditions endorsed hereon on presentation or surrender* of this Bond *the principal sum of One Hundred Pounds and also* in the meantime until such principal moneys shall be fully paid off *to pay in Sterling Interest on the said principal moneys at the rate of 7 per cent. per annum half-yearly on the 1st day of June and the 1st day of December in every year upon presentation and surrender of the coupons attached hereto as they severally become due.*

Payment of principal and interest will be made in Sterling . . . at the offices of Hambros Bank Limited or Erlangers (hereinafter collectively called "the Bankers") in London England or at the option of the holder at the National Bank of Greece in Athens Greece by cheque on London.

This Bond is issued subject to and with the benefit of the Conditions endorsed hereon which are to be deemed part of it.

The National Bank of Greece hereby unconditionally guarantees the due payment of the principal moneys and interest and the due performance of all the conditions of this Bond.

Dated this 1st day of December 1927.

The bond was duly signed on behalf of the National Mortgage Bank of Greece and the National Bank of Greece, S.A.

Among the indorsed conditions the following are or may be relevant:

4. THE Mortgage Bank will pay regularly the coupons and drawn Bonds whether in time of peace or war and whether the holders be subjects of a friendly or hostile country without requiring any declaration or evidence as to the then present or former nationality domicile or residence of such holders or any previous holders or as to the length of time such holders have held such Bonds or coupons.

10. THE Bonds are to be redeemed on or before the 1st day of December 1957 by means of an accumulative amortisation fund payable in half-yearly instalments the first repayment taking place on the 1st day of June 1928. This amortisation fund is to be applied by half-yearly drawings at par in accordance with the amortisation table endorsed hereon.

11. ANY of the Bonds which shall not have been previously redeemed as aforesaid shall be paid off at par on the 1st day of December 1957 with such interest as is properly payable thereon.

13. PAYMENT of interest in respect of drawn Bonds will cease on the date upon which the Bonds become payable out of the amortisation moneys in the hands of the Bankers. Drawn Bonds when presented for payment must be accompanied by all unmatured coupons. The equivalent of any missing unmatured coupons will be deducted from the amount of the Bond. *Coupons not presented for payment within 5 years of their due date* and Bonds not presented within 20 years of the date of redemption *are proscribed and void.* [—The last sentence is "the time-bar clause" which figures largely in this case.—]

17. SHOULD this Bond or any coupon be destroyed from any cause the Mortgage Bank will furnish to the Bankers for delivery to the owner a new Bond and/or coupons upon payment of the expenses occasioned by such substitution after having received satisfactory evidence of the destruction . . .

[1] Parts underlined by learned Judge are shown in italics.

Attached to each of the bonds were 59 half-yearly interest coupons identified by the number of the bond covering the 30 years' life of the bonds (unless drawn) in the following form:

> NATIONAL MORTGAGE BANK OF GREECE 7% STERLING MORTGAGE BONDS.
> *Coupon payable on* [—here is set out the relevant half-yearly due date—] *for £3. 10. 0*
> On the back of each coupon the following appears: **[449]**
> This Coupon is payable in Sterling in London at the offices of Hambros Bank Ltd. or Erlangers, or in Athens at the offices of the National Bank of Greece by Cheque on London. *This coupon will be forfeited if not presented within six years from due date.*

In 1935 the provisions of the bonds were modified by reduction of the interest rate from seven per cent. to 4¾ per cent. and by modification of the cumulative sterling fund provisions and by the following provisions:

> Bondholders permanently resident in Greece to be paid only in Drachmae. Bondholders permanently resident outside Greece to be paid in Sterling upon presentation by such Bondholders of a declaration (a) that coupons presented for payment are detached from Bonds belonging to persons permanently resident outside Greece, and (b) that bonds presented for repayment belong to persons permanently resident outside Greece.

These modifications were superimposed in print upon the bonds and the coupons were overprinted as follows:
RATE OF INTEREST REDUCED TO 4¾%
and £2 7s. 6d. was substiuted for £3 10s.

The second series of bonds was in the same form but ran from Dec. 1, 1930, instead of Dec. 1, 1927.

Up until the year 1941, the National Mortgage Bank of Greece duly honoured the bonds. They provided their agents in London (Hambros Bank, Ltd., and Erlangers, Ltd.) with the funds to pay the coupons as they fell due. Thereupon a notice was inserted on the Stock Exchange, in "The Times" and financial papers saying that payment would be made on the due date. The bearers of the bonds, through their banks, presented the coupons to the agents in London and obtained payment. The last such notice was on Nov. 19, 1940, saying that payment would be made of the coupon falling due on Dec. 1, 1940.

Since 1941, the National Mortgage Bank of Greece have not honoured the bonds. They have not provided their agents in London with any funds with which to pay the coupons. No notice has ever been put up in the Stock Exchange or in the papers saying that payment would be made. So the bearers of the bonds did not present the coupons and the interest was never paid from 1941 onwards. The reason was, of course, due to the war. Greece was invaded and occupied. The consequences on the National Mortgage Bank were adverse and prolonged. They have not had the money with which to pay the interest; or at any rate they have not had the sterling for the purpose. They could only pay in sterling with the permission of the Greek Government and this has never been forthcoming.

On Dec. 6, 1955, one of the bondholders in England, Mr. Metliss, brought an action against the guarantors, for interest from June 1, 1941, to June 1, 1955, inclusive. It was tried before Mr. Justice Sellers, who held that the interest could only be recovered for the six years prior to the issue of the writ (Dec. 6, 1955) and no more (see [1957] 2 Q.B. 33*). Mr. Metliss did not appeal from the decision of Mr. Justice Sellers limiting the claim to the six years before writ. The present action is an attempt by the plaintiffs to upset the decision of Mr. Justice Sellers on this point. They seek to recover interest right back to 1941.

Upon the true construction of these bonds there were two conditions which qualified the obligation to pay interest. First, upon the face of the bond it was a condition precedent that the coupons should be *presented* for payment. They were not payable until presented. And the Statute of Limitations would not run against the holder, or in favour of the Mortgage Bank, until presentation of the coupon. At least, that is how I construe the condition, rather like an account at a bank which is only payable on demand (see *N. Joachimson v. Swiss Bank Corporation*, [1921] 3 K.B. 110; (1921) 6 Ll.L.Rep. 435). No one suggests that this first condition was ever waived. It is accepted by everyone that the holder must present the coupons for payment before he can sue. That is why the plaintiffs allege that the coupons now sued upon were presented. The detached coupons were presented with the bonds on Dec. 12, 1957, and the attached coupons were presented with the bonds on Nov. 2, 1960, and they were not paid.

Second, under the conditions indorsed on the bond, it was a condition subsequent that the coupons should be presented within six years of their due date. They were "proscribed and void" if not presented within six years: or, as the coupons said, "forfeited". There is no doubt that none of these coupons was presented within that **[450]** time. The claims are therefore barred unless the plaintiffs can avoid the condition in some way or other.

The first way in which the plaintiffs try to get round the condition is by saying that, as a matter of construction, it does not apply to these coupons at all. It applies, they say, only to the coupons referred to in the earlier part of Condition 13, that is, missing unmatured coupons.

The effect of the earlier part of Condition 13 is clear. It is set in a group of conditions dealing with drawn bonds, that is, bonds which are redeemed by half-yearly drawings before the 30 years are up. Once a bond is drawn, interest ceases to run on it. The holder has to produce the bond, complete with all unmatured coupons attached to it, and he will get the full principal, but no more. If, by any chance, some of the unmatured coupons are missing, the holder will not get the full principal, but there will be deducted from it the amount of the missing unmatured coupons. If he afterwards produces the missing coupons, he will then get the amount of them paid to him, but not as interest (for that has never accrued due) but only as part of the principal (which was retained pending the production of the missing coupons).

Such being the effect of the first part of Condition 13, the plaintiffs say that the word "coupons" in the last sentence refers only to the coupons in the previous sentence, namely, missing unmatured coupons on drawn bonds. I cannot accept this view. I agree that the last sentence is placed awkwardly among the group of conditions dealing with drawn bonds. But it is quite general in its terms. So far as "bonds" are concerned, it refers not only to drawn bonds, but also to undrawn bonds which run the full term. So far as "coupons" are concerned, the matter is made plain beyond doubt by looking at the coupons themselves which form part of the document and must be construed with it. On the back of every coupon there are the words

> . . . This coupon will be forfeited if not presented within six years from due date.

Seeing that those words are on every coupon, it is impossible to confine them to missing unmatured coupons. They clearly apply to all coupons.

The second way in which the plaintiffs seek to get round the condition is by saying that the defendants were guilty of a fundamental breach of the contract and are on that account disentitled from relying upon the condition. The doctrine of "fundamental breach" is a recent introduction into our law. It has been developed so as to get over an injustice of "standarized contracts". A trader undertakes to warehouse goods, or to carry them, to sell them or to let them on hire purchase, and he issues a printed form of contract which he gets the customer to sign: but somewhere on the form he inserts exemption clauses in which he purports to exempt himself from all liability. No customer has any choice but to accept the form. He must sign on the given line or go without a contract at all. No customer—or not one in a thousand—ever reads the exemption clauses, and it is a fiction to suggest that he agrees to them. So the Courts have held that they cannot be used by the trader so as to avoid the fundamental obligations which he has undertaken.

If you find an obligation, express or implied, which goes to the very core of the contract, and the defendant then seeks by an exemption clause to deny the plaintiff redress for a breach of it, the Courts will not allow him to do so; for the simple reason that an exemption clause can only avail a party when he is carrying out the contract in its essential respects, and not when he is departing from it in a radical manner. This is established by a long series of cases in this Court, of which the chief examples are perhaps *Bontex Knitting Works, Ltd v. St. John's Garage*, (1943) 60 T.L.R. 44, and *Karsales (Harrow), Ltd. v. Wallis* [1956] 1 W.L.R. 936, and by two recent cases in the Privy Council, *Sze Hai Tong Bank, Ltd. v. Rambler Cycle Company, Ltd.*, [1959] A.C. 576; [1959] 2 Lloyd's Rep. 114, and *Adel Bosholi v. Allied Commercial Exporters, Ltd.*, (No. 51 of 1959, unreported).

The doctrine does not depend on the customer electing to disaffirm the contract. Usually he has no option open to him. The contract has been broken irretrievably before he gets to know of it, and the only course for him is to sue for the breach. So the point does not very often arise. But even if he does get to know of it, in time to affirm or disaffirm, he can still treat the contract as in being, and sue for the breach (without being defeated by the exemption clause) provided always that the breach itself is continuing to operate and cause damage to him. That appears from the recent decision of this Court in *Charterhouse Credit Company, Ltd. v. Tolly*, [1963] 2 W.L.R. 1168. It would be different, of **[451]** course, if the breach itself had been waived so that it ceased to be a cause of damage, for that is what happened in *Tate & Lyle, Ltd. v. Hain Steamship Company, Ltd.*, (1936) 55 Ll.L.Rep. 159; (1936) 41 Com. Cas. 350. The ship had deviated, but she had, with the consent of the charterers, resumed the contract voyage. So far as the charterers were concerned, the breach had been waived, so that the shipowners, at the time she stranded, were carrying out the contract in its essential respects and were entitled to the protection of the exceptions.

Let me now try to apply these principles to the present case. The plaintiffs plead that the defendants are precluded from relying on the time-condition

> . . . by reason of the fact that the First Defendants did not at any material time after 1941 pay nor were they ready willing or able to pay any of the coupons sued upon.

In support of this plea they relied on an admission of the defendants that

> . . . the First Defendants could not have paid the coupons of those issues in foreign exchange [—meaning thereby sterling—] if presented at any time since 1941 because they were unable to obtain the necessary foreign currency without the permission of the Greek Government which was not forthcoming but they made every possible effort at all material times to get such permission from the said Government . . .

The effect of this admission is that the defendants were willing, but not able, to pay the coupons.

At the outset I must say I fail to see how the matters alleged amount to a breach, let alone a fundamental breach. The failure to pay after 1941 was not itself a breach. The National Mortgage Bank of Greece was only liable to pay the coupon *on presentation*, and no presentation was made from 1941 onwards. Nor do I see that the inability to pay was itself a breach, there being no presentation to test it. Inability to pay would have only been a breach if the bondholder had treated the inability as equivalent to repudiation and had thereupon elected to treat the contract as at an end and sue for damages (*see Universal Cargo Carriers Corporation v. Citati*, [1957] 2 Q.B. 401, at p. 441; [1957] 1 Lloyd's Rep. 174, at p. 195, by Mr. Justice Devlin). But no bondholder ever did treat the contract as at an end. No one of them sued for damages. It would be the last thing any bondholder would want to do. He wanted to get his money and for that purpose he would have to keep the contract in being. He would therefore have to affirm the contract and present the coupons for payment: just as the holder of a bill of exchange has to do, *Bowes and Others v. Howe*, (1813), 5 Taunt. 30 and Sect. 46 (2) of the Bills of Exchange

Act, 1882. There would be no breach until he presented the coupon for payment and it was not paid.

Seeing that the alleged breaches were not breaches at all, the only way in which this argument about fundamental breach can be put is this. There was implied in the bonds an undertaking by the Mortgage Bank with those who lent money to it (being bondholders permanently resident outside Greece) that there would be, at the time when the interest became payable, money in the shape of sterling in the hands of their bankers in London to pay the amount of the interest (see *Rothschild & Sons v. Commissioners of Inland Revenue*, [1894] 2 Q.B. 142, at p. 146, by Mr. Justice Mathew). By failing to put the bankers in London in funds, the Mortgage Bank of Greece were guilty of a fundamental breach. I will assume for the purposes of the argument that this was so. But what would be the result? Only this: the bondholder could sue for that breach if he thought he could do any good by it. There is no exemption clause to stop him. But if he sued after many years had passed, he would be defaulted, not by Condition 13, but by the Statute of Limitations. Mr. Littman relied on the cases of *Atlantic Shipping and Trading Company, Ltd. v. Louis Dreyfus & Co.*, [1922] 2 A.C. 250; (1922) 10 Ll.L.Rep. 703, and *Smeaton, Hanscomb & Co., Ltd. v. Sassoon I. Setty, Son & Co.*, [1953] 2 Lloyd's Rep. 580, at p. 583; [1953] 1 W.L.R. 1468, at p. 1470, to show that a time-bar clause was an exemption clause. It may be sometimes when it exempts a party from liability for the breach in question. But in the present context Condition 13 is not an exemption clause. It does not exempt the defendants from liability for failing to put the agents in funds. It leaves the bondholder quite free to sue for that breach if he pleases. But when he does, he is met, not by the condition, but by the Statute of Limitations. In my judgment, therefore, the doctrine of fundamental breach has no application to this case.

The third way in which the plaintiffs seek to get round the condition is by the doctrine of waiver. They plead that it has been **[452]** waived by reason of the defendants' "having since the year 1941 evinced an intention not to pay the said coupons even if they had been presented."

There is no doubt that if these coupons had been presented at any time since 1941 they would not have been paid. The defendants never put the paying agent in funds. No announcement was made that payment would be made. And, in the absence of an announcement, it could readily be inferred that the defendants would not be able to pay the coupons, even if presented. Any bondholder in the City of London would know that it was useless to present the coupons and none did so.

The law on this point is simply this: whenever a party makes it plain by his acts or conduct that he will not or cannot perform his part of the contract, the other party is not bound to go on and perform any conditions thereafter on his part to be performed which were contingent on the first party performing his, for the simple reason that "the law will not enforce anyone to do a thing which will be vain and fruitless", see *Sir Anthony Main's case*, (1596) 5 Co. Rep. 20b, at 21a. It is not necessary for him to "do a nugatory act", see *Jones and Another v. Barkley*, (1781) 2 Doug. 684, at p. 694. This is quite a separate doctrine from that of renunciation, as is well shown by a case decided by the High Court of Australia, *Peter Turnbull & Co. Proprietary, Ltd., v. Mundas Trading Company (Australasia) Proprietary, Ltd.*, [1954] 2 Lloyd's Rep. 198, at p. 207, by Sir Owen Dixon, C.J. And it applies here.

I regard the conduct of the defendants as a waiver of the six-year clause. The defendants as good as told the bondholders there was no money available to pay the coupons. I do not see why the bondholders should be required to present the coupons within the six years, when it was obviously a fruitless exercise. The only result of presenting the coupons would be to get nothing, and to start the Statute of Limitations running against the bondholder. But I think that this waiver only operates in favour of those bondholders who were actually influenced by it. If any bondholder had come forward and said: "I did not present these coupons within six years because I knew they would not be paid", he would be entitled to rely on the waiver. But I do not believe that this waiver operates in favour of a subsequent holder. It does not run with the coupon. When a person takes a negotiable instrument (as this bond with coupons) in good faith and for value, he can enforce it according to its tenor. He does not take it subject to equities operating *against* the previous holder. Nor does he take it with the benefit of equities operating *in favour* of a previous holder. There is, as the Judge said, no authority on the point, but I agree with him that

> . . . In principle it would seem to me to be of the essence of negotiability that the instrument in the hands of holders is to be regarded as containing the whole contract the terms of which fall to be determined on a proper contruction of the express words of the document irrespective of any previous dealings between previous holders and the obligor.

Take the plaintiffs here. When they bought the bonds with the *attached* coupons (or when they bought the *detached* coupons) they could see on every coupon the words:

> . . . This coupon will be forfeited if not presented within six years from due date.

They could see, as plain as could be, that it had not been presented within six years. So they were buying coupons which, according to their terms, were already forfeit. I do not believe they can enforce them in the face of such plain notice that they were forfeit.

This disposes of the three ways in which the plaintiffs sought before us to escape from the effect of Condition 13. None of them succeed. If they had succeeded as against the National Mortgage Bank, there would be a nice question whether they could succeed against the National Bank of Greece. I am inclined to think that they would: for after all, the National Bank of Greece guaranteed the due performance of the bonds, and if the National Mortgage Bank were made liable, it would be because they had not duly performed their obligations. As Lord Justice Bowen said in *Mayor of Kingston-upon-Hull v. Harding and Another*, [1892] 2 Q.B. 494, at p. 507:

> . . . the contract of suretyship itself, which provides, not in express terms, but by implication, that the sureties are not in such a case to be discharged in consequence of an act against which they themselves have guaranteed . . .

Again if the plaintiffs had succeeded on the *attached* coupons, there would be a question whether they could succeed on the *detached* coupons. It is clear that bonds **[453]** with attached coupons are negotiable: but not so clear that detached coupons by themselves are negotiable. But we did not go into the evidence on the point, seeing that we were of opinon that even the claim for the attached coupons failed.

For these reasons, I would dismiss the appeal.

Lord Justice HARMAN: I will ask Lord Justice Pearson to read his judgment.

Lord Justice PEARSON: The material provision to be considered is contained in a sentence in Condition 13 of the conditions of each bond:

> . . . Coupons not presented for payment within 6 years of their due date and Bonds not presented within 20 years of the date of redemption are proscribed and void.

The coupons form part of the same document, and each coupon has on its back the words

> . . . This coupon will be forfeited if not presented within six years from due date.

As to the construction of this material provision, which may conveniently be referred to as "the time-bar clause", I agree with the Master of the Rolls and with Lord Justice Harman for the reasons given by them that it should be read as applying to all coupons and not merely to such as may be unmatured and missing from their bond when the bond is presented for payment.

As to the question of "fundamental breach", I think there is a rule of construction that normally an exception or exclusion clause or similar provision in a contract should be construed as not applying to a situation created by a fundamental breach of the contract. This is not an independent rule of law imposed by the Court on the parties willy-nilly in disregard of their contractual intention. On the contrary it is a rule of construction based on the presumed intention of the contracting parties. It involves the implication of a term to give to the contract that business efficacy which the parties as reasonable men must have intended it to have. This rule of construction is not new in principle but it has become prominent in recent years in consequence of the tendency to have standard forms of contract containing exceptions clauses drawn in extravagantly wide terms, which would produce absurd results if applied literally. I will give a very simple example.

Suppose there is a contract for the sale of a ton of cheese, and the seller's contract form is used, and it has an exceptions clause containing, among other exorbitant and oppressive provisions, a provision that no failure of the goods delivered to correspond with the contract description shall entitle the buyer to reject the goods or recover damages. The seller delivers (whether wittingly or unwittingly) a ton of chalk, and claims that the exceptions clause should be applied literally and therefore the buyer must accept the ton of chalk and pay for it the contract price and cannot recover any damages. As that would be an absurd result, which the parties as reasonable men cannot have intended, the Court says: "There is here a fundamental breach of the contract; the exceptions clause does not apply to the situation thereby created; the buyer is entitled to reject."

That the rule is of this nature and is based on the presumed intention of the parties clearly appears from a large number of cases, including *Lilley v. Doubleday*, (1881) 7 Q.B.D. 510; *In re Puckett and Smith's Contract*, [1902] 2 Ch. 258, at p. 263; *Gibaud v. Great Eastern Railway Company*, [1921] 2 K.B. 426, at p. 435; *The Cap Palos* [1921] P. 458, at pp. 470 to 471; *Atlantic Shipping and Trading Company, Ltd. v. Louis Dreyfus & Co.*, [1922] 2 A.C. 250 (at pp. 256 to 257 and 260; (1922) 10 Ll.L.Rep. 703, at pp. 707 and 708; *London and North Western Railway Company v. Neilson*, [1922] 2 A.C. 263, at p. 273; *Bontex Knitting Works, Ltd., v. St. John's Garage*, (1943) 60 T.L.R. 44, Mr. Justice Lewis; (C.A.) (1944) 60 T.L.R. 253; *Alexander v. Railway Executive*, [1951] 2 K.B. 882, at p. 887; *Smeaton, Hanscomb & Co., Ltd. v. Sassoon I. Setty, Son & Co.*, [1953] 2 Lloyd's Rep. 580, at p. 583; [1953] 1 W.L.R. 1468, at p. 1470; *J. Spurling, Ltd. v. Bradshaw*, [1956] 1 Lloyd's Rep. 392, at pp. 396 and 398; [1956] 1 W.L.R. 461, at pp. 465 to 466 and 469; *Karsales (Harrow), Ltd. v. Wallis* [1956] 1 W.L.R. 936, at pp. 939, 942 and 943; *Sze Hai Tong Bank, Ltd. v. Rambler Cycle Company, Ltd*, [1959] A.C. 576, at pp. 587 to 589; [1959] 2 Lloyd's Rep. 114, at pp. 120 to 122. The passages are too long to be conveniently cited in full, but I will give three short extracts. In *Gibauld v. Great Eastern Railway Company*, [1921] 2 K.B. 426, at p. 435, Lord Justice Scrutton said:

> . . . The principle is well known, and perhaps *Lilley v. Doubleday, sup.*, is the best illustration, that if you undertake to **[454]** do a thing in a certain way, or to keep a thing in a certain place, with certain conditions protecting it, and have broken the contract by not doing the thing contracted for in the way contracted for, or not keeping the article in the place in which you have contracted to keep it, you cannot rely on the conditions which were only intended to protect you if you carried out the contract in the way in which you had contracted to do it.

That passage was cited with approval by Lord Justice Atkin in *The Cap Palos, sup.*, at p. 471, and by Lord Atkinson in *London and North Western Railway Company v. Neilson, sup.*, at p. 273.

In *Atlantic Shipping and Trading Company, Ltd. v. Louis Dreyfus & Co., sup.*, Lord Sumner said (ibid., at pp. 260 and 708 of the respective reports):

> . . . Underlying the whole contract of affreightment there is an implied condition upon the operation of the usual exceptions from liability—namely, that the shipowners shall have provided a seaworthy ship. If they have, the exceptions apply and relieve them; if they have not, and damage results in consequence of the unseaworthiness, the exceptions are construed as not being applicable for the shipowners' protection in such a case.

In *Sze Hai Tong Bank, Ltd. v. Rambler Cycle Company, Ltd., sup.,* Lord Denning said (ibid., at pp. 586 to 587 and 120 of the respective reports):

> The exemption, on the face of it, could hardly be more comprehensive, and it is contended that it is wide enough to absolve the shipping company from responsibility for the act of which the Rambler Cycle Company complains, that is to say, the delivery of the goods to a person who, to their knowledge, was not entitled to receive them. If the exemption clause upon its true construction absolved the shipping company from an act such as that, it seems that by parity of reasoning they would have been absolved if they had given the goods away to some passer-by or had burnt them or thrown them into the sea. If it had been suggested to the parties that the condition exempted the shipping company in such a case, they would both have said: "Of course not." There is, therefore, an implied limitation on the clause, which cuts down the extreme width of it: and, as a matter of construction, their Lordships decline to attribute to it the unreasonable effect contended for.

The fundamental breach relied upon in this case by the plaintiffs appears from the defendants' admission, recorded in the judgment of the learned Judge, that

> . . . the [first defendants] could not have paid the coupons on these issues in foreign currency (i.e. sterling currency) if presented at any time since 1941 because they were unable to obtain the necessary foreign exchange without permission of the Greek Government which was not forthcoming though they made every possible effort at all material times to get such permission from the said Government.

The first defendants' ability to pay the amounts of the coupons in sterling was not tested by presentation of coupons for payment until a late stage of the history (I suppose when preparations were being made for the *Metliss** action[2]). I doubt whether the mere inability to pay (not being ready as well as willing to pay) was in itself a breach of the contract. There is the practical objection that difficult and tangled situations would be created if an unconfessed inability to perform a contract, not manifested by any overt act or omission at the time, might be ascertained long afterwards to have been a breach of the contract.

In this case, however, it is reasonable to say that there was an implied term of the contract that the debtor bank would provide the agents with the necessary sterling funds for payment of the coupons, and the long-continued failure to do that constituted a fundamental breach of the contract. It seems clear that the plaintiffs could have elected to treat the contract as repudiated by the continuing default, and so could have terminated the contract and sued for damages, or alternatively perhaps they could have demanded immediate repayment of the outstanding amount of the loan, and could have sued for it as a liquidated sum. The plaintiffs have not taken any such course. They have allowed the contract to remain in force and they have acted under it by presenting coupons for payment. *Prima facie* the whole contract remains in force (*Tate & Lyle, Ltd. v. Hain Steamship Company, Ltd.,* (1936) 55 Ll.L.Rep. 159, at pp. 174 and 178; (1936) **[455]** 41 Com. Cas. 350, at pp. 355 to 356 and 363), and the time-bar clause (Condition 13) defeats the plaintiffs, because they did not present the coupons to which this action relates within the specified time. The plaintiffs, however, contend that, because there was a fundamental breach of

[8] *Metliss v. National Bank of Greece and Athens S.A.,** [1957] 2 Q.B. 33.

contract, the time-bar clause, being similar to an exceptions clause, was rendered void or, alternatively, had its operation suspended so that the six-year period would not begin to run until the debtor bank took some step to resume payment of the interest coupons or became able to do so.

Plaintiffs' Counsel preferred the alternative contention that the operation of the time-bar clause was suspended, though he also kept open the contention that the clause was rendered void. If the time-bar clause were rendered void, all that would be left would be the provision on the face of the bond that interest should be paid upon presentation and surrender of the coupons attached thereto as they severally became due, and there would be no provision allowing the coupons to be presented at any later date, and yet the plaintiffs are relying upon presentation of the coupons at much later dates. Also if the theory of suspended operation is preferred, there is the difficulty of defining with sufficient precision the event that would terminate suspension. In my judgment, however, there is a broad and simple answer to the plaintiffs' contention in either of its alternative versions: As I have demonstrated by citation of authority, the rule on which the plaintiffs seek to rely is a rule of construction and depends upon the contractual intention of the parties.

The plaintiffs are in effect alleging an implied term, an implied proviso to the time-bar clause. They have to show that the parties as reasonable men must have intended, if their attention had been directed to the question at the time when the contract was made, that, if there should be continuing default by the debtor bank in providing funds for payment of the interest, the time-bar clause should be rendered void or have its operation suspended as alleged. The parties included the debtor bank and the guarantor bank. It is not only not a necessary assumption, it is highly improbable that either of the banks would have had any such intention. They would wish to have and to preserve some finality in their obligations, not to have them extended indefinitely. Moreover there is no reason why the time-bar clause should not continue to apply in the event of a protracted default by the debtor bank. There is nothing absurd, unreasonable, burdensome, oppressive or unfair in requiring the couponholder to present his coupon within six years of its due date. That is part of the administration of the contract. It is the drill laid down. The presentation of the coupon brings matters to a head: the debtor bank either pays or makes default: the couponholder either receives payment or becomes entitled to sue. Even in the event of a protracted default by the debtor bank the contract is more practical and workable with the time-bar than without it, because the defendant banks know where they stand, inasmuch as they have to provide for payment of coupons presented within six years but not for payment of coupons not so presented. There is no hardship on the couponholder in having to make a presentation of coupons once in every period of five and a half or six years. I agree with the learned Judge when he said:

> . . . In my judgment, the contract contained in the bonds or in the coupons (if there be an independent contract in the coupons) works perfectly well without any such implication. If the point had been raised by the "officious bystander" referred to by Lord Justice Mackinnon in *Shirlaw v. Southern Foundaries (1926) Ltd.,* [1939] 2 K.B. 206, at p. 227, I have no reason to think that the parties as reasonable men would have said "Of course that goes without saying". In my judgment, to imply the term suggested would involve not construing but rewriting the contract.

The question of waiver in this case can be answered on somewhat similar lines. The contract provided that

> . . . Coupons not presented for payment within 6 years of their due date . . . are proscribed and void.

The couponholder, in order to perfect his own right and the banks' obligations, had to present his coupon for payment within the six years. That was the only requirement. There was no requirement to present the coupon on the due date, which was merely the earliest date on which the holder was entitled to present it. The defendant banks did not expressly or by implication, by words or conduct, intimate to the couponholder that he did not have to present his coupon for payment within the six years. They never intimated that the [**456**] requirement was rendered void and suspended or that the period of six years was extended. It was contended on behalf of the plaintiffs that the presentation would be nugatory, because payment could not be made, and therefore the requirement of presentation within six years was waived. The legal maxim involved is *lex non cogit ad impossibilia aut inutilia.* It seems to me, however, that presentation within the six years was not nugatory or useless, being the necessary step by the couponholder to perfect his own rights and the banks' obligations. It was a simple, inexpensive, formal step required by the contract. It was not a burdensome and expensive requirement such as surrendering an estate (as in *Sir Anthony Main's case,* (1596) 5 Co. Rep. 20b) or providing a ship or providing a cargo, so that an equity dispensing with performance would readily be inferred. Why should not the couponholder present his coupon for payment within the six years, as required by the contract (including the words on the back of each coupon) for the purpose of establishing and preserving his rights, even if the debtor bank is in default? I cannot see any sufficient reason in law or equity or commercial fairness or convenience for relieving him of that requirement, especially as the effect would be to convert the defendant banks' six-year obligations into obligations of perpetual or indefinite duration.

The alleged waiver is beset with other difficulties also. The plaintiffs did not acquire the coupons until they had *prima facie* become time-barred under Condition 13. There was no proof that any person who held any of the coupons within its six-year period knew of or was misled by the defendant banks' failure to provide funds for payment of the coupons. Therefore even the supposed initial waiver in favour of the plaintiffs' predecessors in title must fail to be established for want of evidence. Secondly, even if the evidence were available and were held (contrary to my view) to show a waiver of the time-bar clause, there would still be the problem of whether such a waiver could "run with the coupons" in favour of the plaintiffs as subsequent holders.

I would dismiss the appeal.

Lord Justice Harman: Controversy about these Greek bonds has become a regular feature of the Courts. Two actions concerning them have already been carried to the highest tribunal in the land and there has been a number of other actions on specially indorsed writs in the Queen's Bench Division. The bonds have now all been paid off so far as principal is concerned by the second respondents together with interest for six years from the date when the several bonds were presented. We are here concerned with interest coupons in respect of periods longer ago than six years before presentation.

Mr. Justice Sellers (as he then was) in the earlier of the actions which went to the House of Lords (the *Metliss* action[3]*) ordered that interest for six years be paid and that feature of the case was never made the subject of an appeal. Looking at a transcript of the learned Judge's judgment I am left in some doubt whether that part of it was based on the view that the Statute of Limitations applied or on Condition 13 annexed to the bonds declaring coupons not presented for payment within six years of their due date to be proscribed and void. The plaintiffs in the *Metliss* action were contending for the application of Greek law and therefore, as the Judge says, did not encounter the English statute. The Judge, however, decided that English law applied and that if so, the statute could have been invoked. His decision on the law applicable was upheld in the House of Lords. It would therefore seem that he would have held the statute applicable. However that may be, the point is still open in this Court and has been argued before us.

The first defence consisted of a reliance on the words of Condition 13 which I have mentioned, and the first reply made to that contention was that as a matter of construction of Condition 13, it only applied to missing unmatured

[3] [1957] 2 Q.B. 33.

coupons. It is no doubt a right principle of construction that words will be taken to be limited to their context. The principle is well stated by Lord Justice Devlin (as he then was) in *Akerib v. Booth and Others, Ltd.*, [1961] I W.L.R. 367, at p. 372, in these words:

> . . . my conclusion is based mainly upon the general rule that words, however wide, have to be construed in relation to the subject-matter about which they are used.

Similarly, in *Szymonowski & Co. v. Beck & Co.*, [1923] 1 K.B. 457, it was held that a clause limiting the rights of buyers to reject goods within a limited time, being words of limitation, would deprive the buyers of their right to reject, but left untouched their right to claim damages for breach of contract. These are well-known **[457]** principles but of course a question of construction, as this admittedly is, depends upon the words of the instrument in question. It is argued by the defendants that Clause 13 is one of a fasciculus of conditions dealing with drawing of bonds and that the only coupons to which the words at the end of Condition 13 are intended to apply are "missing unmatured coupons". I think this contention will not hold water. As and when bonds are drawn interest ceases and a coupon unmatured at the date of drawing will therefore never mature and therefore there was no need for a proscription of any such coupon because it never would be payable. This alone seems to me to show that when the condition speaks of coupons not presented for payment within six years, it must refer to coupons unpaid before drawing.

Apart from that, Condition 13 deals not only with coupons but with the bonds themselves which must be presented within 20 years of the date of redemption. This reference quite clearly covers all bonds and I do not see why the immediately preceding reference to coupons not presented within six years of their due date does not equally refer to all coupons. Looking at the coupon itself you find clearly stated on the back the words:

> This Coupon is payable in Sterling . . . This coupon will be forfeited if not presented within six years from due date.

You find the due date stated on the front of the coupon. I am quite unable to see how a bearer of this coupon could possibly receive the impression that the words on the back were limited to interest on missing coupons of drawn bonds.

The next defence to be dealt with was a plea of waiver. The waiver alleged consisted, if I understand it rightly, of the fact that the first defendants, ever since the year 1941, evinced an intention not to pay the interest coupons even if they had been presented. This is an odd way of pleading waiver, but let that pass. It was conceded that in and since 1941 the first defendants were never in a position to pay the interest. It was conceded also that until 1941, up to which time the interest was paid, the defendants half-yearly put their agents in London in funds to pay the interest and that the agents duly advertised in the City of London and elsewhere their willingness to pay coupons on presentation and that anyone who himself or through his agents or bankers was familiar with the practice of the City would appreciate from the absence of advertisement that it was of no use to present the coupons. It is said that the law will never insist on a man doing an act which everybody knows to be useless and that therefore the duty to present cannot be relied upon. I am prepared for the present purpose to agree that this is so. What is the effect of that? It seems to me that it might absolve the holder of a coupon which had become due from presenting it. He could, without going through that formality, sue upon it as a debt due to him, but if that were so the Statute of Limitations would then begin to run and would be available to the debtor six years after the due date. The plaintiffs wish to avoid the obligation to present and argue that in some way or other the debt was deferred until the defendants were in a position to pay. They go on to suggest that the obligation to present would only then arise and that therefore the statute would only start to run from that date. This is an attempt, as it seems to me, to have the best of both worlds. The obligation to present is preserved but the date abolished. I can see no justification at all for this.

There is, as it seems to me, another answer to this plea of waiver. It is said to have been made during the years from 1941 onwards when the defendants were not in a position to pay, but the waiver is not, I think, analogous to a restrictive covenant running with the land under the rule in *Tulk v. Moxhay*, (1848) 2 Ph. 774. The waiver must affect the mind of the holder of the coupon at its due date. Who these were no one knows. What is clear is that the present plaintiffs did not acquire the coupons until long after any relevant date had passed and I do not think it was open to them to rely on a misrepresentation made to some unknown predecessors. No such representation so far as I know was ever made to the plaintiffs, nor was any evidence called that they acted on it.

The third argument was based on what was described as fundamental breach. It was said to be a principle that a party to a contract who had failed to perform some fundamental condition of it was not entitled to rely on clauses limiting his liability or what were called "exception clauses". So, for instance, in *Atlantic Shipping and Trading Company, Ltd. v. Louis Dreyfus & Co.*, [1922] A.C. 250; (1922) 10 Ll.L.Rep. 703, shipowners were held disentitled to rely on a clause limiting the time within which an arbitrator must be appointed as **[458]** a defence to an action based an unseaworthiness. That there is such a principle I do not feel any doubt. An exception clause is one which relieves one party of an obligation and it is said that the defendants, having refused or failed to pay interest on the bonds, are not entitled when sued to rely on the clause which limits the time within which the coupon must be presented.

The first question which arises here is whether the failure to pay interest is a fundamental breach. For myself I think it is not. The promise was a promise to repay the bond at its due date with interest in the meanwhile every six months. During some of these periods of six months the defendants no doubt failed to pay interest and this was a breach of contract, but in the end the principal money and part of the interest has been repaid on these bonds so that the substance of the contract has been performed. A fundamental breach in my understanding of those words means one that in effect makes the bargain something wholly different, as in the instance much cited in argument of the supply of oak logs in a contract which stipulated for mahogany logs.

Let it be supposed, however, that this was a fundamental breach and that the condition about presenting within six years was an exception clause, what is the result? Simply I think that the defendants cannot rely on the obligation to present bonds within six years as specified in the condition, but, as I pointed out before, it would follow that each coupon as it became due represented a debt on which an action could be brought and on which, therefore, the Statute of Limitations would operate. The periods specified in the condition and in the Act happen in the case of coupons to be the same, but this is a mere chance. In the case of bonds themselves, a 20-year period is specified in the condition, which would thus lengthen and not abbreviate the defendants' liability. Supposing the inability to pay interest in 1941 over an indefinite period amounted to a fundamental breach of contract, it entitled bondholders, like any other anticipatory breach, either to sue at once for damages or to wait for the contract to mature and seek to have it performed. It seems to me, however, that couponholders who choose the latter remedy, as they are affirming the contract, must take it as it is with all its faults, that is to say, including the limitation of time for presenting. I think this emerges from the decision of the Court of Appeal in *Tate & Lyle, Ltd. v. Hain Steamship Company, Ltd.*, (1936) 55 Ll.L.Rep. 159; (1936) 41 Com. Cas. 350. It is said that this is not the law and we were referred to a recent decision in this Court under the name of *Charterhouse Credit Company, Ltd. v. Tolly*, [1963] 2 W.L.R. 1168. There it is true the hirer of a motor car was held entitled both to retain the car and to obtain damages for breach of warranty, but in my judgment that case does not show that the principle which I have mentioned is wrong. I should, therefore, hold that the plaintiffs, suing not for damages for breach of contract but in effect for specific performance cannot escape one of the terms of the contract which limits the time for presentation of the coupons.

Having regard to the nature of my conclusions it follows that the glittering superstructure of case law erected before us is quite irrelevant, and much though I admired its construction during the hearing, I hope I shall be excused from not citing any of it. I am quite unable to see how the plaintiffs can remould the contract by deferring the obligation to present until some such time as the defendants or one of them are in a position to pay, thus prolonging the liability on the coupons indefinitely.

So far as the second defendants are concerned, I do not see how they, as guarantors, are affected either by waiver or by fundamental breach on the part of the first defendants. I do not see how the second defendants can be said to have assented to either of these variations of the contract. What they guaranteed was payment of coupons presented within six years of their due date and I, for myself, am unable to see how they can be made liable beyond this.

Having regard to the views I have expressed, I see no point in going on to consider the extra defences raised on what were called the detached coupons or the question whether they ought to be treated as negotiable instruments, and I say no more about it.

Mr. *Roche*: I ask that the appeal be dismissed, with costs.

Lord Justice HARMAN: There does not seem to be any answer to that, Mr. Littman?

Mr. *Littman*: No, my Lord, subject only to this. I was going to ask your Lordships, upon instructions, for leave to appeal and if your Lordships thought it right to grant leave to appeal, I was going to make a suggestion about the form which the order of this Court should take. **[459]**

May I give your Lordships in a word my grounds for asking for leave and then explain what is the suggestion I was going to make? I would remind your Lordships, firstly, that there are a considerable number of other actions by bondholders which will be affected by this—some 30 or 40. It is, therefore, in that sense a matter of principle. Secondly, the case does raise important questions of general principles of law, in my submission, proper to be considered by the House of Lords. Thirdly, I would remind your Lordships that although there are a number of decisions of this Court and two of the Privy Council relating to the nature and extent of the doctrine of fundamental breach, that doctrine has not, so far as I can recollect, been considered by the House of Lords. On those grounds, I would respectfully ask your Lordships to grant leave to appeal.

If your Lordships thought it right to grant leave to appeal, this situation arises, my Lord. If the whole of the appeal is dismissed relating to both the attached and detached coupons, the position is that we shall be obliged to prepare for the appeal by copying all the documents relating to all the issues on the detached coupons, that is to say the evidence, and the House of Lords will then have to consider that matter, assuming they were with us on the first point, without the benefit of the views of this Court upon it.

Your Lordships will recollect Mr. Foster was stopped and my learned friend was not heard on the point. I have considered what suggestion I might make and the only one which seems to me to be a possible one for dealing with that situation is this, to ask your Lordships to dismiss the appeal in so far as it relates to the attached coupons and to leave the matter open with regard to the detached coupons. Then if your Lordships granted leave and there was an appeal, it would go up simply on the attached coupons, and if we lost the appeal, it would go without saying that my friends would only have to come back to ask for a formal order dismissing this appeal in relation to the detached coupons. On the other hand, if the House of Lords allowed the appeal in relation to the attached coupons, the matter in relation to the detached coupons could come back to this Court for the further argument on the point of negotiabilability and so on.

That would then mean that that matter could be decided in this Court and could then go to the House of Lords. This would involve a rather unusual order by this Court. I cannot myself say I have had experience of such an order but I apprehend it would be within the powers of this Court to make an order to that effect dismissing the appeal in relation to the attached coupons and leaving the matter open on that basis.

In regard to costs, I do not think there is anything I can say except—I do not know that it helps me very much—that in regard to the question of negotiability, on which some costs have been incurred in reproducing the evidence and so on, my learned Leader was stopped and that matter has never been decided one way or the other.

Lord Justice HARMAN: Mr. Littman, do you feel you ought to ask that the Court should sit with Lord Denning as a member of it before we decide this matter? I am not sure that we can decide it here with you without the parties assent. What do you feel about it? If you want Lord Denning to be present, we must let it go until the Master of the Rolls' public duties allow him to be present.

Mr. *Littman*: Would your Lordship allow me to take instructions?

Lord Justice HARMAN: We could decide two to one, as we always can, although this Court never has any dissent between its members but it has been known in other Courts. If my brother Pearson and I decide it one way, whatever the Master of the Rolls said, it would be a minority view.

Mr. *Littman*: I consent to your Lordships dealing with it.

Lord Justice HARMAN: As we sit?

Mr. *Littman*: Yes.

Lord Justice HARMAN: Are you content with that, Mr. Roche?

Mr. *Roche*: Yes, my Lord. Would your Lordship hear me if you were thinking of accepting any part of it?

Lord Justice HARMAN: We are not. That is why I did not call upon you. I should have said I did not want to trouble you.

This is a matter upon which four judicial minds have been brought to bear and have come to the same conclusions. We do not think it is a matter which merits more discussion. We therefore refuse leave to appeal.

C.

RECOGNITION

CARL-ZEISS STIFTUNG v. RAYNER & KEELER LIMITED & OTHERS.

([1964] R.P.C. 299)

November 26, 27, 28, 29, December 2, 3, 4, 5, 6, 9, 10, 11, 12, 13, 16, 17, 18, 1963, January 13, 14, 15, 16, 17, 20, 24, March 6, 1964: Chancery Division: Cross J.

Trade mark—Passing-off—*CARL ZEISS*—Procedure summons—Alleged lack of authority to initiate proceedings—Existence of plaintiff in East Germany—Res Judicata—English court not bound by perverse foreign judgment.

An optical works was founded at Jena by Carl Zeiss in 1846. So far as was material to this action, by 1891 his partner Ernst Abbe became the sole owner of the optical works and an associated glass works. These prospering enterprises were transferred to a charitable Foundation. Under a statute which set up the Foundation it was provided inter alia that the Foundation should be presided over by a "Special Board," being the government department responsible for the affairs of the University of Jena, that the Special Board should supervise the "Boards of Management" of the two enterprises, that the Foundation could not dispose of these enterprises but if it became economically impossible to continue them they should be liquidated and the Foundation wound up, and that the works should not be transferred from the vicinity of Jena.

In April, 1945, Jena was occupied by American forces. They set up a provisional government under which Dr. B of the Ministry of Education became the "Special Board." When the members of the Boards of Management left Jena for West Germany upon Jena's incorporation into the Russian Zone, Dr. B appointed in their place six men to act as Boards of Management for a period of two years, it being a term of their appointment that they would resign if those who had departed for West Germany returned before the two years were up. In October, 1945, a Russian order sequestrated certain property in their zone including the plant of the Zeiss enterprises, most of which was taken by the Russians as reparations. Nevertheless the plants were re-equipped in 1948. At the end of 1945 a dispute arose between the members of the Boards of Management in West Germany and Dr. B whether they still had the power to represent the foundation in the West. The position was clarified by their receiving a power of attorney from the officials in the East. Money paid to the Foundation by the Americans in 1946 was used by agreement of all concerned to set up an optical plant in Heidenheim, West Germany. In 1947 the two year appointments to the Boards of Management expired but Dr. B told the existing members to remain in office.

In April, 1948, a further Russian order confiscated property previously covered by the order of sequestration, and the enterprise became owned by "people's own enterprises" (V.E.B.). In fact this involved no change in the persons running the enterprises though the ownership was transferred from the Foundation to the VEBs. However, the VEBs continued to pay their profits to the foundation and the latter continued its social and beneficent functions with the approval of the communist regime. In July, 1948, the Boards of Management in the West asked the West **[300]** German Government to declare Heidenheim to be the legal domicile of the Foundation in the West. In August they met Dr. B. who refused to approve their acts. In February, 1949, the change of domicile was approved by the West German Government, and corresponding changes were made in the registers of patents and trade marks. From then on the West German enterprises and charitable foundation carried on as before the war, regarding themselves as the original Foundation established by Abbe in 1891.

In the East the exact relationship between the VEBs and the Foundation was never clearly defined. The Foundation no longer owned the businesses of the VEBs but it retained other property from which it derived income and continued to pay pensions to ex-employees of the enterprises and later, of the VEBs. In

1952 the Council of Gera became the governing body of the University of Jena and hence the Special Board of the Foundation. In 1953 open competition began between the Eastern and Western Carl Zeiss undertakings, both asserting that they were in law the original business. In West Germany the West German branch was successful in trade mark litigation. The East German branch decided to bring proceedings in West Germany and before doing so obtained an advisory opinion of the East German Supreme Court in April, 1954. That court held that the Foundation remained in Jena unaffected by the confiscation of its principal assets, that the Council of Gera was the Special Board, that a situation envisaged by the articles under which the Foundation should be liquidated had not arisen, that the members of the Boards of Management who had gone to the West resigned on leaving Jena, and that their acts in West Germany were unlawful and invalid.

In April, 1954, the Council of Gera brought an action in Stuttgart Provincial Court against the West German Carl Zeiss firm and its directors seeking an injunction restraining the defendants from using the name "Carl Zeiss" and the rectification of the West German Register of Trade Marks. The action was dismissed on the ground that the Council of Gera had no authority to represent the Foundation then domiciled in Heidenheim. An appeal by the plaintiffs was dismissed in April, 1955, by the Provincial Court of Appeal which held that whether or not the Council of Gera was the Special Board, only the Boards of Management could take action in respect of the trade marks and that no Board of Management had existed since the confiscation of the business. A further appeal to the Federal High Court was allowed in January, 1956. It held that, while leaving open the status of the Council of Gera as the Special Board, only the Board of Management was entitled to represent the Foundation in trade mark litigation. But if there was no board of Management, then the Special Board would have the authority to represent the Foundation. It sent the case back to the Court of Appeal to decide whether the personal defendants had resigned from the Board.

The Court of Appeal gave judgment in October, 1958, in a way which is not easily understood by persons unfamiliar with the relationship of the German courts. It held that even if the domicile of the Foundation remained in Jena and if the personal defendants had resigned, the Foundation was not before the court because, under East German law, either the articles had been inoperative since the confiscation of the business, or the Council of Gera was not capable of functioning as Special Board in the political conditions prevailing in East Germany. Incidentally it held that the personal defendants had not resigned. This judgment was upheld by the Federal High Court in November, 1960.

By these proceedings which were started in 1955, the plaintiff East German Foundation sought to restrain the defendants from passing-off goods in the United Kingdom and other relief. The defendants issued a summons asking that the action be dismissed on the ground that it was commenced without the plaintiff's authority, **[301]** it being their contention that they, the defendants, were the Foundation, the action having been launched in the name of the Foundation. The plaintiffs produced the judgments of the East German courts which held that under East German law the plaintiff was a corporation established in East Germany, and therefore they had prima facie the right to issue proceedings here. The defendants contended that whether the plaintiffs existed depended upon the interpretation of the statute of the Foundation and the effect of the confiscation of its business. This happened before the establishment of either East or West Germany and therefore the East German court had no special competence to decide the matter. They submitted that the issue was res judicata by the judgment of the Federal High Court given in 1960, and that to allow the plaintiffs to sue would be enforcing the confiscation decrees outside East Germany.

Held, (1) that in the light of a letter of 28th January, 1946, by the members of the West German Board of Management which stated unequivocally that as they had vacated office when they left Jena it would be pointless for them to resign, and in the light of all the surrounding circumstances, it appeared that they and the East German Board of Management had accepted that they vacated office. Only in 1948 when they saw potential advantage in maintaining that they had not resigned did they first deny having resigned (p. 37).

(2) That the Foundation remaining the registered proprietor of its land shown in the Land Registers, notwithstanding the confiscation of business assets, was consistent with the expressed intention of the East German authorities that the Foundation should remain in existence as the owner of the rest of its property (p. 39).

(3) That the order confiscating the property of the business and its transfer to the VEBs would have been effective to transfer the trade marks to the VEBs, although these marks had in fact been left on the register as the property of the Foundation and were used by the VEBs under licence (p. 42).

(4) That according to the view of the East German courts, the order of confiscation had extra-territorial effect (p. 43).

(5) That whether or not the confiscation extended to goodwill in this country, the Foundation had an interest in the action either because the decree did not extend to this country, or because though it extended our law will not give it effect (p. 44).

(6) That the effect of the confiscation of the businesses upon the Foundation must be determined according to the law of East Germany. This was the view accepted by the West German courts who then concluded that after confiscation the Articles became totally unworkable in East Germany and the administration passed to the West German Board of Management. It was not established that the Articles were unworkable and it did not follow that if they were unworkable that the Foundation ceased thereupon to exist. Nor was it established that a Special Board within the meaning of the term given to it by the Articles could not exist in East Germany any less than it had during the Hitler regime (p. 49).

(7) That even if it were true that the Special Board as contemplated by the Articles could not exist in East Germany, it did not follow that the West German Board of Management became entitled to represent and administer the Foundation (p. 50).

(8) That the defendants' plea of res judicata arising from the decision of the West German courts was inapplicable because:—(a) it was not a decision on the merits of the case but merely a decision as to whether the Foundation could be represented **[302]** by the Council of Gera; (b) in the present proceedings the Foundation was not represented by the Council of Gera, and the Foundation was not a party to the German judgment; (c) the point at issue was different —there it was to decide whether the Council of Gera could represent the Foundation—here to decide whether the Foundation's solicitors had authority to proceed (p. 52).

(9) That assuming that the parties and issues were the same in the West German proceedings as now before the court, even so the court would not hold itself bound by a foreign decision which was perverse and knowingly failed to give effect to the law of another foreign country that it purported to apply (p. 56).

(10) That although the courts in this country will not give effect to an extra-territorial act of confiscation by a foreign government, it was not established on the facts of this case that the Foundation might not be justified in claiming the ownership of the goodwill of this country to be used for the benefit of the original and intended beneficiaries of the Foundation. Accordingly the summons would be dismissed (p. 58).

Reuter v. *Mulhens* [1954] Ch. 50, (1953) 70 R.P.C. 235, and *Simpson* v. *Fogo* (1863) 1 Hemming and Miller 195, followed. *Thoday* v. *Thoday* [1964] 2 W.L.R. 371 considered.

This was a preliminary hearing on a summons issued by the defendants to an action for passing-off by which they asked that the action be dismissed and all further proceedings stayed because the action had been commenced without the plaintiffs' authority. The plaintiffs were the Carl-Zeiss-Stiftung of Jena, East Germany, and the three defendants were Rayner & Keeler Ltd., of Maddox

Street, W. 1., Degenhardt & Co. Ltd., of New Bond Street, W. 1., and the Carl-Zeiss Stiftung of Heidenheim, West Germany. The remaining facts appear from the arguments of counsel and the judgment.

Guy Aldous, Q.C., *E. Lauterpacht* and *Douglas Falconer* instructed by *Courts & Co*. appeared for the plaintiff. *Sir Milner Holland*, Q.C., *G. A. Rink*, Q.C., and *T. M. Shelford*, instructed by *Dehn & Lauderdale* appeared for the defendants.

Holland, Q.C.—The decisions of the West German courts, which were selected by the plaintiffs for litigation, show that the plaintiffs did not have authority to represent the Carl-Zeiss-Stiftung (called "Stiftung"). If a party selects a forum to litigate an issue and there fails, he cannot litigate the same issue again in England. Where there is an express decision of an exact point by any court, that is binding between the same parties on any subsequent occasion: *Society of Medical Officers of Health* v. *Hope*[1]; *Duedu* v. *Yiboe*[2]; *Hoystead* v. *Taxation Commissioner*[3]. If the question has been in substance decided, or has in substance formed the ratio of, or been fundamental to an earlier decision, that operates as part of the estoppel by *res judicata*: *Duedu* v. *Yiboe*[4]. It extends to any matter which might have been raised in that action, but which was not done for any reason: *Hoystead* v. *Taxation Commissioner*[5].

A judgment given after the commencement of the subsequent proceedings but pronounced before judgment in the subsequent proceedings, operates as an estoppel: *Morrison Rose & Partners* v. *Hillman*[6]. An estoppel operates against all those who take under parties who are estopped: *Spencer* v. *Williams*[7]. It also operates **[303]** against all persons who either authorised another person to bring the proceedings or who stood by and saw the battle fought by others: *Wytcherley* v. *Andrews*[8], and these principles are not confined only to probate and divorce matters: *Nana Ofori Atta II* v. *Nana Abu Bonsra II*[9].

An estoppel operates for the benefit of those who take under the person having the benefit of it (see Spencer Bower on Res Judicata, 1st ed., pp. 125, 193). A judicial decision *inter partes* operates as an estoppel, in favour of and against, parties and privies: *Gray* v. *Lewis*[10]. It makes no difference even it it were a decision of a foreign court (see Spencer Bower on Res Judicata, 1st ed., p. 137). Though a court can disregard a particular judgment of a foreign court, if, for instance, it was inconsistent with another decision on that by the same court; but not merely because the judgment was obtained in a foreign court: *Ricardo* v. *Garcias.*[11] An estoppel operates even if the foreign judgment was wrong in law, wrong according to even English law: *Godard* v. *Gray*[12].

The goodwill in England which belonged to the Stiftung is an item of English property: *Reuter (R. J.) Co. Ltd.* v. *Mulhens*[13] and an English court will not recognise or give assistance to the expropriation of, and an expropriatory decree in respect of, an item of English property: *In re Claim by Helbert Wagg & Co. Ltd.*[14]* This action is an attempt to secure the VEBs the benefit of the goodwill formerly belonging to the Stiftung, and the court is entitled to look behind what is being done: *In re Claim by Helbert Wagg & Co. Ltd.*[14]* An English court will not recognise a discriminatory or penal decree in respect of any property wherever situated: *Frankfurther* v. *W. L. Exener Ltd.*[15]*; *Novello & Co. Ltd.* v. *Hinrichsen Edition Ltd.*[16]* The whole of the two businesses which were the underlying foundation of the Stiftung, and all the assets relating to them, including trade marks and goodwill, have ceased to belong to it and nobody purporting to represent it can use its power to authorise proceedings the benefit of which must pass to the body in whose favour its industrial undertakings have been transferred.

The law by reference to which the effect of the confiscation is to be judged

[1] [1960] A.C. 551.
[2] [1961] 1 W.L.R. 1040.
[3] [1926] A.C. 155, P.C.
[4] [1961] 1 W.L.R. 1040, 1046.
[5] [1926] A.C. 155, 170, P.C.
[6] [1961] 2 Q.B. 226.
[7] (1871) L.R. 2 P. & D. 230.
[8] (1871) L.R. 2 P. & D. 327.
[9] [1958] A.C. 95, P.C.
[10] (1873) 8 Ch. App. 1035.
[11] 12 Cl. F. 368.
[12] (1870) L.R. 6 Q.B. 139.
[13] [1954] Ch. 50; (1953) 70 R.P.C. 235.
[14] [1956] Ch. 323.
[15] [1947] Ch. 629.
[16] [1951] Ch. 1026.

is not the law either of West Germany or of East Germany, and the East German courts have no exclusive jurisdiction on the matter.

Guy Aldous, Q.C.—The decisions of the West German courts do not give rise to any estoppel here. The judgment of the West German Federal High Court given on 15th November, 1960, was not final there, and it was not on the merits of the case, but only on a procedural point. The judgment relied on for *res judicata* must be final on the merits: *Nouvion* v. *Freeman.*[17] Further, it is essential that the causes of action in the foreign tribunal and in the English court must be the same: *Callandar* v. *Dittrich,*[18] but here the causes of action are different from those in West German actions. As estoppels are odious, they are not to be extended to cases not already covered by authority: *Baxendale* v. *Bennett.*[19] They can never be pleaded on the preliminary question like whether the proceedings are brought without authority. They also do not arise where the parties are different and the parties here are different from those in the West German actions. **[304]**

If the West German courts purported to decide the same question as is to be decided here, they came to a decision as to what was the East German law and its effect in disregard of what was in fact the East German law, and hence, the West German judgment is perverse and it cannot be the basis for an estoppel. If the decision of a foreign court is contrary to justice and to the right of comity of nations, as is the case with West German decision, the court would disregard it: *Liverpool Marine Credit Co.* v. *Hunter*;[20] *Simpson* v. *Fogo.*[21]

A foreign judgment *in personam* does not extend to those who are not privy to the judgment. The doctrine of privacy in the case of estoppel cannot arise where the decision is a procedural decision and also where the facts of the cases are different. As the first two defendants were not concerned with the matters in West German action, they cannot be privy to what was decided in that action.

Harris v. *Quine*[22] decided that unless the right itself which was being relied on either as the right which was sought to be enforced or the right which was said to be extinguished had actually been extinguished, it was no bar to an action. The right to prevent passing-off in this country by using the name Carl-Zeiss-Stiftung was not extinguished by the West German judgments. A *res judicata* as to want of authority can never arise either out of English or foreign judgment, because such a judgment can never extinguish any right.

The principle that estoppel operates against persons who stood by and saw the battle fought by others would not extend to any adjudication of the court upon the matter not pleaded and Lord Penzance said in *Wytcherley* v. *Andrews*[23] that this principle was not to be extended. *Nana Ofori Atta II* v. *Nana Abu Bonsra II*[24] was a case of estoppel by conduct and not of estoppel by *res judicata.*

The plaintiffs had selected the West German courts as their forum only to decide the matters that they pleaded and those matters related to West Germany only. Their decisions were not *in rem* and the plaintiffs had never sought there a decision which would bind them in all countries on a matter which they had not raised.

The question whether a foreign juridical person exists is to be decided by the law of the place where such person was created and is said to continue: *Lazard Brothers & Co.* v. *Midland Bank Ltd.*[25]* Whether a person is authorised to represent a foreign juridical person depends upon its articles. The interpretation and operation of those articles is governed by the law from time to time prevailing at the place where the juridical person's home was set up: *Banco de Bilbao* v. *Sancha.*[26]* The foreign law which must have regard is the law as interpreted and enforced by the courts of the foreign country in question, and it is *nihil ad rem* that the English courts would themselves think that the law should be different: *Bankers and Shippers Insurance Co. of New York* v. *Liverpool Marine & General*

[17] (1889) 15 App. Cas. 1.
[18] (1842) 4 Man. & G. 68.
[19] (1878) 3 Q.B.D. 525.
[20] (1868) 3 Ch. App. 479.
[21] 1 Hem. & M. 195, 247.
[22] (1869) L.R. 4 Q.B. 653.
[23] (1871) L.R. 2 P. & D. 327, 329.
[24] [1958] A.C. 95, P.C.
[25] [1933] A.C. 289, 297.
[26] [1938] 2 K.B. 176.
[27] 21 Ll. L.R. 86.

Insurance Co.;[27] *In re Duke of Wellington.*[28]

A corporation has its domicile in the state which has created it and has no domicile anywhere else: *Gasque* v. *Commissioners of Inland Revenue.*[29]

The onus is on the defendants to show that the Stiftung ceased to exist and, therefore, is incapable of maintaining this action: *Russian Commercial & Industrial* **[305]** *Bank* v. *Comptoir d'Escompte de Mulhouse.*[30]* Even if the property of the Stiftung in East Germany was expropriated, yet its management at Jena can take proceedings in this country to protect its goodwill since the expropriation decree had no effect on its property in this country: *A. G. Der Manufacturen I. A. Woronin Leutschig and Cheshire* v. *Frederick Huth & Co.*[31]*

If an action for passing-off between two manufacturers fails and subsequently an action is brought against the retailer, the retailer cannot rely on *res judicata.* An action for passing-off depends on whether the particular transaction in respect of which the suit is brought would deceive anybody: *Goddard* v. *Watford Co-operative Society.*[32] It may be that everybody knows the difference between the two Zeiss's in West Germany and there could not be any passing-off there, but in England the position is different as here any question of having an estoppel in the case of passing-off where there has been a decision in one country could not affect what happened in another country.

If the plaintiffs in an action have got interest which they can protect, it does not matter whether somebody else gets benefit from those proceedings. It is irrelevant who benefits from the action, as for instance, in a case of a trade mark which is registered in the name of one person and others are his licensees, it does not matter if the action will not benefit the registered proprietor but will benefit his licensees.

The question whether or not there has been a confiscation of assets is irrelevant to the question whether or not there was sufficient authorisation to bring the proceedings.

If the judgments of the West German courts give rise to any estoppel, then the judgment of the East German Supreme Court produces a counter-estoppel on the third defendant, even though they did not appear in East German action: *In re Dulles' Settlement* (*No.* 2).[33]

Holland, Q.C.—The real issue of law is the construction of the articles of the Stiftung and it is for this court to construe them according to any principles laid down by the foreign law applicable to it: *Rouyer Guillet Et Compagnie* v. *Rouyer Guillet & Co. Ltd.*[34] *Bankers and Shippers Insurance Co. of New York* v. *Liverpool Marine & General Insurance Co. Ltd.*[35] was a case of construction of a statutory provision forming part of the law of that country and not a case of construction of a private document as here. The case of *Banco de Bilbao* v. *Sancha*[36]* is different from this case because there the question was which of the two express unambiguous legislative enactments governed the matter and there was no difficulty in saying what the law was.

The confiscation covered the whole of the business in Jena and everything having economic connection with it, which included trade marks.

The maxim that the estoppels are odious is out of date: *per* Lord Maugham in *New Brunswick Railway Co.* v. *British & French Trust Corporation Ltd.*[37]; *Canada Dominion Sugar Co. Ltd.* v. *Canadian National* (*West Indies*) *Steamships Ltd.*[38]; per Maugham, J., in *Green* v. *Wetherill.*[39] **[306]**

The causes of action in West Germany and in this action are sufficiently close to make available the whole of the reasoning of the one to the other. The estoppel by *res judicata* covers everything which is naturally part of the reasoning: *Henderson* v. *Henderson.*[40] This is not a procedural matter but it is a

[28] [1947] Ch. 506.
[29] [1940] 2 K.B. 80.
[30] [1925] A.C. 112, H.L.
[31] 79 Ll. L.R. 262.
[32] (1924) 41 R.P.C. 218.
[33] [1951] Ch. 842.
[34] [1949] 1 A11 E.R. 244.
[35] 21 Ll. L.R. 86.
[36] [1938] 2 K.B. 176.
[37] [1939] A.C. 1, 19, 20.
[38] [1947] A.C. 46, 55, P.C.
[39] [1929] 2 Ch. 213, 221.
[40] (1843) 3 Hare 100.

substantive question of right in people to authorise the use of the name of a company. The third defendants are the same as were the defendants in West German courts.

What Denning, L.J., said in *In re Dulles' Settlement* (*No.* 2)[41] was *obiter* and it is not in agreement with the classic cases on the counter-estoppel (see *Emanuel* v. *Symon*[42]) and is contrary to *Harris* v. *Taylor*.[43]

Cross, J.—On the 20th October, 1955, a writ in the Chancery Division of the High Court was issued by Messrs. Courts & Co., solicitors for the plaintiffs, Carl-Zeiss-Stiftung, which was stated to be a corporation under the laws of the German Democratic Republic with a registered office at Carl-Zeiss-Platz, Jena, East Germany. The writ named as defendants Rayner & Keeler Ltd., of 32 Maddox Street, London, W.1, Degenhardt & Co. Ltd., of 100 New Bond Street, London, W.1, and Carl-Zeiss of Heidenheim, Brenz, in Western Germany. The claim was for an injunction to restrain the defendants and each of them from advertising, offering for sale or selling any optical instruments or any articles containing or consisting of glass under or by reference to the name Carl-Zeiss unless such goods be those of the plaintiff or an organisation associated with the plaintiff, and generally from "passing-off" in business goods as and for those of the plaintiff and/or organisation associated with the plaintiff, and for consequential relief.

The writ was served on the first and second defendants at their registered offices in London on the 3rd November, 1955, and both entered appearances to it on the 11th November. On the 1st November the plaintiff had been granted leave under R.S.C. O. 11 r. 1(f) to issue a concurrent writ and serve notice of it on the third defendant at Heidenheim, and on the 26th January, 1956, the third defendant entered appearance as Carl-Zeiss-Stiftung, trading as Carl-Zeiss. Later the writ was amended by changing the name of the third defendant from Carl-Zeiss to Carl-Zeiss-Stiftung and by adding a claim for another injunction restraining the third defendant from using the name Carl-Zeiss-Stiftung or Carl-Zeiss or any name containing Zeiss in relation to its business or goods. On the 7th February, 1956, the three defendants issued a summons asking that all further proceedings in the action be stayed and the action dismissed on the ground that it was commenced and was being maintained without the plaintiff's authority, and for an order that Messrs. Courts pay the costs of the application. This summons was supported by an affidavit of Walter David, the legal adviser of the third defendant, filed on the 6th April, 1956. The plaintiff had meanwhile, on the 23rd December, 1955, delivered a statement of claim. Nothing further was done by either side until the 20th March, 1959, when the defendants gave notice of intention to proceed. This step prompted the plaintiff to file on the 11th May, 1959, two affidavits in answer to the summons, one by Hugo Schrade, who described himself as a member of the Boards of Management of the optical and glassworks of the plaintiff, and the other by Rudolph Reichrath, the legal adviser of the plaintiff. On the 16th May, 1960, the defendants filed a further affidavit by David in reply. On the 1st June they took out a summons to cross-examine Schrade and Reichrath on their affidavits, and on the 27th July another summons for leave to adduce further evidence in the form of affidavits by Paul Henrichs, a member of the Boards of Management of the **[307]** third defendant, and by Richard von Moser, a German lawyer practising in Western Germany. On the 21st March, 1961, the three summonses came before me in court. It soon became clear that the case was not yet ripe for hearing, as the plaintiff wished to put in further evidence in answer to the additional evidence which I gave the defendants leave to adduce. The summons, therefore, stood over for the evidence to be completed.

On the 4th August, 1961, further affidavits were sworn by Schrade and Reichrath. On the 23rd May, 1963, the plaintiff in his turn gave notice to proceed. On the 28th October, 1963, the defendants issued a fourth summons for leave to adduce yet further evidence in the form of an affidavit by Heinz Knoblauch, another lawyer practising in West Germany. Finally, the plaintiff, on the 12th

[41] [1951] 1 Ch. 842. [42] [1908] 1 K.B. 302. [43] [1915] 2 K.B. 580.

and 22nd November, filed further affidavits by Frederick Honig, a doctor of laws of Heidelberg University who is also a member of the English Bar, and by Schrade. The case came before me again on the 26th November. Heinrichs had by then died and counsel for the defendants did not ask leave to read Knoblauch's affidavit. But David and von Moser on one side and Reichrath and Honig, on the other, were cross-examined on their various affidavits. The hearing occupied the court for more than 20 days.

The facts are as follows:—

About 1846, Carl Zeiss founded an optical works at Jena, a University town, in what was then the Grand Duchy of Saxe-Weimar-Eisenach. He later took into partnership with him Ernst Abbe, a mathematician and physicist of Jena University. About 1879, Zeiss and Abbe and Otto Schott became partners in a glass works. Carl Zeiss died in 1888, and his son, Roderick, became for a short time partner with Abbe in the optical business, and with Abbe and Schott in the glass business. But in 1891 he retired and handed over his interests to Abbe, who thus became sole owner of the optical business and part owner of the glass business. At about this time Abbe transferred his interests in the business to a foundation (the German word "Stiftung"), or, as an English lawyer might say, "a charitable corporation." The basic principle was that the two businesses though owned by the Foundation were to be run by two independent Boards of Management, and that the profits were to be paid to a third organ of the Foundation called the "Special Board" (Stiftungs-Verwaltung), which would apply them for certain prescribed objects, and was to be represented on the Boards of Management by an official called "the Deputy" (Stiftung's Kommissar). Articles embodying the constitution of the Foundation were drawn up by Abbe and accepted by the authorities of the Grand Duchy, whose approval was necessary under German law. Schott's share of the glass business did not become vested in the Foundation until 1919, but nothing turns on that fact, and it will be convenient to speak as though the Foundation had become the owner of the whole of both businesses from the start.

Much of the controversy in this case has centred around the construction of the Articles and the effect on them of certain measures taken in 1948 by the Russian Military Administration in Eastern Germany. It is therefore necessary for me to refer to a number of them in detail.

Article 1: "Objects of the Stiftung. The objects of the Carl-Zeiss-Stiftung are:

"A. Within the Works. 1. To cultivate the branches of precise technical industry, which have been introduced into Jena by the optical works and the glass works with the co-operation of the founder of the Stiftung and thereby maintain the said industrial establishments under an impersonal title of proprietorship.

"2. Permanent solicitude for the economic security of the above undertakings as well as for the conservation and further development of their industrial labour organisation—as a source of subsistence for a large number of people and as an efficient member in the service of scientific and practical interests. **[308]**

"3. To fulfil higher social duties than personal proprietors would permanently guarantee towards the totality of co-workers in its employ, in order to better their personal and economic rights.

"B. Outside the works. 1. To promote the general interests of the branches of precise technical industry as indicated above not only within the sphere of action proper of the Stiftung's works but also outside of it.

"2. To take part in organisations and measures designed for the public good of the working population of Jena and its immediate neighbourhood.

"3. To promote study in natural and mathematical sciences both as regards research and teaching.

"The objects of the Stiftung as enumerated under A are to be carried out by the Stiftung by virtue of the statutory administration of its own industrial undertakings exclusively and within the scope of these undertakings.

"Respecting carrying out the objects of this Stiftung as enumerated sub B, these shall be limited to such surplus funds as may be available after the provisions as detailed sub A have been provided for."

Article 3: "Domicile. The legal domicile of the Stiftung shall be Jena."

Article 4: "Organisation of the Stiftung. For representing the Carl-Zeiss-Stiftung as an incorporated body, for the administration of its estate and effects and for the supreme direction of its affairs a 'Special Board of the Stiftung' (Stiftungsverwaltung) shall be formed.

"For directing the industrial operations of the Stiftung and the management of its various establishments there shall be instituted as further organisation of the Stiftung along with the Special Board:

" 'Boards of Management' (Geschaftsleitungen) of the various establishments of the Stiftung for the time being;

"A permanent official, the 'Deputy of the Stiftung' (Stiftungskommissar) appointed to represent the Special Board on the Boards of Management;

"both of which, Boards of Management and the Deputy, shall be nominated by the Special Board in conformity with the articles of this Statute."

Article 5: "Special Board and Deputy of the Stiftung. The rights and duties of the Special Board shall pertain to that Department of the State service of the Grand Duchy of Saxe-Weimar under which the affairs of the University of Jena are, for the time being, placed.

"The office of permanent Deputy to be appointed by the Special Board shall be held in an extra-official capacity by a higher official of the State service of the Grand Duchy of Saxe-Weimar or, failing such, an active higher official of the public service; and he shall receive as remuneration a sum from the funds of the Stiftung fixed from time to time, but no bonuses or similar honoraria.

"It is incumbent on the Special Board and on the Deputy to conduct the affairs of the Carl-Zeiss-Stiftung with due regard to the intentions of the founder thereof, both in accordance with the provisions laid down in this Statute and also in the spirit they suggest. In doing so they are bound to heed interests of State, which are alien to the implied objects of the Stiftung, no more than is legally demanded from private individuals. **[309]**

"Chapter II. Organisation of the Industrial Operations of the Stiftung. Article 6: Present business undertakings. The present commercial undertakings of the Carl-Zeiss-Stiftung—the optical works (the firm of Carl Zeiss) and the glass works (the firm of Schott & Genossen) in Jena—shall each be carried on permanently under the name of their respective firms, with separate assets for their working capital and in independent management under their own Board of Management."

Article 7, so far as relevant: "The number of members composing a Board of Management may not exceed four."

Article 8: "Powers of the Boards of Management. The Board of Management of each business of the Stiftung has control over the entire internal working management, the commercial administration and the whole external trading operations of its own firm, including the appointment of officials empowered to sign in the name of the firm, the appointment and revocation of other attorneys, the appointment, dismissal and pensioning of officials, assistants and working men, defining their duties and their salaries and the regulation of their legal status with the firm in conformity with the articles of this statute.

"In all matters concerning each of the businesses of the Stiftung valid arrangements can only be made by its Board of Management according to the procedure prescribed by the subsequent paragraphs of this statute.

"Each business of the Stiftung can only be represented with respect to a third party in all its affairs, juridical and extra-juridical, by members of its own Board of Management or those authorised by the latter."

Article 9: "Representing the Stiftung externally. In the matter of representing the Stiftung in affairs of the individual firm there shall be either a certain member of the Board of Management appointed by the Special Board as 'Mandatory of the Carl-Zeiss-Stiftung' (Bevollmachtigten der Carl-Zeiss-Stiftung) and a second member appointed as his proxy, and each of these two shall be absolutely empowered in his own person to sign for the firm, or an arrangement shall be made, whereby any two members of the Board of Management shall exercise this function jointly."

Article 10: "Influence of the Special Board on the business directorate. Any influence of the Special Board on the Board of Management of the businesses of the Stiftung may only take place in so far as is prescribed by this statute; and only then through the intermediation of the Deputy of the Stiftung."

Article 11: "Duties of the Deputy. It is the duty of the Deputy of the Stiftung continually to supervise the management of the business in all its branches, to superintend the regularity of the administration and to see that the procedure of the Board of Management is in conformity with this statute, as well as to co-operate in all important acts of the management according to the procedure laid down in 13 to 20 either by way of decision or by ways of advice."

Article 14: "Where the Deputy is to be consulted. All matters and occurrences, which lie outside the ordinary run of business, must, when there is no immediate danger, be submitted before decision to the Deputy of the Stiftung and dealt with before him."

Then Article 16 sets out a number of transactions requiring the consent of the Deputy: "The Boards of Management have to obtain the explicit consent of the Deputy of the Stiftung even in the event of their being unanimous in opinion with regard to the following transactions"—and among them is "Taking part in civil actions or arbitrations in disputes which do not result from the ordinary course of business." **[310]**

Then Article 24 is dealing with pensions, etc.: "The annual payments, which are made on the basis of statutory or contracted pension obligations and on the basis of 77 of this statute are to be considered, even if they be temporarily paid out of the reserve funds of the Stiftung, not as payments of the Carl-Zeiss-Stiftung, but as general expenses of the business and are accordingly to be included in the annual balance sheets and in the statistical reports referred to in 23."

Article 25: "The members of the Boards of Management of the businesses of the Stiftung are to be nominated by the Special Board after consultation with the Deputy of the Stiftung and the members of the Board of Management already actively employed in the said business. No one can be nominated contrary to the unanimous consent of these members."

Then Article 27: "The appointment to a membership of the Boards of Management cannot be effected with the option of revocation, but only either for a fixed period to be determined beforehand, for life or until the term the said member is entitled to a pension according to Statute.

"The retirement of a member from the Board of Management, otherwise than in the event of a voluntary one from his office as accepted by the Special Board, is based solely on the expiration of the period contracted for or by the termination or cancellation of the contract, on the basis of which the nomination was made."

Then Article 37: "From the meaning and purpose of the Stiftung it is absolutely excluded for ever of disposing entirely or partially of its title or ownership of the present businesses of the Stiftung or the rights appertaining thereto by contract, by sale or assignment, or of freeing itself of the responsibility of its administration of the same by leasing, by taking in new partners into the firms affiliated to the Stiftung and such like measures.

"The same is also to be applicable to any new business undertakings established or taken over by the Stiftung in the future within the German Empire, when the said undertaking has once been five or more years in the partial or entire possession of the Stiftung.

"Should at any time the further continuation of a business of the Stiftung falling under the aforesaid provisions be impossible without damaging or endangering the other businesses or even the Stiftung itself, with due regard to the interests concerned the said business shall be finally liquidated, and the said firm finally struck off the registers after the settlement of all its engagements."

Article 39: "The Works of the Stiftung alluded to in 6 shall not be transferred to localities outside the immediate neighbourhood of Jena."

Article 56: "The appointment of officials of the Stiftung and of the businesses of the Stiftung, or clerks and workmen, must always be effected without prejudice as to their parentage, religious or political views."

Article 72: "Rights to Pensions. Claim to pension. Officials, clerks and workmen, who have entered into the service of the businesses of the Stiftung before the completion of their fortieth year are after five years' service entitled to a pension, which can be upheld at law against their firm, not only in their own person in case of becoming incapacitated during their engagement from following their occupation by age or permanent illness or other circumstances not attributable to grave misdemeanours on their own part, but also, in case of death, in favour of their widow and children. **[311]**

"For the settlement of these claims with regard to all those engaged in the business, who are not under special contract, the 'General Pension Statute' of the firms Carl Zeiss and Schott & Gen. dated 1st September, 1897, in its main provisions holds good, namely: "—and then there follow details of pensions to be paid.

Articles 101 to 103 provide for the distribution of the surplus income of the businesses in furtherance of the objects stated in Article 1, B: and Article 104a, which was added, I think, in the early part of this century, runs as follows: "The administration of all organisations in favour of the objects as per 101 to 103 is to be made over to the Jena Board of Management and the Deputy of the Stiftung and is to be executed by these persons in conformity with the provisions in 10 to 15."

Then finally, Article 113: "Should, in consequence of political changes in the State, the provision according to 5 of this statute with reference to the representation of the Stiftung become untenable, this representation including the appointment of the Deputy of the Stiftung within the meaning of 5 and the statutory administration of the Carl-Zeiss-Stiftung shall be made over to that department of State, which with regard to the University of Jena occupies the place of the State Department of the Grand Duchy of Saxe Weimar acting as the Special Board, provided that its seat is in Thuringia, otherwise to the highest administrative authorities in Thuringia."

Article 114. "Should at any time a Special Board corresponding to the provisions of 5 or 113 no longer exist, then until the new formation of such the representation and administration of the Carl-Zeiss-Stiftung is to be taken over forthwith by the executive Board of Management of the optical works and in the event of the latter Board of Management no longer existing, by the Board of Management of the oldest works or the Stiftung in Jena or its neighbourhood."

Then Article 116: "Should the Carl-Zeiss-Stiftung at any time in consequence of dissolution of all its business undertakings, under the suppositions contained in Article 37, paragraph 3, of this statute or through other causes, see no longer any grounds for continuing its activity in the sphere of the higher technical industry profitably and be also in possession of no other organisations of a permanent nature and of sufficient importance, the continuity of which would mean merely administration of its assets, it shall distribute after dissolution of the last works of the Stiftung and liquidation of all its obligations half the remaining value of its assets between the communities of Jena and Weninjena at its discretion, the other half going to the University of Jena: in the event of the latter no longer existing, to another German University to be selected by the Special Board, to be independently employed for purposes in the sense of the Stiftung, and cease to exist as a legal corporation with its own administration."

Article 117: "Up to the expiration of ten years after coming into force of the present statute, any alterations or additions to the same as well as explanatory clauses and where necessary new readings or entire paragraphs are reserved for agreement between the Special Board and the founder."

Article 118: "Later alterations of the statute. Should at a subsequent period important suppositions of the present statute with regard to its legal basis or with regard to technical and economic conditions be altered to such a degree for the effectiveness of the Stiftung, that the further strict observance of all provisions of this statute becomes either directly impossible or in virtue of their consequences impracticable for the future, or in view of the recognisable intentions of the founder palpably inexpedient, the statutory Special Board of the

Carl-[**312**]-Zeiss-Stifftung shall be authorised to amend this statute in compliance with the altered circumstances, as may be deemed necessary, in order to remove the aforesaid drawbacks."

Then Articles 119 and 120 are headed: "Disputing alterations to the statute" and "effect of alteration in the statute." Then follows Article 121: "The provisions of the four 1 to 4 and the four preceding ones above (117 to 120) can, under no circumstances and in no manner, be legally amended or rendered imperative."

It will be seen that one Article which is expressly stated to be incapable of alteration is Article 3, which fixes the domicile of the Stiftung at Jena.

The businesses owned by the Foundation prospered; their products became world famous and very large profits were made. As well as its industrial buildings, the Foundation became the owner of a quantity of property in and around Jena, and substantial capital investments. Details of the property are given in paragraph 11 of Schrade's affidavit. There is, for instance, the People's House at Jena, the Opticians' School, the Ernst Abbe Library, the Children's Hospital, a number of dwelling houses, and so on. Jena is a town of some 80,000 inhabitants, about half of which are composed of persons who are or have been employed in either the optical or glass works, and the families and dependants of such persons.

Article 113 shows that Abbe anticipated that there might be political changes in Germany which would result in changes in the Special Board. His anticipations were fulfilled. First, in 1918, the Grand Duchy and a number of neighbouring principalities were abolished and their territories amalgamated into the State of Thuringia, one of the constitutent States of the German Republic. Thereupon, the Thuringian Minister of Education became the Special Board. Next, in 1935, when the Weimar Republic was replaced by the Third Reich, the sovereign powers of the various States were vested in the Reich, the government of which was represented in each State by a Reich's Deputy (Reichs-Stathalter), subject to the control of the relevant Ministries in Berlin. The Reichs-Stathalter, as the highest administrative authority in Thuringia, therefore became the Special Board of the Foundation.

Then, in April, 1945, the Hitler regime collapsed and the office of Reichs-Stathalter was abolished. Jena was first occupied for some three months by American troops, but by agreement between the Allies, it became part of the Russian zone of occupation, and on the 1st July it was occupied by the Russians. When the American forces left they took with them all the members of the existing Boards of Management of the optical and glass businesses, a number of leading scientists, engineers and senior executives of the businesses and a large quantity of material.

The members of the Boards of Management of the optical business were:— Professor Bauersfeld, who was Mandatory; Mr. Paul Henrichs, who was deputy Mandatory; Dr. Kuppenbender and Professor Joos, each of whom had authority to sign for the firm Carl-Zeiss.

The members of the Board of Management of the glass business were:—Dr. Hirsch, who was Mandatory; Dr. Eric Schott, who was his deputy; and Mr. Henrichs, who had authority to sign for the firm Schott. All these six men had been appointed members of the respective Boards of Management.

The Americans had set up a provincial government in Thuringia and on the 21st June, 1945, the newly constituted Thuringian Ministry of Education, which had become the Special Board, appointed Dr. Barth, the President of the Provincial [**313**] Court, to be the Deputy of the Foundation in place of the former Deputy Professor Esau. He came to Jena on the 23rd June to discuss arrangements for the management of the businesses during the absence of the six gentlemen above mentioned. It was, of course, quite uncertain how long Germany would be occupied by the Allies or when they would be able and willing to return to Jena.

The members of the Board of Management of the optical business had already selected three employees of the Foundation—Dr. Hugo Schrade, Mr. Victor Sandmann and Dr. Friedrich Schomerus—who were staying on in Jena as suitable persons to carry on in their absence. They had thought that the situation could be met if these men had authority to sign for the business; but Barth was firmly of the opinion that this would not suffice, and that those who were going to carry on in Jena must be members of the Board. The six gentlemen left Jena on the 24th and 25th June, and on the 27th Barth, acting on behalf of the Special Board, appointed, or purported to appoint, Schrade, Sandmann and Schomerus to be members of the Board of Management of the optical business for two years. On the same day appointments of Schrade, Mr. Fritz Dunger, Mr. Albert Heintz and Dr. August Klemm to the Board of Management of the glass works were made. All six signed agreements with Barth that they would resign if the gentlemen who had left Jena returned within that period. On the 27th June Barth also asked the District Court to make entries in the Commercial Register to show that for the optical business Schomerus and Sandmann had replaced Bauersfeld and Henrichs as Mandatory and Deputy, and that Schrade had replaced Kuppenbender and Joos as a person authorised to sign on behalf of the Carl-Zeiss, and that for the glass business Dunger and Heintz had replaced Hirsch and Schott as Mandatory and Deputy, and that Klemm and Schrade had replaced Henrichs as persons authorised to sign on behalf of the firm Schott. These changes were made in the Register in the case of the glass business on the 10th October, and in the case of the optical business on the 18th October, 1945. There is a dispute between the parties to which I shall have to return later as to whether the gentlemen who left Jena retired from office at this time or continued to be members of the respective Boards.

On the 2nd August, 1945, the so-called Potsdam Agreement was signed by the representatives of the Allied Powers. Part II set out certain political and economic principles which it was hoped would govern the treatment of Germany in the initial control period. Paragraph 12 ran as follows: "12. At the earliest practicable date, the German economy shall be decentralised for the purposes of eliminating the present excessive concentration of economic power as exemplified in particular by cartels, syndicates, trusts and other monopolistic arrangements."

Part III was headed "Reparations from Germany." Paragraph 1 ran: "1. Reparation claims of the U.S.S.R. shall be met by removals from the zone of Germany occupied by the U.S.S.R. and from appropriate German external assets."

On the 30th October, 1945, Marshal Zhukov, Head of the Russian Military Administration in Germany, made an Order known as "SMAD 124," which provided for the sequestration of certain types of property situated in the Russian Zone. This Order applied to the Foundation. Russian officers were stationed in the works and remained there for some 18 months. Between October, 1946, and March, 1947, some 95 per cent of the machinery and plant was taken to Russia by way of reparations, and a number of workpeople sent to Russia with it; but at the same time great efforts were made on the German side to get the works running again as soon as possible. Machinery which had been damaged in air raids was repaired and fresh machinery was obtained with the aid of funds provided by the Thuringian Government. By the beginning of 1948 the works in Jena had been re-equipped. **[314]**

In the Autumn of 1945 a difference of opinion arose between the old members of the Board of Management who were in Western Germany and Barth and the persons whom he had appointed or purported to appoint as members of the Boards in Jena. The former used language which implied that they considered themselves competent to act as Boards of Management of the Foundation businesses in the Western Zone. Barth objected to this and certain correspondence passed to which I shall have to refer in detail later. All that I need say now is that following on that correspondence, Schomerus, as Mandatory of the Foundation in respect of the optical business, gave to Bauersfeld, Henrichs and Kuppenbender (Joos having by then dropped out of the picture) a power of attorney to represent the optical business in Western Germany, and Dunger, as Mandatory in respect of the glass business, gave a similar power of attorney to Hirsch, Schott and Henrichs in respect of that business. At the same time entries were made in the various commercial registers in Western Germany corresponding to those made in the Commercial Register at Jena in October, 1945.

The American authorities paid the Foundation for the material which they had taken from the optical works at Jena. This money and other funds belonging to the Foundation in the West were employed—with the consent of the Board of the Board of the optical business in Jena—in subscribing for the shares, in a company called "Opton" later named "Zeiss Opton") which was formed at Heidenheim in Wurtemberg in October, 1946, for the manufacture and sale of optical products. The shares belonged, of course, beneficially to the Foundation. Kuppenbender was originally the sole manager; later Bauesfeld and Hirsch joined him on the Board. The Company had works at Oberkochen where it soon began to manufacture Zeiss products, many of the senior employees being in fact employees of the Foundation who had left Jena with the Americans. An organisation similarly related to the glass business at Jena also came into existence at this time at Landshut in Western Germany under the name of "Jenaer Glaswerk Schott & Genossen." The two years for which the new members of the Boards had been appointed expired in the summer of 1947, but the old members could not return to Jena, and Barth, on behalf of the Special Board, told those who he had appointed to carry on for the time. In point of fact, it was becoming more and more doubtful whether the old management would ever be able to return. The Potsdam Agreement envisaged that Germany would be governed as a unit in accordance with a single set of political and economic principles applied by the different governments in their respective zones. But having regard to the wide divergence of view on political and economic questions between the Western Powers on the one hand, and Russia on the other, it is not surprising that the agreement never worked well, and by the end of 1947 it was obvious that it was breaking down. The former allies drifted further and further apart until by the autumn of 1949 a *de facto* division of Germany was brought about by the setting up on the one hand of the German Federal Republic in the West, and on the other of the German Democratic Republic in the East. Meanwhile in the summer of 1948 events occurred which led directly to the controversy of which this action is a product. As I have said, the assets of the Foundation had been sequestrated in October, 1945, under SMAD Order 124. No one suggests that that order in itself affected the existence or constitution of the Foundation. Similar orders were made in the Western Zone which placed large organisations under trusteeship while their future was being decided upon. But the outcome in the two zones was very different, for the powers put different interpretations on Article 12 of the Potsdam Agreement. In the West all that was done was that **[315]** large organisations were broken up. In the East their property was in most cases transferred into public ownership. Between October, 1945, and the spring of 1948 decisions, or, strictly speaking, provisional decisions, as to whether property sequestrated under order 124 was to be confiscated or released were taken locally by district authorities.

In January, 1948, a central body known as the German Economic Council was set up with legislative authority in East Germany, subject to the overriding power of the Russian Military Administration. On the 14th April, 1948, Marshal Zhokov's successor, Marshal Sokolowski, made an order known as SMAD 64, by which he ratified the confiscation set out in lists submitted to him by the German Economic Commission, and brought the system of sequestration started by the order 124 to an end. The chief subject of dispute between the parties is the effect which order 124 had on the Foundation and its property. At the moment I will simply set out the undisputed facts.

On the 1st June, 1948, two documents were signed in Weimar by the Prime Minister and Minister of the Interior of Thuringia. Each was headed "Record of Confiscation." One was directed to the "Optical Mechnical Works, Zeiss, Jena," and read as follows: "The confiscation of your assets which were sequestrated in accordance with order 124 of the Commander-in-Chief of the Soviet Military Administration in Germany dated 30th October, 1945, 'Optical Mechanical Works, Zeiss, Jena, as well as all other assets,' is confirmed by order

No. 64 of the Commander-in-Chief of the Soviet Military Administration in Germany of the 17th April, 1948, and so has become legally effective." The other was directed to the firm Schott, Jena, and was in similar terms.

The confiscated businesses became the "People's Owned Enterprises," "Volks Eigene Betriebe" (for short, VEBs), and were first attached to the Industrial Association for Fine Mechanical and Optical Instruments, called "Optik," without having separate legal personality. Later they were separated from the Association and became separate legal entities known as the VEB, Carl-Zeiss, Jena, and the VEB Schott, Jena. The confiscations did not in fact involve any change in the persons who ran the businesses. Schrade and his colleagues became members of the Boards of Management of the two VEB's. But, like all the other VEB's in Eastern Germany, they had to work—and have to work today—in accordance with plans and guiding instructions laid down by the central authorities.

On the 30th November, 1948, the Commercial Register in Jena was altered by substituting the names of the VEBs for that of the Foundation as the owners of the businesses.

On the 16th June, 1948, the German Economic Commission passed the following resolution: "In recognition and appreciation of the unique nature of the work of Ernst Abbe, and being convinced of the necessity of continuing the existence and operation of the Carl-Zeiss Foundation of Jena, the Secretariat of the German Economic Commission resolved at its meeting of 16th June, 1948, that the two people's owned businesses Carl-Zeiss and Jenaer Glaswerk Schott & Gen., which are members of the Industrial Union for Fine, Mechanical and Optical Instruments, 'Optik' have certain rights and duties in relation to the Carl-Zeiss Foundation, which shall be laid down in the new version to be drawn up of the statute of the Foundation.

"By a Committee to be appointed by the German Economic Commission, a new version of the Statute of the Carl-Zeiss Foundation shall be prepared, taking into consideration the economic and social changes which have meanwhile occurred, and shall be submitted to the German Economic Commission for ratification. **[316]**

"Until the coming into force of the new statute of the Carl-Zeiss Foundation the powers of all the government bodies of the Foundation will be exercised by a Foundation Commissioner to be appointed by the German Economic Commission, who shall decide on the application of the provisions of the old Statute of the Foundation or submit suggestions for such purpose to the German Economic Commission."

The attorneys of the Foundation in the West had been viewing the developments in the East with increasing disquiet, and the confiscation was the last straw. They decided that the time had come for them to act on their own, and on the 30th July, 1948, Bauersfeld, Henrichs, Kuppenbender, Hirsch and Schott addressed a letter to the Minister of Education of Wurtemberg enclosing a memorandum by David on the legal position as he saw it, and requesting the Minister to declare Heidenheim to be the legal domicile of the Foundation in the West, and to appoint the five of them the management of the Foundation with jurisdiction outside the Russian Zone. At the same time they invited Barth to come to Heidenheim to discuss the position. At a long interview on the 13th August they put their point of view before him and sought his approval for the course which they were taking, but he declined to give it. This was the parting of the ways, and relations between Jena and Heidenheim, which hitherto had been reasonably cordial, now became increasingly strained.

I will deal first with the course of events in the West. On 23rd February, 1949, the Minister of State of Wurtemberg ordered first that Article 3 of the Statute of the Foundation should be amended to read: "The legal seat of the Foundation is at Jena and Heidenheim"; and, secondly, that Bauersfeld, Henrichs and Kuppenbender, who were described as members of the Board of Management of the firm Carl-Zeiss since the date of their original appointments, should administer and represent the Carl-Zeiss Foundation in accordance with Article 114 of the statute until a Special Board of the Foundation in accordance with Article 113 should have been reconstituted. On 3rd May, 1949, this order was confirmed by the Minister of Education of Wurtemberg. On 15th January, 1951, on the application of Bauersfeld, Henrichs and Kuppenbender, the District Court of Heidenheim registered the firm Carl-Zeiss in the Commercial Register as a firm owned by the Carl-Zeiss Foundation domiciled at Heidenheim with a statement to the effect that the firm had transferred its seat from Jena to Heidenheim. Following on this registration in the Commercial Register of Heidenheim, Bauersfeld, Henrichs and Kuppenbender were able to have the other Registers in West Germany such as those at Berlin, Hamburg and Cologne, altered by inserting their names as the persons entitled to sign on behalf of the firm Carl-Zeiss in place of the names of the members of the Board of Management at Jena which had hitherto remained on those Registers notwithstanding the confiscation. Similarly, they procured entries to be made on the Registries of Patents and Trade Marks in Western Germany to the effect that the firm Carl-Zeiss, in whose name the optical patents and trade marks owned by the Foundation were registered, had been transferred from Jena to Heidenheim.

On the 28th July, 1953, Henrichs and Kuppenbender, acting on behalf of the Carl-Zeiss Foundation of Heidenheim, held a meeting of Zeiss Opton at which it was resolved that the assets and liabilities of the company be transferred without liquidation to the Carl-Zeiss Foundation of Heidenheim. Finally on 22nd May, 1954, the Minister of Education of Wurtemberg made a further order deleting the word "Jena" altogether from Article 3 of the statute of the Foundation, so that it read: "The legal seat of the Carl-Zeiss Foundation is at Heidenheim." The Carl-Zeiss Foundation of Heidenheim, which considers itself to be and is considered by the West German courts to be, the Foundation established by Abbe in 1891, [**317**] and is the third defendant to this action, has carried on business with success for the last 12 years or so. It applies its profits to various public purposes in Western Germany, such as the University of Tubingen, the Technical Academy of Stuttgart, and the Max Planck Society.

I turn back now to trace the course of events in the East. Professor Rompe of Berlin had been appointed Foundation Commissioner in accordance with the resolution of the German Economic Commission of the 16th June, 1948. But no Committee was set up to revise the articles; Rompe laid down his office without ever doing anything; and the German Economic Commission itself disappeared when the German Democratic Republic came into being in the autumn of 1949. Thus the rights and duties of the VEBs to the Foundation which the resolution had declared to exist have never been precisely defined. In practice, however, the VEBs have always regarded themselves—and have been permitted by the authorities in the East to regard themselves—as being under a duty to provide the funds necessary to supplement the income derived by the Foundation from such of its assets as were not confiscated sufficiently to enable it to carry out its welfare objects. Although the Foundation no longer owned any business—at all events in East Germany—the view was taken that Boards of Management such as were contemplated by the Articles could and did still exist and appointments to them were made—or purported to be made—from time to time. But as for the most part the same people were members of such Boards as were in fact the managers of the VEBs, the position was somewhat artificial. For example, pensions have continued to be paid in accordance with Abbe's "Pensions Statute," both to those who had retired from the service of the Foundation enterprises before the confiscations and to those who were in service in June 1948 and have subsequently retired from the service of the VEBs. Further, there is no doubt that such "Zeiss" pensions are higher than the payments normally made to retired employees in the East. But whether such pensions ought to be regarded as paid directly by the VEBs to their pensioners or as paid by the Foundation to the pensioners out of moneys provided by the VEBs is a question which hardly admits of certain answer. The reason why the relations between the Foundation and the VEBs was left in this somewhat nebulous state was probably because the lawyers in the East feared that if the articles were altered so as expressly to provide for the Foundation continuing to function without running any businesses the lawyers in the West would have a handle for arguing that the juristic person recognised by East German law as the Zeiss Foundation in Jena was a different juristic person from the Foundation founded by Abbe.

I will now supplement this general account with some particulars. Schomerus retired on the 31st March, 1949, and Barth died on the 9th November, 1949. At this stage, therefore, there was no "Deputy", and the board of management of the optical business—if one existed at all—consisted of Sandmann, who was Mandatory, and Schrade who had authority to sign.

On the 24th May, 1951, the Thuringian Minister of Education appointed—or purported to appoint—Dr. Kunz, who was President of the District Court, to be Deputy of the Foundation, and Dr. Harting to be a member of the Board of Management of the optical business. But Harting in fact died on the 21st September, 1951. As a result of an East German law dated the 23rd July, 1952, and an order made under it, the Province of Thuringia was divided into three districts and the governmental functions of the province transferred to the administrative organs of the respective districts. The district in which Jena is situated is the district of Gera, and this body, which stands in the same relation to the University of Jena as the State Department of the Grand Duchy stood to it in **[318]** the old days, is the council (Rat) of Gera. It is common ground that as a matter of political geography the council of Gera would be the Special Board within the meaning of Article 113.

In March 1953 Sandmann went to live in Western Germany, so that Schrade became the only member of the Board of Management of the optical business, and was regarded by Kunz as being the "Mandatory." On the 10th April, 1954, the Council of Gera, acting as the Special Board, authorised, or purported to authorise, Schrade to represent the Foundation as "Mandatory" as from 16th March, 1953, and on the same day appointed, or purported to appoint, Victor Huber and Rudolf Rutter members of the Board of Management of what was described as "the industrial activity." These documents executed on the 10th April, 1954, do not appear to draw any distinction between the optical and glass business. Schrade, however, said in evidence that the Board of Management of the glass business has remained in existence and that its composition had not changed between 1948 and 1954. I shall have to consider later whether the Council of Gera can be regarded as the Special Board, and also whether after the confiscation there can be considered to have been any Boards of Management of any Foundation business within the meaning of the articles.

As a result of the confiscation on the one hand and the action taken by the men at Heidenheim on the other goods made by the VEBs at Jena and sold under the name "Carl Zeiss" and similar goods made by the factory at Oberkochen and also sold under the name "Carl Zeiss" appeared side by side in the market. For some time conflict was averted by a sort of tacit understanding by which the Jena works only sold outside the "Iron Curtain" countries such goods as were not manufactured at all or not manufactured within due times or in sufficient quantities by the plants in West Germany. But this *modus vivendi* broke down in 1953 and a spate of litigation ensued of which this action is a specimen. In West Germany Heidenheim succeeded in several actions brought against the Jena VEBs and persons to whom they were supplying goods. To counter this Jena decided to bring proceedings in West Germany in the name of the Foundation as plaintiffs; but first it was thought wise to obtain an advisory opinion from the East German Supreme Court as to the legal position. This opinion was given on 6th April, 1954.

The views expressed on this chief point at issue may be summarised as follows: First, that the Foundation itself had not been destroyed but continued to exist as a legal entity. Secondly, that the Council of Gera was the Special Board. Thirdly, that though the managers of the VEB's could not strictly be considered as boards of management of the Foundation businesses, nevertheless, having regard to the close economic connection between the VEB's and the Foundation—evidenced by the payments made by the former to the latter—it could not be said that article 116—under which it would be the duty of the Special Board to liquidate the Foundation—had come into play; and, fourthly, that the old members of the Board of Management had retired and that the measures taken in

West Germany with regard to the Foundation were all contrary to law and invalid.

The contemplated action was started on the 28th April, 1954, in the Provincial Court of Stuttgart and was between the Carl-Zeiss Foundation represented by the Council of Gera as plaintiff and Bauersfeld, Henrichs and Kuppenbender and the firm Carl-Zeiss of Heidenheim as defendants.

The plaintiff asked: 1. That the personal defendants should refrain from claiming that they were authorised to administer and represent the Foundation and that all the defendants should refrain from using the names "Zeiss" and "Carl-Zeiss" respectively and from using any of a number of trade marks, details of which were given. **[319]**

2. That the defendants should apply for and consent to the transfer of the trade marks to the plaintiff.

3. That the defendants should apply for and consent to the cancellation of the registration of the firm Carl-Zeiss in the commercial register of Heidenheim.

On the 31st July, 1954, the Provincial Court dismissed the action on the ground that even if the council of Gera was a body capable of being the Special Board, the legal domicile of the Foundation had been transferred from Jena to Heidenheim and the three personal defendants were the only persons authorised to represent it.

The plaintiff appealed from this judgment to the Provincial Court of Appeal and also filed an action in the administrative Court of Stuttgart against the State of Baden-Wurttemberg for the annulment of the orders of the Minister of State of 23rd February, 1949, and of the Minister of Education of 22nd May, 1949. For some reason which was not explained to me, though nearly ten years have elapsed no decision in this action has yet been given by the West German administrative courts.

On 6th April, 1955, the Provincial Court of Appeal gave judgment dismissing the appeal. It held that it could not, pending the decision of the administrative Court, go into the question whether the Council of Gera or the personal defendants were entitled to exercise the functions of the Special Board, but it took the view that under the articles the only organ of the Foundation which could authorise proceedings relating to the trade marks and firm name of the optical business was the Board of Management of that business and that no Board of Management of the business had existed in the East since the confiscation of the businesses.

The plaintiff appealed from this decision to the Federal High Court, which gave judgment on the 28th January allowing the appeal. The Court thought that the Court of Appeal was right in saying that it could not go into the question whether the council of Gera or the personal defendants were entitled to exercise the functions of the Special Board. It further agreed with the Court of Appeal in thinking that under the articles only the Board of Management of the relevant business was entitled to represent the Foundation in litigation relating to the industrial activities of that business. But the Court held that if, as the Court of Appeal had held, there was no Board of Management of the optical business in Jena and if the personal defendants had, as the plaintiff alleged, resigned their office and were claiming to conduct the optical business of the Foundation in the West without any lawful authority, then the Special Board would have authority under the articles to represent the Foundation in litigation directed to preventing such unlawful conduct. It further pointed out that the defendants were claiming to use the name Carl-Zeiss which was the name of the Foundation itself and that the Special Board must have power to represent the Foundation in proceedings to prevent an unauthorised use of its own name. The Court therefore sent the case back to the Court of Appeal for the Court to consider whether or not the personal defendants had resigned from the Board. If the defendants had resigned, then it would follow that they had no authority to claim to act as managers of the optical business and it would not lie in their mouths to say that the council of Gera could not act as the Special Board because of the political and economic conditions prevailing in the German Democratic Republic—whether or not that was in fact the case. If, on the other hand, they had not resigned, then they constituted the only effective Board of Management of the optical business and the action which the council of Gera was causing the Foundation to bring would be an unlawful interference with their lawful activities. **[320]**

When the Provisional Court of Appeal came to give judgment in the case again —which it did on the 29th October, 1958—it took a course which the Federal High Court subsequently decided it was entitled to take though it is somewhat surprising to a foreign lawyer who is ignorant of the precise relations subsisting between the two courts. It treated the view expressed by the Federal High Court that if the personal defendants had in fact resigned it would not lie in their mouths to challenge the competence of the council of Gera to represent the Foundation as an erroneous *obiter dictum* which it was entitled to disregard. It then proceeded to hold that even if the domicile of the Foundation remained at Jena and even if the personal defendants had resigned, yet the Foundation was not properly before the court because under East German law either the articles had been totally inoperative since the confiscation of the business or at all events the council of Gera could not, by reason of the political and economic conditions prevailing in the German Democratic Republic, be considered as being by East German law a body capable of exercising the functions of the Special Board under the articles. Finally, "by way," as it put it, "of precaution" it addressed itself to the question which the Federal High Court had told it to decide and held that Bauersfeld, Henrichs, Kuppenbender and Joos had not resigned. I shall later return to consider the reasoning of this judgment in detail.

The plaintiff appealed from this judgment to the Federal High Court, which dismissed the appeal on the 15th November, 1960. The Court first held that the Provincial Court of Appeal was entitled to deal with the case in the way it did notwithstanding the terms of the earlier judgment of the Federal High Court. It then went on to concur with the views expressed by the Court of Appeal—namely, that the articles became inoperative in East Germany on the confiscation, and further held that under article 114 Bauersfeld, Henrichs and Kuppenbender became entitled to administer the Foundation whether or not they had resigned. They did not express any view on the question whether or not they had in fact retired. I shall return later to the reasoning of the judgment.

After the date of the second judgment of the Provincial Court of Appeal—but before the delivering of the second judgment of the Federal High Court—the plaintiff and the VEB Carl-Zeiss started proceedings in the German Democratic Republic against the three defendants based on their use of the name Carl-Zeiss in correspondence with public authorities (such as the Patent Office) and private individuals in the German Democratic Republic. The three defendants did not enter an appearance in these proceedings.

On the 30th September, 1959, the District Court of Leipzig gave judgment in default against the three defendants so far as concerned the use of the name Carl-Zeiss in correspondence with private individuals but refused the plaintiffs relief in respect of the correspondence with public authorities.

The plaintiffs appealed from this decision to the Supreme Court of the German Democratic Republic, which by a judgment dated 23rd March, 1961, varied the judgment of the District Court by extending the injunctions to include correspondence with public authorities in the German Democratic Republic. The reasoning by which the Supreme Court reached its decision is on the same lines as that contained in its opinion of 6th April, 1954.

This action, as I have said, was started on 20th October, 1955, after the first judgment of the Federal High Court. The long delay which has occurred in bringing on this summons is no doubt in part attributable to the wish of the parties to await the final outcome of the West German action. **[321]**

It appears from paragraphs 19 to 21 of Schrade's first affidavit and the documents exhibited thereto that Messrs. Courts had and have authority to start and prosecute this action on behalf of the plaintiff from the council of Gera purporting to act as the Special Board, from Schrade purporting to act as mandatory and from Schrade, Huber and Muller purporting to act as the Board of Management of the optical business. The question at issue is whether all or any of these persons was entitled to give such instructions on behalf of the plaintiff.

When the plaintiff in an action says that it is a corporation domiciled in a foreign country and the defendants say that the solicitor who issued the writs had no authority from the plaintiff to act for it, the questions for the Court to ask itself would seem to be:

(1) Whether there is, according to the law of the foreign country in question, such a corporation as the plaintiff in existence in its territory, and,

(2) if there is, whether the persons who instructed the solicitor to act had, under the law of the country in question, authority to give such instructions on behalf of the corporation.

As the plaintiff had produced two judgments of the highest court in the German Democratic Republic stating that the plaintiff is a corporation established there, and that the council of Gera and Dr. Schrade have at all times had authority to give instructions to Messrs. Courts to prosecute this action, it might seem at first sight that the answer to the question was easy enough. This was in substance the view taken by the Registrar of Trade Marks in Pakistan in a judgment given on 18th September, 1961, on the question whether the trade mark "Zeiss" should be registered in Pakistan in the name of Carl-Zeiss Stiftung of Jena or in the name of Carl-Zeiss-Stiftung of Heidenheim. The defendants, however, submit that this approach is wrong. They point out that the answer to the question at issue depends largely on the legal effect on the Foundation and its articles of the confiscation of the businesses in 1948. They further point out that at that date neither the German Federal Republic nor the German Democratic Republic was in existence. Germany was then nominally a single unit under the joint control of the Allies operating in their respective zones by their own military administrations. From this the defendants say that it follows that the law by references to which the effect of the confiscation is to be judged is not the law either of West Germany or of East Germany, and that the East German courts have no exclusive jurisdiction or even any special competence to decide on the matter. They further submit that even if the problem is to be regarded as being to any extent one of East German law, the decisions of the East German courts cannot be regarded as reliable indications of what that law is since those courts are in the habit of deciding the same question in different ways on different occasions in accordance with what they think is for the time being the wish of those who wield political power in the German Democratic Republic. Again they submit that the issue is in any case *"res judicata"* by the judgment of the Federal High Court given on 15th November, 1960. Finally they say that to allow the plaintiff to sue would be tantamount to enforcing the confiscation decrees outside East Germany to the benefit of the VEB's.

On the other side the plaintiff submits that the judgments of the West German courts in this matter are perverse and should be disregarded by this Court even if the conditions for the application of the principle of *res judicata* are otherwise satisfied, which they deny. They further submit that if the decisions of the West German courts give rise to any estoppel, the judgment of the East German Supreme Court dated 23rd March, 1961, which is later in date, gives rise to a counter-estoppel even though that judgment was given in default of the defendants' appearance. **[322]**

Finally the defendants say that it would not be contrary to public policy as understood in this country to allow the plaintiff to sue.

In face of these somewhat embarrassing contentions, what I propose to do is first to consider the various points at issue for myself as best I can, paying no more attention to the various judgments than they appear to me to deserve as pieces of legal reasoning. I shall then consider whether any rule of estoppel by *res judicata* or of public policy as understood in these courts applies to the case.

The first question in point of date—though it is far from being the first in importance—is whether Bauersfeld, Henrichs and Kuppenbender were still members of the Board of Management of the optical business when they made their application to the authorities in Wurttenberg in the summer of 1948. Dr. David in his first affidavit in support of the summons deposed that they were, and a good deal of the evidence subsequently put in on either side was directed to the point.

The Provincial Court of Appeal in its judgment dated 29th October, 1958, decided that they had never ceased to be members of the Board; but this finding did not form part of the *ratio decidendi* of the judgment and the Federal High Court did not deal with the point at all. Counsel for the defendants in opening the case said that he did not attach any importance to the point and invited me to deal with the case on the footing that the three men had retired without asking any finding one way or the other. Counsel for the plaintiff pointed out that this might leave it open to the defendants to raise the point in the action supposing that the summons failed. I therefore asked counsel for the defendants whether he was prepared to give an undertaking on behalf of his clients that if the action proceeded they would not seek to raise the point but would allow the action to be fought on the footing that the three men had retired from office. He was not able to give that undertaking and, as I have before me all the material which was before the Provincial Court of Appeal—indeed, somewhat more, since I have heard oral evidence from David and Schrade—I think that it would be better for me to make a finding on the point now rather than to saddle the parties with the trouble and expense of adducing all the evidence, documentary and oral, over again at the trial if the point should eventually turn out to be relevant.

According to David, not only did the existing members of the Board of Management not retire, but the three men who remained in Jena never became members of the Board at all. His view is that their authority stemmed solely from a power of attorney given to them by the existing members of the Board.

The contemporaneous memorandum which Dr. Barth made of his discussions at Jena on 23rd June, 1945 which the Provincial Court of Appeal accepted as accurate, states in terms that he prevailed on the existing Board to recognise that a power of attorney from them would not be adequate, and that new managers must be appointed. The memorandum further makes it clear that the members of the Board of Management of the glass works had not even attempted to deal with the situation by means of a power of attorney.

David's view is, I gather, based on the contention that Dr. Barth's appointment as Deputy of the Foundation by the Thuringian Minister of Education on the 21st June, 1945 (H.S.9) was ineffective because here was not yet any Thuringian Provincial Government in existence. I do not find his reasoning at all convincing. H.S.9—which, incidentally, was initialled by Dr. David, then the legal adviser of the Foundation, without comment at the time—shows that there was at that date a body purporting to act as the Thuringian Ministry of Education. It was obviously operating with the approval of the American Authorities, and I am not prepared **[323]** to hold that it had no legal status because the decree referring to the setting-up of a Provincial Government in Thuringia by the direction of the Americans was not signed by the President of Thuringia until the 2nd July. For a long time after the summer of 1945 everyone concerned proceeded on the footing, and I have no doubt rightly proceeded on the footing, that Barth had been validly appointed Deputy of the Foundation, and Schrade, Sandmann and Schomerus validly appointed members of the Board of Management. The question at issue, as I see it, is what effect did their appointments, which were initially for two years only, have on the position of the existing members of the Board. Did they either expressly or by necessary implication retire from office for the time being, or did they remain as sleeping members of the Board?

The Provincial Court of Appeal favoured the latter view. They attached great importance to the fact that Barth's memorandum does not say that the existing members resigned. I cannot myself see that the fact that there is no express reference to resignation has much significance. Barth may very well have thought that it was the natural consequence of the appointment of new managers that the old ones should temporarily vacate office. On the other hand, if the idea was that there should be six members of the Board, one would have expected the memorandum to have made some reference to Article 4 which limits the membership of the Board to four, and to have said that in the peculiar circumstances this requirement was being waived. Further, I cannot agree with the Court of

Appeal in thinking that the terms of the appointments and collateral agreements executed on 27th June support the view that the old members remained in office. They seem to me to be quite neutral.

Again, I do not think that much light is thrown on the question by the sentence in the memorandum which runs: "It is true that the Board of Management which has so far been in office has been appointed for life in accordance with the Articles. Should it return it has a claim to resume its old office." It is true that the word translated "claim" normally means a legal claim and it may be said that if they would have a legal right to take up their functions again without a fresh appointment they must have been members throughout. On the other hand, the words "resume its old office" suggest that so long as they were absent from Jena they were not members of the Board. The truth, of course, may be that nobody in fact thought out at the time what precisely the legal position of those who were leaving Jena was going to be during their absence. Light must be thrown on the point by the oral evidence of persons who were present at the discussions either at the optical or the glass works and could speak to what the old members and Dr. Barth said to one another. In the proceedings in Stuttgart the plaintiff tendered the evidence of a number of such persons including Joos, and asked to examine Bauersfeld, Henrichs and Kuppenbender, but the Court declined to hear any oral evidence on the ground that it was so clear from the documents that Dr. Barth did not think that the old members were retiring that no oral evidence could possibly affect the position. I must say that I find that a surprising conclusion. Soon after they settled in Western Germany those who had left Jena began to refer to themselves as the "Boards of Management in the West." It is quite clear from a letter dated 12th October, 1945, written by Hirsch, Schott and Henrichs to Jena that they were not claiming that the men in Jena had not been validly appointed to the Board, but only that there were, as it were, two sets of Boards, one functioning in the East and the other in the West. Barth considered that this claim was unjustified and caused those whom he had appointed to the Boards to write to Heidenham enclosing the draft of an application by the Special Board to the President of Thuringia for the removal from office of those who had left Jena on **[324]** the ground of their activities under the Nazi regime with an intimation that this application would be sent in if they did not resign voluntarily. It is argued that the wording of the enclosure shows that Barth cannot have thought that they had already retired from office. I am not much impressed by that argument. Barth's attitude may well have been: "I thought it was implicit in the arrangements made in Jena last June that these men temporarily vacated office; but they may not have said so in terms and now they contend that they are still members. I cannot have that and so if they will not resign expressly now I shall have their removal." If that was his attitude the wording of the application for their removal would be natural enough.

But, however, that may be, the letter of the 12th January, 1964 from the Board in Jena to Henrichs which enclosed the application is absolutely clear. It is headed "To the former Members of the Boards of Management," and it contains the following sentence: "We take the attitude that since on your proposal we were appointed the Board of Management by the Special Board we are the only responsible board of management and you have thereby resigned while we gave the undertaking that we would at the request of the Special Board withdraw in your favour if you should return to Jena and it were possible for you to resume your former office." The letter goes on to refer to the enclosed draft application for their removal by the President of Thuringia and suggests that in order to avoid that unpleasant step they should voluntarily renounce their position.

The answer sent from Heidenheim on 28th January, 1946 which was signed by Bauersfeld and Henrichs and with which Kuppenbender subsequently associated himself, is an unequivocal recognition that the view expressed by the Board in Jena was correct; that is to say, that the appointment of the new Board necessarily involved by implication the retirement of the old, and that, therefore, it I would call particular attention to the words ". . . in order to open for you the way to appointment as regular members of the Board of Management was unnecessary, and indeed inappropriate, for the old members to resign again.

according to the statute we proposed you at the end of June last year to the Deputy as our successors and handed over the business to you," and the words "Consequently we completely agree with you in the judgment of the legal position so you too would agree with us that the recommended resignation was pointless. The position sought after by this recommendation is already in your favour. Consequently we no longer possess any function as Board of Management and therefore such cannot be taken from us not even by the political exclusion procedure."

In arriving at their conclusion that the three men in question remained members of the Board of Management of the optical business the Provincial Court of Appeal attached great weight to the fact that they did not accept the suggestion that they should there and then resign from it. I cannot follow this argument. It would obviously be better, both from the point of view of their eventual return to Jena and from the point of view of their "denazification" in Western Germany that they should accept the position that they had voluntarily retired as a temporary measure rather than that they should resign from office when faced by a threat from Jena to remove them for their activities under the Nazi regime. The important point—which the Provincial Court of Appeal seems to overlook—is that they did unequivocally agree that they had vacated office.

David, who advised the writers on the wording of the letter, told me that the meaning intended was that they were maintaining their claim to be members of the Board but were agreeing that for the time being they would not put forward such a claim publicly. Even if I were disposed to accept his evidence on this point, it **[325]** would not help the defendants because what matters is not what the writers may have intended, but what meaning the recipients would put on the letter. What Dr. David says the writers meant was in effect: "We do not agree that we retired on 23rd June and we take the view that there is now a single Board of six members. We refuse to resign from it. We are prepared, however, for the time being, to act as though we were not members. We invite you to accept this as sufficient for your purpose and not to proceed with the application for our removal."

I do not believe for a moment that anyone would have read the letter in that sense, nor if he had so read it do I think that Dr. Barth, who was sent a copy, would have been content with it. I cannot doubt that he took the letter as an admission that the gentlemen had resigned at the meeting in June and on that footing refrained from proceeding with the application for their removal. In fact, however, I am not prepared to accept David's evidence as to the meaning of the letter. He told me that the reason why it was phrased as it was was that the writers were afraid that it might be read by the Russian officers in the works at Jena. I was not impressed by this explanation. He further said that he explained the sense which was intended orally at a meeting in Jena at which he thinks Dr. Schrade was present. But Schrade denied this, and I prefer his evidence to David's on this point.

The conclusion which I have reached on this point is supported by the fact that the old members accepted powers of attorney from the new Board to act on behalf of the Foundation in Western Germany. In this connection one may further refer to a letter which Henrichs wrote from Heidenheim on the 10th June, 1947, to an insurance company in Munich in which he said in terms that he was no longer a member of the Board of Management of the firm in Jena.

I cannot help thinking that the idea that they were still members of the Board of Management of the optical business first occurred to Bauersfeld, Henrichs and Kuppenbender in August, 1948, when the Minister of Justice of Wurttenberg suggested that Article 114 might possibly apply to the case. The following words in a letter addressed by them on the 12th January, 1949, to the Minister of Education at Wurttenberg are, I think, significant: "To exclude any doubt as to the applicability of Article 114 we confirm that the writers since the date of their appointment have neither resigned from their functions as members of the Board of Management of the firm of Carl-Zeiss nor been dismissed." For the reasons which I have attempted to give, I think that that statement was incorrect.

The second question which arises is whether the Foundation continued to exist as a juristic person after the confiscation of the businesses. The Provincial Court of Appeal and the Federal High Court in fact assumed that it did continue in existence, but they expressed some doubts on the point and Von Moser, the expert called by the defendants, was definitely of the opinion that it had ceased to exist. It is clear that under ordinary German civil law a Foundation continues to exist as a juristic person even if it loses all its property. There is, however, no doubt that the Russian Military administration took the view that when the business of eliminating monopolies enjoined by the Potsdam Agreement included the confiscation of the assets of a corporation, the corporation automatically ceased to exist. Further there is no doubt that this view has been adopted and applied by the Courts of the German Democratic Republic. Von Moser considers that this view should logically be applied to the confiscation of the assets of the Foundation which he says was eminently what the Russians would have described as a "monopolistic organisation." He is of opinion that the words "as well as all other assets" in the records of confiscation covered all the property of the Foundation, **[326]** and that the resolution of the German Economic Commission—passed, as he pointed out, some weeks after the confiscation—was really no more than the expression of an intention to create a new Foundation—which intention, incidentally, was never carried out.

Finally he stressed that this question was not a question of the law of the German Democratic Republic any more than it was a question of the law of the German Federal Republic. It was a question which fell to be decided by the law prevailing in Jena in 1948—which was, in effect, the law laid down by the Russian Military Administration in Eastern Germany. As to the last point, I would go some way with Von Moser. The question whether the German Democratic Republic when it was set up came, so to say, with possession of a juristic person called the Carl-Zeiss Foundation, and if it did whether that Foundation was the same legal entity as the Foundation established by Abbe, is no doubt primarily a question of the law which prevailed in Jena in 1948 before the German Democratic Republic existed. If, however, there is any doubt as to what effect under that law the confiscation had on the existence and character of the Foundation, I should have to accept that the view taken on the point by the courts of the German Democratic Republic, in whose territory Jena is situated, should prevail.

But, however, that may be, I do not myself agree with Von Moser's view as to the effect of the confiscation. In the first place he appears to me to overlook the fact that there was not a single record of confiscation addressed to the Foundation but two documents each addressed to one of the businesses of the Foundation. As well as its two businesses the Foundation owned a great deal of property which, though acquired out of the profits of its businesses—in particular the optical business—were not used for the separate purposes of either business but to further the general objects of the Foundation. I do not think that it was ever the intention of the authorities to confiscate such property. Indeed, the Foundation has remained throughout the registered proprietor of the land in question on the relevant Land Registers.

This conclusion is strongly supported by the terms of the Resolution of the German Economic Commission. I cannot regard that Resolution, as Von Moser seems to do, as a sort of after-thought. The German Economic Commission was the body at whose suggestion Marshal Sokolowski made Order 64. I read the Resolution as part of a consistent policy—namely, that all the business assets of the Foundation should become the property of the people, but that the Foundation should remain in existence as the owner of the rest of its property and that its Constitution should be amended to give effect to this change.

The third question which arises is whether the Foundation is domiciled in Jena. I can deal with that quite shortly. Unless and until the orders made by the authorities in Wurttemberg in 1949 and 1954 are declared invalid by the West German Administrative Courts, it is no doubt the law of West Germany that the Foundation is domiciled in Heidenheim. But for the reasons given by the East German courts and by Reichrath and Honig in their affidavits, there is—to say the least of it—grave doubt whether the authorities in Wurttemberg had any right to make the orders in question. The West German courts, in fact, assumed in favour of the plaintiff that it was domiciled in Jena and counsel for the defendants invited me to proceed on the same footing.

The fourth question which arises is how much of the assets of the Foundation were confiscated. There can be no doubt that all the assets of the two businesses in East Germany were confiscated, and I have already expressed the view that **[327]** any assets which were not assets of one or other of the businesses remained the property of the Foundation. There was, however, a good deal of evidence and argument directed to the question whether (a) the trade marks and (b) the business assets outside East Germany were or were not confiscated. I do not think that the answers to these questions have any very direct bearing on the problem which I have to solve, but in the circumstances I think that I ought to express a view on them.

The trade marks belonging to the Foundation were registered in the German Trade Mark Register in Berlin in the name of the business to the goods of which it related. Thus the trade marks relating to the optical business were registered in the name of the firm Carl-Zeiss. There was no separate East German Trade Mark Register until 1954. Section 47 of the Trade Mark Law, passed in February of that year, provided that paragraphs 1 and 2 of section 71 of the Patent Law of the German Democratic Republic should apply to old trade marks. Section 71(1) of the Patent Law of 1950 ran as follows: "Old patents previously belonging to confiscated enterprises or other persons subjected to confiscation are to be registered in the name of the owner to whom the enterprise or the property of the person subjected to confiscation has been transferred in accordance with the legal measures brought into force after the 8th May, 1945. The same applies to old patents, which were previously owned by the proprietors of or partners in the confiscated enterprises and were used by these enterprises."

One would have thought that there could be no doubt that the trade marks were business assets and that the respective VEB's should have been registered as proprietors of them. In fact, however, they were registered in the name of the Foundation, and on 8th April, 1954, a licence agreement was entered into between the Foundation and the VEB Carl Zeiss which recited that the latter had been using the trade marks in question with the consent of the former without payment since June, 1948 and provided for the continuance of this arrangement.

It may well be that what happened was that the Foundation and the VEB (which, as I have said, are managed by the same persons) thought that it would, or might, be to their advantage in the West German proceedings for the trade marks to be registered in the name of the Foundation rather than that of the VEB and that the Registrar, rightly or wrongly, felt justified in giving effect to their joint request. The East German Supreme Court clearly thought that it was at least arguable that what the Registrar did was wrong, for after seeking to justify it they go on to say that it would make no difference in the case before them whether the trade marks should have been registered in the name of the Foundation or of the VEB since they were both of them plaintiffs.

If it were necessary for me to decide whether the VEB is using the trade marks because it is the beneficial owner of them by East German law as a result of the confiscation or because the Foundation has given it a licence to use them, I should hold that the trade marks belong to the VEB. In fact, however, I cannot see that the point has any relevance to anything which I have to decide.

The question whether the business assets outside East Germany were confiscated divides into two sub-questions, namely: (1) did the confiscation extend to business assets outside East Germany by the law prevailing in the Russian Zone in 1948; and, (2) if it did, did the confiscation have any effect in English law on the ownership of the goodwill the Foundation businesses in this country?

As to the first point, it is clear that nothing was confiscated under order 64 which had not previously been sequestrated under order 124, and order 124 was in terms confined to property situated in the zone occupied by the Russian armed forces. **[328]** The view of the Soviet Military Administration (which was adopted by the courts in East Germany) was that as the Potsdam Agreement contemplated that Germany would be dealt with as a unit—though the different zones were under different administrations—the decisions of the Soviet authorities made in pursuance of the agreement had the force of law throughout Germany and should be given effect to by the authorities in the other zones.

This doctrine was reasonable enough when applied to property situated in the Eastern Zone at the date of the order in question, but it was obviously liable to give rise to difficulty if extended to property not so situate, since different zonal administrations might make contradicting decisions with regard to the same property. Nevertheless, in spite of these difficulties and in spite of the wording of order 124, there seems to be no doubt that the East German courts have always taken the view that a confiscation under order 64 of the property of a corporation situated in the Eastern Zone had extraterritorial effect. Reichrath gave it as his opinion that this doctrine did not apply here because the Foundation was kept alive and not destroyed by the confiscation of the business assets. I cannot myself see the logic of this distinction. What is more, it appears to me to be in conflict with the judgment of the East German Supreme Court in this case. As I read that judgment, the court took the view that the confiscation order bound the business assets in Western Germany though they realised that the West German courts would not agree with that conclusion.

On the whole, therefore, I incline to the view that the decree had extraterritorial effect by East German law—though having regard to the wording of the order 64 and the opinion of Reichrath I feel considerable doubt on the point.

I turn now to the question whether, if the confiscation decree was intended to apply to business assets outside East Germany, it was effective under English law to transfer to the VEB the goodwill of the optical business in this country, which is apparently to be regarded as a separate item of property situated here. (See *Reuter* v. *Mulhens* [1954] Ch. 50 at 95, (1953) 70 R.P.C. 235).

If the rule of English law as to the effect on property here of the acts of a foreign government is correctly stated in Dicey's Rule 130 (see Conflict of Laws, 7th edition, page 667), then it is clear that the confiscation decree had no effect on the English goodwill. I am not, however, by any means satisfied that Dicey's rule does state our law correctly. If, to take a case which is not, indeed, this case but is somewhat analogous to it, a business in Leipzig belonging to a prominent member of the National Socialist Party had been confiscated by the Soviet Military Administration in purported execution of the Potsdam Agreement, it is by no means clear to me that the owner would be entitled, by English law, to retain the goodwill and the benefit of the trade marks in this country.

Fortunately it is not necessary for me—as I see it—to express a concluded opinion either on this question whether the confiscation extended by East German law to the business assets outside East Germany, or on the question whether—if it did—our law would treat it as extending to the goodwill here. All that I need say for present purposes is that the defendants cannot possibly say that it is clear that the Foundation has no interest in the subject-matter of this action. It may have an interest because the decree did not extend to the English goodwill. Alternatively it may have an interest because although the decree extended to the English goodwill our law will not give effect to it. **[329]**

I turn now to the fifth and last question—which is the vital one in the case—namely, what effect this confiscation had on the constitution and organs of the Foundation. If one takes the view—which I am taking—that the Foundation survived the confiscation of its businesses and exists today as a juristic person domiciled in East Germany, then although the answer to the question depends on the effect in law of events which occurred before Germany was divided, the law to which one must look to discover that effect must, as I see it, be the law of the German Democratic Republic.

The West German courts—as I read their judgments—accepted that this was so. They took the view that according to East German law—properly expounded—the result of the confiscation was first that the articles became, and have remained, totally unworkable in East Germany, and, secondly, that under Article 114 the administration of the Foundation passed to Bauersfeld, Henrichs and Kuppenbender who were managing the West German branch of the optical business at the date of the confiscation.

The West German courts gave two reasons for holding that the articles became unworkable on the confiscation of the businesses. The first was that as a matter of construction their working was dependent on the continued ownership of some business by the Foundation; the second that the political and economic conditions prevailing in East Germany were so different from those presupposed by the articles that no "Special Board" or "Board of Management" such as was contemplated by the articles could exist there at all. I will deal with each of these reasons separately.

It is, of course, quite clear that the Foundation envisaged by the articles is a Foundation which runs and carries on a business or businesses. Article 116 expressly provides that if the Foundation ceases to carry on any business it is to be wound up. I can, therefore, fully understand it being said that if the confiscation of the businesses was not followed by a revision of the articles—and in fact it was not—then the Special Board should have taken steps to wind up the Foundation. But the West German courts—as I understand them—go much further than this. They say that on the confiscation of the businesses the Foundation became *ipso facto* incapable of acting. I cannot follow that at all. I should have thought that until the Foundation was in fact wound up the Special Board was entitled—and indeed bound—to take all necessary steps to preserve and recover any of its assets to which the confiscation did not extend.

Suppose, for example, that after the confiscation of the businesses the tenant of a house in Jena which belonged to the Foundation and had not been confiscated left Jena owing some rent to the Foundation and went to live in West Germany. Surely the Special Board would have had power to represent the Foundation in an action brought in the West German courts to recover the arrears?

Suppose, again, that there had been no branch of the optical business in West Germany but that at the date of the confiscation some dealer in West Germany was indebted to the Foundation in respect of goods supplied to him by the business in Jena. Would he have been able to avoid paying for the goods on the ground that the VEB could not sue him because the West German courts would not recognise the confiscation and the Foundation could not sue him because it had become immobilised by the confiscation?

I cannot believe that the West German courts would have given effect to so unmeritorious a plea. Surely they would have said that so long as the Foundation remained in existence the Special Board could represent it for the purpose of recovering business assets to which by West German law the confiscation would not extend. **[330]**

It is, of course, true that although the articles were not revised no steps have ever been taken in East Germany to wind up the Foundation; but I cannot see how that fact can assist the West German argument. The reason why the articles were not revised may well have been that it was feared that by interfering with them might injure the prospects of the Foundation in litigation in the West. As appears from the advising opinion of the East German Supreme Court, the view was taken that having regard to the close economic conection between the VEB's and the Foundation evidenced by the payments made by the former to the latter, it could fairly be said that the conditions envisaged by Article 116 were not fulfilled. I can well understand it being argued that that view was wrong, but the question whether or not the Foundation ought to be wound up is a matter between the Foundation and the East German authorities and cannot, as I see it, justify a court outside East Germany in refusing to accord the Special Board the right to represent the Foundation in litigation so long as it is still in existence.

At this point I ought to notice an argument advanced by Counsel for the defendants before me which was not, I think, mentioned by the West German courts. He submitted that on the true construction of the Resolution of the German Economic Commission of 18th June, 1948, until the articles were revised only Professor Rompe could authorise the bringing of an action by the Foundation, and that as he had in fact laid down his functions no-one could authorise the bringing of an action unless and until somebody with legislative authority in East Germany passed an enactment rescinding the Resolution in question. This is an ingenious construction but, in my view, unsound. Paragraph 3 of the Resolution presupposes that the German Economic Commission will in fact undertake a revision of the articles. If it fails to do so—and indeed passes out of existence without having done so—then the natural implication to make is that paragraphs 2 and 3 of the Resolution both go by the board and that the articles remain in force so far as they are still capable of operating in view of the confiscation of the businesses. As I have said, they are, in my opinion, capable of operating at least to the extent of enabling the Special Board—if one exists at all—to bring actions in respect of any property to which the confiscation did not, or may not have, extended.

I turn now to the alternative argument that no Special Board such as is envisaged by the articles exists or can exist in the German Democratic Republic.

The argument, as I understand it, is that the words of Article 114 "should a Special Board corresponding to the provisions of Article 5 and Article 113 no longer exist," refer not only to political geography but also to political complexion. The council of Gera is indeed "the department of State which with regard to the University of Jena occupies the place of the State department of the Grand Duchy," but it is unable to conduct the affairs of the Foundation with due regard to the intentions of the founder as Article 5(3) directs it to do, and so it is not the Special Board.

To my mind this argument is open to very grave objections. In the first place, if Articles 113 and 114 are to work, the political change which entails a change in the Special Board must be a fact as to the occurrence of which at a particular moment everyone will agree whatever his political views may be. The Grand Duchy is abolished and replaced by the Thuringian Minister of Education; he in his turn is replaced by the Reichstathalter, and so on. There are events which everyone—be he a monarchist, nazi or communist—will admit to have happened, and to have happened on a firm day, and so one knows where one is. But if you begin to enquire whether somebody which under the political and administrative **[331]** arrangements prevailing in East Germany satisfies the letter of Article 113 is nevertheless disqualified from being the Special Board because it is incapable of conducting the affairs of the Foundation with due regard to the intentions of the founder as expressed in the articles, you run into difficulties at once. Politicians do not, generally speaking, experience sudden conversions like that of St. Paul, they change their views gradually under pressure of circumstances. The Thuringian Minister of Education did not go to bed a liberal on the day that Marshal Sokolowski signed order 64 and wake up a Communist next morning. The confiscation was only a symptom of a movement towards the setting up of a communist state which had been gaining ground in East Germany ever since the Russian armies occupied it. But the West German courts accord it a quite unreal importance, because otherwise they have no particular date to which to point as the date on which the power of administering the Foundation passed from Jena to Heidenheim.

But over and above the difficulty of saying precisely when the Special Board in Thuringia forfeited its position, one is faced, on this argument, with the further difficulty of deciding whether the Thuringian authorities have, in fact, ever adopted political or economic views which render them incapable of administering the affairs of the Foundation in accordance with the intentions of the founder. The discussion of this problem in the various judgments both in West and East Germany—going, as it does, into such debatable questions as to what extent, if at all, Abbe was in sympathy with the views of Marx—shows to my mind quite clearly that the only safe course is to read Articles 113 and 114 in their natural sense as referring merely to what I have called political geography as opposed to political complexion, and to read article 5(3) not as a condition which has to be capable of fulfilment by a Special Board if it is to be a Special Board, but simply as the expression of wish to which the founder hoped the Special Board would give effect.

This was apparently the view taken—and I think rightly taken—during the Hitler regime. Whether or not Abbe would have approved of the present East German regime, there can be no doubt that he would have disapproved very strongly of the Third Reich. But the defendants do not suggest that the Reichstathalter of Thuringia had not the powers of the Special Board. Indeed, if he had not Kuppenbender was never validly appointed a member of the Board of Management of the optical business.

Finally, I would say that even if the West German courts are right in thinking that no Special Board such as is contemplated by the articles could exist in East Germany after the confiscation of the businesses, I still cannot see how Bauersfeld, Henrichs and Kuppenbender can have thereupon become entitled to represent and administer the Foundation under Article 114. That article refers to the powers in question being taken over by "the executive Board of Management of the optical works," but these three gentlemen were not even members of that Board of Management at the relevant time. They were—as I have held and as the Federal High Court was prepared to assume—merely attornies of the Board of Management in Jena. It is true that they happened to be the only attornies of the Board in West Germany, but that is irrelevant when one comes to consider the true construction of Article 114. If—as might have happened—the Board in Jena had given one power of attorney to Bauersfeld, Henrichs and Kuppenbender to act for them in one part of Western Germany and another power to Joos to act for them in another part, which of them would have been entitled to administer the Foundation under Article 114 until a new Special Board was constituted? The answer must be neither. I cannot see why the irrelevant circumstance that Bauersfeld, Henrichs and Kuppenbender happened to be the only attornies in the West can justify one in putting an entirely unnatural construction on the language of Article 114. **[332]**

The result to which I come on this branch of the case may, therefore, be summarised as follows: It may be that the confiscation of the businesses put an end to any powers of the Board of Management in Jena to authorise the bringing of legal proceedings in the name of the Foundation. I do not doubt that so-called Boards of Management of the business enterprises—or at all events a single Board of Management of the business activity—have or has continued to exist in Jena. But it may be that the functions of those bodies or that body have been limited to acting under Article 104a—that is to say, to furthering the objects specified in Article 113 by administering the assets of the Foundation which did not belong to either business but also any funds which may be paid to the Foundation by the VEB's. Assuming, however, that that is so, then it must follow that the council of Gera, which in my view is the Special Board of the Foundation, is entitled to represent the Foundation in litigation brought to protect any business property which may remain vested in the Foundation notwithstanding the confiscation, either because the confiscation was not intended to extend to it, or because the law of the place where such property is situated does not recognise the confiscation.

I would add that insofar as the action in question was to restrain the improper use of the name of the Foundation itself I would have thought that the Special Board would have been the proper body to authorise the litigation even in the days when the Foundation owned business enterprises which were run by Boards of Management independent of the Special Board. This, it may be remembered, was the view expressed by the Federation High Court in its first judgment.

I must now turn to consider the plea of *res judicata*. I take the law to be correctly stated in Dicey, 7th edition, pages 1052-53, namely that a foreign judgment *in personam* in favour of the defendant in a foreign action, if it is final and conclusive on the merits is a good defence to an action in England in respect of the same matter by the plaintiff in such action.

I do not see how the defendants can rely on the plea here. In the first place the judgment of the Federal High Court given on the 15th November, 1960, was not a judgment on the merits of the Foundation's case. All that the Court decided was a procedural point, namely, that according to its view of the relevant law, the Foundation was not properly before it. It decided nothing whatever against the Foundation. At most it decided something against the council of Gera which purported to represent the Foundation in the proceedings and against which the court made an order for costs. But even if one treats the judgment as a judgment against the council of Gera on the merits of its claim to represent the Foundation, the present action is not an action by the council of Gera or by the Foundation suing by the Council of Gera but an action by the Foundation suing by Messrs. Courts & Company. If the defendants are right, the action will be struck out and Messrs. Courts will have to pay the costs, but the council of Gera is not before this court, and I cannot see how anything decided by the Federal High Court can be *res judicata* against either the Foundation or Messrs. Courts.

Again, I do not think that the question which was decided by the Federal High Court was the same question as that which I have to decide. What it had to decide was whether the Foundation could be represented by the council of Gera in the proceedings before it at the date when it came to consider the matter. What I have to decide is whether Messrs. Courts have authority to represent the Foundation in this action today. Of course, no one suggests that there has in fact been any material change of circumstances since the decision of the Federal High Court; but, strictly speaking, the two issues are not the same. Counsel for the defendants were, I think, disposed to admit that this was so, but they urged that it was at **[333]** least res judicata that the articles of the Foundation were without force in Eastern Germany in November, 1960, and that unless some evidence of a change of circumstances since that date was adduced, I must hold that they are without force in Eastern Germany today. If that is so, then it would seem to follow that if "A" issues a writ against "B," and "B" succeeds in having the action stayed on the ground that "A" is mentally incapable and should sue by a next friend, and "A" shortly afterwards issues another writ against "B" in respect of the same cause of action, any doctor called to give evidence on "A's" behalf on an application by "B" to stay the second action must assume that "A" was incapable when the first action was stayed and confine his evidence to any improvements which he has observed in his condition since that date. There are apparently no reported cases on the application of this doctrine of *"res judicata"* to a summons to stay proceedings on the ground that the plaintiff is not properly before the Court—but in the absence of authority I have considerable doubt whether on the second application the court would be obliged to assume in "B's" favour that "A" was mentally incapable at the date of the order made on the first application—though I can well understand that the court would stay the second action unless "A" proposed either to adduce fresh evidence as to his condition at the earlier date or evidence as to improvement since then. Furthermore, I am by no means satisfied that the doctrine *res judicata* as applied to foreign judgments extends beyond what Diplock, L.J., in *Thoday* v. *Thoday* [1964] 2 W.L.R. 371 at pages 384 and 385 describes as "cause of action estoppel" to what he describes as "issue estoppel" or "fact estoppel."

But even if I am wrong in thinking that the third defendant cannot invoke the doctrine of *res judicata,* I cannot see how the first and second defendants can avail themselves of it. What is said is that if you look at the statement of claim delivered by the plaintiff you can infer that the case against them will be that they are marketing goods produced by the third defendant. This, it is said, makes them "privies" of the third defendants for the purpose of the operation of the doctrine of *res judicata.* I cannot follow this argument at all. I am not by any means satisfied that if the Federal High Court had in fact decided on the merits that the fourth defendant before them, i.e., the firm, Carl-Zeiss of Heidenheim (which I assume to be the same person as the third defendant in this case) was entitled to trade in Germany under the name of "Zeiss" or "Carl-Zeiss," that this would enable the third defendants to plead *res judicata* as a defence to the plaintiff's claim in this action, which relates to passing-off in this country. Still less am I satisfied that the first and second defendants, even if they are marketing the goods by arrangement with the third defendants, would be entitled to raise the plea. But in fact the Federal High Court did not give any decision on the merits. It only decided a preliminary procedural point against the council of Gera. Whether the first and second defendants can be considered to be "privies" of the third defendant for the purpose of the doctrine of *res judicata* must depend on matters which will fall to be determined in the action but are quite irrelevant to any point which I have to decide now. In fact, one cannot tell from looking at the writ whether or not it is being said that the defendants were acting independently or in concert, and it is only because the plaintiff happens to have delivered a statement of claim amplifying his case that the argument can be got on its legs at all. But there is nothing sacred about a statement of claim; it may be amended and the defendants may deny the allegations contained in it. What matters for this purpose are the facts proved in the action. The contention that the first and second defendants are "privies" of the third defendant for the purpose of the estoppel on the preliminary point seems to me to involve mixing up matters which are logically distinct. **[334]**

Next, I must deal with the argument that even if all the defendants or the third defendants would *prima facie,* be entitled to rely on the judgment of the Federal High Court as establishing a plea of *res judicata,* the character of that judgment is such that I ought not to concede to it the recognition to which it would otherwise have been entitled. This is a delicate question; but as the views which I have hitherto expressed on the application of the doctrine of *res judicata* may be held to be wrong, I ought not to shirk it.

The rule that a foreign judgment "in personam" in favour of the defendant in a foreign action is a good defence to an action in England in respect of the same matter by the plaintiff in such action is not confined to cases in which the foreign court was applying its own law. It extends to cases in which the foreign court was applying the law of England or of some other foreign country. On the other hand, if the foreign court applied—or purported to apply—to the case a system of law which it knew or should have known was not the law which was applicable to the case under the generally recognised rules of private international law, then our courts will not treat such a foreign judgment as founding a plea of *res judicata.* (*Simpson* v. *Fogo* (1863) 1 Hem. and M.195).

Now, in this case the West German courts have, as I read their judgments, purported to apply to the matter in hand the proper system of law, namely, the law of East Germany; but in holding that by East German law the council of Gera is not the Special Board and is incapable of representing the Foundation in litigation they reached a decision which was clean contrary—and which they must have known was clean contrary—to the view of the matter which would have been taken by any court in Eastern Germany. It is no doubt true that the decisions given by the courts of a country—even by its highest courts—are not necessarily an infallible guide to its law. It is conceivable that the law of a country might clearly lay down a certain rule of general application, but that the courts, for some reason or another—government pressure, bribery or what you will—failed to give effect to the rule in some particular case. But I cannot see that the views expressed by the East German courts in this case are in any way contrary to the law of East Germany. Indeed the view of that law as applied to this case which I have formed for myself accords pretty closely with that expressed in the advisory opinion of the East German Supreme Court given on the 6th April, 1954.

In this connection it is relevant to enquire whether or not on those occasions the East German courts have given decisions which are more easily explicable as reflections of what the interests of the German Democratic Republic require than justifiable as pieces of legal reasoning. Even if that were true—and I express no view on the point one way or the other—it could only mean that in this particular case the East German courts were lucky in being able to come by an easy path to a result to which they would have come even if the path had been rougher going for a judge.

But then it is said that the fact that I agree with the view of the law of East Germany expressed by the East German courts and disagree with the view expressed by the West German courts is irrelevant; and so, of course, it would be if I was satisfied that the West German judges had done their "judicial best" to solve the problem before them. I am, however, by no means satisfied of this. The view as to the effect of the confiscation of the businesses on the constitution of the Foundation which the West German courts have declared to be the view required by the law of East Germany has to my mind nothing to be said for it except that it leads to a result which many—perhaps most—of the inhabitants of West Germany **[335]** would consider to be just, and I cannot believe that lawyers of the eminence of the judges of the Federal High Courts would have arrived at such a conclusion if the merits of the case as they saw it did not appear to them imperatively to demand it.

I am anxious not to be self-righteous. If I was a West German judge I dare say that I should have done the same. But as it is, I can view the problem with greater detachment, and, so viewing it, I feel bound to say that if I had thought that the other conditions for this application of the principle of *res judicata* were satisfied, I would still have held that the principle did not apply here because the foreign judgments in question were perverse.

In view of what I have said, it is not necessary for me to express any opinion on the question whether the plaintiff can rely on the East German judgment as a counter estoppel.

Notwithstanding that the third defendant did not appear in the East German proceedings, I must, however, deal in conclusion with the contention that it would be wrong to allow the action to continue because if it succeeds the result will be that the VEB Carl-Zeiss will get the benefit and extraterritorial effect will in substance be given to the confiscation of the optical business. I think that this contention, if sound, ought strictly speaking to be advanced as a matter of defence in the action rather than on this application; but as this point was argued before me, I will deal with it now. For that purpose I shall assume what may well be right, that this confiscation was intended to extend to the business assets outside East Germany, and that our law would not accord extraterritorial effect to it. In considering this contention one must bear in mind that the defendants have not sought to prove that the third defendant is this Foundation established by Abbe. They have argued this application on the footing that the plaintiff is the Foundation established by Abbe and that the third defendants have no title to any of its property. On that footing I can see no merit whatever in the contention in question. Suppose that before the first war a Russian Princess had lent some valuable jewellery to a friend in England; that a Soviet Decree purported to deprive the Princess of her property in the jewellery; that the Princess remained in Russia, became converted to communism and asked her friend to return the jewellery so that she might hand it over to the authority to which the confiscation decree purported to give it; and that the English friend, who detested Lenin and all his works, proposed to sell the jewellery and apply its proceeds in aid of distressed White Russian refugees. Surely it is clear that our courts would order the defendant to return the jewellery to the plaintiff even though the result of that would be in substance to give effect to the decree of confiscation? Counsel for the defendants argued that the analogy between that case and this was not exact because in the case supposed the courts could ascertain, if necessary by examination of the Princess, whether or not she really wished to give effect to the confiscation, whereas here the court cannot be sure that the Foundation wishes the VEB Carl-Zeiss to have the benefit of the English goodwill of the optical business. In considering what are the wishes of a foreign charitable corporation I do not think that the court can really look beyond the wishes of the body—in this case the council of Gera—which the court regards as entitled to speak for the corporation. Assuming, however, that I am entitled to speculate as to the wishes of the beneficiaries, the result is the same. The principal beneficiaries of the Foundation are those persons living in or about Jena who are or have been employed in the optical or glass businesses and their dependants. They must tend to gain by the prosperity of these businesses even though they belong to the VEB's and no longer to the Foundation. If the VEB's prosper they are likely to maintain and even increase the payment which they made towards pensions and **[336]** towards the upkeep of the welfare institutions owned by the Foundation. If on the other hand, the VEB's do not prosper there will be a risk that these payments will be reduced. If one must make a guess, I would suppose that a majority of the people of Jena, whatever their political views, would prefer any profit to be made by the sale of Zeiss products outside East Germany to go to the VEB's rather than to the University of Tubingen and the other bodies benefited by the third defendant.

For these reasons I hold that the summons to stay fails and must be dismissed.

Falconer.—I ask that the summons be dismissed with costs and that your Lordship will certify that this was a proper case for three counsel. The circumstances which justify allowing costs of three counsel are dealt with in *Dunlop Pneumatic Tyre Co. Ltd.* v. *Wapshare Tube Co. Ltd.* (1900) 17 R.P.C. 433 at 459. Complex questions of international law have arisen and it was proper for *Mr. Aldous* to obtain the assistance of *Mr. Lauterpacht.* Three counsel were allowed in similar circumstances in *Adrema Ltd.* v. *Adrema G.m.b.H.* [1958] R.P.C. 323.

Rink, Q.C.—Although this is a passing-off case the issues so far have been entirely of international law. It was not comparable to a patent case involving technical problems in addition to points of international law. Though it started as a passing-off case, it would have been reasonable to engage different counsel to deal with this summons, just as I am instructed on this aspect of the case only. The case is not one of such complexity that on its facts alone it would have called for three counsel specialised in international law.

CROSS, J.—This is the sort of case in which it is very difficult to decide, but on the whole balancing one thing with another, I think this is a case in which I can properly certify for three counsel.

CARL ZEISS STIFTUNG v. RAYNER & KEELER LTD. AND OTHERS

([1965] Ch. 525)

July 27, 1964: Court of Appeal: Lord Denning M.R., Pearson, Salmon L.JJ.

International Law—Recognition—Effect—East and West Germany—Passing-off action begun in England by solicitors on authority of East German organisation —Application by defendants in England and West Germany to stay action as commenced and maintained without the plaintiffs' authority—No request by parties to judge to inquire whether East German government recognised by Her Majesty's Government—Judgment in favour of plaintiffs based on parties' acceptance of legislation of East Germany—Change of defendants' legal representation for pending appeal—Motion by defendants asking Court of Appeal to inquire of H.M. Government whether East Germany recognised de facto or de jure—Whether defendants permitted to raise new point on interlocutory appeal—Whether court required to take judicial note of public matters as to executive policy on recognition of foreign state.
Court of Appeal—Argument not raised below—Discretion of appellate court to entertain— Recognition of foreign state—Whether court under duty to inquire of executive as to recognition for purposes of pending appeal.

In 1955 English solicitors, on behalf of the plaintiffs, Carl Zeiss Stiftung, a charitable foundation founded in 1896 with its domicile in Jena, now in the German Democratic Republic ("East Germany"), began an action against the defendants, two English limited companies and an organisation in the Federal German Republic ("West Germany") calling itself by the same name as the plaintiffs, to restrain them, inter alia, from passing off optical or glass instruments by reference to the name "Carl Zeiss." In 1956 the defendants took out a summons to stay all proceedings in the passing-off action and to have it dismissed on the ground that it had been begun and was being maintained without the plaintiffs' authority.

The summons was not heard until November, 1963; and at that hearing no point was taken by the defendants as to whether or not Her Majesty's Government had recognised the German Democratic Republic Government de facto or de jure nor as to the court having regard to East German legislation and decrees. The judge dismissed the defendants' summons, holding, inter alia, that the body constituted under East German law as the plaintiffs' board was entitled to instruct the English solicitors to proceed in the passing-off action.

The defendants, wishing to appeal against that decision, changed almost all their legal advisers and moved the Court of Appeal, asking that a letter be written on behalf of the court to Her Majesty's Secretary of State for Foreign Affairs, requesting him to certify to the court the answers to seven questions, including **[526]** the question whether Her Majesty's Government had granted recognition de jure or de facto to the German Democratic Republic or its government, and if yes, when? It was submitted for the defendants that though the point had not been taken before the trial judge the court itself was bound to make the inquiry and ought not to proceed to judgment on the appeal on a basis which might conflict with the policy of the executive. For the plaintiffs it was submitted that the defendants, having in the previous proceedings elected not to take the point as to recognition or as to the validity of the East German laws, ought not now to be allowed to raise a new point:—

Held, granting the application in part, that the letter should be written asking for a certificate on the first question, for the court itself should take judicial notice of a public matter, namely, whether Her Majesty's government recognised the German Democratic Republic or its government, and ought not to proceed to judgment on the basis of the validity of foreign laws which might be a false hypothesis; but that only the first question should be asked, for the answer to the second was common knowledge, and the remainder savoured of cross-examination of the Foreign Secretary, which the court would not permit. If, as a result of the answer to that question, the plaintiffs should require further questions to be addressed by the court to the Foreign Secretary, the court would entertain an application for that purpose.

MOTION.

By a writ of summons issued on October 20, 1955, by solicitors, Courts & Co., of London, the plaintiffs, Carl Zeiss Stiftung, whose registered office was at Carl Zeiss Platz 1, Jena, in the German Democratic Republic ("East Germany"), asked for an injunction to restrain the defendants, Rayner & Keeler Ltd., Degenhardt & Co. Ltd., (two companies registered in England) and Carl Zeiss of Heidenheim, Brenz, in the Federal Republic of Germany ("West Germany"), from advertising, offering for sale, or selling any optical instruments or any articles containing or consisting of glass under or by reference to the name "Carl Zeiss" unless such goods were those of the plaintiffs or an organisation associated with the plaintiffs, and generally from passing off any business or goods as and for those of the plaintiffs or an organisation associated with them; for delivery up or destruction on oath of all articles calculated to lead to passing off; for an inquiry as to damages or an account of profits; and further or other relief. By amendments in March, 1960, the plaintiffs by their solicitors asked further for an injunction to restrain the third defendants (by amendment described as "Carl Zeiss Stiftung" of Heidenheim) from using the name "Carl Zeiss **[527]** Stiftung" or "Carl Zeiss" or any name containing "Zeiss" in relation to their business or goods.

By their statement of claim as amended, the plaintiffs stated that they were constituted in about 1896 in accordance with certain Articles of Constitution as drawn up by one Dr. Ernst Abbe in or about August, 1896; and that by article 3 "the legal domicile of the Stiftung" (meaning the plaintiffs) "shall be Jena," which was now in the Eastern Zone of Germany. They claimed further that in pursuance of the provisions of article 113 of the Articles, the administration of the plaintiffs and the appointment of a deputy of the plaintiffs had been transferred to the Council of the District of Gera in which Jena was situated; and that for very many years and at all material times the name "Carl Zeiss" and any name including "Zeiss" had indicated, when used in relation to any business concerned in, or in relation to, any optical instruments or articles containing or consisting of glass, the business and goods of the plaintiffs and none other, or, alternatively, the business and goods of an organisation associated with them, and that the name "Carl Zeiss Stiftung" had indicated them exclusively.

By paragraph 5 it was stated that the first two defendants were retailers of optical instruments but did not deal in the plaintiffs' goods; and that the third defendants were a German organisation with its registered office at Heidenheim, in the Western Zone of Germany, and were competitors of the plaintiffs; that the third defendants, without the plaintiffs' consent, had used the names "Carl Zeiss Stiftung" and "Carl Zeiss" in relation to their business and goods, and that such use was calculated to lead, as the third defendants at all times knew and intended, to their business and goods being thought to be those of the plaintiffs or an organisation associated with them, and to deception, confusion and passing off to the plaintiffs' detriment; and that the third defendants intended to continue to trade under those names whereby the plaintiffs would suffer damage. They claimed further that each of the defendants, acting in concert and with full knowledge of all matters aforesaid, had passed off and intended to pass off the third defendants' business and goods as and for those of the plaintiffs or an associated organisation, whereby the plaintiffs had suffered and were calculated to suffer damage; and, after giving particulars, they claimed the relief set out in the writ.

The defendants on February 7, 1956, following the issue of the writ and the unamended statement of claim, applied to **[528]** Master Neave for an order that all further proceedings in the passing-off action be stayed and that the action be dismissed on the ground that it was commenced and was being maintained without the plaintiffs' authority, and that Messrs. Courts & Co., the solicitors purporting to act for the plaintiffs, should pay the defendants the costs of the action, including the costs of the application. That summons was supported by an affidavit of one Walter David, the legal adviser of the third defendants, filed on April 6, 1956. Nothing further was done by either side until March 20, 1959, when the defendants gave notice of intention to proceed. The plaintiffs filed affidavits in answer to the summons: a further affidavit by David in reply was filed by the defendants; and on June 1, 1960, the defendants took out a summons to cross-examine affidavit witnesses for the plaintiffs. On July 27, 1960, another summons for leave to adduce further evidence on behalf of the third defendants was taken out.

On March 21, 1961, the three summons came before Cross J., when, according to an extract from a contemporary note by junior counsel for the plaintiffs (E. Lauterpacht), leading counsel for the defendants. (B. MacKenna Q.C.) was asked by Cross J.: "Suppose this entity" (namely, the plaintiffs) "exists in East Germany, would it not be a question of East German law?" to which Mr. MacKenna replied: "That would have to be decided by East German law" and that the issue was the application of the proper law. When leading counsel for the plaintiffs (Guy Aldous Q.C.) submitted that East German law must be applied and the judge asked Mr. MacKenna whether he could assume that the relevant law was East German law, Mr. MacKenna replied: "Yes." The judge then asked: "Has any point been taken on recognition?" Mr. MacKenna replied: "East Germany is not recognised de facto, but I take no point." Mr. Aldous said: "One will have to say that everything is done under the aegis of the Soviet authorities."

As the plaintiffs wished to put in further evidence the summons before Cross J. were stood over for evidence to be completed. On October 28, 1963, the defendants issued a fourth summons for leave to adduce yet further evidence and in November the plaintiffs filed further affidavits. The matter came on as interlocutory proceedings for hearing before Cross J. on November 26, 1963, and occupied 20 days. Cross J., in a reserved and closely reasoned judgment on March 6, 1964, dismissed the defendants' summons. In the course of that judgment, most of which is not relevant to the report of the present motion, the judge stated: **[529]** "The question whether the German Democratic Republic when it was set up came, so to say, with possession of a juristic person called the Carl Zeiss Foundation, and if it did, whether that foundation was the same legal entity as the foundation established by Abbe, is no doubt primarily a question of the law which prevailed in Jena in 1948 before the German Democratic Republic existed. If, however, there is any doubt as to what effect under that law the confiscation had on the existence and character of the foundation, I should have to accept that the view taken on the point by the courts of the German Democratic Republic, in whose territory Jena is situated, should prevail." At another point in his judgment, the judge, reviewing the history of the plaintiffs and of the third defendants, stated: "As a result of an East German law dated July 23, 1952, and an order made under it, the Province of Thuringia was divided into three districts and the governmental functions of the Province transferred to the administrative organs of the respective districts. The district in which Jena is situated is the District of Gera, and this body, which stands in the same relation to the University of Jena as the State Department of the Grand Duchy [of Saxe-Weimar] stood to it in the old days, is the Council (Rat) of Gera. It is common ground that as a matter of political geography the Council of Gera would be the Special Board within the meaning of article 113 [of the Carl Zeiss Stiftung articles]."

Later in his judgment the judge said: ". . . It may be that the confiscation of the businesses put an end to any powers of the board of management in Jena to authorise the bringing of legal proceedings in the name of the foundation. I do not doubt that so-called boards of management of the business enterprises —or at all events a single board of management of the business activity—have or has continued to exist in Jena. But it may be that the functions of those bodies or that body have been limited to acting under article 104a—that is to say, to furthering the objects specified in article 113 by administering the assets of the foundation which did not belong to either business but also any funds which may be paid to the foundation by the V.E.B.S. Assuming, however, that that is so, then it must follow that the Council of Gera, which in my view is the special board of the foundation, is entitled to represent the foundation in litigation brought to protect any business property which may remain vested in the foundation notwithstanding the confiscation, either because the confiscation was **[530]** not intended to extend to it, or because the law of the place where such property is situated does not recognise the confiscation. I would add that in so far as the action in question was to restrain the improper use of the name of the foundation itself I would have thought that the special board would have been the proper body to authorise the litigation even in the days when the foundation owned business enterprises which were run by boards of management independent of the special board." He held, therefore, that the Council of Gera who had instructed the English solicitors, Courts & Co., were entitled to represent the plaintiffs as its special board.

Following that decision, the defendants changed their solicitors and instructed new solicitors, Herbert Smith & Co., to act on their behalf on an appeal from Cross J. Those solicitors in turn instructed counsel other than those who had appeared before Cross J. (with the exception of junior counsel T. M. Shelford, who was retained again).

By notice of motion dated July 15, 1964, the Court of Appeal was asked for a direction that a letter be written on behalf of the court to Her Majesty's Secretary of State for Foreign Affairs requesting him (if and in so far and in such manner as he might deem expedient) to certify to the court the answers to the questions set out below, and that if he should certify in response in such request prior to the hearing of the appeal, the contents of such certificate should forthwith be communicated to the parties to the appeal.

The questions were as follows: (1) Has Her Majesty's Government granted any recognition to (a) the German Democratic Republic or (b) its government? If yes, when was such recognition granted, and was it granted de jure or de facto? (2) Has Her Majesty's Government granted any recognition to (a) the Federal Republic of Germany or (b) its government? If yes, when was such recognition granted, and was it granted de jure or de facto? (3) Does Her Majesty's Government now hold the same view of the Federal Republic of Germany as is expressed in a statement of September 19, 1950, made by Her Majesty's Secretary of State for Foreign Affairs, and the Foreign Ministers of the United States of America and France, namely: "Pending the unification of Germany, the three Governments consider the Government of the Federal Republic as the only German government freely and legitimately constituted and therefore entitled to speak for Germany as the representative of the German people in international affairs." (4) Does Her Majesty's Government now **[531]** hold the same view of the Federal Republic of Germany as is expressed in a letter of October 23, 1950, written on behalf of the Allied High Commission in Germany, namely: "The three governments regard the Federal Government as the only German government which can speak for Germany and represent the German people in international affairs pending the reunification of Germany. They consider, therefore, that pending a final peace settlement, and without prejudice to its terms, the Federal Government is the only government entitled to assume the rights and fulfil the obligations of the former German Reich." (5) If the answer to (3) or (4) is "No," in what respects has that view changed? (6) Has the State of Germany as a whole continued in existence since 1945? (7) If so, does it include the territory occupied by the Federal Republic of Germany and the Soviet-occupied zone?

A supporting affidavit by a partner in the firm of Herbert Smith & Co. stated: "It appears from the judgment of Cross J. . . . that he considered himself bound to pay special attention to the judgments of the courts of the German Democratic Republic. It further appears . . . that he founded himself on the legislation and decrees of the German Democratic Republic." The affidavit then referred to the passages in the judgment of Cross J. set out above, and added: "The judge further considered that there were two separate systems of law prevailing in East and West Germany, as appears in many places in his judgment. It appears from the proceedings at the hearing of the summons that the judge took no steps to inform himself of the views held by Her Majesty's Government as to the authority of the German Democratic Republic and the German Federal Republic, or as to the continued existence of Germany as one state. It is respectfully submitted that this Honourable Court would be assisted on matters which are of great importance to this appeal if it were to request Her Majesty's Secretary of State for Foreign Affairs to give a certificate in relation thereto."

Mark Littman Q.C., T. M. Shelford and *P. Lewis* for the defendants. It is plain that the whole hearing before Cross J. proceeded on the footing that there were certain East German laws, and one in particular, which could be recognised and applied by the English court, so that it may be presumed that the defendants' advisers took the view that no letter to or certificate from Her Majesty's Secretary of State for Foreign Affairs would affect **[532]** the position. But now that almost all the legal representation for the defendants has been changed, it is the duty of their counsel to ask the court to take judicial notice of the situation in which a judgment of the English court, proceeding on the basis that there are two Germanys and two systems of law, appear to give recognition to a foreign government which has not, so far as is known, been granted recognition either de facto or de jure by Her Majesty's Government.

It has been laid down time and time again that on grounds of public policy the courts and the executive should speak with one voice in matters within the purview of the Foreign Secretary; and the only method by which the court can inform itself on such a matter is by inquiry of the Foreign Office, whose certificate is conclusive. That is what the court is asked to do by this motion. The answers to the questions set out in the motion could have a profound effect on the appeal, and the application is made now in order to avoid the delay which such an inquiry might involve were it to be raised when the appeal, fixed for November 9, 1964, is ready for hearing. If the reply of the Foreign Office is inconsistent with the way in which Cross J. dealt with the matter, it will have an importance beyond this litigation.

[SALMON L.J. Some of these questions are rather embarrassing.]

The present position is far more embarrassing, for there has gone out to the world an English judicial decision which assumes recognition of the German Democratic Republic, contrary to statements made on behalf of the Western Alliance. [*Rex* v. *Bottrill, Ex parte Kuechenmeister*[1]* was referred to.]

In *Aksionairnoye Obschestvo A. M. Luther* v. *James Sagor & Co.*[2]* the statement of principle by Roche J. was approved in the Court of Appeal by Bankes L.J.,[3] though the situation in regard to recognition of the Soviet Government had in that case changed between the hearing at first instance and in the Court of Appeal: see also Dicey's Conflict of Laws, 7th ed. (1958), at p. 663, that acts of governments not recognised by H.M. Government are devoid of legal effect so far as the English courts are concerned. Other authorities supporting the proposition that the executive and the judiciary should not speak with two voices may be found in *Gdynia-Ameryko Linie Zeglugowe Spolka Akcyjna* v. **[533]** *Boguslawski*,[4]* where an inquiry had been addressed to the Foreign Office on a matter on which the court required further information: and *The Arantzazu Mendi** *per* Lord Atkin[5] *Foster* v. *Globe Venture Syndicate Ltd.*,* per Farwell J.[6]; *Taylor* v. *Barclay** *per* Sir L. Shadwell V.-C.[7] and *The Gagara** *per* Bankes L.J.[8]

Before Cross J. there was some discussion on the basis that even if Her Majesty's Government did not recognise the decrees of the German Democratic Republic in its own right, it might derive authority from the Soviet Government which, of course, is recognised by Her Majesty's Government. But that does not necessarily follow, for the relevant decree was made by what claims to be an independent government. That enhances the desirability of obtaining a certificate from the Foreign Secretary.

Guy Aldous Q.C., E. Lauterpacht and *D. W. Falconer* for the plaintiffs. At all stages of these protracted proceedings and before the judge the question in the minds of both parties was whether any particular law made in the country which is the German Democratic Republic had its legal authority from the Soviet occupation forces and therefore from the Soviet Government, or whether the authority stemmed from the government in East Germany. After discussion with counsel then representing the defendants, it was decided that it was unnecessary to ask the judge to put questions to the Foreign Office, and the judge was so informed. The reason was that the defendants were relying on the particular decree of the German Democratic Republic as the foundation of their submission that the Council of Gera could not act as the Carl Zeiss Special Board *because* it was the organ of a Communist government and it would be contrary to the whole tenor of the "statute" which set up the original Foundation that a Communist organ should be the special Board.

Now the defendants, by their present legal representatives, seek to challenge the validity and effect of laws which they themselves put forward. That is a very important volte face from the plaintiffs' point of view, for if it had been raised at an earlier stage they would have had quite other evidence to show from whence the validity of the laws (hitherto accepted as valid by the defendants) stemmed; and that might have involved evidence from Soviet sources.

[SALMON L.J. If the judge per incuriam has rested his judgment **[534]** on a

[1] [1947] 1 K.B. 41; 62 T.L.R. 570; [1946] 2 All E.R. 434, C.A.
[2] [1921] 1 K.B. 456, 473-475.
[3] [1921] 3 K.B. 532, 540; 37 T.L.R. 777, C.A.
[4] [1953] A.C. 11, 43; [1952] 2 T.L.R. 317; [1952] 2 All E.R. 470, H.L.(E.).
[5] [1939] A.C. 256, 263; 55 T.L.R. 454; [1939] 1 All E.R. 719, H.L.(E.).
[6] [1900] 1 Ch. 811, 812.
[7] (1828) 2 Simon Rep. 213, 220.
[8] [1919] P. 95, 104.

decree of a foreign government which is not recognised by Her Majesty's Government, what ought this court, as a matter of public policy, to do?]

The court would not inquire unless there is an issue on recognition between the parties and that issue is brought to the court's attention by the parties. Where the defendants have themselves put in the decree setting up the Council of Gera and the plaintiffs have put forward their evidence on that footing, the court should not allow the defendants to resile from their position and now raise a matter completely contrary to the case as put and accepted in the court below and quite inconsistent with that case. It is contrary to the settled rules of an appellate court to allow a party to argue a case which is not even mentioned in the notice of appeal, is inconsistent with the case argued below, and is a new point expressly disclaimed below so far as it could be disclaimed, unless all the relevant facts and evidence are before the appellate court. In this case all the facts—all foreign law being a question of fact—are not before this court: see Annual Practice, 1964 (at p. 1675), where it is stated that it is not open to a party to raise a wholly new point on appeal.

Public policy, does not come into this case at all: see *Luigi Monta of Genoa* v. *Cechofracht Co. Ltd.*,[9]* *per* Sellers J. that it is not contrary to public policy for parties to agree to treat the ordinances of a foreign government not recognised by H.M. Government as deciding the rights of the parties to a particular charterparty; and in that case the English court gave effect to the agreement.

[PEARSON L.J. But that was merely a question of contract. Here it is a question of status.]

There was an agreement between the parties that they would treat the laws of East Germany as effective to govern the rights of the parties. The defendants' present proceedings are aimed at getting the plaintiffs' action finally struck out. It was for them to prove that the plaintiffs had no authority to bring the action. They sought to do so by putting in certain laws which they accepted as valid. Now they want to further their proceedings to strike out the action by saying that the laws are invalid and by asking this court to decide on quite a different footing that the plaintiffs did not have proper authority to begin the action. If the court accedes to the application and puts the questions to H.M. Secretary of State, that will be only the first **[535]** stage of the inquiry into the validity of the laws. Nor would the proposed questions be sufficient, for the plaintiffs in their turn would require questions to be put as to recognition of the Soviet occupation forces or other authority and might require to call evidence to establish points on which the defendants relied when they framed their original case.

Mark Littman Q.C. in reply. The practice of the appellate court is, in the exercise of its discretion, to receive fresh evidence, if necessary, where the proceedings are interlocutory. This is not a case in which there are formal pleadings. Though the issues may be adumbrated in affidavits, the mere fact that an East German decree is set out in one of the defendants' affidavits does not mean that the defendants relied on that decree. It would be contrary to authority if this court dealt with this appeal on the hypothesis that the law of the German Democratic Republic, not recognised by Her Majesty's Government, may properly be applied in this case. *Luigi Monta of Genoa* v. *Cechofracht Co. Ltd.*,[10] is distinguishable as a mere matter of contract. It is unthinkable that the English court would, for instance, allow parties to come before it and say: "We have agreed that the court shall deal with this case on the assumption that the Tsarist Government is still the government of Russia." It may be that further evidence will be necessary and that much of the existing paper will become irrelevant; but where a question of public policy is involved the court must proceed in accordance with that public policy. [*The Fagernes*[11]* and *Duff Development Co. Ltd.* v. *Kelantan Government*[12]* were also referred to.]

[9] [1956] 2 Q.B. 552, 565; [1956] 3 W.L.R. 480; [1956] 2 All E.R. 769.
[10] [1956] 2 Q.B. 552.
[11] [1927] P. 311; 43 T.L.R. 746, C.A.
[12] [1924] A.C. 797, 813; 40 T.L.R. 566, H.L.(E.).

Lord Denning M.R. This action is brought in the name, as plaintiffs, of Carl Zeiss Stiftung. The defendants are two English companies and a concern of the same name as the plaintiffs, Carl Zeiss Stiftung. The plaintiffs say that the defendants have passed off their goods, namely, optical instruments and glasses, as the defendants' goods. The defendants say that this action is brought without any proper authority and have applied to stay it on that ground. There has been a very long inquiry already before Cross J. as to the position of the plaintiffs. Are they people who have properly instructed their solicitors to bring this case?

The outline of the facts, as I understand it, is that before the **[536]** war there was in Germany a very big and important foundation called the Carl Zeiss Stiftung, which manufactured cameras, lenses and glass. It had a world-wide trade. Its headquarters apparently were at Jena. After the war some people in Jena, which is in East Germany, purport to have been carrying on the business of the foundation there. These folk in Jena are the plaintiffs. But in West Germany other people have set up a concern at Heidenheim, and they say they are carrying on the business of the Carl-Zeiss Foundation. These folk at Heidenheim are being sued as the defendants in this action.

The question which was debated before Cross J. was whether the plaintiffs have any locus standi before the court at all. In order to determine this question, it is necessary to ask and answer these questions: What law governs the institution known as Carl Zeiss Stiftung? Has the institution continued at all in the new régime in East Germany? Has it been confiscated? Has it been taken over by some other concern altogether? Does the Carl Zeiss Stiftung continue to exist? In order to answer those questions, one must know a good deal about the constitutional position in East Germany. Are the laws in East Germany recognised by this country? In the course of the case the defendants seem to have admitted that there was some legislative authority in East Germany which was able to enact laws which this court would recognise. It might be the new East German Government or the Russians acting through the people there. But it was accepted that there was legislative authority there. Cross J. in the course of his judgment said: "At all events, in some respects the law to which we must look is the law of the German Democratic Republic of East Germany."

In the appeal to this court the defendants want to raise the question here whether or no Her Majesty's Government have recognised the German Democratic Republic and its government. They wish to see whether these laws to which the judge paid attention are to be recognised in this country or not. So they ask that a letter be written on behalf of the court to Her Majesty's Secretary of State for Foreign Affairs asking whether Her Majesty's Government has granted recognition to the German Democratic Republic. That is a matter on which the courts always act on the advice of Her Majesty's Secretary of State for Foreign Affairs. The only way of getting information is for the court to write to the Foreign Secretary.

Mr. Aldous, on behalf of the plaintiffs, said that as this point was not raised before Cross J., it should not be allowed to be **[537]** raised here and we should not ask the question of the Foreign Secretary so as to raise a new point. But I would observe that when a question arises in these courts as to the validity of the laws of a foreign country, it is the duty of the court itself to take notice of it. We ought not to give judgment on a hypothesis that may be false. In *Taylor* v. *Barclay*[13]* Sir L. Shadwell V.-C. said: "I conceive it is the duty of the judge in every court to take notice of public matters which affect the government of the country." So here we ought to take notice of this public matter, namely, whether Her Majesty's Government recognises or not the German Democratic Republic. I think we ought to direct a letter to be written asking some of the questions but not all. Some of them come very near to cross-examining the Secretary of State for Foreign Affairs, which is, of course, a thing the court would not allow. I think that questions 1 and 2 should be allowed but not the others. I doubt whether question 2 is necessary because I should have thought it is plain that Her Majesty's Government has granted recognition to

[13] (1828) 2 Simon Rep. 213, 220.

the Federal Republic of Germany. If this be so, the only question which we should allow to be asked is the first question: "(1) Has Her Majesty's Government granted any recognition to (a) the German Democratic Republic or (b) its government? If yes, when was such recognition granted, and was it granted de jure or de facto?" I do not know what the result will be. It may be that the answer to such question will mean that no further inquiries or further evidence are necessary; but if, as the result of the answers, further matters have to be investigated, then an application must be made for the purpose, but I would grant this application to the extent that I have mentioned.

PEARSON L.J. I agree and have nothing to add.
SALMON L.J. I agree.

Application granted. Costs of application to be costs in appeal. Leave to appeal refused.
Letter to be written accordingly.

Solicitors: *Herbert Smith & Co.; Courts & Co.*

CARL ZEISS STIFTUNG v. RAYNER & KEELER AND OTHERS

(*The Times*, October 3, 1964)

October 2, 1964: Court of Appeal: Lord Denning M.R., Pearson, Salmon L.JJ.

The Court of Appeal, on a summons for directions on behalf of the Carl Zeiss Stiftung of Jena, in the German Democratic Republic, who are the plaintiffs in a proposed passing-off action against two English companies and Carl Zeiss of Heidenheim, Brenz, in the Federal Republic of Germany, intimated that a certificate, dated September 16 had now been received from the Secretary of State for Foreign Affairs, replying to questions put by the Court on July 27 at the request of the defendants* (*The Times*, July 28) and stating that "her Majesty's Government has not granted any recognition *de jure* or *de facto* to (a) the German Democratic Republic or (b) its government".

The Court refused an application by *Mr. Guy Aldous Q.C.* on behalf of the plaintiffs to postpone the date fixed for the hearing of an appeal by the defendants from the judgment of Mr. Justice CROSS* (*The Times*, March 7) by which he dismissed their summons to strike out the plaintiffs' action as having been brought without authority, and the Court directed that the date fixed—November 9—should stand, that any further questions which the plaintiffs might wish to formulate for answer by the Foreign Office should be formulated for the approval of the Court within seven days, and that meanwhile, the application should stand adjourned. If, however, it should prove that as a result of further questions to and answers from the Secretary of State, the plaintiffs required further time, the Court would consider the matter again.

CARL ZEISS STIFTUNG v. RAYNER & KEELER AND OTHERS

(*The Times*, October 30, 1964)

October 29, 1964: Court of Appeal: Harman, Danckwerts, Salmon L.JJ.

Questions to Foreign Secretary.

Their Lordships, on a summons for directions by the Carl Zeiss Stiftung of Jena in the German Democratic Republic, the plaintiffs in a proposed passing-off action, directed that two out of nine questions put forward on behalf of the plaintiffs should be forwarded by the Court for answer by Her Majesty's Secretary of State for Foreign Affairs in connexion with an appeal by the defendants to the passing-off action from the judgment of Mr. Justice Cross* on March 6, 1964 (*The Times*, March 7) in interlocutory proceedings in which the defendants sought to have the proceedings stayed.

The plaintiffs' action was begun in 1955, to restrain the defendants, Rayner & Keeler Ltd. and Degenhardt & Co. Ltd., marketers of products of the third defendants, Carl Zeiss Stiftung of Heidenheim in the Federal Republic of Germany, and the third defendants, from passing off optical or glass instruments by reference to the name "Carl Zeiss". In 1956, the defendants took out a summons to stay all proceedings in the passing-off action and to have it dismissed on the ground that it had begun and was being maintained "without the plaintiffs' authority".

The summons was not heard until November, 1963; and at that hearing, no point was taken by the defendants as to whether or not Her Majesty's Government had recognized the German Democratic Republic or its government, *de facto* or *de jure*, nor as to the propriety of the English Court having regard to East German legislation and decrees. Mr. Justice Cross dismissed the defendants' summons, holding, *inter alia*, that the body constituted under East German law as the Carl Zeiss Foundation's Special Board was entitled to instruct English solicitors to proceed in the passing-off action.

The defendants, wishing to appeal against that decision, changed almost all their legal advisers, filed supplementary notices of appeal, and on July 27,* (*The Times*, July 28) moved the Court of Appeal (The Master of the Rolls, Lord Justice Pearson and Lord Justice Salmon) asking that a letter be written on behalf of the Court to Her Majesty's Secretary of State for Foreign Affairs, requesting him to certify to the Court the answers to seven questions, including the question whether Her Majesty's Government had recognized the German Democratic Republic, and if yes, when? For the East German plaintiffs it was then submitted that as the hearing before Mr. Justice Cross had proceeded on the basis put forward by the defendants that East German law was relevant the defendants ought not now to be permitted to alter the basis of their appeal. The Court of Appeal held that the Court itself should take judicial notice of a public matter, namely, whether Her Majesty's Government recognized the German Democratic Republic or its Government, and directed that a letter should be addressed to the Secretary of State asking that question. The Court intimated that if further questions on behalf of the plaintiffs should prove necessary the Court would entertain such an application.

On October 2, 1964 (*The Times*, October 3), on the plaintiffs' summons for directions,* the Court was informed that the Secretary of State's reply was that Her Majesty's Government had not recognized the German Democratic Republic, or its Government either *de jure* or *de facto*. The summons was adjourned to enable the plaintiffs to frame questions for the consideration and approval of the Court of Appeal to be directed for answer to Her Majesty's Secretary of State for Foreign Affairs.

Mr. Guy Aldous Q.C., Mr. E. Lauterpacht and *Mr. D. W. Falconer* appeared for the Carl Zeiss Foundation of Jena; *Mr. Mark Littman Q.C., Mr. T. M. Shelford* and *Mr. P. Lewis* for the defendants.

Mr. Aldous submitted nine questions for the consideration and approval of the Court. *Mr. Littman* objected to the form of some of the questions and to the substance of others.

LORD JUSTICE HARMAN said that the Court did not propose to give any kind of judgment, but was prepared to allow two of the questions, as follows: "(1) What (a) states or (b) governments or (c) authorities, if any, have since July 1, 1945, up to the present date, been recognized by Her Majesty's Government as (a) entitled to exercise or (b) exercising governing authority in the area of Germany outside the zones allocated to the governments of the United Kingdom, the United States of America and the French Republic by the Protocol of September 12, 1944, and the Agreement of July 26, 1945, concluded between the governments of the said states and the Union of Soviet Socialist Republics (hereinafter called 'the said area'). Has such recognition been *de jure* or *de facto*?"; and "(b) Has Her Majesty's Government granted any recognition to (a) the Federal Republic of Germany or (b) its Government? If yes, when was such recognition granted and was it granted *de jure* or *de facto*? And in respect of what area was such recognition granted *de jure* and in respect of what area *de facto*?"

A letter asking these questions would be directed to the Secretary of State, whose attention should be drawn to the fact that the hearing of the defendants' appeal was fixed for November 9. The parties should have liberty to apply to the Court if they were in trouble over difficulties arising out of any communication from the Secretary of State.

Solicitors: *Messrs. Courts & Co.; Messrs. Herbert Smith & Co.*

CARL ZEISS STIFTUNG v. RAYNER & KEELER LTD. AND OTHERS (No. 2)

([1965] Ch. 596)

November 9, 10, 11, 12, 13, 16, 17, 18, 19, 20, December17, 1964: Court of Appeal: Harman, Danckwerts, Diplock L.JJ.

International Law—Recognition—Effect—Action begun by English solicitors on behalf of East German organisation—Solicitors instructed by governing body of organisation—Governing body authorised by government not recognised by H.M. Government—Unrecognised government set up by de jure government—Whether governing body of organisation competent to institute proceedings.

In 1896 there was established at Jena, in the Grand Duchy of Saxe-Weimar-Eisenach, the Carl Zeiss Stiftung ("the foundation"), an organisation with industrial, scientific and charitable objects. Under the articles of its constitution (or "statute") the legal domicile of the foundation was to be Jena, and for representing it as an incorporate body, for the administration of its estate and effects, and for the supreme direction of its affairs, a "special board" was to be formed, the rights and duties of which were to pertain to that department of the State service of the Grand Duchy under which the affairs of the University of Jena were for the time being placed. In the case of the cessation of the special board in consequence of political changes in the State, the representation of the foundation, and its statutory administration, was to be made over to that department of state which, with regard to the university, occupied the place of the State Department of the Grand Duchy, providing that its seat was in Thuringia, otherwise to "the highest administrative authorities in Thuringia." In 1918 the Grand Duchy was abolished and Jena became part of the "Land" of Thuringia. In 1949 there was set up, in the Russian Zone of Germany, and recognised by the Union of Soviet Socialist Republics, the German Democratic Republic, and the court proceeded on the basis that the Land of Thuringia continued to exist until 1952, when, under a decree of the German Democratic Republic, it was divided into smaller areas, Jena being in the area of Gera, governed by the Rat or Council of Gera, which was itself set up by that decree.

In 1955, English solicitors, on the instructions of an individual authorised by the Rat of Gera as the special board of the foundation, issued a writ against the defendants, two English limited companies and an organisation with its headquarters in the Federal German Republic (West Germany) also calling itself Carl Zeiss Stiftung, to restrain them, inter alia, from passing off optical or glass instruments with reference to the name "Carl Zeiss Stiftung," or "Carl Zeiss," or "Zeiss." In 1956 the defendants took out a summons to stay all proceedings in the action and to have it dismissed on the ground that it had been begun and was being maintained without the authority of the foundation. On March 6, 1964, Cross J. dismissed the summons, holding that under the articles of the foundation the proper body to authorise on its behalf an action such as the present was its "special board," which was at the material time **[597]** the Rat of Gera. No point was taken before Cross J. as to whether Her Majesty's Government had recognised de jure or de facto the German Democratic Republic or its government, or as to the applicability in the English courts of East German legislation or decrees.

The defendants appealed, and moved the Court of Appeal asking that a letter be written to the Foreign Secretary requesting him to certify whether, inter alia, Her Majesty's Government had granted recognition de jure or de facto to the German Democratic Republic or to its government, and, if yes, when. The court, holding that recognition was a matter which the court of its own motion was bound to consider,[1] acceded to that request and the Foreign Secretary subsequently certified that: "Her Majesty's Government have not granted any recognition de jure or de facto to (a) the 'German Democratic Republic' or (b) its 'government.'" In answer to a further letter from the court[2] the Secretary of State certified, inter alia, that since June, 1945, and up to the present date "Her Majesty's Government have recognised the State and Government of the Union of Soviet Socialist Republics as de jure entitled to exercise governing authority in respect of [East Germany]."

On the defendants' contention that, the Rat of Gera having been set up by a decree of the unrecognised government of the German Democratic Republic, it could not be recognised by the English courts as being the special board of the foundation with authority to institute proceedings therein on its behalf:

Held, allowing the appeal, that the "proper law" to be applied in relation to both the construction and application of the constitution of the foundation in determining whether the action had been brought with proper authority was that in force at the place of its incorporation at the date when the instructions were given for the issue of the writ, but only in so far as such law had been made by persons recognised by the Crown as being, or as acting on behalf of, the sovereign government of that place (post, pp. 653, 656, 657, 658, 662); that it was not sufficient, either as a matter of law or on the facts of the present case, that such laws were recognised as valid by the de jure sovereign, since so to hold would mean that the Crown could never differ from another sovereign government in the matter of recognition of a third (post, pp. 615, 663, 664), nor could it be presumed that any law in fact acted upon and enforced in that place had been made by persons authorised by the de jure sovereign so to do (post, p. 663); that while the proper body to authorise the present action was, on the true construction of the articles of the foundation, in the first place the special board (post, pp. 647, 659), the Rat of Gera had been set up by, and owed its existence, its constitution, and whatever powers it possessed, to the unrecognised "government" of the "German Democratic Republic" (post pp. 651, 662, 664, 665); that, on the facts, that "government" could not be considered as having acted, either in that regard or at all, as the agent of the Government of the **[598]** Union of Soviet Socialist Republics (post, p. 651), and, accordingly, the Rat of Gera could not be recognised by the English courts as being competent to set the wheels of justice in motion as the special board of the foundation (post, pp. 653, 662, 665, 666); and that it was not sufficient to constitute the Rat of Gera the "highest administrative authorit[y]" in Thuringia that it should in fact be exercising control in the area, the question being, on a true construction of the articles, whether or not it was performing acts of government. That meant: "according to law" (post, pp. 652-663, 665, 666).

Per Diplock L.J. There was expert evidence of the "proper law" before Cross J. which enabled him to find that the special board, as opposed to the boards of management, was the proper body to bring these proceedings on

[1] *Carl Zeiss Stiftung* v. *Rayner & Keeler Ltd.**; ante, p. 525; [1964] 3 W.L.R. 905; [1964] 3 All E.R. 326, C.A.

[2] See *The Times*, October 30, 1964.

behalf of the foundation, and I see no grounds upon which his decision to that effect can be assailed (post, p. 659).

City of Berne v. *Bank of England** (1804) 9 Ves. 347; *Taylor* v. *Barclay** (1828) 2 Sim. 213; and *Luther* v. *Sagor** [1921] 1 K.B. 456; [1921] 3 K.B. 532; 37 T.L.R. 777, C.A. applied.

Kawasaki Kisen Kabushiki Kaisha v. *Bantham Steamship Co. Ltd.* (*No.* 2) [1939] 2 K.B. 544; and *Luigi Monta of Genoa* v. *Czechofract Co.** [1956] 2 Q.B. 552 distinguished.

Decision of Cross J. reversed on a different basis.

APPEAL from Cross J.

On October 20, 1955, a firm of English solicitors, Courts & Co., issued in the name of Carl Zeiss Stiftung ("Foundation"), of Carl Zeiss Platz 1, Jena, Eastern Germany, a writ in a passing-off action against three defendants, Rayner & Keeler Ltd. and Degenhardt & Co. Ltd., two apparently associated English limited companies with registered offices in London, W.1, and a third defendant with the same name as the proposed plaintiffs, Carl Zeiss [Stiftung], described as being of Heidenheim-Brenz, in the Western Zone of Germany (the Federal German Republic). The writ described the plaintiffs as "a corporation under the laws of the German Democratic Republic," and, as subsequently amended, sought, inter alia, "1. An injunction to restrain the defendants and each of them from advertising, offering for sale, or selling any optical instruments or any articles containing or consisting of glass under or by reference to the name 'Carl Zeiss' or any name containing 'Zeiss' . . . 2. An injunction to restrain the third defendants from using the name 'Carl Zeiss Stiftung' or 'Carl Zeiss' or any name containing 'Zeiss' in relation to their business or goods." The amended writ also changed the nomenclature of the third defendants by adding to the original "Carl Zeiss" the word "Stiftung."

The English solicitors had received their instructions for the [**599**] issue of that writ from one Dr. Hugo Schrade, as appeared from an affidavit sworn by Dr. Schrade on April 17, 1959. By that affidavit, he stated: "By an authority given in writing on September 30, 1955 . . . and acting in my capacities of mandatory of the stiftung and agent of the special board and member of and acting for the board of management of the optical works, I authorised and retained Messrs. Courts & Co. to act (inter alia) as solicitors on behalf of the stiftung in connection with this action. The said authority was given with the full concurrence and approval of the said special board of the stiftung and of the deputy of the stiftung. The members of the board of management of the optical works . . . have known of and approved all the actions I have taken in relation to these proceedings. There is shown to me . . . a resolution passed at a meeting of the stiftung on November 16, 1956, confirming my authority in connection with this action. It appears from . . . [that] resolution . . . that the commencement and carrying on of these proceedings has been ratified and approved by the deputy of the stiftung and by the boards of management of the optical and glass works. Although I am advised and verily believe that no such confirmation is necessary, nevertheless for the better resolution of any doubts which may arise in connection with the said authority I hereby acting in my above mentioned capacities, confirm the same and ratify all and any actions which the said Messrs. Courts & Co. may have taken in pursuance of its terms, including the institution of proceedings in the present action. There is now shown to me . . . a . . . copy of a letter to me dated November 22, 1956, from the chairman of the Council of the District of Gera confirming and ratifying all and any actions which I have taken in instructing Messrs. Courts & Co. to institute and continue the proceedings in the present action."

By their amended statement of claim, as redelivered on March 23, 1960, the plaintiffs stated that the foundation had been constituted in about 1896 in accordance with certain articles of constitution as drawn by one Dr. Ernst Abbé in or about August, 1896. Those articles had from time to time been amended (but not any material to the present proceedings). By article 3, the legal domicile of the foundation was Jena, in the Eastern Zone of Germany. In pursuance of the provisions of articles 113 and 5[3] the administration of the foundation and the appointment of a deputy had been transferred to a body called the Rat **[600]** ("council") of the District of Gera, in which district of Germany Jena was situated. The statement of claim went on to allege that for very many years and at all material times the name "Carl Zeiss" and any name including "Zeiss" had indicated, when used in relation to any business concerned in or in relation to any optical instruments or articles containing or consisting of glass, the business and goods of the foundation and none other or alternatively the business and goods of an organisation connected with the foundation. Further, for very many years and at all material times, the name "Carl Zeiss Stiftung" had indicated the foundation exclusively. The first two defendants were retailers of optical instruments but did not deal in the foundation's goods. The third defendants were a German organisation with its registered office at Heidenheim, which was in the Western Zone of Germany, and were competitors of the foundation. The third defendants had, without the foundation's consent, used the name "Carl Zeiss Stiftung" and "Carl Zeiss" in relation to their business and goods, and such use was calculated to lead, as the third defendants at all times knew and intended, to their business and goods being thought to be those of the foundation or an organisation associated with the foundation and to deception, confusion and passing off to the foundation's detriment. The third defendants intended to continue to trade under the name "Carl Zeiss Stiftung" and "Carl Zeiss" whereby the foundation would suffer damage.

In 1846 Carl Zeiss had founded optical works at Jena, a university town in the Grand Duchy of Saxe-Weimar-Eisenach. Later, a glassworks was founded at Jena, and when the foundation was constituted in 1896 the two businesses were transferred to it. In his judgment, Cross J. summarised the structure of the foundation as follows: "The basic principle was that the two businesses though owned by the foundation were to be run by two independent boards of management, and that the profits were to be paid to a third organ of the foundation called the 'special board' (Stiftungsverwaltung), which would then apply them for certain prescribed objects and was to be represented on the boards of management by an official called the 'deputy' (Stiftungskommissar). Articles embodying the constitution of the foundation were drawn up by Abbé and accepted by the authorities of the Grand Duchy, whose approval was necessary under German law."

Article 1 of the articles of constitution of the foundation (the "statute") laid down the objects of the foundation, which were **[601]** industrial, scientific and charitable. Article 2 provided that the name of the foundation should be for all time "Carl Zeiss Stiftung," in honour of its founder.

Article 4 reads, so far as material: *"Organisation of the stiftung.* For representing the Carl Zeiss Stiftung as an incorporate body, for the administration of its estate and effects and for the supreme direction of its affairs a 'special board' of the stiftung . . . shall be formed. For directing the industrial operations of the stiftung and the management of its various establishments there shall be instituted as further organisation of the stiftung along with the special board: 'boards of management' . . . of the various establishments of the stiftung for the time being; a permanent official, the 'deputy' of the stiftung . . . appointed to represent the special board on the boards of management; both of which, boards of management and the deputy, shall be nominated by the special board in conformity with the articles of this statute."

By article 5: "*Special board and deputy of the stiftung.* The rights and duties of the special board shall pertain to that department of the State service of the Grand Duchy of Saxe-Weimar under which the affairs of the University of Jena are, for the time being, placed. The office of permanent deputy to be appointed by the special board shall be held in an extra-official capacity by a higher official of the State service of the Grand Duchy of Saxe-Weimar or, failing such, an active higher official of the public service. . . ."

[3] See *post,* pp. 602, 601

Articles, inter alia, 6, 7, 8, 9, 10, 11, 16, 25, 26, 27, 28 and 29[4] provided for the constitution and functions of the boards of management.

By article 7: ". . . The number of members composing a board of management may not exceed four. As soon as this number is reduced to two . . . a new member must be co-opted within the interval of one month. . . ."

By article 9: "*Representing the stiftung externally.* In the matter of representing the stiftung in affairs of the individual firm there shall be either a certain member of the board of management appointed by the special board as 'mandatory of the Carl Zeiss Stiftung' . . . and a second member appointed as his proxy, and each of these two shall be absolutely empowered in his own person to sign for the firm, or . . . [the alternative is not relevant]." **[602]**

By article 27: ". . . The appointment to a membership of the boards of management cannot be effected with the option of revocation, but only either for a fixed period to be determined beforehand, for life or until the term the said member is entitled to a pension according to statute. . . ."

By article 28: "*Special duties of members of the boards of management. . . .* Outside the employment of the stiftung they are not to hold any salaried employment. . . ."

By article 113: "*Representation of the stiftung in case of cessation of present special board.* Should, in consequence of political changes in the State, the provision according to 5 of this statute with reference to the representation of the stiftung become untenable, this representation including the appointment of the deputy of the stiftung within the meaning of 5 and the statutory administration of the Carl Zeiss Stiftung shall be made over to that department of State, which with regard to the University of Jena occupies the place of the State Department of the Grand Duchy of Saxe-Weimar acting as the special board, providing that its seat is in Thuringia, otherwise to the highest administrative authorities in Thuringia."

By article 114: "*Procedure until new formation of the special board.* Should at any time a special board corresponding to the provisions of 5 or 113 no longer exist, then until the new formation of such the representation and administration of the Carl Zeiss Stiftung is to be taken over forthwith by the executive board of management of the optical works and in the event of the latter board of management no longer existing, by the board of management of the oldest works of the stiftung in Jena or its neighbourhood. . . ."

By article 121: "The provisions of the four [articles] 1 to 4 and the four preceding ones above (117 to 120 [which concern alterations in the statute]) can, under no circumstances and in no manner, be legally amended or rendered inoperative."

In 1918, the Grand Duchy of Saxe-Weimar-Eisenach was abolished and Jena became part of the Land of Thuringia. In 1923, a Code of Thuringian Law was promulgated, whereupon the Minister of Education of the Land became the special board of the foundation. In 1945 Jena and its neighbourhood was occupied by United States forces, who set up a provisional government of Thuringia. At the end of June, 1945, the United States forces evacuated the area, and Russian forces entered it. In 1949, there was set up in the Russian Zone of Germany the German Democratic Republic. The court proceeded on the basis **[603]** that the Land of Thuringia continued to exist until 1952, when, under a decree of the German Democratic Republic, it was divided into smaller areas, Jena being in the area of Gera, governed by its "Rat" (council), which was itself set up as a result of that decree. The appointment of Dr. Schrade as (deputy) mandatory of the foundation under rule 4 of the articles was made by the Rat. By a document signed by the "Minister of Education" "by proxy," dated June 29, 1951, the management of Carl Zeiss Stiftung at [Jena] conferred on the deputy mandatory, Dr. Schrade, a "power of attorney" on behalf of the Carl Zeiss Stiftung at [Jena] to, inter alia, undertake all legal transactions both in and out of court and to represent the Carl Zeiss Stiftung in law suits.

[4] For articles, or rules 6-11, 16 and 27-9, see the judgments of Harman L.J. (*post*, pp. 640, 641) and Diplock L.J. (*post*, p. 667).

By summons dated February 7, 1956, the defendants applied for "an order that all further proceedings in this action be stayed and that this be dismissed on the ground that the same was commenced and is being maintained without the authority of the foundation and that Messrs. Courts & Co., the solicitors purporting to act for the foundation herein do pay to the defendants the costs of this action including the costs of this application to be taxed as between solicitors and client."

After a hearing occupying 24 days in all, in November and December, 1963, and January, 1964, Cross J. delivered a reserved judgment dismissing the summons on March 6, 1964. After considering the constitution and history of the foundation, and certain other actions which the parties had fought in East and West Germany, he said: "It appears from paragraphs 19 to 21 of Dr. Schrade's first affidavit and the documents exhibited thereto that Messrs. Courts had and have authority to start and prosecute this action from (1) the Council of Gera purporting to act as the special board, (2) from Schrade purporting to act as mandatory, and (3) from Schrade, Huber and Müller purporting to act as the board of management of the optical business. The question at issue is whether all or any of those persons was entitled to give such instructions on behalf of the plaintiff." Subsequently, he held that the Council of Gera, which had instructed the plaintiffs' solicitors, was the special board of the foundation and as such entitled to represent the foundation in any litigation brought to protect business property vested in it. Other extracts from the judgment of Cross J. may be found in the report of the hearing before the Court of Appeal on July 27, 1964.[5] **[604]**

No point was taken before Cross J. that the Government of the German Democratic Republic, by the decree of which the Council of Gera had been set up, had not been recognised by Her Majesty's Government, each side expressly stating that for the purpose of the summons it proposed to regard the courts and legislature of the other side as legally effective.

The defendants appealed against Cross J.'s decision. By their original notice of appeal, dated May 5, 1964, they stated their grounds of appeal, inter alia, as follows: "1. That the persons and bodies . . . who have given instructions to Messrs. Courts & Co. in connection with this action have at no material time in fact had power to give on behalf of the [foundation] instructions to bring this action." The other grounds stated in that notice were concerned with attacking the judgment of Cross J. in the context of the basis on which he had reached it, i.e., no point as to recognition having been taken, and not relevant to this report. On July 27, 1964, the defendants applied by motion to the Court of Appeal asking that a letter be written on behalf of the court to Her Majesty's Principal Secretary of State for Foreign Affairs requesting him to certify the answers to certain questions, including the question whether Her Majesty's Government had recognised de jure or de facto the Government of the German Democratic Republic. The Court of Appeal[6] held that the court itself should take judicial notice of whether Her Majesty's Government recognised the German Democratic Republic or its government and ought not to proceed to judgment on the basis of the validity of foreign laws, which might be a false hypothesis, and a letter was accordingly written to the Secretary of State asking him to certify his answer to that one question, and, by letter dated September 16, 1964, he certified as follows: "Her Majesty's Government have not granted any recognition de jure or de facto to (a) the 'German Democratic Republic' or (b) 'its Government'."

By their amended statement of claim, as redelivered on March 23, 1960, the gave notice that they would rely upon, inter alia, the following grounds of appeal in addition to those contained in their original notice: "1. That Cross J. erred in recognising the existence of the Council of Gera, which was established by a law of the German Democratic Republic, and/or is an organ thereof, notwithstanding that Her Majesty's Government do not recognise the German Democratic Republic as a state or its authorities as a government. 2. That Cross J. erred in

[5] [1965] 1 Ch. 525, 529-537. [6] [1965] 1 Ch. 525.

paying **[605]** attention to decisions of courts which were established by a law of the German Democratic Republic and/or were organs thereof, notwithstanding that Her Majesty's Government do not recognise the German Democratic Republic as a state or its authorities as a government. 3. That in any event the Council of Gera was at no material time either the supreme administrative authority within Thuringia nor had it any authority in respect of the University of Jena." The remainder of the supplemental notice of appeal is not material to this report.

By notice of motion dated September 25, 1964, the plaintiffs applied to the Court of Appeal for further directions. That summons came on for hearing on October 2, 1964,[7] and was adjourned to enable the plaintiffs to frame further questions for the consideration of the court to be directed to the Secretary of State. The adjourned summons was heard on October 29, 1964,[8] a further notice of motion being dated October 22, and as a result two further questions were permitted to be directed to the Secretary of State. The Secretary of State, on November 6, 1964, certified his answers to those questions as follows: "Since [June, 1945] and up to the present date Her Majesty's Government have recognised the State and Government of the Union of Soviet Socialist Republics as de jure entitled to exercise governing authority in respect of [East Germany]. In matters affecting Germany as a whole, the States and Governments of the French Republic, the United Kingdom of Great Britain and Northern Ireland, the United States of America and the Union of Soviet Socialist Republics were jointly entitled to exercise governing authority. . . . In the period from August 30, 1945, to March 20, 1948, they did exercise such joint authority through the Control Council for Germany. Apart from the States, Governments and Control Council aforementioned, Her Majesty's Government have not recognised de jure or de facto any other authority purporting to exercise governing authority in or in respect of that zone."

By a respondents' notice dated November 3, 1964, the plaintiffs gave notice that they might, on the hearing of the appeal, wish to contend "that the decision of Cross J. should be affirmed on the ground that the commencement of the proceedings had been authorised by the boards of management of the [foundation]." In the course of the hearing of the appeal the plaintiffs sought, and obtained, leave to amend that notice by adding the following: "or either of them, or further or alternatively **[606]** by the [foundation] acting by Dr. Hugo Schrade under a power of attorney granted on June 29, 1951, by the Minister of Education of Thuringia as the special board of the plaintiffs."

The facts are more fully stated in the judgments.

Mark Littman Q.C., *T. M. Shelford* and *P. Lewis* for the defendants. The defendants make four submissions: (a) ("The recognition argument") The Council of Gera cannot in English law be regarded as the special board of the foundation, because it is a body which came into existence by virtue of an alleged law of the German Democratic Republic, a government or state not recognised by Her Majesty's Government, either de facto or de jure. In the eyes of English law, the Government of the German Democratic Republic does not exist as a sovereign government, and its laws are nullities. If this submission is correct, it is conclusive in the defendants' favour. (b) Under the Soviet military decree of April 17, 1948 (SMAD 64), all the assets of each of the two foundation businesses were confiscated by the Russian Government, being vested first in a state body called a V.V.B., and subsequently in an organisation called a V.E.B. The effect of this upon the foundation is a matter of German law, and was to deprive the organs of the foundation of the capacity to act. The foundation businesses, and their continuance in the ownership of the foundation, were the whole point of the foundation: see the judgment of the Federal Supreme Court of November 15, 1960. To say that after they had been taken away from it the foundation, or some other organs of it, could continue to function simply as a property-owning entity as distinct from an industrial entity is incompatible with the whole structure of the articles and the whole purpose of the

[7] *The Times*, October 3, 1964. [8] *The Times*, October 30, 1964.

foundation. The effect of the confiscation of the assets would be to render any such organ incapable of acting. (c) The best evidence of this is the judgment of the Federal Supreme Court on November 15, 1960, in an action by the plaintiffs against the third defendants. It is submitted that this issue is res judicata, at all events as regards the third defendants.

[HARMAN L.J. But there is no such thing as German law, is there?]

Yes, there is. The State of Germany, which was created in 1871, has continued to exist in the eyes of Her Majesty's Government ever since. It was not destroyed at the end of the last war. Her Majesty's Government recognises the German Federal Republic as having jurisdiction in all but the Eastern Zone. In **[607]** respect of the Eastern Zone, Her Majesty's Government have never recognised the German Democratic Republic or its government, but continue to recognise the Soviet Union as the government responsible for that zone in accordance with the agreements made in 1945.

(d) The decree of confiscation of April 17, 1948, was penal, confiscatory, and political in character. As a matter of English law, the English courts would not permit effect to be given in this country to a law of that character, either directly or indircetly. This action is, in effect, although brought in the name of the foundation, brought upon the instructions of officials of an organ of the German Democratic Republic (the Council of Gera), and is brought for the purpose of getting into the hands of the East German State the benefit of an English asset, i.e. the English goodwill in the name "Zeiss," for the benefit of another organ of the East German State, the V.E.Bs. That raises questions of law as to the principles underlying such cases as *Frankfurther* v. *Exner* (*W.L.*) *Ltd.*[9]* The courts will not give effect to the confiscatory laws of a foreign state.

There are three questions with which the court will not be troubled, namely, (1) whether the members of the boards of management who left Jena and went to the West did or did not resign; (2) the validity of the two decrees of Bad Wurttemberg, the first varying the statute of the foundation so as to give it a second domicile at Heidenheim, the second making Heidenheim the sole domicile; (3) the question of the existence of the foundation as a corporate body.

[Counsel then outlined the facts and referred to *Banco de Bilbao* v. *Sancha*[10]* and *Rex* v. *Bottrill, Ex parte Kuechenmeister*,[11]* to the judgment of Cross J., and to the answers of the Secretary of State for Foreign Affairs to the court's questions.]

The following submissions are made on the recognition point: (1) The court will take judicial notice of, inter alia, the political and legal existence of states and governments. In case of doubt, the court seeks information from the Foreign Secretary. (2) It is the duty of the court to avoid any decision which is in conflict with the views of the executive as expressed by the Foreign Secretary. (3) If an alleged foreign government is not recognised by Her Majesty's Government either de jure or de facto, it cannot sue in these courts either by itself or by its agents; **[608]** its laws are nullities, and its courts not recognised as such. (4) In the present case, the Council of Gera purports to have been created by a law of the German Democratic Republic. Since the German Democratic Republic is not recognised by Her Majesty's Government, its laws are not recognised in the English courts and will be treated as nullities. To recognise the Council of Gera or the special board of the foundation would involve recognising the sovereign and law-making power of the German Democratic Republic. Not only would recognition of the Council of Gera as the special board involve recognising it as an organ of government—since the articles relied on contemplate that the special board will be a department of state or the highest administrative authority of Thuringia—but the Council of Gera can *only* be the special board under the articles if it is an organ of government. (5) To treat the Council of Gera as an existing body capable of retaining solicitors to institute proceedings in these courts would conflict with the view

[9] [1947] Ch. 629.
[10] [1938] 2 K.B. 176; 54 T.L.R. 603; [1938] 2 All E.R. 253, C.A.
[11] [1947] K.B. 41; 62 T.L.R. 570; [1956] 2 All E.R. 434, C.A.

of Her Majesty's Government. If neither the German Democratic Republic nor the Council of Gera can sue, they cannot authorise a solicitor to issue a writ in the name of the foundation. The court is concerned with this one matter only, namely, whether this action is properly authorised.

[Reference was made to Dicey on Conflict of Laws, 7th ed. (1957), p. 663, r. 130; Oppenheim's International Law, Vol. I, Peace, 8th ed. (1955), p. 765, para. 357A; Lauterpacht's Recognition in International Law (1947), pp. 44, 145; British Year Book of International Law (1931); Court of Chancery and Recognition 1804-1841, Bushe-Fox, p. 63; *City of Berne* v. *Bank of England*[12]*; *Taylor* v. *Barclay*[13]*; *Foster* v. *Globe Venture Syndicate Ltd.*[14]*; *The Gagara*[15]*; *Peru Republic* v. *Dreyfus Brothers & Co.* [16]*] Authority for the proposition that the laws of the unrecognised state have no effect in England is *Luther* v. *Sagor.*[17]* The question whether the decrees of July 23 and 24, 1952, creating the Council of Gera are valid legislative acts which can be recognised by the courts of this country must depend on whether the power from which they purport to emanate is a sovereign power, and that depends on whether the German Democratic Republic is a sovereign power. [Reference was made to *Gelston* v. *Hoyt.*[18]] **[609]**

Thompson v. *Barclay*[19]* has to some extent been overtaken by subsequent cases, but it was much more extreme than the present one, and was dealing with circumstances which were more far-reaching. The question whether an action would lie on a loan for the purpose of supplying funds to an unrecognised foreign government was answered in the negative. The case is really one strand in the authorities leading to the decision of Roche J. in *Luther* v. *Sagor*[20]* that it is for the executive to say whether or not this country recognises a foreign state or government, and that if we do not, then any decrees or laws which it purports to make are not valid or recognised, nor can its agents sue or be sued in the courts of this country.

The present case involves the validity of the actual legislative decree of a foreign government, and, on the existing authorities, there can be no doubt that English courts do not recognise the purported legislative acts of an unrecognised foreign government as having any legal effect in the English courts. The other aspect of this line of authorities is that an unrecognised foreign government cannot come as a plaintiff to these courts and sue, because it just does not exist: *City of Berne* v. *Bank of England.*[21]* [Reference was made to *The Arantzazu Mendi*[22]*; *Gdynia Ameryka Linie* v. *Boguslawski*[23]*; *Banco de Bilbao* v. *Sancha.*[24]*

The decrees creating the Council of Gera should be looked at in the light of the words of Roche J. in *Luther* v. *Sagor.*[25]* The power from which those decrees emanate is the German Democratic Republic. The question whether they can be recognised as valid legislative acts depends upon whether they are the acts of a recognised sovereign power, and on that the first certificate of the Foreign Office is conclusive. No legislative authority has ever purported to say who the special board is, although the plaintiffs contend that it is the highest administrative authority in Thuringia, which they say is the Council of Gera. The defendants say that the Council of Gera is not the highest administrative authority because in the eyes of English law it does not exist, but they prefer

[12] (1804) 9 Ves. 347.
[13] (1828) 2 Sim. 213.
[14] [1900] 1 Ch. 811.
[15] [1919] P. 95; 35 T.L.R. 259, C.A.
[16] (1888) 38 Ch.D. 348; 4 T.L.R. 333.
[17] [1921] 1 K.B. 456, 473; [1921] 3 K.B. 532; 37 T.L.R. 777, C.A.
[18] (1818) 3 Wheat. 246, 324.
[19] (1828) 6 L.J.O.S.Ch. 93; (1831) 9 L.J.O.S.Ch. 215, L.C.
[20] [1921] 1 K.B. 456.
[21] 9 Ves. 347.
[22] [1939] A.C. 256; [1939] 1 All E.R. 719; sub nom. *Spanish Republic Government* v. *Arantzazu Mendi*, 55 T.L.R. 454, H.L.(E.).
[23] [1953] A.C. 11; [1952] 2 T.L.R. 317; [1952] 2 All E.R. 470, H.L.
[24] [1938] 2 K.B. 176.
[25] [1921] 1 K.B. 456, 474.

not to embark upon any positive statement as to who is that authority.

[HARMAN L.J. Do you say they do not exist?]

They do not exist *as a council,* because they claim to exist **[610]** as a council by virtue of a decree which is invalid and a nullity under English law.

That concludes the argument for the appellants on point (a).

[HARMAN L.J. asked the respondents to deal with point (a).]

Guy Aldous Q.C., E. Lauterpacht and *D. W. Falconer* for the plaintiffs. From the end of June, 1945, Her Majesty's Government have recognised the U.S.S.R. as the de jure sovereign power, the only law-making and law-enforcing power, in East Germany, and have recognised no other power either de facto or de jure in that area. When the German Democratic Republic was set up with authority over the whole of East Germany, Her Majesty's Government could either have recognised it as an independent sovereign state or as another governing body of the U.S.S.R., and it was the latter course which they took. It is plain from the second certificate of the Foreign Office that they do not regard any independent authority in East Germany as being an independent de facto or de jure governing authority. The German Democratic Republic does not exercise a governing authority, but is merely an organ of the U.S.S.R. It maintains that it is a sovereign power, but English courts have to look at the matter through the eyes of Her Majesty's Government, who say that the U.S.S.R. is the sole authority in East Germany. Anything which is not obviously unlawful (such as an act of piracy), and which is regarded in East Germany as lawful, should be assumed by these courts as having been done under the aegis of the U.S.S.R. The doctrine of omnia praesumuntur applies. The Foreign Office certificate, however, goes further than this, because by saying that Her Majesty's Government do not recognise de jure or de facto any other authority, it indicates that any "lawful law," or regulation, or rule, which has the effect of controlling other people's acts and has the sanction of the German Democratic Republic must be presumed to have been enacted by or on behalf of the U.S.S.R.

Secondly, the certificates indicate that Her Majesty's Government regard the German Democratic Republic as agents of the U.S.S.R. through whom the U.S.S.R. are governing East Germany. That was common ground below. The opposite view, namely, that all the laws and regulations which have been made in East Germany are regarded as having no effect, is so ridiculous that it is not a view which Her Majesty's Government would take. It cannot be that companies which have been brought into existence under the laws of the German Democratic Republic are to be said not to exist, or that no one can sue or be sued in **[611]** respect of the large trade carried on between this country and East Germany. Such a view would compel the courts to say that, since the formation of the German Democratic Republic, there are no administrative councils, corporations, etc., in East Germany, resulting in a practical vacuum. The plaintiffs submit that the view of Her Majesty's Government is that the law-making power in East Germany is the U.S.S.R., and that the German Democratic Republic is not to be regarded as a sovereign power, but as one of the organs of the U.S.S.R. through which it continues to govern.

Another way of looking at the matter is to consider the validity of the laws of East Germany as seen through the eyes of the de jure sovereign power, the U.S.S.R.; they, no doubt, regard them as valid. If the court accepts the plaintiffs' submissions as to the meaning of the Foreign Office certificates, there is no need to proceed further, but if not, they put their case in four ways:

(1) (a) The defendants put their case below on the footing that all the material laws promulgated in East Germany were valid, and that a certificate from the Foreign Office was unnecessary because there was only one law-making and law-enforcing authority in East Germany (care being taken not to name it). The sovereign power was either the U.S.S.R. acting through the German Democratic Republic or the German Democratic Republic acting independently. The defendants implicitly abandoned any contention that the laws were invalid if the U.S.S.R. was the sovereign authority, and they accepted that the laws, including those setting up the Council of Gera, were valid whoever their author.

[HARMAN L.J. You say that the defendants cannot be heard in this court to impeach the East German laws on which they relied below?]

The defendants cannot resile from the case they put below except in so far as it is inconsistent with the Foreign Office certificates. The certificates mean what they say, but they cannot be construed in a way which produces nonsensical results.

(1) (b) The rule is well established that, where a person wishes to raise a new point on appeal, he may do so only if the court is satisfied beyond doubt that it has before it all the facts bearing on the new contention as completely as would have been the case if the point had arisen at the trial: *The Tasmania*,[26] *per* Lord **[612]** Herschell.[27] Had this matter been raised below, there might have been evidence of the views of the Soviet Government, because their views would appear to be conclusive as to the validity of the laws in the area in which they are recognised as the de jure power. It is only in so far as the certificates impel the court to any conclusion that they should go contrary to the position in the court below. Since the defendants abandoned the point below, and thus relieved the plaintiffs from giving evidence on it, the court should assume that there would have been evidence available which would have been in the plaintiffs' favour—or, in other words, the plaintiffs should be allowed to rely on the defendants' admissions below to fill any gaps in the evidence, though not to contradict the contents of the Foreign Office certificates. The plaintiffs do not need to produce any new evidence, but if new evidence were required, then they would ask for an adjournment.

(2) The defendants cannot discharge the onus of proving that the Council of Gera does not derive authority ultimately from the Soviet. To do that, they have to prove that the law which they put in evidence is invalid, and that, in view of the evidence, their admissions, and their conduct below, they cannot do. The Foreign Office certificates do not prove that the law is invalid. If the court accepts that, in so far as evidence is required to bridge any points in the Foreign Office certificates, the defendants cannot resile from the position which they adopted below, then no further evidence could better the plaintiffs' position. The plaintiffs would want to be in the position of putting in further evidence only if the court said that the defendants were entitled to resile from their position further than the Foreign Office certificates warrant. If a further question were to be put to the Foreign Office, it should be: "Do you consider that the U.S.S.R. is responsible for the conduct of affairs in East Germany, including the laws passed or applied there since 1945?"

(3) The question "Who is the special board under article 113?" has to be decided according to the law subsisting at Jena. That involves ascertaining the *factual* position in the material geographical area without reference to what Her Majesty's Government or any other government might recognise as the sovereign authority in East Germany. In construing a commercial document it is irrelevant what the Foreign Office recognises as a government; what matters is what the parties to **[613]** the document meant by government: *Luigi Monta of Genoa* v. *Czechofracht Co.*[28]* When Abbé drew up the constitution of the foundation, he did not contemplate that the question "Who is the special board?" would be considered through the eyes of a foreign government; the question is a factual one to be decided by the position on the spot. "The highest administrative authorit[y] in Thuringia" in article 113 means the highest administrative authority in that geographical area. It was common ground below that, if one looked to the factual position, the Council of Gera was the highest administrative authority in Thuringia.

(4) The general principle of law (there being one exception to it) is that if in order to prove one's case one has to plead the existence of a foreign government which Her Majesty's Government does not recognise as existing, then one's action or defence fails. Anything in the authorities which appears to go further is mere dictum. The existence of a foreign law is proved by evidence which will, usually, be of an enactment of a government, but there is no reason

[26] (1890) 15 App. Cas. 223, H.L.
[27] 15 App. Cas. 223, 225.
[28] [1956] 2 Q.B. 552.

why it cannot be proved without alleging or proving a sovereign authority. The plaintiffs can prove as a fact that the law appointing the Court of Gera exists, and the court does not need to inquire which sovereign power is responsible for that decree. The fact that it is a law which exists in that area is sufficient. Both parties below accepted that, if Her Majesty's Government did not accept the German Democratic Republic as the law-making power, the laws would be valid as stemming from the U.S.S.R.

[*Littman Q.C.* The defendants took no point below on recognition, but beyond that they are unaware of having made any admission, including any admission, that the German Democratic Republic were agents of the Russian Government. The Court of Appeal has decided that, whatever the position below, recognition is a matter of public policy, and that the case could not be allowed to continue on assumption. They held that the questions should be decided, and it is on that basis that the defendants have prepared their case.]

[The court upheld Mr. Littman's submission.]

Aldous Q.C. continuing. One can prove the law of a foreign country as a fact without having to prove that it was made by a sovereign power. Alternatively, the general principle of law as found in the authorities does not apply to exceptional cases **[614]** such as the present in which non-recognition is based on grounds other than that the unrecognised government is not in control.

The law to be applied in construing the articles of the foundation is that which would be applied by the local courts at Jena, as at the date of the writ, to ascertain Abbé's intention at the time when he drew up the statute. In construing article 113 so as to ascertain, according to the appropriate law, who "the highest administrative authority" is, one has to put oneself in the position of the local court as at the date of the writ, and that court would be the hypothetical Russian court because Russia is the sovereign power.

[DIPLOCK L.J. The statute did not envisage any court at all. You have to ask: "How would a German lawyer, applying the law which was in operation on October 7, 1949 (because that is the date up to which we recognise the laws) answer the question of construction?" The relevant question on construction is: "Does the expression 'highest administrative authority in Thuringia' in article 113 include a body of persons who, de facto, but without any legal right, exercise authority there?"]

[HARMAN L.J. It is really a question of construction. Do you look at the people who are in fact running the university?]

Yes, or, if not running the University, in charge of the sewers, so to speak. That is the plaintiffs' primary submission on the question of construction.

[HARMAN L.J. You say that the article means that the administration of the foundation is to be handed over to whomever has the power to administer. That seems to me quite an intelligible view of article 113. It has nothing to do with the courts of law.]

To go even further, if one is to consider what the factual position is, one may even be bound by the fact that all the courts of East Germany affirm that the Council of Gera is the special board.

The plaintiffs' case is this: (1) Where there is only one government in an area, and that government says that a law is valid in its area, that is conclusive as to the validity of the law. (2) There is only one government in East Germany, namely, the Russian Government (the occupying power). (3) There are laws made in East Germany which the Russian Government recognises as valid. (4) Therefore, such laws are valid. Further, the defendants cannot prove that they are invalid—the onus being on them. Where a party seeks to **[615]** challenge authority for the commencement of an action, the onus lies upon that person: *Russian Commercial and Industrial Bank* v. *Comptoir d'Escompte de Mulhouse*.[29]* It is for the defendants to prove their case. Although one can discharge an onus sufficiently to shift it, even if the defendants were to produce documents appearing to emanate from either the province of Thuringia or the

[29] [1925] A.C. 112, 119, 128, 141, 144, 145, H.L.(E.).

German Democratic Republic, that would not establish that the law or decree in question was not made on behalf of the government in control, namely, the U.S.S.R.

Turning to point (3), that of the proper construction of article 113, it is plain from the constitution of the foundation that Abbé contemplated the possibility of political change. His general purpose was ultimately to benefit the work-people of Jena by maintaining the business so that the profit would go to the people of Jena. "Department of state," in the context of article 113, means something like a municipal department—as opposed to a private body—rather than a department of a sovereign power. "Highest administrative authority" means legal authority, not an authority of usurpers. As a matter of construction of the articles, the views of Her Majesty's Government cannot be relevant since the relevant law is that of Jena. The laws to be applied are the laws of the lex loci contractus: *Banco de Bilbao* v. *Sancha*,[30]* i.e., the laws from time to time prevailing at Jena, and the government responsible for those laws is, according to the Foreign Office, the Russian Government. [Reference was made to *Kawasaki Kisen Kabushiki Kaisha* v. *Bantham Steamship Co. Ltd. (No.* 2)[31]*; *Luigi Monta of Genoa* v. *Czechofracht Co.*[32]*; *Stafford Allen & Sons Ltd.* v. *Pacific Steam Navigation Co.*[33]*] To construe article 113 so that the identity of the special board would vary according to the views from time to time of Her Majesty's Government would be to make nonsense of it. One should not tend towards construing any document in a way which would reduce a plaintiff company to perpetual immobility so as to be unable to contract its property in a country where it owns that property: *A. G. Der Manufacturen I. A. Woronin Leutschig and Cheshire* v. *Frederick Huth & Co.* (*Cheshire* v. *Huth*)[34]*.

Point (4) is divided into two parts, (i) one can prove a law aliunde; (ii) see *M. Salimoff & Co.* v. *Standard Oil Co.*,[35] supported **[616]** by Dr. Lipstein's paper to the Grotius Society,[36] in which his tenth conclusion is: "The regulations of foreign authorities which have not been recognised may be applied as the law of the foreign country if they are in fact enforced in that country, notwithstanding that the authorities have not been recognised by Great Britain."

Littman Q.C. in reply. As a matter of construction of the articles of the foundation, the founder contemplated a *lawful* authority. It is to be emphasised, however, that, whatever the construction of the articles, the present application is to stay these proceedings on the ground that they are brought without authority, and the defendants, on whom (it can be assumed) the onus rests in the first instance, say that, under the articles, the special board has to authorise proceedings, and that the last special board recognised by these courts would have been the Ministry of Education of the Provincial Government of Thuringia established by the Russians. The plaintiffs say that there is a later body which is the special board, namely, the Council of Gera. All that the defendants seek to do in answer is to show that that is not the case. In those circumstances, all the evidence being before the court, the question of onus does not arise. The court has to decide on the evidence before it whether the Council of Gera is the special board of the foundation and entitled to instruct solicitors to bring this action in the name of the foundation. In deciding that, the court is faced, quite apart from the question of construction, with the fact that the Council of Gera, if it exists at all, exists by virtue of a law of the German Democratic Republic. If that law is a law which cannot be treated by these courts as having legal effect, the Council of Gera does not exist in the eyes of English law. In none of the cases which have been cited was the (English) court required to give legal effect to a law of an unrecognised government. In saying that the

30 [1938] 2 K.B. 176, 195.
31 [1939] 2 K.B. 544; 55 T.L.R. 503; [1939] 1 All E.R. 819.
32 [1956] 2 Q.B. 552, 563 et seq.
33 [1956] 1 W.L.R. 629, 630, 631 et seq.; [1956] 2 All E.R. 716, C.A.
34 79 Ll.L.R. 262n., 269.
35 (1933) 262 N.Y.S. 693.
36 *Transactions of the Grotius Society*, 1949, Vol. 35 (1950), p. 157.

Council of Gera does not exist, it is not meant that the *individuals* do not exist, but that the *body* created by the unrecognised law of July, 1952, does not exist. The court cannot recognise the Council of Gera as having had authority to authorise this action without deciding that the law of 1952 is valid in these courts.

Non-recognition of the German Democratic Republic may lead to inconvenience, but that arises only where the laws of the foreign country come into question in these courts. It is true that people who deal with corporations which have been created by the laws of a state not recognised by Her Majesty's **[617]** Government may be taking a risk which they do not take when they deal with corporations created by recognised states, but those inconveniences have to be balanced against the inconveniences which may flow from the recognition of that foreign state. The Foreign Office certificates make it clear that Her Majesty's Government does not recognise the German Democratic Republic either as a sovereign government or as an authority exercising powers of sovereignty on behalf of the Soviet Union. If the plaintiffs can show that the decree on which they rely is a decree of the Soviet Union, then, certainly, it could derive its authority therefrom. The court has to ask itself the question which Roche J. posed in *Luther* v. *Sagor*,[37]* namely: "Whether the decree in question is a valid legislative act which can be recognised as such by the courts this country" which "must, in my judgment, depend upon whether the power from which it purports to emanate is what it apparently claims to be, a sovereign power."

The decree of July 23, 1952, creating the Council of Gera purports to emanate from the German Democratic Republic, and the Foreign Office have said that the German Democratic Republic is not a sovereign state. Other decrees to which the attention of the court has been drawn, such as those of confiscation, were decrees of the Soviet Military Administration and different considerations therefore apply. It is accepted that the U.S.S.R. could delegate some of its governing powers to a local body, but they could not transfer sovereignty in such a way as to make the transfer effective in these courts. The answer to the plaintiffs' point, (1) (a), that the point as to the validity of East German legislation was implicitly abandoned below, is that the position which prevailed below was inconsistent with the Foreign Office certificate which has now been obtained.

The plaintiffs' point (1) (b), that one cannot raise a new case unless all the relevant facts are before the court, ended by their being asked whether they wanted an adjournment, and they have not asked for one.

On the plaintiffs' point (2), on onus, it is conceded that this is at first on the defendants, but then, adopting the approach of Roche J. in *Luther* v. *Sagor*,[38]* one looks at the terms of the decree, and when one finds that it purports by its terms to emanate from one government, it is for anyone who wishes to say that it has been made by that government not as a sovereign power, but in some delegated capacity on behalf of another **[618]** sovereign or some other body, to prove it—and in the present case there is no evidence to that effect.

On the plaintiffs' point (3), it is agreed that the question of construction of a statute is a matter of the proper law of the statute, which in this case is the law of Germany. There is some evidence that, in Germany, one can look at the writings of the maker of the document to see what his intentions were. The document has to be looked at as at the time of its promulgation. One must, however, be careful not to confuse the *meaning* of the document with its *application*.

Dealing first with the question of construction: Abbé contemplated that, in the first instance, the special board would be a department of the state service. It is not material to consider whether that state service was an independent sovereign body or not. The important thing is that it was a department of the public service. Abbé was clearly contemplating, throughout the statute, a public body, lawfully constituted, and exercising lawful authority, not some private

[37] [1921] 1 K.B. 456, 473.

[38] *Ibid.*

body, not even some invading body. Article 113 could never have contemplated any unlawful authority. "Highest authorit[y] in Thuringia" means persons who are entitled to authority—not only somebody who does something, but somebody who has a lawful right to do it. It means a lawful legal authority, and a department of the public service. It may not be the central government itself, but it has to derive authority directly or indirectly from the sovereign power.

[HARMAN L.J. Supposing this body is governing with the approval of the de jure government?]

That would be asking the court to treat the question who is the sovereign government of the country to be decided not only by Her Majesty's Government but by the Soviet Union.

In considering the meaning of the articles of the foundation, the courts of this country, will treat the relevant law as being that which prevailed at Jena. That law is, so far as we know, the same as it would be in England.

Having construed the article referring to lawful authority, one has to decide who is the lawful authority governing this area. That has to be decided, in these courts, by reference to what Her Majesty's Government regards as being the authority entitled to govern there. "Lawful authority" means either that body or a body deriving its authority from that body. When *construing* the documents, one does not consider the views of Her Majesty's Government, but when seeking to *apply* that construction to the facts by ascertaining who is the lawful government of the area **[619]** in question, one is constrained by the authorities to conclude that this has to be a government which Her Majesty's Government recognises, and no other. The identity of the lawful government is a matter of English public policy, in respect of which the courts of this country have always treated themselves as bound by the views of Her Majesty's Government as expressed through the Foreign Secretary. On this point, *Luigi Monta of Genoa Ltd.* v. *Czechofracht Ltd.*[39]* should be distinguished on its facts: there, the parties were not in any sense concerned with public international law. Further, whatever may have been the proper construction of the charterparty in *White, Child & Beney Ltd.* v. *Eagle Star and British Dominions Insurance Co.* (*White* v. *Simmons*),[40]* on a proper construction of the statute of the foundation "highest administrative authority" does not signify persons simply exercising power but means persons who exercise power derived from the order of a lawful government.

Even if, as a matter of construction, the words "department of state" or "highest administrative authority" are capable of extending to an unlawful or unrecognised government, they still only apply to a government or organ of government of some kind, i.e., only to a public body exercising public functions as distinct from, for example, mere private individuals, or bandits. The Council of Gera cannot be shown to exist as an organ of government or public body except by reference to the three decrees of the German Democratic Republic which have been relied upon in this court by the plaintiffs as constituting, or creating, its pedigree or authority. This contention does not conflict with the decision of Sellers J. in *Luigi Monta*.[41]* The point did not arise in that case, because it was not there necessary for the shipowners to rely upon any law of the unrecognised government as a law valid in these courts. The question was not whether there had been a *law* of a government but whether there had been an *act*—"orders or directions"—of a government. In the present case, the plaintiffs have to show that the decrees constituting the Council of Gera are effective in the English courts as a matter of law.

[HARMAN L.J. In *Luther* v. *Sagor*[42]* the Government appear to have recognised the trade delegation. It entered into relations with that organ, whatever it was an organ of, before it had officially recognised it.] **[620]**

The laws of the Russian Soviet Government were not treated as valid laws

[39] [1956] 2 Q.B. 552.
[40] [1922] 38 T.L.R. 616, C.A.
[41] [1956] 2 Q.B. 552.
[42] [1921] 1 K.B. 456; [1921] 3 K.B. 532, C.A.

in these courts. Its law-making power was not recognised. The certificate of the Foreign Office was construed by Roche J. as meaning that, notwithstanding that the trade delegation had been received, implying perhaps a degree of recognition, its government had not de facto been recognised. The degree of recognition which may have existed was overridden by the statement in the certificate. In the present case there is not even the degree of recognition which there was in *Luther* v. *Sagor*[42]*, the present case is thus a fortiori. The delegation in *Luther* v. *Sagor*[42]* were, moreover, treated as almost total strangers—not as a government at all, but as traders.

It is submitted that "department of state" means a public body which is either part of the central government or derives its authority from it.

The decision of Sellers J. in *Luigi Monta*[43]* was contrary to the weight of authority. The courts will not, in any event, enforce any instrument or give effect to any enactment the enforcement of which or the giving effect to which would involve the recognition of a government which has not been recognised by Her Majesty's Government.

[HARMAN L.J. The court is concerned at present only with the question of capacity to sue, not with whether these decrees can be enforced.]

"Enforced" may or may not be the right word; what is referred to is the giving of effect to the decree of 1952.

In *Luigi Monta*,[43]* the general colour of the war risks clause was that it was concerned with the possibility that, during the ship's voyage, someone claiming to exercise governmental powers might interfere with that voyage, giving the ship orders or directions which it would be compelled to obey. It was contention (vi)[44] advanced on behalf of the shipowners which particularly impressed Sellers J. There are certain notable omissions in the list of cases referred to: the earlier decisions of Lord Eldon, to some of which the defendants have referred the court, and cases such as *City of Berne* v. *Bank of England*[45]*; *Taylor* v. *Barclay*[46]*; *Foster* v. *Globe Venture Syndicate Ltd.*[47]*; also *The Arantzazu Mendi.*[48]* What Sellers J.[49] held was that, in that commercial contract, what the parties were concerned **[621]** with was not the meaning of the word "government" in any sense of public international law, but something which was in fact carrying on a government, actually acting as a government, lawful or unlawful, recognised or unrecognised, whatever legality or authority it had or did not have, and had made an order diverting the ship. Sellers J. held that this was a matter of construction of the document in question. He said[50] that it was a very different question from that of a sovereign seeking immunity from the jurisdiction of our courts. It is, the defendants would agree, different in form, though it is not accepted that there are not certain common principles underlying the matter. All the earlier cases, in their submission, indicate that the principle goes much wider than merely to be applicable to a sovereign claiming immunity or even to direct enforcement of a foreign law; *Luther* v. *Sagor*[51]* goes much further. Sellers J.'s decision[52] is inconsistent with *White* v. *Simmons.*[53]* There, the Court of Appeal treated the Foreign Office certificate as conclusive as to whether or not the Russian Government was a government under the policy. It is to be noted that that case, too, concerned an ordinary commercial contract. The Foreign Office certificate expressed no view as to when the government had actually been constituted, and the court held that it was accordingly entitled to determine as a matter of fact on the evidence from what date the retrospectivity of the certificate was to operate. The question of what was a government was, however, treated as conclusively determined by the certificate. It is difficult to see how the decision of Sellers J. in *Luigi Monta*[54]* can be reconciled with that. If it is to be reconciled, it can only be upon the

[43] [1956] 2 Q.B. 552.
[44] See ibid. 558-559.
[45] (1804) 9 Ves. 347.
[46] (1828) 2 Sim. 213.
[47] [1900] 1 Ch. 811.
[48] [1939] A.C. 256, H.L.(E.).
[49] [1956] 2 Q.B. 552.
[50] [1956] 2 Q.B. 552, 566.
[51] [1921] 1 K.B. 456; [1921] 3 K.B. 532, C.A.
[52] [1956] 2 Q.B. 552.
[53] (1922) 38 T.L.R. 616, C.A.
[54] [1956] 2 Q.B. 552.

footing that, whereas in *White* v. *Simmons*[55]* the document was to be construed as referring to the lawful government, in *Luigi Monta*[56]* it was to be construed as meaning not merely the lawful government but anybody who was in fact purporting to be the government or acting as such. That is not a legitimate distinction; alternatively, the present case is governed by *White* v. *Simmons*[57]* rather than by *Luigi Monta,*[58]* the concepts involved being "administrative authority" and "department of state." One is thus concerned, as a pure matter of construction, with a lawful body.

[HARMAN L.J. What the court is looking for in the present **[622]** case is not "government" but "authority." Are we not to look for who was exercising authority at the relevant date? That is the point of construction—not whether it was a government within the Foreign Office use of the word or not.]

See *Luigi Monta.*[58]* The defendants refer to *White* v. *Simmons*[59]* to show that, in another case involving a commercial document, the court treated the Foreign Office certificate as conclusive. If the present case is approached from the point of view of what is an "administrative authority," it is submitted that those words mean someone occupying a public office: see above. "Authority" means a lawful authority, but, further, it means a governmental authority—not a private authority, like that of the board of a company, or of a father over his children. What is referred to in the articles is an organ of government. *White* v. *Simmons*[59]* indicates that where there is a reference, albeit in a private commercial contract, to "government," the courts will treat the question what is a government as falling to be determined by the Foreign Office. In the present case, there is not in fact the word "government," but there are the words "administrative authority" and "department of state," within which it is submitted there is no way in which the plaintiffs can bring themselves, it being essential to their case that they should do so.

In White v. *Simmons*[59]* Atkin L.J. held that, in considering whether the acts in question were the acts of the Russian Government, he was bound by *Luther* v. *Sagor,*[60]* where it had been held that that government had been recognised in 1921. He held himself bound by the view of the Foreign Office on the question whether the Russian Government had been the government of the country. He then went on to consider from what date it had in fact come into existence. The decision is important as showing the breadth of the principle which has been applied, and it is very doubtful whether the decision of Sellers J.[61] can be reconciled with what Atkin L.J. said.

[HARMAN L.J. I do not understand how one case of construction can govern another. The principles apply, but the words, or the context, are always rather different.]

The defendants agree.

Sellers J. in *Luigi Monta*[61]* seems to have left out of his mind the element of retroactivity. The evidence in *White* v. *Simmons*[62]* was not inconsistent with the opinion of the Foreign **[623]** Office, who had expressed no opinion as to the date when the Russian Government had come into existence. If it had done, its view would probably have been treated as conclusive. That was the conclusion of Atkin L.J. See also *per* Warrington L.J. Sellers J.[63] does not seem to have had in mind that, in *White* v. *Simmons,*[64]* the question whether the Russian Government was a government or not had been held to be determined by the Foreign Office certificate. He said rightly, however, that, had the British Government never recognised the Russian Government, as they had in *White* v. *Simmons,*[64]* the court could never have found that the exception in the policy applied. The conclusion which follows inevitably from that is that it was only if the Foreign Office did recognise the Russian Government that it could be treated as a government under the policy. Only then could the court go into

[55] 38 T.L.R. 616, C.A.
[56] [1956] 2 Q.B. 552.
[57] 38 T.L.R. 616.
[58] [1956] 2 Q.B. 552.
[59] 38 T.L.R. 616.
[60] [1921] 3 K.B. 532.
[61] [1956] 2 Q.B. 552.
[62] 38 T.L.R. 616.
[63] [1956] 2 Q.B. 552.
[64] 38 T.L.R. 616.

the question of retroactivity. That is what Sellers L.J.[65] was saying. His statement that *White* v. *Simmons*[66]* was no authority for the proposition that if there was no recognition there was no government is, however, wrong; that is exactly what it is an authority for. It is impossible to suppose that the court in *White* v. *Simmons*[66]* would have reached the conclusion which they did except on the basis of what had been established in *Luther* v. *Sagor*,[67]* namely, that the Russian Government had received de facto recognition, and that this operated retrospectively.

Kawasaki Kisen Kabushiki Kaisha v. *Bantham Steamship Co. Ltd.* (*No.* 2)[68] was a very different case from the present. The word "war" can clearly be used in a purely factual sense to describe people, so to speak, shooting at one another. One could quite understand the court taking the view that the parties had used the word in that sense. Indeed, the Foreign Office letter in the case in effect invited the court to deal with the question on that factual basis. That is very different from a reference in a document to "organs of government" or "authorities" or "departments of state," or matters of that kind, which by their very nature are concerned not only with people doing things but with their having the right to do them.

To sum up, *Luigi Monta*[69]* is distinguished from the present on the following grounds: (1) Sellers J. was able to take, or did take, the view, rightly or wrongly, that "government" in **[624]** that particular charterparty could be construed to mean persons carrying on the functions of government lawfully or unlawfully, whereas in the present case the articles of the foundation contemplate a lawful authority; (2) it was unnecessary in that case for the defendants to ask the court to recognise as valid a law of the foreign government; (3) *Luigi Monta*[69]* is not consistent with *White* v. *Simmons*[70]*; (4) certain cases were not referred to in *Luigi Monta*[71]* (see above). It is probably not necessary for the defendants to go so far as *Taylor* v. *Barclay*,[72]* but the case does show the width to which the principle has been taken. It is a matter of public policy. The judges in those earlier cases would have been surprised at the decision in *Luigi Monta*[73]*; they would have said that, in asking to be allowed to escape from liability under an insurance policy because the decree was the decree of the government, albeit unrecognised, they were being asked to recognise that government.

In *Foster* v. *Globe Venture Syndicate Ltd.*,[74]* even though there was no question of applying the laws of a foreign state, as there was in *City of Berne*,[75]* and the question was one of a private, commercial contract, it was held that, in deciding what were the facts relevant to the implementing of the contract, the views of the Foreign Office were to be looked at and nothing else. See also *per* Atkin L.J. in *The Arantzazu Mendi*,[76]* where he expressed his disapproval of an observation of Lord Sumner in *Duff Development Co. Ltd.* v. *Kelantan Government*.[77]* It is interesting, in this context, to note the reference of Sellers J. in *Luigi Monta*[78]* to that passage in the speech of Lord Sumner.[79] Sellers J.[80] had not been referred to Atkin L.J.'s criticism of it.[81]

Articles 53 and 55 are additional indications that Abbé, in connection with the words "administrative authority or department of state," had in mind a public body, an organ of government. Regulations relating to the administering of state funds apply more naturally to a public body.

The answer to the plaintiffs' point (4) (i) is that one may have customary laws in a tribe, and, in an appropriate case, one could prove a foreign law by establishing that it was part of the custom of that tribe; cf. the common law. In the present case, however **[625]** there is no evidence that the Council of Gera is a

[65] [1956] 2 Q.B. 552.
[66] 38 T.L.R. 616.
[67] [1921] 3 K.B. 532, C.A.
[68] [1939] 2 K.B. 544.
[69] [1956] 2 Q.B. 552.
[70] 38 T.L.R. 616.
[71] [1956] 2 Q.B. 552.
[72] (1828) 2 Sim. 213.
[73] [1956] 2 Q.B. 552.
[74] [1900] 1 Ch. 811.
[75] 9 Ves. 347.
[76] [1939] A.C. 256, 263-264.
[77] [1924] A.C. 797; 40 T.L.R. 566, H.L.(E).
[78] [1956] 2 Q.B. 552.
[79] [1924] A.C. 797.
[80] [1956] 2 Q.B. 552.
[81] [1939] A.C. 256.

body created or existing by the common or customary law prevailing in the area in question. It derives its authority and existence from the decrees of 1952. It is not a common law but a statutory body.

The plaintiffs' submission, point (4) (ii), that the general principle does not apply to exceptional cases where the ground of non-recognition is that the unrecognised government is not in control is, as the defendants understand it, based on the American case of *Salimoff*[82] and on the views of Dr. Lipstein.[83] In *Salimoff*,[84] however, de facto recognition had been given, and Dr. Lipstein's approach[85] is not really from the point of view of English, but of international, law.

The plaintiffs' suggestion, based on *Cheshire* v. *Huth*,[86]* that the courts will tend to construe a document against producing perpetual immobility, does not assist where the prime question is the impinging upon that document of certain principles of public policy. Although to reduce a going concern to impotence so far as protecting its rights in this country are concerned is something which the courts of this country would do with great reluctance, this raises many other aspects of the case. It hardly assists the court on the construction of these articles and on their application to the events which have supervened in this case. There are no provisions in the articles as to what is to happen if there is no special board; indeed, it has not been established that the special board has ceased to exist; presumably it goes on until there is evidence that it has done so. The only reason put forward for its having ceased to exist—on the plaintiffs' case—is that it was replaced by the Council of Gera. Although the intervention of public policy may sometimes produce results which are anomalous and disrupting under ordinary commercial, trading and legal conditions, that is something which, in the present case, flows from public policy, not from the meaning of the articles, and one cannot put a special construction on the articles, which were adopted long before the question of the intervention of public policy arose, to meet the effects of that intervention. In any event, the appellants do not accept that the intervention of public policy in the present case would have the effect of reducing the foundation to perpetual immobility. Quite apart from the question of the position in the West, there **[626]** is the possibility of winding-up proceedings with respect to the assets in this country, and if one is to look at the realities they are that these businesses in the East no longer exist and that this action is for the benefit of the V.E.B.

Aldous Q.C. replying. In *White* v. *Simmons*[87]* Bankes L.J.[88] pointed out that one might have a government, not being the de jure government, which did the act in question. A question might then arise as to the effect and meaning of the policy. That case, and others which have been referred to, are instances of the application of the normal principle of construction of commercial documents: one looks at the intention of the makers. To construe one document from another, except in relation to general principles, may lead to wrong results. In a case such as *White* v. *Simmons*,[89]* where the agreement was between two English companies, it might well be that a court would conclude that by "government" the parties meant government as recognised by Her Majesty's Government. Such a conclusion, however, would seem odd in a case such as *Luigi Monta*,[90]* where the contract was between an Italian and a Czechoslovak. A fortiori in construing the words of the constitution of a German corporation made a considerable time ago, the words being: "In that authority." In such a case, it is nonsense to read in the words "lawfully recognised by Her Majesty's Government." That is the step which Sellers J., in *Luigi Monta*,[90]* would not take. One does not want, in a case of this kind, to go into the niceties of international law: see *per* Goddard J. in *Kawasaki*,[91] or into the niceties of diplomacy: see

[82] (1933) 262 N.Y.S. 693.

[83] *Transactions of the Grotius Society*, 1949, Vol. 35 (1950), p. 157.

[84] 262 N.Y.S. 693.

[85] *Transactions of the Grotius Society*, 1949, Vol. 35 (1950), p. 157.

[86] 79 Ll.L.R. 262n.

[87] 38 T.L.R. 616.

[88] Ibid. 617-618.

[89] 38 T.L.R. 616.

[90] [1956] 2 Q.B. 552.

[91] [1939] 2 K.B. 544, 549.

per Sellers J. in *Luigi Monta*.[92]* One wants to stick to the recognised principles of construction, and, on that basis, the question here is: what would a German lawyer say that article 113 means? To come to the answer, by whatever circuity, that he would read into "lawful" the qualification "as recognised by the English courts" is ridiculous.

[Counsel continued his address on the other grounds advanced by the plaintiffs in their respondents' notice, which do not call for a full report here. In the course of that address, he applied to amend the plaintiffs' notice, in the following circumstances:]

Aldous Q.C. Assuming, therefore, that the Council of Gera should be disregarded as the special board, these proceedings are nevertheless properly authorised, on the ground, first, that they **[627]** were authorised by Dr. Schrade in his capacities as a member of the board of management of the optical works, alternatively, or additionally, under the power of attorney of June 29, 1951.

Littman Q.C. (intervening). Cross J. found that these proceedings had been authorised by the Council of Gera as the special board. That was the sole ground of his decision. Nothing in his judgment refers to this power of attorney of 1951, and the plaintiffs' respondents' notice does not entitle them to rely on it. The contention that it gave additional powers to Dr. Schrade as a member of the board of management—that it had, so to speak, extended his power as mandatory or deputy mandatory—may be open to them, but not the argument that its effect was to give him a special authority on behalf of the foundation. It would be wrong for the court to consider any such argument without cross-examination of the plaintiffs' witnesses on the question of the position of powers of attorney under German law.

Aldous Q.C. No point was taken by the defendants below as to the various ways in which the present action could have been authorised. The plaintiffs, on the other hand, indicated that they intended to rely upon any authorisation upon which it was open to them on the evidence to rely. If their notice is inadequate, they ask leave to amend it. They wish to rely on the power of attorney by itself, quite apart from any authorisation which it might constitute under article 39 to act as mandatory.

[HARMAN L.J. They wish to add "by the boards of management, or, alternatively, by the foundation, acting under the document dated June 29, 1951"?]

Yes.

[HARMAN L.J. The court could not allow that amendment without giving the defendants the chance to supplement the evidence as to what happened to the Ministry of Education of Thuringia between 1949 and 1952.]

There is evidence as to this: see the first affidavit of Dr. David, paragraph 28, and the point was taken below; in the plaintiffs' submission, no further evidence should be allowed to be called. The sole purpose of the amendment is to put the notice in a position to raise a point which was dealt with in evidence below and taken below.

[HARMAN L.J. The court will allow the amendment, and the defendants will consider what further evidence they wish to file.]

Aldous Q.C. continued his address, and concluded: The first part of the plaintiffs' case is that the proper persons to bring proceedings to protect the name "Carl Zeiss Stiftung" are the **[628]** foundation itself acting through the special board. This was the view which succeeded before Cross J.

Littman Q.C. The defendants do not contend that Cross J. was wrong in the view which he took that the proper body of the foundation to authorise these proceedings to protect its name was the special board.

In connection with the plaintiffs' amendment of their cross-notice, the defendants now apply to adduce fresh evidence to show that the Ministry of Education of Thuringia, when it gave the power of attorney relied upon by the plaintiffs, was an organ of the German Democratic Republic and, therefore, so to speak, tarred with the same brush as the Council of Gera. The fresh evidence which the defendants seek leave to adduce is the constitution of the

[92] [1956] 2 Q.B. 552, 568.

German Democratic Republic and the decree which adopted it.

[HARMAN L.J. We will admit the evidence. The plaintiffs may put in evidence in answer if they wish.]

Littman Q.C. replied on the plaintiffs' other grounds, and concluded: There are further arguments which the defendants would wish to address to the court on article [114], but these would take the matter beyond that which the court has indicated that they wish dealt with at this stage. Under their point (B), they wish to contend that, in any event, the effect of the confiscation was to render the organs of the foundation incapable of functioning.

[HARMAN L.J. We do not want to go into that now.]

What the defendants have not dealt with is the question of the constitution of the German Democratic Republic. On the formation of the German Democratic Republic the special board became an organ of this, and thereupon ceased to be the special board.

[DIPLOCK L.J. This is a difficult horse to ride with their first contention—that the German Democratic Republic does not exist!]

There may be an intermediate position. It may be reasonable to draw an inference of fact—rather than of law—that the special board was, from the time that the German Democratic Republic came into existence, under its control, and acting as an organ of it.

[DIPLOCK L.J. "Was under the control of some people whom we cannot recognise as being a government"!]

The defendants have made the point, and do take it.

[Counsel then put in affidavits relating to the points on which **[629]** the court gave leave to the defendants to adduce fresh evidence and said:] If the court were to come to a conclusion adverse to the defendants on the point in respect of which these affidavits are adduced, they would undertake not to object to any fresh evidence which the plaintiffs might seek to adduce in answer before the House of Lords, assuming that the case goes as far.

Aldous Q.C. I have that evidence now, and seek leave to adduce it. It is evidence concerning the constitution of the Land of Thuringia—the constitution itself, of 1946, and the decree which appointed the Council of Gera.

Littman Q.C. The defendants will not press the point on which it is sought to adduce all these new facts, and will, accordingly, object to their admission on an issue which was not before Cross J. The only reason why further evidence was allowed to be adduced by this court was as an indulgence granted to the defendants in return for that granted to the plaintiffs in their being allowed to amend their notice of appeal so as to raise, inter alia, the contention relying upon the power of attorney of 1951 as an authority from the special board. In return, the defendants were permitted to raise the point that the Ministry of Education of Thuringia was in the same position as the Rat of Gera. That was the only ground on which the defendants were allowed to adduce further evidence, and it does not justify the plaintiffs in seeking to adduce this further evidence.

[HARMAN L.J. The right course is for the defendants to withdraw the affidavits which they have put in altogether, and push this point out of the way. It is not a good point, in our view.]

Aldous Q.C. There is authority that, once an affidavit has been put in, it cannot be withdrawn. That may, perhaps, be done with leave. The real point, however, is that this point is being tried for the first time in this court.

[HARMAN L.J. That is because of your cross-notice.]

No—*all* the matters which have been argued have been argued for the first time in this court. There was very little time to prepare to meet them.

Littman Q.C. The plaintiffs were given the opportunity of applying for an adjournment.

Aldous Q.C. On the footing only that, it being a question of what the Russians would say, the court indicated that it would assume it.[93] Having looked into this matter, the matters which the plaintiffs wish to adduce are of supreme impor-

[93] See *post*, p. 664.

tance, and it **[630]** would be a negation of justice that they should be shut out, especially when they are foreigners. They wish to show how the Council of Gera was appointed under the constitution of Thuringia.

[HARMAN L.J. This is a new point.]

It is the same point. The defendants have asked the court to draw all sorts of inferences from documents with "German Democratic Republic" at the top of them. The plaintiffs do not want the court to draw inferences which would be contrary to the facts.

[HARMAN L.J. The case was fought both here and below on the footing that the Council of Gera was the child of the decree of July, 1952.]

It was not. The admission below was that the Council of Gera was accepted as being the special board, subject to questions of confiscation and so on, because it had been appointed by a properly authorised government.

[HARMAN L.J. By the decree of 1952.]

That was an appointment by the government of Thuringia. It is vital for the court to see how the Council of Gera came to be appointed.

[HARMAN L.J. I said to counsel for the defendants at one stage [i.e., during that part of the argument not reported here] that the law of July 23, 1952, and the order thereunder of July 24, 1952, did not say exactly how it was created. The plaintiffs could have put this evidence forward then if they had wanted to. The whole case has been presented on the basis that the order of July 24, 1952, was the document under which the Council of Gera was set up.]

It does not say so. It is not an original. That is only how the case was presented by the plaintiffs for the first time in this court.

[HARMAN L.J. Cross J. came to his decision on the footing that the Council of Gera was the special board. He based that on concessions to this extent—that if the point of estoppel, and of the Council being a communist organisation,[94] were out, then, as a matter of geography, it would be the special board. Then came the answers of the Foreign Office to the effect that the German Democratic Republic was not recognised here and that the only authority in that area which was recognised was the Russian Government. That is where we start in this case. If the plaintiffs had wished to say that it was not true that the **[631]** Council of Gera was the creature of the German Democratic Republic, it was for them to say so at that stage—not now, when all the arguments have been adduced.]

The plaintiffs do not seek to say that the Council of Gera was not the proper body to authorise these proceedings, but that it was properly constituted. They are not seeking to go back on what they have argued so far, but to fill in gaps. These are gaps which the court should allow to be filled in, otherwise it will be deciding the matter contrary to the true position. The plaintiffs wish to adduce the constitution of the German Democratic Republic.

[HARMAN L.J. If the plaintiffs are going to say that the Council of Gera is not the creature of the German Democratic Republic that might be relevant.]

They are going to say that. They are going to show that it was appointed by the Government of Thuringia, and that the Government of Thuringia was appointed by the Russians. They also wish to show the correct date for the establishment of the German Democratic Republic. There was no German Democratic Republic in existence as an independent body in 1952. The Council of Gera was appointed by the Government of Thuringia, whose authority stemmed from the Russians. There may have been directions which purported to come from the so-called German Democratic Republic, but that was then under the control and supervision of the Russians.

[HARMAN L.J. The plaintiffs had the opportunity of an adjournment to deal with the Russian position.]

Only for the purpose of showing what the Russians themselves would have said. The present point, however, is a different one. The plaintiffs wish to show how the Council of Gera was appointed by the Ministry of Thuringia, whose authority stemmed from the Russians. The Council of Gera therefore stems

[94] Points taken before Cross J.

from a body which the court should recognise.

[Harman L.J. Did you not say that the plaintiffs' first point was that the German Democratic Republic, if it was not itself recognised, was really the agent of the Russian Government?]

Yes.

[Harman L.J. That is the same point as they are now putting.]

No. This is a separate point: that the Council of Gera was appointed, not by a law of the German Democratic Republic, but by a law of the Government of Thuringia. **[632]**

[Diplock L.J. The plaintiffs wish to contradict the affidavit of Honig.]

They do not wish to contradict it, only to put forward the factual situation as it is now discovered by them to be.

[Harman, L.J. That affidavit shows that all this material was well known to the plaintiffs' advisers. This was done by the Government of Thuringia because that is how the decree says it was to be done. There does not seem to be any substance in this point.]

It is not shown in this affidavit that the Government of Thuringia was set up by the Russians with a constitution, and that it remained in being until 1954. The question of the Government of Thuringia being controlled by some other independent government in Germany can be dealt with by evidence.

Littman Q.C. The defendants have until now had no intimation whatever of what the nature of this fresh evidence, now disclosed for the first time, would be. The plaintiffs knew at the time whether or not it would be to their advantage to proceed on the basis that certain facts were the case, and they did so, electing not to ask for an adjournment. Their present application has been made on a sidewind. They want to put in this evidence on this new, broad, point after the defendants asked leave to put in evidence on an entirely narrow aspect of the case.[95] They want to make an entirely new case, and should not be allowed to do so. There must be some finality. The defendants would have to answer the new case. They would have to ask for an adjournment, and they might have to ask for cross-examination, and matters of that kind. Honig's affidavit, in any event, makes it clear that the Council of Gera owed its birth to a decree of the German Democratic Republic, so that it is doubtful, in any event, whether the new point will make any difference in the result. The application should be refused.

[Harman L.J. This is the 10th day of hearing of this so-called interlocutory appeal. It has taken an unprecedented course, so far as I know, in that it has all been argued upon a footing which both sides in their affidavits below disclaimed.]

Another division of this court, as it felt bound to do, this being a question of public policy, has allowed the question of the political recognition of the East German régime to come into it, and that is the only matter which we have discussed over this long period.

There has been a respondents' notice on the part of the **[633]** plaintiffs, and an amendment thereto. An opportunity was given, quite early on, to the plaintiffs to call further evidence and the matter yesterday gradually wound itself, as I thought, to a standstill. At that point, counsel for the plaintiffs asked, in effect, to tear up the whole case which he had made so far and to start a new one, and he said with candour that he did not shrink from the view that it might be necessary to tear up all that had been deposed to and open a new set of submissions.

When one looks at the evidence, one sees that the plaintiffs' witnesses give a certain account of the creation of the Council of Gera, which has been the object of so much controversy, and until a late hour yesterday afternoon that stood. Now counsel for the plaintiffs says he wishes to provide a whole new series of facts to show that that is all nonsense, and that really an entirely different set-up was in existence.

The court has considered that application—as, indeed, it must—anxiously,

[95] *Ante*, p. 628.

having regard to the extraordinary nature of these proceedings, and has come to the conclusion that there must be an end somewhere to this litigation. We do not propose now to adjourn the whole case so that it may be refashioned to come on again in a month's time, with new evidence, new cross-examination, new affidavits and new thoughts. I see no end to the matter at this rate. We think we must make an end to it.

We therefore refuse the request that has been made to us to refashion the evidence at this stage, and propose that we should now consider the matter so far as we have gone and give judgment upon it in due course, because if we come to one conclusion on it that may put an end to the matter and lighten the burden of all the other points canvassed before Cross J., which were the subject of his lengthy and careful judgment.

We propose, therefore, to rise at this point, and consider what our judgment will be.

DANCKWERTS L.J. I agree.

DIPLOCK L.J. I agree.

Littman Q.C. submitted that the court had jurisdiction to permit the defendants' affidavits[96] to be taken off the file.

[HARMAN L.J. The defendants will leave their affidavit on the file, having abandoned the point based upon it.]

Aldous Q.C. The plaintiffs ask leave to cross-examine Dr. Mann [the deponent] on that affidavit. **[634]**

[HARMAN L.J. No. The point has been abandoned. Therefore the object for which it was put on the file is out of the case.]

Cur. adv. vult.

1964. December 17. The following judgments were read.

HARMAN L.J. The writ in this action was issued as long ago as October 20, 1955, the plaintiff being styled Carl Zeiss Stiftung, describing itself as having a registered office at Jena in Eastern Germany and as being a corporation under the laws of the (Eastern) German Democratic Republic. The defendants are two English limited liability companies (apparently associated); the third defendant has the same style as the plaintiff, but is described as being of Heidenheim in the Western Zone of Germany. That there is a corporation of this name is not for present purposes in dispute, which is whether its seat is on the west or the east side of the so-called "Iron Curtain." The present application on the part of the defendants is at least competent to the first two defendants, whatever the status of the third; it is to stay all proceedings in the action upon the ground that those who purported to make use of the plaintiff corporation's name and to instruct English solicitors to bring these proceedings had no authority so to do and that, in accordance with the ordinary practice, the solicitors, having acted without authority, ought personally to pay the costs. This is the proper, and indeed the only, way in which this point can be taken. See the *Mulhouse* case.[97]*

The writ, as I have said, was issued in October, 1955, and a statement of claim was delivered at the end of that year and redelivered in March, 1960, but no other step in the action has ever been taken except the present one. This is apparently due to the fact that the protagonists have been busy with litigation in other parts of the world, notably in the Western Zone of Germany where the third defendant has been successful, and in the Eastern Zone of Germany where the plaintiff has been successful. The relief sought in the action is an injunction to restrain all the defendants from using the name Carl Zeiss or any name containing the word "Zeiss," and from sale of optical or glass instruments under that name unless the goods be those of the plaintiffs; in fine, **[635]** this is a passing-off action. The plaintiff claims to be the only and true Carl Zeiss Stiftung; the third defendant makes a like claim. The first two defendants are agents for the sale of the third defendant's products. Both the plaintiff and the third defen-

[96] See *ante*, p. 629.

[97] *Russian Commercial and Industrial Bank* v. *Comptoir d'Escompte de Mulhouse** [1925] A.C. 112, 130, H.L.(E.).

dant do, as I understand, flourishing businesses in this country in so-called "Zeiss" optical instruments.

The present summons was issued on February 7, 1956, and was, as I have said, a summons to stay on the ground that the action was being prosecuted without the plaintiff's authority. A large mass of evidence was filed on both sides; leave to cross-examine was given, and the matter came into court and occupied some 25 days of Cross J.'s time at the end of 1963 and the beginning of the present year. Cross J. eventually delivered an elaborate and closely reasoned judgment on March 6, 1964, refusing the defendants any relief and allowing the action to go forward. It is against that decision that this appeal is brought.

A number of points were discussed before Cross J., notably whether the judgments of the courts of Western or of Eastern Germany created an estoppel between the parties, whether the action ought to be entertained, being, it was said, brought in aid of a confiscatory decree and to enlarge the area over which that confiscation had effect beyond the territorial bounds of the German Democratic Republic, and whether on the true construction of the statute, which is the charter, so to speak, of the corporation, the body which was the motive force behind the action had, as a matter of construction, the requisite authority.

It is a noteworthy point that before Cross J. each side expressly stated that for the present purpose it proposed to regard the courts and the legislature of the other side as legally effective. For instance, in the leading affidavit filed on behalf of the defendants, that of Dr. Walter David, sworn on April 6 and filed on April 9, 1956, the following is to be found in paragraph 4: "The status and powers of the persons and bodies making, or purporting to make, laws and decrees in East Germany, and consequently the validity of those laws and decrees, are controversial and the defendants may wish to challenge the validity of such laws and decrees in future proceedings in Germany and elsewhere. On their instructions however, this affidavit has been made on the assumption that the laws and decrees made in East Germany and hereinafter referred to were valid and effective in East Germany (though not that they can have had any effect outside East Germany)." And in the evidence filed on behalf of the plaintiffs I find in the affidavit of Dr. Hugo Schrade, sworn on **[636]** April 12 and filed May 11, 1959, precisely the corresponding assumption expressly made. I find also in the Law Reports of this year[98] this passage: ". . . according to an extract from a contemporary note by junior counsel for the plaintiffs (E. Lauterpacht), leading counsel for the defendants (B. MacKenna Q.C.) was asked by Cross J.: 'Suppose this entity' (namely, the plaintiffs) 'exists in East Germany, would it not be a question of East German law?' to which Mr. MacKenna replied: 'That would have to be decided by East German law' and that the issue was the application of the proper law. When leading counsel for the plaintiffs (Guy Aldous Q.C.) submitted that East German law must be applied and the judge asked Mr. MacKenna whether he could assume that the relevant law was East German law, Mr. MacKenna replied: 'Yes.' The judge then asked: 'Has any point been taken on recognition?' Mr. MacKenna replied: 'East Germany is not recognised de facto but I take no point.' Mr. Aldous said: 'One will have to say that everything is done under the aegis of the Soviet authorities.'"

It was upon this footing that Cross J. reached his conclusions. He specifically inquired at one point whether any question as to recognition in this country of the German Democratic Republic was involved, and he was informed that no such question arose.

Notice of appeal, with the leave of the judge, was lodged on May 5, 1964, and covered much of the ground on which the judgment was based. Shortly afterwards, the defendants changed their legal advisers and at the same time lodged a supplemental notice of appeal in which, for the first time, it was alleged that Cross J. had erred in recognising the existence of the German Democratic Republic or its organisations or the decisions of its courts, they not being recognised by Her Majesty's Government. On July 15, 1964, the

[98] In *Carl Zeiss Stiftung* v. *Rayner & Keeler Ltd.*,* [1965] 1 Ch. 525; [1964] 3 W.L.R. 905, 908, [1964] 3 All E.R. 326, C.A.

defendants moved the Court of Appeal[99] asking for a letter to be written to Her Majesty's Secretary of State for Foreign Affairs requesting him to certify to the court certain answers. At the hearing of this motion it was objected on behalf of the plaintiff that no such point ought to be allowed to be taken having regard to the position taken up in the court below, but it was held (see the judgment of Lord Denning M.R.[1]) that this was a question on which the court of its own motion was **[637]** bound to seek proper information, in order that judgment be not given on a false hypothesis, and as a matter of public policy. The Secretary of State's answer to the question posed by the court was dated September 16, and was in these terms: "Her Majesty's Government have not granted any recognition de jure or de facto to (a) the 'German Democratic Republic' or (b) its 'Government.'" Thereafter, on October 2, 1964,[2] the plaintiff applied to the Court of Appeal for further directions, asking that further questions be put to Her Majesty's Secretary of State, and, as a result, an order was made, dated October 29, 1964,[3] in these terms, so far as material: "This court doth order that a letter be written on behalf of this court to Her Majesty's Secretary of State for Foreign Affairs requesting him . . . to certify to this court the answer to the following questions namely 1. What (a) States or (b) Governments or (c) authorities (if any) have since July 1, 1945, up to the present date been recognised by Her Majesty's Government as (a) entitled to exercise or (b) exercising governing authority in the area of Germany outside the zones allocated to the Governments of the United Kingdom the United States of America and the French Republic by the protocol of September 12, 1944, and the agreement of July 26, 1945, concluded between" those governments, that is, the Potsdam Agreement. I need not read the other question because it does not arise. Those questions were answered by Her Majesty's Secretary of State on November 6, 1964, wherein, after defining the area allocated to the Union of Soviet Socialist Republics by the Potsdam Agreement, the following answer was given: "Since that time," that is to say, since June, 1945, "and up to the present date Her Majesty's Government have recognised the State and Government of the Union of Soviet Socialist Republics as de jure entitled to exercise governing authority in respect of that zone. In matters affecting Germany as a whole, the States and Governments of the French Republic, the United Kingdom of Great Britain and Northern Ireland, the United States of America and the Union of Soviet Socialist Republics were jointly entitled to exercise governing authority. In the period from August 30, 1945, to March 20, 1948, they did exercise such joint authority through the Control Council for Germany. Apart from the States, Governments and Control Council aforementioned, Her Majesty's Government have not recognised **[638]** either de jure or de facto any other authority purporting to exercise governing authority in or in respect of the zone."

By a respondents' notice dated November 3, 1964, as amended by leave during the course of the hearing, the plaintiff gave notice raising new points in terms which will be better understood when I have stated the facts.

The appeal came before this court on November 9, 1964, when counsel for the appellant defendants opened his case by stating broadly four points on which he desired to rest his appeal. Of these the first is what he called the "recognition" argument, that is to say, the argument arising out of the Foreign Office answers. This, as I have said, was a point never canvassed in the court below, but which is open to the appellant in my judgment having regard to the decision of this court in July last.[4] It seemed to us that this was the fundamental point in the case, and, if answered according to the appellants' contention, conclusive. We have therefore spent some 10 days in hearing argument on this point and have taken time to consider our judgment upon it without proceeding to the rest of the questions on the appeal. This is an unusual course to take, but if we should come to a conclusion that the point is a good one it would be

[99] *Ante,* p. 525.
[1] Ibid. ante, p. 537.
[2] *The Times,* October 3, 1964.
[3] *The Times,* October 30, 1964.
[4] [1965] 1 Ch. 525.

sufficient by itself to justify a stay of the whole action. Accordingly, we have thought it right not to proceed at this stage with the consideration of the arguments addressed to Cross J. If, therefore, we do not further canvass his judgment, it is because it is almost entirely concerned with matters outside our consideration. Having regard to the attitude of the parties before him, the judge had no alternative but to take the course which he did.

Counsel for the appellants stated that there were certain points agitated below which he did not desire to take in this court, and it may be convenient to state them here. The first was whether the members of the governing board of the optical business (a part of the corporation), who left the Eastern Zone and went to the West when the American Forces left Jena, did or did not resign from the board. He conceded, for present purposes only, that they did. The second was the validity, or otherwise, of certain decrees made by the government of Baden-Württemberg in the Western Zone: This question does not arise here. Thirdly, the existence of the Stiftung (or foundation, as I may call it) as a corporate body. For the present purpose its continued corporate existence is assumed. Cross J.'s judgment contained a detailed statement of the origin, progress and history of the foundation. I **[639]** shall only repeat so much of it as will, I hope, make the present question intelligible.

The optical works were founded in 1846 by Carl Zeiss at Jena, a university town in the Grand Duchy of Saxe-Weimar-Eisenach. One Ernest Abbé, a university professor, became associated with Zeiss in the optical works, and these two, later in the century, founded at Jena a glassworks in conjunction with one Schott. The two businesses prospered, and were in about 1890 transferred to what I have called the foundation. This is an odd body to the eye of an English lawyer. It embraced the two commercial firms which continued to exist as firms each with its own board of management and capable of suing and being sued in its business name, but having no legal entity separately from the foundation, a kind of overlord or supreme authority governed by what is called in translation "the special board," consisting of an official in the State service acting through a "deputy" (Stiftungskommissar) who was to sit in, so to speak, on the boards of the two businesses and decide questions of difficulty or doubt. It has been a question between the parties what matters the boards of management of each of the businesses were to control and what was left to the overriding authority of the special board. The function of the foundation, acting through the special board, was to receive the net profits of the two commercial businesses and to use them for various charitable and benevolent purposes connected with the University of Jena, the employees, and the inhabitants of the district.

In 1896 there were promulgated, with State approval, articles of constitution of the foundation, and these, as varied from time to time, constitute the key instrument in this case. It is a great pity that the parties did not have them competently translated, for the instrument as we have it seems to be the work of a German with a dictionary in his hands and hardly more knowledge of the English language than the dictionary will furnish. The articles form a kind of charter for the foundation, combining the functions of the memorandum and articles of association of an English limited company. I must state the effect of some of these articles, which are extremely detailed, but shall omit most of them as not relevant to the present inquiry.

Article 1 states the objects of the foundation, which are, in the first place, to carry on the two businesses, that is to say, the optical business and the glassworks, and next to serve philanthropic ends among the workers and the population of Jena and its neighbourhood and to promote through the university, out **[640]** of surplus profits of the industrial undertakings, the study of the sciences. Article 2 gives the name "Carl Zeiss Stiftung" to the foundation. Article 3 provides that the legal domicile (Sitz) of the foundation shall be Jena. Article 4, which is headed *"Organisation of the* [*foundation*]," provides, first, for the so-called "special board," which is to represent the foundation as a corporate body in the direction of its affairs; secondly, along with the special board, there are to be the boards of management of the businesses to direct their industrial operations; thirdly, there is to be the before-mentioned deputy appointed to represent the special board on the boards of management. Both the boards of management and the deputy are to be nominated by the special board. Article 5 provides that the rights and duties of the special board are to be vested in that department of the State service of the Grand Duchy under which the affairs of the University of Jena are from time to time placed. It also provides that the office of deputy is to be held by an official of the State service, or, failing that, of the public service, who is to be paid by the foundation. The rule ordains that the special board and the deputy are to conduct the affairs of the foundation with due regard to the intentions of the foundation and to pay no more heed to the interests of the State than a private individual is bound to have. Article 6 provides that the optical works (the firm of Carl Zeiss) and the glassworks (the firm of Schott und Genossen) in Jena shall be carried on permanently under their respective firm names each with separate working capital and independent management under its own board. Article 7 provides that the number of members of a board of management is not to exceed four nor be less than three and that within a month of the number being reduced to two, a new member is to be appointed. At least one member of the board of the optical works must have a seat on the board of the glassworks. Article 8 provides that the internal control of each business, and its commercial administration, trading operations, and staffing, is to be vested in its board subject to the articles. Each business is to be represented as against third parties, in all its affairs, legal and otherwise, by members of its own board. Article 9 provides that one member of each board is to be appointed by the special board as "mandatory," and a second to be his "proxy," and that each of these two may sign on behalf of the firm. Article 10 limits the influence of the special board on the boards of management to such as the rules provide and to be operative only through the deputy. Article 11 provides that the deputy is to supervise the management of **[641]** the business in all its branches and ensure that the boards of management comply with the articles. Article 13 provides that each member of the boards of management may act on behalf of his board in day-to-day matters, but that otherwise the decisions of the boards must be unanimous. Articles 14, 15 and 16 provide for reference of various important questions to the decision of the deputy. There follow a number of very detailed articles relating to the control of the businesses which I can omit.

Article 27, as translated, provides that members of a board of management may not be appointed "with the option of revocation" (which must I think mean revocable at the will of the deputy) but only for a fixed period determined beforehand, or for life, or until pensionable age under the rules (that is to say, 60). A member of a board may resign his office if the special board accepts. Articles 28 and 29 provide that members of boards are to give their whole time to the business and may not hold any outside salaried post. Article 37 forbids the sale or disposal of the foundation's business. Article 56 provides that in making appointments no regard should be had to the parentage, religion or political views of the appointee. The same injunction is contained in article 104. These have an ironic ring. Article 105 provides that the surplus funds arising from trading activities are to be applied to encourage scientific study and research in the whole region of natural science and mathematics, these to be carried out through payments to the University of Jena.

Chapter 9 of the articles is headed "Final Provisions" and is perhaps the most important part of the articles so far as this case is concerned. Articles 113, 114 and 116, as translated, read as follows: "113. *Representation of the Stiftung in case of cessation of present special board.* Should, in consequence of political changes in the State, the provision according to 5 of this statute with reference to the representation of the Stiftung become untenable, this representation including the appointment of the deputy of the Stiftung within the meaning of 5 and the statutory administration of the Carl Zeiss Stiftung shall be made over to that department of State, which with regard to the Universiy of Jena occupies the place of the State Department of the Grand Duchy of Saxe-Weimar acting as the special board, providing that its seat is in Thuringia, otherwise to the highest administrative authorities in Thuringia." "114. *Procedure until new formation of the special board.* Should at any time a special board corresponding to the provisions of 5 or 113 no longer exist, then until the new **[642]** formation of such the representation and administration of the Carl Zeiss Stiftung is to be taken over forthwith by the executive board of management of the optical works and in the event of the latter board of management no longer existing, by the board of management of the oldest works of the Stiftung in Jena or its neighbourhood. . . ." I will leave out the rest of that article. "116. *Dissolution of the Stiftung.* Should the Carl Zeiss Stiftung at any time in consequence of dissolution of all its business undertakings, under the suppositions contained in 37, section 3, of this statute or through other causes, see no longer any grounds for continuing its activity in the sphere of the higher technical industry profitably and be also in possession of no other organisation of a permanent nature and of sufficient importance, the continuity of which would [not] mean merely administration of its assets, it shall distribute after dissolution of the last works of the Stiftung and liquidation of all obligations half the remaining value of its assets between the communities of Jena and Wenigenjena at its discretion, the other half going to the University of Jena: in the event of the latter no longer existing, to another German University to be selected by the special board, to be independently employed for purposes in the sense of the Stiftung, and cease to exist as a legal corporation with its own administration."

Articles 117 to 120 provide for the manner in which the articles may be altered. Article 121 provides that articles 1 to 4 and 117 to 120 may under no circumstances be amended or abolished.

Thus, the special board under these rules was the Minister of Education from time to time of the Grand Duchy, a constituent state of the German Empire founded by Bismarck which lasted till 1918 when, at the armistice of that year, there came into existence the Second Reich, the so-called Weimar Republic. The Grand Duchy was then abolished, and Jena and its neighbourhood became part of the "Land" of Thuringia. A Code of Thuringian law was promulgated in 1923, and thereupon the Minister of Education of the Land became the special board. The Weimar Republic was destroyed by Hitler, who set up the Third Reich in 1935; this was a highly centralised organisation. An official calling himself the Statthalter and directly responsible to the Minister of Kultur in Berlin affected to have the authority of the special board. This period may be ignored. The Third Reich collapsed in 1945, and Jena and its neighbourhood were occupied on June 2 by United States forces, who set up a provisional government of Thuringia. A Dr. Wolff, Minister of Education of this govern-**[643]**-ment, and as such entitled to exercise the powers of the special board, appointed one Dr. Barth as deputy under the rules. The United States forces evacuated the area at the end of the month and the Russian forces entered it, and shortly afterwards by decree provided for a new provisional government of Thuringia; Drs. Wolff and Barth retained their offices. When the Americans left they took with them to the West the entire managing boards of both the optical works and the glassworks. For the present purpose it may be taken that all these gentlemen resigned their offices on leaving, and at the end of June Dr. Barth, as deputy of the special board and with its authority, made fresh appointments to each board for a period of two years, it being expected that the members of the original boards would be able to return and resume their offices. Those appointed to the optical board were Drs. Schomerus, Sandmann and Schrade, and to the glassworks Drs. Dunger, Heinz, Klemm and Schrade, the last named being on both boards in accordance with rule 7. Those appointments were duly registered in the commercial registry of the Land.

In October, 1945, Field Marshal Zhukov, as Russian commander-in-chief, made a decree sequestrating the property of both businesses and a great part of the plant, and some of the employees were carried off to Russia by way of reparations. Dr. Barth gave powers of attorney to the former directors who had gone to the West to carry on the business in that area, and there was there formed a limited company subsequently styled Zeiss-Opton to carry on that part of the business. The two-year period for which Dr. Barth had appointed Drs. Schrade, Sandmann and Schomerus to be members of the optical board ended in 1947. The former directors who had gone to the West were, of course, unable to return, but Dr. Barth appears to have made no new appointments, merely telling the three above-named to carry on for the time being. In January, 1948, the Russians set up a body called the German Economic Commission, and issued under the advice of that body decrees of confiscation of both businesses. These were made in pursuance of an order known as SMAD 64, and bear the date April 28, 1948. The two businesses were transferred to two nationalised organisations called V.E.B.s (Volks eigene Betriebe) which are still carrying them on at Jena at the present time. Dr. Schrade turns up once more as works manager of the optical V.E.B.

The German Economic Commission seems to have contemplated a reconstitution of the rules of the foundation, which it **[644]** assumed to continue in existence, and appointed a certain Dr. Rompe to be Foundation Commissar, but this individual, if he ever got into the saddle, soon fell out of it, and of him no more is heard. On November 30, 1948, the firm name of Carl Zeiss was struck off the register in Eastern Germany and the Zeiss V.E.B. was registered as proprietor. In March, 1949, Dr. Schomerus resigned from the board of management of the optical business (which of course had no business any more) and in November, 1949, Dr. Barth died. He was not replaced till May, 1951, when the Minister of Education of the Land of Thuringia appointed one Kunz to be deputy. The same official, or Kunz as his deputy, appointed, or affected to reappoint, Drs. Schrade and Sandmann to the optical board and one Harting to make up the quorum, but he died in the year 1951, since when there has been no quorum of that board. In the year 1949 the division of Germany became an accomplished fact; the Potsdam arrangement broke down. The Russians set up and recognised in their zone the German Democratic Republic, which, as appears from the Foreign Office certificate, Her Majesty's Government has never recognised either de jure or de facto. Our Government still regards the Russian authority as de jure in control. In the Western Zone the Federal German Republic was recognised by Her Majesty's Government and by the Governments of France and the United States of America.

In my judgment, on the information at present before us, it may be taken that the Land of Thuringia continued to exist after the declaration of the German Democratic Republic in 1949, and, consequently, for the present purpose I should be inclined to hold the appointments made in 1951 of Kunz as deputy and Harting as director as valid, though, as will appear in a moment, the so-called government of the Land was subject to the orders of the German Democratic Republic. It was in fact formally abolished, or abolished itself, in July, 1952, as a result of a law of the German Democratic Republic dated July 23, which provided for the reorganisation of the executive public authorities of the area and ordered the Land to effect a new organisation of its territory by dividing it into smaller districts, Kreise and Bezirke, and to transfer all the duties of the government of the Land to those districts. Details of this reorganisation were embodied in an order made by the Council of Ministers of the German Democratic Republic on the next day. In obedience to those laws, the Land of Thuringia was divided into smaller areas, that in which Jena was situated being called Gera, which was to be **[645]** governed by a council called a Rat. The actual document by which this Rat was set up was not before us, but we were told on the last day of the hearing that it was a document published by the government of the Land of Thuringia on the same July 24, and it was rather faintly suggested that the Rat had therefore been set up by the expiring Land of Thuringia (which derived some authority from the Russian Government) rather than by the German Democratic Republic. This suggestion had no documentary backing, and though we were asked at the close of the hearing to grant an adjournment to see if evidence could be found to support it, we felt unable to reopen the matter at that stage. All the evidence so far filed either stated or assumed that the Rat of Gera was set up by the laws of the German Democratic Republic. Statements to this effect are to be found in both the affidavit of Dr. David filed on April 9, 1956, on the defendants' behalf (see paragraph 29), and of Mr. Honig (see paragraph 38) filed on the plaintiff's behalf, and in the judgments of the East German courts referred to in that paragraph, and the case has been argued throughout on that footing.

From this time onwards the newly created Rat asserted that it was the special board under the rules of the foundation. The two businesses had, of course, been confiscated, and were being carried on as the state-owned V.E.B.s. Dr. Schrade was the works manager of the optical V.E.B., thus acting in contravention of rule 29. The V.E.B.s were paying at least a part of the pensions formerly paid by the foundation, as appears from a document of July 31, 1953, signed by Dr. Schrade as works manager of the V.E.B. and announcing to a retiring workman that a part of his "Zeiss pension" will be paid.

In 1954 the Rat, affecting to act as the special board, appointed two new members of the board of management, Drs. Müller and Hüber. It also purported to appoint Dr. Schrade to be mandatory on the board under rule 4. The documents in question do not specify which board is meant. The appointments are expressed to be "for the management of the industrial activity," but as there was at this time no such activity by either board it does not, I suppose, matter which one is intended. On April 8, 1954, the foundation, represented by Schrade, purported to make an agreement with the V.E.B.s (Schrade himself being manager of one of them) licensing the V.E.B.s to make use of the trade marks of the foundation without charge.

Preparations for the present action were now begun, and a letter retaining Courts & Co., of 15, Wimpole Street, as solicitors **[646]** on behalf of the foundation and the Carl Zeiss V.E.B.s was sent on September 30, 1955, under the signature of Dr. Schrade holding himself out as mandatory of the foundation and works director of the optical V.E.B. On October 5, 1955, the council of the Rat acting as the special board purported to appoint once more Drs. Schrade, Hüber and Müller as "members of the board of management," and Dr. Schrade as mandatory, without distinguishing one board from the other. There was a further meeting on November 16, 1956, where what purported to be a resolution of the foundation in Jena was passed approving the present action. This meeting was attended by Kunz as deputy and by Drs. Schrade, Dunge, Heinz and Klemm, that is to say, the board of management of the glassworks. All signed it, and it was afterwards ratified by Drs. Hüber and Müller as "members of the board of management."

In addition, the council of the Rat on November 22, 1956, addressed a further letter of authority to Dr. Schrade.

In order to complete the documentary evidence connected with the authority required to start the action, I must mention a document dated June 29, 1951, called a "power of attorney," which is in the following terms: "The management of the Carl Zeiss Stiftung, at Weimar (sic.) hereby confers on the deputy mandatory of the Stiftung, Herr Dr. Hugo Schrade, works manager at the V.E.B. Carl Zeiss Optical Works at Jena power of attorney on behalf of the Carl Zeiss Stiftung at Jena to undertake all legal transactions, both in and out of court and in particular 1. To acquire and sell real property 2. To execute mortgage and other legal claims and to carry out and to grant their discharge 3. To receive money or money's worth 4. To represent the Carl Zeiss Stiftung in law suits and at compulsory sales, and sequestrations of realty. Herr Dr. Schrade is also empowered to transfer to a third party the power of attorney hereby conferred for the execution of individual transactions. Herr Dr. Schrade may not undertake legal matters on behalf of the Carl Zeiss Stiftung in his own name or as representative of a third party (s. 181 of the Statute Book of the Civil Code)." That document is signed by the "Ministry of Education. By proxy."

By the statement of claim, the plaintiff claims that the office of special board and the power to appoint a deputy has been transferred under rule 113 to the Rat, which is therefore alleged to be the body competent to use the foundation's name and start this action. In addition or alternatively to this, Dr. Schrade **[647]** claims to have had authority to instruct solicitors on behalf of the plaintiff under the document which I last read. He also claims a like right as a member of the board of management of the optical works and as mandatory or deputy mandatory of that board. These alternative claims are inconsistent with the statement of claim, but that document can be amended. They arise on the amended respondents' notice alluded to earlier in this judgment.

The first task is to construe the articles, for it is only when the court has arrived at a view of their true meaning that it can approach the questions of law which arise out of them. It was not argued before us that in this broad respect there were any rules of construction peculiarly applicable to German instruments, and I therefore approach the articles having regard to the familiar English principles of construction. Translation, it is true, draws a veil, but I hope not an impenetrable one. Rule 4 sets up the special board as the representative of the foundation in its corporate capacity "for the administration of its estates and effects and for the supreme direction of its affairs." The two boards of management were set up by the same rule to manage and superintend the industrial concerns of the foundation. These boards under rule 8 control the internal trading operations of each firm through the mandatory and his deputy provided for by rule 9. The special board remains an advisory body acting through its deputy, who, however, has to be consulted in all matters outside the ordinary course of business, as shown by rule 14 and those which follow. It has been argued by the defendants that the present action, being in the nature of a passing-off action, ought to be brought in the name of the optical works because it is a matter of the trading activities of the foundation. The answer to that is that there are no such trading activities since the Russian confiscation. These are all carried on by the V.E.B.s. So much is this so that it has been argued both in the court below and in the German courts that the foundation has ceased to exist altogether.

Upon the footing which here prevails that the foundation is still an existing body, though only something in the nature of a holding company controlling assets remaining unconfiscated, it seems to me that the special board, if there be one, is the right person to authorise the action, the object of which is to preserve the goodwill of the foundation. The licence agreement of April 8, 1954, which I have mentioned[5] indicates that the confiscation **[648]** only touched the physical trading assets of the businesses and not the trade marks, and, if so, clearly the foundation through the special board has the duty to protect the remaining assets. Even if, as is I suppose arguable, the only thing that remains for the foundation is to dissolve itself under article 116 (a process which I believe under German law precedes winding up) it is clearly the duty of the special board to preserve the assets in the meanwhile.

It remains then to seek for the special board in the present circumstances. Rule 5 vests the office in an official of the Grand Duchy of Saxe-Weimar. That clearly became ineffective in 1918 when the Grand Duchy disappeared, and it becomes necessary to turn to article 113; this shows that the framer of the articles envisaged political changes in the State. The special board was then to pass to that department of State which should be in control of the university. This, apparently, under the Weimar Republic was the Ministry of Education of the Land of Thuringia. Alternatively, the same result is reached by reference to "the highest administrative authorities in Thuringia." Who are these? Clearly enough, under the Weimar Republic, the authorities of the Land. These were abolished by Hitler, but his régime may be ignored. The U.S.A. Command in 1945 reconstituted the government of the Land, and either this was confirmed by the Russian Government when it came in or a similar organisation was set up. As long as this lasted, there was, I consider, a properly constituted special board, namely, the Minister of Justice or Education of the Land acting through his deputy, Dr. Barth, on whose death, in November, 1949, there was an interregnum until May, 1951, when the then Education Minister of the Land purported to appoint Dr. Kunz as deputy. I am content for the present purpose to assume that this appointment was valid. The Land Government, however, was abolished by the German Democratic Republic law of July, 1952, and with it disappeared the special board which consisted of the Minister of Education of the Land and his deputy, Dr. Kunz. By the same law there came into existence the Rat, and the

[5] *Ante,* p. 645

question before us is whether that body is or is to be deemed to be the special board as being the "highest administrative authorit[y] in Thuringia."

The plaintiff's first point on this is that as a matter of construction all that need be sought for to fulfil this description is the body in fact controlling the area in question. Before Cross J. it was admitted that as a matter of political geography the **[649]** Rat did perform this function, that is to say, it was in control of the area.

The defendants took the point that rules 5 and 113 both point to an organ of government as fulfilling the function of the special board, and that anyone reading the two together must at once conclude that the "highest administrative authorities" alluded to in article 113 must of necessity mean the highest administrative authorities according to law. A mere usurping power, they say, is not within the meaning of the article, and they go on to say that, having regard to the fact that Her Majesty's Government has not recognised the German Democratic Republic, the English courts must ignore the decrees of that body and the organ it has created, and that the Rat is, accordingly, in the eye of an English court, a mere nullity.

The authorities which support this proposition may be said to begin with *City of Berne* v. *Bank of England*,[6]* where the sidenote reads: "A judicial court cannot take notice of a foreign government, not acknowledged by the government of the country, in which that court sits." It was a decision of Lord Eldon L.C. who declined relief to the City of Berne on the ground that the then existing government in Switzerland had not been acknowledged by Her Majesty's Government. To the same effect is the decision of Sir Lancelot Shadwell V.-C. in *Taylor* v. *Barclay*,[7]* where he made the following observations[8]: "The judgment"—that is, the judgment below—"proceeded, not on the question whether the court should give relief or not, or give a discovery or not, or give discovery, and withhold relief; but upon the question whether the King's courts should attend to the case of a party who founded his case on the representation that certain persons did form an independent government, recognised by this country, when the government of this country did not so recognise them. It appears to me that sound policy requires that the courts of the King should act in unison with the government of the King. Now I apprehend that what Lord Eldon proceeded upon was a general doctrine of policy, that is, that he would not allow a person to sue, at least as a plaintiff, in the Court of Chancery, who founded his case upon the representation that there was that existing as an independent government, acknowledged by this country, which, in fact, was not so. It is impossible for me to suppose that any other than some such general principle as that influenced him, **[650]** when I observe what his Lordship did in the case of *Biré* v. *Thompson*.[9]"

Coming down to modern times, the decision of Roche J. in *Aksionairnoye Obschestvo A. M. Luther* v. *Sagor (James) Co.* (*Luther* v. *Sagor*)[10]* was cited. In that case, the Soviet authority had confiscated certain timber and sold it to the defendants in this country. The plaintiff, a Russian company, claimed that no property had passed to the defendants, and Roche J. assented to that proposition on the ground that the Soviet Government had not been recognised by His Majesty's Government. The last paragraph of the headnote reads as follows: "*Held*, that if a foreign government or its sovereignty is not recognised by His Majesty's Government the courts of this country will not recognise such foreign government or its sovereignty: that on the facts the Russian Soviet Government had not been recognised by His Majesty's Government as the government of a Russian Federative Republic or of any sovereign state or power: that accordingly the court was unable to recognise any such Russian Government or to hold that it had sovereignty or was able by its decree to deprive the plaintiff company of their propery."

[6] (1804) 9 Ves. 347.
[7] (1828) 2 Sim. 213.
[8] Ibid. 221, 222.
[9] Unreported; see *per* Shadwell V.-C., loc. cit.
[10] [1921] 1 K.B. 456.

Roche J. read Lord Curzon's statement on the subject and said[11]: "It was said on behalf of the defendants that these communications were vague and ambiguous. I should rather say that they were guarded, but as clear as the indeterminate position of affairs in connection with the subject-matter of the communications enabled them to be; but lest it should be deemed that ampler or further information might now be available, I caused communication to be made by a Master of the Crown Office to His Majesty's Secretary of State for Foreign Affairs, asking whether there was in addition to the letters to the parties or their solicitors further matter or information which should be placed before me. The reply of the Secretary of State was that he had no further information which he desired to place before me. On these materials I am not satisfied that His Majesty's Government has recognised the Soviet Government as the Government of a Russian Federative Republic or of any sovereign state or power. I therefore am unable to recognise it, or to hold it has sovereignty, or is able by decree to deprive the plaintiff company of its property. Accordingly I decide this point against the defendants." **[651]**

The case went to the Court of Appeal.[12] By the time it reached that court the situation had altered in that His Majesty's Government had recognised the Soviet Government as the de facto government of Russia and as having existed at a date before the decree of confiscation. The court therefore held that the decree and the sale to the defendants could not be impeached. The court also held that Roche J. had been quite right in the result he reached at the time, there having then been no recognition.

There can be no doubt that no recognition has been accorded to the German Democratic Republic. It is said to follow that that body and its laws must be ignored in an English court. Upon that footing its creature, the Rat, must also be ignored and can have no authority to authorise the start of proceedings here. The plaintiffs started their argument by submitting that the defendants ought not to be allowed to argue a case inconsistent with that made below except in so far as the Foreign Office certificates have brought about a change. So far I agree. Starting from there, the plaintiffs pointed out that the case had been argued in the court below upon the footing that all governmental decrees on the east side of the "curtain" were either those of the German Democratic Republic or of the Russian occupying power, and that it was immaterial which was the true authority. This was well enough so long as East German laws were accepted as valid by both sides as they then were. In this court the position is quite altered, for we know now that Her Majesty's Government recognises no authority in the eastern zone but that of Russia. The plaintiffs then submit that all laws made by the German Democratic Republic must be taken to have been so made as agents of the Russians and are to be accepted accordingly as the acts of the de jure sovereign. This I am unable to accept. It is in fact notorious that the U.S.S.R. has recognised the German Democratic Republic as a sovereign state and treats its law-making capacity accordingly. The court offered counsel for the plaintiffs an opportunity to adduce evidence to the contrary, but he did not avail himself of it.

The plaintiff's second point was that on the footing that there was only one sovereign power in East Germany, namely, the U.S.S.R., the laws which that sovereign power regarded as valid must be respected under international law. This I reject; it would entail the consequence that no state could ever disagree with another on a question of recognition of a third.

The plaintiff next argued that in a commercial document, such **[652]** as the statute of the foundation, words ought to be given the meaning which commercial people would give them, and that the "highest administrative authorities" are what would be meant by those words by commercial people. In support of this proposition two cases were cited: first, a decision of Goddard J. and the Court of Appeal in *Kawasaki Kisen Kabushiki Kaisha* v. *Bantham Steamship Co. Ltd.* (*No.* 2).[13] Here the court was construing a charterparty which could

[11] Ibid. 477, 478.
[12] [1921] 3 K.B. 532; 37 T.L.R. 777, C.A.
[13] [1939] 2 K.B. 544; 55 T.L.R. 503; [1939] 1 All E.R. 819.

be cancelled "if war breaks out involving Japan." The Foreign Office, in response to a question, were not prepared to say that in their view a state of war existed. Goddard J. and the Court of Appeal held that this was not conclusive, and that it had been open to the umpire on the facts to find as he had found that war had broken out. In effect, it was held that the word "war" in that charterparty was used in the sense in which the ordinary commercial man would use it.

Similar is a decision of Sellers J. in *Luigi Monta of Genoa* v. *Czechofracht Co.*,[14]* where the question was whether freight was payable having regard to orders given by "any other government." This was again a case of a commercial document, the parties to it being an Italian and a Czecho-Slovak. The so-called government in question was the Chinese Government of Formosa, which was not recognised by Her Majesty's Government. Nevertheless, Sellers J. held, as a matter of construction, that it was not essential that it should be so recognised, and that in a commercial document it was enough to conclude on the facts that those who gave the order were in control of the country.

Those decisions, in my judgment, merely turn on the true construction of the commercial documents in question. Contracting parties are at liberty to express their meaning in such terms as they choose. This meaning is not controlled by the attitude of governments.

Apart from this, the plaintiff argues that the proper law of the articles is the law of Germany, and that any German, whether in West or East Germany, would, as indeed the actions between the parties in those countries show, recognise the Rat as being the relevant authority. Cf. *Banco de Bilbao* v. *Sancha*,[15]* where Clauson L.J., giving the judgment of the court, said[16]: "The question what body of directors have the legal right of representing the Banco de Bilbao, a commercial entity **[653]** organised under the laws prevailing in Bilbao and having its corporate home in Bilbao, must depend in the first place on the articles under which it is constituted. The interpretation of those articles and the operation of them, having regard to the general law, must be governed by the lex loci contractus (see *per* Lord Wrenbury in *Russian Commercial and Industrial Bank* v. *Comptoir d'Escompte de Mulhouse*),[17]* i.e., by the law from time to time prevailing at the place where the corporate home (domicilio social) was set up. It seems clear that (for example) a law of the French legislature cannot have (at all events outside France) any operation in regard to the relations between an English company established in England under English law, and its shareholders on the one hand, and persons claiming as a board of directors to have control over the affairs of that company on the other. The question accordingly resolves itself into this: What is the Government whose laws govern in such a matter the Banco de Bilbao? The answer would seem necessarily to be: the laws of the government of the territory in which Bilbao is situate. Should the question arise as to what government must be recognised in this court as the government of the territory in which Bilbao is situate, the question must, in case of doubt, be resolved by a statement made by His Majesty to this court through the appropriate channel."

Moreover, says the plaintiff, it is absurd to read into this contract, even if the word "lawful" be properly employed, a reference to recognition by Her Majesty's Government.

I feel the force of these arguments, but I do not think that they can prevail. The plaintiff, through the Rat, is seeking to sue in the English courts, and, therefore, it seems to me, the English law as to recognition must prevail, and in our courts the Rat is not a body which can be recognised as competent to set the wheels of justice in motion.

There remain the plaintiff's alternative claims. The first depends on the "power of attorney" which I have already read.[18] This purports to have emanated from the Ministry of Education in Thuringia on June 29, 1951, and so far is

[14] [1956] 2 Q.B. 552; [1956] 3 W.L.R. 480; [1956] 2 All E.R. 769.
[15] [1938] 2 K.B. 176; 54 T.L.R. 603; [1938] 2 All E.R. 253, C.A.
[16] [1938] 2 K.B. 176, 194.
[17] [1925] A.C. 112, 149.
[18] Ante, p. 646.

unexceptionable as being a power granted by the special board, but when one turns to the subject-matter and reads the four special spheres in which the power is given to the attorney, it seems to me that on its true construction the document is no more than an appointment of Dr. Schrade to act in the several spheres defined *if* the special board **[654]** authorises him so to do. On any other view this would be a complete delegation of the main powers which the rules entrust to the special board. It is to be observed that Dr. Schrade may transfer his powers to a third party, and it cannot be supposed that he could, for instance, transfer to a third party the right to acquire real property anywhere at any time and to any amount. This document does not in my judgment carry Dr. Schrade's powers any further than such powers as he would have as mandatory of a board of management under the rules. In other words, it defines the scope of Dr. Schrade's powers but does not sanction his use of them except in a properly authorised instance.

Secondly, Dr. Schrade claimed to be entitled to authorise the action as a member of the board of management of the optical works. The first question here is whether he was such a member when the writ was issued in 1955. For present purposes I assume that he was well appointed as a member of the board by Dr. Barth in 1945, but this appointment only lasted two years, and Dr. Barth's subsequent direction to carry on for an indefinite period seems to me ineffective having regard to rule 27, which forbids an appointment "with the option of revocation." It follows that he ceased to be a member of the board in 1947. He was, however, re-appointed for life in 1951, and he may therefore have been a member of the board of management in 1955. I feel much doubt about this, because in 1951 he was disqualified from being a member under rule 28, being already in the salaried service of the V.E.B. However this may be, there was in 1955 no quorum of this board. Of the three appointed in 1945, only Dr. Schrade remained; Dr. Schomerus had retired in 1949, and Dr. Sandmann had died in 1954. The appointments of Drs. Hüber and Müller by the Rat in 1954 are to be ignored, as is the purported appointment of Dr. Schrade in 1954 to be mandatory under rule 4. The board of management was as a result incapable of acting. It was argued by the plaintiff that there was no doctrine of ultra vires in German law and that, therefore, the fact that there was no quorum was not an obstacle. This has nothing to do with the doctrine of ultra vires, in my opinion.

Thirdly, Dr. Schrade alleged that he had authority as mandatory of the board under rule 9. In an affidavit filed on May 11, 1959, he said that he "began to act" as mandatory in 1953, but no evidence of appointment is forthcoming until the document of 1954 above mentioned. Anyhow, a mandatory does not have a general authority to start actions by the foundation. In my judgment there is nothing in this point. **[655]**

An argument was also raised for the plaintiff under rule 114. It was said that on the footing that no special board existed within rule 113, rule 114 empowered the executive board of management of the optical works to take over the functions of the special board. The answer to this is that there was at the relevant time no "executive board of management" of the optical works, first of all because there was no quorum and, secondly, because there were no functions of management to perform and the board was thus not "executive."

Rule 114 goes on to provide for the event of the optical board no longer existing, in which case the function is to be taken over by the board of management of the oldest works of the foundation in Jena. It was argued that this pointed to the board of management of the glassworks, all the members of which signed the authority of November 16, 1956. This point, however, was abandoned by the plaintiff. There were, when the writ was issued, no "works" of the foundation existing in Jena or the neighbourhood.

I would, therefore, allow the appeal.

DANCKWERTS L.J. I have had the advantage of reading the exhaustive judgments of my two brethren, and, as I agree with them, I cannot find any valid reason for adding to the volume.

DIPLOCK L.J. The Carl Zeiss Stiftung, which both parties to this appeal assert is still in existence, is an artificial person; its legal personality is the creation of the law of a foreign sovereign State. It can act only through the agency of natural persons. The sole issue in this appeal is whether or not any of those natural persons who purported to give or to ratify instructions to Courts & Co., a firm of English solicitors, to issue a writ in the name of Carl Zeiss Stiftung were entitled according to English law to give such instructions on its behalf. I say "according to English law" because that is the only law which we are entitled to apply—"the law and customs of this realm" of our judicial oaths. English courts are concerned only with the legal consequences in England of things which happen, whether they happen in England or out of England. That is the limit of our jurisdiction. When it is claimed that things which have happened outside England have legal consequences in England to which an English court ought to give effect we ascertain those consequences by applying rules of English law, in particular, those rules which are called indifferently "conflict of laws" or "private international law." But because, despite this latter name, the rules are rules of English law, it by no means follows that the legal consequences in England of a **[656]** thing which happened abroad will be the same as the legal consequences of that happening in the State in which it happened, or as its legal consequences in any other State.

In determining what are the legal consequences in England of a thing which has happened outside England, the first inquiry usually is to ascertain what would be the legal consequences of that happening under that system of law which is regarded in English law as the "proper law" applicable to that happening, i.e., the law which the parties by whom the thing was done contemplated would regulate its legal consequences. This is often the law of the place where the thing happened—the lex loci actus. Although there are many exceptions to this rule, the proper law of the only happenings with which we are concerned in the present appeal, viz., the creation and constitution of the Carl Zeiss Stiftung and the authority of various natural persons to authorise the institution of legal proceedings in its name in England, is the lex loci actus.

In cases where the proper law of a thing which has happened outside England is the lex loci actus, the English courts will normally treat that happening as having the same legal consequences in England as it would have under the lex loci actus unless there is some rule of English law to the contrary. In many cases there is, such as the anomalous rule as to the legal consequences in England of "torts" committed abroad. Where English courts do treat a thing which has happened abroad as having the same consequences in England as it would have under the lex loci actus, they do this because the sovereign Government of the United Kingdom, of which the courts in England, Scotland and Northern Ireland are the judicial branch, recognises the right of other sovereign governments to lay down what shall be the legal consequences of things which happen within their territorial jurisdiction. The lex loci actus to the consequences of which English courts will give effect is thus limited to laws made by or under the authority of those persons who are recognised by the Government of the United Kingdom as being the sovereign government of the place where the thing happens, and the English courts will not treat the happening as having in England any legal consequences which are claimed to result from a law made by persons who are not recognised as being either the sovereign government of that place or persons authorised by that sovereign government to make laws for that place.

The granting or withholding of recognition of persons as being the sovereign government of any territory by the Government of **[657]** the United Kingdom is a prerogative of the Crown: that is to say, a function of the executive branch of the Government of the United Kingdom. The English courts as part of the judicial branch of the United Kingdom Government are bound of their own motion to give effect to such recognition or non-recognition and, if they are in any doubt as to the facts of recognition, must inform themselves by inquiry from that branch of government, the executive, through which the prerogative power to grant or withhold recognition is exercised. The courts are bound to give effect to any statement as to recognition or non-recognition received from the executive, for the Crown cannot speak with two contradictory voices through its executive and its judiciary. That is what was decided by the Court of Appeal in the earlier application in the present appeal.[19]

As a result of that decision, it is now apparent that the hearing before Cross J. was conducted upon the erroneous assumption that the "German Democratic Republic" was recognised by the Crown as a sovereign State whose territory included Jena, and the "Government of the German Democratic Republic" as the sovereign government of that territory. Both parties to this appeal combined to lead the judge into making that assumption; nevertheless, the fact that it was not so recognised was a matter of which, in English law, he was bound to take judicial notice even though he was ignorant of it—and we, who are not ignorant of it, are bound to take judicial notice of it in this appeal. If we did not, we should decide this case on an erroneous basis of law. This we are not entitled knowingly to do. It would be contrary to public policy for us to do so, for recognition is a political act from which many political consequences flow.

In English law, the creation of a corporation with an artificial legal personality distinct from that of the natural persons who compose it or act on its behalf is regarded as an act of sovereign power. Only a sovereign can create a corporate personality or make laws authorising its creation. Once created, its continued existence, its constitution and its powers are regulated and can be altered in accordance with the law of the sovereign State by which it was created, or of a State recognised by Her Majesty's Government as the successor of that State. In English law the "proper law" to be applied in ascertaining what are the legal consequences of its creation, constitution and powers is the law of the State which created it or the recognised successor State.

To determine whether particular natural persons are entitled **[658]** in English law to instruct solicitors to issue a writ in the name of the Carl Zeiss Stiftung involves two distinct questions. The first is a question of construction of the constitution of the corporation: "What qualifications are laid down by that constitution as requisite to entitle a natural person to commence legal proceedings in its name?" The second question is a question of application: "Did those persons who in fact authorised or ratified the issue of the writ in the present action possess those qualifications?" The "proper law" for determining both these questions is the law which was in force in the place in which the Stiftung was incorporated at the date at which instructions to issue the writ in its name were given in the autumn of 1955, but only in so far as such law was made by persons recognised by the Crown as being the sovereign government of that place.

The Question of Construction

The relevant articles of the constitution (statute) of the Stiftung have already been set out by Harman L.J. The Carl-Zeiss Stiftung was created at Jena under the law of the Grand Duchy of Saxe-Weimar, which was then a federated state forming part of the German Empire. The German Empire was the sovereign State, and the Government of the Grand Duchy of Saxe-Weimar was a subordinate government authorised under the constitutional law of the German Empire to make laws, inter alia, creating and regulating corporations within the territorial area of the Grand Duchy, in which Jena was situated. The statute of the Carl Zeiss Stiftung has been amended from time to time since its incorporation in 1896 pursuant to laws made by the sovereign government of Germany from time to time recognised by the Government of the United Kingdom, or by the subordinate governments authorised by that sovereign government to make laws for the geographical area, Thuringia, in which Jena is situated, but no alteration has been made to it under any purported law of the Government of the "German Democratic Republic" or of a subordinate government established or authorised by that government. On the question of construction, therefore, no problem as to recognition of the "German Democratic Republic" or of its

[19] [1965] 1 Ch. 525.

"Government" arises. Furthermore, the relevant articles have remained unaltered since the creation of the Stiftung in 1896. They fall to be construed according to the law in force in Jena at that date. Their construction, as distinct from their application, does not change with the passsage of time. The evidence discloses a controversy as to **[659]** whether, upon the true construction of the statute in accordance with that law, the right to authorise the commencement of proceedings for the protection of trade marks belonging to the Stiftung or for "passing off" was vested in the board of management of the respective businesses of the Stiftung in which the trade marks were used or was vested in the special board if there is one. Cross J. decided that controversy in favour of the special board. There was expert evidence of the "proper law" which entitled him to do so, and I see no grounds upon which his decision to that effect can be assailed.

As he found, upon the question of application, that the special board did exist in 1955 when the writ was issued and did in fact ratify its issue, it was unnecessary for him to consider who, if anyone, had the right to authorise the commencement of proceedings in the name of the Stiftung if there were no special board in existence. Under the respondents' cross-notice, it is necessary for us to consider this. I agree with Harman L.J. that under article 113 the appropriate persons would be the board of management of the optical works, or, if they too had ceased to exist, the board of management of the last works of the Stiftung existing in Jena or its neighbourhood.

The Question of Application

(a) *The special board.* The Grand Duchy of Saxe-Weimar ceased to exist in 1918. The provisions of article 5 as to the constitution of the special board thereupon became, in the language of the translator of the statutes, "untenable," and the functions of the special board thereupon devolved upon "that department of State which, with regard to the University of Jena, occupies the place of the State Department of the Grand Duchy of Saxe-Weimar acting as the special board, providing that its seat is in Thuringia," or, if there is no such department of State, "the highest administrative authorities in Thuringia."

The ratification by the "special board" of the issue of the writ in the present action which is relied upon by the respondents was given on November 22, 1956, by a natural person called Lechmann describing himself as "Deputy of the Chairman" and purporting to act on behalf of the "Rat" or Council of the District of Gera. The first questions for our determination are: (1) Did those natural persons who in November, 1956, were purporting to act as the Council of Gera constitute that department of State which at that date exercised in relation to the University of Jena the same functions as those which were exercised in 1896 **[660]** by the State Department of the Grand Duchy of Saxe-Weimar, or (2) if there were no such department of State, did they constitute the highest administrative authorities in Thuringia?

These questions we have to answer according to English law. A department of State is a natural person or body of natural persons, with or without separate artificial legal personality, who exercise executive or administrative functions of government, and who are authorised to do so (a) by the government of the sovereign State in which they exercise those functions, or (b) by laws made by the government of that sovereign State, or (c) by a person or body of persons authorised by such government to make laws conferring executive or administrative powers. We have, therefore, to investigate the source from which the Council of Gera derived its executive or administrative powers. This is dealt with in the affidavit of Mr. Honig filed on behalf of the respondents.

Prior to July 25, or possibly August 9, 1952, there was a provincial government of the Land of Thuringia. It exercised executive and administrative functions of government and, it may be, also some legislative functions. It was originally authorised to do so by the Government of the United States of America as the occupying power of the zone of Germany in which Thuringia was situate, and its authority was confirmed by the Government of the U.S.S.R. when that state became the occupying power of the zone. Despite the purported creation of a new sovereign state, the "German Democratic Republic," with a territory consisting of the zone of Germany theretofore occupied by the U.S.S.R., the provincial government of the Land of Thuringia continued to function as the executive and administrative authority in Thuringia. As its authority had been confirmed by the government of the U.S.S.R., which has at all material times been recognised by Her Majesty's Government as de jure entitled to exercise governing authority in respect of Thuringia, the purported establishment of the "German Democratic Republic" with a "government" which claims to be a sovereign government as an independent successor government not subordinate to the U.S.S.R., did not, according to English law, have any legal effect upon the executive or administrative powers of the government of the Land of Thuringia, nor did it terminate, according to English law, the authority conferred upon the government of the Land of Thuringia by the Government of the U.S.S.R. to exercise executive and administrative functions of government. The Ministry of Education of the **[661]** Government of the Land of Thuringia exercised in relation to the University of Jena the same functions as those which were exercised in 1896 by the State Department of the Grand Duchy of Saxe-Weimar, and so long as the Government of the Land of Thuringia continued to exist, at any rate in the form in which it was constituted under the aegis of the Government of the U.S.S.R., its Ministry of Education would in English law be a special board of the Carl Zeiss Stiftung. It ceased to exist, however, in 1952, in the following circumstances. On July 23, 1952, a body of persons describing themselves as "The People's Chamber of the German Democratic Republic" passed a purported "law relating to the further democratisation in the "development and working of public authorities in the Länder [States] of the German Democratic Republic." This purported law provided for the substitution for the existing governments of the Länder of a two-tiered system of administration subordinate to the government of the German Democratic Republic. The territories hitherto administered by the governments of the Länder were to be divided into large districts (Bezirke) which were in turn to be subdivided into smaller districts (Kreise). It was provided by clause 4 of this law that the functions, executive, administrative and legislative, previously exercised by the governments of the Länder, were to be transferred to the authorities of the new Bezirke and Kreise. The "Cabinet," or Council of Ministers, of the German Democratic Republic was authorised by clause 3 of the law to make orders regulating the constitution and powers of the executive authorities of the new Bezirke and Kreise. Such an order was purportedly made on July 24, 1952, providing for the creation in each Bezirke of a District Diet (Bezirkstag) with legislative powers subordinate to those of the People's Chamber of the German Democratic Republic and a District Council (Bezirksrat) as "the executive and administrative authority of the District Diet." The decrees of the Bezirksrat were to be subject to repeal by the Cabinet of the German Democratic Republic. On July 25, 1952, in pursuance of the above-mentioned law and order, a further law was passed, the full text of which is not in evidence, purporting to divide Thuringia into three districts (Bezirke), of which Gera was one. Jena was geographically in the District of Gera. By clause 4 of this further law, all functions hitherto performed by the government of the Land of Thuringia were transferred to the executive and administrative authorities of the new districts pursuant to clause 4 of the law of July 23, 1952. It is not stated in the evidence by what body this further **[662]** law of July 25, 1952, was passed, but I will assume in favour of the respondents that it was passed by the expiring provincial government of Thuringia, as would appear to be contemplated by clause 1 of the purported law of July 23, 1952. It is, however, clear upon the evidence that after July 25 or August 9, when the further law was published in the Gazette of the Land of Thuringia, those persons who had up till then constituted the provincial government of Thuringia in fact ceased to exercise any executive or administrative functions in that territory, and thereafter all acts of administration were done by the persons constituting the purported new executive and administrative authorities in the new districts, viz., the district councils (Bezirksräte). In particular, the acts of administration in relation to the University of Jena which were formerly performed by the Ministry of Education of the provincial government of the Land of Thuringia were done by the Council of Gera.

The Council of Gera owes its existence, its constitution, and whatever powers it possesses, to the purported exercise of sovereign powers by persons claiming to be the "government" of the "German Democratic Republic," to wit, a law passed by the People's Chamber or legislature of that "government" and an order made by the cabinet or executive of that "government." Her Majesty's Government does not recognise the "German Democratic Republic" as a sovereign, nor its "government" as a sovereign government. It recognises the government of the U.S.S.R. alone as entitled de jure to exercise governing authority in the area in which Jena is situated.

It follows that, in applying the lex loci actus for the purpose of deciding what natural persons were qualified under the statutes of the Carl Zeiss Stiftung in 1955 or thereafter to authorise or to ratify the issue of a writ in England in its name, we as an English court must ignore any laws passed or orders made by persons purporting to act as the government of the German Democratic Republic. The English cases which established this rule, in particular *Luther* v. *Sagor*,[20]* have already been cited by Harman L.J. I will content myself with adopting the succinct expression of the consequences of non-recognition by Storey J. in the United States case of *Gelston* v. *Hoyt*[21]: "No doctrine is better established than that it belongs exclusively to governments to recognise new states in the revolutions which may occur in the world: and until such recognition either by our own government **[663]** or the government to which the new state belonged *Courts of Justice are bound to consider the ancient state of things as remaining unaltered*"—although, as the law has developed in England by 1964, recognition by our own government alone is the decisive factor.

This principle is in no way eroded by the decisions in *Kawasaki Kisem Kabushiki Kaisha* v. *Bantham Steamship Co. Ltd.* (*No. 2*)[22] and *Luigi Monta of Genoa* v. *Cechofracht Co.*,[23]* relied on by counsel for the respondents. Parties to contracts may, in general, agree on whatever terms they please. They may agree that certain contractual consequences may flow from acts of force which take place in circumstances which the Government of the United Kingdom does not recognise as a "state of war" or from acts of force instigated by persons whom the Government of the United Kingdom does not recognise as a "government." In giving effect to such a contract, the English court is not recognising the existence of a state of war or the existence of a foreign sovereign government. Nor is it doing so when, as in the above-mentioned cases, it is construing what in the result it decides is a contract of this kind. It is simply finding out what the parties meant by the words used in the document. This is what we are doing when we are answering the question of construction. It is quite different from what we are doing when we are answering the question of application.

Counsel for the respondents has argued that, in view of Her Majesty's Government's recognition of the Government of the U.S.S.R. as entitled de jure to exercise governing authority in the area in which Jena is situate, any law, by whomever it purports to be made, which is in fact acted upon and enforced in that area, must be presumed by an English court to have been made by persons who were authorised to make it by the Government of the U.S.S.R. This contention thus badly stated seems to me to be in flat contradiction of the value of English Law, for it would involve treating the recognition of a new sovereign state by the Government of the U.S.S.R. as binding upon the English courts rather than recognition of such new state by the Government of the United Kingdom. Furthermore, in this particular case it is not as if the Eastern Zone of Germany ever "belonged," in Storey J.'s phrase, "to the U.S.S.R."; the carving out of a new state, the "German Democratic Republic," affected Germany as a whole, **[664]** and the Foreign Office certificate makes it clear that Her Majesty's Government does not recognise the authority of the Government of the U.S.S.R. to do that. But counsel further asked us to assume—as I am prepared to

[20] [1921] 1 K.B. 456; [1921] 3 K.B. 532, C.A.
[21] (1818) 3 Wheat. 246, 324.
[22] [1939] 2 K.B. 544.
[23] [1956] 2 Q.B. 552.

do—that the Government of the U.S.S.R. would recognise the validity of laws made by the "Government of the German Democratic Republic." If, he said, a law is for any reason recognised as valid by the government which is itself recognised by Her Majesty's Government as entitled to exercise governing authority in the geographical area to which the law purports to apply, the English courts must also recognise it as a valid law.

For my part I cannot accept this contention either. It is, I think, merely another way of formulating the contention just discussed. If the Government of the U.S.S.R. recognised the "Government of the German Democratic Republic" as a subordinate government deriving its powers from the Government of the U.S.S.R. and exercising them on its behalf in an area in respect of which the Government of the U.S.S.R. is recognised by the United Kingdom Government as entitled to make laws—as was the case with the provincial government of the Land of Thuringia before 1949—such recognition would be relevant, but there is no evidence, and Mr. Aldous does not seek to adduce it, that the Government of the U.S.S.R. does so recognise the "Government of the German Democratic Republic." All that I am prepared to assume—and I think it is a matter of which I can take judicial notice—is that the Government of the U.S.S.R. recognises the "Government of the German Democratic Republic" as the independent sovereign government of an independent sovereign state for whose territory the Government of the U.S.S.R. claims no power to make laws. It recognises the laws of the "Government of the German Democratic Republic" as valid under its own rules of private international law for the purpose of determining the legal consequences in the U.S.S.R. of things which happen in another independent sovereign state. This kind of recognition by the U.S.S.R. of the validity of the laws of the "German Democratic Republic" is irrelevant to the issues which we have to decide in this case.

We are thus compelled to approach the question whether the "Council of Gera" was the special board of the Carl Zeiss Stiftung under article 113 of its statute on the basis that the purported laws and order of July 23-25, 1952, had never been passed. The Council of Gera owes its very existence to that legislation and order. So far as English courts are concerned it **[665]** is not merely not a "Department of State"; it is nothing, and the natural persons who purport to act as the "Council of Gera" have no powers in that capacity which we are entitled to recognise.

Counsel for the respondents has, however, argued that, if the "Council of Gera" is not a "Department of State," then there was no longer in existence after 1952 any department of State which with regard to the University of Jena occupied the position of the State Department of the Grand Duchy of Saxe-Weimar. Accordingly, he contended, the second part of article 113 applies, and the Council of Gera is in fact exercising the highest administrative functions in Thuringia whether or not it is recognised by Her Majesty's Government. In construing article 113 of the statute, he says, it would be absurd to construe it so as to limit the "highest administrative authorities in Thuringia" to the highest administrative authorities in Thuringia who are recognised as such by the Government of the United Kingdom. The draftsman of the statute in 1896 cannot have intended this.

Like Harman L.J., I recognise the force of this argument, but I think that it is fallacious. Its fallacy lies in confusing the question of construction with the question of application. I agree that when construing the statutes of the Stiftung the question whether Her Majesty's Government has recognised any body of persons as the "highest administrative authorities in Thuringia" is wholly irrelevant. But the question of application is one of fact: who were the highest administrative authorities in Thuringia in 1956? This is a fact which, so far as an English court is concerned, is determined conclusively by the certificate of the Foreign Office. That certificate states specifically that apart from the States and Governments of the French Republic, the United Kingdom, the United States of America and the U.S.S.R., and the Control Council, Her Majesty's Government has not recognised either "de jure or de facto any other authority purporting to exercise governing authority in or in respect of that zone," i.e., the area which includes Thuringia. We, therefore, as an English court, are precluded from holding that the Council of Gera was in fact in 1956 exercising any governmental powers in the district in which Jena is situate.

There is an air of unreality about this because there was before this court evidence which was admitted in the court below before the certificate of the Foreign Office was obtained, and this contradicts the conclusive evidence which that certificate represents. Evidence to show that the Council of Gera was de facto exercising administrative powers in Gera would not, however, have been **[666]** admissable if the certificate of the Foreign Office had been obtained earlier. The unreality would have been kept behind the curtain. We, who have a certificate in the terms quoted above, are bound to disregard this evidence which contradicts it.

Finally, it was argued that this court would not be precluded by the Foreign Office certificate from finding as a fact that the natural persons who call themselves the Council of Gera were in fact doing acts of administration in the District in which Jena is situated, and that even if the court was bound to hold that they had had no authority to do so, nevertheless on the true construction of article 113 they fell within the description "the highest administrative authorities in Thuringia." I think that this is merely another way of inviting us to say that the Foreign Office certificate is not conclusive as to the relevant factual situation in Thuringia. The certificate is, of course, not conclusive as to the actual things which natural persons are doing in a foreign state, but it is conclusive as to whether those things are being done as acts of government. The question of application does not depend upon what actual things natural persons are doing in Thuringia but upon who are "the highest administrative authorities," i.e., are entitled to perform or are in fact performing acts of government. We are precluded by the Foreign Office certificate from holding that the natural persons who call themselves the "Council of Gera" are performing any acts of government even de facto, and it is not, I think, arguable on the construction of article 113 that "the highest administrative authorities in Thuringia" means persons who are not performing and are not entitled to perform any acts of government.

It remains to consider the alternative arguments raised by the respondents' cross-notice in support of their contention that the issue of the writ in the name of the Stiftung was properly authorised either by the board of management of the optical works under article 114 or by Dr. Schrade as agent of the special board under a written power of attorney of June 20, 1951, or as mandatory of the stiftung under article 9.

(b) *The board of management of the optical works.* As, for the reasons already discussed, we are bound to hold that the Council of Gera was not an administrative authority, and as the evidence discloses that the provincial government of the Land of Thuringia in fact ceased to exist in 1952 when the so-called District of Gera was constituted, it follows that at the relevant time the state of affairs contemplated by the draftsman of the statutes had occurred, and a special board corresponding to the provisions of **[667]** article 5 or 113 no longer existed. Accordingly, the provisions of article 114 apply. Under those provisions the board of management of the optical works was entitled to exercise the powers of the special board. There is no evidence of any resolution of any persons describing themselves as the board of management of the optical works purporting to authorise or to ratify the issue of the writ. The meeting of November 16, 1956, which purported to ratify the issue of the writ in the name of the Stiftung was described as a meeting of the Stiftung, not of the board of management of either of its works. Those present were all members of the board of management of the glass works, which, it is now conceded, had no power to authorise the issue of the writ. Dr. Schrade was also a purported member of the board of management of the optical works, but the claim of Hüber and Müller to be members of that board was based on their appointment as such by the Council of Gera acting as special board on April 10, 1954, and these appointments we are bound to treat as a nullity.

The claim that the issue of the writ was authorised by the board of management of the optical works thus rests upon the contention that Dr. Schrade acting alone was that board. The answers to this contention are: (1) that by article 7 of the statute of the Stiftung a board of management must consist of at least three members, although two may act temporarily pending the appointment of a third. In no circumstances, however, may a board of management consist of one person only; (2) that although Dr. Schrade was validly appointed in 1945 for two years, his subsequent reappointment in 1947 for an indefinite period terminable by notice appears to be invalid under article 27 of the statute. I may add that, since he was manager of the V.E.B., he was disqualified as from the date in 1948 when he took up that post under article 28. There is, however, conflicting evidence as to the effect of this disqualification in German law. The judge made no finding about it, and I accordingly base my conclusion that Dr. Schrade acting alone could not be the board of management of the optical works upon the two other grounds. It was never suggested in the evidence that Dr. Schrade, acting alone, could constitute the board of management of the optical works. Reliance was placed upon the concurrence of Hüber and Müller, whose appointments we are bound to hold were invalid.

(c) *The power of attorney.* On June 20, 1951, Dr. Schrade was given a power of attorney by the Ministry of Education of the **[668]** provisional government of the Land of Thuringia which, it is conceded, was then the special board. The terms of this document have been recited by Harman L.J. I agree with what he says as to the effect of this document, and need do no more than point out that if it had the effect contended for by the respondents, and conferred upon Dr. Schrade the right to do acts of the kind referred to in the document upon his own initiative and at his own discretion on behalf of the Stiftung without any further authority from any of its organs of management, this would render nugatory all the elaborate provisions of the statutes apportioning the spheres of management between the special board, the boards of management of the works, and the deputy. I need only draw attention to articles 4,[24] 6, 8, 10, 14, 15,[25] and particularly to article 16, which contains express provisions as to the persons who are alone entitled to authorise, inter alia, the sale or incumbrance of real property, the mortgaging of personal property, and the taking part by the Stiftung in civil actions in relation to disputes which do not result from the ordinary course of business. This power of attorney does no more, in my view, that constitute Dr. Schrade the proper officer of the Stiftung to do such specific acts of the classes described as are duly decided upon by the person or persons upon whom the statute confers the power of making such decisions.

(d) *The mandatory of the Stiftung.* For the same reasons, even if Dr. Schrade had been validly appointed as mandatory of the Stiftung under article 9 of the statute, this, in my view, would give him no authority to decide at his own discretion to commence proceedings in the name of the Stiftung. This article merely provides who is to be the proper officer of the Stiftung whose signature will bind the Stiftung in transactions with third parties. A German corporation has no seal; there must be a person, whose name and description is in fact registered in the commercial register open to inspection by the public, whose signature will bind it. But although this may estop the corporation from denying to a third party that an act done by its mandatory, whose name is registered on the commercial register, was done without its authority, it cannot in my view prevent a third party from asserting that the purported act of the corporation was in fact done without authority, particularly where, as in the present case, the third party claims, whether rightly or wrongly (as to which I express no view), to be acting on behalf of the corporation. **[669]**

For these reasons, and for those already so much better expressed by Harman L.J., I would allow this appeal. This relieves us of the necessity of considering the arguments which commended themselves to Cross J. in his careful and closely reasoned judgment, for they were all based upon an erroneous though excusable assumption of fact upon which, in the light of the Foreign Office

[24] See *ante*, p. 601.
[25] See *ante*, pp. 640-641.

certificates, it would be contrary to public policy for this court to base its decision.

Appeal allowed.
Writ and all subsequent proceedings struck out.
No costs of either side down to date of present hearing; plaintiff's solicitors to pay defendants' costs of present hearing on common fund basis.
Certificate for three counsel.
Leave to appeal to the House of Lords.

Solicitors: *Herbert Smith & Co.; Courts & Co.*

CARL ZEISS STIFTUNG v. RAYNER & KEELER LTD. AND OTHERS
(Original-Appeal)

RAYNER AND KEELER LTD. AND OTHERS v. COURTS AND OTHERS
(Cross-Appeal)

([1967] A.C. 853)

December 1, 2, 6, 7, 8, 9, 13, 14, 15, 16, 1965; January 24, 25, 27, 31, February, 1, 2, 3, 7, 8, 9, 13, 14, 15, 16, May 18, 1966: House of Lords: Lords Reid, Hodson, Guest, Upjohn, Wilberforce.

International Law—Recognition—Effect—Action begun by English solicitors on behalf of East German organisation—Solicitors instructed by governing body of organisation—Governing body authorised by government not recognised by H.M. Government—Unrecognised government set up by de jure government—Whether governing body of organisation competent to institute proceedings.
Conflict of Laws—Foreign judgment—Issue estoppel—Judgment by court of country with unrecognised government.

In 1891 there was established at Jena, in the Grand Duchy of Saxe-Weimar, the Carl-Zeiss-Stiftung ("the foundation"), an organisation with industrial, scientific and charitable objects. Under the articles of its constitution (or "statute") the legal domicile of the foundation was to be Jena, and for representing it as an incorporate body, for the administration of its estate and effects, and for the supreme direction of its affairs, a "special board" was to be formed, the rights and duties of which were to pertain to that department of the state service of the Grand Duchy under which the affairs of the University of Jena were for the time being placed. In the case of the cessation of the special board in consequence of political changes in the state, the representation of the foundation, and its statutory administration, were to be made over to the department of state which, with regard to the University, occupied the place of the State Department of the Grand Duchy, provided that its seat was in Thuringia, otherwise to "the highest administrative authorities in Thuringia." In 1918 the Grand Duchy was abolished and Jena became part of the "Land" of Thuringia. In 1949 there was set up in the Russian-administered zone of Germany, the German Democratic Republic, **[854]** and the court in the present case proceeded on the basis that the Land of Thuringia continued to exist until 1952, when under a decree of the German Democratic Republic, it was divided into smaller areas, Jena being in the area of Gera, governed by the Rat (or Council) of Gera, which was itself set up by that decree.

In 1955 English solicitors, on the instruction of an individual authorised by the Council of Gera as the special board of the foundation, issued a writ against the defendants, two English limited companies and an organisation with its headquarters in the Federal German Republic (West Germany) also calling itself Carl-Zeiss-Stiftung, to restrain them (inter alia) from passing off optical and glass instruments with reference to the name "Carl-Zeiss-Stiftung" or "Carl Zeiss" or "Zeiss." Meanwhile proceedings had also been brought in West Germany to restrain this organisation and the persons appointed to administer it from administrative and representative activities on behalf of the foundation; in 1960 the Federal Supreme Court dismissed the action. In 1956 the defendants in the English proceedings took out a summons to stay all proceedings in the action and to have it dismissed on the ground that it had been begun, and was being maintained, without the authority of the foundation. On March 6, 1964, Cross J. dismissed the summons, holding that under the articles of the foundation the proper body to authorise on its behalf an action such as the present was its "special board," which was at the material time the Council of Gera. No point was taken before Cross J. as to whether Her Majesty's Government had recognised de jure or de facto the German Democratic Republic or its Government, or as to the application in the English courts of East German legislation or decrees. The defendants appealed and moved the Court of Appeal, asking that a letter be written to the Foreign Secretary requesting him to certify whether (inter alia) Her Majesty's Government had granted recognition de jure or de facto to the German Democratic Republic or to its Government and, if yes, when. The court,[1] holding that recognition was a matter which the court of its own motion was bound to consider, acceded to that request, and the Foreign Secretary subsequently certified that:

"Her Majesty's Government have not granted any recognition de jure or de facto to (a) the 'German Democratic Republic' or (b) its 'Government.'"

In answer to a further letter from the court,[2] the Secretary of State certified (inter alia) that since June, 1945, and up to the present date

"Her Majesty's Government have recognised the State and Government of the Union of Soviet Socialist Republics as de jure entitled to exercise governing authority in respect of [East Germany]." **[855]**

On the defendants' contention that the council of Gera, having been set up by a decree of the unrecognised government of the German Democratic Republic, could not be recognised by the English courts as being the special board of the foundation with authority to institute proceedings therein on its behalf:—

Held, (1) that, although the German Democratic Republic is not recognised by Her Majesty's Government, its acts should be recognised by the English courts as lawful, not as the acts of a sovereign state, but as acts done by a subordinate body which the U.S.S.R. set up to act on its behalf, since a de jure governing body cannot disclaim responsibility for the acts of subordinate bodies set up by it.

City of Berne v. *Bank of England** (1804) 9 Ves. 347; *Taylor* v. *Barclay** (1828) 2 Sim. 213; and *Aksionairnoye Obschestvo A.M. Luther* v. *James Sagor & Co.** [1921] 1 K.B. 456; [1921] 3 K.B. 532; 37 T.L.R. 777, C.A. considered.

(2) That the decision of the West German courts does not fulfil the requirements for the application of the doctrine of issue estoppel and accordingly has not made the subject-matter of the present issue res judicata, so that the defendant solicitors are not estoppel from contending that they have authority to bring the action in the name of the foundation.

(3) That questions relating to the constitution of a foreign corporation should be decided according to the law of the place where it is incorporated and since, on the evidence, every court in the Eastern Zone of Germany would hold that the Council of Gera was the special board of the foundation, the courts of another jurisdiction are debarred from deciding the question in any other way.

Per Lord Reid, Lord Hodson, Lord Upjohn and Lord Wilberforce. Issue

[1] *Carl Zeiss Stiftung* v. *Rayner & Keeler Ltd.** [1965] Ch. 525; [1964] 3 W.L.R. 905; [1964] 3 All E.R. 326, C.A.

[2] *The Times*, October 30, 1964.

estoppel can be based on a foreign judgment, although in such a case the doctrine should be applied with caution because of the uncertainties arising from the differences of procedure in foreign countries (post, pp. 918, 927, 948, 966, 967).

Simpson v. *Fogo* (1862) 1 H. & M. 195 distinguished.

Per Lord Reid, Lord Hodson, Lord Guest and Lord Upjohn. There was no complete identity between the parties in the proceedings in West Germany and in the present case, since the solicitors in the present case had no connection with or interest in the German litigation and could not be estopped from now defending themselves and showing that they had authority to act (post, pp. 911, 929, 937, 946).

Per Lord Wilberforce. There is identity of parties in the two sets of proceedings. The reality behind the action is that the Council of Gera is seeking in these proceedings to set up the foundation as plaintiff. To treat the solicitors as parties is lacking in reality and is unduly technical (post, pp. 968, 969).

Per Lord Reid. There was no identity of issues in the two sets of proceedings. The question before the West German courts was whether the Council of Gera were the legal representatives of **[856]** the foundation at one date. The question here is whether at a different date the solicitors had the authority of the foundation to bring the action. An answer, yes or no, to the first question does not necessarily imply an answer to the second (post, p. 913).

Per Lord Upjohn and Lord Wilberforce. The issue whether the Council of Gera had authority to give instructions to start proceedings in England in the name of the foundation or whether the foundation had become paralysed and could not act depends on precisely the same facts, circumstances and arguments as were relied on in the West German courts and rejected by them (post, pp. 943-944, 967-968, 972).

Per Lord Guest, Lord Upjohn and Lord Wilberforce. It was not established that the judgment of the West German courts was final and conclusive in West Germany as regards other proceedings between the same parties (post, pp. 936, 949, 971).

Per Lord Hodson and Lord Wilberforce. There is no ground for concluding from a communiqué issued on September 19, 1950, by the Foreign Ministers of France, Great Britain and the United States of America that the views of the courts of the Federal German Republic are conclusive as to the law of Germany as a whole (including the German Democratic Republic), the communiqué being only concerned with political representation (post, pp. 929-930, 974).

Decision of the Court of Appeal* [1965] Ch. 596; [1965] 2 W.L.R. 277; [1965] 1 All E.R. 300, C.A. reversed.

APPEAL from the Court of Appeal (Harman, Danckwerts and Diplock L.JJ.).

This was an appeal by leave of the Court of Appeal by the present appellants, the plaintiffs in the action, Carl-Zeiss-Stiftung of Jena, from an order of that court dated December 17, 1964, whereby it allowed the appeal of the respondents, the defendants in the action, Rayner & Keeler Ltd., Degenhardt & Co. Ltd. and Carl-Zeiss-Stiftung of Heidenheim, Brenz, from the order of Cross J. dated March 6, 1964.

On March 17, 1965, the respondents presented a petition of appeal naming as sole respondents thereto Louis Courts, Philip Max Skelskey, Martin Roy Kagan, Montague Cohen, David Michael Blackburn and William Hollis, the present individual partners of the firm of Courts & Co., which firm, but not all the individual partners, had throughout acted in this litigation as solicitors for the appellants.

On April 12, 1965, the Appellate Committee of the House of Lords ordered that the respondents should be permitted to present that appeal by way of cross-appeal in the original appeal by the **[857]** appellants, the individual partners being respondents to that cross-appeal, with liberty to lodge a case in answer to the cross-appeal and without prejudice to any other contentions, to object therein to the competency of the cross-appeal. The respondents were to have liberty to proceed with the cross-appeal in the event of the original appeal not being proceeded with. The individual partners lodged a case in the cross-appeal.

Carl-Zeiss-Stiftung (Jena) and Carl-Zeiss-Stiftung (Heidenheim, Brenz) are so referred to in order to distinguish by their respective seats the rival organisations claiming to be entitled to the name of the original foundation.

This action for passing off was commenced by writ dated October 20, 1955, in the Chancery Division of the High Court of Justice by the appellants on the footing that they were a German foundation, founded in 1891, and had their registered office and seat ("Sitz") at Jena which was in that part of Germany now constituting the territory of the German Democratic Republic. Originally the third defendants (the third respondents) were sued in the name of Carl-Zeiss, but on service on them of notice of a concurrent writ, issued by leave under R.S.C., Ord. 11, r. 1 (*f*), they entered an appearance as "Carl-Zeiss-Stiftung trading as Carl Zeiss." Subsequently the writ was amended by changing their name to Carl-Zeiss-Stiftung and extending the relief claimed. As amended, the writ claimed:

> "(1) An injunction to restrain the defendants and each of them from advertising offering for sale or selling any optical instruments or any articles containing or consisting of glass under or by reference to the name 'Carl Zeiss' or any name containing 'Zeiss' unless such goods be those of the plaintiffs or an organisation associated with the plaintiffs and generally from passing off any business or goods as and for those of the plaintiffs or an organisation associated with the plaintiffs. (2) An injunction to restrain the third defendants from using the name 'Carl-Zeiss-Stiftung' or 'Carl Zeiss' or any name containing 'Zeiss' in relation to their business or goods. (3) Delivery up or destruction upon oath of all articles calculated to lead to passing off. (4) An inquiry as to damages or an account of profits. (5) Further and other relief. (6) Costs."

The facts are stated in the opinions of Lord Reid and Lord Guest and are also fully set out in the report of the case in the Court of Appeal.[3]* **[858]**

The relevant transactions in relation to the foundation at and after the end of the war may be summarised as follows: Jena was first occupied by the Americans but it subsequently became part of the Russian Zone of occupation on July 1, 1945. When the Americans left they took with them all the members of the existing boards of management of the foundation. The members of the board of management of the optical business had selected three employees of the foundation, Dr. Hugo Schrade and two others, who stayed in Jena, as suitable persons to carry on in their absence.

On October 30, 1945, Marshal Zhukov, head of the Russian Military Administration in Germany, made an order (SMAD 124), providing for the sequestration of certain types of property in the Russian Zone. On June 1, 1948, documents were signed recording the confiscation of the Zeiss optical works at Jena, and this was confirmed by the Soviet Military Administration. The confiscated businesses became known as Volks Eigene Betriebe (VEBs), "People's Owned Enterprises." The confiscation did not involve change in the persons who ran the businesses.

On July 30, 1948, a request was made to the Minister of Education of Wurtemburg to declare Heidenheim to be the legal domicile of the foundation in the West and appoint five named persons the management of the foundation, with jurisdiction outside the Russian Zone. On February 23, 1949, the Minister of State of Wurtemburg ordered that article 3 of the Statute of the foundation should be amended to read: "The legal seat of the foundation is at Jena and Heidenheim." Three named persons were appointed to administer and represent the foundation in accordance with article 114 until a special board in accordance with article 113 should have been reconstituted. This order was confirmed by the Minister of Education on May 3, 1949, and on January 15, 1951, the District

[3] [1965] Ch. 596, 598-606, 637; [1965] 2 W.L.R. 277, 279-286, 289-290, C.A.

Court of Heidenheim registered the firm of Carl-Zeiss in the commercial register as a firm owned by the Carl-Zeiss-Stiftung domiciled at Heidenheim, with a statement to the effect that it had transferred its seat from Jena. By a document signed by the Minister of Education "by proxy" on June 25, 1951, the management of Carl-Zeiss-Stiftung at Jena conferred on Dr. Schrade a "power of attorney" on behalf of the Stiftung to undertake all legal proceedings and represent it in law suits.

Meanwhile in 1949 there had been set up in the Russian Zone of Germany the German Democratic Republic. On September 16, 1964 the Foreign Secretary certified: **[859]**

> "Her Majesty's Government have not granted any recognition de jure or de facto to (a) the 'German Democratic Republic' or (b) its 'Government.' "

On November 6, 1964, the Foreign Secretary further certified:

> "From the area allocated to the Union of Soviet Socialist Republics, Allied forces under the Supreme Allied Commander, General Eisenhower, withdrew at or about the end of June, 1945. Since that time and up to the present date Her Majesty's Government have recognised the State and Government of the Union of Soviet Socialist Republics as de jure entitled to exercise governing authority in respect of that zone . . . In the area comprised in the zones allocated to the Governments of the French Republic, the United Kingdom of Great Britain and Northern Ireland and the United States of America in pursuance of the protocol of September 12, 1944, and the agreement of July 26, 1945, . . . the Government of the Federal Republic of Germany was established on September 21, 1949. In a communiqué issued by the Foreign Ministers of the French Republic, the United Kingdom of Great Britain and Northern Ireland and the United States of America on September 19, 1950, it was stated that 'Pending the unification of Germany, the three Governments consider the Government of the Federal Republic as the only German Government freely and legitimately constituted and, therefore, entitled to speak for Germany as the representative of the German people in international affairs.' This statement does not constitute recognition of the Government of the Federal Republic as the de jure Government of all Germany."

There was litigation in West Germany relating to the foundation. The Carl-Zeiss-Stiftung of Jena was represented therein by the Council of Gera, in the area of which Jena was situated. The council had been set up by a decree of the German Democratic Republic in 1952 and had appointed Dr. Schrade as deputy (or mandatory) of the foundation under article 4 of its statute. In an action in the courts of the Federal Republic of Germany in West Germany against the firm Carl-Zeiss of Heidenheim, Brenz, and the three persons who had been appointed to administer it, the relief claimed was that the defendants should desist from administrative and representative activities on behalf of the foundation and from the use of the name Zeiss and the style Carl-Zeiss. On November 15, 1960, the Federal Supreme Court held that the action should be dismissed.

Meanwhile there had been litigation in the Russian Zone and on March 23, 1961, the Supreme Court of the German Democratic Republic determined an action brought by Carl-Zeiss-Stiftung of Jena, represented by the Council of Gera in its capacity as special **[860]** board and Dr. Schrade as mandatory, against the firm of Carl-Zeiss in West Germany. It held that the defendants should refrain from using the firm name of Carl-Zeiss.

In the present proceedings in England the defendants in the action applied by summons dated February 7, 1956, for

> "an order that all further proceedings in the action be stayed and that this action be dismissed on the ground that the same was commenced and is being maintained without the plaintiffs' authority and that Messrs. Courts & Co. the solicitors purporting to act for the plaintiffs herein do pay to the defendants the costs of this action."

Cross J. dismissed the summons. The Court of Appeal having reversed this decision, the plaintiffs appealed to the House of Lords.

Guy Aldous Q.C., *D. Falconer* and *E. Lauterpacht* for the appellants. It does not matter whether the U.S.S.R. or the German Democratic Republic is the sovereign of the East German territory. In neither event can the laws enacted there be treated as a nullity in this country, for, if the German Democratic Republic is not independent, then the U.S.S.R. is the sovereign there. Thus there is no possible point at issue on which the certificate of the Foreign Secretary can have any effect. The law as to the effect of such a certificate is stated in *Duff Development Co. Ltd.* v. *Government of Kelantan.*[4]*

Finding out what is the law of a foreign country means finding out what is the law which the courts of that country in fact enforce. There might conceivably be a country in which there was no sovereign at all recognised by Her Majesty's Government de jure or de facto and the law of that country would be the law in fact enforced there. On this aspect of the case the judgment of Cross J. was right in every respect.

As to the Foreign Secretary's certificate of November 6, 1964, it is only paragraph (*a*) which is of any materiality. The U.S.S.R. are in de jure control of the East German Zone as the occupying power and, so far as the British Government are concerned, only the U.S.S.R. exercises control there. The German Democratic Republic is a mere creature of the U.S.S.R., subservient to it. The House of Lords must interpret the certificate and it should not be interpreted so as to produce an unreasonable result. One must presume that everything is rightly and properly done, unless the contrary is proved, and that the laws of East Germany are **[861]** validly enacted. The U.S.S.R. is responsible for whatever has happened there; whatever the German Democratic Republic did, it did as a dependent entity. If an occupying power allows an existing government to pass laws, that is done under the aegis of the occupying power, and the only government operative in East Germany is the occupying power. The appellants argue this case on the footing that what the Foreign Secretary says is the case is indeed the case.

In the case of the construction of a document the local law is found by considering how the local courts would interpret it. In construing a foreign contract one must give it the sense which the parties would have understood it to have, and to do that one must go to the foreign law. That has nothing to do with the question whether or not the foreign country has been recognised by our government. Nor has it anything to do with the question in the present case what article 113 of the statute of the Stiftung means to a German. So long as courts are operating in a country, the law of it can be ascertained, even if no government at all is recognised by Her Majesty's Government, and it is to that law that one goes to understand what the parties meant.

It is first submitted that the onus of proof is on the defendants in every respect: *Russian Commercial and Industrial Bank* v. *Comptoir d'Escompte de Mulhouse.*[5]* A person who brings an action is assumed in English law to have authority to do so. The appellants say that the power of attorney under which this action was brought was a good power. The onus is on the respondents to prove the contrary.

The second submission is that what foreign law is must be proved by proper evidence: *Lazard Brothers & Co.* v. *Midland Bank Ltd.*[6]* The present case must depend on the interpretation of the statute of the Stiftung in the light of German law at the material time. See *Banco de Bilbao* v. *Sancha.*[7]*

Here there is a recognised government in de facto control of East Germany, the U.S.S.R. The statute of the Stiftung and its operation must be interpreted so as to have regard to the law prevailing from time to time at Jena. That is the law which the U.S.S.R. has applied. If an occupying power does not suspend the law operating in the territory which it occupies, the courts validly administer

[4] [1924] A.C. 797, 813, 823-4, 830; 40 T.L.R. 866, H.L.(E.).

[5] [1925] A.C. 112, 119, 129, 140; 40 T.L.R. 837, H.L.(E.).

[6] [1933] A.C. 289, 297-8; 49 T.L.R. 94, H.L.(E.).

[7] [1938] 2 K.B. 176, 194-5; 54 T.L.R. 603; [1938] 2 All E.R. 253, C.A.

the law under the authority of that sovereign, **[862]** who permits it to continue. In East Germany there are courts of law, whose authority stems from the fact that the U.S.S.R. permits them to operate. Whatever the U.S.S.R. might say to the contrary, that is the factual position. The source of the law which the courts administer is irrelevant. That law may be judge-made or customary and need not be enacted. There is evidence that under East German law the Council of Gera was the appropriate party to give the relevant authority. There was evidence that any East German court would hold that the relevant acts were properly authorised under the statute of the Stiftung. That law can be proved as a fact and the English courts will accept the proof. The law of Formosa could be proved in order to interpret a contract, even though since 1952 Her Majesty's Government has recognised no government there.

Properly understood, *Aksionairnoye Obschestvo A. M. Luther* v. *James Sagor & Co.*[8]* is not contrary to the appellants' submissions: see "Judiciary and Executive in Foreign Affairs" by F. A. Mann in the Transactions of the Grotius Society, 1943, Vol. XXIX, pp. 143, 156-9. That case was rightly decided on the facts, but if there had been courts of law in Russia at the time and place in question and it could have been proved what their ruling would have been, the decision might have been the other way: see also *U.S.* v. *Insurance Companies,*[9] and *Sokoloff* v. *National City Bank of New York.*[10] The American approach could mitigate the consequences of the extreme application of non-recognition. The courts of a country give validity to those acts which are necessary to preserve peace and good government and what is lawful is ascertained by the decisions of the local courts at the particular time in question.

As to de facto and de jure recognition: see "Recognition" by Sir John Fischer Williams K.C., Transactions of the Grotius Society, 1929, Vol. XV, pp. 53, 66-70; Oppenheim's International Law, 8th ed. (1955) Vol. 1, pp. 134-6, para. 74 and *Upright* v. *Business Machines Co. Inc.*[11]

If the House of Lords rejected the appellants' submissions on this part of the case, it would mean that every judgment in the courts in East Germany for the last ten years had been a nullity, including decisions on divorces and contracts, and that all officials appointed had been unlawfully appointed and that, for example, all **[863]** marriages before those officials were invalid. This is avoided by accepting that the laws are valid because they derive their authority from the only valid government in East Germany, the U.S.S.R.

The recognition point, which was not taken in the court of first instance, should be jealously scrutinised: see *Tasmania* (*Owners*) v. *City of Corinth* (*Owners*).[12] There was no evidence before the court that the German Democratic Republic was independent. The evidence was all one way that it was dependent on the U.S.S.R. which remained the occupying power. The respondents have not proved that the laws in question did not validly stem from the U.S.S.R. In their case they make no distinction between governments which are subservient and those which are not.

Alternatively to the recognition point there is the question whether the Council of Gera was the special board of the Stiftung at the relevant date. That involves a question of the law in force at Jena. There is no doubt that it is, according to the law in force in East Germany. But if one is to go outside what the courts there would say, the matter is one of construction of the statute of the Stiftung, especially article 113, and in construing it no question of the recognition of the German Democratic Republic arises. The views of Her Majesty's Government on that point have nothing to do with identifying the special board. Once it is identified, it can sue in this country as the appropriate body to do so: see *Luigi Monta of Genoa* v. *Cechofracht Co. Ltd.*[13]* In East Germany the occupy-

[8] [1921] 1 K.B. 456, 469-72; 37 T.L.R. 282; [1921] 3 K.B. 532, 546-7; 37 T.L.R. 777, C.A.
[9] (1874) 89 U.S. 99.
[10] (1924) 145 N.E. 917.
[11] (1961) 13 App.Div. 2nd 36; 213 N.Y. 2nd 417.
[12] (1890) 15 App.Cas. 223, 225, H.L.(E.).
[13] [1956] 2 Q.B. 552; [1956] 3 W.L.R. 480; [1956] 2 All E.R. 769.

ing power is still there and the government there is not independent but is subservient. The situation is different from that which prevailed in *Salimoff & Co.* v. *Standard Oil Co. of New York,*[14] but that case is relied on.

The case for the appellants is summarised in their reasons in their printed case. (1) This action was properly authorised by the Council of Gera as the special board of the Stiftung and the respondents have not proved the contrary. (2) This action was properly authorised by Dr. Schrade under his power of attorney dated June 29, 1951, from the Ministry of Education, Thuringia, as the special board of the Stiftung at that time, and the respondents have not proved the contrary. (3) This action was properly authorised by the board of management of the optical works of the Stiftung under article 114 of the statute, acting by Dr. Schrade **[864]** as the sole member of that board, and the respondents have not proved the contrary. (4) This action was properly authorised by Dr. Schrade as the mandatory or proxy mandatory of that board under the provisions of article 9 of the statute, and the respondents have not proved the contrary. (5) The respondents ought not to have been allowed to argue in the Court of Appeal a case inconsistent with, and contrary to, the case which they put forward in the High Court. (6) The respondents ought not to have been allowed to take any point in the Court of Appeal which they had not taken in the High Court and on which all the material facts were not before the court as completely as would have been the case if the controversy had arisen in the High Court. (7) The respondents had expressly disclaimed the non-recognition point in the hearings before the High Court, and the Court of Appeal ought not to have allowed them to take that point in the appeal. (8) It is implicit in, or, alternatively, not inconsistent with, the Foreign Office certificate that, so far as laws are recognised by the East German courts as valid and have not been, or purported to have been, made by the German Democratic Republic over the last fifteen years, those laws are to be regarded as having been made by, or with the authority of, the U.S.S.R. and accordingly those laws are to be regarded as valid. (9) It is not disputed that the U.S.S.R., which is regarded by Her Majesty's Government as de jure sovereign authority of East Germany, would regard the laws in question as valid. (10) Only the U.S.S.R. as the de jure sovereign in East Germany can say that the laws in question are not valid, and the U.S.S.R. has not done so. (11) If the validity of the laws in question had been put in issue by the respondents in the High Court, the appellants might have been able to adduce evidence to establish that such laws did in fact derive their authority from the U.S.S.R. as the de jure sovereign power in East Germany, and the House of Lords should assume that those laws did in fact so derive their authority. (12) There was no issue in the High Court as to the validity of the laws in East Germany and it is unnecessary for the House of Lords to take notice of the non-recognition point, since recognition of the laws of East Germany as valid does not involve taking any view contrary to that of Her Majesty's Government. (13) The laws of East Germany can and should be proved as matters of fact without it being necessary to inquire as to who is the sovereign power. (14) Diplock L.J. was in error in holding that the hearing before Cross J. was conducted on the erroneous assumption that the German Democratic Republic was recognised **[865]** by the Crown as a sovereign state and its government as a sovereign government. (15) In the circumstances and having regard to the evidence filed by them in this application the respondents cannot discharge the onus upon them. (16) The statute of the Stiftung is a private document of a commercial nature and the attitude of Her Majesty's Government as to the recognition or non-recognition of any particular authority is irrelevant to its construction or the intention of the founder. (17) The "highest administrative authorities in Thuringia" for the purposes of article 113 of the statute of the Stiftung are to be ascertained according to the laws of East Germany, and, as a matter of fact, the Council of Gera is the highest administrative authority in that part of Thüringia in which Jena is situate.

Mark Littman Q.C., Michael Kerr Q.C. and *T. M. Shelford* for the respon-

[14] (1933) 186 N.E. 179.

dents. The constitutional background of Germany since the war appears from *Rex* v. *Bottrill, Ex parte Kuechenmeister.*[15]* Since 1871 Her Majesty's Government has recognised only one German state. Germany is still one, and there are no West German nationals or East German nationals; all are Germans. So the domicile of the foundation, which was incorporated before 1945, is Germany as a whole and the determination of its status and the right to represent it are matters which affect Germany as a whole and which, if arising outside Germany, are within the scope of the Foreign Office communiqué set out in the certificate of November 6, 1964. In the determination of such matters the decisions of the courts of the Federal Republic are paramount. The West German decrees to the effect that Heidenheim is the domicile of the foundation are not relied on for the purposes of this summons: see also *Preston* (*orse Putynski*) v. *Preston* (*orse Putynska*) (*orse Basinska*)[16] and Selected Documents on Germany and the Question of Berlin 1944-61 (Cmnd. 1961 No. 1552), p. 43, document No. 9.

Luther v. *Sagor*[17]* was right in holding that the laws of a state not recognised by His Majesty's Government have no legal effect in an English court which cannot give any effect to them. The law of a subservient state not so recognised does not become the law of the dominant state because it is made under pressure and control of the dominant state. If the new laws of the unrecognised German Democratic Republic are not given any legal effect, hardship, inconvenience or injustice may result in some cases, but there is not a vacuum. The old laws would remain in force, whether **[866]** customary, statutory or judge-made. Appointments of judges under the old laws would be valid, though appointments under the new laws would be invalid.

The question to be decided now is not whether those in West Germany represent the Stiftung, but whether those in East Germany represent it. It might conceivably be held that neither do.

The following propositions are submitted: (1) It is an established rule of constitutional law that it is the sovereign's prerogative to act as the representative of the nation in international affairs. This comes within the province of the sovereign acting through the executive. The matters covered include the question which states and which governments are to be recognised as having sovereign authority in foreign lands.

(2) On such matters the views of the sovereign, given through the executive, are decisive. The courts will take judicial notice of the attitude of the executive and, when any doubt exists, will seek information from the executive, and that information is conclusive.

(3) In matters thus within the province of the executive there is a principle established over the last hundred and fifty years that the courts will not speak with a different voice from that of the executive. This principle has been applied to a wide variety of different situations, which include the following: (i) laws purporting to emanate from states or governments unrecognised by Her Majesty have no legal effect in an English court; (ii) an unrecognised government cannot initiate proceedings in an English court; (iii) a party cannot found his case on any contention which involves recognition by an English court of the existence of such a body as having sovereign powers; (iv) these are matters of public policy of which the court will take notice of its own motion, and the court will not decide such matters except on the basis of what it knows or believes to be the true facts.

(4) These principles are probably founded, as a matter of constitutional law, on the fact that in law the courts are the Queen's courts and that she will not speak with one voice through the executive and another through the judges.

(5) Whatever its constitutional origins, this is founded on practical policy. Her Majesty's Government must consider many matters besides legal questions, such as injustice to individuals, treaty obligations and political consequences, as also the boundaries and functions of states, for example, whether or not to recognise a division of Germany. This is recognised by the authorities. **[867]**

15 [1947] K.B. 41; 62 T.L.R. 570; [1946] 2 All E.R. 434, C.A.
16 [1963] P. 141, 151-2; [1963] 2 W.L.R. 1401; [1962] 3 All E.R. 1057.
17 [1921] 1 K.B. 456, 473-474.

(6) Non-recognition may create a practical vacuum so far as enforcement in an English court is concerned. But all the law already established in the area goes on in the country itself. The law in the Eastern Zone is the law at the end of the Hitler regime, save so far as it has been changed by the United States or the Soviet military administrations; for example, the German Civil Code continues in force.

(7) As to retroactivity: (a) When a non-recognised state becomes recognised, the English courts are bound to treat the acts of the government as valid, with retroactive effect. (b) The judiciary is dependent on the Crown and in effect the act of recognition compels the courts to apply a different set of laws from that which they would otherwise apply. (c) The recognition brings in acts emanating from a state which was formerly unrecognised. It is wrong to say that if there is a sovereign recognised de jure, the courts regard everything done in that territory as having been done by that sovereign. In the present case three possible positions can be put forward: (i) that everything in East Germany is done by the U.S.S.R.; (ii) that what exists there is a usurping government purporting to be making laws but in fact acting without the consent of the de jure government; or (iii) that the de facto power is acting with the consent of the de jure government.

(8) The court cannot let this action continue for these reasons: (i) The appellants cannot rely on the Council of Gera as giving authority for this action as the special board of the Stiftung without showing that it is indeed the special board. They have to show that the Council of Gera exists and exercises governmental functions. It is essential for them to set up the decree of 1952, but that decree purports to be a decree of the German Democratic Republic and the appellants do not rely on it because it emanates from a state not recognised by Her Majesty's government either de jure or de facto. (ii) This case goes further than *Luther* v. *Sagor*[18]* and is a fortiori because the recognition of the Council of Gera as a governmental body would involve the recognition of an organ of an unrecognised state. (iii) To allow that the Council of Gera was a proper body to institute proceedings for the Stiftung would be to recognise the authority of an unrecognised state to institute proceedings in English courts. (iv) Such proceedings as the present would not only be brought by an unrecognised state or government but would be for its benefit, because the effect of the action succeeding would be that the organs of the unrecognised [868] state could run the Stiftung's affairs. (v) There is no justification for holding that the decree of 1952 is to be treated as a law of the U.S.S.R. or otherwise as deriving legislative authority from the U.S.S.R. That would be contrary to the terms of the Foreign Secretary's certificate and the decree itself. In substance and effect this would put the German Democratic Republic on a par with a recognised state.

The authorities on the general law are Dicey's Conflict of Laws, 7th ed. (1958), pp. 662-4; Oppenheim's International law, 8th ed. (1955), Vol. I, pp. 765-6; Lauterpacht's Recognition in International Law (1947), pp. 44, 70-1, 72-3, 145-50, 154, 156-7. *City of Berne* v. *Bank of England*[19]*; *Jones* v. *Garcia del Rio*[20]*; *Thompson* v. *Powles*[21]*; *Taylor* v. *Barclay*[22]*; *Republic of Peru* v. *Dreyfus Brothers & Co.*[23]*; *Mighell* v. *Sultan of Johore*[24]*; *Foster* v. *Globe Venture Syndicate Ltd.*[25]*; *The Gagara*[26]*; *The Annette*[27]*; *The Lomonsoff*[28]*; *Luther* v. *Sagor*[29]*; *White, Child & Beney Ltd.* v. *Simmons*[30]*; *Banque Internationale*

[18] [1921] 1 K.B. 456; [1921] 3 K.B. 532.
[19] (1804) 9 Ves. 347.
[20] (1825) Turn. & R. 297.
[21] (1828) 2 Sim. 194.
[22] (1828) 2 Sim. 213, 220-1.
[23] (1888) 38 Ch.D. 348, 358-9; 4 T.L.R. 333.
[24] [1894] 1 Q.B. 149; 10 T.L.R. 115, C.A.
[25] [1900] 1 Ch. 811, 814-5.
[26] [1919] P. 95; 35 T.L.R. 259, C.A.
[27] [1919] P. 105.
[28] [1921] P. 97, 105; 37 T.L.R. 151.
[29] [1921] 1 K.B. 456; [1921] 3 K.B. 532, 540, 545, 546-7, 547-8, 549, 551, 559.
[30] (1922) 127 L.T. 571, 583; 38 T.L.R. 616, C.A.

de Commerce de Petrograd v. *Goukassow*[31]*; *Duff Development Co. Ltd.* v. *Government of Kelantan*[32]*; *Russian Commercial and Industrial Bank* v. *Comptoir d'Escompte de Mulhouse*[33]*; *Lazard Brothers & Co.* v. *Midland Bank Ltd.*[34]*; *Banco de Bilbao* v. *Sancha*[35]* *The Arantzazu Mendi*[36]*; *Gdynia Ameryka Linie Zeglugowe Spolka Akcyjna* v. *Boguslawski.*[37]*

There is nothing in English law which raises the possibility of an exception to the rule stated by the respondents.

As to the American position: see Professor D. P. O'Connell on International Law (1965), Vol. I, pp. 189-99. American law on this point is not wholly settled or clear, but it is not established that it is different from English law in this respect: see *The Maret*[38]; *Russian Socialist Federated Soviet Republics* v. **[869]** *Cibrario*[39]; *Banco Nacional de Cuba* v. *Sabbatino*[40]; *Petrogradsky Mejdunarodny Kom. Merchesky Bank* v. *National City Bank of New York*[41]; and *In the Estate of Luks.*[42] In cases in which the courts have refused recognition of a foreign law, it was not because of the objectionable character of the law, but because the body which made it had no power to do so. This applied equally to a marriage law and a confiscatory law.

By refusing recognition to a foreign government for a prolonged period one is sending the government to Coventry and putting it to inconvenience which may produce hardship for individual persons, including British subjects, but this may be in accordance with the policy of Her Majesty's Government and follows from the doctrine of non-recognition.

As to the American cases cited for the appellants, see how *U.S.* v. *Insurance Companies*[43] was dealt with in O'Connell on International Law (1965) Vol. I, pp. 189-90. Lauterpacht on Recognition, p. 146, shows that this case is not an authority for the exception contended for by the appellants. *Sokoloff's* case,[44] also relied on by the appellants, indicates no more than the possibility of an exception. Too much must not be extracted from *Salimoff's* case[45]: see Lauterpacht on Recognition, pp. 147-8. It is very far away from the present case, which stands on its own in view of the form of the certificate. *Uprights* case[46] was not concerned with the validity or invalidity of foreign legislation: see also *Baldy* v. *Hunter*[47]; *MacLeod* v. *United States*[48]; *Fred S. James & Co.* v. *Second Russian Insurance Co.*[49]; *Banque de France* v. *Equitable Trust Co. of New York.*[50]

Once there is recognition, the American courts will not inquire into the validity of a foreign act of state, unless the United States Government intimates that it has no objection to their doing so.

Foreign laws will only be enforced on the ground of comity and, in the absence of recognition of the foreign state, there is no comity. The inconveniences of non-recognition are always urged in favour of recognition. During the last 150 years the principle has been worked out that not recognising a state necessarily involves not recognising any laws which it has purported to make.

[31] [1923] 2 K.B. 682; 691-2, C.A.
[32] [1924] A.C. 797, 827-8.
[33] [1923] 2 K.B. 630, 636, 663; 39 T.L.R. 574, C.A.; [1925] A.C. 112, 123-4.
[34] [1933] A.C. 289, 297-8.
[35] [1938] 2 K.B. 176, 195-6.
[36] [1939] A.C. 256, 264; 55 T.L.R. 455; [1939] 1 All E.R. 719, H.L.(E.).
[37] [1953] A.C. 11, 30, 44-5; [1952] 2 T.L.R. 317; [1952] 2 All E.R. 470, H.L.(E.).
[38] (1944) 145 Fed. 2nd 431.
[39] (1923) 139 N.E. 259.
[40] (1964) 376 U.S. 398, 410-411.
[41] (1930) 170 N.E. 479, 481 et seq.
[42] (1965) 45 Misc. 2nd 72; 256 N.Y. 2nd 194.
[43] 89 U.S. 99.
[44] 145 N.E. 917.
[45] 186 N.E. 179.
[46] 13 App.Div. 2nd 36; 213 N.Y. 2nd 417.
[47] (1898) 171 U.S. 388.
[48] (1913) 229 U.S. 416.
[49] (1925) 146 N.E. 369.
[50] (1929) 33 Fed. 2nd 202.

[870] An unrecognised government is not always evil nor a recognised government always good.

As to the respondents' submission (8), in order to bring the action the appellants must show that they have the characteristics specified in the statute of the Stiftung and that they have been appointed in accordance with it. In order to do this, they must rely on the decree of 1952. But that decree was part of the setting up of the new order in East Germany and indicates the highly political character of the special board so appointed. The members of the Council of Gera are bound as communists to obey the directions of the East German government. The courts of East Germany are also influenced by political considerations. As to this aspect of the case: see what Cardozo C.J. said in the *Petrogradsky* case.[51] Even if the respondents are wrong in submitting that *Luther* v. *Sagor*[52]* is subject to no exception, a law of this character cannot come within that case. Here there is an unrecognised decree by an unrecognised government, relating to that government. There is no authority in English or United States law for treating it as an exception to the principle that such laws have no effect in an English court. This action is in effect an attempt by an unrecognised government to extend the original confiscations of 1945. English courts will not help to enforce foreign confiscatory laws and therefore will not give the appellants the relief they seek.

As to the *Luigi Monta* case,[53]* that was correctly dealt with in the Court of Appeal in the present case.[54]

No inference is to be drawn from the evidence that Her Majesty's Government regards any body purporting to act as a law-making body in Eastern Germany as the alter ego of the U.S.S.R. It does not regard the U.S.S.R. as governing through the German Democratic Republic. Accordingly, the English courts should not treat whatever is done by that body as being done on behalf of the U.S.S.R. That government is nothing at all if it does not draw its authority from the U.S.S.R. But there is no evidence of any delegation to it from the U.S.S.R. On the contrary, both claim that it is absolutely independent. There is no principle which would allow the English courts to say that, although the law in question is not a law of the U.S.S.R., it is to be treated as such. In the eyes of the U.S.S.R. this is not a law of the Soviet Government nor of the Soviet occupying authority. **[871]**

The appellants have contended that, even if the Council of Gera could not be relied on as providing authority to bring the action, Dr. Schrade had sufficient authority under his power of attorney. But, in the absence of special rules of construction, that foreign document must be construed according to English principles, since prima facie foreign law is presumed to be the same as English law. On that approach, the relevant organ of the Stiftung could not make a wholesale delegation of its powers to an individual any more than an English board of directors could so delegate its powers unless there was in the articles of association power to do so: see Dicey's Conflict of Laws, 7th ed., p. 1107; *In re Parana Plantations Ltd.*[55] and *Rouyer Guillet et Cie* v. *Rouyer Guillet & Co. Ltd.*[56] In the statute of the Stiftung there is no contemplation of a board consisting of one person and Dr. Schrade could not constitute a quorum capable of making a resolution on behalf of the board.

Michael Kerr Q.C. following: The argument that the German Democratic Republic acted as agent for the U.S.S.R. is unacceptable. (1) It rests on no basis of legal principle known to the law and is not a necessary consequence of the Foreign Office certificate. (2) Its acceptance would involve the drawing of inferences, unsupported by any evidence, which are of a political nature and an indeterminate character. (3) Its acceptance would have far reaching and unintended consequences. (4) There is no ground of law or public policy which

[51] 170 N.E. 479, 481.
[52] [1921] 3 K.B. 532.
[53] [1956] 2 Q.B. 552.
[54] [1965] Ch. 596, 652, 663; [1965] 2 W.L.R. 227; [1965] 1 All E.R. 300, C.A.
[55] [1946] 2 All E.R. 214, 217, C.A.
[56] [1949] 1 All E.R. 244, C.A.

should incline the courts to give effect to it.

As to (1), the act of A cannot be attributed to B or deemed to be the act of B unless there exists one of two factual situations, either (a) that B expressly or impliedly authorised A to act on his behalf, in which case the court must be satisfied that the authority has been proved and also that the intention of the parties to stand in a principal and agent relationship is proved, or (b) that when A performed the act on behalf of B he had no authority to do so but that B subsequently ratified his act. It is not sufficient that A intends to act on B's behalf if he does not say so and if there is no ratification. A power of control and domination, however great, does not in English law result in a legal attribution of A's acts to B. In international law there is no principle which entitles a court to attribute to a de jure sovereign acts done within his territory. His attitude is quite irrelevant. That follows **[872]** from the principle in *Luther* v. *Sagor*.[57]* The argument that an ostensible situation is a sham has never been used to validate an act; it has only been used to invalidate what the parties have done.

As to (2), if the House of Lords were to hold that the substance was different from the appearance in relation to the grant of independence to the German Democratic Republic, that would be a political inference in a manner not dealt with in the evidence of either party to this case. The House of Lords could ask the Foreign Secretary whether the indirect rule in East Germany which is suggested is factual.

(3) As to the consequences of accepting the submission, in this situation the English courts would be obliged to accord to the laws of the unrecognised East German Republic the same recognition as is accorded to those of a recognised state. Laws made by the U.S.S.R. in this indirect way would be quite different from laws which they were entitled to make under the Berlin Declaration, and the English courts would have to recognise as valid any laws so made, whether or not they fall within the province of the rights of the U.S.S.R. Under that declaration the U.S.S.R. had no power to set up the German Democratic Republic. The phenomenon of powerful states dominating small states is world wide, for example, Hungary or Panama. The only question is: does the law in question purport to be that of the duly recognised de jure government? If it purports to be, then it is recognised as the law of that government. But, if that government says that it did not make that law and the subordinate government says that it made the law, then here is no principle by which it can be treated as a law made by the de jure government merely because the latter would be entitled to legislate. There is no presumption that any act which takes place in the territory of a de jure sovereign is his act. On the basis of the appellants' argument the English courts might have to recognise the legislation of any unrecognised government. The present position is analogous to that which arises when rebels have gained control of part of a sovereign's territory. The government they set up can derive no authority from the de jure sovereign and its acts and those of its officers must be treated as nullities until Her Majesty's Government have given it de facto recognition.

(4) The only safe legal basis is to ask: has this been proved to be the act of the U.S.S.R.? If the answer is "No," there is no way in which this law can be attributed to the U.S.S.R. **[873]**

Guy Aldous Q.C. in reply. One must see exactly what the Foreign Office certificate proves: see J. L. Brierley's Law of Nations, 6th ed. (1963), pp. 146-8. The practice of the British Government in recognising Governments de jure or de facto is stated. Recognition does not depend on whether or not Her Majesty's Government likes the particular foreign government. The certificate of September 16, 1964, shows that the German Democratic Republic is not so recognised, and that as a fact there has been no abdication by the U.S.S.R. The factual position shown by the Foreign Office certificate must be accepted. The U.S.S.R. cannot, by setting up what in the eyes of Her Majesty's Government is a sham régime force other countries to accept that the laws made in the name of that régime,

[57] [1921] 3 K.B. 532.

were not the act of the U.S.S.R., which is responsible for all that goes on in Eastern Germany. When a hired servant gives orders to under-servants, his orders are valid because they stem from the master.

The Stiftung is entitled to institute proceedings to protect its name and goodwill. Under article 4 of its statute the special board has a general power in this connection, which is not restricted by anything in article 8. The boards of management of the optical works and glass works continue to exist at Jena and have approved the institution of these proceedings. The meaning of the statute is not controlled by the attitude of Her Majesty's Government on the question of recognition and should be construed without regard to it.

The relevant law is the German law in force at Jena.

Mark Littman Q.C. submitted that the following questions should be put to the Foreign Office: "(1) (a) Does Her Majesty's Government recognise the U.S.S.R. as being not only de jure entitled to exercise governing authority in the said zone but also as in fact doing so? (b) Does Her Majesty's Government recognise the U.S.S.R. as exercising such authority in the said zone, if at all, (inter alia) through the instrumentality of the so-called 'German Democratic Republic'? (2) Does Her Majesty's Government recognise the purported legislation of the 'German Democratic Republic' as lawful acts done by or on behalf of the U.S.S.R. as de jure entitled to exercise governing authority in the said zone?"

Guy Aldous Q.C. Questions of law which arise from recognition are for the court and not for the Foreign Office to determine. The answers already given by the Foreign Office go as far as they can go. The situation is clearly defined in Selected Documents on Germany and the Question of Berlin 1944-1961 (Cmnd. 1961 No. [**874**] 1552) at p. 188 (Document No. 67 Joint Declaration of the Allied High Commission on the Status of East Germany, April 8, 1954). This indicates that the U.S.S.R. is the only sovereign in East Germany. The further questions should not be put to the Foreign Office.

[LORD REID intimated that in the opinion of their lordships the further questions should not be put.]

[The hearing of arguments arising on the cross-notice were adjourned to the next sittings.]

January 21, 1966. *Guy Aldous Q.C.* It is submitted that the appellants have the right to open this point.

Mark Littman Q.C. The respondents appealed against the cross-notice by the other side. The Court of Appeal considered only the recognition point and delivered no decision on the other points, which were not argued. This is the respondents' first opportunity to appeal on this point.

[LORD REID. In the special circumstances, it is better that the respondents should open this point and reply.]

Mark Littman Q.C. For the purposes of this part of the argument, it must be assumed that the Council of Gera exists and is the highest legal authority in Thuringia and is capable of acting as the special board.

There have been conflicting decisions of the courts in West and East Germany, the former in effect deciding in favour of the respondents' contentions and the latter deciding in favour of those of the appellants. This is a question of foreign law and the relative priority of the two decisions must be considered. The judgment of the West German court should be given priority as res judicata or by estoppel.

As to estoppel, it is submitted, that the West German court had jurisdiction, since all the parties submitted to it. The eventual decision was framed in the sense required by the law of estoppel and it cannot be challenged on the ground that it was wrong or applied the wrong law. No estoppel arises from the decision in East Germany because the respondents were not parties to the proceedings there and the judgment was a default judgment. The courts there had no jurisdiction and the respondents never purported to submit to their jurisdiction.

Secondly, the judicial system of a country is an aspect of its sovereignty, as much so as its legislature. One must contrast the recognition afforded to the U.S.S.R. in relation to East Germany and that accorded to the Federal Republic of West Germany. [**875**] The U.S.S.R. is recognised as the occupying power and it exercises governing power within its zone in zonal matters, but it is not recognised as having power to act or speak in any matter affecting Germany as a whole. But the Federal Republic is recognised as a fully sovereign state, the state of Germany, which has been uninterruptedly recognised by the Foreign Office since 1871. It is entitled to speak for Germany as a whole in international affairs: see the communiqué of September 19, 1950, referred to in the Foreign Office certificate of November 6, 1964. The present dispute is not a purely zonal matter, but affects Germany as a whole and is, moreover, an international matter. The basic issue concerns the interpretation of German law, as distinct from zonal law. It concerns the right to represent a foundation which was established not during the occupation under a new U.S.S.R. law, but many years ago under the laws of Germany. This foundation has operated, not only in the Soviet Zone but throughout Germany and the world. This dispute concerns the right to represent the foundation outside the Soviet Zone and outside Germany altogether. It concerns assets in England and not in the Soviet Zone. It concerns the relative authority of the Supreme Court of the Soviet Zone and the Supreme Court of the Federal Republic when dealing with such matters. The views of the Supreme Court of the Federal Republic should be treated in England as authoritative. The courts in East Germany are influenced by political considerations.

In English law the question who is entitled to represent a corporation depends on the law of the country where it is domiciled, that is, to which it owes its existence. The law of the domicile of this foundation is German law.

The issues in this application are res judicata as between the parties thereto by reason of the judgment of the Supreme Court of the Federal Republic, because the issue is the same as the issue which was decided by the court. As to res judicata, see Halsbury's Laws of England, 3rd ed., Vol. 15 (1956), p. 168, para. 334; p. 181, para. 355; p. 210, para. 393; Dicey's Conflict of Laws, 7th ed., p. 196 et seq. and Spencer Bower on Res Judicata, p. 91, para. 141.

The issue on the summons of February 7, 1956, now in question is between the defendants and some other person. But who is that person? Not the nominal plaintiff, the Stiftung, because if the issue were decided in favour of the defendants, it would establish that the nominal plaintiff was never before the court at all. The Council of Gera was a party to the German proceedings [**876**] and can be regarded as parties to the present proceedings. This is not a narrow technical point; it bears on the policy of the courts to see that there is an end of litigation. Suppose the Council of Gera was not a party and the solicitors were, estoppel affects, not only the parties to proceedings, but also their privies, and in the present case the solicitors were privies to the Council of Gera. They claim the rights they are asserting because they derive them from the Council of Gera: see Halsbury's Laws of England, 3rd ed., Vol. 15, p. 196, para. 372; *Hancock* v. *Welsh*[58]; *Kinnersley* v. *Orpe*[59] and Spencer Bower on Res Judicata pp. 130-1, paras. 205, 206.

There is privity of interest between the solicitors and the Council of Gera, since they are representing its interests. The object of estoppel is to prevent substantially the same people litigating the same matter twice. Here the very same issue has already been decided by the courts in both East and West Germany. That issue was whether the events of 1948 paralysed the organs of the foundation in East Germany. The solicitors have no authority to conduct these proceedings on behalf of the appellants, because they are estopped by the judgment of the Supreme Court of the Federal Republic in an action brought in the name of the present appellants against the present respondents.

As to res judicata, see *Connelly* v. *Director of Public Prosecutions*[60] and *Fidelitas Shipping Co. Ltd.* v. *V.O. Exportchleb.*[61]

[58] (1816) 1 Stark. 347.
[59] (1780) 2 Dougl. 517.
[60] [1964] A.C. 1254; 1353 et seq; [1964] 2 W.L.R. 1145; [1964] 2 All E.R. 401, H.L.(E.).
[61] [1966] 1 Q.B. 630, 641-2; [1965] 2 W.L.R. 1059; [1965] 2 All E.R. 4, C.A.

If it is necessary to look behind the judgment of the West German court to the underlying issue. That can be done, since issue estoppel is part of the law of England. It is submitted (1) that res judicata applies not only to the cause of action but also to the issues; (2) that one is not restricted to looking at the formal order and (3) that the other material to be looked at includes the pleadings and the reasons of the judge. The matter often arises in the Divorce Division: see Spencer Bower on Res Judicata, p. 3, para. 6; pp. 8-9, para. 13; p. 102, para. 158; p. 112, para. 170; pp. 113-5, paras. 173-5. It is not suggested that there are special facts applicable in England which were not applicable in West Germany, so that one can look to see whether the decision there rested on any such special facts.

The principle of res judicata is correctly set out in Phipson on Evidence, 10th ed., (1963), p. 518, para. 1363. The relevant **[877]** authorities are *Reg.* v. *Inhabitants of the Township Hartington Middle Quarter*[62]; *Flitters* v. *Allfrey*[63]; *Hunter* v. *Stewart*[64]; *Hoystead* v. *Commissioner of Taxation*[65]; *Marginson* v. *Blackburn Borough Council*[66]; *Bright* v. *Bright*[67]; *Thompson* v. *Thompson*[68]; *Warren* v. *Warren*[69]; *Thoday* v. *Thoday*[70]; *Fidelitas Shipping Co. Ltd.* v. *V.O. Exportchleb*[71]; *Randolph* v. *Tuck*[72]; *Penn-Texas Corporation* v. *Murat Anstaldt* (*No. 2*)[73]; *Henderson* v. *Henderson*[74]; *Ellis* v. *M. Henry*[75]; *Castrique* v. *Imrie*[76]; *New Brunswick Railway Co.* v. *British & French Trust Corporation Ltd.*[77]; *In re Dulles' Settlement* (*No. 2*)[78] and *Ricardo* v. *Garcias.*[79]

As to the question who are parties or privies, see Spencer Bower on Res Judicata, pp. 126-7, paras. 197-8, and the summary of the American authorities in the American Restatement of the Law (Judgments) (1943), ss. 79, 83, 84 and 85. "Privy" covers a person who is in control of the proceedings. If the Council of Gera would have been estopped from putting forward this claim, the solicitors whom they have instructed are also estopped. It is enough that they have been professionally employed; they are representing the same interest. The term "party" includes servants. *Laidlaw* v. *Blackwood*[80] is distinguishable on the facts.

As to foreign judgments, see *Henderson* v. *Henderson*[81]; *Kok Hoong* v. *Leong Cheong Kwang Mines Ltd.*[82] and *Bank of Australasia* v. *Nias.*[83] The English courts will not treat a foreign judgment as ineffective for the purposes of estoppel just because, in the opinion of the English court, it is wrong, or a wrong system of law was applied according to foreign rules on conflict of laws, or the foreign court adopted an incorrect view on some point of **[878]** English law. But if the proceedings of the foreign court were contrary to natural justice, that would justify an English court in refusing to have regard to its judgment. Or, if the English court were satisfied that the foreign court was not trying to apply

[62] (1855) 4 E. & B. 780.
[63] (1874) L.R. 10 C.P. 29, 40.
[64] (1861) 4 De G. F. & J. 168, 178.
[65] [1926] A.C. 155, 163-8; 42 T.L.R. 207, P.C.
[66] [1939] 2 K.B. 426, 435-6; 55 T.L.R. 389; [1939] 1 All E.R. 273, C.A.
[67] [1954] P. 270, 272-4, 280-1; [1953] 3 W.L.R. 659; [1953] 2 All E.R. 939.
[68] [1957] P. 19, 28-9, 36-7, 38, 44; [1957] 2 W.L.R. 138; [1957] 1 All E.R. 161, C.A.
[69] [1962] 1 W.L.R. 1310, 1312, 1313; [1962] 3 All E.R. 1031.
[70] [1964] P. 181; [1964] 2 W.L.R. 371; [1964] 1 All E.R. 341, C.A.
[71] [1966] 1 Q.B. 630, 640, 641-2.
[72] [1962]1 Q.B. 175, 182-3, 184; [1961] 2 W.L.R. 855; [1961] 1 All E.R. 814.
[73] [1964] 2 Q.B. 647; [1964] 3 W.L.R. 131; [1964] 2 All E.R. 594, C.A.
[74] (1843) 3 Hare 100.
[75] (1871) L.R. 6 C.P. 228.
[76] (1869) L.R. 4 H.L. 414, H.L.(E.).
[77] [1939] A.C. 1, 19-20, 20-21, 23, 35; T.L.R. 360; [1938] 4 All E.R. 747, H.L.(E.).
[78] [1951] Ch. 842, 851; [1951] 2 T.L.R. 145; [1951] 2 All E.R. 9.
[79] (1845) 12 Cl. & F. 368, 387, H.L.(E.) 69, C.A.
[80] (1843) 15 Sc. Jur. 484.
[81] 3 Hare 100, 113-15; (1844) 6 Q.B. 288, 296 et seq.
[82] [1964] A.C. 993, 1010-11; [1964] 2 W.L.R. 150; [1964] 1 All E.R. 300, P.C.
[83] (1851) 16 Q.B. 717, 734-5.

the law, it would take that into account. But none of these considerations are relevant to the present case: see Spencer Bower on Res Judicata, p. 162, para. 272; *Luther* v. *Sagor*[84]* and *Godard* v. *Gray*.[85]

As to the position of the first and second defendants, Cross J. said in his judgment[86] that they could not invoke the doctrine of res judicata. But the defendants and each of them have been acting in concert and jointly and they are within the category of privity. The principle is broad enough to cover this case. The action is brought against the three defendants as joint tortfeasors in respect of a matter in which they have acted in concert and they have identical interests so as to come within the rule, the object of which is to prevent a plaintiff from relitigating a matter with the person with whom he has already litigated it and also to prevent him getting in by the back door by suing persons who are jointly liable with the person he has already sued: see Spencer Bower on Res Judicata, p. 126, para. 197; pp. 127-8, para. 198; pp. 130-1, para. 206; and *Flitters* v. *Allfrey*.[87]

So far as the opinion delivered by the East German Court is concerned, the respondents were not parties to it and it was delivered without jurisdiction. Dicey on Conflict of Laws, 7th ed., pp. 1016-7, rule 189, sets out the five cases in which a foreign court has jurisdiction to give a judgment in personam which is capable of enforcement or recognition in England. That judgment comes within none of them: see also pp. 1018-9, 1027-8. The relevant cases are *Emanuel* v. *Symon*[88]; *In re Dulles' Settlement* (*No. 2*)[89] and *In re Trepca Mines Ltd.*[90]

The judgment of the Federal Supreme Court was delivered on November 15, 1960. That of the Supreme Court of the German Democratic Republic was delivered on March 23, 1961. Therefore, it was too late for the latter judgment to create an estoppel since there cannot be two estoppels per rem judicatam: see Spencer Bower on Res Judicata, pp. 160-1, paras. 266, 267.

The West German judgment should be preferred to the East German judgment (1) on the ground of estoppel; (2) on the ground **[879]** of the Foreign Office certificate and (3) on the ground of the intrinsic merit of the judgment.

The following questions should be put to the Foreign Office: (1) Does Her Majesty's Government recognise that the determination of the status of and the right to represent a body under the law of the State of Germany prior to 1945 and now having its Sitz in the territory of the zone allocated to the U.S.S.R. are matters (a) which affect Germany as a whole and (b) which, if arising outside Germany, are within the scope of the communiqué dated September 19, 1950, as referred to in the answer to question 2 in the certificate dated November 6, 1964? (2) What states, governments or authorities now functioning in Germany or any parts of it does Her Majesty's Government recognise as entitled to determine any such matter as is referred to in question 1?

[LORD REID intimated that in the opinion of their Lordships these questions should not be put.]

As to the effect which English courts should give to decisions of foreign courts on a matter of foreign law, see *Guaranty Trust Co. of New York* v. *Hannay & Co.*[91]; *Bankers and Shippers Insurance Co. of New York* v. *Liverpool Marine & General Insurance Co. Ltd.*[92] and *Evera S.A. Commercial* v. *Bank Line Ltd.*[93]

Her Majesty's Government recognises the Soviet Government as de jure entitled to govern in East Germany. The government of West Germany is recognised as a sovereign body. The situation is that the courts in East Germany are saying one thing and those in West Germany another. There are no special

[84] [1921] 3 K.B. 532, 558-9.
[85] (1870) L.R. 6 Q.B. 139, 148-9.
[86] [1964] R.P.C. 299, 333.
[87] L.R. 10 C.P. 29, 41.
[88] [1908] 1 K.B. 302, 309-10; 24 T.L.R. 85, C.A.
[89] [1951] Ch. 842.
[90] [1960] 1 W.L.R. 1273, 1280-1; [1960] 3 All E.R. 304, C.A.
[91] [1918] 2 K.B. 623, 637-8; 34 T.L.R. 427, C.A.
[92] (1926) 24 Ll. L.R. 85, 87, 92, 93, H.L.(E.).
[93] [1961] 1 Lloyd's Rep. 231, H.L.(E.).

statutes in the Eastern Zone applying to this matter and so the law which should be applied there is the German Civil Code and the articles of association of the Stiftung. The English courts are here concerned with the law of Germany as to the right to represent a German corporation. This depends on the law of the domicile of the corporation as understood in English private international law: see Dicey's Conflict of Laws, 7th ed., p. 477, rule 76. If a French corporation was required to have its central office in Burgundy, it would be regarded as incorporated under the law of France, not of Burgundy. Since the incorporation of the Stiftung the original principalities have become part of the single state of Germany and, when the German Civil Code came into existence, **[880]** it applied to existing foundations and still applies. This foundation was not domiciled in one part of Germany, as distinct from Germany as a whole. Even if the Stiftung has its centre of gravity at Jena, that did not so locate it there that its capacity to act through its organs depended on the law of that particular part of Germany. The law which governs the whole of Germany must be distinguished from the local laws passed in the different zones, for example, the Soviet Zone.

The English courts recognise the U.S.S.R. as the occupying power in their Zone but their authority is restricted to matters not affecting Germany as a whole. But they recognise the Federal Republic of Germany as a fully sovereign state, the only German government entitled to speak as representative of the German people in international affairs and the successor of the Weimar Republic. The present matter is not purely zonal, but concerns Germany as a whole and comes within the category of an international affair within the declaration of September 19, 1950. There is no question of the meaning and effect of zonal law and it concerns an old foundation, not established under the authority of the U.S.S.R., which operated throughout Germany and the world and not just in the Soviet Zone. The question is not as to the right to represent that body in the Soviet Zone but as to the right to represent it in the international sphere outside Germany. It concerns its assets in the international sphere and not just in the Soviet Zone. It raises the problem of the relative authority of the courts in East Germany and of those of the Federal Republic of Germany. The latter have the higher claim to authority in these matters: see the Reciprocal Enforcement of Judgments (Germany) Order, 1961 (S.O. 1961 No. 1199) Schedule, articles I (3), III, IV and V (1). There is no comparable arrangement for the recognition of the courts and judgments of East Germany. There is another indication of the high degree of recognition granted by Her Majesty's Government to the Federal Republic of Germany. If there is any doubt or ambiguity in the Foreign Office certificate already given, it can be resolved by inviting a further answer from the Foreign Office.

In the case before the Federal Supreme Court the right questions were put and the contentions were fairly stated and understood. The reasoning of the judgment was cogent and its conclusions were correct. But, whether they were correct or not, the court was entitled to treat the law of East Germany, not as foreign law but as something of which it could take judicial notice. **[881]**

As to the confiscation point, a decree made in East Germany has purported to extend the confiscation of all the property of the Stiftung to its assets in England. The English courts will not give effect to such legislation: see *Lecouturier* v. *Rey*.[94] They will look behind the formal relationships of the parties to the action. So that if a decision of a foreign court giving effect to confiscatory legislation is on the face of it delivered in relation to a contract or a liquidation, the English courts will look behind these to the reality of the situation: see *Banco de Vizcaya* v. *Don Alfonso de Bourbon y Austria*[95]*. *Government of India, Ministry of Finance* (*Revenue Division*) v. *Taylor*[96]* and an article on "Prerogative Rights of Foreign States and the Conflict of Laws" by Dr. F. A. Mann (1954), Transaction of the Grotius Society, Vol. 40, pp. 25,

[94] [1910] A.C. 262; 26 T.L.R. 368, H.L.(E.).
[95] [1935] 1 K.B. 140; 50 T.L.R. 282.
[96] [1955] A.C. 491, 509-10; [1955] 2 W.L.R. 303; [1955] 1 All E.R. 292, H.L.(E.).

34 et seq., 46-47. In the present case the claim is for the enforcement of confiscatory legislation, either directly or indirectly.

[Their Lordships indicated that the latter contentions raised a substantive defence which should not be argued on the summons, but remained open to the respondents in the action.]

Michael Kerr Q.C. following. There are two aspects of the jurisdiction point on which there are several authorities: (1) the application of issue estoppel, the question whether one looks at the formal order or the record and (2) the meaning and scope of the expressions "parties" and "privies" in connection with res judicata.

Starting with issue estoppel regarded from the point of view of the common law in civil mattters, once an issue of fact or law or mixed fact and law has been litigated and determined by the court of competent jurisdiction the parties and their privies are estopped from relitigating it. The questions arise: (a) What material may be looked at to determine the existence of the estoppel? (b) Are foreign judgments treated differently from English judgments? It is a question of evidence whether an issue has been litigated and determined. When the judgment shows what issues have been determined, the court will look at that. "It is the res judicata, not the record of it, which creates the estoppel": Spencer Bower on Res Judicata, p. 5 and see *Reimers* v. *Druce*[97] and *In re Trufort.*[98]* A judgment can only be impeached if the court **[882]** which pronounced it had no jurisdiction or if it offends against natural justice. In *Kalc Krishna Tagore* v. *Secretary of State for India*[99] the court looked at the actual judgment and not merely at the order. Spencer Bower on Res Judicata, pp. 175 et seq., distinguishes between res judicata in the ordinary sense and res judicata as a bar to subsequent recovery: see also *Sri Raja Rao Lakshmi Kontaiyammi* v. *Sri Raja Inuganti Rejagopa Rao.*[1] These cases were followed in a line of Australian authorities: *Gray* v. *Dalgetty & Co. Ltd*[2]; *Rex* v. *Wilkes*[3]; *Mraz* v. *The Queen* (*No. 2*)[4] and *Brown* v. *Robinson,*[5] and see *Sealfon* v. *United States*[6]; Spencer Bower on Res Judicata, p. 47, para. 64, and *Connelly* v. *Director of Public Prosecutions.*[7]

No distinction can be drawn between foreign judgments and English judgments.

As to the next point, the meaning and scope of the expressions "parties" and "privies," there are few decisions in England. It is not possible to get any definition of the terms which is both concise and exhaustive; there are too many permutations. A "privy" is a person so situated in relation to a party in the earlier proceedings and the new proceedings that further proceedings by him as agent would amount in substance to the relitigation of one or more of the issues already decided in the earlier proceedings, a relitigation between the real parties and interests. A party or privy includes any person who is a real party in interest to the claim or defence in question, that is, any person who participates in the conduct of the proceedings, whether alone or with other persons, or as a representative on the record, who is acting in the interest of a party, whether or not that representative has a personal interest in the proceedings. The Council of Gera is covered by this definition, being in opposition to the respondents' claim, and they cannot shelter behind the solicitors on the record. Conversely, there is included any person on the record who represents anyone who is a real party or has a real interest, and who acts on that person's behalf so as to be in privity with that person, whether or not he himself has any personal interest in the proceedings. A principal and agent are in privity.

[97] (1857) 26 L.J.Ch. 196.
[98] (1887) 36 Ch. D. 600, 613-17; 3 T.L.R. 798.
[99] (1888) L.R. 15 Ind.App. 186, P.C.
[1] (1898) L.R. 25 Ind.App. 102, 107-8, P.C.
[2] (1916) 21 C.L.R. 509, 543.
[3] (1948) 77 C.L.R. 511, 518-19.
[4] (1956) 96 C.L.R. 62, 69-70.
[5] (1960) S.R.(N.S.W.) 297, 301-2.
[6] (1948) 332 U.S. 575, 578, 579.
[7] [1964] A.C. 1254, 1321, 1333-4, 1343 et seq., 1366.

One may illustrate the position with three cases. In the first case take Action 1 (*Company* v. *C and D*): A and B instruct **[883]** solicitors to issue a writ in the name of the company against C and D for a declaration that C and D are not directors of the company, and other ancillary relief. C and D issue a summons to stay the action on the ground that it is brought without the company's authority. (C and D may also add a claim that their costs are to be paid by the solicitors personally, but whether or not they do so is irrelevant.) A and B file evidence in answer to the summons to the effect that A and B authorised the action and that they are entitled to do so as directors of the company. (The solicitors may also file evidence that they received their instructions from A and B and believe A and B to be entitled to act as directors of the company, but it is submitted that whether or not they do so is irrelevant). C and D file evidence denying that A and B are directors and asserting that C and D are the directors. On the hearing of the summons the judge decides that A and B are not directors and that C and D are directors. The summons therefore succeeds and he stays the action. (He may or may not also order the solicitors to pay C and D's costs, but it is submitted that whether or not he does so is irrelevant.) Action 2 (i) (*C and D* v. *the Company*), C and D sue the company for directors' fees. On the instructions of A and B, a solicitor enters an appearance for the company and pleads that C and D are not directors. C and D plead estoppel per rem judicatam on the basis of the issue raised and determined in their favour in the summons in Action 1. This plea must succeed, for the simple reason that the issues in, and the formal parties to, Action 1 and 2 (i) are identical. Alternatively, Action 2 (ii) (*C and D* v. *A and B*). Since A and B continue to assert that they are directors, C and D bring an action to restrain them from claiming to be entitled to act as directors of the company. A and B plead that they are directors and C and D are not. C and D plead that A and B are estopped per rem judicatam from raising this issue on the ground that it has already been determined in the summons in Action 1. Their estoppel could be upheld on the grounds that: (i) this issue was raised and litigated in that summons, (ii) C and D were parties to this issue, (iii) A and B were parties to this issue. They were not parties to Action 1, but upon the trial of the summons they became the opposing party to the issue raised and litigated by that summons, the "real party in interest" to the summons. (iv) The conclusion that they were the real party in interest to that summons can also be stated by saying that the solicitors (who may be regarded as the formal parties to the summons) represented A and **[884]** B in this issue litigated in that summons and that accordingly there was privity between A and B and the solicitors. (It should be noted in this connection that in all these illustrations A and B are clients of the solicitors on that side: compare the definition of "clients" in section 86 (1) of the Solicitors Act, 1957, formerly section 81 of the Solicitors Act, 1932.) (v) The same conclusion can also be stated by saying that in the summons in Action 1 the issue which was litigated was between the company and C and D, namely, that the company cannot be represented by A and B, and that A and B are the real parties in interest or privy to that issue. These are semantic differences, not real distinctions. (vi) It would be contrary to common sense that there should be an estoppel in Action 2 (i) but not in this action, when the issue and the real parties to that issue were precisely the same in Actions 1, 2 (i) and 2 (ii), and a relitigation of that issue would in substance be a relitigation between precisely the same parties.

In the second case Action 1 (*Company* v. *C and D*): As in the first case, but C and D's summons fails. On the summons the judge decides that C and D are not the directors and that A and B are. The action proceeds and an injunction is given against C and D to restrain them from acting as directors of the company. Action 2: C and D are not put off and sue A and B for a declaration that A and B are not directors of the company. A and B plead estoppel on the basis of the summons in Action 1. C and D plead that there is no estoppel because (a) A and B were not parties to Action 1; (b) the decision in Action 1 was merely that C and D were not directors, not that A and B were. The plea of estoppel would succeed because (a) A and B were parties or privies to the issue tried in the summons in Action 1 for the same reasons as those submitted in relation to Action 2 (ii) in the first case; (b) the evidence that the issue raised and decided in the summons in Action 1 was not only that C and D were not directors, but also that A and B were.

The third case may be considered in two parts: I. Action 1 (*Company* v. *C and D* in Jurisdiction X): As in Action 1 in the second case, C and D's summons to stay fails and it is held that A and B are entitled to represent the company. Action 2 (*Company* v. *C and D* in Jurisdiction Y): Upon C and D issuing the summons to stay, A and B plead that C and D are estopped by the issue raised and decided in the summons in Action 1. It is submitted that (as in Action 2 (i) in the first case) the plea of estoppel must succeed because the issue and the formal parties are **[885]** identical. II. (the present case Action 1 (*Company* v. *C and D* in Jurisdiction X): Proceedings as in Action 1 in the first case. The summons to stay the action succeeds and it is held that A and B are not entitled to represent the company, the converse result of Action 1 in I. above. Action 2 (*Company* v. *C and D* in Jurisdiction Y): Upon C and D issuing a summons to stay on the ground that A and B have no right to represent the company and that this issue has been decided in the summons in Action 1, C and D would be entitled to rely upon the estoppel in the same way as A and B are entitled to rely on it in I. above. The only difference is that in I. the summons to stay fails in Jurisdiction X, thus raising an estoppel in favour of A and B in Jurisdiction Y; whereas in this case the summons to stay succeeds in Jurisdiction X, thus raising an estoppel in favour of C and D in Jurisdiction Y. Further, it makes no difference in either I. or II. above whether the solicitors on either side in Jurisdictions X and Y are identical or not; in either event the estoppel will operate in favour of, or against (as the case may be) the real parties to the issue raised and determined in the summons, for the reasons submitted in relation to Action 2 (ii) in the first case.

As to estoppel: see *In re Defries*.[8] As to the position of the solicitors, see *Myers* v. *Rothfield*,[9] reversed in the House of Lords sub nom. *Myers* v. *Elman*.[10] In this litigation if the Stiftung is not a party against the respondents, it must be the Council of Gera. But the council cannot be heard to argue the same point that has already been decided in West Germany, nor can the solicitors of whom the council are the clients: see the definition of "client" in section 86 (1) of the Solicitors Act, 1957.

It is enough to show that the persons instituting these proceedings have already instituted previous proceedings in which they have failed. Privity is a wide concept, wide enough to embrace such a case as this. The solicitors are parties to these proceedings and privies of the Council of Gera. It does not matter whether or not they are protagonists: see Spencer Bower on Res Judicata, p. 126, para. 197. An estoppel would have been created if the West German case had been decided the other way.

The American authorities on this point are the Corpus Juris, Vol. 50 (Judgments), pp. 275-7, para. 756; p. 281, para. 757; p. 297, para. 768; *Bruszewski* v. *United States*[11]; *Gibson* v. *United* **[886]** *States*[12]; *Chicago Rock Island and Pacific Railway Co.* v. *Schendel*[13]; *Warren Featherbone Co.* v. *De Camp*[14]; *Cuneo Importing Co.* v. *American Transportation Co.*[15]; *Cutler* v. *Jennings*[16] and *Don Chemical Co.* v. *Benton*.[17] The conclusions to be deducted from those cases are: (1) Where there is a judgment against A upon an issue with B, B can rely on the judgment as creating an estoppel when the same issue arises in

[8] (1883) 48 L.T. 703.
[9] [1939] 1 K.B. 109, 124-5; [1938] 3 All E.R. 498, C.A.
[10] [1940] A.C. 282, 336; 56 T.L.R. 177; [1939] 4 All E.R. 484, H.L.(E.).
[11] (1950) 181 Fed. 2nd 419.
[12] (1954) 211 Fed. 2nd 425.
[13] (1926) 270 U.S. 611, 617.
[14] (1907) 154 Fed. 198.
[15] (1917) 241 Fed. 421; 247 Fed. 413.
[16] (1925) 130 A. 583.
[17] (1962) 357 S.W. 2nd 565.

proceedings instituted by C where C is in a significant relationship with A. (2) There is a significant relationship where C is a person who institutes the proceedings upon the instructions of A or conducts the proceedings under the control of A or derives his alleged authority to bring the proceedings from A. For "significant relationship" one can say "privity." None of these principles would have applied to *Laidlaw's* case.[18]

Guy Aldous Q.C. Counsel on the appeal are instructed to appear on behalf of the Carl-Zeiss-Stiftung, neither for the Council of Gera nor for the solicitors. On the cross-appeal they are instructed on behalf of the six individual partners of the firm of solicitors.

Two points arise on the cross-appeal: (1) Whether under German law the effect of the confiscation of the assets of the two businesses of the foundation under the Soviet military decree of 1948 was to deprive the organs of the foundation of their capacity to act, so that the Council of Gera was not capable of acting as the special board of the foundation, and (2) whether because of the Federal Supreme Court's decision in November, 1960, it was res judicata, at least against the third defendants in the present action (the third respondents), that the Council of Gera could not represent the foundation and therefore the Council of Gera were estopped from bringing this action as against at least the third defendants. The cause of action is misappropriation by passing off the name and marks of the Carl-Zeiss-Stiftung and the question is whether the plaintiffs in the action are the persons to take proceedings to protect the name and trade marks.

The appellants put their case thus: (1) The Carl-Zeiss-Stiftung is an existing corporation domiciled at Jena. (2) Therefore the law governing the question whether it has validly authorised these proceedings in the law in force at Jena at the date of the authorisation. (3) According to that law these proceedings are validly **[887]** authorised and on this point every court in East Germany would follow the decision of the East German Supreme Court. To establish these matters proves the appellants' case.

The vital question is: what is the local law? That must be decided as a fact on the evidence before the court. The local law is proved by the evidence of persons who know how that law is interpreted in the local courts. It is common ground that every court in East Germany would hold these proceedings properly brought. The relevant law is the law which would be applied there, not the law which the courts in England or West Germany think ought to be applied: see *Lazard Brothers.*[19]*

It is conceded that Carl-Zeiss-Stiftung is an existing corporation. The key to the case is its place of domicile. It is contrary to the evidence to say that its domicile is in Germany as a whole and not at Jena. Every Stiftung had to be established according to the laws of a particular "land" and on those laws the control of it depended. The legal domicile of this Stiftung has always been at Jena and the relevant law in this case is the law governing there at the date of authorisation of the legal proceedings. This is recognised in English law. In its judgment the West German court was purporting to administer the law in force in East Germany. A similar question as to which board of directors of a Spanish bank had the legal right to represent it during the Spanish Civil war arose in *Banco de Bilbao* v. *Sancha.*[20]* The only way of proving the law of East Germany is to call expert witnesses to prove how the courts there would interpret the code. It is irrelevant to call experts from West Germany to say how they think the East German courts would decide. Even if the judges in East Germany decide according to the wishes of the state, that is equivalent to a state decree and is accordingly the law.

As to the ascertainment of the law of a foreign country on a point which has already been the subject of a decision by a court of that country: see the

[18] 15 Sc.Jur. 484.
[19] [1933] A.C. 289, 296 et seq., 302.
[20] [1938] 2 K.B. 176, 194-5.

Bankers and Shippers case[21]; the *Guaranty Trust* case[22]; the *Evera* case[23]; *Baron de Bode's* case[24]*; *The Sussex Peerage* case[25] and *Buerger* v. *New York Life Assurance Co.*[26] The court would revolt against a conclusion which would put the foundation into a state of perpetual **[888]** immobility: *A.G. Der Manufacturen D.A. Woronin Leutchig* v. *Frederick Huth & Co.*[27]* The findings of Cross J. are correct. They involve the conclusion that the board of management in East Germany was properly appointed.

As to the question of res judicata, counsel on this side are appearing for the Carl-Zeiss-Stiftung and they are not affected by the pleadings of other persons for whom they do not appear; they are not putting forward arguments on behalf of anyone else. Success on the main part of the case would involve success in proving that the Carl-Zeiss-Stiftung are the right parties. There can be no estoppel against the Carl-Zeiss-Stiftung by reason of the proceedings in West Germany to which they were not parties: see *Buerger's* case.[28] *Nana Ofori Atta II* v. *Nana Abu Bonsra II*[29] does not help in this case.

On this part of the case it is submitted: (1) Since there is no estoppel against the Stiftung, counsel can put forward contentions on their behalf, because they were parties to the summons of February 7, 1956. This summons was sent both to the plaintiffs and to the solicitors: compare the form in the Encyclopedia of Forms and Precedents, Vol. V, p. 241.

(2) The submission by the defendants that the Council of Gera are the parties to these proceedings is wrong. On the footing that the solicitors are parties to these proceedings and that counsel on this side represent them (although they deny it), the solicitors are not privies of the Council of Gera. Not being privies to the Council of Gera, they are not bound by the West German judgment.

(3) Issue estoppel has no application in foreign judgments. It is quite different from res judicata in the case of English judgments.

(4) The judgments of the West German courts are perverse in that they purported to apply as the law of East Germany, that which they knew perfectly well was not the law there.

(5) The appellants do not put forward any counter estoppel.

Estoppel is a rule of law or evidence which prevents a party from proving facts which would be in his favour. Here no estoppel is alleged against the Stiftung and it cannot be estopped from proving such facts as it may wish.

The Council of Gera are not parties to these proceedings, and it is contrary to all accepted ideas or jurisprudence that a person **[889]** should be held to be a party who has never received any documents and is not named as a party and has had no opportunity to address the court: see *Daimler Co. Ltd.* v. *Continental Tyre & Rubber Co.* (*Great Britain*) *Ltd.*[30]* The solicitors are only brought in for the purpose of making them pay costs. They could leave it to the Stiftung to argue, and abide by the result. Their only interest is to defend themselves against the claim for costs made against them personally on the basis of a breach of warranty of authority: see *Yonge* v. *Toynbee*.[31]

It is argued by the respondents that the solicitors are privies of the Council of Gera, because the council were in control of the previous proceedings. But, in the first place, privity is limited to privity of interest and there is no such privity between the two. In the second place, no one was in control but the Stiftung.

As to the question of privity, there can be privity of interest or privity of

[21] 24 Ll.L.Rep. 85, 87-8, 90-1, 92, 94.
[22] [1918] 2 K.B. 623, 637-41, 644.
[23] [1961] 1 Lloyd's Rep. 231.
[24] (1845) 8 Q.B. 208, 250-1.
[25] (1844) 11 Cl. & F. 85.
[26] (1927) 96 L.J.K.B. 930; 43 T.L.R. 60, C.A.
[27] (1941) 70 Ll.L. Rep. 262, 269.
[28] 96 L.J.K.B. 930.
[29] [1958] A.C. 95; [1957] 3 W.L.R. 830; [1957] 3 All E.R. 559, P.C.
[30] [1916] 2 A.C. 307, 336-7, 348; 32 T.L.R. 624, H.L.(E.).
[31] [1910] 1 K.B. 215, 227, 233-4; 26 T.L.R. 211, C.A.

contract, but only the former need be considered here. The interest which was the subject of the West German proceedings was a claim by the present appellants that the trade marks registered in West Germany should be assigned to them. There was also an issue whether certain entries in the commercial register should be altered. The solicitors had no interest in any of these things at all; their only interest now is to be paid their fees and to resist an order against them for costs. They have no interest in the question whether or not their clients have any power to institute any proceedings. So far as the Council of Gera are concerned, their interest is quite different from that of the solicitors. The solicitors are looking to the authority of the special board in representing the stiftung and they represent nobody else. There is no privity between the Stiftung and the Council of Gera in the capacity of special board. As to who are privies, see Spencer Bower on Res Judicata, pp. 130-1, paras. 205 and 206; Halsbury's Laws of England, 3rd ed., Vol. 15, p. 196, para. 372 and *Mercantile Investment and General Trust Co.* v. *River Plate Trust, Loan & Agency Co.*[32]

A decision was made against the Council of Gera in the West German courts. In those proceedings the solicitors had no opportunity of being heard and accordingly they cannot now be estopped from being heard for the purpose of resisting an order that they should pay costs in the present proceedings. **[890]**

Take the case of a servant, a chauffeur who having been injured in a road accident brings an action against the driver of the other car. His master backs him, undertaking to be responsible for his costs. The action fails on the ground that the accident was caused by a defect in the car which the chauffeur was driving. Afterwards the insurance company brings an action against the same defendant in respect of damage to the car which the chauffeur was driving. The insurance company would not be estopped from proving that the car was not defective. The servant's action would not bind the master because the servant's cause of action was not the master's. *Kinnersley* v. *Orpe*[33] and *Hancock* v. *Welsh and Cooper*[34] do not support the respondents' case: see *Outram* v. *Morewood*[35] and Spencer Bower on Res Judicata, pp. 199-200, para. 339. The real parties to an issue are those who can be heard and who can oppose it. There is no proof that the Council of Gera were ever in control of the proceedings.

As to the effect of foreign judgments, it was common ground before Cross J. that if there was to be estoppel per rem judicatam, it could only arise by reason of a decision of the prior court which was a final conclusion on the merits of the matter submitted to it for adjudication, so that the judgment either gives rise to a legal right or obligation or extinguishes such a right or obligation. If the West German judgment had been of that character, there might have been an estoppel, but that was not the case: see Halsbury's Laws of England, 3rd ed., Vol. 7 (1954), p. 140, para. 249; p. 150, para. 267, and Dicey's Conflict of Laws, 7th ed., pp. 981-985, r. 182; p. 1052, r. 196.

The reason for recognising a foreign judgment is that it gives rise to an obligation: *Godard* v. *Gray*.[36] From this case it appears that, for example, a foreign judgment on the meaning of the Sale of Goods Act might be challenged in an English court.

A foreign judgment does not merge the original cause of action as does an English judgment, and the principles on which we treat a foreign judgment are not the same as the principle of res judicata in England: *Nouvion* v. *Freeman*.[37]

If the West German proceedings had gone to finality and the courts there had decided that there was no passing off and that the trade marks should remain in the hands of the organisation in West Germany, that decision would establish res judicata, since the **[891]** courts would have been deciding finally on matters within their jurisdiction. But in the present case the English courts are not

[32] [1894] 1 Ch. 578; 10 T.L.R. 186.
[33] 2 Dougl. 517.
[34] 1 Stark, 347.
[35] (1803) 3 East 346, 366.
[36] L.R. 6 Q.B. 139, 148-9, 152.
[37] (1887) 37 Ch.D. 244, 250, 254-5, 258, C.A.; (1889) 15 App. Cas. 1, 8-9, 13, H.L.(E.).

bound to give effect to the decision of the West Germany courts: see *Harris and Adams* v. *Quine*[38]; *In re Low*[39] and *Henderson* v *Henderson*,[40] which illustrate the basis on which res judicata operates in relation to foreign judgments. Issue estoppel does not come into the matter. There can be no estoppel in relation to foreign judgments unless there is a final and conclusive judgment on the merits on a precise cause of action: see *New Brunswick Railway Co.* v. *British and French Trust Corporation Ltd.*[41] and *Callandar* v. *Dittrich*.[42]

It is submitted: (1) The basis of the enforcement of a foreign judgment is the arising or extinction of a legal right by that judgment. (2) The foreign judgment does not merge the cause of action. It is possible to rely either on it (res judicata) or on the original cause of action. (3) The right in question must have been entirely extinguished by the foreign judgment before there can be res judicata. (4) The foreign judgment cannot have a greater effect in England than it has under the foreign law. Thus the West German judgment in the present case cannot prevent this matter being relitigated in England because it would not prevent it being relitigated in West Germany.

Issue estoppel does not come into play in the case of foreign judgment. But, if it be held that it does, it is limited to the extent suggested by the opinion of Lord Romer in the *New Brunswick* case.[43] If issue estoppel were applied blindly to foreign judgments, the effects would be startling. Thus often foreign lawyers will not take a particular point because their courts will not consider it sympathetically, possibly for political reasons. It cannot be that, in such circumstances, the matter will be taken to have been decided finally for ever. In some countries there might be extra-ordinary procedures which would create situations in which it would be anomalous and unfair to allow estoppel.

Further, the West German judgment was perverse in the sense that the court purported to apply, as being the law of East Germany, a law which it knew to be contrary to that which every court in East Germany would apply. This case comes within the ratio of *Simpson* v. *Fogo*.[44] The decision of the West German **[892]** court should be treated on the same footing as that of the Louisiana court in that case: see also *Castrique* v. *Imrie*[45] and *Liverpool Marine Credit Co.* v. *Hunter*.[46] There must come a point when the English courts will refuse to allow estoppel to operate in relation to a foreign judgment. Long before the point at which a judgment must be treated as perverse in an unpleasant sense the English courts will refuse to have regard to it. If necessary, it is submitted that the West German decision was perverse in the full sense.

As to estoppel: see also *Hall* v. *Odber*[47]; *Smith* v. *Nicholls*[48] and *Bank of Australia* v. *Harding*.[49] Canadian authorities on the subject are *Clergue* v. *Humphrey*[50]; *State Bank of Butler* v. *Benzonson*[51] and *Davidson* v. *Sharpe*.[52]

The reason why English courts recognise foreign judgments is that under such a judgment an obligation has arisen. If the foreign judgment has dismissed a claim it shows that the defendant is free from any obligation. A foreign declaratory judgment should be recognised in the English courts: see Dicey's Conflict of Laws, 7th ed., r. 183, pp. 492, 996; r. 196, p. 1052; r. 197, p. 1054. The West German judgment, however, is not final and conclusive on the merits.

[38] (1869) L.R. 4 Q.B. 653, 657, D.C.
[39] [1894] 1 Ch. 147, 162-3; 10 T.L.R. 106, C.A.
[40] 3 Hare 100, 110 et seq.
[41] [1939] A.C. 1, 19-20, 28, 37, 41-2.
[42] (1842) 4 Man. & G. 68, 76-7.
[43] [1939] A.C. 1, 42-3.
[44] (1861) 1 H. & M. 195, 240-1, 247.
[45] L.R. 4, H.L. 414.
[46] (1868) 3 Ch.App. 479.
[47] (1809) 11 East 118.
[48] (1859) 5 Bing.N.C. 208.
[49] (1850) 9 C.B. 661.
[50] (1900) 31 Can.S.C.R. 166.
[51] (1914) 16 D.L.R. 848.
[52] (1920) 60 Can.S.C.R. 72.

A foreign judgment is only prima facie evidence and is not conclusive. What Lord Brougham L.C. said in *Houlditch* v. *Donegal*[53] is unanswerable. What Lord Lyndhurst L.C., said in *Ricardo* v. *Garcias*[54] is not inconsistent with the previous case. Reliance is placed on *Liverpool, Brazil and River Plate Steam Navigation Co. Ltd.* v. *Benham*.[55] In *In re Queensland Mercantile and Agency Co.*[56] the Court of Appeal distinguished *Simpson* v. *Fogo*[57] but recognised it as good law: see Dicey's Conflict of Laws, 7th ed., p. 549; *London & Mediterranean Bank* v. *Strutton*[58]; *Luther* v. *Sagor*.[59]*

In summary: (1) There is no estoppel against the Stiftung and counsel are entitled to appear on its behalf in the summons to which it is respondent. (2) (a) if (which is denied) counsel on this side are appearing not for the Stiftung, but for the solicitors, then the solicitors are not privies of the Council of Gera; (b) if (which is **[893]** denied) the term "privy" can include a person who is under the control of another, then it has not been proved that the respondents are under the control of the Council of Gera. (3) Even assuming that the solicitors are the servants of the Council of Gera, they are not estopped from defending themselves against this summons which seeks an order against them personally. No estoppel arises from the West German proceedings in which they had no chance of appearing. (4) The first and second defendants are not privies of the third defendant and cannot take advantage of any estoppel arising from the West German judgment. (5) The West German judgment cannot prevent anyone from contending now that these proceedings are not authorised by the Council of Gera because that judgment did not extinguish any cause of action. (6) The West German judgment did not estop anyone from commencing any proceedings in West Germany. (7) The causes of action in West Germany are different from the causes of action in England: see *Callandar's* case.[60] (8) The law of issue estoppel does not apply to foreign judgments. (9) If (which is denied) issue estoppel does apply to foreign judgments it is only to the extent stated by Lord Romer in the *New Brunswick* case.[61] (10) The West German decisions should not be recognised as foreign judgments capable of giving rise to estoppel because they applied, not East German law, but West German law in relation to the Stiftung of Jena. (11) The West German courts did not do their best to come to a judicial decision but, while purporting to apply the law of East Germany, applied a law which they knew was not that law. (12) The West German judgment was not judicial, but political, and had no validity outside West Germany.

Mark Littman Q.C. in reply. Since the application that all proceedings be stayed for want of authority in Courts & Co. the courts have been engaged in deciding that issue between whatever persons were parties to the proceedings. The appellants contend that the proceedings were brought without the authority of the Stiftung because, as a result of the confiscation in East Germany, its organs were paralysed. The respondents contend that Courts & Co. received their authority from the Council of Gera. The appellants say that the matter has been clearly decided in Germany between the same parties or parties so closely connected with them that estoppel arises.

As to estoppel, it is contended (1) that the Council of Gera was a party to the proceedings in West Germany; (2) that an issue **[894]** identical to the present issue (namely, whether or not the confiscation paralysed the organs of the Stiftung) was decided in West Germany; (3) that this decision was final and conclusive, since it was embodied in an order to determine the case; (4) that in English law it bound the Council of Gera and their privies, and (5) that the

[53] (1834) 8 Bligh (N.S.) 301, 338 et seq.
[54] (1845) 12 Cl. & F. 368, 397 et seq.
[55] (1868) L.R. 2 P.C. 193, 202.
[56] [1892] 1 Ch. 219, 224 et seq.; 8 T.L.R. 177, C.A.
[57] 1 H. & M. 195.
[58] (1869) 21 L.T. 415.
[59] [1921] 3 K.B. 532, 558-9.
[60] 4 Man. & G. 68.
[61] [1939] A.C. 1, 41-2.

contentions sought to be made against the respondents are sought to be made by the Council of Gera or their privies and accordingly estoppel arises: see the *New Brunswick* case[62] and the *Fidelitas* case.[63]

It is not contended that a determination by a judge on a point of fact, which was not a necessary link in his chain of reasoning would be res judicata. The point of the principle of res judicata is that there is a public interest in not relitigating the same matters, so that, if any matter raised in an action is an issue which has already been fought between the parties and decided by the court, this doctrine of public policy applies. In the present case the decision on the effect of the confiscation was a question which had in substance been decided in the earlier case. In considering this matter one is not confined to the formal cause of action; one must look behind it and see what were the matters raised: see Halsbury's Laws of England, 3rd ed., Vol. 15, pp. 186-7, paras. 360, 362. Where it can be shown that a particular issue was in fact raised and decided, the earlier judgment is conclusive. Here the issue which was decided was whether or not the Council of Gera ever had authority to act as the special board of the Stiftung. On that depends the question whether or not the confiscation paralysed the Stiftung and whether the Council of Gera is competent to bring the present action. In *Brown* v. *Robinson*[64] the approach of the court was perfectly reasonable and consistent with the underlying doctrine of public policy. It is not inconsistent with what Lord Romer said in the *New Brunswick* case.[65] The cases of *Hartington*[66] *Marginson*[67]; *Bright*[68]; *Hoystead*[69] and *Fidelitas*[70] and the passages cited from Spencer Bower's book are to be particularly noted and see *Callandar's* case.[71]

Assuming that there is such a thing as issue estoppel, it is reasonable that it should apply when the parties have litigated in England and also when they have litigated abroad and the matter **[895]** has been determined by a court of competent jurisdiction: see *Henderson* v. *Henderson*[72]; *Ricardo* v. *Garcias*[73]; *In re Dulles' Settlement (No. 2)*[74]; *Bell* v. *Holmes*[75]; *Ord* v. *Ord*[76] and Spencer Bower on Res Judicata, pp. 175-7, paras. 294 to 297; see particularly note (*m*).

When the underlying issues have been decided in a foreign court they should be treated in the same way as if they had been decided in an English court: see *Randolph* v. *Tuck*[77]; *Wood* v. *Luscombe*[78] *Duedu* v. *Yiboe*[79] and *Kok Hoong* v. *Leong Cheong Kwang Mines Ltd.*[80] It is conceded that issue estoppel is defeated if one party discovers a fresh point of law or discovers some new evidence.

The appellants have submitted that foreign judgments differ from English judgments in that an English judgment merges a debt but a foreign judgment does not. But it is extremely doubtful whether this old distinction is still part of English law: see Dicey's Conflict of Laws, 7th ed., rule 182, p. 981, rule 183, p. 992; sub-rule 183, p. 996; rule 185, p. 1002; rule 186, p. 1007 and Professor Horace Emerson Read's Recognition and Enforcement of Foreign Judgments (1938), pp. 116-8, 120-1.

[62] Ibid. 19-20, 21, 28, 36-37, 38, 43.
[63] [1966] 1 Q.B. 630, 639-40, 640-1.
[64] [1960] S.R.(N.S.W.) 297, 302.
[65] [1939] A.C. 1, 43.
[66] 6 E. & B. 780.
[67] [1939] 2 K.B. 426.
[68] [1954] P. 270.
[69] [1926] A.C. 155.
[70] [1966] 1 Q.B. 630.
[71] 4 Man. & G. 68, 91, 93.
[72] 3 Hare 100, 115.
[73] 12 Cl. & F. 368, 401.
[74] [1951] Ch. 842, 849, 851.
[75] [1956] 1 W.L.R. 1359; [1956] 3 All E.R. 449.
[76] [1923] 2 K.B. 432; 39 T.L.R. 437, D.C.
[77] [1962] 1 Q.B. 175.
[78] [1966] 1 Q.B. 169, 172; [1965] 3 W.L.R. 996; [1964] 3 All E.R. 972.
[79] [1961] 1 W.L.R. 1040, 1044-5, P.C.
[80] [1964] A.C. 993, 1010-11.

The appellants also contended that foreign judgments are only prima facie evidence of the facts which they find. But see Spencer Bower on Res Judicata, pp. 37-40, paras. 53-5. It is hard to see how that rule, unless it is purely technical and has nothing to do with the substance of res judicata, can be consistent with the rule that a final judgment of a foreign court is conclusive, as it is, save in certain circumstances, for example, where there is want of jurisdiction: see *Ricardo* v. *Garcias*[81] and *Barber* v. *Lamb*.[82]

The appellants referred to *Calandar's* case[83] and *Hull* v. *Odber*[84] but they are not applicable to the present case. The latter is of doubtful validity and does not help on the point of res judicata. They also referred to *In re Low*[85] and *Harris and Adams* v. *Quine*[86] as supporting the proposition that the earlier judgment must be final and conclusive in the merits. But both these cases were decided on the ground that all that had been decided **[896]** at the first trial was that no action lay in the foreign court by reason of the foreign law of limitations which was part of lex fori: see *In re Low*.[87]

The appellants cannot say that they did not intend to submit the matter to the foreign court before which the matter was fought out and by which it was decided, whatever may have been in the appellants' minds initially. The parties here are the same as the parties to the case in West Germany or their privies and estoppel should be held to apply.

It was submitted that the only party for whom counsel were appearing here was the Stiftung. But this is fallacious. It is not disputed that the Council of Gera were parties to the proceedings in West Germany. Who are the parties to the present proceedings? Clearly not the solicitors. Is the Stiftung, then, represented before the court in the present proceedings? If counsel are making representations on behalf of the Stiftung, it can only be because they are instructed by solicitors who have its authority. But if the respondents are right in their contentions the Stiftung have never been parties to these proceedings in any form. Over the period of this litigation counsel have been making submissions on behalf of someone other than the Stiftung. The only lay client whom they claim to have is not theirs. Either they are on a frolic of their own or they are representing someone else. In this context the word "party" has a special meaning. A person who is not a party on the record is yet a party if he allows someone else to fight his battles for him: see *Bruszewski* v. *United States*.[88] What is the relationship to be established for persons to be treated as affected by an estoppel? Here there is a close enough relationship to make it fair and just for those who directly instruct counsel on the other side, namely, the solicitors of the Council of Gera, to be bound by the West German decision. The latter are the clients of the former: see the definition in section 86 (1) of the Solicitors Act, 1957. The Council of Gera should be responsible for the costs of this action and the solicitors should likewise be liable on the principle of breach of warranty of authority if that turns out to be the case. The solicitors are in the same position vis-á-vis the Council of Gera who might be liable for the solicitors' costs if they allowed them to hold themselves out as having their authority. The right inference is that the Council of Gera controls the solicitors in these proceedings. If it does not, who does? On it the solicitors rely for their authority to issue the writ and **[897]** conduct the proceedings. It was really the council which fought the proceedings in West Germany: see Spencer Bower on Res Judicata, p. 127, para. 198, *Kinnersley* v. *Orpe*[89] and *Hancock* v. *Welsh and Cooper*.[90]

In order to show that a matter is res judicata by local law, it must be established that the judgment was final and conclusive, that is, that it was not reversible by the court which pronounced it.

The appellants relied on what Lord Watson said in *Nouvion's* case[91] but see

[81] 12 Ch. & F. 368.
[82] (1860) 8 C.B.(N.S.) 95.
[83] 4 Man. & G. 68.
[84] 11 East 118.
[85] [1894] 1 Ch. 147.
[86] L.R. 4 Q.B. 653.
[87] [1894] 1 Ch. 147, 161, 162-3.
[88] 181 Fed. 2nd 419, 422.
[89] 2 Dougl.K.B. 517.
[90] 1 Stark, 347.
[91] 15 App.Cas. 1, 13.

what was said by Lord Herschell[92]; see also *Pemberton* v. *Hughes.*[93] What has been fought out and decided between the parties binds them. That can be the case even in interlocutory proceedings: *Thoday* v. *Thoday.*[94]

In summary: (1) The domicile of the Stiftung, in the relevant sense, is not Jena. (2) Even if one must look to the law in force at Jena, that law is the law of all Germany, the old law which formerly prevailed there. (3) In normal circumstances when dealing with a sovereign state with its own judicial system and Supreme Court a decision of that court on a matter of its own law is the best evidence of the law of that place and it will be accepted as such, save in unusual or special circumstances. (4) What one has here is not a usual case but a highly exceptional case and, taking the circumstances as a whole, it is right that the judgments both of the West German and the East German Supreme Courts should be examined, with the aid of expert evidence, to find what is the relevant law. (5) The sitz of the Stiftung must be taken to be at Jena, but, for the purposes of English conflict rules, that is not the same as domicile. A piece of domestic law gave the Stiftung its seat or principal place of business, but the fact that this is a particular "land" does not prevent the overriding consideration that the law applicable is the law of Germany, for the Stiftung's domicile in the relevant sense was Germany, so the law which was to be applied in East Germany was the law of the Federal Republic, the old law before Germany was divided. (6) The law is not just what the courts say; the courts are applying themselves to something outside themselves, which they apply or interpret. Here one is dealing with the provisions of a code, and, though the decisions of a court are usually the best evidence of what the law is, the English courts are not bound to accept them. (7) The decision of the East German Supreme Court goes very little way to **[898]** showing what the law of Germany really is and it cannot be accepted as conclusive without accepting the postulate behind it that there is a state in East Germany established by the East Germans and not by the occupying power. This is not the ordinary type of case where one can look at the decision of the Supreme Court to see what the law is. (8) The decision of the Federal Supreme Court can be looked at on its merits, whereas the East German court made its decision politically. (9) On the facts the Stiftung could not continue to act in East Germany, where it was immobilised. (10) Accordingly the House of Lords should adopt the law laid down by the Supreme Court in West Germany.

Guy Aldous Q.C. on the new cases cited in reply. As to *Bell* v. *Holmes,*[95] a parallel might be suggested. Suppose an English driver in Ruritania carrying a Ruritanian passenger is involved in a collision in which his passenger is slightly injured but the driver of the other car is seriously injured. The passenger sues him in Ruritania and he lets judgment be given against him in default of defence. If the other driver sues him in England, he is not estopped from contesting the liability. As to *Ord* v. *Ord,*[96] the real distinction is between fact estoppel and cause of action estoppel. As to *Barber* v. *Lamb,*[97] that is explained in Spencer Bower on Res Judicata, p. 183, n. (o) and Professor Read on Recognition and Enforcement of Foreign Judgments, p. 117.

[The cross-appeal was ordered to stand over until the decision on the points argued was formulated.]

Their Lordships took time for consideration.

May 18. LORD REID. My Lords, in this action the appellants are seeking an injunction against the respondents to restrain them from selling optical instruments under the name Carl Zeiss and for other relief. The present appeal arises out of a summons taken out by the respondents on February 7, 1956, for an

92 Ibid. 6-7, 9.
93 (1899) 1 Ch. 781; 15 T.L.R. 211, C.A.
94 [1964] P. 181; [1964] 2 W.L.R. 371; [1964] 1 All E.R. 341, C.A.
95 [1956] 1 W.L.R. 1359.
96 [1923] 2 K.B. 432.
97 8 C.B.N.S. 195.

order for a stay of proceedings and dismissal of the action on the ground that it was commenced and is being maintained without the plaintiffs' (the appellants') authority. At various dates thereafter lengthy affidavits were filed and after long cross-examination Cross J. on March 6, 1964, refused to stay the proceedings, having decided against the respondents on the three grounds then put forward by them. The respondents appealed and, having **[899]** received new advice, put forward a new quite different ground based on the non-recognition by Her Majesty's Government of the German Democratic Republic. The Court of Appeal on December 17, 1964, allowed the respondents' appeal on this new ground and so found it unnecessary to reach any decision on the grounds maintained before Cross J.

I think that it will be convenient first to deal with the new point raised for the first time in the Court of Appeal and then to deal separately with the other grounds. The issues raised are complex and difficult and your Lordships are confronted with some 1,500 pages of affidavits, cross-examination and documents. I shall therefore try to restrict my narrative to those matters which are directly relevant to the issues to be decided.

It is necessary to have the appellants' history in mind. About 1846 Carl Zeiss founded an optical business in Jena. He later assumed as a partner Ernst Abbe of Jena University. Then they and Otto Schott founded a glass works. By 1891 Abbe was the owner of the whole (subject to Schott's interest) and he decided to set up a Stiftung or charitable foundation to own and carry on the two businesses under the name of the Carl-Zeiss-Stiftung. The main objects were to promote "precise technical industry" (which may not be an adequate translation) and to benefit the employees and the working population of Jena.

The constitution of the Stiftung was elaborately set out. First there was to be a special board for the administration of its estate and the supreme direction of its affairs and the rights and duties of the special board were to pertain to "that department of the state service of the Grand Duchy of Saxe-Weimar under which the affairs of the University of Jena are for the time being placed." Then "for directing the industrial operations of the Stiftung" there were to be "boards of management of the various establishments of the Stiftung for the time being" and a permanent official, the Deputy (Stiftungs Kommissar), was to be appointed to represent the special board on the boards of management, and finally article 113 provided:

> "Should, in consequence of political changes in the state, the provision according to 5 of this statute with reference to the representation of the Stiftung become untenable, this representation including the appointment of the Deputy of the Stiftung within the meaning of 5 and the statutory administration of the Carl-Zeiss-Stiftung shall be made over to that department of state, which with regard to the University of Jena occupies the place of the State Department of the Grand Duchy of Saxe-Weimar acting as special board, **[900]** provided that its seat is in Thuringia, otherwise to the highest administrative authorities in Thuringia."

In 1918 under the Weimar Republic the Grand Duchy was abolished and a new state of Thüringia was set up: thereupon the Minister of Education of that state became the special board. Then after 1935 under the National Socialist régime his place was taken by a Reichs-Stathalter. And when Thuringia was occupied by American forces in 1945 a new provincial government of Thuringia was set up by them and its Ministry of Education became the special board. On July 1, 1945, by agreement between the allied powers Thuringia came under Russian occupation and the present controversy turns on what happened thereafter.

We do not have precise evidence about this, but it is said that in 1949 the U.S.S.R. set up the German Democratic Republic to govern that part of Germany then occupied by Russia, and purported to make it an independent state. And it is further said that thereafter the German Democratic Republic purported to act as an independent state in legislating for and administering the Russian zone of Germany. That there is a body calling itself the German

Democratic Republic and that it does operate in that zone is, I think, common knowledge. I do not think that common knowledge goes farther than that, but, for the purposes of this appeal, I am prepared to assume that the U.S.S.R. did purport to confer independence on the Democratic Republic and that that body does purport to act as if it were an independent state.

Shortly stated, the respondents' case is that we are bound to have regard to the basis on which the Democratic Republic purports to act, and that as Her Majesty's Government has never granted recognition de jure or de facto to that Republic or its Government, we must refuse to recognise as effective all legislation emanating from it, and all acts done under such legislation. For reasons which I shall give later I do not think that that is right, but first I shall explain why, if it were right, it would be decisive of the point I am now dealing with.

In 1952 the Democratic Republic passed legislation re-organising local government in its "territory," and in fact this legislation was put into effect. The old state or land of Thuringia was abolished and in its place Districts were created, each with a Diet and a Council or Rat. Jena fell within the District of Gera, and the Council of Gera did in fact operate as the special board **[901]** of the appellants, and did in fact authorise the raising of the present action. If the respondents' argument based on non-recognition is well founded, then it must follow that British courts cannot recognise either the existence of the Council of Gera or the validity of anything done by it, and in particular cannot recognise any authority given by it for the raising of the present action. So I must now examine the principle on which this argument is founded.

In the normal case a law is made either by the sovereign directly or by some body entitled under the constitution of the country to make it or by some person or body to which the sovereign has delegated authority to make it. On the other hand, there are many cases where laws have been made against the will of the sovereign by persons engaged in a rebellion or revolution: then until such persons or the government which they set up have been granted de facto recognition by the Government of this country, their laws cannot be recognised by the courts of this country, but after de facto recognition such laws will be recognised. So far there is no difficulty. But the present case does not fit neatly into any of these categories. We are considering whether the law of 1952 under which the Council of Gera was set up can be recognised by our courts and therefore we must ascertain what was the situation in East Germany in 1952.

It is a firmly established principle that the question whether a foreign state ruler or government is or is not sovereign is one on which our courts accept as conclusive information provided by Her Majesty's Government: no evidence is admissable to contradict that information.

> "It has for some time been the practice of our courts . . . to take judicial notice of the sovereignty of a state, and for that purpose (in any case of uncertainty) to seek information from a Secretary of State; and when information is so obtained the court does not permit it to be questioned by the parties" (*per* Lord Cave in *Duff Development Co. Ltd.* v. *Government of Kelantan*[98*]).
>
> "Such information is not in the nature of evidence; it is a statement by the sovereign of this country through one of his ministers upon a matter which is peculiarly within his cognizance" (*per* Lord Finlay[99]).

In the present case the Court of Appeal twice received such information from the Foreign Secretary. First on September 16, 1964, it was stated: "Her Majesty's Government has not granted **[902]** any recognition de jure or de facto to (a) the 'German Democratic Republic' or (b) its 'Government,'" and secondly on November 6, 1964, a further answer was given to questions which had been asked on October 29.

In my opinion, this latter answer is decisive on the question which I am now considering and I must therefore quote the relevant question and the

[98] [1924] A.C. 797, 805-806; 40 T.L.R. 566, H.L.(E.).
[99] [1924] A.C. 797, 813.

relevant parts of the answer or certificate given by the Foreign Secretary. The question was:

"What (a) states or (b) governments or (c) authorities (if any) have since July 1, 1945, up to the present date been recognised by Her Majesty's Government as (a) entitled to exercise or (b) exercising governing authority in the area of Germany outside the zones allocated to the Governments of the United Kingdom, the United States of America and the French Republic by the protocol of September 12, 1944, and the agreement of July 26, 1945, concluded between the Governments of the said states and the Union of Soviet Socialist Republics. Has such recognition been de jure or de facto."

The relevant parts of the certificate are as follows:

"The area of Germany to which the question is understood to refer comprises (a) the zone of occupation allocated to the Union of Soviet Socialist Republics under the protocol of September 12, 1944, and the agreement of July 26, 1945, as modified by the protocol of the proceedings of the Berlin Conference of August 2, 1945, and (b) the 'Greater Berlin' area. The question is understood not to relate to the areas of Germany placed under Soviet or Polish administration in pursuance of the aforesaid protocol of August 2, 1945.

'(a) From the zone allocated to the Union of Soviet Socialist Republics Allied forces under the Supreme Allied Commander, General Eisenhower, withdrew at or about the end of June, 1945. Since that time and up to the present date Her Majesty's Government have recognised the state and Government of the Union of Soviet Socialist Republics as de jure entitled to exercise governing authority in respect of that zone. In matters affecting Germany as a whole, the states and Governments of the French Republic, the United Kingdom of Great Britain and Northern Ireland, the United States of America and the Union of Soviet Socialist Republics were jointly entitled to exercise governing authority. In the period from August 30, 1945, to March 20, 1948, they did exercise such joint authority through the Control Council for Germany. Apart from the states, Governments and Control Council aforementioned, Her Majesty's Government have not recognised either de jure or de facto any other authority purporting to exercise governing authority in or in respect of the zone. Her Majesty's Government, however, regard the **[903]** aforementioned Governments as retaining rights and responsibilities in respect of Germany as a whole."

It was not argued that the matter which I am now considering is one affecting Germany as a whole; so the rights of the other three allied Governments do not affect this question, and I need only consider what the certificate says with regard to the U.S.S.R. and the inferences which must be drawn from it.

The purpose of a certificate is to provide information about the status of foreign governments and states and therefore the statement that since July, 1945, "Her Majesty's Government have recognised the state and Government of the Union of Soviet Socialist Republics as de jure entitled to exercise governing authority in respect of that zone" cannot merely mean that Her Majesty's Government have granted this recognition so as to leave the courts of this country free to receive evidence as to whether in fact the U.S.S.R. are still entitled to exercise governing authority there. The courts of this country are no more entitled to hold that a sovereign, still recognised by our Government, has ceased in fact to be sovereign de jure, than they are entitled to hold that a government not yet recognised has acquired sovereign status. So this certificate requires that we must take it as a fact that the U.S.S.R. have been since 1945 and still are de jure entitled to exercise that governing authority. The certificate makes no distinction between the period before and the period after the German Democratic Republic was set up. So we are bound to hold that the setting up of that Republic made no difference in the right of the U.S.S.R. to exercise governing authority in the zone. And it must follow from that that the U.S.S.R. could at any time lawfully bring to an end the German Democratic Republic and its Government and could then resume direct rule of the zone.

But that is quite inconsistent with there having in fact been any abdication by the U.S.S.R. of its rights when the German Democratic Republic was set up.

The judgment of the Court of Appeal appears to me to be based on the view that the courts of this country can and must accept the position that the U.S.S.R. have recognised the German Democratic Republic as an independent sovereign state. Harman L.J. says[1]: "It is in fact notorious that the U.S.S.R. has recognised the German Democratic Republic as a sovereign state **[904]** and treats its law-making capacity accordingly." And Diplock L.J. says[2]:

> "All that I am prepared to assume—and I think it is a matter of which I can take judicial note—is that the Government of the U.S.S.R. recognises the 'Government of the German Democratic Republic' as the independent sovereign government of an independent sovereign state for whose territory the Government of the U.S.S.R. claims no power to make laws."

But the learned judges of the Court of Appeal do not appear to have had their attention directed to the true import of the certificate of the Secretary of State. The U.S.S.R. may have purported to confer independence or sovereignty on the German Democratic Republic but, in my judgment, that certificate clearly requires us to hold that, whatever the U.S.S.R. may have purported to do, they did not in fact set up the German Democratic Republic as a sovereign or independent state. If they retained their right to govern its territory, they could not possibly have done so; and the certificate requires us to hold that they did retain that right.

If we are bound to hold that the German Democratic Republic was not in fact set up as a sovereign independent state, the only other possibility is that it was set up as a dependent or subordinate organisation through which the U.S.S.R. is entitled to exercise indirect rule. I do not think that we are concerned to enquire or to know to what extent the U.S.S.R. in fact exercise their right of control. At a late stage in the argument before your Lordships counsel for the respondents made an application that further questions should be addressed to Her Majesty's Government. That would be a perfectly proper thing to do if your lordships were of the opinion that the existing certificate is ambiguous or insufficient. But I can see no ambiguity or insufficiency in this certificate and therefore I agree that this application was properly refused.

It was argued that the present case is analogous to cases where subjects of an existing sovereign have rebelled and have succeeded in gaining control of a part of the old sovereign's dominions. When they set up a new government in opposition to the de jure sovereign that new government does not and cannot derive any authority or right from the de jure sovereign, and our courts must regard its acts and the acts of its organs or officers as nullities until it has established and consolidated its position to such an extent as to warrant our government according de facto recognition of it. **[905]** The case of *Banco de Bilbao* v. *Sancha*[3]* affords a fairly recent example of this: there General Franco's adherents had succeeded in gaining control of a large part of Spain and the government which they set up in opposition to the Republican Government was recognised de facto by the British Government. Giving the judgment of the Court of Appeal, Clauson L.J. said[4]:

> ". . . this court is bound to treat the acts of the government which His Majesty's Government recognise as the de facto government of the area in question as acts which cannot be impugned as the acts of an usurping government, and conversely the court must be bound to treat the acts of a rival government claiming jurisdiction over the same area, even if the latter government be recognised by His Majesty's Government as the de jure government of the area, as a mere nullity, and as matters which cannot be taken into account in any way in any of His Majesty's courts."

Aksionairnoye Obschestvo A.M. Luther v. *James Sagor & Co.*[5]* is another

[1] [1965] Ch. 596, 651; [1965] 2 W.L.R. 277; [1965] 1 All E.R. 300, C.A.
[2] [1965] Ch. 596, 664.
[3] [1938] 2 K.B. 176; 54 T.L.R. 603; [1938] 2 All E.R. 253, C.A.
[4] [1938] 2 K.B. 176, 195-196.
[5] [1921] 1 K.B. 456; 37 T.L.R. 282; [1921] 3 K.B. 532; 37 T.L.R. 777, C.A.

good example. The case turned on whether the courts of this country could recognise a decree made in 1918 by officers of the U.S.S.R. which had by revolutionary means assumed power in Russia. At the time when the case came before Roche J. His Majesty's Government had not recognised the U.S.S.R. and therefore Roche J. properly held that he could not give effect to that decree. But before the case was decided by the Court of Appeal the court were informed by the Secretary of State that His Majesty's Government recognised the Soviet Government as the de facto government of Russia. Accordingly the Court of Appeal were able to give effect to the decree.

But the present case is essentially different. The German Democratic Republic was set up by the U.S.S.R. and it derived its authority and status from the Government of the U.S.S.R. So the only question could be whether or not it was set up as a sovereign state. But the certificate of our Government requires us to hold that it was not set up as a sovereign state because it requires us to hold that the U.S.S.R. remained de jure sovereign and therefore did not voluntarily transfer its sovereignty to the Democratic Republic. And, if the Democratic Republic did not become a sovereign state at its inception, there is no suggestion that it has at any subsequent time attempted to deprive the U.S.S.R. of rights which were not granted to it at its inception. The courts of this country must disregard any declarations of the Government **[906]** of the U.S.S.R. in so far as they conflict with the certificate of Her Majesty's Secretary of State, and we must therefore hold that the U.S.S.R. set up the German Democratic Republic, not as a sovereign state, but as an organisation subordinate to the U.S.S.R. If that is so, then mere declarations by the Government of the Democratic Republic that it is acting as the government of an independent state cannot be regarded as proof that its initial status has been altered, and we must regard the acts of the German Democratic Republic, its government organs and officers as acts done with the consent of the Government of the U.S.S.R. as the government entitled to exercise governing authority.

It appears to me to be impossible for any de jure sovereign governing authority to disclaim responsibility for acts done by subordinate bodies which it has set up and which have not attempted to usurp its sovereignty. So, in my opinion, the courts of this country cannot treat as nullities acts done by or on behalf of the German Democratic Republic. De facto recognition is appropriate —and, in my view, is only appropriate—where the new government have usurped power against the will of the de jure sovereign. I would think that where a sovereign has granted independence to a dependency any recognition of the new state would be a recognition de jure.

The general practice of the British Government was stated in Parliament on March 21, 1951, by the Secretary of State for Foreign Affairs (Hansard, Vol. 485, col. 2410) as follows:

> ". . . it is international law which defines the conditions under which a government should be recognised de jure or de facto, and it is a matter of judgment in each particular case whether a régime fulfils the conditions. The conditions under international law for the recognition of a new régime as the de facto government of a state are that the new régime has in fact effective control over most of the state's territory and that this control seems likely to continue. The conditions for the recognition of a new régime as the de jure government of a state are that the new régime should not merely have effective control over most of the state's territory, but that it should, in fact, be firmly established. His Majesty's Government consider that recognition should be accorded when the conditions specified by international law are, in fact, fulfilled and that recognition should not be given when these conditions are not fulfilled. The recognition of a government de jure or de facto should not depend on whether the character of the régime is such as to command His Majesty's Government's approval."

Recognition implies independence and refusal to recognise **[907]** the German Democratic Republic or its Government is entirely consistent with that statement if independence was never in fact granted by the U.S.S.R., for no one suggests that the Democratic Republic has, or could have, seized independence in defiance of the U.S.S.R. So there can, in my view, be no question of awaiting de facto recognition before we can recognise as lawful the acts of the German Democratic Republic. We recognise them, not because they are acts of a sovereign state, but because they are acts done by a subordinate body which the U.S.S.R. set up to act on its behalf.

I am reinforced in my opinion by a consideration of the consequences which would follow if the view taken by the Court of Appeal were correct. Counsel for the respondents did not dispute that in that case we must not only disregard all new laws and decrees made by the Democratic Republic or its Government, but we must also disregard all executive and judicial acts done by persons appointed by that Government because we must regard their appointments as invalid. The result of that would be far-reaching. Trade with the Eastern Zone of Germany is not discouraged. But the incorporation of every company in East Germany under any new law made by the Democratic Republic or by the official act of any official appointed by its Government would have to be regarded as a nullity, so that any such company could neither sue nor be sued in this country. And any civil marriage under any such new law, or owing its validity to the act of any such official, would also have to be treated as a nullity, so that we should have to regard the children as illegitimate. And the same would apply to divorces and all manner of judicial decisions, whether in family or commercial questions. And that would affect not only status of persons formerly domiciled in East Germany but property in this country the devolution of which depended on East German law.

It was suggested that these consequences might be mitigated if the courts of this country could adopt doctrines which have found some support in the United States of America. Difficult questions arose there with regard to acts of administration in the Confederate states during the Civil War and again out of the delay in recognition of the U.S.S.R. A solution of the earlier difficulty was found by the Supreme Court in *U.S.* v. *Insurance Companies*[6] and other similar cases. And for the latter difficulty solutions were suggested, particularly by Cardozo C.J. in such **[908]** cases as *Sokoloff* v. *National City Bank of New York*[7] and *Petrogradsky Mejdunarodny Kom. Merchesky Bank* v. *National City Bank of New York.*[8] In the view which I take of the present case, it is unnecessary to express any opinion whether it would be possible to adopt any similar solutions in this country, if the need should ever arise.

Finally, on this branch of the case I must deal briefly with three grounds on which the appellants argued that the raising of this action should be held to have been properly authorised, even if the actions of the Council of Gera must be disregarded. These grounds involved the interpretation and effect of a power of attorney granted to Dr. Schrade in 1951 and questions as to his powers by virtue of appointments in the Stiftung which he then held. These matters involve German law. They only became important after the respondents put forward their new case in the Court of Appeal, so they were only dealt with cursorily, if at all, in the affidavits and in the evidence led before Cross J. The Court of Appeal found it possible to decide these questions without receiving further evidence of German law, which the appellants wished to adduce. In my opinion, these questions could not properly be decided on the evidence as it stands, and, if they should ever arise in any other litigation, the judgment of the Court of Appeal cannot be regarded as res judicata or as having binding effect.

The next question for consideration is whether by reason of a decision of the Federal Supreme Court of West Germany the subject-matter of the issue now before this House is res judicata so that the respondents must succeed without further inquiry. I can deal briefly with the events which led up to that decision. When the American forces left Jena in 1945 a number of officers of the Stiftung and of the firm Carl Zeiss went with them to West Germany. The Stiftung and the firm already had interests there and these were developed in particular by three of these officers. After a time relations between them and

[6] (1874) 89 U.S. 99. [7] (1924) 145 N.E. 917. [8] (1930) 170 N.E. 479.

Jena became strained and legal proceedings of various kinds were begun. Decrees were obtained in West Germany to the effect that the domicile of the Stiftung was removed from Jena to Heidenheim in Würthemberg, and goods were manfactured and sold under the name Carl Zeiss. Then the West German firm Carl Zeiss sought to prevent sale in West Germany of the products made in Jena, and in 1953 an action was commenced at Stuttgart by "the **[909]** Carl-Zeiss-Stiftung of Jena represented by the Council of the District of Gera" against the firm Carl Zeiss of Heidenheim and the three individuals who were directing it. The main purpose of this action was to restrain these defendants from using the name Carl Zeiss.

Those defendants at once raised the preliminary objection that the Stiftung was not properly before the court, as the Council of Gera was not the legal representative of the Stiftung. The proceedings on this objection were elaborate and prolonged, but ultimately on November 15, 1960, it was sustained by the Federal Supreme Court. I do not attempt at this point even to summarise the reasons: the various judgments given in this action occupy over 200 closely typed pages of which the final judgment occupies more than 30.

The respondents maintain that this decision must be held decisive of the question now before this House, because the issue in this appeal is the same as that which was decided by the Federal Supreme Court. So, in the first place, it is necessary to make clear what is the question now before this House. On February 7, 1956, the respondents took out a summons

> "for an order that all further proceedings in this action be stayed and that this action be dismissed on the ground that the same was commenced and is being maintained without the plaintiffs' authority and that Messrs. Courts & Co., the solicitors purporting to act for the plaintiffs herein, do pay to the defendants the costs of this action . . . to be taxed as between solicitor and client."

This question, whether these solicitors are maintaining this action without the authority of the Stiftung, is the sole question which your Lordships now have to determine.

There is a vast amount of authority on estoppel per rem judicatam.

> "The object of the rule of res judicata is always put upon two grounds—the one public policy, that it is the interest of the state that there should be an end of litigation, and the other, the hardship on the individual, that he should be vexed twice for the same cause" (*per* Lord Blackburn in *Lockyer* v. *Ferryman.*[9])

And the general principle is clear that the earlier judgment relied on must have been a final judgment, and that there must be identity of parties and of subject matter in the former and in the **[910]** present litigation. But each of these three requirements can give rise—and in the present case does give rise—to difficult questions.

Let me take first identity of parties. In this preliminary or interlocutory matter the issue is whether the nominal plaintiff is before the court at all. If it is decided in favour of the defendant, that establishes that the nominal plaintiff never was before the court. So I do not see how the nominal plaintiff, here the Stiftung, can be a party to that issue. And it is admitted that the Stiftung was not a party to the German proceedings. The defendants are of course parties —they raise the issue. But who is their opponent? We are not told the precise implications of the requirement of German procedure as to "representation," but I am content to assume that the Council of Gera was a party to the German proceedings: that council was ordered to pay the costs. But who is the appellant in this House? Again, I think, not the Stiftung. The issue is whether the solicitors are maintaining the action without authority and surely they must be parties—how else could they be made personally liable to the respondents in costs. And I can see no other party—no other appellant. It was argued that the Council

[9] (1877) 2 App.Cas. 519, 530, H.L.(Sc.).

of Gera can be regarded as parties but I can see no ground for that. There may be a question when I come to deal with privity. But the Council of Gera has never sought to be a party and no one has sought to make them a party.

Again there is no doubt that the requirement of identity of parties is satisfied if there is privity between a party to the former litigation and a party to the present litigation. The only way in which that could be satisfied in this case would be if there were privity between the Council of Gera and the solicitors. We have a letter from the Council of Gera in their capacity of special board of the Stiftung authorising the raising of this action, but we do not know whether that council has taken any further part, whether it has given any further instructions, or whether it is using the funds of the Stiftung to finance this litigation. The most that can be said is that the council is the "client" instructing the solicitors, though I doubt whether that is proved; the real question may be whether there is a "client" at all. Does this make them privies? It has always been said that there must be privity of blood, title or interest: here it would have to be privity of interest. That can arise in many ways, but it seems to me to be essential that the person now to be estopped from defending himself must have had some kind of interest in the previous litigation or its subject-matter. I have found no English case to the contrary. If that is **[911]** right, then there can be no privity here because these solicitors had no connection with and certainly no interest in the German litigation.

There does, however, seem to me to be a possible extension of the doctrine of privity as commonly understood. A party against whom a previous decision was pronounced may employ a servant or engage a third party to do something which infringes the right established in the earlier litigation and so raise the whole matter again in his interest. Then, if the other party to the earlier litigation brings an action against the servant or agent, the real defendant could be said to be the employer, who alone has the real interest, and it might well be thought unjust if he could vex his opponent by relitigating the original question by means of the device of putting forward his servant. But this is not a case of that character. The Council of Gera has no substantial interest in this litigation. If the plaintiff succeeds, the only persons who can benefit are the Stiftung or the two nationalised firms in Jena to which I shall refer later. The Council of Gera is merely a local public authority, like a county council, on which there has been imposed the duty of acting as the special board of the Stiftung and there is nothing to show that the council or any of its members will gain anything if the plaintiff wins, or lose anything if the plaintiff loses this case. And here the respondents are seeking to make these solicitors personally liable to them in solicitor and client costs—in effect seeking damages against them for breach of warranty of authority. In my view, the solicitors cannot properly be held to be estopped from defending themselves, and showing that they have authority to act, by a judgment which had nothing to do with them.

There is little authority bearing on a question of this kind. The only modern English case cited was *Mercantile Investment and General Trust Co.* v. *River Plate Trust, Loan and Agency Co.*[10] The facts were complicated but it is sufficient, for present purposes, to say that the plaintiffs in this action had obtained a judgment against another company ("the American company") and they maintained this as an estoppel against the defendants in this action ("the English company") on the ground that, by reason of an indemnity given by the English company, the English company had assisted the American company in the previous action and had paid their costs, so that they were virtually parties **[912]** to the previous action. Romer J. dealt with this point very briefly and held that there was no estoppel.

I should also refer to *Kinnersley* v. *Orpe*[11] which was cited as relevant on privity. There Dr. Cotton claimed a right to fish and sent a servant, Orpe, to assert it. Kinnersley brought an action of trespass and succeeded. Then Dr. Cotton sent another servant, also called Orpe, to fish and this action was brought

[10] [1894] 1 Ch. 578; 10 T.L.R. 186.
[11] (1780) 2 Dougl.K.B. 517, 518.

against him. The plaintiff simply produced the record in the former case and Perryn B. held this evidence conclusive, "both the Orpes having acted under the authority of Cotton, who was the real defendant in both cases." On a rule "the court also thought that the record in the former cause, though admissible evidence, was not conclusive." With regard to this case Lord Ellenborough C.J. said in *Outram* v. *Morewood*[12]:

> "As to the case of *Kinnersley* v. *Orpe,*[13] it is extraordinary that it should ever have been for a moment supposed that there could be an estoppel in such a case. It was not pleaded as such; neither were the parties in the second suit the same with those in the first."

And a little later he referred to "the defendant, who was no party to the former action."

One should not attach too much weight to this, because it was a very minor point in Lord Ellenborough's elaborate and learned judgment. But at least it never occurred to him that the doctrine of privity could be stretched to affect a defendant from whom a penalty was claimed and who had no connection with the previous case, merely because his employer had been concerned with it.

The respondent sought to rely on American authorities. Their effect is summarised in the American Restatement (Judgments), Chap. IV. The only section which seemed to me to come near to applying to the appellant solicitors is at pp. 402-403, s. 85 (2):

> "Where a person is bound by or entitled to the benefit of the rules of res judicata because of a judgment for or against him with reference to a particular subject-matter, such rules apply in a subsequent acton brought or defended by another on his account."

With that I would agree; and, if these solicitors were bringing this action on account of or for the benefit of the Council of Gera, I would hold that res judicata could be pleaded against them. **[913]** But I have already stated my view that this action is not brought on account of or for the benefit of the Council of Gera and, in particular, these solicitors are not contesting the issue now before your Lordships for the benefit of that council. In so far as they are not acting to protect their own interests they are seeking to act for the benefit of the Stiftung, and it is not alleged that the plea of res judicata would be good against the Stiftung.

The second requirement for res judicata is identity of subject-matter. As to this, it has become common to distinguish between cause of action estoppel and issue estoppel. There is certainly no cause of action estoppel here. The question before the German court was whether the Council of Gera were the legal representatives of the Stiftung at one date. The question here is whether at a different date the solicitors had the authority of the Stiftung to raise this action. An answer, yes or no, to the first question does not necessarily imply a similar answer to the second. What the respondents maintain is that the grounds on which the German court in fact decided the first question are such that we cannot decide this case in favour of the solicitors without disagreeing with at least some of the findings on which the German court based their decision. I think that that is true and the question is whether we are entitled to do that.

Issue estoppel may be a comparatively new phrase, but I think that the law of England—unlike the law of some other countries—has always recognised that estoppel per rem judicatam includes more than merely cause of action estoppel. The earliest case commonly referred to on res judicata is *The Duchess of Kingston's* case[14] in 1776. The Duchess of Kingston was prosecuted for bigamy in this House. She put forward in defence a decision of an ecclesiastical court that her first marriage was invalid. The first question put to the judges who were in attendance was whether a sentence of the spiritual court against

[12] (1803) 3 East 346, 366. [13] 2 Dougl.K.B. 517. [14] (1776) 20 St. Tr. 355.

the marriage was conclusive evidence. The unanimous opinion of the judges was given by De Grey C.J. and in the course of it he said[15]:

> "From the variety of cases relative to judgments being given in evidence in civil suits, these two deductions seem to follow as generally true: first, that the judgment of a court of concurrent jurisdiction, directly upon the point, is as a plea, a bar, or as evidence, conclusive, between the same parties, upon the same matter, directly in question in another court: **[914]** secondly, that the judgment of a court of exclusive jurisdiction, directly upon the point, is, in like manner, conclusive upon the same matter, between the same parties, coming incidentally in question in another court, for a different purpose. But neither the judgment of a concurrent or exclusive jurisdiction is evidence, of any matter which comes collaterally in question, though within their jurisdiction; nor of any matter incidentally cognizable: nor of any matter to be inferred by argument from the judgment."

In referring to a judgment being conclusive on the same matter "coming incidentally in question in another court for a different purpose" the judges were clearly going beyond cause of action estoppel, but I need not attempt to discover just how far they meant to go because this has been developed in many later decisions.

In *Reg.* v. *Inhabitants of the Township of Hartington Middle Quarter*[16] it appeared that in a previous litigation it had been decided that two young children had a settlement in the defendants' township. The question at issue in this case was the settlement of their mother and it was held that the defendants were estopped from denying that she had the same settlement. The cause of action was obviously not the same. Coleridge J., in delivering the judgment of the court, said[17]:

> "The question then is, whether the [former] judgment concludes, not merely as to the point actually decided, but as to a matter which it was necessary to decide, and which was actually decided, as the groundwork of the decision itself, though not then directly the point at issue. And we think it does conclude to that extent. . . . Now, it cannot be said that the facts we are considering were merely collateral to the decision in the former case. The question then was where two unemancipated children were settled: and it was answered by showing that they were the legitimate issue of William and Esther, that is, that these two were lawfully married, and the children born after, and that William was settled with the now appellants. Strike either of these facts out, and there is no ground for the decision: these facts therefore were necessarily and directly matter of enquiry. The question now is, where is Esther settled: and this is answered by showing the same two facts, the marriage of Esther and William, and the settlement of William, the two facts already decided. The judgments in the two cases therefore rest on the same foundation; which, having been settled in the first, cannot be, as between the same parties, unsettled in the latter." **[915]**

In *Flitters* v. *Allfrey*[18] a landlord alleging a weekly tenancy obtained a warrant for the eviction of the tenant and then sued him in the county court for 29 weeks' rent. He failed in this action because the judge held there was a yearly tenancy. Then the tenant sued for damages for eviction. Lord Coleridge C.J. said[19]:

> "The now plaintiff succeeded upon the trial of a plaint in the county court which involved the same question of fact as that which was in issue in this cause, viz., whether his tenancy under the defendant was a weekly or a yearly tenancy. The defendant thought the decision of the county court wrong. Upon the trial of this cause, the jury thought so too; and I agreed with them: but the plaintiff, against the right, succeeded upon an estoppel."

[15] Ibid. 538 n.
[16] (1855) 4 E. & B. 780.
[17] Ibid. 794-795.
[18] (1874) L.R. 10 C.P. 29.
[19] Ibid. 43

Counsel had pointed out that failure to succeed in the action for rent did not on the face of it or necessarily involve any decision that the tenancy was yearly and not weekly: but that was in fact the ground on which the county court judge decided the case and the landlord was not allowed to relitigate that issue in the tenant's subsequent action for damages.

These two cases appear to me to be authorities directly in favour of issue estoppel, but the complications in each were such that it is easy to miss the point, and little attention seems to have been paid to this form of estoppel until comparatively recently.

A case which has given rise to some difficulties is *Hoystead* v. *Commissioner of Taxation.*[20] There an appeal with regard to income tax for an earlier year had been decided on an assumption that certain beneficiaries under a will were joint owners. Then in a case as to liability to tax in a later year the commissioner tried to maintain that that assumption had been wrong but he was held to be estopped. Lord Shaw in delivering the judgment of the board, after citing numerous authorities, including the judgment of Lord Ellenborough C.J. in *Outram* v. *Morewood,*[21] said[22]:

> "It is seen from this citation of authority that if in any court of competent jurisdiction a decision is reached, a party is estopped from questioning it in a new legal proceeding. But the principle also extends to any point, whether of assumption or admission, which was in substance the ratio of and fundamental to the decision." **[916]**

Comments were made on that passage in *New Brunswick Railway Co.* v. *British and French Trust Corporation Ltd.*[23] by Lord Russell[24] and Lord Romer[25] and in *Society of Medical Officers of Health* v. *Hope*[26] by Lord Radcliffe. And there may well be a difference between a case where an issue was in fact decided in the earlier case and a case where it was not in fact decided because the earlier judgment went by default or was founded on an assumption. Indeed, I think that some confusion has been introduced by applying to issue estoppel without modification rules which have been evolved to deal with cause of action estoppel, such as the oft-quoted passage from the judgment of Wigram V.-C. in *Henderson* v. *Henderson.*[27] But it is unnecessary to pursue that matter because in the present case the issues with regard to which the respondents plead estoppel were fully litigated in the West German court.

In *Marginson* v. *Blackburn Borough Council*[28] both the parties had been defendants in a county court action in which a plaintiff claimed damages for negligence and they had been held both to blame. This was held to estop the plaintiff in this action from maintaining (in his personal capacity) that he was not to blame.

> "In such a case the question arises, what was the question of law or fact which was decided [in the earlier case]? And for this purpose, it may be vital in many cases to consider the actual history of the proceedings" (*per* Slesser L.J., delivering the judgment of the court).[29]

Thoday v. *Thoday*[30] is the most recent of a series of matrimonial cases raising this question. There are special considerations in this field, so Willmer L.J. only says[31]:

[20] [1926] A.C. 155; 42 T.L.R. 207, P.C.
[21] 3 East 346.
[22] [1926] A.C. 155, 170.
[23] [1939] A.C. 1; 55 T.L.R. 260; [1938] 4 All E.R. 747, H.L.(E.).
[24] [1939] A.C. 1, 28.
[25] Ibid. 42.
[26] [1960] A.C. 551, 566; [1960] 2 W.L.R. 404; [1960] 1 All E.R. 317, H.L.(E.).
[27] (1843) 3 Hare 100.
[28] [1939] 2 K.B. 426; 55 T.L.R. 389; [1939] 1 All E.R. 273, C.A.
[29] [1939] 2 K.B. 426, 437.
[30] [1964] P. 181; [1964] 2 W.L.R. 371; [1964] 1 All E.R. 341, C.A.
[31] [1964] P. 181, 191.

". . . there may be cases in which a party may be held to be estopped from raising particular issues, if those issues are precisely the same as issues which have been previously raised and have been the subject of adjudication."

But Diplock L.J. dealt with the matter on more general lines and what he says is further explained in *Fidelitas Shipping Co. Ltd.* v. *V. O. Exportchleb.*[32] He draws a distinction between issue estoppel and fact estoppel which I find difficult to understand **[917]** Suppose that as an essential step towards the judgment in an earlier case it was decided (a) that on a particular date A owed B £100 or (b) that on that date A was alive. The first is, or at least probably is, a question of law, the second is a pure question of fact. Are these findings to be treated differently when issue estoppel is pleaded in a later case? Or take marriage—an issue in the earlier case may have been whether there ever was a ceremony (a pure question of fact) or it may have been whether the ceremony created a marriage (a question of law). I cannot think that this would make any difference if in a later case about quite different subject matter the earlier finding for or against marriage was pleaded as creating issue estoppel.

The difficulty which I see about issue estoppel is a practical one. Suppose the first case is one of trifling importance but it involves for one party proof of facts which would be expensive and troublesome; and that party can see the possibility that the same point may arise if his opponent later raises a much more important claim. What is he to do? The second case may never be brought. Must he go to great trouble and expense to forestall a possible plea of issue estoppel if the second case is brought? This does not arise in cause of action estoppel: if the cause of action is important, he will incur the expense: if it is not, he will take the chance of winning on some other point. It seems to me that there is room for a good deal more thought before we settle the limits of issue estoppel. But I have no doubt that issue estoppel does exist in the law of England. And, if it does, it would apply in the present case, if the earlier judgment had been a final judgment of an English court.

Next I must consider whether it makes any difference that the former judgment was the judgment of a foreign court. At one time foreign judgments were regarded as being only evidence and not conclusive. But at least since the decision in *Godard* v. *Gray*[33] they have been regarded as equally conclusive with English judgments (subject to any difference there may be resulting from there being no merger of a cause of action in a foreign judgment). The same pleas, for example, fraud or lack of jurisdiction, are good against both. It would seem that the only plea which may be available against foreign judgments alone is perversity, if *Simpson* v. *Fogo*[34] was rightly decided. In that case Page Wood V.-C. refused to give effect to a judgment of the Supreme Court of Louisiana. There was no question of perversity in the ordinary **[918]** sense of obstinately or dishonestly shutting one's eyes to what one knows to be right. The Supreme Court had applied what they believed to be their common law, but it was at variance with a generally accepted rule of private international law, which required foreign (in this case, English) law to be applied in the circumstances of that case. Page Wood V.-C. called[35] this "a perverse and deliberate refusal to recognise the law of the country by which title has been validly conferred." I shall have to return to this case later.

I can see no reason in principle why we should deny the possibility of issue estoppel based on a foreign judgment, but there appear to me to be at least three reasons for being cautious in any particular case. In the first place, we are not familiar with modes of procedure in many foreign countries, and it may not be easy to be sure that a particular issue has been decided or that its decision was a basis of the foreign judgment and not merely collateral or obiter. Secondly, I have already alluded to the practical difficulties of a defendant in deciding whether, even in this country, he should incur the trouble

[32] [1966] 1 Q.B. 630; [1965] 2 W.L.R. 1059; [1965] 2 All E.R. 4, C.A.
[33] (1870) L.R. 6 Q.B. 139.
[34] (1862) 1 H. & M. 195.
[35] 1 H. & M. 195, 247.

and expense of deploying his full case in a trivial case: it might be most unjust to hold that a litigant here should be estopped from putting forward his case because it was impracticable for him to do so in an earlier case of a trivial character abroad, with the result that the decision in that case went against him. These two reasons do not apply in the present case. The case for the Stiftung, or on this issue those who purported to represent it, was fought as tenaciously in West Germany as this case has been fought here, and it is not difficult to see what were the grounds on which the West German judgment was based. But the third reason for caution does raise a difficult problem with which I must now deal.

It is clear that there can be no estoppel of this character unless the former judgment was a final judgment on the merits. But what does that mean in connection with issue estoppel? When we are dealing with cause of action estoppel it means that the merits of the cause of action must be finally disposed of so that the matter cannot be raised again in the foreign country. In this connection the case of *Nouvion* v. *Freeman*[36] is important. There had been in Spain a final judgment in a summary form of procedure. But that was not necessarily the end of the matter, because it was possible to reopen the whole question by commencing a different kind of action: so the summary judgment was not res **[919]** judicata in Spain. I do not find it surprising that the House unanimously refused to give effect in England to that summary judgment.

When we come to issue estoppel I think that, by parity of reasoning, we should have to be satisfied that the issues in question cannot be relitigated in the foreign country. In other words, it would have to be proved in this case that the courts of the German Federal Republic would not allow the re-opening in any new case between the same parties of the issues decided by the Supreme Court in 1960, which are now said to found an estoppel here. There would seem to be no authority of any kind on this matter, but it seems to me to verge on absurdity that we should regard as conclusive something in a German judgment which the German courts themselves would not regard as conclusive. It is quite true that estoppel is a matter for the lex fori but the lex fori ought to be developed in a manner consistent with good sense.

The need to prove whether West German law would permit these issues to be re-opened there appears to have escaped the notice of the appellants' advisers and your Lordships are left in considerable difficulty. On the one hand, there is always a presumption that the foreign law on any particular question is the same as English law unless the contrary is proved. On the other hand, it would be remarkable if German law had reached precisely the same stage of development on issue estoppel as the law of England has, and there are some indications in the German judgments that it has not. I have had an opportunity of reading the views of my noble and learned friend, Lord Wilberforce, on this matter. I do not dissent from them. But I must rest my judgment that there is here no res judicata or estoppel on there being no sufficient identity of parties in the West German proceedings and in the matter now before your Lordships.

As I am of opinion that the respondents do not succeed on these preliminary pleas I must now turn to the substantial question in this appeal—have the respondents proved that the plaintiff's solicitors have commenced and are maintaining this action without the plaintiff's authority? The plaintiff is a foreign corporation and it is not maintained that it has ceased to exist. Further, it is not disputed that the capacity of a foreign corporation and the functions and powers of its organs or officers are matters for the law of its domicile. So the first question is—what is the legal domicile of the Stiftung? Its constitution provides in article 3: **[920]** "The legal domicile of the Stiftung shall be Jena." I have mentioned West German decrees to the effect that the domicile shall be Heidenheim, but counsel for the respondents stated that he did not rely on these decrees in the present appeal. He did, however, argue that, according to German law, its domicile is in Germany as a whole. But Germany is, for the time being at least, divided; the Federal Republic being sovereign in West

[36] (1889) 15 App.Cas. 1, H.L.

Germany, and the U.S.S.R. having sovereign authority in the Eastern Zone. And the law in those two parts of Germany may now not be the same.

The respondents submitted in argument that we must regard the law of West Germany as paramount. They relied on the language of the second Foreign Office certificate given on November 6, 1964. This contained an extract from a Foreign Minister's communiqué which stated:

> "Pending the unification of Germany, the three Governments consider the Government of the Federal German Republic as the only German government freely and legitimately constituted and, therefore, entitled to speak for Germany as the representative of the German people in international affairs."

This is followed in the certificate by the following words: "This statement does not constitute recognition of the Government of the Federal Republic of Germany as the de jure Government of all Germany." It was argued that the determination of the status of and the right to represent a body incorporated under the law of the State of Germany prior to 1945 are matters which affect Germany as a whole and which, if arising outside Germany, are within the scope of the Foreign Office communiqué. But for the reason given by my noble and learned friend, Lord Hodson, I cannot accept this argument.

What, then, is the law of the Eastern Zone with regard to these matters? It is well settled that you do not take the code of statutes or other sources of law and construe them according to English ideas. Foreign law is a question of fact to be decided by evidence.

> "The evidence it is clear must be that of qualified experts in the foreign law. If the law is contained in a code or written form, the question is not as to the language of the written law, but what the law is as shown by its exposition, interpretation and adjudication" (*per* Lord Wright in *Lazard Brothers & Co.* v. *Midland Bank Ltd.*[37]*). **[921]**

On several occasions it has been necessary to decide in a case here what is the law of a foreign country on a point which has already been the subject of a decision by a court of that country. A good example is *Bankers and Shippers Insurance Co. of New York* v. *Liverpool Marine and General Insurance Co. Ltd.*[38]

In that case the question was whether according to the law of New York State it was necessary to the validity of an award that an order of court should have been obtained. The Court of Appeal in England held that it was not. Then in another case, *Bullard* v. *Morgan H. Grace & Co.*[39] the Court of Appeal of New York decided that it was necessary. Then this House reversed the decision of the Court of Appeal and followed the American decision. Lord Buckmaster said[40]: "Unaided by that authority your Lordships would, I think, have supported the judgment appealed from." Lord Sumner said[41]:

> "Evidence of the opinion of the highest court of the foreign state whose law happens to form the subject matter of proof in this country, is obviously for an English court the best available evidence upon the question, and is such that, if it is clearly directed to the point in dispute and is insusceptible of any but one interpretation, other evidence of that law could hardly be set against it."

There is a quotation with approval of what Scrutton L.J. had said in the Court of Appeal[42]:

37 [1933] A.C. 289, 298; 49 T.L.R. 94, H.L.(E.).
38 (1926) 24 Ll.L.R. 85 H.L.(E.).
39 (1924) 206 N.Y.S. 335.
40 24 Ll.L.R. 85, 88.
41 Ibid. 94.
42 (1925) 21 Ll.L.R. 86, 91, C.A.

"I agree with the view of Lord Sterndale in *Hannay's* case[43] that while it is almost certain that an English court would not differ from a decision of the Supreme Court of the state on the law of that state, the decision of a subordinate court is only an 'opinion of an expert on the fact, to be treated with respect, but not necessarily conclusive'."

In the present case we have not only two judgments of the Supreme Court of the Eastern Zone but also uncontradicted evidence of skilled witnesses that every court in the Eastern Zone would hold that the Council of Gera is entitled to act as the special board of the Stiftung. And we have evidence that the Stiftung has brought a number of actions in recent years in East Germany and has obtained judgments in its favour. How, then, did the West German courts come to decide as they did? **[922]**

Cross J. was inclined to hold that the West German courts were acting perversely in disregarding the judgments of the Eastern courts. I do not take that view. I am certainly not prepared to hold that the West German courts gave judgments which they knew to be wrong. They may have erred, but honest error is a very different thing from perversity. Counsel for the appellants argued that this case fell within the ratio of *Simpson* v. *Fogo*,[44] to which I have already referred. That case was cited more than once with approval in the nineteenth century but in *Aksionairnoye Obschestvo A.M. Luther* v. *James Sagor & Co.*[45]* Scrutton L.J. said that it had been the subject of considerable adverse comment. In my view, if *Simpson* v. *Fogo*[46] can stand at all it must be limited to cases where the law of the foreign country applied in the foreign judgment is at variance with generally accepted doctrines of private international law. But then one must bear in mind what was said by Lindley L.J. in *In re Queensland Mercantile and Agency Co.*[47] about different countries taking different views on international law. And Page Wood V.-C. himself indicates that there might be a difference if the foreign judgment were founded on a statute[48] or on mistake[49] —distinctions which I have difficulty in appreciating. To distinguish *Simpson* v. *Fogo*[50] it is sufficient to say that the West German courts did not refuse to apply the law of East Germany: they applied what they thought was the law of East Germany.

It is not easy to summarise the long judgment of the Federal Supreme Court, but it appears to me to be based on the view that Germany is still one country and that the law of Germany applies equally in the East as in the West, subject only to new local enactments, of which there are none relevant to this case. On that view the West German courts hold themselves entitled to override the decisions of the East German courts, if they regard those decisions as wrong in law.

The main question which has given rise to this conflict in the present case is the effect of confiscatory decrees of the Russian Military Administration. It is not disputed that as a result there was confiscation of the assets of the two firms Carl Zeiss and Schott & Co., and these two businesses were then carried on as nationalised industries—Volks Eigene Betriebe, referred to as VEBs. But it is not clear how far this affected other assets of **[923]** the Stiftung, and it is proved that in recent years the Stiftung has been treated by the East German authorities as owning a large amount of property; it has an annual revenue of some £180,000 and employs a staff of about 170. And the Council of Gera has in

[43] [1918] 2 K.B. 623, 667; 34 T.L.R. 427, C.A. (In the report of the *Bankers and Shippers Insurance* case (supra) the dictum from *Guaranty Trust Co. of New York* v. *Hannay & Co.* (*supra*) is erroneously attributed to Lord Sterndale and in fact appears in the judgment of Scrutton L.J. in the latter case.)

[44] 1 H. & M. 195.

[45] [1921] 3 K.B. 532.

[46] 1 H. & M. 195.

[47] [1892] 1 Ch. 219, 226; 8 T.L.R. 177, C.A.

[48] 1 H. & M. 195, 234.

[49] Ibid. 242.

[50] 1 H. & M. 195.

fact acted as the special board and in particular has authorised the raising of various local proceedings in the Eastern Zone.

The main ground of the West German judgment is that after the businesses of these two firms were separated from the Stiftung by confiscation it became legally impossible under its constitution for the Stiftung to carry on any activities. The only lawful course was to wind up the Stiftung as provided in its constitution, and neither the Stiftung nor any of its organs had any power to carry on any other activity; so the Council of Gera could not authorise the proceedings in West Germany which were brought to an end by the judgment of the Supreme Court. That court was aware that the East German Supreme Court had reached a decision to the contrary, but in effect it held that the East German court had wrongly applied the law of Germany.

I am not impressed by the reasoning in this judgment but, even if it were convincing, I cannot see how it would be relevant. The West German courts have no jurisdiction over East Germany. The two parts of Germany are at present under different sovereignties: they have separate legal systems and are separate jurisdictions. According to the commonly accepted doctrine of private international law, the courts of one state or jurisdiction cannot of their own knowledge determine what is the law in a different state or jurisdiction. That has to be proved by evidence and, if it is clear, as in this case it was, and is, that all courts in one state or jurisdiction have decided and will decide a particular question in one way, the courts of another state or jurisdiction have no right to decide that that question ought to have been decided in a different way.

Let me take an analogy. Many countries formerly under the British Crown still follow the common law. Suppose that this House were to reach a decision on a point of common law which did not meet with general acceptance. All courts in this country must follow that decision, but courts in other common law jurisdictions are free to decide otherwise. Suppose, however, that in one of those other countries a question arose as to what is the law of England on that point: the principles of private international law would require the courts of that other country to **[924]** decide that the law of England is what the House of Lords has said it is, and they could not say that the House of Lords had reached a wrong decision on this point of common law, however much they might disagree with it. If they did substitute their own view for that of the supreme authority in England, they would then be deciding what they thought the law of England ought to be and not what in fact it is. It appears to me that the only legitimate ground for rejecting a decision of a foreign court as to its own law is an expectation that, if the point arose again in the foreign country and were carried to the Supreme Court, it would be decided differently. The West German courts appear to take a different view of the principles of private international law. The German Federal Republic is a sovereign state and its courts are entitled to their own view. But so are we. And I would not accept their view.

But then it is said that the courts of East Germany are influenced by political considerations. It is true that when one examines the judgments of the East German Supreme Court—and particularly the second of them—one finds them plentifully sprinkled with Communist clichés. No doubt professing Communists find it necessary to adopt this form of embellishment. But going behind this ornamentation I find a judicial approach and a reasonable result. And, even if political considerations were apparent, it would remain true that what the courts have decided is in fact the law which is being enforced in the foreign country.

And finally it is said that because the members of the Council of Gera are Communists and bound to act as Communist theory and government directions require, therefore they cannot act as the special board in the interests of the Stiftung as the constitution of the Stiftung requires. This may be common knowledge in West Germany, but I cannot agree that it is common knowledge here. On the contrary, it is common knowledge here that individuals often fail to live up to—or to live down to—their principles. This is an action to vindicate the right of the Stiftung to its own property: this Communist body has authorised it, whatever view Communist theory might take about it.

That brings me to an important question which was raised in the West German case and before Cross J. The respondents found on the principle that English courts will not assist the enforcement of foreign confiscatory laws, and argue that therefore the appellants cannot be given the relief which they seek in this **[925]** case. Your Lordships did not permit that matter to be argued in this appeal because it is not relevant on the only question now before this House—the authority of the solicitors to act for the Stiftung. But the respondents will be free to raise that issue in their pleadings and at the trial of this action, and nothing that Cross J. may have said on this matter can hamper or limit the power of the trial judge to deal with it.

On the whole matter I would allow this appeal and restore the order of Cross J.

LORD HODSON. My Lords, on the first part of the case I agree entirely with the opinion which has been given by my noble and learned friend, Lord Reid. In my view, the Foreign Office certificate was conclusive against the view taken by the Court of Appeal. The U.S.S.R. having the de jure sovereignty over the so-called German Democratic Republic there is no room for any other de facto recognition and the courts of this country must hold that the U.S.S.R. is still entitled to exercise authority over the territory and to bring to an end the German Democratic Republic which only exists on sufferance. This effect of the certificate holds good so far as this country is concerned and is not affected by any pronouncement of the U.S.S.R. itself as to whether or not it recognises the German Democratic Republic as a sovereign state.

On the second part of the case, the respondents have argued that the solicitors, Messrs. Courts & Co., who have the conduct of these proceedings on behalf of the appellant have no authority to do so, since they are estopped by the judgment of the Supreme Court of the Federal Republic of Germany in an action brought in the name of the appellants as plaintiffs against the respondents in this action. This is a formidable argument and involves consideration of the operation and effect of foreign judgments.

The courts have moved a long way since the opinion was expressed by Lord Brougham L.C. in 1834 in the Irish appeal of *Houlditch* v. *Donegal*[51] that "the judgment of a foreign court in courts of this country is only prima facie evidence—is liable to be averred against, and not conclusive." The modern doctrine accepted since the decision of *Godard* v. *Gray*[52] is that a foreign judgment may be pleaded and is conclusive.

If this is so, I see no reason why the rule of estoppel per rem judicatam should not be applied, subject to the caution contained **[926]** in Lord Brougham's observations in *Houlditch* v. *Donegal*[53] as to the difficulties which arise from the differences in the course of procedure as between one jurisdiction and another.

Although estoppel operates most commonly in those cases which cover "cause of action," the English rule has always been wide enough to cover "issue estoppel"—see *The Duchess of Kingston's* case,[54] a passage from which has been quoted by my noble and learned friend, Lord Reid, and *Reg.* v. *Inhabitants of the Township of Hartington Middle Quarter*,[55] likewise quoted by my noble and learned friend. The estoppel here, if any, must be issue estoppel, the issue being that of want of authority to bring an action. Upon this the respondent succeeded in the West German action in which judgment was delivered by the Federal Supreme Court on November 15, 1960. On principle the judgment should be binding on the parties and their privies, to whom I will later refer. There may be difficulties in applying the principle through the necessity of following the course of procedure when pleadings and evidence have to be examined to ascertain what issues have been determined. There may be cases of manifest injustice, that is, in a case, perhaps, where a defendant having a minimal interest in a matter allows a case to go by default, exposing himself to the risk of

[51] (1834) 8 Bligh (N.S.) 301, 338, H.L.(Ir.).
[52] L.R. 6 Q.B. 139.
[53] 8 Bligh (N.S.) 301, 338.
[54] 20 St.Tr. 355, 538n.
[55] 4 E. & B. 780, 794-795.

being bound by the judgment when the issue turns out to be more serious for him. None of these difficulties appears to exist in this case. The West German judgment is detailed and elaborate and leaves no doubt as to the precise issue about which the parties were contending, an issue which was regarded as of prime importance by both sides.

In order to comply with rule 183 as stated in Dicey's Conflict of Laws, 7th ed. (1958), p. 992, the judgment must be conclusive in order to create an estoppel. In section 1 (2) (*a*) of the Foreign Judgments (Reciprocal Enforcement) Act, 1933, the expression "final and conclusive" is to be found, but these words are repetitive and "conclusive" in the sense of the rule must mean that it cannot, although it may be subject to appeal, be varied by the court which made it, as are, for example, some maintenance or alimony orders. *Nouvion* v. *Freeman*[56] is an example of an action which had been tried in Spain under a summary form of procedure leading to a "remate" judgment but held by this House not to amount to res judicata, since it was possible to reopen the matter which had been tried and obtain a "plenary" judgment **[927]** rendering the "remate" judgment inoperative. One asks, about what is the judgment to be final and conclusive? The answer is that it must be on the merits and not only as to some interlocutory matter not affecting the merits. The question here may, I think, properly be described as "on the merits," the issue being whether or not there was authority to proceed in an action representing the foundation.

On this point I would respectfully dissent from the opinion expressed by Cross J., although I do not disagree with his main conclusion which distinguishes this action from that commenced by the foundation suing by the Council of Gera. There was, in my opinion, a decision against the Council of Gera on the merits of its claim to represent the foundation.

There is admittedly a gap in the evidence as to whether the judgment was final and conclusive. It is for the defendants to show the estoppel and, to prove it, they must establish as a matter of German law that the judgment is final and conclusive. This they have failed to do by express evidence and, as my noble and learned friend, Lord Wilberforce, points out in his opinion, there are passages in the evidence which at least suggest the possibility of want of authority being relitigated in the German courts.

For my part, I think it would be legitimate to rely on the assumption commonly made in English courts that in the absence of evidence of foreign law it is taken to be the same as English law and to hold that the judgment relied on for the estoppel is final and conclusive.

Another argument against the estoppel was put forward by the appellants which I do not find it possible to accept. It was based on the rule which still subsists in English law, notwithstanding animadversions which have been passed on it, that the cause of action in a foreign case does not merge in the judgment but remains available to be sued upon, the foreign judgment being only evidence of the cause of action not, as in this country, that in which the cause of action has merged. It seems to me that this argument does not logically involve that there can be no estoppel in the case of a foreign judgment. Indeed, the cases are consistent in admitting that there may be an estoppel notwithstanding the absence of merger.

If the fact that the cause of action does not merge prevents the estoppel where issue estoppel is concerned, it must similarly, **[928]** one would suppose, do so where cause of action is in question. No one has suggested that the latter contention is sound.

There was a further contention, accepted by the learned judge, that there could be no estoppel because the judgment of the West German court was perverse in that they knowingly and wilfully declined to give effect to the relevant law, that of East Germany. Like others of your Lordships, I find this conclusion too difficult to sustain, although, in fairness to the learned judge, it should be said that there was strong support for this conclusion in the case of *Simpson* v. *Fogo*,[57] upon which reliance was placed on behalf of the appellants. "Perverse"

[56] 15 App.Cas. 1.

[57] 1 H. & M. 195.

is a strong word in this context, meaning, I would say, "obstinate in error" and inappropriate to describe the reasoning of the West German court.

There remains only the question of privity. On this I am in agreement with the learned judge. There was here no privity in estate. The only privity could be privity in interest. The action in West Germany was begun by the Council of Gera claiming to represent the foundation and, upon the issue of the right to represent, judgment was given against the Council of Gera, which was ordered to pay the costs. The Council of Gera itself never had any interest in the subject-matter of the action. It was only required to act in order that the foundation might seek to enforce its rights, that is to say, the rights of the foundation itself.

This action is in truth an action by the foundation suing by Messrs. Courts & Co., a firm of solicitors, who again have themselves no interest in the subject-matter of the action. The Council of Gera is not itself before the court. The way in which the respondents seek to put the matter of privity is founded on an extended view of privity taken in America, where authorities show a broader concept of the privity necessary to establish estoppel. This is to be found in the American Restatement (Judgments), Chap. IV, s. 85 (2) which reads:

> "Where a person is bound by or entitled to the benefit of the rules of res judicata . . . such rules apply in a subsequent action brought or defended by another on his account."

The argument is that the solicitors are bringing this action on account of the Council of Gera but this is not my view of the case. They are acting on behalf of the foundation, and the judgment given in the West German court against the Council of **[929]** Gera on their claim to represent the foundation does not raise an estoppel against the solicitors acting in this action.

It is upon this last ground, namely, absence of privity, that I would hold that there is no estoppel against the solicitors, preventing them from representing the foundation in this action.

If there is no estoppel, there remains to be considered whether the effect of the confiscation of the foundation's business was to make it legally impossible to carry on under its constitution. On this question I am in entire agreement with the learned judge, and would accept his finding that the foundation still maintained its existence so as to enable it to give authority to the solicitors to sue on its behalf. This is partly a question of law and partly one of fact. If it is right to apply the law of the domicile of the foundation—Jena is in East Germany and the law applicable is that administered in the court of that part of Germany. The respondents argued that the law applicable to the matters in dispute between the parties should, in any event, by the law of the Federal German Republic. They relied on the language of the second Foreign Office certificate given on November 5, 1964. This contained an extract from a Foreign Ministers' communiqué which stated:

> "Pending the unification of Germany, the three Governments consider the Government of the Federal German Republic as the only German government freely and legitimately constituted and, therefore, entitled to speak for Germany as the representative of the German people in international affairs."

This is followed in the certificate by the following words: "This statement does not constitute recognition of the Government of the Federal Republic of Germany as the de jure government of all Germany."

It was argued that the determination of the status of and the right to represent a body incorporated under the law of the State of Germany prior to 1945 and now having its "Sitz" in the territory of the zone allocated to the U.S.S.R. are matters which affect Germany as a whole and, if arising outside Germany, are within the scope of the Foreign Office communiqué.

True that the judicial system is an organ of the sovereign power, but the explanatory footnote to the communiqué indicates the limits to be put on the Foreign Office certificate and does not support the contention that the West German courts, as courts of the Federal German Republic, are entitled to speak for Germany as a whole. That the communiqué is directed to **[930]** political representation only is, I think, clear from the language of the certificate, which makes clear that the Government of the Federal Republic is not thereby to be regarded as being recognised as the de jure government of all Germany. There are in the two parts of Germany two separate legal systems operating independently of one another, the East German courts deriving their authority from the sovereignty of the U.S.S.R. and the West German courts from the sovereignty which lies in the Federal Republic of Germany as at present constituted. I do not think that there is any justification for the view that the law common to the whole of Germany as distinguished from zonal law should be applied on the ground that the Carl-Zeiss-Stiftung came into existence many years ago before Germany was divided and that this case concerns operations and issues outside Germany as a whole, namely, in England and not in the Soviet Zone itself. The law in the two parts of Germany not being the same, we must apply the law of the Eastern Zone.

The facts as to the activities of the foundation are not in dispute, and if the law in operation in the Eastern Zone is applied to those facts the appellant must succeed on this issue.

I would allow the appeal.

Lord Guest. My Lords, the somewhat complicated facts out of which this appeal arises have been so fully rehearsed in the courts below that I find it necessary only to state them in broad outline in order to decide the various points at present in issue between the parties.

The history of Carl-Zeiss-Stiftung begins in 1846, when optical works at Jena were founded by Carl Zeiss. Thereafter, glass works were founded and Zeiss was joined by Ernst Abbe and Otto Schott. In 1891 a "Stiftung" or foundation was formed which was administered by a special board, the optical business and the glass business being run by two separate boards of management. The articles of the Stiftung and constitution have been set out in the courts below, and it is only necessary now to state that the legal domicile of the Stiftung was Jena (article 3) and that the organisation of the Stiftung was to be, by article 4, by a special board for representing the Stiftung as an incorporated body, for the administration of its estate and effects and for the supreme direction of its affairs. Article 113 is in the following terms:

> "Should, in consequence of political changes in the state, the provision according to 5 of this statute with reference to [**931**] the representation of the Stiftung become untenable, this representation including the appointment of the Deputy of the Stiftung within the meaning of 5 and the statutory administration of the Carl-Zeiss-Stiftung shall be made over to that department of state, which with regard to the University of Jena occupies the place of the State Department of the Grand Duchy of Saxe-Weimar acting as special board, provided that its seat is in Thuringia, otherwise to the highest administrative authorities in Thuringia."

The business owned by the Stiftung prospered and their products have become world famous. Besides the business the Stiftung owned a large amount of property and substantial capital investments.

In terms of article 113, owing to the changing political situation in Germany, certain changes in the constitution of the special board took place. Upon the amalgamation in 1918 of certain States in Germany, including the Grand Duchy of Saxe-Weimar-Eisanach, in which Jena was situated, into the state of Thuringia, the Thuringia Minister of Education became the special board. In 1935, when the Weimar Republic was replaced by the Third Reich, the "Reichs-Stathalter" as the highest administrative authority in Thuringia became the special board of the Stiftung.

In April, 1945, when the Hitler régime collapsed, the office of Reichs-Stathalter was abolished. Jena was first occupied by American troops, but shortly after it became part of the Russian Zone of Occupation and on July 1, 1945, it was occupied by the Soviet forces. When the Americans left they took with them all the members of the boards of management, a number of leading scientists, engineers and senior executives and a large amount of material.

On October 30, 1945, Marshal Zhukov, Head of the Russian Military Administration, made an order, "SMAD 124," providing for the sequestration of certain types of property within the Russian Zone which included the foundation. Russian officers were stationed in the works until March, 1947, and nearly all the machinery and plant was taken to Russia by way of reparations, together with a number of workpeople. At the same time great efforts were made on the German side to get the works running again, and by the beginning of 1948 the works at Jena had been re-equipped.

In January, 1948, a central body known as the German Economic Council was set up with legislative authority in East Germany, subject to the overriding power of the Russian Military **[932]** Administration. Between April and June, 1948, orders were made by the Russian authorities confiscating the optical and glass business of the Stiftung. The confiscated business became the "People's Owned Enterprises"—"Volks Eigene Betriebe" (VEBs)—and became known as VEB Carl-Zeiss Jena and VEB Schott Jena respectively.

It is now possible to pass over a great amount of history recited in the opinion of Cross J. and come to 1949. In that year the German Democratic Republic came into being. As a result of an East German law dated July 23, 1952, and an order made under it, the Province of Thüringia was divided into three districts and the governmental functions of the province transferred to the administrative organs of the respective districts. The district in which Jena is situated is the District of Gera, and this body, which stands in the same relation to the University of Jena as the State Department of the Grand Duchy stood to it in the old days, is the Council (Rat) of Gera. It is common ground that, as a matter of political geography, the Council of Gera would be the special board within the meaning of article 113.

This action, which is an action for passing off, was commenced on October 20, 1955, by the appellants. On February 7, 1956, the respondents issued a summons against the appellants asking that all further proceedings in the action be stayed and the action dismissed on the ground that it had been commenced and was being maintained without the appellants' authority. Affidavits were lodged by both parties and the application to stay was heard by Cross J. with cross-examination during November and December, 1963, and January, 1964. The judge gave judgment on March 6, 1964, dismissing the summons. When the case came before the Court of Appeal the respondents applied for an order that a letter be addressed to Her Majesty's Secretary of State for Foreign Affairs concerning the recognition of the German Democratic Republic, a point which had not been taken in the court below, and had been expressly disclaimed before Cross J.

The Court of Appeal accepted the respondents' arguments based upon the non-recognition by Her Majesty's Government of the German Democratic Republic and ordered that the writ and all subsequent proceedings be set aside on the grounds that the action was instituted and all subsequent proceedings on behalf of the appellants have been taken without the authority of the appellants.

The position, accordingly, is that the special board of the **[933]** Stiftung is now, as a matter of geography, the Council of Gera, established by the law passed on July 23, 1952, by the German Democratic Republic. The decision of the Court of Appeal was that as the Council of Gera was set up by the German Democratic Republic, a government not recognised by Her Majesty's Government, the special board has no locus to commence proceedings in the English courts, and the action accordingly was commenced without authority.

Several arguments not including the non-recognition point were taken before Cross J. and decided adversely to the respondents. The Court of Appeal, in view of their decision on the non-recognition point, did not deal with these other points.

I have had the advantage of reading in advance the speech prepared by my noble and learned friend, Lord Reid, on the question of the recognition by the

English courts of the Council of Gera as authorising the present action. I agree with his opinion, and I have nothing to add.

The first question which arises on what may conveniently be described as the second stage of the case is whether the appellants are estopped per rem judicatam by the judgment of the West German court from arguing, in answer to the respondents' summons to stay the proceedings, that the appellants have authority to raise this action in name of the Carl-Zeiss-Stiftung. A considerable part of the argument was devoted to this question, which is not without difficulty and raises a number of complicated issues.

The doctrine of estoppel per rem judicatam is reflected in two Latin maxims, (1) interest rei publicae ut sit finis litium, and (2) nemo debet bis vexari pro una et eadem causa. The former is public policy and the latter is private justice. The rule of estoppel by res judicata, which is a rule of evidence, is that where a final decision has been pronounced by a judicial tribunal of competent jurisdiction over the parties to and the subject-matter of the litigation, any party or privy to such litigation as against any other party or privy is estopped in any subsequent litigation from disputing or questioning such decision on the merits (Spencer Bower on Res Judicata, p, 3).

As originally categorised, res judicata was known as "estoppel by record." But as it is now quite immaterial whether the judicial decision is pronounced by a tribunal which is required to keep a written record of its decisions, this nomenclature has disappeared and it may be convenient to describe res judicata in its true and **[934]** original form as "cause of action estoppel." This has long been recognised as operating as a complete bar if the necessary conditions are present. Within recent years the principle has developed so as to extend to what is now described as "issue estoppel," that is to say, where in a judicial decision between the same parties some issue which was in controversy between the parties and was incidental to the main decision has been decided, then that may create an estoppel per rem judicatam. The issue arising upon the summons to stay the proceedings is whether Messrs. Courts, purporting to act for the plaintiffs, the Carl-Zeiss-Stiftung, have the necessary authority to raise the action in name of the Carl-Zeiss-Stiftung. The estoppel which is alleged to have been created is by the decision of the West German courts where in an action between the Carl-Zeiss-Stiftung of Jena, represented by the Council of the District of Gera, and the Carl-Zeiss-Stiftung Heidenheim, Brenz, the present respondents, to restrain the defendants from, inter alia, using the name of Zeiss or Carl Zeiss and from using certain trade marks, it was held that the action was inadmissible on the ground that the constitution of the Stiftung is no longer effective, so that the legal basis for administration of the Stiftung in accordance with the article has been removed and that the Council of Gera has no authority to represent the Carl-Zeiss-Stiftung before the court. The English action is of a different character, namely, a summons to stay proceedings on the ground of lack of authority. It is, therefore, plain that there is no cause of action estoppel because the cause of action in each case is different. Accordingly, if there is estoppel it must be "issue estoppel."

The law on the matter is not altogether clear, but I am prepared to assume that, at any rate in relation to estoppel founded on an English judgment there may be issue estoppel. This was referred to as early as 1776 in *The Duchess of Kingston's Case*,[58] as interpreted in *Reg.* v. *Hartington Middle Quarter* (*Inhabitants*).[59] It has been approved recently by Lord Denning M.R. and Diplock L.J. in *Fidelitas Shipping Co. Ltd.* v. *V/O Exportchleb*.[60] (See also *Thoday* v. *Thoday*,[61] Diplock L.J.) Although not described as "issue estoppel," it is inferentially approved in the most recent textbook on Res Judicata by Spencer Bower at p. 9, where he speaks of a judicial decision which involved "a determination of the same question as that sought to be contraverted in **[935]** the litigation in which the estoppel is raised." The doctrine of issue estoppel has also been accepted as good law by the courts in Australia for a number of years.

[58] 20 St.Tr. 355.
[59] 4 E. & B. 780.
[60] [1966] 1 Q.B. 630, 640-1.
[61] [1964] P. 181, 197-198.

The requirements of issue estoppel still remain (1) that the same question has been decided; (2) that the judicial decision which is said to create the estoppel was final; and, (3) that the parties to the judicial decision or their privies were the same persons as the parties to the proceedings in which the estoppel is raised or their privies. I have for the moment postponed the question whether issue estoppel, if valid in relation to an English judgment, applies to a foreign judgment. There is little doubt that the same question was incidentally decided in the West German action as arises in the present summons, namely, whether the Council of Gera have authority to raise the action in name of the Carl-Zeiss-Stiftung.

I turn, therefore, at once to the question of finality. This is understood to mean "final and conclusive on the merits" of the cause (Dicey, Conflict of Laws, 7th ed., r. 196, p. 1052). The decision upon which the issue estoppel arises must itself be final in this sense. In other words, the cause of action must be extinguished by the decision which is said to create the estoppel (see *Nouvion* v. *Freeman,*[62] Lord Herschell: "It puts an end to and absolutely concludes that particular action.") The West German judgment was not a judgment on the merits, but on a preliminary point relating to the capacity of the Carl-Zeiss-Stiftung to sue and it was there held that the Council of Gera had no authority to raise the action in name of the Carl-Zeiss-Stiftung. I have difficulty in seeing how a decision on capacity to sue can ever be final or conclusive. The West German judgment related to the position in 1960 when it was pronounced, but non constat the position is the same when the English action was tried. The appellants would clearly be entitled to show that a change of circumstances had occurred to affect their capacity to sue. If this is so, it would defeat the whole purpose of estoppel which is to preclude them from leading evidence to that effect. I can best illustrate the position by reference to what would happen if the decision in West Germany had been given by the Scots courts. The decision would have been to sustain the plea of "No title to sue," but this would not have been final and conclusive as the interlocutor sustaining the plea would have been one of dismissal. A subsequent action would not be barred per rem judicatam. **[936]**

Another aspect of finality relates to the requirement that the decision relied upon as estoppel must itself be res judicata in the country in which it is made. This is made clear in *Nouvion* v. *Freeman.*[63] (See also Cheshire, Private International Law, 7th ed. (1965), p. 562; Dicey, Conflict of Laws 7th ed., p. 1036.) It would, indeed, be illogical if the decision were to be res judicata in England, if it were not also res judicata in the foreign jurisdiction. I am not satisfied that the respondents have discharged the burden of proof upon them of establishing that the West German judgment is res judicata in West Germany. I would, accordingly, hold that the West German judgment is not final and conclusive and for these reasons does not create an estoppel.

The next requirement is that the judgment should have been between the same parties or their privies. The parties to the West German judgment, it is conceded, were the Council of Gera, on the one hand, and the respondents on the other hand. The parties to the present proceedings are the respondents and the Carl-Zeiss-Stiftung. As the question is whether the Carl-Zeiss-Stiftung is properly a party to the proceedings, the Stiftung is plainly not the other party for the purposes of res judicata, notwithstanding Mr. Aldous's ingenious argument that the only party he appears for is the Stiftung. Who are the other parties? I am unable to agree that the Council of Gera are parties. They do not appear on the proceedings as parties, they are not represented, and no order for costs could be made against them. They have no interest in the subject-matter of these proceedings. They only come into the picture as the body who, according to article 4 of the Code, are entitled to represent the Carl-Zeiss-Stiftung. In these circumstances, the only other possible parties to the proceedings are the solicitors, Messrs. Courts, to whom the summons is directed. As they were not parties to the West German proceedings, they would only be obnoxious to the plea of

[62] 15 App.Cas. 1, 9.

[63] 15 App.Cas. 1.

res judicata, if they were the privies of the Council of Gera. There is a dearth of authority in England upon the question of privies. The two cases of *Kinnersley* v. *Orpe*[64] and *Hancock* v. *Welsh and Cooper*,[65] referred to by the respondents are, in my opinion, of no assistance. "Privies" have been described as those who are "privy to [the party] in estate or interest" (Spencer Bower on Res Judicata, p. 130). Before a person can be privy to a party there must be community or privity of interest between them. Messrs. Courts **[937]** have no interest in the merits of this action. Their interest is merely to defend themselves against the claim made against them for costs by the respondents which is on the basis of breach of warranty of authority (see *Yonge* v. *Toynbee*[66]). In this matter the Council of Gera have no interest. It is only, as I understand, by the form of procedure chosen by the respondents that Messrs. Courts have been made parties to these proceedings. Assuming that the summons had not been directed to them, but that the respondents had been successful in the West German proceedings and in this summons, the latter would then have been entitled on the authorities to raise an action against the solicitors for breach of warranty of authority claiming the costs in the action. Could it possibly have been said in these circumstances that the solicitors were estopped by the West German judgment, of which they had no knowledge, from arguing that they had authority to raise the present action? I apprehend not, and this must be on the basis that they are not privies to the Council of Gera. It was argued for the respondents, although without clear authority in this country, that "privy" covers a person who is in control of the proceedings. Reference was made to the American Restatement of the Law (Judgments) (1942), s. 84, where it is said that a person who is not a party but who controls an action is bound by the judgment as if he were a party if he has a proprietary or financial interest in the judgment as a privy. But this cannot apply to the solicitors who are not in control of the proceedings and have no proprietary or financial interest in the judgment. They are instructed by the Carl-Zeiss-Stiftung who, on their side, control the proceedings. No case has been referred to in England in which a solicitor has been held privy to the party instructing him. In Scotland an attempt to make a solicitor a party for the purpose of res judicata failed (*Laidlaw* v. *Blackwood*[67]). We were referred to a number of American cases dealing with privies. I am not prepared in this country to extend the doctrine to the extent which it apparently has reached in that country.

I now pass to the question reserved in an earlier part of my speech, namely, whether issue estoppel can ever be operated by a foreign judgment. This was doubted by Cross J. It is clear that a foreign judgment can operate as res judicata in a cause of action estoppel properly so called (Dicey's Conflict of Laws, 7th ed. rr. 182 and 183, pp. 981 and 992). But different considerations **[938]** may, I apprehend, apply to issue estoppel. The first matter to be observed is that a foreign judgment does not have the same finality and conclusiveness as an English judgment. In the case of the latter the cause of action is merged with the judgment, so that action can only be brought to enforce the judgment. Not so in the case of foreign judgments. Sub-rule 183 of Dicey's Conflict of Laws, p. 996, states: "A foreign judgment does not of itself extinguish the original cause of action in respect of which the judgment was given." The plaintiff, therefore, has the option either of suing on the judgment or on the original cause of action. The doctrine of non-merger stated in *Nouvion* v. *Freeman*[68] is still, as I understand it, good law, notwithstanding the animadversions of Professor Horace Emerson Read in his book, Recognition and Enforcement of Foreign Judgments (1938), pp. 120-121 and the doubt expressed by Dicey in his Conflict of Laws on p. 997. If this be sound, it means that the unsuccessful litigant can, if he is defendant, table fresh defences to the original cause of action. From this it follows that "issue estoppel" could never operate to shut out the defendant from litigating issues which may have incidentally been determined in the foreign suit.

[64] 2 Dougl.K.B. 517.
[65] (1816) 1 Stark. 347.
[66] [1910] 1 K.B. 215; 26 T.L.R. 211, C.A.
[67] (1843) 15 Sc.Jur. 484.
[68] 15 App.Cas. 1.

There are, in my view, moreover, considerations of policy and expediency which make it undesirable that the doctrine of issue estoppel should be introduced in the case of foreign judgments. There has been no case in which it has been applied in England and while, perhaps, not all estoppels are odious, considerable caution, in my view, should be exercised before the principle is extended any further. In operating issue estoppel it may be necessary, in order to ascertain what issues have been inferentially or incidentally decided, to look, not only at the judgment, but also at the pleadings and, it may be, at the evidence. We are not familiar in this country with the practice and procedure in foreign countries, and it may be a matter of considerable nicety in certain cases to find out what issues were determined and whether they were incidental or collateral to the main decision.

For all these reasons I would concur with Cross J. in holding that the plea of res judicata is not open to the respondents.

If the appellants are not estopped per rem judicatam by the West German judgment from arguing that the Council of Gera are entitled to represent the Carl-Zeiss-Stiftung, then the matter is at large for the decision of this House. Whether this action is properly authorised by the Carl-Zeiss-Stiftung is a question of **[939]** foreign law to be decided as a question of fact. The law to be applied is the law of the domicile of the Stiftung, which is in Jena, and the law is that of East Germany as shown by "its exposition, interpretation and adjudication" (*Lazard Brothers & Co.* v. *Midland Bank Ltd.*)[69]* It must be the law as in practice interpreted and enforced by the courts of law of the foreign country. A considerable volume of expert evidence on both sides was devoted to the question. But in this case one starts with the judgment of the East German courts that the Carl-Zeiss-Stiftung still exists as a juristic person, notwithstanding the confiscation of its assets in East Germany by the Soviet authorities. This judgment is embodied in the opinion of the Supreme Court of the German Democratic Republic, dated April 6, 1954, as confirmed by the judgment of the German Democratic Republic Supreme Court, dated March 23, 1961, affirming the judgment of the District Court of Leipzig. Technically, no foreign judgment would bind the courts of this country, but prima facie a judgment would be accepted by the English courts as representing the law: ". . . the comity of international affairs would require special and unusual circumstances to lead this House away from the clear decision of a final court" (*Bankers and Shippers Insurance Co. of New York* v. *Liverpool Marine and General Insurance Co. Ltd.*,[70] Lord Buckmaster).

> "Evidence of the opinion of the highest court of the foreign state whose law happens to form the subject-matter of proof in this country, is obviously for an English court the best available evidence upon the question, and is such that, if it is clearly directed to the point in dispute and is unsusceptible of any but one interpretation, other evidence of that law could hardly be set against it" (Lord Sumner[71]).

The experts on foreign law from both sides were unanimous that all East German courts would follow the decision of the Supreme Court of the German Democratic Republic that the Carl-Zeiss-Stiftung still exists as a juristic person with domicile at Jena, and that the Carl-Zeiss-Stifting had the capacity to sue for the protection of its name, trade-marks and goodwill. The only criticism which is made by the West German lawyers of the East German judgment is that there are no free judges in East Germany and that no East German court would dare come to a contrary conclusion. But this is only the opinion of the West German lawyers, and there is not a shred of evidence to support it. Upon **[940]** the question of fact as to what the East German law is, the evidence is really all the one way, consisting of the judgment of the highest court in East Germany and the opinion of the East and West German lawyers who gave evidence.

In this state of evidence there is no need to examine further the decisions of the West German courts or the East German courts. Indeed, in this state of

[69] [1933] A.C. 289, 298. [70] 24 Ll.L.Rep. 85, 87. [71] Ibid. 94.

affairs the English courts would not be entitled, in my view, to express their views as to the soundness or otherwise of either decision (see *Buerger* v. *New York Life Assurance Co.*)[72] The English courts must accept the East German decision as being the law of East Germany.

Upon the whole matter, I would allow the appeal and restore the judgment of Cross J.

LORD UPJOHN. My Lords, the issues between the parties in this singularly complicated appeal fall into two watertight compartments.

Into the first compartment falls an issue which has been described in argument as the "non-recognition" point. It has been admirably and elaborately argued before your Lordships, but in the end the point may shortly be stated: whether the English courts will recognise the legislative and other acts of the German Democratic Republic which operates in the Russian Zone of Germany, having regard to the fact that Her Majesty's Government has not granted any de jure or de facto recognition to that Republic or its Government. This issue was raised for the first time in the Court of Appeal, who held that, as it was common knowledge that the U.S.S.R. had recognised the German Democratic Republic as an independent sovereign state but Her Majesty's Government had not done so, the courts of this country would not recognise any acts done by that Government or by any person appointed by it. This conclusion necessarily led to the result on the facts of this case, to which I shall refer later, that the action was not properly authorised and that the solicitors who issued the writ were acting without authority to do so. The result of the decision of the Court of Appeal is of course to deny in the courts of this country to the inhabitants, organisations and institutions of East Germany any lawful origin to any acts or events based on any executive, judicial or legislative acts or directions of the Government of the German Democratic Republic since it was set up by the U.S.S.R.: a most deplorable result in **[941]** respect of any highly civilised community, with which we have substantial trading relationships, I believe, which should be avoided unless our law compels that conclusion.

My Lords, my noble and learned friend, Lord Reid, whose opinion I have had an opportunity of reading, has advanced very powerful reasons for preferring the view that the answers of Her Majesty's Secretary of State for Foreign Affairs, to the requests for information submitted to him by the Court of Appeal in accordance with the well-settled practice, must lead to the conclusion that, so far as the courts of this country are concerned, we ought to assume that, whatever may be thought to be common knowledge on this point, the German Democratic Republic is a subordinate body set up by the U.S.S.R. as the de jure Government of East Germany to act upon its behalf, and that its legislative executive and judicial acts must receive recognition. I agree entirely with the reasons and conclusions of my noble and learned friend, and I cannot usefully add anything upon this issue.

It, therefore, becomes necessary to examine the second compartment with which the Court of Appeal quite reasonably did not deal, having regard to their decision on the non-recognition point.

The issues here are even more complex, and are threefold. Taking them in the order which I think is most convenient, they may be described (as in the arguments addressed to your Lordships) as (1) the confiscation point, (2) the estoppel point, (3) the Supreme Court point.

The confiscation point depends on proof of the fact that the commercial assets of the Stiftung (Jena) abroad have been confiscated by legislation in East Germany and upon the respondents' argument that in such event the English courts would not assist the enforcement of expropriatory or penal legislation outside the territorial jurisdiction of that country.

But that plainly is an issue in the action itself; it is a matter for allegation in the pleadings and goes to the question of the relief (if any) that should be granted.

It is not a matter which can be dealt with on this appeal, which is concerned

[72] (1927) 96 L.J.K.B. 930; 43 T.L.R. 601, C.A.

solely with the authority of Courts & Co. to issue a writ in the courts of this country on behalf of the Stiftung, which has nothing to do with the issues in the action, a matter I shall develop later.

Apart from this, I should be very reluctant to deal with this matter, even if it were open to your Lordships to do so, on the **[942]** materials at present available. Plainly there is much scope for further exploration of the relevant facts before this issue in the action can be satisfactorily decided. When (if pleaded) the matter comes on for trial the learned trial judge must not consider himself hampered, restricted or in any way bound by any findings or observations of Cross J. on this matter.

I turn, then, to the estoppel point. This raises a matter of some general importance.

This is an appeal based on a summons dated February 7, 1956, whereby the respondents claimed against the solicitors, Courts & Co. (respondents to the summons), that they issued a writ in the name of the Stiftung as plaintiffs without authority to do so and that, therefore, the action should be stayed and Courts & Co. ordered to pay the respondents' costs on a common fund basis.

This form of summons is well known and is based not on any misconduct on the part of the solicitor, as was at one time thought to be necessary to empower the court to exercise its summary jurisdiction over a solicitor, but, as was pointed out by Lord Porter in *Myers* v. *Elman*,[73] is based on the proposition that the solicitor is not party to the action, but that the court exercises its summary powers over the solicitor who by issuing a writ warrants his authority to do so, and so if he has no authority, may I add, commits a tort against the so-called defendants; he therefore has to pay them damages by indemnifying them against the expenses to which they have been put by paying costs taxed on the common fund basis rather than on a party and party basis.

It is alleged by the respondents that upon this summons Courts & Co. cannot contest this issue, for it has already been tried conclusively between the parties or their privies in earlier proceedings in the West German Federal Court so that they are estopped per rem judicatam, or more shortly this matter is res judicata. It is clear that a party relying on such a plea must at least prove that the earlier proceedings were determinative of the issues arising in the second proceedings; that the same parties or their privies are common to both proceedings and that the earlier proceedings were within the jurisdiction of the court and were final and conclusive of the relevant issues.

This makes it necessary to answer to a number of questions: 1. Are the issues in the former proceedings the same as in the latter? 2. Who are the parties to the earlier proceedings? 3. Who are the parties to these subsequent proceedings? 4. If there is no **[943]** complete identity of parties in (2) and (3) above, are the different parties properly described as in privity one with another for the purpose of the doctrine? 5. Even if the answer to question (1) is yes, is the matter of the lis between the parties such as to give rise to res judicata? 6. Does the doctrine if applicable between two sets of English proceedings apply where the former proceedings were in a foreign court? And, if so, 7. Were these proceedings final and conclusive between the parties?

To answer these questions some facts must necessarily be set out but I shall be as brief as I can. For this purpose it may be taken as common ground that a local government body acting in that part of Eastern Germany known as Thuringia and called the Council of Gera (to which I will refer as "the council") is the special board within the meaning of article 113 of the articles of association of the Stiftung and, as such (as provided by article 4), entitled to represent the Stiftung in the supreme direction of its affairs, including, of course, the power and right to instruct its legal advisers to bring or defend actions on its behalf. However, in proceedings culminating in the Supreme Court of the Federal Republic of West Germany it was held that the council had no right to instruct anyone to act for the Stiftung in proceedings in those courts because, since the confiscation of its industrial assets by certain decrees of the Russian

[73] [1940] A.C. 282, 336; 56 T.L.R. 177; [1939] 4 All E.R. 484, H.L.

occupying forces in 1948, the Stiftung, though continuing as a legal entity, became an empty shell incapable of giving any instructions and the council was in effect divested of its powers to act on its behalf. Whether this is a correct conclusion is the Supreme Court point which I shall examine later, though with extreme brevity.

It must be noted that in contrast to our procedure it appears that in the West German courts the person giving the instructions on the part of a purely juridical person appears on the record; at all events, in the West German proceedings in the Supreme Court the plaintiff is described as "the Carl Zeiss Foundation of Jena represented by the Council of the District of Gera plaintiffs and appellant."

In the proceedings before your Lordships Courts & Co. at once concede that they have received instructions to issue the writ in the name of the Stiftung from the council. That is a sufficient statement of the facts to answer the first two questions: 1. The issue whether the council had authority to give instructions to begin proceedings in the name of the Stiftung in this country depends on precisely the same facts, circumstances and arguments **[944]** as were advanced before the West German courts and decided against it. It is not suggested that there has been any relevant change in those facts or circumstances since 1960, when judgment was delivered in the Supreme Court. 2. The parties to the West German proceedings, I am prepared to assume, are (a) the council and, (b), the third respondents.

The third question has given rise to much argument and some difference of opinion among your Lordships. Counsel for the appellants has argued that the Stiftung are parties to the summons; a somewhat dangerous argument, I would have thought, for it seems to presuppose that, regardless of the question of Courts & Co.'s authority to sue, they are parties and so the same argument must apply to the West German proceedings and, if so, identity of parties seems to be established.

However, I reject the argument. If the summons succeeds it does so on the footing that the Stiftung is not a party to the writ or the summons and for that reason the action is stayed and the solicitor made personally liable for breach of warranty of authority. Under our procedure in such circumstances no order of any kind, even for costs, can be made against the Stiftung.

Secondly, it seems to me clear that the council are not, under our procedure, parties to the writ or the summons. It can make no difference that in this case in some earlier proceedings in another country they are named in the record of those proceedings. The solicitor is in a special position, for, in respect of a purely juridical person, only a solicitor can issue a writ. He does not thereby, become a party to the proceedings but, for the reasons already mentioned, as an officer of the court, he can be made a respondent to a summons to strike out the writ. His liability depends not on agency, for if the summons succeeds he has no principal; it depends solely upon his position as a solicitor issuing a writ and thereby warranting his authority to do so to the defendants named in the writ. I am quite unable to understand the argument that those de facto instructing him become parties to the writ or to the summons seeking to strike out the writ. It may be that such body of persons may be liable to the solicitor for breach of warranty of authority, if they have no principal, but that does not make them party to the proceedings nor liable for breach of warranty to the defendants for they, unlike the solicitor who has issued the writ, have warranted nothing to them. To hold the contrary would make all those along the line who may have given instructions to the solicitors to **[945]** issue a writ from a junior clerk of the instructing body upwards liable as parties to the defendants; but this has never been the law of our country.

So I answer this question by saying that the parties to the summons under appeal are (a) the third respondents, (b) Courts & Co.

As to question four, the third respondents are parties to both proceedings but there is no identity between the Council and Courts & Co.; so the next question is whether they are in privity one with another for the purpose of the doctrine.

The position of the solicitor in proceedings such as these is clear-cut; as I have already pointed out, he is no party to the proceedings; the sole question is as to his authority to initiate proceedings. It is not an issue in the action at all, and that is why it cannot be taken as a plea in defence in contrast to the confiscation point.

This House in *Russian Commercial and Industrial Bank* v. *Comptoir D'Escompte de Mulhouse*[74]* approved the decision of Warrington J. in *Richmond* v. *Branson & Son*[75] where he said:

"But the real question is the authority of the solicitor. Is that a question which can be raised as a relevant issue in the action and at the trial? . . . it is impossible, according to the ordinary practice and procedure of the court, to justify that proposition."

The solicitor has no interest in the action as such, nor under our system (unlike that pertaining, for example, in the U.S.A.) is he permitted even to participate in the proceeds of a successful judgment. His duty is to render his services to his client in the litigation to the best of his skill and ability and his sole reward is the costs which by law he may charge.

I can see nothing in the solicitor's relationship with his client which renders them privy to one another in the ordinary sense in which privy or privity is used for the purposes of the doctrine.

As has been said in Halsbury's Laws of England, 3rd ed., Vol. 15 (1956), pp. 196-197, para. 372, privies are of three classes: (1) privies in blood, (2) privies in law and (3) privies in estate, but they all have an interest in the subject-matter of the action. Though your Lordships have been referred to a number of authorities in other courts which may expand the meaning of privy, none touch on the question before your Lordships, where the lis has nothing to do with the substance of the action itself. **[946]**

In my opinion, Courts & Co. cannot be described as privy to the council so as to preclude them from trying to establish their authority to issue the writ, unless, by reason of some requirement of the law to meet new conditions, a greatly extended meaning beyond anything it has borne before is to be given to the word, a matter to which I shall return later.

I turn to the fifth question I have posed. Res judicata may be divided into a number of classes or branches. The most ancient is estoppel by record, strictly so called. It still exists, though is usually overtaken by the broader principles I shall next discuss. A defendant who has failed even to enter an appearance and who has taken no part in the earlier litigation may be estopped by record if his defence in the second action was necessarily and with complete precision decided by the previous judgment (see per Lord Maugham L.C. in *New Brunswick Railway Co.* v. *British & French Trust Corporation Ltd.*).[76] How narrow is the estoppel in such a case is shown by the actual decision there. This narrow concept of estoppel has no application to the present case, for the questions are different; the first is as to the authority of the council to initiate proceedings on behalf of the Stiftung in West Germany, and the second as to the authority to initiate proceedings in these courts. Nor is the judgment of the foreign court one of record.

The broader principle of res judicata is founded upon the twin principles so frequently expressed in Latin that there should be an end to litigation and justice demands that the same party shall not be harassed twice for the same cause. It goes beyond the mere record; it is part of the law of evidence for, to see whether it applies, the facts established and reasons given by the judge, his judgment, the pleadings, the evidence and even the history of the matter may be taken into account (see *Marginson* v. *Blackburn Borough Council*[77]). Res judicata itself has two branches: (1) cause of action estoppel

[74] [1925] A.C. 112; 40 T.L.R. 837, H.L.(E.).
[75] [1914] 1 Ch. 968, 974.
[76] [1939] A.C. 1, 21.
[77] [1939] 2 K.B. 426.

—that is where the cause of action in the second case has already been determined in the first. To such a case the observations of Wigram V.-C. in *Henderson* v. *Henderson*[78] apply in their full rigour. These observations have been so often approved by your Lordships' House that I will not repeat them. I need not pursue this matter further for the alleged res judicata with which your Lordships are concerned certainly has nothing to do with any cause of action in the proceedings. (2) Issue **[947]** estoppel—a convenient phrase first coined apparently by Higgins J. in the High Court of Australia in *Hoystead* v. *Federal Commissioner of Taxation*,[79] whose dissenting judgment was upheld by the Privy Council in 1926.[80] But issue estoppel has been recognised ever since *The Duchess of Kingston's Case*[81] and there are many quite early examples of it, see, for example, *Reg.* v. *Inhabitants of the Township of Hartington Middle Quarter*[82] and many others.

Recently in *Thoday* v. *Thoday*[83] and in *Fidelitas Shipping Co. Ltd.* v. *V.O. Exportchleb*[84] the Court of Appeal applied to issue estoppel the full breadth of the observations of Wigram V.-C. in *Henderson* v. *Henderson*.[85] While in this case it is not necessary to decide whether that is right, because for the reasons given in the answer to the first question that I posed for myself it does not arise, I should be reluctant to support that view. As my noble and learned friend, Lord Reid, has already pointed out there may be many reasons why a litigant in the earlier litigation has not pressed or may even for good reason have abandoned a particular issue. It may be most unjust to hold him precluded from raising that issue in subsequent litigation and see Lord Maugham's observations in the *New Brunswick* case.[86] All estoppels are not odious but must be applied so as to work justice and not injustice and I think the principle of issue estoppel must be applied to the circumstances of the subsequent case with this overriding consideration in mind.

My Lords, I only desire to add one observation upon these cases; once it is clear that the principle of res judicata is part of the law of evidence I find it difficult to understand the distinction drawn by Diplock L.J. in *Thoday* v. *Thoday*[87] between issue estoppel and fact estoppel, but that does not call for further consideration here.

So if Courts & Co. are debarred from arguing their authority to issue the writ, it is because of an issue estoppel. But I have already shown that this lis is not and cannot be an issue in the action at all. It is a matter which would seem, to paraphrase the words of De Grey C.J. in *The Duchess of Kingston's Case*[88] quoted by Lord Reid, to be a matter collateral or incidentally cognisable and therefore not the subject of estoppel. No authority **[948]** has been cited to your Lordships which bears any resemblance to the present case.

All the authorities we have examined on issue estoppel have been cases where the earlier action dealt with issues or points which, however inferentially or incidentally, arose in the course of trying the substance of the issues between the parties to the action; not with a lis having nothing to do with those issues, which arises only between the defendant and the solicitor issuing the writ.

Ought the principles of issue estoppel to be extended to a case such as this? I can see no reason for doing so. Under our system the respondent to the summons is necessarily a solicitor, an officer of the court. It would require strong reasons to preclude him from defending his issue of a writ by reason of some decision to which he was no party and of which he may be in complete ignorance. Justice does not require the invocation of the doctrine to protect the defendant from being doubly harassed, for if an officer of the court with full knowledge of some earlier proceedings in these courts which covers exactly and precisely the question of his authority issues a writ, the arm of the court

[78] 3 Hare 100, 115.
[79] (1921) 29 C.L.R. 537, 561.
[80] [1926] A.C. 155; 42 T.L.R. 207, P.C.
[81] 20 St.Tr. 355.
[82] 4 E. & B. 780.
[83] [1964] P. 181.
[84] [1966] 1 Q.B. 630.
[85] 3 Hare 100.
[86] [1939] A.C. 1, 21.
[87] [1964] P. 181.
[88] 20 St.Tr. 355, 538 n.

is long enough and strong enough to prevent an abuse of its process without resort to the doctrine.

The application of the doctrine may, on the other hand, lead to much injustice. Such summonses are normally heard at a very early stage of the proceedings on evidence frequently hurriedly prepared (in marked contrast to this most exceptional case) and some point may have been overlooked or misunderstood in the earlier proceedings.

I would deny to these purely incidental proceedings in the action the doctrine of issue estoppel and for the same reasons I would refuse to extend the meaning of the word privy to cover the case of two successive solicitors (for that is what it amounts to) who have issued writs in the name of a common principal; the only so called privity between them is that they have successively issued writs upon the instructions of some persons purporting to act for the principal but that person cannot himself or itself be a party to any proceedings. So I would regard the doctrine as entirely inappropriate to this form of proceedings.

My Lords, in these circumstances, I can answer the remaining questions nos. 6 and 7 very shortly.

I accept at once that for the purpose of the doctrine of res judicata in general a prior foreign judgment may be just as effective as an English one. But, even if I had come to the **[949]** conclusion that the doctrine applied to successive summonses, the first of which was decided in our courts, raising the question of authority to issue a writ, I would deny the benefit of the doctrine to a prior foreign judgment, for the simple reason that I do not think it is necessary in the interests of justice to do so and it may easily be productive of grave injustice. Questions of authority and, indeed, the very concept of authority for this purpose depend so much on matters of procedure in each court and on the precise rules governing the issue of writs therein by persons other than the parties themselves that it is difficult to apply a judgment in the one case to another under a different jurisprudence. This case provides a good example; under our system the council could never be a party to the writ or the summons.

Finally, with regard to question no. 7, the respondents have failed to prove that the proceedings in West Germany were final and conclusive as must necessarily be proved for an estoppel to be successfully established (see *Nouvion* v. *Freeman*[89]).

In conclusion upon the estoppel point, even if I had reached a contrary conclusion as between the third respondents and Messrs. Courts & Co., I should require much persuasion that the first and second respondents who are alleged to be passing off the goods of the third respondents as and for the goods of the Stiftung and thus committing independent torts in this country, are entitled to the benefit of the alleged estoppel, but the point is not an important one.

So it is necessary to turn to the Supreme Court point. I have already set out very briefly the grounds upon which the West German Federal Court held that the council had not authority to act for the Stiftung, and the real issue is whether that decision is right or whether on the same facts the decision of the Supreme Court of the East German Republic deciding that the council had authority to issue a writ is to be preferred. This is a question of foreign law which by the law of this country is essentially a matter of fact. It has been discussed very fully by my noble and learned friend, Lord Reid, in his opinion and by Cross J. in the court of first instance. I agree entirely with what my noble and learned friend has said and also with what Cross J. said, though I think he went too far in describing the judgment of the West German Supreme Court as perverse. As a piece of legal reasoning the decision of the West German courts seems to me quite unconvincing and, for my part, I can see no ground for holding that the **[950]** council ceased to have any authority to act on behalf of the Stiftung or that the Stiftung itself was but an empty shell in existence but incapable of acting when all the known facts indicate the contrary. I only desire to add that the respondents, in inviting us to prefer the decision of

[89] 15 App.Cas. 1.

the West German Federal Supreme Court, advanced an argument based on the certificate dated November 6, 1964, given by Her Majesty's Secretary of State for Foreign Affairs when in answer to question (2) submitted to him he quoted a communiqué dated September 19, 1950, where it was stated that

> "Pending the unification of Germany the three Governments consider the Government of the Federal Republic as the only German Government freely and legitimately constituted and therefore entitled to speak for Germany as the representative of the German people, in international affairs."

It was said that this statement authorised the West German Government to speak in the name of the whole German people and this gave a superior sanctity to the decision of the West German Supreme Court over the decision of the East German Supreme Court. The argument seems to me to be fallacious. It has never been the practice of Her Majesty's Secretaries of State to express any views upon the law. While they constantly express views on recognition in answer to questions submitted to them by the courts, the legal consequences that flow from recognition is a matter which is always left to these courts.

My Lords, for these reasons, I would allow this appeal and restore the order of Cross J.

LORD WILBERFORCE. My Lords, the substantive issue in this litigation is whether the right to use in this country the name of Carl Zeiss, or Zeiss, in relation to certain glass, or optical, goods, and to profit from the goodwill attached to those names, belongs to a body of persons in the West German Federal Republic, or to a body of persons in that part of Germany which is outside of, and to the east of the Republic, which I will call for convenience "East Germany." The rights in question are claimed by both sides to belong to a corporate entity called Carl-Zeiss-Stiftung (the word "Stiftung" denotes approximately a foundation with corporate status), the contest being as to which body of persons is entitled to control that corporate entity. The writ in the action was issued in the name of the Stiftung through English solicitors on the authority of a Dr. Schrade, who in turn claimed to act on the authority of the Council of Gera (alleged to be **[951]** the "special board" of the Stiftung), and also in other capacities and in accordance with accepted procedure, the issue must be tested in limine, whether the Stiftung is legally before the court. This procedure has some inconveniences, both because it normally (and here) takes the form of an application against the solicitors (the difficulty as to which will hereafter appear) and also in that it is traditionally carried out by a motion or summons, supported by affidavit evidence, but without pleadings defining the precise matters in dispute. In a case such as the present, where important and difficult questions of law, including foreign law, arise this may result in some confusion, and I think that it would be advantageous if some method could be found in such cases of defining the issues to be presented to the court.

The issues as to the right or otherwise of Dr. Schrade to authorise the proceedings on behalf of the Carl-Zeiss-Stiftung, as these were debated before Cross J. in the Chancery Division, and to which the evidence was directed, were issues, under several headings, of German law and no question arose as to the status, internationally, of East Germany or of the "government" which claims authority in Eastern Germany. The affidavits on either side were drafted on the basis that, for the purpose of the summons to stay the proceedings, no challenge was made to the validity of East German legislation, and before the court leading counsel for the defendants (the respondents in this appeal) disclaimed any intention to question the status of that government, or to inquire whether it was recognised by Her Majesty's Government. The facts with regard to, or bearing upon recognition, were therefore not examined at that stage. But in the Court of Appeal the respondents sought to base their case upon non-recognition of the "government" in East Germany and that court, inevitably, as I think, because of the public interest involved, allowed them to take the point. Inquiry was made in the usual manner of the Secretary of State and, certificates given by him having shown that Her Majesty's Government does not recognise the "government" of East Germany either de jure or de facto, the respondents argued, and the Court of Appeal accepted, that the ground on which Cross J. held the action to be validly commenced no longer existed. The Court of Appeal also decided against various alternative claims by the appellants as to the authorisation of the proceedings, which Cross J. had not found it necessary to consider. Correspondingly, the Court of Appeal did not find it necessary to deal with some difficult issues decided in the **[952]** appellants' favour by Cross J. I leave all these aside for the moment in order to concentrate upon the contention which is affected by the non-recognition argument.

First, I must explain how the right of Dr. Schrade to authorise the proceedings is connected with the question of non-recognition. I can do this quite summarily, since the history and the constitution of the Carl-Zeiss-Stiftung have already been fully explained.

Since the establishment of the Carl-Zeiss-Stiftung in 1891 at Jena as a charitable foundation, it has by its constitution been linked with the public administration of that district in Germany in which Jena lies. This was at that time the Grand Duchy of Saxe-Weimar. The "special board" of the foundation, which is the organ of the Stiftung which (under the issue I am now considering) authorised the present action to be brought, was then the department responsible for the University of Jena. Later, under the Weimar Republic, the appropriate district was the state of Thuringia and the authority its Minister of Education. There was a displacement during the National Socialist régime but in 1945, when American forces occupied this part of Germany, Thuringia was restored as a province or Land and its Minister again became the special board. It is interesting, and relevant to a later argument, to note that this reconstitution of the regional administration in this part of Germany was apparently accomplished without any formality; it simply took place under the authority of the occupant and, as one of the expert witnesses said, I think correctly, the fact, that the occupation authorities allowed the Ministry of Education to operate, endowed the acts of that Ministry with legal validity. This factual state of affairs seems to have continued without change when in July, 1945, East Germany, including Thuringia, was taken over by the forces of the U.S.S.R. The local administration continued: the Minister continued to act as the special board and, as regards this period which lasted until 1952, no challenge has been made to the validity of that board or to action taken by it. Its legal life-blood can only have been derived from the Minister of Thuringia, who in turn derived authority either from the U.S.S.R. as the holder of sovereign power (I shall explain this later) or possibly from the previous authority of the U.S.A.

It is upon events occurring in 1952 that the respondents rely for their contention that the special board which authorised this action had, so far as the courts of this country are concerned, no legal existence. On July 23, 1952, under a "law" passed by the **[953]** "government" of the German Democratic Republic (as East Germany is called by those in control of it) and an order made on the following day under that law, the Province or Land of Thüringia was divided into three districts and its functions were transferred to the administrative organs of the respective districts. The district in which Jena is situated is that of Gera and the body which (admittedly) assumed the position corresponding to the former Minister of Thuringia was the Council of Gera.

On these facts, the respondents contend that, since the Council of Gera depends for its creation upon a legislative act of the "government of the German Democratic Republic" and as no such government is recognised in this country, there is no legal basis for the Council of Gera as the special board, so that the purported authority is simply a nullity.

It is as well, before considering the legal consequences of non-recognition, to appreciate what the respondents' contention involves. The Stiftung is a corporate body established for industrial and trading purposes under the law of Germany; one of whose constitutional organs—the special board—is an administrative authority exercising power at the place of the body's operations. As a fact, there is no doubt that at the relevant date this authority was there, that it was exercising its functions, that it was operating as the special board, that (this is proved by the evidence) it would be recognised by the local courts as so doing. Yet, so it is said, because the law and the order which set it up are derived from a body not recognised as a lawful government, this authority qua organ of the Stiftung, has no legal existence: all its transactions in private law are void, as are presumably all other transactions carried out under its authority or by persons who derive their authority from it. By logical extension it seems to follow, and counsel for the respondents accepted, that there is, for many years has been and, until the attitude of Her Majesty's Government changes, will be, in East Germany a legal vacuum; subject only, it may be, to the qualification that pre-existing German law, so far as it can continue to be operated or have effect, may continue in force. Whether in fact it can continue to be operated to any great extent if its operation depends upon administrative or judicial authorities set up by the non-existent "government" must be doubtful. But the respondents, so far from shrinking from these consequences, insist upon them as the necessary and, as they say, intended consequences of non-recognition. And correspondingly, they argue that if recognition were to be **[954]** given by the courts to legislative acts of the non-recognised "government" that would be tantamount to recognition of that government, and so in conflict with the policy of the executive.

My Lords, if the consequences of non-recognition of the East German "government" were to bring in question the validity of its legislative acts, I should wish seriously to consider whether the invalidity so brought about is total, or whether some mitigation of the severity of this result can be found. As Locke said: "A government without laws is, I suppose, a mystery in politics, inconceivable to human capacity and inconsistent with human society," and this must be true of a society—at least a civilised and organised society—such as we know to exist in East Germany. In the United States some glimmerings can be found of the idea that non-recognition cannot be pressed to its ultimate logical limit, and that where private rights, or acts of everyday occurrence, or perfunctory acts of administration are concerned (the scope of these exceptions has never been precisely defined) the courts may, in the interests of justice and common sense, where no consideration of public policy to the contrary has to prevail, give recognition to the actual facts or realities found to exist in the territory in question. These ideas began to take shape on the termination of the Civil War (see *U.S.* v. *Insurance Companies*[90]), and have been developed and reformulated, admittedly as no more than dicta, but dicta by judges of high authority, in later cases. I mention two of these, *Sokoloff* v. *National City Bank*[91] and *Upright* v. *Mercury Business Machines Co. Inc.*,[92] a case which was concerned with a corporate body under East German law. Other references can be found conveniently assembled in Professor D. P. O'Connell's International Law (1965) vol. 1, pp. 189 et seq. No trace of any such doctrine is yet to be found in English law, but equally, in my opinion, there is nothing in those English decisions, in which recognition has been refused to particular acts of non-recognised governments, which would prevent its acceptance or which prescribes the absolute and total invalidity of all laws and acts flowing from unrecognised governments. In view of the conclusion I have reached on the effect to be attributed to non-recognition in this case, it is not necessary here to resort to this doctrine but, for my part, I should wish to regard it as an open question, in English law, in any future case whether and to what extent it can be invoked. **[955]**

I return now to consideration of the effect of the refusal to recognise the "government" of East Germany. The respondents, claiming that non-recognition of a government entails automatically non-recognition of all laws enacted by that government, rely upon the well-known line of cases following upon *Aksionairnoye Obschestvo A.M. Luther* v. *James Sagor & Co.*,[93]* where non-recognition had these consequences.

[90] 89 U.S. 99.
[91] 145 N.E. 917.
[92] (1961) 13 App.Div. 2d 36; 213 N.Y. 2d 417.
[93] [1921] 1 K.B. 456; [1921] 3 K.B. 532, C.A.

But before their argument can be made good, they must show that the present refusal of recognition is given in a situation comparable with that which is found in the cases. This is the critical issue here and it is on this that the respondents' argument, in my opinion, breaks down. For the present situation, as regards sovereignty in Germany, is incomparable with any that has previously come before our courts and, as I shall hope to show, gives rise to different consequences.

The classic cases of non-recognition of governments arise in two types of situation: first, where some new state comes into existence, as by separation from another state or states (in such a case there may be a question of non-recognition of the state itself as well as of the government); instances of this are cases concerned with breakaway Spanish colonies—*Jones* v. *Garcia del Rio*[94]* (Peru); *Thompson* v. *Powles*[95]* (Guatemala); *Taylor* v. *Barclay*[96]* (Colombia); secondly, where a new government claims authority over an existing state, or part of it. Instances of this are *City of Berne* v. *Bank of England*[97]*; *Aksionairnoye Obschestvo A.M. Luther* v. *James Sagor & Co.*[98]* (U.S.S.R.); *White, Child & Beney Ltd.* v. *Simmons*[99]* (U.S.S.R.) and numerous cases relating to Russian banks. But neither of these is the situation in East Germany. When Germany surrendered unconditionally to the Allied Powers in 1945, instead of proceeding to the traditional status of belligerent occupancy, they brought a novel legal situation into being. The state of Germany remained (and remains) in existence; governing authority or supreme authority in respect of Germany as a whole was reserved to the four Allied Powers acting jointly, and governing authority in respect of each zone was left to be exercisable by that one of the Allied Powers to which the zone was allocated; in the Eastern part of Germany in which Jena is situated by the U.S.S.R. There is no controversy about this: the facts were so stated by the executive and accepted by the courts **[956]** in the case of *Rex* v. *Bottrill, Ex parte Kuechenmeister*[1]* and *Preston* (*orse. Putynski*) v. *Preston* (*orse. Putynska*) (*orse. Basinska*).[2] It is against this background that the certificates of the Secretary of State were given in these proceedings in September and November, 1964. The certificate of November 6, 1964, and the questions to which it was directed have been set out in the opinion of my noble and learned friend, Lord Reid, and I shall not repeat them here. The following are, in my opinion, the conclusions to be drawn from the certificate:

(1) The governments of the four Allied Powers retain rights and responsibilities in respect of Germany as a whole;

(2) In respect of the Eastern Zone—called "the zone of occupation allocated to the U.S.S.R." in which Jena is—the state and Government of the U.S.S.R. are recognised as de jure entitled to exercise governing authority;

(3) This recognition is stated to extend to the period since "at or about the end of June, 1945" to the "present date," that is, November, 6, 1964;

(4) Apart from the four Allied states and their Governments and the Control Council for Germany (an organ of the four Allied Governments) Her Majesty's Government have not recognised de jure or de facto any other authority purporting to exercise governing authority in or in respect of the Eastern Zone.

There should be added to these facts that stated by the earlier certificate dated September 16, 1964, that

(5) Her Majesty's Government have not granted any recognition de jure

[94] (1823) Turn. & R. 297.
[95] (1828) 2 Sim. 194.
[96] (1828) 2 Sim. 213.
[97] (1804) 9 Ves. 347.
[98] [1921] 3 K.B. 532.
[99] (1922) 127 L.T. 571; 38 T.L.R. 616, C.A.
[1] [1947] K.B. 41; 62 T.L.R. 570; [1946] 2 All E.R. 434, C.A.
[2] [1936] P. 141; [1963] 2 W.L.R. 1435; [1963] 2 All E.R. 405, C.A.

or de facto to the "German Democratic Republic" or its "Government"—the inverted commas are as in the certificate itself.

The first question for a court when presented with this certificate (for convenience I treat the two as a single statement) is to consider whether it completely states the facts and whether there is any ambiguity in it. If so, it may be appropriate to ask the Secretary of State for a supplementary statement. There are only two questions which might arise in relation to the Eastern Zone. The first is whether it is admissable in the courts of this country to take account of the fact (if such be the case, as to which I shall make some observation later) that the U.S.S.R. itself considers that there is in existence in the Eastern Zone a government independent of the U.S.S.R., viz., the "government" of the "German Democratic Republic." In my opinion, the **[957]** answer to this must be negative: to make any such assertion would be in direct contradiction to the certificate which states without qualification that the U.S.S.R. and its Government is entitled de jure to exercise governing authority there and that nobody else is, either de jure or de facto. What view another state may take as to the legal and factual situation in any territory is irrelevant to the recognising (or non-recognising) state and, after the latter has defined its own attitude, is inadmissible in its courts. As a well-known international law authority puts it: "The recognising state is not concerned with the question whether the state of things which it is recognising"—and I add "or not recognising"—"is legal by the national law of another state" (The Law of Nations (1963) Brierly/Waldock, p. 147). The second question is whether consistently with the certificate it is possible to assert that the U.S.S.R. is not de facto exercising governing authority or control in the Eastern Zone. It was, indeed, suggested by the respondents that there was a deliberate and significant abstention in the certificate from any positive assertion to this effect, two points being particularly relied on. First it was said that although the question was put what state or governments have been recognised as "exercising governing authority" in the Eastern Zone, no answer to this was specifically given. Secondly, although in relation to Germany as a whole it was said that until March 20, 1948, the four Allied Powers "did exercise . . . joint authority through the Control Council for Germany" no comparable statement was made concerning the Eastern Zone. Either, therefore, the inference should be drawn that Her Majesty's Government did not regard the U.S.S.R. as "exercising governing authority" in the Eastern Zone, or at least the certificates were ambiguous and further inquiry ought to be made.

I have no temptation, in a matter of this kind, to speculate or to read into the certificate anything which is not there, but I cannot find that the certificate is either incomplete or ambiguous. In stating that the U.S.S.R. is exercising de jure governing authority and that no other body is exercising de facto authority, the two certificates to my mind say all that need or can be said. De jure recognition in all cases but one is the fullest recognition which can be given: the one exception is the case where there is concurrently some other body de facto exercising a rival authority to that of the "de jure" sovereign (as in the case of *Banco de Bilbao* v. *Sancha*[3]*). But any such possibility as this is **[958]** excluded by the terms of the certificates. Moreover, some more enlightenment (if any be needed) as to what is meant by de jure recognition may be drawn from the official statement made by Mr. Secretary Morrison on March 21, 1921, (quoted in full by my noble and learned friend, Lord Reid) in which he said:

> "The conditions for the recognition of a new régime as the de jure government of a state are that the new régime should not merely have effective control over most of the state territory, but that it should, in fact, be firmly established."

—a statement which is not necessarily binding on successor Secretaries of State but which is reproduced, as still effective, in the 1963 edition of Brierly's Law of Nations (p. 148). This shows that, if nothing more is said, de jure recognition presupposes effective control in fact. It is consistent with this approach that Mr.

[3] [1938] 2 K.B. 176; 54 T.L.R. 603; [1938] 2 All E.R. 253, C.A.

Secretary Gordon Walker, when asked what states or governments are recognised as (a) entitled to exercise or (b) exercising governing authority, answered only the first question: after doing so there was no occasion to go further. That in doing so there was no intention to deny effective control in fact to the de jure sovereign is shown by the fact that the reply relates, without distinction, to the whole period from 1945-1964. For at any rate for some years after 1945, it would not be possible to dispute that the U.S.S.R. was directly governing the Eastern Zone, which must dispose of any conjecture that in the words he has used for the period as a whole the Secretary of State is distinguishing between what could be done and the actuality of the situation. The certificates therefore in my opinion establish the U.S.S.R. as de jure entitled to exercise governing authority and in full control of the area of the Eastern Zone.

This makes possible a determination of what is the legal character of enactments by the "German Democratic Republic." To say that this is an unrecognised government, though in a sense correct, may be misleading: it is so in a sense quite different from the sense in which the expression was used of, for example, the Russian revolutionary government prior to (de facto) recognition in 1921, whose status and the validity of whose legislation was considered in *Aksionairnoye Obschestvo A.M. Luther* v. *James Sagor & Co.*[4]* If that government was not recognised, there was nothing which could give international validity to its laws. But the "German Democratic Republic" is making laws in and as to a territory where a recognised **[959]** "sovereign" exists. Is there, then, any reason for denying validity to its acts? The respondents say that there is: that no documentary authority has been proved to show that the "German Democratic Republic" had power, under the U.S.S.R., to make the law in question, or any law: that there must be either a constitution, or some enabling provision, or some express authority from the "sovereign" or proof positive of some other connection with the government, to avoid the consequences that the law is simply a nullity, and that none such has been proved.

This argument, in my opinion, is unduly formalistic. The U.S.S.R. and the other Allied Powers assumed power in Germany after a military collapse followed by a declaration that they had done so: an exceptional, if not unprecedented step which, and the consequences of which, however, we are bound to recognise. Thereafter, for a period, they exercised their power directly through their military commanders-in-chief. After a time they set up or allowed to be set up zonal or regional authorities to carry out tasks of government or administration. The United States military authorities, as we know, set up or allowed a "government" in the Land of Thuringia, which was continued by the U.S.S.R. when they took over. It is unnecessary in circumstances such as these to seek for a formal constitutional chain of power. Given the continuance of de jure authority and complete control, it follows that acts done by what are (as we are bound to hold) necessarily subordinate bodies are done under the governing authority of the occupying power. The argument to the contrary becomes all the more unrealistic when it is seen that the respondents themselves, in the evidence filed in these proceedings, have gone to considerable pains to demonstrate the subservient, or puppet, character of the "German Democratic Republic" and its Government. Thus Dr. Walter David, after stating that the Eastern section of Germany (including Jena) remains under the occupation of a foreign power, Russia, continues that the intentions of Dr. Abbé, the founder of the Carl-Zeiss-Stiftung, "cannot be implemented if the Council of Gera (*or indeed any authority under Russian or communist control*) were the special board." And Dr. Richard Moser von Filseck says:

> "In East Germany a centralised régime *has been set up by the Soviet Union to which it is subservient* . . . The Council of Gera is, therefore, the *representative of that political power* which carried out the expropriation of the assets of the foundation enterprises." **[960]**

The latter power was the U.S.S.R. Other passages are to a similar effect.

[4] [1921] 3 K.B. 532.

Together with the certificate they present a consistent picture of subordinate central and local authorities exercising authority under the sovereignty or control of the U.S.S.R. as occupying power.

I must notice here two arguments:

(i) In the Court of Appeal, it was assumed, as a matter of which judicial notice should be taken, that the "German Democratic Republic" was independent of the U.S.S.R., the conclusion from this being that its acts could not be derived from or attributed to the authority of the latter. Thus Harman L.J. said[5]:

> "It is in fact notorious that the U.S.S.R. has recognised the German Democratic Republic as a sovereign state and treats its law-making capacity accordingly."

And Diplock L.J.[6] thought that he could take judicial notice that

> ". . . the Government of the U.S.S.R. recognises the 'Government of the German Democratic Republic' as the independent sovereign government of an independent sovereign state for whose territory the Government of the U.S.S.R. claims no power to make laws."

I have already stated my opinion that, in the face of the Foreign Office certificate, recognition (if given) by the U.S.S.R. of the German Democratic Republic is something of which the courts of this country cannot take account. But, in addition, as to judicial knowledge, or notoriety, it is not shown, at any rate to my satisfaction, that *in 1952* when the critical "law" was enacted even the U.S.S.R. was claiming that the German Democratic Republic was independent of it or was disclaiming its own authority. Without elaboration, it is sufficient to say that from official documents to be found in Command Paper 1552, which the respondents made available to us, the contrary is seen to be clearly the case, and such is also the effect of the respondents' evidence. There is only one piece of evidence to the contrary, a single answer given by Professor von Moser in cross examination to the effect that sovereignty was transferred to the German Democratic Republic in 1949. But this was not directed to the issue now being considered (which had not at that time been raised) and its true meaning was not explored; its apparent meaning seems to be contradicted both by the facts and by the considered evidence on **[961]** affidavit of the same witness to which I have referred. The Court of Appeal did not rely on it and it should be disregarded.

(ii) It was said by the respondents that to recognise the law setting up the Council of Gera of July 23, 1952, would in effect be to recognise the Government of East Germany and to create a conflict with the views of the executive. The principle is well established that the courts of Her Majesty do not speak with a different voice from that of Her Majesty's executive government (it was stated as early as *Taylor* v. *Barclay*[7]* and has been accepted ever since) but we are not here under the risk of committing the courts to action of this kind. Merely because in the class of case, of which *Aksionairnoye Obschestvo A.M. Luther* v. *James Sagor & Co.*[8]* is an example, non-recognition of a "government" entails non-recognition of its laws, or some of them, it does not follow that in a different situation this is so, nor that recognition of a law entails recognition of the law-maker as a government with sovereign power. The primary effect and intention of non-recognition by the executive is that the non-recognised "government" has no standing to represent the state concerned whether in public or private matters. Whether this entails non-recognition of its so-called laws, or acts, is a matter for the courts to pronounce on, having due regard to the situation as regards sovereignty in the territory where the "laws" are enacted and, no doubt, to any relevant consideration of public policy. I can see no inconsistency in (a) accepting the view of the executive that there is no recognised (that is, independent) government in the Eastern Zone apart from the de jure governing authority of the U.S.S.R. and (b) attributing legal validity, if

[5] [1965] Ch. 596, 651.
[6] Ibid. 664.
[7] 2 Sim. 213.
[8] [1921] 3 K.B. 532.

no other legal obstacle exists, to a "law" or act of that "government" as a subordinate or dependent body.

On consideration, therefore, of the whole of the situation in the Eastern Zone of Germany I reach the conclusion that the challenge to the validity of the law of July 23, 1952, setting up the Council of Gera fails. I should add that, even if there was a change in the situation in the Eastern Zone between 1952 and the issue of the writ in 1955 (in the direction of a discontinuance of Russian control), it has not been suggested that this would have invalidated a law already passed.

I must next mention the alternative contentions of the appellants with regard to the right to institute the present proceedings. **[962]** These are three, namely, that Dr. Schrade (who instructed solicitors on behalf of the plaintiffs) had authority so to do (i) under a power of attorney granted on June 29, 1951, by the then special board, namely the Ministry of Education of the Land of Thüringia, (ii) as mandatory or proxy mandatory under article 9 of the constitution, (iii) as the (i.e., the sole member of the) board of management of the optical works, entitled to act, under article 114, in the absence of a special board.

These alternative contentions were not dealt with by Cross J. because he held that the action was validly authorised by the Council of Gera as the special board so that the alternatives did not arise. They were considered by the Court of Appeal and rejected there after careful examination by both Harman L.J. and Diplock L.J. It was complained by counsel for the appellants that the learned Lords Justices, on certain points, came to conclusions on what were essentially matters of German law without sufficient evidence, and your Lordships were invited to receive fresh affidavits as to these matters. In my opinion, the expert evidence filed at the trial by either side was on some points incomplete and obscure, and if these three points had to be decided it would be unsafe to agree or disagree with the conclusions of the Court of Appeal on the existing material.

If, however, the appellants are entitled to succeed on the other points raised in this appeal, it would be unnecessary for them to rely on these alternatives or to call any further evidence, and they could be left undetermined, as they were left by Cross J. I proceed, therefore, to consider the issues which Cross J. decided in favour of the appellants, and which the respondents now contest. These are: (1) Whether the appellants are estopped from contending that the Council of Gera had authority to commence this action on behalf of the Stiftung by certain judgments given in the Federal Republic of Germany; (2) Whether, if there is no estoppel, it has been established on the evidence that the Council of Gera had such authority; (3) Whether the appellants are entitled to bring the present proceedings in view of the confiscation in East Germany of the optical business. The third question was dealt with briefly by Cross J. but he expressed some doubt whether it was not more properly one which should be left for decision at the trial rather than decided at the present preliminary stage. In my opinion, this doubt was justified and the issue, which may be a substantial and difficult one, cannot properly be decided on this appeal. It should be left to the trial as an open issue on **[963]** which the parties can put their case unfettered by the tentative conclusions of Cross J. The remaining two questions require decision:

(1) *Estoppel*: The judgment mainly relied on by way of estoppel is the judgment in West Germany of the Federal High Court (I take the translation which was used before Cross J.) of November 15, 1960. There are other decisions, but they carry the matter no further. This judgment was given in proceedings commenced in the Provincial Court (Landgericht) at Stuttgart on April 28, 1954, the parties to which were the Carl-Zeiss-Stiftung represented by the Council of Gera as plaintiff and three individuals (Bauersfeld, Heinrichs and Kuppenbender) and the firm of Carl Zeiss of Heidenheim as defendants. As regards these parties it is not disputed (a) that the Carl-Zeiss-Stiftung named as plaintiff is the same as the body named as plaintiff in this action, (b) that the firm Carl-Zeiss of Heidenheim named as defendant is the same body as that named as the third defendant to this action. It was also accepted that the

effective plaintiff in those proceedings was the Council of Gera and that the substantive claim sought to be brought for trial related to the use of the names Zeiss or Carl-Zeiss and of certain trade marks in the Federal Republic of Germany, so differing from the substantive claim in the present action, which relates to similar matters in this country.

Objection was taken, before the West German action could be tried on the merits, to the right of the Council of Gera to represent the Stiftung and proceedings on this preliminary issue went through a number of stages and appeals. Finally, the Federal High Court, by its judgment of November 15, 1960, held that the action was inadmissible, on the ground that the Council of Gera had no authority to represent the Carl-Zeiss-Stiftung. The action was, therefore, dismissed and the Council of Gera was ordered to pay the costs.

Several questions, some of difficulty, arise in considering whether the respondents in the present action can rely on the judgment of the Federal High Court by way of estoppel or as res judicata. The first question arises from the fact that what is relied on here is not the mere fact of a judgment and not a decision on the substantive "cause of action" or claim which the Carl-Zeiss-Stiftung was trying to make good, but only a decision on a particular issue: in other words, what has come to be called an "issue estoppel." I must begin by ascertaining what is meant by **[964]** "issue estoppel" in English law and then consider how far this kind of estoppel, or something analogous to it, may be applied to judgments of foreign courts.

A convenient starting point, as regards the English doctrine, is to be found in the judgments of the Court of Appeal in *Fidelitas Shipping Co. Ltd.* v. *V/O Exportchleb.*[9] The case was concerned with an interim award made in a commercial dispute embodied in a special case on which the court had given a decision and it was held that an issue raised by the special case so determined was the subject of "issue estoppel" so that it could not be raised again. Lord Denning M.R. said this[10]:

> "The law, as I understand it, is this: if one party brings an action against another for a particular cause and judgment is given on it, there is a strict rule of law that he cannot bring another action against the same party for the same cause. Transit in rem judicatam; see *King* v. *Hoare.*[11] But within one cause of action, there may be several issues raised which are necessary for the determination of the whole case. The rule then is that, once an issue has been raised and distinctly determined between the parties, then, as a general rule, neither party can be allowed to fight that issue all over again . . ."

He goes on to deal with "points" within issues, including those which though not actually raised could have been raised, as argument which is not material here, and which I prefer to leave open.

Similarly in the judgment of Diplock L.J. there is a useful passage which contains these words.[12]

> "The final resolution of a dispute between parties as to their respective legal rights or duties may involve the determination of a number of different 'issues,' that is to say, a number of decisions as to the legal consequences of particular facts, each of which decisions constitutes a necessary step in determining what are the legal rights and duties of the parties resulting from the totality of the facts . . ."

He continues by making a distinction between issue estoppel and fact estoppel which may deserve some further exploration, but it does not arise here.

The doctrine of issue estoppel generally is not a new one. It can certainly be found in the opinion of the judges delivered by De Grey C.J. in *The Duchess of Kingston's Case,*[13] a passage from which has been quoted by my noble and learned friend **[965]** Lord Reid, and an accepted re-statement of it was given by

[9] [1966] 1 Q.B. 630.
[10] Ibid. 640.
[11] (1844) 13 M. & W. 494, 504.
[12] [1966] 1 Q.B. 630, 641-2.
[13] 20 St.Tr. 355, 538n.

Coleridge J. in *Reg.* v. *Inhabitants of the Township of Hartington Middle Quarter*,[14] which is also quoted by my noble and learned friend. Mr. Spencer Bower, in his work on Res Judicata states the principle as being "that the judicial decision *was, or involved,* a determination of the same question as that sought to be controverted in the litigation in which the estoppel is raised" (Res Judicata, p. 9)—a formulation which invites the inquiry how what is "involved" in a decision is to be ascertained. One way of answering this is to say that any determination is involved in a decision if it is a "necessary step" to the decision or a "matter which it was necessary to decide, and which was actually decided, as the groundwork of the decision" (*Reg.* v. *Inhabitants of Hartington Middle Quarter Township*[14]). And from this it follows that it is permissible to look not merely at the record of the judgment relied on, but at the reasons for it, the pleadings, the evidence (*Brunsden* v. *Humphrey*[15]) and if necessary other material to show what was the issue decided (*Flitters* v. *Allfrey*[16]). The fact that the pleadings and the evidence may be referred to, suggests that the task of the court in the subsequent proceeding must include that of satisfying itself that the party against whom the estoppel is set did actually raise the critical issue, or possibly, though I do not think that this point has yet been decided, that he had a fair opportunity, or that he ought, to have raised it.

This being the position as regards English judgments, one must next inquire whether a similar principle should apply as regards foreign judgments. It has taken some time before the recognition of foreign judgments by English courts was placed on a logical footing. Unlike English judgments, they were not considered to be judgments of a court of record so that the simplest form of estoppel—by record—could not be applied to them. They were, in the early stages of private international law, considered only to be prima facie evidence of the rights of the parties and were examinable on the merits. This attitude can be found as late as 1834 in the Irish appeal of *Houlditch* v. *Donegal*[17] where Lord Brougham L.C. expressed his disagreement with the opinion of the Lord Chancellor of Ireland that an English Chancery decree was conclusive, in strong terms. He said:

> "The leaning of my opinion is so strong that I can hardly call it the inclination of an opinion; and we know it is the **[966]** general sense of lawyers in Westminster Hall (notwithstanding dicta of considerable weight coming from very learned judges' obiter dicta to the contrary) that the judgment of a foreign court in courts of this country is only prima facie evidence—is liable to be averred against and not conclusive. One argument is clear—that the law in the course of procedure abroad sometimes differs so mainly from ours in the principles upon which it is bottomed, that it would seem a strong thing to hold that our courts were bound conclusively to give execution to the sentence of foreign courts. . . ."

But the Lord Chancellor's remarks showed that the tide was running in the direction of recognition and in *Ricardo* v. *Garcias*[18] this House assented to the view that when a foreign judgment comes in collaterally, or the defendant relies upon it under the exceptio rei judicatae, it is then received as conclusive and Lord Brougham's earlier remarks came to be explained as referring only to the limited grounds on which foreign judgments may be examined such as fraud, public policy or want of jurisdiction (see Spencer Bower on Res Judicata, p. 38). In this respect, foreign judgments retain their distinction from English judgments. But, these limitations apart, the modern doctrine (usually derived from *Godard* v. *Gray*[19]) is that a foreign judgment may be pleaded and is conclusive.

Is, then, what may be pleaded in defence to a claim limited to what may be called "cause of action" estoppel, that is, a judgment which negatives the plaintiff's cause of action, or does it extend to any matter raised between the parties necessary to the decision and actually decided? There is no clear

[14] 4 E. & B. 780, 794.
[15] (1884) 14 Q.B.D. 141, C.A.
[16] L.R. 10 C.P. 29.
[17] 8 Bligh(N.S.) 301, 338.
[18] (1845) 12 Cl. & F. 368 H.L.(E.).
[19] L.R. 6 Q.B. 139.

authority on the point. *Henderson* v. *Henderson*,[20] in any event a decision of a colonial court, was a simple example of cause of action estoppel, and the same appears to be true of the more complicated case of *Callandar* v. *Dittrich*.[21]

The appellants, arguing against issue estoppel in the case of foreign judgments, invoke a rule by which it appears that a plaintiff who has obtained a foreign judgment may sue here either on that judgment or on his original cause of action, a rule vouched by a number of decided cases, which maintains a precarious foothold as a sub-rule in Dicey's Conflict of Laws, 7th ed., p. 996. But this rule, which, if surviving at all, is an illogical survival, affords no sound basis for denying a defendant the benefit of a decision on an issue; if it proves anything it proves that much, and **[967]** would deny both parties to a foreign proceeding the benefit of any estoppel at all.

As a matter of principle (and we are really thrown back upon principle), whether the recognition of judgments is based upon a recognition of vested rights, or upon considerations of public interest in limiting relitigation, there seems to be no acceptable reason why the recognition of foreign judgments should not extend to the recognition of issue decisions. From the nature of things (and here it is right to recall Lord Brougham's warning) this, in the case of foreign judgments, may involve difficulties and necessitate caution. The right to ascertain the precise issue decided, by examination of the court's judgment, of the pleadings and possibly of the evidence, may well, in the case of courts whose procedure, decision-making technique, and substantive law is not the same as our own, make it difficult or even impossible to establish the identity of the issue there decided with that attempted here to be raised, or the necessity for the foreign decision. And I think that it would be right for a court in this country, when faced with a claim of issue estoppel arising out of foreign proceedings, to receive the claim with caution in circumstances where the party against whom the estoppel is raised might not have had occasion to raise the particular issue. The fact that the court can (as I have stated) examine the pleadings, evidence and other material, seems fully consistent with its right to take a broad view of the result of the foreign decision. But with these reservations, where after careful examination there appears to have been a full contestation and a clear decision on an issue, it would in my opinion be unfortunate to exclude estoppel by issue decision from the sphere of recognition. If that is so, in this case where an explicit statement is available of the decision of the Federal High Court, of the reasons for it, and of the issue as defined between the parties to it, and where the English court has the assistance of expert witnesses to explain the foreign decision, the difficulty should not be too great in ascertaining whether the same issues as were there decided are involved in the present action.

The appellants, indeed, say that the issue is not the same: that in the German proceedings it was whether the Council of Gera representing the Carl-Zeiss-Stiftung could sue in respect of certain matters in Germany and that here the issue is whether this can be done in respect of matters arising here. But that is to argue for "cause of action" estoppel only: if issue estoppel exists, the issue is whether (briefly) the Carl-Zeiss-Stiftung has **[968]** become paralysed or its organs rendered ineffective so that it cannot act in the manner in which it is purporting to act. Identity of issue is, to my mind, clearly shown.

Next as to identity of parties. Normally to establish this should be the simplest part of the case. But there is a peculiar difficulty here because of the way in which the present issue arises. The proceedings profess to be brought by the Carl-Zeiss-Stiftung but since it is a legal person there must be some actual person, or persons, to bring it before the court, who has or have power to do so. The Council of Gera claims to be the relevant organ for this purpose; and it is clear that it is on their authority that the action was started. The question to be decided is whether the Carl-Zeiss-Stiftung is before the court or whether it is not: so according to the eventual decision the plaintiff may or may not be the Carl-Zeiss-Stiftung. Obviously in these circumstances the test of identity of

[20] 3 Hare 100.

[21] (1842) 4 Man. & G. 68.

parties cannot be the formal test of identity on the record, so what is it to be? Cross J. decided that there was not identity of parties and I understand that the majority of your Lordships agree with him. I regret that I cannot share this view. The point, no doubt, merits longer argument, but in view of the numerous points discussed in this appeal I shall abstain from giving at any length the reasons why I think identity of parties exists. Briefly, in my opinion, one must look to see who in reality is behind the action: and the reality is that a body of persons, namely, the Council of Gera, is seeking in these proceedings, precisely as in Germany they sought, to set the Carl-Zeiss-Stiftung as plaintiff in motion before the court. One may consider the simpler case of a limited company. If certain persons, claiming to be its directors, start an action in the company's name, the defendant may seek and may obtain a decision that the company is not properly before the court because the persons concerned had no right to commit the company to the action. As a result the action is struck out. Can it be that those same persons may start another action in the company's name against the same defendant making the same claim? According to the appellants' argument the relevant party as regards the application to strike out the action is the solicitors, so that if the directors started their second action through the same firm there would be an estoppel; but if they employed a second—or a third—firm there would not be. I can hardly think so bizarre an argument can be correct. There must surely be an estoppel in the second action for the reason that the effective party to the decided issue (not to the action) is the same **[969]** in each case—namely the directors. Admittedly, as I mentioned at the start of this opinion, the involvement of the solicitors in the proceedings, according to our practice, introduces a complication. But this does not, to my mind, prevent the party to the proceedings (who is behind the solicitors as we know) being the Council of Gera. To treat the solicitors as the parties to these proceedings seems to me, with respect to the argument, both lacking in reality and unduly technical. There is naturally no authority which deals with such a situation as this but I find of assistance a passage from the American Restatement (Judgments), s. 85 (2), which reads:

> "Where a person is bound by or entitled to the benefit of the rules of res judicata . . . such rules apply in a subsequent action brought or defended by another on his account."

We were also referred to passages from the Corpus Juris Secundum, Tit. Judgments, ss. 756 et. seq., and to American authorities there cited which show that U.S. courts take a flexible view of the requirements of these estoppel rules. The present case seems to me one which does not require much, if any, adjustment, to fit into the rules as to parties. If the Council of Gera is not itself the party, then the case seems to fall within the "Restatement" rule. So I do not think that the estoppel fails on this ground.

To my mind, a more serious obstacle to the efficacy of the estoppel is to be found in the requirement that the foreign judgment should be final and conclusive or, as it is sometimes put, conclusive on the merits. I have no difficulty as to the latter element, for I cannot accept the argument that, for this purpose, the merits means the merits of the action as stated in the plaintiff's claim. The defendants' contention that the Stiftung's ability to act has been fatally impaired is just as much an argument on the merits: indeed, the issue which group of persons is entitled to control the Stiftung is at the root of the present dispute. But the remaining requirement is more difficult.

The textbooks are in agreement in stating that for a foreign judgment to be set up as a bar in this country it must be res judicata in the country in which it is given (see Dicey, Conflict of Laws, 7th ed., p. 1036; Cheshire Private International Law, 7th ed., p. 562). The chief authority cited for this is *Nouvion* v. *Freeman*,[22] in which both Lindley L.J. in the Court of Appeal and Lord Herschell in this House expressed themselves strongly in this sense. No doubt that was rather a special case since the **[970]** remate judgment was no more than

[22] (1887) 37 Ch.D. 244; 3 T.L.R. 566, C.A.; 15 App.Cas. 1, H.L.

provisional, but, generally, it would seem unacceptable to give to a foreign judgment a more conclusive force in this country than it has where it was given. In relation to the present case I think that "conclusive" must be taken in the sense that if the Stiftung represented by the Council of Gera were to attempt to commence another action in West Germany against the same defendants as were parties to the previous action they would, by the force of the previous judgment, be prevented from proceeding with it. Moreover, I think that it is for the defendant, who sets up the bar, to establish the conclusive character of the judgment. This must be so on principle and there is support for it in *Behrens* v. *Sieveking*.[23] Unfortunately there is no clear evidence whether the judgment of the Federal High Court is res judicata (in the sense I have mentioned) in Germany or not. The respondents rely on the accepted presumption that the foreign law is the same as English law, but this presumption, never more than a fragile support, is less than ever reliable here when the question is what is the effect of a particular judgment which has no exact parallel in English law. There are in fact indications in the evidence to the contrary.

In 1957 an action, commenced in Dusseldorf in West Germany, came on appeal before the Federal High Court. The parties to that action were "the firm Carl Zeiss of Heidenheim, represented by Dr. Bauersfeld" as plaintiff and (inter alios) V.E.B. Carl Zeiss Jena as defendants. The defendants took the point that the plaintiff lacked capacity to sue and was not properly represented, alleging that Dr. Bauersfeld had resigned from the board of management of the Stiftung. The Federal High Court in its decision on July 24, 1957, rejected this objection, on the ground that it was not satisfied that Dr. Bauersfeld had resigned.

In 1959 another action, also commenced in Dusseldorf in West Germany, came on appeal before the Federal High Court with the same plaintiff and (inter alios) the same defendants as in the 1957 appeal. The defendants again took the point that the plaintiff had not the capacity to sue and was not properly represented because Dr. Bauersfeld had resigned from the board of management of the Stiftung. The Federal High Court again rejected the objection and in doing so used these words:

> "It had already negatived the questions by its judgment dated July 24, 1957, with detailed reasons. This must stand even after repeated examination and assessment of the objections raised against it by the appeal"; **[971]**

and later: "The court maintains its view even after a re-examination." The significance of these two judgments in relation to the conclusive effect, in a subsequent action, of a decision, by way of objection, that a plaintiff was not properly represented in an earlier proceeding between the same parties, was not explored at the trial. But, if the fate of the estoppel turned on this point (as it would on my view as to identity of parties) I should be strongly inclined to hold that the defendants (the present respondents) had not established to the satisfaction of the court that the judgment of November 15, 1960, was conclusive in West Germany as regards other proceedings, even between the same parties, and that consequently it could not be conclusive as regards other proceedings here. The estoppel fails in any event in view of the conclusion reached by your Lordships as to identity of parties. This being so, it is not necessary to consider whether the appellants, for their part, could set up the judgments given in East Germany as a counter-estoppel, or to decide on the effect of an estoppel as regards the first and second defendants to the present action.

(2) I now consider, free from any estoppel, whether the Council of Gera had authority to commence these proceedings on behalf of the Stiftung. The evidence before the learned judge consisted in the main, of decisions of courts in both East and West Germany. There were also affidavits by experts on each side, on which extensive cross-examination took place. On the appellants' side most reliance was placed on two judgments of the Supreme Court in East Germany, an advisory opinion given on April 6, 1954, and a judgment on appeal from the District Court of Leipzig dated March 23, 1961. This judgment was given in proceedings brought by the Stiftung (represented by the Council of Gera as

[23] (1837) 2 Myl. & Cr. 602.

the special board and by its mandatory, Dr. Schrade) and V.E.B. Carl Zeiss (the public body which had taken over the optical works in 1940) against "the firm Carl Zeiss of Oberkochen" (a description intended to apply to the present third defendants) to restrain them from using the name Carl-Zeiss in the German Democratic Republic. Notice of these proceedings was apparently given to the defendants but they did not appear or take any part in the action. These two decisions, which enter in great detail into both the facts and the law, state as the conclusions of the Supreme Court, (i) that the Stiftung continued to exist as a legal entity, (ii) that the Council of Gera was the special board of the **[972]** Stiftung, (iii) that article 116, which provided for liquidation of the Stiftung, had not come into play.

On the side of the respondents, reliance was in the main placed on the judgment of the Federal High Court of West Germany of November 15, 1960, coupled with that of the Provincial Court of Appeal of Stuttgart dated October 29, 1958, the reasoning of which was approved by the Federal High Court. The effect of these judgments was that, under East German law, the articles of the Stiftung had been inoperable since and by reason of the confiscations of the undertakings of the Stiftung in 1948 and that in any event the Council of Gera was not capable of exercising the functions of the special board by reason (inter alia) of the political and economic conditions in the "German Democratic Republic."

There is thus a direct conflict between the views of the two highest courts. The expert evidence divides itself similarly into two sides supporting the one or the other set of judgments. The existence of the Stiftung as a legal entity, though at one time disputed, is now accepted by both sides and the essential questions which have to be decided may be summarised as being (1) whether the Stiftung, from 1948 onwards, was incapable of acting and its articles were inoperative and (2) whether the Council of Gera was capable or incapable of fulfilling the functions conferred by the articles on the special board.

Each of these questions may be "classified" as questions relating to the constitution of a foreign corporation, and so, according to English private international law, to be decided according to the law prevailing at the place where the Stiftung was incorporated (see Dicey, Conflict of Laws, 7th ed. r. 78 (2)). So far as German private international law is concerned, it appears that account is taken of the law prevailing at the place of the "domicile" of the corporation. There is no dispute that the place of incorporation was Jena, and although an attempt has been made to transfer the domicile or seat of the Stiftung to West Germany, the courts of West Germany have been prepared to assume for the purpose of their decisions (rightly in my opinion) that this remains in Jena. The question, then, on either approach, is, what is the relevant applicable law prevailing at Jena? The expert evidence establishes, in my opinion, that the law applicable to Stiftungen in Germany rests on the triple foundation of (i) the German Civil Code (BGB) of 1900 and in particular articles 80-88; (ii) the Legal Code of the Land of Thuringia of 1923, and (iii) the articles. From this it would seem to follow **[973]** that the relevant law should be that stated by the courts having jurisdiction in Thuringia, or whatever geographical area corresponds to Thuringia, namely, the Provincial Court at Leipzig and on appeal the Supreme Court in East Germany.

In general, it may be taken to be the case that the best evidence as to the law of a foreign country is the law as stated by its court of last resort. All five speeches in this House in *Bankers and Shippers Insurance Co. of New York* v. *Liverpool Marine & General Insurance Co.*[24] accepted this. Lord Buckmaster, after pointing out that no foreign judgment is technically binding, said that[25] it would require "special and unusual circumstances" to lead the House away from a clear decision of a final court. His opinion was expressed in relation to a matter of construction of a statute, but the principle must apply equally to other matters of foreign law. I need not quote from the other speeches which were, if anything, expressed in still stronger terms. Similarly, in *Lazard Brothers*

[24] 24 Ll.L.R. 85.

[25] Ibid. 87.

& Co. v. *Midland Bank Ltd.*,[26]* Lord Wright said that the question is what the foreign law is shown to be by its exposition, interpretation and adjudication. So it would seem that there are strong reasons—if not quite conclusive—why courts in this country should accept the East German judgments as stating the relevant law.

The respondents contest this conclusion on several grounds. They submit that the questions of law, as to the constitution of the Stiftung, should properly be considered to be questions not of East German law but of German law. The questions relate, they say, to the issue how the Stiftung may be represented in Germany as a whole and internationally and how, if at all, it may protect assets outside the Eastern Zone. Formally, the questions of law concern the interpretation, or application of the German Civil Code, under which the Stiftung was formed, not of any zonal law. As to such a legal question the decisions of courts of the Federal Republic of Germany have a superior or (alternatively) an equal right to international recognition as compared with those of East German courts.

The claim for superior status was based principally upon the terms of the certificate of the Secretary of State given on November 6, 1964, already considered in another context and set out in the opinion of my noble and learned friend, Lord Reid. This certificate makes it clear, so it is said, that the rights of the **[974]** U.S.S.R. as de jure "sovereign" in the Eastern Zone are confined to that zone and explicitly recognises (following a communiqué of the Western Allies on September 19, 1950) the Government of the Federal Republic as "entitled to speak for Germany as the representative of the German people in international affairs." So, it is argued, in what is essentially an international matter, the courts of the Federal Republic should be accepted as the proper organ to declare what the law of Germany is.

I recognise the ingenuity of this argument but I am not convinced by it. Read as a whole, the certificate gives recognition to the U.S.S.R. as de jure entitled to exercise governing authority in respect of the Eastern Zone; and (negatively) the certificate also states, after the passage on which the respondents rely, that the communiqué of 1950 does not constitute recognition of the Government of the Federal Republic as the de jure Government of all Germany. The right to exercise governing authority includes, in my opinion, the right to set up or maintain courts and the recognition of the one carries with it the recognition, as a source of law, of the decisions of the courts. The right to "speak for Germany as the representative of the German people in international affairs" is a right of diplomatic representation which is not coincident with, and does not impinge upon, the right of the governing authority in each part of Germany to make and state the law in the part over which it has power. Furthermore, it by no means follows from the fact that the present claim of the Stiftung extends beyonds the frontiers of East Germany that the legal question we are considering is one of international or interzonal concern. The legal question relates to the constitution of the Stiftung, which depends on the law of the place where it is localised. Your Lordships were invited by the respondents to consult the Secretary of State on the matters discussed above, and to seek a further certificate as to the proper authority to determine the status of and right to represent the Stiftung. This course, in my opinion, should not be followed. The questions, which it was suggested should be asked, were questions of law which it is the function of the courts to determine and which they are in a position to determine on the basis of the certificate previously given, the terms of which are sufficiently clear.

The argument, therefore, that superior recognition should be given to the West German judgments, in my opinion, should not be accepted. But there remains the further submission that the West German judgments should at least be considered side by **[975]** side with those of the East German courts—as rival pieces of evidence entitled to equal weight—and a decision reached on their respective merits. The arguments for this are that the circumstances

[26] [1933] A.C. 289, 298.

prevailing in Germany are unusual, that the legal questions involved are common to both parts of divided Germany, that the East German judgments consist of an advisory opinion and a default judgment, whereas those of West Germany were given in contested proceedings brought at the present appellants' choice in the courts of West Germany, and (ultimately if the comparison is admissible) that the West German judgments are superior in legal reasoning.

These are difficult questions indeed. I am prepared to go so far with the respondents as to agree that it may be right in the present circumstances to look beyond the decisions of the East German courts and to consider, and at least to test them by, the rival decisions in West Germany. But, in making this comparison, there are two points to bear in mind. First: the question to be resolved is not merely one of interpretation of a common code—the Civil Code of 1900—(I pass over for this purpose the Thüringian Law of 1923, whose provisions are of a general character with no direct bearing on the issues). It is a question of the application of the somewhat general provisions of the Civil Code to a factual situation peculiar to the Eastern Zone, the answer to which, by agreement of both sets of courts, depends upon a consideration of the effect of the 1948 (Eastern Zone) decrees on the actual business undertaking in Jena of the Stiftung. Both sets of courts in fact give considerable attention to the factual situation prevailing in Jena since 1948. On such matters, prima facie, preference should be given to the East German courts, as the appropriate tribunal to deal with the impact of East German legislation on an organisation in their zone. Secondly: in so far as the questions for decision are general questions of law, rather than questions depending on local considerations, there is no reason why, given a separation of de jure sovereignty between the two parts of Germany, there should not be differences of interpretation and application of rules of law formerly common to the whole of Germany. The respondents' experts, indeed, asserted that there were such differences: their contentions were that decisions in East Germany were those appropriate to a centralised socialist state whose courts were guided by considerations of policy. If this argument could have been carried to the point of showing that the courts of East Germany are not courts **[976]** of law at all or that their decisions were corrupt or perverse, that might (I do not say would) be a ground for disregarding them in favour of decisions of other courts shown to act more judicially. But the evidence did not, in my opinion, approach this point, and a mere difference in philosophy, or even of method, so far from entitling us to prefer the West German approach, on the contrary gives support to those who argue that the East German variety of German law should be taken as being the law in East Germany. With these considerations in mind, I consider the two sets of judgments. They have been analysed in detail by Cross J. and (subject to the one point to which I return later) I am satisfied to accept his analysis. I only make some observations of my own in recognition of their careful re-examination by counsel in the present appeal and because these issues have not been considered by the Court of Appeal.

The East German Supreme Court bases its decisions on the following main points: (1) the confiscations which took place in 1948 were not of the whole business of the Stiftung but were separate acts of confiscation of the assets of the two individual businesses—the optical works and the glass works; (2) the Stiftung as such retains considerable assets: these produce an income of some £180,000 per annum. It is able with these assets to fulfil many of the charitable functions for which it was created. The Supreme Court refers to establishments for the development and training of optical personnel, for the promotion of studies, research and training in natural sciences and mathematics, as well as for social and health care of the employees of the plants of the foundation, for example, schools for opticians, libraries, clinics, recreation and rest homes, and their findings as to these matters were supported by evidence before Cross J. There was also evidence as to the ownership of trade marks and other industrial property and as to assets of the Stiftung outside East Germany, but this was perhaps controversial and it is safer to leave these matters out of account; (3) the Stiftung employs over 400 persons and there are about 4,000 pensioners who are paid according to the pensions statute of the Stiftung. There remain also other beneficiaries within the purposes of the Stiftung; (4) the Stiftung is in a position to take and does take legal action for the protection of its assets; (5) the resolution of the German Economic Commission of June 16, 1948, contemplated that the Stiftung should remain in existence and that its constitution should be amended to reflect its changed position. This was not done, but **[977]** it is consistent with the resolution to hold that the original articles continue in effect.

The principal reasons for the judgment of the West German Supreme Court are (1) that the articles became unworkable after 1948 because they were dependent for their working on the continued ownership of some business by the Stiftung. After 1948 the Foundation ceased to have any interest in its former businesses which became nationalised undertakings. According to the "Soviet Zone view," as interpreted by the Federal High Court, this interfered with the organisation of the Stiftung to such a far-reaching effect that in the Eastern Zone the Stiftung no longer had capacity to act as a juristic person; (2) that the centre of gravity of the Stiftung's organisation lay in the industrial enterprises and the removal of these destroyed the balance on which the organisation of the governing bodies of the Stiftung depended; (3) that the Council of Gera, because of its political complexion, cannot act as a special board or represent the interests of the Stiftung or carry on the affairs of the Stiftung consistently with the intentions of the founder, Abbé.

As between these opinions, and taking also into account the expert evidence on them, much of which was not challenged, and certain supplementary evidence (particularly of Dr. Schrade) regarding the factual position at Jena, I think that the learned judge was fully justified in coming to the conclusion that the East German decisions should be preferred. The decisions of the West German courts carry less conviction: on points (1) and (2) because they were less fully informed than the East German courts as to the existing activity and assets of the Stiftung and because they based their decisions on a view as to the law in the Eastern Zone which is not in agreement with that law as declared by the Supreme Court in that zone; on point (3) because it is really impossible to say that, and if so when, the authority designated as the special board diverged from the intentions of the founder so radically that it ceased to be capable of acting. In fact both Supreme Courts claimed that the intentions of the founder were reflected in the very different philosophies prevailing in their respective zones so that, as Cross J. observed, the only safe course is to keep to the natural sense of the articles which base the constitution of the special board on considerations of administrative geography.

I must add one point as to the respective merits of the judgments. The learned judge, in that part of his judgment dealing **[978]** with res judicata, after a careful analysis of the West German judgments, expressed the view that these were perverse, and so in any case ought to be disregarded. He, of course, had the advantage of hearing the expert witnesses which we have not, but even allowing for this, I do not think that a finding of perversity ought to stand. In my opinion, the case amounts to this: (1) that the law prevailing in East Germany should be taken to be that declared by the East German courts; (2) that the West German decisions proceeded on a view as to the law in East Germany which, for reasons I have given, ought not to be accepted in preference to the view of the East German courts themselves. Further than this I do not think that the evidence requires or indeed entitles us to go. For my part, I accept the West German decisions as judicial in the fullest sense, which could readily be accepted if they stood alone. This being so, I do not consider it necessary (as on some future occasion it may be) to examine the limits in law of the doctrine of perversity, some of the authorities on which (for example, *Simpson* v. *Fogo*[27]) seem to me to present difficulties.

My Lords, in this long and involved case we have heard many arguments from counsel on either side and many authorities have been referred to. It

[27] 1 H. & M. 195.

involves I hope no disrespect to those arguments not to examine them all. In the end, and on the whole of the case, the conclusion emerges that the respondents' preliminary attack on the validity of the action fails: I would allow the appeal and restore the judgment of Cross J.

Appeal allowed.

Solicitors: *Courts & Co.; Herbert Smith & Co.*

2

STATE TERRITORY

A.

IN GENERAL

1

OCCUPATION AND SETTLEMENT

SABALLY AND N'JIE v. H.M. ATTORNEY-GENERAL

([1965] 1 Q.B. 273)

July 2, 1964: Queen's Bench Division: Salmon L.J.
July 16, 17, 20, 1964: Court of Appeal, Lord Denning M.R., Harman, Russell L.JJ.

Crown—Prerogative—Protectorate—Settled Colony—Statute, application of—Grant of constitution with representative legislature to settled colony and protectorate by Order in Council—Order made in exercise of statutory powers "and all other powers enabling" Her Majesty in Council "in that behalf"—No reservation of constituent powers to Crown—Power to legislate reserved to Crown—Elections to representative legislature invalidated by use of unauthorised register of voters—Representative government unable to function—Retrospective validation of elections by Order in Council—Whether retrospective validation in excess of powers of Crown conferred by statute—Whether royal prerogative surviving statutory power to "make, and when made to alter and revoke, Orders for the purposes of this Act"—British Settlements Act, 1887 (50 & 51 *Vict. c.* 54), *ss.* 2, 5—*Foreign Jurisdiction Act,* 1890 (53 & 54 *Vict. c.* 37), *s.* 10.
Gambia—Constitution—Orders in Council—Powers of Her Majesty in Council.
Statute—Retroactive effect—Order in Council—Act giving power to Crown in Council to alter or revoke Orders previously made—Whether conferring power to do so with retroactive effect—British Settlements Act, 1887, *ss.* 2, 5.

In April, 1960, the Gambia, a territory consisting of a former settled British colony and a British protectorate, was granted a representative legislature by Order in Council, expressed to be made **[274]** "by virtue and in exercise of the powers vested in" Her Majesty in Council "by the British Settlements Acts, 1887[1] and 1945, and by the Foreign Jurisdiction Act, 1890, and of all other powers enabling Her in that behalf." Section 63 of the Order reserved (a) power to revoke or amend that constitution and (b) power to legislate for the peace, order and good government of the Gambia.

An electoral register ("the 1959 register") was compiled for the elections to be held under that constitution, in accordance with local ordinances, which provided that that register, brought up to date, should be used for any election held in, inter alia, 1962.

By a further Order in Council of May, 1962, made in exercise of the same powers, a further constitution was granted to the Gambia, giving a more representative legislature. Section 74 reserved to Her Majesty in Council power to legislate but no power was reserved to revoke or amend the con-

[1] British Settlements Act, 1887, s. 2: "It shall be lawful for Her Majesty the Queen in Council from time to time to establish all such laws and institutions, and constitute such courts and officers, and make such provisions and regulations for the proceedings in the said courts and for the administration of justice, as may appear to Her Majesty in Council to be necessary for the peace, order, and good government of Her Majesty's subjects and others within any British settlement."
S. 5: "It shall be lawful for Her Majesty the Queen in Council from time to time to make, and when made to alter and revoke, Orders for the purposes of this Act."

stitution. By section 28 of the Order it was provided that at the elections to be held under the new constitution the "1959 register," brought up to date, should be used. The registering officer in the former Protectorate territory, instead of bringing the 1959 register up to date and certifying it for use, compiled and certified an entirely new register ("the 1961 register") and that new register was used at elections held in May, 1962.

M. S., an unsuccessful candidate in a Protectorate constituency, in a test action in the courts of the Gambia, obtained a declaration that the election held in his constituency on the basis of the 1961 register was invalid. As a result of that decision it was conceded that the election of 25 of the 36 members of the representative legislature was invalid, and, there being no quorum of the House of Representatives, the constitution could not function. To remedy the impasse, Her Majesty in Council in London, on May 30, 1963, made the Gambia (Validation) Order in Council, 1963, by section 4 of which the invalid elections of May, 1962, were validated retrospectively.

M. S., and E. D. N. (a person elected at the 1962 elections) thereupon brought an action in the High Court in England claiming against the Crown a declaration that the validating Order of 1963 was in excess of the powers of Her Majesty in Council and void.

The trial judge dismissed the action, holding that the constitution of 1962 had been granted not only in the exercise of the royal prerogative but also by virtue of the powers vested in Her Majesty in Council by the British Settlements Act, 1887,[1] in respect of the **[275]** settled colony, and by the Foreign Jurisdiction Act, 1890, in respect of the Protectorate, and that the language of section 5 of the Act of 1887 and section 10 of the Act of 1890 was wide enough to warrant the making of the Validation Order in Council of 1963 with retrospective effect. The trial judge expressed the view that if the representative legislature had been granted solely in the exercise of the royal prerogative, the plaintiffs' action must have succeeded. On appeal by the plaintiffs:—

Held, dismissing the appeal, that the Gambia (Validation) Order in Council, 1963, was intra vires Her Majesty in Council exercising the powers conferred by the British Settlements Act, 1887, pursuant to which the Order was made. That Act empowered Her Majesty in Council to make laws, with retroactive effect where necessary, for any British settlement, and by section 5 gave powers to make the Validation Order in question (post, pp. 295, 297, 298, 299).

Per Harman and Russell L.JJ. The Order of 1963, being merely the validation of electoral machinery, was not an exercise of the power (not reserved) to alter the 1962 Constitution but was an exercise of the power to legislate which had been expressly reserved to the Queen in Council by section 74 of the 1962 Constitution (post, pp. 297, 300).

Per Lord Denning M.R. The Constitution of 1962 was not granted in the exercise of the royal prerogative, but was granted in the exercise of the powers taken by Parliament in the Act of 1887 to enable the Crown in Council to grant non-representative as well as representative legislatures to British settled colonies. The Act of 1887 completely swallowed up the royal prerogative, based on the common law, to grant representative legislatures to British settled colonies, so that all acts done thereafter in relation to a British settlement by the Crown in Council were done under the powers contained in that Act; and in the circumstances of this case those powers included the power to alter or amend the constitution (post, pp. 293, 294-295).

Per Lord Denning M.R. and Russell L.J. Even if the 1962 Constitution had been granted solely in the exercise of the royal prerogative, and despite the deliberate omission to reserve to the Crown power to alter or amend the constitution, the Crown would not thereby be rendered impotent if by reason of supervening events an impasse were reached such that the constitution granted could not function or, as here, had been rendered a nullity. In such circumstances the Crown could resort to its prerogative to put matters right and could in this case have intervened to validate the elections retrospectively in order that the intended representative government might function. An Act of the Imperial Parliament would therefore not have been the only method of restoring representative government to the Gambia (post, pp. 293, 299-300).

Campbell v. *Hall** (1774) 1 Cowp. 204, and *Sammut* v. *Strickland** [1938] A.C. 678; 54 T.L.R. 1080; [1938] 3 All E.R. 693, P.C. considered.

Decision of Salmon L.J. (infra) affirmed. **[276]**

APPEAL from Salmon L.J. (sitting as an additional judge of the Queen's Bench Division).

By the Gambia (Constitution) Order in Council, 1960 [S.I. 1960, No. 701], made on April 8, 1960, a new constitution was granted to the integrated territories on the West Coast of Africa consisting of the settled Colony of Gambia and the Protectorate of Gambia. That Order, by sections 23 and 27, provided, among other things, for a House of Representatives, to consist of the Governor, a Speaker, four ex-officio members, not more than three nominated members, and 27 elected members. Seven of the elected members were to represent the Colony and 20 (of whom eight were to be elected by the head chiefs) were to represent the Protectorate. The Order made no provision as to the manner in which the election was to be held, save that it was to be in accordance with the local laws. Section 63 of the Order of 1960 provided: "(1) Her Majesty hereby reserves to Herself, power, with the advice of Her Privy Council to revoke or amend this Order. (2) Nothing in this Order shall affect the power of Her Majesty in Council to make laws from time to time for the peace, order and good government of the Gambia."

In contemplation of that Order, and of the fact that elections would be held under the new constitution in 1960, the Protectorate Elections Ordinance, 1959, was enacted, receiving the Governor's assent on December 31, 1959, to make provision for regulating the procedure at such elections. It provided that a fresh register of voters should be prepared in 1959, and in every tenth year thereafter, and that in every other year save 1960 the then current register should be brought up to date. A register was prepared in 1959 ("the 1959 register") and was used for the elections which were held in 1960. By the Protectorate Elections (Amendment) Ordinance, 1961, the Ordinance of 1959 was amended by providing that for the year 1962 there should be no revision of the register, but that for that year the registering officer should certify the accuracy of the 1959 register as revised in 1961.

In 1962, a further step was taken along the constitutional road to independence for the Gambia, and the Gambia (Constitution) Order in Council, 1962 [S.I. 1962, No. 826], was enacted. That provided for a new constitution under which there was to be a House of Representatives consisting of the Speaker, the Attorney-General, 36 elected members, of whom seven were to be elected for the Colony, 25 for the Protectorate and four by the head chiefs; and two nominated members. Section 28 (3) of that **[277]** Order provided that the register of voters compiled in accordance with the local Ordinance should be the valid register for the purpose of the elections to be held in 1962 under the new constitution.

By section 74, the power reserved to Her Majesty provided only that: "Nothing in this Order shall affect the power of Her Majesty in Council to make laws from time to time for the peace, order and good government of the Gambia."

Had the procedure laid down in the 1959 Election Ordinance, as amended, been complied with, the 1959 register would have been revised in 1961. In that year, however, instead of a revision of the 1959 register, a completely new register was compiled ("the 1961 register"). That register had no legal basis, but it was that register which was certified in 1962 and used for the election held in that year.

Mamadi Sabally, one of the present plaintiffs, who was an unsuccessful candidate for the Sabach-Sanjal constituency in the Lower River Division of the Protectorate at the elections held in May, 1962, brought a test action by which he sought a declaration from the High Court of the Protectorate that the register of voters compiled by the defendant to his action, Ian Coghill, as registering officer for the constituencies in the Lower River Division in 1961, and certified by him, was invalid. His claim was dismissed by Wiseham C.J. on December 24, 1962; but on appeal the Gambia Court of Appeal, on March 16, 1963, unanimously upheld Mr. Sabally's claim to the declaratory judgment that the register used in his constituency was invalid. It was conceded that, as a result of that decision, the election of 25 of the persons returned to the House to represent the Protectorate was invalid, thereby making it impossible for representative government to function in the Gambia, either by reason of the fact that there was no House as designated by the constitution, since none of the 25 electoral districts in the Protectorate was represented in the House, or because there was no quorum in the House; (a quorum, by section 44 of the Order in Council of 1962, consisted of 14 members besides the person presiding at any sitting).

The resulting situation was dealt with by the Gambia (Validation) Order in Council, 1963 [S.I. 1963, No. 1051], made on May 30, 1963, by Her Majesty in Council at the Court at Buckingham Palace, for the declared purpose of validating retrospectively the invalid elections of May, 1962, and provided by section 4, as follows: "Section 6A of the Protectorate Elections Ordinance 1959 (as inserted by section 4 of the Protectorate Elections **[278]** (Amendment) Ordinance 1961) shall have effect, and shall be deemed always to have had effect, as if the references therein to registers of voters included references to the 1961 registers."

Each of the Orders in Council of 1960, 1962, and 1963, were expressed to have been made by Her Majesty "by virtue and in exercise of the powers vested in Her by the British Settlements Acts, 1887 and 1945, by the Foreign Jurisdiction Act, 1890, and of all other powers enabling her in that behalf."

On September 19, 1963, the first plaintiff, Mamadi Sabally, the unsuccessful candidate at the 1962 elections whose appeal had succeeded before the Gambia Court of Appeal, and the second plaintiff, Ebrima Daour N'Jie, an official of the United Party in the Gambia who had been elected at the 1962 elections to represent the Saloum Constituency in the MacCarthy Island Division of the Protectorate, issued a writ against Her Majesty's Attorney-General, claiming a declaration that the Gambia (Validation) Order in Council, 1963, was ultra vires, invalid, null and void or of no effect in law.

By their statement of claim they drew attention in paragraph 1 to the fact that while the 1960 Order in Council reserved to Her Majesty in Council the power to amend the constitution of the Gambia, the 1962 Constitution Order in Council reserved only the power to make laws from time to time for the peace, order and good government of the Gambia. Having set out the provisions of the constitution in regard to the elections register, the effect of the decision of the Court of Appeal in the Gambia, and the terms of the Validation Order in Council of 1963, they humbly submitted and contended that "notwithstanding the declared purpose, the Gambia (Validation) Order in Council, in excess of the powers of Her Majesty in Council, is void and of no effect whether to validate the said elections or at all." Following a summons on behalf of the Attorney-General, and the delivery of further and better particulars of the matters in respect of which it was alleged that the Validation Order in Council exceeded the powers of Her Majesty in Council, the defence, dated December 5, 1963, was delivered by which the defendant joined issue on each point pleaded and denied that the plaintiffs were entitled to the relief claimed, or to any relief.

Salmon L.J., in a reserved judgment given on July 2, 1964, having stated the facts substantially as set out above, referred to the powers by virtue of which the Orders in Council of 1960, 1962 and 1963 were expressed to be made, and continued: "'All other powers enabling her in that behalf' are the powers **[279]** vested in the Crown by virtue of the royal prerogative. The Crown by virtue of the royal prerogative is prima facie entitled to legislate for colonies acquired by conquest or cession, but has no general power to legislate for colonies acquired by settlement. The Crown by virtue of its prerogative cannot legislate for a settled colony otherwise than by appointing a governor, establishing courts of justice, and making provision for the summoning of a representative legislature. This is because 'English settlers wherever they went carried with them the principles of English law and . . . English common law necessarily applied in so far as such laws were applicable to the conditions of the colony.' *Sammut* v. *Strickland.*[2]*"

"The British Settlement Acts, to which I must later refer in detail, conferred very wide powers on the Crown to legislate in settled colonies, and the Foreign Jurisdiction Act regulated similar powers of the Crown to legislate in foreign territories, including protectorates. Since the Gambia is partly a settled colony and partly protectorate, and the Orders in Council of 1960 and 1962 made provision for the summoning of a representative legislature, these Orders in Council could have been made solely by virtue of the royal prerogative. But they were not so made: they were made by virtue of the powers vested in Her Majesty by the prerogative and the statutes to which I have referred. Had the Orders been made solely by virtue of the prerogative, this action would in my judgment have been successful. The Order in Council of 1960 provides by section 63 (1): 'Her Majesty hereby reserves to Herself, power, with the advice of Her Privy Council to revoke or amend this Order. (2) Nothing in this Order shall affect the power of Her Majesty in Council to make laws from time to time, for the peace, order and good government of the Gambia.'"

"The corresponding section in the Order in Council of 1962 is section 74. This section reserves power to make laws from time to time for the peace, order and good government of the Gambia, but it omits the reservation contained in section 63 (1), that is to say, it makes no reservation of the powers to revoke or amend the constitution. It is well settled that where the Crown grants a constitution, it divests itself of the power to revoke or amend the constitution unless it expressly reserves that power in the instrument granting the constitution: *Campbell* v. *Hall*[3]* and *Sammut* v. *Strickland.*[4]* A reservation to **[280]** make laws for peace, order and good government does not reserve the power to revoke or amend the constitution: *Chenard & Co.* v. *Joachim Arissol.*[5]

"Accordingly, in 1963 the Crown had no residual powers under the royal prerogative to alter or revoke the Gambia Constitution. The Order in Council of 1963 does purport to alter the effect of section 28 (3) of the Gambia (Constitution) Order in Council of 1962. This section, to my mind, is clearly part of the Gambia Constitution. It must therefore follow that, if the Order in Council of 1963 rested on the royal prerogative alone, it would clearly be ultra vires. But, as I have already said, it does not rest on the royal prerogative alone. It rests also on the British Settlements Act, 1887, and the Foreign Jurisdiction Act, 1890. The relevant sections are sections 2 and 5 of the Act of 1887, and sections 1 and 10 of the Act of 1890, and I must read those sections.

"Section 2 of the Act of 1887 reads as follows: 'It shall be lawful for Her Majesty the Queen in Council from time to time to establish all such laws and institutions, and constitute such courts and officers, and make such provisions and regulations for the proceedings in the said courts and for the administration of justice, as may appear to Her Majesty in Council to be necessary for the peace, order, and good government of Her Majesty's subjects and others within any British settlement.' Section 5 reads: 'It shall be lawful for Her Majesty the Queen in Council from time to time to make, and when made to alter and revoke, Orders for the purposes of this Act.'

"Section 1 of the Foreign Jurisdiction Act reads as follows: 'It is and shall be lawful for Her Majesty the Queen to hold, exercise, and enjoy any jurisdiction which Her Majesty now has or may at any time hereafter have within a foreign country in the same and as ample a manner as if Her Majesty had acquired that jurisdiction by the cession or conquest of territory.' Section 10 reads: 'It shall be lawful for Her Majesty the Queen in Council to revoke or vary any Order in Council made in pursuance of this Act.'

"It is not disputed that under section 5 of the Act of 1887 and section 10 of the Act of 1890, Her Majesty had power to amend the constitution; but it is

[2] [1938] A.C. 678, 701; 54 T.L.R. 1080; [1938] 3 All E.R. 693, P.C.
[3] (1774) 1 Cowp. 204.
[4] [1938] A.C. 678.
[5] [1949] A.C. 127; 65 T.L.R. 72, P.C.

argued on behalf of the plaintiffs that these sections did not empower Her Majesty to make any amendment with retrospective effect. It is, of course, **[281]** trite law that no statute shall be considered so as to have retrospective operation unless such a construction appears very clearly in the terms of the Act or arises by necessary implication from it: *Main* v. *Stark*[6]; *In re Athlumney, Ex parte Wilson.*[7]

"There is here, however, no question of giving retrospective effect to the provisions of this statute. We are dealing with events which occurred more than 70 years after the last of the relevant statutes came into operation. The only question is as to whether the powers which these statutes vested in the Crown to make and alter laws included a power to make a law or an alteration to it which would have restrospective effect as from the day on which such law or alteration was made.

"It seems to me that the language used in the sections which I have read is amply wide enough to confer such a power. The object of the statutes seems clearly to have been to vest in the Crown plenary powers to legislate in the territories to which the statutes referred. Retrospective legislation, although rarely resorted to, is well known under the British system.

"There is a passage which seems to me to be much in point in the judgment of Higgins J., and in which the other judges in the High Court of Australia concurred, in *Rex* v. *Kidman.*[8] That reads as follows: 'The British Parliament, admittedly, has power to make its laws retroactive; and I know of no instance in which a legislature created by the British Parliament has been held to have overstepped its powers by making legislation retroactive. There are plenty of passages that can be cited showing the inexpediency, and the injustice, in most cases, of legislating for the past, of interfering with vested rights, and of making acts unlawful which were lawful when done; but these passages do not raise any doubt as to the power of the legislature to pass retroactive legislation, if it see fit.'

"It is true that in the present case I am not concerned with a legislature created by Parliament, but with legislative powers created and vested in the Crown by Parliament. It seems clear that the powers intended to be vested in the Crown were at least as plenary as any that might be vested in a legislature. Plenary legislative powers include the power to legislate retrospectively, seldom though such a power in practice may be used. I can see no reason for reading into the statutes the **[282]** limitations for which the plaintiffs contend. Had Parliament intended to impose any such limitation, in my judgment it would have done so in express language. The words of the statute are very wide, and do not expressly, or by implication, impose any such limitation.

"Great stress has naturally been laid on behalf of the plaintiffs on the omission from the Gambia (Constitution) Order in Council, 1962, of the reservation of the power to amend the Constitution. It is pointed out that this omission must have been made deliberately, since such a reservation was included in the Gambia (Constitution) Order in Council, 1960. This omission may well have been deliberate. Possibly it was thought that the Gambia had so far developed by 1962 that it would, in no foreseeable circumstances, be necessary for the Crown in future to make any further amendment to the constitution. What was not foreseen, and could hardly have been foreseen, was that by an unfortunate mistake of the officers responsible for the register of voters, the inhabitants of the Gambia would be deprived of representative government unless Her Majesty in Council or the Imperial Parliament intervened on their behalf by means of retrospective legislation. No doubt it would have taken too long for Parliament to do so.

"For the reasons I have stated earlier in my judgment, Her Majesty had lost her prerogative powers so to intervene, but in my opinion she had ample statutory power to do so. Certainly nothing that was included in, or omitted

[6] (1890) 15 App.Cas. 384, 387, P.C.
[7] [1898] 2 Q.B. 547.
[8] (1915) 20 C.L.R. 425, 451.

from, Orders in Council made in 1960 and 1962 can affect the construction of statutes passed in 1887 and 1890, under which these powers are given. In my judgment, there is no legal basis for this claim, and I give judgment for the defendant."

Judgment was entered for the defendant, the order for costs being that the defendant should have three-quarters of the costs of the action, on the ground that a number of issues were raised by the defendant on the pleadings on which the plaintiffs had succeeded.

The plaintiffs entered notice of appeal and on July 10, 1964, applied for and obtained leave from the Court of Appeal to have the hearing of the appeal expedited and the decision of the court obtained before the opening of the Gambia Independence Conference in London fixed for July 22, 1964.

The grounds of appeal were (1) that the judge was wrong in holding that section 5 of the British Settlements Act, 1887, gave Her Majesty in Council power to amend the Gambia (Constitu-**[283]**-tion) Order in Council, 1962, since that section conferred no right to alter, amend or revoke the Gambia constitution: (2) that the judge was wrong in holding that on the true construction of section 5 of the Act of 1887 the Crown had power to pass an Order in Council retrospectively validating the 1962 election, either in relation to a constituent power or a legislative power; (3) that the judge applied the wrong principles in testing whether section 5 of the Act of 1887 gave Her Majesty in Council the right or power to pass retrospective legislation; and (4) that the judge was wrong in holding that Her Majesty in Council had, by virtue of section 5 of the Act of 1887, plenary legislative powers (including the power to legislate retrospectively) in as ample a manner as had the Gambia House of Representatives under its powers conferred by the Gambia (Constitution) Order in Council, 1962.

Morris Finer Q.C. and *L. J. Blom-Cooper* for the plaintiffs. The first issue is whether the Validation Order of 1963 was validly made in the exercise of the royal prerogative. That Order was a purported exercise of a constituent power because it contradicts section 28 of the Constitution of 1962; and as there was a deliberate omission of the reservation of constituent powers to Her Majesty in Council in the 1962 Constitution, there was no longer any prerogative remaining in Her Majesty in Council to define, with retrospective effect, what were to be the valid registers for the 1962 elections. It follows that the Validation Order of 1963 is ultra vires and void.

The situation which arose after the Gambia Court of Appeal had decided that the election in Sabally's constituency was invalid could have been remedied (*a*) by an Act of the United Kingdom Parliament at Westminster, legislating for British possessions; or possibly (*b*) by Her Majesty in Council directing that fresh elections should be held on the basis of the register defined in section 28 of the 1962 Constitution. But there was no power to remedy the situation by the exercise of the prerogative.

The second issue is whether the Validation Order of 1963 was a valid exercise of the powers of Her Majesty in Council under the British Settlements Act, 1887, as Salmon L.J. held it to be. That Act, the third of its kind enacted in the 19th century, has never before been judicially considered. The situation in which that Act and its predecessors in 1843 and 1860 (6 & 7 Vict. c. 13 and 23 & 24 Vict. c. 121) were enacted was as follows: At common law the only kind of legislature which the Crown could grant to a *settled* colony was a representative legislature: **[284]** *Campbell* v. *Hall.*[9]* Once such a legislature had been granted, the Crown could no longer exercise constituent powers within the colony unless such powers had been expressly reserved to the Crown. A problem then arose over settled colonies which were not yet suited for representative government. In order to grant such colonies non-representative governments, it became necessary to legislate. The Act of 1843 was passed in relation to the Falkland Islands and the Act of 1860 in relation to settlements on the West Coast of Africa. Those Acts were repealed by the British Settlements Act, 1887, and re-enacted in a

[9] (1774) 1 Cowp. 204.

generalised form to permit the Crown to do that which it had no power to do under the prerogative at common law, namely, to grant non-representative legislatures to British-settled colonies.

It is submitted—though admittedly as a new point not argued before Salmon L.J.—that, having regard to the definition of "British settlement" in section 6 of the Act of 1887, that Act does not apply to the Gambia, because the Act only applies where there is a grant of a non-representative legislature to a settled colony. When, therefore, the Crown granted a representative legislature to the Gambia in 1960, it did so in the exercise of its ancient prerogative power and not by virtue of the Act of 1887. Therefore the Gambia is "constituted otherwise than by virtue of" the Act of 1887, and the Validation Order of 1963, stated to be made by virtue and in exercise of the powers vested in Her Majesty by the Act of 1887, is ultra vires.

[*Sir Peter Rawlinson Q.C., S.-G.* for the Crown. This point was not only not raised below but it does not appear from the pleadings nor in the notice of appeal Where a plaintiff makes a complaint against the Crown, it is important that the case should be stated and argued in precise form because of the repercussions it may have in other directions. If the court permits this point to be argued, the Crown reserves its right to seek an adjournment to answer it if necessary.]

Finer Q.C. continuing. The court ought to consider this new point, because Salmon L.J.'s decision that the Act vested in the Crown plenary powers sufficient to enable the Crown to make the Validation Order of 1963 would have far-reaching and serious results, as follows:

(1) *The quasi-political result.* The whole modern process of Commonwealth democratic evolution is a process of transferring responsibility from the Crown to the colony stage by stage, **[285]** subject to reservations of powers. The precise extent and nature of the reserved powers tend to be the most excitedly debated subjects at every constitutional conference. At the penultimate stage before independence, the Crown in the most formal and solemn manner takes the step of abandoning its constituent powers. If it is correct that there remain all the time up the sleeve of the Crown plenary powers conferred by the Act of 1887 to do that which the Crown has solemnly renounced, the whole procedure of abandoning the reserved power becomes a meaningless charade, and the political consequences might be startling. In particular, if the Act of 1887 enables the Crown to make any laws it likes for a settled colony with a representative government, the inclusion and later abandonment of powers of the kind reserved by section 63 of the Gambia Constitution of 1960 becomes pointless.

(2) *The strictly legal result.* If the Act of 1887 confers plenary powers on Her Majesty in Council, that Act is coextensive with the royal prerogative, and there would be nothing which the Crown could do in a settled colony under the prerogative which it could not also do under the Act. It would follow from the decision in *Attorney-General* v. *De Keyser's Royal Hotel Ltd.*[10] that the Act has swallowed up the prerogative; and one may ask rhetorically what the Crown has been doing for nearly 100 years in making, in constitutional instruments which govern the future of millions of people, these solemn reservations of powers appropriate only to the continuing existence of a prerogative power.

If, however, the court accepts that the Act of 1887 permits only the grant of non-representative legislatures, that the grant of representative legislatures is still an act of the prerogative, and that the words in section 6 of that Act "constituted otherwise than by virtue of this Act" should be construed as meaning "constituted under the prerogative," so that the Act of 1887 does not apply to the Gambia, that would give some meaning to the careful reservation of powers in the constitutional instruments. But as Her Majesty abandoned her constituent prerogative powers in relation to the Gambia in the 1962 Constitution, the Order of 1963 would still be void as purporting to change section 28 of that Constitution by the exercise of a constituent power. [British Rule and Jurisdiction Beyond the Seas, by Sir Henry Jenkyns (1902), p. 4, on the purpose of the **[286]**

[10] [1920] A.C. 508; 36 T.L.R. 600, H.L.(E.).

Act of 1887 and its predecessors; and *Ex parte Mwenya*[11]* were referred to.]

It is not open to the plaintiffs to raise any point in relation to the Foreign Jurisdiction Act, 1890, for acts done by Her Majesty in foreign territory are acts of State not justiciable in these courts: *Nyali Ltd.* v. *Attorney-General, per* Denning L.J.[12]*

[RUSSELL L.J. If there had been an Act of the Parliament at Westminster authorising the Queen in Council to do what has been done by the Validation Order in Council, it could not be challenged in these courts?]

That is so; but the court has jurisdiction to make a declaration, against the Crown, that this Order in Council is ultra vires.

In *Sammut* v. *Strickland*[13]* it was held that the United Kingdom Parliament could take away the representative government which had been granted to Malta; but that decision is distinguishable from the present case, for here the continuing policy is that the Gambia shall have representative government, though the House of Representatives is defectively constituted. *Sammut* v. *Strickland*[13]* is not authority for the proposition that after representative institutions have been granted by law and that law has not been revoked, the prerogative remains as a kind of barrel of power into which one can dip in order to put right any serious trouble that may arise in the future. So to hold would go a long way towards destroying the doctrine laid down in *Campbell* v. *Hall*[14]*: see also *Re Lord Bishop of Natal*,[15] which decided that once representative institutions had been established in a settled colony, the Crown had only the same powers in relation to that colony as it has in the United Kingdom. [*Kielley* v. *Carson-Kent*[16] was also referred to.]

If the reservation of powers in constitutional instruments has any meaning, they are clearly reservations of the prerogative power; and if there is still a prerogative existing which has not been swallowed up by the Act of 1887, the problem for the court will be to define the area of distinction between the prerogative power and the powers under the Act. If the main submissions made on this appeal are rejected, it is suggested that such an area of distinction might be found by holding that while it is permissible to legislate with retrospective effect when exercising **[287]** the prerogative power, it is not permissible to do so when exercising the statutory powers under section 5 of the British Settlements Act, 1887.

[LORD DENNING M.R. Section 5 provides that the Queen in Council may "alter" or "revoke." Prima facie that includes power to legislate with retrospective effect.]

But on the ordinary canons of construction the law hesitates long before implying a power to legislate with retrospective effect. Though in 1964 we have become used to legislation having retrospective effect, it would have been regarded with horror in 1887 and if power to legislate retrospectively was intended, one would expect section 5 to have so provided by express words. [*Chenard & Co.* v. *Joachim Arissol*[17]; *West* v. *Gwynne*[18]; *Re Athlumley, Ex parte Wilson*[19]; and Maxwell on the Interpretation of Statutes, 11th ed. (1962), p. 204, were also referred to.]

Sir Peter Rawlinson Q.C., S.-G., Sir Kenneth Roberts-Wray Q.C. and *Nigel Bridge* for the Crown. The sin, vice, or mischief of which the plaintiffs complain in these proceedings is the erroneous act of registering officers in certain constituencies in the protectorate who, in excess of zeal, went to the labour of preparing a full new register instead of merely, and with less labour, revising the old. Once the mistake had been established in the test action in the courts

[11] [1960] 1 Q.B. 241, 305; [1959] 3 W.L.R. 747; [1959] 3 All E.R. 525, C.A.
[12] [1956] 1 Q.B. 1, 14; [1955] 2 W.L.R. 649; [1955] 1 All E.R. 646, C.A.
[13] [1938] A.C. 678; 54 T.L.R. 1080; [1938] 3 All E.R. 693, P.C.
[14] 1 Cowp. 204.
[15] (1865) 3 Moo.P.C.(N.S.) 115.
[16] (1842) 4 Moo.P.C. 63.
[17] [1949] A.C. 127; 65 T.L.R. 72, P.C.
[18] [1911] 2 Ch. 1; 27 T.L.R. 444, C.A.
[19] [1898] 2 Q.B. 547.

of the Gambia, only two alternatives were open to remedy the situation: (1) an Act of the Parliament at Westminster; or (2) an Order by Her Majesty in Council—the Order which was in fact made. The possibility of new elections has been exhausted. The issue for the court is the validity of that Order in Council, which recites that it is made "by virtue of powers vested in Her Majesty in Council by the Acts of 1887 and 1890" and "all other powers remaining in her in that behalf." No new problem arises from the fact that the Gambia is composed of a settled colony and a protectorate in light of the decision of Wilberforce J. in *Buck* v. *Attorney-General*[20]* as to the meaning of "otherwise in Her Majesty vested." The statutory powers are contained in the two Acts; the third "power" is included merely to cover the possibility that a settled colony may at some time have acquired a portion of land which was not settled territory and in respect of which a prerogative power may be necessary. **[288]**

Where, as here, there has been integration of a settled colony and a protectorate, the powers vested in Her Majesty in Council by the Acts of 1887 and 1890 are sufficient to justify the making of the Validation Order of 1963. It has been conceded that the Act of 1890 cannot assist the plaintiffs. The question for the court, therefore, is whether what has been done has been validly done in exercise of the powers conferred by sections 2, 3 and 5 of the Act of 1887. Section 5 provides that "it shall be lawful for Her Majesty . . . in Council . . . to make . . . alter and revoke Orders in Council." That enabled Her to legislate in the form in which Her Majesty in fact legislated in this case. The effect of the Act is that where the Queen in Council has established a representative legislature in a settled colony, Her Majesty retains to herself power to legislate.

[HARMAN L.J. But not to amend the constitution; for if that were possible there would be no significance in abandoning in 1962 the first of the powers reserved in the 1960 Constitution.]

Under the Act of 1887 Her Majesty can do everything.

[HARMAN L.J. Then *Campbell* v. *Hall*[21]* is a dead letter?]

Campbell v. *Hall*[21] was concerned with conquered territory. It is not authority for the proposition that the Crown could not amend the constitution of a representative legislature. Under the Act of 1887 Her Majesty is given power to do everything there set out, and under it Her Majesty will have power to legislate in the future.

[HARMAN L.J. Then why all these elaborate reservations?]

The reasons, which it is hoped will not sound too jejune, are that where there is an Order in Council setting up a constitution for territories new to constitutions and political development, the constitutional instrument does recite that there are such powers still remaining in the Queen in Council.

[HARMAN L.J. So the Crown submits that after the grant of the 1962 Constitution Her Majesty retained a perfectly general power to revoke or amend the constitution under the Act? If I were a Gambian I should be rather surprised if I were told that.]

It was not disguised from the Gambia that this power to alter the constitution was retained.

[LORD DENNING M.R. I can understand a limited power to put right what has gone wrong; but surely once it has been put right the power to interfere would be gone?]

The Queen in Council is still exercising that power: see the **[289]** new Constitution Order of 1963 [S.I. 1963, No. 1629] laid before Parliament on October 23, 1963.

[RUSSELL L.J. Then on any footing this abandonment of the reserved powers is so much waste paper. I should have thought that by the 1962 Constitution the Crown abandoned its prerogative right to legislate on constitutional matters and can now only rely on the Act of 1887.]

The Crown relies on the Act as opposed to the prerogative and the reserved powers.

[20] [1964] 3 W.L.R. 850; [1964] 2 All E.R. 663.
[21] 1 Cowp. 204.

Salmon L.J. held that the Validation Order of 1963 was the exercise of a constituent power under the Act of 1887. There is no cross-notice of appeal against that holding, but leave is now sought to submit that this was not the exercise of a constituent power but was legislation for the peace, order and good government of the colony, which was expressly reserved under section 74 of the 1962 Constitution. The test whether a provision is constituent or for peace, order and good government is whether such a provision could be revised or altered; and electoral machinery can be altered. It is really no more than transitional machinery in force for the time being in Gambia.

The Crown's submissions may be summarised as follows: (1) The powers exercised in making the Validation Order of 1963 were the powers conferred by the Act of 1887. (2) If the Order was made in exercise of the prerogative, then it is submitted that where a situation has arisen through a mistake by civil servants such that an intended grant of representative government has wholly failed, there is and must be power remaining under the prerogative to put the matter right; and (3) if this Order was made in exercise of prerogative powers, it was in any event not constituent legislation but legislation for peace, order and good government reserved under the 1962 Constitution.

Finally, on the retrospective effect of the Order in Council, Her Majesty in Council is a colonial legislature and as such has plenary power to legislate, including the power to make laws with retrospective effect: see *Rex* v. *Kidman*[22]; and the Act of 1887 also gives power to legislate retrospectively by prerogative instrument.

Finer Q.C. replied.

LORD DENNING M.R. Towards the westernmost point of the bulge of Africa, there is the little Colony of the Gambia. It **[290]** was settled by the English a couple of centuries ago. It was, I believe, the earliest settlement on the West Coast. Its principal town is Bathurst. This little colony is, in constitutional law, a settled colony. It has from the beginning been one of the possessions of the British Crown. The Crown exercises its jurisdiction over the colony either under the prerogative powers of the Crown or under the British Settlements Act of 1887. If the Crown exceeds its jurisdiction over the colony, its conduct can be challenged in these courts.

Stretching inland from the Colony is the Protectorate of the Gambia. This is a territory some 200 miles in length on either side of the River Gambia. It is not a possession of the British Crown, but it has been under its protection for over 100 years. The Crown exercises its jurisdiction over the Protectorate by virtue of its exercise in fact, coupled with the Foreign Jurisdiction Act, 1890. Its jurisdiction over the Protectorate is in the eye of the law complete, because it cannot be challenged in any court of law. It is an Act of State: see *Nyali Ltd.* v. *Attorney-General.*[23]*

The Crown has for many years administered the Colony and Protectorate together. It has done so by means of a governor and a nominated council. There was for a long time no elected assembly. In recent years, however, steps have been taken towards representative government and thence self-government with the ultimate objective perhaps of independence. Orders in Council have been made providing for a constitution consisting of the governor, the executive council, and an elected assembly. We are here concerned with the existing assembly which is called the House of Representatives. Were the members of it validly elected or not?

Under the 1962 Constitution, contained in the Gambia (Constitution) Order in Council [S.I. 1962, No. 826], the House of Representatives was to consist of a Speaker; the Attorney-General; 36 elected members, of whom seven were to be elected for the Colony, 25 for the Protectorate and four elected by the head chiefs; and two nominated members. In holding the elections the registering officers were to use the register of voters prescribed by section 28 (3) of the Order

[22] (1915) 20 C.L.R. 425.
[23] [1956] 1 Q.B. 1; [1955] 2 W.L.R. 649; [1955] 1 All E.R. 646, C.A.

in Council. These were registers compiled in accordance with the local ordinances of 1959 and 1961. According to these ordinances the registers for the Protectorate ought to have been compiled in this way: during the month of **[291]** May, 1959, a list of voters should have been compiled for every town and village in the Protectorate: and in the year 1961 the lists so compiled should have been revised by deleting or adding names as required. The list so compiled in 1959 and revised in 1961 should have been certified by the registering officer by January 16, 1962. Then it would be available as a valid register of voters for the electors for the 1962 election.

Unfortunately the machinery, so provided by the ordinances, was not strictly complied with. The registering officers for the Protectorate compiled the list of voters satisfactorily in 1959. But in 1961, instead of revising that list as they should have done, they compiled a new list for the Protectorate altogether, and in 1962 they certified that new list as the register of voters. It may have been a better list by being newly compiled. But it was not the prescribed list. Hence all the trouble, as I will show.

On April 27, 1962, the 1962 Constitution came into operation. In May, 1962, elections for the Protectorate were held on the basis of the new 1961 register. Members were returned for the House of Representatives and acted as such. But then someone discovered the mistake. The wrong list of voters had been used. It should have been, *not the new 1961 register, but the old 1959 register as revised*. Thereupon one of the candidates, Mr. Mamadi Sabally, who had been unsuccessful in the election, brought an action in the High Court of the Protectorate against the registering officer, Mr. Coghill. He sought a declaration that the register of voters, which had been used at the election, was invalid. The Chief Justice of the Gambia [Wiseham C.J.] on December 24, 1962, dismissed the claim; but the Gambia Court of Appeal on March 16, 1963, allowed the appeal and declared that the register was invalid. This decision was accepted as correct by the Governor and by Her Majesty's Government in the United Kingdom. The result was that the election of the 25 members was invalid. There were no members validly elected for the Protectorate. So the House of Representatives was never properly constituted. At any rate, it could not act. The quorum was 14 members besides the Speaker, and no quorum could be achieved with 25 members absent.

The Crown acted quickly to put things right. The decision of the Gambia Court of Appeal was given on March 16, 1963. Ten weeks later, on May 30, 1963, a new Order in Council was passed [S.I. 1963, No. 1051] called the Gambia (Validation) Order in Council. It retrospectively validated the register. It did so by saying that the new 1961 register (which was in fact **[292]** certified and used for the Protectorate) should be deemed to have been lawfully compiled in respect of the election for the year 1962 and should not be open to challenge. This Validation Order was expressed to concern the Protectorate only: for it was only the election of the 25 members for the Protectorate which was invalid. But nevertheless the Order indirectly affected the Colony as well: for so long as the 25 members for the Protectorate were unseated, there was no House of Representatives at all, not even for the Colony.

The plaintiffs in this action now challenge the validity of the Validation Order. One of the plaintiffs, Mr. Sabally, is a candidate who was defeated in the 1962 elections for the Protectorate. The other, Mr. E. D. N'Jie, is a candidate who was successful. If this challenge to the Order in Council had concerned the Protectorate only, they could not have challenged it in the courts at all. But as the Order indirectly concerned the Colony also, they can, I think, and they do, challenge it in these courts. They seek a declaration that the Validation Order itself is ultra vires, invalid, null and void and of no effect in law.

This involves a consideration of the powers under which the Crown enacted the Orders in Council. When Her Majesty made the Orders in Council, She did so in each case expressly "by virtue and in exercise of the powers vested in Her by the British Settlements Acts, 1887 and 1945 and by the Foreign Jurisdiction Act, 1890 and of all other powers enabling Her in that behalf." There are only two bases on which the Crown can be said to have enacted a constitution for the Colony. One is by virtue of the prerogative. The other is by virtue of the British Settlements Act, 1887. I will consider these in order: (1) *By virtue of the prerogative*: The plaintiffs say that it is a general principle of constitutional law that when the Crown, by virtue of its prerogative, grants to a colony a representative legislature, it thereby deprives itself of any right to legislate for the colony thereafter, except in so far as it expressly reserves such power. It impliedly renounces all those powers which are not reserved. They rely for this principle on the famous case of *Campbell* v. *Hall.*[24]* The plaintiffs then point out that in an earlier Order in Council made in 1960 [S.I. 1960, No. 701] granting a constitution to the Gambia, the Crown expressly reserved a power to alter that 1960 constitution in these two specific reservations in section 63: "(1) Her Majesty hereby reserves to Herself, power, with the **[293]** advice to Her Privy Council to revoke or amend this Order. (2) Nothing in this Order shall affect the power of Her Majesty in Council to make laws from time to time for the peace, order and good government of the Gambia." The first reservation in that 1960 Order authorised the Queen to revoke or alter the constitution. The second reservation authorised the Queen to enact laws for the Gambia so long as they did not impinge on the constitution: see *Chenard & Co.* v. *Joachim Arissol.*[25]

But the plaintiffs then go on to point out that when the Order in Council was made in 1962 granting a new 1962 constitution to the Gambia, the first reservation was omitted and only the second reservation was retained: see section 74. That meant, they say, that the Crown impliedly renounced any power to revoke or alter the constitution, as set out in the 1962 Order; and the Crown retained only the right to enact laws so long as they did not interfere with the constitution. The plaintiffs then go on to say that in making this Validation Order, the Crown attempted to alter the constitution, and that is the thing they renounced. They cannot do, therefore, what they have attempted to do.

I think that there is one short answer to the whole of this argument. The doctrine of *Campbell* v. *Hall*[26]* must be read subject to the qualification indicated in *Sammut and Another* v. *Strickland.*[27]* The implied renunciation of the Crown only applies while the legislative institutions are in existence and capable of functioning. If the legislative institutions set up by the Crown cease to exist, or are for any reason incapable of functioning, then the Crown must be able to resolve the impasse. It can in that event resort to its prerogative power to amend the constitution or set up a new one. So here when it turned out that there was no House of Representatives (because of the invalidity of the elections) the Crown could resort to its prerogative power to put the matter right. It could legislate itself to validate the elections by means of the Order in Council; and it could do so retrospectively.

(2) *By virtue of the British Settlements Act*, 1887: But in truth I think the plaintiffs are wrong in saying that when the Crown granted the constitution of 1962 to the Colony, it did so by virtue of the prerogative power. On the contrary, it did so, I think, by virtue of the statutory power contained in the British Settlements Act, 1887. This is a point of some importance and **[294]** needs some consideration of the position of a settled colony like the Gambia.

When English folk settled in a colony (as distinct from conquest or cession) they took their English law with them, that is to say, the common law and the statute law as it existed at that time. They took with them, too, the Crown prerogative, in this sense, that the Crown could give them a representative legislature in which they elected their own representatives: but the Crown could not impose on the settlers a legislature on which they were not represented. It could not impose on them a non-representative legislature. The usual practice in a settled colony was for the Crown to issue a Royal Commission providing for a governor and council and an assembly elected by the people. The assembly, with the consent of the governor and council, had legislative authority over the colony. A

[24] (1774) 1 Cowp. 204.
[25] [1949] A.C. 127; 65 T.L.R. 72, P.C.
[26] (1774) 1 Cowp. 204.
[27] [1938] A.C. 678; 54 T.L.R. 1080; [1938] 3 All E.R. 693, P.C.

good instance will be found set out in the case of Newfoundland, which was a settled colony, in *Kielley* v. *Carson-Kent.*[28] Thenceforward the legislative authority could only be exercised by the assembly or by any Act of Parliament of Great Britain: see the case of Jamaica discussed by Lord Mansfield in *Campbell* v. *Hall.*[29]* There were, however, some settled colonies for which a representative legislature was unsuitable. The population was too sparse: the inhabitants too little educated. Such were the Falkland Islands and the colonies on the West Coast of Africa, including the Gambia. For these colonies it was desirable to set up in those days a non-representative legislature; and as the Crown could not do it by its prerogative for a settled colony, Parliament intervened so as to enable the Crown to do it by statutory authority. It passed Acts in 1843 and 1860, which were repealed and replaced by the British Settlements Act, 1887. Under these Acts the Crown had power to, and did, appoint a governor to legislate with a nominated council but no elected assembly. This was the form of legislature in the Colony of the Gambia until recent times. It was a non-representative legislature constituted under the British Settlements Act, 1887, and nothing else.

Although the Act of 1887 was passed so as to enable the Crown to set up non-representative legislatures, nevertheless it was expressed in wide comprehensive terms, such as to enable the Crown to set up representative institutions as well. The terms of the statute (especially section 2) cover the pre-existing prerogative power (to set up representative legislatures) and also **[295]** the new power which did not exist before (to set up non-representative legislatures). It seems to me that this new wide statutory power swallowed up the old prerogative power. Thenceforward there was clearly no object in the Queen in Council exercising the prerogative power. The statutory power covered all, and more than all, covered by the prerogative. As Lord Sumner said in *Attorney-General* v. *De Keyser's Royal Hotel*[30]: "There is no object in dealing by statute with the same subject-matter as is already dealt with by the prerogative, unless it be either to limit or at least to vary its exercise, or to provide an additional mode of attaining the same object."

Some question was raised whether the Gambia Colony was a "settlement" within the Act of 1887. It clearly was. It was a British possession. It had not been acquired by cession or conquest. It was not within the jurisdiction of the legislature of a British possession, save for the legislature constituted by virtue of the Act. It was, therefore, within the Act; and under that Act the jurisdiction extended to the Protectorate also: see *Buck and Others* v. *Attorney-General.*[31]*

Once it is held, as I think it should be held, that, in granting the new constitution in 1962 to the Gambia, the Crown acted under the statutory powers contained in the Act of 1887, the rest is clear. Section 5 of the Act of 1887 says that "It shall be lawful for Her Majesty the Queen in Council from time to time to make, and when made to alter and revoke, Orders for the purposes of this Act." Under this section it is clear that the Queen in Council can amend the constitution from time to time as she thinks best. Indeed, she has recently done so in an important amendment in 1963 [S.I. 1963, No. 1629] which has made express provision in the Gambia for the protection of human rights and the freedom of the individual.

Mr. Finer says that section 5 gives the Queen in Council power to alter the orders prospectively but not retrospectively. I can see no basis for this limitation. I agree with Salmon L.J. that "the powers intended to be vested in the Crown were at least as plenary as any that might be vested in the legislature. Plenary legislative powers include the power to legislate retrospectively, seldom though such a power in practice may be used."

I come to the conclusion, therefore, that the Crown exercised its jurisdiction within the Gambia Colony under the British **[296]** Settlements Act, 1887, and that its jurisdiction thereunder is amply sufficient to warrant the Validation Order of 1963. I would therefore dismiss the appeal.

28 (1842) 4 Moo.P.C.C. 63, 84-86, P.C.
29 (1774) 1 Cowp. 204, 212-214.
30 [1920] A.C. 508, 561; 36 T.L.R. 600, H.L.(E).
31 [1964] 3 W.L.R. 850; [1964] 2 All E.R. 663.

HARMAN L.J. I confess to moving uneasily in the avenues of constitutional law. Nonetheless I should have listened with less dis-ease to this appeal had I been able to appreciate what end it was intended to serve. The first appellant was a defeated candidate in the elections which the Gambian Court of Appeal has found to be unconstitutionally held. If his object in attacking the order which rectified the mistake had been to oblige the authorities to hold new elections in which he might hope to be more successful, I could at least have understood his point: but it was conceded during the argument that no new elections could be called to put the matter right, and that the only recourse was to an Act of the Imperial Parliament which it was admitted could rectify the blunder. This expedient would confirm the position as it is and leave the first plaintiff precisely where he stands today.

As to the second plaintiff, he was successful in the elections declared void and confirmed by the order he now attacks, so he apparently is seeking to destroy his own position. We were assured by plaintiffs' counsel that the plaintiffs' motive was pure zeal for the rule of law. This I take with "a pinch of salt." Their apparent object is to produce chaos and thus set back the progress towards that independence which I should have supposed every politically minded Gambian is set on achieving.

However that may be, I am of opinion that the course taken by the Order in Council of 1963 is an effective one and that there is no substance in this appeal. My reasons for this view admit of concise statement. In 1959 the Colony and the Protectorate of the Gambia had progressed some way towards responsible government, but there is no doubt that Her Majesty in Council had extensive reserved powers. These were, first, the Royal Prerogative giving the right to proceed by letters patent or by Order in Council, and, secondly, as to the Protectorate, the Foreign Jurisdiction Act, 1890, and as to the Colony, the British Settlements Act, 1887.

In 1960, by the Order in Council of that year, a step forward in the establishment of a responsible legislature was made. Her Majesty, by section 63, expressly reserved two powers: (1) to revoke or amend the Order; (2) to legislate for the peace, order and good government of the Gambia, that is to say, the Colony **[297]** combined with the Protectorate. I take it that (*a*) reserved the prerogative right and (*b*) the legislative rights of Her Majesty. In 1962 a further step forward was taken but in this Order the only expressly reserved power was (*b*) above. It is on this point that the appellants really rely. Be it assumed (although I do not necessarily accept it) that not having been expressly reserved, the prerogative power to revoke the order is deemed to have been surrendered, this leaves the legislative power outstanding, and it is under this that the Order of 1963 is expressed to be made. So the judge held, and he seems to me to have been right.

What are the arguments against? First, a point not taken below, that the Act of 1887 does not, having regard to its definition section, apply to the Colony. This is a false point. It is not the fact that the creation of the new state is due entirely to the prerogative: only so would the Act of 1887 not apply. Secondly, it is said that the Order of 1962 is a constitutional instrument which may not be interfered with by the legislative powers. Assuming for this purpose that what are called constituent powers can only be subject to the prerogative, I am of opinion that section 28 (3) of the Order of 1962, with which alone it is sought to interfere, has nothing to do with constitutional matters: it deals merely with the machinery for setting up voting registers and has no concern at all with the constitution or membership of the House of Representatives. It is exactly the sort of matter with which ordinary legislation would concern itself. The Order of 1963 affects to be made under the Foreign Jurisdiction Act, 1890 (which, and not the British Settlements Act, applies to the Protectorate), and in my opinion is an exercise of the legislative power reserved by the Order of 1962.

This assumes that the judge was right, as I think he was, in the only point he decided, namely, that the Order of 1963 has retrospective effect. Grant that Her Majesty in Council had effectually reserved her rights to legislate, then it seems to me to follow that Her Majesty in Council is a legislature and, like any other legislature in the Commonwealth, has a right to legislate retrospectively. I would therefore dismiss the appeal.

RUSSELL L.J. I do not myself criticise the attitude of the appellants in this litigation. They appear to take a purist's stand to no obviously useful purpose; but they may have, or think they have, some wider grievance or complaint or purpose beyond the mere legal façade, and it is only the legal façade that can be presented to us. **[298]**

The Crown bases its case for the validity of the Validation Order in Council of 1963 primarily on the powers conferred by the Act of 1887, and in so doing accepts that what was done affects the settled colony of the Gambia, though both the defect and the attempted cure relate directly only to elections in the Protectorate, to which territory the Act of 1887 has no application. This is right: for the point at issue was whether there ever was a properly elected quorum sufficient for the House of Representatives, which was to be as much part of the legislature for the Colony as for the Protectorate.

At the trial it was accepted that the situation was covered by the Act of 1887, but it was argued that section 5 of that Act, in giving power to alter or revoke, should not be construed as conferring a power to do so with retroactive effect. Salmon L.J. held otherwise. For my part I entirely agree with him. Section 5 is dealing with a legislative body—the Queen in Council—which in its legislative capacity is naturally to be expected to have the ability to introduce retroactive legislation. I see no ground for construing section 5 in those circumstances as not conferring power to introduce by alteration a retroactive result.

Before this court, however, further arguments were put forward. It was pointed out that in the 1960 Order in Council there was reserved a power to the Queen in Council to revoke or amend it, and it was also provided that nothing in the Order in Council should affect the power of Her Majesty in Council to make laws from time to time for the peace, order and good government of the Gambia. Moreover, though the latter provision was found in the 1962 Order in Council, the former had been markedly dropped. These provisions, it was argued, can have related only to prerogative powers; so that it appeared that the Crown, notwithstanding that it purported expressly to be acting by virtue and in exercise of the powers vested in the Crown by (inter alia) the Act of 1887, must have considered the prerogative power to be alive. This was ground for asserting that the powers given by the Act of 1887 must be different from the prerogative power, since if co-extensive the prerogative would have been superseded by the Act of 1887. The end of the argument was that the difference must lie either in holding that the Act of 1887 was limited to the operation of conferring on the Crown the ability which under the prerogative it lacked, namely, that of imposing on a settled colony a non-representative system of government, or in holding that section 5 did not authorise an Order in Council retroactive in operation. If either was the **[299]** correct conclusion, the Validation Order of 1963 was ultra vires the Act of 1887. I cannot accept that argument. First, an assumption by the Crown cannot alter the construction and effect of the statute. Secondly, the mere fact that a statute, in conferring powers on the Crown which it previously lacked, uses language which embraces also powers which already exist under the prerogative, does not in my view necessarily suspend the prerogative in respect of those latter powers: if, in conferring expressly on the Crown powers within its prerogative, a statute imposes restrictions, limitations, conditions or a required modus operandi, then the prerogative is superseded and the powers cannot be exercised otherwise than subject to such restrictions, limitations or conditions or in accordance with that modus operandi. I do not think the cases establish more than that.

I consider, therefore, that the Validation Order of 1963 was intra vires the Act of 1887. It is complained that if this be so, the dropping from the 1962 Order in Council of the first of the reservations found in the 1960 Order in Council is a farce calculated to mislead. I do not accept that: but even if it were so, the complaint is not a matter of law for this court. For myself I would alternatively have decided this question on a different ground. Suppose it were the case that the 1963 Validation Order in Council must rely for its validity on the exercise of the prerogative, I would still hold it valid. The argument against is that once the Crown in the exercise of its prerogative has conferred on a colony a representative constitution, then, unless it simultaneously reserves power to legislate in relation to the constitution, the prerogative power to do so is gone: and in the 1962 Order in Council, in contrast to the 1960 Order in Council, there was no such reservation. Reference was made to *Campbell* v. *Hall*[32]* and *Sammut* v. *Strickland*.[33]* Let this be so. But in my judgment the ground for this principle must be that a representative constitution has been effectively granted and is not to be whittled down or taken away. In the present case it was finally admitted, after close inspection of the relevant instruments, that the work of supererogation undertaken by the registration officers prior to the 1962 Order in Council, unknown to Her Majesty in Council, had in advance made the representative constitution envisaged and intended by the Order in Council a nullity. It was wholly ab initio unworkable. The 1962 Order in Council conferred on the Gambia no representative constitution at all. **[300]** I entirely decline to accept the proposition that an instrument which was relevantly a nullity has this effect on the prerogative. It does not make sense, and I see no reason to declare it to be the law. Nor am I persuaded otherwise by the fact that the impasse which would otherwise exist (assuming that the Act of 1887 was not available) could be avoided by an Act of the Imperial Parliament.

I add finally that I think there is much to be said for the view that the 1963 Validation Order in Council is not really to be regarded as an exercise of what is referred to as a constituent power. Section 28 is in its relevant parts really a transitional provision: it deals with the mechanics of the production of electoral lists in the Protectorate: these mechanics are committed by the 1962 Order in Council to the local legislature and are not, so to speak, enshrined in the constitution. But I need not enlarge further on that subject. In the result I agree that the appeal fails.

Appeal dismissed with costs.
Leave to appeal refused.

Solicitors: *Bryden & Williams; Treasury Solicitor.*

[32] (1774) 1 Cowp. 204.
[33] [1938] A.C. 678.

2

ANNEXATION AND CESSION

DON JOHN FRANCIS DOUGLAS LIYANAGE AND OTHERS v. THE QUEEN

([1967] A.C. 259)

October 27, 28, November 1, 2, 3, December 2, 21, 1965: Judicial Committee of the Privy Council (on Appeal from the Supreme Court of Ceylon): Lords Macdermott, Morris of Borth-y-Gest, Guest, Pearce, Pearson.

Ceylon—Constitution—Legislation—Validity—Whether contrary to fundamental principles of justice—Legislation ad hominem and ex post facto directed to particular criminal proceedings—Severance of powers between legislature, executive and judiciary—Whether intra vires—Ceylon Charter of Justice, 1833 *—Courts Ordinance,* 1890 (*Legislative Enactments of Ceylon,* 1956, *Rev. c.* 6) *Evidence Ordinance,* 1896 (*Legislative Enactments of Ceylon, Rev.* 1956, *c.* 14)*— Colonial Laws Validity Act,* 1865 (28 & 29 *Vict. c.* 63), *ss.* 2, 3*—Ceylon* (*Constitution and Independence*) *Orders in Council,* 1946 *and* 1947*—Ceylon Independence Act,* 1947 (11 & 12 *Geo.* 6, *c.* 7), *ss.* 1 (1) (2) (3), *Sch.* 1, 1 (2), 2*— Criminal Law* (*Special Provisions*) *Act, No.* 1 *of* 1962*—Criminal Law Act, No.* 31 *of* 1962.

Colony—Ordinance—Validity—Whether natural justice relevant—Colonial Laws Validity Act, 1865, *ss.* 2, 3.

The Criminal Law (Special Provisions) Act, No. 1 of 1962, passed by the Parliament of Ceylon on March 16, 1962, contained substantial modifications of the Criminal Procedure Code, inter alia, by purporting to legalise ex post facto the detention for 60 days of any person suspected of having committed an offence against the State, by widening the class of offences for which trial without a jury by three judges nominated by the Minister of Justice could be ordered, by allowing arrest without a warrant for waging war against the Queen and prescribing new minimum penalties for that offence and for conspiring to wage war against the Queen and overawe the government by criminal force, and by widening the scope of that offence. The Act also provided for the admission in evidence of certain confessions and statements to the police inadmissible under the Evidence Code.

The Act was expressed to be retrospective to cover an abortive coup d'etat on January 27, 1962, in which the appellants took part, and was to cease to be operative after the conclusion of all legal proceedings connected with or incidental to any offence **[260]** against the state committed on or about the date of the coup or from one year after the date of the commencement of the Act, whichever was later.

The Criminal Law Act, No. 31 of 1962, substituted the Chief Justice for the Minister of Justice as the person to nominate the three judges before whom trial without a jury might be ordered, but left unaffected other provisions of the former Act, including those above summarised.

In April, 1965, the Supreme Court of Ceylon, consisting of three judges nominated by the Chief Justice, convicted the appellants of (1) conspiring to wage war against the Queen; (2) conspiring to overawe, by means of criminal force or the show of criminal force, the Government of Ceylon; and (3) conspiring to overthrow otherwise than by lawful means the Government of Ceylon by law established, and sentenced them to ten years' rigorous imprisonment and forfeiture of all goods, the minimum prescribed by the Act No. 1 of 1962.

On appeal to the Privy Council on the ground that the legislation of 1962 was ultra vires.

Held, (1) that the Acts could not be challenged on the ground that they were contrary to the fundamental principles of justice. The Colonial Laws Validity Act, 1865, which provided that colonial laws should be void to the extent that they were repugnant to an Act of the United Kingdom applicable to the colony but not otherwise and should not be void on the grounds of repugnancy to the law of England, did not leave in existence a fetter of repugnancy to some vague and unspecified law of natural justice; those liberalising provisions were incorporated in, and enlarged by, the Ceylon Independence Act, 1947, of the British Parliament, the joint effect of which, with the Ceylon (Constitution) Order in Council, 1946, was to confer on the Ceylon Parliament the full legislative powers of a sovereign independent state (post, pp. 284-285, 286).

Ibralebbe v. *The Queen* [1964] A.C. 900; [1964] 2 W.L.R. 76; [1964] 1 All E.R. 251, P.C., applied.

Campbell v. *Hall** (1774) 1 Cowp. 204 considered.

(2) That the Acts, directed as they were to the trial of particular prisoners charged with particular offences on a particular occasion, involved a usurpation and infringement by the legislature of judicial powers inconsistent with the written Constitution of Ceylon, which, while not in terms vesting judicial functions in the judiciary, manifested an intention to secure in the judiciary a freedom from political, legislative and executive control and, in effect, left untouched the judicial system established by the Charter of Justice, 1833. The silence of the Constitution as to the vesting of judicial power was consistent with its remaining where it was and inconsistent with any intention that it should pass to or be shared by the executive or the legislature (post, pp. 287-288, 290-292). The Acts were accordingly ultra vires and void, and the convictions could not stand. **[261]**

Bribery Commissioner v. *Ranasinghe* [1965] A.C. 172; [1964] 2 W.L.R. 1301; [1964] 2 All E.R. 785, P.C. applied.

Decision of the Supreme Court of Ceylon (1965) 67 N.L.R. 193 reversed.

APPEAL (No. 25 of 1965) by special leave in forma pauperis from the judgment and sentence of the Supreme Court of Ceylon (Sansoni C.J., Fernando and de Silva JJ.) (April 6, 1965) whereby the appellant, Don John Francis Douglas Liyanage, and ten others were each convicted under section 115 of the Penal Code (as amended by the Criminal Law (Special Provisions) Act, No. 1 of 1962) of three offences: (1) of conspiring to wage war against the Queen; (2) of conspiring to overawe, by means of criminal force or the show of criminal force, the Government of Ceylon; and (3) of conspiring to overthrow otherwise than by lawful means the Government of Ceylon by law established. Each of the appellants was sentenced to ten years' rigorous imprisonment and to forfeit all his property, as required by Act No. 1 of 1962.

1965. October 27, 28. November 1, 2, 3. *E. F. N. Gratiaen Q.C., H. W. Jayewardene Q.C.* (Ceylon), *Dick Taverne Q.C., Walter Jayawardena, Montague Solomon* and *S. J. Kadirgamar* (Ceylon) for the appellants. The appellants were tried for three offences committed in respect of an abortive coup d'etat on January 27, 1962. The Ceylon legislature passed the Criminal Law (Special Provisions) Act, No. 1 of 1962 conferring upon the Minister of Justice the power of nominating three judges to try the appellants (s. 9). The Supreme Court held in *Reg.* v. *Liyanage*[1] that the power given by that section was ultra vires the Constitution on the grounds: (*a*) that the power of nomination conferred on the Minister was an interference with the exercise by the judges of the supreme court of the strict judicial power of the state vested in

[1] (1963) 64 N.L.R. 313.

them by virtue of their appointment in terms of section 52 of the Ceylon (Constitution) Order in Council, 1946, or was in derogation thereof; (*b*) that the power of nomination was one which had hitherto been invariably exercised by the judicature as part of the exercise of the judicial power of the state and could not be reposed in anyone outside the judicature; and (*c*) that the power of nomination conferred on the Minister offended against the cardinal principle that nothing was to be done which created even a suspicion that there had been an improper interference with the course of justice as restated by Lord Hewart in *Rex* v. *Sussex* **[262]** *Justices, Ex parte McCarthy.*[2] The Supreme Court accordingly held that the invalidity of the power conferred by section 9 deprived them of jurisdiction to enter upon a trial of the appellants. Before the Supreme Court the appellants contended that the Constitution recognised a separation of powers of government similar to the constitutions of the United States of America, Australia, Canada, South Africa and India. The Crown contended that no separation of powers existed under the Ceylon constitution, and that, if a separation of powers existed dehors the written constitution, it was a separation on the lines of the British constitution, as Ceylon had been accustomed to that kind of separation throughout British occupation. The judges of the supreme court held that their nomination by the Minister was ultra vires the Constitution and therefore they could not try the case. That judgment held further that a separation of the three powers or functions of government was embodied in the Constitution given by the Ceylon (Constitution) Order in Council, 1946, and that judicial power, in the sense of the judicial power of the state, was vested in the judicature, the established civil courts of the country.

The Criminal Law (Special Provisions) Act, No. 1 of 1962 purported, ex post facto, to create new offences after the acts complained of had been committed, and to alter the rules of evidence and criminal procedure obtaining under the general law at the time when the offences were committed in a context where the intention was manifest to do away with the prohibitions under the general law of certain kinds of evidence, and purporting further to impose enhanced punishments even up to the sentence of death and a compulsory confiscation of property. [Reference was made to sections 4, 5, 6, 11, 12, 17, 19, 21, 36, 37, 38.] Thus the Act swept away the protections given by the general criminal law to all accused persons to ensure them a fair trial.

The appellants and the other accused at the time were all remanded again to custody by those judges, and a new amendment repealing the offending Act was passed in November, 1962 (the Criminal Law Act, No. 31 of 1962) whereby a court properly qualified under the law was appointed by the Chief Justice to try the appellants. The trial commenced on June 3, 1963, and judgment was pronounced on April 6, 1965.

The principal question for determination was whether the ex post facto legislation introduced by the legislature in 1962 especially in order to deal with the trial of the appellants was valid or not. **[263]** This turned upon the language of the Constitution itself which conferred legislative power, and upon the consideration of that language in the light of the status of Ceylon as a Crown Colony, and, in the light of the source from which that legislative power was derived.

Since 1833 the judicial functions were declared by the Charter of 1833 to be for the future entirely separate from the legislature and the executive in regard to the performance of judicial functions. In accordance with the established principles of dispensing justice and in accordance with the judicial oath, which every member of the judiciary takes before entering upon his duties, the judge's duty is to do justice to all men equally. Since 1833, the separation of the judiciary from the legislature was apparent in all legislative enactments which were relevant. It was recognised and further protected by the Ceylon (Constitution) Order in Council, 1946. That Order conferred on the parliament of Ceylon a purely legislative function, something which was in its very nature very much less than the general powers which vested in Britain in a sovereign parlia-

[2] [1924] 1 K.B. 256; 40 T.L.R. 80.

ment. One of the principal reasons for impugning the ex post facto legislation was that it sought under the guise of legislation to direct the judges to try a particular case in a different way from the way in which they would try a similar case in accordance with the general rules of evidence and procedure; and, further, that it sought under the guise of legislation to direct them to impose new punishments and to administer new criminal laws which were not in force at the time.

It was therefore necessary to consider not merely the language of the Constitution itself which conferred legislative power but to consider that language in the light of (1) the status of Ceylon as a Crown Colony until it was granted full independence in 1947; (2) the source from which that legislative power was derived, whether it was derived from an Act of the Imperial Parliament, or from the Crown in the exercise of its prerogative right to legislate in respect of colonies by way of transfer; and (3) what was "law" or what were "laws" in the context of a strictly legislative power. In the case of a conquered or ceded colony one would have regard to the former laws of that colony which continued to have validity after the conquest or cession.

Until 1796, immediately preceding the conquest, Ceylon was a Dutch colony as far as the Maritime Provinces were concerned; while in the centre of Ceylon the Kandyan Kingdom survived as a separate kingdom. The history of the matter was set out in The Laws of Ceylon by Walter Pereira, pp. 1-6. The Dutch **[264]** as the rulers of the Maritime Provinces capitulated on February 15, 1796, and the terms of capitulation were set out in an Instrument.

One of the requests made by the Dutch was: "The citizens and other inhabitants shall be allowed to follow their employments, and enjoy all liberties and privileges as subjects of His Majesty," i.e., of England (Article 19). In accordance with those arrangements the British Proclamation of 1799 adopted the general Roman-Dutch law for certain purposes, in particular, for the administration of justice and police, which was to be "exercised by all courts of judicature, civil and criminal, ministers and ministerial officers according to the laws and institutions that subsisted under the ancient Government of the United Provinces," the Dutch Government.

By a Convention of March 2, 1815, the Kingdom of Kandy which survived the earlier conquest was ceded to England. Subject to the limited operation of special native laws of certain inhabitants of the country, such as Kandyans and Tamils, the Roman-Dutch law was considered and acted upon as the law of the land: The Laws of Ceylon, Pereira, p. 4. From time to time thereafter there had been various Charters of Justice entrusting the Governor of Ceylon as representing the Queen with judicial powers, legislative powers and executive powers. Under his judicial powers the Governor was the final court of appeal in the country. There were some very unpleasant collisions between the Governor, who was invested with judicial powers, and the British judges, who administered justice, and it was in that situation that the Ceylon Charter of Justice, 1833, came into law. It was an historic document because it was the first occasion on which it was decreed that the judicial functions of the judges should be completely separated from the legislative and executive functions of government. Together with the Charter, the Imperial Government sent instructions to the Governor calling upon him to "rigidly adhere to the rules by which the Charter separates the functions of the judges from your own," i.e., the Governor as head of the executive and the legislative authority. Ever since 1833 there had been similar provisions for the separation of the courts as courts of judicature and nothing to indicate at any time that the rule for a separation of those functions was to be altered in any way. In 1946 the judge's functions were given very much greater protection.

The 1946 constitution, whilst retaining the status of Ceylon as a Crown Colony, granted internal self-government. This constitution was laid down by an Order in Council and not by an Act of the Imperial Parliament. It was passed by the Crown in the **[265]** exercise of its legislative powers. Part III, section 7 provided for a legislature. Section 29 provided for the power to make laws for peace, order and good government but so as not to discriminate against races or religions. That express prohibition against discrimination as far as racial or religious groups were concerned applied equally to discriminating against individuals by legislative enactment. Section 52 dealt with the functions of the judicature. The holding of office at will was abolished and the judges of the Supreme Court were given the same protection as the judges in England had enjoyed for many years. There was a special protection with regard to the minor judiciary, also to assist them in the preservation of their independence; they were placed under the Judicial Service Commission upon whose recommendation the Governor would act in dealing with matters of appointments, transfer, dismissal and disciplinary control (s. 55). Section 56 expressly made it a criminal offence to interfere with the Judicial Service Commission. This constitution was intended for an interim period until the grant of full independence.

The law, which defined the Crown's powers of legislation in regard to conquered and ceded colonies and the limits of those powers, was laid down by Lord Mansfield in *Campbell* v. *Hall.*[3]* The sixth proposition laid down by Lord Mansfield was important for the purpose of this case, because it laid down that when the King passed legislation by virtue of his prerogative, his legislative powers were subordinate to the powers of the Imperial Parliament of which he formed a part, and, further, that in regard to a conquered colony he could not make any new law contrary to fundamental principles. One of the questions in this case was what were those fundamental principles which limited the legislative powers of the Crown and which did not in any way limit the powers of the Imperial Parliament which, within its own sphere, was quite supreme. Accordingly, so far as the Crown and the conquered or ceded colony were concerned, no law contrary to fundamental principles could survive the conquest, and no laws contrary to fundamental principles could be enacted by the Crown in the exercise of its subordinate legislative authority. In *Abeyesekera* v. *Jayatilake*[4] the Judicial Committee accepted *Campbell* v. *Hall*[5]* as the leading case on the question of the legislative powers of the Crown. All retrospective legislation is not bad, it is perfectly valid in certain circumstances to grant a person an indemnity even **[266]** retrospectively; but in the present case ex post facto legislation in regard to criminal matters was contrary to fundamental principles where it sought to make persons liable to punishment for new crimes and to higher punishment for old crimes, and to pass legislation which purported to deprive them of the protection of the earlier laws ex post facto in order that evidence which at the relevant point of time was inadmissible to prove their guilt should be made retrospectively admissible to secure their conviction in a matter which the legislature had directly in mind: Chitty's Prerogatives of the Crown; *Blankard* v. *Galdy*[6]*; *Fabrigas* v. *Mostyn*[7]*; *Reg.* v. *Picton.*[8] The appellants adopted the arguments of Mr. Nolan in *Reg.* v. *Picton*[8] in so far as he equated the limitations on the power to legislate as far as the Crown was concerned with the power to allow something fundamentally contrary to fundamental principles to continue.

In the Proclamation of 1799 the civilized parts of the principles of Roman-Dutch law were allowed to continue. Reliance was strongly placed on the well-established principles of the Roman-Dutch law as to what in truth "law" and legislation was; the first principle being that there could be no law which was not of general application or of application at least to groups of people in similar circumstances, so that a law against an individual alone, operating with special importance against an individual alone, was not law at all: Voet's Commentary on the Pandects, vol. 1, s. 5, p. 34, s. 11, p. 39; Pereira's Laws of Ceylon, p. 135.

Even if it was very difficult to find a complete and comprehensive definition of what kind of legislation would be contrary to fundamental principles, in the

[3] (1774) 1 Cowp. 204; 98 E.R. 1045.
[4] [1932] A.C. 260, 262, 263.
[5] 1 Cowp. 204.
[6] (1693) 2 Salk. 411; 91 E.R. 356.
[7] (1773) 20 St.T. 82, 179, 180-182.
[8] (1805) 30 St.T. 225, 865, 890, 903, 905, 906, 933, 934, 956; 2 East 195.

average case it was extremely easy to decide in accordance with the accepted notions of justice on which side of the line a particular kind of legislation fell: *Ridge* v. *Baldwin*[9]; *Phillips* v. *Eyre*[10]; *Calder* v. *Bull.*[11]

The words "peace, order and good government" in section 29 had been interpreted to indicate a very conclusive discretion in regard to matters of policy; and, provided the legislative enactment was something which was not against fundamental principles, the question whether it was calculated to promote peace, order and good government was not a matter which was justiciable; **[267]** otherwise there would be a conflict between judges and parliament as to whether something was good for the country or not, and the whole machinery of justice was not appropriate for that consideration. It was quite a different thing to say, and quite wrong to say, that the well-known "peace, order and good government" policy was something which enlarged the power which the Crown had no right to assign at all.

Where the Imperial Parliament transferred a legislative power without words of limitation, then that passed the full plenary powers which the Imperial Parliament could bestow. The same applied to the Queen, save that, in the case of the Queen's legislative powers, she only had power to bestow the limited power which she herself possessed.

Legislation directed against selected individuals or against one individual is not law at all, but an exercise of judicial power or an interference with judicial power, which is equally invalid. The legislature had purported to direct the judges by the terms of the impugned legislation to ignore the general law applicable to the kind of cases similar to the case of the appellants, and to substitute rules as to admissibility of evidence which deprived the appellants of the protection given by the general law to other subjects: Coke's Institutes, vol. 2, p. 46; Blackstone's Commentaries, 2nd ed., vol. 1, p. 44; Schwartz's Analysis of the American Constitution, vol. 1, pp. 116, 117; *Holden* v. *James*[12]; *Vanzant* v. *Waddel*[13]; *Bank of the State* v. *Cooper.*[14]

The Colonial Laws Validity Act, 1865 (28 & 29 Vict. c. 63), provided that a law passed by a colonial legislature was not bad law merely because it was repugnant to the common law of England (s. 3). The Ceylon Independence Order in Council 1947 (Legislative Enactments of Ceylon, Rev. 1956, c. 377) removed the reserve power of the Crown to make any further amendments. The Ceylon Independence Act, 1947, s. 1 (3) provided that the provisions of Schedule 1 to the Act should have effect with regard to the legislative powers of Ceylon. Schedule 1 was of considerable importance. Paragraph 1 (2) provided that no law and no provision of any law made after the appointed day by the parliament of Ceylon should be void or inoperative on the ground that it was repugnant to the law of England. The law of England would include the common law of England. That merely said that any **[268]** Ceylon law made by virtue of the powers vested in the Ceylon parliament under the Ceylon (Constitution) Order in Council, 1946, s. 29, should not be invalidated on the ground that it was repugnant to the common law of England. That did not touch the present case because the invalidity of the impugned legislation was referable not to repugnancy as far as the common law was concerned, but because it proceeded from an exercise of power derived from the subordinate legislative power of the Crown. It was because the Crown's legislative power, which was the source of Ceylon's legislative power, was limited; the Crown had the power to confer only as much as the Crown itself possessed, but no more. If the true position was that the Crown had as unfettered a legislative power as the Imperial Parliament, then the whole of that part of the appellants' argument fell to the ground.

H. W. Jayewardene Q.C. following. The concept of making laws for peace, order and good government existed before 1946 and was given by the Ceylon

[9] [1964] A.C. 40, 64; [1963] 2 W.L.R. 935; [1963] 2 All E.R. 66, H.L.(E.).
[10] (1871) 6 Q.B. 1, 23; 10 B. & S. 1004.
[11] (1798) 3 Dallas 386, 389; 1 Curtis 269, 272.
[12] (1814) 11 Mass. 396, 403, 404; 6 A.D. 174.
[13] (1829) 2 Yerger's Rep. 230, 239.
[14] (1831) 2 Yerger 529, 534-543; 24 A.D. 517.

State Council Order in Council, 1931, and that power was to be found in all Orders in Council from the moment the legislature was established in Ceylon in 1931. It vested in the Governor who acted with the advice and consent of the legislature.

In regard to the grant of independence to all other countries the Queen acted under the powers given to her by the Foreign Jurisdiction Act, 1890. Ceylon was unique in this respect that the Order in Council, 1946, and the Order in Council, 1947, were purely in the exercise of the Queen's prerogative. It was not enacted under the Foreign Jurisdiction Act, 1890, and therefore could not be regarded as having been derived from an Act of Parliament. The Federal Court of Pakistan had drawn the distinction between countries which had been granted their constitutions by Order in Council and made particular reference to the fact that the Crown did not have a power to permit any country to cease to be a Dominion of the Crown; that could be done only by Act of Parliament. The Crown's rights in that respect were controlled by the powers of Parliament: Jennings' Constitutional Problems in Pakistan, 3rd ed. (1954), p. 89; *Wilkinson* v. *Leyland*.[15] The powers of the Crown to legislate were restricted by the terms of the surrender, and the Crown could not, by the exercise of the prerogative, pass laws which were against fundamental principles and against the terms of cession. If the Crown could not do that, then the Crown could not grant a power of legislation under **[269]** article 29 which gave the legislature a wider power than the Crown had.

When interpreting a written constitution one must look at the whole scheme of the legislation. The Order in Council 1946, article 29, gave the Ceylon parliament the power of legislation for the first time; it took away the legislative power that was in the Governor-General under the Order in Council, 1931, and placed it in parliament. By Article 45 the executive power continued to be vested in the Crown and was exercised through the cabinet of ministers who were responsible to parliament. There was no reference at all to the vesting of judicial power in the judicature because that had already vested in the judicature by the Charter of 1833 which set up the Supreme Court, the District Courts and the Courts of Request which were in existence today and derived their authority from the Charter.

The judicial power rested, since 1833, in the courts. Neither the Crown nor the legislature had power to tell the judicature that it should adjudicate in respect of one section of its subjects in a manner different from another section of its subjects. Judicial power implies a totality of power, and, once vested in the courts, it cannot be taken away: *Le Mesurier* v. *Connor*.[16]

The impugned legislation was not legislation applicable to all persons and was ad hominem and therefore ultra vires. [Reference was made to Act No. 1 of 1962 in full: *Ervine's Appeal*[17]; *Lewis* v. *Webb*.[18]] The pith and substance of the impugned legislation was that it only affected the appellants, and as they were entitled to even-handed justice the courts would disregard the impugned legislation as ultra vires the constitution.

Victor Tennekoon Q.C. (Solicitor General of Ceylon), *R. K. Handoo* and *V. S. A. Pullenayegum* for the Crown. The first complaint or information received by the authorities was that the most senior deputy inspector of police and other senior police officers were planning to overthrow or take over the Government, and in that situation the Prime Minister would have been completely foolish, to have entrusted the investigation to the police under the normal procedure provided by the Criminal Procedure Code. That was a situation in which it was impossible to comply with the normal provisions of the criminal law. If the investigation had been handed over to the police, the very people who were **[270]** attempting the coup d'etat would have easily carried out their purposes. The provisions of sections 11, 12, 13, 15 and 17 [LORD MACDERMOTT. We need not hear you on section 17.] while they might be ad hoc, i.e., provided

15 (1829) 2 Peter's S.C.R. 627, 656.
16 (1929) 42 C.L.R. 481, 510.
17 (1851) 16 Penn. S.R. 256, 263, 266, 268.
18 (1825) 3 Maine S.R. 298, 306.

for a particular incident, were not provided for particular persons; they were directed towards the trial of any person or persons who might have been found to have associated in the conspiracy to overthrow the government. The prosecution was free to find other people concerned in the conspiracy. The provisions in the impugned legislation could properly be described as ad hoc, but not ad hominem. The legislation was aimed at those who had taken part in the attempted coup of January 27. It was important to bear in mind that the judgment appealed from was brought from a court which was not constituted under the repealed sections 8, 9 and 10 of Act No. 1 of 1962, which were no longer on the statute book. If it was suggested that those were provisions of law by which the legislature sought to ensure a conviction, they had now disappeared. The law to be examined was the law under which they were tried actually.

It would be extremely dangerous if the courts were given such a wide power to strike down legislation where "fundamental principles" were incapable of definition. If one approached the Constitution in that way, one arrived at a position in which Ceylon had not parliamentary supremacy, but supremacy of the judiciary, where according to its view of fundamental principles it could strike down laws passed by parliament: Berriedale Keith's Sovereignty of the British Dominions, 1929 ed., p. 45; and Responsible Government in the Dominions. 2nd ed. (1928), vol. 1, p. 333.

Quite irrespective of whether the colonial legislation was created by an Act of the Imperial Parliament or by Order in Council, the legislative powers of a colonial legislature were set out in the Colonial Laws Validity Act, 1865. As from 1865, the only two limitations on the legislative powers of a colonial legislature were, first, any limitation in the document granting the constitution, and, secondly, by section 2 of the Colonial Laws Validity Act: *Phillips* v. *Eyre,*[19] *per* Willes J.[20] That was an argument which was not based on Lord Mansfield's dictum in *Campbell* v. *Hall*[21]* of it being contrary to fundamental principles of English law, but was being applied to foreign laws which the parties sought to have applied in England, and the courts refused to apply such a law if they felt it was contrary to natural justice. But the courts **[271]** were not referring to the supremacy of parliament, because it was not a law of the parliament but of some other authority. The Judicial Committee is a civil court and is being asked to strike down a law of the Ceylon parliament on the ground that it is contrary to natural justice. That certainly was never done by the English courts. [Reference was made to *Calder* v. *Bull*[22]; *Li Hong Mi* v. *Attorney-General for Hong Kong*[23]; *Abeyesekera* v. *Jayatilake.*[24]]

The provisions of the Statute of Westminster, 1931, ss. 2 and 3 were almost verbatim those of the Schedule to the Ceylon Independence Act, 1947. There was no difference between the present case and *British Coal Corporation* v. *The King*[25] for the reason that the Colonial Laws Validity Act equated colonial legislation, whether created by Act of Parliament or by the Crown, in the exercise of its prerogative. The Colonial Laws Validity Act was an Act of Parliament, and it was that which said that, if there was a defect in the exercise of the prerogative, the statute was intended to fill up the gap. Section 3 said that no such law should be void or invalid if it was repugnant to English law; it was a very positive statement that hereafter you could never declare a colonial law invalid on the ground that it was repugnant to the law of England. Wheare's Statute of Westminster and Dominion Status, 5th ed. (1953), p. 75, said that the law officers were unable to lay down any rule to fix the dividing line between fundamental and non-fundamental rules of English law. It was for that very reason that in the recital of the Colonial Laws Validity Act it was set out that

19 (1871) L.R. 6 Q.B. 1.
20 Ibid. 23.
21 (1774) 1 Cowp. 204, 209.
22 (1798) 3 Dallas 386.
23 [1920] A.C. 735, 737.
24 [1932] A.C. 260, 262, 264.
25 [1935] A.C. 500, 516, 517; 51 T.L.R. 508, P.C.

the matter was in such great doubt as to what these principles were that it was necessary for the Imperial Parliament to step in itself and to fill in anything lacking in the powers of the colonial legislatures.

By the Ceylon (Constitution and Independence) Order in Council, 1946, the Ceylon (Constitution and Independence) Order in Council, 1947, and the Ceylon Independence Act, 1947, where it was suggested that any law passed by the Ceylon parliament was void or inoperative, it could only be contested on the grounds that it conflicted with section 29 (2) or that it did not follow the manner and form set out in section 29 (4). The effect of the Independence Order in Council and the Independence Act of 1947 was to create a parliament with as wide powers of legislation in its proper field as the British parliament had in any field. The **[272]** main purpose of the Independence Act, 1947, was to ensure that the new parliament to be set up in Ceylon was not to be in any sense a subordinate legislature but was to have the full legislative powers of a sovereign independent state: *Ibralebbe* v. *The Queen.*[26] It is too late to say that Ceylon is to be regarded as having only a colonial legislature. The words "peace, order and good government" in section 29 connoted the widest law-making powers appropriate to a sovereign legislature. But those words did not stand alone, the whole phrase was "Parliament shall have power to make laws for the peace, order and good government of the Island." It was in the context of a grant of legislative power that it had been said in all the cases that it was the grant of legislative power of the greatest amplitude, and it was now too late in the day to take those words separately and to find out their dictionary meaning or their Roman-Dutch meaning. [Reference was made to Voet's Commentaries on the Pandects, Book 1, Tit. 3, ss. 2 and 5; Salmond's Jurisprudence, 11th ed. (1957), p. 38.]

The word "laws" in section 29 certainly included laws which dealt with particular cases, particular individuals, particular geographical areas, particular classes of people. Indeed the statute books were full of particular pieces of legislation which did not apply generally: e.g., Niall MacPherson Indemnity Act, 1954; Mr. Speaker Morrison's Retirement Act, 1959; the War Damage Act, 1965, which interfered with cases pending in court and directed the courts to dismiss claims for war damage compensation, than which nothing could be more particular.

[LORD GUEST. Do you say that in a criminal case a law could say to the judges that they must find the accused guilty? Do you say that you could be incorporated in a law?]

However shocking it might be, the answer was yes. The concept of sovereignty was so wide. In fact it was called an awful power and no doubt it must be exercised with responsibility. In this case, looking at the proceedings and the judgment, the appellants had had one of the fairest trials that any democracy could give to any people.

The appellants submitted an inference was to be drawn from section 29 (2). [LORD McDERMOTT. We need not trouble you about the argument on section 29 (2).]

Lastly, the legislation was attacked on the basis of a separation of powers in the Ceylon constitution; that parliament could not exercise the judicial power of the state, and that this legislation was **[273]** in reality an exercise of such judicial power. The Ceylon constitution was not even remotely supposed to be based on the American constitution. It was clearly stated by Lord Soulbury that the object was to create in Ceylon a constitution similar to the British constitution. In this constitution the formula of separation was not used, there were no words which said that the legislative power was vested in Parliament, the executive power was vested in the Crown, and the judicial power was vested in the Supreme Court. Indeed the only time the word "vested" was used was when it came to deal with the executive power by section 45. The legislative power was given by section 29. There was no reference to the judicial power at all. Part VI, section 52, dealt with the appointment of the Chief Justice and puisne judges of the Supreme Court. Part VI, section 55, dealt with the Judicial Service Commission.

[26] [1964] A.C. 900; [1964] 2 W.L.R. 76; [1964] 1 All E.R. 251, P.C.

[LORD MCDERMOTT. The point made against you was not so much that there was any analogy to be drawn from the United States constitution, but that here, on the true construction of the Ceylon Constitution, one should imply that the judicial functions were intended to be vested in the judiciary. The substance of the reasoning in the first decision of the Supreme Court[27] was that that was so, and that the nomination of the judges was ultra vires because the executive was purporting to usurp its judicial function.]

That decision[27] proceeded upon the statement that the Attorney-General accepted that there was vesting of the judicial power of the state in the judicature, but that was a misunderstanding of what the Attorney-General said, because in other parts of the judgment it is perfectly plain that the Attorney-General did not concede that. By judicial power was meant of course that it was recognized that in every civilised state the state must provide the institutions for the final decision of disputes between subject and subject, and subject and the state. It was vested in those institutions mentioned in Part VI. That submission would not stand one moment's examination for the reason that, if the whole of the judicial power was vested in those institutions alone, the appeal was not competent, because on that argument the board was exercising the judicial power on behalf of the state of Ceylon.

[LORD GUEST. Is not the power of this Board that in respect of Her Majesty's prerogative at present?]

The theory of separation excluded even that kind of extension because the appellants' contention was the Crown in section 45 **[274]** was given only executive power, no other power could be exercised by the Crown, no other function could be exercised and no law passed by parliament could give it to the Crown.

At the time when the Constitution came into operation judicial powers were being exercised by other persons and bodies. In certain areas divorce could be granted by the government officer of the district though he was not a member of the judicature. Other public bodies were exercising what were clearly admitted to be judicial functions. There were Boards who heard income tax appeals which nobody would argue were part of the judicature. They were settling matters appropriate to courts, but nevertheless the Constitution did not deal with them. In fact in one section of the Constitution it said that all such laws should continue to operate. Under the strict application of the theory of separation of powers no body or no person other than those designated in the Constitution could decide a case, whether original or an appeal. It meant then that there was no right of appeal to the Board because the judicial power must be monopolistically exercised by those persons in whom it was vested, in the same way that the legislative power could be exercised by nobody except parliament, just as it was said that the executive power can only be exercised by the Governor-General. Reliance was placed on the passage in Viscount Radcliffe's judgment in *Ibralebbe* v. *The Queen*[28] dealing with the words "peace, order and good government."

Under section 29 (1) the legislative power was as wide as it could be. Section 29 (2) brought in a limitation. Section 29 (4) said that parliament could amend even this Order in Council but must follow a particular manner and form. Thus any law passed by the parliament of Ceylon could be struck down for only two reasons; first, that it was made in contravention of section 29 (2), or secondly, that it purported to amend the Order in Council and therefore must have been passed by a two-thirds majority as required by section 29 (4).

[LORD GUEST. You must say then that the Supreme Court was wrong in holding that the previous law was invalid, and that parliament could do what the Supreme Court said they could not do.]

Yes.

[LORD PEARSON. What is the position if there is an amendment of any of the provisions of this Order? Suppose that in addition to express provisions, there were held to be some implied provisions in this Order in Council.] **[275]**

27 [1965] 64 N.L.R. 313.
28 [1964] A.C. 900, 923.

That was decided in *Bribery Commissioner* v. *Ranasinghe*,[29] where unwittingly parliament had said, in a law passed by a simple majority, that members of bribery tribunals would be appointed by the Governor-General. It conflicted with section 55 which said that judicial officers should be appointed by the Judicial Service Commission. There was a conflict of laws.

[LORD PEARCE. If you are right in saying that there can be interference with the process of the judiciary, although the appointment of the judiciary is protected, there is really no limitation to the lengths to which interference with the judiciary can go. Could you direct all the judges to find all their prisoners guilty by Act of Parliament, or not to find any contravention of the statute void?]

It was necessary to look at the chapter dealing with the judiciary, Part VI, ss. 52, 53, 55. There were no express provisions in this Order in Council which had been contravened by the impugned legislation. The Constitution did not seek to invest the judicial power of the state in a set of institutions. The expression "judicial powers" was not used anywhere in the constitution document. Even if the impugned legislation was regarded as impinging on the exercise of the judicial functions of the Supreme Court, what did it do? It certainly altered the rules of evidence. That all parliaments did. That did not interfere with the provisions which said that judges should be appointed by the government. It did not interfere with their independence. Judges had to administer justice according to the law. There was nothing in the Constitution from which it could be inferred that the legislature was prohibited from interfering with the judge's judicial functions and judicial powers. It would be travelling very far from the mere power to appoint judges to infer that you could not alter rules of evidence and the constitution of the courts. The amplitude of legislative power was sufficient to give power to parliament to pass the legislation which was impugned.

V. S. A. Pullenayegum followed.

E. F. N. Gratiaen Q.C. in reply. The pith and substance of Act No. 1 of 1962 was that there was a legislative plan designed ex post facto to facilitate, if not ensure, the conviction and enhanced punishment of the appellants, and for that purpose parliament purported ex post facto to create new laws or at least to create aggravated crimes by making them greater than they **[276]** were. The laws purported to change ex post facto the punishment to be inflicted under the general law. The legislature had altered in fundamental matters the general rules of evidence which would facilitate the proof of guilt. Parliament had legalised conditions of detention of the appellants while they were awaiting their trial, which were illegal under the general law and which were criticised by the trial judges as disgraceful. This being a criminal case, the appellants complained of the deviation from all the general rules of the general law which were established to ensure a fair trial and to guarantee and give special protection in regard to matters of admissibility of evidence which had been and were on the statute book for over a century. Having regard to the conditions which obtained in Ceylon, the importance of that protection was that the parliament that passed this very enactment themselves recognised the value and importance of those general laws, because those general laws which remained in force for all other offences during the relevant period had been restored in toto and were intended to be restored in toto at the end of this prosecution.

From the days of the Charter in 1833 the separation of judicial functions of the courts from the executive and legislative functions was emphasised as of great importance to the country and to good government. Certainly there was no express provision in the Constitution taking away that fundamental separation which was considered so important in 1833. Where there is an express separation of two parts of the government, and by necessary implication recognition of the separation of the third important compartment of government, then that necessarily gives a limited meaning to the legislative power conferred by section 29. Parliament can make general laws regarding evidence, courts, and so on; and the judges administer those laws. Only criminal laws were in issue here. Having regard to the judicial oath which every judge takes and

[29] [1965] A.C. 172; [1964] 2 W.L.R. 1301; [1964] 2 All E.R. 785, P.C.

to the protection which he recognises as essential under the constitution, his duty in exercising his judicial function is to dispense even handed justice to all men according to the laws of the country. From that it follows that in the exercise of what is merely a legislative power parliament cannot under the guise of what is called legislation either usurp the judicial function of the judges or interfere with them. That is the fundamental distinction which flows from the constitutional position which arises when there is expressly or by necessary implication a complete separation of judicial functions. That submission is basic to the appellants' argument. **[277]**

1965. December 2. LORD PEARCE announced that their Lordships would humbly advise Her Majesty that the appeals should be allowed and that the convictions should be quashed.

1965. December 21. The reasons of their Lordships for allowing the appeal were delivered by LORD PEARCE.

This is an appeal against the judgment and sentence of the Supreme Court of Ceylon. The eleven appellants were each convicted of three offences in respect of an abortive coup d'etat on January 27, 1962. The offences were, first, that they conspired to wage war against the Queen, secondly, that they conspired to overawe by means of criminal force or the show of criminal force the Government of Ceylon and, thirdly, that they conspired to overthrow otherwise than by lawful means the Government of Ceylon by law established. Thirteen other defendants who were tried with the appellants were acquitted. Each of the appellants was sentenced to ten years' rigorous imprisonment and forfeiture of all his property.

The appellants were not tried by a judge and jury in accordance with the normal criminal procedure, but by three judges of the Supreme Court sitting without a jury. The trial was very long and complicated since so many defendants were involved, playing, as was alleged, different parts in the attempted coup. Indeed, the judgment of the court occupies more than 200 pages of the law reports (*Reg.* v. *Liyanage*[30]). The individual appeals raise many points which demand a very extensive consideration of evidence and factual detail.

All the appeals however share a common submission that, whatever be the details of fact or evidence, these convictions must be quashed owing to the invalidity of certain legislation in 1962 passed especially in order to deal with the trial of those persons who partook in the abortive coup. This legislation affected the mode of trial, the offences, the admissibility of evidence and the sentences. It was rightly agreed between the parties that, if this legislation was invalid, the convictions cannot be sustained. Their Lordships therefore decided that before embarking on a detailed investigation of the facts and evidence they should first decide, as a preliminary point, whether the legislation in question was invalid.

The detailed story of the coup d'etat of January 27, 1962, and how it was foiled at the very last moment, is set out in a **[278]** White Paper of the Ceylon Government issued on February 13, 1962. This sets out the names of thirty alleged conspirators and the parts played by them. All the accused were named in it. It alleges that the coup was planned by certain police and army officers with the object of overthrowing the Government and arresting, inter alios, the Parliamentary Secretary for Defence and External Affairs since he could give orders to the Service Commanders which might frustrate the coup. The White Paper stated what the participants intended to do and gave descriptions of their interrogation by Ministers immediately after their arrest. It concluded with the observation:

> "It is also essential that a deterrent punishment of a severe character must be imposed on all those who are guilty of this attempt to inflict violence and bloodshed on innocent people throughout the country for the pursuit of reactionary aims and objectives. The investigation must proceed to its logical end and the people of this country may rest assured that the Government will do its duty by them."

[30] (1965) 67 N.L.R. 193.

From about January 27 all the accused were in custody (except one who gave himself up on July 31, 1962), and they remained thereafter in very rigorous custody. (See *Reg.* v. *Liyanage*[31]). They were questioned both on the night of January 27, 1962, and thereafter while in custody.

On March 16, 1962, there was passed the Criminal Law (Special Provisions) Act, No. 1 of 1962 ("the first Act"). That it was directed towards the participants in the coup is clear. It was given retrospective force and section 19 read:

> "The provisions of this Act, other than the provisions of section 17, shall be deemed, for all purposes, to have come into operation on January 1, 1962:
>
> Provided, however, that the provisions of Part I of this Act shall be limited in its application to any offence against the State alleged to have been committed on or about January 27, 1962, or any matter, act, or thing connected therewith or incidental thereto."

Part I was directed towards legalising the detention of the persons who had been imprisoned in respect of the attempted coup. Under the general criminal law an arrested person has the following protective provisions. Under the Criminal Procedure Code he must without unreasonable delay be taken or sent before a magistrate (s. 36). If he is arrested without a warrant, the reasonable period shall not exceed 24 hours (s. 37). The police **[279]** must report the arrest to the magistrate's court (s. 38). Part I of the first Act legalised ex post facto the detention for 60 days of any person suspected of having committed offences against the State, but the fact of his having been arrested had to be notified to the magistrate's court.

In Part II of the first Act section 4 altered the mode of trial for the offences in question in the following manner. Under section 440A of the Criminal Procedure Code the Minister of Justice could direct that the defendant be tried by three judges without a jury in the case of the offence of sedition and any other offence in which such a mode of trial would be appropriate by reason of civil commotion, disturbance of public feeling or any other similar cause. That clause was amended so as to apply expressly not only to sedition but to any other offence under Part VI of the Penal Code, the part which dealt with offences against the State, the offences with which the appellants were charged. Thus the Minister could direct that the appellants should be tried by three judges without a jury. With this section one may conveniently read section 9 of the first Act, whereby in cases in which the Minister directs a trial by three judges without a jury, the three judges should be nominated by the Minister of Justice, and section 17 which provided for the addition of two more judges to the Supreme Court, such provision to come into operation on such date as the Minister might appoint.

Section 5 retrospectively allowed arrest without a warrant for the offence of waging war against the Queen whereas previously a warrant had been necessary.

Section 6 altered the penalty for an offence under section 114 of the Penal Code, namely for waging war against the Queen, by inserting a minimum punishment of not less than ten years' imprisonment. It altered the penalty for an offence under section 115 of the Penal Code, namely for conspiring to wage war against the Queen and overawe the Government by criminal force, by inserting a minimum punishment of ten years' imprisonment and a forfeiture of all property. It also altered the offence itself. Section 115 had read previously as follows:

> "Whoever conspires to commit any of the offences punishable by the next preceding section, or to deprive the Queen of the sovereignty of Ceylon or of any part thereof, or of any of Her Majesty's Realms and Territories, or conspires to overawe, by means of criminal force or the show of criminal force, the Government of Ceylon, shall be punished with imprisonment of either description which may extend to twenty years, and shall also be liable to fine." **[280]**

[31] 67 N.L.R. 193, 259.

This was amended as follows:

"By the substitution, for all the words from 'Ceylon, shall' to 'to fine,' of the following:

"Ceylon, or conspires to overthrow, or attempts or prepares to overthrow, or does any act, or conspires to do, or attempts or prepares to do any act, calculated to overthrow, or with the object or intention of overthrowing, or as a means of overthrowing, otherwise than by lawful means, the Government of Ceylon by law established, or conspires to murder, or attempts to murder, or wrongfully confines, or conspires or attempts or prepares to wrongfully confine, the Governor-General or the Prime Minister or any other member of the Cabinet of Ministers, with the intention of inducing or compelling him to exercise or refrain from exercising in any manner any of the lawful powers of such Governor-General, Prime Minister or Cabinet Minister, shall be punished with death, or imprisonment of either description which shall extend to at least ten years but shall not extend to more than twenty years, and shall forfeit all his property."

Thus a new offence was added ex post facto to meet the circumstances of the abortive coup.

Section 11 of the first Act provided that the Attorney-General might before or at any stage during the trial pardon any accomplice with a view to obtaining his evidence.

Section 12 altered the laws of evidence in the case of offences against the State. The general criminal law gave the following protections to an accused person.

It provided "No confession made to a police officer shall be proved as against a person accused of any offence" (Evidence Code, s. 25 (1)). It further provided that no confession made by an accused in the custody of a police officer could be proved against him, unless made in the immediate presence of a magistrate (Evidence Code, s. 26 (1)). And it forbade that a confession by one of several co-defendants should be used against the other (Evidence Code, s. 30). It excluded from admission all statements to a police officer in the course of an investigation (Criminal Procedure Code, s. 122 (3)). Further, the onus of proving a confession to be voluntary was on the prosecution.

The first Act swept these protections away. It allowed statements made in the custody of a police officer to be admitted, provided that police officer was not below the rank of Assistant Superintendent (s. 12 (1)). It laid on the accused the burden of proving that a statement made by him was not voluntary (s. 12 [**281**](3)). It removed the effect of sections 25, 26 and 30 of the Evidence Ordinance above referred to (s. 12 (4)).

Section 12 (2) provided:

"In the case of an offence against the State, a statement made by any person which may be proved under subsection (1) of this section" (i.e., whether or not in the custody of a police officer) "as against himself may be proved as against any other person jointly charged with such person if, but only if, such statement is corroborated in material particulars by evidence other than a statement proved under that subsection."

Thus a vital and age old protective rule of evidence was removed.

Section 12 (5) removed the protection of section 122 (3) of the Criminal Procedure Code which prohibited the admission of statements made to a police officer in the course of an inquiry. Section 15 removed the right of appeal to the Court of Criminal Appeal in the case of trials before three judges without a jury.

Finally section 21 provided as follows:

"The preceding provisions of this Act, save and except Part I and section 17, shall cease to be operative after the conclusion of all legal proceedings connected with or incidental to any offence against the State committed on or about 27th January, 1962, or from one year after the date of commencement of this Act, whichever is later, provided that the Senate and the House of

Representatives may, by resolution setting out the grounds therefor, extend the operation of this Act from time to time for further periods not exceeding one year at a time."

In the circumstances the reference to one year after the commencement of the Act cannot be read as indicating any intention that the provisions in question should continue in force beyond the conclusion of the proceedings mentioned. Thus, apart from the increase in the number of judges by section 17 (which obviously could not be temporary), and apart from Part I (which gives the right to arrest and detain persons suspected of having committed an offence against the State and which in itself is limited to any offence against the State alleged to have been committed on or about January 27, 1962, and matters incidental thereto), the whole of these elaborate provisions for altering the nature of the offence, for providing a trial without a jury, and for allowing the admission of otherwise inadmissible statements and confessions is to end when the proceedings based on the coup come to an end. By that time it would have served its purpose **[282]** which would appear to be the fulfilment of the promise implied in the last two sentences of the White Paper, quoted above.

The Minister of Justice then nominated three judges to try the accused. Preliminary objection was taken that the nomination and the section under which it was made were ultra vires the Constitution. In October, 1962, the three learned judges of the Supreme Court in a full and careful judgment in which they examined the relevant authorities unanimously upheld the objection (*Reg.* v. *Liyanage*[32]). They concluded[33]:

"For reasons which we have endeavoured to indicate above, we are of opinion that because

(*a*) the power of nomination conferred on the Minister is an interference with the exercise by the Judges of the Supreme Court of the strict judicial power of the State vested in them by virtue of their appointment in terms of section 52 of the Ceylon (Constitution) Order in Council, 1946, or is in derogation thereof, and

(*b*) the power of nomination is one which has hitherto been invariably exercised by the Judicature as being part of the exercise of the judicial power of the State, and cannot be reposed in anyone outside the Judicature,

section 9 of the Criminal Law (Special Provisions) Act, No. 1 of 1962, is ultra vires the Constitution."

This conclusion was not challenged by an appeal to this board. But in November, 1962, there was passed the Criminal Law Act, No. 31 of 1962 (for convenience referred to as the "second Act"). This repealed those provisions of the first Act which dealt with section 440A of the Criminal Procedure Code, and amended that section anew by providing as respects offences under certain sections of the Penal Code, including section 115, for a trial before three judges without a jury; but instead of the nomination by the Minister which had been rejected by the Supreme Court, there was inserted a new subsection whereby the Chief Justice could nominate three judges before whom the trial should be held. It was also provided that the determination should be according to the majority. Further the second Act (s. 6) nullified the Minister's earlier direction, information and nomination in the proceedings (setting them out in schedules), and it deemed that the Minister had never had any power to nominate the judges for the trial without a jury, and any action proceeding or thing instituted by virtue of the said direction, information or nomination was deemed for all purposes never to have been instituted or commenced. **[283]**

All the other elaborate provisions of the first Act were left untouched.

The trial proceeded before three judges nominated by the Chief Justice. In April, 1965, after a very extensive trial the appellants were convicted and sentenced.

[32] (1963) 64 N.L.R. 313.
[33] Ibid. at 359.

Mr. Gratiaen on behalf of the appellants attacks the validity of the convictions on three main grounds.

The first is that the Ceylon Parliament is limited by an inability to pass legislation which is contrary to fundamental principles of justice. The 1962 Acts, it is said, are contrary to such principles in that they not only are directed against individuals but also ex post facto create crimes and punishments, and destroy fair safeguards by which those individuals would otherwise be protected.

The appellants' second contention is that the 1962 Acts offended against the Constitution in that they amounted to a direction to convict the appellants or to a legislative plan to secure the conviction and severe punishment of the appellants and thus constituted an unjustifiable assumption of judicial power by the legislature, or an interference with judicial power, which is outside the legislature's competence and is inconsistent with the severance of power between legislature, executive, and judiciary which the Constitution ordains.

The appellants' third argument is that the language of the 1962 Acts did not suffice "in the absence of an express provision to that effect" (Interpretation Ordinance, s. 6 (3)) to deprive the appellants of the right to a jury which they had acquired previous to the passing of those Acts.

The first argument starts with a judgment of Lord Mansfield L.C.J. In *Campbell* v. *Hall*[34]* he laid down as a clear proposition that

> "if the King (and when I say the King, I always mean the King without the concurrence of Parliament,) has a power to alter the old and to introduce new laws in a conquered country, this legislation being subordinate, that is, subordinate to his own authority in Parliament, he cannot make any new change contrary to fundamental principles."

The Crown having, therefore (it is said), no power over Ceylon as a colony to make laws which offended against fundamental principles, could not hand over to Ceylon a higher power than it possessed itself. The Constitution of Ceylon was not laid down **[284]** as in the case of many other colonies by an Act of Parliament but by an Order in Council (The Ceylon (Constitution) Order in Council, 1946) which gave power to the Ceylon Parliament to make laws for the peace, order and good government of the island. This was followed by the Ceylon Independence Act, 1947, a United Kingdom Act. But Parliament, it is contended, did not in terms transfer to Ceylon the Sovereign right of the United Kingdom Parliament. Therefore the legislative power of Ceylon is still limited by the inability (which it inherits from the Crown) to pass laws which offend against fundamental principles. This vague and uncertain phrase might arguably be called in aid against some of the statutes passed by any Sovereign power. And it would be regrettable if the procedure adopted in giving independence to Ceylon has produced the situation for which the appellants contend.

In view of their Lordships, however, such a contention is not maintainable. Before the passing of the Colonial Laws Validity Act, 1865, considerable difficulties had been caused by the over-insistence of a Colonial judge in South Australia that colonial legislative Acts must not be repugnant to English law ("The Statute of Westminster and Dominion Status" by K.C. Wheare[35]). That Act was intended to and did overcome the difficulties. It provided that colonial laws should be void to the extent in which they were repugnant to an Act of the United Kingdom parliament applicable to that colony, "but not otherwise" (s. 2) and that they should not be void or inoperative on the ground of repugnancy to the law of England (s. 3).

> "The essential feature of this measure is that it abolished once and for all the vague doctrine of repugnancy to the principles of English law as a source of invalidity of any colonial Act. . . . The boon thus secured was enormous; it was now necessary only for the colonial legislator to ascertain that there was no Imperial Act applicable and his field of action and choice of means

[34] (1774) 1 Cowp. 204, 209.
[35] 4th Ed. 75, 76, 77.

became unfettered." ("The Sovereignty of the British Dominions" by Prof. Keith.[36])

Their Lordships cannot accept the view that the legislature while removing the fetter of repugnancy to English law, left in existence a fetter of repugnancy to some vague unspecified law of natural justice. The terms of the Colonial Laws Validity Act and especially the words "but not otherwise" in section 2 make it clear that Parliament was intending to deal with the whole **[285]** question of repugnancy. Moreover their Lordships doubt whether Lord Mansfield was intending to say that what was not repugnant to English law might yet be repugnant to fundamental principles or to set up the latter as a different test from the former. Whatever may have been the possible arguments in this matter prior to the passing of the Colonial Laws Validity Act, they are not maintainable at the present date. No case has been cited in which during the last 100 years any judgment (or, so far as one can see, any argument) has been founded on that portion of Lord Mansfield's judgment. And in *Abeyesekera* v. *Jayatilake,*[37] a case from Ceylon dealing with the validity of a retrospective Order in Council and therefore a fertile field for the germination of arguments about fundamental principles, Lord Mansfield's judgment in *Campbell* v. *Hall*[38]* was only referred to in the Board's judgment as authority on a wholly different point.

The Ceylon Independence Act, 1947, of the British Parliament provided:

"1.—(1) No Act of the Parliament of the United Kingdom passed on or after the appointed day shall extend, or be deemed to extend, to Ceylon as part of the law of Ceylon, unless it is expressly declared in that Act that Ceylon has requested, and consented to, the enactment thereof.

(2) As from the appointed day His Majesty's Government in the United Kingdom shall have no responsibility for the government of Ceylon.

(3) As from the appointed day the provisions of the First Schedule to this Act shall have effect with respect to the legislative powers of Ceylon."

* * *

"First Schedule

Legislative Powers of Ceylon

1. (1) The Colonial Laws Validity Act, 1865, shall not apply to any law made after the appointed day by the Parliament of Ceylon.

(2) No law and no provision of any law made after the appointed day by the Parliament of Ceylon shall be void or inoperative on the ground that it is repugnant to the law of England, or to the provisions of any existing or future Act of Parliament of the United Kingdom, or to any order, rule or regulation made under any such Act, and the powers of the Parliament of Ceylon shall include the power to repeal or amend any such Act, order, rule or regulation in so far as the same is part of the law of Ceylon. **[286]**

2. The Parliament of Ceylon shall have full power to make laws having extra-territorial operation."

These liberating provisions thus incorporated and enlarged the enabling terms of the Act of 1865, and it is clear that the joint effect of the Order in Council of 1946 and the Act of 1947 was intended to and did have the result of giving to the Ceylon Parliament the full legislative powers of a sovereign independent State. (See *Ibralebbe* v. *The Queen.*[39])

Accordingly the appellants' first argument fails.

Those powers, however, as in the case of all countries with written constitutions, must be exercised in accordance with the terms of the constitution from which the power derives. The appellants' second argument maintains that the

[36] 1929 Ed. 45.
[37] [1932] A.C. 260; 48 T.L.R. 71, P.C.
[38] (1774) 1 Cowp. 204.
[39] [1964] A.C. 900; [1964] 2 W.L.R. 76; [1964] 1 All E.R. 251, P.C.

powers of Parliament were not so exercised in the passing of the Acts which are here in question.

The learned Solicitor-General in his clear, fair and forceful argument strongly relied on the fact that there is no express vesting of judicial power in the courts, such as one finds for example in the case of the United States of America or Australia. But that is not necessarily decisive. For in the two latter instances there were no federal courts apart from the Constitution. Unless such courts were created and invested with power by the Constitution they had no existence or power.

In Ceylon, however, the position was different. The change of sovereignty did not in itself produce any apparent change in the constituents or the functioning of the Judicature. So far as the courts were concerned their work continued unaffected by the new Constitution, and the Ordinances under which they functioned remained in force. The judicial system had been established in Ceylon by the Charter of Justice in 1833. Clause 4 of the Charter read:

> "And to provide for the administration of justice hereafter in Our said Island Our will and pleasure is, and We do hereby direct that the entire administration of justice, civil and criminal therein, shall be vested exclusively in the courts erected and constituted by this Our Charter . . . And it is Our pleasure and We hereby declare, that it is not, and shall not be competent to the Governor of Our said Island by any Law or Ordinance to be by him made, with the advice of the Legislative Council thereof or otherwise howsoever, to constitute or establish any court for the administration of justice in any case civil or criminal, save as hereinafter is expressly saved and provided." **[287]**

Clause 5 established the Supreme Court and clause 6 a Chief Justice and two puisne judges. Clause 7 gave the Governor powers of appointing their successors. There follow many clauses with regard to administrative, procedural and jurisdictional matters. Some half a century later Ordinances (in particular the Courts Ordinance) continued the jurisdiction and procedure of the courts. Thereunder the courts have functioned continuously up to the present day.

There was no compelling need therefore to make any specific reference to the judicial power of the courts when the legislative and executive powers changed hands.

> "But the importance of securing the independence of judges and maintaining the dividing line between the judiciary and the executive" (and also, one should add, the legislature) "was appreciated by those who framed the Constitution" (*Bribery Commissioner* v. *Ranasinghe*[40]).

The Constitution is significantly divided into parts:

> "Part 2 The Governor-General," "Part 3 The Legislature," "Part 4 Delimitation of Electoral Districts," "Part 5 The Executive," "Part 6 The Judicature," "Part 7 The Public Service," "Part 8 Finance."

And although no express mention is made of vesting in the judicature the judicial power which it already had and was wielding in its daily process under the Courts Ordinance, there is provision under Part 6 for the appointment of judges by a Judicial Service Commission which shall not contain a member of either House but shall be composed of the Chief Justice and a judge and another person who is or shall have been a judge. Any attempt to influence any decision of the Commission is made a criminal offence. There is also provision that judges shall not be removable except by the Governor-General on an address of both Houses.

These provisions manifest an intention to secure in the judiciary a freedom from political, legislative and executive control. They are wholly appropriate in a Constitution which intends that judicial power shall be vested only in the judicature. They would be inappropriate in a Constitution by which it was

[40] [1965] A.C. 172, 190; [1964] 2 W.L.R. 1301; [1964] 2 All E.R. 785, P.C.

intended that judicial power should be shared by the executive or the legislature. The Constitution's silence as to the vesting of judicial power is consistent with its remaining, where it had lain for more than a century, in the hands of the judicature. It is not consistent **[288]** with any intention that henceforth it should pass to or be shared by, the executive or the legislature.

During the argument analogies were naturally sought to be drawn from the British Constitution. But any analogy must be very indirect, and provides no helpful guidance. The British Constitution is unwritten whereas in the case of Ceylon their Lordships have to interpret a written document from which alone the legislature derives its legislative power.

The difficult question as to the separation of powers was carefully argued before the learned judges on the hearing of the interlocutory application which successfully challenged the Minister's nomination of three judges to try the accused. (*Reg.* v. *Liyanage.*[41]) The learned Attorney-General there contended that[42]

"no separation of powers exists under our Constitution, and that, if a separation of powers exists dehors the written constitution, it is a separation after the British method because we have been accustomed to that kind of separation throughout the British occupation of this country."

But he conceded that there was a recognised separation of functions. As the court itself said[43]:

"That a division of the three main functions of Government is recognised in our Constitution was indeed conceded by the learned Attorney-General himself. For the purposes of the present case it is sufficient to say that he did not contest that judicial power in the sense of the judicial power of the State is vested in the Judicature, i.e. the established civil courts of this country. There is no dispute that the three of us, as constituting, for the purposes of this Trial at Bar, the Supreme Court are called upon to exercise the strict judicial power of the State, and, in fact, we have, all three of us, received at one time or another, but in each case before the Supreme Court was so called upon to exercise judicial power, appointment by the Governor-General acting under section 52 (1) of the 1946 Order in Council."

After a careful review of authorities the three learned judges came to the conclusions quoted previously and decided that the Minister's nomination of judges was an infringement of the judicial power of the State which cannot be reposed in anyone outside the judicature.

The learned Solicitor-General before the Board has contended that the decision was wrong and that there was no separation **[289]** of powers such as would justify it. But in their Lordships' view that decision was correct and there exists a separate power in the judicature which under the Constitution as it stands cannot be usurped or infringed by the executive or the legislature.

Section 29 (1) of the Constitution says: "Subject to the provisions of this Order Parliament shall have power to make laws for the peace order and good government of the Island." These words have habitually been construed in their fullest scope. Section 29 (4) provides that Parliament may amend the Constitution on a two-thirds majority with a certificate of the Speaker. Their Lordships however cannot read the words of section 29 (1) as entitling Parliament to pass legislation which usurps the judicial power of the judicature—e.g., by passing an Act of attainder against some person or instructing a judge to bring in a verdict of guilty against someone who is being tried—if in law such usurpation would otherwise be contrary to the Constitution. There was speculation during the argument as to what the position would be if Parliament sought to procure such a result by first amending the Constitution by a two-thirds majority. But such a situation does not arise here. In so far as any Act passed without recourse to section 29 (4) of the Constitution purports to usurp or infringe the judicial power it is ultra vires.

[41] (1963) 64 N.L.R. 313.
[42] Ibid. 348.
[43] Ibid. 350.

But do the Acts of 1962, otherwise than in respect of the Minister's nomination, usurp or infringe that power? It goes without saying that the legislature may legislate, for the generality of its subjects, by the creation of crimes and penalties or by enacting rules relating to evidence. But the Acts of 1962 had no such general intention. They were clearly aimed at particular known individuals who had been named in a White Paper and were in prison awaiting their fate. The fact that the learned judges declined to convict some of the prisoners is not to the point. That the alterations in the law were not intended for the generality of the citizens or designed as any improvement of the general law is shown by the fact that the effect of those alterations was to be limited to the participants in the January coup and that, after these had been dealt with by the judges, the law should revert to its normal state.

But such a lack of generality in criminal legislation need not, of itself, involve the judicial function, and their Lordships are not prepared to hold that every enactment in this field which can be described as ad hominem and ex post facto must inevitably usurp or infringe the judicial power. Nor do they find it necessary to attempt the almost impossible task of tracing where the line **[290]** is to be drawn between what will and what will not constitute such an interference. Each case must be decided in the light of its own facts and circumstances, including the true purpose of the legislation, the situation to which it was directed, the existence (where several enactments are impugned) of a common design, and the extent to which the legislation affects, by way of direction or restriction, the discretion or judgment of the judiciary in specific proceedings. It is therefore necessary to consider more closely the nature of the legislation challenged in this appeal.

Mr. Gratiaen succinctly summarises his attack on the Acts in question as follows. The first Act was wholly bad in that it was a special direction to the judiciary as to the trial of particular prisoners who were identifiable (in view of the White Paper) and charged with particular offences on a particular occasion. The pith and substance of both Acts was a legislative plan ex post facto to secure the conviction and enhance the punishment of those particular individuals. It legalised their imprisonment while they were awaiting trial. It made admissible their statements inadmissibly obtained during that period. It altered the fundamental law of evidence so as to facilitate their conviction. And finally it altered ex post facto the punishment to be imposed on them.

In their Lordships' view that cogent summary fairly describes the effect of the Acts. As has been indicated already, legislation ad hominem which is thus directed to the course of particular proceedings may not always amount to an interference with the functions of the judiciary. But in the present case their Lordships have no doubt that there was such interference; that it was not only the likely but the intended effect of the impugned enactments; and that it is fatal to their validity. The true nature and purpose of these enactments are revealed by their conjoint impact on the specific proceedings in respect of which they were designed, and they take their colour, in particular, from the alterations they purported to make as to their ultimate objective, the punishment of those convicted. These alterations constituted a grave and deliberate incursion into the judicial sphere. Quite bluntly, their aim was to ensure that the judges in dealing with these particular persons on these particular charges were deprived of their normal discretion as respects appropriate sentences. They were compelled to sentence each offender on conviction to not less than ten years' imprisonment, and compelled to order con-**[291]**-fiscation of his possessions, even though his part in the conspiracy might have been trivial.

The trial court concluded its long and careful judgment with these words[44]:

> "But we must draw attention to the fact that the Act of 1962 radically altered ex post facto the punishment to which the defendants are rendered liable. The Act removed the discretion of the court as to the period of the sentence to be imposed, and compels the court to impose a term of 10 years' imprisonment, although we would have wished to differentiate in the matter

[44] (1965) 67 N.L.R. 193, 424.

of sentence between those who organised the conspiracy and those who were induced to join it. It also imposes a compulsory forfeiture of property. These amendments were not merely retroactive: they were also ad hoc, applicable only to the conspiracy which was the subject of the charges we have tried. We are unable to understand this discrimination. To the courts, which must be free of political bias, treasonable offences are equally heinous, whatever be the complexion of the Government in power or whoever be the offenders."

Their Lordships sympathise with that protest and wholly agree with it.

One might fairly apply to these Acts the words of Chase J., in the Supreme Court of the United States in *Calder* v. *Bull*[45]: "These acts were legislative judgments; and an exercise of judicial power."

Blackstone in his Commentaries[46] said:

"Therefore a particular act of the legislature to confiscate the goods of Titius, or to attaint him of high treason, does not enter into the idea of a municipal law: for the operation of this act is spent upon Titius only and has no relation to the community in general: it is rather a sentence than a law."

If such Acts as these were valid the judicial power could be wholly absorbed by the legislature and taken out of the hands of the judges. It is appreciated that the legislature had no such general intention. It was beset by a grave situation and it took grave measures to deal with it, thinking, one must presume, that it had power to do so and was acting rightly. But that consideration is irrelevant, and gives no validity to acts which infringe the Constitution. What is done once, if it be allowed, may be done again and in a lesser crisis and less serious circumstances. And thus judicial power may be eroded. Such **[292]** an erosion is contrary to the clear intention of the Constitution. In their Lordships' view the Acts were ultra vires and invalid.

The appellants' third argument as to the appellants' right to a jury does not therefore arise and their Lordships express no opinion on the matter.

It may be that section 17 of the first Act can escape from its context and survive under the authority of *Thambiayah* v. *Kulasingham*,[47] but as their Lordships had no argument on this point they prefer to express no opinion.

It was agreed between the parties that if the Acts were ultra vires and invalid, the convictions cannot stand. Their Lordships have therefore humbly advised Her Majesty that these appeals should be allowed and that the convictions should be quashed.

Solicitors: *Fisher, Dowson & Wasbrough; T. L. Wilson & Co.*

[45] (1799) 3 Dallas 386.
[46] Vol. 1, p. 44.
[47] (1949) 50 N.L.R. 25, 37.

B.

PARTS OF STATE TERRITORY

1

BOUNDARIES

NAVIGATORS AND GENERAL INSURANCE CO. LTD. v. RINGROSE

([1962] 1 W.L.R. 173)

November 16, 1961: Court of Appeal: Holroyd Pearce, Willmer, Davies L.JJ.

Insurance—Marine—Geographical limits—Vessel covered "whilst within the United Kingdom, ashore or afloat"—Voyage from England to Channel Islands—Dismasted in mid-Channel—Whether insurers liable—Whether Channel Islands within United Kingdom—Interpretation Act, 1889 (52 & 53 *Vict. c.* 63), *s.* 18 (1).
Channel Islands—United Kingdom, whether part of—Marine insurance policy—Craft insured "whilst within the United Kingdom"— "United Kingdom"—Meaning—Interpretation Act, 1889, *s.* 18 (1).
Ships' Names—Chanticleer.

The plaintiffs insured the defendant's 16-foot catamaran "whilst within the United Kingdom, ashore or afloat or in transit by road or by rail." While on a voyage from Teignmouth, England, to the Channel Islands, the defendant's craft was dismasted in mid-Channel about 28 miles south of Portland Bill, and was salved by an Italian steamer. The plaintiffs paid the salvage claimed without any admission of liability and on the defendant's express promise to repay if on investigation the plaintiffs should prove not to be liable for the loss. On the plaintiffs' claim for the money paid on the defendant's behalf for the salvage services, the county court judge gave the plaintiffs judgment for £52. 15s. 8d. The defendant appealed:—

Held, that the plaintiffs' liability under the insurance policy was to be determined solely by the place where the accident occurred, and whatever meaning was given to the words "within the United Kingdom ashore or afloat" they could not include a point in the English Channel mid-way between England and France, 28 miles south of Portland Bill, and, accordingly, the defendant was not covered under the policy and his appeal failed.

Per Holroyd Pearce and Willmer L.JJ.: (1) As section 18 of the Interpretation Act, 1889, shows that the Channel Islands are not part of the United Kingdom, and as there was no evidence from which the court could deduce that there was any special meaning to be given to the words "United Kingdom" in commercial documents, it seems that the Channel Islands cannot be covered by the words of the policy "within the United Kingdom."

Stoneham v. *Ocean Railway & General Accident Insurance Co.* (1887) 19 Q.B.D. 237; 3 T.L.R. 695 considered.

Semble, that the words "within the United Kingdom, ashore or afloat" covers the waters over which the Crown claims jurisdiction.

APPEAL from Judge Block at the Mayor's and City of London Court.

The plaintiffs, Navigators and General Insurance Co., insured the 16-foot catamaran "Chanticleer," belonging to the defendant, Nigel J. Ringrose, and valued at £200 against certain risks and perils. The insurance policy was headed "Dinghy Insurance **[174]** Policy" provided inter alia: "The Company will at their option pay for, replace or make good accidental loss of or damage to the insured craft, her machinery, gear, and equipment whilst within the United Kingdom, ashore or afloat or in transit by road or by rail."

The defendant set sail from Teignmouth in Devonshire, intending to sail to Guernsey in the Channel Islands. He got to a point in mid-Channel about 28 miles south of Portland Bill when his craft was dismasted. He was rescued by an Italian tramp steamer, and both he and his catamaran were taken on board and conveyed to Genoa; on arrival the Italian steamer claimed salvage. The defendant got in touch with the plaintiffs, his insurers, who agreed to pay him the sum claimed as salvage, but without any admission of liability and on his promise to repay, if, on investigation, they proved not to be liable therefor.

The plaintiffs by specially indorsed writ issued on January 28, 1960, claimed £114 0s. 8d. as money advanced on the defendant's behalf in respect of salvage services and repairs to the defendant's catamaran "Chanticleer." The defendant entered an appearance on February 12, 1960, and on February 14, 1960, wrote to the defendants a letter as follows: "Dear Sir, This is to inform you that I entered an appearance at the law courts on February 12. My defence is as follows: (1) When the Navigators and General asked to see me on my return from the Navidad in July, they accepted the claim, saying they would write to Lloyd's agent in Genoa and ask for the repairs to be put in hand (the matter was fairly urgent) and for the salvage claim to be settled, if it was nominal; (2) I took the trouble to read the Navigators Dinghy Insurance Policy carefully before leaving Devon for Guernsey, and I feel it was more than I could be reasonably expected to know that, for the purposes of the Navigators Dinghy Insurance Policy, Guernsey was *not* included in the United Kingdom, yours faithfully, Nigel Ringrose."

On March 21, 1960, the defendant delivered a further pleading by post which read: "Plaintiffs at one stage admitted liability, and secondly, it is more than the defendant can be reasonably expected to know that for this particular policy, the Channel Islands are excluded."

On July 14, 1960, the action was transferred to the Mayor's and City of London Court. On November 29, 1960, it was adjourned until February 1961 to enable the defendant to apply for legal aid, the judge certifying that an interesting point of law was to be argued. It was again adjourned on January 31, 1961, until April 11, 1961, when the matter was heard by Judge Block who gave judgment for the plaintiffs for £52 15s. 8d. with costs, the judge holding that the middle of the English Channel could not be included in the United Kingdom within the meaning of the insurance policy.

The defendant appealed arguing (1) that for the purposes of the policy the Channel Islands were in the United Kingdom; (2) **[175]** for the purposes of the policy the plaintiffs do cover passages made across open water provided the passage starts and finishes at points in the United Kingdom.

The defendant appeared in person.
R. F. Stone for the plaintiffs, the insurers.

The case cited in argument is referred to in the judgment.

Holroyd Pearce L.J. This is an appeal from a judgment of Judge Block, in favour of the plaintiffs for £52 15s. 8d. The plaintiffs issued a policy of insurance to the defendant in respect of his 16-foot catamaran, valued at £200. The defendant set sail in his catamaran from England bound for the Channel Islands, and in the course of his voyage he suffered a misadventure in respect of which he claims to be covered under the terms of the policy. The policy is headed "Dinghy Insurance Policy" and provides: "The company will at their option pay for, replace or make good accidental loss of or damage to the insured craft, her machinery gear and equipment whilst within the United Kingdom, ashore or afloat, or in transit by road or by rail."

The defendant's craft was dismasted about 28 miles south of Portland Bill. He was rescued by an Italian tramp steamer which took him and his catamaran on board. On arrival at Genoa she laid claim to salvage. The defendant got in touch with his insurers and ultimately it was agreed that they should pay him the sum now claimed without admission of liability, on his promise to repay if on investigation they proved not to be liable. They now sue him on his promise to repay. If his accident was within the terms of the policy this claim for repayment fails. The defendant contends that his accident occurred "whilst within the United Kingdom, ashore or afloat." He bases his argument on two grounds. First, he argues that the Channel Islands are part of the United Kingdom and that, since he was setting out from England to the Channel Islands, it is reasonable that he should be covered by the insurance policy for the whole of that journey between two places in the United Kingdom. It would, he said, be artificial to suggest that he was covered for a while when he left England and covered for a while before he arrived at the Channel Islands but was not covered in mid-Channel.

In my view, that first argument cannot stand. A case was very fairly produced by Mr. Stone, who appears for the plaintiffs, in which a divisional court held that the Channel Islands were within the United Kingdom. It is *Stoneham* v. *Ocean Railway and General Accident Insurance Co.*[1] in which Mathew J. said[2]: ". . . I think it is sufficiently apparent that the question which the parties intended to leave to the court as a question of law **[176]** is whether Jersey is, in popular language, a part of the United Kingdom. I have no hesitation in saying that it is: I can give no other answer to the question." Cave J. said[3]: "As to the first point, I think it is very clear that Jersey is within the United Kingdom within the meaning of the words of this policy." He continues in words which show that the court was much influenced in their view by the complete absence of merit in the contrary contention[4]: "Some light is thrown on this question by one of the conditions indorsed on the policy: 'This policy shall be void if the assured shall travel beyond the limits of Europe, or shall embark in any vessel with the intention of going beyond such limits.' That provision means that the policy shall be in force in Europe, and Jersey is in Europe. In my judgment it is also within the United Kingdom."

Two years after that case the Interpretation Act, 1889, was passed, and section 18 provided that in every Act passed after that date ". . . the following expressions shall, unless the contrary intention appears, have the meanings hereby respectively assigned to them, namely:—(1) The expression 'British Islands' shall mean the United Kingdom, the Channel Islands, and the Isle of Man."

The language of that subsection clearly shows that the Act does not include the Channel Islands in the United Kingdom. The fact that the Interpretation Act assigns a meaning to a word in Acts of Parliament does not necessarily mean that it has that meaning in commercial documents. Nevertheless, it is of some guidance in ascertaining their true construction.

In Halsbury's Laws of England, 3rd ed., vol. 5, at p. 647, there appears this paragraph: "Constitutional status. The Channel Islands and the Isle of Man occupy an anomalous position, for they are neither parts of the United Kingdom nor colonies. They differ considerably from each other in powers and practice. With the United Kingdom they make up the British Islands. Citizens of the Channel Islands and the Isle of Man are citizens of the United Kingdom and colonies, but may be known, if they so desire, as citizens of the United Kingdom, Islands and Colonies. In matters relating to the Channel Islands and the Isle of Man, the Queen is advised by the Home Secretary." There is no evidence in this case from which we can deduce that there is a special meaning by custom to be given to the words "United Kingdom" in commercial documents of this or any other nature. In my view, therefore, the Channel Islands cannot be said to be covered by the words of this policy, "within the United Kingdom."

Nor do I assent to the second part of the proposition, namely that assuming the Channel Islands to be part of the United **[177]** Kingdom, the insured is covered for the whole of his journey of 50 miles or so from the coast of England to the Channel Islands.

The place where the casualty occurred must determine whether there was a

[1] (1887) 19 Q.B.D. 237; 3 T.L.R. 695, D.C.
[2] 19 Q.B.D. 237, 239.
[3] 19 Q.B.D. 237, 240.
[4] Ibid. 241.

claim for accidental loss "whilst within the United Kingdom, ashore or afloat." The destination to which the craft is going is not the deciding factor.

Secondly, it is argued that even if the Channel Islands are not included in the United Kingdom, the words "within the United Kingdom, ashore or afloat" covers a wide area stretching out from the actual shore of the United Kingdom. One must bear in mind that the words occur in the context of a "Dinghy Insurance Policy" and not of a "Yacht Policy."

It was suggested in argument that the limit might be the area within sight of land, a wide area which differs greatly according to the type of land, the size of the ship and various physical conditions. In the context of this policy, that is a possible contention.

It was also suggested that it covered the waters over which Her Majesty claims jurisdiction. In the context this seems to provide the most clear and ascertainable limitation of the area included in the policy.

But it is not necessary to decide that matter finally. Here the accident happened 28 miles from the shore of England in mid-Channel in a spot that was nearer to the Channel Islands than to England. Clearly the place where the casualty occurred is not covered by the words "within the United Kingdom, ashore or afloat."

For those reasons the defendant was not covered by the policy in respect of this accident and the plaintiffs are entitled to succeed on their claim. I would therefore dismiss the appeal.

WILLMER L.J. I have come to the same conclusion. The question raised in this case is an extremely interesting and not unimportant one. It is whether the liability which the defendant incurred by reason of the casualty to his craft falls within a policy which insures against accidental loss of or to his craft "within the United Kingdom, ashore or afloat."

There is no issue as to where the casualty happened. The position has been marked, for convenience, on a chart for us to see, and it is sufficient to say that it is somewhere between 25 and 30 miles to the south of Portland Bill, i.e., a position which can fairly be described as about in the middle of the English Channel.

In my judgment, it is the place where the casualty happened that must determine whether the loss falls within the policy or not. The destination to which the craft was bound, namely, the Channel Islands, only becomes important, as I see it, in relation to an argument addressed to us, to the effect that anything happening within the course of a voyage from one place in the United Kingdom to another place in the United Kingdom must itself be within the United Kingdom. The Channel Islands, it is **[178]** said, are within the United Kingdom; therefore, since this was a voyage from Teignmouth in the United Kingdom to the Channel Islands in the United Kingdom, the casualty must be covered by the policy.

I do not think, however, that that argument can prevail. For one thing I am far from satisfied that the Channel Islands do come within the United Kingdom. I do not refer again to the authorities to which Holroyd Pearce L.J. has already referred; I am content to express my concurrence with the conclusions which my Lord has drawn therefrom. Furthermore, I should not be prepared to subscribe to the argument even if it could be shown that both the point of departure and the destination were within the United Kingdom. I can conceive of a number of possible voyages starting from port A in the United Kingdom and leading to port B in the United Kingdom which could well take a vessel far, far away from any of the coasts of the United Kingdom. I should have difficulty in holding that merely because a voyage begins and ends in the United Kingdom, everything that happens during it happens within the United Kingdom.

I do not think it is necessary in this case to reach any final conclusion as to what exactly is embraced within the expression "within the United Kingdom, ashore or afloat." For myself, I think there is much to be said for the view that the expression covers the area over which Her Majesty claims jurisdiction. But, as I have said, I do not think it is necessary to reach a final conclusion on that point, because I am satisfied that, wherever the line is drawn, the place where this casualty happened, being substantially mid-way between England and France, must fall outside it, and could not by any test be held to be within the United Kingdom.

In those circumstances it seems to me that the loss which the defendant had the misfortune to sustain is not a loss within the policy, and that the plaintiffs rightly succeeded in the court below. Accordingly, I agree that the appeal fails.

DAVIES L.J. I agree. I do not think that it is necessary for the court to express any view as to the correctness of the decision of the Queen's Bench Division in *Stoneham* v. *Ocean Railway and General Accident Insurance Co.*[5] to which Holroyd Pearce L.J. has referred.

Speaking for myself, I am unable to see that any assistance can be derived in this case from the provisions of the Interpretation Act, even if they could possibly be said to apply to a policy of insurance as opposed to a statute. Section 18 refers to the United Kingdom, the Channel Islands and the Isle of Man; and it is therefore argued that those three places are mutually exclusive. But I find it very difficult to believe that an insured yachtsman in the Isle of Man, if he had this policy issued to him, **[179]** would not be covered by it as being afloat within the United Kingdom in the terms of the policy. The passage from Halsbury's Laws of England, to which we have been referred, is based on no other authority than the deduction made from the words in the Interpretation Act.

But all these matters are, in my opinion, as my Lords have said, irrelevant. Even if the Channel Islands are part of the United Kingdom, it is impossible, as I see it, to deduce from the fact that the port of departure was an English port and the intended destination was a Channel Islands port the conclusion that throughout the whole of that voyage the defendant's vessel was within the United Kingdom.

An example that was referred to in the argument, I think, makes this plain from a common sense point of view. Supposing the holder of a "Dinghy Policy," such as this, were minded to sail from Liverpool to Belfast, both of those ports being unquestionably within the United Kingdom, and suffered a loss while out at sea, it seems to me that by no stretch of the imagination could it possibly be said that at that time he was within the United Kingdom.

It is quite plain, as I think, that the place where this loss occurred was not within the United Kingdom.

What that phrase in the policy does mean is, as my Lords have indicated, a very much more difficult matter to pronounce upon. Indeed, it is not necessary for us to pronounce upon it at all. All I would say about it in addition to what has been said is this. Whatever test one chooses gives rise, one would think, to anomalies. If the test of "the waters over which Her Majesty claims jurisdiction" is applied, one would, I think, encounter anomalies. On a straight line of coast, presumably, those waters would mean waters within the three-mile limit. If, in the course of a voyage intended to be within that three-mile limit or in the course of a race intended to be within the three-mile limit, a vessel were carried, say, a quarter of a mile beyond the three-mile limit owing to conditions of wind or tide, to say that in those circumstances she would cease to be insured when she sailed more than three miles from the shore would seem to me to be an affront to common sense. But, as I say, it is not necessary to decide what the words mean. I agree that, as my Lords have said, whatever they mean, this loss is not within them. I therefore agree that the appeal fails.

Appeal dismissed with costs.

Solicitors: *Ingledew, Brown, Bennison & Garrett.*

[5] (1887) 19 Q.B.D. 237.

3

TERRITORIAL WATERS

JOSEPH JOHNSTON & SON LTD. v. MORRISON AND OTHERS

([1962] S.L.T. 322)

July 17, 1962: Court of Session (Outer House): Lord Cameron.

Fishings—Salmon fishings—Crown—Extent of Crown rights to salmon fishings in the sea—Whether Crown's right limited to fishing by apparatus attached to or connected with the shore.

In an action of interdict at the instance of lessees from the Crown of salmon fishing rights within territorial waters it was contended, on the authority of *Commissioners of Woods and Forest* v. *Gammell* (1859) 3 Macq. 419, that the right of the Crown to salmon fishings in the sea was limited to fishing by stake nets, bag nets, or net and coble or by means which implied either connection of the apparatus with the shore or use and possession of the coast. **[323]**

Held that *Gammell's* case did not introduce into the law of Scotland any limitation on the previously understood generality of the right of the Crown in salmon fishing in territorial waters, and that a grant or lease of salmon fishing in territorial waters by the Crown, unless specifically limited, was a grant or lease of the exclusive right to fish by all lawful anl legitimate means.

Petition

Joseph Johnston & Son Ltd. presented a petition for suspension and interdict against Stephen Summer Morrison and Others.

Interim interdict was granted on an *ex parte* statement on 5th July, 1962.

The respondents pleaded, *inter alia*, "no title to sue," and lodged a motion for the recall of the interim interdict.

Counsel were heard on the motion for recall before Lord Cameron.

The circumstances out of which the petition arose and the contentions of parties are sufficiently set forth in his Lordship's opinion.

On 17th July 1962 his Lordship *refused* the respondents' motion for recall *in hoc statu* and *continued* the interim interdict.

LORD CAMERON.—This is a motion for recall of an interim interdict granted *ex parte* on 5th July. Answers have now been lodged and counsel for the respondents has moved me to recall the interim order and dismiss the petition, alternatively, to recall and sist the proceedings.

The petitioners are lessees from the Crown of certain salmon fishings in the sea *ex adverso* of the coast of Kincardine. The first and second respondents are fishermen and the third is their father who is called as their curator, they being in minority. They are the owners of a fishing boat named the *Quest*. It is not disputed that the petitioners had a lease or that the respondents are fishermen and own a boat. The petitioners aver that they are a company which carries on business as salmon fishers and has its registered office at 3 America Street, Montrose. They are lessees from the Crown Estate Commissioners (formerly the Commissioners of Crown Lands) of salmon fishings in the sea *ex adverso* the lands extending from the southern boundary of the Estate of Kinneff in the Parish of Kinneff to Hog's Holes near Crawton Ness in the Parish of Dunnottar and County of Kincardine as the sea boundaries of the lands are set out on a map which is annexed to the lease. This lease was granted in February 1934, and was originally for a period of nine years from Martinmas 1934, but it has been extended from time to time under minutes of agreement dated respectively 25th November and 1st December 1942, 19th and 30th November 1951 and 30th November and 5th December 1960. The lease is presently current until Martinmas 1970. By minute of confirmation dated 24th April 1962 it is declared and confirmed by the lessors that by the lease there was let to the petitioners "the exclusive right to the fishing for salmon and fish of the salmon kind belonging to the Crown in the sea within territorial water, *ex adverso* the lands described in the lease." The petitioners claim in terms of that lease that they are entitled to prosecute and pursue any other person or persons who shall fish for, catch or destroy at any time of the year any salmon or other fish of the salmon kind within the bounds of the fishing let. The petitioners go on to aver that about 1.15 p.m. on 21st June 1962 the first and second-named respondents were, without the permission or approval of the petitioners, fishing for and attempting to catch salmon or fish of the salmon kind by drift net from the vessel *Quest* at a point inside the limit of territorial waters and within the boundaries of the Kinneff salmon fishings. They aver that the fishing boat *Quest* is owned by the first and second-named respondents who were aboard her at the time. The petitioners go on to allege that the first and second-named respondents have been fishing for salmon within the Kinneff salmon fishings leased by the petitioners from the Crown Estate Commissioners. They go on to state that on a previous occasion, namely 9th May 1962, the first and second respondents fished for salmon within the Lauriston salmon fishings which are also leased by the petitioners from the Crown Estate Commissioners and in respect of that action the petitioners raised an action for interdict and interim interdict in the Sheriff Court at Stonehaven. That action is still in Court but interim interdict was refused by the sheriff-substitute on 9th June 1962. The petitioners go on in their averments to explain that the practice of drift-netting for salmon within territorial waters without the consent of the legal owner or lessee of the salmon fishing has become widespread in the north-east of Scotland and they aver that the first and second-named respondents have caught considerable quantities of salmon within the Kinneff salmon fishings leased by them, and that they will continue to catch salmon there to the loss, injury and damage of the petitioners unless interdicted, and they reserve their right to claim damages. The interdict which they seek is to interdict the first and second respondents and all others acting for them or under their instructions from fishing for, catching or destroying at any time of the year and in any manner of way salmon, and any fish of the salmon kind within three miles *ex adverso* of the lands within bounds of the salmon fishing described in the body of the petition. The respondents do not deny that they have been at sea on a date alleged or that they were fishing in the sea from a fishing boat owned by them without permission of the petitioners although they deny that they were fishing for or attempting to catch salmon in the precise position alleged. It is to be noted at this stage that the terms of the lease in favour of the petitioners show that the grant is one of the exclusive rights to fish for or take salmon.

The respondents plead in the first place *lis alibi* **[324]** *pendens* and "no title to sue." In support of his argument on title, counsel for the respondents maintained boldly that the law of Scotland has been settled for over one hundred years and that the petitioners' present claim was clearly contrary to that law. Indeed, he described the petitioners' claim as based on a "naive" view of the law. The authority on which he based this attack is the well-known case of the *Commissioners of Woods and Forests* v. *Gammell* (1859) 3 Macq. 419, also reported in the Court of Session (1851) 13 D. 854. As I understood counsel's argument it was this; it is admitted that the Crown possesses the right to salmon fishings in territorial waters, but this is a limited right as the measure of the right is limited to fishing by certain means, that is, by stake nets, bag nets, or net and coble, or other similar means all of which imply either connection of the apparatus with the shore or use and possession of the coast. Therefore, counsel said, the only right obtained by the petitioners under their lease was the right to fish by these means and no other, because the

Crown could not give them any wider right. As a necessary corollary to this fishing for salmon by any other means would be free in territorial waters to anyone who cared to prosecute it except in so far as struck at by statute. Now, whatever may be the rights of the Crown, there is no doubt that the petitioners possessed the whole of these under their lease and its renewals, and it is equally clear that the plain intention of the lease was to give the exclusive right, as appears plain from the express licence, to pursue and prosecute any person who shall fish for, catch or destroy at any time of the year any salmon or other fish of the salmon kind within the bounds of the fishings let. It is equally without doubt that the respondents have no such right nor have they any permission from the petitioners. This latter point means that whatever their rights *vis-à-vis* the petitioners, the respondents would be liable to the penalty provided for breach of section 1 of the Salmon and Freshwater Fisheries (Protection) (Scotland) Act, 1951 if they were to attempt to fish for salmon within one mile of the shore *ex adverso* of the lands referred to in the petitioners' lease.

For the petitioners, counsel maintained that the right of salmon fishing in the sea was not measured or limited in the way counsel for the respondents contended, and that by the law of Scotland a grant of salmon fishing included the right to exercise it by all or any lawful means and was not limited to such methods as were either known in 1859 or enumerated in the judgment in the case of *Gammell.* It has for centuries been recognised in Scotland that salmon fishings are *inter regalia* whether they are in rivers, estuaries, lochs or that part of the open sea over which the Crown claims sovereignty, at present three miles. I have examined the authorities to which I was referred by counsel as well as the institutional writers to see whether, apart from the case of *Gammell,* it has ever been suggested that the Crown's right is limited in the way counsel for the respondents submitted. Craig is silent as to any limitation on the form or manner in which salmon might be caught under a Crown grant of salmon fishings; Stair does not suggest any such limitation nor does Erskine nor does Bell in his reference to salmon fishing grants. Later writers of authority such as Rankine on *Land-ownership* (4th edition), page 305 are to the same effect, while the most recent edition of the *Encyclopaedia of the Laws of Scotland* contains a statement to the same effect. That article was from the pen of the late Lord Blades. The sole apparent authority for the proposition relied on by counsel for the respondents in attacking the petitioners' title is *Gammell.* But the issue which was raised in *Gammell's* case was not as to the total extent of the Crown's right in territorial waters, it was a dispute as to the right of a seabound proprietor to fish for salmon and to lease the right to do so by means of certain engines or by net and coble, modes in which use and possession of the coast was essential to the operation. And it is to be noted that the declarator sought by the Crown in that case went further. It was in these terms: "that the salmon fishings around the sea coast of Scotland belong to the Crown and form part of its hereditary revenue and that the defenders have no right or title to fish for salmon *ex adverso* of the lands of Portlethen or in any part of the sea coast adjoining by means of stake-nets or bag-nets or by net and coble, or *in any other manner or way*" as appears from the Court of Session Report, at page 859. The interdict sought by the Crown was in similar terms. The pleas-in-law in *Gammell's* case *hinc inde* are instructive as to the wider issues which were argued and discussed in that case. They are quoted on page 858. The Lord Ordinary in that case granted decree in terms of the first declarator of the summons. The case went to the Second Division but in view of the substantial character of the issues involved was sent to the Whole Court. The Court by a majority adhered to the Lord Ordinary's interlocutor and that interlocutor was affirmed in the House of Lords. Now the declarator and the only declarator which was covered by the Lord Ordinary's interlocutor and, therefore, was subjected to appeal to the Whole Court and to the House of Lords was in the following terms: "that the salmon-fishings around the sea-coast of Scotland belong exclusively to us and our royal successors, and form part of the hereditary revenues of the Crown in Scotland, so far as the said salmon-fishings have not been expressly granted to any of our subjects or vassals by charter or otherwise:". The Lord Ordinary having decerned and declared in terms of that first conclusion appointed parties to be heard on the first defence for the defenders, namely that the principal defender was proprietor of the lands erected into a barony and, therefore, had a right of salmon fishing adjoining thereto. The speech of the Lord Chancellor, Lord Chelmsford, in (1859) 3 Macq. 419, shows clearly that the House of Lords was only concerned at that stage with the interlocutor dealing with this first conclusion of the summons. The quotation from the opinion of the majority of the consulted judges in the **[325]** speech of the Lord Chancellor quoted at page 454, and on which counsel for the respondents placed great reliance, is clearly not intended to limit the terms of the declarator which was under review far less to prejudge a determination on the immediately succeeding declaratory conclusion. I think it is desirable to see what was the precise context of this quotation as it appears in the Court of Session Report (1851) 13 D. 854. That will be found at page 859. This is from the opinion of the majority of consulted judges who returned a single opinion. The summons stated "that the defender has recently, without any right or title, granted a pretended lease of the salmon-fishings *ex adverso* of the said estate, in favour of the other defenders; and these parties have illegally and unwarrantably erected or used stake-nets, bag-nets, or other destructive engines for catching salmon in the sea opposite or nearly opposite to the said estate of Portlethen: That these nets or engines are placed in the sea along the sea-coast, and remain stationary in the water, where they are fixed by stakes, anchors, or other moorings, so as to intercept the passage of the salmon, and force and decoy them into courts or enclosures of netting, where they are caught; and although the pursuers maintained their willingness to grant a lease, etc., the defenders continued illegally to persist in fishing for salmon by means of bag-nets, and stake-nets, and other apparatus; and the conclusion is, to have it found and declared, 'that the salmon-fishings round the sea-coast of Scotland belong to the Crown, and form part of its hereditary revenues; and that the defenders have no right or title to fish for salmon etc., *ex adverso* of the lands of Portlethen, or in any part of the sea-coast adjoining, by means of stake-nets or bag-nets, or by net and coble, or in any other way.' The conclusion for interdict is expressed in similar terms. The defences, too, show that the meaning of the summons was perfectly understood. 'It is admitted,' they say, 'that the defender, Mr. Gammell, has granted a lease of the right to fish to the other defenders, and that they have been at great expense in placing nets in the public seas, for the purpose of catching the fish therein.' And again, 'in the year 1827, the fishings opposite the defender, Mr. Gammell's lands were wrought by bag-nets, and a large sum of money was expended in procuring and placing them; they have been improved since, and the defenders have laid out very considerable capital in their establishment and especially at the commencement of each fishing season. These fisheries not having the shelter of any bay or creek, but being exposed in the open sea, require a stock of strong, heavy, and expensive material and implements.' And the same statement is repeated on page four of the case for the defenders.

"It has been thought right to quote these passages at length; because in the absence of any condescendence they form the record of the facts by which the respective claims of the parties are to be ascertained. From these facts it is obvious that the right of fishing in dispute—the right which is asserted on the part of the Crown, and denied to the defenders in the summons—is the right of fishing in the 'open sea;' when by that term is meant the sea on an open coast, as distinguished from estuaries and inlets; but still by stake-nets, bag-nets, and by net and coble, and other similar modes, all of which, it is matter of notoriety, imply either the connection of the apparatus with the coast, as in the case of stake-nets, and bag-nets, or the use and possession of the coast, as in the case of net and coble. In short, the modes of fishing on the coast, which it is the object of the summons to deny to the defenders, and to claim for the Crown, are those modes of fishing in which the use and possession of the coast is essential to the operation." Thus the passage quoted by Lord Chelmsford from the opinion of the consulted judges was designed to focus the particular issue which was in dispute between the parties in the case of *Gammell* at that stage and not to limit by definition the extent of the total Crown right to salmon fishing in territorial waters. It is nowhere suggested in the opinion of the consulted judges or in argument or in the speeches in the House of Lords that, if the Crown had a right to salmon fishings in territorial waters, that was a right which was limited to certain specific modes of exercise. This point which would arise on the second declarator as I have shown was not before the Court, though an observation of the Lord Chancellor at the foot of page 462 in (1859) 3 Macq. 419 would seem to express approval of the implications contained in the second conclusion of the summons. There is no doubt that there is no such limitation as the respondents contend for here in the case of the Crown's right to salmon fishing in rivers, inlets or estuaries and no obvious reason suggests itself as to why there should be such in the open sea. If that were the meaning of the judgment in *Gammell's* case, as counsel for the respondents maintained it was, it would not be easy to reconcile that decision with the later case in the House of Lords of *McDouall* v. *Lord Advocate* (1875) 2 R. (H.L.) 49. The observations of the Lord Chancellor (Lord Cairns) in his speech, at pages 56 and 57, in moving that the decision of the First Division of this Court should be reversed and of Lord Hatherley in concurring at page 60, would seem to make it clear that it is not the manner in which the right is exercised which is limitative of the extent of the right itself. The ground of judgment of the First Division led by Lord Ardmillan was that the pursuers' claim based on prescription could not succeed because the only method of fishing which would support a prescriptive claim had been known and practised for less than the relevant period of time. This was rejected by the unanimous judgment of the House of Lords. I read the observations of their Lordships in that case as indicating that any lawful means of taking salmon may suffice to establish a prescriptive title to salmon fishing in the open sea. If this is so, then it must clearly follow that a specific grant by the Crown or a lease of the royal right must include the right to fish by all lawful means unless specifically limited. I would recall that **[326]** while in the early part of the last century a prescriptive right to salmon fishing could not be established on evidence of fishing with rod and line alone, the law has developed as habits have changed and values have altered and that under certain conditions such a mode of fishing, if persisted in for the prescriptive period, may suffice to establish such a title.

The observations of Lord Neaves and the Lord Justice-General in the case of *Anderson* v. *Anderson* (1867) 6 M. 117, as they appear at pages 119 and 120, seems to me equally clear to the same effect as the observations of Lord Cairns and Lord Hatherley in the case of *McDouall*. In my opinion, properly and fairly read, the case of *Gammell* does not introduce into the law of Scotland such a limitation on the previously understood generality of the right of the Crown in the matter of salmon fishing in territorial waters as counsel for the respondents maintained. In my judgment the passages on which his argument rested are insufficient to bear the weight that he sought to lay upon them. I am, therefore, of opinion that where a grant of salmon fishing in territorial waters is made by the Crown or a lease given, that is a grant or lease of an exclusive right to fish by all lawful and legitimate means, unless specifically limited. There is no such limitation here. On the contrary, the provision is to use net and coble and other legal engines. If then the petitioners are correct in their averments, and at this stage I must take them *pro veritate*, the respondents have infringed their right of property. The challenge to title which has been made by the respondents is in fact a positive assertion of a contrary right or liberty in the respondents to fish for and take salmon or fish of the salmon kind within territorial waters up to at least the one mile from shore prescribed by the Act of 1951 which, in this respect, is a re-enactment of the earlier and now repealed statute of 1844. The terms of that Act also appear to me to lend support to the petitioners. If the right of the grant were limited as the respondents suggest, then there would be no one *in titulo* to give permission to fish within one mile of the shore by any other means than those which they say are the only methods covered by a grant or lease of salmon fishing—it being a feudal estate vested in the Crown in so far as not granted out or leased or acquired on a proper prescriptive title.

This is enough to dispose of the argument on title and also of *lis alibi pendens* because the plea relates to other proceedings in another court in respect of other alleged infringements at a different time of the petitioners' rights in a different area. But counsel for the respondents maintained that on balance of convenience and for maintenance of the *status quo* it was proper that the interim order should be recalled. As regards balance of convenience, I think that the balance of convenience lies in the preservation of the petitioners' rights. I was informed that this was a matter in which local feeling had been aroused. Assuming that to be so, I do not see why this should be a good reason for permitting the continuance of the unlawful invasion of an undoubted right of property even if the actual injury sustained was small, but I am not at all convinced that in a matter such as salmon fishing the damage to be done by invasion of the petitioners' rights is necessarily to be measured by the instant loss that can be verified. Future as well as present damage has to be looked to and the damage to be apprehended for the future may well be out of all proportion to the real damage done by the present interference with the petitioner's rights. As regards the point as to the maintenance of the *status quo*, I have no information before me to suggest that the petitioners did in fact lie by inactive in face of verifiable interference with their rights, and no such concession is made by the petitioners or by their counsel, nor indeed do the respondents claim in their answers that they have been acting in the way alleged by the petitioners for any length of time throughout the occasion specified in the petition. On the other hand, they make a somewhat significant concession that they believe it to be true that the practice of which they are accused (and which they incidentally deny they were guilty of) "is widespread in the north-east of Scotland." Being of this opinion, I shall refuse the respondents' motion for recall *in hoc statu* and continue the interim interdict.

Counsel for Petitioners, Grieve, Q.C., Stewart; Solicitors, Shiels & Macintosh, S.S.C.—Counsel for Respondents, Davidson; Solicitors, Drummond & Reid, S.S.C.

3

JURISDICTION

A.

TERRITORIAL JURISDICTION

1

OVER TERRITORY AND PERSONS AND PROPERTY THEREIN

REGINA v. HARDEN

([1963] 1 Q.B. 8)

November 27, 28, 29, 30, December 19, 1961: Court of Criminal Appeal: Lord Parker, C.J., Ashworth, Widgery JJ.

Crime—False pretences—Abroad, obtaining—Whether offence completed when cheque posted in Jersey.
Crime—Practice—Indictment—Amendment—Whether amendment can charge new offence after arraignment—False pretences—"Valuable security" for "money"—"Procuring of delivery" for "obtaining."
Crime—Evidence—Handwriting—No expert witness called—Comments on handwriting during summing-up—Issue of handwriting left to jury—Whether proper course. **[9]**
Crime—Attempt—Substantive offence only charged—Attempt in jurisdiction to obtain abroad by false pretences—Substantive offence completed—Criminal Procedure Act, 1851 (14 & 15 *Vict. c.* 100), *s.* 9.

The appellant sold refrigerators and refrigeration equipment both as a director of a company and on his own account. A number of the sales were on hire-purchase terms. In 1958, this side of his business was financed by a Jersey company. The practice was for the appellant to post a batch of completed hire-purchase forms to the Jersey company and for that company to send a cheque made payable to the appellant for the net amount. One of the terms of the agreement was that "This offer may be accepted by you at any time within one month of the date hereof by sending your cheque for the net amount." In January, 1959, the Jersey company refused to do any further business with the appellant and the appellant then made a similar arrangement with a company in England (referred to as the Berkshire company), but the cheques, with one exception, were made payable to the appellant's company. Some of the hire-purchase agreements were fictitious and the appellant was indicted on 19 counts. Counts 1-13 charged him with obtaining money by false pretences from the Jersey company for and on behalf of the appellant's company; counts 14-19 were similar but charged him with offences against the Berkshire company.

At the trial, the appellant pleaded not guilty to all counts. At the close of the case for the prosecution, it was submitted for the appellant; (1) that there was no evidence that he had obtained money; (2) that the offence of obtaining for and on behalf of another was bad in law; (3) that in counts 14-18 the appellant had obtained nothing as the cheques had been made payable to the company; (4) that the court had no jurisdiction to try offences committed in Jersey. The prosecution then sought leave to amend all counts. The deputy chairman refused to allow an amendment in respect of 10 counts and later directed the jury to acquit on those counts. The remaining counts were amended, and except for count 14, the material amendment was the substitution of "obtaining a valuable security" for "obtaining money." The allegations that the appellant had obtained for and on behalf of the company were deleted. The amendment of count 14 was "procuring delivery of a valuable security by false pretences." The trial then proceeded and the chairman during the trial and in his summing-up invited the jury to compare the handwriting on a number of documents. No handwriting expert had given evidence. The appellant was found guilty on the remaining nine counts and he appealed against his conviction:—

Held, allowing the appeal, (1) that the gist of the offence of obtaining lay in the act of obtaining which must be within the jurisdiction; and that there was no single rule which decided whether a cheque transmitted by the victim through the post was to be treated as having been obtained by the prisoner at the moment of posting; but that it would be so if the prisoner had agreed with his victim **[10]** that receipt by the postmaster would be equivalent to receipt by himself. In this case the agreement entered into by the appellant was that the transaction should be completed by the victim posting the cheque in Jersey; therefore the offence of obtaining had taken place in Jersey and the court had no jurisdiction to try the appellant in respect of the Jersey counts (post, p. 21.)

(2) That, since the offences were in fact completed, the alternative verdict of guilty of an attempt was not open to the court under section 9 of the Criminal Procedure Act, 1851 (post, pp. 21, 22).

(3) That the amendment of the indictment by the substitution of "a valuable security" for "money" was a correction of a mis-description of the thing obtained: the same offence had been charged throughout and such an amendment could be validly made after arraignment (post, pp. 22, 23).

(4) That an amendment that went beyond a correction of a misdescription and substituted a new offence could not be made after the arraignment. The alteration of count 14 to charging the procuring of the delivery of a valuable security to a third party from charging the obtaining by the appellant himself was an amendment which charged a new offence and could not be made as the appellant had not pleaded to it (post, p. 23).

(5) That the jury should not be invited to compare handwriting in documents unless expert evidence as to the genuineness of the handwriting had been called, and in the circumstances the proviso could not be applied.

Dicta in *Reg.* v. *Martin* [1962] 1 Q.B. 221; [1961] 3 W.L.R. 17; 45 Cr.App.R. 199; [1961] 2 All E.R. 747, C.C.A. approved.

Reg v. *Tilley* [1961] 1 W.L.R. 1309; [1961] 3 All E.R. 406, C.C.A. applied.

APPEAL against conviction.

The appellant, Alan Goldstone Harden, carried on the business of selling refrigerators and refrigeration equipment in Eastbourne. He traded under his own name and that of a company, the Refrigeration Investments Ltd. In this company he held a majority of the shares and was the only active director. In 1958 he entered into an agreement with a Jersey company, the Guarantee Trust of Jersey Ltd., for that company to finance the hire-purchase side of his business. The practice was for the appellant to send to the Jersey company a batch of hire-purchase agreements, which included a form of assignment and a signed letter called an "offer for sale." The last sentence of this letter was "This offer may be accepted by you at any time within one month of the date hereof by sending your cheque for the net amount." Normally the Jersey company would post in Jersey a cheque for the total amount, the cheque being made payable to the appellant.

In January, 1959, the Jersey company refused to finance any **[11]** more of the appellant's hire-purchase agreements and the appellant entered into an agreement of a similar nature with an English company, the Berkshire Finance Co. Ltd. The practice again was for the appellant to forward a batch of hire-purchase forms and for the Berkshire company to send a cheque for the total amount, but with one exception the cheques were made payable to the appellant's company. All the cheques were paid into the company's bank account but the appellant did not always keep his personal affairs separate from the affairs of the company.

Some of the proposal forms forwarded to the two companies were fictitious and the appellant was committed for trial on 10 charges of obtaining cheques by false pretences. A bill of indictment was preferred against him containing 19 counts of obtaining money by false pretences. The reason for the alteration was that the prosecution had decided to allege the different false hire-purchase agreements in separate counts and had split the amount of the cheque to correspond with the amount of money obtained on each agreement. All the counts also alleged that he had obtained the money for and on behalf of his company. Counts 1-13 alleged offences against the Jersey company and the remainder against the Berkshire company. Count 19 referred to the one transaction between the appellant and the Berkshire company when the cheque had been made payable to the appellant.

The appellant was tried in May, 1961, at East Kent Quarter Sessions before the deputy chairman, Sir Reginald Sharpe Q.C., and a jury. At the trial he pleaded not guilty to all the counts, and at the close of the case for the prosecution a number of submissions were made on his behalf. The submissions were, inter alia, (1) that there was no evidence of the appellant having obtained money: if he had obtained anything by false pretences then it was cheques; (2) that the charge of obtaining money on behalf of a third party was bad in law; (3) that there was no jurisdiction to try the appellant on the first 13 counts as the offences had been committed abroad in Jersey; (4) that in counts 14-18 the appellant had not obtained anything as the cheques had been made payable to the appellant's company. The prosecution then sought leave to amend all the counts. The deputy chairman gave leave to amend nine counts; the jury were later directed to acquit the appellant on the remaining 10 counts.

Seven of the amended counts referred to offences alleged to have been committed against the Jersey company and counts 14 and 19 referred to offences against the Berkshire company. The **[12]** material amendment in all the counts, except count 14, was the substitution of "obtaining a valuable security" for "obtaining money" in the statement of the offence, and in the particulars of the offence the substitution of "obtained . . . a cheque for the payment of . . ." for "obtained . . . the sum of . . ." The words "for and on behalf of Refrigeration Investment Company" were deleted from the particulars of the offence. Count 14 was amended to "procuring delivery of a valuable security by false pretences" from "obtaining money by false pretences." In some of the counts the value of the property was amended so as to correspond with the amount of the relevant cheque and there were also other minor amendments.

The trial then proceeded and the deputy chairman during the trial and in his summing-up invited the jury to compare the handwriting in a number of documents, the defence to count 19 being that a number of the hire-purchase agreements had been completed by the appellant's salesmen and one of these documents, which was material to count 19, had been witnessed by what purported to be the signature of the appellant's wife. The prosecution had called no handwriting expert to give evidence. On May 11, 1961, the appellant was convicted on all the nine counts and was sentenced to three years' imprisonment on all counts, the sentences to be concurrent.

The appellant appealed on the grounds, inter alia: (1) that in respect of seven counts the court had no jurisdiction to try the appellant because the offences took place in Jersey; (2) that in respect of all nine counts the original indictment had not merely misdescribed the property obtained but had charged different offences from those in the amended indictment, therefore the court had no jurisdiction to allow the amendments; (3) that all nine counts and the convictions based upon them ought to be quashed as the indictment was not preferred in accordance with the provisions of section 2 of the Administration of Justice (Miscellaneous Provisions) Act, 1933; (4) that evidence had been wrongly admitted; (5) that the deputy chairman in summing up had misdirected the jury in that, inter alia, he had wrongly invited the jury to draw inferences from the form of the handwriting on certain documents although no expert evidence had been called.

M. D. L. Worsley for the appellant. The court had no jurisdiction to try the appellant on seven of the counts because those offences were committed abroad. The duty of the English courts is the preservation of the Queen's Peace within her realm: *Board* **[13]** *of Trade* v. *Owen*[1]*; *Reg.* v. *Page.*[2]* There are certain exceptions to that rule but those exceptions do not include the offence of obtaining property by false pretences and that offence is committed at the place where the property is obtained: *Reg.* v. *Ellis.*[3] In this case cheques were obtained and went into the account of the Refrigeration Investments Ltd., but a cheque in the bank is not money: *Reg.* v. *Davenport.*[4] If the property is posted it is obtained at the place of posting: *Rex* v. *Stoddart*[5]; *Reg.* v. *Jones*[6]; *Reg.* v. *Cryer.*[7] Against that submission is *Rex* v. *Marston,*[8] but in that case the dicta were per incuriam. The obtaining is not a continuous action but takes place at an instant of time and is comparable in that respect to the offence of receiving stolen property: *Reg.* v. *Stanbury.*[9] The false representations were also made in Jersey for that was where the hire-purchase documents were received: *Reg.* v. *Ellis*[10]; *Reg.* v. *Leech*[11]; *Reg.* v. *Allington.*[12] In *Reg.* v. *Holmes*[13]* the court's attention was not drawn to *Reg.* v. *Leech*[14]; if it had been, that decision was binding on the court. Not only was the property obtained and the false representations made abroad but the victim was a foreign company and the loss was incurred abroad and therefore the court had no jurisdiction to try those seven counts.

Next, the court of trial had no jurisdiction to amend the indictment. The appellant was committed on charges of obtaining a valuable security but in the indictment preferred the counts alleged sums of money which were fractions of the cheques obtained and the sums of money were the particular proceeds of specific hire-purchase agreements. There is a vital difference between the cheques and their proceeds and unless money includes a valuable security there was no committal for the offences alleged in the indictment within the meaning of section 2 (2) (*a*) of the Administration of Justice (Miscellaneous Provisions) Act, 1933; the proviso to that section does not apply because there was a substitution of a new offence of obtaining **[14]** money and there was no evidence of any obtaining of money on the depositions and the indictment was liable to be quashed under section 3 of the Act. Lord Goddard C.J. dealt with the distinction between a count based on a committal charge and a count added or substituted under the proviso in *Reg.* v. *Chairman, County of London Sessions, Ex parte Downes.*[15] This case is distinguishable from *Reg.* v. *Martin,*[16] because in this case there had been no committal for trial for the offence charged in the indictment and every count substituted a new offence.

A valuable security is defined by section 46 of the Larceny Act, 1916, as including bills of exchange and a cheque is a bill of exchange by virtue of section 73 of the Bills of Exchange Act, 1882, and a cheque cannot be money. A distinction is made between a valuable security and money in sections 32 (1) and 17 of the Larceny Act, 1916. In *Reg.* v. *Keena*[17] a conviction was quashed where

[1] [1957] A.C. 602; [1957] 2 W.L.R. 351; 41 Cr.App.R. 11; [1957] 1 All E.R. 411, H.L.
[2] [1954] 1 Q.B. 170; [1953] 3 W.L.R. 895; 37 Cr.App.R. 189; [1953] 2 All E.R. 1355, Cts.-M.A.C.
[3] [1899] 1 Q.B. 230; 15 T.L.R. 57, C.C.R.
[4] [1954] 1 W.L.R. 569; 38 Cr.App.R. 37; [1954] 1 All E.R. 602, C.C.A.
[5] (1909) 2 Cr.App.R. 217; 25 T.L.R. 612, C.C.A
[6] (1850) 4 Cox C.C. 198, C.C.R.
[7] (1857) 7 Cox C.C. 335, C.C.R.
[8] (1918) 13 Cr.App.R. 203, C.C.A.
[9] (1862) 9 Cox C.C. 94, C.C.R.
[10] [1899] 1 Q.B. 230.
[11] (1856) 7 Cox C.C. 100, C.C.R.
[12] (1893) 9 T.L.R. 199, C.C.R.
[13] (1883) 12 Q.B.D. 23, C.C.R.
[14] 7 Cox C.C. 100.
[15] [1954] 1 Q.B. 1; [1953] 3 W.L.R. 586; [1953] 2 All E.R. 750, D.C.
[16] [1962] 1 Q.B. 221; [1961] 3 W.L.R. 17; 45 Cr.App.R. 199; [1961] 2 All E.R. 747, C.C.A.
[17] (1868) L.R.C.C.R. 113.

the indictment alleged the embezzlement of money and a cheque had been obtained.

There is a distinction between an amendment of a misdescription of the object passing from the victim to the defendant and an amendment from a charge of obtaining the object passing from the victim to the defendant to a charge of obtaining the proceeds of that object or vice versa. A mere misdescription or slip in an indictment may be amended, *Rex* v. *Smith*,[18] but here there was a deliberate alteration from the offence charged to another offence, *Reg.* v. *Keena*,[19] *Rex* v. *Clarke*.[20] The appellant was convicted of offences on which he had not been arraigned. The court has power to amend an indictment by section 5 (1) of the Indictments Act, 1915, but, if an indictment is amended in the course of a trial to allege a new offence, the question arises whether the defendant has to plead to the amended count. If he does so he will still be in the charge of the jury in respect of the charges alleged in the counts before they were amended, but a prisoner must be arraigned on all charges and therefore there must be a re-arraignment in the middle of the trial which is unknown in practice. Where an alteration of a count alleges a new offence the court has no jurisdiction to allow the amendment: Even if there had been jurisdiction here there should be no amendment **[15]** at that late stage. *Reg.* v. *Martin*[21] does not apply because there was there an addition of a new count, which was made before arraignment, and there was no alteration in the substance of the charge.

Count 14 was originally in the same form as all the other counts but was amended to allege the procuring of a valuable security on behalf of the Refrigeration Investments Ltd. and the value of the thing obtained was altered. The offence of procuring is not the same offence as obtaining and the amendment was one of substance: *Rex* v. *Lurie*.[22] If in that case it had been a mere misdescription of the offence then the proviso might have been applied: *Reg.* v. *Miller and Hanoman Ltd.*[23]

The court allowed the evidence of the appellant's subsequent bankruptcy to be given in evidence in order to rebut a remark in the appellant's statement that he fully expected to be able to repay the money obtained from the finance company. The evidence was irrelevant—the appellant had not put his character in issue—and it could have implied to the jury that he was dishonest and might commit the crime of false pretences: *Rex* v. *Cohen*.[24] Whether the appellant intended to repay later if he could is irrelevant: *Reg.* v. *Naylor*.[25] The statement made by the appellant to the Berkshire Company should not have been admitted in evidence for if, at the worst, it showed an intention to defraud, it did not show a systematic course of fraud of the type charged in the indictment: *Rex* v. *Fisher*[26]; *Rex* v. *Ellis*.[27]

Bankers' books are not public documents and they can only be used to refresh the memory of a witness, but the copies are evidence against a party to an action: *Harding* v. *Williams*.[28] [Reference was also made to *Arnott* v. *Hayes*.[29]] The evidence of a witness, who had been conditionally bound over, was read at the trial, although notice had been given by the appellant to the clerk of the justices that he required the presence of the witness at the trial. The evidence of another witness was also read although it was apparent that all his evidence was hearsay [*Reg.* v. *Schaffer*[30] was referred to.]

[18] [1951] 1 K.B. 53, sub nom. *Rex* v. *Pople*; 66 T.L.R. (Pt. 2) 319; 34 Cr.App.R. 168; [1950] 2 All E.R. 679, C.C.A.
[19] L.R.C.C.R. 113.
[20] (1905) 69 J.P. 150, C.C.R.
[21] [1962] 1 Q.B. 221.
[22] [1951] 2 T.L.R. 686; 35 Cr.App.R. 113; [1951] 2 All E.R. 704, C.C.A.
[23] [1959] Crim. L.R. 50, C.C.A.
[24] (1938) 26 Cr.App.R. 190; [1938] 3 All. E.R. 380, C.C.A.
[25] (1865) L.R. 1 C.C.R. 4.
[26] [1910] 1 K.B. 149; 26 T.L.R. 122; 3 Cr.App.R. 176, C.C.A.
[27] [1910] 2 K.B. 746; 26 T.L.R. 535; 5 Cr.App.R. 41, C.C.A.
[28] (1880) 14 Ch.D. 197.
[29] (1887) 36 Ch.D. 731; 3 T.L.R. 807; 56 L.J.Ch. 842, C.A.
[30] [1960] Crim.L.R. 124.

With regard to count 19, the case for the appellant was that **[16]** one of his salesman had forged the appellant's wife's signature as a witness to the hire-purchase agreement. No handwriting expert was called nor was the appellant questioned as to the validity of the signature, but the deputy chairman invited the jury to study and compare the writing on different exhibits with that of the agreement. If the jury decided that one document was forged by the appellant, the natural conclusion would be to find that all the documents had been forged by him; see *Reg.* v. *Tilley*.[31]

A. Harmsworth and *B. C. G. Whitaker* for the Crown. The submission that the appellant obtained the cheques in Jersey is artificial and contrary to common sense. He wanted money in England and the cheque was useless to him at the time of posting in Jersey. *Reg.* v. *Stanbury*[32] can be distinguished, for in that case the defendant drove the sheep he had obtained from one county to another and he had obtained them before he moved them. The appellant would only obtain the cheques when he received them himself or had sent his agent to collect them. He had no control over the post office and it is fallacious to say that he had appointed the post office as his agent.

The offence is not only obtaining but the gaining of control over the property, and the offence is continuous and not instantaneous: *Rex* v. *Marston*;[33] *Reg.* v. *Holmes*.[34]* The facts in *Reg.* v. *Holmes*[35] were similar to those here and it was held that the false pretences were committed in this country because the letter was posted here and he received the banker's draft from France through the post and cashed it in England. In that case *Reg.* v. *Cooke*[36] and *Rex* v. *Burdett*[37] were referred to and the material parts of these offences were committed in England. None of the cases relied on by the appellant laid down an exclusive jurisdiction, but it was said that there must be a sufficient act of obtaining, and neither *Reg.* v. *Allington*[38] nor *Reg.* v. *Leech*[39] overruled the decision in *Reg.* v. *Holmes*.[48]* The obtaining is not the only matter on which jurisdiction is based, but it is the kernel of the offence. *Reg.* v. *Ellis*[41] decided that there was jurisdiction to try the offence in the country where the **[17]** obtaining took place even though the false representation was made abroad; the case decided only that, and Wills J.[42] was not saying that there was jurisdiction to try the offence only at the place where the goods were obtained. It is an offence to attempt to obtain goods and there must be jurisdiction to try the offence at the place where the representation was made.

By section 21 of the Bills of Exchange Act, 1882, a cheque has to be delivered and, before delivery to the post office is delivery to the appellant, he must have expressly or impliedly adopted the post office as his agent, otherwise the post office is the agent of the sender and the property does not pass till it is received in England by the appellant: *Baker* v. *Lipton Ltd.*[43] The inference that there is an implied agency is not lightly drawn and there must be some evidence of it: *Pennington* v. *Crossley & Son Ltd.*[44]; *Mitchell-Henry* v. *Norwich Union Life Assurance Society*[45]; *Norman* v. *Rickett*.[46] The appellant sent hire-purchase agreements to Jersey and in return he wanted money, and how that money was sent was immaterial to him. If this argument is unacceptable then the appellant

[31] [1961] 1 W.L.R. 1309; [1961] 3 All E.R. 406, C.C.A.
[32] 9 Cox C.C. 94.
[33] 13 Cr.App.R. 203, C.C.A.
[34] 12 Q.B.D. 23, C.C.R.
[35] Ibid.
[36] (1858) 1 F. & F. 64.
[37] (1820) 4 B. & A. 95.
[38] 9 T.L.R. 199.
[39] 7 Cox C.C. 100.
[40] 12 Q.B.D. 23.
[41] [1899] 1 Q.B. 230; 15 T.L.R. 57, C.C.R.
[42] [1899] 1 Q.B. 230, 234.
[43] (1899) 15 T.L.R. 435.
[44] (1897) 13 T.L.R. 513.
[45] [1918] 2 K.B. 67; 34 T.L.R. 359, C.A.
[46] (1886-7) 3 T.L.R. 182, C.A.

could be convicted of attempting to commit the offence for the attempt was made in England. A person cannot be convicted of an attempt if he has been acquitted of the offence, but here the appellant was convicted and the Court of Criminal Appeal has the power to substitute a conviction of attempting to obtain for that of the offence itself: *Reg.* v. *Males.*[47] The fact that he carried out the offence outside the jurisdiction does not alter the fact that he could have been convicted of the attempt: *Rex* v. *Waugh.*[48]

An indictment which does not charge the offence shown on the depositions is defective and must either be amended or quashed. Such an indictment has a latent defect which may be amended provided there is no injustice to the accused: *Reg.* v. *Martin*[49]—in that case the court held that a count could be added before arraignment. A misdescription in the indictment can be amended at any stage provided there is no injustice to the defendant: *Reg.* v. *Smith.*[50] If a cheque cannot be money then there was a misdescription of the thing obtained, and in Reg. v. Smith[50] the court held that the charge of obtaining a sum of money by **[18]** false pretences was the same in substance as obtaining a cheque, and that case is indistinguishable from this case.

The obtaining of the cheque was a necessary part of the transaction and there could be no proof of obtaining money until it was proved that a cheque had been received. The prosecution were saying, in effect, that in the transactions the appellant received money and that was the charge, but the money was received in the form of a cheque and therefore misdescribed in the indictment as money. It was essentially a matter of misdescription, for money was obtained, but there was a stage when the money was in the form of a cheque. It would be impossible to say that if the description had been "valuable security" the accused would have pleaded differently. The object of an amendment is to ensure both that the accused has a fair trial and that he does not escape conviction on a technicality. In this case the appellant was not prejudiced nor did he suffer any injustice.

There is power to amend at any stage in the trial and certainly to the close of the prosecution's case. If an amendment could be made only before arraignment there would be a severe restraint on the court's discretion to allow an indictment to be amended. A more elaborate amendment was made to count 14 because the cheque had been made payable to the appellant's company: the offence was committed in the same type of transaction and if it was not in substance the same offence it was basically an offence of obtaining by false pretences and was so closely related to the other counts that an amendment could be made.

There is nothing wrong in principle in cross-examination as to a person's bankruptcy providing there is no imputation of dishonesty: *Rex* v. *Cohen.*[51] There was no such implication in the cross-examination of the appellant. The statement of the appellant was given in evidence because it was a statement that he had made willingly and was his explanation of the facts; it was not put in to show a systematic defrauding of hire-purchase companies nor to rebut the defence of mistake. An interpretation of the Bankers' Books Evidence Act, 1879, which makes the production of a Photostat copy evidence but not the original is contrary to common sense.

Reg. v. *Tilley*[52] shows that it is wrong to invite a jury to compare handwriting in a case where there is no expert evidence, and to that extent the appellant was prejudiced. The prosecution **[19]** could have proved that the signature was a forgery, but the appellant had admitted it to be so, and the handwriting was never a major issue in the trial. The jury could not have been affected by the wife's signature because of the appellant's admission that the documents were false and the jury would assume the signatures to be as false as the document.

Worsley in reply. The documents, known as the offer of sale, sent to the

[47] [1961] 3 W.L.R. 1297; [1961] 3 All E.R. 705, C.C.A.
[48] [1909] V.L.R. 379.
[49] [1962] 1 Q.B. 221.
[50] 34 Cr.App.R. 168.
[51] 26 Cr.App.R. 190.
[52] [1961] 1 W.L.R. 1309.

Jersey company with the hire-purchase agreements and signed by the appellant, read "This offer may be accepted by you at any time within one month of the date hereof by sending your cheque for the net amount." If my submission on jurisdiction is correct, then it is not possible to substitute a verdict of attempt because here the appellant succeeded and failure is the essence of an attempt. Although that point was left open in *Reg.* v. *Males*,[53] see *Commonwealth* v. *Crow*[54] and section 9 of the Criminal Procedure Act, 1851.

At the close of the argument the court told the appellant that his appeal would be allowed and he was then discharged.

Cur. adv. vult.

Dec. 19. WIDGERY J. read the following judgment of the court which stated the facts and continued: In this court the grounds of appeal put forward by Mr. Worsley for the appellant can conveniently be grouped under three heads: first, as to counts 1, 2, 3, 4, 9, 10 and 13, that the court of trial had no jurisdiction because the offences were committed in Jersey; secondly, as to all counts, that there was no jurisdiction to amend the indictment in the manner already described at the stage in the trial at which the amendment was made or, alternatively, that the deputy chairman was wrong in exercising his discretion to allow amendment, and, thirdly, as to all counts that evidence had been wrongly admitted and certain misdirections given to the jury in the summing-up. We will deal first with the objection to the jurisdiction in the Jersey counts.

It appears from *Reg.* v. *Ellis*[55] that the gist of the offence of obtaining by false pretences lies in the act of obtaining, and that if this act is done within the jurisdiction it matters not that the false pretence was made abroad. To support the charge, the **[20]** obtaining relied upon must be an obtaining of the property in the thing charged, and not merely possession or control of it; and when this principle is applied to a cheque it means that the accused obtains the cheque when the victim makes actual delivery of it to him, or makes constructive delivery by handing the cheque to an agent duly appointed by the accused to receive it on his behalf.

In the present case the cheques charged did not come into the physical possession of the appellant until they were received by him in the post at Eastbourne, and Mr. Worsley's submission must fail unless the postmaster can properly be regarded as the agent of the appellant for the purpose of accepting delivery of the cheques in Jersey.

We have been referred to numerous authorities in both civil and criminal cases where the agency of the postmaster to receive postal packets on behalf of the addressee has been considered, and counsel on both sides have severally drawn our attention to decisions which they claim to be decisive in their favour. In *Rex* v. *Stoddart*[56] the prisoner was charged with obtaining money by false pretences on evidence that he had organised a competition in Holland which required competitors to predict the results of certain football matches and to post their entries and stake money so as to reach him at Middelburg on the evening of the day on which the matches were played. The fraud consisted in the prisoner pretending that prizes had been allotted and paid to non-existent competitors to the prejudice of the genuine competitors, and it was argued that there was no obtaining within the jurisdiction because the stake money was received in Holland. The full Court of Criminal Appeal rejected this argument and held that when the letters containing money were posted in London for transmission to Middelburg the offence was complete. In the earlier case of *Reg.* v. *T. S. Jones*[57] jurisdiction in a charge of false pretences had been based on the authority of the postmaster to receive postal packets on behalf of the prisoner, and this decision was mentioned with approval in *Rex* v. *Stoddart*.[58]

[53] [1961] 3 W.L.R. 1297; [1961] 3 All E.R. 705, C.C.A.
[54] (1931) 303 Penn. 91.
[55] [1899] 1 Q.B. 230; 15 T.L.R. 57, C.C.R.
[56] (1909) 2 Cr.App.R. 217; 25 T.L.R. 612, C.C.A.
[57] (1850) 4 Cox C.C. 198, C.C.R.
[58] (1909) 2 Cr.App.R. 217; 25 T.L.R. 612, C.C.A.

Counsel for the prosecution relied on *Reg.* v. *Holmes*[59]* and *Rex* v. *Marston.*[60] In *Holmes*[61]* the prisoner wrote a letter from Nottingham to the victim in France and by means of a false **[21]** pretence in the letter induced the victim to send a draft by post from France which the prisoner received in Nottingham and there cashed. The prisoner was held to have been rightly convicted in Nottingham but as the indictment charged the obtaining of money and not the obtaining of the draft, the agency of the postal authorities to receive the draft on behalf of the prisoner was not in issue. In *Marston*[62] the prisoner by a false pretence induced the victim to send him the sum of £1 by post but the letter was intercepted by the police at the prisoner's address before it actually came into his hands, and it was held that no more than an attempt to obtain by a false pretence had been established. The report does not indicate that the prisoner had directed the victim to send the money by post.

There are also a number of civil authorities which concern the date at which the property in a cheque, transmitted by post, will pass from the sender to the recipient. We find it unnecessary to refer to them all, but it appears from *Pennington* v. *Crossley & Son*[63] that a course of dealing over many years in which the postal service has been the medium of transmission between the parties is not in itself enough to justify the inference that the postmaster has been appointed the agent of the addressee so as to make the property in a cheque pass on posting. If however, the addressee has given instructions in a particular case which imply that the post is to be used, this may suffice: *Mitchell-Henry* v. *Norwich Union Life Assurance Society.*[64]

In our judgment, there is no single and universal rule which decides that a cheque transmitted by the victim through the post is to be treated as having been obtained by the prisoner at the moment of posting, but it is clear that this will be the case if the prisoner has agreed with the victim that receipt by the post-master should be equivalent to the receipt by himself.

In the present case, the appellant, when transmitting a hire-purchase agreement to the Guarantee Trust, completed a form of assignment of the agreement and also signed a form of letter called an offer for sale, in which he offered to make the assignment for the purchase price therein set out. The final sentence of this letter reads: "This offer may be accepted by you at any time within one month of the date hereof by sending your cheque for the net amount." In our judgment, the appellant was thus agreeing that the "sending" of the cheque should **[22]** complete the transaction, and since the parties obviously contemplated that it should be sent by post, this act of posting by the victim passed the property in the cheque to the appellant and completed the act of obtaining by him. There was, accordingly, no jurisdiction to try the appellant on counts 1, 2, 3, 4, 9, 10 and 13, and the conviction on those counts must be quashed. Counsel for the prosecution contended that the false pretence was nevertheless made within the jurisdiction, and that it was open to the court to substitute a verdict of guilty of an attempt on each of these counts, but as the offences were in fact completed the alternative verdict of guilty of an attempt is not open to us under section 9 of the Criminal Procedure Act, 1851.

Mr. Worsley's second main ground of appeal, namely, that the deputy chairman erred in giving leave to amend the indictment, is based on the proposition that the obtaining of a valuable security by a false pretence is a wholly different offence from that of obtaining money. *A fortiori* the procuring delivery of a valuable security is also a wholly different offence. Given this premise he puts his argument in two ways. First, he submits that the counts alleging the obtaining of money were bad and incapable of amendment because they failed to comply with section 2 (2) of the Administration of Justice (Miscellaneous Provisions) Act, 1933, in that the obtaining of money was not a charge upon

[59] (1883) 12 Q.B.D. 23, C.C.R.
[60] (1918) 13 Cr.App.R. 203, C.C.A.
[61] (1883) 12 Q.B.D. 23, C.C.R.
[62] 13 Cr.App.R. 203.
[63] (1897) 13 T.L.R. 513, C.A.
[64] [1918] 2 K.B. 67; 34 T.L.R. 359, C.A.

which the appellant was committed, nor was it a charge founded upon facts and evidence disclosed in the depositions. Alternatively, he submits that an amendment charging a wholly different offence cannot be made after arraignment.

The wide powers of amendment conferred by section 5 (1) of the Indictments Act, 1915, can never be exercised so as to cause injustice to the prisoner and, as this court recently pointed out in *Reg.* v. *Martin*[65]: "After arraignment it is doubtful whether a new count can be added at all as the defendant will not have pleaded to it nor, if the trial has started, have been put in charge of the jury on it; and if it were made, injustice . . . would almost certainly be caused." We think that the same observations apply to an amendment of an existing count if the result is to substitute a new offence for that originally charged, but the distinction between an amendment which charges a new offence and one which merely corrects a misdescription of the original offence may be one of degree depending on the **[23]** circumstances of the particular case. In *Rex* v. *Smith*[66] various accused were charged with obtaining money from a building society by false pretences. The method was for one accused to buy a house and purport to sell it to another for an enhanced price, whereupon the second accused would purport to sell the house again to a third, at a still higher price, thus enabling the third accused to represent to the building society that the market price had been increasing and obtain a larger loan than the true value justified. The payments made by the building society were made by cheque and not in cash, and on a submission by the defence at the close of the case for the prosecution that there was no evidence of obtaining money, the trial judge gave leave to amend the relevant counts by substituting for "money" the words "a valuable security, to wit, a cheque." This court held that the amendment was properly made, and Humphreys J. said[67]: "It is to be observed that in this case the matter in respect of which the prosecution suggested that the indictment was defective was in the mere description of the thing obtained. In substance, the charge was the same, but in the view of the prosecution it was necessary to show that what was referred to in the count was not the actual sum of money obtained but the cheque, that is, the valuable security with which in fact the building society parted. We have no hesitation in this case in supporting the action of the judge in amending the indictment." So far as count 19 in the present case is concerned, we are unable to distinguish the amendment allowed from that which was allowed in *Smith*,[67] and accordingly hold that in substance the same offence has been charged throughout in respect of the transaction therein referred to.

In count 14, however, the amendment allowed went beyond a correction of a misdescription of the thing obtained, and substituted the procuring of delivery to a third party for an obtaining by the appellant himself, and in our judgment it cannot on any view be said that the substituted offence is in substance the same as that originally charged. Such an amendment was not permissible at that late stage in the trial at which it was made, and the conviction on this count must be quashed.

Those grounds of appeal which relate to the wrongful admission of evidence and misdirection of the jury need be considered **[24]** only in relation to the last remaining count, count 19. Of these grounds the most serious is that which relates to the deputy chairman's invitation to the jury to compare the handwriting in one exhibit with that in another as a guide to the genuineness of the documents themselves. It is necessary to explain that the defence on the merits to many of the counts was that the hire-purchase agreement in question had been brought to the appellant by one of his salesmen and transmitted by the appellant to the finance company concerned in ignorance that the agreement was not genuine, but in the case of at least six counts the appellant maintained

[65] [1962] 1 Q.B. 221; [1961] 3 W.L.R. 17, 22; 45 Cr.App.R. 199; [1961] 2 All E.R. 747, C.C.A.

[66] [1951] 1 K.B. 53; 66 T.L.R. (Pt. 2) 319; sub nom. *Rex* v. *Pople*, 34 Cr.App.R. 168; [1950] 2 All E.R. 679, C.C.A.

[67] [1951] 1 K.B. 53, 54.

that the agreement had been completed in his presence, was a genuine agreement, and that no false pretence had been made at all. The jury were supplied with photographs of the various exhibits, but no expert evidence as to handwriting was called, and neither side made any significant point on the handwriting at the trial. In the course of his summing-up, however, the deputy chairman repeatedly drew the attention of the jury to particular features of the signatures of customers or witnesses on the hire-purchase agreements in question, and invited them to draw conclusions therefrom as to the genuineness of those signatures. It is fair to say that the deputy chairman had not then had the guidance given by this court in *Reg.* v. *Tilley*,[68] but in the light of that decision he erred in inviting the jury to reach their conclusions without the assistance of expert evidence. On the face of it, this error would not be particularly serious in relation to count 19, where the appellant's case was that the agreement was brought in by one of his salesmen and that any forgery was carried out without his knowledge, but it so happened that in this case the witness to the hirer's signature was the appellant's wife, "K. Harden." If in response to the deputy chairman's invitation the jury had concluded that this signature purporting to be that of the appellant's wife, was a forgery, they might have concluded that the appellant must have been aware of this because no salesman who wished to perpetrate a fraud behind the appeallant's back would have been so foolish as to forge the signature of the appellant's wife on a document which the appellant was bound to see.

There were a number of other complaints of misdirection which we do not think it necessary to set out in detail, as even in their cumulative effect they would not be likely to cause a **[25]** substantial miscarriage of justice in view of the fact that the appellant had made a statement to the police which deeply implicated him and made the general case for the prosecution a formidable one. After considering all the circumstances, however, and having particular regard to the misdirection on handwriting, we feel unable to say that no substantial miscarriage of justice occurred with regard to the conviction on count 19, and we have accordingly decided that that conviction must also be quashed. At the close of the argument we informed the appellant that his appeal would be allowed, and he was then discharged.

Appeal allowed.

Solicitors: *Registrar, Court of Criminal Appeal; F. H. Busby, Town Clerk of Eastbourne.*

REGINA v. SMITH

([1962] 2 Q.B. 317)

March 21, 1962: Court of Criminal Appeal: Ashworth, Hinchcliffe, Phillimore JJ.

Crime—Receiving—Abroad, property stolen—No proceedings against principal offender—Charge of receiving stolen property—Alternative count of possessing property stolen abroad—No proceedings in respect of actual theft—Whether properly charged with receiving—Whether proceedings against "principal offender" necessary prerequisite to charge of possession of property stolen abroad—"Principal offender"—Larceny Act, 1916 (6 & 7 *Geo.* 5, *c.* 50), *s.* 33 (1) (3) (4). *Crime—Court of Criminal Appeal—Substitution of verdict—Alternative counts—Conviction of receiving—Facts satisfying jurors of guilt of receiving property stolen abroad—Jury discharged from giving verdict on alternative count—Appeal—Substitution of verdict—Variation of sentence—Criminal Appeal Act,* 1907 (7 *Edw.* 7, *c.* 23), *s.* 5 (2).

The appellant was convicted on a count under subsection (1) of section 33

[68] [1961] 1 W.L.R. 1309; [1961] 3 All E.R. 406, C.C.A.

of the Larceny Act, 1916,[1] charging him with receiving in Surrey property which, on the uncontested facts, had been stolen abroad, and was sentenced to three years' imprisonment. The indictment contained an alternative count under subsection (4) of **[318]** section 33. No proceedings had been taken in respect of the theft itself. On appeal against conviction, in which it was conceded that the jury must have been satisfied of the facts necessary to establish a case under subsection (4) of section 33 and the prosecution sought a substituted verdict on the alternative count pursuant to section 5 (2) of the Criminal Appeal Act, 1907[2]:—

Held, (1) that the appellant was not properly charged with receiving under subsection (1) of section 33 of the Larceny Act, 1916, when the uncontested facts showed that the theft had taken place abroad (post, p. 325).

Reg. v. *Debruiel* (1861) 11 Cox C.C. 207 followed.

(2) That the "principal offender" referred to in subsection (3) of section 33 was the person who had, so to speak, started the business which ended with the receiver, and started it in nearly every case by stealing the goods in question, and contemplated a person amenable to the jurisdiction of the English courts; and that, viewed from that angle, there could not be such a principal offender for the purposes of subsection (4) of section 33 which created a special offence to deal with a special situation, so that, if the ingredients set out in that subsection were established, it was immaterial whether the person who originally stole the goods had been brought to justice or not (post, p. 329).

Rex v. *Graham* (1901) 65 J.P. 248 explained.

(3) That, since the jury were satisfied of the facts necessary to establish guilt under subsection (4) of section 33, it was a case in which the court should exercise its jurisdiction under section 5 (2) of the Criminal Appeal Act, 1907, and substitute a verdict of guilty on that alternative count.

Reg. v. *Caslin* [1961] 1 W.L.R. 59; 45 Cr.App.R. 47; [1961] 1 All E.R. 246, C.C.A. applied.

(4) That the court would substitute a verdict under subsection (4) notwithstanding that the need for substitution had arisen through the fault of the prosecution; but there were good grounds for not imposing exactly the same sentence on the substituted verdict as had been passed in respect of the verdict on the count under subsection (1). Accordingly, instead of allowing or dismissing the appeal, the court would substitute a verdict of guilty on the alternative count and would pass on that substituted verdict a sentence of two years' imprisonment.

APPEAL against conviction.

On August 24, 1961, a considerable quantity of jewellery was **[319]** stolen at Cap d'Antibes in France. On October 13, 1961, at Wimbledon Greyhound

[1] Larceny Act, 1916, s. 33: "(1) Every person who receives any property knowing the same to have been stolen or obtained in any way whatsoever under circumstances which amount to felony or misdemeanour, shall be guilty of an offence of the like degree . . . (2) Every person who receives any mail bag . . . shall be guilty of felony. (3) Every such person may be indicted and convicted, whether the principal offender has or has not been previously convicted, or is or is not amenable to justice. (4) Every person who, without lawful excuse, knowing the same to have been stolen or obtained in any way whatsoever under such circumstances that if the act had been committed in the United Kingdom the person committing it would have been guilty of felony or misdemeanour, receives or has in his possession any property so stolen or obtained outside the United Kingdom, shall be guilty of an offence of the like degree. . . ."

[2] Criminal Appeal Act, 1907, s. 5 (2): "Where an appellant has been convicted of an offence and the jury could on the indictment have found him guilty of some other offence, and on the finding of the jury it appears to the Court of Criminal Appeal that the jury must have been satisfied of facts which proved him guilty of that other offence, the court may, instead of allowing or dismissing the appeal, substitute for the verdict found by the jury a verdict of guilty of that other offence, and pass such sentence in substitution for the sentence passed at the trial as may be warranted in law for that other offence, not being a sentence of greater severity."

Stadium, in London, police officers keeping observation saw the appellant, Duncan James Smith, with a small white packet which was subsequently found to contain two pieces of the stolen jewellery; two other pieces of the stolen jewellery were later found on the appellant; their total value was about £400. The appellant was tried on November 27 and 28, 1961, at Surrey Quarter Sessions on an indictment containing two counts in the alternative: count 1 charged him with receiving the four pieces of jewellery knowing the same to have been stolen contrary to subsection (1) of section 33 of the Larceny Act, 1916, and count 2 charged that, without lawful authority or excuse, knowing the same to have been obtained under such circumstances that if the act had been committed in the United Kingdom the person committing it would have been guilty of larceny, he had in his possession the four pieces of jewellery so obtained by larceny contrary to subsection (4) of section 33 of the Larceny Act, 1916. The appellant pleaded not guilty to both counts. He gave evidence and put forward an explanation which the jury obviously rejected, and he was found guilty on count 1. The chairman (Brigadier A. C. C. Willway) discharged the jury from giving a verdict on count 2. The appellant was sentenced to three years' imprisonment.

He appealed against his conviction, it being contended that he had been wrongly charged under subsection (1) of section 33 and that, as no proceedings had been taken in respect of the actual theft, the court had no jurisdiction under section 5 (2) of the Criminal Appeal Act, 1907, to substitute a verdict of guilty on the alternative count under subsection (4).

Ian Percival and *Miss Nemone Lethbridge* for the appellant. The original dishonest taking was abroad, and the trial was conducted on the hypothesis that, nevertheless, if the receiving was in England the relevant count was count 1, and that count 2 was relevant only if the receiving was abroad. That was wrong and the conviction on count 1 cannot stand.

At common law the courts took no cognisance of offences committed abroad and would not inquire whether acts abroad amounted to crimes according to foreign law. The courts will take cognisance of dishonest acts abroad only if required by statute so to do. Section 33 of the Larceny Act, 1916, is to be interpreted against that background. As a matter of interpretation subsection (1) of section 33 is applicable only if the original **[320]** taking is in England because it could not "amount to felony or misdemeanour" unless committed in England; they are English crimes. This is confirmed by a comparison with the words of subsection (4) which are clearly designed, and are the appropriate words to cover the case where the original dishonest taking is abroad. Support for that view is to be found in the relevant history and decided cases. Unless there has been a material change in the statute or case law since the Larceny Act, 1827, and the case of *Reg.* v. *Debruiel,*[3] that case covers the position here. Section 91 of the Larceny Act, 1861, replaced the relevant sections of the Act of 1827, but made no material change. In *Reg.* v. *Carr and Wilson,*[4]* the Crown accepted the proposition now advanced but argued that the ship was within or part of the jurisdiction. The Larceny Act, 1896, introduced for the first time provisions applicable where the dishonest taking was abroad. This was specifically to cover the deficiency and created the offence of receiving or having in possession within the jurisdiction property stolen (sic) abroad. [*Reg.* v. *Panse,*[5] was referred to.] The Larceny Act, 1896, is now incorporated in subsection (4) of section 33 of the Larceny Act, 1916. If any offence was committed here it was an offence under subsection (4). The appeal should be allowed.

This court cannot substitute a verdict on count 2 under the provisions of the Criminal Appeal Act, 1907, s. 5 (2). It is conceded that in so far as the issue is whether the jury must have been satisfied of the facts necessary to support a conviction under subsection (4) of section 33 of the Larceny Act, 1916, the answer is adverse to the appellant [see *Reg.* v. *Caslin*[6]] and accordingly that, subject to the one point following, there is power to substitute a verdict on count

[3] (1861) 11 Cox C.C. 207.
[4] (1882) 10 Q.B.D. 76.
[5] (1897) 61 J.P. 536.
[6] [1961] 1 W.L.R. 59.

2. There cannot be a conviction under subsection (4) unless the principal offender has been convicted or is amenable to justice. As a matter of interpretation section 33 must be considered as a whole. Subsection (1) and subsection (2) apply to receiving where the "theft" took place within the jurisdiction. The words "every such person" in subsection (3) make it clear that that subsection applies only to the persons referred to in subsections (1) and (2). Subsection (3), therefore, makes the conviction or amenability to justice of the principal offender immaterial in the case of prosecutions under subsections (1) and (2)—and it must be inferred that those considerations **[321]** would have been material but for subsection (3). Subsection (4) extends the provisions of subsection (1) in two ways; first to the receipt in England of goods dishonestly acquired abroad; and secondly to possession in England of goods dishonestly acquired and received abroad. Prima facie if it would be necessary but for subsection (3) to consider conviction or amenability in connection with receiving under subsections (1) or (2), a fortiori in the case of the extensions made under subsection (4). If it had been intended to make conviction or amenability of the principal offender immaterial in all cases covered by section 33 nothing could have been simpler than to do so than by reversing the order of subsections (3) and (4). The provisions of subsection (3) having been inserted between subsections (2) and (4) the interpretation of the section as a whole is that conviction and amenability are immaterial in cases under subsections (1) or (2) but material in cases under subsection (4). If it could be said that the principal offender in a case under subsection (4) could never be convicted or amenable to justice, that would provide an alternative explanation for the order of the subsections; but that is not so. For example, if the "thief" brought the goods to England, or if he sent them to England and resumed possession of them in England, he would be amenable to justice under subsection (4) [*Rex* v. *Graham,*[7] was referred to]. It may be true that he is less likely to become amenable to justice but that is all the more reason for specifically making amenability immaterial if it is intended to be immaterial. Support for the foregoing propositions, arrived at as a matter of interpretation, is to be found in the history of the law relating to receivers and other accessories. [Reference was made to Foster's Discourses on Crown Law, 1st ed. (1762), Discourse No. 3, sec. 6, p. 373; section 54 of the Larceny Act, 1827, section 3 of the Accessories and Abettors Act, 1861, and the Larceny Act, 1861.] Conviction or amenability of the principal felon was expressly made immaterial by statute because prior to and but for the statutory provisions to that effect there could not be a conviction of a receiver or accessory unless the principal felon was convicted or amenable to justice. Such provisions were re-enacted in the Larceny Act, 1861, and it must be assumed that that was because such provisions were necessary. The Larceny Act, 1896, which created by extension further offences in the nature of receiving or accessory, contained no such provisions and it must be assumed that that was because it was **[322]** not intended to make conviction and amenability immaterial in cases under that Act. Section 33 of the Larceny Act, 1916, consolidates the "receiving" provisions of the Act of 1861 and the provisions of the Act of 1896 into one section. It re-enacts the provisions in the Act of 1861 as to conviction and amenability by taking them out of the text of the sections and putting them into a separate subsection—subsection (3). That subsection, which could readily have been made applicable to all subsections of section 33 if so intended, is by design made applicable only to subsections (1) and (2) and not to subsection (4). The conviction or amenability to justice of the principal offender are therefore material in the case of a prosecution under subsection (4). There was no evidence as to either in this case. Therefore there could not have been a conviction on count 2 and this court cannot substitute one for the conviction under count 1.

If, contrary to this contention, the court has jurisdiction to substitute a verdict, there is a discretion, and a verdict should not be substituted because the trial was conducted by the Crown on an incorrect hypothesis. If the court does substitute a verdict, the sentence must be not greater in severity, and the court should be generous and pass a lesser sentence.

[7] (1901) 65 J.P. 248.

Henry Pownall for the Crown. It is conceded that the conviction on count 1 cannot stand and that the trial was conducted on a mistaken basis. That, however, in this case makes little difference; such difference as exists constitutes merely a different label, because the jury were clearly satisfied of the facts necessary to establish a case under subsection (4). The court should, therefore, substitute a verdict under the Criminal Appeal Act, 1907, s. 5 (2).

The Larceny Act, 1896 (now subsection (4) of the Act of 1916), created a new offence; it stopped a gap and prevented international trafficking in stolen property. Subsection (3) contemplates a thief amenable to justice; subsection (4) contemplates a thief not amenable to justice. *Rex* v. *Graham*[7] supports the Crown's contention; the persons concerned were charged in this country with possessing the stolen property, not with stealing it.

Ashworth J. stated the facts substantially as set out above, and continued: Subject to the question of law, it is quite plain that the appellant was in unlawful possession of stolen jewellery, and if the theft had taken place in England the propriety of his conviction of receiving could not have been challenged. **[323]**

The point that is taken is that the count of the indictment on which he was convicted was a count alleging receiving under subsection (1) of section 33 of the Larceny Act, 1916. The indictment also contained a second count under subsection (4) of that same section which deals, to put it compendiously, with the receipt or unlawful possession of property stolen abroad in circumstances which would have amounted to larceny in this country if the theft had taken place here. The two charges were alternative, and, therefore, the jury were absolved from giving a verdict on the second count, having returned a verdict of guilty on the first.

[His Lordship read subsection (1) of section 33 of the Larceny Act, 1916, and continued:] What is said is that the principal felony of theft can have been committed only in this country in order to be the foundation of a charge of receiving under that subsection. It is argued that, for the avoidance of doubt, subsection (4) of section 33 makes it plain that when the theft takes place abroad in circumstances contemplated in that section it gives rise to a charge under that subsection and not under subsection (1). Counsel for the appellant said that, as a matter of construction, that is plain from the section itself, but he finds support from the decision in *Reg.* v. *Debruiel,*[8] where the headnote reads: "Indictment for larceny and receiving. The prisoner had stolen goods in Guernsey, and brought them to England, where he was taken and committed for trial: *Held*, that Guernsey not being a part of the United Kingdom, the prisoner could not be convicted of larceny, for having them in his possession here, nor of receiving in England the goods so stolen in Guernsey." That case was decided in 1861, and in giving judgment Byles J., who had consulted Channell B., said[9]: "Nor could the prisoner be convicted of receiving, because that crime consisted in the guilty receipt of stolen goods; that is to say, goods stolen according to the law of England, and that law does not recognise a stealing in a foreign country as a crime which it will punish."

In the course of his argument counsel for the appellant referred us, on this point, to the terms of the Larceny Act, 1827, and the Larceny Act, 1861, which re-enacted in effect the Act of 1827, for the purpose of pointing out that in neither Act was there any provision corresponding with what is now subsection (4) of section 33 of the Larceny Act, 1916.

The next case which has a bearing on this matter is *Reg.* v. **[324]** *Carr and Wilson.*[10]* The matter in issue there arose out of the fact that a British ocean-going merchant ship was lying afloat in the river at Rotterdam, Holland, and the question was whether the defendants could be properly tried and convicted at the Central Criminal Court in this country on the ground that the court had jurisdiction since the offence took place within the jurisdiction of the Admiralty in England. That was the main issue, but in the course of the case, as appears

[7] (1901) 65 J.P. 248.
[8] (1861) 11 Cox C.C. 207.
[9] Ibid. 208.
[10] (1882) 10 Q.B.D. 76.

from the argument for the defendant Carr, this submission was put forward[11]: "The direction is, that if a Dutchman stole from the ship where she lay in Holland, an English subject here may be guilty of receiving. This cannot be, unless the Dutchman who stole can be tried here. The prisoners are British subjects, but that is quite immaterial—nationality does not give jurisdiction. The question is whether the stealing is a felony triable here. If the stealing is not within the jurisdiction, the receivers are not triable here." That particular contention does not seem to have been controverted by counsel for the Crown, and in giving judgment Lord Coleridge C.J. said[12]: "The conviction is for the offence of feloniously receiving these bonds knowing them to have been stolen. Now it is obvious that the prisoners cannot be convicted here unless the stealing took place within the jurisdiction of our courts. The question has therefore to be considered whether the ship was, when the bonds were stolen, within the jurisdiction of the Admiralty, so that the thief, if he had been caught, could have been tried at the Old Bailey. The exact point has never yet, it would seem, been decided. None of the cases cited absolutely covers the precise question now before us. There are, indeed, two questions involved: first, was the ship within the jurisdiction of the Admiralty, so that the stealing took place locally within the jurisdiction of the court which tried the prisoners; and, secondly, was the person who stole a person subject to the jurisdiction of that court."

That was in 1882, and the matter received the attention of Parliament in 1896, when the Larceny Act, 1896, was passed, consisting of two sections only, of which the long title is: "An Act to amend the law with respect to the jurisdiction exerciseable in cases relating to the receipt or possession of stolen property." Without reading the provisions of section 1 in detail, it is sufficient to say that that Act was the forerunner of **[325]** what is now subsection (4) of section 33 of the Larceny Act, 1916, and for the first time created the offence of receiving or having in possession in this country property stolen outside the United Kingdom, such receipt or possession being accompanied by knowledge that the property had been stolen.

In *Reg.* v. *Panse*[13] a case was argued arising out of the Larceny Act, 1896, and the headnote reads: "Where a person has in his possession property stolen outside the United Kingdom, he is liable to be convicted under the Larceny Act, 1896, although he had received and had been in possession of that property before the Larceny Act, 1896, came into operation."

The Larceny Act, 1916, was, in substance, a codifying Act, and section 33 reproduced, in somewhat altered form but substantially with the same content, the provisions theretofore in force relating to receiving, that is to say, the provisions which originally found their origin in the Larceny Act, 1827, together with the provisions enacted in the Larceny Act, 1896. Section 33 of the Larceny Act, 1916, is divided into four subsections, subsection (1) dealing, as already indicated, with the receipt of stolen property which has been stolen in this country, and subsection (4) dealing with property which has been stolen abroad, of which the courts first took cognisance by virtue of the Larceny Act, 1896.

Pausing there, one may profitably return to this present case and ask the question: In the light of those enactments and those authorities was this present appellant properly charged under subsection (1) of section 33 of the Larceny Act, 1916, with receiving when the uncontested facts showed that the theft of the jewellery took place in France? To that question there can be only one answer, and the court is indebted to counsel for the Crown for not seeking to suggest any other. Having regard to *Reg.* v. *Debruiel*[14] and the terms of the Larceny Act, 1896, with its modern counterpart in subsection (4) of section 33 of the Act of 1916, he conceded that the conviction under subsection (1) of section 33 of the Larceny Act, 1916, could not be upheld and, as he said, the trial at Surrey Quarter Sessions was conducted on a mistaken basis. To that extent, therefore, the appeal certainly succeeds.

The question which then arises, which was brought to the notice of counsel for the appellant when he obtained leave to appeal, is whether this court, in

[11] Ibid. 80.
[12] Ibid. 84.
[13] (1897) 61 J.P. 536.
[14] 11 Cox C.C. 207.

the circumstances, could or should **[326]** exercise the jurisdiction conferred on it under subsection (2) of section 5 of the Criminal Appeal Act, 1907.

[His Lordship read that subsection, and continued:] In approaching this branch of the case, counsel for the appellant was again of assistance to the court because he frankly conceded that, in so far as the issue is whether the jury must have been satisfied of the facts necessary to establish a case under subsection (4) of section 33 of the Larceny Act, 1916, the answer is adverse to the appellant. In other words, if the only count in the indictment had been the second count and the jury had returned a verdict of guilty, subject to the point about to be discussed, their verdict could not have been challenged.

In considering whether a verdict should be substituted, this court has recently laid down the basis that should be applied in *Reg.* v. *Caslin,*[15] where Lord Parker C.J., after reading subsection (2) of section 5 of the Criminal Appeal Act, 1907, said[16]: "The jurisdiction of this court under that subsection does not depend on whether the judge did in fact sum up on the alternative basis, but upon whether the jury must have been satisfied of facts which proved him guilty of that other offence. No doubt, therefore, this is a jurisdiction which must be exercised with great caution, and the fact that the jury never had a proper direction as to the alternative offence, in this case false pretences, is a very relevant consideration."

The argument that this court has no jurisdiction to substitute a verdict of guilty under the second count of the indictment is based in the first place upon a consideration of the whole of section 33 of the Larceny Act, 1916. It is pointed out that the first two subsections of that section deal with forms of receiving where the original theft has occurred in this country. There then follows subsection (3) in these words: "Every such person may be indicted and convicted, whether the principal offender has or has not been previously convicted, or is or is not amenable to justice." The terms of subsection (3) are a reproduction, in the form of a separate subsection, of words that found a place both in the Larceny Act, 1827, and in the Larceny Act, 1861. The difference now is that they have been put in a separate subsection, but it is pointed out that subsection (3) applies only to a person who is charged with receiving within subsection (1) of the section. Accordingly, a person who is charged under **[327]** subsection (4) with receiving property stolen abroad is not any "such person" as is referred to in subsection (3). Accordingly, it is said that this setting out of section 33 of the Larceny Act, 1916, is quite deliberate, and while considerations affecting the principal offender are rendered immaterial for the purposes of subsection (1) and subsection (2), they remain material and important in regard to subsection (4). The argument proceeds that, because in effect this form of receiving is akin to the position of accessories after the fact, the old principle is still relevant and applicable: that until the principal offender, namely, the man who has stolen abroad, has been convicted or brought to justice, there is no room for a conviction of the receiver under subsection (4). As counsel for the appellant put it, subsection (4) is extending the preceding subsections, (a) by covering thefts abroad, and (b) by covering receipt abroad and possession in England; and if it would be necessary, but for subsection (3), to consider the principal offender in relation to subsections (1) and (2), a fortiori it is necessary to consider him in regard to subsection (4). It is to be noted in passing that when the Larceny Act, 1896, was passed, although the situation in regard to principal offenders had been made plain both in the Larceny Act, 1827, and the Larceny Act, 1861, Parliament did not think it necessary to include in the Larceny Act, 1896, any provision regarding the amenability to justice or conviction of the principal offender, and it would seem at first sight as if the Larceny Act, 1896, was in effect creating a new statutory offence designed to close a gap which the cases to which reference has been made had shown to exist. Counsel for the appellant went on to argue that, of course, if the principal offender in respect of a charge under subsection (4) of section 33 of the Larceny Act, 1916, could never be convicted in this country, it might well be understood

[15] [1961] 1 W.L.R. 59; 45 Cr. App. R. 47; [1961] 1 All E.R. 246, C.C.A.
[16] [1961] 1 W.L.R. 59, 63.

why there was no corresponding section to subsection (3) either in the Larceny Act, 1896, or following subsection (4) of section 33 of the Act of 1916, because, on that approach to the problem, the existence of a corresponding section would be unnecessary; but he said that that argument loses all force when it is appreciated that there can be proceedings under subsection (4) of section 33 of the Act of 1916 in respect of articles stolen abroad in which the principal offender is the accused person. For that purpose he cited *Rex* v. *Graham*,[17] where the headnote reads: "The prisoners, whilst living in expensive rooms in an hotel in Paris, ordered a fur jacket to be **[328]** made for one of them by the prosecutor. Before this fur jacket was delivered, they ordered and received at their hotel various other fur articles. They were not asked to pay for any of these articles, but the prosecutor said that he regarded it as a cash transaction and did not ask for payment because other goods were in order, and the transaction would not be complete till the delivery of the fur jacket. The prisoners brought the furs to London, where they were arrested and indicted under the Larceny Act, 1896. *Held*: (1) That there was evidence of larceny according to English law. (2) That the Larceny Act, 1896, applied to a case such as this, where the property was alleged to have been stolen by the same person in whose possession it was afterwards found in England."

One matter of importance arises at once from that reading of the headnote and from the decision itself. The persons charged in that case were not charged, nor could they be charged, with what I venture to call the principal offence of larceny. The larceny was committed in Paris, but what they were charged with under the Larceny Act, 1896—now subsection (4) of section 33 of the Larceny Act, 1916—was being in possession of goods knowing them to have been stolen outside the United Kingdom. That case does not lend, in the view of this court, any support to the view that, before proceedings can be brought under subsection (4) of section 33 of the Act of 1916, the principal offender has to be brought to justice and convicted for the principal offence. The two words "principal offender" used in subsection (3) of section 33 are, in the view of this court, applicable to the person who has, so to speak, started the business which ends with the receiver, and started it in nearly every case by stealing the goods in question. The principal offence which is rendered immaterial for the purposes of subsection (3) of section 33 is the offence of theft. Counsel for the Crown says that, approached from this point of view, section 33 is perfectly easy to understand. Subsection (3) contemplates someone who would be, or should be, amenable to the jurisdiction of the English courts, that is to say, the thief who has stolen the goods of which the accused is thereafter charged with being the receiver, but that is a theft in England. Subsection (4) contemplates someone not amenable to justice, in other words, the man who has stolen abroad whether he be a foreigner or a British subject; and counsel for the Crown says that viewed from this angle there never can be a principal **[329]** offender for the purposes of subsection (4), using the words "principal offender" in the sense in which they are used in subsection (3).

The conclusion to which this court has come is that the answer put forward by counsel for the Crown to the persuasive argument ably put forward on behalf of the appellant is completely convincing. There was, in the view of this court, no need at all for the principal offender to be brought to justice or convicted in this country or, indeed, anywhere, before a charge could properly be preferred under subsection (4) of section 33 of the Larceny Act, 1916. Subsection (4) of section 33 creates a special offence to deal with a special situation, and if the ingredients set out in that subsection are established, it is immaterial whether the person who originally stole the goods has been brought to justice or not.

If the matter stopped there, this court would feel not only entitled but in justice bound to substitute a verdict of guilty under the second count of the indictment. Counsel for the appellant has said that, even if he is wrong in his main submission, the power to substitute should not in this case be exercised because the fault lay largely with the Crown for pursuing the matter under the

[17] (1901) 65 J.P. 248.

wrong subsection, and this present appellant should not be penalised by, so to speak, a side wind and found guilty of an offence which was never really before the jury. But full effect can be given to that line of argument when one comes to his last point, which is that, in any event, the court should be generous, if that is the right word, in considering its duty under the last words of section 5 (2) of the Criminal Appeal Act, 1907, namely, "passing such sentence in respect of the substituted offence as may be warranted in law." The appellant has 18 previous convictions, but that bare statement does not truly reflect his behaviour over the past 10 years. Until 1953 he was in constant trouble, but he then seems to have spent eight years or thereabouts free of trouble until, in November, 1961, in connection with a quite different matter, he was sent to prison, and he is now serving that other sentence. This court feels that, for the reasons put forward on the appellant's behalf, there are good grounds for not imposing exactly the same sentence on the substituted verdict as was passed in respect of the verdict under count 1.

Accordingly, the result of this appeal is that this court, instead of allowing or dismissing the appeal, will substitute for the verdict **[330]** found by the jury of guilty on count 2, and will pass upon that substituted verdict a sentence of two years' imprisonment.

Verdict substituted and sentence varied accordingly.

Solicitors: *Alan Isaacs & Co.; Solicitor, Metropolitan Police.*

5

EXCEPTIONS FROM AND RESTRICTIONS ON TERRITORIAL JURISDICTION

V.

OTHER PUBLIC VESSELS

THE BULGARIA

([1964] 2 Ll. Rep. 524)

October 29, 1964: Probate, Divorce and Admiralty Division: Sir J. Simon, P.

Admiralty practice—Bail bond—Application to file qualified bail bond.

Writ *in rem* issued on Oct. 9, 1964, as result of collision between plaintiffs' steamship *Aurum* and defendants' steamship *Bulgaria*—Writ served and *Bulgaria* arrested on Oct. 14—Conditional appearance entered by defendants (intending to claim sovereign immunity) on Oct. 20—Application by defendants on Oct. 29 to file bail bond qualified by addition of

> . . . This bail is put up without prejudice to the right of the owners of the *Bulgaria* to move the Court to set aside the writ in the action on the grounds that the ship is the property of the Government of a recognized foreign Sovereign State and that the said State decline to sanction the institution of these proceedings in this Court.

————*Held*, by SIR JOCELYN SIMON, P., that defendants were anxious lest, if bond were in usual form, it might be construed as a step in the action, converting the conditional appearance into an unconditional appearance amounting to a submission to the jurisdiction; that plaintiffs would not be prejudiced by the addition; and that, accordingly, defendants should have leave to file bond with the addition.

The following cases were referred to:
*Jassy,** [1906] P. 270;
Rosina, (1921) 6 Ll.L.Rep. 346.

In this application, Navigation Maritime Bulgare, the owners of the steamship *Bulgaria* and the defendants in an action *in rem* by the plaintiffs, the owners of the steamship *Aurum*, sought leave to file a bail bond, without thereby submitting to the jurisdiction of the Court or, alternatively, to file a bail bond which stated that it was filed under protest and without prejudice to the right of the defendants to apply to have the writ set aside. They also applied for the release of the *Bulgaria*, which was arrested in the port of London on Oct. 14, 1964.

Mr. J. D. H. Rochford (instructed by Messrs. Middleton, Lewis & Co.) appeared for the applicants; Mr. Gerald Darling (instructed by Messrs. Thomas Cooper & Co.) represented the respondents. **[525]**

Mr. *Rochford*, for the applicant defendants, said that the writ in the action was issued on Oct. 9, and subsequently the *Bulgaria* was arrested and the writ served upon her. A conditional appearance was entered on Oct. 20. It was intended to apply to have the writ set aside on the ground that the vessel was owned by the Bulgarian Government, which was a sovereign state. The application was of some urgency because the vessel hoped to sail that night or the next day. Counsel said that if the bail bond was filed in the prescribed form, it might amount to a submission to the jurisdiction.

After citing *The Rosina*, (1921) 6 Ll.L.Rep. 545, COUNSEL said that the bond was being put up by the Moscow Narodny Bank, Ltd.

Mr. *Darling*, for the respondent plaintiffs, submitted that the matter was not urgent. The conditional appearance had been entered on Oct. 20, and the defendants had had nine days in which the defence of sovereign immunity could have been raised. If it had been successful the action would have come to an end.

Counsel submitted that the practice in the Admiralty Court was that the vessel could be released only by giving an unqualified bail bond. There was no reason in the present case for a departure from the established practice.

When Sir JOCELYN SIMON, P., suggested that the words "under protest and" in the bail bond should be deleted, COUNSEL said that the plantiffs had offered to accept an undertaking but that the defendants could not accept it without instructions.

Mr. *Rochford* said that he was instructed that that form had been approved many miles away from England, and if it was altered it would have to be approved again.

Mr. *Darling* said that he feared that the bond would not be honoured on the pretext that it was given under protest. Any departure from the standard form was likely to lead to difficulties either in securing payment, or non-payment. Counsel cited *The Jassy*,* [1906] P. 270 and *Coughlin* v. *Navigation Maritime Bulgare*, [1963] 1 Lloyd's Rep. 113.

JUDGMENT

Sir JOCELYN SIMON, P.: This application is in an Admiralty action *in rem* arising out of a collision. The plaintiffs issued a writ on Oct. 1964. The defendants' vessel, the *Bulgaria*, was arrested on Oct. 14, and on Oct. 20, the defendants entered a conditional appearance, that is to say, an appearance which does not amount to a submission to the jurisdiction of the Court, provided the defendants moved the Court within 28 days to set aside the writ. The defendants intend, I am told, to claim that the writ should be set aside on the ground that the vessel in question is the property of a foreign Sovereign, who is immune from the process of the Court.

The present application has been made to-day because the defendants desired that the *Bulgaria* should sail either tonight or tomorrow. The defendants are prepared to procure the execution of a bond as a condition of the release of the ship from arrest; but they are anxious lest, if the bond is in the usual form, that might be construed as a step in the action, converting the conditional appearance into an unconditional appearance amounting to a submission to the jurisdiction: see *The Rosina*, (1921) 6 Ll.L.Rep. 346. They therefore wish that the bond should vary from the usual form as set out in the Appendices to the White Book, by adding: "This bail is put up without prejudice to the right of the owners of the *Bulgaria* to move the Court to set aside the writ in the action on the grounds that the ship is the property of the Government of a recognized foreign sovereign state and that the said State decline to sanction the institution of these proceedings in this Court". The plaintiffs object to the bond being in anything other than the standard form prescribed in the Rules. R.S.C. Order 1, r. 7, however, states:

> The forms in the Appendices shall be used where applicable with such variations as the circumstances of the particular case require.

I cannot myself see in what way the plaintiffs would be prejudiced by the addition to the bond of the proviso that I have recited. It may be that in any event the giving of bail unconditionally by the defendants would not prevent them thereafter claiming to be released from the process of this Court on the ground that the vessel in question was the property of a foreign Sovereign: see

The Jassy [1906] P. 270.* But the matter cannot be regarded as free from doubt; and it seems to me reasonable that the defendants should not feel embarrassed in laying before the Court grounds for releasing them from the process of the Court. There being, as far as I can **[526]** see, no prejudice to the plaintiffs by the bond being in the form that the defendants offer, in my view the reasonable course is to give the defendants leave to file a bond in the form to which I have referred and to order that, on doing so, the vessel may be released from arrest.

Mr. *Rochford*: There does remain the question of costs, my Lord. Would your Lordship order that they be left to be dealt with when the motion comes on?

Sir JOCELYN SIMON, P.: What do you say, Mr. Darling?

Mr. *Darling*: My Lord, this is a special application, aside from the question which will be at issue in the motion. It is obviously also a question aside from the main issues in the collision action, if there ever was one. My friend has come here to ask for a special privilege for himself. He has succeeded in getting it, but his coming here has been the occasion of these costs. As I was pointing out in my argument, it would have been open to him at any time during the last nine days to have moved the Court, and this application would have then been entirely unnecessary. In those circumstances, I would submit that it is only fair that the plaintiffs should have these costs; and I would ask your Lordship to so order.

Sir JOCELYN SIMON, P.: Costs in the cause.

vii

VISITING FORCES

UREY v. LUMMIS

([1962] 1 W.L.R. 826)

April 6, 1962: Queen's Bench Division, Lord Parker C.J., Ashworth, Hinchcliffe JJ.

Road Traffic—Licence—Driving licence—Driving permit issued to serviceman of visiting force—No British driving licence—Serviceman supervising learner driver—Whether aiding and abetting learner to commit offence—Whether driving permit equivalent to driving licence—Road Traffic Act, (8 & 9 *Eliz.* 2, *c.* 16), *ss.* 98 (1) (2), 102, 115—*Magistrates' Courts Act,* 1952 (15 & 16 *Geo.* 6 & 1 *Eliz.* 2, *c.* 55), *s.* 35—*Motor Vehicles* (*International Circulation*) *Act,* 1952 (15 & 16 *Geo.* 6 & 1 *Eliz.* 2, *c.* 39), *s.* 1 (2) (*b*)—*Motor Vehicles* **[827]** (*Driving Licences*) *Regulations,* 1950 (*S.I.* 1950, *No.* 333), *regs.* 3, 16 (3) (*a*)—*Motor Vehicles* (*International Circulation*) *Order,* 1957 (*S.I.* 1957, *No.* 1074), *art.* 3 (1) (*a*).

The defendant, an airman serving in the United States Air Force, a visiting force within the Visiting Forces Act, 1952, was the holder of a driving permit issued under article 3 of the Motor Vehicles (International Circulation) Order, 1957,[1] authorising him to drive or be employed in driving motor-vehicles in Great Britain. He held no British driving licence. On April 30, 1961, the defendant acted as the driving instructor of a learner driver who held a provisional licence. The defendant was charged with aiding and abetting the learner driver to commit an offence contrary to section 35 of the Magistrates' Courts Act, 1952,[2] in that she, the learner driver, used the provisional licence to drive a motor-car when not under the supervision of a person present in the vehicle with her who held a licence authorising him to drive a motor-car, contrary to section 102 (3) of the Road Traffic Act, 1960.[3] The justices were of the opinion that the driving permit was not a driving licence for the purposes of the Motor

[1] Motor Vehicles (International Circulation) Order, 1957, art. 3: "(1) It shall be lawful—(*a*) for a member of a visiting force of a country to which Part I of the Visiting Forces Act, 1952, for the time being applies who holds a driving permit issued under the law of any part of the sending country or issued by the service authorities of the visiting force, or (*b*) for a member of a civilian component of such a visiting force who holds such a driving permit, to drive, and be employed in driving, in Great Britain a motor vehicle of any class or description which he is authorised by that permit to drive, notwithstanding that he is not the holder of a driving licence under Part I of the Road Traffic Act, 1930."

[2] Magistrates' Courts Act, 1952, s. 35: "A person who aids, abets, counsels or procures the commission by another person of a summary offence shall be guilty of the like offence. . . ."

[3] Road Traffic Act, 1960, s. 102: "(3) If a person to whom a provisional licence is granted fails to comply with any of the conditions subject to which it is granted, he shall be liable on summary conviction to a fine not exceeding £20, or on a second or subsequent conviction to a fine not exceeding £50 or to imprisonment for a term not exceeding three months."

S. 115: "'licence' means a licence to drive a motor vehicle granted under this Part of this Act:"

Vehicles (Driving Licences) Regulations, 1950,[4] or of Part II of the Road Traffic Act, 1960,[3] and convicted the defendant of the offence charged. On appeal by the defendant:—

Held, that the defendant was not the holder of a driving licence for the purposes of section 102 of the Road Traffic Act, 1960, or of regulation 16 of the Motor Vehicles (Driving Licences) Regulations, 1950; that on its true construction article 3 of the Motor Vehicles (International Circulation) Order, 1957, merely permitted the holder of a driving permit to drive in Great Britain notwithstanding that he had no licence and was not intended to make a driving permit equivalent to a driving licence; that, where it was intended to equate a permit with a licence, it was expressly so provided in schedule 3 to the Order; and that, therefore, the **[828]** defendant was not entitled to supervise the learner driver and the justices were right in convicting him of the offence charged.

CASE STATED by West Suffolk justices sitting at Mildenhall.

On July 4, 1961, an information was preferred by the prosecutor, Reginald John Henry Lummis, against the defendant, Ray William Urey, that, on April 30, 1961, at Eriswell, Suffolk, he did aid, abet, counsel and procure one Mrs. Margaret Plover to commit a certain offence, that is to say, that Mrs. Plover being a person to whom a provisional licence to drive a motor-vehicle had been granted, failed to comply with the condition subject to which it was granted, in that, on the Eriswell to Lakenheath road, she used the licence to drive a motor-car when not under the supervision of a person present in the vehicle with her, who held a licence (other than a provisional licence) authorising him to drive a motor-car and who had been the holder of a licence for at least two years or had passed a test under section 99 of the Road Traffic Act, 1960, contrary to section 102 (3) of the Road Traffic Act, 1960, and section 35 of the Magistrates' Courts Act, 1952.

At the hearing of the information on July 31, 1961, the following were among the facts found by the justices: At 3.25 p.m. on Sunday, April 30, 1961, Police Constable Johnson was on motor-cycle patrol duty on the Eriswell/Lakenheath road and travelling towards Lakenheath when he saw a Morris Minor motor-car coming towards him from the opposite direction. It transpired that this vehicle was then being driven by Mrs. Margaret Plover and as it turned off towards Holywell Row the police constable noticed that the driver did not appear to be performing that manoeuvre very competently. He overtook and stopped the vehicle, and asked Mrs. Plover for her driving licence. She produced a provisional licence issued by the West Suffolk county council which was current and in order. In the car was a passenger, the defendant, who was an airman in the United States Air Force, a visiting force within the meaning of the Visiting Forces Act, 1952. When asked to produce his driving licence, the defendant produced a United States Forces United Kingdom driving permit which had been issued on May 16, 1958, and expired on May 16, 1962. When asked if he had a British driving licence, he replied that he had not. He agreed that he was teaching Mrs. Plover to drive. The defendant had come to the United Kingdom in December, 1955, and during the whole of that period had held what he described as a "Stateside" driving licence, had undergone instruction in driving on English roads and had obtained a good report from his Unit Commander.

It was contended on behalf of the defendant that the driving permit issued to the defendant by the United States Air Force authorities was a licence for the

[4] Motor Vehicles (Driving Licences) Regulations, 1950, reg. 3: "'licence' means a licence to drive a motor vehicle . . . and includes a provisional licence."

Reg. 16: "(3) A provisional licence shall be granted only subject to the condition that until the holder thereof has passed the appropriate test:—(*a*) he shall . . . use it only when under the supervision of a person who is present in the vehicle with him and holds a licence . . . authorising him to drive a vehicle of the same class as the vehicle being driven by the holder of the provisional licence, and who has been the holder of a licence for at least two years or has passed a test under section 6 of the Act of 1934; . . ."

purposes of the Motor Vehicles (Driving Licences) Regulations, 1950, and that the permit was and/or had the full force and effect of a licence for the purposes of Part II of the Road Traffic Act, 1960. **[829]**

It was contended on behalf of the prosecutor that the driving permit issued to the defendant by the United States Air Force authorities was not a driving licence nor had it the force or effect of a driving licence for the purposes of the Motor Vehicles (Driving Licences) Regulations, 1950, or of Part II of the Road Traffic Act, 1960.

The justices were of the opinion that a driving permit held by a United States serviceman was not a licence for the purposes of the Motor Vehicles (Driving Licences) Regulations, 1950, and that it did not have the force and effect of a licence for the purposes of Part II of the Road Traffic Act, 1960. Accordingly, the defendant was found guilty and convicted of the offence charged. He was conditionally discharged under section 7 of the Criminal Justice Act, 1948, for 12 months.

The question for the opinion of the High Court was whether a driving permit issued in those circumstances to a member of a visiting force was a licence for the purposes of the Motor Vehicles (Driving Licences) Regulations, 1950, and whether, accordingly, it had the full force and effect of or in the alternative was a licence for the purposes of Part II of the Road Traffic Act, 1960.

D. S. Hunter for the defendant.
L. K. E. Boreham for the prosecutor.

No cases were cited in argument.

LORD PARKER C.J. stated the facts and continued: Section 98 of the Road Traffic Act, 1960, provides: "(1) A person shall not drive on a road a motor vehicle of any class or description unless he is the holder of a licence authorising him to drive a motor vehicle of that class or description. (2) A person shall not employ a person to drive on a road a motor vehicle of any class or description unless the person employed is the holder of a licence authorising him to drive a motor vehicle of that class or description." Subsequent sections make provision for tests and for the requirement of physical fitness, and by section 101 the form of licence, the duration thereof and the fees payable are dealt with. Then by section 102 it is provided: "(1) For the purpose of enabling an applicant for the grant of a licence to learn to drive a motor vehicle with a view to passing a test of competence to drive or a test of fitness to drive, the licensing authority may, if so requested by him and on payment of such fee not exceeding ten shillings as may be prescribed, grant him a provisional licence to be in force for a period of six months. (2) A provisional licence shall be in the prescribed form and granted subject to the prescribed conditions." Section 113 gives the Minister power to make regulations, and by section 115 "licence" is defined as meaning "a licence to drive a motor vehicle granted under this Part of this Act."

The relevant regulations in regard to provisional licences **[830]** having effect under the Act of 1960 are the Motor Vehicles (Driving Licences) Regulations, 1950, as amended by the Motor Vehicles (Driving Licences) (Amendment) Regulations, 1957. By regulation 16 (3), it is provided: "A provisional licence shall be granted only subject to the condition that until the holder thereof has passed the appropriate test:— (*a*) he shall ". . . use it only when under the supervision of a person who is present in the vehicle with him and holds a licence, not being a provisional licence, authorising him to drive a vehicle of the same class as the vehicle being driven by the holder of the provisional licence," . . . and by regulation 3, the interpretation regulation, "licence" is defined, always of course subject to whether the context otherwise requires, as meaning "a licence to drive a motor vehicle . . . and includes a provisional licence." So far, therefore, as the Road Traffic Act, 1960, is concerned, and the regulations thereunder, it is quite clear that the defendant was not the holder of a licence for the purposes of regulation 16 of the Motor Vehicles (Driving Licences) Regulations, 1950, or of section 102 of the Road Traffic Act, 1960.

When the policeman came up to him, the defendant very frankly said: "I have not got such a licence," but he then produced another document, and that document is what has been referred to as a United States Air Force United Kingdom driving permit. For my part, I find it unnecessary to go further back than the agreement of 1955[5] in regard to the North Atlantic Alliance. Article 4 thereof says: "The receiving State shall either (*a*) accept as valid, without a driving test or fee, the driving permit or licence or military driving permit issued by the sending State or a sub-division thereof to a member of a force or of a civilian component; or (*b*) issue its own driving permit or licence to any member of a force or civilian component who holds a driving permit or a licence or military driving permit issued by the sending State or a sub-division thereof, provided that no driving test shall be required." It seems clear that, in order to give effect to that treaty agreement, this country in the first instance availed itself of article 4 (*b*); in other words, we issued licences to members of the visiting forces, and we did that pursuant to article 5 of the Motor Car (International Circulation) Order, 1930. That continued until the coming into force of the Motor Vehicles (International Circulation) Act, 1952, which provided that Her Majesty might by order in council make provision for modifying, in relation to persons so resident who are temporarily in Great Britain, any enactment relating to the drivers of vehicles. Although that was an Act of 1952, it did not come into force until August 1957, and by an order in council entitled the Motor Vehicles (International Circulation) Order, 1957, it is clear that provision was being made to implement article 4 (*a*) of the treaty agreement. **[831]**

By article 3 (1) of the Motor Vehicles (International Circulation) Order, 1957, it was provided as follows: "It shall be lawful—(*a*) for a member of a visiting force of a country to which Part I of the Visiting Forces Act, 1952, for the time being applies who holds a driving permit issued under the law of any part of the sending country or issued by the service authorities of the visiting force, or (*b*) for a member of a civilian component of such a visiting force who holds such a driving permit, to drive, and be employed in driving, in Great Britain a motor vehicle of any class or description which he is authorised by that permit to drive, notwithstanding that he is not the holder of a driving licence under Part I of the Road Traffic Act, 1930." In other words, the defendant, when he was accosted by the police, was able to say: "I have not one of your English licences, but I have a driving permit which, by reason of article 3 of the Order of 1957, makes it lawful for me to drive and be employed in driving, notwithstanding that I am not the holder of an English driving licence."

The argument in the present case for which the court is indebted to Mr. Hunter for the defendant, is that article 3 of the Motor Vehicles (International Circulation) Order 1957, modifies section 98 of the Road Traffic Act, 1960, and that one must read some words into section 98 (1) and (2) to the effect that the licence there referred to includes such a driving permit as is referred to in article 3 of the Order of 1957, and that, thereupon, when one comes to section 102 and the regulations prescribing the conditions on which a provisional licence is granted, a person is entitled to sit next to the holder of a provisional licence and supervise him if he is the holder not merely of one of our licences but of such a driving permit. I am quite unable to accept that argument. It would have been easy for the draftsman, no doubt, to deal with it in that way and to provide by article 3 that a driving permit of the nature there referred to should be deemed for all purposes to be a licence for the purposes of the Road Traffic Act, 1960. Observe that the draftsman has carefully avoided doing that; he has merely said that it will be lawful for the holder of such a document to drive on our roads notwithstanding that he has not got a licence. When the draftsman desires to equate such a driving permit with a licence he does so expressly by the third schedule. By article 4, "The Third Schedule to this Order shall have effect as respects the driving permits referred to in Article 2 and 3 of this Order" and by paragraph 5 of the third schedule it is specifically provided: "In the following provisions of the Road Traffic Act, 1930, [that being the relevant Act at that time] references to a driving licence shall include references to a driving permit."

[5] Cmd. 9363, Treaty Series No. 3 (1955).

Thereafter in the next paragraph are set out three instances where a driving licence referred to in the Road Traffic Act is to include **[832]** a driving permit of the nature referred to in article 3. That, as it seems to me, puts the matter beyond doubt.

Mr. Hunter has urged us to say that any such interpretation would show that we have not implemented the treaty agreement of 1955. It is not for me to consider whether we have implemented the treaty agreement or not. It seems to me quite reasonable to say that visiting forces may drive on our roads and be employed in driving on our roads, but, when it comes to acting as supervisors for a learner, we will not treat them as eligible for that purpose. That is not a matter for this court, but it seems to me a reasonable attitude.

ASHWORTH J. I agree.

HINCHCLIFFE J. I also agree.

Appeal dismissed with costs.

Solicitors: *Vizard, Oldham, Crowther & Cash for Wild, Hewitson & Shaw, Cambridge; Moodie, Randall, Carr & Miles for Bankes, Ashton & Co., Bury St. Edmunds.*

B.

PERSONAL JURISDICTION

REGINA v. NAYLOR

([1962] 2 Q.B. 527)

July 18, 1962: Central Criminal Court: Lord Parker C.J.

Crime—Aircraft—Offence on—Jurisdiction—Larceny—Alleged offence on British aircraft over high seas—Whether accused could be tried for offence in England—Civil Aviation Act, 1949 (12, 13 & 14 *Geo.* 6, *c.* 67), *s.* 62 (1).

N. on the first count of an indictment was charged with larceny. The particulars alleged that while on a British aircraft in flight over the high seas she stole three rings. A motion to quash the count was made on the ground that it did not allege an offence known to English law for which N. could be tried in England:—

Held, dismissing the motion to quash, that any act or omission which would constitute an offence if done in England was made by section 62 (1) of the Civil Aviation Act, 1949,[1] an offence if committed on a British aircraft, unless the offence in question was clearly one of domestic application only, in which case section 62 (1) did not apply; and that section 62 (1) covered the present offence.

Reg. v. *Martin** [1956] 2 Q.B. 272; [1956] 2 W.L.R. 975; [1956] 2 All E.R. 86, C.C.C. distinguished.

MOTION.

The accused, Inga Monica Maria Naylor, was charged in count one of an indictment with larceny, contrary to section 2 of the Larceny Act, 1916. The particulars of that count were that the accused on June 30, 1960, on a British aircraft in flight over the high seas stole three rings. Her counsel moved to quash the count on the ground that that was not an offence known to English law for which this accused could be tried in England.

E. J. P. Cussen and *Alastair Morton* for the Crown.
Victor Durand, Q.C. and *James Burge* for the accused.

No case was cited during argument other than that referred to in the judgment.

LORD PARKER C.J. Mr. Durand moves to quash count one of the indictment in this case under which the accused is charged **[528]** with larceny, contrary to section 2 of the Larceny Act, 1916. The particulars of that count are that the accused on June 30, 1960, on a British aircraft in flight over the high seas stole three rings. The motion to quash is on the ground that that is not an offence known to English law for which this accused can be tried in this country.

The matter depends on the true construction of section 62 (1) of the Civil Aviation Act, 1949. That section, which has the sidenote "Jurisdiction," provides that: "Any offence whatever committed on a British aircraft shall, for the purpose of conferring jurisdiction, be deemed to have been committed in any place where the offender may for the time being be." It is on any view rather unfortunate language.

The two rival contentions are, on the one hand, that the subsection is saying in a shortened form what has already been provided in regard to British ships on the high seas, namely, that any act or omission which constituted an offence if committed in England constitutes an offence if committed on a British aircraft.

[1] Civil Aviation Act, 1949, s. 62 (1): "Any offence whatever committed on a British aircraft shall, for the purpose of conferring jurisdiction, be deemed to have been committed in any place where the offender may for the time being be."

On the other hand, it is said that it is only dealing with a matter of jurisdiction and venue, and that you must first of all find that under English law the acts complained of constitute offences if committed on a British aircraft.

The matter was considered by Devlin J. in *Reg.* v. *Martin*,[2]* on a motion to quash an indictment containing counts concerning regulation 3 of the Dangerous Drugs Regulations, 1953.

Before considering that case, I should say that I have come to the clear conclusion that the wide construction contended for should be put on section 62 of the Civil Aviation Act. Although, as I have said, the language is not altogether as clear as it should be, I have little doubt that it does cover any acts or omissions which would constitute offences if committed in this country unless, and this is, I think, where Devlin J.'s case is in point, they are contrary to some purely domestic legislation.

I need not repeat the arguments which were adduced in *Martin's* case[1] as to the narrow scope that there would be for the operation of section 62 on the limited construction, since offences under the Treachery Act, 1940, bigamy (if one can imagine it taking place), and murder, by reason of the Offences against the Persons Act, 1861, are the only possible offences to which that section could apply. **[529]**

I have been referred to McNair's Law of the Air, 2nd ed., p. 118, in which, after setting out the rival contentions, this passage occurs: "It is submitted, however, that their effect is not limited to questions of venue but is to render amenable to trial, wherever in the United Kingdom the offender may be, any person, whether British, foreign or stateless, who commits any offence on board an aircraft registered in the United Kingdom, or contravenes any of the relevant statutory provisions on civil aviation."

I confess that for my part I would approach the matter in that way. What happened in *Martin's* case[3]* was that the offences concerned the Dangerous Drugs Regulations, which were clearly regulations to prevent the possession of dangerous drugs in this country. Thus, apart from certain duly qualified medical practitioners and registered veterinary surgeons on the English registers, any other person, unless so authorised, who had possession of one of the drugs was guilty of an offence.

Devlin J. took the view, for which there is considerable support, that that in effect is a purely domestic regulation, and went on to say that crimes conceived by the common law—which are mostly offences against the moral law, such as murder and theft—are not thought of as having territorial limits. Although he stated expressly that he was not saying that section 62 did apply to offences at common law, it is quite clear from his judgment that he was taking the view that there was ample scope for the operation of section 62, in that common law offences might well be covered by the section.

In my judgment, the approach to this matter is that any act or omission which would constitute an offence if done in England is made an offence if done on a British aircraft, subject to this, that if the offence in question is clearly one of domestic application only, then, as in *Martin's* case[3]* section 62 does not cover that sort of offence. Accordingly I would dismiss the motion to quash.

Motion to quash dismissed.

Solicitors: *Director of Public Prosecutions; Turberville Smith & Co., Uxbridge.*

[2] [1956] 2 Q.B. 272; [1956] 2 W.L.R. 975; [1956] 2 All E.R. 86; 40 Cr.App.R. 68, C.C.C.

[3] [1956] 2 Q.B. 272.

COX v. ARMY COUNCIL

([1963] A.C. 48)

October 20, November 7, 27: Courts-Martial Appeal Court: Slade, Glyn-Jones, Thompson JJ.

February 14, 15, March 15, 1962: House of Lords: Viscount Simonds, Lords Reid, Radcliffe Morris of Borth-y-Gest, Jenkins.

Military Law—Civil offence—Abroad, committed—Driving without due care and attention—Whether civil offence within meaning of Army Act—Army Act, 1955 (3 *&* 4 *Eliz.* 2, *c.* 18), *s.* 70—*Road Traffic Act,* 1960 (8 *&* 9 *Eliz.* 2, *c.* 16), *ss.* 3 (1), 257 (1).
Road Traffic—"Road"—Meaning—Overseas road—Road Traffic Act, 1960, *ss.* 3 (1), 257 (1).

By section 70 of the Army Act, 1955: "(1) Any person subject to military law who commits a civil offence, whether in the United Kingdom or elsewhere, shall be guilty of an offence against this section. (2) In this Act the expression 'civil offence' means any act or omission punishable by the law of England or which, if committed in England, would be punishable by that law; and in this Act the expression 'the corresponding civil offence' means the civil offence the commission of which constitutes the offence against this section. . . ."

By section 3 (1) of the Road Traffic Act, 1960: "If a person drives a motor vehicle on a road without due care and attention, or without reasonable consideration for other persons using the road, he shall be liable on summary conviction to a fine not exceeding £40. . . ."

By section 257 (1): ". . . 'road' means any highway and any other road to which the public has access, and includes bridges over which a road passes. . . ."

The appellant, while serving with the British Army in Germany, was charged before a district court-martial held there with "committing a civil offence contrary to section 70 of the Army Act, 1955, that is to say, driving without due care and attention contrary to section 3 (1) of the Road Traffic Act, 1960, in that he at Sundern on September 15, 1960, drove a motor vehicle on a road without due care and attention." He was convicted:—

Held, (1) that section 70 of the Act of 1955 is an offence-creating section, providing that acts or omissions which apart from it would not be offences become offences by virtue of it (post, pp. 67, 71, 72).

(2) That if the offence charged is one of a nature that can be committed only in England the section cannot operate (post, pp. 68, 72).

(3) That, even though the Road Traffic Act, 1960, had no application except to acts done on the roads of England (post, p. 72), the offence charged had a character of universality which brought it within the scope of section 70 of the Act of 1955 (post, pp. 68, 72).

Per Lord Reid. The question is not whether the road on which **[49]** the appellant was driving was a road within the meaning of the Road Traffic Act, but whether there was the requisite degree of similarity between what he did and an act done in England which would have been contrary to section 3 (1) of that Act (post, p. 70).

Reg. v. *Martin** [1956] 2 Q.B. 272; [1956] 2 W.L.R. 975; [1956] 2 All E.R. 86 and *Reg.* v. *Naylor** [1962] 2 Q.B. 527; [1961] 3 W.L.R. 898; [1961] 2 All E.R. 932 considered.

Attorney-General for Hongkong v. *Kwok-a-Sing** (1873), L.R. 5 P.C. 179 distinguished.

Decision of the Courts-Martial Appeal Court, sub. nom. *Reg.* v. *Cox,* infra [1962] 2 W.L.R.; [1961] 3 All E.R. 1194 affirmed.

The appellant, Sergeant Roy Ewart Cox, Royal Army Pay Corps, serving with the British Army of the Rhine, was convicted of a civil offence by a district court-martial held on January 20, 1961, at R.A.F. Sundern, Germany. He was charged with "committing a civil offence contrary to section 70 of the Army Act, 1955, that is to say, driving without due care and attention contrary to section 3 (1) of the Road Traffic Act, 1960, in that he at Sundern on September 15, 1960, drove a motor vehicle on a road without due care and attention." He was sentenced to be severely reprimanded and appealed to the Courts-Martial Appeal Court.

George Heseltine for the appellant.
David Lloyd for the Crown.

Cur. adv. vult.

1961. Nov. 27. SLADE J. read the judgment of the court: On January 20, 1961, the appellant, Sergeant Roy Ewart Cox, Royal Army Pay Corps, serving with the British Army of the Rhine, was convicted in Germany by a district court-martial of "committing a civil offence contrary to section 70 of the Army Act, 1955, that is to say, driving a motor vehicle contrary to section 3 (1) of the Road Traffic Act, 1960, in that he at Sundern [Germany] on September 15, 1960, drove a motor vehicle on a road without due care and attention." He was sentenced to be severely reprimanded. From that conviction he appeals to this court by leave of the single judge.

His grounds of appeal are as follows: (1) that the charge as laid is not correct in law because it does not disclose an offence under section 70 of the Army Act, 1955, in that the act particularised is not an act contrary to section 3 (1) of the Road Traffic Act, 1960, nor is it an act which can be committed in England. **[50]** (2) that the charge as laid is not a civil offence within the meaning of section 70 of the Army Act, 1955.

Neither of these points was taken in *Reg.* v. *Jennings*,[1] which was an appeal to this court in similar circumstances. Indeed in that case it seems to have been assumed that the then corresponding section to the present section 70 of the Army Act, 1955, namely, section 41 (5) of the Army Act, 1881, was applicable to the Road Traffic Act of 1930, and the sole ground of appeal was that the conviction was invalid because the appellant had not received the warning of intended prosecution required by section 21 of that Act.

In addition to his grounds of appeal, Mr. Heseltine, who appeared for the appellant, urged that it was not a military necessity to frame the charge against the appellant under section 70 of the Act of 1955 in that the charge could have been laid under section 36, but the question which this court has to decide is whether the appellant was rightly convicted of the charge laid under section 70, and not whether he could have been convicted on some other charge.

In support of his grounds of appeal Mr. Heseltine made the following submissions: (1) that section 70 was not an "offence-creating" section. In support of this submission Mr. Heseltine cited *Reg.* v. *Martin.*[2]* (2) that the Road Traffic Act, 1960, is in any event mere "domestic legislation" in the sense in which that expression was used by Lord Parker C.J. in *Reg.* v. *Naylor.*[3]* (3) that if, contrary to his contention, section 70 did create a new offence, the words in section 70 "if committed in England" precluded it from applying to an act which was incapable of being committed in England. (4) that if, contrary to his contention, the words of section 70 are capable of the construction put forward by the prosecution nevertheless so many and such strange anomalies would result from their being held to apply to the Road Traffic Act, 1960, that the court should hold that Parliament cannot have intended them to be so construed, and accordingly should put a narrower construction upon them. In support of

[1] [1956] 1 W.L.R. 1497; [1956] 3 All E.R. 429.
[2] [1956] 2 Q.B. 272; [1956] 2 W.L.R. 975; [1956] 2 All E.R. 86; 40 Cr. App.R. 68.
[3] [1962] 2 Q.B. 527; [1961] 3 W.L.R. 898; [1961] 2 All E.R. 932; 45 Cr.App.R. 69.

this submission Mr. Heseltine cited *Attorney-General for Hong Kong* v. *Kwok-a-Sing.*[4]* **[51]**

Martin's[5]* and *Naylor's*[6]* cases were both decided upon the construction of section 62 (1) of the Civil Aviation Act, 1949, which reads as follows: "(1) Any offence whatever committed on a British aircraft shall, for the purpose of conferring jurisdiction, be deemed to have been committed in any place where the offender may for the time being be." In *Martin's*[7]* case the defendants were charged on indictment with being in possession of raw opium on a British aircraft flying between Bahrein and Singapore contrary to regulation (3) of the Dangerous Drugs Regulations, 1953, made under the Dangerous Drugs Act, 1951.

In *Naylor's*[8]* case the defendant was charged on indictment with larceny on a British aircraft in flight over the high seas. In each case counsel for the defence moved to quash the indictment upon the ground that the court had no jurisdiction to try the offence charged. In *Martin's*[9]* case the prosecution conceded that the possession of raw opium was outside the United Kingdom, and further that regulation (3) of the Regulations of 1953 did not in itself make it an offence to have possession of drugs in a British aircraft abroad. The prosecution contended, however, that whenever an act which is an offence under English law if committed in England is committed on a British aircraft anywhere in the world, such act was made an offence under English law justiciable in this country by virtue of section 62 of the Act of 1949.

Counsel for the defendant in presenting his argument stated succinctly that the only question to be decided was whether section 62 was a "venue-creating" or an "offence-creating" section. Devlin J., in the course of the prosecution's argument, said[10]: "The question is what is meant by 'offence.' What about a confidence trick; that is not an offence unless committed in England. Really you say that 'offence' means any act which if done in England would be an offence."

In the course of his judgment quashing the indictment, Devlin J. said[11]: "The prosecution say that, apart from these few statutes," (for example, the Offences against the Persons Act, 1861, sections 9 and 57, the Offences at Sea Act, 1536, section 1) "section 62 is the only enactment that can make a criminal act done in the air an offence. Accordingly, the prosecution say that section 62 must be given a construction which is wide enough to make it an offence-creating section. Since it starts **[52]** off by apparently assuming that the act to be considered is an offence before the words of the section operate on it—because it begins by saying: 'Any offence whatever committed on a British aircraft'—the prosecution say the word 'offence' must be construed as if it read 'any act which if done in England would be an offence.' No doubt so wide a construction would sustain the prosecution's submission." Again Devlin J. said[12]: "In my judgment, if the prosecution are to succeed, it can only be if a very free construction is applied to the words of the statute. It can only be if, as I say, in lieu of the words: 'any offence whatever' there is read 'any act which if done in England would be an offence.' That is a free construction. It is not a construction which emerges from the grammar of the Act and it is not one which I find myself willing to accept."

Later, Devlin J. said[13]: "I am not saying that section 62 applies to offences at common law. I have not heard that point argued and it may have to be argued hereafter. What I am saying is that section 62 does not apply to a statutory offence which by the terms of the statute that creates it is local and not universal in character, . . . I wish, therefore, to make it clear that the decision which I have given is a decision which is to be regarded as applying to the particular offence which I have had to consider under the Dangerous Drugs Regulations."

In *Naylor's* case,[14]* Lord Parker C.J. said: "The two rival contentions are,

[4] (1873) L.R. 5 P.C. 179.
[5] [1956] 2 Q.B. 272.
[6] [1962] 2 Q.B. 527.
[7] [1956] 2 Q.B. 272.
[8] [1962] 2 Q.B. 527.
[9] [1956] 2 Q.B. 272.
[10] Ibid. 278.
[11] Ibid. 283.
[12] [1956] 2 Q.B. 272, 284-285.
[13] Ibid. 287, 288.
[14] [1962] 2 Q.B. 527, 528.

on the one hand, that the subsection is saying in a shortened form what has already been provided in regard to British ships on the high seas, namely, that any act or omission which constituted an offence if committed in England constitutes an offence if committed on a British aircraft. On the other hand, it is said that it is only dealing with a matter of jurisdiction and venue, and that you must first of all find that under English law the acts complained of constitute offences if committed on a British aircraft.

"The matter was considered by Devlin J. in *Reg.* v. *Martin*,[15*] on a motion to quash an indictment containing counts concerning regulation 3 of the Dangerous Drugs Regulations, 1953. Before considering that case, I should say that I have come to the clear conclusion that the wide construction contended for should be put on section 62 of the Civil Aviation **[53]** Act. Although as I have said the language is not altogether as clear as it should be, I have little doubt that it does cover any acts or omissions which would constitute offences if committed in this country unless, as this is, I think, where Devlin J.'s case is in point, they are contrary to some purely domestic legislation."

Further on Lord Parker C.J. said[16]: "In my judgment the approach to this matter is that any act or omission which would constitute an offence if done in England is made an offence if done on a British aircraft, subject to this, that if the offence in question is clearly one of domestic application only, then, as in *Martin's* case,[17*] section 62 does not cover that sort of offence. Accordingly I would dismiss the motion to quash." (An interesting note on *Martin's* case[17*] appears in 72 Law Quarterly Review, p. 318.)

Mr. Heseltine's next argument was that the words in section 70 "if committed in England" cannot apply to an act such as driving on a German road which is incapable of being committed in England. He says it is an essential ingredient of the offence under section 3 (1) of the Road Traffic Act, 1960, that the motor-vehicle should be driven on a road, and that "road" as defined by section 257 of the Act, means a road to which the public, i.e. the public in England, has access. It is self-evident that you cannot drive a motor-vehicle on a German road in England, but if that argument is carried to its logical conclusion it would seem that simple larceny in Germany would be a "civil offence" within the meaning of section 70, but larceny in a German dwelling-house would not. Before dealing with this argument, it is desirable to analyse section 70, which provides as follows: "(1) Any person subject to military law who commits a civil offence, whether in the United Kingdom or elsewhere, shall be guilty of an offence against this section. (2) In this Act the expression 'civil offence' means any act or omission, (a) punishable by the law of England, or (b) which, if committed in England, would be punishable by that law; and in this Act the expression 'the corresponding civil offence' means the civil offence the commission of which constitutes the offence against this section." The letters (a) and (b) have been introduced by this court to facilitate reference hereafter. "Civil offence" means, of course, a civil as opposed to a purely military offence. The words in (a) cover any act or omission **[54]** punishable by the law of England whether committed in the United Kingdom or abroad. The words in (b) "if committed in England would be punishable by that law" necessarily presuppose that the act or omission relied upon as constituting the civil offence (1) was committed abroad, and (2) but for those words could not be punishable by the law of England.

Indeed, if this were not so the act or omission would fall within (a) which covers acts or omissions punishable by the law of England whether committed in or outside the United Kingdom: (b) therefore necessarily involves the supposition that an act or omission was committed in England which in fact was not so committed.

Unless therefore (b) is mere surplusage as being covered by (a) it must create a new offence, namely, an act or omission committed abroad and not punishable by the law of England, but which if it had been committed in England would have been so punishable. That new offence necessarily involves the notional

[15] [1956] 2 Q.B. 272.
[16] [1962] 2 Q.B. 527, 529.
[17] [1956] 2 Q.B. 272.

transfer to England of all the relevant circumstances surrounding the act or omission so that it may be determined whether the act or omission, if it had been committed in England, would have been punishable by English law. There are, no doubt, acts and omissions committed abroad which are by their very nature incapable of being committed in England, and vice versa, e.g., acts which relate solely to some specific place or object or which are indigenous to or inseparably connected with a particular locality. Illustrations of such would be, abroad, smoking in the Louvre, and at home, exceeding the speed limits in the Royal Parks. There may well be sections of the Road Traffic Act, 1960, which fall within this category. In the present case, however, the essence of the act alleged to constitute the civil offence is the driving of a motor-vehicle without due care and attention on a road to which members of the public have access. It is akin to the more serious acts of dangerous driving (section 2) causing death by dangerous driving (section 1) and driving under the influence of drink (section 6).

The definition of "road" in the Road Traffic Act, 1960, takes the form it does because Parliament was of course legislating for the roads of this country. It is to be observed that there are very few acts committed abroad even by a British subject which are punishable by the law of England and which would thus fall within the language of (a); moreover, as Mr. Heseltine pointed out, there are persons subject to military law who are not British subjects, and with the exception of piracy, which jure gentium **[55]** is justiciable anywhere, there is no offence committed by an alien abroad which is punishable in England.

To hold therefore that the language of (b) is not apt to cover acts or omissions abroad which if committed in England would constitute offences against, for example, sections 1, 2, 3 and 6 of the Road Traffic Act, 1960, would seem to deprive section 70 of the effect which, in the opinion of this court, Parliament in enacting it must have intended that it should have in order to regulate the conduct of persons subject to military law who are for the time being stationed abroad.

In construing section 70 of the Act of 1955 it is not irrelevant to observe that the corresponding section of the Army Act, 1881, namely, section 41 (5), uses the words "Any offence . . . which when committed in England is punishable by the law of England" instead of the words "any act or omission" which are found in section 70.

We now turn to Mr. Heseltine's final submission. As instances of anomalies which would flow from holding that section 70 was applicable to the Road Traffic Act, 1960, and cognate legislation, Mr. Heseltine referred us to the Road Traffic Act, 1960, s. 4 (1). He said that speed limits in Germany might differ from those in England (Road Traffic Act, 1960, ss. 19 and 20: speeding on restricted roads) and he emphasised particularly the definition of a restricted road in section 20 (1). Road Traffic Act, 1960, s. 98—driving without a licence issued by a British licensing authority. Road Traffic Act, 1960, ss. 201 and 203 (2)—driving without insurance against third-party risks. Mr. Heseltine says rightly that the policy so required must by section 203 (2) be issued by an authorised insurer, that is to say, a person or body of persons carrying on motor-vehicle insurance business in Great Britain. Highways Act, 1835, s. 78—which requires drivers of wagons or carts, etc., to keep to the left or near side of the road. He says rightly that the rule of the road in Germany is to keep to the right.

The court recognises the force of Mr. Heseltine's argument based upon these anomalies. We have no doubt that if the scope of the inquiry were extended beyond the Road Traffic laws many more anomalies could be found of which it is unnecessary to give further examples. As I have already said, it may be that the Road Traffic Act, 1960, and the Highways Act, 1835, do contain provisions which are purely domestic in their application and which by their very nature are intrinsically incapable of being **[56]** committed abroad, or of being notionally transferred to England for the purpose of applying section 70 of the Army Act.

Any such provisions will fall to be dealt with if and when the need should arise. At the moment this court is concerned, and concerned only, with section 3 of the Road Traffic Act, 1960. In this connection it may be observed that when a statute requires that something shall be deemed to be that which it is not, it is frequently not difficult to conjure up illustrations which may seem to reduce to absurdity the requirement of the statute, but that does not relieve a court of its duty to make the hypothesis which the statute demands, that is, in the present case, that this motor-vehicle was being driven on a road in England whereas it was in fact being driven on a road in Germany.

Finally, in support of his argument on this point Mr. Heseltine cited to us the decision of the Privy Council in *Attorney-General for Hong Kong* v. *Kwok-a-Sing.*[18]* He asked us to apply the principle underlying that decision by substituting "and" for "or" in section 70 (2) of the Army Act, 1955, or by leaving the section as it stands, but placing a narrow construction upon it.

As to his first suggestion, it is true that there are cases in which the word "or" in an Act of Parliament has been construed as "and," and where "and" has been construed as "or," but to substitute "and" for "or" in the definition clause of section 70 of the Act of 1955 would seem to make nonsense of the expression "civil offence."

As to the second suggestion, it is to be borne in mind that the decision in *Kwok-a-Sing's* case[18] was based upon the peculiar relationship of Hongkong to the mainland of China, and the reasoning underlying the judgment of the Board in that case seems to this court to be wholly inapplicable to the control of Her Majesty's Forces abroad through the instrumentality of military law.

Parliament may well have thought it better to give wide powers to those responsible for the maintenance of discipline and right conduct in the Army abroad, trusting them to act fairly and reasonably in the exercise of them, than to attempt what would have been the most difficult task of seeking to define with precision each of the acts which if committed abroad should be triable by court-martial as a civil offence.

This court accordingly holds that section 70 is upon its true **[57]** construction an offence-creating section, and that it covers an act committed abroad by a person subject to military law which, if committed in England, would have constituted an offence under section 3 (1) of the Road Traffic Act, 1960. The appellant was, therefore, rightly convicted of the civil offence with which he was charged.

We have accordingly dismissed this appeal, but having regard first, to the importance of the points raised in it, secondly to the number of trials by courts-martial in which these points have been raised by the defence, and thirdly, to the opinion of the judge-advocate-general that these points deserved consideration by this court, we have already given leave to appeal to the House of Lords, and have certified in manner required by section 1 (2) of the Administration of Justice Act, 1960, as applied to this court by section 10 of that Act.

Appeal dismissed.
Certificate under section 1 (2) *of the Administration of Justice Act.*
Leave to appeal to House of Lords.

The appellant appealed to the House of Lords.

Mark Littman Q.C. and *George Heseltine* for the appellant. The Army Act, 1955, applies to every person subject to military law: see section 205 and the sections following. As to offences relating to property, see sections 44 to 46. As to disobedience to standing orders, see section 36. See also sections 59, 63 and 98 (4) and the definitions of "constable" and "civil offence" in section 225 (1). In the Road Traffic Act, 1960, see sections 3 (1), 253 and 254 and the definition of "road" in section 257 (1). Reliance is placed on *Reg.* v. *Jennings*[19]; *Reg.* v. *Martin*[20]* and *Reg.* v. *Naylor.*[21]* Offences such as larceny are brought by the

[18] L.R. 5 P.C. 179.
[19] [1956] 1 W.L.R. 1497, 1498; [1956] 3 All E.R. 429.
[20] [1956] 2 Q.B. 272; [1956] 2 W.L.R. 975; [1956] 2 All E.R. 86.
[21] [1962] 2 Q.B. 527; [1961] 3 W.L.R. 898; [1961] 2 All E.R. 932.

Act within the province of military law, but section 70 of the Army Act does not apply to purely domestic legislation or to acts which are not wrong in themselves. That is the result of the cases just cited. There is no material difference between the **[58]** effect of section 70 and that of section 62 of the Civil Aviation Act, 1949. In Acts of Parliament there are frequent changes of language, though substantially the same subject-matter is referred to.

The background of this branch of the law is that at common law offences committed outside the realm are not punishable in England, save in the case of treason. The reason lay in the difficulties arising from jursidiction. Originally every offence was triable only in the county where it was alleged to have been committed, by a jury who had knowledge of the facts. Treason was within the jurisdiction of the Court of the High Constable, essentially a military tribunal and the precursor of courts-martial. This court applied the Civil Law and not the common law. It was abolished in 1521 when on the attainder of the last hereditary holder of the office, Edward Stafford, Duke of Buckingham, it became forfeited to the Crown. There was also the concurrent jurisdiction of the Court of Admiralty which also applied the Civil Law. See also the Offences at Sea Act, 1536 (28 Hen. 8, c. 15). Generally, a statute enacting offences will not be construed as having extraterritorial effect unless it is so expressed. But over the years there have been many Acts giving extraterritorial jurisdiction. See, for example, the Act 11 Will. 3, c. 12, to punish oppressions by colonial governors, the Dockyards, etc., Protection Act, 1772 (12 Geo. 3, c. 24), and sections 9 and 57 of the Offences against the Persons Act, 1861 (24 & 25 Vict. c. 100). In such Acts there may be certain differences of language in referring to the same thing. Thus "theft" might be called "larceny" or "an act which, if done in England, would have amounted to theft." See also section 33 (4) of the Larceny Act, 1916 (6 & 7 Geo. 5, c. 50). As to offences committed afloat, see sections 286 and 287 of the Merchant Shipping Act, 1894 (57 & 58 Vict. c. 60), and *Reg.* v. *Dudley and Stephens.*[22]*

The predecessor of the Army Act, 1955, was the Army Act, 1881 (44 & 45 Vict. c. 58), of which the relevant subsection is section 41 (4). Compare section 70 of the Act of 1955, which contemplates that there shall be brought within the definition of civil offence an act which would not be punishable by the law of England unless it were committed in England. It also contemplates an act which can be performed either in or out of **[59]** England. Therefore, if the relevant act is that of driving carelessly on an English road, the section does not apply because it is not an act which is capable of being done outside England. The Road Traffic Act, 1960, has no application except to acts done on the roads of England: see sections 5, 7, 8, 12, 19, 20 (1), 22, 23, 24, 26-35, 41, 68, 98, 201-216, 241, 271. The whole system is inapplicable anywhere but in the United Kingdom. The Act is a system of road regulations rather than a part of the criminal law. In some sections roads can only mean roads in England, and other provisions (as those relating to the Menai Bridge) can only apply to a particular subject-matter.

There is no legitimate principle of construction on which it can be held that while the word "road" as used in some of the sections of the Act can comprise only roads inside Great Britain, in section 3 (1) it must be held to apply to roads both inside and outside Great Britain. In certain respects section 3 is linked up with other provisions of the Act. See, for example, the system of punishments, including the indorsement of driving licences. The correct approach is not to look at each individual legislation or offence-creating section on its own, but to look at the legislation as a whole, of which each section forms a part, and see whether it is domestic and whether the Act which creates the offence is local or universal in character. It makes no difference that one may find one particular compartment of the Act dealing with a certain subject-matter which might be applied abroad. Larceny in a dwelling-house is not a localised offence so as to tie the meaning of "dwelling-house" to a dwelling-house in England; the Larceny Act is not domestic legislation in the same sense as the Road Traffic Act.

Section 36 (2) of the Army Act enables the army by standing orders to

[22] (1884) 14 Q.B.D. 273, 280-281; 1 T.L.R. 118.

regulate the conduct of its troops in foreign territory. There are difficulties in applying to it sections 2 and 3 of the Road Traffic Act, which must be read against the background of the decisions of the courts. Under the English authorities no mens rea is required as an ingredient in the offence of careless driving and the degree of the driver's skill cannot be taken into consideration. The defence of error of judgment is not open any more than unskilfulness. Different views may be taken abroad about that sort of thing, for example, in some countries the traffic approaching from the right always has absolute priority. Again, the Highway Code, authorised by section 74 of the Road Traffic Act, prescribes many things which would be contrary to safety on a foreign road. The army can control the driving of **[60]** its soldiers under standing orders authorised by section 36 of the Army Act, whereby it can be ensured that they obey the German road traffic laws. See the Bonn Conventions of May 26, 1952 (Cmd. 8571), article 17 (3) of the Convention on the Rights and Obligations of Foreign Forces and their Members in the Federal Republic of Germany, whereby German traffic laws are to apply to the forces and their members. Under the relevant standing orders it is an offence to drive a vehicle otherwise than in accordance with German traffic laws. It is not to be assumed that the members of the British forces should not be obliged to obey German traffic laws. Under the Bonn Conventions it is for the British Government to see that its soldiers obey the German traffic laws and, although the Road Traffic Act does not apply, there are adequate alternative provisions for safeguarding the public in Germany. As to the incompatibility of the English and German road traffic systems, see the note to section 78 of the Highways Act, 1835 (5 & 6 Will. 4, c. 50), in Halsbury's Statutes of England, 2nd ed., vol. XI, p. 86.

The appellant does not press the argument unsuccessfully submitted in *Reg.* v. *Martin,*[23]* but where there is a definition clause like section 70 (2) of the Army Act the proper practice is similar to that applicable where under a statute something which is not a fact is to be deemed to be a fact: see *Ex parte Walton.*[24] Section 70 should be given a construction which avoids absurdity. The acts referred to by the Road Traffic Act cannot be done outside the United Kingdom. Alternatively, one should understand an exception to the definition of "civil offence" in section 70 (2) of the Army Act to the following effect: ". . . except such part of that law which is merely made for the better order or government of England." That would leave out the Public Health Acts and the Merchandise Marks Acts. As to crimes which are limited territorially, see *Reg.* v. *Martin.*[25]* The right approach to the interpretation of general enactments is found in *Attorney-General for Hong Kong* v. *Kwok-a-Sing,*[26]* which shows that the extreme generality of words may be narrowed by surrounding circumstances. See also sections 104, 111 and 112 of the Road Traffic Act, which indicate that the provisions as to the withdrawal of driving licences may not be applicable where an English driving licence is not held.

The following are the appellant's submissions: (1) Section 70 of the Army Act does not on its true construction enable persons **[61]** to which it applies to be punished by court-martial for every breach of every English law, for that would lead to many absurdities.

(2) It is accepted that it is not limited in its application to acts punishable by the law of England, but it covers by reason of its last words ("if committed in England, would be punishable by that law") offences, such as larceny, which are not purely domestic.

(3) The statute contemplates that the act in question is one which can be done inside or outside England. If, therefore, upon a true view, the legislation creating the offences only applies to acts done inside England, it follows that section 70 will not take effect.

(4) The act in question in this case is driving carelessly on a road and the word "road" should be read as restricted to an English road, because the same word is used in other sections of the Road Traffic Act where it is inconceivable that they could have any sensible application outside England. There is nothing

[23] [1956] 2 Q.B. 272.
[24] (1881) 17 Ch.D. 746, 756, C.A.
[25] [1956] 2 Q.B. 272, 285-286.
[26] (1873) L.R. 5 P.C. 179, 197.

in this legislation which enables one to give a different interpretation to "road" in those sections. That legislation is only dealing with England. It is unlikely that such an expression would be used by Parliament to cover foreign roads, where different laws and standards for regulating traffic would prevail.

(5) *Reg.* v. *Martin*[27]* and *Reg.* v. *Naylor*[28]* support this. They decided that comparable words in the Civil Aviation Act, 1949, must be construed to exclude offences against purely domestic legislation. They were correctly decided and there is no distinction between those cases and the present one.

(6) It is not sufficient to say that the only exclusions from section 70 are acts intrinsically incapable of being committed abroad in a factual sense, since that would not cover cases where the act is capable of being factually committed abroad but it would yet be anomalous to punish it.

(7) A construction of the general words should be adopted so as not to relate to purely domestic legislation. If, contrary to the appellant's contention, some qualification of the literal meaning is needed, it should be given.

(8) The appellant's contentions cause no practical inconvenience, because there are plenty of ways of dealing with situations which might arise in such a case as this. **[62]**

George Heseltine following. Section 3 (1) of the Road Traffic Act, being a penal section, must be construed strictly. In so doing "road" is an essential ingredient of the offence. No such offence is known to English law as careless or dangerous driving. It must be careless or dangerous driving on a road within the meaning of the Act. A public road can only mean an English public road, unless there is a qualifying phrase to the contrary. The charge here is driving without due care on a public road at Sundern in Germany. It must be shown that it is a road within the meaning of the Act. A German policeman's conception of a public road will not be the same as a public road within section 3 (1) of the Road Traffic Act. A road leading to a farm may or may not be a public road. Consider also the roads in docks or in Aldershot barracks. In an English court the difficulty of proving whether or not a particular road in Germany is a public road would be almost insuperable.

As an example of the difficulties arising from the contrasting laws of road traffic, take a charge of causing death by dangerous driving within section 1 of the Road Traffic Act, where a railway train at a level crossing in Germany hits a British motor-car driven by a soldier on duty, killing his passenger. The Germans give evidence from their point of view of the precautions necessary at the crossing and the engine driver is held blameless because he had the right of way.

In England, a charge under section 2 (1) of the Road Traffic Act is triable at quarter sessions, but, if it is held that it can be tried by court-martial, the accused may not be tried by the highest criminal tribunal, which is what the Act provides for, but by the lower, the nearest equivalent to quarter sessions. Thus the soldier would be deprived of the standard of justice to which the legislature considered a person so charged to be entitled.

There are great difficulties in applying a domestic statute under the Army Act. It is sought to apply the rules and regulations of the Road Traffic Act to a man who is bound under the Army Act by others, namely, the German traffic regulations. One has the case of a young soldier who learnt to drive in Germany and knows only the German traffic laws. Again, a soldier's wife, although subject to military law may be a German who has never been in England. A British soldier is bound by the law of England, by military law and, when he is in Germany, by German law. If it were right to say that the Road Traffic Act can be imported into Germany, then the game laws, the Shops Acts and English law regulating the employment of foreign servants should also be **[63]** imported. Thus if a member of the British forces or his German wife employed a German girl he or she might be charged with employing her without a proper permit. Again the game laws of Germany provide proper control there and it would not be right if, at the whim of a commanding officer, a soldier were charged

[27] [1956] 2 Q.B. 272.
[28] [1962] 2 Q.B. 527.

with an offence arising out of the English game laws relating to close seasons. It becomes manifestly absurd if our laws of a domestic and regulatory character are to be imported into Germany.

Then there was the question of the differentiation of punishment under the Act. Until this year it was not possible to fine a soldier, so the court had no alternative but to apply Army Act penalties, not for a military offence but for a civil offence. Loss of seniority or rank might well amount to a fine of enormous proportions, since, if a sergeant was reduced to a corporal's rank, that might affect his pension rights for the rest of his life and set his career back for an offence for which in English law no mens rea was necessary, for example, careless or dangerous driving, for which the law provides a limited punishment much less severe.

If the Road Traffic Act were imported into Germany, a British soldier would have to have in mind both that Act and the German highway code, but he would be tried on the basis of the Act. There is no rule that there must be a Judge Advocate at his trial and the matter would be determined by a court composed of persons who were not in so good a position as even lay magistrates in England, who have the benefit of legal advice. It is important that such an extra disadvantage should not be put on a soldier. He and other persons subject to military law should be protected. Section 70 of the Army Act calls for definition and qualification on some principle and the principle on which *Reg.* v. *Martin*[29]* and *Reg.* v. *Naylor*[30]* were decided is sound, whatever the form of words used.

John Hobson Q.C., S.-G. and *David Lloyd* for the respondent. There is only one short question on the interpretation of section 70 of the Army Act, namely, the extent to which it incorporates section 3 of the Road Traffic Act. The argument based on *Reg.* v. *Martin*[31]* and *Reg.* v. *Naylor*[32]* is not in point, because there the question was the extent to which English criminal law could be given extraterritorial effect. Here one is considering a domestic tribunal, a court-martial, which is analogous to professional bodies which have to apply a special **[64]** law of their own. For example, the General Medical Council applies to all doctors, wherever they may be in the world, English law and the rules of professional conduct. The Road Traffic Act prescribes punishments for offences against the ordinary criminal law. Courts-martial apply their own military punishments, just as professional bodies have their own penalties. Soldiers are subject to special scales of penalties under the Army Act: see section 72.

Under section 70 a person subject to military law can only be tried for an act which would be an offence under English law, not the law of any other place. If the appellant's arguments were right, he could not be tried by court-martial in Scotland for an act contrary to the Road Traffic Act. The position would be the same in Northern Ireland and Commonwealth territories, some of which do not have the English system of law. Troops may be serving in countries with a system of criminal law different from the English or with different moral concepts or in uncivilised countries with no system of law at all, or in countries occupied by right of conquest or under agreement, for example, West Germany under the Bonn Conventions. See, for example, articles 2 and 6 of the Convention on the Rights and Obligations of Foreign Forces. Article 17 (3), of that Convention deals with liability under German traffic laws, but applies only for civil and not for criminal purposes. One of the ingredients of reckless driving under section 1 (1) of the Road Traffic Act is "having regard to all the circumstances of the case," and one of the circumstances is the regulation of German traffic under their laws. Germany is only one aspect of the problem. Courts-martial are the courts which enforce the criminal law on persons accompanying the British forces. Section 70 of the Army Act must be applied in diverse circumstances, and it should therefore be interpreted in the widest possible sense, so that no limitation is imposed on the words of the section. If one departs from that principle difficulties arise. This is an offence-creating section. English troops are expected to obey all the criminal law of their own country. If one tries to distinguish certain types of offences which British forces abroad can commit

[29] [1956] 2 Q.B. 272.
[30] [1962] 2 Q.B. 527.
[31] [1956] 2 Q.B. 272.
[32] [1962] 2 Q.B. 527.

from others which they cannot, that would amount to reading into section 70 something which is not there. If one is driven to apply a limitation one must ask: What is the essential nature and quality of the English offence? What are the acts and omissions that are essential ingredients? Are any of those acts or omissions incapable of being committed outside England? Something of that sort **[65]** might properly have a limiting effect, but in this case one should not seek to draw a definite line. Under the Town and Country Planning Acts there are some offences created which could not be committed overseas, for example, failure to get licences from a local authority. In *Reg.* v. *Martin*[33]* Devlin J. held that regulation 3 of the Dangerous Drugs Regulations, 1953, only created an offence if the act constituting the offence was committed in England and that section 62 of the Civil Aviation Act, 1949, did not apply. But in the case of British forces serving overseas it might be sensible that the dangerous drugs legislation should apply. No reasonable line can be drawn which would put section 3 of the Road Traffic Act on the wrong side of it. The act of driving a motor vehicle on a road without due care and attention falls precisely within section 70 of the Army Act.

Mark Littman Q.C. in reply. There should be no shrinking from the construction of section 70. If the House of Lords takes the view that some classes of statutory offences are not punishable by courts-martial under section 70, one must ask on what principle they are excluded. The suggestion that one should examine the essential ingredients of each particular offence to see whether it could be committed outside England, is not satisfactory. There must be many offences excluded which would not fall within that test. For example, it is physically possible to drive outside England without a licence. Again, under the Shops Acts or the Factory Acts the essential ingredient of an offence may be said to be the employer's failure to take particular care in regard to a particular piece of machinery, and on the Solicitor-General's test one could not exclude a factory outside England. But his basis is not satisfactory and this matter should be dealt with as one of principle. The principle enunciated in *Reg.* v. *Martin*[34]* is sound, namely, to look at the Act under which the offence in question arises and ask whether that Act is meant to do more than deal with offences in England. That is sound in principle and gives rise to no difficulties in practice. On the Solicitor-General's contentions a foreign doctor helping the British forces abroad could be prosecuted for being in possession of drugs contrary to British drugs legislation.

The British forces serve in varying conditions all over the world. That is an argument for confining the transfer of English statutes abroad to such of them as may fairly be said to be applicable in general conditions. **[66]**

One should not start with the hypothesis that wherever the line is drawn, section 3 of the Road Traffic Act will be on the wrong side of it. An essential ingredient of an offence under that Act is that the road must be in England. Accordingly, there can be no offence under section 3 in driving without due care and attention on a German road and no civil offence is committed under section 70 of the Army Act.

Their Lordships took time for consideration.

1962. Mar. 15. VISCOUNT SIMONDS. My Lords, this appeal, the first that has been brought to this House under the Administration of Justice Act, 1960, on appeal from the Courts-Martial Appeal Court, raises an important question upon section 70 of the Army Act, 1955.

The appellant, a sergeant in the Royal Army Pay Corps serving with the British Army of the Rhine, was on January 20, 1961, convicted by a District Court-Martial sitting in Germany of an offence which was charged in these terms: "Committing a civil offence contrary to section 70 of the Army Act, 1955, that is to say, driving a motor vehicle contrary to section 3 (1) of the Road Traffic Act, 1960, in that he at Sundern [Germany] on September 15, 1960,

[33] [1956] 2 Q.B. 272.
[34] Ibid.

drove a motor vehicle on a road without due care and attention." He was sentenced to be severely reprimanded.

He appealed to the Courts-Martial Appeal Court on the grounds that the charge as laid was not correct in law because it did not disclose an offence under section 70 of the Army Act, 1955, in that the act particularised in the charge was not an act contrary to section 3 (1) of the Road Traffic Act, 1960, and was not an act which could be committed in England, and further was not a civil offence within the meaning of section 70 of the Army Act. I have stated the further ground of appeal, but it appears to add nothing to the first ground. The appeal was dismissed by the Courts-Martial Appeal Court on November 7, 1961, the reasons being given at a later date by the late Slade J.

Section 70 of the Army Act, 1955, provides as follows: "(1) Any person subject to military law who commits a civil offence, whether in the United Kingdom or elsewhere, shall be guilty of an offence against this section. (2) In this Act the expression 'civil offence' means any act or omission punishable by the law of England or which, if committed in England, would be punishable by that law; and in this Act the expression 'the **[67]** corresponding civil offence' means the civil offence the commission of which constitutes the offence against this section . . ."

I have already indicated the nature of the offence charged, but it is necessary, in order to understand the case for the appellant, to state the relevant section of the Road Traffic Act, 1960, more fully. It is as follows: "If a person drives a motor vehicle on a road without due care and attention, or without reasonable consideration for other persons using the road, he shall be liable on summary conviction to a fine not exceeding £40 . . ." With this section must be read the definition of "road" in section 257 of the Act, which is: ". . . . 'road' means any highway and any other road to which the public has access, and includes bridges over which a road passes . . ." The argument for the appellant is then a very simple one. He says that "road" in section 3 of the Road Traffic Act, 1960, means a road in England, therefore he cannot have contravened the section by driving on a road in Germany with or without due care and attention. This argument did not prevail in the Courts-Martial Appeal Court and is, in my opinion, unsound.

We may in the first place dispose of a contention which was raised in the cases of *Reg.* v. *Martin*[35]* and *Reg.* v. *Naylor*[36]* (to which I shall again refer) upon an essentially different section of the Civil Aviation Act, 1949, and was at one time raised also upon section 70 of the Army Act, namely, that the relevant section is not what has been called an "offence-creating section." It is clear that, whatever may be said of section 62 of the Civil Aviation Act, section 70 of the Army Act in the plainest terms provides that acts or omissions which apart from it would not be offences become by virtue of it offences which are punishable in the manner prescribed.

The question, then, is what are the acts or omissions for which the section thus provides. In construing the section two things must be borne in mind. First, apart from those exceptional cases in which specific provision is made in regard to acts committed abroad, the whole body of the criminal law of England deals only with acts committed in England. Secondly, section 70 and the following sections have to be applied in diverse circumstances wherever the armed forces of the Crown happen to be, in developed or undeveloped countries, as conquerors or guests, and their purpose is, as the title to that Part of the Act in which they are to be found shows, disciplinary. **[68]**

Bearing these considerations in mind, I cannot accept the simple argument that, if an act is committed on a German road, it cannot be a civil offence within section 70. Such a construction gives no content to the words "or which, if committed in England, would be punishable by that law," and frustrates the clear purpose of the Army Act, namely, to make those persons subject to military law who are serving abroad liable to punishment for offences which, though not military offences in a narrow sense, are yet prejudicial to discipline. Amongst

[35] [1956] 2 Q.B. 272; [1956] 2 W.L.R. 975; [1956] 2 All E.R. 86.
[36] [1962] 2 Q.B. 527; [1961] 3 W.L.R. 898; [1961] 2 All E.R. 932.

these must be placed those acts which fall short of the standard of behaviour towards each other and the inhabitants of the occupied territory which military discipline traditionally demands. I know of no better way of describing such acts than that which I find in section 70—"which, if committed in England, would be punishable by that law."

But it is, of course, obvious that the whole body of our criminal law cannot be thus translated to a foreign country, and attempts were made in the course of the argument to formulate a qualification which would be a guide to courts-martial before which a similar question might arise. The learned Solicitor-General deprecated any such attempt. He was content to urge that at any rate the act of driving a motor vehicle on a road without due care and attention fell precisely within the language of section 70. In this he was, in my opinion, clearly right. It is true that in the Road Traffic Act, "road" means a road in England. But the essence of the offence lies in driving without due care and attention on a road to which the public have access. I see no difficulty in at least this degree of translation. Nor should the issue be confused by saying that in England and (say) Germany the traffic regulations are different. A driver shows due care and attention by observing the regulations which prevail in the country where he is driving. Nor, again, does it appear to be relevant that the Road Traffic Act contains numerous provisions in which "road" can only have a sensible meaning if it is confined to roads in England, and other provisions, for example, in regard to the Menai Bridge, which by their nature can have no application except to a particular subject-matter. It appears to me that here at least in a negative sense is the test of the applicability of the section. If the act is of its nature one that can only be committed in England the section cannot operate. I need say no more than that it is otherwise with such acts as driving without due care or, it may be, dangerously on a highway or larceny from a dwellinghouse or an offence against the person. All such acts have what, for want of a better expression, I will call a character of universality **[69]** which makes it sensible to bring them within the scope of section 70. I mean the same thing whether I refer to them being done at Sundern or at Surbiton.

I have mentioned the cases of *Reg.* v. *Martin*[37]* and *Reg.* v. *Naylor*.[38]* Both cases were decided on the construction of section 62 of the Civil Aviation Act, 1949, which differs materially from section 70 of the Army Act. I will therefore say no more about the former case than that, assuming that Devlin J. correctly decided in that case that the possession of raw opium on a British aircraft flying between Bahrein and Singapore was not rendered an offence by the Civil Aviation Act, it by no means follows that a similar result would follow if a person serving in the British Army of the Rhine and therefore subject to military law was found to be in possession of dangerous drugs within the meaning of the Dangerous Drugs Act, 1951, and the regulations made thereunder. As to the latter case I would make only one comment. With great respect to the learned Lord Chief Justice, I doubt whether the distinction which he makes between "purely domestic" and other legislation is a valid one. Or perhaps I should rather say that it is capable of being misunderstood. For, as I have already pointed out, with rare exceptions the whole body of our criminal law is "domestic" in the sense that it is made for the order and good government of this country and is applicable only to acts done on English soil. It is not necessary for your Lordships to review this decision and I would myself reserve consideration of it.

Reference was also made to the case of *Attorney-General for Hongkong* v. *Kwok-a-Sing*,[39]* but I do not get any assistance from this case for the purpose of construing section 70 of the Army Act. No authority is needed for the proposition that the extreme generality of words in a statute may be narrowed by the context.

I have made no mention of a point which may deserve consideration in some future case. It will have been observed that "civil offence" is defined by section 70 (2) as meaning not only any "act" but also any "omission" which, if committed

[37] [1956] 2 Q.B. 272.
[38] [1962] 2 Q.B. 527.
[39] (1873) L.R. 5 P.C. 179.

in England would be punishable by the law of England. Committing an omission is not a happy phrase though it may suggest an intelligible idea. In any event it does not in any way reflect upon the meaning which the words "act committed" must bear.

I move that the appeal be dismissed. **[70]**

My noble and learned friend, Lord Jenkins, who is unable to be here, asks me to say that he has read and concurs in the opinion which I have just given.

LORD REID. My Lords, I agree that this appeal must be dismissed. The appellant is guilty of a "civil offence" within the meaning of section 70 of the Army Act, 1955, if his act or omission in Germany was of such a character that "if committed in England" it would be punishable by the law of England. Any act or omission committed abroad was committed there and nowhere else. So the statute requires us to imagine another act committed in England. It cannot require that that other act should be precisely the same in every detail because that would be impossible. So it must require that we can imagine another act committed in England which is similar in all relevant respects. With many types of offence that is easy. For example, murder and theft are the same all the world over. At the other end of the scale there are acts or omissions so closely connected with conditions which are peculiar to England, or at least which are absent in the place where the act was committed, that it would be impossible to find the necessary degree of similarity between the act or omission committed abroad and any act or omission which could be committed in England.

The requisite degree of similarity must depend on the nature of the offence. In this case the appellant was found guilty of driving a motor-vehicle on a road without due care and attention contrary to section 3 (1) of the Road Traffic Act, 1960. But the question is not whether that Act applies to Germany, or whether the road on which he was driving was a road within the meaning of that Act. The question is whether there is the requisite degree of similarity between what the appellant did and an act done in England which would be contrary to that section. I can see no relevant difference between the two. No doubt traffic regulations are different in Germany from those in England. But conditions vary greatly in England and the essence of the offence is failure to drive with due care and attention having regard to all the circumstances at the particular place and time. I therefore find no difficulty in equating failure to drive with due care and attention in particular circumstances in Germany with a similar failure in England. And that is sufficient to dispose of this case.

I would only add that the cases of *Reg.* v. *Martin*[40]* and *Reg.* v. *Naylor*[41]* were dealing with an entirely different question and I **[71]** express no opinion as to whether or not these cases were rightly decided.

LORD RADCLIFFE. My Lords, I am in full agreement with the speech that has been delivered by my noble and learned friend, Viscount Simonds. I think that it demonstrates clearly why it is that this appeal cannot succeed. I add a few words only because the ambit of section 70 of the Army Act, 1955, is so very wide and yet we are forced to leave the line of its boundaries undefined.

It is, I think, beyond question that this is an "offence creating" section. It would be impossible to read it otherwise, having regard to the words of subsection (2), "any act or omission . . . which, if committed in England, would be punishable by that law." Therefore, what we have in this section is the general application of the entire corpus of the law of England as to punishable offences, subject to the necessary qualification (1) that there must be some acts or omissions punishable if done in England which cannot be reproduced by any equivalent occurrence taking place outside this country, and (2) there must be some acts or omissions occurring outside England which are so much identified with their locality that they cannot be translated into any equivalent English offence.

It is a formidable thought that this great body of criminal law is thus made potentially applicable without it being possible to find or lay down any useful

[40] [1956] 2 Q.B. 272.

[41] [1962] 2 Q.B. 527.

definition of what is to be excluded, which will aid those whose duty is to frame charges under this section. I agree that the situation is unavoidable, but it is nonetheless unfortunate.

It may help, perhaps, to stress one or two points that seem to me to be involved in the requirements of section 70. First, we can put on one side the act or omission which is punishable by the law of England anyway. This must denote either offences actually committed in England or those very few offences which we punish wherever committed. Then there come the "created" offences, and these can only be ascertained by a process of translation; as in all translations, the problem is to find a fair and proper equivalent, since there cannot be literal reproduction. Secondly, the occurrence that is said to constitute the offence is always the actual occurrence itself as it took place outside England and that means importing into the hypothetical English occurrence the circumstances and conditions that prevailed at the place where and the time when the thing that is complained of was done or omitted. The difficult question, as I see it, is to **[72]** decide in any particular case how far those circumstances and conditions are an essential element of the act which it is said would have constituted an offence if committed in England, and how far the English offence is capable of being applied to the non-English occurrence.

For instance, in the present case, the appellant must be envisaged as driving along a German road, possibly observing the local rule to be on the right of the road, and under whatever system of traffic control and direction may have been locally operative on that road. Do these circumstances or conditions make it wrong to say that if he had shown in England the lack of care and attention which he showed in Germany he would have been punished in England? In my opinion, they do not, for there is nothing in the case to suggest that what occurred in Germany is not fairly translatable into the conditions of the equivalent English offence.

The appellant's argument centred round the proposition that in the Road Traffic Act, 1960, the word "road" means by construction English road or the Queen's highway, and therefore the offence of driving on it without due care and attention could not be committed in Germany. This is perhaps a picturesque way of putting his position but, logically, it is, I think, indefensible. First, it is, in my opinion, an abuse of language to say that in this statute "road" means English road "as a matter of construction." It means, I think, road pure and simple, as defined by the Road Traffic Act, and the more correct proposition is to say that the statute itself has no application except to acts done on the roads of England. But, secondly, it is just because the Road Traffic Act, in common with virtually every other offence-creating enactment, has this limited application that section 70 requires the making of the hypothesis that the act, which did not in fact take place on an English road, was committed in England where what takes place on roads is subject to the provisions of the Road Traffic Act.

Lord Morris of Borth-y-Gest. My Lords, I entertain no doubt that section 70 of the Army Act, 1955, is an offence-creating section. A person who is subject to military law will be guilty of an offence against that section if either in the United Kingdom or elsewhere he commits an act punishable by the law of England or if either in the United Kingdom or elsewhere he commits an act which if committed in England would be punishable by the law of England. It follows that a person who is subject to military **[73]** law may commit an act outside England and be guilty of an offence under section 70 if, had the act been committed in England, he would have been punishable by the law of England. It is to be observed that the section does not contain words of exception.

My Lords, I can see no reason for excluding from its operation an act which if it had been committed in England would have been punishable under section 3 (1) of the Road Traffic Act, 1960. The appellant drove a motor vehicle at Sundern. If he drove it at Sundern on a road (meaning by that word any highway and any other road to which the public had access including any bridge over which a road passes—see section 257) and if having regard to all relevant circumstances he drove it without due care and attention then, on the assumption that the road had been in England, there would have been an offence under section 3 (1) and on that basis there was an offence under section 70 of the Army Act of 1955.

My Lords, I cannot think that this reasoning is refuted by observing that the Road Traffic Act was enacted in reference to traffic on roads in this country. It clearly was. In the same way most penal statutory provisions have reference to offences committed in the United Kingdom and there are but few acts committed abroad which are punishable by the law of England. For the purposes of applying section 70, which requires an assumption or may involve a notional transfer, I can see no difficulty either in assuming that a road in some other territory had been in England or, for example, in assuming that a dwellinghouse in some other territory had been in England.

As section 70 does not contain any words of exception I see no justification for the submission that the Road Traffic Act as a whole must be excluded from the operation of the section. A perusal of that Act shows, however, that there are certain offences which could only be committed in or by reference to some particular place in the United Kingdom. This circumstance does not warrant a failure to apply section 70 to the present case or to other situations in which the section can operate.

I would dismiss the appeal.

Appeal dismissed.

Solicitors: *Church, Adams, Tatham & Co.; The Director of Army Legal Services.*

IN RE P. (G.E.) (AN INFANT)

([1964] Ch. 575)

May 6, 7, 1964. Chancery Division: Plowman J.

Infant—Ward of court—Jurisdiction—Infant abroad—Infant born in Egypt—Father stateless—Migration to England—English domicile acquired but not naturalised—Infant taken out of jurisdiction—Application to make infant ward of court—Whether court had jurisdiction.

An infant born in Egypt on February 15, 1956, of a stateless father and an Egyptian mother was brought to England by its parents in February, 1957. In order to obtain an exit visa the mother gave up her Egyptian nationality and became stateless. **[576]** While in this country they lived with the mother's relatives until January, 1962, when they bought a house. In April, 1962, each signed an application for naturalisation, stating that his, and her, intention was to live in the United Kingdom, but those applications were not proceeded with and neither of them became a British subject. In August, 1962, the mother left the matrimonial home, leaving the infant there with the father. Subsequently the infant spent part of the week, when the father was working, with the mother and the week-ends with the father. On November 9, 1962, the father collected the infant as usual but the next day he flew to Israel with him and both had lived there ever since. The father's evidence was that he went to Israel with the intention of making his permanent home there. On January 4, 1963, the mother issued a summons under the Law Reform (Miscellaneous Provisions) Act, 1949, and the Guardianship of Infants Acts, 1886 and 1925, seeking, inter alia, to make the infant a ward of court. No appointment for the hearing of that summons was obtained within 21 days after its issue. The infant was, therefore, not a ward of court. On February 13, 1963, the mother obtained leave to serve the father out of the jurisdiction. The father was served in Israel and entered appearance under protest.

On a summons by the father seeking to have the mother's summons set aside for lack of jurisdiction:—

Held, that the court had no jurisdiction to order that an infant should become or remain a ward of court unless either the infant was a British subject or was physically present within the jurisdiction at the time when the proceedings were commenced; and that it was not enough in the case of a foreign infant that he had been within the jurisdiction at some earlier date (post, p. 581). Accordingly, the mother's summons ought to be set aside for lack of jurisdiction.

Brown v. *Collins* (1884) 25 Ch.D. 56 and *Harben* v. *Harben* [1957] 1 W.L.R. 261; [1957] 1 All E.R. 379 distinguished.

Per curiam. If the contrary conclusion had been reached then, in the circumstances of the case, the disputes as to the domicile of the infant before November, 1962, and since, and as to the date when there was a change of domicile, if change there was, were matters which could only properly be decided at the hearing of the mother's originating summons (post, p. 584).

ADJOURNED SUMMONS.

The following statement of facts is taken from the judgment.

The father of the infant was born in 1915 in Jerusalem, which was then part of the Ottoman Empire. His father was a White Russian and his mother stateless. At birth the father acquired Turkish nationality, but he lost that in early infancy when his parents moved to Egypt. The father lived in Egypt as a stateless person till 1957. From 1926 until he left the country he was registered as a White Russian. He married the mother of the **[577]** infant in Egypt in 1954. She had been born in Egypt in 1927 of an Egyptian father.

The infant, a boy, was born in Egypt on February 15, 1956, and was now eight years old.

In February, 1957, as a result of the Suez crisis, the father and mother left Egypt with the infant and came to England, where the mother's own mother and brothers were living. In order to obtain an exit visa the mother gave up her Egyptian nationality and became stateless.

For a few years the father, mother and infant shared accommodation with the mother's relatives, and then, in January, 1962, they bought a house and moved into it.

In April, 1962, each signed an application under the British Nationality Act, 1948, for a certificate of naturalisation stating that, if the application was granted, his, and her, intention was to live in the United Kingdom. Those applications were not proceeded with and neither the father, the mother nor the infant became a British subject.

In August or September, 1962, as a result of quarrels, the mother left the matrimonial home, leaving the infant there with the father. Subsequently, arrangements were made whereby the infant spent part of the week, when the father was working, with the mother at her mother's flat and the week-ends with the father. On November 9, 1962, the father collected the infant for the week-end in the usual way, and on the following day he flew with the infant to Israel, where they had lived ever since. On November 11 the mother received a cable from the father informing her that they were both in Jerusalem.

The father's evidence was that he went to Israel with the intention of making it his permanent home. He was now working in that country as a government official and about three months before the hearing of this summons he and the infant obtained Israeli nationality.

On January 4, 1963, the mother issued an originating summons asking for relief under the Law Reform (Miscellaneous Provisions) Act, 1949, and the Guardianship of Infants Acts, 1886 and 1925. The infant was not, at the time of hearing, a ward of court, by virtue of section 9 of the Act of 1949, since an appointment for the hearing of the originating summons was not obtained within 21 days after its issue in accordance with R.S.C., Ord. 54P, r. 3. On February 13, 1963, the mother obtained leave to serve the father out of the jurisdiction. He was served in Israel and had entered appearance under protest. **[578]**

On October 2, 1963, the father issued the present summons asking for an order that the mother's originating summons should be set aside for lack of jurisdiction; and, alternatively, that the service on the father of notice of the mother's summons should be set aside and the order authorising that service should be discharged on the grounds that it was not authorised by R.S.C., Ord. 11.

A. J. Balcombe for the father. The court has no jurisdiction to make an infant a ward of court unless the infant is either a British subject or is resident within the jurisdiction or, possibly, is domiciled in England: Dicey on Conflict of Laws, 7th ed. (1958), p. 387. It is a well established principle of law that the domicile of an infant follows the domicile of the father: Halsbury's Laws of England, 3rd ed., Vol. 7, p. 23. The question, therefore, is what was the father's domicile at the date of the issue of the mother's summons? It is common ground that when the parties left Egypt they left for good. The father had been born in the Turkish Empire. On giving up his Egyptian domicile of choice there is a conflict of evidence whether he acquired English domicile, but when he left England in November, 1962, he left with the intention of living in Israel permanently. Therefore, even if he had acquired an English domicile that was destroyed by his leaving the country with the intention of settling elsewhere: Dicey on Conflict of Laws, 7th ed., p. 112. The jurisdiction of the court to make an infant a ward of court is a delegation of the sovereign's power as parens patriae. It would be very odd if the sovereign exercised that power over foreign children. The Court of Chancery has jurisdiction over the children of a British subject even though they are resident or even born abroad: *Hope* v. *Hope*[1]; *Brown* v. *Collins*[2]; *In re Willoughby*.[3] It was at one time doubted whether proceedings which sought to make an infant a ward of court ought to allege some right of the infant to property within the court's jurisdiction: *Johnstone* v. *Beattie*.[4] But that doubt has been put to rest and it is now clear that the court's jurisdiction is exercised to protect the infant and not his property: *In re D.* (*An Infant*)[5]. The court has refused, on the ground of lack of jurisdiction, to appoint an English guardian of French children who were in France: *In re Bourgoise*.[6]* [Reference **[579]** was also made to *Nugent* v. *Vetzera*,[7] *In re E.* (*An Infant*)[8] and *In re C.* (*An Infant*).[9]] The only view that can be extracted from those authorities is that the court only exercises its parental jurisdiction over infants who owe allegiance to the sovereign or, being foreign infants, are resident here and owe allegiance temporarily.

A. A. Baden Fuller for the mother. The court has jurisdiction to entertain wardship proceedings whenever an infant is domiciled or ordinarily resident within the jurisdiction. The infant here was domiciled in England when the mother commenced proceedings. The father in his evidence does not say where he is domiciled—he only says where he is not. The inference which can be drawn from the circumstances is that the infant acquired a domicile of choice in Egypt because his father settled there. The father left Egypt for good and came to England. Thus he acquired a domicile of choice in England. The infant, therefore, also became domiciled here. The infant is thus subject to the protection of the courts of this country: see the observations of Kay J. in *Brown* v. *Collins*.[10] From here the infant's domicile was not changed, because the rule that the domicile of an infant changes with the father's or guardian's is subject to qualification that it is not affected where the change is for a wrongful purpose: Cheshire on Private International Law, 6th ed. (1961), p. 191; *In re Beaumont*.[11]

[1] (1854) 4 De G.M. & G. 328.
[2] (1884) 25 Ch.D. 56.
[3] (1885) 30 Ch.D. 324; 1 T.L.R. 652, C.A.
[4] (1843) 10 Cl. & F. 42, H.L.
[5] [1943] Ch. 305; 59 T.L.R. 354; [1943] 2 All E.R. 411.
[6] (1889) 41 Ch.D. 310, 318, C.A.
[7] (1866) L.R. 2 Eq. 704.
[8] [1956] Ch. 23; [1955] 3 W.L.R. 493; [1955] 3 All E.R. 174.
[9] [1959] Ch. 363; [1958] 2 All E.R. 656.
[10] (1884) 25 Ch.D. 56, 62.
[11] [1893] 3 Ch. 490.

In this respect there is no distinction whether the change is effected by the father or by the mother if the father is dead. A wrongful purpose may be presumed where there is no reasonable cause for the change and it appears that the change has been effected by the parent to take advantage of law: *Potinger* v. *Wightman*.[12] Here, not only had the father no reasonable cause to remove the infant, but he obtained an advantage in law by removing the infant. Where an infant has been wrongfully removed from the court's jurisdiction and the remover claims a change of jurisdiction the court would order him to deliver up the infant here: *Harben* v. *Harben*.[13] The court has jurisdiction in relation to guardianship and custody if the infant is domiciled in England: Dicey on Conflict of Laws, 7th ed. (1958), pp. 387-388. The editors' "semble" there is unduly cautious. Their **[580]** statement is an example of the general principle that the domestic affairs of individuals are regulated by the law of their domicile. The courts administering such law necessarily have jurisdiction. The absence of authority should not prevent the court from giving effect to this principle.

Balcombe in reply. There is no authority which states that the English domicile of an infant gives jurisdiction to the court. The court's jurisdiction depends on subjection to the Crown, i.e., nationality or physical presence. That power is exercised by the court by delegation.

PLOWMAN J. The question which arises in this case is a novel one; it is whether the parental jurisdiction of this court over infants extends to infants who are neither British subjects nor present within the jurisdiction of the court. It is suggested on behalf of the mother of the infant with whom I am concerned that it does if the infant is domiciled or ordinarily resident in this country.

The question arises on an application by the father for an order setting aside, for lack of jurisdiction, an originating summons under the Law Reform (Miscellaneous Provisions) Act, 1949, issued by the mother. [His Lordship stated the facts set out above, observing that he assumed that by 1962, before the marriage had broken up, both parents and the infant had acquired an English domicile. His Lordship continued:] It is now conceded by Mr. Balcombe on behalf of the father that, if the father fails under paragraph 1 of the summons [on the issue as to the jurisdiction], he cannot succeed under paragraph 2 [on the issue of the validity of the service on him], and I need not consider that paragraph further.

The position, therefore, is this: that since a time some two months prior to the issue of the originating summons in this matter, the infant, who is not a British subject, has been living outside the jurisdiction of this court, and the question arises whether, in those circumstances, I have jurisdiction to entertain wardship proceedings.

For this purpose, the question whether the court would be likely to accede to the mother's application, if it ultimately came to be determined, is irrelevant.

Mr. Baden Fuller, for the mother, submits that the court has jurisdiction to entertain wardship proceedings whenever an infant is domiciled or ordinarily resident within the jurisdiction of the **[581]** court, as he submits that this infant is or was when the originating summons was issued.

Mr. Balcombe, for the father, disputes that the infant is, or was, when the originating summons was issued, either domiciled or ordinarily resident in this country, but for the purpose of determining the question of jurisdiction I propose to assume, without deciding, that Mr. Balcombe is wrong about that.

What, then, is the result? In my judgment, this court has no jurisdiction to order that an infant shall become or remain a ward of court unless either the infant is a British subject or is physically present within the jurisdiction of the court at the time when the proceedings are commenced. It is not, in my judgment, enough, in the case of a foreign child, that he has been within the jurisdiction of the court at some earlier date.

I have been referred to what I take to be all the relevant authorities over the past 120 years and in no single case has the court assumed its parental jurisdiction unless the infant either was a British subject or was actually within the

[12] (1817) 3 Mer. 67.
[13] [1957] 1 W.L.R. 261; [1957] 1 All E.R. 379.

jurisdiction. It would not, I think, serve any useful purpose to refer to all the cases cited in order merely to demonstrate this purely negative proposition, but I desire to refer briefly to some of them.

In *Hope* v. *Hope*,[14] Lord Cranworth L.C. held that the Court of Chancery had jurisdiction over the custody of British children though they were born or resident abroad. In a well-known judgment he had this to say about the basis of the court's jurisdiction[15]: "The jurisdiction of this court, which is entrusted to the holder of the great seal as the representative of the Crown, with regard to the custody of infants rests upon this ground, that it is the interest of the state and of the sovereign that children should be properly brought up and educated; and according to the principle of our law, the sovereign, as parens patriae, is bound to look to the maintenance and education (so far as it has the means of judging) of all his subjects." Then, after referring to the court's jurisdiction over foreign children in this country, Lord Cranworth says[16]: "The reason why such a jurisdiction exists over foreign children in this country is, because foreign children, like adult foreigners while here, are to a certain extent the subjects of the Crown of England, and it has been decided that they are so for many purposes." Those passages in my judgment show that the jurisdiction is based on nationality or on presence within the jurisdiction. **[582]**

In *In re Willoughby*,[17] Cotton L.J. said that the court would exercise its jurisdiction over British children who were outside the jurisdiction and had no property within the jurisdiction only under "extraordinary circumstances." I refer to that case because, in *Harben* v. *Harben*,[18] to which I shall refer in a moment, Sachs J. had to consider whether the circumstances there prevailing were "extraordinary."

In *In re Bourgoise*,[19]* Kay J. held that he had no jurisdiction to appoint English guardians of French children resident in France. The case went to the Court of Appeal,[19] who decided the appeal on another point.

Mr. Baden Fuller referred to the decision of Sachs J. in *Harben* v. *Harben*.[20] The headnote to that case, so far as relevant, is as follows: "A husband of English nationality and domicile of origin kidnapped the children of the marriage from the matrimonial home in Eire and took them to Jersey where he alleged that he had acquired a domicile of choice. He entered an appearance under protest to the wife's subsequent petition for divorce and resisted her application for an injunction to restrain him from removing the children from Jersey and for an order that they should be delivered up to her in England. *Held*, . . . (2) The court had jurisdiction to deal with applications relating to children who were British subjects although they were outside its jurisdiction. *Hope* v. *Hope*[21] and *In re Willoughby*[22] applied. (3) Orders relating to children outside the jurisdiction would only be made in exceptional circumstances . . ." It is clear that in that case[23] the court was concerned with British children and that the jurisdiction of the court was conceded. The question with which Sachs J. was concerned was, therefore, not one of jurisdiction but whether the circumstances, including the so-called kidnapping, were such as to constitute what Cotton L.J. called "extraordinary circumstances" so as to induce the court to exercise its jurisdiction notwithstanding the fact that the children were not present within the jurisdiction of the court.

Mr. Baden Fuller also prayed in aid an obiter dictum of Kay J. in *Brown* v. *Collins*.[24] That was a very different case from **[583]** anything with which I am

[14] (1854) 4 De G.M. & G. 328.
[15] Ibid. 344.
[16] Ibid. 346.
[17] (1885) 30 Ch.D. 324, 331; 1 T.L.R. 652, C.A.
[18] [1957] 1 W.L.R. 261; [1957] 1 All E.R. 379.
[19] (1889) 41 Ch.D. 310, 316, 318, C.A.
[20] [1957] 1 W.L.R. 261.
[21] 4 De G.M. & G. 328.
[22] 30 Ch.D. 324.
[23] [1957] 1 W.L.R. 261.
[24] (1884) 25 Ch.D. 56.

concerned, as the headnote shows. It is as follows: "A fund was carried over in an administration action to a separate account, intituled, 'The account of A.B., and of X.Y., and his issue,' to answer a settled legacy under the will of the testator, wherein A.B. and X.Y. had life interests. X.Y. was a domiciled Frenchman, and he died leaving issue three daughters only, who were all French and married to Frenchmen, two of them having married under age, and one being still an infant. A.B. having also died, these three daughters and their husbands petitioned for payment out to them of their respective shares. *Held*, that the court would not in the exercise of its discretion treat the two daughters who had married under age as wards of court. *Semble*, the carrying of a fund to separate account of an infant in an action to which the infant is not a party will not constitute such infant a ward of court, and even if such carrying over would have constituted a natural born British subject a ward of court, it would not have that effect in the case of an alien not resident in this country." My attention was particularly called to a passage where Kay J. said[25]: "In this case . . . the infant is an alien; and although it seems clear that if an alien were domiciled in this country, and therefore subject to the protection of the law of this country while resident and domiciled here, she might be made a ward of court; yet this infant is not domiciled here, and she is not and never has been resident here, and the only circumstance rendering it possible to treat her as a ward of court is the fact that this money has been paid to this account in the Court of Chancery." I think that, in that passage, Kay J. had *Hope* v. *Hope*[26] in mind, which had been cited to him, and he in fact referred to it in the very next sentence. However that may be, he was not, in my opinion, intending to lay down any principle wider than had previously been established.

A reference was also made to a passage in Dicey on the Conflict of Laws, 7th ed. (1958), on p. 387, which reads: "The court has jurisdiction (a) to appoint a guardian for an infant (i) (*Semble*) where the infant is domiciled in England, or (ii) where the infant is resident in England, (b) to make a custody order in respect of an infant (i) (*Semble*) where the infant is domiciled in England, or (ii) where the infant is present in England, or (iii) where the court exercises its jurisdiction to pronounce a decree of **[584]** divorce or of nullity or for judicial separation or for restitution of conjugal rights in respect of the marriage of the parents of the infant, and the fact that the infant possesses no property in England is immaterial."

Then in a comment on that passage the editor on p. 390 says: "It is submitted further that the English courts have jurisdiction over any infant, whether a British subject or an alien, who is domiciled in England. This rule is supported, as regards guardianship proper, by an obiter dictum which gives equal prominence to the English domicile and residence of the infant." The reference in that comment is to the passage in the judgment of Kay J. in *Brown* v. *Collins*[27] which I have just read. It seems to me that the text and the comment on the text give more weight to that obiter dictum than it properly bears, and, as I have already indicated, I can find no foundation in any authority which has been cited to me for the view which is indicated by those passages in Dicey.

To sum up, it does not appear that the jurisdiction of the sovereign as parens patriae over its own subjects has ever been extended to foreign children unless they happen to be present within the jurisdiction of the court, and, as in this case, the infant concerned is neither a British subject nor present in this country, I feel bound to hold that the court has no jurisdiction to make this infant a ward of court, and I must make the order asked for in paragraph 1 of the father's summons.

I should perhaps add this. If I had reached the contrary conclusion, I should have been disposed to the view that, in the circumstances of this case, the disputes as to the domicile of the infant before November, 1962, and since, and as to the date when there was a change of domicile, if change there was, were

[25] 25 Ch.D. 56, 62.
[26] 4 De G.M. & G. 328.
[27] 25 Ch.D. 56, 62.

matters which could only properly be decided at the hearing of the originating summons. In the circumstances, however, that does not arise.

Declaration accordingly.
No order as to costs.
Leave to appeal granted on the main issue but refused on the question of costs.

Solicitors: *Birkbeck, Julius, Coburn & Broad; Hickson & Parish.*

IN RE P. (G.E.) (AN INFANT)

([1965] Ch. 568)

October 5, 6, 7, November 9, 1964: Court of Appeal: Lord Denning M.R., Pearson, Russell L.JJ.

Infant—Ward of court—Jurisdiction—Infant abroad—Alien infant ordinarily resident in England—Infant removed from jurisdiction by father without knowledge of mother—Stateless father furnished with travel document permitting return to United Kingdom within three months—Travel document covering both father and infant—Application by mother to make infant ward of court—Summons by father to set aside mother's application for lack of jurisdiction— **[569]** *Whether father and infant "ordinarily resident" in England—Whether allegiance owed to Crown—Whether infant entitled to Crown protection as parens patriae—Jurisdiction of Court of Chancery.*
Crown—Allegiance to—Ordinary residence in England—Travel document giving stateless person right to return to United Kingdom—Whether allegiance owed to Crown—Whether infant entitled to protection of Crown.

An infant born in Egypt of Jewish parents in 1956, the father being stateless and the mother Egyptian, was brought to England after the Suez crisis in February, 1957, by his parents, the mother having relatives in England. In January, 1962, they set up a matrimonial home at Brighton, and in April of that year each signed an application for naturalisation, stating that each intended to live in the United Kingdom; but those applications were not brought to a conclusion and neither parent became a British subject. In August, 1962, the mother left the matrimonial home and went to live with her own mother at Hendon. By arrangement between the parents, the infant lived with his mother and went to school in Hendon during the week, and spent the weekends with his father at Brighton.

On November 9, 1962, the father collected the infant as usual; but on the following day he flew to Israel with the infant, and on November 11 sent a cable to the mother saying that they were in Israel. They had remained there ever since.

On January 4, 1963, the mother issued a summons under the Law Reform (Miscellaneous Provisions) Act, 1949, and the Guardianship of Infants Acts, 1886 and 1925, seeking, *inter alia*, to make the infant a ward of court; but as she did not make the necessary appointment, the infant was not made a ward of court. The mother having obtained leave to serve the father out of the jurisdiction, he entered appearance under protest, and on October 2, 1963, took out a summons seeking to have the mother's summons set aside for lack of jurisdiction.

The evidence before the court showed that the father and the infant had left England under the aegis of a travel document issued to stateless persons by the Home Office, the document in form affording no diplomatic or consular protection to the holder while abroad but entitling him (unless the contrary were stated) to return to the United Kingdom within three months. The father also had a tourist visa for three months from the Israeli government; but in his own affidavit he stated that when he went to Israel with the infant he did so with the intention of making his permanent home there. At the date of the hearing of his summons he and the infant had acquired Israeli nationality.

Plowman J., assuming without deciding that the infant was at the date of the mother's summons either domiciled or ordinarily resident in England, held that the court had no jurisdiction in wardship proceedings over an alien infant not physically present in England, and set aside the mother's summons. On appeal by the mother, the court was asked to decide on the available evidence **[570]** whether or not the infant at the relevant date was ordinarily resident in this country:—

Held, allowing the appeal, (1) that the English Court of Chancery, representing the Crown as parens patriae, has jurisdiction to make an order for the custody, education and maintenance of a child ordinarily resident within the jurisdiction, although the child is neither a British subject nor physically present in this country when the proceedings are taken out. An alien infant ordinarily resident in this country owes an allegance to the Crown, and, as a corollary to that allegiance, has a right to protection from the Crown and therefore to the parental jurisdiction of the Crown exercised through the High Court (post, pp. 584, 585, 590, 593).

Per curiam. The test of ordinary residence is to be preferred to that of domicile, for the tests of domicile are archaic and artificial and would produce strange results if applied in the context of a jurisdiction which historically is closely connected with allegiance (post, pp. 583, 589, 592-593).

(2) That, on the available evidence, the father, and a fortiori the infant, were ordinarily resident within the jurisdiction when the mother took out her summons, for (*a*) the infant's home was with his mother in this country; (*b*) the father and son had left the jurisdiction on a travel document issued by Her Majesty's Government which entitled them to return, which had not been surrendered, and by virtue of which they were admitted to the foreign jurisdiction on a temporary tourist basis; and (*c*) they had left family and effects in England; and by reason of those factors, by analogy with the law of treason, the infant continued to owe sufficient allegiance to the Crown to found jurisdiction in the Court of Chancery (post, pp. 585, 590-591, 595).

Joyce v. *Director of Public Prosecutions** [1946] A.C. 347; 62 T.L.R. 208; [1946] 1 All E.R. 186, H.L.(E.) applied.

Per Lord Denning M.R. and Pearson L.J. Where an infant ordinarily resident in this country has been taken out of the country in circumstances where some element of force, deception or secrecy is involved, justice, convenience and the trend of authority require that the wronged parent or parents should be able to obtain relief in the English High Court of Justice (post, pp. 585, 588-589).

Per Lord Denning M.R. An infant of tender years is ordinarily resident where he has his home, and that ordinary residence cannot be changed by kidnapping him or by one parent taking him from that home without the consent or acquiescence of the other (post, p. 586).

(3) That although the court had established jurisdiction over the infant, the question whether that jurisdiction should as a matter of discretion be exercised to make the child a ward of court must be determined in other proceedings, when all the circumstances were before the court, and in the light of what was now best for the infant (post, pp. 586-587, 591, 595). **[571]**

Decision of Plowman J.* [1964] Ch. 575; [1964] 3 W.L.R. 191; [1964] 2 All E.R. 482 reversed.

APPEAL from Plowman J.[1]*

The following statement of the facts is taken from the judgment of Plowman J. supplemented by evidence considered by the Court of Appeal as relevant to the

[1] [1964] Ch. 575; [1964] 3 W.L.R. 191; [1964] 2 All E.R. 482.

issue for its decision and set out in the judgments of the court.

The father of the infant was born in 1915 in Jerusalem, which was then part of the Ottoman Empire. His father was a White Russian and his mother stateless. At birth the father acquired Turkish nationality but he lost that in early infancy when his parents moved to Egypt. The father lived in Egypt as a stateless person till 1957. From 1926 until he left the country he was registered as a White Russian. He married the mother of the infant in Egypt in 1954. She had been born in Egypt in 1927, her father being Egyptian. Both father and mother were Jewish and were married in accordance with Rabbinic law. The infant, a boy, was born in Egypt on February 15, 1956, and was now eight years old.

In February, 1957, as a result of the Suez crisis, the father and mother left Egypt with the infant and came to England, where the mother's own mother and brothers were living. In order to obtain an exit visa the mother gave up her Egyptian nationality and became stateless.

For a few years the father, mother and infant shared accommodation with the mother's relatives, and then, in January, 1962, they bought and moved into a house at Brighton.

In April, 1962, each signed an application under the British Nationality Act, 1948, for a certificate of naturalisation, stating that, if the application was granted, his, and her, intention was to live in the United Kingdom. Those applications were not proceeded with, and neither became a British subject.

In August or September, 1962, as a result of quarrels, the mother left the matrimonial home, leaving the infant there with the father. Subsequently, arrangements were made whereby the infant spent part of the week, when the father was working, with the mother at her mother's flat and the week-ends with the father. On Friday, November 9, 1962, the father collected the infant for the week-end in the usual way. On the following day, November 10, he flew with the infant to Israel; and on November 11, when the mother was expecting the son's return, she **[572]** received a cable from the father informing her that they were both in Jerusalem. They had remained there ever since. The father later sent letters giving their address in Jerusalem, saying that the boy was attending school there, and asking the mother to join them.

The evidence before the court and considered by the Court of Appeal was that when the father took the son to Israel he, having no British passport, had been furnished with a travel document for himself and his son of the kind issued by the Home Office to stateless persons, pursuant to the Convention relating to the Status of Stateless Persons, 1954 (Cmd. 9509, Article 28), which, unless the contrary were stated, gave the holder an absolute right of re-entry to the United Kingdom within not less than three months, though the travel document stated expressly that it did not entitle the holder to any diplomatic or consular protection while abroad. There was no suggestion in the evidence that the right of re-entry had been denied to the holder of the travel document in this case; and so far as the Israeli Republic was concerned, he and his son had at the relevant time only a three months' tourist visa.

The father's evidence on affidavit was that he went to Israel with the intention of making it his permanent home. He was now working in that country as a government official and about three months before the hearing of this summons he and the infant obtained Israeli nationality.

On January 4, 1963, the mother issued an originating summons asking for relief under the Law Reform (Miscellaneous Provisions) Act, 1949, and the Guardianship of Infants Acts, 1886 and 1925. The infant was not, at the time of the hearing, a ward of court, by virtue of section 9 of the Act of 1949, since an appointment for the hearing of the originating summons was not obtained within 21 days after its issue in accordance with R.S.C., Ord. 54P, r. 3. On February 13, 1963, the mother obtained leave to serve the father out of the jurisdiction. He was served in Israel and entered appearance under protest.

On October 2, 1963, the father issued the present summons asking for an order that the mother's originating summons should be set aside for lack of jurisdiction; and, alternatively, that the service on him of notice of the mother's summons should be set aside and the order authorising that service discharged on the grounds that it was not authorised by R.S.C., Ord. 11.

Plowman J., giving judgment on May 7, 1964,[2]* said that he **[573]** was prepared, for the purpose of determining the question of jurisdiction, to assume, without deciding, that when the originating summons was issued by the mother on January 4, 1963, the infant was either domiciled or ordinarily resident in this country; but he went on to hold that the Court of Chancery had no jurisdiction to order that an infant should become or remain a ward of the court unless either the infant was a British subject or was physically present within the jurisdiction of the court at the time when the proceedings were commenced; that it was not enough, in the case of a foreign child, that he should have been within the jurisdiction of the court at some earlier date; and that therefore the mother's summons should be set aside for lack of jurisdiction. The judge added that if he had reached the contrary conclusion, he would have been disposed to the view that in the circumstances of the case the disputes as to the domicile of the infant before November, 1962, and since, and as to the date when there was a change of domicile, if change there were, were matters which could only properly be decided at the hearing of the mother's originating summons.

The judge granted leave to the mother to appeal on the issue of jurisdiction, the grounds of appeal being as follows: (1) That the judge should have held that the court had jurisdiction to grant all or some of the relief claimed in the originating summons (*a*) because the infant was domiciled or ordinarily resident in England on January 4, 1963, when the summons was issued; or alternatively (*b*) because the infant was domiciled or ordinarily resident in England on or about November 10, 1962, when the father wrongfully against the wish of the mother took the infant out of England; or alternatively (*c*) because the infant on and since January 4, 1963, although not physically present in England, owed allegiance to and was under the protection of the Crown. (2) That the judge should have held that the court had jurisdiction in respect of all or some of the relief claimed in the originating summons because the father was domiciled or ordinarily resident in England on January 4, 1963, or alternatively on November 10, 1962, or alternatively because on January 4, 1963, and since that date he, though not physically present in England, owed allegiance to and was under the protection of the Crown. (3) That the judge was wrong in holding that the jurisdiction of the Court of Chancery in relation to the infant was dependent on the infant being in England at the time when the originating summons was issued. **[574]**

R. S. Lazarus Q.C. and *A. A. Baden Fuller* for the mother. The question on the appeal is the extent of the court's jurisdiction to make an infant a ward of court, or to make a custody order under the Guardianship of Infants Acts, where the infant is neither a citizen of the United Kingdom and Colonies under the British Nationality Act, 1948 (or a "British subject" under the pre-1948 description), nor physically present within the realm of England.

There is undoubted authority that if the child is a "British subject," it is subject to the special jurisdiction of the Crown as parens patriae, wherever the infant may be, the basis of the jurisdiction being the need to provide protection: see *Hope* v. *Hope*[3]; *In re Willoughby, per* Cotton and Lindley L.JJ.[4]; and *In re Liddell's Settlement Trusts.*[5] There is also ample authority that the court has jurisdiction over alien infants physically present within the jurisdiction of the English Court of Chancery: *Johnstone* v. *Beattie*[6]; *Brown* v. *Collins*[7]; *In re D. (An Infant).*[8]

It is also undoubted that in matrimonial proceedings the court has jurisdiction to deal with the custody of an infant, whether or not it is physically present in the jurisdiction, if the mother, being ordinarily resident here, has brought

[2] [1964] Ch. 575; [1964] 3 W.L.R. 191; [1964] 2 All E.R. 482.
[3] (1854) 4 De G.M. & G. 328, 344-346.
[4] (1885) 30 Ch.D. 324, 332, 335.
[5] [1936] Ch. 365; 52 T.L.R. 308; [1936] 1 All E.R. 239, C.A.
[6] (1843) 10 Cl. & Fin. 42, H.L.
[7] (1883) 25 Ch.D. 56.
[8] [1943] Ch. 305; 59 T.L.R. 354; [1943] 2 All E.R. 411.

divorce proceedings: see section 18 of the Matrimonial Causes Act, 1950; Dicey on Conflict of Laws, 7th ed., (1958) p. 392; and *Harben* v. *Harben*,[9] a case of a kidnapping where Sachs J. said that it would be wrong if the mother had to follow the kidnapping father to another part of the globe. It is anomalous that if the mother in this case went through the procedure of divorce, the Divorce Division would have jurisdiction, and yet she cannot go straight to the Court of Chancery. [Cheshire on Private International Law, 6th ed. (1961), p. 447 et seq., was also referred to.] This court is invited to remove such anomalies.

It is submitted that the Court of Chancery, representing the Crown as parens patriae, also had jurisdiction over this infant either because it was domiciled or because it was ordinarily resident in England on January 4, 1963, when the mother's originating summons was issued, or on November 10, 1962, when the father, against the will of the mother, took the child out of England. **[575]**

On domicile as the test of jurisdiction, a person by living here places himself under the law of this country, and cannot divest himself of liability under that law immediately he goes outside the territory. A fortiori an infant domiciled here cannot be removed from the jurisdiction by the very act of kidnapping which raises the need for protection. Although at common law the father was the lawful guardian of the child, what he has done in this case is a moral, if not a legal wrong, which the law should be able to rectify.

[RUSSELL L.J. If domicile is suggested as a possible test of jurisdiction, it is relevant that a father has power to alter the domicile of his child, but the mother has no such power.]

The courts of Scotland have accepted domicile as the test. [*Stuart* v. *Bute* (*Marquis of*)[10]; *Ponder* v. *Ponder*[11]; *Kitson* v. *Kitson*[12] and *M'Lean* v. *M'Lean*[13] were referred to.] Where a conflict of jurisdiction has arisen or may arise, the English courts have made it clear that they will give weight to the order of the foreign court but will not treat it as conclusive. [*Stuart* v. *Bute* (*Marquis of*)[14]; *Nugent* v. *Vetzera*[15]; *Mark T. McKee* v. *Evelyn McKee*[16]; *In re R.* (*An Infant*)[17] and *Babington* v. *Babington*[18] were referred to.] The Scots rule has always been that the court of the domicile has paramount but not exclusive jurisdiction; and the Canadian rule appears to be similar: see *In re McGibbon*.[19]

[RUSSELL L.J. This question of jurisdiction as between provinces or states within the general jurisdiction of the Crown is really a sort of internal family arrangement, because in all of them the Crown's jurisdiction as parens patriae is undoubted.]

It has yet to be decided whether under the British Nationality Act, 1948, the old term "British subject" will have to be interpreted in the light of being a citizen of some particular part of the Commonwealth; but nothing in that Act takes away the Crown's jurisdiction as parens patriae over "British subjects." Throughout the civilised world domicile confers jurisdiction in matrimonial matters; and the old ecclesiastical law took domicile as its basis. It is conceded that if jurisdiction is extended to protect infants domiciled or ordinarily resident in England but **[576]** not physically present at the relevant date, the range of possible conflict is extended; but justice demands that that risk be taken in particular cases: see the Report of the Committee on Conflicts of Jurisdiction Affecting Children (Cmnd. No. 842 of 1959). Where in these days infants are snatched across national boundaries, conflicts are bound to arise and must be resolved in a sensible and reasonable manner. Whatever test is adopted, conflicts cannot be wholly avoided. Some assistance may be derived from divorce cases

[9] [1957] 1 W.L.R. 261, 266; [1957] 1 All E.R. 379.
[10] (1861) 9 H.L.Cas. 440, H.L. (Sc.)
[11] 1932 S.C. 233, 238.
[12] 1945 S.C. 434, 439.
[13] 1947 S.C. 79.
[14] 9 H.L.Cas. 440, H.L.
[15] (1866) L.R. 2 Eq. 704.
[16] [1951] A.C. 352; [1951] 1 T.L.R. 755; [1951] 1 All E.R. 942, P.C.
[17] [1962] 1 W.L.R. 1147; [1962] 3 All E.R. 238, C.A.
[18] 1955 S.C. 115.
[19] (1918) 39 D.L.R. 177 (Alberta C.A.).

in the United States: *Daugherty* v. *Nelson*[20]; *Dawson* v. *Dawson*[21] and *Descollonges* v. *Descollonges.*[22] In the last-named case the jurisdiction taken was based on the *residence* of the father, though not of the child

The major defect of the doctrine of domicile is that it depends on the intention of a person to establish a permanent home. Domicile cases have been much criticised because of their artificial results, though the latest editor of Dicey (at p. 390) seems to prefer domicile as the test.

An alternative submission is that the court has jurisdiction to make this child a ward of court on the ground that it was at the date of the issue of the summons ordinarily resident here, and therefore owed allegiance to, and had a corresponding right to protection by, the Crown. That is based on the observations of the House of Lords in *Joyce* v. *Director of Public Prosecutions.*[23]* For this submission, which was not made to Plowman J., reliance is placed on the fact that this father, being a stateless person, was travelling on a travel document issued by Her Majesty's Government; and so long as it remained valid his allegiance remained owing to the Crown. In *Joyce's* case[23] the argument that Joyce's local allegiance, based on his holding a British passport, ended when he left the territory, was rejected; and it was also pointed out that allegiance continues if the person himself goes out of the country but leaves his family and effects here. This child, being either domiciled or ordinarily resident in England, left not only his effects but also his mother and his home here, so that he continued to owe allegiance and had a right to protection at least until January 4, 1963. Though it may appear artificial to speak of infants of tender years owing allegiance to the Sovereign, that is the way in which judges have **[577]** approached the subject throughout the history of wardship jurisdiction, so that the submission that a person ordinarily resident here continues to owe some form of allegiance, even during periods when he is not physically present, has the merit of going back to the roots of the Crown's jurisdiction as parens patriae. If there is a finding that the child was ordinarily resident when the proceedings were begun, that is a finding that the child owes allegiance and is entitled to protection. In this case there was more than a theoretical assumption of ordinary residence, for the father had only a three-month tourist visa for Israel so that he could not by the relevant date have formed any intention to make a permanent change.

Finally, the court has jurisdiction to deal with the custody of this child, although it is outside the jurisdiction, under the Guardianship of Infants Acts, 1886 and 1925, as interpreted in the cases: see *Harris* v. *Harris*[24]; *Rex* v. *Sandbach Justices, Ex parte Smith, per* Lord Goddard C.J.[25]; *In re Dulles' Settlement, Dulles* v. *Vidler*[26] and *In re Dulles' Settlement* (*No.* 2), *Dulles* v. *Vidler.*[27] The extent of the jurisdiction under the Acts appears to be limited to proceedings properly constituted. No words in the Act show what is required for the proceedings to be properly constituted, but it is submitted that a mother ordinarily resident here could apply to the English court, even if the father were not here. Though the jurisdiction is to be used sparingly, the Acts are for the protection of infants, and, in the circumstances of this case, they give jurisdiction to make this infant a ward of court.

Gerald Godfrey for the father. On the assumption that at the dates of the kidnapping and of the originating summons both father and child were ordinarily resident or domiciled in this country, the first question is: Is there any authority which supports the submission that the English courts have parental jurisdiction over the infant until some point of time not yet defined, but at any rate some time after ordinary residence has been determined? The answer is that there

20 (1950) 234 S.W. 2d 353 (Kansas City C.A.).
21 (1951) 241 S.W. 2d 725.
22 (1959) 183 N.Y.S. 2d 943; 190 N.Y.S. 314 (C.A.).
23 [1946] A.C. 347, 366-367, 368; 62 T.L.R. 208; [1946] 1 All E.R. 186, H.L.(E.).
24 (1949) 65 T.L.R. 519; [1949] 2 All E.R. 318, 322.
25 [1951] 1 K.B. 62, 67-68; 66 T.L.R. (Pt. 2) 1028; [1950] 2 All E.R. 781, D.C.
26 [1951] Ch. 265; [1951] 2 T.L.R. 1028; [1951] 2 All E.R. 1013, C.A.
27 [1951] Ch. 842; [1951] 2 T.L.R. 145; [1951] 2 All E.R. 69, C.A.

is no such authority. The court's jurisdiction over infants derives from the doctrine that the Crown is the father of its people, and all the cases show that the only circumstances in which the Crown assumes that parental duty and obligation are (1) when the child is in this country and **[578]** (2) where the child is a "British subject." The only support for any extension of those circumstances is derived from two lines of cases: (a) those where it is said that there is a duty of allegiance through some connection with the country; and (b) those containing dicta by judges of the Queen's Bench or the Divorce Division indicating that there may be jurisdiction to make awards of custody in respect of children who are not within the jurisdiction. Neither (a) nor (b) are in pari materia with the concept of the Crown as parens patraie. Even if it were good sense to make ordinary residence the test for founding jurisdiction it is not open to this court to introduce such an extension.

[LORD DENNING M.R. But if the parents of a child have their home here and the father kidnaps the child, do you say that these courts can do nothing?]

The courts of equity can act in personam, and if the father were here it might be possible to exercise the jurisdiction. If the protection of the Crown as parens patriae is to be extended to those who have at some time been ordinarily resident or who at the relevant date may be described as ordinarily resident though not physically within the sovereign territory, it would be necessary to decide the limit in time of that ordinary residence. It is conceded that if the court is satisfied that when the summons was issued on January 4, 1963, the father of this child still owed allegiance to the British Crown, then, on the basis of the decision in *Joyce* v. *Director of Public Prosecutions*,[28]* that would deter mine the point of law on jurisdiction, were it not for the difficulty of reconciling questions of allegiance derived from the law of treason with questions of the custody of infants by the Crown, for they are so far apart. There is no ground in authority for importing into English law the concept of "ordinary residence" as a test of *this* particular jurisdiction.

On the suggested test of domicile, that has been accepted in Scots law, but Scots law treats the custody of infants as a matter of status; domicile is not an English test and in any event it is so artificial that academic lawyers prefer the test of nationality. Though "ordinary residence" has been introduced into matrimonial and taxation law by Parliament, no such concept has been introduced in relation to infants under the parental jurisdiction of the Crown. If the court applies that test, it will have to define carefully what "ordinary residence" means and when it begins and ends.

[RUSSELL L.J. If it is admitted that on the authority of **[579]** *Joyce's* case[28]* the appeal succeeds on the point of law, why should the court be concerned with what in any particular case is properly to be described as "ordinarily resident"?]

This is a summons asking that the mother's summons be set aside for lack of jurisdiction. There are two ways of succeeding: (1) to show that ordinary residence is not a test at all; and (2) to show that, if it is a test, it does not apply in this case. The second issue should not be left outstanding until the trial of the mother's originating summons, and the court is therefore asked to decide it on the available evidence.

It is conceded that "ordinary residence" is not destroyed by simple physical absence, and that before it is determined there must be something more. The question is what that something is. Where an adult, being capable of a conscious act of will, leaves this country to commit an act of treason, leaving behind him his furniture, effects, or family, or holding a British passport entitling him to protection, ordinary residence cannot be said to have been determined and allegiance continues. That follows from the resolution of the judges of January 12, 1707, as stated in Foster's Crown Cases[29] and *Joyce's* case.[30] But in the case of a child too young to be capable of an act of will who is taken out of the jurisdiction by an alien parent, what happens to his ordinary residence? Does it change after three months, or after three years? The test of ordinary residence

[28] [1946] A.C. 347.
[29] (1792) (3rd ed.) 185.
[30] [1946] A.C. 347.

is too vague to be invoked as a ground for founding the parental jurisdiction of the Crown.

[PEARSON L.J. It would not be difficult in this case to find that this child has his ordinary residence where he had his settled home with his mother at Hendon.]

The question where an infant is ordinarily resident is a simple question of fact at any particular moment of time, and the court should not import into it the lawyer's notion of "settled home." Prima facie where a child has not been made a ward of court it is the father who decides where the child should reside, and he may withdraw an infant ordinarily resident here from the protection of the Crown if he chooses to do so.

On the available evidence, the court is asked to infer that when this father took this infant to Israel in November, 1962, he intended to settle permanently in Israel, and though that was dependent on his obtaining employment in Israel, the fact that he had not obtained such employment by January 4, 1963, is not **[580]** sufficient to require the court to find that the infant was still ordinarily resident in England on that date.

[LORD DENNING M.R. Why not? The child still had his permanent home and his mother in England.]

The fact that a child has a permanent home in one place has nothing to do with where he is ordinarily resident at a particular moment of time. If "ordinarily resident" is given a natural and not an artificial meaning, the father is entitled to succeed on the facts.

Lazarus Q.C. in reply. All that is sought in these proceedings is a general definition of the jurisdiction in wardship. The test of "ordinarily resident" is to be preferred to that of domicile because it is factual and does not depend on intention. All that is necessary is to look at the external circumstances of the person concerned; and his state of mind is only relevant if it is necessary to consider whether he has abandoned his ordinary residence. It is better not to lay down any general rule as to the period at which abandonment may be inferred, but to decide each case on its own facts.

On the question of fact which the court has been asked to decide, the father's two statements in evidence are inadequate to displace the presumption of continued ordinary residence in England. The form of travel document issued to stateless persons gives the holder a right to re-enter the United Kingdom within three months, so that prima facie this father's right to come back may be assumed to have lasted at least until February, 1963. That factor is relevant on the question whether he and the infant owed allegiance to the Crown as persons maintaining their right to live in England on the relevant date in January, 1963. The travel document establishes sufficient reliance on the Crown's protection to put the father in a state of allegiance at that date; and his son must have been in the same state of allegiance, with a corresponding right to protection. [*De Manneville* v. *De Manneville*[31] was also referred to.]

Cur. adv. vult.

November 9, 1964. The following judgments were read:

LORD DENNING M.R. The father and mother in this case are both Jewish people. They were married at the Synagogue at Alexandria on December 5, 1954. A son was born to them on **[581]** February 15, 1956. After the Suez affair they had no wish to stay in Egypt. In February, 1957, when the boy was one year old, they came to England where the mother had relatives. They were stateless persons and we received them and gave them shelter here. In April, 1962, having been here the necessary five years, they applied for naturalisation. They said they intended to stay here and make England their home. Before the papers went through, however, the marriage broke up. In August, 1962, the mother left their home at Brighton and went to her mother at Hendon. They made arrangements about the son, who was then aged six. The mother had

[31] Unreported, 1952, May 10.

him with her at Hendon and he went to school there. But at week-ends the father had him at Brighton. He used to take him down to Brighton on the Friday and return him on the Sunday.

On Friday, November 9, 1962, the father had the child out, as usual, for the week-end. He was to bring him back on the Sunday in time to go to a party. But this time he did not return him to the mother. Without a word to the mother, on Saturday November 10, 1962, the father took the son by aircraft to Israel. On Sunday, November 11, 1962, the father cabled to the mother from Jerusalem telling her they were there. Within two months, namely, on January 4, 1963, the mother took out a summons in the Chancery Division of the High Court here in England asking that the son be made a ward of court and for custody of him. The father entered a conditional appearance and applied to dismiss the summons on the ground that the courts here in England have no jurisdiction over the son. Plowman J. has held that the court has no jurisdiction. The mother appeals to this court.

I say nothing about the merits of the case—nothing as to whether it is best for the son to be with his father in Jerusalem or to be brought back to his mother here. We are concerned only with the question whether the court here has jurisdiction to hear the mother's case. And this is a matter which must be determined as at the time when the mother issued her summons on January 4, 1963. The father has recently issued a summons in the courts of Israel. Those courts would, I should think, clearly have jurisdiction as the boy is there. But the question is whether the courts here also have jurisdiction over the custody of the child.

Let me say at once that if the mother had instituted proceedings here for divorce, the Divorce Court would clearly have jurisdiction over the child. If the mother had any ground for saying that the father had committed a matrimonial offence, she **[582]** could bring a petition for divorce, and the Divorce Court here would have jurisdiction over the marriage. If the father retained his English domicile, she could rely on the English domicile as a ground of jurisdiction in the English court; or, if the father had taken up his domicile in Israel, she could rely on the ground that she was herself resident here and had been "ordinarily resident" here for three years before the proceedings: see section 18 (1) (*b*) of the Matrimonial Causes Act, 1950. Once the divorce proceedings were properly brought here, the Divorce Court would have jurisdiction to make provision for the custody, maintenance and education of the child, even though the child was far away in Israel: see section 26 (1) of the Act of 1950 and *Harben* v. *Harben*.[32]

No divorce proceedings have, however, been taken. The mother has simply applied to the Chancery Division to make the child a ward of court under section 9 of the Law Reform (Miscellaneous Provisions) Act, 1949, and for custody under the Guardianship of Infants Acts, 1886 and 1925. And the question is whether the Court of Chancery has jurisdiction. Those Acts give no guidance as to the geographical jurisdiction of the court; and we have to determine it on principle by reference to the inherent jurisdiction.

It is quite plain that if the child had been a *British subject*, the Court of Chancery would have had jurisdiction to make an order as to its custody, maintenance or education, even though the child itself was out of the country and in a foreign land. The court here always retains a jurisdiction over a British subject wherever he may be, though it will only exercise it abroad where the circumstances clearly warrant it: see *Hope* v. *Hope*[33]; *In re Willoughby*[34]; *Rex* v. *Sandbach Justices, Ex p. Smith*.[35] So also if the child was *physically present* here, the Court of Chancery would have jurisdiction over it (just as the Queen's Bench would on habeas corpus), even though the child was not living here and only passing through on a journey. That happened recently when a child in transit was stopped in England from being taken to Russia and was sent back

[32] [1957] 1 W.L.R. 261; [1957] 1 All E.R. 379.
[33] (1854) 4 De G.M. & G. 328.
[34] (1885) 30 Ch.D. 324; 1 T.L.R. 652, C.A.
[35] [1951] 1 K.B. 62; 66 T.L.R. (Pt. 2) 1028; [1950] 2 All E.R. 781, D.C.

to America. See such cases as *Johnstone* v. *Beattie*[36] and *In re D. (An Infant)*.[37]

Mr. Godfrey submitted to us that the jurisdiction of the **[583]** court was limited to those two cases—a child who is a British subject and a child who is physically present here—and could not be extended further. No case could be found, he said, to warrant any extension. That is the sort of argument we have heard many times, and as often as not we have rejected it. When we come upon a situation which has not arisen before, we must say what we believe the law to be upon the matter. We are not to be deterred by the absence of authority in the books. Our forefathers always held that the law was locked in the breasts of the judges, ready to be unlocked whenever the need arose.

Mr. Lazarus invited us to hold that the Court of Chancery has jurisdiction over any child who is *domiciled* here. He asked us to follow the Scottish law, supported by the latest edition of Dicey's Conflict of Laws (7th ed., (1958), p. 390). It appears that the Scottish courts hold that they have jurisdiction over any child under 16 who is *domiciled* in Scotland even though the child is not resident in Scotland nor physically present there. The custody of a child, say the Scotsmen, is a matter of status, and is governed by the law of the *domicile*. An order for custody, made by the court of the *domicile*, is, they say, a judgment in rem and should be recognised everywhere. Inasmuch as the child takes the *domicile* of its father, this means that, in Scottish eyes, the pre-eminent jurisdiction rests in the courts of the domicile of the father of the child: see *Ponder* v. *Ponder*.[38]

I do not think that we should follow the Scottish courts in this matter. The tests of *domicile* are far too unsatisfactory. In order to find out a person's domicile, you have to apply a lot of archaic rules. They ought to have been done away with long ago. But they still survive. Particularly the rule that a wife takes the domicile of her husband. And the rule that a child takes the domicile of its father. If you were to ask what was the domicile of the child in this case, you would have a pretty problem. The child would take the domicile of the father. But what was the father's domicile? His domicile of origin was Palestine. His domicile of choice was England. But in November, 1962, he left England for Israel, taking the child with him. What was the father's domicile then? It all depends on his intention. Goodness knows how you are to find that out. His intention may at first have been to go to Israel for a short time. Later, when he found work there, he may have intended to make his home there permanently. When did his domicile change? Are you to take **[584]** his word for it? If so, he could always defeat the jurisdiction of the court by saying that, from the very outset, he intended never to return to England, and abandoned his English domicile.

As an alternative to *domicile*, Mr. Lazarus invited us to apply the test of *ordinary residence*, and supported it by references to some cases where the word "residence" was used and also to a case in the State of New York: *Descollonges* v. *Descollonges*.[39] I think this is the right test. The fount of the jurisdiction of the Court of Chancery is the Crown which, as parens patriae, takes under its protection every infant child who is ordinarily resident within the realm, whether he is a British subject or an alien. As Lord Campbell said in *Johnstone* v. *Beattie*,[40] "I do not doubt the jurisdiction of the Court of Chancery on this subject, whether the infant be domiciled in England or not. The Lord Chancellor, representing the Crown as parens patriae, has a clear right to interpose the authority of the court for the protection of the person and property of *all infants resident* in England."

The Crown protects every child who has his home here and will protect him in respect of his home. It will not permit anyone to kidnap the child and spirit it out of the realm. Not even its father or mother can be allowed to do so without the consent of the other. The kidnapper cannot escape the jurisdiction of

[36] (1843) 10 Cl. & Fin. 42, H.L.
[37] [1943] Ch. 305; 59 T.L.R. 354; [1943] 2 All E.R. 411.
[38] 1932 S.C. 233.
[39] (1959) 183 N.Y.S. 2d 943; 190 N.Y.S. 314.
[40] 10 Cl. & Fin. 42, 119-120.

the court by such a stratagem. If, as in this case, it is the father who flies away with the child, the mother is not bound to follow him to a foreign clime. She can bring her proceedings against him in England. I know that it will be difficult for her to enforce any order the court may make. But it is not impossible. The father may have assets here. Or he may return here for a visit. And if she has eventually to apply to the courts of the foreign country, they will surely respect an order made by the courts of the ordinary residence—just as we should—for the simple reason that it is his home and, as such, is entitled to special consideration.

There is some support for the test of *ordinary residence*. It comes from a strange quarter—from the law of treason. An alien who comes here, whether adult or babe in arms, owes *allegiance* to the Crown from the moment that he comes within the realm. So long as he is here, or is *ordinarily resident* here, he owes allegiance to the Crown and correspondingly comes under its protection. He cannot throw off his allegiance simply by departing from the country. Suppose he departs, leaving his family **[585]** and effects here, and then adheres to the enemy. He is guilty of treason. That was laid down in 1707 by all the judges: see Foster's Crown Cases.[41] Suppose he departs and holds a British passport, and then broadcasts on behalf of the enemy, as Joyce did. He is guilty of treason: see *Joyce* v. *Director of Public Prosecutions.*[42]* The reason in either case is that he has still a call on the protection of the Crown—in the one case for his family and effects—in the other case by the passport. And as he has a call on the protection of the Crown, he is held to owe allegiance to it. I think this principle applies equally to the father in this case. For one thing he left his wife here. For another, although he did not hold a British passport, he held a travel document for himself and his son of the kind issued by this country to stateless persons. These travel documents are issued pursuant to the Final Act and Convention relating to the Status of Statelesss Persons, 1954 (Cmd. No. 9509 of 1954, Art. 28). They serve a stateless person in lieu of a passport and entitle the holder to return within three months or more: see the schedule, paragraph 13. In these circumstances I think the father still owed allegiance within those three months at least; and if we were at war and, while still holding this document, he adhered to the Queen's enemies, he would be guilty of treason. As for the child, he clearly had a call on the protection of the Crown, because he was too young to protect himself. He had a right to the protection of the Crown by reason of having his mother here and his home here. And he, too, had a travel document entitling him to return within three months. It would be a strange thing if he could be deprived of the protection of the Crown by being kidnapped and taken out of the realm, without being able to say "aye" or "nay" to it.

I hold therefore that the Court of Chancery has jurisdiction to make an order for the custody, education and maintenance of an alien child who is ordinarily resident in this country, even though the child is for the time being absent from this country or taken out of it. But then we are faced with the question, what is the ordinary residence of a child of tender years who cannot decide for himself where to live, let us say under the age of 16? So long as the father and mother are *living together in the matrimonial home*, the child's ordinary residence is the home—and it is still his ordinary residence, even while he is away at boarding school. It is his base, from whence he goes out and to which he returns. When father and mother are at variance and living **[586]** *separate and apart* and by arrangement the child resides *in the house of one of them*—then that home is his ordinary residence, even though the other parent has access and the child goes to see him from time to time. I do not see that a child's ordinary residence, so found, can be changed by kidnapping him and taking him from his home, even if one of his parents is the kidnapper. Quite generally, I do not think a child's ordinary residence can be changed by one parent without the consent of the other. It will not be changed until the parent who is left at home, childless, acquiesces in the change, or delays so long in bringing proceedings that he or

[41] (1792) (3rd ed) 185.
[42] [1946] A.C. 347; 62 T.L.R. 208; [1946] 1 All E.R. 186, H.L.(E.).

she must be taken to acquiesce. Six months' delay would, I should have thought, go far to show acquiescence. Even three months might in some circumstances. But not less.

I would say a word about *Babington* v. *Babington*,[43] which was mentioned to us. I should have thought that the girl (aged 11) had her ordinary residence in the matrimonial home in Scotland: and this could not be changed by the unilateral act of the wife in leaving the father and having the child in London. The father in no way acquiesced, and brought his proceedings in good time. The pre-eminent jurisdiction rested with the Scottish courts, and the courts of England should have recognised this. I would myself support the view stated by Lord Hodson and the majority of his committee in 1959 [Report of the Committee on Conflicts of Jurisdiction Affecting Children, Cmnd. No. 842 of 1959] that "there should be a pre-eminent jurisdiction which should be the ordinary residence of the child at the time of the application." It is not an exclusive jurisdiction. Other courts may have jurisdiction too. But, in case of conflict, much respect should be paid to the decision of the courts of the country where the child is ordinarily resident.

Applied to this case, it is plain that the child's ordinary residence was at Hendon. That was his home, so arranged by both mother and father. The father broke the arrangement and took him off to Israel. That did not mean that his ordinary residence ceased to be in England. The father could not change his home without the mother's consent. His ordinary residence was still in England when the mother took out the summons two months later. That means that the English court has jurisdiction over him. I do not say that the court would exercise that jurisdiction in the special circumstances of the case. I do not suggest that it would order the child to be brought back to England. The father says that in these two years he has settled down well in **[587]** Jerusalem. The court will consider what is best for the child. Suffice it for us to hold that the court has jurisdiction. I would allow the appeal accordingly.

PEARSON L.J. The main question in this appeal is whether it was rightly decided by the judge that he had no jurisdiction to make a wardship order in respect of an infant who was not physically present in this country at the date when the relevant proceedings were instituted, although the judge assumed, without deciding, that the infant was at that date domiciled or ordinarily resident in this country.

To avoid the confusion that might arise from using the same word "jurisdiction" in two different senses, I am using that word "jurisdiction" as meaning the court's power to adjudicate and the word "country" as meaning the geographical area in relation to which the power is exercisable. It is not necessary in this case to consider any complication arising (1) from the existence of citizenship of the United Kingdom and Colonies under the British Nationality Act, 1948, or (2) from the existence of different courts having jurisdiction in relation to different parts of the United Kingdom. The father, mother and infant came from Egypt to England in 1957, and the father took the infant from England to Israel in 1962, and no other country is concerned. It is convenient and permissible in this case to use the phrases "British nationality" and "this country" without precise definition. There is no evidence of the infant having any property in this country.

It is clear from the authorities that the English court has, by delegation from the Sovereign, jurisdiction to make a wardship order whenever the Sovereign as parens patriae has a quasi-parental relationship towards the infant. The infant owes a duty of allegiance and has a corresponding right to protection and therefore may be made a ward of court: *Hope* v. *Hope*.[44] Subsequent cases confirm that that is the basis of the jurisdiction.

An infant of British nationality, whether he is in or outside this country, owes a duty of allegiance to the Sovereign and so is entitled to protection, and the English court has jurisdiction to make him a ward of court; *Hope* v. *Hope*[45]; *In*

[43] 1955 S.C. 115.
[44] 4 De G.M. & G. 328, 344-345.
[45] Ibid.

re Willoughby[46] *per* Kay J. and *per* Cotton L.J.; and *Harben* v. *Harben*.[47]

The jurisdiction should be sparingly exercised when the infant is abroad, even if he is of British nationality. The courts of **[588]** different countries are expected to collaborate for the benefit of the infant, but there may be difficulties of enforcement and there is the risk of conflict between an order of the English court and the order of a court of the country in which the infant is present and resident: *Nugent* v. *Vetzera*[48]; *In re Willoughby*,[49] *per* Kay J., *per* Cotton L.J., *per* Lindley L.J.; *In re B's Settlement*[50]; *Harben* v. *Harben*.[51] Compare *Harris* v. *Harris*[52] and *Rex* v. *Sandbach Justices, Ex parte Smith*.[53]

An infant of foreign nationality owes a duty of allegiance to the Sovereign and is entitled to protection and so may be made a ward of court, if he is in some sense in this country. *Hope* v. *Hope*[54]; *Nugent* v. *Vetzera*[55]; *Brown* v. *Collins*[56] and *In re D.* (*An Infant*).[57]

There are two classes of cases to be considered: (*a*) The infant may be only temporarily present in this country. It would be unusual for the English court to exercise wardship jurisdiction in such cases, but there might be some occasion for it, for example, in a case of emergency to prevent some grievous wrong being committed, or in a case where an order of the English court could usefully and in furtherance of justice support or supplement an order of the foreign court having jurisdiction by virtue of the nationality or residence of the infant. However seldom it may be proper to exercise the jurisdiction in such a case, I think there must be jurisdiction by virtue of local allegiance. (*b*) Suppose, however, that the infant is, at the time when the relevant proceedings are instituted, ordinarily resident in this country but temporarily present in some foreign country. He may be there on holiday, or accompanying his father on a business trip, or he may have been "kidnapped" from this country and taken to a foreign country. "Kidnapping" may include any case of a child being taken out of this country by some person against the wishes of the parents, or by one parent against the wishes of the other parent, at any rate where some element of force or deception or secrecy is involved. In my judgment there must be jurisdiction in such cases for several reasons. First, justice and convenience require it. It would be absurd and unjust if the wronged parents or parent were prevented from **[589]** obtaining relief in the English court by the accident of the child being abroad on holiday at a particular date, or by the wrongful act of "kidnapping." Secondly, there is support in the authorities for residence conferring jurisdiction: *Johnstone* v. *Beattie, per* Lord Campbell[58]; *Brown* v. *Collins, per* Kay J.[59]; *In re Bourgoise, per* Cotton L.J.[60]* Thirdly, *Joyce* v. *Director of Public Prosecutions*,[61]* shows that an alien resident in this country does not necessarily free himself from his allegiance by the mere act of departure from this country. He may continue to owe allegiance because he has left his family and property in this country under the protection of the Crown, or because he has applied for and obtained a British passport, or because his "residence" may not cease immediately on his quitting the country.

It has been suggested in argument that the jurisdiction to make a wardship order should depend on the domicile of the infant. That suggestion is supported

46 30 Ch.D. 324, 328, 332.
47 [1957] 1 W.L.R. 261.
48 (1866) L.R. 2 Eq. 704, 713, 714.
49 30 Ch.D. 324, 329, 331-334, 335-336.
50 [1940] Ch. 54; 56 T.L.R. 30.
51 [1957] 1 W.L.R. 261, 265-266.
52 (1949) 65 T.L.R. 519; [1949] 2 All E.R. 318, 322, D.C.
53 [1951] 1 K.B. 62.
54 4 De G.M. & G. 328, 346.
55 L.R. 2 Eq. 704, 714.
56 (1883) 25 Ch.D. 56, 62.
57 [1943] Ch. 305.
58 10 Cl. & Fin. 42, 120.
59 25 Ch.D. 56, 62.
60 (1889) 41 Ch.D. 310, 319.
61 [1946] A.C. 347, 366-369.

by some Scottish authority (*Ponder* v. *Ponder*,[62] *Kitson* v. *Kitson*[63] and *M'Lean* v. *M'Lean*[64]), and by a passage in the current (7th) edition of Dicey on Conflict of Laws at pp. 387-388. In my view this suggestion should not be accepted as part of English law. First, there is no English authority for it. The cases cited in the relevant footnote on page 387 of Dicey seem to me not to support the suggestion. The nearest is the passage in the judgment of Kay J. in *Brown* v. *Collins*,[65] but that passage, on the face of it, requires residence as well as domicile, though I do not think it was intended as a precise formulation. Secondly, the rules for ascertaining domicile are in some respects artificial and unrealistic and would produce strange results if domicile were taken as the basis of jurisdiction to make a wardship order. A child of foreign nationality but English domicile of origin might have lived abroad for many years and have no intention of returning to England, and yet have his English domicile of origin surviving or reviving if he had not acquired or had lost a domicile of choice. The answer made in argument is that the jurisdiction would not be exercised if the infant, though technically domiciled in this country, had ceased to have any real connection with this country. That answer, however, does not wholly remove the objection to a theory which asserts the **[590]** existence of jurisdiction in a case where its existence would be absurd.

In my view residence of an infant in England at the time of the institution of the relevant proceedings does confer on the English court jurisdiction to make a wardship order. I would reverse the decision of the judge on that point.

The judge assumed, without deciding, that the infant was domiciled or ordinarily resident in this country at the date of the institution of the relevant proceedings. If he had taken a different view of the law he would have deferred the decision of the question of fact, as to the actual domicile or ordinary residence, until the hearing of the originating summons. That would have been a reasonable course to take. However, we are now invited by counsel to decide the question of fact on the available evidence, and, as that may help to save costs and the evidence is not manifestly incomplete, I think we should do so.

The date of the instiution of the relevant proceedings was January 4, 1963, more than seven weeks after the father and son had arrived in Israel. On the question whether they had by that date ceased to be ordinarily resident in England there are points on both sides. The son was in the father's charge. The father after the failure of his marriage had no compelling reason to remain in or return to England, and he had gone himself and taken his son to the land of his own birth, the land of their religion, and the land where his family lived. He seems to have sent his son to school as soon as possible. It is not unlikely that the father already by that time wished to settle in Israel if that proved to be possible. On the other hand, he may not have been able to make up his mind firmly by January 4, 1963. He had initially only a tourist visa from the Israeli Government: immigrant status and naturalisation came later. Being a stateless person, he had a travel permit from the British Government. That did not have the effect of a passport, because it stated expressly that it did not entitle the holder to any diplomatic or consular protection. On the other hand, it gave permission to the holder to return to England, and while he still might need to use that permission and had only a tourist visa from the Israeli Government, it is hard to say that he had abandoned his ordinary residence in England or acquired one in Israel. A fortiori, it is hard to say that he had deprived his son of ordinary residence in England. The ordinary residence of the son while in the father's charge would naturally tend to be the same as that of the father, but is not necessarily **[591]** at all times the same. In any case, both the father and the son undoubtedly had a well-established ordinary residence in England before they went to Israel on November 10, 1962, and on balance I think the right inference from the available evidence is that such residence had not been terminated by January 4, 1963.

There will remain for consideration at the hearing of the originating summons the question whether the jurisdiction, held to exist, ought, as a matter of

[62] 1932 S.C. 233.
[63] 1945 S.C. 434.
[64] 1947 S.C. 79.
[65] 25 Ch.D. 56, 62.

discretion, to be exercised in this case. Should this child now, towards the end of the year 1964, be made a ward of the English court? The course of events, not only before but also after January 4, 1963, and the present situation will have to be taken into account. I agree that the appeal should be allowed.

RUSSELL L.J. Plowman J. assumed in favour of the mother—without deciding—that the boy was at the date of the originating summons either domiciled or ordinarily resident in England, but nevertheless held there was no jurisdiction. On a review of authority he concluded that in the case of an alien infant his physical presence within the jurisdiction was necessary to found jurisdiction. From that decision on the law the mother appeals: for her it is argued that either domicile or ordinary residence at the initiation of the proceedings suffices for jurisdiction: an additional argument for jurisdiction was put forward based on the existence of a travel document provided by the English Home Office for the father and the boy as something which involved a degree of continuing allegiance to the Crown with its corollary of a right and duty in the Crown to protect the infant. Should the mother succeed on the point of law either on an assumption of domicile or of ordinary residence or of both, it was contended for her that the father's summons should be adjourned to come on with the originating summons, when all the facts could be investigated—a course which the judge intimated he would have been minded to adopt had he found it necessary to come to a decision on those heads. The father, however, contended that in that event he was entitled to a present conclusion on those matters, since he asserted that the proceedings were in effect a nullity and should at once be struck out if the evidence before the court did not establish facts (whether domicile or ordinary residence) which alone supported the jurisdiction. Moreover, he contended, this court should arrive at the conclusion, and not remit the matter to the judge, since no oral evidence was involved. **[592]** If the stage is reached at which it is necessary to arrive at a conclusion on domicile or ordinary residence I consider that these contentions of the father are correct.

It is clear on authority that wardship jurisdiction exists (a) in the case of any infant, whether alien or not, who at the time of the initiation of the proceedings is within the territorial jurisdiction of the court, and (b) in the case of any infant who is a British subject wherever that infant may be. Under heading (a) I add that I should have thought that presence within the territorial jurisdiction at the time of an order might mend any defect due to absence at the initiation of the proceedings, unless they had already been struck out on the grounds of that defect. Under heading (b) I have used the phrase "British subject" appearing in authority. We now have the conception of citizens of the United Kingdom and Colonies and citizens of other parts of the Commonwealth. I do not propose to examine the jurisdiction of the court in England in relation to infant citizens of the Commonwealth countries or even of the colonies. Nor in connection with the relevance of domicile or ordinary residence to the jurisdiction of the English court over an alien infant do I propose to consider domicile or ordinary residence other than in England and Wales. Nor do I propose to consider the situation should an alien infant be outside the territorial jurisdiction of the English court but within the United Kingdom or a colony or a Commonwealth country.

Here, then, is a stateless alien infant assumed to be domiciled in England at the relevant date but outside the territorial jurisdiction in a foreign state. Does that domicile confer jurisdiction by itself? In my judgment it does not. The scant references to domicile in the cases are wholly insufficient—even as obiter dicta—to support that conclusion. The whole trend of English authority on the parental jurisdiction of the Crown over infants bases the jurisdiction on protection as a corollary of allegiance in some shape or form. Domicile is an artificial conception which may well involve no possible connection with allegiance. I need not condescend to particular illustrations to demonstrate this. It is true that in Scottish decisions there is a strong tendency to attribute this jurisdiction to domicile, though there is something to be said for the view that this approach derives from an attempt to resolve internal conflicts in the United Kingdom. But it would seem that the Scottish view of orders affecting custody, care and control of infants relates such matters to status: and in this I am not prepared to follow it. **[593]** Accordingly, despite those views and those expressed by the editors of Dicey, I am unable to accept the view that English domicile per se will confer the relevant jurisdiction in respect of an alien infant in a foreign land at the relevant time.

What, then, of "ordinary residence"? In relation to alien infants the authorities speak of jurisdiction over such if "residing" within the territorial jurisdiction, or sometimes "being within" it. The judge concluded, quite rightly, that there was nothing in these authorities which could be regarded as deciding that any but actual physical presence produced that degree of allegiance which involves the corollary of entitlement to protection. On the other hand, authority decides nothing to the contrary. It is true to say that there is no ground for asserting a jurisdiction to protect an alien infant merely here in transit once it has left the territorial jurisdiction, although during its brief sojourn it owes a local allegiance, even if the infant be "kidnapped" to a foreign land. There is no ground for asserting any continuance of that local allegiance. But there is ground for considering whether an alien infant who is ordinarily resident in England may not be considered as sometimes remaining within allegiance after leaving the shores of this country, and therefore still within the protection of the Crown. At this stage in the case we must assume that at the relevant time the infant was still ordinarily resident in England. This, so to speak, assumes that his settlement was in England, and that his absence was out of the ordinary run of his life, which was to live with his mother in Hendon, where he was at school. Does such an alien child maintain his local allegiance to the Crown to a degree sufficient to support a right in the Crown (and therefore a jurisdiction in the court) to protect him? I think so. I refer here to the treason case of *Joyce* v. *Director of Public Prosecutions.*[66]* I leave aside the ultimate basis of that decision, which was the retention of the United Kingdom passport. The views of Lord Jowitt L.C.,[67] approved by the majority, make it plain that mere physical absence of an alien from the territorial jurisdiction does not necessarily and inevitably denude an alien, for purposes of treason, of all his allegiance. The example is given of an alien settled here who cannot, by brief visits overseas, divest himself while overseas of allegiance, irrespective of any question of passport: he cannot, it was said, come and go at will, and, while gone for the time being, deny all allegiance to the Crown or duty of fidelity to the Crown. I think it would accord with the views there expressed **[594]** that an alien, settled in the territorial jurisdiction, retains his local allegiance while temporarily outside the jurisdiction. I am conscious that the application of the law of treason is peculiarly susceptible to the temper of the moment. Nevertheless, I cannot but find sympathetic to my mind an approach which is not prepared to accept a theory of allegiance (or loyalty) which depends on a sort of Tom Tiddler's ground concept. In my judgment it is right and just that if it can be said of an alien that at a particular moment of time he is still ordinarily resident in England he continues in his local allegiance to the Crown, though for the moment absent from the territorial jurisdiction of England, and as such he continues (if an infant) in theory entitled to the protection of the Crown, and therefore to the parental jurisdiction of the Crown exercised through the High Court.

I would therefore respectfully differ from the judge's view that, assuming this alien boy was, though at the relevant time actually in Israel, nevertheless ordinarily resident in England, there was no jurisdiction to adjudicate on his control by wardship or otherwise. I remark that the aspects of the problem involving the *Joyce* case[68]* were not presented to the judge.

I turn now to the new point raised for the mother, which in a different way relates to the Joyce case.[68]* Under an international treaty relating to stateless people it was arranged that states in which they were resident should, if they wished to travel, give them a travel document, since they could not have a national passport. The father and the infant had such when they left this

[66] [1946] A.C. 347.
[67] Ibid. 369 et seq.
[68] [1946] A.C. 347.

country. It expressly gave them no advantages or right to protection while abroad. But it did operate as an authenticated identity card, and, unless the contrary were stated, gave an absolute right of re-entry to this country. Under the treaty, such right, if not expressly denied, must give right of re-entry within not less than three months. The evidence does not suggest that the travel document given to the father and the infant denied the right of re-entry, nor that at the date of the originating summons it was not still preserved by the father in case it was needed by them. So far as the Israeli Republic is concerned, they had at the relevant time (so far as the evidence goes) only a three months' tourist visa. We therefore have the situation that father and son, previously settled in England, were in the Israeli Republic on a three months' permit because they had an English Crown document which absolutely entitled them to return to England to live, which had not been destroyed or handed in to an **[595]** English representative as no longer wanted or relevant to their lives or futures. By analogy with the case of a passport in the *Joyce* case, [69]* I for my part do not think that aliens in such a case can be said to have divested themselves of all semblance of allegiance to the Crown. Accordingly in my view the infant at the time retained sufficient allegiance to the Crown to found jurisdiction in the present case.

If this be correct, the father's summons must be dismissed. Whether the jurisdiction should be exercised is a totally different matter. That question is not for us. We are told that both father and son are now accepted as citizens of the Israeli Republic, and that infancy proceedings are now pending there. It would be exceptional for the court here to pronounce on the matter; but this is not for us, and must depend on the ultimate evidence.

It is right that we should decide whether in our view the infant was on the evidence ordinarily resident in England when the originating summons was issued on January 4, 1963. I think that he was. He has a home with his mother in Hendon, where he was at school, and had been settled in England for several years. He had left England with his father on an English travel document which provided for a right of return within three months, and this he still had: his presence in Israel at the time of the summons was still precarious, since he was there only on a tourist visa valid for three months. His actual residence in Israel was in those circumstances still to be regarded as insecure and unsettled, and his ordinary residence remained at the relevant time in England, even if his father had already formed the intention to remain and settle in Israel if he could.

Accordingly, even if my view of the effect of the travel document alone is wrong, jurisdiction existed founded on the fact of ordinary residence—to which fact the travel document was a contribution—and the appeal should be allowed and the father's summons dimissed.

Appeal allowed with costs.
Summons by father dismissed.
Costs to be taxed and paid forthwith.
Leave to appeal refused.

Solicitors: *Hickson & Parish; Birkbeck, Julius, Coburn & Broad.*

[69] [1946] A.C. 347.

4

THE INDIVIDUAL IN INTERNATIONAL LAW

A.

NATIONALITY

1

THE STATUS OF A BRITISH SUBJECT

(A) Acquisition and Effects

vii

Adoption

IN RE A. (AN INFANT)

([1963] 1 W.L.R. 231)

January 16, 17, 21 1963: Chancery Division: Cross J.

Adoption—Discretion of court—Object of naturalising infant—Infant alien aged 20 years—Statutory conditions fulfilled—Order for infant's benefit—Whether discretion should be exercised in infant's favour.

An application was made by a married couple to adopt a French boy who was born on February 8, 1942. The boy's father died soon after his birth and he was adopted by his mother's step-father under French law. He lived with his mother up to 1952. From then onwards he was educated in boarding schools in England, visiting his mother during holidays until she came to live largely in England. Both the boy and his mother had temporary permits to live here. The boy was the second cousin of the male applicant and, at the time of the application, was a trainee in a company of which the male applicant was a director. The evidence showed that he went to live with the applicants and their children in July, 1962, in order to fulfil the conditions prescribed by section 3 (1) of the Adoption Act, 1958, and that the object of adoption was to enable him to acquire British nationality under section 19 (1) of the Act[1] and to receive consequential benefits:—

Held, (1) that where the person to be adopted was 19 or 20 years **[232]** of age, the words "care and possession" in section 3 (1) of the Act of 1958 must bear a somewhat artificial meaning, but they at least required that the applicants with whom the adoptee was living should be really in loco parentis to him, and this was not the position here.

(2) That such an adoption would be open to objection on the grounds of public policy because an alien infant, who wished to live in the United Kingdom for the purpose of carrying on some undesirable activity, might

[1] Adoption Act, 1958, s. 3 (1): "An adoption order shall not be made in respect of any infant unless he has been continuously in the care and possession of the applicant for at least three consecutive months immediately preceding the date of the order . . ."

S. 19 (1): "Where an adoption order is made in respect of an infant who is not a citizen of the United Kingdom and Colonies; then, if the adopter, or in the case of a joint adoption the male adopter, is a citizen of the United Kingdom and Colonies, the infant shall be a citizen of the United Kingdom and Colonies as from the date of the order."

arrange to be adopted by friends in order to secure his position and put forward a plausible case that the order was for his benefit, and as a consequence in an application of that nature the court would be taking on itself functions similar to those of the Home Secretary on an application for naturalisation, and such functions were not within the purview of the Act. Accordingly, in the exercise of the discretion vested in the court the order ought to be refused.

In re D. (*An Infant*) [1959] 1 Q.B. 229; [1959] 2 W.L.R. 26; [1958] 3 All E.R. 716, C.A. distinguished.

In re K., Petitioner, 1949 S.C. 140 and *In re L., Petitioner*, 1951 S.C. 605 considered.

ADJOURNED SUMMONS.

The following statement of facts is taken from the judgment.

The applicants who were a married couple with children of their own were British subjects domiciled and resident here. The infant whom they wished to adopt was a second cousin of the male applicant. He was a French national, born in France of French parents on February 8, 1942, and so was nearly 21 years old. Soon after the infant's birth his father died and for the first 10 years of his life he lived with his mother in France. In 1951 he was adopted under French law by his mother's stepfather. From 1952 onwards he was educated in boarding schools in England. For some years he spent his holidays with his mother in France, but later she herself came to live largely in this country. The permits to reside here, which the mother and the infant had were only temporary permits.

At the time of the application the infant was a trainee with a company of which the male applicant was a director, and he was taking a course at London University. The infant went to live with the applicants and their children in July, 1962, and, apart from a short period during the summer holidays, he had been living with them ever since. The applicants had taken an interest in the infant ever since he began to be educated over here; but the reason why they wished to adopt him and he wished to be adopted by them was not that they should become his parents in the true sense of the word. The object was that the infant should acquire British nationality. That would benefit him in two ways. First, his right to go on living in this country, as he wished to do, would cease to be precarious as it was at present. Secondly, he would be freed from certain difficulties **[233]** which the Exchange Control legislation placed in his way as an alien with regard to his interest under certain English settlements.

Peter Oliver for the appellant.
Bryan Clauson for the Attorney-General.

The following cases, in addition to those referred to in the judgment, were cited in argument: *In re S., Petitioner*[2]; *Skinner* v. *Carter*.[3]

Cur. adv. vult.

January 21. CROSS J. read the following judgment: This application under the Adoption Act, 1958, came before me in chambers at the end of last term. The facts are unusual and seem to me to raise a question of principle with regard to the exercise of the discretion which the Act gives the judge to make or to refuse to make an adoption order. I therefore adjourned the case into court for argument, and directed that notice of it should be given to the Treasury Solicitor so that counsel for the Attorney-General might assist me by saying anything that could properly be said against the propriety of the order sought being made. Mr. Clauson appeared in response to that invitation, and I am grateful to him and also to Mr. Oliver, who appeared for the applicants, for the assistance which they have given me. [His Lordship stated the facts substantially as set out

[2] 1953 S.L.T. 220.
[3] [1948] Ch. 387; [1948] 1 All E.R. 917, C.A.

above and continued:] It is, of course, true if no order is made, this young man will be able in a few weeks' time to apply to the Home Office to be naturalised as a British subject, but it will be in the discretion of the authorities whether or not to accede to the application and, in any case, there may be some question whether or not he will have fulfilled the necessary residence qualification. In those circumstances, I think that it can fairly be said that it will be for his benefit that the order should be made.

Section 1 (1) of the Act of 1958 runs as follows: "Subject to the provisions of this Act, the court may, upon an application made in the prescribed manner by a person domiciled in England or Scotland, make an order (in this Act referred to as an adoption order) authorising the applicant to adopt an infant." "Infant" is defined in section 57 as "a person under twenty-one years of age, but does not include a person who is or has been married." Section 3 (1) reads: "An adoption order shall not be made in respect of any infant unless he has been continuously in the care and possession of the applicant for at least three consecutive months immediately preceding the date of the order, not counting any time before the date which appears to the court to be the date on which the infant attained the age of six weeks." Sections 4 to 6 deal with consents. In **[234]** this case the mother and her step-father both consent to the proposed order. Section 7 (1) prescribes certain matters of which the court must be satisfied before it makes an order. The first by paragraph (a) is that the necessary consents have been given. As I have said, no question arises on that head in this case. The second matter under paragraph (b) is that the order, if made, will be for the welfare of the infant. The word "welfare" might perhaps be thought to point rather to the physical or moral well-being of the infant than to such a benefit as he will secure here if the order is made. But in the light of *In re D. (An Infant)*,[4] to which I shall be referring in a moment, I think that "welfare" means simply "benefit," and, as I have said, I am satisfied that it will be for the benefit of this young man that I should make the order. The third matter under section 7 (1) (c) is that the applicants should not have received or been promised any consideration for the adoption. No question under that head arises in this case.

Section 7 (2) directs the court to pay regard, inter alia, to the wishes of the infant if he is of an age to express any. This young man, of course, wishes the order to be made.

Sections 13 and 19 are headed "Effects of adoption orders." Section 13 provides: "(1) Upon an adoption order being made, all rights, duties, obligations and liabilities of the parents or guardians of the infant in relation to the future custody, maintenance and education of the infant, including all rights to appoint a guardian and (in England) to consent or give notice of dissent to marriage, shall be extinguished, and all such rights, duties, obligations and liabilities shall vest in and be exercisable by and enforceable against the adopter as if the infant were a child born to the adopter in lawful wedlock; and in respect of the matters aforesaid (and, in Scotland, in respect of the liability of a child to maintain his parents) the infant shall stand to the adopter exclusively in the position of a child born to the adopter in lawful wedlock." Section 16 provides: "(1) Where, at any time after the making of an adoption order, the adopter or the adopted person or any other person dies intestate in respect of any real or personal property (other than property subject to an entailed interest under a disposition to which subsection (2) of this section does not apply), that property shall devolve in all respects as if the adopted person were the child of the adopter born in lawful wedlock and were not the child of any other person (2) In any disposition of real or personal property made, whether by instrument inter vivos or by will (including codicil) after the date of an adoption order—(*a*) any reference (whether express or implied) to the child or children of the adopter shall, unless the contrary intention appears, be construed as, or as including, a reference to the adopted person; (*b*) any reference (whether express or implied) to the child or children of the adopted person's natural parents or either of them shall, unless the contrary intention

[4] [1959] 1 Q.B. 229; [1959] 2 W.L.R. 26; [1958] 3 All E.R. 716, C.A.

appears, **[235]** be construed as not being, or as not including, a reference to the adopted person; and (*c*) any reference (whether express or implied) to a person related to the adopted person in any degree shall, unless the contrary intention appears, be construed as a reference to the person who would be related to him in that degree if he were the child of the adopter born in lawful wedlock and were not the child of any other person. . . ." Finally, section 19 (1) provides: "Where an adoption order is made in respect of an infant who is not a citizen of the United Kingdom and Colonies, then, if the adopter, or in the case of a joint adoption the male adopter, is a citizen of the United Kingdom and Colonies, the infant shall be a citizen of the United Kingdom and Colonies as from the date of the order." It is, of course, under that section that benefits will arise to this infant if the order is made. In the great majority of cases the benefit which will accrue to the infant from the making of the order consists in the operation of section 13 (1); that is to say, in the substitution of a statutory parent who will be a real father or mother to the child in place of a natural parent who is unable or unwilling to perform his or her parental duties. But the wording of the Act and the decisions under it show that the benefit to the infant need not necessarily take this form. *In re D.* (*An Infant*),[5] to which I have referred, the mother of an illegitimate child of three applied to the county court for an adoption order. She was looking after her child herself satisfactorily and the life of the infant was not going to be affected in any way by the order. It was not suggested that the substitution under section 13 (1) for the rights and duties which the mother had towards the child at common law as her illegitimate child of such rights and duties as she would have had if the child had been legitimate would make any difference whatever to the infant. The reason for which the Court of Appeal, reversing the decision of the county court judge, made an adoption order was that several sections of the Act indicated that the mother of an illegitimate child could apply to adopt it and that a sufficient benefit to the child to satisfy section 7 (1) (*b*) was to be found in the provisions with regard to wills and intestacies in section 16 (1) and (2) and in the fact that the child's birth would henceforth be registered in the Adopted Children's Register. Of course, as the child was only three, it was necessary for the court in that case to be satisfied that the conditions in which the child was being brought up were satisfactory. But the reasoning of the judges would apply with equal force to an application by the mother of an illegitimate child of twenty, provided he or she had not been married. Indeed, I do not see why it should make any difference that the child in question had been living away from his mother and supporting himself by his own exertions for some years and had only come back to live with his mother for a few months in order to fulfil **[236]** the conditions for the making of the order laid down by section 3 (1) and without any intention of remaining with her after the order was made.

In reliance on that case counsel for the applicants in this case submits that if, as the decision in *In re D.* (*An Infant*)[6] shows, an adoption order can properly be made simply in order to secure to the child the rather shadowy advantages in the field of succession which are contained in section 16 and without his relation to his natural parent or his mode of life being affected in any way, there is no reason why an order should not be made to secure to this infant the very real benefit of becoming a British subject.

But there is to my mind a great difference between such a case as *In re D.* (*An Infant*)[6] and this case. In this case the benefit to the child flows simply from the fact that it is being adopted, not from the fact that it is being adopted by the particular adopters. Any adopters, provided that they were British subjects, would do. No doubt the applicants would become the statutory parents of this young man. The parental rights of the mother would be extinguished and the consequences in the field of succession provided by section 16 would ensue. But there would be no reality in those changes. He is, so far as I know, on the best of terms with his mother. The applicants do not—and would not—stand to him

[5] [1959] 1 Q.B. 229.
[6] [1959] 1 Q.B. 229.

in the relation of parents and one may guess that in practice each party would take care to see that section 16 did not operate. Indeed, it is to my mind perhaps doubtful whether this young man can really be said to be in the "care and possession" of the applicants at this moment within the meaning of section 3 (1). Of course, in any case where the person to be adopted is 19 or 20 years of age —and there is no doubt that the court can and sometimes does make adoption orders in such cases—the words "care and possession" must bear a somewhat artificial meaning; but it might be said that at least they require that the applicants with whom the infant is living should be really in loco parentis to him, and this can hardly be said here. In truth, this adoption would be an "accommodation" adoption, and it is not difficult to envisage cases in which such adoption would be open to objection on the grounds of public policy. An alien infant who wished to live here for the purpose of carrying on some undesirable activity might arrange to be adopted by friends in order to secure his position and put forward a plausible case that the order was for his benefit. I do not, of course, suggest for a moment that this is such a case, and counsel for the applicants argued that fears of this sort were really groundless because the judge would always have a discretion to refuse to make the order even though the statutory conditions were fulfilled, and he said it would be the duty of the guardian ad litem—who is normally the Official Solicitor—to put before the court any objection of this sort **[237]** which occurred to him. But that would mean that in this sort of application the court would be taking on itself functions similar to those of the Home Secretary on an application for naturalisation. I do not think that the Act intended the court to embark upon such inquiries.

Mr. Oliver cited in support of his argument two Scottish cases, *In re K., Petitioner*[7] and *In re L., Petitioner,*[8] to which I ought to refer. They arose under section 10 of the Adoption of Children (Scotland) Act, 1930, which corresponded to section 10 of the English Adoption of Children Act, 1926, and was in the following terms: "Where at the date of the commencement of this Act any child under the age of twenty-one years is in the custody of, and being brought up, maintained and educated by any person or two spouses jointly as his, her or their own child under any de facto adoption, and has for a period of not less than two years before such commencement been in such custody and been so brought up, maintained and educated, the court may, upon the application of such person or spouses, and notwithstanding that the applicant is a male and the child a female, make an adoption order authorising him, her or them to adopt the child without requiring the consent of any parent or guardian of the child to be obtained, upon being satisfied that in all the circumstances of the case it is just and equitable and for the welfare of the child that no such consent should be required and that an adoption order should be made."

The Acts of 1926 and 1930 were subsequently repealed and replaced in 1950 by a single Adoption Act applying both to England and Scotland; but section 10 of both the old Acts remained in force until 1958, when they were repealed, presumably because it was thought that there would not any longer be any case to which they could apply.

In *In re G., Petitioner,*[9] it was held by the Court of Session that section 10 of the Act of 1930 enabled the court to make an adoption order in the case of a person over 21 years of age, provided that he was under 21 when the Act came into force and had been in the de facto custody of the adopters for two years before that date. In *In re L., Petitioner,*[10] the Lord President (Lord Cooper) expressed a doubt—which I share to the full—whether this construction of the section was right. But he did not think that he was justified in refusing to follow *In re G., Petitioner*[11]; and in *In re K., Petitioner*[12] and *In re L., Petitioner*[13] adoption orders were made in the case of adults under section 10, which the court treated as a code of its own standing apart from the rest of the Adoption Act. The reason for which counsel cited those two cases in this case was that

[7] 1949 S.C. 140.
[8] 1951 S.C. 605.
[9] 1939 S.C. 782.
[10] 1951 S.C. 605.
[11] 1939 S.C. 782.
[12] 1949 S.C. 140.
[13] 1951 S.C. 605.

in each of them the benefit which was sought and gained by the application had nothing to **[238]** do with the upbringing of the person adopted—in one case the infant would be included in a superannuation scheme, and in the other case he would avoid the embarrassment caused to him by the form of his birth certificate.

But I do not think that those decisions help the applicants or the infant here. In the first place, they were under a section which—as construed by the court—stood apart from the rest of the Act. But in any case I fully accept that the benefit to the person adopted need not consist in the statutory transfer of parental rights and duties but may consist solely in what I may call some collateral consequence of the making of the order. The basic objection which I feel to this application is, as I have tried to explain, that the applicants are not really in loco parentis to the infant, whereas in the Scottish cases they had at least satisfied that condition in the past.

For these reasons, even assuming, as for present purposes I am prepared to do that, all the statutory requirements have been complied with, I feel obliged in the exercise of my discretion to refuse to make the order.

There will be no order for costs.

Order accordingly.

Solicitors: *Herbert Smith & Co.; Treasury Solicitor.*

2

LOCAL BRITISH NATIONALITY AND CITIZENSHIP

(E) CITIZENSHIP OF OTHER COUNTRIES OF THE COMMONWEALTH

i

Ceylon Citizenship

NALLA KARUMBURU KAYAMBU SHANMUGAM
v.
COMMISSIONER FOR REGISTRATION OF INDIAN AND PAKISTANI RESIDENTS

([1962] A.C. 515)

January 29, 30, 31, May 7, 1962: Judicial Committee of the Privy Council (on Appeal from the Supreme Court of Ceylon): Lords Radcliffe, Keith of Avonholm, Hodson, Devlin, Rt. Hon. L. M. D. de Silva.

Ceylon—Citizenship—Indian resident—Married male Indian resident—Qualification of wife—Whether interruption of continuity of residence—Statutory requirement not satisfied **[516]**
Statute—Retroactive effect—Retrospective amending legislation—Whether amended provisions regarding wife's residence applicable—"Express provision", meaning of—Applicability of provision not to arise by inference—Arising directly from language used—Indian and Pakistani Residents (Citizenship) Act, No. 3 *of* 1949 (*as amended by Act No.* 45 *of* 1952), *ss.* 5 (1), 6 (2) (ii), 22—*Interpretation Ordinance (Legislative Enactments of Ceylon,* 1938 *Rev., c.* 2), *s.* 6 (3) (*c*).

The appellant, who was married in India in March, 1944, alleging that he was continuously resident in Ceylon for the requisite period, applied in July, 1951, to be registered as a citizen of Ceylon under the Indian and Pakistani Residents (Citizenship) Act, 1949. His wife first arrived in Ceylon in October, 1945, and the respondent commissioner in May, 1957, refused the application on the ground that the appellant's wife was not "uninterruptedly resident in Ceylon from a date not later than the first anniversary of the date of her marriage and until the date of the application" as required by sections 6 (2) (ii) of the Act as amended by Act No. 45 of 1952, which changed the requirements of residence of a wife. Section 6, as amended, also provided that the continuity of residence of the wife should not be deemed to have been interrupted by reason that she was not resident in Ceylon during the period from December 1, 1941, to December 31, 1945, if the commissioner was satisfied that she did not reside in Ceylon during that period owing to special difficulties caused by the existence of a state of war. It was contended for the appellant that his wife did not arrive in Ceylon until October, 1945, owing to reasons covered by the above amendment and that for that reason the Act excused her absence from Ceylon until that date although she had never resided previously in Ceylon:—

Held, that the appellant's wife did not satisfy the provisions of section 6 (2) (ii). It could not be said that continuity of residence had been interrupted when the wife had never been resident in Ceylon.

Fakrudeen v. *Commissioner for Registration of Indian and Pakistani Residents* (1955) 57 N.L.R. 111 disapproved.

By section 6 (3) of the Interpretation Ordinance of Ceylon: "Whenever any written law repeals . . . a former written law, such repeal shall not, in the absence of any express provision to that effect, affect or be deemed to have affected— . . . (*c*) any action, proceeding, or thing pending or incompleted when the repealing written law comes into operation, but every such action, proceeding, or thing may be carried on and completed as if there had been no such repeal."

The amendments effected by Act No. 45 of 1952 were, by section 5 (1) thereof, made retrospective to the date of the principal Act, but it was contended by the appellant that by reason of section 6 (3) of the Interpretation Ordinance the provision regarding the residence of the wife was inapplicable in that the Act did not contain the "express provision" required by the Interpretation Ordinance to make it applicable as no reference had been made to pending proceedings:—**[517]**

Held, that while express provision was provision the applicability of which did not arise by inference, the applicability of the provision here did not arise by inference; it arose directly from the language used. To be "express provision" with regard to something it was not necessary that that thing should be specially mentioned; it was sufficient that it was directly covered by the language, however broad the language might be which covered it, so long as the applicability arose directly from the language used and not by inference therefrom.

Though facts had to be proved by an applicant for registration justifying a finding that there was a permanent settlement, it was not required that they should be subjected to the same very strict tests as English law had applied to any claim of a changed domicile.

Tennekoon v. *Duraisamy** [1958] A.C. 354; [1958] 2 W.L.R. 994; [1958] 2 All E.R. 479, P.C. considered.

Judgment of the Supreme Court of Ceylon affirmed.

APPEAL (No. 62 of 1960), by special leave, from a judgment of the Supreme Court of Ceylon (August 8, 1958) dismissing an appeal by the present appellant from an order of the Deputy Commissioner for the Registration of Indian and Pakistani Residents (respondent to this appeal) (May 23, 1957) by which he had refused an application by the appellant to be registered as a citizen of Ceylon under the Indian and Pakistani Residents (Citizenship) Act, No. 3 of 1949.

The following introductory statement is taken from the judgment of the Judicial Committee: The Act came into force on August 5, 1949. It made provision for granting the status of a citizen of Ceylon to Indian and Pakistani residents in Ceylon who were possessed of the residential qualifications specified in the Act if they satisfied certain conditions set out in it. Those residential qualifications and the conditions just mentioned were discussed in the judgment of the Board in *Tennekoon* v. *Duraisamy*.[1]*

In section 22 of the Act, as amended, Indian or Pakistani resident was defined thus: "'Indian or Pakistani resident' means a person—(*a*) whose origin was in any territory which, immediately prior to the passing of the Indian Independence Act, 1947, of the Parliament of the United Kingdom, formed part of British India or any Indian State, and (*b*) who has emigrated therefrom and permanently settled in Ceylon, and includes—(i) a descendant of any such person, and (ii) any person permanently settled in Ceylon who is a descendant of **[518]** a person whose origin was in any territory referred to in the preceding paragraph (*a*)."

In section 6 as amended by Act No. 45 of 1952 the following, among other conditions that have to be satisfied, appeared: "6 (2) (ii) . . . that his wife was uninterruptedly resident in Ceylon from a date not later than the first anniversary of the date of her marriage and until the date of the application, and in addition, that each minor child dependent on the applicant was uninter-

[1] [1958] A.C. 354; [1958] 2 W.L.R. 994; [1958] 2 All E.R. 479; 59 N.L.R. 481, P.C.

ruptedly resident in Ceylon from a date not later than the first anniversary of the date of the child's birth and until the date of the application. . . ."

The application was refused by the commissioner on the grounds that (a) the applicant's wife had not resided in Ceylon as required by section 6 (2) (ii) and (b) that the applicant had not satisfied him that he was "permanently settled" in Ceylon as required by section 22. As would be seen from the section, permanent settlement by a person in Ceylon was necessary before he could claim to be an "Indian or Pakistani resident." On appeal the Supreme Court affirmed the order of the commissioner without giving reasons.

The applicant was married in India on March 16, 1944. The wife did not arrive in Ceylon till October, 1945, later than "the first anniversary of the date of her marriage." Section 6 as amended contained the following provision: "For the purposes of the preceding paragraph (2) (ii), [above] the continuity of residence of the wife or a minor child of an applicant shall not be deemed to have been interrupted by reason that she or he was not resident in Ceylon during the period commencing on December 1, 1941, and ending on December 31, 1945, or during any part of that period, if the commissioner is satisfied that she or he did not reside in Ceylon during that period or part thereof owing to apprehension of enemy action in or against Ceylon or owing to special difficulties caused by the existence of a state of war."

1962. Jan. 29, 30, 31. *E. F. N. Gratiaen Q.C.* (Ceylon) and *Walter Jayawardena* for the appellant. So far as concerns the residential qualification of the appellant himself, he, being a married man, had uninterrupted residence from January 1, 1939, to January 1, 1946, and also uninterrupted residence within the meaning of the Ordinance from January 1, 1946, to the date of his application, which was July 13, 1951. It was held at the end of the inquiry that he did possess the necessary residential **[519]** qualification. With regard to his wife, the law at the time of the application has been the subject of a Privy Council decision when it was held that the words "ordinarily resident" in respect of a wife and child meant not, as the Crown maintained, resident for a long period of time, but actual residence at the date of the application: *Wirasinha, Commissioner for Registration of Indian and Pakistani Residents* v. *Badurdeen.*[2]* The date of that judgment is interesting, October 6, 1952. On November 28, 1952, the Governor-General's assent was given to the amending Ordinance, No. 45 of 1952, and the submission will be that section 6 (2) (ii) as amended, which came into force after the appellant's application, did not refer to the wife and children; the section which applied to them is the original section 6 (2) (ii), and it is nowhere suggested that that was not satisfied. If that submission is rejected, then it will be contended that the wife has in fact satisfied the new test under the 1952 Ordinance. On the true interpretation the wife did delay her return owing to a genuine apprehension of enemy action, and the deputy commissioner completely misdirected himself in rejecting that.

The position is that they were married in India on March 16, 1944, and the date of her anniversary would be March 16, 1945. She did not come to Ceylon until October, 1945—some months after the date of the anniversary. There is a definite ruling of the Supreme Court of Ceylon to the effect that the new section 6 (2) (ii) does not mean that the wife should have been in Ceylon at the latest on the date of the anniversary of her wedding; it was held that if her delay in coming to Ceylon for the *first time* was owing to the matters referred to in the section, then she could claim the benefit of the subsection: *Fakrudeen* v. *Commissioner for Registration of Indian and Pakistani Residents.*[3] That decision was given on September 8, 1955, and the commissioner's order here was made on May 23, 1957. There was no legislative amendment subsequent to that decision.

The words "permanently settled" in section 22 (*b*)—the interpretation section of the Ordinance—have been considered by this Board in *Tennekoon* v. *Durai-*

[2] [1952] A.C. 623, 629; [1952] 2 T.L.R. 610, P.C.
[3] (1955) 57 N.L.R. 111.

samy,[4]* and it is now quite clearly ruled that an applicant must prove at the time of his application that he genuinely intends to live permanently in Ceylon; it is not an issue of domicile or anything like that. The deputy commissioner has treated it as a question of domicile. **[520]** The Board's judgment was after the commissioner's determination, but they affirmed the view of the Supreme Court which was before the commissioner's decision. The commissioner is under a duty to take the investigator's report into consideration, but it does not bind him.

The first complaint in regard to the deputy commissioner's finding of no permanent settlement is that when the appellant was asked to show cause, the only reason why it was suggested that he had failed to establish permanent settlement was that he had signed applications when remitting moneys abroad that he was a temporary resident; but he denied it and it has not been proved against him; instead, without any notice to him, he has been held to have failed to prove a domicile of choice. On the law, a domicile of choice need not be proved at all; whether a man has changed his domicile is a matter of inference to be drawn from conduct over a long period of time. In the present case, as in *Tennekoon* v. *Duraisamy,*[5]* the deputy commissioner made a completely wrong approach to the question of permanent settlement, he considered it a question in which there was a burden to prove change of domicile, whereas the only question was whether a prima facie case had been made out of a genuine intention to settle in Ceylon. It would appear from *Tennekoon's* case[5]* that the Board does not regard the question of change of domicile as coming into the matter at all.

The moment the applicant (having the residence qualification) makes a genuine decision to make Ceylon his home, then he is entitled as of right to be registered, because he has by his decision elected now permanently to settle in Ceylon, and what had happened in the past—such as visiting India—is insignificant compared with the enormous weight which must be given to his decision. The initial burden is discharged by proving certain facts. *Tennekoon* v. *Panjan*[6] is in line with the above submissions on proof of permanent settlement. Further, from the scheme of the legislation there are good reasons supporting the view that "permanently settled" does not necessarily involve a finding that the applicant has changed his domicile of origin. "Permanently settled" means has elected by forming a solemn decision just before the time of the application to settle down permanently in Ceylon. He then makes his application and demonstrates the genuineness of his intention by satisfying the authorities that he clearly understands the consequences set out in section 6 (2) (iv). **[521]** There is a prima facie case at the time of the application unless there is ground for doubting whether the intention permanently to settle in Ceylon is genuine. Here, on the facts, the appellant has prima facie proved his case. He has categorically denied the one ground which was urged against him, and the judgment below cannot stand, for there is no material which displaces that prima facie case.

With regard to the wife's residence, the deputy commissioner's finding must be set aside because if *Fakrudeen's* case[7] is right, and section 6 (2) (ii) applied, the deputy commissioner was wrong on a very vital matter, the interpretation of subsection (2) (ii), and he completely misdirected himself on a question of fact and did not direct himself on a relevant question of fact and therefore came to the conclusion that the excuse for the wife's absence was belated.

The final point is that through the provisions of the amending Ordinance, No. 45 of 1952, are in certain respects retrospective, the legal position is, nevertheless, that the appellant's pending proceeding—his application for registration—which had been made in 1951, had to be disposed of in accordance with the law as it stood at that time. The Interpretation Ordinance of Ceylon, s. 6 (3), provides that "Whenever any written law repeals either in whole or part a former written law, such repeal shall not, in the absence of any express provision

[4] [1958] A.C. 354; [1958] 2 W.L.R. 994; [1958] 2 All E.R. 479, P.C.
[5] [1958] A.C. 354.
[6] (1958) 59 N.L.R. 512, P.C.
[7] 57 N.L.R. 111.

to that effect, affect or be deemed to have affected—(*c*) any . . . proceeding . . . pending . . . but every such . . . proceeding . . . may be carried on and completed as if there had been no such repeal." The words "in the absence of any express provision to that effect" in section 6 (3) have taken the place of "unless the contrary intention appears" in section 38 (2) of the English Interpretation Act, 1889. In this case the appellant made his application at the time when the Ordinance of 1949 was unamended, and at that time all that he had to prove was that his wife was ordinarily resident in Ceylon at the time of the application: *Wirasinha's* case.[8]* While the application was pending the Ordinance of 1952 came into force on November 28, 1952, and substituted stricter residential qualifications than had been laid down in the earlier Ordinance. The question is whether section 5 of the amending Ordinance has express provision to the effect that what was the appellant's vested right, under section 4, of exercising the privilege of procuring registration has been **[522]** limited or reduced in any way, and also whether there is, while the disposal of his application in accordance with the procedure laid down is pending, express provision that the amendment shall apply even to his pending proceeding. The expression in section 6 (3) of the Interpretation Ordinance merely says something which is obvious, because the amendment could not on a proper interpretation prejudice any rights which had already been vested in litigants, and certainly not in cases where there had been finality reached. [Reference was made to *Abbott* v. *Minister for Lands.*[9]] Here it is not merely a right to take advantage of the provision, it is a right which has been exercised—that the appellant should be registered. To affect his accrued rights there must be an express provision to that effect. Whether or not what was said in *In re Joseph Suche & Co. Ltd.*[10] would be correct law in England today, those words perfectly suit the very precise words of the Ceylon Ordinance. The proposition in *Hutchinson* v. *Jauncey*[11] is not quarrelled with, but where one has a different rule for interpretation of statutes, then the only way in which an accrued right or rights in a pending action can be affected by amending legislation would be where there is express reference to accrued rights and express reference to pending actions. The Ceylon legislation insists on an express provision if the normal rule laid down in section 6 (3) of the Interpretation Ordinance is to be departed from: see also sections 3, 4, 6 (1), (2) and (3) and 10 of that Ordinance. On the meaning of "express" see *In re Meredith.*[12] The question is whether section 5 (1) of the amending Ordinance of 1952 contains an express provision to the effect that even accrued rights are affected—that is the test one extracts from section 6 (3) of the Interpretation Ordinance. [*Akilandanayaki* v. *Sothinagaratnam*[13] was referred to.] If this argument on the retrospective question is right, there is no question that the wife was ordinarily resident under the earlier Ordinance.

Jayawardena following. The facts are not inconsistent with the appellant's declaration that he was permanently settled in Ceylon. The idea of a matrimonial home in Ceylon is fully established in a real and practical sense. Further, he has an established business of his own in Ceylon and was thus in no **[523]** danger as an employee of losing his employment. Those are factors to be taken into consideration. There is no evidence on which any court can say that his declaration was insincere—there is positive evidence of its truth.

On the question of how the wife can be said to have uninterrupted residence in Ceylon when she did not come there until over a year after the marriage, the submission is that the words "uninterrupted residence" in this Ordinance have not been used with a special meaning attached to them. Admittedly, there cannot be interruption of the period if the wife was not there, but she is nevertheless deemed to be resident in Ceylon if the continuity is deemed not to be interrupted. The section gives her a sort of notional residence: *Fakrudeen's* case.[14]

[8] [1952] A.C. 623.
[9] [1895] A.C. 425, P.C.
[10] (1875) 1 Ch.D. 48, 50.
[11] [1950] 1 K.B. 574, 578; 66 T.L.R. (Pt. 1) 195; [1950] 1 All E.R. 165, C.A.
[12] (1898) 67 L.J.Ch. 409.
[13] (1952) 53 N.L.R. 385, 386.
[14] 57 N.L.R. 111.

Dingle Foot Q.C. and *Montague Solomon* for the respondent. There are three issues: (1) Whether the amending Ordinance of 1952 operated retrospectively so as to affect pending applications. (2) If so, whether the appellant can claim the benefit of section 6 (2) (ii) of the Ordinance of 1952 on the ground that his wife was not residing in Ceylon on March 16, 1945, owing to apprehension of enemy action or owing to special difficulties caused by the war. (3) Whether the deputy commissioner's order was made in the proper exercise of his discretion. With regard to (1) (supra), Mr. Gratiaen relied on section 6 (3) of the Interpretation Ordinance. It is submitted that "express provision" has been made; it is difficult to imagine words wider than those to be found here—to find more sweeping retrospective legislation than that. There are a number of amendments which will affect pending claims. When one looks at the actual words in subsection (1) of section 5, or at the whole of section 5 of the Act of 1952, or at the purpose and structure of the Ordinance itself, or at the chronology, one is driven to the conclusion that these words are plainly retrospective and that they must cover applications which had already been filed before the Ordinance of 1952.

As to point (2) (supra), *Fakrudeen's* case[15] is really doing violence to the language of the section because it is giving no effect to the words of the last paragraph. If it had been intended that that form of extension should apply to the original period of grace, that is, the 12 months following the wedding day, it would have been a perfectly simple matter for the legislature to have said so —it would have used entirely different words. **[524]**

As to (3) (supra)—whether the deputy commissioner was wrong—there were matters affecting the credibility of the appellant which entitled the deputy commissioner to take an adverse view of the appellant's evidence.

With regard to the prima facie case point, Mr. Gratiaen relied on *Tennekoon* v. *Panjan.*[16] It is submitted that that case does not avail him at all. Before the question of the genuineness of intention can arise at all, before the commissioner really begins to inquire into that aspect of the matter, conditions have to be satisfied before the question of prima facie case can begin. If the appellant has failed in this case to satisfy the conditions in relation to his wife the other issues—whether he has made up his mind to settle permanently and apply for citizenship—do not arise in this case.

It is a very fine distinction between domicile and the requirements of this statute. If the Board finds that the deputy commissioner arrived at the right conclusion—and the submission is that there was material on which he could so find—it does not really matter that he brought in the concept of domicile. It is not necessary for the purposes of this Ordinance to introduce the question of domicile at all—the statute is complete in itself.

Gratiaen Q.C. in reply. *Tennekoon's* case[17]* makes it clear that it is wrong to approach the issue of permanent settlement as a court of law would approach the question of change of domicile. Here there are these somewhat artificial rules and heavy onus where it is necessary for the court to assess intention. [Reference was made to Cheshire's Private International Law, 4th ed., pp. 155, 161.] In the present case the standard has virtually been fixed by the Ordinance itself. The deputy commissioner misdirected himself in saying that the burden of proof was a heavy one and the domicile of origin was not easily displaced. On the legislative plan, see *Pillai* v. *Mudanayake.*[18]* Ignoring the misdirection as to onus of proof, the findings of fact on permanent settlement cannot stand.

As to the retrospective effect of the Ordinance of 1952, one is left with the question whether section 5 (1) contains an express provision to the effect that vested rights under the old Ordinance are taken away, and that vested rights of a pending applicant are also retrospectively taken away in respect of a status which he was entitled to claim at the time of the application. It could **[525]** have been made clear in section 5 (1) that in all these pending proceedings the old

[15] Ibid.
[16] 59 N.L.R. 512.
[17] [1958] A.C. 354.
[18] [1953] A.C. 514, 529-530; [1952] 2 W.L.R. 1142; [1955] 2 All E.R. 833, P.C

qualification was to be taken away and a new one imposed; that would be an express provision.

May 7. The judgment of their Lordships was delivered by LORD RADCLIFFE, who stated the facts set out above and continued: It was argued before the commissioner and before their Lordships that the wife did not arrive in Ceylon till October, 1945, owing to reasons covered by the last words of the passage in section 6 as amended, set out above, and that for this reason the Act excused her absence from Ceylon till October, 1945, although she had never resided previously in Ceylon.

In *Fakrudeen* v. *Commissioner for Registration of Indian and Pakistani Residents*[19] this view of the law was taken by the Supreme Court. The commissioner rejected this argument saying amongst other things: "It cannot be said that continuity of residence has been interrupted if a person has never been resident in this country." His order, as already stated, was affirmed by the Supreme Court in this case. Their Lordships are of the opinion that the commissioner was right. In *Fakrudeen's* case the Supreme Court, commenting on the words of the Act relied on by the appellant, said[20]: "The legislature here has in mind not *occasional absence* or mere interruptions of a period of residence, but *non-residence* during the war period, an expression which can fairly include *any* failure to reside attributable to war conditions, *whether or not* the period of non-residence constituted an interruption of a period of residence." With all respect to the Supreme Court their Lordships think that such a view strains language beyond permissible limits.

The commissioner also held that even if the argument mentioned above be accepted he was not satisfied that during the period in question the applicant's wife remained in India because of war conditions. He gave two reasons for this view, first, that it was a belated piece of evidence given in May, 1957, of a state of things which had never been mentioned before. In this he was wrong because the record shows that on September 25, 1953, the applicant had said to an investigating officer that the delay in bringing the wife over was "due to special circumstances created by the war." The second reason was that in his application he had stated that during 1944 and 1945 his wife had resided at No. 9 Puppurasa Bazaar. Confronted with this statement the **[526]** applicant said: "That entry is a mistake—my wife never lived at Puppurasa." It is difficult to see how a positive statement such as that made by the applicant could be an inadvertent mistake. The commissioner appears to think it was a false statement which the applicant had forgotten having made. There appears to be substance in the commissioner's second reason, but as on the point in question the commissioner had made an error of fact (in his view that certain evidence was belated) their Lordships prefer not to place reliance on his finding. It is not necessary to do so for the reason, expressed earlier, that the applicant's wife did not satisfy the provisions of section 6 (2) (ii). Upon this view alone the application would fail.

There arises, however, a question whether the Act of 1952 affects the appellant's application. The application was made in July, 1951, and the provision set out above relating to the residence of the wife was made by Act No. 45 of 1952 which also contains provision in section 5 making it retrospective to the following effect: "(1) The amendments effected by the preceding sections of this Act shall be deemed to have come into force on the date appointed under section 1 of the principal Act; and accordingly, but subject to the provisions of subsection (3) of this section, the principal Act shall be deemed on and after that date to have had effect, and shall have effect, in like manner as though it had on that date been amended in the manner provided by this Act."

It has been argued that the provision regarding the residence of the wife is inapplicable to this case. It has been said that the application was pending when Act No. 45 of 1952 was passed and that by reason of the provisions of section 6 (3) of the Interpretation Ordinance (chapter 2, Legislative Enactments of

19 (1955) 57 N.L.R. 111.
20 Ibid. 113.

Ceylon) the Act is not applicable. Section 6 (3) is to the following effect: "Whenever any written law repeals either in whole or part a former written law, such repeal shall not, in the absence of any express provision to that effect, affect or be deemed to have affected— . . . (*c*) any action, proceeding, or thing pending or incompleted when the repealing written law comes into operation, but every such action, proceeding, or thing may be carried on and completed as if there had been no such repeal."

Subsections (*a*) and (*b*) have no bearing on this case.

It is argued that the Act does not contain the "express provision" required by the Interpretation Ordinance to make it applicable. Their Lordships do not agree. Upon the meaning of the **[527]** words "express provision" counsel relied upon *In re Meredith*[21] and stated that it must be provision the applicability of which did not arise by inference. He argued that there was no "express provision" as no reference had been made to pending proceedings. Their Lordships are of the view that it is correct to state that express provision is provision the applicability of which does not arise by inference. The applicability, however, of the provision under discussion to the present case does not arise by inference; it arises directly from the language used. The fact that the language used is wide and comprehensive and covers many points other than the one immediately under discussion does not make it possible to say that its application can arise by inference only. To be "express provision" with regard to something it is not necessary that that thing should be specially mentioned; it is sufficient that it is directly covered by the language however broad the language may be which covers it so long as the applicability arises directly from the language used and not by inference therefrom. The argument fails.

In the circumstances their Lordships do not find it necessary to give any decision upon the other ground of appeal that was argued before them, viz., that the commissioner had erred in law in his finding that the applicant was not permanently settled in Ceylon at the date of application. It was said that his error consisted in introducing a reference to "change of domicile" into his stated reasons for holding that there was no permanent settlement.

Their Lordships think, however, that it may be helpful for the future if they make one observation about the decision of the Board in *Tennekoon* v. *Duraisamy*[22]* which was much relied upon in argument before them. In their opinion it would be a misunderstanding to suppose that, in considering whether a person had acquired a permanent settlement in Ceylon prior to application, the tribunal of inquiry would not have to investigate and assess virtually the same facts as those normally regarded as relevant in considering a question of change of domicile. The respective fields of inquiry necessarily contain the same sorts of facts. The importance of the decision of *Tennekoon* v. *Duraisamy*[22]* is that it emphasises that, though facts have to be proved by the applicant justifying a finding that there was a permanent settlement, it is not required that they should be subjected to the same very strict tests as English law has applied to any claim **[528]** of a changed domicile as, for instance, that strong presumption in favour of the retention of the domicile of origin which has not infrequently been attributed to English decisions on this subject.

For the reasons which they have given their Lordships will humbly advise Her Majesty that the appeal be dismissed. The appellant must pay the costs of this appeal.

Solicitors: *A. L. Bryden & Williams; T. L. Wilson & Co.*

[21] (1898) 67 L.J.Ch. 409.
[22] [1958] A.C. 354.

M. K. S. SEYED MOHAMED SHAREEF
v.
COMMISSIONER FOR REGISTRATION OF INDIAN AND PAKISTANI RESIDENTS

([1966] A.C. 47)

May 11, 12, 13, June 30, 1966: Judicial Committee of the Privy Council (on appeal from the Supreme Court of Ceylon): Lords Morris of Borth-y-Gest, Guest, Pearce, Wilberforce, Pearson.

Ceylon—Citizenship—Indian and Pakistani residents—Application for registration as citizen—Inquiry by commissioner—Whether commissioner acting in semi-judicial capacity—Investigations into authenticity of document made without knowledge of applicant—Examination of witness on report not disclosed to applicant—Whether a failure to comply with principles of natural justice—Indian and Pakistani Residents (Citizenship) Act, No. 3 *of* 1949 (*as amended by Act No.* 37 *of* 1950 *and Act No.* 45 *of* 1952) (*Legislative Enactments of Ceylon,* 1956 *Rev., c.* 350), *s.* 15.
Natural Justice—Opportunity to meet charge—Registration as citizen—Investigations into authenticity of document—Report of investigating officer not disclosed to applicant—Whether compliance with principles of natural justice—Ceylon.

The Indian and Pakistani Residents (Citizenship) Act, No. 3 of 1949 (as amended by Act No. 37 of 1950 and Act No. 45 of 1952), **[48]** provides by section 4 (1) that any Indian or Pakistani resident possessed of certain residential qualifications may apply for registration as a citizen of Ceylon; section 8 (1) provides that the Commissioner for Registration of Indian and Pakistani Residents or his deputy shall refer any such application for verification of the particulars and statements therein to the area investigating officer, and section 8 (4) that the report of the investigating officer shall be taken into consideration in dealing with the application. Section 10, by subsection (1), provides that where the commissioner is of opinion that a prima facie case has not been established he shall serve a notice on the applicant setting out the grounds on which the application would be refused and giving the applicant an opportunity to show cause to the contrary and, by subsection (3), where cause is shown the commissioner may either hold an inquiry, serving notice on the applicant, or take the steps authorised to be taken where there was a prima facie case for allowing the application. Section 13 relates to the holding of an inquiry in the case of an objection.

By section 14:

"Where, in considering any application, the commissioner is of opinion that any matter or matters arising therefrom or connected therewith should be further investigated, he may of his own motion order an inquiry. . . . A copy of such order shall in every case be served on the applicant."

By section 15 (4):

"The proceedings at an inquiry shall as far as possible be free from the formalities and technicalities of the rules of procedure and evidence applicable to a court of law, and may be conducted by the commissioner in any manner, not inconsistent with the principles of natural justice, which to him may seem best adapted to elicit proof concerning the matters that are investigated."

On August 4, 1951, the appellant applied under section 4 of the Indian and Pakistani Residents (Citizenship) Act, No. 3 of 1949, for registration as a citizen of Ceylon, setting out as his residential qualifications, inter alia, uninterrupted residence in Ceylon from January 1, 1936, to January 1, 1946, and uninterrupted residence from that date until the application. On July 31, 1956, the Commissioner for Registration of Indian and Pakistani Residents informed the appellant pursuant to section 10 (1) of the Act that he had decided to refuse the application unless the appellant showed cause to the contrary. On October 25, 1956, the appellant showed cause and asked for an inquiry. The inquiry lasted from April 22, 1957, until August 29, 1958. In support of his claim the appellant relied on his school certificate. The deputy commissioner, mistakenly thinking that the school certificate purported to be issued in 1943, formed the view that the freshness of the writing was suspicious and accordingly initiated an investigation into its genuineness. On September 2, 1957, the investigating officer reported to the deputy commissioner that the school certificate was not a true copy of the original and must have been issued sometime between **[49]** January 1, 1952, and September 1, 1953. On September 19, 1957, the commissioner requested the Director of Education to direct an officer to report on the genuineness of the school certificate. On September 21, 1957, the head teacher who had signed the school certificate was examined by the deputy commissioner, on material taken from the report made by the investigating officer. On January 20, 1958, the Director of Education by letter reported that the school certificate in question had been issued under false pretexts and was not genuine. At a hearing on February 18, 1958, the appellant was confronted with the contents of the investigating officer's report, whereupon his advocate asked for attendance of the officer who made the report. After further investigation by an officer of the Ministry of Education, the Director of Education informed the deputy commissioner on May 19, 1958, that the school certificate was genuine. At the resumed hearing on August 29, 1958, the officer who had made the superseded report against the genuineness of the school certificate gave evidence and the deputy commissioner for the first time disclosed to the appellant the letters received from the Director of Education. In his written submissions the appellant's advocate relied upon the letter of May 19, 1958, submitting, inter alia, that the matter was now put beyond all doubt by the authoritative letter of the Director of Education, and that it followed from the terms of the letter that the school certificate was genuine. On September 15, 1958, the deputy commissioner made an order refusing the application. Only after the order was made and the record of proceedings was made available to him did the appellant become aware of the investigations made by the deputy commissioner without his knowledge. The appellant appealed to the Supreme Court, who dismissed the appeal without giving reasons.

On appeal:—

Held, that when conducting an inquiry under section 10, 13 or 14 of the Act of 1949 the commissioner was acting in a semi-judicial capacity in which he was bound to observe the principles of natural justice, which required that a party should be given fair notice of the case made against him and an adequate opportunity at the proper time to meet that case (post, p. 60); that, although under section 15 (4) the commissioner had wide powers of inquiry and investigation not enjoyed by a judge in a civil or criminal trial and was not bound to conduct the inquiry according to the normal rules of evidence, it would have been in accordance with normal fair conduct of an inquiry to disclose the report of the investigating officer of September 2, 1957, and the report on which the letter from the Director of Education of January 20, 1958, was made, nor was it fair that the school teacher should have been examined by the deputy commissioner on the details of the investigating officer's report without disclosing the report to the appellant's advocate, for it was almost impossible for the appellant's advocate to re-examine the witness and clear up any difficulties raised (post, **[50]** p. 61); that, during the whole conduct of the inquiry, the appellant was never told the details of the case against the genuineness of the document and was never given a proper opportunity of answering it, and the failure to disclose the Director of Education's letters at an earlier date may have misled the appellant's advocate into thinking that no further argument or evidence was required as to the genuineness of the certificate; and that, in all the circumstances, the principles of natural justice were not complied with (post, p. 62). Accordingly, the orders of the Supreme Court and of the deputy commissioner must be quashed and the case remitted to the Supreme Court for the purpose of placing de novo the appellant's application before the commissioner, preferably for hearing by a different deputy commissioner (post. p. 63).

Ridge v. *Baldwin* [1964] A.C. 40; [1963] 2 W.L.R. 935; [1963] 2 All E.R. 66, H.L.(E.) applied.

Per curiam. It is a matter of regret that there was not the assistance of the reasons of the Supreme Court in dismissing the appeal (post, p. 62).

Judgment of the Supreme Court of Ceylon set aside.

Order of the deputy commissioner quashed.

APPEAL (No. 4 of 1963) by special leave from an order of the Supreme Court of Ceylon (de Silva J.) (December 14, 1960) dismissing the appellant's appeal from an order of the Deputy Commissioner for the Registration of Indian and Pakistani Residents (September 15, 1958) refusing the appellant's application for registration as a citizen of Ceylon under the Indian and Pakistani Residents (Citizenship) Act, No. 3 of 1949.

The following statement of facts is taken from the judgment of the Judicial Committee: the appellant, M. K. S. Seyed Mohamed Shareef, duly made application to the respondent, the Commissioner for the Registration of Indian and Pakistani Residents, for registration as a citizen of Ceylon under section 4 of the Pakistani Residents (Citizenship) Act, No. 3 of 1949. In his application dated August 4, 1951, he stated, inter alia, that he had been continuously resident in Ceylon for a period of 10 years from January 1, 1936, to December 31, 1945, and that he had been continuously resident in Ceylon from January 1, 1946, to the date of the application. The deputy commissioner gave notice to the appellant on July 31, 1956, under section 10 (1) of the Act (then section 9 (1)) that he had decided to refuse the application, unless the appellant showed cause to the contrary, on various grounds, inter alia, that the applicant had failed to prove (1) that he was resident in Ceylon during the period January 1, 1936, to August 4, 1951, without absence exceeding 12 months on any single occasion and (2) that he had permanently settled in Ceylon. The appellant by letter dated **[51]** October 25, 1956, showed cause and asked for an inquiry. The inquiry opened on April 22, 1957, and on various dates between then and August 29, 1958, the deputy commissioner heard evidence and caused investigations to be conducted into various details connected with the application.

On April 22, 1957, when the appellant gave evidence before the deputy commissioner he produced his school certificate known as a "Q Schedule" which was in the following terms:

"Name of School.	K. Boputuya Estate, Tamil Mixed School
Full Name of Pupil	M. K. S. Muhamed Sharrif, Neen Thurugala, Girindi Ella Rangala
Full Name of Parent	Seyed Ahamed Thamby
Admission number of Pupil . . .	8 Date of Admission 17.11.1935
Age of Admission	8. Passed fifth standard (Vth)
Last standard passed in	Reading X Sp. x. Writing X — Arithmetic X —
	Sgd. S. Ponniah Signature of Head Teacher
Date of Withdrawal	1.12.1943."

The deputy commissioner, mistakenly thinking that the certificate purported to be issued in 1943, formed the view that the freshness of the writing was suspicious and he accordingly initiated an investigation into the genuineness of the school certificate. No notice of that investigation was given to the appellant. On September 2, 1957, the investigating officer sent a report to the deputy commissioner stating that, in his opinion, inter alia, the certificate was not a true copy of the original and that the certificate must have been issued sometime between January 1, 1952, and September 1, 1953. That report was in the following terms:

> "*Report on copy of School Schedule (Q)—INO/9.C.*8009/*G/C.* I examined the original of the schedule Q in the Q Schedule Book of the K/Boputuya Estate Tamil School. The following is a copy of the original. Name. M. K. S. Muhamed Sharrif. Date of withdrawal. 1.12.43. Admission number. 8. ...... 1935. Signature of Teacher. It would appear from the above that the copy handed over to you is not a true copy of the original which does not contain the date of admission except the year. The pupil's age is not given nor the standard passed with subjects. The head teacher could not have issued this Q schedule on 1.12.43 because the Q schedule leaf prior to this gives the date of withdrawal of a student as 1.1.52 and the Q schedule following this gives the date of withdrawal as 1.9.53. Therefore he should have issued this Q schedule sometime **[52]** between 1.1.52 and 1.9.53. When I asked the head teacher for the examination Schedule Book from which he would have taken these particulars he told me that it was lost in December, 1953. *Admission and Withdrawal Register.* The first 23 pages of the old admission and withdrawal register are missing. On page 25 is a fresh registration which is not in chronological order. There are two other fresh registrations on p. 24 and p. 67. This name appears on p. 37, which is towards the end of the book giving the admission No. 8 and the date of admission and withdrawal as 17.11.35 and 1.12.43 respectively. It does not give the last standard passed. The writing appears to be fresh. On asking the teacher from where he obtained these particulars he said it was from the old register whose pages are missing."

Neither the fact that that report had been obtained nor the terms of the report were at any time disclosed to the appellant. The deputy commissioner on September 19, 1957, requested the Director of Education to direct an officer to report on the genuineness of the school certificate. No notice was given to the appellant of the fact that that investigation was being made.

On September 21, 1957, the head teacher, S. Ponniah, who signed the school certificate was examined at length by the deputy commissioner. The witness said that he had issued the school certificate in 1951 when the pupil asked for it. He stated that the documents from which the information on the certificate was obtained had been lost. The material upon which the examination by the deputy commissioner was made was evidently taken from the report of the investigating officer, dated September 2, 1957.

On January 20, 1958, the Director of Education wrote to the deputy commissioner as follows: "In continuation of my letter of 2.1.58, it is reported that Q schedules in question have been issued under false pretexts and that they are not genuine." The deputy commissioner did not at any stage call for the report on which that letter was based, but at the resumed inquiry on February 18, 1958, the appellant was confronted by the deputy commissioner with the contents of that letter from the Director of Education. He persisted that he attended the Boputuya Estate Tamil School from 1935 to 1943. His advocate then asked for the attendance of the officer who made the report, Sandarasegaram. Before the next hearing on August 29, 1958, when the officer who made the report gave evidence, the deputy commissioner had been told, on April 11, 1958, by the Director of Education that the matter was being further investigated, and on May 19, 1958, he had received a letter from the Director of Education informing him that **[53]** the Q schedules, i.e., the school certificates, were genuine. The deputy commissioner was informed on June 20, 1958, that the further inquiries which resulted in the opinion by the director that the certificates were genuine were conducted by M. J. M. Mushsin, C.C.S., Assistant Secretary, Ministry of Education, Colombo. Neither the communication of May 19, 1958, nor the communication of June 20, 1958, were disclosed to the appellant prior to the resumed hearing on August 29, 1958.

At this resumed hearing Sandarasegaram was examined by the deputy commissioner. He said that he had visited the school and that he found by circumstantial evidence that the schedules were not genuine. He did not say what that circumstantial evidence was. He did not know of the assistant secretary's finding that the schedules were genuine, but he understood that the benefit of the doubt had been given to the head teacher of the school and that the officer who made the inquiry took into account his report and "the meritorious record of the teacher and the documents produced of which I am unaware." During the course of that hearing the deputy commissioner for the first time disclosed to the appellant the letter dated January 20, 1958, from the Director of Education to the deputy commissioner in which he stated that the Q schedules had been issued under false pretences and were not genuine.

At the conclusion of the evidence the deputy commissioner read out the correspondence between him and the Director of Education in which the director informed the deputy commissioner that the schedules were genuine and disclosed that the name of the officer who conducted the inquiries was Mushsin. The deputy commissioner then recorded the following addendum:

> "Mr. Aluwihare mentions that he does not want the head teacher of the school called in, although he was summoned at his request as no questions for clarification arose from the evidence of the inspector of schools. Mr. Aluwihare does not wish to examine the applicant any further."

He then recalled the appellant and asked him some questions about a temporary residence permit in which it was stated he was resident in Ceylon since 1944.

The appellant's advocate then handed in a statement signed embodying his submission on behalf of the appellant. That statement included, inter alia, the following:

> "We have to prove (1) residence from 1.1.36 to date of application without absence from the Island more than a year on any single occasion. (2)........ (3)........(1) We **[54]** have produced school registers and 'Q' schedules, covering the period 1.1.36 to 1944 i.e. for 10 years' period to 1946. The 'Q' schedules were admitted to be genuine i.e. the school certificate. The Education Officer stated that if the 'Q' schedules were genuine, the supplementary documents, i.e. the school register must be genuine. Even on the inspector's own reasoning, the school register, the genuineness of which he originally said was in doubt, has to be taken as genuine. The matter is now put beyond doubt by the authoritative letter of the Director of Education which was issued after the inspector took and had agreed [sic]. The terms of the letter are that the 'Q' schedules are genuine. No qualification is mentioned. It follows that all supplementary documents are genuine. . . ."

On September 15, 1958, the deputy commissioner refused the applicant. After the order was made and the record made available to the appellant, the appellant became aware of the investigations which had been made without his knowledge. His appeal to the Supreme Court of Ceylon was dismissed by de Silva J. without reasons.

The appellant appealed to the Board submitting that the order of the Supreme Court should be set aside and the finding of the deputy commissioner quashed on the ground that in the conduct of the inquiry the deputy commissioner contravened the principles of natural justice.

1965. May 11, 12 and 13. *E. F. N. Gratiaen Q.C.* and *Walter Jaywardena* for the appellant. The course adopted by the deputy commissioner was contrary to the provisions of the Act of 1949 and in breach of the principles of natural justice. The investigations instituted by the deputy commissioner on July 20, 1957, were unauthorised by the Act. The investigating officer, whom at this date the deputy commissioner requested to carry out investigations, had already furnished his report, as provided by section 8 (2) (*b*) of the Act. This report appears nowhere in the record on the deputy commissioner's file. The officer must have investigated and reported at an earlier stage before the deputy commissioner served notice under section 9 (1) of a refusal of the appellant's application. The investigating officer was therefore functus officio, and the deputy commissioner was not entitled to send his investigating officer to make further investigations.

If the deputy commissioner thought that there were matters which required further investigation, he could only act under section 14 of the Act of 1949. This would have necessitated an inquiry, specifying the matter or matters to be inquired into, and **[55]** thereby giving the appellant an opportunity of dealing with the matter or matters as to which the deputy commissioner was not satisfied. The suspicion of the deputy commissioner was aroused by a misunderstanding on his part in that he thought that the school leaving certificate purported to show the date of issue as December 1, 1943, whereas this was merely stated to be the date of withdrawal. The deputy commissioner laboured under another misconception, namely, that the "foil" of the school leaving certificate would be an exact copy of the counterfoil kept in the school. These misconceptions persisted throughout the deputy commissioner's investigations.

Throughout the investigations no indication was given to the appellant or his advocate as to what was in the mind of the deputy commissioner. Although the matters which the deputy commissioner was investigating were disclosed to the appellant before the end of the inquiry, they were disclosed at such a late stage and in such circumstances that the appellant had no real opportunity of dealing with them. The deputy commissioner did not call for documents. When the head teacher, S. Ponniah, was in the witness-box, he was virtually cross-examined by the deputy commissioner, who put to him the various matters of complaint arising out of the documents without his having the documents to refer to, or thus being able to meet the cross-examination by reference to the documents.

With regard to the communications received from the Department of Education, the deputy commissioner, having called the official who made the adverse report, ought to have called the senior official who overruled the adverse report. Having sought the opinion of the Department of Education, who were the proper authority to investigate the matter and who had investigated it, the deputy commissioner should have accepted that department's exoneration of Ponniah. The appellant's advocate having said that he did not wish to call Ponniah as no questions for clarification arose from the evidence of the inspector of schools, the deputy commissioner's failure to point out at that stage that he was not satisfied by the final conclusion of the Department of Education exonerating Ponniah was tantamount to stopping the appellant's advocate on this point, and thereby misled him.

To sum up: the investigations conducted by the deputy commissioner in the course of the hearing are referable to section 14 of the Act of 1949; the failure to give notice to the appellant of the matters investigated by the deputy commissioner deprived the **[56]** appellant of a fair opportunity to present his case and to meet the case made out on the further inquiry; in particular, the deputy commissioner obtained an adverse report from the investigating officer without the appellant's knowledge; he did not disclose to the appellant the contents of that report; he wrote to the Director of Education without the appellant's knowledge; he asked the Director of Education to get the genuineness of the document investigated without the appellant's knowledge, and finally he cross-examined the schoolmaster called by the appellant on material not disclosed to the appellant. Section 14 includes an inquiry within an inquiry. Where the deputy commissioner finds that there is a subsidiary issue which requires further inquiry, he himself must consider that further inquiry and decide upon it, so that the decision is his decision. By withholding from the appellant the points made against him in the report of the investigating officer, the deputy commissioner virtually deprived the appellant of a fair opportunity of cross-examining the witnesses on the matters which were vitally material to his case. The deputy commissioner's omission to indicate to the appellant that the adverse report of Sandarasegaram had been reversed, his suggestion to the appellant, as late as August 15, 1958, that Sandarasegaram should be summoned at the appellant's expense and his omission to tell the appellant the point he was intending to make against the appellant by calling the clerk from the Immigration Department are some of the matters which indicate that he did not appreciate the need to approach his duty judicially and to distinguish his duty as judge from his administrative functions under the Act.

Finally, the deputy commissioner, in rejecting the school leaving certificate as a forgery, was basing his conclusions upon the report made earlier by his investigating officer and by the inspector of schools, whose actual report had even now not been disclosed, and did not appear in the record of proceedings of this appeal. The deputy commissioner had acted in the proceedings as an advocate hostile to the appellant, had conducted investigations behind the appellant's back, had not given the appellant a real opportunity of dealing with the matters upon which his application was eventually refused, and in the result had founded himself upon reports and documents which the appellant had never seen, and the contents of which he had not had notice in time or circumstances which would have enabled him to meet them. He totally failed to comply with the principles of natural justice.

Montague Solomon for the respondent. The view that further **[57]** investigations could only be by means of a formal inquiry under section 14 of the Act of 1949 was based upon the premise that the duties and powers of an investigating officer and of the deputy commissioner are particularised and specified in the Act. This was a false premise. Section 19 (4) shows that the investigating officer can be assigned other duties and other functions. Section 19 (1) imposes a general duty to administer the provisions of the Act; thus the commissioner and deputy commissioner have, apart from their duty of holding inquiries under sections 9, 13 and 14, other functions ancillary and incidental thereto. For example, under section 7 (1), an applicant furnishes names of persons who have direct knowledge of the matters set out in his application; plainly the commissioner and deputy commissioner are entitled to write to them and find out whether they can give evidence about any relevant matters, and to procure their attendance. Section 15 (4) empowers the commissioner and deputy commissioner "to elicit proof concerning the matters that are investigated." This shows they have the power to make inquiries and investigations which are ancillary to the holding or conduct of a formal inquiry. Section 14 makes provision merely for one of the contingencies in which a formal inquiry may be held. It is a misconception to argue that there has to be a formal inquiry under section 14 whenever any further investigation is required.

It cannot be said that once an inquiry has started a commissioner who investigates or causes investigations to be carried out has infringed the principles of natural justice, unless it can be established that the investigations remained undisclosed throughout the proceedings so as to deny the applicant an opportunity of dealing with the matters revealed by the investigations. The proceedings in a case like the present are governed by the following principles: (1) courts, in considering whether the proceeding of a tribunal has infringed the principles of natural justice, will take cognisance of the fact that a tribunal other than a court of law is entitled to follow its own procedure; *Ridge* v. *Baldwin*[1]; the express provisions of section 15 (4) authorise a procedure other than that appropriate in a court of law: (2) in proceedings of this nature there is no prosecuting solicitor or counsel, and therefore the commissioner and deputy commissioner necessarily have to act not only as judge but also as counsel presenting the facts of the **[58]** case: (3) the onus is always on the applicant to prove his case affirmatively: s. 6 (1).

The evidence, oral and documentary, established that the documentary evidence adduced by the appellant in support of an important aspect of his case raised grave suspicion and invited thorough scrutiny such as to justify the deputy

[1] [1964] A.C. 40, 132; [1963] 2 W.L.R. 935; [1963] 2 All E.R. 66, H.L.(E.).

commissioner in making further investigation and inquiries; that the result of these further investigation and inquiries were disclosed to the appellant in the course of the proceedings and the appellant had ample opportunity to meet the matters arising from the investigation and inquiries and to adduce evidence to meet them; that there was abundant evidence before the deputy commissioner upon which he might and did found his decision and which justified him in rejecting the school leaving certificate and finding against the appellant; and that his decision was upheld by the Supreme Court.

The judgment of their Lordships was delivered by LORD GUEST. This is an appeal by special leave of the board from an order of the Supreme Court of Ceylon (de Silva J.) dismissing without reasons the appellant's appeal from an order of the Deputy Commissioner for the Registration of Indian and Pakistani Residents (referred to hereafter as "the deputy commissioner") dated September 15, 1958, refusing the appellant's application for registration as a citizen of Ceylon under the provisions of the Indian and Pakistani Residents (Citizenship) Act, No. 3 of 1949.

Under this Act, Indian or Pakistani residents may be granted the status of citizenship of Ceylon provided they fulfil certain residential qualifications. These were in the appellant's case (1) uninterrupted residence in Ceylon for 10 years prior to January 1, 1946, and (2) uninterrupted residence from January 1, 1946, till the date of the application for residence, which, in the appellant's case, was August 4, 1951. Occasional absence for less than 12 months on any one occasion does not interrupt the continuity of residence (s. 3). The application for registration is made to the commissioner under section 4 (1) of the Act. The procedure under the Act is that the commissioner refers the application for verification of the particulars to the investigating officer who makes a report to the commissioner. This report must be taken into consideration by the commissioner in dealing with the application (s. 8). If the commissioner is of opinion that a prima facie case has not been established he serves on the applicant a notice setting forth the grounds upon which the application will **[59]** be refused unless the applicant shows cause within three months of the notice. If no cause is shown, the commissioner refuses the application. If, however, cause is shown by the applicant he may hold an inquiry (s. 10). The commissioner may also hold an inquiry of his own motion (s. 14). Provisions for inquiries are contained in section 15. Subsections (3) and (4) are in the following terms:

> "(3) The commissioner shall, for the purposes of any inquiry under this Act, have all the powers of a District Court—(*a*) to summon witnesses, (*b*) to compel the production of documents, and (*c*) to administer any oath or affirmation to witnesses. (4) The proceedings at an inquiry shall as far as possible be free from the formalities and technicalities of the rules of procedure and evidence applicable to a court of law, and may be conducted by the commissioner in any manner, not inconsistent with the principles of natural justice, which to him may seem best adapted to elicit proof concerning the matters that are investigated."

At the close of the inquiry the commissioner shall either proceed as if a prima facie case for allowing an application had been made out or make an order refusing the application (s. 15 (7)). There is provision in section 16 for an appeal against an order refusing or allowing an application to the Supreme Court.

[His Lordship stated the facts set out above and continued:] It is necessary to detail quite shortly the grounds on which the deputy commissioner arrived at his decision which were given in his order. Having detailed the issues before him the deputy commissioner stated that the report of his investigating officer impelled him to make further inquiries. He detailed the evidence of S. Ponniah, the school teacher, who signed the school certificate which he found most unsatisfactory and "almost confirmed the report of the investigating officer." He then referred to the report of the Director of Education that the school schedules were not genuine and stated that Sandarasegaram, the officer who made the inquiry, confirmed the report of the Director. His order then proceeds as follows:

"Before I proceed to discuss the foregoing evidence, I should refer to a subsequent letter of the Director of Education dated May 19, 1958 (folio 160), who informed me that the Q schedules in question were genuine. On my inquiry from the director, I was informed by letter of June 20, 1958 (folio 164), that the further inquiries were made by the Assistant Secretary, Ministry of Education. I have not been informed of the reasons for making further inquiries on the basis on which this finding was **[60]** carried out. I myself might have made the inquiry but it appeared to me that no purpose would be served by doing so, especially in view of the reports earlier made by my Investigating Officer and the Inspector of Schools from which I could myself arrive at an independent decision. In fact that was the only course left to me. It appears to me from the evidence of the Inspector of Schools (folio 174) that the decision of the Assistant Secretary, Ministry of Education, to regard the Q schedules as genuine, was prompted by a meritorious record of the teacher. For my part, I would not be content to abide by that decision, and as I have stated earlier, the evidence before me is sufficient to take an independent decision."

Having considered the school teacher's evidence further he concluded that his story was a fabrication. He finally rejected the school schedules produced as not genuine and stated that the applicant had failed in his proof of residence in Ceylon between 1936 and 1943. The other matters in issue he determined in the applicant's favour except that in view of his determination of failure to prove residence from 1936 to 1943 he was unable to say that the applicant was permanently settled in Ceylon.

The deputy commissioner in fulfilling his duties under the Act occupies an anomalous position. In his position as a member of the executive he regulates the investigation into the matters into which he considers it his duty to inquire and as an officer of state he must take such steps as he thinks necessary to ascertain the truth. When conducting an inquiry under section 10, 13 or 14 he is acting in a semi-judicial capacity. In this capacity he is bound to observe the principles of natural justice (s. 15 (4)). In view of his dual position his responsibility is increased to avoid any conduct which is contrary to the rules of natural justice. These principles have often been defined and it is only necessary to state that they require that the party should be given fair notice of the case made against him and that he should be given adequate opportunity at the proper time to meet the case against him (*Ridge* v. *Baldwin*[2]).

It is against these principles that the deputy commissioner's conduct must be examined. It is noteworthy that the initial suspicion engendered in the deputy commissioner's mind was ill-founded. He thought the school certificate to be dated December 1, 1943, whereas "1.12.43" was expressly stated to be the "date of withdrawal." The freshness of the writing had in these circumstances not the same significance. The investigation therefore **[61]** started so to speak "on the wrong foot" with the deputy commissioner entertaining an erroneous suspicion against the appellant. It is not doubted that under section 15 the deputy commissioner has wide powers of inquiry and investigation not enjoyed by a judge in a civil or criminal trial, and that he is not bound to conduct the inquiry according to the normal rules of evidence. But the appellant complains that information which was obtained behind his back was in some cases not disclosed to him until the last moment and in others was never disclosed to him at all. Counsel for the appellant argued that it was unfair not to disclose the report of the investigating officer dated September 2, 1957, and that the report upon which the letter from the Director of Education dated January 20, 1958, was made should have been obtained by the deputy commissioner and disclosed to the appellant. Their Lordships consider that it would have been in accordance

[2] [1964] A.C. 40; [1963] 2 W.L.R. 935; [1963] 2 All E.R. 66, H.L.(E.).

with normal fair conduct of an inquiry that this should have been done, and what was scarcely fair to the appellant was that the school teacher, Ponniah, should have been examined, or rather cross-examined, by the deputy commissioner, who had the details of the investigation officer's report without disclosing this report to the appellant's advocate.

Such procedure made it almost impossible for the appellant's advocate, who had no direct knowledge of the terms of the report, to re-examine the witness and clear up any difficulties raised. It is also to be noted that it was apparently never put to the witness that his report was a fabrication, which was the conclusion ultimately reached by the deputy commissioner.

Their Lordships now pass to February 18, 1958, when at the conclusion of the inquiry the appellant was confronted with the opinion of the Director of Education that the Q schedule was not genuine. His advocate not unnaturally asked that the reporter should be called to give evidence. As a result, Sandarasegaram was examined by the deputy commissioner on August 29, 1958, the last day of the inquiry. In the meantime, the deputy commissioner had received information from the Director of Education that the Q schedules were considered genuine, that his previous opinion was cancelled and that this was the result of inquiries made by a senior official in the C.C.S. But Sandarasegaram's evidence proceeded on the basis of his report that the Q schedules were not genuine, and it was only at the conclusion of his evidence that the deputy commissioner read the letters from the Director of Education to the effect that the Q **[62]** schedules were genuine. It is in the light of these developments that the appellant's advocate's statements and submissions have to be considered.

The impression which would naturally have been left upon his advocate, in view of the course of the proceedings, was that the last report of the Director of Education concluded the matter of the genuineness of the Q schedules in his client's favour. By the deputy commissioner's failure to point out to him that he was by no means convinced of their genuineness and that he proposed to rely on the superseded report of Sandarasegaram, he may well have been misled into thinking that the deputy commissioner did not require any further argument or evidence on this aspect of the matter. During the whole conduct of the inquiry the appellant was never told the details of the case against the genuineness of the document and he was never given a proper opportunity of answering that case.

Counsel for the appellant claimed that the deputy commissioner should have called Mushsin to explain his reasons for concluding that the Q schedules were genuine. No doubt the appellant could have asked for him to be called. But the deputy commissioner in holding the inquiry was under a duty to ascertain the truth and in any event the appellant's advocate at that stage was under the impression that Mushsin's opinion was being accepted by the deputy commissioner. However this may be, it is apparent from the passage from the deputy commissioner's order previously quoted that he was prepared to disregard the opinion of Mushsin without hearing his evidence and to prefer the investigating officer's report and the evidence of Sandarasegaram, the inspector of schools, to the effect that the schedules were not genuine, which opinion had been cancelled by the Director of Education. In the whole circumstances their Lordships are satisfied that the appellant was not fairly treated and that the principles of natural justice were not complied with by the deputy commissioner.

Their Lordships must record their regret that they did not have the assistance of the reasons of the Supreme Court in dismissing the appeal, a decision reached, as they understand, after two days' hearing.

It follows that the order of the deputy commissioner must be quashed. Their Lordships have had to consider what further orders should be made. It would not be proper in their view upon the state of the evidence to make a finding that the appellant had **[63]** made out a prima facie case. It would, however, in their Lordships' opinion be preferable, in accordance with the usual practice in such cases, that the appellant's application should be heard by a different deputy commissioner. It will of course be for the respondent to decide whether upon the existing state of the evidence he is prepared to admit the appellant's claim or whether a further inquiry is to take place.

Their Lordships will therefore humbly advise Her Majesty that the order of the Supreme Court dated December 14, 1960, should be set aside, that the order of the deputy commissioner dated September 15, 1958, should be quashed, and that the case should be remitted to the Supreme Court for the purpose of placing de novo the appellant's application for registration before the respondent under the Indian and Pakistani Residents (Citizenship) Act, 1949.

The respondent must pay the appellant's costs before the Board and the Supreme Court.

Solicitors: *Rexworthy, Bonser & Simons; T. L. Wilson & Co.*

ii

Malayan Citizenship

LIM LIAN GEOK v. MINISTER OF THE INTERIOR, FEDERATION OF MALAYA

([1964] 1 W.L.R. 554)

February 26, 27, March 23, 1964: Judicial Committee of the Privy Council (on Appeal from the Court of Appeal of the Supreme Court of the Federation of Malaya): Lords Cohen, Evershed, Morris of Borth-y-Gest, Hodson, Donovan.

Malaya—Citizenship—Intention to deprive of—Preliminary order stating statutory ground—Validity—No necessity for detailed particulars—To be furnished at subsequent statutory inquiry—Federation of Malaya Independence Order in Council (*S.I.* 1957 *No.* 1533), *arts.* 25 (1) (*a*), 27 (1) (2).

Article 25 of the Constitution of the Federation of Malaya provides: "(1) . . . the Federal Government may by order deprive of his citizenship any person who is a citizen by registration . . . if satisfied—(a) that he has shown himself by an act or speech to be disloyal or disaffected towards the Federation; . . ."

By article 27 (1): "Before making an order under article . . . 25 . . . the Federal Government shall give the person . . . notice . . . of the ground on which the order is proposed to be made and of his right to have the case referred to a committee of inquiry under [subsection (2) of] this article."

A notice issued by the Registrar-General of citizens of the Federation of Malaya under article 27 (1) of the Constitution informed the appellant, a Chinese-born school teacher and a citizen by registration of the then Federation, that the Federal Government proposed to make an order under article 25 of the Constitution depriving him of his citizenship on the ground, specified in article 25 (1) (*a*), that he had shown himself by act and speech to be disloyal and disaffected towards the Federation. The notice proceeded to particularise the allegations against the appellant, which included "deliberate misrepresentation and inversion of Government education policy" and "emotional appeals of an extreme communal nature calculated to promote feelings of ill-will and hostility between different races in the Federation. . . ." The appellant was given one month in which to claim to have his case referred to a committee of inquiry pursuant to article 27 (2) of the Constitution. He did not do so, but by motion applied ex parte to the High Court for an order nisi prohibiting the respondent, the Minister of the Interior, from referring his case to a committee of inquiry. He contended that the allegations in the notice, even if true, could not reasonably be said to amount to disloyalty or disaffection within the meaning of articles 25 (1) (*a*). He obtained the order nisi, but it was discharged on a motion by the respondent, and that decision was affirmed on appeal:—

Held, dismissing the appellant's further appeal, that he was not entitled to the order sought by his motion. The word "ground" in article 27 (1) referred to that part of article 25 which was being invoked—that "by act or speech" he had shown **[555]** himself "to be disloyal or disaffected towards the Federation." While, where desirable, the giving of further particulars in a notice under article 27 (1) was not to be discouraged, the notice would have been effective without them—full and elaborate particulars need not at that stage be given.

It was implicit in the procedure—though not expressly so stated—that any particulars reasonably desired should be given at any inquiry held pursuant to article 27 (2) so as to enable the citizen then to make his representations (post, pp. 563, 564, 565).

Order of the Court of Appeal of the Supreme Court of the Federation of Malaya affirmed.

APPEAL (No. 23 of 1962) from a judgment and order of the Supreme Court of the Federation of Malaya, Court of Appeal at Kuala Lumpur (January 4, 1962) dismissing an appeal from a judgment and order of the High Court of Kuala Lumpur (October 13, 1961) whereby an order of prohibition nisi, made against the respondent Minister of the Interior, on the appellant's application, was discharged.

The following introductory statement is taken from the judgment of the Judicial Committee: The main question which arose in this appeal concerned the validity of a notice which was served upon the appellant and which was issued by the Registrar-General of Citizens of the Federation of Malaya and dated August 12, 1961. The notice informed the appellant that the Federal Government proposed to make an order under article 25 of the Federation of Malaya Constitution depriving him of his citizenship of the Federation of Malaya and gave him notice that unless within a period of one month from the date of serving upon him of the notice he claimed to have his case referred to a committee of inquiry the Federal Government would "proceed to make" an order. The appellant on an ex parte application to the High Court at Kuala Lumpur obtained, on September 13, 1961, an order nisi prohibiting the respondent from referring the appellant's case to a committee of inquiry under clause 2 of article 27 of the Constitution until the order nisi should be made absolute or discharged and ordering the respondent to show good cause on or before October 4, 1961, why the said prohibition should not be made absolute. On October 13, 1961, the order nisi was, on the respondent's motion, discharged by an order made by Thomson C.J. The appellant appealed to the Court of Appeal of the Supreme Court of the Federation of Malaya. By order dated January 4, 1962, the appeal was dismissed. By order of the Supreme Court of the Federation of Malaya dated May 15, 1962, the appellant was granted final leave to appeal to His Majesty the Yang di-Pertuan Agong.

1964. February 26, 27. *E. F. N. Gratiaen Q.C.* and *T. O. Kellock* for the appellant.

Lord Bledisloe Q.C. and *P. G. Clough* for the respondent. **[556]**

The following case was cited in argument: *Liversidge* v. *Anderson.*[1]

March 23. The judgment of their Lordships was delivered by Lord Morris of Borth-y-Gest, who after making the statement set out above continued: The appellant was born in China and went to Malaya in 1929. In 1951 he became by registration a citizen of the then Federation of Malaya. By reason of article 28 of the Constitution, which had the force of law as from August 31, 1957 (see S.I. 1957, No. 1533), the appellant was treated as a citizen by registration under article 17 of the Constitution.

Article 24 of the Constitution contains certain provisions enabling the Federal Government to make an order depriving a person of his citizenship if, as set out in the article, he has acquired or exercised foreign citizenship.

Article 25 of the Constitution is in the following terms: "25. (1) Subject to clause (3), the Federal Government may by order deprive of his citizenship any person who is a citizen by registration under Article 17 or a citizen by naturalisation if satisfied—(*a*) that he has shown himself by act or speech to be disloyal or disaffected towards the Federation; or (*b*) that he has, during any war in which the Federation is or was engaged, unlawfully traded or communicated with an enemy or been engaged in or associated with any business which to his knowledge was carried on in such manner as to assist an enemy in that war; or (*c*) that he has, within the period of five years beginning

[1] [1942] A.C. 206; 58 T.L.R. 35; [1941] 3 All E.R. 338, H.L.(E.).

with the date of the registration or the grant of the certificate, been sentenced in any country to imprisonment for a term of not less than twelve months or to a fine of not less than five thousand dollars or the equivalent in the currency of that country, and has not received a free pardon in respect of the offence for which he was so sentenced.

"(2) Subject to clause (3), the Federal Government may by order deprive of his citizenship any person who is a citizen by registration under Article 17 or a citizen by naturalisation if satisfied that he has been ordinarily resident in foreign countries for a continuous period of seven years and during that period has neither—(*a*) been at any time in the service of the Federation or of an international organisation of which the Federal Government was a member; nor (*b*) registered annually at a Malayan Consulate his intention to retain his citizenship.

"(3) No person shall be deprived of citizenship under this Article unless the Federal Government is satisfied that it is not conducive to the public good that that person should continue to be a citizen; and no person shall be deprived of citizenship under clause (1) if, as the result of the deprivation, he would not be a citizen of any country outside the Federation."

Article 26 of the Constitution contains provisions for deprivation of citizenship and is in the following terms: "26. (1) Subject **[557]** to clause (3), the Federal Government may by order deprive of his citizenship any citizen by registration or by naturalisation if satisfied that the registration or certificate of naturalisation—(*a*) was obtained by means of fraud, false representation or the concealment of any material fact; (*b*) was effected or granted by mistake.

"(2) Subject to clause (3), the Federal Government may by order deprive of her citizenship any woman who is a citizen by registration under clause (1) of Article 15 if satisfied that the marriage by virtue of which she was registered has been dissolved, otherwise than by death, within the period of two years beginning with the date of the marriage.

"(3) No person shall be deprived of citizenship under this Article unless the Federal Government is satisfied that it is not conducive to the public good that that person should continue to be a citizen; and no person shall be deprived of citizenship under paragraph (*b*) of clause (1) unless the notice required by Article 27 is given within the period of twelve months beginning with the date of the registration or of the grant of the certificate, as the case may be.

"(4) Except as provided by this Article, the registration of a person as a citizen or the grant of a certificate of naturalisation to any person shall not be called in question on the ground of mistake."

Article 27 prescribes certain procedure in regard to deprivation. It is in the following terms:— "27. (1) Before making an order under Article 24, 25 or 26, the Federal Government shall give to the person against whom the order is proposed to be made notice in writing informing him of the ground on which the order is proposed to be made and of his right to have the case referred to a committee of inquiry under this Article.

"(2) If any person to whom such notice is given applies to have the case referred as aforesaid the Federal Government shall, and in any other case the Federal Government may, refer the case to a committee of inquiry consisting of a chairman (being a person possessing judicial experience) and two other members appointed by that Government for the purpose.

"(3) In the case of any such reference, the committee shall hold an inquiry in such manner as the Federal Government may direct, and submit its report to that Government; and the Federal Government shall have regard to the report in determining whether to make the order."

The articles above referred to are contained in Part III of the Constitution and article 31 provided for the application of the provisions contained in the Second Schedule. Included in that Schedule are the following provisions: "1. The functions of the Federal Government under Part III shall be exercised by such Minister of that Government as the Yang di-Pertuan Agong may from time to time direct, and references in this Schedule to **[558]** the Minister shall be construed accordingly. 2. A decision of the Federal Government under Part III shall not be subject to appeal or review in any court. 6. Subject to Federal law, the Minister and the registration authority may make rules and prescribe forms for that purpose of the exercise of their respective functions under Part III and this Schedule."

The Yang di-Pertuan Agong directed that the functions of the Federal Government under Part III should be exercised by the Minister of Interior and Justice—who is the respondent. (Legal Notification (New Series) No. 33 of 1957 as amended by Legal Notification No. 40 of 1959). Pursuant to his power under 6 above the respondent did make rules, viz., Citizenship Rules, 1960 (Legal Notification 310 of 1960). Rule 3 (1) of these rules is as follows: "3. (1) The Minister may appoint a Registrar-General of Citizens of the Federation of Malaya and as many Registrars, Deputy Registrars and Assistant Registrars as he deems necessary in order to give effect to the objects of Part III of the Constitution and the Second Schedule thereto."

Rule 22 of these rules is as follows: "22. The notice given by the Federal Government to a person against whom the deprivation order is proposed to be made under the provisions of Article 27 of the Constitution shall be in the form Q set out in the Schedule to these Rules."

The notice that was served upon the appellant was undoubtedly in the prescribed form. The prescribed "Form Q" concluded with a space for the signature of the "Registrar-General of Citizens of the Federation of Malaya." The notice read as follows: "To Mr. Lim Lian Geok alias Lim Chai Koo of 52/2, Jalan Raja Muda Musa, Kampong Bahru, Kuala Lumpur. WHEREAS it has been represented to the Federal Government that you LIM LIAN GEOK a Citizen of the Federation of Malaya, have shown yourself, since 1957, by act and speech to be disloyal and disaffected towards the Federation of Malaya, in that you did make: (*a*) deliberate misrepresentation and inversion of Government education policy in a manner calculated to excite disaffection against the Yang di-Pertuan Agong and the Government of the Federation: and (*b*) emotional appeals of an extreme communal nature calculated to promote feelings of ill-will and hostility between different races in the Federation likely to cause violence. AND WHEREAS the Federal Government proposes to make an Order under Article 25 of the Federation of Malaya Constitution depriving you of your citizenship of the Federation of Malaya. NOW, THEREFORE, I Ibrahim bin Ali, the Registrar-General of Citizens of the Federation of Malaya acting on behalf of the Federal Government DO HEREBY GIVE YOU NOTICE that unless within one calendar month from the date of service upon you of this notice, you inform me in writing that you claim that your case be referred to a committee of inquiry constituted for that purpose by the Federal Government under article 27 (2) of the said Constitution, **[559]** the Federal Government will proceed to make the Order of depriving you of your citizenship of the Federation of Malaya. Dated this 12th day of August, 1961. Registrar-General of Citizens to the Federation of Malaya. (SEAL)"

The notice was served upon the appellant by registered post on August 14, 1961. He did not make claim, within the period of one month thereafter, to have his case referred to a committee of inquiry. What he did, as already stated, was to apply ex parte for an order prohibiting the respondent from referring the case to a committee of inquiry. His notice of motion was dated September 12, 1961. He had previously, i.e., on September 5, written a letter to the Registrar-General of Citizens saying that he was advised that the power to deprive of citizenship was vested in the Minister alone who had no power to delegate that function to any other official or authority: in his letter the appellant asked that the notice should be withdrawn and a proper notice served if it was the Federal Government's intention to deprive him of his citizenship. To that letter a reply had been sent on September 6, 1961, pointing out that the notice that had been served was a notice which was in accord with rule 22. The appellant was also reminded of the fact that the period of one month ran from August 14.

The appellant's notice of motion set out two reasons for his application for an order prohibiting the Minister from referring the case to a committee of inquiry under article 27 (2). The first was that it was not competent for the

Registrar-General to issue the notice that he purported to have issued under rule 22 of the Citizenship Rules. This reason was based upon the view that there had been a delegation by the Minister of his powers to a Registrar-General and that there could not be any such delegation. The second reason was that the allegations made as to the basis for the notice of August 12, 1961, were not, assuming them to be true, "a sufficient compliance with the requirements of paragraph (*a*) of article 25 (1) of the Constitution." It is to be noted that the reference was to article 25 and not to article 27. The complaint appears to have been, not that the particulars given in the notice of August 12, 1961, were insufficient, but that, assuming the truth of what was alleged in the particulars, the Federal Government could not on that basis have been satisfied that the appellant had shown himself by act or speech to be disloyal or disaffected towards the Federation. The complaint, therefore, was not that inadequate particulars had been given but that the weight of the allegations was inadequate to prove disloyalty or disaffection towards the Federation. The complaint was that the particulars lacked substance and not that they lacked detailed statement. Paragraph 6 of the appellant's affidavit in support of his notice of motion was as follows: "6. I am further advised that the acts and conduct alleged against me, as being the cause of the proposed deprivation of my citizenship are not in their very statement capable of falling within para (a) of Article 25 (1) **[560]** and the notice therefore, even assuming it was issued by the proper authority, is not in its content sufficient for the exercise by the Federal Government of its powers under the Constitution."

On the appellant's ex parte application, Ong J. made an order nisi of prohibition on September 13, 1961. Until the order was either made absolute or discharged the respondent was "prohibited from referring the case of the above-named applicant to a committee of inquiry under Article 27 (2) of the Constitution."

The respondent gave notice of motion (dated September 18, 1961) to have the order nisi of prohibition discharged. Included in the grounds for the motion were that: (*a*) the notice issued "by the Registrar-General of Citizens was in the form prescribed by and upon the instructions of the Minister of the Interior and was in compliance with the requirements of Article 27 of the Constitution; (*b*) the grounds shown in the notice are a sufficient compliance with the requirements of paragraph (*a*) of Clause (1) of Article 25 of the Constitution." In an affidavit in support of his motion the respondent said that upon his own decision he had caused the notice of August 12, 1961, to be sent and that the notice (in the form prescribed by him in rule 22 of the Citizenship Rules 1960) had been sent to the appellant by the Registrar-General of Citizens of the Federation of Malaya, a civil servant in the respondent's Ministry.

No challenge was made as to the truth of what the respondent said. It would seem to follow that no further reliance could be placed by the appellant upon the first of his two reasons above referred to for applying for an order of prohibition. It was clear that the notice of August 12, 1961, was not signed by the Registrar-General in the purported exercise of any powers delegated to him.

In his affidavit the respondent, whose good faith was in no way challenged, further said: "I am satisfied that the act and speech of the applicant justify my decision to proceed under Article 27 of the Federal Constitution." The appellant in an affidavit in reply dated October 2, 1961, said that he was born in China and that when he went to Malaya in 1929 he had qualified at Amoy in China as a Chinese school teacher. He set out, inter alia, his record as a teacher and in the field of education. He said that he had actively taken part in public debates and discussions relating to Chinese education and the Government policy thereon but that he had not taken part in any other public activity nor had acted in any way suggestive of disloyalty or disaffection to the Government. He said that he had always striven to instil a sense of loyalty to the country in Chinese students and had always urged their learning the national language as a means of promoting unity among the several races in the country. He said that his speeches in that connection had been repeatedly broadcast by Radio Malaya.

It is to be observed that the appellant, possibly because of his **[561]** mistaken belief that there had been some unauthorised delegation of power to the Registrar-General, allowed the period of one month to pass by from August 14 without claiming to have his case referred to a committee of inquiry. It is further to be observed that there does not appear to have been (down to October, 1961) any request for further information or any suggestions that the appellant was or had been in any sort of difficulty by reason of any lack of fuller particularity in the notice of August 12. The submission was made, among others, that if the allegations set out under (*a*) and (*b*) of the notice of August 12 were made out in fact, they did not amount to and furthermore were incapable of amounting to proof of disloyalty or disaffection within the meaning of Article 25.

After hearing argument on October 4 and 5 Thomson C.J. by a judgment delivered on October 13, 1961, discharged the order nisi. In considering article 25 (1) (*a*) he said that the Minister must have certain grounds of fact in his mind: that these grounds must consist of acts or speech: that the person against whom the order is proposed to be made should be informed what the grounds are: and that the grounds of fact should be capable, if made out, of showing, as a matter of law, disloyalty or disaffection towards the Federation. He said that the question (under article 25 (3)) whether or not it was conducive to the public good that the person concerned should continue to be a citizen would arise for decision if it was made out that there had been acts or speeches which showed disloyalty or disaffection.

It is clear from the judgment of the Chief Justice that the main question which was argued before him was whether the grounds as stated in the notice of August 12, 1961, were such as to be capable in law of showing disloyalty or disaffection. There is no reference to any question as to whether the notice was deficient as being lacking in adequate particularity. Though the Chief Justice appears to have proceeded on the assumption that an inquiry was going to be held or had to be held (whereas article 27 (2) only obliges the Federal Government to refer a case if the person concerned applies to have it referred, the matter being otherwise in the discretion of the Federal Government) the basis of his view is not as a result invalidated. His view in effect was that the grounds as stated in the notice of August 12, 1961 were capable in law, if made out, of showing disloyalty or disaffection. It does not appear that at the hearing before the Chief Justice there was consideration of any differentiation between the grounds on which a deprivation order is proposed and particulars of such grounds.

The appellant then appealed to the Court of Appeal. It appears from the memorandum of appeal that it was still being maintained that there had been a delegation of powers by the respondent to the Registrar-General. Among the grounds of appeal it was said that the Chief Justice ought to have held that both in its form and in its content the notice was bad in law and that "the matters of **[562]** complaint stated therein, even assuming them to be true, were not such as to be capable of attracting the altogether excessive penalty of deprivation of citizenship, having regard to the provisions of Article 25 of the Constitution." It was further said in the grounds of appeal that the Chief Justice ought to have held "that the Minister's affidavit not having condescended to any particulars setting out the facts and circumstances on the faith of which he attained the requisite satisfaction" it was not possible to say whether there were good grounds or any grounds for such satisfaction. It is to be observed that the reference just quoted was to the Minister's affidavit and not to the notice of August 12, 1961. Among other matters raised in the memorandum of appeal it was said that "in any event the second ground stated in the notice" was by itself incapable of providing the required satisfaction on the part of the Minister because it alleged criminal offences against him which, if proved, would have no more effect than to render him liable to punishment in accordance with the law. It is to be observed that the matters referred to under (*b*) in the notice were treated as being a "ground" on which the proposed order was to be made.

After hearing argument on December 14, 1961, the Court of Appeal (Hill J.A.,

Good J.A., Hepworth J.) gave judgment on January 4, 1962, dismissing the appeal. In his judgment Hill J.A. held that there had not either in fact or in law been any delegation of the Minister's functions. He held that all that article 27 (1) requires is that the notice should state the ground on which an order is proposed so that the requirement involved setting out, for example, whether it was ground (*a*) or ground (*b*) or ground (*c*) as respectively referred to in article 25 (1), but did not involve or necessitate the giving of particulars or details or circumstances or allegations as in fact had been done in the notice of August 12, 1961, under the headings (*a*) and (*b*) Though he felt that what was set out under those headings in the notice could have been more happily worded, he considered that the appellant was in fact left in no sort of doubt and was in fact clearly and unequivocally informed by the notice that the "ground" on which the Federal Government proposed to make the order was ground (*a*) of article 25 (1).

In his judgment, agreeing with that of Hill J.A., Good J.A., pointed out that "ground" (*a*) of article 25 (1) involved that a person might be deprived of citizenship by reason either of his actions or his words where such actions or words had shown him to be either disloyal or disaffected towards the Federation. He said that at the stage of the issue of a notice the only purpose for which the supervisory jurisdiction of the court could be invoked was to ascertain whether the essential preliminary steps had been properly taken according to law. He said: "The Government is not yet committed to depriving the appellant of his citizenship: it has only announced its intention of doing so if the appellant does not within a specified time claim that his case be referred **[563]** to a committee of inquiry as provided by article 27." He held that the making and issuing of the notice was the Minister's own act and not that of the Registrar-General. He held that the notice was not invalidated so long as it gave, at that stage, sufficient notice of the ground upon which the Government proposed to rely: he said that "it would have been sufficient if the notice had merely informed the appellant that it was proposed to deprive him of his citizenship on the ground of acts (or speech) showing him to be disloyal (or disaffected) towards the Federation. Anything further is surplusage, but there could be no misunderstanding in the mind of any person reading the contents of the notice that what was intended was deprivation on ground (*a*) in Article 25 (1). In my opinion that is sufficient. The particular allegations will emerge at the inquiry if the appellant elects to ask for one. This is nowhere explicitly stated, but it is implicit in the procedure: there cannot be an inquiry unless there is something to inquire into, and it cannot be a proper inquiry unless the appellant is told what is alleged against him."

Hepworth J. agreed with the judgments of the President and of Good J.A.

Their Lordships have reached the conclusion that the Court of Appeal were correct in dismissing the appeal and that the appellant was not entitled to the order which, by his motion, he had sought. Before their Lordships it was not argued that the notice was in any way invalid because it was signed by the Registrar-General and it was no longer contended that there had been any delegation by the Minister. The main submissions which were presented to their Lordships related to the content and form of the notice. It was said that the notice was defective because it was lacking in particulars. It was said that before a person could or ought to be called upon to decide whether he would claim to have his case referred to a committee of inquiry he should be informed in the notice as to the details of what was alleged against him. It was furthermore submitted that the notice, though purporting to follow a prescribed form, was in disregard of the rules of natural justice and expressed an unwarranted threat or indication. It was additionally submitted that though the particulars contained in the notice were inadequate they revealed the general nature of the complaints and that, even if the complaints were true, they could not reasonably be said to amount to disloyalty or disaffection within the meaning of those words in article 25 (1) (*a*).

It is to be observed that article 27 is a procedure article. Orders of deprivation of citizenship may be made under article 24 or 25 or 26. The procedure under article 27 relates to the preceding three articles. Under the provisions of these three articles there are many and varied circumstances under which the Federal Government if satisfied as to any of them may make an order. Thus if a citizen after Merdeka Day had by voluntary and formal act acquired the citizenship of a country outside the Federation the **[564]** provisions of article 24 might be brought into play. By way of further example if a citizen had obtained a certificate of naturalisation by means of fraud the provisions of article 26 might apply. Other circumstances are covered by those two articles. Various circumstances are covered by article 25, such as unlawful trading with an enemy during a war or being sentenced (as specified in the article) to a term of imprisonment. The scheme of the article seems therefore to be that in certain circumstances the Federal Government may make an order of deprivation of citizenship but may only do so if certain conditions are fulfilled. In the present case it is quite clear that the provisions of article 25 (1) (*a*) are the primarily operative ones. There is no suggestion that the circumstances contemplated in article 25 (1) (*b*) or (*c*) existed nor those indicated by articles 24 and 26. In the present case the stage of actually making a deprivation could not be reached unless the Federal Government (whose functions are to be exercised by the Minister directed to exercise them) was satisfied (1) that the appellant had shown himself by act or speech to be disloyal or disaffected towards the Federation and (2) that it was not conducive to the public good that the appellant should continue to be a citizen and (3) that deprivation would not have the consequential result that the appellant would not be a citizen of any country outside the Federation. No question arises in this case under (3), and it has been common ground as regards (2) that a decision as to whether it would not be conducive to the public good that the appellant should continue to be a citizen is purely a policy decision for the Government. It is in regard to (1) that the issues arise in the present case. The machinery and procedure laid down by article 27 apply in reference to the process of being satisfied in regard to one or more of the grounds for deprivation which are set out in articles 24, 25, 26. It is not suggested that the machinery of giving a notice applies as such to the question whether a deprivation would be conducive to the public good. The provisions of article 25 (3) and of article 26 (3) do not contain grounds for deprivation but contain conditions to which regard must be had before an order is made.

As regards being satisfied that a person has shown himself by act or speech to be disloyal or disaffected towards the Federation, it would seem clear that if the Federal Government received information to which they gave no credence then no further question would arise. If, on the other hand, the information as to the act or speech of a person seemed to the Government to establish disloyalty or disaffection, the Government would in the first place only be satisfied as to this in a conditional or provisional way. Article 27 would then come into play. A notice must be given informing the person "of the ground on which the order is proposed to be made and of his right to have the case referred to a committee of inquiry." In agreement with the Court of Appeal, their Lordships consider that the word "ground" in article 27 refers to that part (or those parts) of article 24 or 25 **[565]** or 26 which is (or are) being invoked. In the present case the appellant was informed by the notice that (according to what had been represented to the Government) he had shown himself by act and speech to be disloyal and disaffected towards the Federation of Malaya. That was "the ground." What followed, under the headings (*a*) and (*b*), consisted of particulars of the "ground" which had been previously stated. In holding, as their Lordships do, that the notice would have been effective even if the particulars had not been included, their Lordships do not wish in any way to discourage the giving of particulars in a notice whenever it is thought to be desirable to give them. Their Lordships cannot, however, accede to the submission that full and elaborate particulars must at that stage be given or that a person concerned cannot without them decide whether to exercise his right to have his case referred. If there is an inquiry (which might come about either because a person concerned required one or because the Government decided to have one) then the necessity for giving particulars might arise. Though there are no express provisions which require that any particulars that are reasonably desired should at that stage be given, their Lordships agree that the view expressed by Good J.A., that it is implicit in the procedure that this should be so. If an inquiry is held, it will be presided over by a chairman (possessing legal experience) sitting with two appointed members. The committee will report and thereafter "the Federal Government shall have regard to the report in determining whether to make the order." This involves that the citizen concerned is to have every reasonable and proper opportunity to deal with the "ground" (or "grounds") on which a deprivation order is proposed. This in turn involves that he must have such reasonable information as he may seek to have in regard to the case against him so as to enable him to deal with it or to answer it or to make such representations in regard to it as he may wish. There would not be a proper inquiry if the citizen concerned was denied such particulars as he might need to have or as he might reasonably request in order to be able to protect his interests.

The fact that in the event of an inquiry being held the Federal Government is to have regard to the report of the inquiry "in determining whether to make" an order shows that any provisional conclusions which may have been formed after receiving information as to any of the "grounds" for a deprivation order must remain provisional until after the receipt of a report or until after it is known that no inquiry is to be held. Only then, under article 25, can the complete stage of "satisfaction" as denoted by article 25 (1) be reached. The making of an order requires that additionally there must be satisfaction, in the manner hereinbefore mentioned, concerning the matters referred to in article 25 (3). It must be pointed out, however, that a citizen concerned cannot safely neglect the opportunity which is presented to him when a notice under article 27 (1) is given to him. If he decides **[566]** to ignore such a notice their Lordships see nothing in the Constitution which obliges the Federal Government to give him some later or further or different opportunity to be heard. The Constitution prescribes a form of procedure which seems reasonable and fair and just. A citizen could not spurn his proferred right to have an inquiry and then later complain, if a deprivation order were made, that the Federal Government could not properly have been satisfied because he had not been heard.

In the light of what has been said above their Lordships can deal shortly with the submission that the wording of the prescribed Form Q is open to the objection that it offends the rules of natural justice because it announces a result that would have not been reached by proper process. It was said that its concluding words to the effect that unless an inquiry was claimed the Government "will proceed to make the order depriving you of your citizenship of the Federation of Malaya" were minatory in tone and unfortunate in expression. Their Lordships consider, however, that in the context of the notice as a whole the words are not calculated to mislead. It cannot reasonably be said that the Government are announcing settled conclusions which will not be affected even if there is an inquiry. Nor do the words bear the meaning that the Government will proceed to make an order whether or not they are "satisfied" as required by the articles in question. The notice denotes that following upon the receipt of representations the Federal Government are proposing to make an order or, in other words, have reached the stage of being provisionally satisfied as to certain things. There is nothing in the notice, however, which in any way suggests that the spirit and the letter of the relevant articles in the Constitution are not being or will not be followed. The statement that if an inquiry is not claimed the Federal Government will proceed to make an order does not involve that they will proceed in any irregular manner or in defiance of any requirement of law or otherwise than in due and proper course.

The further contention that was advanced was that the matter set out under headings (*a*) and (*b*) of the notice, even if true, could not reasonably be said to amount to disloyalty or disaffection. Their Lordships cannot accept this. The complaint was that the appellant had "shown" himself by act and speech to be disloyal and disaffected. All, therefore, that their Lordships have to decide is whether such conduct as is denoted under the headings (*a*) and (*b*) was capable of demonstrating disloyalty or disaffection. If there were an inquiry much would depend upon the details and circumstances, but their Lordships cannot hold that the allegations denoted by the wording under headings (*a*) and (*b*) were not capable of warranting the view that a person had shown himself by act and speech to be disloyal and disaffected towards the Federation.

For the reasons which have been stated their Lordships cannot accept the submissions made on behalf of the appellant. Though **[567]** he could have claimed an inquiry but did not do so, and though he took legal action which has wholly failed and though his time for claiming an inquiry has long since gone by, the respondent has stated that he will, if so requested in writing by the appellant within one calendar month after the conclusion of this appeal, himself refer the case to a committee of inquiry.

Their Lordships will therefore report to the Head of Malaysia their opinion that the appeal should be dismissed and that the appellant should pay the respondent his costs of this appeal.

Solicitors: *Graham Page & Co.; Wray, Smith & Co.*

C.

ALIENS

1

ADMISSION

REGINA v. SECRETARY OF STATE FOR HOME AFFAIRS EX PARTE SOBLEN

([1963] 1 Q.B. 829)

July 17, 18, 1962: Queen's Bench Division: Lord Parker C.J., Winn, Widgery JJ.
July 26, 1962: Court of Appeal: Lord Denning M.R., Donovan, Pearson L.JJ.

Alien—Landing or embarkation—Airport—Leave to land—Meaning—Hospital treatment required to save alien's life—Acquiescence of immigration authority in landing subject to continuous police supervision—Service of notice of refusal of landing permission after unavoidable delay—Effect—Aliens Order, 1953 (*S.I.* 1953, *No.* 1671), *arts.* 1, 8 (4).

Immigration authorities, knowing of the intended arrival at London Airport of an alien, prepared a notice of refusal of leave to land expressed to be on the grounds of article 1 (1) of the Aliens Order, 1953.[1] Before the aircraft landed, the alien inflicted severe **[830]** wounds upon himself with the object of making it necessary for him to be landed in England. The pilot sent a radio message, as a result of which an ambulance and doctor were available at landing on July 1, 1962. The doctor and an immigration officer boarded the aircraft at about the same time, the immigration officer having with him, and intending to serve on the alien, the notice of refusal of leave to land. The immigration officer took the view that the alien was in such a physical condition that he was incapable of appreciating any communication of the refusal, and therefore the notice was not then served on him, but similar notices were served on another passenger claiming the alien as his prisoner and on the owners of the aircraft. The doctor took the view that there was a real danger of death if the alien was not at once removed to hospital, and he was conveyed

[1] Aliens Order, 1953. art. 1: "(1) Subject to the provisions of this order, an alien shall not land . . . in the United Kingdom except with the leave of an immigration officer, . . ."

Art. 8: "(1) Where leave to land is refused to an alien, an immigration officer may, subject to paragraph (2) of this article, give directions . . . (2) No directions shall be given under this article in respect of an alien after the expiration of two months from the date on which he last arrived in the United Kingdom. . . . (4) An alien to whom leave to land is refused may be detained, under the authority of an immigration officer, pending the giving of directions in his case under paragraph (1) of this article and pending his removal in pursuance of directions so given; and where any such alien is on board a ship or aircraft he may, under the like authority, be removed therefrom for detention under this paragraph."

Art. 25: "(1) If any person acts in contravention of, or fails to comply with, any provision of this order or of any order made or conditions imposed or directions given thereunder, he shall be guilty of an offence against this order. . . ."

Art. 29: "Any power conferred by this order to make orders or give directions shall include power to revoke or vary such orders or directions."

Art. 31: ". . . (2) . . . 'leave to land', except where the context otherwise requires, means leave to land in the United Kingdom granted under article 1 of this order. . . ."

there by the ambulance under the supervision of a police constable and with the knowledge and acquiescence of the immigration authorities. The alien's condition had somewhat improved on the following day when an immigration officer sought, but was refused, permission to see him in order to serve the notice; however, on the third day, July 3, 1962, it was served on and read to him. Very early on the sixth day successful application was made on behalf of the alien for a writ of habeas corpus. Before it was served the immigration authorities signed an authority for his detention as an alien to whom leave to land had been refused under article 8 (4) of the Aliens Order. The alien, still under the supervision of the police, was transferred to the prison hospital. The alien contended that what in fact happened at the airport constituted an implied grant to him of leave to land, and that the notice of refusal of leave to land could not form the basis of any authority of detention under article 8 (4) since that could be made only if leave to land had been refused.

The Divisional Court of the Queen's Bench Division discharged the writ, holding that leave to land, in the relevant sense, had not been impliedly granted to the alien and that the refusal to grant leave had been validly communicated. The alien appealed:—

Held, (1) that on the facts there was no ground for any implication that the alien was given leave to land in the relevant sense of **[831]** landing as a free man, free to move about in this country, either subject to conditions or not.

(2) That it was not necessary that leave to land should be granted or refused to an alien immediately on arrival in this country, but it might be in suspense. In the present case leave was refused on July 3.

(3) That the immigration officer was entitled to direct that the alien should be detained, and that he was, accordingly, detained lawfully.

Decision of Divisional Court of the Queen's Bench Division, post, p. 833; [1962] 2 All E.R. 373, affirmed.

Application for writ of habeas corpus.

The applicant, Robert Soblen, was born in Lithuania and lived there and in other places practising as a doctor of medicine until 1941. Thereafter he lived in the United States of America. In 1961 he was tried in New York State and on July 13 he was found guilty on two charges of conspiracy to obtain information valuable to a foreign power (the Soviet Union) and of conspiracy to hand over such information. On August 7, 1961, he was sentenced to life imprisonment but pending an appeal he was released on bail in the sum of $100,000. He appealed to the United States Court of Appeals for the Second Circuit and his appeal was dismissed on March 13, 1962. He and others submitted briefs for the consideration of the Supreme Court and they were rejected on June 25, 1962. He was then still on bail, and heard that the Supreme Court had rejected the briefs at 4 p.m. on June 25, 1962. At 9 o'clock that night he flew to Tel Aviv from the Idlewild Airport using the passport of a deceased brother of his. He landed in Tel Aviv, but a few days later, on July 1, a Sunday, he was removed from the State of Israel. He was taken first to Athens on a specially chartered aircraft of the El Al (The Israeli State) Airline, and there he was transferred to a regular aircraft of the same airline flying on commercial routes. This aircraft was due to stop at London en route for New York. About 20 minutes out of London he inflicted severe wounds upon himself with a knife. He said subsequently that his object was to make it necessary for him to be landed in England. He inflicted upon his wrist a longitudinal cut and he cut his abdomen, ripping through the skin and the belly muscles. The captain of the aircraft communicated with London Airport and asked for an ambulance to be ready when the aircraft landed. A Dr. Miller came with an ambulance and at the same time an immigration officer, Hargreaves, came to the **[832]** aircraft. Hargreaves had with him, already prepared, a notice refusing any permission for the alien to land in England. The form was dated July 1, 1962, and read: "Leave to land has been refused to Robert Soblen of doubtful nationality[2]

[2] It subsequently appeared that he became a nationalised citizen of the United States of America in 1947 and had not been deprived of that citizenship.

brought to the port of London Airport" in an aircraft, and directions were given that he was to be removed by the aircraft by which he arrived. When the aircraft arrived, Hargreaves was not able to serve the notice upon him because of the condition of the applicant at that time. Hargreaves said in evidence that the applicant was either unconscious, or at least in such a physical condition that he was incapable of appreciating himself any communication of the refusal of leave to land. So Hargreaves served the notice of refusal of leave on a United States marshal, one McShane, who was in attendance on the applicant; and as soon as he could he also served on the owners of the aircraft notice of the refusal to land. But he did not serve it on the applicant because he was not in a condition then, owing to the injuries which he had inflicted upon himself, to receive any legal notice of any kind. And indeed the condition of the applicant at that time was such that, in the opinion of Dr. Miller at the airport, it was essential, in order to save his life, that he should be removed at once to hospital. He was removed, accordingly, to Hillingdon Hospital, where the surgeon, Duncan, said it was a case of saving his life that he was brought to hospital. He was given blood transfusions that day and eventually, not on the Sunday or Monday, but on the Tuesday, he was in a position to receive a legal notice. At 9 o'clock on the Tuesday morning, July 3, an immigration officer attended and served him with notice refusing him leave to land. That was the earliest moment at which he was fit to receive a notice. On July 6 he was sufficiently well to be able to be taken to an aircraft (in accordance with the undertaking which the airline had given) to be taken to New York. But before that could happen, very early in the morning he applied to Mocatta J. for a writ of habeas corpus claiming his freedom and saying his detention was unjustified.

Mocatta J., on counsel undertaking that the facts stated by him would be put on affidavit, ordered the issue of a writ of habeas corpus ad subjiciendum directed to the Secretary of State for Home Affairs returnable to the Divisional Court of the Queen's Bench Division on July 17, 1962. [**833**]

Before that writ was served, on the morning of July 6, authority for the alien's detention was signed pursuant to article 8 (4) of the Aliens Order, 1953. It was headed as from Her Majesty's immigration office at London Airport and read: "Robert Soblen. The above-named being an alien to whom leave to land has been refused, I have authorised his detention under article 8 (4) of the Aliens Order, 1953. A copy of the refusal of leave to land notice is attached. I accordingly request you to see the said alien pending the completion of arrangements for dealing with him under article 8 of the order." It was signed by one of the chief immigration officers and was addressed to the commissioners of police of the metropolis and the governor of Her Majesty's prison at Brixton. As stated in that authority there was attached another copy of the form setting out the refusal to allow landing (Home Office Form 1B31). The directions in the form served on the alien differed from the directions in the copy form attached to the authority for detention. The latter was relied on in the return to the writ of habeas corpus, referred to below, as authority for the alien's detention in Brixton prison.

The return to the writ was made by Karlo Bruce Paice, an assistant Under-Secretary of State, on behalf of the Home Secretary. It certified that on July 6, 1962, the applicant was taken to Brixton prison, and had since been detained there under and by virtue of the authority of an immigration officer issued on instructions which he, Paice, on July 6, had given on behalf of the Home Secretary.

F. Elwyn Jones Q.C. and *Peter Solomon* for the applicant.

Sir John Hobson Q.C., A.-G. and *J. R. Cumming-Bruce* for the Secretary of State for Home Affairs.

The following cases, in addition to those cited in the judgment, were referred to in argument: *Liversidge* v. *Anderson*[3]; *Kuchenmeister* v. *Home Office*.[4]*

[3] [1942] A.C. 206; 58 T.L.R. 35; [1941] 3 All E.R. 338, H.L.
[4] [1958] 1 Q.B. 496; [1958] 2 W.L.R. 453; [1958] 1 All E.R. 485.

LORD PARKER C.J. In these proceedings Mr. Elwyn Jones moves for the discharge of one Robert Soblen, now detained in Her Majesty's prison at Brixton, in respect of whom a writ of habeas corpus was issued on the order of Mocatta J.

[His Lordship stated the facts and the articles of the Aliens **[834]** Order, 1953, and continued:] The applicant's main contention is that article 8 (4) authorises the detention of an alien only when the alien has been refused leave to land; that the refusal of leave to land served on July 8 cannot form the basis for any authority for his detention, since he had been granted leave to land on July 1. The applicant recognises that all that was done at London Airport was done, and undoubtedly done, in his own interests and for the purpose of saving his life, but nevertheless he says that in fact what happened at London Airport amounted to a granting to him of leave to land. Accordingly, if in those circumstances he was to be removed from this country, then some different machinery, the deportation machinery, alone would be available.

It seems to me that the first question that arises is whether he was granted leave to land within the meaning of article 1 (1) of the order. Several things are, I think, clear with regard to that article. First, it seems to me clear that the grant of leave envisaged under that article is not merely the grant of leave to land physically, but involves the grant of leave to land and go as a free man anywhere in this country or subject to such conditions as are imposed. Secondly —perhaps it is looking at it in the same way— the mere acquiescence in the physical landing of an alien is not enough, there must be something which amounts to the grant of leave to him to go as a free man throughout the country. Thirdly, no provision is made for the giving of notice, written or otherwise, providing for the grant of leave to land. Whether leave has been granted or not in any particular case must depend upon all circumstances of the case, the object of investigation being to see whether there has been a grant of leave given either expressly or impliedly. Lastly, I think it is important to bear in mind what Lord Greene M.R. said in *Rex* v. *Governor of Brixton Prison; Ex parte Lannoy*.[5]* This is a useful judgment on a number of points, in particular as to what he said[6] about the approach to article 1 (1): "Under article 1 (1) (*a*) landing without leave is prohibited. The giving of leave is merely the lifting of this prohibition. The refusal of leave is merely an intimation that the prohibition will not be lifted."

In these circumstances, it is necessary to see from all the circumstances, there being no express grant here of leave to land, **[835]** whether a grant can be implied. The position at London Airport was this: here was a man in urgent need of medical treatment, thought to be dying. When notice had been given to London Airport as to the imminent arrival of the aeroplane, Hargreaves, one of the immigration officers, was instructed to board the aircraft and to refuse the applicant leave to land. He had prepared notices of refusal and, armed with those notices, he went on board at about the same time as Dr. Miller. He said that when he went on board he took the view that the applicant "was either unconscious or at least in such a physical condition that he was incapable himself of appreciating any communication to him of my refusal of leave to land." He went on to say: "I served notice of refusal of leave to Soblen to land upon the said McShane [the United States marshal] who claimed to be in charge of Soblen. As soon as was practicable I served upon the owners of the aircraft, El Al Israel Airline, notice of refusal of leave to Soblen to land in the form of Home Office Form, 1B31." There is a dispute on the evidence as to the exact condition of the applicant. The applicant himself said that he was conscious, that at all times he could have understood if any notice of refusal had been given to him and, indeed, he said that he talked to Dr. Miller. For my part, I unhesitatingly prefer the evidence of the immigration officer, Hargreaves, as to his condition, supported as it undoubtedly is by the evidence of Dr. Miller.

On the same day the immigration officer obtained from the airline an undertaking "to remove [the applicant] from the United Kingdom at the earliest

[5] [1942] 2 K.B. 281; 58 T.L.R. 350; sub nom. *R.* v. *Lannoy* [1942] 2 All E.R. 232, C.A.

[6] [1942] 2 K.B. 281, 285.

opportunity in accordance with article 8 (1) (*b*) or 8 (1) (*c*) of the order under arrangements to be notified to and approved by you." Undoubtedly, therefore, the authorities at London Airport were minded to refuse leave and were doing all they could do to communicate that refusal to the applicant. There followed the attempts of an immigration officer, Saunders, to see the applicant on July 2, and finally when he got leave to interview the applicant on July 3 he served the notice of refusal. Thereafter, the authority of detention was made as soon as the applicant was ready to leave the hospital, and throughout the whole period from the moment he landed till the moment he went to Brixton Prison he was under the supervision of a police constable.

In those circumstances I find it quite impossible to imply a grant of leave to land in the sense I have indicated. The evidence points all the other way, that there never was any **[836]** intention to grant such leave, and that he was merely allowed to land physically for the purpose of saving his life.

The fact, as I find, that he was not granted leave to land of course is not an end of the matter because article 8 (4) depends upon refusal. It is true that the refusal was not communicated until July 3, but, in my judgment, such a refusal is a perfectly valid refusal if it is communicated so soon as is reasonably practicable. Owing to the applicant's condition it was clearly impracticable to serve him with any notice of refusal until July 3, when it was done. The Attorney-General has raised an alternative contention that no communication of a refusal is necessary. I should hesitate to come to that conclusion. I should only do so after further argument on the matter. So far as this case is concerned, I find it unnecessary to deal with that point.

A further point was taken by Mr. Elwyn Jones, a point that I am afraid I still do not fully understand. It is really an alternative, and it is something to this effect: that article 8 (4) can only come into force when there has been a refusal; that a refusal can only be given to somebody who is in breach of article 1 (1) of the order; that article 1 (1) of the order coupled with article 25 makes landing without leave an offence; that here the applicant never intended to land without leave, he was landed involuntarily without leave, and accordingly he himself, applying ordinary principles of criminal law, was not committing an offence. I imagine the argument continues that if he was not committing an offence and not contravening article 1 (1), he could not be the subject of a notice of refusal. I confess I do not pretend to have fully understood it. As stated, I should have thought myself it contained a non sequitur, and in any event I take the view that this applicant, as he himself said, did what he did with the sole object of being landed, and that that was his object regardless of whether he was refused or granted permission to land.

Finally, if it is necessary, I would rely on *Rex* v. *Larsonneur*,[7]* and, indeed, *Rex* v. *Governor of Brixton Prison, Ex parte Lannoy*,[8]* for the proposition that a contravention of article 1 (1) was an absolute offence and did not depend upon mens rea.

Finally, an argument was put before this court based on the documents themselves and, in particular, on the fact that the notice of refusal attached to the authority of detention differs from the notice of refusal which was served on the applicant. They bear different stamps of different immigration officers, and **[837]** the directions in the two notices differ, but in my judgment those matters cannot affect the validity of the refusal itself. Directions can be given at any time within two months of landing. They need not be given at the time of refusal. They can be varied at any time, and the mere fact that those notices contain different directions cannot, I think, invalidate the refusal which is contained in them, nor, indeed, can the fact that in both notices the aircraft was described as being LY 213, whereas in fact that was not the number of the aircraft at all but merely the number of the flight.

In my judgment, accordingly, there is no validity in the applicant's contentions, and the writ should be discharged. Before leaving the case I would only point out that this court is in no way concerned with questions whether or not, as

[7] (1933) 24 Cr.App.R. 74, C.C.A.

[8] [1942] 2 K.B. 281.

the applicant contends, he is innocent of the charges of which he has been found guilty, nor with any question as to his physical condition today and whether, if he serves his sentence, he will die in prison. Those matters, whatever we may think of them, are not for us.

WINN J. I agree.

WIDGERY J. I also agree.

Writ discharged with costs.

The applicant appealed.

F. Elwyn Jones Q.C. and *Peter Solomon* for the applicant. If, as it is submitted the applicant was given leave to land a deportation order will have to be made if it is now desired to remove him. Whether leave to land was given is a question of fact. [Reference was made to *Rex* v. *Governor of Brixton Prison*; *Ex parte Lannoy.*[9]*]

There is an issue of fact as to the applicant's condition when he arrived at the airport. He says that he was then in a fit state to receive notice of refusal of leave to land. He was not served with notice of the refusal but he was given implied leave; thus **[838]** the purported application on July 6 of the provisions of section 8 (4) came too late.

The first question is whether the applicant is an "alien" for the purposes of the Aliens Order, 1953. The expression is not defined in the Order or in either of the enabling Acts under which the Order was issued (Aliens Restriction Act, 1914, amended by the Aliens Restriction Act, 1919), but it is defined in the British Nationality and Status of Aliens Act, 1914, as "not of British nationality." This definition is not in terms incorporated into the other Acts. It would, however, be difficult to resist the contention that it does apply. The applicant was born in Lithuania and in the notice of refusal of leave to land he was described as of doubtful nationality. If he is an alien, it cannot be disputed that as such he has no right to enter the United Kingdom, but while he is here he is entitled to the protection of British law: *Liversidge* v. *Anderson.*[10] The primary concern at the airport was, doubtless, to save the applicant's life, but a mistake of law has nevertheless been made. The landing officer must act strictly within the powers conferred by the Order: *Kuchenmeister* v. *Home Office.*[11]*

Article 1 of the Aliens Order, 1953, provides that an alien is not to land except with leave, but leave to land must be implied in the present case from the conduct of the persons attending at the airport. Article 2 makes the provision for temporary landing, but it is dealing with a special matter and it has been conceded that it has no reference to the circumstances of this case. The only power expressly given to the landing officer to refuse leave to land to an alien who is already in the United Kingdom is under article 2 (2) (*b*), but that does not apply here. It is a condition precedent to the exercise of the powers of removal under article 8 (1) that there has been an express refusal of leave to land. Landing without leave must be distinguished from being subject to an expressed refusal.

If a power to refuse leave is implicit in article 1 (1), there would have been no need for specific provision in article 2 (2) (*b*). If leave to land has been refused then the applicant would not be within the United Kingdom, but this alien has landed in fact because he has physically left the airport precincts and once he has done that the landing officer has no power to deal with the situation by a purported notice of refusal to land. The **[839]** authorities would then have

[9] [1942] 2 K.B. 281; 58 T.L.R. 350; sub nom. *R.* v. *Lannoy* [1942] 2 All E.R. 232, C.A.
[10] [1942] A.C. 206; 58 T.L.R. 35; [1941] 3 All E.R. 338, H.L.
[11] [1958] 1 Q.B. 496; [1958] 2 W.L.R. 453; [1958] 1 All E.R. 485.

to rely on the powers of deportation conferred by article 20, which do not apply here because it cannot be said that it is "conducive to the public good" that this alien should be deported.

Article 3 sets out the matters which are relevant to the question whether leave to land should be granted. It is not known whether they are applicable in the present case. Article 5 provides that leave to land be granted subject to conditions of which notice is given. In the present case the implied leave was unconditional. Article 9 deals with aliens who have landed unlawfully, and covers the only case where the powers conferred by article 8 are not dependent on leave to land having been previously refused, but in this case there was no purported exercise of authority under that article and it is not open to the Crown to call it in aid now. Article 25 deals with offences under the Order. A breach of article 1 is a criminal offence and the ordinary standards of proof must be applied. The onus is on the authorities to show that within the ordinary meaning of the phrase, an alien has "landed without the leave" of the landing officer. If the Crown are right in saying that the applicant was unconscious when he was landed, the landing was an involuntary act on his part carried out by others for which he cannot be held responsible. Preparatory arrangements were made to serve notice of refusal of leave to land and there was a clear intention that he should not land, but a new situation arose and it was necessary that he should land for the humanitarian reason of saving his life. This transformed the circumstances of the case, and although disembarkation was necessary and the landing officer was influenced by humanitarian reasons to do what he did, it nevertheless amounted to leave to land.

There were the following elements of an implied grant: (1) the landing officer was not merely passively acquiescent. He went on board the aircraft intending to serve notice of refusal but did not in fact serve it. (2) The landing officer permitted the applicant to be taken off the plane though the American marshal said that he was his prisoner. (3) The landing officer did not, as he could have, purport to act under paragraph 5 (1) of the Aliens Order and to give conditional leave to land. (4) The failure to communicate leave to land constituted a failure to refuse leave. Refusal must be communicated at the moment of landing except where article 2 (2) (*b*) applies. Nothing in the Aliens Order suggests that landing with the approval of the **[840]** landing officer for the purpose of medical treatment is not landing without leave.

If an alien is brought ashore unconscious with the permission of the landing officer then under the terms of the Order there is no power to refuse leave to land. The only power available in these circumstances would be that expressed in article 2 (2) (*b*). Power to refuse leave to land should not be implied in article 1 (1) because this is a matter which involves the liberty of the subject. If the ground on which to land was refused is stated, the authority is committed to that ground and cannot rely on others. There has been no application to amend the terms of the writ and that relies on the terms of the Order and the notice of refusal to land. In the circumstances of this case there has been no contravention of article 1 (1) and no grounds arise under article 8 (1) and (4) justifying the detention. The onus is on the Crown to justify the detention for, as Lord Atkin said in *Liversidge* v. *Anderson*[12] (in a dissenting opinion but on a point not controverted by the majority opinions) any imprisonment is prima facie unlawful.

Rex v. *Larsonneur*[13]* and *Rex* v. *Governor of Brixton Prison Ex parte Lannoy*[14]* are both distinguishable on the facts. They concerned the Emergency Regulations. In *Ex parte Lannoy*[15]* the issue was whether there could be a request to land having been made. All the rest is obiter and in any case it turned on a different Aliens Order.

Sir John Hobson Q.C., A.-G. and *J. R. Cumming-Bruce* for the Home Secretary. It is a short question of fact whether there has been a refusal of leave to land for the purpose of the Aliens Order, 1953. The Divisional Court

[12] [1942] A.C. 206, H.L.
[13] (1933) 24 Cr.App.R. 74, C.C.A.
[14] [1942] 2 K.B. 281, C.A.
[15] Ibid.

found against the submission that a grant of leave should be implied from the facts.

It is conceded that the conduct of a landing officer might be equivalent and tantamount to granting leave to land, and leave to land could be implied if the landing officer indicated that he was allowing the alien to proceed as if he was a free man. But the illness of the applicant negatives any idea that leave to land was impliedly granted by the landing officer. He only acquiesced reasonably and humanely allowed the removal of the applicant to hospital. He had brought with him to the airport the notice of refusal to land but he could not serve it. He took an undertaking from the airline company that the applicant would be removed as soon as possible. **[841]**

The second question is whether refusal of leave to land is a condition precedent to the exercise of the powers under article 8 (1) and (4). Power to refuse leave to land is to be implied in article 1 (1). It is incorrect that it is found only in article 2. If so, and lawful refusal to land was in fact served before July 6, the detention was lawful. As the Divisional Court said, the question of the grant and refusal of leave to land is a question of status. If he has landed with leave he is a free man subject to any conditions attached to the leave. It is not sufficient to show that the body of an alien is on this soil. He must be lawfully within the realm and free within the context of the conditions, if any. It is obvious that a person who has physically landed can be subsequently granted or refused leave to land. An unlawful arriving can be converted to a lawful remaining. There can be a state of suspense before leave is either given or refused, as with a forced landing of an aircraft or where a shipwrecked mariner is assisted ashore. In such cases the question whether leave to land should be granted or refused may have to be postponed.

Even if the landing officer assisted an alien ashore that could never be held to amount to implied leave to land. It is unnecessary to decide here whether refusal of leave must be communicated to the alien before it is effective. If the notice is effective from the date of the making of the order then it operated from the arrival of the aircraft, but if it is effective only on communication then it operated from the date when the order was communicated in hospital. Communication is not essential to the effectiveness of a grant of leave to land. A general class order may be issued, to permit, for example, the landing of refugees from a particular area to land, but an alien should not arrive unless he has assured himself that he has leave to land. If he has not found out, he must take the consequences. So the original refusal would be sufficient though not enforced pending the medical recovery of the applicant. It is conceded that there must be two parties to a refusal, the person applying and the person refusing. An alien may make application by presenting himself in the United Kingdom. The applicant was clearly anxious to get into this country. It is not necessary that the other party should be present for the refusal to be complete. Refusal was made before or at the time when the applicant was landed. It was available throughout though it was not exercised except to the extent of providing police supervision. Alternatively, if communication **[842]** was necessary, the refusal was comunicated on Tuesday, July 3, at the first moment when, according to the evidence, the applicant was in a state that he could receive the notice. Plainly he is an "alien." The Aliens Order, 1953, was made under the powers of the Aliens Restriction Act, 1914, s. 1 (4). The onus of proof is on the person alleging that he is not an alien. In the affidavit he said that he was born in Lithuania and for the last 20 years has been in America.

Elwyn Jones Q.C. replied.

Lord Denning M.R. In this case Robert Soblen applies for a writ of habeas corpus, he being a person at present detained in Her Majesty's prison at Brixton, and he is of course entitled to call on those detaining him to justify their detention in point of law so as to show whether he is being unlawfully detained or no. Those who detain him claim to do so by virtue of an order made under the Aliens Restriction Act, 1914. The chief immigration officer on July 6, 1962, said that the applicant was an alien to whom leave to land had been refused and accordingly he authorised his detention under article 8 (4) of the Aliens Order, 1953. There is no doubt that if he is "An alien to whom leave to land is refused," he is properly detained. The whole question in the case, therefore, is whether he is such an alien to whom leave to land has been refused.

That he is an alien there can be no question. He is a doctor of medicine. He was born in Lithuania and lived there practising as a doctor of medicine until 1941, but for the last 20 years or thereabouts he has been in the United States of America. So he is not a British subject; he is an alien.

Now is he an alien to whom leave to land has been refused? [His Lordship stated the facts as set out above and continued:] It is on these facts that the alien says he had "leave to land" in this country and on which those detaining him say he was "refused" leave to land.

It seems to me that in essence this question is one of fact. Mr. Elwyn Jones is quite right in saying that leave to land can in some circumstances be implied, but I must say on the facts of this case I see no possible ground for any implication that the applicant was ever given leave to land in the proper sense of the word. To "land" does not mean physically to land a body on the land of this country. To "land" in these articles means to land as a free man, free to move about in this country, either **[843]** subject to conditions or not. The applicant was certainly not given leave to land in that sense at all.

This is really the end of the case. I agree that it is necessary that leave to land should be "refused," but I am quite clear that it was refused him on July 3. When a man presents himself at an airport in this country seeking leave to land here, it is not necessary for the immigration officer to grant or refuse it at once. The matter may be in suspense whilst inquiries are made, or, as here, when he is not fit to receive a communication. So in the case of a shipwrecked mariner who was rescued from the sea, the question of leave to land might not be determined for a few days. The leave to land might be in suspense, but eventually when it is refused, it is refused, and that is all that matters. So here there may have been an intervening time from July 1 to July 3, when it was in suspense, but I am quite clear that on July 3, when he was served with this notice, leave to land was refused to him. I need not, therefore, go into the question which the Attorney-General raised as to whether in point of law it is necessary for a refusal to be communicated. In this case it was in fact refused on July 3. Therefore, under the provisions of article 8 (4) the immigration officer was entitled to direct that he should be detained. He was so detained, and lawfully detained, and I see no reason whatever to suggest the contrary.

I think this appeal should be dismissed.

DONOVAN L.J. I agree. I add only this, that, as Lord Parker C.J. said in the Divisional Court, we have nothing at all to do with the merits of the applicant's conviction in America.

PEARSON L.J. I agree.

Appeal dismissed.
Leave to appeal refused.

Solicitors: *Kaufman & Seigal; Treasury Solicitor.*

LIM CHIN AIK v. THE QUEEN

([1963] A.C. 160)

October 30, 31, November 1, 2, 9, 1962: Judicial Committee of the Privy Council (on appeal from the High Court of the State of Singapore): Viscount Radcliffe, Lords Evershed, Devlin.

Singapore—Immigration—Statutory provisions, contravention of—Presumption that mens rea an essential ingredient of every offence—Not displaced by words

of statute or by subject-matter—Absence of "knowingly"—Maxim that "ignorance of the law is no excuse" inapplicable—Immigration Ordinance, 1952 (*Singapore*) (*as amended by Ordinance No.* 22 *of* 1959), *ss.* 6 (2) (3), 9 (1) (3).
Crime—Mens rea—Statutory offence—Entering Singapore when prohibited by order—No notice of order given to defendant—Whether offence committed.
Ignorantia Juris Neminem Excusat—Unpublished law—Entry prohibition—Not served on defendant—Whether guilty of entry as a probibited person.

By section 6 of the Immigration Ordinance, 1952, of the State of Singapore (as amended by the Amendment Ordinance of 1959): ". . . (2) It shall not be lawful for any person other than a citizen of Singapore to enter the colony from the Federation or having entered the colony from the Federation to remain in the colony if— . . . (*b*) such person has been prohibited by order made under section 9 of this Ordinance from entering the colony; . . .

"(3) Any person who contravenes the provisions of subsection . . . (2) of this section shall be guilty of an offence against this Ordinance."

Section 9, in the case of an order directed to a single individual, contained no provision for publishing the order or for otherwise bringing it to the attention of the person named.

The appellant was charged with and convicted of contravening section 6 (2) of the Immigration Ordinance by remaining in Singapore (after having entered) when he had been prohibited from entering by an order made by the Minister under section 9. At the trial there was no evidence from which it could properly be inferred that the order had in fact come to the notice or attention of the appellant:—

Held, that there is a presumption that mens rea or knowledge of the wrongfulness of the act is an essential ingredient of every offence, but that presumption is liable to be displaced either by the words of the statute creating the offence or by the subject-matter with which it deals and both must be considered. Here, first, the sense of the language in question required, for the commission of a crime thereunder, mens rea as a constituent of such crime, or at least there was nothing in the language used which sufficed to **[161]** exclude the ordinary presumption. The absence of the word "knowingly" or the phrase "without reasonable excuse" from section 6 (3) was not sufficient to prevail against the conclusion which the language as a whole suggested. Secondly—with regard to the inference to be drawn from the subject-matter with which the Ordinance dealt—where it could be shown that the imposition of strict liability would result in the prosecution and conviction of a class of persons whose conduct could not in any way affect the observance of the law then, even where a statute was dealing with a grave social evil, strict liability was not likely to be intended. Here there was nothing that the appellant could possibly have done so as to ensure that he complied with the regulations—it would not, for example, have been practicable for him to make continuous inquiry to see whether an order had been made against him.

Accordingly, the application of the rule that mens rea is an essential ingredient in every offence had not in this case been ousted by the terms or the subject-matter of the Ordinance and the conviction must be quashed.

Sherras v. *De Rutzen* [1895] 1 Q.B. 918; 11 T.L.R. 369, D.C. (approved in *Srinivas Mall Bairoliya* v. *King-Emperor* (1947) I.L.R. 26 Pat 460) and *Brend* v. *Wood* (1946) 62 T.L.R. 462, D.C. approved and applied.

Reynolds v. *G. H. Austin & Sons Ltd.* [1951] 2 K.B. 135; [1951] 1 T.L.R. 614; [1951] 1 All E.R. 606, D.C. considered.

Per curiam: Even if the making of the order by the Minister were regarded as an exercise of the legislative as distinct from the executive or administrative function (which the Board did not concede) the maxim that "ignorance of the law is no excuse" could not apply here where there was not in Singapore any provision for the publication in any form of an order of the kind made in this case or any other provision designed to enable a man by appropriate inquiry to find out what "the law" was.

Order of the High Court of the State of Singapore reversed.

APPEAL (No. 1 of 1962), by special leave, from an order of the High Court of the State of Singapore (February 24, 1960) dismissing the appellant's appeal against his conviction by the Magistrate's Court of Singapore (August 17, 1959) for an offence under the Immigration Ordinance.

The following introductory statement is taken from the judgment of the Judicial Committee: The appellant, Lim Chin Aik (who appeared to have been known by several other names but who will hereafter be referred to as "the appellant"), appealed to the Board by special leave from the dismissal by the High Court of Singapore of his appeal against conviction by a magistrate for an offence under section 6 of the Immigration Ordinance of 1952 (c. 102) of the State of Singapore (as later amended) and the sentence then imposed of a fine of $1,250 or three months' imprisonment. **[162]**

The appellant appeared to have been born in China about the year 1900. It is unnecessary to relate his history beyond stating that, after living in Singapore with his wives and children, he left Singapore in 1954 in circumstances apparently of some suspicion. At the beginning of 1959 he was living in the Federation of Malaya. He then began to visit Singapore and his family daily, returning each night to the Federation. At some time, according to a statement made by the appellant to the police, "more than 10 days before June 29, 1959," the appellant began to live in Singapore with his wives and children. On June 29 the appellant was discovered by a police officer of Singapore who was making a search for narcotics and he was then arrested.

The appellant was first charged on July 1, 1959, with having entered the State of Singapore about May 17, 1959, without a valid permit, thereby contravening section 6 (1) of the Immigration Ordinance. At the trial of the appellant that charge was abandoned by the prosecution and it need not therefore further be considered.

A second charge was dated August 15, 1959 (two days in fact before the appellant's trial). That charge was in the following terms: ". . . you . . . having entered Singapore from the Federation of Malaya in May, 1959, did remain therein whilst prohibited by an order made by the Minister under section 9 prohibiting you from entering Singapore and have thereby contravened section 6 (2) of the Immigration Ordinance, an offence under section 6 (3) punishable under section 57 thereof."

The relevant terms of the Ordinance of 1952 (as amended by the Amendment Ordinance of 1959 (c. 22), which came into operation on May 1, 1959), will now be referred to. Section 9 (1) of the (amended) Ordinance so far as relevant was in the following terms:

"9.—(1) The Minister may, by order—(*a*) where he deems it expedient to do so in the interests of public security or by reason of any economic, industrial, social, educational or other conditions in Malaya—(i) prohibit, either for a stated period or permanently, the entry or re-entry into the Colony of any person or class of persons; . . ."

Subsection (3) of the same section stated: "(3)—(*a*) Every order made under subsection (1) of this section shall unless it be otherwise provided in such order take effect and come into operation on the date on which it is made. (*b*) Every order made under subsection (1) of this section which relates to a class of persons shall be published in the Gazette and, except **[163]** an order made in the interests of public security, shall be presented to the Legislative Assembly as soon as may be after publication and if a resolution is passed pursuant to a motion . . . annulling the order or any part thereof as from a specified date, such order or such part thereof, as the case may be, shall thereupon become void as from such date but without prejudice to the validity of anything previously done thereunder or to the making of a new order."

It would be noticed that in the case of an order directed to a single person as distinct from one directed to a class of persons there was not in the section (nor was there elsewhere in the Ordinance) and any provision for publishing the order or for otherwise bringing it (actually or notionally) to the attention of the person named.

By section 6 (2) of the (amended) Ordinance it was provided—(2) It shall not be lawful for any person other than a citizen of Singapore to enter the colony from the Federation or having entered the colony from the Federation to remain in the colony if . . . (*b*) such person has been prohibited by order made under section 9 of this Ordinance from entering the colony."

By subsection (3) of the same section it was provided that—"Any person who contravenes the provisions of subsection . . . (2) of this section shall be guilty of an offence against this Ordinance."

Finally, section 57 of the Ordinance provided that any person guilty of an offence under the Ordinance for which no special penalty was provided should be liable on conviction to imprisonment for a term not exceeding six months or to a fine not exceeding $2,000 or to both such imprisonment and fine.

It was not in dispute that pursuant to section 9 of the Ordinance above recited the Minister of Labour and Welfare did make, on May 28, 1959, an order prohibiting the appellant from entering Singapore.

At the trial (which as already stated took place on August 17, 1959) it was proved by the Deputy Assistant Controller of Immigration that the Minister's order was received by him on the day on which it was made; but there was no evidence of what was done with the order thereafter and no evidence of any step having been taken by way of publication or otherwise so as to bring the order to the attention of the appellant—or indeed of anyone else.

The appellant at his trial did not personally give any evidence at all. **[164]**

It followed from the above recital of facts that there was at the trial no evidence at all from which it could be properly inferred that the order had in fact come to the notice or attention of the appellant. It was therefore said on the appellant's behalf before the magistrate that, since there was no evidence of guilty intent on his part and that since such a guilty intent on general principles must be an ingredient of any criminal offence, it therefore followed that no offence had been proved against the appellant under the Ordinance. That plea was rejected by the magistrate who, basing himself upon the terms of the relevant section of the Ordinance, held that there was in this case no need for any evidence of mens rea.

The appellant then appealed to the High Court of Singapore, but that court dismissed his appeal without stating any reasons for the dismissal.

1962. October 30, 31; November 1. *E. F. N. Gratiaen Q.C.* and *Dick Taverne* for the appellant. The questions are, (1) whether mens rea is an essential ingredient of the particular offence under the Immigration Ordinance; (2) whether the burden of proving imputed knowledge is on the prosecution. If mens rea is an essential ingredient, and if the burden on that issue is on the prosecution, it is admitted that the prosecution has failed to prove mens rea. There is no charge of unlawful entry into Singapore, the gist of the charge is remaining in Singapore during the period when there was a prohibition. The order made by the Minister under section 9 was sent by him to the Immigration Department and remained with them. That order was in the form of the communication prescribed for a class—not for an individual—and that strengthens the argument about the question of knowledge being brought home to the individual.

The main submissions are, first, that on a proper interpretation the words "such person has been prohibited by order made under section 9 of this Ordinance from entering the colony" in section 6 (2) (*b*) mean that an order to that effect has to his knowledge been made. The second submission, which is allied to the question of interpretation, is that in construing the section the proper rule of interpretation is that there is a presumption that mens rea is an essential part of the statutory offence unless that be ruled out either expressly or by necessary implication by the language of the statute or by the subject-matter with which the statute deals. Thirdly, it is submitted that if there is a presumption, then the presumption has not been rebutted either **[165]** by the provisions of the Ordinance or by its subject-matter. Lastly, if knowledge is an essential ingredient, then the burden is on the prosecution to prove guilty knowledge.

As to the first submission—whether the order has to his knowledge been made

—see *Sambasivam* v. *Public Prosecutor, Federation of Malaya,*[1] where it was conceded for the Crown that "carries" in the relevant regulation meant "carries to his knowledge." Knowledge of the relevant fact had also to be established in *Reg.* v. *Cugullere.*[2]

On the question whether there is a presumption that mens rea is an essential ingredient or not, the correct approach is to be found in the judgment of Wright J. in *Sherras* v. *De Rutzen*[3] where he said: "There is a presumption that mens rea, an evil intention, or knowledge of the wrongfulness of the act, is an essential ingredient in every offence; but that presumption is liable to be displaced either by the words of the statute creating the offence or by the subject-matter with which it deals, and both must be considered." That was expressly approved by the Judicial Committee in *Srinivas Mall Bairoliya* v. *King-Emperor.*[4] It is sufficient for the appellant here to rely on the words of Lord Goddard C.J. in *Brend* v. *Wood*[5] and referred to in the *Srinivas* case: "It is of the utmost importance for the protection of the liberty of the subject that a court should always bear in mind that, unless a statute, either clearly or by necessary implication rules out mens rea as a constituent part of a crime, the court should not find a man guilty of an offence against the criminal law unless he has a guilty mind." There does not appear to be a single case since 1947 in which the *Srinivas* case[6] has been considered. Again, *Reynolds* v. *G. H. Austin & Sons Ltd.*[7] deals with the presumption in words which are completely applicable to the present case. The most recent case which supports a different approach is *Reg.* v. *St. Margaret's Trust Ltd.,*[8] but the court was not there referred to the *Srinivas* case.[9]

With regard to the burden of proof; if the presumption of mens rea has not been rebutted the question then arises as to where the burden of proof lies, and reliance is placed on *Reg.* v. *Cugullere.*[10] **[166]** The only evidence is that the Minister signed the order and sent it to the Immigration Department from whose custody it was produced at the trial. There is no evidence that the appellant was in fact told of, or had any knowledge of, the prohibition. The burden was on the prosecution to prove knowledge, and at the end of the case the magistrate should have asked himself whether he was satisfied beyond reasonable doubt that the appellant knew that the prohibition order had been made—that is the effect of *Reg.* v. *Cugullere.*[11] The quantum of the evidence would depend on the very nature of the facts which they have to establish—it is almost a case of res ipsa loquitur raising a presumption. As to shifting of the burden of proving reasonable doubt, see Stephen's Digest of Evidence, 12th ed., (1936), art. 104, which must be read in the light of article 103. There is a correct statement of the law in *Elkin* v. *Janson.*[12] Reliance is also placed on *Roper* v. *Taylor's Central Garages (Exeter) Ltd.*[13] in regard to shifting the burden to the defence. If the true view of the statute is that mens rea is an ingredient of the offence—whether expressly or by implication makes no difference—the burden is on the prosecution to lead some evidence at least which would constitute a prima facie case. If mens rea is not an ingredient of the offence then one is left with an absolute prohibition, and in that case as a matter of construction ignorance of the offence would not constitute a defence. [Reference was made to *Harding* v. *Price.*[14]]

1 [1950] A.C. 458, 469; 66 T.L.R. (Pt. 2) 254, P.C.
2 [1961] 1 W.L.R. 858; [1961] 2 All E.R. 343, C.C.A.
3 [1895] 1 Q.B. 918, 921; 11 T.L.R. 369, D.C.
4 (1947) I.L.R. 26 Pat. 460, 468.
5 (1946) 62 T.L.R. 462, 463, D.C.
6 (1947) I.L.R. 26 Pat. 460.
7 [1951] 2 K.B. 135, 147, 150; [1951] 1 T.L.R. 614; [1951] 1 All E.R. 606, D.C.
8 [1958] 1 W.L.R. 522;]1958] 2 All E.R. 289, C.C.A.
9 I.L.R. 26 Pat. 460.
10 [1961] 1 W.L.R. 858, 859-861.
11 [1961] 1 W.L.R. 858, 861.
12 (1845) 13 M. & W. 655, 661
13 [1951] 2 T.L.R. 284, 287, D.C.
14 [1948] 1 K.B. 695; 64 T.L.R. 111; [1948] 1 All E.R. 283, D.C.

The prosecution must prove every ingredient of the case unless the statute expressly or by necessary implication places the burden of disproving one of the ingredients on the defence, and that, again, is a matter of construction. The question is, does the law intend that the signing of this order by a person over whom the accused has no control make him a guilty man automatically as from the moment of the signing of the document? If so, it would be useless even for him to spend his whole time outside the Minister's door asking for information as to whether he has been subject to a prohibition order, because the answer would be that the moment he was told "Yes, I have just signed an order," there was nothing he could do to prevent it. [Reference was made to *Attygalle* v. *The King.*[15]] There is nothing in the Ordinance or in its object which leads to such an offensive result. If mens rea is an ingredient there is nothing as a matter of construction from which it can **[167]** safely be inferred that the burden of proof has been placed fairly and squarely on the accused. It is not sought to deny that the appellant is a prohibited immigrant, the only question is whether at a particular point of time he was guilty of an offence.

Taverne following. On the question of onus of proof and the absence of the word "knowingly," see *Roper's* case,[16] *Harding* v. *Price*[17] and *Rex* v. *Banks.*[18] There is no authority which would constrain the court to hold that the absence of the word "knowingly" as a general rule placed the burden of proof on the defence. There is nothing in *Fowler* v. *Padget*[19] which has any relation to the burden of proof. So *Harding* v. *Price*[20] must be based on what Day J. said in *Sherras.*[21] The principle is put rather too broadly in the *Reynolds* case.[22] *Nichols* v. *Hall*[23] shows that the absence of the word "knowingly" does not transfer the burden of proving the absence of knowledge to the defence. There is no general rule that the absence of "knowingly" places the onus on the defence; it must depend on the nature of the offences prohibited and the context of the particular provisions of the statute, and in certain cases where knowledge is an ingredient of the crime a prima facie case can be established from proof of other ingredients of the crime. [Reference was made to Glanville Williams on the Criminal Law, 2nd ed. (1961), p. 289.] The principle in *Burns* v. *Nowell*[24] is relied on and applied to the present case. On a proper construction of the Immigration Ordinance, no one can be convicted of an offence under section 6 (3) until it is proved that a prohibition order has been served on him or otherwise brought to his notice, mens rea being an essential element of such an offence.

J. G. Le Quesne Q.C. and *Mervyn Heald* for the Crown. Here the knowledge is of that which can be regarded as not fact but law, and it means that this is not really a case of guilty knowledge at all, because neither mens rea nor guilty knowledge in this context can properly be applied to knowledge of law as opposed to knowledge of fact. What was made here was an order by the Minister under his power conferred by section 9 of the Ordinance. It was an order according to its terms prohibiting the appellant from entering Singapore. When such an order had been made the result was that it became part of the **[168]** law of Singapore that the person named in the order was prohibited from entering nonetheless that it was applied to one person and was not of general application. That order is law. Ignorance of this particular kind of law is not a defence to the particular charge. There is no trace of any authority in which it has ever been suggested that ignorance of any kind of law will constitute a defence. The submission comes to this: it was said that the fact that this appellant was ignorant of this order excuses him from the offence under section 6; that is wrong, because the maxim that ignorance of the law is no defence applies here as it does in any other case. There appears to be no authority dealing with this point. It has to be shown that the result of the Minister's action under section 9

[15] [1936] A.C. 338; 52 T.L.R. 390; [1936] 2 All E.R. 116, P.C.
[16] [1951] 2 T.L.R. 284, 288.
[17] [1948] 1 K.B. 695, 700.
[18] (1794) 1 Esp. 144, 146.
[19] (1798) 7 T.R. 509, 513.
[20] [1948] 1 K.B. 695.
[21] [1895] 1 Q.B. 918, 921.
[22] [1951] 2 K.B. 135, 145.
[23] (1873) L.R. 8 C.P. 322, 325.
[24] (1880) L.R. 5 Q.B.D. 444, 453.

was to make law. His order that a particular person is prohibited from entering Singapore can only be described as making law, because when it has been done it is contrary to the law of the country for the named individual to enter. It is not shown that it would have been impossible to discover that the order had been made. If this first submission is right, that should be an end of the case.

Next, as to the general rule which is to be applied in deciding with regard to any statutory offence whether guilty knowledge is a necessary constituent or not, the proper approach to the interpretation of a section which creates a statutory offence is to examine the language and the subject-matter of the section. As a result of that one may find some indication that guilty knowledge is not intended to be an ingredient of the offence—it may be an express statement or an implication either from the language or the subject-matter. On the authorities there is really no difference between them—they require examination of the language of the statute: see *Cundy* v. *Le Cocq*[25]; the statement is put in much the same way in *Toppin* v. *Marcus.*[26] In *Hobbs* v. *Winchester Corporation*[27] the presumption is put the other way round, and it is said that unless one can find some positive indication in the statute that guilty knowledge is required then the presumption is that it is not. That is the opposite approach to that of Wright J. in the *Sherras* case.[28] *Reg.* v. *St. Margaret's Trust Ltd.*[29] is important as showing the view which was there taken of Kennedy L.J.'s judgment in *Hobbs.*[30] Both ways of approaching the statute depend on the existence of **[169]** a presumption. Unless one finds a clear indication in the language of the statute one has to depend on the application of a rebuttable presumption.

It is accepted that if mens rea is a constituent part of the offence then the prosecution must produce evidence of it. Both the language and the subject-matter of this Ordinance, however, contain material upon which the only possible implication is that under section 6 (2) guilty knowledge was not intended to be a constituent of the offence; by that, of course, is meant knowledge that the order had been made. Where it was intended that knowledge should be an ingredient of the offence the legislature says so expressly.

In the case of an order made under section 9 in respect of a person outside Singapore there can be no question of bringing it to his notice, but it operates straight away to make that person a prohibited immigrant. Where an order is made under section 9 in respect of someone already in Singapore, that order can take effect straight away to the extent of making the man a prohibited immigrant; before he can be prosecuted he has, of course, to be found. If the legislature had wanted to say that knowledge of the offence under section 6 (2) (*b*) was a necessary ingredient they would have said so. The offence under that subsection is committed on entering the colony; it cannot have been the intention of the legislature that knowledge of the making of the order should have been conveyed to him before he entered the colony at all. The subject-matter of the statute, which according to the authorities must be taken into account, leads to the same conclusion.

The question in its simplest terms is whether subsection (3) of section 6 is to be read as though it said "any person who *knowingly* contravenes," etc. When statutes contain in some sections the word "knowingly" and there are other sections creating offences without using it, there is only one explanation other than that Parliament omitted "knowingly" because they did not think it necessary, and it is that of Day J. in *Sherras*[31] that the effect of the word is to shift the onus of proof to the defence. It is submitted that that explanation of "knowingly" cannot be supported, and that the explanation that it was meant to shift the burden of proof can no longer be adopted.

One finds in the language of the Ordinance and its subject-matter that the

[25] (1884) L.R. 13 Q.B.D. 207, D.C.
[26] [1908] 2 Ir.R. 423.
[27] [1910] 2 K.B. 471, 482, 485; 26 T.L.R. 557, C.A.
[28] [1895] 1 Q.B. 918, 921.
[29] [1958] 1 W.L.R. 522, 527.
[30] [1910] 2 K.B. 471, 482.
[31] [1895] 1 Q.B. 918, 921.

offence under section 6 (2) would be complete **[170]** without guilty knowledge. If guilty knowledge were required, it is quite clear that in considering the particular offence charged in this case the guilty knowledge required would be knowledge that the order under section 9 had been made. It is conceded that if that is the position under the Ordinance, then the burden is on the prosecution to provide some evidence from which the existence of that guilty knowledge can be established, and it is further conceded that there is no such evidence here.

This Ordinance is obviously directed to a matter of great public importance to a country in the situation of Singapore—to protect the country from the presence of undesirable people from outside.

Heald following. On the point that ignorance of the law is no excuse, see *Blackpool Corporation* v. *Locker*,[32] which shows that in considering the possible application of the maxim one has to define what the law is; Scott L.J.'s definition is that it is something which affects the right of a member of the community; whether it be by circular, order or statutory rule does not matter—it is the nature of the act which has been prohibited that is important. The prohibition order made here was exactly within that definition, and therefore for the purposes of the maxim there was a piece of law enacted by the Minister just as much as if the legislature had passed a separate Ordinance saying that the appellant was prohibited from entering Singapore.

Gratiaen Q.C. in reply. *The Blackpool Corporation* case[33] is not a direct authority on the question; this order of the Minister is something which falls far short of the exercise of a legislative power. There is no question of ignorance of the law arising here.

As the main question, mens rea is presumed to be a part of the offence, and the only question is, when one examines the statute, is that presumption expressly or by necessary implication ruled out to such an extent that section 6 (2) (*b*) means that it is unlawful for a person to remain in Singapore if, whether he knew it or not, an order has been made? The presumption has certainly not been rebutted. As Channell J. said in the *Hobbs* case,[34] mens rea must be an element and the burden of proving it lies on the prosecution. The conviction and sentence should be quashed and the fine which the appellant has paid should be remitted to him.

1962. November 29. The judgment of their Lordships was **[171]** delivered by LORD EVERSHED. The relevant facts fall within a small compass but the point involved in the appeal is one, as their Lordships think, of no little importance. [His Lordship stated the facts as set out above and continued:] Mr. Gratiaen, who appeared for the appellant before their Lordships, took as his first point the contention which had been rejected in the courts below, namely, that the absence of any evidence of the guilty intent of the appellant was fatal to the validity of his conviction. He argued, secondly, that if, as he contended, mens rea was an essential ingredient of an offence under section 6 (3) of the Ordinance, then the onus of proof of its existence lay upon the prosecution. Mr. Le Quesne, for the respondent, challenged the first of Mr. Gratiaen's submissions but conceded the validity of his second point upon the hypothesis that the first was well founded. In the event, therefore, it is with the question whether a guilty mind is a necessary requisite for the establishment of an offence under the relevant section that their Lordships are alone concerned and, as their Lordships have already observed, the question is one, as they venture to think, of substance and importance.

It is convenient to dispose at once of Mr. Le Quesne's first suggested answer to this question which was an invocation of the precept that ignorance of the law is no excuse. It was said on the respondent's part that the order made by the Minister under the powers conferred by section 9 of the Ordinance was an instance of the exercise of delegated legislation and therefore that the order, once made, became part of the law of Singapore of which ignorance could

[32] [1948] 1 K.B. 349, 361, 367, 381; [1948] 1 All E.R. 85, C.A.
[33] Ibid.
[34] [1910] 2 K.B. 46, 55.

provide an excuse upon a charge of contravention of the section. Their Lordships are unable to accept this contention. In their Lordships' opinion, even if the making of the order by the Minister be regarded as an exercise of the legislative as distinct from the executive or administrative function (as they do not concede), the maxim cannot apply to such case as the present where it appears that there is in the State of Singapore no provision, corresponding, for example, to that contained in section 3 (2) of the English Statutory Instruments Act of 1946, for the publication in any form of an order of the kind made in the present case or any other provision designed to enable a man by appropriate inquiry to find out what "the law" is. In this connection it is to be observed that a distinction is drawn in the Ordinance itself between an order directed to a particular individual on the one hand and an order directed to a class of persons on the other; for subsection (3) (*b*) of section 9 provides **[172]** in the latter case both for publication in the Gazette and presentation to the Legislative Assembly.

Their Lordships return accordingly to the main question. That proof of the existence of a guilty intent is an essential ingredient of a crime at common law is not at all in doubt. The problem is of the extent to which the same rule is applicable in the case of offences created and defined by statute or statutory instrument. Their Lordships were very properly referred to a number of cases, including the often-cited *Nichols* v. *Hall*[35] and *Cundy* v. *Le Cocq*,[36] and covering a considerable period ending with the decision last year of the Court of Criminal Appeal in *Reg.* v. *Cugullere*.[37] As was observed by Wright J. at the beginning of his judgment in the case of *Sherras* v. *De Rutzen*,[38] to which their Lordships will presently make further reference, the difficulty of the problem is enhanced by the fact that many of the cases are not easy to reconcile. Thus it has been held that a licensee of a public house commits an offence under the licensing legislation of serving alcoholic liquor to a drunken man even though he was unaware of the customer's condition (*Cundy* v. *Le Cocq*[39]): but that a licensee does not commit the offence under the same legislation of serving drinks to a police constable on duty if he reasonably supposed that the constable was in fact off duty (see *Sherras's* case above mentioned): and in the latest case above cited the Court of Criminal Appeal held that the terms of section 1 of the Prevention of Crime Act, 1953, "Any person who without lawful authority or reasonable excuse, the proof whereof shall lie on him, has with him in any public place any offensive weapon shall be guilty of an offence" must be read as if the word "knowingly" were written before the word "has."

Mr. Gratiaen founded his argument upon the formulation of the problem contained in the judgment of Wright J. in *Sherras's* case.[40] The language of that learned and experienced judge was as follows: "There is a presumption that mens rea, or evil intention, or knowledge of the wrongfulness of the act, is an essential ingredient in every offence; but that presumption is liable to be displaced either by the words of the statute creating the offence or by the subject-matter with which it deals, and both must be considered." **[173]**

It is to be observed that in that case the court held the presumption not to be displaced even though the word "knowingly" which was not found in the subsection involved in the case did appear in another subsection of the same section. Their Lordships add that the circumstance last mentioned was regarded by Day J. in his judgment in the same case as shifting the onus of proof to the defendant (which onus the learned judge held to have been discharged). The question of onus does not, as already stated, arise in the present case. Their Lordships think it right, however, to say that they should not be thought to assent to Day J.'s proposition—and they have in this respect noted that Mr. Le Quesne has not so contended.

Their Lordships accept as correct the formulation cited from the judgment

[35] (1873) L.R. 8 C.P. 322.
[36] (1884) L.R. 13 Q.B.D. 207, D.C.
[37] [1961] 1 W.L.R. 858; [1961] 2 All E.R. 343, C.C.A.
[38] [1895] 1 Q.B. 918; 11 T.L.R. 369, D.C.
[39] L.R. 13 Q.B.D. 207.
[40] [1895] 1 Q.B. 918, 921.

of Wright J. They are fortified in that view by the fact that such formulation was expressly accepted by Lord du Parcq in delivering the judgment of the Board in the case in 1947 of *Srinivas Mall Bairoliya* v. *King-Emperor*[41]—a case which unfortunately has not found its way into the Law Reports. That was a case in which one of the appellants had been charged with an offence under the rules made by virtue of the Defence of India Act, 1939, consisting of the sale of salt at prices exceeding those prescribed under the rules, the sales having in fact been made without that appellant's knowledge by one of his servants. The Indian High Court had held the appellant to be nonetheless liable upon the terms of the rules; but the Board rejected the view of the High Court. Lord du Parcq, after citing with approval the judgment already quoted of Wright J., also adopted the language of Lord Goddard C.J. in the case of *Brend* v. *Wood*.[42] "It is in my opinion of the utmost importance for the protection of the liberty of the subject that a court should always bear in mind that unless a statute either clearly or by necessary implication rules out mens rea as a constituent part of a crime a defendant should not be found guilty of an offence against the criminal law unless he has got a guilty mind."

The adoption of these formulations of principle does not, however, dispose of the matter. Mr. Le Quesne, indeed, as their Lordships understood, did not challenge the formulations. But the difficulty remains of their application. What should be the proper inferences to be drawn from the language of the statute or statutory instrument under review—in this case of sections 6 and 9 of the Immigration Ordinance? More difficult, perhaps, still, **[174]** what are the inferences to be drawn in a given case from the subject-matter with which [the statute or statutory instrument] deals?"

Where the subject-matter of the statute is the regulation for the public welfare of a particular activity—statutes regulating the sale of food and drink are to be found among the earliest examples—it can be and frequently has been inferred that the legislature intended that such activities should be carried out under conditions of strict liability. The presumption is that the statute or statutory instrument can be effectively enforced only if those in charge of the relevant activities are made responsible for seeing that they are complied with. When such a presumption is to be inferred, it displaces the ordinary presumption of mens rea. Thus sellers of meat may be made responsible for seeing that the meat is fit for human consumption and it is no answer for them to say that they were not aware that it was polluted. If that were a satisfactory answer, then as Kennedy L.J. pointed out in *Hobbs* v. *Winchester Corporation*,[43] the distribution of bad meat (and its far-reaching consequences) would not be effectively prevented. So a publican may be made responsible for observing the condition of his customers: *Cundy* v. *Le Cocq*.[44]

But it is not enough in their Lordships' opinion merely to label the statute as one dealing with a grave social evil and from that to infer that strict liability was intended. It is pertinent also to inquire whether putting the defendant under strict liability will assist in the enforcement of the regulations. That means that there must be something he can do, directly or indirectly, by supervision or inspection, by improvement of his business methods or by exhorting those whom he may be expected to influence or control, which will promote the observance of the regulations. Unless this is so, there is no reason in penalising him, and it cannot be inferred that the legislature imposed strict liability merely in order to find a luckless victim. This principle has been expressed and applied in *Reynolds* v. *G. H. Austin & Sons Ltd.*[45] and *James & Son Ltd.* v. *Smee*.[46] Their Lordships prefer it to the alternative view that strict liability follows simply from the nature of the subject-matter and that persons whose conduct is beyond any sort of criticism can be dealt with by the imposition **[175]** of a nominal penalty.

[41] (1947) I.L.R. 26 Pat. 460.
[42] (1946) 62 T.L.R. 462, D.C.
[43] [1910] 2 K.B. 471; 26 T.L.R. 557, C.A.
[44] L.R. 13 Q.B.D. 207.
[45] [1951] 2 K.B. 135; [1951] 1 T.L.R. 614; [1951] 1 All E.R. 606, D.C.
[46] [1955] 1 Q.B. 78; [1954] 3 W.L.R. 631; [1954] 3 All E.R. 273, D.C.

This latter view can perhaps be supported to some extent by the dicta of Kennedy L.J. in *Hobbs* v. *Winchester Corporation*,[47] and of Donovan J. in *Reg.* v. *St. Margaret's Trust Ltd.*[48] But though a nominal penalty may be appropriate in an individual case where exceptional lenience is called for, their Lordships cannot, with respect, suppose that it is envisaged by the legislature as a way of dealing with offenders generally. Where it can be shown that the imposition of strict liability would result in the prosecution and conviction of a class of persons whose conduct could not in any way affect the observance of the law, their Lordships consider that, even where the statute is dealing with a grave social evil, strict liability is not likely to be intended.

Their Lordships apply these general observations to the Ordinance in the present case. The subject-matter, the control of immigration, is not one in which the presumption of strict liability has generally been made. Nevertheless, if the courts of Singapore were of the view that unrestricted immigration is a social evil which it is the object of the Ordinance to control most rigorously, their Lordships would hesitate to disagree. That is a matter peculiarly within the cognisance of the local courts. But Mr. Le Quesne was unable to point to anything that the appellant could possibly have done so as to ensure that he complied with the regulations. It was not, for example, suggested that it would be practicable for him to make continuous inquiry to see whether an order had been made against him. Clearly one of the objects of the Ordinance is the expulsion of prohibited persons from Singapore, but there is nothing that a man can do about it if, before the commission of the offence, there is no practical or sensible way in which he can ascertain whether he is a prohibited person or not.

Mr. Le Quesne, therefore, relied chiefly on the text of the Ordinance and their Lordships return, accordingly, to the language of the two material sections. It is to be observed that the Board is here concerned with one who is said (within the terms of section 6 (3) to have "contravened" the subsection by "remaining" in Singapore (after having entered) when he had been "prohibited" from entering by an "order" made by the Minister containing such prohibition. It seems to their Lordships that, where a man is said to have contravened an order or an order of prohibition, the common sense of the language presumes that **[176]** he was aware of the order before he can be said to have contravened it. Their Lordships realise that this statement is something of an oversimplification when applied to the present case; for the "contravention" alleged is of the unlawful act, prescribed by subsection (2) of the section, of remaining in Singapore after the date of the order of prohibition. Nonetheless it is their Lordships' view that, applying the test of ordinary sense to the language used, the notion of contravention here alleged is more consistent with the assumption that the person charged had knowledge of the order than the converse. But such a conclusion is in their Lordships' view much reinforced by the use of the word "remains" in its context. It is to be observed that if the respondent is right a man could lawfully enter Singapore and could thereafter lawfully remain in Singapore until the moment when an order of prohibition against his entering was made; that then, instanter, his purely passive conduct in remaining—that is, the mere continuance, quite unchanged, of his previous behaviour, hitherto perfectly lawful—would become criminal. These considerations bring their Lordships clearly to the conclusion that the sense of the language here in question requires for the commission of a crime thereunder mens rea as a constituent of such crime; or at least that there is nothing in the language used which suffices to exclude the ordinary presumption. Their Lordships do not forget the emphasis placed by Mr. Le Quesne on the fact that the word "knowingly" or the phrases "without reasonable cause" or "without reasonable excuse" are found in various sections of the Ordinance (as amended) but find no place in the section now under consideration—see, for example, sections 16 (4), 18 (4), 19 (2), 29, 31 (2), 41 (2) and 56 (*d*) and (*e*) of the Ordinance. In their Lordships' view the absence of such a word or phrase in the relevant section is not sufficient in the present case

[47] [1910] 2 K.B. 471.
[48] [1958] 1 W.L.R. 522; [1958] 2 All E.R. 289, C.C.A.

to prevail against the conclusion which the language as a whole suggests. In the first place, it is to be noted that to have inserted such words as "knowingly" or "without lawful excuse" in the relevant part of section 6 (3) of the Act would in any case not have been sensible. Further, in all the various instances where the word or phrase is used in the other sections of the Ordinance before-mentioned the use is with reference to the doing of some specific act or the failure to do some specific act as distinct from the mere passive continuance of behaviour theretofore perfectly lawful. Finally, their Lordships are mindful that **[177]** in the *Sherras* case[49] itself the fact that the word "knowingly" was not found in the subsection under consideration by the court but was found in another subsection of the same section was not there regarded as sufficient to displace the ordinary rule.

Their Lordships have accordingly reached the clear conclusion, with all respect to the view taken in the courts below, that the application of the rule that mens rea is an essential ingredient in every offence has not in the present case been ousted by the terms or subject-matter of the Ordinance, and that the appellant's conviction and sentence cannot stand.

Their Lordships will, accordingly, humbly advise Her Majesty that this appeal ought to be allowed, and the conviction of the appellant and the sentence imposed upon him ought to be quashed. Their Lordships also are of opinion that the respondent ought to pay the costs of the appellant's appeal to the Board.

Solicitors: *T. L. Wilson & Co.; Charles Russell & Co.*

[49] [1895] 1 Q.B. 918.

3

EXPULSION

REGINA v. GOVERNOR OF BRIXTON PRISON EX PARTE SOBLEN

([1963] 2 Q.B. 243)

August 14, 22, 23, 24, 1962: Queen's Bench Division: Stephenson J.
August 29, 30, 31, 1962: Court of Appeal: Lord Denning M.R., Donovan Pearson L.JJ.

Alien—Deportation order—Validity—Refusal of leave to land—United States citizen convicted of spying in United States—Wounds inflicted on himself on aircraft bound for United States—Taken off aerodrome for medical treatment—Order for deportation by aircraft to United States—Whether Aliens Order, 1953, *ultra vires—Whether alien refused leave to land may be deported—Whether deportation a judicial or quasi-judicial act requiring inquiry—Whether political character of deportation relevant matter for court—Whether power to deport alien to own country—Aliens Restriction Act,* 1914 (4 & 5 *Geo.* 5, *c.* 12), *s.* 1 (1)—*Aliens Restriction (Amendment) Act,* 1919 (9 & 10 *Geo.* 5, *c.* 92), *s.* 1 (1)—*Aliens Order,* 1953 (*S.I.* 1953 *No.* 1671), *arts.* 8 (1), 20 (1), (2), 21 (4).
Extradition—Common law—Illegality at—Extradition by deportation order—Whether valid—Aliens Order, 1953, *art.* 20 (2) (*b*).
Crown—Minister, determination by—Whether subject to review by courts—Deportation order—Bona fides—Aliens Order, 1953, *art.* 20 (2) (*b*).
Habeas Corpus—Alien—Jurisdiction—Alien refused leave to land—Physical presence within realm—Entry gained by subterfuge—Whether entitled to apply for writ—Whether Crown can rely on "Act of State."
Crown—Privilege—Evidence—Habeas corpus—Communications from foreign government regarding alien—Addressed to British Government—Minister's certificate that disclosure injurious to good diplomatic relations—Whether documents disclosable—Whether Crown privilege applies in habeas corpus proceedings.

S., an American citizen, was convicted in the United States of conspiring to obtain and deliver defence information to the Soviet **[244]** Union, and sentenced to life imprisonment. He was released on bail pending an application to the Supreme Court for a new trial. On hearing that his application had been rejected he fled to Israel, from where he was forcibly expelled in an aircraft which took him to Athens. There he was transferred on to a regular flight of El Al [the Israeli state airline] bound for New York via London. In order to gain entry into the United Kingdom S. deliberately inflicted severe knife wounds on himself while on the aeroplane, so that when it landed at London Airport he had to be taken to hospital for medical treatment.

Before S. had ever arrived at London Airport, the Home Secretary genuinely considered that S.'s presence in this country was undesirable and not in the public interest, and, on instructions from the Home Office, the immigration officer at London Airport drew up a notice of refusal of leave to land, pursuant to articles 1 (1) and 2 (2) (*a*) of the Aliens Order, 1953.[1] The notice **[245]** was not served on S. on his arrival because of his physical condition but it was served on him in hospital a few days later. S. challenged the validity of the notice in habeas corpus proceedings; its validity was upheld by the Divisional

[1] Aliens Restriction Act, 1914, s. 1: "(1) His Majesty may at any time when a state of war exists between His Majesty and any foreign power, or when it appears that an occasion of imminent national danger or great emergency has arisen, by Order in Council impose restrictions on aliens, and provision may be made by the Order—(*a*) for prohibiting aliens from landing in the United Kingdom, . . . (*c*) for the deportation of aliens from the United Kingdom."

Aliens Restriction (Amendment) Act, 1919, s. 1: "(1) The powers which under subsection (1) of section 1 of the Aliens Restriction Act, 1914 (. . . the principal Act), are exercisable with respect to aliens at any time when a state of war exists between His Majesty and any foreign power, or when it appears that an occasion of imminent national danger or great emergency has arisen, shall, for a period of one year after the passing of this Act, be exercisable, not only in those circumstances, but at any time; and accordingly that subsection shall, for such period as aforesaid, have effect as though the words 'at any time when a state of war exists between His Majesty and any foreign power, or when it appears that an occasion of imminent national danger or great emergency has arisen' were omitted. . . ."

Aliens Order, 1953, art. 1: "(1) Subject to the provisions of this Order, an alien shall not land or embark in the United Kingdom except with the leave of an immigration officer. . . ."

Art. 2 (2): ". . . . an immigration officer may at any time—(*a*) give notice to an alien who is for the time being on board a ship or aircraft prohibiting him from landing without leave thereunder; or (*b*) grant or refuse leave to land to an alien who is within the United Kingdom after landing without leave thereunder; . . . ."

Art. 8: "(1) Where leave to land is refused to an alien, an immigration officer may . . . give directions—(*a*) to the master of the ship or commander of the aircraft in which the alien arrived in the United Kingdom, requiring him to remove the alien from the United Kingdom in that ship or aircraft; (*b*) to the owners or agents of the said ship or aircraft, requiring them to remove the alien from the United Kingdom in any ship or aircraft specified in the directions, being a ship or aircraft of which they are the owners or agents; (*c*) to the said owners or agents, requiring them to make arrangements for the removal of the alien from the United Kingdom in any ship or aircraft bound for a country specified in the directions, being either—(i) a country of which the alien is a national or in which he embarked for the United Kingdom; or (ii) a country to which there is reason to believe that the alien will be admitted, and for securing him a passage to that country . . . (3) An alien in respect of whom directions are given under paragraph (1) of this article may be placed, under the authority of an immigration officer, on board any ship or aircraft in which he is to be removed in accordance with the directions. (4) An alien to whom leave to land is refused may be detained, under the authority of an immigration officer, pending the giving of directions in his case under paragraph (1) of this article and pending his removal in pursuance of directions so given; . . ."

Art. 20: "(1) The Secretary of State may, if he thinks fit, in any such case as is mentioned in paragraph (2) of this article make an order (in this Order referred to as a 'deportation order') requiring an alien to leave and to remain thereafter out of the United Kingdom. (2) A deportation order may be made in the case of an alien in the following circumstances, that is to say,—(*a*) if any court certifies to the Secretary of State that the alien has been convicted either by that court . . . of any of the offences specified in the Fourth Schedule to this Order and that the court recommends that a deportation order be made in his case; or (*b*) if the Secretary of State deems it to be conducive to the public good to make a deportation order against the alien. . . ."

Art. 21: "(1) An alien in whose case a deportation order has been made may be placed, under the authority of the Secretary of State, on board any ship or aircraft which is about to leave the United Kingdom; and the master of the ship or commander of the aircraft shall, if so required by an immigration officer, take such steps as may be necessary for preventing the alien from landing from the ship or aircraft before it leaves the United Kingdom, and may for that purpose detain the alien in custody on board the ship or aircraft. . . . (4) An alien in whose case a deportation order has been made may be detained, under the authority of the Secretary of State, until he is dealt with under paragraph (1) of this article."

Court,[2] whose decision was affirmed by the Court of Appeal.[3]

Subsequently, on four different occasions directions were given to El Al, pursuant to article 8 (1) (*b*) and (*c*) of the Order 1953, to remove S. in one of its aircraft to the United States, but it failed to comply with those directions and ultimately they were revoked. At about the same time "The Times" newspaper reported that the American Government had requested the British Government to return S. to the United States.

Just before the revocation of the fourth direction served on El Al, a deportation order made by the Home Secretary, pursuant to article 20 (2) (*b*) of the Order of 1953, was served on S., requiring him to leave the United Kingdom and thereafter to remain out of the United Kingdom. The Home Office in a press statement announced that it was the Home Secretary's intention to deport S. by an aircraft expected to go to the United States. Pursuant to **[246]** article 21 (4) of the Order of 1953, the Home Secretary ordered that S. be detained at Brixton Prison pending deportation.

On an application by S. for a writ of habeas corpus, S. issued a subpoena duces tecum addressed to the Home Secretary requiring the production of all communications passing from the American Government to the British Government requesting his return to the United States. The Foreign Secretary objected to their production on the ground that it would be injurious to good diplomatic relations and claimed Crown privilege in respect of them.

S. contended that the deportation order was invalid on the grounds that (1) the Aliens Order, 1953, was ultra vires because it was made under the Aliens Restriction Act, 1914 and the Aliens Restriction (Amendment) Act, 1919, which themselves had become dormant during peacetime; (2) that an alien subject to a notice of refusal of leave to land was not subject to deportation; (3) that deportation, being a quasi-judicial proceeding, he should have been given the opportunity to submit representations against the making of the order; (4) that even if it be valid on its face, the order was being used for the unlawful purpose of extraditing a political fugitive convicted of a non-extraditable offence and that the order was a sham and not made bona fide.

Stephenson J. held (1) that an alien physically within the realm, even though refused leave to land, could apply for a writ of habeas corpus (post, p. 282); (2) that Crown privilege applied to habeas corpus proceedings and that the communications passing from the American Government to the British Government were not disclosable (post, p. 274); (3) that none of the objections to the deportation order could be sustained, and that, therefore, it was a valid order made in the bona fide exercise of the Home Secretary's powers; accordingly, he refused the application.

On appeal:—

Held, (1) that although by section 1 (1) of the Aliens Restriction Act, 1914, the powers contained in that Act were exercisable only in times of war or national emergency, section 1 (1) of the Aliens Restriction (Amendment) Act, 1919, had amended the Act of 1914 by making its powers exercisable at any time, and, therefore, the Aliens Order, 1953, was intra vires the Act of 1914 (post, pp. 297, 305).

(2) That, on their true construction, the Articles of the Aliens Order, 1953, were cumulative and complementary, so that the Home Secretary could, under article 20 (2) (*b*), order the deportation of an alien refused leave to land under article 1 without having to cancel the refusal of leave (post, pp. 297, 305).

(3) That deportation was an act of an executive, not of a judicial or quasi-judicial, character and, accordingly, an alien was not entitled to an opportunity of submitting representations against the making of the order (post, pp. 298, 306, 315).

Rex v. *Leman Street Police Station Inspector, Ex parte Venicoff** [1920] 3 K.B. 72; 36 T.L.R. 677, D.C., approved.

Quaere per Lord Denning M.R.: Whether, after the order was made and

[2] *Reg.* v. *Secretary of State for Home Affairs, Ex parte Soblen**; [1963] 1 Q.B. 829; [1962] 3 W.L.R. 1145; [1962] 3 All E.R. 373, C.A.

[3] [1963] 1 Q.B. 829, 842.

before it was executed, the alien was not entitled in some **[247]** cases to an opportunity of making representations against its execution (post, p. 298).

(4) That the Home Secretary could deport an alien to the country of his nationality, even though he had fled from it when convicted of a non-extraditable offence and even though a request had been made by its government for his return. His discretion could not be questioned in any court, unless it were shown that the deportation order was a sham in that the Home Secretary did not genuinely consider it in the public interest to expel the alien. In the present case, there not even being prima facie evidence that the Home Secretary had not acted bona fide, the appeal of S. against refusal of his application for a writ of habeas corpus would be dismissed (post, pp. 300, 301, 302, 305, 307, 311, 312, 314, 315).

Rex v. *Secretary of State for Home Affairs, Ex parte Duke of Chateau Thierry** [1917] 1 K.B. 922; 33 T.L.R. 264, C.A., and *Rex* v. *Chiswick Police Station Superintendent, Ex parte Sacksteder** [1918] 1 K.B. 578; 34 T.L.R. 279, C.A., applied.

Decision of Stephenson J., post, p. 268; [1962] 3 W.L.R. 1154; [1962] 3 All E.R. 641, affirmed.

APPLICATION for a writ of habeas corpus.

The following statement of facts is taken substantially from the judgment of Stephenson J.: On June 19, 1961, the applicant, Dr. Robert Soblen, was tried in the United States of America on two charges. One of those was the charge of "conspiring to obtain information, records, documents, photographs, respecting the national defence of the United States of America, with intention and having reason to believe that such information was to be used to the advantage of the Union of Soviet Socialist Republics." The second charge was one of conspiring to deliver and transmit to the Union of Soviet Socialist Republics such information with such intention and having reason to believe that such information was to be used to the advantage of the Union of Soviet Socialist Republics. On July 13, 1961, the applicant was found guilty on both counts and sentenced on the first to imprisonment for 10 years and on the second to imprisonment for the term of his natural life, with a recommendation for commitment to the medical centre for federal prisoners in Missouri in view of the lymphatic leucaemia from which he was suffering. He was released on bail on August 7, the day on which those sentences were pronounced.

On October 5 he moved for a new trial on the ground that he had obtained fresh evidence, and on November 3 that motion was denied. On February 6, 1962, his appeal to the United States Court of Appeals for the Second Circuit against his conviction and **[248]** sentence was heard, and on March 13 it was dismissed. On June 25 the Supreme Court of the United States rejected three briefs applying for a new trial which had been filed on his behalf, and, on hearing of the rejection, the applicant flew to Tel Aviv, Israel, on his dead brother's passport. On July 1 he was put on a specially chartered aircraft and taken to Athens where he was transferred to a regular flight of an aircraft of El Al, the Israeli state airline, for carriage to the United States via London. In the course of that flight he inflicted severe knife wounds on himself with the sole object of making it necessary for him to be landed in England.

On arrival in England at London Airport he was seen by a doctor and removed to hospital. There, on July 3, he was served with a notice dated July 1 refusing him leave to land in this country. The terms of that notice were as follows: "Aliens Order, 1953. To the alien. Leave to land has been refused to Robert Soblen of doubtful nationality"—the words "citizen of U.S.A." had been crossed out—"brought to the port of London Airport in the aircraft 17 213"—which was, in fact, the description of the flight, not the aircraft—"from the port of Tel Aviv. Grounds for refusal: Aliens Order, 1953, article 1 (1). Directions have been given to the master/commander of the aircraft, in which you arrived, to remove you from the United Kingdom in the aircraft in which you arrived"—that is stamped with the immigration officer's stamp.

On July 6 the applicant applied to Mocatta J. for leave to issue a writ of habeas corpus, and his application was successful. The same day his detention was authorised under article 8 (4) of the Order of 1953. On July 18 his motion for his discharge was refused by the Divisional Court,[4] who also discharged the writ of habeas corpus. On July 26 the Court of Appeal[5] dismissed his appeal from that decision. On July 21, between the decision of the Divisional Court and the decision of the Court of Appeal, the applicant had sent a petition to the Secretary of State for Home Affairs. On July 23 the applicant's solicitors had received a letter from the embassy of the Czechoslovak Socialist Republic informing them that a visa for the applicant to enter and stay in Czechoslovakia had been granted.

On August 3 and August 4 directions were served upon El Al **[249]** Airlines by William Henry Daw, one of Her Majesty's inspectors of the Immigration Branch of the Home Office, on instructions from the Home Office. Those directions were in these terms: the first of them, dated August 3, read: "To El Al Israel Airlines, Whereas Dr. Robert Soblen, an alien who has been refused leave to land, is now detained in Brixton Prison pending the giving of directions under article 8 (1) of the Aliens Order, 1953, and his removal in pursuance of directions so given: and whereas the said alien arrived in the United Kingdom on July 1, 1962, in an aircraft of which you are the owners or agents; now, therefore, in pursuance of the powers conferred on me by articles 8 (1) and 29 of the Aliens Order,1953, I hereby revoke all directions previously given under the said article 8 (1) in respect of the said alien and I hereby direct you to make arrangements for the removal from the United Kingdom in an aircraft leaving London Airport before August 6, 1962, bound for the United States of America, being a country of which he is a national and to which there is reason to believe that he will be admitted, and for securing him a passage to that country."

It is to be noted that, although the applicant was described in the notice refusing him leave to land as of doubtful nationality, he was in fact a naturalised citizen of the United States of America, having been admitted a citizen of the United States by a certificate of naturalisation dated May 5, 1947.

The direction of August 4, after reciting the same two matters as were recited in the first notice, went on to add: "And whereas by directions dated August 3, 1962, you were required to make arrangements for the removal of the said alien from the United Kingdom in an aircraft leaving London Airport before August 6, 1962, bound for the United States of America, being a country of which he is a national and to which there is reason to believe that he will be admitted, and for securing him a passage to that country: and whereas it is expedient to vary the said directions by extending the period during which the said alien is required to be removed thereunder: now, therefore, in pursuance of the powers conferred on me by articles 8 (1) and 29 of the Aliens Order, 1953, I hereby vary the said directions and direct you to make arrangements for the removal of the said alien from the United Kingdom in an aircraft leaving London Airport before August 9, 1962, bound for the United States of America, being a country of which he is a national, and to which there is reason to believe he will be admitted, and for securing him a passage **[250]** to that country," and that direction like the first is signed by an immigration officer.

On August 5 the Israeli Government announced that in no circumstances would the applicant be carried in the direction of the United States of America by an Israeli aircraft, and that if placed on an aircraft of El Al, the aircraft would be ordered to return the applicant to Israel. On August 8 another direction was given by an immigration officer in the terms of the direction of August 4 further extending the time.

On August 8 "The Times" newspaper stated in its columns: "An official of the American Embassy in London said last night that the political counsellor at the Embassy had made representations to the British Government about Dr. Robert Soblen, the convicted spy. The official said it had been represented 'that the United States would like very much to have Dr. Soblen returned to the

[4] *Reg.* v. *Secretary of State for Home Affairs, Ex parte Soblen** [1963] 1 Q.B. 829; [1962] 3 W.L.R. 1145; [1962] 3 All E.R. 373, C.A.

[5] [1963] 1 Q.B. 842.

United States.' The British Government had been requested to do everything possible to facilitate his speedy return." The article concluded with the words: "In Washington, Reuter reports, the State Department said it had 'emphatically' reiterated to both Britain and Israel that the United States wanted Dr. Soblen returned to America."

On August 11 a fourth direction was given, this time for the removal of the applicant by El Al flight No. 265. After reciting that the alien had not been removed in accordance with the directions previously given, this direction concluded: "Now, therefore, in pursuance of the powers conferred on me by" the articles previously relied on "I hereby revoke all directions previously given under the said article 8 (1) in respect of the said alien, and I hereby direct you to remove the said alien from the United Kingdom in the aircraft hereinafter specified, being an aircraft of which you are the owners or agents, that is to say El Al Israel Airlines flight No. 265, which was scheduled to leave London Airport on August 10, 1962, and the departure of which has been delayed until August 11, 1962." That direction was served on representatives of the airline at 7 a.m., and again by the immigration officer, Daw, about 10.45 a.m. and at about that time he was informed that flight No. 265 had been cancelled.

On the same day a deportation order was drawn up providing for the deportation of the applicant and his detention under article 20 (2) (*b*) and article 21 (1) and (4) of the Order of 1953. At 8.25 p.m. that order was served on the applicant and some **[251]** 10 minutes later all the directions which had previously been given were revoked by the service of the last direction by Harold Brown, an immigration officer, on a representative of El Al. It was this order of deportation and detention pending deportation which was the alleged justification for the applicant's detention and which was the subject of this application.

The order reads as follows: "Aliens Order, 1953. Deportation order. Whereas I deem it to be conducive to the public good to make a deportation order against Robert Soblen, an alien: now, therefore, in pursuance of the power conferred upon me by paragraph (2) (*b*) of article 20 of the Aliens Order, 1953, I hereby order that the said Robert Soblen shall leave and thereafter remain out of the United Kingdom; and in pursuance of the powers conferred on me by paragraphs (1) and (4) of article 21 of the said Aliens Order, 1953, I hereby authorise any immigration officer, at any time after this order is served on the said Robert Soblen, to place him on board a ship or aircraft, which is about to leave the United Kingdom, and I hereby authorise the Governor of Her Majesty's Prison at Brixton to detain him until arrangements are completed for so placing him on board." It was signed by Henry Brooke, one of Her Majesty's Principal Secretaries of State, Home Office, Whitehall, August 11, 1962.

At or about the same time as the revocation of all previous directions given under article 8 of the Order of 1953 was served upon El Al Airlines a statement was issued to the Press in this country. That statement read as follows: "The Home Secretary, Mr. Henry Brooke, M.P., this afternoon made an order for the deportation of Dr. Robert Soblen. The order was served on Dr. Soblen in Brixton Prison by the police" [in fact by Police Constable Guy]. "As announced this morning, directions were given to El Al Airlines under article 8 (1) of the Aliens Order, 1953, requiring them to remove Dr. Soblen from the United Kingdom on the flight which had been scheduled to leave London Airport for the U.S.A. at 8 p.m. yesterday but was delayed until today. These directions superseded directions previously given to El Al, and twice extended but not complied with, to arrange for Dr. Soblen's removal on an aircraft bound for the United States. The scheduled flight specified in the new directions was cancelled by El Al. The Secretary of State has given very careful consideration to all the circumstances of the case and has come to the conclusion that he should order Dr. Soblen's deportation. The deportation order authorises any **[252]** immigration officer to place Dr. Soblen on board a ship or aircraft which is about to leave the United Kingdom, and it is the Home Secretary's intention to give instructions for Dr. Soblen to be placed on an aircraft leaving the United Kingdom for the U.S.A."

On August 14 an application for a writ of habeas corpus was made ex parte by Mr. Elwyn Jones Q.C. on behalf of the applicant. That application was adjourned so that notice of it could be given under R.S.C., Ord. 56, r. 16 (*b*). On August 15 the applicant's solicitors made a request to the Treasury Solicitor in the following terms: "We should be grateful if we could be supplied, as soon as possible, with copies of the following documents:—1. All directions made by the Home Secretary relating to the removal from this country of Robert Soblen addressed to the El Al Airline. 2. Statement of the Home Office issued to the Press on Saturday, the 11th instant in the evening, in which it was stated, inter alia, that it was the Home Secretary's intention to give instructions to an immigration officer to have Soblen placed on an aircraft about to leave the United Kingdom for the United States. In view of the very early return date fixed for the adjourned hearing, we should be glad if the requested documents can be supplied to us by midday tomorrow." The adjourned hearing had been fixed for August 22.

On August 16 the Treasury Solicitor replied as follows: "I thank you for your letter of the 15th instant and now enclose herewith:—1. A copy of all the directions made by the Home Secretary relating to the removal from this country of Robert Soblen addressed to El Al Airline. 2. A copy of the statement issued by the Home Office to the Press on Saturday the 11th instant."

On August 17 the applicant's solicitors made to the Treasury Solicitor a further request in these terms: "In the issue of 'The Times' newspaper for August 8, 1962, it was stated (inter alia), as follows, . . ." [then the letter set out the report, to which reference has already been made, in "The Times" newspaper]. The letter went on: "In the light of these reported statements, we should indeed be grateful, if you would kindly indicate to us, whether Her Majesty's Government did, in fact, receive any written communication from the U.S. Government, or from some person recognised by either the Home Secretary, or the Foreign Secretary, as a diplomatic representative of the United States Government, requesting the delivery up to them of the body of Dr. Soblen. If such communications were **[253]** received, please furnish us with copies thereof. If such communications were made to Her Majesty's Government orally, may we please be informed of the contents and substance thereof, by whom the said communications were made, and to whom they were made. May we kindly hear from you, on this matter, at your earliest convenience."

On August 21 the Treasury Solicitor made this reply: "I am in receipt of your letter of 17th instant requesting information about certain communications alleged to have passed between the United States Government and Her Majesty's Government. I confirm that representations have been made on behalf of the United States Government to Her Majesty's Government, but I have to inform you that Her Majesty's Government is not prepared to disclose the nature thereof or the other particulars for which you ask." The day after that reply was written the hearing of this application began.

On the second day of the hearing a subpoena duces tecum was issued. His Lordship gave leave for it to be issued,[6] if leave were required, and it was served in court on a representative of the Treasury Solicitor. The subpoena was addressed to Her Majesty's Principal Secretary of State for the Home Department, the Rt. Hon. Henry Brooke, M.P.; it was dated August 23, and it required him to bring with him and produce before this court: "1. All written communications addressed to Her Majesty's Government or any representative thereof from the United States Government or from some person recognised by either the Home Secretary or the Foreign Secretary as a diplomatic representative of the United States Government requesting the delivery up to them of the body of Dr. Robert Soblen." The subpoena went on with a request for documents referred to in a paragraph of another exhibit, but leave was refused to issue that part of the subpoena and counsel for the applicant was content to accept that refusal and not to press for the inclusion of that part of the subpoena. The

[6] There was some argument as to whether leave was required for the issue of the subpoena under R.S.C., Ord. 59, r. 43 (2), see note thereto in Annual Practice, 1963, p. 1762. His Lordship indicated that he considered that leave was required. See, *post*, p. 260.

ground of refusal was that the documents requested were not in the possession or power of the British Government.

The Crown was forearmed to meet that subpoena with a certificate claiming Crown Privilege for the documents which the Home Secretary was required to produce. That certificate was **[254]** in these terms: "Certificate by the Secretary of State for Foreign Affairs to the honourable court above mentioned. 1. I have read a letter dated August 17, 1962, from Messrs. Kaufman & Seigal to the Treasury Solicitor. 2. I have formed the opinion that on grounds of public interest, evidence, oral or documentary, ought not to be given in these proceedings as to whether or not there was any communication, oral or documentary, or the contents thereof from the Government of the United States of America, or from any representative of that Government, to Her Majesty's Government in the United Kingdom, or to any person acting on behalf of Her Majesty's Government, relating to the applicant in these proceedings, since it is necessary in the public interest that such evidence should be withheld because disclosure would be injurious to good diplomatic relations. 3. Accordingly, I object to any such evidence being given," and the certificate was signed by the Earl of Home, one of Her Majesty's Principal Secretaries of State, Foreign Office, August 22, 1962. His Lordship upheld the claim to Crown Privilege.

Further facts are stated in the judgments given in the Court of Appeal.

F. Elwyn Jones Q.C., Peter Solomon and *Louis Blom-Cooper* for the applicant. This application raises constitutional issues of the highest importance. It concerns the very nature of deportation. Deportation consists of an order by the Government of a country to an alien "to get out of the country and to stay out." That is the object, purpose and limit of deportation. It is a form of punishment which has been classified by Archbold, Criminal Pleading, Evidence and Practice, 35th ed. (1962), p. 234, between those crimes meriting death and those meriting imprisonment. Its gravity was thus eloquently expressed by Judge Learned Hand in *United States, Ex rel. Klonis* v. *Davis*[7] "however heinous his [the alien's] crimes, deportation is to him exile, a dreadful punishment abandoned by the common consent of all civilised people. Such indeed it would be to anybody. . . ."

The deportation order in the present case is invalid on four grounds. First, even if the order is on its face valid, nevertheless the court can go behind it and can and should declare it invalid if it is being used for a collateral purpose. Deportation is **[255]** the proper machinery to be invoked for ordering an alien to get out of the country and to stay out. Extradition is the only machinery for handing over an alien to the custody of a foreign power. In the present case the Secretary is purporting to use the machinery of deportation for the purpose of handing over the applicant, who is a political fugitive, to the government of the United States of America. That is an improper, illegal and collateral use of the Home Secretary's power to deport. The order is a sham, for the Home Secretary under the guise of deportation is seeking to extradite the applicant for a non-extraditable offence. Secondly, the Home Secretary can make a deportation order under article 20 (2) (*b*) of the Aliens Order, 1953, only if he "deems" it conducive to the public good. That implies that he must allow the alien an opportunity to make representations against the making of an order; otherwise the word "deems" would not have been used. The applicant has not been afforded that opportunity and, therefore, the order is invalid. Thirdly, articles 8 and 20 of the Order of 1953 are mutually exclusive. Since the notice of refusal of leave to land has never been revoked, the applicant's position is dealt with exclusively by article 8. From the legal point of view the applicant is the man who never was. He is not here except for the purpose of being removed by the carrier who brought him pursuant to the directions of the immigration authorities under article 8. An alien subject to the provisions of article 8 cannot be dealt with under article 20. Fourthly, the Order of 1953 is wholly ultra vires, since the principal Act from which it purports to derive its validity, the Aliens Restriction Act, 1914, is defunct and inoperative and was

[7] (1926) 13 Fed. Reporter (2nd Series) 630, 631.

so defunct and inoperative in 1953 when the Order was made.

The court can go behind a deportation order to see if it is being used for a collateral purpose and, if it is, the court can quash the order: see *per* Pickford L.J.[8] and *per* Warrington L.J.[9] in *Rex* v. *Chiswick Police Station Superintendent, Ex parte Sacksteder.** If the order is a mere sham and not made bona fide, the court can quash it. A sham, *per* Warrington L.J.,[10] covers up something which would be illegal or enables an illegal act to be committed. In the present case the deportation order is being used to cover up the illegal act of extraditing the applicant to a foreign country when the offence for which he is sought to be **[256]** transported is non-extraditable and of a political character. The order is being used to circumvent the rule that political fugitives shall not be surrendered. This rule received statutory recognition in section 3 (1) of the Extradition Act, 1870. The order is an attempt to deprive the applicant of the benefits he would have if extradition proceedings were taken against him. Since the government of the United States cannot ask for him to be extradited, because espionage is a non-extraditable offence, resort is had to the subterfuge of a deportation order to achieve the same illegal object. It is an intrinsic part of the order that the applicant is being deported to a named country. Although the order does not state the destination on its face, the press notice issued by the Home Office has stated the Home Secretary's intention specifically and there has been no attempt on his part to resile from that statement. Whatever else can be done by way of deportation, an alien cannot be deported to a selected country. It was conceded by the then Attorney-General in *C* v. *E.*[11]* that there was no power to deport to a named country. There is power expressly given under article 8 to remove an alien to a named country, but there is no such power under article 20. Halsbury's Laws of England, 3rd ed. (1952), Vol. 1, p. 691, refers to the power of deportation simply as deportation from the United Kingdom. It is not described as a power to deport to a particular place. If it were otherwise there would be a confusion between deportation and extradition. The moment the United States government indicated that it wanted the applicant it made what was tantamount to a requisition by a foreign power, which could be dealt with only by the machinery set out in the Extradition Acts, 1870 to 1935.

The power of the court to go behind apparently lawful orders derives from the jurisdiction of the courts to see that delegated legislation is being used bona fide for its proper purpose and not in fraud legis. The principle was stated in *Municipal Council of Sydney* v. *Campbell.*[12] See, too, Rowlatt J., arguendo, in *Marshall Shipping Co. Ltd.* (*In Liquidation*) v. *The King,*[13] *Van Eck, N.O. and Van Rensburg N.O.* v. *Etna Stores,*[14] and *Arthur Yates & Co. Proprietary Ltd.* v. *Vegetable Seeds Committee.*[15] Article 21 (2) in no way impinges on the rule that an alien cannot be deported to a particular place. The article authorises the Home Secretary to direct any immigration officer to "afford" **[257]** to any alien or his dependants a passage to a port in any ship. "Afford" there implies a request by an alien that he be given a choice. Since his dependants cannot be deported the reference in the article to his "dependants" shows that the Home Secretary is empowered to accede to a request from the alien that he be put off at a port chosen by himself. The article emphasises the protection given to the alien at common law and indicates that consideration should be given to his wishes.

In *Rex* v. *Secretary of State for Home Affairs, Ex parte Duke of Chateau Thierry*[16]* the proceedings were solely by certiorari and the court was limited by the form of proceedings to deciding whether on its face the deportation order

[8] [1918] 1 K.B. 578, 586; 34 T.L.R. 279, C.A.
[9] [1918] 1 K.B. 578, 589.
[10] Ibid.
[11] (1946) 62 T.L.R. 326.
[12] [1925] A.C. 338, P.C.
[13] (1925) 41 T.L.R. 285.
[14] [1947] 2 S.A.L.R. 984.
[15] (1946) 72 C.L.R. 37.
[16] [1917] 1 K.B. 922; 33 T.L.R. 264, C.A.

was valid. The same limitation does not apply in habeas corpus proceedings. It was also a wartime case which arose pursuant to a Franco-British treaty, which may have become part of the municipal law. The same consideration was also present in *Rex* v. *Chiswick Police Station Superintendent, Ex parte Sacksteder*.[17*]

The question whether it was the Home Secretary or the alien who could choose the destination to which the alien was to be deported was left open in *Rex* v. *Governor of Brixton Prison, Ex parte Sarno*.[18*] Low J.[19] considered that political refugees could not be deported. In the present case the applicant is a genuine political refugee and the deportation order is an attempt to enforce the return of a genuine political offender to the country of his origin which wants him for political reasons. If extradition is sought, the formalities of extradition must be complied with: *Muller* v. *Superintendent, Presidency Jail, Calcutta*.[20]

Deportation is not an absolute power to be exercised by the mere ipse dixit of the Home Secretary but must be exercised judicially. It is a quasi-judicial act; that is shown by the use of "deem" in article 20 (2) (*b*). Accordingly, the Home Secretary must give the alien an opportunity of making representations directed to the issue of whether it is conducive to the public good that a deportation order be made. The representations which the applicant made to the Home Secretary in his petition in July, 1962, were directed to a different issue. In the *Sacksteder* case[21*] Scrutton L.J.[22] referred to the powers given under the Act of 1914 as powers of a judicial character which **[258]** could not be delegated. If deportation was not meant to be a quasi-judicial act but a purely executive act the phraseology of article 20 (2) (*b*) would have been different. Compare *Liversidge* v. *Sir John Anderson*[23] where the terms of the relevant order were "if the Secretary of State has reasonable cause to believe." In other statutory instruments the Secretary of State is empowered to act if he is "satisfied." A deemster was a judge and "deem" connotes the conception of judgment. Parliament by using that word in the article intended the Home Secretary to act in a quasi-judicial capacity and to hear the representations of the alien before deciding whether to make an order. This matter is of particular importance in this case because the applicant desires to protest his innocence.

[STEPHENSON J. That is not a relevant matter for this court. Am I not bound by *Rex* v. *Leman Street Police Station Inspector, Ex parte Venicoff*[24*] to reject the submission that deportation is a quasi-judicial act?]

It is distinguishable for two reasons. First, the attention of the Divisional Court was not drawn to the need for parity of treatment between article 20 (2) (*a*) and (*b*). Under (*a*) an alien cannot be deported on account of a criminal offence without the benefit of a court hearing; it would be anomalous if under (*b*) when he has committed no criminal offence he was to be in a worse position. Secondly, since the decision of the Divisional Court, an administrative concession[25] has been introduced whereby certain cases of proposed deportation are referred to the chief metropolitan magistrate sitting at Bow Street for an advisory opinion. That concession is in law no more than a recognition of the right of the alien to be heard. The right to be heard, audi alteram partem, is one of two fundamental principles applicable to all judicial inquiries. The deportation order is invalid by reason of the absence of the judicial process.

[STEPHENSON J. I cannot see how the two considerations on which you rely entitle me to disregard *Rex* v. *Leman Street Police Station Inspector, Ex parte Venicoff*.[26*]]

17 [1918] 1 K.B. 578.
18 [1916] 2 K.B. 742; 32 T.L.R. 717, D.C.
19 [1916] 2 K.B. 742, 752.
20 [1955] Internat.L.R. 497; (1955) S.C.J. 324.
21 [1918] 1 K.B. 578.
22 Ibid. 591.
23 [1942] A.C. 206; 58 T.L.R. 35; [1941] 3 All E.R. 338, H.L.
24 [1920] 3 K.B. 72; 36 T.L.R. 677, D.C.
25 Made pursuant to European Convention on Establishment, 1955. See (1955) 559 H.C.Deb., col. 1349.
26 [1920] 3 K.B. 72.

It is conceded that that decision is binding, but the right to challenge it in a higher court is reserved. **[259]**

In the previous proceedings relating to the applicant[27] Donovan L.J. said that the applicant had done nothing to justify deportation. The whole conception of deportation is that it is a punishment for misconduct and misbehaviour by a person resident in this country. It is not, therefore, appropriate in the case of an alien who has been refused leave to land and held in custody pending his proposed removal from this country under article 8, which contains the appropriate machinery for dealing with such a case. Article 8 deals with the precise situation which has arisen in the present case. It gives far greater powers than can be obtained by deportation—since it confers express authority to order the transportation of an alien to a named destination. Article 20 empowers the deportation of aliens who are resident in the United Kingdom or at the very least physically present in the United Kingdom in the eyes of the law. Deportation is an order to an alien to depart from the place where he is. But the applicant has never been allowed to land and it is quite illogical to order him to depart from a place where he is not. An alien refused leave to land can be dealt with only under article 8. The notice of refusal to land and a deportation order are mutually contradictory, for the very fact of deportation assumes the lawful presence in this country of the alien, which is denied by the notice of refusal of leave to land. Until the notice of refusal is revoked the Home Secretary is precluded from invoking the machinery of deportation. If articles 8 and 20 were not mutually exclusive, but were complementary, and conferred the same power to transport to a selected destination, article 8 would be otiose.

The onus is on the executive to establish the validity of the Order of 1953. The executive must prove that it is intra vires the Act of 1914, which is the enabling Act. Every imprisonment is prima facie illegal: *per* Lord Atkin in *Liversidge* v. *Sir John Anderson*.[28] The Order of 1953 is wholly ultra vires since the Act of 1914 from which it purports to derive its validity was defunct and inoperative in 1953 when the Order of 1953 was made. At that time the Act of 1914 was in abeyance. The peculiarity of the Act of 1914 is that it is alive and effective only when there is a state of war or imminent national emergency: see section 1 (1). The Aliens Restriction (Amendment) Act, 1919, did not **[260]** re-enact the powers created by the Act of 1914, as should have been done if they were to be applicable in peacetime, but only made them exercisable in a wider set of circumstances than those mentioned in the Act of 1914. Therefore, the legal status of the powers to impose restrictions on aliens depends entirely on the Act of 1914, and that Act restricts the existence of these powers to times of war or imminent national emergency. Except for the Second World War, the Act of 1914 was dormant since the end of the First World War and had spent its legislative force. It could still be revived by another war or by some imminent national emergency; otherwise it remains dormant, defunct and inoperative. There was no war or occasion of national emergency in 1953: compare *Willcock* v. *Muckle*.[29]

The applicant desires to prove that there has been a requisition by the government of the United States to Her Majesty's government for his return to the United States. A subpoena duces tecum[30] has therefore been served on the Home Secretary. No leave is required for the issue of the subpoena under R.S.C., Ord. 59, r. 43 (2). In the note thereto in the Annual Practice (1963), p. 1763, certain courts, which do permit the issue of a subpoena duces tecum, are mentioned, but the Vacation Court is not included among them and accordingly the normal practice pertains so that no leave is required in the present case.

[STEPHENSON J. If I were sitting in chambers leave would be required. If the application came before a Divisional Court it would be required. I can hardly

[27] *Reg.* v. *Secretary of State for Home Affairs, Ex parte Soblen**; [1963] 1 Q.B. 829, 837; [1962] 3 W.L.R. 1145; [1962] 3 All E.R. 373, C.A. Reporter's note: see now post, p. 311.

[28] [1942] A.C. 206, 245.

[29] [1951] 2 K.B. 844; [1951] 2 T.L.R. 373; [1951] 2 All E.R. 367, D.C.

[30] The contents of the subpoena are set out, *ante*, p. 253.

think that a judge sitting alone in vacation is in a better position than the Divisional Court. I think leave is required.]

Sir John Hobson Q.C., A.-G. and *R. A. Barr* for the Governor of Brixton Prison. Leave ought not to be given. The discretion of the Home Secretary to deport the applicant is absolute and this court does not sit as a court of appeal from the exercise of his discretion. It is therefore not proper to place before the court material on which the Home Secretary exercised his discretion. In any event, the documents mentioned in the second part of the subpoena are not in the possession of Her Majesty's government. They are exhibits to judicial proceedings in the United States and are not in this country.

[STEPHENSON J. I cannot decide on the Attorney-General's submission that the Home Secretary's discretion is absolute until **[261]** I have heard full argument. I think that in this case I should grant leave to issue the first part of the subpoena. I do not grant leave to issue the second part.]

F. Elwyn Jones Q.C. It is not now sought to have the documents referred to in the second part of the subpoena.

[The Attorney-General produced a certificate[31] from the Foreign Secretary claiming Crown Privilege in respect of the documents for which leave to issue the subpoena had been given.]

F. Elwyn Jones Q.C. In habeas corpus proceedings Crown Privilege does not lie. All the circumstances point to a requisition for the return of the applicant having been made by the United States government: see the report in "The Times" of August 8, 1962.[32] The applicant should be entitled to probe the matter further. *Duncan* v. *Cammell Laird & Co. Ltd.*[33] is distinguishable because it was a civil dispute inter partes. Habeas corpus is a special procedure to safeguard the liberty of the subject where the court is always eager to assist the applicant. When the fundamental liberties of the subject are concerned the Crown cannot shelter behind the plea of Crown Privilege. Crown Privilege is repugnant to the principle of habeas corpus that it is for the Crown to justify its arbitrary interference with the liberties of the subject. At the very least, if public disclosure of governmental communications would be injurious to the public interest, the documents should be disclosed privately to the judge.

[STEPHENSON J. In my view, Crown Privilege can be claimed in habeas corpus proceedings. I do not think that, even if I had power to look at the documents privately, this is a case where I should exercise my discretion to do so.]

Sir John Hobson Q.C., A.-G. and *R. Barr* for the Governor of Brixton Prison. The whole of the applicant's argument assumes that the Home Secretary's intention is to surrender the applicant to the custody of the United States government. But there is no evidence to support that assumption. The Home Secretary's intention from the outset has been to ensure that the applicant did not land here, because his presence in this country is undesirable, and to ensure that he continued his journey on the aircraft on which he came here. In taking that decision the Home Secretary was acting in an executive capacity on material not before the court and he is answerable only to Parliament, to whom he had already announced his decision. When the Home **[262]** Secretary was defeated in his original intention to keep the applicant out by the applicant's stratagem and when he was then frustrated in his intention to ensure that the applicant continue on the same journey as that which he was on by the carrier's refusal to comply with the directions given under article 8, the Home Secretary resorted to the use of a deportation order so as to achieve his *original* intention. Before ever the applicant had landed here the Home Secretary intended to keep him out of the country. The desire to expel the applicant preceded any possible question of handing him over to the United States Government. Moreover, there is no evidence of any requisition by the United States Government for the surrender of the applicant. The report in "The Times"[34] is not evidence of the truth of the statements contained in it. What a newspaper correspondent says

[31] The contents of the certificate are set out, *ante*, p. 254.
[32] *Ante*, p. 250.
[33] [1942] A.C. 624; 58 T.L.R. 242; [1942] 1 All E.R. 587, H.L
[34] *Ante*, p. 250.

someone else said is hearsay, and merely because it is not denied by the Home Office it does not become any the less hearsay inadmissible as evidence. There are many matters on which the United States Government might wish to communicate with Her Majesty's Government about the applicant which would not involve a request for his extradition. Espionage is not an extraditable offence and no government should be assumed to be so inefficient as to make a requisition for a non-extraditable offence which it knows could not be granted.

The question is whether a deportation and a detention order otherwise valid on their face are rendered invalid because of the Home Secretary's intention to place the applicant on board an aircraft about to leave the United Kingdom and expected to go to the United States. It might be objectionable to the applicant, but the deportation of the applicant in this matter is wholly within the Home Secretary's powers. It is a matter solely for his executive discretion and this court will not sit as a court of appeal from the exercise of his discretion nor will it inquire into the basis of the exercise of his discretion provided that he acted in good faith and within the limits of the authority conferred on him. There is no evidence in the present case to suggest mala fides or an improper use of power.

By international law every sovereign state has the power to prevent aliens from entering its territory and the power to expel them on arrival, without which the power to prohibit entry would be nugatory: *Attorney-General for Canada* v. *Cain.*[35]* The power **[263]** to deport includes the ancillary powers of selecting the aircraft or ship on which the alien should be put and of authorising his detention pending his removal on board the selected aircraft or ship. It does not include the power to direct another sovereign state to take the deportee. A sovereign state cannot enforce its directions on the deportee once he is outside its territory because he is not expected to return and therefore there is no sanction for the enforcement of directions on him. It can enforce its directions for the removal of the alien on the masters of aircraft and ships who are expected to return. On their return they might find themselves prosecuted for the offence of failing to comply with the directions given to them. It is not for the protection of the alien that there is any limitation on the power to direct the alien to a particular destination and that such express power is not given in article 20. It is simply because of the lack of sanction if the alien failed to obey the direction owing to the limited nature of territorial jurisdiction. The concession in *C.* v. *E.*[36]* was only that in that case there was no power to deport the alien to Czechoslovakia because she was no longer a Czech national and that country did not want her.

By international and national law an alien can be deported to the country of his origin or his nationality or to the country from where he embarked or to any country willing to receive him. The Act of 1914 gives power to deport to a particular destination. There is no such direct power in the Order of 1953 because it was considered ludicrous to authorise directions on an alien when there was no sanction for their enforcement once he was outside territorial jurisdiction. But there is no juristic principle to prevent such power being given in the order. In practice the same result is achieved by the selection of a specified ship or aircraft: see *Rex* v. *Secretary of State for Home Affairs, Ex parte Duke of Chateau Thierry*[37]* and *Rex* v. *Chiswick Police Station Superintendent, Ex parte Sacksteder.*[38]* It would be absurd if it was the alien and not the Home Secretary who could choose the destination to which the alien was to be deported. The alien might choose some remote country to which there was no ready access and to which there were only infrequent journeys by ships or aircraft. It would be ridiculous that the alien could stay here for quite some time until his deportation could be made effective because of his choice of destination. It would not be **[264]** practicable to operate the machinery of deportation if the choice of destination was to be the privilege of the alien. *Rex* v. *Secretary of State for Home Affairs,*

[35] [1906] A.C. 542, 546; 22 T.L.R. 757, P.C.
[36] 62 T.L.R. 326.
[37] [1917] 1 K.B. 922.
[38] [1918] 1 K.B. 578.

Ex parte Duke of Chateau Thierry[39]* is an exact parallel with the present case and is binding authority for the rejection of the applicant's argument. The then Attorney-General admitted[40] that the object and intention of the deportation order in that case was to send the alien to France to perform his military obligations there. Nevertheless the order was held to be valid. That case decided three things: first, that the selection of the ship for deportation and hence choice of destination was a matter for the Home Secretary; secondly, that in exercising his discretion he was acting in an executive capacity and the courts could not inquire into the exercise of his discretion or sit as a court of appeal therefrom; thirdly, that the political character of a deportation is not a relevant consideration for the courts but entirely one for the Home Secretary who in his discretion can grant asylum to political refugees. That is a concession he makes for which he is answerable only to Parliament. The protection given against political deportation by section 3 of the Aliens Act, 1905, was removed by the Act of 1914 and has never been restored. The observations of Low J. in *Rex* v. *Governor of Brixton Prison, Ex parte Sarno*[41]* were obiter, for the alien there was not a political refugee, and they were expressly disapproved by Pickford L.J. in *Rex* v. *Chiswick Police Station Superintendent, Ex parte Sacksteder.*[42]*

The following authorities on the previous Alien Orders are relied on: *Rex* v. *Chiswick Police Station Superintendent, Ex parte Sacksteder,*[43]* *Rex* v. *Leman Police Station Inspector, Ex parte Venicoff,*[44]* *Rex* v. *Governor of Brixton Prison, Ex parte Bloom,*[45]* *Rex* v. *Home Secretary, Ex parte Bressler*[46]* and *Rex* v. *Secretary of State for Foreign Affairs and Secretary of State for the Colonies, Ex parte Greenberg,*[47]* which decides that a degree of extraterritorial effect must be attributable to a deportation order.

See, too, *Rex* v. *Governor of Brixton Prison and Secretary of State for Home Affairs, Ex parte Pawel Sliwa.*[48]* It follows from those authorities: (1) that the Home Secretary and not the **[265]** deportee can choose the ship or aircraft for deportation; article 21 (1) of the Order of 1953 makes that even clearer than the Order of 1919; (2) that he acts as an executive officer under powers delegated to him by Parliament; (3) that the courts cannot review the exercise of his discretion nor inquire into the way in which or the grounds on which he exercises his discretion, provided that he has exercised them under and in accordance with the Order of 1953; (4) that the Home Secretary is for this purpose in the same position as when he exercises his emergency powers of detention in wartime: compare *Greene* v. *Secretary of State for Home Affairs,*[49] in particular the speeches of Lord Macmillan[50] and Lord Wright.[51]

The present case has nothing to do with extradition. *Muller* v. *Superintendent, Presidency Jail, Calcutta*[52] shows that extradition and deportation are two completely separate and different processes. Deportation only applies to aliens and arises from the unilateral act of the domestic government; extradition applies to both alien and British subjects and arises from the request of a foreign government to the domestic authorities for the surrender of a particular person. The mere fact that in different circumstances a similar result could have been achieved by extradition in no way makes what is otherwise lawful deportation unlawful. There is not an iota of evidence to suggest that the Home Secretary

[39] [1917] 1 K.B. 922.
[40] [1917] 1 K.B. 552, 553, D.C.
[41] [1916] 2 K.B. 742, 752.
[42] [1918] 1 K.B. 578, 586.
[43] [1918] 1 K.B. 578, 590.
[44] [1920] 3 K.B. 72, 78.
[45] (1920) 124 L.T. 375, 378, D.C.
[46] (1924) 131 L.T. 386, C.A.
[47] [1947] 2 All E.R. 550.
[48] [1952] 1 K.B. 169; [1952] 1 T.L.R. 61; [1952] 1 All E.R. 187, C.A.
[49] [1942] A.C. 284; 58 T.L.R. 53; sub nom. *R.* v. *Home Secretary, Ex parte Greene* [1942] 2 All E.R. 338, H.L.
[50] [1942] A.C. 284, 297.
[51] Ibid. 304, 307.
[52] [1955] Internat.L.R. 497.

has not exercised his powers bona fide and otherwise than in the discharge of his public duties. He had to consider the relations of Her Majesty's Government with friendly powers, the security risks of the applicant travelling about this country or other countries, the international consequences of his going east or west, and the desirability of getting him out of this country or allowing him to remain here. Those were proper and relevant considerations for him to bear in mind in determining the public good. No court, reflecting on those considerations, could conclude on the evidence that the public interest cannot require the expulsion of the applicant. The references to "sham" in *Rex* v. *Chiswick Police Station Superintendent, Ex parte Sacksteder*[53]* were intended to cover the use of deportation orders for private purposes. If the Home Secretary loved a modern Bethsheeba, his deportation of Uriah would be a sham in that he was using his public office for a private purpose. Those dicta were not intended **[266]** to give the courts power to question the making of a deportation order by the Home Secretary for public purposes.

Even if the courts could give protection against deportation of a political character, the offence in the present case (espionage) was not a political offence. A political offence requires the existence of two or more contending parties within the state and the act relied on must be committed on behalf of one of those parties in the course of its struggle with the other: *In re Meunier*[54]* *In re Castioni*[55]*; *Reg.* v. *Governor of Brixton Prison, Ex parte Schtraks.*[56]* It is not enough that the offence might have a political context. The espionage in the present case was not an attempt to influence the government of the United States by one party against another, but was an act on behalf of a foreign government which was designed to violate the sovereignty of the United States.

The second ground of alleged invalidity is not made out.

[STEPHENSON J. You need not trouble about that submission.]

On their true construction the articles of the Order of 1953 are cumulative and complementary. There is no logical reason why articles 8 and 20 should be mutually exclusive. It would be nonsensical if an alien who arrived illegally in the country without leave had to be granted leave to land before he could be expelled. Again, if the owner of an airline only had one aeroplane which broke down when it was embarked at an airport in this country the undesirable alien on board would have to be granted leave, if the applicant is right, to land before he could be deported. No action could be taken under article 8 because the carrier would have no means of removing the alien. These absurd results demonstrate the fallacy of the applicant's interpretation of the Order of 1953. It would be ridiculous if in this case the Home Secretary had to go through the motions of granting the applicant leave to land simply to deport him immediately the notice of refusal was cancelled.

It is for the executive to establish that a deportation order is valid on its face. Once that is shown the burden is on the applicant to prove that for some reason the order is not valid or that it does not apply to him.

The Aliens Order, 1953, is intra vires the Act of 1914. **[267]**

[STEPHENSON J. You need not trouble about the contention that it is ultra vires.]

Even if the deportation order in this case was invalid, what was done was an "Act of State" against a non-resident alien and, therefore, there is no jurisdiction to entertain the present application. It is conceded that "Act of State" is no defence in the case of a friendly alien resident in the United Kingdom. It is clear that an alien who is abroad cannot sue the Crown in respect of an "Act of State" except for an interference with his goods within the realm. The position of a non-resident alien unlawfully present within the realm has never been decided. An alien who is unlawfully here and has not received permission to land is in precisely the same position as a friendly alien who is abroad. He cannot sue

[53] [1918] 1 K.B. 578, 586, 589.
[54] [1894] 2 Q.B. 415, D.C.
[55] [1891] 1 Q.B. 149; 7 T.L.R. 50, D.C.
[56] [1963] 1 Q.B. 55; [1962] 2 W.L.R. 976; [1962] 2 All E.R. 176, D.C.; affd. [1962] 3 W.L.R. 1013; [1962] 3 All E.R. 589, H.L.

the Crown and he cannot improve his position by securing entry by stealth or stratagem. The right of an alien to sue the Crown is based on his lawful residence in this country: *Poll* v. *Lord Advocate*[57]*; *Johnstone* v. *Pedlar*.[58]* See in particular the speeches of Viscount Finlay,[59] Viscount Cave, [60] Lord Sumner[61] and Lord Phillimore.[62] The applicant is not lawfully resident here and he cannot sue the Crown. Habeas corpus is to protect the liberty of the subject. A friendly alien resident here owes temporary allegiance to the Crown and is for this purpose treated as a British subject, but an alien refused leave to land can have no rights as against the Crown. It is true that Atkin L.J. in *Commercial and Estates Co. of Egypt* v. *The Board of Trade*[63] said that an "Act of State" only related to acts done outside the realm, but he based himself on *Johnstone* v. *Pedlar*[64]* and misconceived the basis of that decision. [Reference was also made to *Rex* v. *Governor of Brixton Prison, Ex parte Lannoy*.[65]*]

F. Elwyn Jones Q.C. in reply. Even if the representations of the United States Government do not amount to a requisition for the return of the applicant under section 7 of the Extradition Act, 1870, at the very least they constitute or evidence "an arrangement" for the surrender of the applicant under section 2 of the Act of 1870. The language of that section is wide enough to cover an agreement between two states to deal with a fugitive **[268]** alien otherwise than by the procedure laid down in the Act of 1870 and extradition treaties made thereunder.

The definition of a political offence in the earlier authorities is not an exhaustive one. Whether an offence is one of a political character is something which has to be considered in the circumstances of the time: there is no rigid definition; in *Reg.* v. *Governor of Brixton Prison, Ex parte Kolczynski*[66]* Cassels J.[67] said that treason could be a political offence. If treason can be a political offence, so can espionage.

The deportation order is tainted with the illegality of returning a fugitive political offender to the country from where he came and to where, if the law took its proper course, he could not be returned.

The remedy of habeas corpus is available to the meanest subject against the most powerful. *Rex* v. *Earl Crewe, ex parte Sekgome*.[68]* It is available not only to subjects of the Crown but to aliens physically present within the realm: Halsbury's Laws of England, 3rd ed. (1955), Vol. II, p. 25. The applicant is physically present within the realm and therefore entitled to apply for a writ of habeas corpus. The references in the authorities to "residence" relate to residence in its purely factual sense of physical presence; residence was not being used in any technical sense. It is fantastic to suppose that, if the Home Secretary took leave of his senses and began torturing the applicant, any such action could be met with a plea of "Act of State."

STEPHENSON J. stated the facts as set out above and continued: I take the submissions made by Mr. Elwyn Jones, on behalf of the applicant, in an order which is the reverse of that in which he argued them, because the reverse order seems to me to be the logical order. His first submission was this—I am not surprised that he made it last or that he puts in the forefront of his argument the submission with which I shall deal last—that the Aliens Order, 1953, is wholly ultra vires, since the Aliens Restriction Act, 1914, under which it purports to

57 (1899) 1 F. 823, 827, 828.
58 [1921] 2 A.C. 262; 37 T.L.R. 870, H.L.
59 [1921] 2 A.C. 262, 274.
60 Ibid. 277.
61 Ibid. 289.
62 Ibid. 297.
63 [1925] 1 K.B. 271, 297, C.A.
64 [1921] 2 A.C. 262; 37 T.L.R. 870, H.L.
65 [1942] 2 K.B. 281; 58 T.L.R. 350; sub nom. *R.* v. *Lannoy* [1942] 2 All E.R. 232, C.A.
66 [1955] 1 Q.B. 540; [1955] 2 W.L.R. 116; [1955] 1 All E.R. 31, D.C.
67 [1955] 1 Q.B. 540, 549.
68 [1910] 2 K.B. 576; 26 T.L.R. 439, C.A.

have been made, is now defunct and inoperative, and was so in 1953 when the Order purported to be made.

The Act of 1914, says Mr. Elwyn Jones, has this peculiarity, that it is only alive and awake "when a state of war exists between His Majesty and any foreign power, or when it appears **[269]** that an occasion of imminent national danger or great emergency has arisen." Only then may provision be made by order under that Act for such matters as "prohibiting aliens from landing in the United Kingdom" or "the deportation of aliens from the United Kingdom," under section 1 (1), and the powers exerciseable under section 1 (1) of the Act of 1914, notwithstanding their continuance by section 1 of the Aliens Restriction (Amendment) Act, 1919, "for a period of one year" from the passing of the Act of 1919, "not only in those circumstances, but at any time," and notwithstanding the continuance of section 1 of the Act of 1919 from year to year by successive Expiring Laws Continuance Acts ending with the Expiring Laws Continuance Act, 1961, died or fell asleep with the end of the 1914-1918 war, officially declared as August 31, 1921, by the Termination of the Present War (Definition) Act, 1918, and the Termination of War Order in Council, 1921 (S.R. & O. 1921 No. 1276).

The Act of 1914, he submits, was called out of abeyance by the blast of the 1939-45 war, but on October 8, 1949, that emergency ended (cf. *Willcock* v. *Muckle*[69]) and by 1953 it was again defunct or dormant and awaiting resuscitation by a third world war or comparable emergency. Its waking life would have been prolonged if the Expiring Laws Continuance Acts had continued the principal Act of 1914, but as they only continued the amending Act of 1919, the Act of 1914 and all its powers expired on August 31, 1921, and all subsequent Aliens Orders, save those made during the 1939-45 war emergency, were ultra vires because made under an inoperative statute.

I find it difficult to do justice to this argument, but must not be deterred from trying by its novelty or by the consideration that, if successful, it would establish that this country would have been without any principal Aliens Act for long periods, since section 16 (2) of the Act of 1919 repealed in terms the Aliens Act, 1905.

The argument appears to me to ignore the plain terms of section 1 (1) of the Act of 1919, which not only continues the emergency powers exerciseable under section 1 of the Act of 1914 in times which are not those of emergency, but declares that section 1 "shall, for a period of one year . . . have effect as though the words 'at any time when a state of war exists between His Majesty and any foreign power, or when it appears that an occasion of imminent national danger or great **[270]** emergency has arisen' were omitted." Therefore, section 1 (1) of the Act of 1914 so amended is continued annually by the continuation of the Act of 1919. The law in reference to the deportation of aliens is still contained in the Acts of 1914 and 1919 as extended by the Expiring Laws Continuance Acts, 1920-61; the Court of Appeal so held in 1924 (see *Rex* v. *The Home Secretary, Ex parte Bressler*[70]*) and again by implication at any rate in 1952 (see *Rex* v. *Governor of Brixton Prison and Secretary of State for Home Affairs, Ex parte Pawel Sliwa*[71]*). This bold argument, therefore, fails, and I have to consider Mr. Elwyn Jones' next submission.

This is that the deportation order is invalid because it purports to be made in respect of an alien who has been refused leave to land. As long as the notice refusing him leave to land under article 8 (1) of the Order of 1953 remains neither revoked nor withdrawn, the applicant is not here except for the purpose of being detained under article 8 (4) of the Order of 1953, and can only be removed by directions given under article 8 (1) of that Order. Articles 8 and 20 are mutually exclusive, not complementary, and the applicant cannot be deported under article 20 or detained under article 21 (4) or removed under article 21 (1), at least until the notice refusing him leave to land has been revoked under

[69] [1951] 2 K.B. 844; [1951] 2 T.L.R. 373; [1951] 2 All E.R. 367, D.C.
[70] (1924) 131 L.T. 386, C.A.
[71] [1952] 1 K.B. 169; [1952] 1 T.L.R. 61; [1952] 1 All E.R. 187, C.A.

article 29 (if it is an "order" within the meaning of that article) or in some manner withdrawn.

Further, deportation under article 20 is inapplicable to an alien who has done nothing to justify deportation (as Donovan L.J. is reported to have said of this applicant during the hearing of his appeal to the Court of Appeal in the previous proceedings[72]), nor committed any offence nor otherwise misbehaved himself so as to justify his removal from the United Kingdom, but has merely been refused leave to land and, in fact, been landed for medical treatment and detention pending removal under article 8.

I find nothing in the terms of the Order of 1953, or in logic, or common sense, to support this at first sight attractive, submission. Article 20 (1) refers to "an alien" without qualification, and empowers the Secretary of State to require any alien not merely to go away but to stay away, as the Attorney-General contends. **[271]**

I see no reason why it should not apply not only to aliens lawfully residing in the United Kingdom, but to aliens refused leave to land in the United Kingdom under article 8, or to aliens landing in the United Kingdom without leave, unlawfully, because of the restrictions imposed by article 1, to which article 8 is applied by article 9. An alien found in the United Kingdom after landing without leave might have been convicted of a specified offence in the United Kingdom and recommended for deportation under article 20 (2) (*a*). Where leave to land is refused to an alien, information may reach the Secretary of State on which he deems it to be conducive to the public good to make a deportation order against the alien under article 20 (2) (*b*).

An alien cannot well be detained at one and the same time both under article 8 (4) and under article 21 (4), but I cannot see why the Secretary of State should not decide to deport under article 20 and detain under article 21 an alien who has been detained under article 8 (4) after landing unlawfully, or (as here) being refused leave to land, without the technicality of revoking or withdrawing the notice of refusal as well as the directions given under it.

In my judgment, the provisions of these articles are cumulative and complementary, not mutually exclusive; it is not necessary for the Secretary of State to lift the ban on landing before making a deportation order, whether the alien has in fact been admitted as an act of mercy, or is in fact in the United Kingdom by remaining on board the ship or aircraft which brought him into the territorial waters of the United Kingdom or landed him on a United Kingdom airfield. This submission must also fail.

I have, therefore, next to consider Mr. Elwyn Jones' third submission. This is that the deportation order is invalid because the Secretary of State purported to deem it to be conducive to the public good to make it against the applicant, but purported to make it under article 20 (1) and (2) (*b*) without first hearing representations from the applicant directed to the issue whether it was conducive to the public good to make the order.

This branch of Mr. Elwyn Jones' argument repeated the argument for the applicant Venicoff in *Rex* v. *Leman Street Police Station Inspector, Ex parte Venicoff*,[73]* which was rejected by the Divisional Court.

Mr. Elwyn Jones sought to strengthen that argument and distinguish that decision by calling my attention, first, to the **[272]** anomaly that an alien would be worse off if deported under article 20 (2) (*b*) than if deported under article 20 (2) (*a*) [which deals with deportation of criminals] and, secondly, to the administrative concession since made by the Home Secretary, pursuant to a European Convention,[74] by which he refers certain cases of aliens, which would not include the applicant's case, whom he was proposing to deport, to the chief metropolitan magistrate sitting at Bow Street. He ultimately conceded that the

[72] *Reg.* v. *Secretary of State for Home Affairs, Ex parte Soblen**; [1963] 1 Q.B. 829, 837; [1962] 3 W.L.R. 1145; [1962] 3 All E.R. 373, C.A. Reporter's note: see now *post*, p. 311.

[73] [1920] 3 K.B. 72; 36 T.L.R. 677, D.C.

[74] European Convention on Establishment, 1955. See (1955) 559 H.C. Deb., col. 1349.

decision in *Venicoff's* case[75]* was binding on me, even if wrongly decided, and he reserved his right to take the point that it was wrongly decided in a court with jurisdiction to overrule it. I am not persuaded that these two new considerations would have weighed any more heavily with the Divisional Court in 1920 than they would with me were I free to consider them. But whatever their weight, I feel bound by the decision of the Divisional Court in *Venicoff's* case[76]* to reject that argument.

This brings me to the argument which was put, and in my judgment rightly put, by counsel for the applicant, in the forefront of his case. Even if the deportation order is on its face valid, says Mr. Elwyn Jones, the court can and should look behind it and declare it invalid if being used for a collateral purpose, particularly if that purpose is illegal or leads to illegality. If the court does look behind this order and in particular at the revoked directions of August 3, 4 and 8, the press statement of August 11 and the letter from the Treasury Solicitor of August 21, it sees that the real object and purpose of this deportation order is to extradite the applicant to the United States of America in response to representations made by the United States Government, so that he may serve his sentence there and for a political offence in breach of section 3 of the Extradition Act, 1870, and article 6 of the United States of America (Extradition) Order in Council, 1935 (S.R. & O. 1935, No. 574).

The crime or offence of which the applicant has been convicted, runs the argument, is not one of those specified as extraditable in article 3 of that Order in Council, but is of a political character, and so not extraditable by reason of the Act of 1870 and article 6 of the Order in Council. To avoid the illegality of surrendering a political offender of United States nationality to the requisition of the United States Government and surrendering him without the necessity of a prima facie case against him being established before **[273]** the chief metropolitan magistrate, the Secretary of State has resorted to the device of a deportation order admittedly to be carried into effect by placing the applicant on an aircraft which is about to leave the United Kingdom and is expected to go to the United States of America. Deportation and extradition are completely different and should be kept separate (cf. *Muller* v. *Superintendent, Presidency Jail, Calcutta*[77]). An exercise of the power to deport for the purpose of extradition is an abuse of it which the court can and should restrain. The order is ultra vires the Secretary of State in that it is in effect nominating the place to which the applicant is to be deported; it is not made in good faith because it is made for the purpose of extraditing the applicant to the United States of America; it is not genuine or bona fide, but a sham and would be so even if the offences of which the applicant had been convicted were extraditable; as they are political, it is a device to enable an illegal act to be done.

This I have found a formidable argument. It rests first on the facts, mostly admitted by the respondent or on his behalf; then on matters which have been left by the Crown's successful claim for privilege in the unsatisfactory realm of speculation, and, finally, on the authority of judicial decisions, and in particular the dicta of Pickford L.J.[78] and Warrington L.J.[79] in *Rex* v. *Chiswick Police Station Superintendent, Ex parte Sacksteder.*[78]* I was referred to several cases where the courts both of this country and of the Dominions had declared acts which were done under statutory powers ultra vires because done for a purpose not specified by the statutes. I refer only to *Municipal Council of Sydney* v. *Campbell.*[80] I have no doubt that one of the court's most important duties is to see so far as possible that the great officers of State and those who act under their orders, no less than public bodies and private individuals, act lawfully in the exercise of their powers; and the greater the power which is exercised, and the higher the authority exercising it, the more important is the discharge by

[75] [1920] 3 K.B. 72.
[76] *Ibid.*
[77] [1955] Internat.L.R. 497; (1955) S.C.J. 324.
[78] [1918] 1 K.B. 578, 586; 34 T.L.R. 279, C.A.
[79] [1918] 1 K.B. 578, 589.
[80] [1925] A.C. 338, P.C.

the court of this duty and the more difficult.

This case illustrates both the importance and the difficulty. Mr. Elwyn Jones asks me to accept the truth of the statements printed by "The Times." The Attorney-General asks me to reject them as inadmissible. Mr. Elwyn Jones submits that the representations admitted to have been made by the United States **[274]** Government amounted to a requisition antecedent to the deportation order for the surrender of the applicant under section 7 of the Extradition Act, 1870, and even that the action taken by the United States Government and the Secretary of State amounts to or evidences an arrangement within section 2 of that Act. The Attorney-General submits that it is most unlikely that the United States Government would ask Her Majesty's Government to extradite the applicant for an offence which is not extraditable, and that the Secretary of State may well have formed the intention to deport him to the United States of America before ever he received the representations of the United States Government; and the Crown claims privilege for the relevant communications, a claim I felt bound to uphold without requiring the attendance of the certifying Secretary of State, rejecting Mr. Elwyn Jones's submissions that the Crown cannot claim privilege in habeas corpus proceedings and that, if it could, I should look at the documents before upholding the claim. Mr. Elwyn Jones contended that the Secretary of State's mind was primarily directed not to getting the applicant out of this country, but to getting him into the hands of the United States authorities. The Attorney-General contended that the Secretary of State was entitled to consider the relations of Her Majesty's Government with friendly powers, the security risks of the applicant travelling about this country or other countries, the international consequences of his going east or west, and the desirability of getting him out of this country or allowing him to remain here; but that the courts could not inquire whether he had those considerations in mind or what his intention was so long as he was not acting altogether outside his capacity of Home Secretary for some personal advantage or some private end.

Sacksteder's case[81]* was the second of two cases in the Court of Appeal concerning the deportation of French subjects liable to military obligations in consequence of an arrangement between the French and British Governments of the day by which such subjects resident in this country were sent to France. The other case was *Rex* v. *Secretary of State for Home Affairs, Ex parte Duke of Chateau Thierry*,[82]* the effect of which was stated by Scrutton L.J. in *Sacksteder's* case.[83]*

Referring to that case, Scrutton L.J. said[83]: "I understand **[275]** all the members of the court to have said that this court is not a Court of Appeal from the discretion of the Secretary of State in making an order of deportation. I understand all the members of the court to have said that article 12 of the Order in Council"—which is in much the same terms as articles 20 and 21 of the Order of 1953 which I have to consider—"gives the Secretary of State a power to select the ship on which the alien shall be deported, so that, while they all say the Secretary of State cannot in terms make an order that an alien shall be deported to a specific country, yet he has power to select the ship on which the alien may be placed, with the probable result that, unless the alien manages to get overboard onto some other ship, he will go to the country to which the ship on which he is placed is sailing. That has been decided for me by the Court of Appeal, and I am bound by it." Mr. Elwyn Jones contends that what is true of a ship is even truer of an aircraft, and the result which Scrutton L.J. describes as probable, namely, that the deported alien will go to the country to which the ship on which he is placed is sailing, becomes a certainty in the case of an alien put on board an aircraft, because his means of escaping from it are more limited and more dangerous.

In giving judgment in *Sacksteder's* case,[84]* Pickford L.J., who was a party to the decision in the *Chateau Thierry* case,[85]* said, speaking of a direction given

[81] [1918] 1 K.B. 578.
[82] [1917] 1 K.B. 922; 33 T.L.R. 264, C.A.
[83] [1918] 1 K.B. 578, 591.
[84] [1918] 1 K.B. 578.
[85] [1917] 1 K.B. 922.

under the then Aliens Order[86]: "In my opinion it is not possible for us to go behind that. I wish to guard myself in this way. I am not prepared to go quite so far as I think Low J. was inclined to go in the case of *Rex* v. *Governor of Brixton Prison, Ex parte Sarno.*[87]* I am not prepared to say that in every case where there is an order of detention or imprisonment the court is entitled to go behind that and see what the motives for making that order were. But I certainly am not inclined to say that in no case can the court go behind an order which on the face of it is valid ordering detention or custody. If that order is, if I may say so, practically a sham, if the purpose behind it is such as to show that the order is not a genuine or bona fide order, it seems to me the court can go behind it. Therefore I wish to guard myself against being supposed to say there are no circumstances in which the court can go behind on order for detention **[276]** valid on the face of it." Then he added: "In this case I do not think there are any grounds for doing so."

Warrington L.J. entered his caveat in these words[88]: "Then can the court in this case go behind the order, which is a legal order, for arrest? I am far from saying that there may not be cases in which that can be done. If, for example, the order, though on the face of it a valid order, was a mere sham to cover up something which would be illegal or to enable some subsequent act to be done which would itself be illegal. In the first case I am far from saying that the court could not go behind the apparently valid order and say that it was no order at all. In the second case, I am far from saying that the court might not find means of preventing the subsequent illegal act from being done. But in the present case there is nothing of that sort. The order is on the face of it valid, and there is no pretence for saying that it is a sham order or anything of the kind, nor is there any pretence for saying that under it or in consequence of it something illegal is going to be done by any of the officers of the executive government."

To see how far Low J. was inclined to go I have to look at *Rex* v. *Governor of Brixton Prison, Ex parte Sarno.*[89]* In giving the last judgment, Low J., though agreeing with the decision of the Divisional Court that the particular article under consideration was within the power conferred by the Act of 1914, said[89]: "I wish, before parting with this case, emphatically to protect myself from being supposed to assent to some of the arguments which have been used at the Bar. For instance, I do not agree that if the executive were to come into this court and simply say 'A person is in our custody, and therefore the writ of habeas corpus does not apply because the custody is at the moment technically legal,' the court would have no power to consider the matter and, if necessary, deal with the application for the writ. In my judgment that answer from the Crown in reply to an application for the writ would not be sufficient if this court were satisfied that what was really in contemplation was the exercise of an abuse of power. The arm of the law in this country would have grown very short, and the power of this court very feeble, if it were subject to such a restriction in the exercise of its power to protect the liberty of the subject as that proposition involves.

"I agree that article 12 is within the powers conferred by the **[277]** statute, and it is therefore only necessary to add that this decision must not be thought to determine the question as to what this court could do if there were a deliberate attempt by the exercise of the powers conferred by the statute and regulations to enforce the return of a real, genuine, political refugee to the country of his origin. In the present case I am not satisfied that the applicant is really a political refugee at all."

The question how far the courts can go behind a technically valid order has been raised in a number of cases and I have been referred to many, perhaps all, the authorities dealing with article 12 of the then Aliens Order which was under consideration in *Sarno's* case[90]* and the articles or orders in substantially the same terms which have replaced it. I do not think it would be helpful for me to

[86] [1918] 1 K.B. 578, 586.
[87] [1916] 2 K.B. 742, 752; 32 T.L.R. 717.
[88] [1918] 1 K.B. 578, 589.
[89] [1916] 2 K.B. 742, 752.
[90] [1916] 2 K.B. 742.

embark upon an exhaustive review of those authorities, particularly as I understand that, whatever my decision, it is the intention of the unsuccessful party to take the matter higher.

In the *Chateau Thierry* case[91]* the Divisional Court had looked behind an order, which was valid on the face of it, but the Court of Appeal said that the Divisional Court were wrong to do so. I was referred to *Venicoff's* case[92]* and *Sacksteder's* case[93]* which I have already mentioned. I was also referred to *Rex* v. *Governor of Brixton Prison, Ex parte Bloom.*[94]* In that case the respondent was the same officer as in this case; it does contain some observations in the judgment of Lord Reading C.J.,[95] with which Darling J. and Sankey J.[96] agreed, which bear upon this submission of Mr. Elwyn Jones and which are relied upon not only by him but also by the Attorney-General: "The second point is one that may be dismissed in very few words. It is said that on the facts there was a misuse by the Home Secretary of his executive powers, but, in my opinion, there is not the faintest ground for that suggestion, which was that there was a misuse of those powers in the sense to which I referred in using that expression in *Sarno's* case.* It was contended that the Home Secretary ought not to have exercised his discretion by making the order, but that is an appeal from the order. We have no right to sit on appeal from the Home Secretary when he has used the executive powers conferred upon him, provided that he has used them in a lawful way in accordance with the Act. If he **[278]** has come to a conclusion from which we might differ (and there is no ground for suggesting that we should), we could not interfere. So far from there having been a misuse of the Home Secretary's powers, all that we have before us is that the applicant, it is said, seems to have lived peaceably and lawfully in this country until the offences in question were committed by him. We do not know for what reason the Home Secretary thought it right to make the order. He may have considered particular circumstances which are not present to our minds. He may have information which we have not. He may think that the condition of the country required him to take action, although on the facts before us we might not think so. It is sufficient to say that there is no evidence whatever of any misuse by the Home Secretary of his executive powers, and therefore the second ground fails."

The next case to which I was referred was *Rex* v. *Home Secretary, Ex parte Bressler,*[97]* a case in which Bankes L.J.[98] advised that when future deportation orders were made by the Home Secretary deeming it to be conducive to the public good to make the order, he should recite that fact in his order and there would be an end to the questioning of the order; and that policy has been adopted in this case as no doubt in many previous cases.

Then there was *Rex* v. *Secretary of State for Foreign Affairs and Secretary of State for the Colonies, Ex parte Greenberg,*[99]* and finally *Rex* v. *Governor of Brixton Prison and Secretary of State for Home Affairs, Ex parte Pawel Sliwa,*[1]* to which I have already referred.

Bearing in mind that there has been no material change in the terms of the relevant provisions of the Aliens Orders, I think that the effect of the authorities to which I have been referred was accurately summed up by the Attorney-General. First, it follows from those authorities that the Secretary of State, not the deportee, is the person who may choose the ship or aircraft by which the deportee has to leave these shores; secondly, the Secretary of State in making the deportation order is acting as an executive and not as a judicial officer, and the power of so acting has been delegated to him by Parliament; thirdly, the courts

[91] [1917] 1 K.B. 522; 33 T.L.R. 757, D.C.
[92] [1920] 3 K.B. 72.
[93] [1918] 1 K.B. 578.
[94] (1920) 124 L.T. 375; 90 L.J. K.B. 574, D.C.
[95] 124 L.T. 375, 378.
[96] Ibid. 378.
[97] 131 L.T. 386.
[98] Ibid. 387.
[99] [1947] 2 All E.R. 550.
[1] [1952] 1 K.B. 169.

cannot review or interfere with his discretion, exercised either under article 20 or under article 21 of the Order of 1953, or act as a court of appeal from him and substitute its decision for his as **[279]** to how he should exercise his powers, or inquire into the way in which or the grounds on which he has exercised his discretion provided it appears that he has purported to exercise those powers under and in accordance with the Order of 1953 or, as I should prefer to put it in the words of Lord Reading C.J.,[2] "provided that he has used them in a lawful way in accordance with the Act."

The Attorney-General submitted on the authorities that the Secretary of State exercising this statutory power is really in the same position as a Secretary of State acting under wartime powers such as were given him by defence regulations during the last war, or under the rather similar powers conferred on him in the First World War, and he referred me to observations of Lord Macmillan[3] and Lord Wright[4] in their speeches in *Greene* v. *Secretary of State for Home Affairs.*

It is also clear, I think, from the authorities that the question of an alien being a political refugee or a fugitive offender convicted of or wanted for an offence of a political character, appears to be one which is for the Home Secretary a matter to be taken into consideration by him; and for that the principal authorities are the observations of Swinfen Eady L.J.,[5] Pickford L.J.[6] and Bankes L.J.[7] in the *Chateau Thierry* case.*

The Attorney-General was authorised to assure the court that it is still the position, as it was according to the *Chateau Thierry* case,[8]* that the Secretary of State would not deport those who are entitled to political asylum in this country, an assurance he has already given to the House of Commons. The Attorney-General further stated that the Secretary of State in this case had not merely received the applicant's petition of July 21, made of course before the deportation order of August 11 and not, therefore, specifically directed to the issue raised by an order for deportation, but other representations made by and on behalf of the applicant and is willing to receive any further representations that may be made by him or on his behalf.

If the argument of the Attorney-General is right, and his submission as to the effect of the decided cases, most of them binding on me, goes as far as he says, the court is prevented from getting **[280]** to the point of considering whether the applicant has a claim to be treated as a political refugee, any suggestion by Low J. in *Sarno's* case[9]* that that was a matter for the courts is wrong, and it is a matter for the Home Secretary and for Parliament; the court is equally prevented from considering whether the applicant has a claim to be treated as a fugitive offender convicted for an offence of a political character, but if that point is reached, the Attorney-General says, further, that the applicant's offences were clearly not of a political character as that phrase has been interpreted in *In re Meunier*[10]* and *Reg.* v. *Governor of Brixton Prison, Ex parte Schtraks,*[11]* a case at this moment under consideration by the House of Lords.[12] As a matter of first impression and ordinary language, many in the twentieth century might regard espionage, or at least such espionage as the applicant was convicted of committing, as a political offence, and that view would, perhaps, be fortified by the observations of Cassels J. in *Reg.* v. *Governor of Brixton Prison, Ex parte Kolczynski,*[13]* that treason would be an offence of a political character. But I do not feel able to hold it to be an offence of that character on the facts as they

[2] *In Rex* v. *Governor of Brixton Prison, Ex parte Bloom** (1920) 124 L.T. 375, 378.
[3] [1942] A.C. 284, 297; 58 T.L.R. 53; sub nom. *R.* v. *Home Secretary, Ex parte Greene* [1942] 3 All E.R. 388, H.L.
[4] [1942] A.C. 284, 304, 307.
[5] [1917] 1 K.B. 922, 929.
[6] Ibid. 933.
[7] Ibid. 936.
[8] Ibid.
[9] [1916] 2 K.B. 742, 752.
[10] [1894] 2 Q.B. 415, D.C.
[11] [1963] 1 Q.B. 55; [1962] 2 W.L.R. 976; [1962] 2 All E.R. 176, D.C.
[12] Affirmed* [1962] 3 W.L.R. 1013; [1962] 3 All E.R. 529, H.L.
[13] [1955] 1 Q.B. 540, 549; [1955] 2 W.L.R. 116; [1955] 1 All E.R. 31, D.C.

appear in the affidavits in the present case, and on the interpretation which the courts have put upon the language of the Extradition Act, 1870, and the Fugitive Offenders Act, 1881.

I think, too, that if the question were free from authority, I might have taken a more generous view of the court's power of challenging the Home Secretary's exercise of his discretion in this case than I feel able to take. But the cases cited, and especially the decision and observations of the Court of Appeal in the *Chateau Thierry* case,[14]* make it impossible for me to hold that the Home Secretary has abused his powers under the Acts of 1914 and 1919, and Order of 1953, in making the deportation order of August 11, 1962, or that the order was invalid and the applicant's detention under it is illegal.

By international law, every State has the power to prevent aliens, whether friendly or enemy, from entering its territory, and the power to expel them on arrival: *Attorney-General for Canada* v. *Cain.*[15]* And that power includes the ancillary powers of detention within its jurisdiction, and of determining the method of **[281]** conveyance outside its jurisdiction, which are necessary to the effective exercise of that power of expulsion. All that the Secretary of State is proved to have done is to exercise that power of expulsion and to put in motion the machinery necessary to carry it out in accordance with the provisions of the Acts of 1914 and 1919, and articles 20 and 21 of the Order of 1953. How far the Acts or the Order empower the Secretary of State to deport to a particular place on the face of the deportation order, and how far the form of deportation order may confine that power within unnecessarily narrow limits, are questions which I do not find it necessary to decide. I am not able to accept the limitation put upon the court's power to go behind a deportation order valid on its face for which the Attorney-General contends, as I do accept the observations of Pickford and Warrington L.JJ. in *Sacksteder's* case[16]* as a guide to the measure of the court's power. It may be possible for a detained alien to show that the deportation order is a sham or illegal in its consequences, although it is not made for other than public purposes. All I am saying is that this applicant has not done so. When I accept Mr. Elwyn Jones' invitation to look behind the order of August 11, I find nothing which enables me to say that the order is not genuine or lawful, or made in the honest belief that the good of this country requires the deportation of the applicant, whether or not it has been asked for or pressed for by the United States Government. I certainly do not find a requisition for surrender or a compliance with a requisition. What I should find if the veil imposed by the claim for Crown privilege were removed, I know not. In my view, the Attorney-General is right in contending, and Mr. Elwyn Jones wrong in denying, that the onus of proving this prima facie valid deportation order to be a sham, or not bona fide, or unlawful, is on the applicant who alleges it, however difficult it may be for him to discharge the onus. I must, therefore, reject this last contention of counsel for the applicant.

The arguments put forward by the applicant's counsel all seem to me at once to recognise, and to ask the court to ignore, the fundamental fact that what the Acts of 1914 and 1919 and the Orders made thereunder give the Secretary of State are emergency powers conferred at a time, and only for a time, when the legislature considered that the executive, in its treatment of aliens, should be almost out of reach of the control of the judiciary, and **[282]** the judiciary was unwilling and unable to interfere with the executive's treatment of aliens. What began as a temporary expedient has been continued for nearly half a century, and the protection given to political offenders by section 3 (i) (*b*) (ii) of the Aliens Act, 1905, removed in 1914, has never been restored. Mr. Elwyn Jones' argument that the arm of the law should be extended further to protect aliens in peace than it was in two wars, and that in peace the alien and not the Secretary of State should be allowed to choose the place to which he will go if deported, is one which should be addressed not to the court, but to Parliament.

I conclude that the writ of habeas corpus must be refused without having any

[14] [1917] 1 K.B. 922.
[15] [1906] A.C. 542; 22 T.L.R. 757, P.C.
[16] [1918] 1 K.B. 578, 586, 589.

regard either to the question whether the applicant is guilty or innocent of the offences of which he has been convicted, or to the state of the applicant's health and his expectation of life. I was informed by the Attorney-General that the latest medical opinion indicates that the applicant may live for several years, but like the Divisional Court[17] who have already considered one application for this writ, I regard such matters as irrelevant to my decision.

I must not omit to notice an argument, put forward by the Attorney-General at the end of his submissions, that the Home Secretary's deportation of the applicant was an Act of State of which the applicant, as a friendly alien not resident in this country has no right to complain in the courts of this country. I find nothing in the opinion of Lord Kyllarchy in *Poll* v. *Lord Advocate*,[18]* or in the comments of Viscount Cave and Lord Sumner on that case in *Johnstone* v. *Pedlar*,[19]* which compels me to hold that an alien in the exceptional situation of the applicant is shut out from trying to win his freedom by the right, denied to few hitherto, of applying for the historic safeguard of a writ of habeas corpus.

For the reasons I have tried to give, this application for the writ is refused.

Application refused.
Legal aid taxation of the applicant's costs.

The applicant appealed. **[283]**

F. Elwyn Jones Q.C., *Peter Solomon* and *Louis Blom-Cooper* for the applicant. The deportation order is not being used for the lawful purpose of expelling an alien—telling him to get out of the country and to stay out, which is all that a deportation order can properly achieve. It is being used to surrender the applicant to the United States Government to serve a sentence of imprisonment. That is not a lawful use of the machinery of deportation. It cannot be employed to surrender an alien to the custody of another country. The Crown could not surrender an alien at common law. The only way it can surrender him is by invoking the machinery of the Extradition Acts, 1870 to 1935. The machinery of the Aliens Restriction Act, 1914, is combined to deportation simpliciter.

[LORD DENNING M.R. Cannot an alien be sent back to his own country?]

No, not as a procedure of surrender. The deportation order and the detention order made under it are tainted with the illegality of surrender. Political offenders have always been in a special category; the principle has long been established that there should be no extradition of political fugitives: see Oppenheim, International Law, 8th ed. (1958), Vol I, p. 704. Such a person cannot be extradited. In the present case the applicant is a political fugitive who committed a non-extraditable offence.

[PEARSON L.J. You do not have to establish that the applicant is a political fugitive. He has committed a non-extraditable offence and therefore cannot be extradited on that ground. Why should we consider if it is also a political offence?]

It is sufficient for the applicant's purpose that he has committed a non-extraditable offence. Having committed a non-extraditable offence he cannot be extradited or surrendered on account of it. At common law an alien could not be surrendered or expelled once he set foot in this realm no matter how dangerous he might be and no matter how desirable his removal would be: see Dicey on the Law of the Constitution, 10th ed. (1958), p. 224, Oppenheim on International Law, 8th ed. (1955), Vol. I, p. 697, Lord McNair,[20] International Law Opinions, (1956), Vol. 2, p. 41, British Yearbook of International Law, (1928), Vol. 9, p. 60 and Clark on Extradition, 4th ed. (1903), p. 26. The early English authorities on the power of the Crown to surrender aliens were considered in the Australian case of **[284]** *Brown* v. *Lizars*,[21] which held that the only existing powers to

[17] [1963] 1 Q.B. 829, 837.
[18] (1899) 1 F. 823, 827, 828.
[19] [1921] 2 A.C. 262, 277, 289; 37 T.L.R. 870, H.L.
[20] Formerly President of the International Court of Justice.
[21] (1905) 2 C.L.R. 837.

surrender aliens suspected of criminal offences were such as were embodied in legislation.

[LORD DENNING M.R. Assuming that the common law is as you say, it has now been superseded by statute which gives power to deport.]

The power to deport has in no way affected the common law principle that alien fugitives are not to be surrendered except in accordance with powers conferred by Parliament. If deportation is being used for a collateral purpose, the court can go behind the deportation order and declare it invalid: *per* Pickford L.J. and Warrington L.J. in *Rex* v. *Chiswick Police Station Superintendent, Ex parte Sacksteder.*[22]* Deportation cannot be used to circumvent the common law rule that fugitives are not to be surrendered except by proper use of the machinery of extradition. On the evidence in the present case it is clear that representations have been made to Her Majesty's Government by the United States Government for the surrender of the applicant. It is also clear that deportation is being employed to give effect to the request of the United States Government. The reality of this case is that the Home Secretary is attempting to surrender the applicant to the United States Government. That is an improper and illegal use of the deportation machinery—it is an abuse of the power vested in the Home Secretary. Deportation and extradition are two different processes which should be kept separate: *Muller* v. *Superintendent, Presidency Jail, Calcutta.*[23] *Kanadzole et Al* v. *Artukovic*[24] is recent confirmation of the general principle that those convicted of non-extraditable offences cannot be surrendered.

[PEARSON L.J. Such a person cannot be extradited. It does not in the least follow that he cannot be deported in the usual way. It must be the usual way to deport an alien to his own country.]

But in the present case the deportation order is a sham. It is being used to cover up the illegal act of surrendering the applicant to a foreign power without employing the proper procedure.

[DONOVAN L.J. Your argument is that because deportation will lead to surrender, therefore it is surrender. As a matter of logic that is a non-sequitur. It confuses cause with effect.] **[285]**

The only fit or appropriate word to describe the action of the Home Secretary is "surrender." His whole object has been to surrender the applicant to the United States Government and the effect of what he is doing is simply to achieve what has always been his object. The issue in the present case, whether a deportation order can be used to surrender an alien to a foreign government, did not arise in *Rex* v. *Secretary of State for Home Affairs, Ex parte Duke of Chateau Thierry*[25]* or in *Rex* v. *Chiswick Police Station Superintendent, Ex parte Sacksteder.*[26]* In the former case the alien was never detained and the only point for decision was whether certiorari lay to quash the deportation order as such. In the latter case the issue was academic because at the material time the alien was allowed to enlist in the British army. Therefore, both those cases are distinguishable. In any event, they were cases in wartime in which the return of the alien was sought not because of a request for their return from the French Government but because of the obligation of the British Government under an international treaty, which might well have become part of municipal law, to secure their return to France.

Article 20 of the Aliens Order, 1953, has to be construed and read subject to the implied limitation imported from the common law that it is not to be used so as to surrender an alien to a foreign power. If the inevitable or the intended effect of deportation is surrender of an alien to a country which wants him, it is not lawful deportation. The principle that every man must be presumed to intend the natural and probable consequences of his acts applies in this sphere of the law. Short of actually handing over the applicant to the physical custody of two United States marshals at Brixton prison, there could not be a clearer

[22] [1918] 1 K.B. 578, 586, 589; 34 T.L.R. 279, C.A.
[23] [1955] Internat.L.R. 497; (1955) S.C.J. 324.
[24] [1957] Internat.L.R. 510; 247 Fed. (2nd Series) 198.
[25] [1917] 1 K.B. 922; 33 T.L.R. 264, C.A.
[26] [1918] 1 K.B. 578; 34 T.L.R. 279, C.A.

attempt to surrender the applicant than the action taken by the Home Secretary. It is conceded that the Home Secretary can choose the ship or aircraft for deportation subject to the rule that in so doing he must not surrender the alien to a foreign power. *Rex* v. *Governor of Brixton Prison, Ex parte Bloom,*[27]* *Rex* v. *Home Secretary, Ex parte Bressler,*[28]* *Rex* v. *Secretary of State for Foreign Affairs and Secretary of State for Colonies, Ex parte Greenberg*[29]* and *Rex* v. *Governor of Brixton Prison, Ex parte Pawel Sliwa*[30]* were not cases of the surrender of aliens. **[286]**

The Home Secretary has not an unfettered discretion when acting under article 20 (2) (*b*); otherwise "deems" would not have been used. "Deems" in this context means that there must be something in the nature of a judicial inquiry. Deportation is therefore a quasi-judicial act which requires that an opportunity be given to the applicant to make representations directed to the issue of whether it is for the public good to make a deportation order. It is a fundamental principle of all judicial inquiries that a man has the right to be heard, audi alteram partem. The applicant was not given an opportunity of submitting representations against the making of the deportation order. There has, therefore, been a breach of a fundamental principle of natural justice which vitiates the decision of the Home Secretary. The judge felt bound by *Rex* v. *Leman Street Police Station Inspector, Ex parte Venicoff,*[31]* but that decision does not bind this court and ought to be overruled.

[Lord Denning M.R. It has stood for a long time.]

Longevity is no indication of its correctness. The House of Lords in *St. Marylebone Property Co. Ltd.* v. *Fairweather*[32] recently overruled a case which had stood for 60 years.

It would be anomalous if an alien liable to deportation under article 20 (2) (*b*) was not given the opportunity of at least submitting representations against the making of a deportation order before it was finally made. He would be in a worse position than an alien deported under article 20 (2) (*a*) for having committed a criminal offence, since such an alien has the benefit of a court hearing before he can be deported. The principle of audi alteram partem is deep rooted in English jurisprudence and it is not to be excluded unless Parliament has expressly or impliedly said so or there are exceptional circumstances of an immediate emergency to justify its exclusion: see the South African cases of *Jeewa* v. *Donges N.O.*[33] and *Reg.* v. *Ngwevela.*[34] The modern tendency is expressly to exclude the principle where Parliament so intends: see, for example, section 26 of the British Nationality Act, 1948. See, too, *De Verteuil* v. *Knaggs*[35] and the observations of Lord Radcliffe in *Nakkuda Ali* v. *Jayaratne*[36] on the **[287]** limitations of *Liversidge* v. *Sir John Anderson.*[37] There is no reason why this fundamental principle of natural justice should not apply to the present case.

The argument that an alien subject to a notice of refusal of leave to land cannot be deported is not now pursued in this court. The submission was based on the concept that until the notice of refusal was cancelled the alien in law was not here, and if he was not here, he could not be deported.

The final submission is that the Order of 1953 is ultra vires the Aliens Restriction Act, 1914. The Order purports to derive its validity from the Act of 1914, which is the principal Act, but that Act was defunct and inoperative in 1953 when the Order was made and, consequently, the Order is not authorised by the Act of 1914. The powers given by the Act of 1914 exist only in times of war or imminent national emergency. At any other time they are dormant and

27 (1920) 124 L.T. 375; 90 L.J. K.B. 574, D.C.
28 (1924) 131 L.T. 386, C.A.
29 [1947] 2 All E.R. 550.
30 [1952] 1 K.B. 169; [1951] 1 T.L.R. 61; [1951] 1 All E.R. 187, C.A.
31 [1920] 3 K.B. 72; 36 T.L.R. 677, D.C.
32 [1962] 1 Q.B. 498; [1962] 2 W.L.R. 1020; [1962] 2 All E.R. 288, H.L.
33 [1953] 1 S.A.L.R. 414.
34 [1954] 1 S.A.L.R. 123.
35 [1918] A.C. 557; 34 T.L.R. 325, P.C.
36 [1951] A.C. 66, 76; 66 T.L.R. (Pt. 2) 214, P.C.
37 [1942] A.C. 206; 58 T.L.R. 35; [1941] 3 All E.R. 338, H.L.

ineffective; 1953 was not a time of war or national emergency, and therefore in 1953 the powers given by the Act of 1914 did not in law exist and were of no effect. They could be revived by a state of war or national emergency if such conditions should arise. The Aliens Restriction (Amendment) Act, 1919, did not re-enact or recreate the powers given by the Act of 1914, as should have been done if they were to be applicable in peacetime. Accordingly, the Act of 1919 cannot affect the legal situation if on the true construction of the Act of 1914 the powers given under it were non-existent and dormant. The judge failed to distinguish between the valid existence of powers and the exercisability of existing powers. If a power does not exist under a principal Act it cannot be given an existence by a later Act saying that it shall be exerciseable at any time. The Act of 1919 only dealt with the exercisability of powers, not their existence.

Peter Solomon following. In none of the cases was the burden of proof argued. It seems to have been assumed that the onus is on the applicant to show that the deportation order is a sham. But the fundamental issue is whether the detention of the applicant is lawful. As to that, initially the onus is on the respondent, for prima facie every imprisonment is unlawful and the person who detains must justify his action: *per* Lord Atkin in *Liversidge* v. *Sir John Anderson*.[38] See, too, the observations of Lord Atkin in *Eshugbayi Eleko* v. *Officer* **[288]** *Administering the Government of Nigeria*.[39] The court always has power to investigate the truth of the allegations contained in the return to a writ of habeas corpus: *Reg.* v. *Board of Control, Ex parte Rutty*.[40]

There is no evidence in justification of the detention other than the deportation order itself. Admittedly that is enough to shift the onus. But if the applicant then adduces prima facie evidence which in the opinion of the court requires an answer, the onus will once again be upon the respondent: *Rex* v. *Chiswick Police Station Superintendent, Ex parte Sacksteder*.[41]* The evidence filed on behalf of the applicant raises matters which call for an answer. The Home Secretary has failed to give one. The proper inference to be drawn from the evidence is that he has not acted bona fide. The court must investigate whether the Home Secretary has exercised his discretion without pressure by the United States authorities. If the exercise of his discretion has been subject to pressure the deportation order is a sham. On the facts of this case the cause of the deportation order was the pressure of the United States authorities. Reliance is placed on the following factors: there was no denial of the truth of what "The Times" said in its report[42] of August 8, 1962; the Home Secretary repeatedly gave directions under article 8 to El Al to remove the applicant to the United States although he knew that the airline would not comply with them, thereafter he did not exhaust his powers under article 8 and direct the airline to remove the applicant to another destination. Had it been the Home Secretary's policy simply to expel the applicant he could have deported him to Czechoslovakia which was willing to receive him or he could have sent him back to Israel where the airline was willing to transport him. Throughout the Home Secretary has insisted on removing the applicant to the United States. The only rational explanation of the Home Secretary's conduct is that he was seeking to appease American pressure for the surrender of the applicant. That is further borne out by the press statement of August 11, 1962, when the order was made, and by the other events of that day. The Home Secretary has been motivated by a desire to surrender the applicant to the United States Government. He has resorted to the expedient of a **[289]** deportation order to achieve that illegal purpose. On the evidence the detention of the applicant is prima facie unlawful. Hence, the deportation order is a sham.

Sir John Hobson Q.C., A.-G. and *R.A. Barr* for the Governor of Brixton Prison. The Order of 1953 is intra vires the Act of 1914.

[LORD DENNING M.R. You need not trouble about the contrary submission.]

Although it is now conceded that articles 8 and 20 of 1953 are cumulative and

[38] [1942] A.C. 206, 245.
[39] [1931] A.C. 662, 670, P.C.
[40] [1956] 2 Q.B. 109; [1956] 2 W.L.R. 822; [1956] 1 All E.R. 769, D.C.
[41] [1918] 1 K.B. 578.
[42] The contents of the report are set out, *ante*, p. 250.

complementary, it is desired to make it clear for future cases that an alien can be detained under both articles 8 (4) and 21 (4) at the same time. The judge accepted that articles 8 and 20 were cumulative and complementary, but erroneously considered[43] that an alien could only be detained under one article at any given time.

"Deem" in current parlance means "is of the opinion that" or "consider." Its ordinary and natural meaning according to the Shorter Oxford English Dictionary (1944) 3rd ed., p. 468, is to form an opinion, to conclude, to consider, or to hold, or to think of something as existing when it is not. It originally meant to judge, to estimate, and to sentence but that is an archaic meaning which no longer applies in modern times. The use of the word "deems" in article 20 (2) (*b*) does not, therefore, give rise to the implication that there must be a judicial inquiry. One can deem that something exists or is without holding any inquiry. "Deems" simply refers to the belief or opinion of the person who takes a certain view.

Rex v. *Leman Street Police Station Inspector, Ex parte Venicoff*[44]* has not only stood for a long time but subsequent legislation has been based on it. Parliament re-enacted the material part of the Aliens Order, 1919, on which that decision was given, in the same terms in the Order of 1953 knowing of the meaning which had been given to it in *Rex* v. *Leman Street Police Station Inspector, Ex parte Venicoff*.[45]* Had Parliament disapproved of that decision it would have altered the language of the Order of 1953. It must be assumed that when Parliament chose the same language for the Order of 1953 as had been used in the Order of 1919 it was giving the impress of its authority to the judicial interpretation of the Order of 1919 in the *Venicoff* case.

The principle of audi alteram partem cannot apply because **[290]** the reality of a deportation order does not permit of a judicial hearing. The Home Secretary when making a deportation order is acting in a purely executive capacity: see *per* Scott L.J. in *Rex* v. *Secretary of State for Home Affairs, Ex parte Greene*,[46] adopting the judgment of Earl Reading C.J. in *Rex* v. *Leman Street Police Station Inspector, Ex parte Venicoff*.[47]* Parliament has committed a purely executive discretion to a Minister to decide what is in the public interest. The principle of audi alteram partem is appropriate to a civil dispute inter partes, but it is not appropriate to the exercise of an executive power which must be based on considerations of policy and also on material that is not available to the courts. If there could be no deportation before a judicial inquiry has been held, deportation in many cases would be rendered ineffective. If it were proposed to deport a spy, the last thing that the Home Secretary would wish would be to warn him of what was proposed, for he would take the opportunity to disappear. If a spy were entitled to a judicial hearing, the whole purpose of deportation would be rendered nugatory. If an alien, who landed here unlawfully without leave, was entitled to a judicial hearing when the authorities discovered his whereabouts, he might take the opportunity to disappear and conceal his presence in this country more effectively. Until a deportation order was made there would be no power of arresting and detaining him. Deportation would become quite impractical and nonsensical if an alien were entitled to a judicial inquiry.

The history of the right to expel aliens is set out in Holdsworth, History of English Law (1938), Vol. 10, pp. 393, 396, 397.

The right to expel an alien is historically a prerogative right of the Crown in respect of which the alien has no remedy, whatever: see *per* Lord Atkinson in *Johnstone* v. *Pedlar*,[48]* and Holdsworth, History of English Law (1938), Vol. 10, p. 396. An "Act of State" cannot be a defence against a British subject or a

[43] *Ante*, p. 271.
[44] [1920] 3 K.B. 72.
[45] Ibid.
[46] [1942] 1 K.B. 87, 98; [1941] 3 All E.R. 104, C.A.; affd. sub nom. *Greene* v. *Secretary of State for Home Affairs* [1942] A.C. 284; 58 T.L.R. 53; [1941] 3 All E.R. 388, H.L.
[47] [1920] 3 K.B. 72; 36 T.L.R. 677, D.C.
[48] [1921] 2 A.C. 262, 283; 37 T.L.R. 870, H.L.

resident alien. Whether it can be a defence against a non-resident was left open in *Johnstone* v. *Pedlar.*[48]* It is clear, however, that a non-resident alien has no right to enter the country and no grounds for complaint if he is refused admission: see the observations of Lord Atkinson[49] and of Lord Sumner[50] **[291]** in *Johnstone* v. *Pedlar** and *Poll* v. *Lord Advocate.*[51]* The Crown has a prerogative right not only to expel but also to exclude an alien. Accordingly, a non-resident alien in respect of whom the Crown exercises that prerogative right has no remedy whatever. It is an "Act of State." In the present case, however, the point does not arise for decision, since it was not stated in the deportation order that the Home Secretary was relying on the royal prerogative. The point must, therefore, be regarded as left open in this case and the Crown reserves its position on it.

The argument for the applicant in this court, which is not what was put below, is that article 20 must be read subject to a limitation derived from the common law that the power to deport is not to be exercised in such a way that the effect of the deportation would be the surrender of the alien. There is no authority for that proposition and it is plainly not tenable. In any event, there is no evidence of any surrender in the present case. There is no evidence of any surrender in the sense of a direct handing over of the applicant to the United States authorities. The Home Secretary is not concerned with making any arrangements other than arranging with an airline to transport the applicant on board an aircraft about to leave the United Kingdom and expected to go to the United States. That is not a surrender of the applicant though the effect of it will be surrendered. The Home Secretary is entitled to expel an alien in such circumstances that the inevitable result of his expulsion will be his return to the country where he was convicted of an offence. A request for the return of an alien by a foreign government does not fetter the discretion of the domestic government to deport him: *Muller* v. *Superintendent, Presidency Jail, Calcutta.*[52]

Although there may be no obligation to extradite an alien, yet the Home Secretary can expel him in conformity with the principle of territorial supremacy. There is no shackle on the power to expel aliens. If there were any such fetter on the power to deport as has been suggested, it would produce the most appalling consequences. It is contrary to the comity of nations and the spirit of international law that one country should receive another country's criminals unless they are nationals of the country receiving them. Suppose that the world's most wanted criminal, who would obviously be most suitable for deportation, arrived here when wanted by every other country in the world **[292]** so that he might receive punishment. If there was the suggested fetter on the power to deport, the Home Secretary could never deport him, for the inevitable result would be his surrender to a foreign power, and he would be entitled to remain here for ever, notwithstanding that he was the most undesirable alien there could be. Again, if the applicant were right, it would be impossible to expel war criminals who managed to enter the country and bring them to justice. The result of the applicant's construction of article 20 is that those who committed crimes in their own country would have a private right of asylum in this country. Neither international law nor English law has ever recognised any right of asylum: see Morgenstern on "The Right of Asylum," British Yearbook of International Law (1949), Vol. 26, pp. 327, 345, citing the following statement of Lord Simon[53] when Lord Chancellor: "There is not, as many people suppose, any private right, recognised in international law, called the right of asylum. That is to say the fugitive—the criminal who manages to get over the border into some other country—is not thereby entitled to claim to stay there. . . . It is perfectly competent for the country which receives the criminal, whether there is an extradition treaty or not, if that country thinks it will be fulfilling its duty to the world, or if its conception of public policy requires and justifies it,

[49] Ibid. 283.
[50] Ibid. 289.
[51] (1899) 1 F. 823.
[52] [1955] Internat.L.R. 497; (1955) S.C.J. 324.
[53] (1942) Hansard, Parliamentary Debates, 5th Series, H.L., Vol. 124, col. 582.

to hand the criminal over." That statement of the then Lord Chancellor correctly summarises the law. There is no limitation in the Home Secretary's power to deport under article 20 (2) (*b*). If any limitation had been intended, it would have been expressed in the Order of 1953. There is no reason at all to imply a limitation which is not there. The courts ought not to imply limitations on statutory powers unless they are absolutely necessary for the operation of the statute or plainly intended from its context. The Aliens Act, 1905, contained severe limitations on the power to refuse admission to aliens: see section 1 of the Act of 1905. It protected aliens convicted of political offences from deportation: see section 3 of that Act. The Act of 1905 was repealed in toto by section 16 (2) of the Aliens Restriction (Amendment) Act, 1919. Neither the Act of 1914 nor the Act of 1919 contained any of the limitations or protection conferred on aliens by the Act of 1905. It is plain, therefore, that when Parliament seeks to limit the Home Secretary's powers, it does so expressly. It is plain, too, from the later Acts that Parliament expressly and deliberately abolished **[293]** such protection as aliens then enjoyed by existing legislation. Parliament clearly intended the Home Secretary to have an unlimited and unfettered discretion as to the exclusion and expulsion of aliens.

By international law the only country which is bound to receive an expelled alien is the country of which he is a national: Oppenheim, International Law, 8th ed. (1955), Vol. I, p. 645. Whatever the alien's nationality, he can be sent back to the country from which he embarked: *Rex* v. *Secretary of State for Foreign Affairs and Secretary of State for Colonies, Ex parte Greenberg.*[54]* The country of his nationality and the country whence he embarked are the only two countries which can be required to receive him. By international law and by national law the power to deport includes such ancilliary powers, such as the selection of the ship or aircraft, as are required to make the deportation effective: *Rex* v. *Secretary of State for Home Affairs, Ex parte Duke of Chateau Thierry*[55]* and *Rex* v. *Chiswick Police Station Superintendent, Ex parte Sacksteder.*[56]* Therefore, it is the Home Secretary and not the deportee who can choose the means of deportation and choice of destination; were it otherwise the whole purpose of deportation could be rendered ineffective, for the deportee might choose some remote country to which there was no ready access and to which infrequent journeys were made by ships and aircraft. Not only has the Home Secretary the right to select the ship or aircraft but he also has the right to authorise the alien's detention outside territorial waters so as to make the deportation effective: *Rex* v. *Secretary of State for Foreign Affairs and Secretary of State for Colonies, Ex parte Greenberg.*[57]* There is no power to direct the alien to any particular destination, not because of any juristic principle giving protection to the alien, but because of the lack of sanction in enforcing such a direction on the alien once he is outside the territorial jurisdiction. Therefore, the Order of 1953 does not confer such a power on the Home Secretary but it would be competent to do so if it were thought desirable or practical. Directions can be given to the carriers who are expected to return to the territorial jurisdiction and therefore amenable to judicial sanction for non-compliance with the directions given to them. They can be prosecuted for failing to obey the directions given to them under article 8. **[294]**

[DONOVAN L.J. Have proceedings been taken against El Al?]

Not as yet, but they might be taken.

The present case has nothing to do with extradition. The fact that the applicant could or could not in similar circumstances be extradited is immaterial. Deportation and extradition are wholly different and separate processes: *Muller* v. *Superintendent, Presidency Jail, Calcutta.*[58] As to extradition, first, it is part of the criminal law of a foreign country; secondly, it involves the surrender of the fugitive to the custody of the foreign power; thirdly, it is a special branch of the

[54] [1947] 2 All E.R. 550.
[55] [1917] 1 K.B. 922.
[56] [1918] 1 K.B. 578.
[57] [1947] 2 All E.R. 550.
[58] [1955] Internat.L.R. 497; (1955) S.C.J. 324.

law of criminal procedure; fourthly, it applies to British subjects as well as aliens. As to deportation, first, it applies to aliens only; secondly, it does not depend on the commission of criminal offences; thirdly, it is based on an administrative decision by the domestic authorities; fourthly, the discretion to deport is absolute and unfettered and not affected by the fact that the alien could be extradited.

The only statutory duty on the Home Secretary is to decide whether it is conducive to the public good to deport the applicant. There is no evidence in the present case of any mala fides or that the order was a sham. The order would be a sham if the Home Secretary was using it for a purely private purpose such as the deportation of the rival to the woman he loved. If there was overwhelming evidence that no reasonable Home Secretary could believe it in the public interest to deport the applicant, it might be possible by analogy to *Associated Provincial Picture Houses Ltd.* v. *Wednesbury Corporation*[59] to show bad faith or that the Home Secretary's real purpose was improper. But no such situation arises in the present case. There was evidence on which a reasonable Home Secretary could say that it was desirable to deport the applicant to the United States.

He was entitled to consider, first, the nationality of the applicant; secondly, the desirability that an alien should derive no advantage from a stratagem by which he gained unlawful admission; thirdly, the security risks of the applicant going east or west; fourthly, the need for good diplomatic relations with friendly powers; and, fifthly, the undesirability of having convicted spies in this country. Before the applicant had ever landed here, the Home Secretary had formed the intention that the applicant should continue on his journey to the United States. The intention to expel preceded any possible question of surrender **[295]** of the applicant to the United States authorities. Moreover, the Home Secretary has stayed his hand pending these proceedings when he was not bound to do so. He would have acted otherwise if his intention had been to surrender the applicant. The proper place to send a deportee is the country of his nationality. See the case of *Tom Mann.*[60]

Rex v. *Secretary of State for Home Affairs, Ex parte Duke of Chateau Thierry*[61]* is an authority which exactly covers the present case. It was there admitted by the Home Secretary[62] that the order was made with the intention of sending the alien to France to perform his military service. It could have been said that his real object was not to expel the alien but to surrender him to the French military authorities, yet the deportation was held to be valid. Counsel for the applicant in *Rex* v. *Chiswick Police Station Superintendent, Ex parte Sacksteder*[63]* contended that the Home Secretary intended to surrender the applicant to the French authorities and, therefore, that the deportation order was illegal, but that contention was rejected.

The discretion of the Home Secretary to make a deportation order is absolute and unfettered, and the courts cannot interfere with the exercise of his discretion nor inquire into the basis on which it was exercised, provided that the order is made under and in accordance with statutory powers delegated by Parliament: *Rex* v. *Secretary of State for Home Affairs, Ex parte Duke of Chateau Thierry*[64]*; *Rex* v. *Chiswick Police Station Superintendent, Ex parte Sacksteder*[65]*; *Rex* v. *Leman Street Police Station Inspector, Ex parte Venicoff*[66]*; *Rex* v. *Governor of Brixton Prison, Ex parte Bloom*[67]*; *Rex* v. *Home Secretary, Ex parte Bressler.*[68]* The Home Secretary when making a deportation order is acting in a similar capacity and under the same type of executive discretionary

[59] [1948] 1 K.B. 223; 63 T.L.R. 623; [1947] 2 All E.R. 680, C.A.

[60] Unreported (recorded in Lord McNair's International Law Opinions (1956), Vol. 2, p. 111; see Tom Mann, Memoirs (1923), pp. 135-138).

[61] [1917] 1 K.B. 922.

[62] Ibid. 924, note (1), 927, 930, 932.

[63] [1918] 1 K.B. 578, 582.

[64] [1917] 1 K.B. 922.

[65] [1918] 1 K.B. 578.

[66] [1920] 3 K.B. 72.

[67] (1920) 124 L.T. 375; 90 L.J. K.B. 574.

[68] (1924) 131 L.T. 386.

power as when he made a detention order under the wartime emergency regulations given in regulation 18 (*b*): see *Liversidge* v. *Sir John Anderson*[69] and *Greene* v. *Secretary of State for Home Affairs.*[70]

F. Elwyn Jones Q.C. in reply. The principles of natural justice are often inconvenient to the executive and may well **[296]** cause practical difficulties in some cases. But that is no reason for dispensing with the fundamental right of every person to be heard. The importance of this principle was recently emphasised in *Kanda* v. *Government of Malaya.*[71] It is a time-honoured maxim of English law that not only should justice be done, but also that it should manifestly be seen to be done. The assertion by the courts of the principles of natural justice in the heat of the cold war would be a notable contribution to the British way of life.

It is conceded that the three procedures of exclusion, expulsion and extradition are separate processes which do not impinge on each other. Exclusion is dealt with by article 8, expulsion by article 20, and extradition by the Act of 1870. But when the United States Government made a request for the return of the applicant, the present case was removed from the sphere of exclusion and expulsion to that of extradition. In the present case there is evidence at the very least of an "arrangement" for the return of the applicant within the meaning of that term in section 2 of the Act of 1870. The point of the present case, that a surrender otherwise than by extradition proceedings is contrary to the common law and that article 20 must not be exercised so as to effect such a surrender, was never argued nor decided on in *Rex* v. *Secretary of State for Home Affairs, Ex parte Duke of Chateau Thierry*[72]* or in *Rex* v. *Chiswick Police Station Superintendent, Ex parte Sacksteder*[73]* In any event, there was no bilateral surrender in those cases. In the former there was no request by the French Government for the return of the alien and in the latter the request had been abandoned. But in the present case the court is in the presence of an illegal bilateral surrender. The deportation order is being used for that illegal purpose and the whole transaction is tainted with the illegality. [Reference was also made to *Rex* v. *Governor of Brixton Prison, Ex parte Sarno*[74]* and *Kader* v. *Minister of the Interior.*[75]]

LORD DENNING M.R. In this case Dr. Soblen applies for a writ of habeas corpus. He is an alien, but the writ of habeas corpus is available to anyone within this country who is being detained. **[297]** By means of it he can call upon those who are detaining him to show that his detention is justified by law.

In this case a deportation order of the Home Secretary, dated August 11, 1962, is produced by way of justification. It reads: "Whereas I deem it to be conducive to the public good to make a deportation order against Robert Soblen an alien: now, therefore, in pursuance of the power conferred upon me by paragraph (2) (*b*) of article 20 of the Aliens Order, 1953, I hereby order that the said Robert Soblen shall leave and thereafter remain out of the United Kingdom: and in pursuance of the powers conferred on me by paragraphs (1) and (4) of article 21 of the said Aliens Order, 1953, I hereby authorise any immigration officer, at any time after this order is served on the said Robert Soblen to place him on board a ship or aircraft, which is about to leave the United Kingdom, and I hereby authorise the Governor of Her Majesty's Prison at Brixton to detain him until arrangements are completed for so placing him on board."

That deportation order is good on the face of it, and affords prima facie a justification for the detention of Robert Soblen. It has been challenged before us on four grounds. The first ground of challenge was that the Aliens Order,

[69] [1942] A.C. 206.
[70] [1942] 1 K.B. 87; affd. [1942] A.C. 284.
[71] [1962] A.C. 322; [1962] 2 W.L.R. 1153, P.C.
[72] [1917] 1 K.B. 922.
[73] [1918] 1 K.B. 578.
[74] [1916] 2 K.B. 742; 32 T.L.R. 717, D.C.
[75] [1954] 2 S.A.R. 510.

1953, was invalid because there was no war or emergency at the time it was made. It was said that on the true construction of the Aliens Restriction Act, 1914, the authority to impose restrictions on aliens only applied in time of war or on an occasion of imminent national danger or great emergency. The plain answer to that contention is given by section 1 of the Aliens Restriction (Amendment) Act, 1919. The authority to impose restrictions is not so confined. It can be exercised "at any time." And the section has been continued every year since that time.[76] It is too plain for argument.

The second ground of challenge was that the Home Secretary had already put into force the provisions of article 8 of the Order of 1953, whereby Dr. Soblen was refused leave to land and the carrier was ordered to remove him. It was said that so long as those directions remained unwithdrawn, there was no power in the Home Secretary to make a deportation order under article 20. That challenge was rejected by the judge and not pursued before us. The fact that the carrier disobeys the directions which are given to him, cannot prevent the Home Secretary from acting under the deportation provisions if he so thinks fit. I agree with **[298]** the judgment of Stephenson J. on this point,[77] save that it must not be taken that a person could not be detained at one and the same time under the provisions of article 8 (4) and 21 (4) of the Order.

The third ground of challenge was that it was said that the Home Secretary could not make a deportation order unless he had first given the person affected the opportunity to be heard, and in this case the Home Secretary had made this deportation order against Dr. Soblen without any such opportunity being given. I quite agree that when a public officer is given the power to deprive a person of his liberty or his property, the general principle of our law is that that is not to be done without his first being given an opportunity of being heard and of making representations on his own behalf. That has been the tenor of the decisions of these courts for nearly 100 years. But there are exceptions. A statute may expressly or by necessary implication provide that the person affected is not to be given a right to be heard. Such an exception has been held to exist in the case of deportation orders. In 1920 it was held by a Divisional Court in *Rex* v. *Leman Street Police Station Inspector, Ex parte Venicoff*[78]* that an alien has no right to be heard before a deportation order is made against him. That case has been questioned before us and it has been suggested that it was wrongly decided.

All I need say about it is that in 1953, without any dissent in Parliament, an Order was made in the very self-same words as the Order considered in *Venicoff's* case.[79]* It is a reasonable assumption that Parliament proceeded on the assumption that *Venicoff's* case[79]* was good law. And when I look to the objects of this legislation, it seems to me that much of the purpose of it would be defeated, if it were necessary for the Home Secretary always to give every alien the right of being heard before a deportation order is made. Reasons of security themselves might be such as to make it unwise and undesirable to give him advance notice of the intention to make a deportation order. He might well take advantage of it so as to absent himself and to avoid apprehension. I think, therefore, that there is no right to be heard before a deportation order is made. I reserve my opinion, however, on the following point: It may be a question whether, after a deportation order is made and before it comes to be executed (by his being expelled from the realm), an alien may not in some circumstances **[299]** have a right to be heard. It does not arise here because, as in *Venicoff's* case,[79]* so in this case, the Home Secretary has stated his willingness to hear and consider any representations which the person affected desires to be made. It may, indeed, never arise at all because of the many circumstances in which

[76] Expiring Laws Continuance Acts, 1920-1961.
[77] *Ante*, p. 271.
[78] [1920] 3 K.B. 72; 36 T.L.R. 677, D.C.
[79] [1920] 3 K.B. 72.

it is now open to an alien to ask for a hearing by the Chief Magistrate at Bow Street.[80]

This brings me to the principal ground of challenge. It is said that the Home Secretary in making this deportation order is using it as a means of achieving an ulterior object; his real object, it is said, is to surrender a fugitive criminal to the United States of America. It is being done, it is said, at the request of the United States of America; and that by our law no fugitive criminal is to be surrendered to another country except in accordance with legislation in that behalf; and in particular, in accordance with extradition provisions duly complied with.

On this point I desire to say that the law of extradition is one thing; the law of deportation is another. For myself, I go a great way with Mr. Elwyn Jones' argument on the law of extradition. As I understand it, by the common law of England (affirmed by implication in the Extradition Acts, 1870-1935), every person coming from abroad, as soon as he sets foot lawfully in this country, is free; and, so long as he commits no offence here, he is not to be arrested or detained for any offence that he may have committed in some other country. If any attempt were made to arrest him in order to surrender him to that other country, he would at once be entitled to be set free. The writ of habeas corpus is available to him for the purpose. In the absence of an extradition treaty, it is no answer for the Crown, or any officer of the Crown, to say that he wishes to send him off to another country to meet a charge there. That this is the law is clearly stated in Sir Edward Clark's book on Extradition (1903), 4th ed., p. 26:

"If any magistrate were now to arrest a person on this ground"—that is on the ground that it is desired to surrender him to a foreign country for trial—"the validity of the commitment would certainly be tested, and, in the absence of special legislative provisions, the prisoner as certainly discharged upon application **[300]** to one of the superior courts." Lord McNair,[81] in his volume of International Law Opinions (1956), Vol. 2, p. 41, says the same: "For some time the law was doubtful, but later it became recognised that the Crown could not surrender an alleged criminal even if it wished to do so, unless the surrender was authorised by legislation." It is unlawful, therefore, for the Crown to surrender a fugitive criminal to a foreign country unless it is warranted by an extradition treaty with that country. If there is an extradition treaty, the Crown can surrender him for an extraditable offence if the requisite steps are taken; but it cannot surrender him for a non-extraditable offence. Now the offence for which the applicant was convicted in the United States is not an extraditable offence. If, therefore, this case were one of extradition, that is, if the purpose of the Home Secretary was simply to surrender him as a fugitive criminal in response to a request of the United States, that purpose would be unlawful. That is the force of Mr. Elwyn Jones' argument.

But although such is the law of extradition, there is another side to the picture, that is, the law of deportation. Here we come upon another principle of our law. Although every alien, as soon as he lawfully sets foot in this country, is free, nevertheless the Crown is entitled at any time to send him home to his own country, if in its opinion his presence here is not conducive to the public good; and it may for this purpose arrest him and put him on board a ship or aircraft bound for his home country. That was clearly the law under the Aliens Order, 1916, as interpreted by this court in 1917 in *Rex* v. *Secretary of State for Home Affairs, Ex parte Duke of Chateau Thierry*[82]* and in 1918 in *Rex* v. *Chiswick Police Station Superintendent, Ex parte Sacksteder*,[83]* and it is clear now under the Aliens Order of 1953. It is unnecessary to go into the state of the law before the Aliens Orders. I always understood that the Crown had a Royal Prerogative to expel an alien and send him home whenever it considered that his presence here was not conducive to the public good. Sir

[80] Pursuant to an administrative concession made under the European Convention on Establishment, 1955. See (1955) 559 H.C.Deb., col. 1349.

[81] Formerly President of the International Court of Justice.

[82] [1917] 1 K.B. 922; 33 T.L.R. 264, C.A.

[83] [1918] 1 K.B. 578; 34 T.L.R. 279, C.A.

William Blackstone certainly said in his Commentaries—(1765), vol. 1, pp. 259-260: "Strangers who come spontaneously" are "liable to be sent home whenever the King sees occasion." And this view is in accord with international law as stated by the law officers of the Crown (Sir Richard Webster, A.-G., and Sir Robert Finlay, S.-G.) in 1896 in *Thomas* **[301]** *Mann's* case.[84] It seems clear from that case that by international law any country is entitled to expel an alien if his presence is for any reason obnoxious to it; and as incidental to this right, it can arrest him, detain him, and put him on board a ship bound for his own country.

I know that Professor Dicey said that the Crown has no means of arresting even the most dangerous aliens or of expelling them from the country (Law of the Constitution (1958), 10th ed., p. 224), and Professor Oppenheim (International Law (1955), vol. 1, 8th ed., p. 697) said the same. I am not at all sure that I agree with them. The matter was never tested in the courts. But it is not necessary to go into it now; for it is quite plain that the Royal Prerogative in this matter is now supplanted and replaced by the Aliens Order, 1953 (articles 20 and 21), under which there is power in the Crown to deport an alien "if the Secretary of State deems it to be conducive to the public good"; and for this purpose to detain him, and place him "on board any ship or aircraft which is about to leave the United Kingdom." Those words make it clear that the Home Secretary may choose the ship or aircraft and thus his destination.

It was suggested before us that there was a common law shackle on this power of deportation. It was said that a man could not be deported, even to his own country, if he was a criminal who had fled from it. No authority was cited for this proposition. It can not stand examination for one moment. Supposing no other country but his own is willing to take him. Are we to keep him here against our will simply because he is in his country a wanted man? Clearly not. If a fugitive criminal is here and the Secretary of State thinks that in the public good he ought to be deported, there is no reason why he should not be deported to his own country, even though he is there a wanted criminal. The Supreme Court of India considered this very point in 1955 in *Muller* v. *Superintendent, Presidency Jail, Calcutta,*[85] and in an instructive judgment made it quite clear that in their opinion the right to expel an alien could be exercised, even though he was wanted by his own country for a criminal offence. Even though his home country has requested that he should be sent back to them, I see no reason why the Home Secretary should not still deport him there, if his presence here is not conducive to the public good. The **[302]** power to deport is not taken away by the fact that he is a fugitive from the justice of his own country, or by the fact that his own country wants him back and has made a request for him.

So there we have in this case the two principles: on the one hand the principle arising out of the law of extradition, under which the officers of the Crown cannot and must not surrender a fugitive criminal to another country at its request except in accordance with the Extradition Acts, 1870-1935, duly fulfilled; on the other hand, the principle arising out of the law of deportation, under which the Secretary of State can deport an alien and put him on board a ship or aircraft for his own country if he considers it conducive to the public good that that should be done. How are we to decide between these two principles? It seems to me that it depends on the purpose with which the act is done. If it was done for an authorised purpose, it was lawful. If it was done professedly for an authorised purpose, but in fact for a different purpose with an ulterior object, it was unlawful.

If, therefore, the purpose of the Home Secretary in this case was to surrender the applicant as a fugitive criminal to the United States of America because they had asked for him, then it would be unlawful. But if the Home Secretary's purpose was to deport him to his own country because the Home Secretary considered his presence here to be not conducive to the public good, then the Home Secretary's action is lawful. It is open to these courts to inquire whether

[84] Unreported (recorded in Lord McNair's International Law Opinions (1956), Vol. 2, p. 111; see Tom Mann, Memoirs (1923), pp. 135-138).
[85] [1955] Internat.L.R. 497; (1955) S.C.J. 324.

the purpose of the Home Secretary was a lawful or an unlawful purpose. Was there a misuse of the power or not? The courts can always go behind the face of the deportation order in order to see whether the powers entrusted by Parliament have been exercised lawfully or no. That follows from *Reg.* v. *Board of Control, Ex parte Rutty*.[86]

Then how does it rest in this case? The court cannot compel the Home Secretary to disclose the materials on which he acted, but if there is evidence on which it could reasonably be supposed that the Home Secretary was using the power of deportation for an ulterior purpose, then the court can call on the Home Secretary for an answer: and if he fails to give it, it can upset his order. But on the facts of this case I can find no such evidence. It seems to me that there was reasonable ground on which the Home Secretary could consider that the applicant's presence here was not conducive to the public good.

Just let me recapitulate for this purpose the salient facts. [**303**] The applicant is a naturalised citizen of the United States of America, having been naturalised on May 5, 1947. A charge was made against him in the United States alleging that he had conspired to deliver to the Union of Socialist Soviet Republics information concerning the defence of the United States of America. We were told that the overt acts of that conspiracy were as long ago as 1944 and 1945. On July 13, 1961, he was convicted of the conspiracy and he was sentenced to be imprisoned for life. It was suggested before us that he was innocent, but it was never suggested that the trial was unfair. He was released on bail pending an application for a new trial. On June 25, 1962, the Supreme Court of the United States finally rejected a motion for a new trial made on his behalf. On that very day, but later in the day, breaking his bail, he flew off to Israel using his brother's passport. When he arrived in Israel, no application was made to the courts of that country, so far as we know, for a writ of habeas corpus. On July 1, 1962, the Israeli authorities sent him back by aircraft en route for the United States of America. The aircraft was due to stop for a short while at London Airport. On his way, he inflicted severe wounds on himself with the sole object of making it necessary for him to be landed in this country. He had no leave to land. He was refused permission to land. He forced himself on our attention and he was only taken in for humanity's sake. As soon as he was fit to travel, directions were given to the airline to remove him in the aircraft in which he arrived. It did not do so. And he was detained as being an alien to whom leave to land had been refused. He applied for a writ of habeas corpus on the ground that he had been given leave impliedly. We rejected that application on the ground that he had never been given leave to land.[87] He applied to the Home Secretary for political asylum, a matter which is entirely in the discretion of the Home Secretary; and his request was refused. He applied to the Czechoslovakian authorities for leave to go to Czechoslovakia, and he obtained a visa for that country. But the Home Secretary, it may be presumed, did not wish him to go there. On August 3 and 4 directions were given by an immigration officer that El Al was to take him to the United States of America. But the Israeli Government said that its airline was not to take him there. Then on August 8 it was reported in "The Times" newspaper that representations had [**304**] been made by the United States Government to the British Government desiring him to be sent to the United States. We do not know the actual terms of those representations; discovery has been refused of them; but, nevertheless, in the circumstances of this case I am prepared to assume that the report in "The Times" was correct, for it has never been contradicted.

We do not know whether the Home Secretary was influenced by those representations, but we do know that he continued his efforts to get El Al to take the applicant to the United States. On August 11, the immigration officers gave directions to El Al to take him to the United States of America by a particular flight. But then that flight was cancelled. So the Home Secretary,

[86] [1956] 2 Q.B. 109; [1956] 2 W.L.R. 822; [1956] 1 All E.R. 769, D.C.

[87] *Reg.* v. *Secretary of State for Home Affairs, Ex parte Soblen** [1963] 1 Q.B. 829, 842; [1962] 3 W.L.R. 1145; [1962] 3 All E.R. 373, C.A.

having tried time after time to get the airline to take him to the United States and having failed, made this deportation order.

What in those circumstances was the purpose of the Home Secretary? It is quite plain that at the outset he refused the applicant leave to land, because in his opinion the presence of the applicant in this country was not conducive to the public good; and it seems to me that throughout his purpose has been to see that this refusal of leave was implemented. The applicant cannot complain of the refusal of leave to land. The Crown has the right to exclude any alien from this country without reason given. And the applicant cannot better his position by means of his device, his contrivance, of self-mutilation by which he arrived here. He never lawfully set foot in this country. Time after time the Home Secretary tried, by directions to El Al, to get it to take the applicant to the destination where he was going, the United States, which, be it noted, was his own home country and the only country which is obliged by international law to receive him. If the applicant had never mutilated himself—or if El Al had taken him to the United States as it was directed to do—no one could suggest that the Home Secretary was guilty of an illegal extradition. And it seems to me that all that the Home Secretary has done by the deportation order is to see that his original refusal of leave was implemented. It was the only means open to him once the airline refused to take the applicant. He might well think it not conducive to the public good that a person should be able to enter this country in such a way and to stay here. The applicant was in no better position than a stowaway.

I need not go into the many other matters which might weigh with the Home Secretary. Suffice it to say that, in my judgment, **[305]** the fact that the applicant was a wanted criminal in the eyes of the United States, and the fact that the United States asked for him, does not take away the power of the Home Secretary to make a deportation order. I see no ground for attributing to the Home Secretary anything in the nature of a sham or want of bona fides or any unlawful or ulterior purpose.

I think, therefore, that this deportation order is good, and I would dismiss this appeal.

DONOVAN L.J. On the issue whether the Aliens Order, 1953, is ultra vires, I have nothing to add to what Lord Denning M.R. has said. I agree with it, and I think that Stephenson J. was right in the conclusion to which he came. I, further, think that the powers contained in articles 8 and 20 of the Order are not mutually exclusive, although no doubt the cases are few where the powers under article 8 having been frustrated, the Home Secretary finds himself obliged to resort to article 20. But the two powers are, I think, complementary and cumulative, as the judge held. And I also think, although it is not necessary to decide the point, that a person could be detained under the authority of both powers at one and the same time.

As to the alleged obligation on the part of the Home Secretary to allow representations, oral or written, to be made by or on behalf of any person, whom he proposes to deport, before he makes the order, I think the question should be approached from the standpoint that ordinarily a man shall be heard in his own defence before his liberty is interfered with in this drastic way, and that he should be denied that elementary requirement of natural justice only if the statute, or regulations properly made under it, when fairly construed, either expressly or by necessary implication exclude the right. There is no express provision excluding the right to make prior representations in the Aliens Restriction Act, 1914, which is the enabling Act, nor in the Order of 1953 which has been made thereunder. But a Divisional Court in 1920 held in effect that a denial of a prior right to be heard was implicit in the Act of 1914 and in the regulations then current, which differ in no material respect for this purpose from the regulations in the Order of 1953: see *Venicoff's* case,[88]* already cited. Since that time Parliament has on numerous occasions made fresh Orders concerning aliens and their possible deportation without attempting to alter the law laid down in

[88] [1920] 3 K.B. 72.

Venicoff's case,[88]* **[306]** and this is a weighty reason why we should not overrule the case now, unless we were quite clear that it had been wrongly decided.

For myself, I do not think that it was. The power vested in the Home Secretary to order deportation is a power to do an executive or administrative and not a judicial act. While in most cases no doubt the grant to the alien of an opportunity to be heard before a deportation order were made would involve little administrative inconvenience, there would undoubtedly be cases where the intimation of proposed deportation would make the power to do so almost useless. This possibility would have to be reckoned with and provided against in any condition which the court were to read into article 20 of the kind now contended for; and the careful and detailed language which any such condition would require leads me to the view that Parliament did not intend that it should be imposed, for otherwise the task of such definition would not have been left to the courts. I, accordingly, concur with the view that such a condition is not to be implied, but rather that the absence of any express provision for some preliminary hearing was deliberate and is to be justified by the necessities of the case. We are told that in practice the Home Secretary does refer such cases to the Chief Metropolitan Magistrate before whom the proposed deportee can appear and urge reasons against his deportation. This is done by way of an administrative concession,[89] and obviously it is a wise one. But it is not granted to aliens who have been refused leave to land, as the applicant has, and it seems to me that that exception is beyond criticism.

The main argument for the applicant is that the deportation order is illegal on a wider ground. Mr. Elwyn Jones puts it in this way. The common law forbids the surrender of a fugitive criminal to a foreign Power. Such a surrender is legal only when the case comes within the limited provisions of the Extradition Acts, 1870-1935, and this case admittedly does not do so. It is true that article 20 of the Order of 1953 on its face is general in its terms, and it is also true that this court has held[90] that the Home Secretary can select the ship on which the deportee is to be placed and thus indirectly, but effectively, determine his destination. But the article must be read and construed as if it implied conformably with the common law a prohibition against surrendering a fugitive criminal to a foreign Power. As Pearson L.J. **[307]** pointed out in the course of the argument, this seems to confer a privilege upon an alien because he is a criminal. In the end, Mr. Elwyn Jones said that the limitation implicit in article 20 was to this effect: that the power of deportation could not be exercised if the inevitable result would be that the alien would get into the hands of a foreign Power which wanted him for the purpose of making him serve a term of imprisonment which its authorities had imposed upon him. For that, said counsel, is surrender, and you may surrender only pursuant to the Extradition Acts, 1870-1935.

I say it with all respect, but I think that the fundamental defect in this argument is that it concentrates attention on what will happen when the alien arrives at the foreign country and then relates that consequence back, so that the consequence is regarded as if it existed from the outset as the purpose of the operation, and thus gives it its true quality. In my opinion, the fact that the present applicant will serve an existing sentence of imprisonment, if he is sent to the United States, does not mean that an act which otherwise would be deportation and nothing else becomes instead not deportation but the surrender of a fugitive criminal. To hold otherwise would be to give assent to the proposition that the quality of an act is determined by its consequence, which is obviously untrue; otherwise cause would become the same thing as effect. There may, it is true, be no practical difference from the applicant's point of view between a deportation which gives the United States authorities the power to make him serve his sentence, and an illegal surrender having the same effect. But that cannot involve that in law the two things must be regarded as the

[89] Pursuant to European Convention on Establishment, 1955. See (1955) 559 H.C. Deb., col. 1349.

[90] *Rex* v. *Secretary of State for Home Affairs, Ex parte Duke of Chateau Thierry** [1917] 1 K.B. 922.

same. If, therefore, this deportation order is to be regarded as invalid, it must be for some other reason than the consequence to which it will lead. Further, I think the history of the legislation regarding aliens, to which the Attorney-General drew our attention this morning, is antagonistic to the implied restriction for which Mr. Elwyn Jones contends.

Mr. Solomon asserted that the order was invalid for a different reason, namely, because it was a sham. The Home Secretary had not genuinely formed the opinion that it was conducive to the public good to deport the applicant; he simply wanted to comply with a United States request to surrender the applicant to them notwithstanding that the offences occurred as far back as 1944 and 1945, and had resorted to the device of a deportation order simply to give the look of legality to that compliance.

The task of the subject who seeks to establish such an **[308]** allegation as this is indeed heavy. On the face of it the order which he wishes the court to quash will look perfectly valid, and to get behind it and to demonstrate its alleged true character he will need to have revealed to him the communications, oral and written, which have passed between the home and the foreign authorities. But if the appropriate Minister here certifies, as he has done in this case, that such disclosure will be contrary to the public interest, then as a general rule the subject will not obtain it. He will be left to do his best without such assistance, and in the nature of things, therefore, he will seldom be able to do more than raise a prima facie case, or alternatively to sow such substantial and disquieting doubts in the mind of the court about the bona fides of the order he is challenging that the court will consider that some answer is called for. If that answer is withheld, or, being furnished, is found unsatisfactory, then, in my view, the order challenged ought not to be upheld, for otherwise there would be virtually no protection for the subject against some illegal order which had been clothed with the garments of legality simply for the sake of appearances and where discovery was resisted on the ground of privilege. I think that what I have just said conforms to what this court said in *Sacksteder's* case[91]* by Pickford L.J.[92] and Warrington L.J.[93]

I look, therefore, to see what evidence there is tending to suggest that this is such a case. The applicant stresses that mere deportation does not involve more than that he shall leave this country and stay away, and this he is perfectly willing to do. He is willing to go to Czechoslovakia, and that country is willing to receive him. Why, therefore, is it being insisted upon that he shall go to the United States of America and nowhere else? Then it has not been denied that the United States authorities have asked for him to be returned to them, and the only rational conclusion from the facts is, it is said, that the true object of the Home Secretary is simply to surrender the alien as a fugitive offender to the Power which has asked for him, in other words, to effect an illegal extradition.

The Attorney-General, contesting this allegation, pointed out that, even before the applicant arrived in this country, the British immigration authorities had decided to refuse him permission to land and had prepared a written notice to that effect, the notice saying in addition, and by way of anticipation, that directions had **[309]** been given to the owners of the aircraft to remove him in the same aircraft in which he arrived, and that aircraft was bound for America. These moves were frustrated by the applicant's self-inflicted injuries on board the aircraft, and later by El Al's breach of its undertaking to remove him under arrangements which the Home Office would notify to it. But from the outset the intention had been to send the applicant on to the United States, and that intention was not the result of some change of front after he had arrived here.

One asks, however, how the original intention came to be formed. We know from an affidavit filed in the previous proceedings[94]* by Hargreaves, an immigration officer at London Airport, that while the aircraft was still in the air on the way here he was told by the chief immigration officer at the airport that the

[91] [1918] 1 K.B. 578.
[92] Ibid. 586.
[93] Ibid. 589.
[94] [1963] 1 Q.B. 829, 831, 832.

applicant was on the aircraft and was to be refused permission to land. This direction must obviously have come from higher authority still, and one may safely assume, I think, that it was the appropriate department of the Home Office. The applicant was a national of the United States of America, where he had been convicted of espionage, and where he had broken his bail and whence he had fled to Israel. Clearly, he was followed there by a United States marshal, and when Israel summarily expelled him on an aircraft bound for Athens, where he was to be transferred to an El Al aeroplane bound for the United States via London, the United States marshal was on board in charge of him. Clearly some precaution was called for on the part of the United States authorities that they did not lose their prisoner in London, and it would be the most natural thing in the world that they should seek the co-operation of our own authorities to that end. It is not, therefore, mere speculation or conjecture but a wholly reasonable inference from the known facts that while the applicant was on his way here originally, our home authorities were asked to refuse him leave to land, and to see that he continued on his way to the United States. Hence the notice of refusal to land being made out while he was still in the air on his way here. But in all this there was nothing unreasonable or sinister at all; and the only way it helps the applicant is to show that from the outset the intention was that he should go to the United States.

But does that in any way tend to establish that the subsequent deportation order was a sham? It might well be that when the **[310]** Home Secretary came to make it, he would find that the United States was the right place for the applicant to go, anyway; and that whether the United States authorities had previously asked for him or not. It was, after all, his home country. In other words, the Home Secretary's idea of the alien's proper destination might simply coincide with what the United States authorities wanted to happen; and even if the Home Secretary welcomed such coincidence, it could have no effect upon the validity of the order. In the circumstances, I cannot see that the mere fact that all along it has been the intention to send the applicant to the United States is, of itself, any evidence to show that the deportation order is a mere pretence or sham or illegal extradition in disguise.

Next, what evidence is there for the allegation that the Home Secretary never genuinely came to the conclusion that it was conducive to the public good to deport the applicant? Here the applicant relies again on the facts I have already narrated. But the evidence the other way is indeed formidable. In the first place, he gained admittance by a stratagem which relied for its success on the humanity of our immigration officials. That reliance was justified in the event, and the success of the stratagem has produced for the home authorities an extremely troublesome problem, and, as it now transpires, substantial expense for the taxpayer. I venture to think it would be the duty of the Home Secretary in the interests of the public to do whatever he could to prevent such a stratagem from achieving its ultimate end, lest its success should set a precedent for others to copy.

Next, if country A is an ally of country B, each of them may well think it conducive to the public good of their own citizens that they should co-operate to see that a national of one of them, who gives defence information to a common potential enemy, should not escape the consequences inflicted upon him by due process of law.

Finally, if the real object of the Home Secretary were simply surrender, his actions have been strangely at variance with that purpose, for such purpose could have been effected weeks ago immediately upon the making of the deportation order. Instead the Home Secretary stayed his hand in order that the applicant should have the opportunity of challenging his action in court, just as he stayed the operation of the previous order of expulsion under article 8 when he learned that the applicant wished to contest it by means of an application for a writ of habeas corpus. **[311]**

I reach the conclusion, therefore, that there is no evidence which would justify the court forming even a provisional opinion that the Home Secretary has not genuinely deemed it to be conducive to the public good that the applicant should be deported. I have gone into the matter in this detail because I think that when such an allegation of bad faith is made and the liberty of the subject is involved, the court should examine the grounds of the allegation with the help of such material as is before it, and drawing any reasonable inferences of fact therefrom. The alternative would be to say that the claim for privilege made by the Crown precludes a really satisfactory inquiry and therefore none should be attempted. This, I think, would be wrong. But since this allegation has been made, I think it is proper to say not merely that it fails, but that there appears to be no valid ground of criticism of anything the Home Secretary or his officers have done in this case.

During the hearing of the previous proceedings in this court,[95] it was suggested at one stage in the argument for the applicant that the power of expulsion under article 8 of the Order of 1953 was no longer available, and that the only power left, if any were left at all, was the power to deport. I intervened to say that the applicant had done nothing to deserve deportation. I had in mind, of course, that he had committed no criminal offence here. The question of public good had not then arisen and what I said had no reference to this.

For the rest, I agree with what Lord Denning M.R. has said, and I agree that this appeal must be dismissed.

PEARSON L.J. Under articles 20 and 21 of the Order of 1953 the Secretary of State has very wide powers. He can make an order for the deportation of an alien if he deems it conducive to the public good, and he can cause the alien to be detained and be placed on board any ship or aircraft which is about to leave the United Kingdom. He can select the ship or aircraft: *Rex* v. *Secretary of State for Home Affairs, Ex parte Chateau Thierry*[96]* and *Rex* v. *Chiswick Police Station Superintendent, Ex parte Sacksteder.*[97]* The selection of the ship or aircraft must in most cases determine the destination at which the alien will arrive. The Extradition Acts, 1870-1935, impose limitations and restrictions on the extradition of fugitive criminals to prosecuting **[312]** governments. There is an area in which the deportation procedure, when it includes detention of the alien and placing him on board a ship or aircraft, and de facto extradition overlap, inasmuch as the effect of the deportation procedure applied to an alien may be that he arrives in the country of the prosecuting government and can be arrested by them. Accordingly, it can at any rate be suggested that the wide powers of the Secretary of State under the Order of 1953 might be misused for the purpose of surrendering a fugitive criminal to the prosecuting government in a case where the extradition procedure was not available, so as to evade the limitations and restrictions imposed by the Extradition Acts, 1870-1935. Is that being done in this case?

One of the contentions put forward on behalf of the applicant would make the effect rather than the purpose the determining factor. According to this contention, the deportation procedure, though in all other respects admissible and appropriate, cannot lawfully be used in a case where the effect would be to send a fugitive criminal to a place where he comes within the power of the prosecuting government. This contention seems to me to be clearly wrong. It would have the odd result that a person, by committing a crime in a foreign country, would gain the privilege of exemption from deportation from the United Kingdom to that country, and if that country was his own country and no other country would receive him, his criminal activity would have rendered him immune from deportation from the United Kingdom. That cannot be right. The powers of the Secretary of State to use the deportation procedure in any case where he deems it conducive to the public good are not fettered in the way suggested by this contention.

There is, however, another contention put forward on behalf of the applicant. It is that the detention procedure is in this case a mere sham being unlawfully used for the indirect and improper purpose of bringing about an unlawful

[95] [1963] 1 Q.B. 829, 837.
[96] [1917] 1 K.B. 922, 931, 934, 937.
[97] [1918] 1 K.B. 578, 584, 588, 591.

extradition. Reference was made to *Sacksteder's* case,[98]* in particular to the observations of Pickford L.J.[99] and Warrington L.J.[1]

Assuming that this contention is sound in law, I have come to the conclusion that it fails on the facts of the case. The evidence does not show that there is anything other than a genuine deportation. The United Kingdom Government were from the beginning for good reasons wishing and trying to procure **[313]** removal of the applicant from the United Kingdom to the United States, being the country to which he belongs. The United Kingdom had good reasons, apart from any representations eventually made, or indeed made at any time, by the United States Government.

The applicant's own conduct in this case is material. Being on bail in the sum of 100,000 dollars he absconded from the United States, acting evidently in breach of the trust that had been reposed in him, and he made use of his dead brother's passport, falsely pretending that it was his own. A few days later being in an aircraft of the El Al Airline bound for the United States via London Airport, he gained an entry into the United Kingdom by the subterfuge of inflicting serious wounds on himself, so that for reasons of humanity he had to be taken off the aircraft and taken to a hospital for treatment. That was undoubtedly a courageous act, but it was dangerous to his own safety, and a dishonest subterfuge in relation to the United Kingdom authorities. The United Kingdom authorities were at all stages wishing and trying to have him removed from the United Kingdom to the United States. On July 1, when the aircraft arrived at London Airport, an immigration officer went on board for the purpose of refusing permission to land but was unable to communicate the refusal to the applicant owing to his condition. On the same day a direction was given to the El Al Airlines to remove the applicant in the aircraft in which he had come, and that aircraft was bound for the United States. On July 3 the refusal of permission to land was communicated to the applicant in hospital by the service of a written notice, and that written notice referred to the direction which had been given. Then the United Kingdom authorities gave repeated directions to El Al Airlines requiring them to remove the applicant from the United Kingdom. [His Lordship read the direction and continued:] Directions different in detail but similar in principle were given on August 4, 8 and 11. None of those directions was complied with. The last of them was revoked on August 11, and on that day a deportation order was made, and it was announced in a Press notice that it was the Home Secretary's intention to give instructions for the applicant to be placed on an aircraft leaving the United Kingdom for the United States.

Thus, when the United Kingdom Government abandoned the attempt to secure the removal of the applicant from the United Kingdom to the United States under article 8 of the Order of **[314]** 1953, they immediately began the attempt to secure such removal under article 20. Clearly, there was no change of attitude or intention or policy, and no new departure except in the sphere of procedure. It was taking further steps along the same road.

Whether or not there may have been any earlier representations made, as Donovan L.J. has suggested there may have been, it appears from the evidence that on or about August 8 representations were made by the United States Government to the United Kingdom Government to the effect that the United States Government would very much like to have the applicant sent to the United States. It may well be that those representations caused some acceleration of the procedure, but there is no indication or ground for inferring that those representations induced the United Kingdom Government to take any steps which it would not otherwise have taken.

Independently of any such representation, the United Kingdom Government has good reasons for deporting the applicant from this country, especially as he gained admission to it by a subterfuge. It, also, has at least two good reasons for intending to place him on an aircraft bound for the United States. First, he is a naturalised citizen of that country, so that it is his home and the country to

[98] [1918] 1 K.B. 578.
[99] Ibid. 586.
[1] Ibid. 589.

which he belongs, and that which by International Law is bound to receive him: Oppenheim's International Law (1955), 8th ed., Vol. I, at pp. 645 and 646. Secondly, for the purpose of discouraging others from following his example, it is desirable that he should not gain any ultimate advantage by his subterfuge. But for his subterfuge he would have arrived in the United States on July 1. If the intention of the United Kingdom Government is fulfilled, he will still in the end arrive in the United States.

There are also the broader considerations referred to in the judgment of Stephenson J. in this case, where he said[2]: "The Attorney-General contended that the Secretary of State was entitled to consider the relations of Her Majesty's Government with friendly powers, the security risks of the applicant travelling about this country or other countries, the international consequences of his going east or west, and the desirability of getting him out of this country or allowing him to remain here." The admissibility of these considerations has not been disputed in this appeal.

Having regard to the matters which I have mentioned, I am **[315]** unable to find the necessary foundation of fact for the applicant's contention that there is in this case a misuse of the powers under the Order of 1953. The intended deportation appears to be in every way a genuine deportation, not a sham, and not a device for bringing about an unlawful extradition.

I am not expressing any concluded opinion on the difficult questions whether any, and if so, what, facts would show a misuse of the deportation procedure for the purpose of bringing about an unlawful extradition. The fact that an alien has committed crimes in another country, whether or not they are extraditable crimes, is a factor which can legitimately be taken into account in deciding whether he is an undesirable alien who ought to be deported. Political factors also can properly be taken into account. The decision and reasoning of this court in the *Chateau Thierry* case[3]* and the *Sacksteder* case[4]* show the wide extent of the discretion conferred on the Secretary of State. Also the Indian case of *Muller* v. *Superintendent, Presidency Jail, Calcutta*,[5] which has been referred to, may have an important bearing on those questions. I wish to leave those questions entirely open for future consideration.

It was also contended on behalf of the applicant that upon the true construction of article 20 there is no power to make a deportation order until after an inquiry has been held, or at any rate some opportunity has been given to the alien concerned to make representations against the proposal for the making of the deportation order. The suggested construction is based on the use in article 20 (2) (*b*) of the word "deems" and also a suggested implication of a requirement to hear the other side, audi alteram partem. This is an interesting contention, especially as it has involved citation of South African authorities[6] on the principle of audi alteram partem. In my judgment, however, the contention cannot succeed in relation to the provision with which we are concerned in this case, article 20 (2) (*b*). The word "deems" normally means only "is of opinion" or "considers," or at most "decides," and there is no implication of steps to be taken before the opinion is formed or the decision is taken. To some extent the word "deems" can take its meaning from its context and the provision here is "if the Secretary of State deems it to be **[316]** conducive to the public good," referring unmistakably to an executive policy decision to be taken by a Minister of the Crown as to what is expedient to be done, and not to an issue to be determined judicially or semi-judicially between parties. The maxim audi alteram partem is no doubt a sound and valuable maxim of administration as well as of adjudication, but it may not be suitable for insertion as an implied condition in the terms of a particular statutory instrument.

In this case there are numerous problems. Does the hearing have to be oral

[2] *Ante*, p. 274.
[3] [1917] 1 K.B. 922.
[4] [1918] 1 K.B. 578.
[5] [1955] Internat.L.R. 497; (1955) S.C.J. 324.
[6] *Reg.* v. *Ngwevela* [1954] 1 S.A.L.R. 123 and *Jeewa* v. *Donges N.O.* [1950] 3 S.A.L.R. 414; [1953] 1 S.A.L.R. 414.

or is an opportunity to make representations sufficient? Is the alien entitled to know the reasons for which the deportation order is proposed to be made? Does the hearing have to be given before the deportation order is made or is it sufficient if given before the deportation order is executed?: *De Verteuil* v. *Knaggs.*[7] Should there be exceptions, for instance for emergencies or for security reasons in particular cases, or for obstructive conduct on the part of the alien.[8] Having regard to these problems, I seriously doubt whether it would be possible to draft any condition precedent so certain and so obvious that it could be read into article 20 (2) (*b*) by necessary intendment. Moreover, there is the rule of construction, expressum facit cessare tacitum. Here a condition precedent to the making of a deportation order is expressed, namely, "if the Secretary of State deems it to be conducive to the public good to make a deportation order against the alien." That express condition excludes the supposed implied condition that a hearing must be given.

Finally, there is the very formidable point that in *Rex* v. *Leman Street Police Station Inspector, Ex parte Venicoff,*[9]* a construction was placed on the same words as they were used in the Aliens Order, 1919, and the same words were repeated in the Order of 1953, and presumably were intended to bear the same construction.

As to the validity of the Order of 1953 and as to the relation between action under article 8 and action under article 20 I have nothing to add to what has been said. I agree that the appeal should be dismissed.

Appeal dismissed. **[317]**

[Counsel for the applicant stated that he had been authorised by the Attorney-General to say that the Secretary of State for Home Affairs would not execute the deportation order until the applicant had been given an opportunity of making representations in regard to the matter.]

Solicitors: *Kaufman & Seigal; Treasury Solicitor.*

R. v. THURNLACKH

([1963] Crim. L.R. 582)

1963: Court of Criminal Appeal: Lord Parker C.J., Havers, Widgery JJ.

Age: thirty-nine (male). *Facts*: pleaded guilty to eight counts of obtaining credit by fraud to the amount of £4,000. He got into financial difficulties in connection with his business. *Previous history*: no convictions. Came to England from Austria in 1950; married an Englishwoman and had children by her. *Decision*: not a case for a recommendation. Further, not the worst case of its kind: four years' imprisonment reduced to two and a half years.

[7] [1918] A.C. 557, 562; 34 T.L.R. 325, P.C.
[8] [1918] A.C. 557, 561.
[9] [1920] 3 K.B. 72.

R. v. RELISH

((1964) 108 Sol. Jo. 201)

February 24, 1964: Court of Criminal Appeal: Lord Parker C.J., Paull, Widgery JJ.

Criminal Law—Leave to call fresh evidence—Deportation order—U.S. Serviceman—Aliens Order, 1953.

Application for leave to appeal against conviction and sentence.

At about 6.15 a.m. on 2nd November, 1963, police officers detected the smell of Indian hemp in a parked car in which were the defendant, a member of the United States Air Force, and two other persons. Subsequently all three were charged with being in possession of a dangerous drug. They pleaded not guilty but were convicted; the defendant was sentenced to six months' imprisonment, and an order recommending his deportation was made. The defendant applied for leave to appeal against his conviction and sentence, seeking, *inter alia,* leave to call fresh evidence, viz., that of his two co-accused, now in prison, who, it was alleged, had since denied that the defendant had any of the Indian hemp in his possession.

LORD PARKER, C.J., said that, whilst the court had ample powers to call fresh evidence, it fettered those powers by admitting the evidence only of witnesses who were not available at the trial. The discretion was elastic and it could be accepted that the evidence of the co-accused would be fresh evidence, having regard to the fact that they had pleaded not guilty at the trial, and thus their evidence was not available for the applicant at the trial. The court, however. had no powers to investigate the matter and the most expedient course for the applicant was to petition the Home Secretary. With regard to the deportation order, there were grounds for **[202]** thinking that the Aliens Order, 1953, did not apply to members of visiting forces stationed in the United Kingdom as a result of arrangements with Her Majesty's Government, and in those circumstances it appeared that there would be no power to make a deportation order. In any event the order was inapt because it was understood that the applicant would be discharged from the service—taken back to the United States and discharged there. The ultimate decision would be in the hands of the commanding officer of the Air Force. The court, therefore, adopted the wording of para. 3 of art. 20 of the Aliens Order, 1953, and would merely signify that it did not concur with the order recommending deportation. Save for the order recommending deportation, the applications were refused.

APPEARANCES: *R. N. Titheridge* (*Hunnybun & Sons,* Huntingdon).

REGINA v. BIMBO
REGINA v. WILSON

(*The Times,* December 5, 1964)

December 4, 1964: Court of Criminal Appeal: Ashworth, Brabin, Lyell JJ.

The Court granted these applications for leave to appeal and, treating the hearing of the applications as the hearing of the appeals, allowed the appeals against sentence of Rose Bimbo, aged 54 and her daughter, Susan Wilson, aged 21, American gypsy women, who, after pleading guilty to charges of theft at County of London Sessions (Chairman: R. E. Seaton, Esq.), on November 19, 1964, were each sentenced to eight weeks' imprisonment, with recommendations for deportation, were ordered to make restitution of £48, and were each ordered to pay 50 guineas towards the costs of the prosecutions.

The Court today, substituted sentences of a fine of £20 on Bimbo and £10 on Wilson, and ordered each to pay 10 guineas towards the costs of the prosecutions, accepting from counsel the information that the money was available and would be paid. The recommendations for deportation were set aside.

Mr. Kenneth Richardson, for the applicants, said that the women came to this country from the United States in March on a fortune-telling business trip, bringing £2,500 with them and wanting to buy a Rolls Royce motor car. It was bought for £1,800 and shipped back to America. Bimbo had obtained £13 from a justice of the peace to whom she went for a certificate after losing a pawn ticket. She offered to tell his fortune, saying that to do so, she needed to hold his money and bless it. She handed back the notes, and after she left, he discovered that some were missing. Both women went into a gown shop, and Wilson engaged the attention of the proprietor's wife, while Bimbo offered to tell his fortune and the money she handed back was £35 short. Bimbo had a bizarre belief that if gypsies were shut up for 60 days, they died and when she was imprisoned for six months in New York, a tent was put up for her in the prison yard. Wilson had given birth to a daughter in hospital at Holloway.

Mr. JUSTICE ASHWORTH, giving the judgment of the Court said that on November 18, the applicants had appeared at East Sussex Quarter Sessions on seven charges of larceny—and, after a prolonged hearing, that Court took an understandable and right view, the effect of the order being that, subject to a quite considerable financial penalty, each was bound over to come up for judgment, if still within reach of the Court, by November 24. That Court expressed the view that they should be permitted to leave the country at the earliest possible moment. The Chairman of London Sessions was under the mistaken impression that the East Sussex order would be ineffective if the object of the exercise was to prevent either woman returning to this country. This Court agreed that the sooner these women were out of the country, the better. The Court did not intend to substitute or add to its order and requirement regarding their departure, and it was said that they hoped to leave this very evening by air. The Court hoped so too. If they changed their minds, there was no reason why steps should not be taken to implement the Sussex order.

Solicitors: *Messrs. Sampson & Co.*

D.

EXTRADITION

1

PRACTICE AND PROCEDURE

REGINA v. GOVERNOR OF BRIXTON PRISON. *EX PARTE* LENNON

(*The Times*, October 13, 1962)

October 12, 1962: Queen's Bench Division: Lord Parker C.J., Gorman, Salmon JJ.

New York Bank "Imaginary".

The Divisional Court granted this application by Percy Frederick Lennon, detained in Brixton prison for a writ of *habeas corpus* and ordered that he be released. The applicant had been committed at Bow Street Magistrates' Court (Sir Robert Blundell) pursuant to the Extradition Acts, on charges of false pretences and forgery.

Mr. Neil Butter appeared for the applicant; *Mr. M. Koenig* for the Government of the Republic of France; *Mr. J. H. Buzzard* and *Mr. John Leonard* for the Governor of Brixton Prison.

The Lord Chief Justice said that the substantial point raised in the present case was whether there had been evidence before the magistrate which would justify the committal. If a strong and probable presumption had been raised, the Court would not interfere, as this was not an appeal from the magistrate.

The charges arose out of two transactions both of which were concerned with false pretences and forgery. The first transaction occurred on September 27, 1959, when the applicant went into a confectionary shop in Boulogne, and there bought a box of chocolates, giving a traveller's cheque for $100 drawn on the Chase National Bank of New York. It turned out that the cheque was not accepted by the banks in France and the charge was that the cheque was drawn on an imaginary bank. That was puzzling, as there was a well-known bank of such a name. It might be that there was some defect in the spelling of the name. It was the whole basis of the present case that the cheque was drawn on an imaginary bank and that its form was a complete forgery. The second transaction occurred on October 1, 1959, when the applicant bought some jewellery in a shop again tendering a traveller's cheque for $100 drawn on the Chase National Bank of New York. Again, the charge was that the cheque was a forgery as it was drawn on an imaginary bank. The basis of both charges was that the cheques were forgeries.

In each case, in the depositions, the persons in the shop described the transaction and then stated that a bank official later informed them that the cheques were bad. In both transactions the evidence was partly hearsay. It was right to say that it was to be expected that the cheques would be produced and identified by the person in the shop and the official in the bank who took them. A bank official should also have stated why the cheques were not accepted. Without going into the question whether the magistrate was entitled to rely on hearsay evidence in France, it was clear that there was not a scrap of evidence that the cheques were drawn on an imaginary bank. They might have been genuine cheques which had been stolen by the applicant, signed by him twice and then refused by the bank because a customer had informed the bank of the theft. There was, therefore, no evidence that the cheques were forgeries because they were drawn on an imaginary bank, which was the whole basis of the charges. On the ground that there was no evidence as to that fundamental fact, the magistrate was not justified in committing the applicant.

There was, apparently, a further bundle of documents from France which were not translated. It was said that those documents concerned a police inquiry which showed that the bank was an imaginary bank. The Court was in doubt as to whether the documents could be looked at, as they were not statements on oath. It had been argued that, by section 14 of the Extradition Act, the bundle could be looked at as it consisted of judicial documents the contents of which need not be on oath. But that section referred only to cases where the applicant had been convicted of an offence. In the present case, therefore, the Court had refused to look at them.

This was another case of which there had already been two, where the requisitioning country had really not taken the trouble to put their tackle in order. In cases involving the liberty of the subject, the Court while anxious to observe treaty obligations, regarded the matter strictly. Therefore, the writ of *habeas corpus* would be issued and the applicant discharged.

Mr. JUSTICE GORMAN agreed.

Mr. JUSTICE SALMON said that he agreed with reluctance. The applicant was a rogue who had been allowed to go free because the requisitioning country had not put their tackle in order.

Solicitors: *Official Solicitors; Messrs. Barnet, Tuson & Co.; Director of Public Prosecutions.*

3

EXTRADITION CRIMES IN GENERAL

IN RE KRONENBERG

((1965) 109 Sol. Jo. 933)

November 10, 1965: Queen's Bench Division: Lord Parker C.J., Ashworth, Widgery JJ.

Criminal Law—Fraudulant Conversion—Whether Bill of Exchange 'Property'—Aided Litigant with Nil Contribution—Order for Payment of £1 Costs 'Without Prejudice to Future Application' for Further Order.

Motion for habeas corpus.

The applicant (a foreign woman married to a foreigner), in respect of whom a request for extradition had been made in relation to charges of offences against the laws of the Federal Republic of Germany, was brought before a magistrate, under s. 10 of the Extradition Act, 1870, on equivalent English charges of, *inter alia*, fraudulent conversion, in that she had fraudulently converted to the use and benefit of herself and her husband bills of exchange entrusted to her and her husband by the alleged victims for retention by her and her husband in safe custody. The evidence was that the alleged victims had been induced to indorse the bills of exchange by pretences which were false, that the bills had been entrusted on terms that they were to be retained by the applicant and her husband in safe custody, that the bills had got into circulation and had been discounted. The magistrate was satisfied that a prima facie case had been made out and committed the applicant to prison to await extradition. She moved for habeas corpus contending, *inter alia*, that since what had been handed over was a mere promise to pay, that did not constitute property which could be the subject of fraudulent conversion. She was in receipt of legal aid with a nil contribution, and the government applying for extradition, a respondent to her motion, applied for an order for costs against her *de bene esse*.

LORD PARKER, C.J., said that the definition of 'property' in s. 46 of the Larceny Act, 1916, including 'all . . . instruments relating to or evidencing the title or right to any property, or giving a right to recover or receive any money or goods', was very wide, and was apt to cover bills of exchange, which were property entrusted to the applicant and her husband, if the evidence was accepted, on certain terms, and could be the subject of fraudulent conversion. Accordingly there was no reason to interfere with the order of committal. The motion for habeas corpus would be refused and an order made for payment of £1 by way of costs without prejudice to any further application in the future which the extraditing government might care to make.

ASHWORTH and WIDGERY JJ., agreed. Motion dismissed.

APPEARANCES: *Michael Beckman* (*Ivor Denfield*); *Claud Allen* (*Buckeridge & Braune*); *John Buzzard* (*Director of Public Prosecutions*).

5

POLITICAL OFFENCES

REGINA v. GOVERNOR OF BRIXTON PRISON *EX PARTE* SCHTRAKS

([1963] 1 Q.B. 55)

February 20, 21, 22, 23, 27, 1962; Queen's Bench Division: Lord Parker C.J., Ashworth, Atkinson JJ.

Extradition—Extent of treaty—"Territory"—Israel—Non-recognition of Israel's sovereignty over Jerusalem—De facto authority recognised—Whether Jerusalem "territory" of Israel Government—Israel (Extradition) Order, 1960 (*S.I.* 1960, *No.* 1660).
Extradition—Offence of political character—Offence in itself not political—Subsequently becoming political—Whether offence of political character at the time of commission—Burden of proof—Extradition Act, 1870 (33 & 34 *Vict. c.* 52), *s.* 3.

In September, 1959, in Israel, the grandfather of a boy, Yossele, aged seven, refused to return the boy to his parents because he feared that the child would not be given the religious education of an orthodox Jew. The parents brought proceedings in the High Court of Israel in Jerusalem, and on February 10, 1960, the court ordered the return of Yossele to his parents by February 15, 1960. That order was not complied with. The parents brought proceedings against both grandparents and the applicant, the uncle of Yossele, for contempt of court. At the hearing the applicant, having affirmed, said that he had not seen Yossele since the feast of Hanukka which, that year, was from December 25, 1959, to January 1, 1960, at Rishon Le-Zion. On May 12, 1960, the court ordered that the grandfather be imprisoned but made no order against the applicant, who, shortly afterwards, came to live in England.

The boy was not found and in August, 1961, in the course of their enquiries, the police arrested Shlomo Kot, his wife and his brother Reuben. They were all imprisoned and the men were not released until after they had made their declarations. In those declarations all three alleged that the applicant and Yossele had come to the settlement after the Feast of Hanukka and Yossele had stayed with Shlomo and his wife. Shlomo also stated that the applicant had told him that the boy had to be kept from his father who desired his conversion to another religion and asked that the boy should remain in the settlement until after the dispute was over. Shlomo's wife gave evidence of the boy staying with them until the applicant came for him three weeks later. On that evidence, the Government of Israel asked for the extradition of the applicant in pursuance of an agreement dated April 4, 1960, between the two Governments that the Extradition Act, 1870,[1] should apply, **[56]** subject to

[1] Extradition Act, 1870, s. 2: "Where an arrangement has been made with any foreign state with respect to the surrender to such state of any fugitive criminals, Her Majesty may, by Order in Council, direct that this Act shall apply in the case of such foreign state. Her Majesty may . . . limit the operation of the order . . . and render the operation thereof subject to such conditions, exceptions, and qualifications as may be deemed expedient."

the terms of the Israel (Extradition) Order, 1960.[2] The charges against the applicant were for perjury and child stealing. On January 12, 1962, the applicant was committed to prison by order of the chief magistrate to await extradition to Israel.

The applicant applied for a writ of habeas corpus on the grounds, inter alia, that (1) Jerusalem was not "territory" of Israel within the meaning of the agreement since the United Kingdom Government did not recognise the Israel Government as having de jure sovereignty in Jerusalem but only de facto authority, so that, there was no power to order his extradition on a charge of perjury committed in Jerusalem, nor, in that the declarations were made in that city was there jurisdiction to extradite him on any of the charges; and (2) that the offences were of a political character:—

Held, (1) that "territory" in the agreement of April 4, 1960, must be construed in its context, namely, that of an extradition treaty in which the important consideration was whether the writ of a contracting party ran in a particular area; and that, as the Israel Government had de facto authority and exercised jurisdiction over Jerusalem and no other State was recognised as having de jure sovereignty, Jerusalem was within the "territory" of Israel within the meaning of the agreement (post, p. 74).

(2) That the function of the magistrate was the same under section 10 of the Extradition Act, 1870, as it was under section 5 of the Fugitive Offenders Act, 1881, despite the difference of wording between those sections, that was, to commit if there were such **[57]** evidence that, if it were uncontradicted at the trial, a reasonably minded jury might convict on it. The function of the Divisional Court was to review the evidence before the magistrate and interfere only if satisfied that no magistrate properly directing his mind to the question could reasonably have been satisfied that the evidence justified committal (post, p. 78).

Dictum of Swift J. in *Rex* v. *Governor of Brixton Prison, Ex parte Bidwell** [1937] 1 K.B. 305, 313; 53 T.L.R. 1; [1936] 3 All E.R. 1, D.C. applied.

(3) That, although under section 3 (1) of the Extradition Act, 1870, a person could not be extradited for an offence of a political character where the offences charged were prima facie included in the treaty of extradition, it was for a person alleging that his extradition was in fact sought in order that he might be tried or punished for an offence of a political character, to prove its political character (post, p. 83).

Reg. v. *Governor of Brixton Prison, Ex parte Kolczynski** [1955] 1 Q.B. 540; [1955] 2 W.L.R. 116; [1955] 1 All E.R. 31, D.C. considered.

(4) That an offence was not of a political character unless it was of such a character when committed; it was not enough, therefore, that the issues

S. 3: "The following restrictions shall be observed with respect to the surrender of fugitive criminals: (1) A fugitive criminal shall not be surrendered if the offence in respect of which his surrender is demanded is one of a political character, or if he prove to the satisfaction of the police magistrate or the court before whom he is brought on habeas corpus, or to the Secretary of State, that the requisition for his surrender has in fact been made with a view to try or punish him for an offence of a political character: . . ."

[2] Israel (Extradition) Order, 1960, para. 1: "The Extradition Acts, 1870 to 1935, shall apply in the case of the State of Israel under and in accordance with the said agreement."

Art. 1: "The contracting parties agree to extradite to each other, in the circumstances stated in the present agreement, those persons who, being accused or convicted of any of the offences enumerated in article 3 and committed within the territory of the one party . . . shall be found within the territory of the other party."

Art. 6: "A person claimed shall not be extradited if the offence in respect of which his extradition is requested is one of a political character, or if he proves that the request for his extradition has, in fact, been made with a view to try or punish him for an offence of a political character."

Art. 12: "In the examinations which they have to make in accordance with the foregoing stipulations, the authorities of the requested party shall admit as valid evidence the sworn depositions or the affirmations of witnesses taken in the territory of the requesting party, or copies thereof."

subsequently became political, and it must have been committed not merely in the context of a movement or struggle of a political nature, but as part of it and with the object of advancing it. Accordingly, since the applicant had acted in furtherance of a private and domestic matter, the fact that his offences may have become a political issue did not make them offences of a political character (post, p. 88).

APPLICATION for write of habeas corpus ad subjiciendum.

The following statement of facts is taken from the judgment of the court and the affidavits cited in support of the action. Ida and Alter Schuchmacher emigrated from Russia to Israel with their two children, a daughter, Zina, and their son, Yosef, known as Yossele; who was born on March 2, 1952. The parents had difficulty in finding work and accommodation and therefore, early in 1959, they left their children with the grandparents, the wife's parents, Nachman and Miriam Schtraks. The parents had no difficulty in getting their daughter back but when they asked for the return of Yossele, in about September, 1959, the grandfather refused to return him because he thought that the parents would not give Yossele the religious education of an orthodox Jew.

The parents began proceedings in the High Court of Israel, in Jerusalem, and on January 16, 1960, obtained an order nisi addressed to the grandparents to show cause why they should not bring the boy to the court so that he might be dealt with as the court ordered. On January 28, 1960, the grandparents made **[58]** a declaration that it was in the interest of Yossele that he should remain with them, that the boy wished to do so, and that they feared the parents would take the child back to Russia. The case was heard on February 10, 1960, when the order was made absolute and the grandparents ordered to return Yossele by February 15, 1960.

The grandparents did not return the child and the parents then brought proceedings for contempt of court against the grandparents and their son, the applicant, Shalom Schtraks. They alleged that the applicant was making common cause with the grandparents, assisting and encouraging them in the withholding of Yossele, when he knew of the order of the court. On February 25, 1960, the applicant, in an affidavit, denied the allegation.

On May 12, 1960, the case was heard. The applicant gave evidence and, according to a police officer of the Israeli police, Sergeant Tishler, affirmed "I last saw [Yossele] before Hanukka this year. I saw him in Rishon Le-Zion. It was at the Yeshiva in Rishon Le-Zion. I was with my father, Nachman Schtraks. I study at a Yeshiva in Lod and my father came to me and asked me to go with him to Rishon Le-Zion . . . Since then I have not seen the boy . . . I do not know from my father or from another source that the child is hidden from his father." The feast of Hanukka that year was from December 25, 1959, to January 1, 1960, and in one translation of this passage "Yeshiva" was translated as a college of religion. According to the notes of evidence of the trial, the applicant later said: "I do not remember whether I spoke to the child between Hanukka and the trial." The court committed the grandfather to prison for contempt, the parents withdrew their application against the grandmother and the court, not being satisfied that the applicant had rendered any assistance, made no order against him. The applicant came to England on May 23, 1960 and, at the time of the hearing of this application, the grandfather was still in prison and the whereabouts of Yossele was still unknown.

In August, 1961, as a result of extensive police inquiries and searches for Yossele, three people were arrested by the police from the Komemiyut Settlement. They were Shlomo Kot, his wife Rachel and his brother, Reuben. On August 2, Shlomo and his wife were arrested and charged. On August 9, their application for bail was refused but Sergeant Tishler said that Rachel would be released next day; Reuben was arrested on that day. On August 10, Rachel was released and on August 17, they all made declarations in Jerusalem and Reuben was released; **[59]** Shlomo was released the following day. Reuben was never charged.

Shlomo Kot, in his declaration, affirmed that "A few weeks after the Feast of Hanukka about a year and a half ago, that is after the Feast of Hanukka of the year 5720, which fell on the days December 25, 1959, to Janury 1, 1960, approximately in the month of Tevet, 5720, while I was, towards evening, in the synagogue of the said Komemiyut Settlement, there appeared a young man with a boy about seven years of age. The young man and the boy who arrived together were unknown to me and were not local residents." The young man and the boy were referred to Shlomo Kot as the rabbi of the settlement was not present and by paragraph 5 of his declarations "The young man and the boy came up to me, and I asked the young man what he wanted. The young man said that he was the boy's uncle and that there was a family quarrel about the boy who was with him, namely, the boy's father wanted to remove him from the Jewish fold and convert him to another religion while the mother was opposed to this and the boy, therefore, had to be saved by keeping him away from his father for a short period until the matter was settled. The young man informed me that he had a letter in this matter from Rabbi Meisels of Jerusalem to the rabbi of the said Komemiyut Settlement. As the said rabbi was not present and as the young man asked that the boy who had come with him should remain in the said Komemiyut Settlement that very night, I agreed that the boy should remain at my house. The young man then told me that the name of the boy was Israel Hazan . . ." He then went on to affirm that the boy stayed at his house for two to three weeks and that during that time the young man came to see the boy and that the boy confided to him that his real name was Yossele. He identified, from photographs, Yossele and the applicant as being the boy and the young man.

Rachel Kot, in her declaration, affirmed that one evening her husband brought home the young man and the boy and that the boy stayed with them. By paragraph 5 of her declaration, she affirmed that "One day, after about three weeks had elapsed from the day on which the boy had been brought to my house, the boy came to me and told me joyfully that his uncle had come to take him with him. I packed the boy's things; he took them with him, travelling in a car driven by a man named Menahem Moses, of the Komemiyut Smallholders' Settlement. In that car, I saw two other persons, one of whom was Rappaport **[60]** Meir, who lives at the said Komemiyut Smallholders' Settlement." She also stated that the young man came to see the boy twice and identified them as being the applicant and Yossele from photographs.

Reuben Kot, in his declaration, affirmed that he saw the young man and the boy near the synagogue and that one or two days later he visited the house of his brother and saw the boy there. He also identified the boy as Yossele and the young man as the applicant from photographs.

On the evidence of the three Kots and of Sergeant Tishler, who deposed to the applicant's evidence in the High Court of Israel, the Government of Israel asked for the extradition of the applicant. The applicant was arrested on August 28, 1961, and during the proceedings for his extradition an inquiry was made of the Foreign Office concerning the recognition afforded the State of Israel by the Government of the United Kingdom. On October 4, 1961, a letter was received from the Foreign Office stating "(1) His Majesty's Government accorded de facto recognition to the State of Israel on January 29, 1949. (2) His Majesty's Government accorded de jure recognition to the State of Israel on April 27, 1950. In according such de jure recognition His Majesty's Government made certain reservations which, in relation to the status of Jerusalem, were explained as follows by the then Minister of State in a statement to the House of Commons on April 27, of that year:— 'His Majesty's Government are unable to recognise the sovereignty of Israel over that part of Jerusalem which she occupies, though, pending a final determination of the status of the area, they recognise that Israel exercise de facto authority in it.' (3) In according recognition on the same date of the Union of the Kingdom of Jordan and of that part of Palestine under Jordan occupation and control His Majesty's Government made a similar reservation in respect of that part of Jerusalem occupied and controlled by Jordan. (4) Her Majesty's Government continue to maintain, as regards the status of that part of Jerusalem occupied by Israel, the attitude which they adopted when according de jure recognition to the State of Israel on April 27, 1950."

On January 12, 1962, the chief magistrate (Sir Robert Blundell) committed the applicant to Brixton Prison to await extradition to Israel on the following charges: "1. Perjury for that he on May 12, 1960, during proceedings in an application No. 52/60 in the High Court of Justice of Israel knowingly gave false evidence touching a matter material in those proceedings **[61]** contrary to section 117 of the Criminal Code Ordinance. 1936. 2. Child stealing: (*a*) on a date between January 1 and February 15, 1960, with intent to deprive Alter and Ida Schuchmacher of their son Joseph (born in 1952) fraudulently detained him in the house of Shlomo Zalman Kot at Komemiuth, contrary to section 188 of the said Ordinance; (*b*) on a date between January 1 and February 15, 1960, wrongfully confined the said Joseph Schuchmacher in the said house knowing that he was an abducted person, contrary to section 259 of the said Ordinance."

The applicant applied for a writ of habeas corpus. In an affidavit he stated that "The application for my extradition by the Government of Israel has arisen out of the struggle between the orthodox right wing and the non-orthodox left wing parties, a conflict which started even before the establishment of the State of Israel and has continued unabated ever since then. Politics and religion are in fact inseparable. . . ."

The grounds of the application were (1) that the agreement of April 4, 1960, did not apply to any part of Jerusalem. (2) That the method by which the affidavits of all three witnesses for the prosecution where obtained raised a presumption of duress which was not rebutted by the prosecution. (3) That two of the three witnesses were accomplices to two of the alleged offences and the rules which govern the admissibility of the evidence of accomplices in this country were not observed; neither was it taken into consideration that, where all three witnesses were concerned, there was both the element of fear and the hope of reward. (4) That an examination of the dates when it was alleged the offences of child stealing and harbouring were committed showed that these charges could not be maintained. Thus both those charges and the perjury which arose from those charges could not stand. (5) That by article 11 of the Israel (Extradition) Order, 1960, it was necessary before an extradition order was made that "the evidence be found sufficient, according to the laws of the territory from which extradition is desired, either to justify the committal of the person claimed for trial, if the offence of which he is accused had been committed in that territory." The magistrate failed to find that as a fact the evidence was sufficient to justify the applicant's committal according to the laws of this country and in the absence of such finding there was no jurisdiction for the issue of the warrant. (6) That the charges against the applicant were brought and the request for his extradition made in furtherance of a struggle between the various political parties in Israel arising out of the **[62]** conflict between the religious and secular forces in the state. The religious conflicts had at all material times assumed a political character, and accordingly the State of Israel were preferring charges against the applicant for offences, which, though the offences themselves were not political in character, arose from the conflict, and it was thought thereby to placate the secular parties in the struggle against the orthodox elements. Considered as they must be in the framework of the background of political and religious conflicts in the State of Israel, the charges and the request for the applicant's extradition must therefore be regarded as political in character and they were accordingly contrary to article 6 of the Order. They were brought by the Government of Israel on false evidence in furtherance of their campaign against the strict orthodox parties in Israel, who had aroused the enmity of the party of Mr. Ben Gurion, the Prime Minister, because they were not Zionists and opposed the secular State of Israel, an attitude which was much resented by that Government.

John Foster Q.C., M. A. B. King-Hamilton Q.C. and *Esther Iwi* for the applicant. The Israel (Extradition) Order, 1960, limits the Extradition Act, 1870 (*Reg. v. Wilson*[3]*); the Order limits the Act so that they apply only to offences com-

[3] (1877) 3 Q.B.D. 42, D.C.

mitted in the territories of the contracting parties and not to offences committed in the area of their jurisdiction. The offences must have been committed in the area over which the sovereignty of the State of Israel is recognised by Her Majesty's Government. The area over which the sovereignty of Israel is recognised is a matter for the executive and not for the judiciary. The Foreign Office has certified that Her Majesty's Government does not recognise the de jure sovereignty of Israel over part of Jerusalem but only recognises her authority de facto and that certificate is binding on the court. In article 2 of the Israel (Extradition) Order, 1960, the territories outside the United Kingdom to which the agreement applies are carefully enumerated, but there is no such enumeration in the case of territories outside Israel. By article 12 the sworn depositions or affidavits of the evidence on which a contracting party seeks extradition must be taken within that party's territory. In this case the examination of witnesses and the affidavits were affirmed in Jerusalem and outside the territory of Israel. The question is whether an area which is occupied **[63]** by a state is the territory of that state. The Channel Islands, Isle of Man and the colonies are all outside the territory of the United Kingdom but Her Majesty's Government exercises jurisdiction therein. Areas which are outside the territory of the United Kingdom but within her jurisdiction are carefully enumerated in article 2 of the Order. Jurisdiction is a wide term, unlike territory, and is the term used in the Extradition Act, 1870, but the more precise term is used in the Order. That there is de facto recognition by Her Majesty's Government of the jurisdiction of the State of Israel over Jerusalem does not alter the fact that the territory of Israel is the area over which she is recognised to have de jure sovereignty. The terms "de facto" and "de jure" are not merely concepts of international law but a recognition of the existence of the jurisdiction and territory of another state.

The Order must be construed in the ordinary meaning of the words used and not in the political circumstances in which the agreement was made. The fact that there is a lacuna in the Order does not affect the construction and the word "territory" must be given its plain meaning, for nowhere in the Order is there anything to suggest that it should be given a wider meaning. Article 2 of the Order recognises that certain areas of jurisdiction are to be included and therefore there can be no intention of using the word "territory" to include the meaning of jurisdiction: *Reg.* v. *Governor of Brixton Prison, Ex parte Minervini.*[4]* Article 1 specifically includes the contracting parties' ships on the high seas as being in their territories. The territory of a nation always does include her ships on the high seas (*per* Lord Cockburn C.J. in *Reg.* v. *Keyn*[5]*), and the Territorial Waters Jurisdiction Act, 1878, enacts that the territorial jurisdiction and the territory of Her Majesty should co-terminate. There may be outside a country's territory areas of territorial jurisdiction and there are numerous territories in which Her Majesty's Government exercises the full rights of sovereignty and jurisdiction but those areas are not in the territory of the United Kingdom: *Ex parte Mwenya.*[6]*

In respect of the charge of perjury the committal charge did not allege that the applicant "knowingly gave false evidence." **[64]** A charge where the word "knowingly" is omitted is bad: *Reg.* v. *Stewart*[7]; *Reg.* v. *McVitie.*[8] By article 11 of the Order the extradition of the applicant is not permissible unless there is evidence which would justify a committal of the applicant for trial in this country. The statement made by the applicant in the proceedings of May 12, 1960, was not a material statement in those proceedings. He said that he could not remember if he had spoken to the child between Hanukka and the trial, which shows that his mind was not directed to the matter. His attention should have been directed to the matter if it was to be the basis of a charge of perjury. The statement was ambiguous and as such cannot be the basis for a charge of perjury:

[4] [1959] 1 Q.B. 155, 162; [1958] 3 W.L.R. 559; [1958] 3 All E.R. 318, D.C.
[5] (1876) 2 Ex.D. 63, C.C.R.
[6] [1960] 1 Q.B. 241; [1959] 3 W.L.R. 767; [1959] 3 All E.R. 525, C.A.
[7] (1960) 44 Cr.App.R. 29.
[8] (1960) 44 Cr.App.R. 201.

Reg. v. *Bird.*[9] The material witnesses had a purpose of their own in giving evidence, and a warning should be given to the jury in such cases: *Reg.* v. *Prater.*[10] In a case where a jury would not convict there should not be an extradition of a defendant: *Reg.* v. *Governor of H.M. Prison, Brixton.*[11]* The material evidence against the applicant is that of the three Kots, who are accomplices, and there is a strong presumption that their evidence was obtained by duress. They were all detained in custody and two of them were not released until all had made their declarations, and that was in circumstances in which there were political issues and a desire by the state to obtain a conviction. No magistrate would convict the applicant on evidence that raised a presumption of duress which had not been rebutted. All three witnesses had a purpose to placate the police, which, although not the same as duress, makes the evidence unreliable. The photograph, by which Reuben Kot purported to identify Yossele, is very unsatisfactory. There is no evidence supporting the Kots' evidence, and it should have been possible to obtain evidence from other people in the settlement —the driver and the men who accompanied the applicant when Yossele was taken from the settlement. The evidence of the Kots is also unreliable in that it speaks of happenings nearly 18 months previous to the making of the declarations.

This is not a case of child stealing but of custody proceedings—a civil matter. The position is that the grandfather had the control and custody of the child and the parents asked to be given the care and custody; there is nothing illegal in the fact that **[65]** the grandfather refused their request. When the matter came before the court on February 10, 1960, the court ordered the return of Yossele to his parents by February 15, 1960; until the latter date the grandparents could not steal the child nor detain him illegally since he was in their care and custody. Therefore, whatever the applicant did before that date, he could not have deprived the grandparents of the control and custody of the child if he acted with their consent. It is a defence to a charge of detaining a child that he was detained by lawful excuse. The child was detained on religious grounds and according to the Torah, for the grandparents feared that he would be taken to an atheist country and be brought up in an atheistic atmosphere. The grandparents have never been charged with such detention, and there is no evidence that Yossele was abducted by force or deceit.

This matter arose out of the conflict between the orthodox religious parties and the secular. That there was such a conflict and that religion and politics were inseparable in Israel is shown by the evidence of Bishop Stewart, who was Bishop in Jerusalem in 1957, of Emile Marmorstein and of Guy Eden. In Israel and the Middle East religious leaders have also political duties, and the Knesset reports show the bitterness of the religious issue which had become a political movement inside the Knesset. The commissioner of police had stated that the grandfather recognised no secular authority and was anxious that Yossele should receive a religious education. Education was part of the struggle between the religious and secular parties and there had been a campaign over the last 10 years to wean young Jews from their religious practices. The fact that the child was being taken back to Russia had a political undertone which in itself would not be a political offence but is an added factor. The grandfather's action had been supported by the members of the settlement and the police had been hindered in their search for Yossele. The Chief Rabbi in Jerusalem had stated that according to the law of the Torah the grandfather was as a father to the boy. The disappearance of Yossele had become a political matter and the subject-matter of questions in the Knesset and, as such, it was a political offence. An offence takes on a political character when it is committed in furtherance or in execution of a political movement which has expressed itself in the legislature, it is a movement against the government or a movement that cuts across the parties. A political offence may occur in a police state where **[66]** persons are persecuted for their personal views and when there is no such division in the

[9] (1891) 17 Cox C.C. 387.
[10] [1960] 2 Q.B. 464; [1960] 2 W.L.R. 343; [1960] 1 All E.R. 298, C.C.A.
[11] *The Times*, March 19, 1952.

legislature: *Reg.* v. *Governor of Brixton Prison, Ex parte Kolczynski.*[12]* An offence may assume a political character when a state punishes for political motives. If a movement is purely religious in nature its activities would not amount to a political offence, but in the State of Israel the political parties are involved in a religious struggle and this struggle is reflected in the legislature: *In re Castioni.*[13]*

Sir Reginald Manningham-Buller Q.C., A.-G., and *J. R. Cumming-Bruce* for the Home Secretary. The offences with which the applicant is charged are offences to which article 3 of the Israel (Extradition) Order, 1960, applies. To interpret article 1 of the Order so that Jerusalem is excluded renders the Agreement between the United Kingdom and Israel largely ineffective. Section 25 of the Extradition Act, 1870, indicates that the relevant test whether an extradition treaty applies in an area is whether the government, which seeks extradition, controls, occupies and exercises jurisdiction in that area. The term "territory of Israel" is not confined to the area over which Her Majesty's Government recognises the State of Israel as having de jure sovereignty but also includes the area where her de facto authority is recognised. Such a construction gives a meaning to the whole Agreement; the applicant's suggested construction does not —his suggested construction is based on the letter from the Foreign Office and not on the Order. The appropriate test for the meaning of "territory" is the area in which a state exercises jurisdiction: *Aksionairnoye Obschestvo Dlia Mechanicheskoyi Obrabotky Diereva (1) A. M. Luther* v. *James Sagor & Co.*[14]*; *Banco de Bilbao* v. *Sancha.*[15]* The Home Secretary, in considering whether the request of the applicant's extradition is lawful, must ask the question. Do the laws of the Government of Israel apply in that part of Jerusalem? The answer is that they do, and the applicant can therefore be lawfully extradited.

Leonard Caplan Q.C. and *R. L. Goff* for the Government of Israel. The Chief Magistrate's decision that Jerusalem was included in the territory of the State of Israel is consistent with authorities in which no distinction has been drawn as to the legal consequences of Her Majesty's Government recognising a state's **[67]** authority as being de jure or de facto. Whenever territory is recognised as being under the control of a foreign state the court recognises that territory as being part of the territory of that state. The certificates of the Foreign Office vary in their wording and such certificates must be construed in the usual way. The wording of this certificate is plain, and Her Majesty's Government recognises Israeli authority in Jerusalem. The authority is recognised de facto, which means that the Government of Israel exercises the power of government in Jerusalem. The reason for the de facto recognition is that the boundaries of Israel were not fixed by international agreement but were agreed under the armistice, and the sole reason for the reservation as to Israel having full sovereignty is that the boundaries might eventually be altered. The word "sovereignty" in the Foreign Office certificate means de jure sovereignty. Where the Foreign Office states that it recognises the authority of a government to exist de facto, it means that the state's sovereignty is recognised and that it is recognised to govern in a certain area: *Bank of Ethiopia* v. *National Bank of Egypt and Liguori.*[16]* In the one apparently contrary authority the facts were exceptional as there were two competing governments, one of which was recognised de jure and the other de facto, and the property in question was outside the area over which either form of sovereignty was recognised: *Haile Selassie* v. *Cable and Wireless Ltd.* (*No. 2*).[17]*

The Chief Magistrate was also correct in the view that he took that the treaty must be given its true construction according to its language, object and intent: *per* Lord Russell C.J. in *In re Arton* (*No. 2*).[18]* The whole purpose of the treaty

[12] [1955] 1 Q.B. 540; [1955] 2 W.L.R. 116; [1955] 1 All E.R. 31, D.C.
[13] [1891] 1 Q.B. 149; 7 T.L.R. 50, D.C.
[14] [1921] 3 K.B. 532; 37 T.L.R. 777, C.A.
[15] [1938] 2 K.B. 176; 54 T.L.R. 603; [1938] 2 All E.R 253, C.A.
[16] [1937] Ch. 513; 53 T.L.R. 751; [1937] 3 All E.R. 8.
[17] [1939] 1 Ch. 182; 54 T.L.R. 996; [1938] 3 All E.R. 384, C.A.
[18] [1896] 1 Q.B. 509, 517; 12 T.L.R. 189, D.C.

is the reciprocal extradition of criminals. A construction which excludes Jerusalem from the Israel (Extradition) Order, 1960, stultifies the intention of the parties. One of the offences included in the Order is perjury and if Jerusalem is not included in the territory of Israel then the courts in Jerusalem are excluded, and those courts include the Supreme Court and the High Court. The courts of Israel would not give an interpretation that excluded crimes committed in Jerusalem and the interpretation must be the same for both contracting parties. The court is entitled to consider the matters which must have been in the minds of both parties. On one construction of the term "territory" there would be a [**68**] boundary round the perimeter of Jerusalem and on the other construction the boundary would divide the city; either construction is consistent with the meaning that might be given by the United Kingdom, but it is inconceivable that the State of Israel would have considered that the part of the city of Jerusalem which they controlled would be excluded from the treaty. Once the State of Israel exercises authority and her writ runs in an area that area is recognised as her territory: *Arab Bank* v. *Barclays Bank* (*Dominion, Colonial and Overseas*) *Ltd.*[19] "Territory of Israel" means any area over which the State of Israel has power and control, otherwise there would be established a sort of "Tom Tiddler's Ground" from which the extradition of British fugitive offenders could not be sought.

This court has not to consider the weight of the evidence but whether there was evidence before the Chief Magistrate sufficient for the defendant to be committed for trial: *Rex* v. *Governor of Brixton Prison, Ex parte Perry.*[20]* The facts concerning the detention of the Kots were before the Chief Magistrate and he was entitled to commit the applicant on that evidence. The uncorroborated evidence of accomplices is not a bar to the committal of a defendent: *In re Meunier.*[21]* The same applies under the Fugitive Offenders Act, 1881, where the standard of proof is higher: *Rex* v. *Secretary of State for India, Ex parte Ezekiel.*[22]* Reuben Kot was never charged and was merely a person in the settlement who knew what had occurred; he was not an accomplice and his evidence was corroborative evidence. None of the Kots were accomplices to the charge of perjury. They were all in custody for various periods, but it does not follow that there was anything improper in their imprisonment or that any inducement was held out to them to make their declarations before a magistrate. Their evidence has been said to be unsatisfactory in that it speaks of things that happened nearly 18 months before. That goes to the weight to be attached to the evidence, but not to a very great extent because the boy was in the village for three weeks—his disappearance was a cause célèbre and the people at the settlement would know all about it. The date on which the offence of child stealing is alleged to have taken place may affect the argument in respect of the grandparents but not the applicant. The grandparents had the care of the child by the [**69**] consent of the parents and that consent was withdrawn sometime towards the end of 1959 and, if the child was taken to the settlement to deprive the parents of their care and control, the offence of child stealing was then committed. The applicant is not asserting that he took the child under a legal right, but even if he was that is a matter of defence only. There is no evidence that the child was abducted by force, but the evidence of Shlomo Kot shows that the boy was deceived into believing that his parents had had a quarrel and that the father wanted his conversion to another religion; that was contrary to the depositions made by the mother when she had said that the grandfather feared that the boy would not receive a religious education from his parents.

[ASHWORTH J. Why is the applicant charged under section 188 and under section 259 of the Criminal Code Ordinance, 1936?]

[LORD PARKER C.J. It is very artificial to say that there were two offences.]

The charge of abduction is alternative to that of child stealing and the Government of Israel does not now seek extradition on both charges. I abandon the

[19] [1954] A.C. 495.
[20] [1924] 1 K.B. 455; 40 T.L.R. 181, D.C.
[21] [1894] 2 Q.B. 415, D.C.
[22] [1941] 2 K.B. 169; [1941] 2 All E.R. 546, D.C.

charge of abduction on the footing that the charge of child stealing stands.

There has never been a satisfactory authority on what is an offence of a political character, and under section 3 (1) of the Extradition Act, 1870, the onus of proving that it is a political offence is on the applicant. The court has to consider whether this is a political offence; it has not to consider what is a political offence. There has never been a case where an offence was held to be political that did not contain an element of violence. On the authorities a definition of a political crime is a crime of violence committed with the object of influencing the policy of, or supplanting or escaping from the political control of, the governing party in a state. With the new techniques used to exert political pressure that definition may not go far enough, nor perhaps need it be a crime of violence, for blackmailing a prime minister or impersonation may be political offences. Sir Charles Russell Q.C., in argument in *In re Castioni*,[23]* refers to the definitions of J. S. Mill and of Stephen J. If *Reg.* v. *Governor of Brixton Prison, Ex parte Kolczynski*[24]* did not extend the definition to Stephen J. which was approved in the former case, that definition has stood for 60 years. Sir Hartley Shawcross Q.C., in *Reg.* v. *Governor of Brixton Prison, Ex parte Kolczynski*,[24]* **[70]** expressly put that case within the definition of a political offence given in *In re Castioni*.[25]* The ratio decidendi in *Reg.* v. *Governor of Brixton Prison, Ex parte Kolczynski*[26]* was not that they were going to be tried for a political offence but that they were going to be punished for a political offence.

In the present case there is no need to choose between the two definitions of a political offence, for whether violence is included or not there must be an object of influencing, supplanting or escaping from the political control of the governing party in the state. The applicant never gives one word of his motives, and it is not enough to say that there were strong religious feelings in the country, for however great the volume of feeling in a country in which a non-political crime is committed it will not make that crime into a political offence.

J. H. Buzzard for the Governor of Brixton Prison. This court has the same powers to review an order for extradition as under the Fugitive Offenders Act, 1881; *Rex* v. *Governor of Brixton Prison, Ex parte Bidwell*.[27]* This court has to decide whether upon the depositions a reasonable magistrate could find that there was evidence upon which, if it was not contradicted, a jury might reasonably convict: *Reg.* v. *Governor of Brixton Prison, Ex parte Mourat Mehmet*.[28]*

The definition of a political offence as an act done with the object of influencing the policy of the governing party is wider than is stated in the authorities, and under that definition bribery might be included. The Extradition Act, 1906, added bribery to the list of crimes which could be extraditable. A definition that includes only crimes of violence is too narrow, but the definition given by Mr. Caplan would protect only the revolutionary. The movement must be to some extent a disturbance: *In re Castioni*.[29]* The lack of good faith by the party asking for extradition is not per see a ground for relief: *In re Arton, No. 1*.[30]* An offence is of a political character (1) if it is incidental to and forms part of a political disturbance resulting from an attempt to overthrow one form of government and substitute another, or (2) it is incidental to or forms part of an attempt to prevent the trial or punishment **[71]** of someone for treason, sedition or other offences of a like nature. This is not a comprehensive definition, but it is based on decided cases.

Foster Q.C. replied.

[23] [1891] 1 Q.B. 149.
[24] [1955] 1 Q.B. 540, 545.
[25] [1891] 1 Q.B. 149.
[26] [1955] 1 Q.B. 540.
[27] [1937] 1 K.B. 305; 54 T.L.R. 1; [1936] 3 All E.R. 1, D.C.
[28] [1962] 2 Q.B. 1; [1962] 2 W.L.R. 686; [1962] 1 All E.R. 463, D.C.
[29] [1891] 1 Q.B. 149.
[30] [1896] 1 Q.B. 108; 12 T.L.R. 131, D.C.

Cur. adv. vult.

February 27. Lord Parker C.J. In these proceedings Mr. Foster moves on behalf of one Shalom Schtraks, the applicant, now detained in Her Majesty's Prison at Brixton, for a writ of habeas corpus. The applicant is so detained in pursuance of a warrant of committal dated January 12, 1962, awaiting delivery to the State of Israel pursuant to the Extradition Acts, 1870 to 1935.

The charges on which he was so committed by the chief magistrate were as follows: "1. Perjury for that he on May 12, 1960, during proceedings in an application No. 52/60 in the High Court of Justice of Israel knowingly gave false evidence touching a matter material in those proceedings contrary to section 117 of the Criminal Code Ordinance, 1936. 2. Child stealing: (*a*) on a date between January 1 and February 15, 1960, with intent to deprive Alter and Ida Schuchmacher of their son Joseph (born in 1952) fraudulently detained him in the house of Shlomo Zalman Kot at Komemiuth, contrary to section 188 of the said Ordinance; (*b*) on a date between January 1 and February 15, 1960, wrongfully confined the said Joseph Schuchmacher in the said house knowing that he was an abducted person, contrary to section 259 of the said Ordinance." All those alleged offences are offences which are extraditable offences under an agreement concluded on April 4, 1960, between Her Majesty's Government in the United Kingdom and the government of the State of Israel, to which the Extradition Acts were made to apply by an Order in Council entitled "The Israel (Extradition) Order, 1960" (S.I. 1960, No. 1660).

Before dealing with the facts of the case it is convenient to deal with a point of jurisdiction which has been raised on behalf of the applicant. The offence of perjury, the subject of the first charge, is alleged to have been committed in the High Court of Israel sitting in that part of Jerusalem occupied by the State of Israel. I will for convenience hereafter refer to that part occupied by Israel as "Jerusalem." It is said that Jerusalem does not, on a true construction of the agreement between the governments, come within the territory of the State of Israel to **[72]** which the agreement applies. Moreover, by article 12 of the agreement it is provided as follows: "In the examinations which they have to make in accordance with the foregoing stipulations, the authorities of the requested party shall admit as valid evidence the sworn depositions or the affirmations of witnesses taken in the territory of the requesting party." Since the depositions in the case on all charges were taken in Jerusalem, it is said that they are inadmissable in this country if, as is contended, Jerusalem is not in the territory of the State of Israel. The question, as it seems to me, falls to be determined by a construction of the agreement to which I have referred of April 4, 1960, the Order in Council, and of course the Extradition Act, 1870.

Looking first at the Act, it is provided by section 2 as follows: "Where an arrangement has been made with any foreign state with respect to the surrender to such state of any fugitive criminals, Her Majesty may, by Order in Council, direct that this Act shall apply in the case of such foreign state. Her Majesty may, by the same or any subsequent order, limit the operation of the order, and restrict the same to fugitive criminals who are in or suspected of being in the part of Her Majesty's dominions specified in the order, and render the operation thereof subject to such conditions, exceptions, and qualifications as may be deemed expedient."

By section 26, the interpretation section, "fugitive criminal" is thus defined: "The term 'fugitive criminal' means any person accused or convicted of an extradition crime committed within the jurisdiction of any foreign state who is in or is suspected of being in some part of Her Majesty's dominions; and the term 'fugitive criminal of a foreign state' means a fugitive criminal accused or convicted of an extradition crime committed within the jurisdiction of that state." In passing, it is convenient to refer also to section 25, which provides that: "For the purposes of this Act, every colony, dependency, and constituent part of a foreign state, and every vessel of that state, shall (except where expressly mentioned as distinct in this Act) be deemed to be within the jurisdiction of and to be part of such foreign state."

The Order in Council provides by article 1 that: "The Extradition Acts, 1870 to 1935, shall apply in the case of the State of Israel under and in accordance with the said agreement," that is the agreement of April 4, 1960, which was recited in the order. That agreement, so far as it is relevant here, provides **[73]** as follows: "The Government of the United Kingdom of Great Britain and Northern Ireland and the Government of the State of Israel; desiring to make provision for the reciprocal extradition of criminals; have agreed as follows:— article 1. The contracting parties agree to extradite to each other, in the circumstances stated in the present agreement, those persons who, being accused or convicted of any of the offences enumerated in article 3 and committed within the territory of the one party, or on the high seas on board a vessel registered in the territory of that party, shall be found within the territory of the other party." Article 2 then provides that: "In relation to the Government of the United Kingdom of Great Britain and Northern Ireland, the territories to which the present agreement shall apply are"—there are then set out some eight sub-headings whereby there are included in the territory of the Government of the United Kingdom and Northern Ireland, the Channel Islands and the Isle of Man, the colonies, Southern Rhodesia, Northern Rhodesia and Nyasaland, British protectorates, British-protected states, territories administered under trusteeship of the United Nations and certain others.

In the course of these proceedings inquiries were made of the Foreign Office as to the status of Jerusalem in relation to the jurisdiction and territory of the State of Israel. In their reply of October 4, 1961, the following is stated: "(1) His Majesty's Government accorded de facto recognition to the State of Israel on January 29, 1949; (2) His Majesty's Government accorded de jure recognition to the State of Israel on April 27, 1950. In according such de jure recognition His Majesty's Government made certain reservations which, in relation to the status of Jerusalem, were explained as follows by the then Minister of State in a statement to the House of Commons on April 27 of that year:— 'His Majesty's Government are unable to recognise the sovereignty of Israel over that part of Jerusalem which she occupies, though, pending a final determination of the status of the area, they recognise that Israel exercises de facto authority in it.' (3) In according recognition on the same date of the Union of the Kingdom of Jordan and of that part of Palestine under Jordan occupation and control His Majesty's Government made a similar reservation in respect of that part of Jerusalem occupied and controlled by Jordan."

Accordingly, the first question to be answered is whether Jerusalem, over which Israel exercises de facto authority, is part of the territory of Israel within the agreement of April 4, 1960. **[74]** The contentions on behalf of the applicant can be summarised I think as follows: (1) That the word "territory" has acquired a meaning in international law which must be applied unless in the agreement some different meaning is provided, which is not the case here except as provided in article 2 in relation to Her Majesty's Government of the United Kingdom; (2) that applying that meaning the territory of Israel means that geographical area over which Israel exercises sovereignty recognised by Her Majesty's Government; (3) that the court must accept the answer of the executive, which states that Her Majesty's Government are unable to recognise the sovereignty of Israel over that part of Jerusalem which she occupies; and (4) that if the above interpretation of "territory" is correct, the agreement may in certain respects become ineffective, but the fact that there is a lacuna in the agreement does not entitle the court to give an extended meaning to the word "territory."

It is contended on the other hand by the Attorney-General, to whom the court is indebted for his assistance, and by the Government of Israel, first, that, as it can be taken for granted that the parties intended the provisions of the agreement to be effective for the reciprocal extradition of criminals, an interpretation of "territory" which would render the agreement largely ineffective is not readily to be adopted; secondly, that in its context "territory" includes not only territory in respect of which Her Majesty's Government recognises the right of Israel to exercise sovereignty de jure, but also territory over which Her Majesty's

Government recognises that Israel exercises de facto authority, there being no distinction to be drawn so far as extradition is concerned between the legal consequences of those two conceptions; thirdly, that although one cannot enlarge the scope of the agreement by looking at the Extradition Act, 1870, the Act may nevertheless provide assistance in construing the agreement, and that having regard to the preamble of the Act, section 25 and the definition of fugitive criminal in section 26, the relevant test is: who exercises jurisdiction in the area.

For my part I am clearly of opinion that although as an abstract proposition of international law "territory" has the meaning advanced by the applicant, the context in which it is used here is an extradition treaty in which the important consideration is whether the writ of a contracting party runs in a particular area. At the date of this agreement Israel had for 10 years and had throughout been recognised by Her Majesty's **[75]** Government as exercising de facto authority and control in Jerusalem, and plainly at the date of the agreement exercised jurisdiction over that area. Moreover, there has never been and is not today any question of competing sovereignty in the area. No other state is recognised as having de jure sovereignty. Again, Jerusalem is the capital, the seat of government, the seat of the High Court of Israel, and to exclude Jerusalem from the territory of Israel in this context would render the agreement wholly ineffective. It would indeed produce the absurd proposition that whereas a British subject in Jerusalem could be extradited to this country, a citizen of Israel in this country could not be extradited to Israel if the alleged offence had been committed in Jerusalem, and yet the whole object of the agreement is to provide reciprocal rights and obligations. Moreover, when both contracting parties are agreed that for this purpose Jerusalem is within the jurisdiction of the State of Israel, it seems to me quite unrealistic to adopt a construction of the word "territory" which would limit the plain object of the agreement. Indeed, a similar interpretation was placed on the Anglo-Norwegian treaty by this court in *Reg.* v. *Governor of Brixton Prison, Ex parte Minervini*,[31]* where this passage occurs[32]: "This treaty is not treating 'territory' in its strict sense, but in a sense which is equivalent to jurisdiction, and it is only in that way that one can make sense of the treaty. Indeed, it is to be observed that in many of these treaties reference is made not to territory but to jurisdiction, and, in my view, in this treaty 'territory' is equivalent to jurisdiction."

Some emphasis was naturally laid on the fact that whereas article 2 in relation to Her Majesty's Government in the United Kingdom gave an extended meaning to "territory," in particular it included protectorates over which there was only de facto control, yet there was no such definition clause in regard to the State of Israel. I am far from satisfied, however, that that consideration is conclusive. Indeed, it may well be that any such definition would have met with strong objection from the Government of Israel. It should also be mentioned that we were referred to a number of other agreements between the same high contracting parties in which different terms were used, such as "the territory administered by the State of Israel." For my **[76]** part I get no help from such agreements. The importance to my mind is the context in question, and in this case it is an extradition treaty.

I come next, therefore, to a consideration of the facts alleged by the prosecution as giving rise to the charges. [His Lordship stated the facts set out above and continued:] It is the evidence of the three witnesses, Shlomo Kot, his wife Rachel and his brother Reuben, which is the foundation of the present case in respect of all the charges against the present application. If the Kots are believed, then clearly the applicant committed perjury in saying that he had not seen Yossele since January 1, 1960. Again, so it is said, if the Kots are believed, the present applicant was assisting the grandparents to conceal Yossele and to prevent the parents obtaining possession of him, matters which it is said amount to child stealing. Mr. Foster has made a number of forceful criticisms of their evidence. Thus, as he points out, Shlomo was arrested and charged

[31] [1959] 1 Q.B. 155; [1958] 3 W.L.R. 559; [1958] 3 All E.R. 318, D.C.
[32] [1959] 1 Q.B. 155, 162.

and made his declaration while under arrest and while in custody, and indeed was not granted bail until August 18, 1961, the day after he made his declaration. Rachel, his wife, also had been arrested and charged, though she was in fact released on bail before she made her declaration. Reuben was arrested but not charged, but it is to be observed that he was not released until he had made his declaration. In those circumstances it is said that there was strong evidence that these declarations had been made under duress or as the result of promises of bail. It is also said that at any rate Shlomo and Rachel, who were charged, were accomplices and Reuben's evidence afforded little or no corroboration. It is pointed out further that the evidence of all three is as to events nearly 18 months previous, and that it is vague in many respects. In particular Reuben's evidence was unsatisfactory as to identification, having taken place during the evening when it was probably dark, and that, having regard to the size of the photograph by which he purported to identify Yossele, his identification is clearly suspect. Again, it is pointed out that there is no supporting evidence from the driver and those whom Rachel speaks of as being in the car when the boy was taken away from the settlement.

As against these criticisms, it was pointed out on behalf of the Government of Israel that though Shlomo and Reuben were charged, and were in custody, it does not follow that anything improper took place in the manner of the taking of the declarations, which were in fact given before a magistrate. Further, it is **[77]** said that even if Shlomo and Rachel were accomplices, it does not of itself prevent the chief magistrate here from committing.

In *In re Meunier*[33]* Cave J., in dealing with such a matter said[34]: "In my judgment the fact that there is not corroborative evidence is not conclusive in favour of the accused; but the magistrate must exercise his discretion in each case in arriving at a conclusion as to whether there ought to be a committal or not. It is not the law that a prisoner must necessarily be acquitted in the absence of corroborative evidence; for the evidence must be laid before the jury in each case. No doubt, it is the practice to warn the jury that they ought not to convict unless they think that the evidence of the accomplice is corroborated; but I know of no power to withdraw the case from the jury for want of corroborative evidence, and I know of no power to set aside a verdict of guilty on that ground. The magistrate has a discretion in each case, as to whether the evidence is or is not sufficient to justify a committal." To the same effect is a passage in *Rex* v. *Secretary of State for India, Ex parte Ezekiel,*[35]* which was a case under the Fugitive Offenders Act, 1881, in which Humphreys J. said[36]: "It was admitted in argument before us that the depositions did disclose the existence of the conspiracy alleged, and, further, that the evidence of one witness, Medhora, clearly implicated the applicant. Counsel for the applicant did, indeed, draw our attention to the fact that Medhora was an admitted accomplice, but, since the law of India with regard to the evidence of accomplices does not differ from that of England, that fact would not even tend to invalidate the magistrate's findings." Further, it is agreed that Reuben's evidence does afford some corroboration, although for my part I think it is only right to say that he may well have had a motive of his own to be released, and should accordingly be treated as an accomplice within the principle laid down in *Reg.* v. *Prater.*[37] Again, it is said that it is difficult to see how these witnesses could be said to be accomplices to the perjury charge. In answer to the criticism as to the difficulty of identifying somebody that you have only seen for a short period some 18 months before, it is pointed out that the disappearance of Yossele was a matter of very considerable publicity in Israel. It resulted, as **[78]** I have said, in these extensive inquiries and searches, and therefore the Kots may well have been in a position to remember even though the matter was so long ago.

In considering these rival contentions it is important, I think, to bear in

[33] [1894] 2 Q.B. 415, D.C.
[34] Ibid. 418.
[35] [1941] 2 K.B. 169; [1941] 2 All E.R. 546, D.C.
[36] [1941] 2 All E.R. 545, 549.
[37] [1960] 2 Q.B. 464; [1960] 2 W.L.R. 343; [1960] 1 All E.R. 298, C.C.A.

mind the function of the magistrate in the first instance, and then the function of this court. Under section 10 of the Extradition Act, 1870, it is provided that: "In the case of a fugitive criminal accused of an extradition crime if the foreign warrant authorising the arrest of such criminal is duly authenticated, and such evidence is produced as (subject to the provisions of this Act) would, according to the law of England, justify the committal for trial of the prisoner if the crime of which he is accused had been committed in England, the police magistrate shall commit him to prison, but otherwise shall order him to be discharged." It is to be observed that that formula is slightly different from that which appears in section 5 of the Fugitive Offenders Act, 1881, where the magistrate must be satisfied that the evidence raises a "strong or probable presumption" that the fugitive committed the offence mentioned in the warrant.

I am prepared to accept that there is no real distinction between those two. Indeed, it was pointed out by Swift J. in *Rex* v. *Governor of Brixton Prison, Ex parte Bidwell*,[38]* as follows[39]: "As to the third ground, it is said that before the magistrate can commit an alleged fugitive under section 5 of the [Fugitive Offenders] Act of 1881 the evidence produced must raise a strong or probable presumption that he is guilty of the offence mentioned in the warrant, and that here the evidence did not disclose a strong or probable presumption that the accused was guilty of the offence with which he is charged. The language of section 5 (1), however, was not new in 1881, but is the same as that on which our courts have been accustomed to act when committing persons for trial, at any rate since the passing of section 25 of the Indictable Offences Act, 1848. The section means that there must be such evidence that, if it be uncontradicted at the trial, a reasonably minded jury may convict upon it." That, as it seems to me, is the test, whichever formula is adopted.

So far as this court is concerned, we proceed, as I conceive it, on the basis that we are entitled to review the evidence before the chief magistrate, but that we will only interfere if satisfied **[79]** that no magistrate properly directing his mind to the question could reasonably have felt satisfied that the evidence produced would justify committal in the sense to which I have just referred. Approaching the matter in this way, I am quite unable to hold that the magistrate could not reasonably have felt so satisfied. No one individual criticism of the evidence leads me to a contrary conclusion. Nor does the cumulative effect of all the points that Mr. Foster has so ably argued.

I turn, accordingly, to the other points which have been raised on behalf of the applicant. First, in regard to the perjury charge, it is said that if one looks at the notes of evidence, one will find after the passages to which I have already referred a further passage in which the present applicant said: "I do not remember whether I spoke to the child between Hanukka and the trial." Based on that, it is contended that the applicant's mind was really not on the point, and that in such a case perjury would not lie. So far as that contention is concerned, I am quite unable to come to that conclusion, even if, which I doubt, we are entitled to look at the notes of evidence.

Secondly, in regard to perjury, it is said that the evidence given, which is said to be perjured evidence, was not a material particular in the issue then being determined, since the present applicant was only being charged with disobedience to a court order after February 15, 1960. I cannot accept this contention. It seems to me plain that if the court had known, if it be the truth, that the present applicant had taken and concealed Yossele in the settlement, they might well, if not have been bound to come to the conclusion that not only before but after February 15, 1960, the applicant was still concerned in assisting the grandparents to conceal the child and deprive the parents of possession of him.

I come now to child stealing. Assuming that the Kots' evidence is acceptable, is is contended that there is no evidence of the offence charged, which is an offence committed between January 1, 1960, and February 15, 1960. The definition of the offence of child stealing by section 188 of the Criminal Code

[38] [1937] 1 K.B. 305, 313; 53 T.L.R. 1; [1936] 3 All E.R. 1, D.C.
[39] [1937] 1 K.B. 305, 313.

Ordinance, 1936, is as follows: "Any person who, with intent to deprive any parent, guardian or other person who has the lawful care or charge of a child under the age of fourteen years, of the possession of such child:—(*a*) forcibly or fraudulently takes or entices away, or detains the child; or (*b*) receives or harbours the child, knowing it have have been so taken or enticed away or detained: is guilty of a felony." It is to be observed **[80]** before leaving that section of the Ordinance that it goes on to provide that: "It is a defence to a charge of any of the offences defined in this section to prove that the accused person claimed in good faith a right to the possession of the child."

What is said first is that up to February 15, 1960, inclusive the grandparents had the possession of Yossele, and that he was in their lawful care and custody. Accordingly, the present applicant, so it is said, could not be convicted of any action taken with intent to deprive the parents. For my part, I am unable to accept these contentions. It seems to me that action taken with an intent to deprive a parent of possession may include action taken with an intent to deprive the parent not merely of actual possession, but of the right to possession. It is to be observed that the action of detaining the child is made an offence if with intent to deprive the parent of possession. Accordingly, in that context at any rate, "possession" must mean "right to possession."

Further, I think that as a result of the judgment of February 10, 1960, in Israel, the right to possession was at all times in the parents from the time when the child was demanded. According to the mother, this was in September, 1959, but at latest, it would have been in December, 1959, according to the grandfather's evidence. After that, the grandparents were holding the child contrary to law. At any rate, as it seems to me, the right to possession could not have arisen later than the date of the order nisi of January 16, 1960, and that, too, would have been at a time when, if the Kots' evidence is true, Yossele was being concealed by the present applicant in the settlement.

Finally, it was said that the defence here was one of claim of right in that it was the grandfather's duty according to the laws of his religion to ensure that the child was educated and brought up according to his religion. Whether that would have been a defence or not for the grandfather, if charged, it does not follow that the present applicant has any such defence. But in any event it is a defence, and does not fall to be considered at this stage of the proceedings.

A somewhat similar point was argued in regard to the word "fraudulently." There was no question of Yossele having been forcibly taken, and it was said that there was no prima facie evidence that he had been fraudulently taken or detained. It is sufficient for me to say that in my judgment "fraudulently" there is merely equivalent to an intent to prejudice the parents' right to possession. **[81]**

Lastly, with regard to the second part of the charge of child stealing, it is said that in any event Yossele could not be said to be an abducted person within the meaning given to that word in section 254 of the Israeli Ordinance. I find it quite unnecessary to go into that matter, since Mr. Caplan has quite properly told the court that the Government of Israel does not desire to proceed with that charge, assuming that they had satisfied the court in regard to the first part of the charge of child stealing.

I come now to the last matter, and a matter which I have always felt from the start was the real point in this case. It is whether it has been shown that the offence with which the present applicant is charged is an offence of a political character. Section 3 of the Extradition Act, 1870, is in these terms: "The following restrictions shall be observed with respect to the surrender of fugitive criminals: (1) A fugitive criminal shall not be surrendered if the offence in respect of which his surrender is demanded is one of a political character, or if he prove to the satisfaction of the police magistrate or the court before whom he is brought on habeas corpus, or to the Secretary of State, that the requisition for his surrender has in fact been made with a view to try or punish him for an offence of a political character."

I think I should also read paragraph (2), which says that: "A fugitive criminal shall not be surrendered to a foreign state unless provision is made by the law of that state, or by arrangement, that the fugitive criminal shall not, until he has been restored or had an opportunity of returning to Her Majesty's dominions, be detained or tried in that foreign state for any offence committed prior to his surrender other than the extradition crime proved by the facts on which the surrender is grounded," and the agreement of April 4, 1960, by article 7 so provides.

The true construction of paragraph (1) of section 3 is far from clear. As long ago as 1896, in *Arton No. 1*,[40]* Lord Russell of Killowen C.J. expressed this view on the matter[41]: "I . . . come to the fourth ground . . . namely, that the offences for which the prisoner was committed were political in their character, and that his surrender was demanded from political motives. No doubt if the learned counsel were able to show that the surrender was demanded for an offence of a political character, **[82]** or that it was demanded in order that the prisoner might be tried or punished for an offence of a political character, it would furnish ground for the intervention of this court, and for a declaration by this court that for such an offence extradition could not legally be granted. Let us consider whether there is any real ground for either of the suggestions made. First, is this offence, or is any of the offences in respect of which the order of committal was made, one of a political character? The bare enumeration of them seems to afford a sufficient answer to that suggestion: they are falsification of accounts and using falsified accounts, fraud by an agent, fraud by a trustee, fraud by a director of a company and by a public officer; obtaining money and goods by false pretences, offences against the bankruptcy laws, larceny, and embezzlement. The mere enumeration of these offences shows that they are completely divested of any trace of a political character. Then, can it be said that the application for extradition has been made with a view to try or punish the prisoner for an offence of a political character? It is clear what this suggestion means: it means that a person having committed an offence of a political character, another and wholly different charge (which does come within both the Extradition Act and the treaty) is resorted to as a pretence and excuse for demanding his extradition in order that he may be tried and punished for the offence of a political character which he has already committed."

So Lord Russell of Killowen C.J. there is treating what I may call the second limb of paragraph (1) of section 3, as a case where the extraditable offence in question is a mere excuse to get the prisoner back to his own country where he could be tried and punished for an offence of a political character. I have found, and still find, considerable difficulty in that construction, in that it does seem to overlook the provision which I have read in paragraph (2) of section 3 of the Act, and the equivalent provision, as there has to be, in any extradition treaty. Under such a provision the prisoner has to be returned or given an opportunity of being returned to this country before he is tried for any offence other than that for which he is extradited, and this court, it seems to me, must always proceed on the basis that a foreign state is going to honour the treaty that they have entered into.

If Lord Russell of Killowen C.J. had merely dealt with it as a matter of punishment as opposed to trial, one can see that that construction would be possible, but here the words are "tried and punished," and bearing that in mind, I find it difficult to follow **[83]** that construction. It was no doubt for that reason that Lord Goddard C.J., in what is always called the *Polish Seamen's* case in fact *Reg.* v. *Governor of Brixton Prison, Ex parte Kolczynski*,[42]* adopted a different construction.

Lord Goddard C.J. refers to the fact that the court must not assume that a foreign state will not observe the terms of the treaty, and he goes on[43]: "The second limb of the section"—that is the second limb of paragraph (1) of the section—"cannot, therefore, in my opinion, mean that the court can say that if extradition is sought for crime A we believe that if surrendered he will be

[40] [1896] 1 Q.B. 108; 12 T.L.R. 131, D.C.
[41] [1896] 1 Q.B. 108, 113.
[42] [1955] 1 Q.B. 540; [1955] 2 W.L.R. 116; [1955] 1 All E.R. 31, D.C.
[43] [1955] 1 Q.B. 540, 549.

tried or punished for crime B. None of the offences in the schedule to the Act are prima facie political. The precise meaning of this difficult section has not yet been made the subject of judicial decision and textwriters have found it difficult of explanation, but in my opinion the meaning is this: if in proving the facts necessary to obtain extradition the evidence adduced in support shows that the offence has a political character the application must be refused, but although the evidence in support appears to disclose merely one of the scheduled offences, the prisoner may show that in fact the offence is of a political character. Let me try to illustrate this by taking a charge of murder. The evidence adduced by the requisitioning state shows that the killing was committed in the course of a rebellion. This at once shows the offence to be political; but if the evidence merely shows that the prisoner killed another person by shooting him on a certain day, evidence may be given, and under section 9 the magistrate is bound to receive it, to show that the shooting took place in the course of a rebellion. Then if either the magistrate or the High Court on habeas corpus or the Secretary of State is satisfied by that evidence that the offence is of a political character, surrender is to be refused. In other words, the political character of the offence may emerge either from the evidence in support of the requisition or from the evidence adduced in answer."

Adopting, as I do, that construction put on the section by Lord Goddard C.J., the approach must be to ask oneself the question: Has this applicant proved, whether to the magistrate or, if need be by further evidence to this court, that the requisition of his surrender has been made to try or punish him for an offence of a **[84]** political character, in other words, that one or more of the charges on which he is committed are offences of a political character?

Quite shortly what is said here is this. It is said this grandfather is an orthodox Jew. He is described by the Minister of Police in a statement in the Knesset: "I am describing the man. He does not recognise the authority of any secular administration. He is fully convinced and fully believes that if it has been granted to him to remain alive and go up to the Holy Land then it has been given to him to enable him to educate his grandson who has been handed over to him, in the spirit of the Torah, in religious piety; that is his belief. As he is in his character also a stubborn person he has not listened and he has refused to return the child." The beliefs of the sect to which the grandfather belongs can be clearly seen from a further statement of the Minister of Police in the Knesset in which he read what purported to be a ruling by Rabbi Frank, the Chief Rabbi of Jerusalem. It is to this effect: "Whereas Mr. Nachman Schtraks is preventing his grandson Josef Schuchmacher from being taken out of the country; that is to say this, his son-in-law wishes to travel to Russia, and there he will be estranged from Judaism as is known; now, in accordance with the law of the Torah, Mr. Nachman Schtraks is in duty bound to prevent his grandson from leaving the land of Israel for such a place where apostasy is decreed on Jews, and grandchildren are as children in accordance with the laws of the Torah and he is in duty bound to prevent with all his strength that he should not come to apostasy and go in evil ways and whosoever can render him help in this matter is in duty bound to help him with all his strength."

Not only is it a matter, so it is said, of religious belief, but it is said to be political, in that there is a struggle between this sect and the secular element in the state, as disclosed in a number of the Knesset reports which have been supplied to this court. It can be perhaps conveniently put in this way by referring to the applicant's affidavit in the present proceedings. In paragraph 24 he says: "The application for my extradition by the Government of Israel has arisen out of the struggle between the orthodox right wing and the non-orthodox left wing parties, a conflict which started even before the establishment of the State of Israel and has continued unabated ever since then. Politics and religion are in fact inseparable." Then a little further on: "My family, with the exception of my sister and brother-in-law, belong to the orthodox section of the Jewish **[85]** community. Although some of the orthodox parties join in the coalitions which are the usual form of government in Israel, bargaining is always going on and the friction between the parties is never far below the surface. . . . The intolerant attitude of the Government of Israel towards its orthodox subjects and its resentment of the desire on the part of these subjects to educate their children on religious lines has been made manifest by the statement they presumably instructed their counsel to make in the course of the proceedings at the magistrates' court on November 13, 1961; 'It is religious bigotry and fanaticism, in which the participants thought it was right to take the child away from its parents because they disapprove of the religious views of the parents'."

That was undoubtedly supported before the chief magistrate by the evidence of a great expert on the Middle East, Emile Marmorstein, who said this, taking a few statements from his deposition: "For the last 10 years I have been writing a book about the political struggle between the religious and the secularists in the State of Israel. There are in Israel many people who have come there since the state was created. . . . The main effect of the establishment of the state was to intensify the struggle between the orthodox and the secular. There are parties in the government which are openly hostile to religion. Normally the majority of the government are in various degrees of hostility to religion—there are no neutrals in this struggle. There is a tremendous campaign—especially during the last ten years—to wean young Jews away from orthodox practices. If orthodox immigrants find themselves in a secular village they would have a hard time of it, especially with regard to the religious education of their children. Religious education has been the subject of cabinet crises, and recently hard bargaining about it brought about the formation of a coalition. There are state orthodox and state secular schools. . . . I have studied the Knesset reports and the court decisions in this case therein referred to. The boy"—that is Yossele—"is a symbol in this case: both political sides regard his destiny as influencing their prospects of victory."

With that background, it is said that this court should hold that the offence, if an offence there be, was committed in consequence of the struggle, and presumably to advance the cause of the sect to which the applicant belonged. In deciding this issue, the first question is to determine what is meant by the expression [**86**] "offence of a political character" in section 3 of the Extradition Act, 1870. There is not a great deal of authority on the matter, but I should refer to one or two of the cases.

The first is *In re Castioni.*[44]* The facts there, of course, are a long way from this case, but an attempt was made to provide some definition of that expression "offence of a political character." Denman J. gave his views on the matter in these terms[45]: "I think that in order to bring the case within the words of the Act and to exclude extradition for such an act as murder, which is one of the extradition offences, it must at least be shown that the act is done in furtherance of, done with the intention of assistance, as a sort of overt act in the course of acting in a political matter, a political rising, or a dispute between two parties in the state as to which is to have the government in its hands, before it can be brought within the meaning of the words used in the Act."

Hawkins J.[46] deals with the matter in a passage in which he adopts the definition used by Stephen J. "I think, therefore, that the expression in the Extradition Act ought (unless some better interpretation of it can be suggested) to be interpreted to mean that fugitive criminals are not to be surrendered for extradition crimes, if those crimes were incidental to and formed a part of political disturbances." It so happened that Stephen J. was a member of the court, and he adhered to the definition already given.

In other words—it is only fair to say it was not necessary to go further for the purpose of that case—it was laid down there that some form of disturbance was necessary before it would be said that it was an offence of a political character. *In re Meunier*,[47]* to which I have already referred, and which was a case of an offence committed by an anarchist, shows that to be of a political character it must be aimed against the government of the state and not merely, as in that case, against all government.

44 [1891] 1 Q.B. 149; 7 T.L.R. 50, D.C.
45 [1891] 1 Q.B. 149, 156.
46 Ibid. 166.
47 [1894] 2 Q.B. 415.

Finally I must refer again to the *Polish Seamen's* case.[48]* In that case, as appears from the headnote, seven Polish nationals, who were members of the crew of a trawler fishing in the North Sea as part of the Polish fishing fleet, decided to seek political asylum **[87]** in England. Apparently, according to evidence which the magistrate accepted, they had been overheard while at sea by a political officer giving their political opinions, which were against the government of the state. The magistrate came to the conclusion that the only object the prisoners had in mind in seizing the trawler was to leave their country in which they suffered an intolerable sense of frustration and repression, and that they achieved their object with the smallest amount of injury to persons and property. In other words, extradition was there sought for an extradition crime which came within the schedule of the treaty in question, which included assaults on board a ship on the high seas with intent to destroy life or to do grievous bodily harm, revolt or conspiracy to revolt by two or more persons on board a ship on the high seas against the authority of the master. It was held that that offence in the circumstances of that case was an offence of a political character. It is not altogether clear exactly on what ground the court was arriving at that conclusion. Cassels J. gave the first judgment, and said[49]: "It is submitted on behalf of the men that if they should be extradited they may well only be tried for the offences for which their extradition is requested, but they will be punished as for an offence of a political character, and that offence is treason in going over to the capitalistic enemies. Everything in the case points that way and for that reason I agree that the writ of habeas corpus should issue." Again he says[50]: "They committed an offence of a political character, and if they were surrendered there could be no doubt that, while they would be tried for the particular offence mentioned, they would be punished as for a political crime."

Lord Goddard C.J. as I understand it, however, does not really deal with the matter on that ground but on a very broad basis. He says[51]: "The evidence about the law prevalent in the Republic of Poland today shows that it is necessary, if only for reasons of humanity, to give a wider and more generous meaning to the words we are now construing, which we can do without in any way encouraging the idea that ordinary crimes which have no political significance will be thereby excused."

One thing at any rate is clear, that the court in the *Polish* **[88]** *Seamen's* case[52]* were clearly extending, and considerably extending, the definition of "political offence" which had heretofore held the day. I find it quite unnecessary, and indeed impossible, to lay down any exclusive definition. So far as this case is concerned there is no question of rebellion, insurrection, supplanting the government of the day, or, as in the *Polish Seamen's* case,[52]* escaping from political control. So far as this case is concerned, no one has suggested any definition in wider terms than the following: A crime of a political character is a crime committed as part of a political movement with the object of influencing the policy of the governing party of the state. This clearly is wider than any definition has so far gone, and I am far from saying that it is a possible definition. But assuming for the moment that it is, I have come to the conclusion that it has not been shown to my satisfaction that the offence, if offence there was, was of that character. I say that for a number of reasons, which I can express shortly. First, the offence must have been of a political character when committed. It is not enough that the issues involved have since become political. Secondly, it is not enough in my judgment that the offence was committed at a time when there was a political movement of the character in question. It must have been done not merely in the context of a movement or struggle of a political nature but as part of it and with the object of advancing it.

This applicant has nowhere stated what his motives were; indeed, he is in the familiar difficulty in which many an accused finds himself of seeking to deny that he has ever committed the offence, and at the same time to say that if he did he did it for a particular reason. Here we are completely ignorant as to what

[48] [1955] 1 Q.B. 540.
[49] [1955] 1 Q.B. 540, 548.
[50] Ibid. 549.
[51] Ibid. 551.
[52] [1955] 1 Q.B. 540.

his motives were in concealing Yossele, if he ever did so. Even, however, if it can be inferred that his motives were the same as his father, the grandfather, there is nothing to suggest that the grandfather's action and this applicant's action was done as part of the movement or struggle rather than as part of a domestic and purely religious dispute within the family, albeit it occurred at a time when a political struggle was in being. Indeed, it may have been done, as was suggested by the grandfather himself, in order to prevent the child being taken to Russia.

In all these circumstances, I am quite unable to say that the crime, if crime there be, was of a political character, even within the suggested wider definition. Accordingly, I have come [89] to the conclusion that this application fails, and that it must be dismissed insofar as the committal on charge 1 and charge 2 (a) are concerned. As I have said, that in respect of charge 2 (b) has been withdrawn.

ASHWORTH J. I agree.

ATKINSON J. I also agree.

Application dismissed.
Leave to appeal to the House of Lords.
Bail refused.

Solicitors: *E. F. Iwi; Treasury Solicitor; Herbert Oppenheimer, Nathan & Vandyk; Director of Public Prosecutions.*

SCHTRAKS v. GOVERNMENT OF ISRAEL AND OTHERS

[On appeal from Regina v. Governor of Brixton Prison, *Ex parte* Schtraks]

([1964] A.C. 556)

July 25, 26, 30, 31, September 6, 1962: House of Lords: Lord Reid, Viscount Radcliffe, Lords Evershed, Jenkins, Hodson.

Extradition—Extent of treaty—"Territory"—Israel—Non-recognition of Israel's sovereignty over Jerusalem—De facto authority recognised—Whether Jerusalem "territory" of Israel Government—Israel (Extradition) Order, 1960 (*S.I.* 1960, *No.* 1660).
Extradition—Habeas corpus—Appeal—House of Lords—Ambit of jurisdiction to review magistrate's decision—Fresh evidence—Whether [557] *admissible—Admissibility a question of jurisdiction—Whether offence political.*
Extradition—Offence of a political character—Meaning—Extradition Act, 1870 (33 & 34 *Vict. c.* 52), *s.* 3 (1).

In September, 1959, in Israel, the grandfather of a boy, Yossele, aged seven, refused to return the boy to his parents because he feared that the child would not be given the religious education of an orthodox Jew. The parents brought proceedings in the High Court of Israel, in Jerusalem, and on February 10, 1960, the court ordered the return of Yossele to his parents by February 15, 1960. That order was not complied with. The parents brought proceedings against both grandparents and the appellant, the uncle of Yossele, for contempt of court. At the hearing the appellant, having affirmed, said that he had not seen Yossele since the feast of Hanukka which, that year, was from December 25, 1959, to January 1, 1960, at Rishon Le-Zion. On May 12, 1960, the court ordered that the grandfather be imprisoned but made no order against the appellant, who, shortly afterwards, came to live in England.

The boy was not found and in August, 1961, in the course of their inquiries, the police arrested Shlomo Kot, his wife and his brother Reuben. They were all imprisoned and the men were not released until after they had made their declarations. In those declarations all three alleged that the appellant and Yossele had come to the settlement after the Feast of Hanukka and Yossele had stayed with Shlomo and his wife. Shlomo also stated that the appellant had told him that the boy had to be kept from his father who desired his conversion to another religion and asked that the boy should remain in the settlement until after the dispute was over. Shlomo's wife gave evidence of the boy staying with them until the appellant came for him three weeks later. On that evidence, the Government of Israel asked for the extradition of the appellant in pursuance of an agreement dated April 4, 1960, between the two Governments that the Extradition Act, 1870,[1] should apply **[558]** subject to the terms of the Israel (Extradition) Order, 1960.[2] The charges against the appellant were for perjury and child stealing. On January 12, 1962, the appellant was committed to prison by order of the chief magistrate to await extradition to Israel.

The appellant applied for a writ of habeas corpus on the grounds, inter alia, that (1) Jerusalem was not "territory" of Israel within the meaning of the agreement since the United Kingdom Government did not recognise the Israel Government as having de jure sovereignty in Jerusalem, but only de facto authority, so that, there was no power to order his extradition on a charge of perjury committed in Jerusalem, nor, in that the declarations were made in that city was there jurisdiction to extradite him on any of the charges; and (2) that the offences were of a political character.

The Divisional Court dismissed the application.

On appeal to the House of Lords the appellant sought to adduce additional evidence in order (a) to discredit the evidence on which the magistrate had reached his conclusion, and (b) to supplement the evidence which was before the magistrate to the effect that the crimes with which the appellant had been charged were "of a political character" within the meaning of section 3 (1) of the Extradition Act, 1870:—

Held, (1) that "territory" in the context of the agreement of April 4, 1960, included any area over which a contracting party exercised effective jurisdiction; and that, accordingly, since the Israeli Government had de facto authority and exercised jurisdiction over Jerusalem, and no other State was recognised as having de jure sovereignty, Jerusalem was within the "territory" of Israel within the meaning of the agreement (post, pp. 579, 587, 593, 604).

[1] Extradition Act, 1870, s. 2: "Where an arrangement has been made with any foreign state with respect to the surrender to such state of any fugitive criminals, Her Majesty may, by Order in Council, direct that this Act shall apply in the case of such foreign state. Her Majesty may . . . limit the operation of the order . . . and render the operation thereof subject to such conditions, exceptions, and qualifications as may be deemed expedient."

S. 3: "The following restrictions shall be observed with respect to the surrender of fugitive criminals: (1) A fugitive criminal shall not be surrendered if the offence in respect of which his surrender is demanded is one of a political character, or if he prove to the satisfaction of the police magistrate or the court before whom he is brought on habeas corpus, or to the Secretary of State, that the requisition for his surrender has in fact been made with a view to try or punish him for an offence of a political character:"

[2] Israel (Extradition) Order, 1960, para. 1: "The Extradition Acts, 1870 to 1935, shall apply in the case of the State of Israel under and in accordance with the said agreement."

Art. 1: "The contracting parties agree to extradite to each other, in the circumstances stated in the present agreement, those persons who, being accused or convicted of any of the offences enumerated in article 3 and committed within the territory of the one party, or on the high seas on board a vessel registered in the territory of that party, shall be found within the territory of the other party."

Art. 6: "A person claimed shall not be extradited if the offence in respect of which his extradition is requested is one of a political character, or if he proves that the request for his extradition has, in fact, been made with a view to try or punish him for an offence of a political character."

Art. 12: "In the examinations which they have to make in accordance with the foregoing stipulations, the authorities of the requested party shall admit as valid evidence the sworn depositions or the affirmations of witnesses taken in the territory of the requesting party, or copies thereof. . . ."

(2) That in habeas corpus proceedings which arose out of a committal order under the Extradition Act, 1870, the court did not rehear the case that was before the magistrate or hear an appeal from his order, but its function, apart from considering any issue raised as to the offence charged being a political one, was to see that **[559]** the prisoner was lawfully detained by his gaoler. Further, that the House of Lords had in this respect no wider powers than that of the lower courts. Thus, the court, and on appeal therefrom the House of Lords, could and must consider whether on the material before the magistrate a reasonable magistrate would have been entitled to commit the prisoner, but neither a court nor the House of Lords could retry the case so as to substitute its discretion for that of the magistrate (post, pp. 579, 585, 596).

(3) That, accordingly, the right and competence of the court to take cognisance of additional evidence was limited to cases where such evidence went to the question of the magistrate's jurisdiction at the date of the committal order. That in so far as the additional evidence here related to the political character of the crimes charged, it went not to the question of the exercise by the magistrate of his discretionary powers and duties, but to his jurisdiction; and that, accordingly, the House was both competent and bound to receive that part of it, but only that part, which tended to show that the crimes charged were altogether outside the scope of the agreement (post, pp. 597, 605).

Rex v. *Governor of Holloway Prison, Ex parte Siletti** (1902) 20 Cox C.C. 353; 18 T.L.R. 771, D.C., and *Rex* v. *Governor of Brixton Prison, Ex parte Perry** [1924] 1 K.B. 455; 40 T.L.R. 181, D.C. approved and applied.

Per Viscount Radcliffe. On the issue whether the offence charged is an offence of a political character, it seems to be the evident intention of the Extradition Act, 1870, that the issue should be considered as a substantive matter at any stage by any authority, magistrate, court or Secretary of State, which has a duty to perform in relation to the extradition. If it is so regarded, it seems to me proper to consider on its merits any evidence that is available at the time when consideration is required. I should not treat this procedure so much as depending upon the court's duty to inquire into the magistrate's jurisdiction as upon the special conditions laid down by the Act for the carrying out of an extradition request (post, pp. 585-586).

(4) That whilst no precise definition could or ought to be laid down of the phrase "offence of a political character" in section 3 (1) of the Extradition Act, 1870, nevertheless it was plain that the offences charged against the appellant did not come within the ambit of that phrase as used in that subsection, since the charges if made good showed no more than that the appellant had involved himself in a family quarrel. The fact that his offences had become a political issue did not make them offences of a political character.

Per Lord Reid. It appears to me that the provisions of section 3 of the Act of 1870 are clearly intended to give effect to the principle that there should in this country be asylum for political refugees, and I do not think that it is possible, or that the Act evinces any intention to define the circumstances in which an offence can properly be held to be of a political character (post, p. 584).

Per Viscount Radcliffe. In my opinion the idea that lies behind the phrase "offence of a political character" is that the fugitive is at odds with the State that applies for his extradition on some **[560]** issue connected with the political control or government of the country. The analogy of "political" in this context is with "political" in such phrases as "political refugee," "political asylum" or "political prisoner." It does indicate, I think, that the requesting State is after him for reasons other than the enforcement of the criminal law in its ordinary, what I may call its common or international, aspect (post, p. 591).

Decision of the Divisional Court* [1963] 1 Q.B. 55; [1962] 2 W.L.R. 976; [1962] 2 All E.R. 176, D.C. affirmed.

APPEAL from the Divisional Court (Lord Parker C.J., Ashworth and Atkinson JJ.).

This was an appeal by leave of the Divisional Court of the Queen's Bench Division by the appellant, Shalom Schtraks, from the dismissal by the Divisional Court of the appellant's application for a writ of habeas corpus ad subjiciendum.

The facts giving rise to the proceedings were as follows: Ida and Alter Schuchmacher emigrated from Russia to Israel with their two children, a daughter, Zina, and their son, Yosef, known as Yossele, who was born on March 2, 1952. The parents had difficulty in finding work and accommodation and therefore, early in 1959, they left their children with the grandparents, the wife's parents, Nachman and Miriam Schtraks. The parents had no difficulty in getting their daughter back but when they asked for the return of Yossele, in about September, 1959, the grandfather refused to return him because he thought that the parents would not give Yossele the religious education of an orthodox Jew.

The parents began proceedings in the High Court of Israel, in Jerusalem, and on January 16, 1960, obtained an order nisi addressed to the grandparents to show cause why they should not bring the boy to the court so that he might be dealt with as the court ordered. On January 28, 1960, the grandparents made a declaration that it was in the interest of Yossele that he should remain with them, that the boy wished to do so, and that they feared the parents would take the child back to Russia. The case was heard on February 10, 1960, when the order was made absolute and the grandparents ordered to return Yossele by February 15, 1960.

The grandparents did not return the child and the parents then brought proceedings for contempt of court against the grandparents and their son, the appellant. They alleged that the appellant was making common cause with the grandparents, assisting and encouraging them in the withholding of Yossele, when he knew of the order of the court. On February 25, 1960, the appellant, in an affidavit, denied the allegation. **[561]**

On May 12, 1960, the case was heard. The appellant gave evidence and, according to a police officer of the Israeli police, Sergeant Tishler, affirmed: "I last saw [Yossele] before Hanukka this year. I saw him in Rishon Le-Zion. It was at the Yeshiva in Rishon Le-Zion. I was with my father, Nachman Schtraks. I study at a Yeshiva in Lod and my father came to me and asked me to go with him to Rishon Le-Zion . . . Since then I have not seen the boy . . . I do not know from my father or from another source that the child is hidden from his father." The feast of Hanukka that year was from December 25, 1959, to January 1, 1960, and in one translation of this passage, "Yeshiva" was translated as a college of religion. According to the notes of evidence of the trial, the appellant later said: "I do not remember whether I spoke to the child between Hanukka and the trial." The court committed the grandfather to prison for contempt, the parents withdrew their application against the grandmother and the court, not being satisfied that the appellant had rendered any assistance, made no order against him. The appellant came to England on May 23, 1960, and, at the time of the hearing of the application before the Divisional Court, the grandfather was still in prison and the whereabouts of Yossele was still unknown. Subsequently Yossele was found in New York, U.S.A.

In August, 1961, as a result of extensive police inquiries and searches for Yossele, three people were arrested by the police from the Komemiyut Settlement. They were Shlomo Kot, his wife Rachel and his brother Reuben. On August 2, Shlomo and his wife were arrested and charged. On August 9, their application for bail was refused but Sergeant Tishler said that Rachel would be released next day; Reuben was arrested on that day. On August 10, Rachel was released and on August 17 they all made declarations in Jerusalem and Reuben was released; Shlomo was released the following day. Reuben was never charged.

Shlomo Kot, in his declaration, affirmed that, "A few weeks after the Feast of Hanukka about a year and a half ago, that is, after the Feast of Hanukka of the year 5720, which fell on the days December 25, 1959, to

January 1, 1960, approximately in the month of Tevet, 5720, while I was, towards evening, in the synagogue of the said Komemiyut Settlement, there appeared a young man with a boy about seven years of age. The young man and the boy who arrived together were unknown to me and were not local residents." The young man and the boy were referred to Shlomo Kot as the rabbi of the settlement **[562]** was not present and by paragraph 5 of his declaration, "The young man and the boy came up to me, and I asked the young man what he wanted. The young man said that he was the boy's uncle and that there was a family quarrel about the boy who was with him, namely, the boy's father wanted to remove him from the Jewish fold and convert him to another religion while the mother was opposed to this and the boy, therefore, had to be saved by keeping him away from his father for a short period until the matter was settled. The young man informed me that he had a letter in this matter from Rabbi Meisels of Jerusalem to the rabbi of the said Komemiyut Settlement. As the said rabbi was not present and as the young man asked that the boy who had come with him should remain in the said Komemiyut Settlement that very night, I agreed that the boy should remain at my house. The young man then told me that the name of the boy was Israel Hazan . . ." He then went on to affirm that the boy stayed at his house for two to three weeks and that during that time the young man came to see the boy and that the boy confided to him that his real name was Yossele. He identified, from photographs, Yossele and the appellant as being the boy and the young man.

Rachel Kot, in her declaration, affirmed that one evening her husband brought home the young man and the boy and that the boy stayed with them. By paragraph 5 of her declaration, she affirmed that, "One day, after about three weeks had elapsed from the day on which the boy had been brought to my house, the boy came to me and told me joyfully that his uncle had come to take him with him. I packed the boy's things; he took them with him, travelling in a car driven by a man named Menahem Moses, of the Komemiyut Smallholders' Settlement. In that car, I saw two other persons, one of whom was Rappaport Meir, who lives at the said Komemiyut Smallholders' Settlement." She also stated that the young man came to see the boy twice and identified them as being the appellant and Yossele from photographs.

Reuben Kot, in his declaration, affirmed that he saw the young man and the boy near the synagogue and that one or two days later he visited the house of his brother and saw the boy there. He also identified the boy as Yossele and the young man as the appellant from photographs.

On the evidence of the three Kots and of Sergeant Tishler, who deposed to the appellant's evidence in the High Court of Israel, the Government of Israel asked for the extradition of the **[563]** appellant. The appellant was arrested on August 28, 1961, and during the proceedings for his extradition an inquiry was made of the Foreign Office concerning the recognition afforded the State of Israel by the Government of the United Kingdom. On October 4, 1961, a letter was received from the Foreign Office stating: "(1) His Majesty's Government accorded de facto recognition to the State of Israel on January 29, 1949. (2) His Majesty's Government accorded de jure recognition to the State of Israel on April 27, 1950. In according such de jure recognition His Majesty's Government made certain reservations which, in relation to the status of Jerusalem, were explained as follows by the then Minister of State in a statement to the House of Commons on April 27, of that year: — 'His Majesty's Government are unable to recognise the sovereignty of Israel over that part of Jerusalem which she occupies, though, pending a final determination of the status of the area, they recognise that Israel exercises de facto authority in it.' (3) In according recognition on the same date of the Union of the Kingdom of Jordan and of that part of Palestine under Jordan occupation and control His Majesty's Government made a similar reservation in respect of that part of Jerusalem occupied and controlled by Jordan. (4) Her Majesty's Government continue to maintain, as regards the status of that part of Jerusalem occupied by Israel, the attitude which they adopted when according de jure recognition to the State of Israel on April 27, 1950."

On January 12, 1962, the chief magistrate (Sir Robert Blundell) committed the appellant to Brixton Prison to await extradition to Israel on the following charges: "1. Perjury for that he on May 12, 1960, during proceedings in an application No. 52/60 in the High Court of Justice of Israel knowingly gave false evidence touching a matter material in those proceedings contrary to section 117 of the Criminal Code Ordinance, 1936. 2. Child stealing: (*a*) on a date between January 1 and February 15, 1960, with intent to deprive Alter and Ida Schuchmacher of their son Joseph (born in 1952) fraudulently detained him in the house of Shlomo Zalman Kot at Komemiyut, contrary to section 188 of the said Ordinance; (*b*) on a date between January 1 and February 15, 1960, wrongfully confined the said Joseph Schuchmacher in the said house knowing that he was an abducted person, contrary to section 259 of the said Ordinance."

The appellant applied for a writ of habeas corpus. In an **[564]** affidavit he stated that, "The application for my extradition by the Government of Israel has arisen out of the struggle between the orthodox right wing and the non-orthodox left wing parties, a conflict which started even before the establishment of the State of Israel and has continued unabated ever since then. Politics and religion are in fact inseparable. . . ."

The grounds of the application were (1) that the agreement of April 4, 1960, did not apply to any part of Jerusalem. (2) That the method by which the affidavits of all three witnesses for the prosecution were obtained raised a presumption of duress which was not rebutted by the prosecution. (3) That two of the three witnesses were accomplices of two of the alleged offences and the rules which govern the admissibility of the evidence of accomplices in this country were not observed; neither was it taken into consideration that, where all three witnesses were concerned, there was both the element of fear and the hope of reward. (4) That an examination of the dates when it was alleged the offences of child stealing and harbouring were committed showed that these charges could not be maintained. Thus both those charges and the perjury which arose from those charges could not stand. (5) That by article 11 of the Israel (Extradition) Order, 1960, it was necessary before an extradition order was made that, "the evidence be found sufficient, according to the laws of the territory from which extradition is desired, either to justify the committal of the person claimed for trial, if the offence of which he is accused had been committed in that territory." The magistrate failed to find that as a fact the evidence was sufficient to justify the appellant's committal according to the laws of this country and in the absence of such finding there was no jurisdiction for the issue of the warrant. (6) That the charges against the appellant were brought and the request for his extradition made in furtherance of a struggle between the various political parties in Israel arising out of the conflict between the religious and secular forces in the State. The religious conflicts had at all material times assumed a political character, and accordingly the State of Israel were preferring charges against the appellant for offences, which, though the offences themselves were not political in character, arose from the conflict, and it was thought thereby to placate the secular parties in the struggle against the orthodox elements. Considered as they must be in the framework of the background of political and religious conflicts in the State of Israel, the charges and the request for the applicant's extradition must therefore be regarded as political in **[565]** character and they were accordingly contrary to article 6 of the Order. They were brought by the Government of Israel on false evidence in furtherance of their campaign against the strict orthodox parties in Israel, who had aroused the enmity of the party of Mr. Ben Gurion, the Prime Minister, because they were not Zionists and opposed the secular state of Israel, an attitude which was much resented by that Government.

John Foster Q.C. and *R. D. L. Du Cann* for the appellant. There is a preliminary point of jurisdiction, namely, whether that part of Jerusalem occupied by the State of Israel comes within the terms of the Israel (Extradition) Order, 1960. The question of jurisdiction is relevant to (i) the charge of perjury; (ii) the charge of child stealing, and (iii) the admissibility in the courts of this country of the depositions, all of which were taken in Jerusalem. The submission, put compendiously, is that the Israel extradition treaty only applies to the territory of Israel and that Jerusalem is not in the territory of Israel. The decision of the Divisional Court was that in the present context territory equals jurisdiction; that Israel exercises jurisdiction in Jerusalem and that, therefore, Jerusalem is in the territory of Israel. But if the terms of the Israel (Extradition) Order, 1960, are examined it will be seen that in many places "territory" cannot be equivalent to jurisdiction. The Order of 1960 limits the Extradition Act, 1870 (*Reg.* v. *Wilson*[3]*); the Order limits the Act so that it applies only to offences committed in the territories of the contracting parties. The offences must have been committed in the area over which the sovereignty of the State of Israel is recognised by Her Majesty's Government. The Foreign Office has certified that Her Majesty's Government does not recognise the de jure sovereignty of Israel over part of Jerusalem but only recognises her authority de facto, and that certificate is binding on the courts.

In article 2 of the Order of 1960 the territory to which the agreement applies and over which the United Kingdom does not have sovereignty is included, and, therefore, if the Order had meant to cover territory over which Israel did not have sovereignty such territory would have had to be specifically included therein. The territory of a state is the area over which the state exercises sovereignty; an area over which a state, in the view of another state, does not exercise sovereignty does not **[566]** form part of its territory for the purposes of recognition in international law by that other state. It is to be observed that article 2 of the Order includes territories where the United Kingdom does not have sovereignty but does exercise jurisdiction. That is precisely parallel to the situation in respect of Jerusalem save that Jerusalem is not included in this Order. For the context in which "territory" is used: see articles 1, 4, 7, 11, 12, 14, 15 and 17.

If the judgment of the Divisional Court[4]* on this question is accepted it would have the following consequences. Suppose a treaty of extradition with France. Subsequently France annexes a Pacific island which belongs to Japan. France makes it part of the territory of metropolitan France and exercises jurisdiction there. It would follow that the extradition treaty would apply to that area although the Foreign Office would certify that Her Majesty's Government did not recognise the sovereignty of France over that area.

It should be assumed that an extradition treaty comprises all the territory recognised by the United Kingdom at the time the offence was committed. It follows that any territory which is acquired "unlawfully" cannot form part of the territory of the requesting state, for otherwise it would mean that a state's territory would be ascertained by means of an entirely subjective test and whatever the requesting state declared was its territory—whatever jurisdiction it exercised in the areas in question—would, according to the decision of the Divisional Court, be recognised by the United Kingdom.

It is emphasised that a state's territory is confined to that area over which sovereignty is exercised. The essential element of sovereignty is that it is to be exercised within territorial limits. Territory is co-terminous with sovereignty: see the definition of "territorial waters" in the Territorial Waters Jurisdiction Act, 1878. It is plain from the certificate of the Foreign Office that Her Majesty's Government does not recognise Israel's sovereignty over Jerusalem.

The fact that there is a lacuna in the Order does not affect the construction and the word "territory" must be given its plain meaning. Article 2 of the Order recognises that certain areas of jurisdiction are to be included and therefore there can be no intention of using the word "territory" to include the **[567]** meaning of jurisdiction. [Reference was made to *Reg.* v. *Governor of Brixton Prison, Ex parte Minervini.*[5]*] Article 1 specifically includes the contracting parties' ships on the high seas as being in their territories.

[3] (1877) 3 Q.B.D. 42, 45, D.C.
[4] [1963] 1 Q.B. 55, 71-76.
[5] [1959] 1 Q.B. 155, 161, 162; [1958] 3 W.L.R. 559; [1958] 3 All E.R. 318, D.C.

In fine, if the decision of the Divisional Court was right it would not have been necessary to include the protectorates in article 2 because the United Kingdom exercises exclusive jurisdiction there and therefore they are part of the territory of the United Kingdom. But cases such as *Ex parte Mwenya*[6]* show clearly that the fact that Her Majesty's Government exercises exclusive jurisdiction over an area outside the United Kingdom does not make that area part of the territory of the United Kingdom.

When there is, as here, a treaty, which is the subject of international law, between two sovereign states, and one sovereign state does not recognise the sovereignty of the other state over a particular area, then it is impossible to maintain that the area in question is part of the territory of the other state. Accordingly, it cannot be maintained that Jerusalem forms part of the State of Israel. [Reference was also made to *Kossekechatko* v. *Attorney-General for Trinidad*.[7]*]

Sir Peter Rawlinson Q.C., S.-G. and *R. A. Barr* for the Home Secretary were not called upon to argue the question of jurisdiction and took no further part in the appeal.

John Foster Q.C. There is a supplementary petition which seeks to lay additional evidence before the House. This additional evidence is of two kinds: (a) evidence which shows that on the whole material now available it would be improper to commit the appellant; (b) evidence to supplement that given before the chief magistrate to the effect that the crimes of which the appellant is charged are of a political character.

Leonard Caplan Q.C. and *R. L. Goff* for the Government of Israel. In so far as the additional evidence relates to the political nature of the offences the Government of Israel does not wish to take the position most adverse to the appellant and, therefore, the adducing of additional evidence on this question is not opposed. **[568]**

As to the additional evidence it is proposed to adduce in relation to the habeas corpus point, it is submitted that it should not be allowed unless the House is given all the available evidence from both sides so that the House may be fully apprised of the position.

J. H. Buzzard for the Governor of Brixton Prison raised objection to the competency of the supplementary petition.

John Foster Q.C. The Governor of Brixton Prison has no locus standi to take this objection. The true respondents, the Government of Israel, are before the House. The task of the Governor of Brixton Prison is to deal with any return to a writ of habeas corpus. It cannot be anything to do with him whether, in regard to a person who is in his custody and who is seeking release on habeas corpus, certain evidence is or is not admissible in those proceedings.

It is conceded that where in proceedings such as these the requesting government has not appeared, then, instead of the Governor of Brixton Prison those who appear on behalf of the Secretary of State for Home Affairs can speak on behalf of the requesting state. But where, as here, the requesting government appears and makes no objection to the additional evidence it is not for the Governor of Brixton Prison to make an objection, for by so doing he is abandoning the neutral attitude of the gaoler, which he should maintain. Further, such a situation could lead to abuse in that the requesting government could shelter behind the Governor of Brixton Prison and not come forward and state what its real attitude was in relation to an application made by the fugitive.

J. H. Buzzard. The only person who is entitled as of right to be heard against the petition is in fact the Governor of Brixton Prison. This is an application for habeas corpus, it is a common law application, and the one person who must be heard and is entitled to be heard is the person in whose custody the prisoner is, and, indeed, it has never been decided that the foreign government is entitled as of right to be heard. The Governor is here to see that all the relevant facts are put before the House and to assist as to the principles of law to be applied,

[6] [1960] 1 Q.B. 241; [1959] 3 W.L.R. 767; [1959] 3 All E.R. 525, C.A.
[7] [1932] A.C. 78, 95; 48 T.L.R. 27, P.C.

and that includes what evidence should be received or not received. That is the extent of the Governor's interest; it is no function of those who appear on his behalf to enter into the merits of whether or not there was a prima facie case made out against the appellant. **[569]**

This additional evidence is not receivable at all for the purpose for which it is tendered. For the purpose of disposing of an appeal section 1 (4) of the Administration of Justice Act, 1960, provides that the House may exercise any of the powers of the court below. Accordingly, the House can only receive fresh evidence in those circumstances in which the Divisional Court may do so. The Divisional Court and, therefore, this House can only receive fresh evidence (a) to show lack of jurisdiction in the magistrate at the start of the proceedings before him; (b) though this is doubtful, to cure a technical omission in the chain of evidence in support of the request for extradition; (c) to prove that the real reason for bringing the extradition proceedings is to try or punish the fugitive for some offence of a political character and not for the offence for which the requisition is ostensibly made (section 3 (1) of the Extradition Act, 1870).

It is to be remembered that an application for habeas corpus is at common law and is not under the Extradition Act, 1870: see *Rex* v. *Governor of Holloway Prison, Ex parte Siletti*[8]* and Piggott on Extradition (1910), p. 155. It follows that the usual rules as to a habeas corpus application apply here, apart from any extra powers which may be conferred by section 3 (1) of the Act of 1870. As to the position at common law apart from section 3 (1), the issue is whether the custody by the Governor of Brixton Prison is lawful, and that depends solely on the validity of the committal by the magistrate. This is not an appeal in the ordinary course at all and is never so regarded. The court merely looks to see whether the detention is lawful, that is, whether the committal was valid. The Divisional Court can only hear fresh evidence—evidence which was not before the magistrate—going to the want of jurisdiction at the start of the proceedings before the magistrate: see Short and Mellor's Crown Practice, 2nd ed. (1908), p. 328, where it is stated: "Even under the foregoing Act [Habeas Corpus Act, 1816] affidavits are not admissible to controvert facts found by the judgment of a court of competent jurisdiction, though they may be received to show some extrinsic collateral matter essential to the jurisdiction, or to show a total want or excess of jurisdiction". Thus, assuming that the magistrate was acting within his jurisdiction and had depositions before him justifying the committal, that is, disclosing a prima facie case, **[570]** the fact that it later transpires that such evidence was perjured or entirely mistaken does not enable the Divisional Court to admit fresh evidence to that effect. [Reference was made to sections 11 and 12 of the Extradition Act, 1870, and article 11 of the Order of 1960.]

It is submitted that here, just as in proceedings by certiorari to remove a conviction, further evidence on the merits cannot be looked at by any court. As to certiorari: see *Reg.* v. *Bolton*.[9] These proceedings by habeas corpus are analogous to certiorari proceedings: see Short and Mellor's Crown Practice, 2nd ed., pp. 319, 47. The principle of *Reg.* v. *Bolton*[9] was specifically applied to habeas corpus proceedings in *Rex* v. *Morn Hill Camp Commanding Officer, Ex parte Ferguson*.[10] Further, *Rex* v. *Nat Bell Liquors Ltd.*[11] makes it plain that on certiorari fresh evidence on the merits can never be entertained. As to the other authorities, in *In re Guerin*[12]* the Divisional Court held on an application for habeas corpus that since the question there went to the jurisdiction at the commencement of the inquiry fresh evidence could be heard. Darling J.'s observations in *Rex* v. *Governor of Holloway Prison, Ex parte Siletti*[13]* are correct. When the depositions are examined on habeas corpus upon their return with the committal order this is because it is a speaking order and the court is

[8] (1902) 20 Cox C.C. 353, 357; 18 T.L.R. 771, D.C.
[9] (1841) 1 Q.B. 66, 71-73, 75, 76.
[10] [1917] 1 K.B. 176; 33 T.L.R. 47, D.C.
[11] [1922] 2 A.C. 128, 154, 155, 159, 160; 38 T.L.R. 541, P.C.
[12] (1888) 16 Cox C.C. 596, D.C.
[13] 20 Cox C.C. 353, 358.

entitled so to do to ascertain whether as a matter of law there was any evidence to found the committal. In *Rex* v. *Governor of Brixton Prison, Ex parte Perry*[14]* the Divisional Court followed *Ex parte Siletti*[15]* and held that on a question of fact within the jurisdiction of the magistrate the court would not review his conclusion upon evidence subsequently arising. *Greene* v. *Secretary of State for Home Affairs*[16] is an a fortiori case for it involved a non-criminal matter and therefore the Habeas Corpus Act, 1816, applied, and it is plainly implicit in the opinions of the House that there can be no question of fresh evidence to contravene the magistrate's decision on the merits.

On the question whether the court can hear fresh evidence to cure an irregularity or an omission: see *Rex* v. *Governor of* **[571]** *Brixton Prison, Ex parte Percival*[17]*; *Rex* v. *Governor of Brixton Prison Ex parte Servini*[18]* and *Reg.* v. *Governor of Brixton Prison, Ex parte Shuter.*[19]* These authorities appear to establish that the writ of habeas corpus being a prerogative writ the court will decline to issue it if it is satisfied that there are absolutely no merits and the omission or irregularity is merely a formal matter that can easily be rectified. [Reference was made to *Kossekechatko* v. *Attorney-General for Trinidad*[20]* and *In re Arton* (*No.* 2).[21]*]

As to the political aspect, there have been conflicting decisions on the construction of section 3 (1) of the Extradition Act, 1870. It is submitted that the subsection falls into two parts: "A fugitive criminal shall not be surrendered if the offence in respect of which his surrender is demanded is one of a political character . . ." forms the first part, and on that issue there is nothing to indicate that the Divisional Court can hear fresh evidence. The remainder of the subsection forms a different and separate issue and it is plain on its language that the fugitive must be allowed to adduce evidence on that issue to any one of the three bodies there mentioned to whom he is allowed to prove it. The conflicting opinions as to the meaning of the second limb of section 3 (1) are set out by Lord Parker C.J.[22] It is submitted that Lord Russell of Killowen C.J.'s construction of the second limb of the subsection in *In re Arton* (*No.* 1)[23]* is right on the plain language of the subsection and that the second limb thereof contemplates the possibility that the foreign government might act in bad faith. In other words, it is concerned with an indirect motive on the part of the foreign government. [Reference was made to *Zacharia* v. *Republic of Cyprus.*[24]*]

As to the statements it is proposed to tender, these are habeas corpus proceedings and if the ordinary rules apply the evidence must be on oath and should be in the form of affidavits. The difficulty about receiving these statements is that they are not statements on oath by those making them. Under Lord Denman's Act if a witness gives evidence and he has made statements **[572]** which conflict with it he can be cross-examined whether he made the statements and if he does not admit making them those statements can be proved against him. But the difficulty here is that the foundation for putting in the contrary statements has not been laid, and cannot be laid because the evidence of the witnesses is in the form of an affidavit from Palestine and the witnesses cannot be cross-examined. There is no rule of law which allows in this kind of proceeding proof of a statement, however contradictory, by a witness, who is not on oath, unless the foundation has been laid for its reception under Lord Denman's Act.

It is conceded that if affidavit evidence, deposition or statement on oath is given in the form laid down in sections 14 and 15 of the Extradition Act, 1870,

14 [1924] 1 K.B. 455; 40 T.L.R. 181, D.C.
15 20 Cox C.C. 353.
16 [1942] A.C. 284, 303; 58 T.L.R. 53; [1941] 3 All E.R. 388, H.L.
17 [1907] 1 K.B. 696, 705, 707, 708; 23 T.L.R. 238, D.C.
18 [1914] 1 K.B. 77, 80, 81, 84; 30 T.L.R. 35, D.C.
19 [1960] 2 Q.B. 89, 94, 95; [1959] 3 W.L.R. 603; [1959] 2 All E.R. 782, D.C.
20 [1932] A.C. 78, 95.
21 [1896] 1 Q.B. 509, 516, 518; 12 T.L.R. 189, D.C.
22 [1963] 1 Q.B. 55, 81-83.
23 [1896] 1 Q.B. 108, 113; 12 T.L.R. 131, D.C.
24 [1962] 2 W.L.R. 1163, 1181-1184; [1962] 2 All E.R. 438, H.L.

it can be received under section 3 (1) of that Act on the political issue because that is for the purposes of the Act and is over and above what the court can take cognisance of on the general provisions of habeas corpus. [Reference was also made to sections 7, 9 and 10 of the Extradition Act, 1870.]

John Foster Q.C. In ordinary committal proceedings before a magistrate there is no appeal from his decision; it is not a question that can be put before a superior court by prerogative right. Where, however, there is a committal in extradition proceedings by virtue of the provisions of the Extradition Act, 1870 (and in the present case by article 14 of the Order of 1960), the fugitive is given a right of appeal by way of habeas corpus—a branch of habeas corpus peculiar to extradition. Accordingly, since it is an appeal, on the hearing of the habeas corpus application, which deals with questions which do not go to jurisdiction, further evidence can be admitted and the matter is at large. There have been a number of reported cases where fresh evidence was admitted or where there appear dicta which envisage that possibility: see *In re Guerin*[25]*; *in re Arton* (*No.* 2)[26]*; *Rex* v. *Governor of Brixton Prison, Ex parte Percival*[27]*; *Rex* v. *Governor of Brixton Prison, Ex parte Servini*[28]*; *Kossekechatko* v. *Attorney-General for Trinidad*[29]*; *Reg.* v. *Governor of Brixton Prison, Ex parte Shuter.*[30]*

The evidence in the supplemental petition should be admitted. In respect of the non-authentication of that part of it which **[573]** relates to whether there is here a political offence it is to be observed that the rules of evidence are relaxed in favour of the accused where it is within the knowledge of the prosecution that a particular statement was made. That is akin to the position here. [Reference was also made to Piggott on Extradition, p. 156; *In re Galwey*[31]*; *Rex* v. *Governor of Holloway Prison, Ex parte Siletti*[32]*; *In re Castioni*[33]*; *Colonial Bank of Australasia* v. *Willan.*[34]]

[Their Lordships conferred.]

LORD REID. Their Lordships will allow the petition so far as regards material which bears upon the issue whether this is a political offence and they will refuse the petition so far as the other material is concerned. If any of the material bears on both issues, their Lordships will consider it with regard to the political offence but not with regard to the other points made on behalf of the appellant.

John Foster Q.C. With regard to the charge of child stealing, the facts here do not fall within section 188 of the Criminal Code. At all relevant times Yossele's grandparents still had—or were at least entitled in good faith to claim that they had—the right to "possession" of the child; at all events Yossele's parents in the circumstances did not have his "lawful care or charge." It cannot be said, therefore, that the appellant had the intent to deprive them of Yossele's "possession" within the meaning of section 188.

In considering whether an offence takes on a political character it is first necessary to ascertain whether the offence was committed in a political context. No precise definition can be given of "political." If a crime is committed within the context of an acute political struggle within the state then it is a crime of a political character. This matter of stealing the child arose out of the conflict between the orthodox religious parties and the secular. That there was such a conflict and that religion and politics are inseparable in Israel is shown by the evidence of Bishop Stewart, who was Bishop in Jerusalem in 1957, of Emile Marmorstein and of Guy Eden. In Israel and the Middle East religious leaders have also political duties, and the Knesset reports show the bitterness of the religious issue which had **[574]** become a political movement inside the Knesset.

[25] 16 Cox C.C. 596.
[26] [1896] 1 Q.B. 509.
[27] [1907] 1 K.B. 696.
[28] [1914] 1 K.B. 77.
[29] [1932] A.C. 78.
[30] [1960] 2 Q.B. 89.
[31] [1896] 1 Q.B. 230, 236; 12 T.L.R. 150.
[32] 20 Cox C.C. 353.
[33] [1891] 1 Q.B. 149, 164; 7 T.L.R. 50, D.C.
[34] (1874) L.R. 5 P.C. 417, 446, P.C.

The commissioner of police had stated that the grandfather recognised no secular authority and was anxious that Yossele should receive a religious education. Education was part of the struggle between the religious and secular parties and there had been a campaign over the last 10 years to wean young Jews from their religious practices. The grandfather's action had been supported by the members of the settlement and the police had been hindered in their search for Yossele. The Chief Rabbi in Jerusalem had stated that according to the law of the Torah the grandfather was as a father to the boy. The disappearance of Yossele had become a political matter and the subject-matter of questions in the Knesset and, as such, it was a political offence. Further, the perjury was part of the whole offence of resisting the authorities.

Du Cann following. On the question of the charge of child stealing it is pertinent to observe that this is a case where persons who are blood relations (the grandparents) have had the child to all intents and purposes from the day he was born. An offence can only be committed under section 188 of the Israeli Criminal Code—a penal code based on English law—to the detriment of the parent if that offence is committed at the time when the parent has the lawful care or charge of the child. If some other person has the lawful care or charge of the child at the relevant time, then the offence is committed to their detriment, but not to the detriment of the parent. The detaining, the receiving or the harbouring of the child must be to the prejudice of the parent, guardian or other person who has the lawful care or charge of the child. The parents here at all relevant times had neither the lawful care nor charge of Yossele. [Reference was made to *Reg.* v. *Manktelow.*[35]]

As to the word "fraudulently" in section 188 of the Code, in the context it must mean a fraud, deceit, practised either upon the parent or guardian or the person having lawful charge or control, or a fraud perpetrated upon the child. The evidence here does not show that either force or fraud was brought to bear upon either the child or upon the parents in order to secure the child's going with the appellant. [Reference was also made to sections 55 and 56 of the Offences against the Person Act, 1861; section 55 of the Sexual Offences Act, 1956; *Reg.* v. *Miller*[36]; *Reg.* v. *Bellis*[37]; *Reg.* v. *Barrett.*[38]] **[575]**

Leonard Caplan Q.C. The first contention for the appellant was that even if the evidence adduced is taken at its face value there is no evidence of the offence charged. The second contention is that the evidence should not be taken at its face value because for a variety of reasons it is suspect and not such as the magistrate should have acted upon.

The arguments on the first question in relation to the charge of child stealing stem from the same concept of the difference between a parent's right to possession and actual possession. However important that concept may be in considering the offence of taking away a child with an intent to deprive some person of possession it is not important when the question is whether a child has been *detained* with that intent. The evidence establishes that the parents sought the return of the child some time at the end of 1959, that the grandparents failed and refused to return the child although the court in Israel has decided there was no justification for so failing and refusing. Accordingly, from the time when they did so fail and refuse after request, the parents were entitled to possession of the child and they had a right to that possession as from some time at the end of 1959. If parents have a right to possession of a child, and some person with intent to defeat that right places the child somewhere under a false name, it cannot be said that that intent was not to deprive the parents of possession to which they had a right and which in the ordinary way would have ripened into actual possession. Further, if the detaining of a child is accompanied by any circumstances of deceit for the purpose of misleading the parents or those who on behalf of the parents may be seeking the child, that is a detainer fraudulently within section 188 of the Code. Any form of deceit, such as a change of name, dyeing the child's hair or practising some other kind of camouflage such as hiding the child, is fraud within the section.

35 (1853) 6 Cox C.C. 143, 147.
36 (1876) 13 Cox C.C. 179.
37 (1893) 17 Cox C.C. 660.
38 (1885) 15 Cox C.C. 658.

As to the contention that the evidence should not be accepted at its face value, the totality of the appellant's objections is that there exists material on which the Kots could be cross-examined for the purpose of attempting to discredit their evidence. Suggestions could be made to them in cross-examination that they had not told the truth because they wanted to get out of custody, because they had had inducements held out to them and because they had suffered duress. But it does not in the least follow that that cross-examination when it took place would be in any degree successful in achieving its purpose and, **[576]** therefore, there is no good reason why the appellant should not be extradited to stand his trial. [Reference was made to section 25 of the Indictable Offences Act, 1848; sections 9 and 10 of the Extradition Act, 1870; *In re Meunier*[39]*; *Rex* v. *Secretary of State for India, Ex parte Ezekiel*[40]*; *Windsor* v. *The Queen*[41]*; *Reg.* v. *Norfolk Quarter Sessions, Ex parte Brunson*[42]; *Rex* v. *Zossenheim.*[43]*]

As to what constitutes an "offence of a political character," it is to be observed that there has not been any comprehensive and satisfactory definition of that expression as it occurs in the Act of 1870. The term "political crime" is capable on one view of covering so wide a field of criminal activities that it is pertinent to consider whether the legislature in 1870 intended that that expression should have its widest possible meaning. In construing the statute it is permissible to have regard to the historical context in which it was passed for the purpose of ascertaining the true meaning of any doubtful parts thereof.

The exception from extradition of certain crimes of a political character has its origin in the political and humanitarian concepts that prevailed in England at the time of the passing of the Act of 1870. The liberal tradition of the nineteenth century viewed with sympathy the plight of those peoples who were oppressed by a government in whose choice they had played no part and who were left with no alternative, if they desired to supplant that government, but violence and civil disturbance. Thus when such persons took the only course open to them to supplant the government the sentiment of the time was that they should not be treated as criminals but should enjoy the right of political asylum in this country. This gives a clue to what under this Act was intended to be covered by the expression "offence of a political character." On the other hand, it cannot be supposed that it was intended to protect, for example, persons who in elections conducted on democratic lines organised personation of voters on a large scale, or a thief who stole a large sum of money for the purpose of donating it to the political party of his choice. [Reference was made to *In re Castioni.*[44]*]

It is impossible, and would, indeed, be wrong to attempt to define for all time what constitutes an offence of a political **[577]** character. All that can be said is that any definition, if ever one is finally achieved, must involve the element that the person who committed the crime in question must have had a political motive: see *In re Meunier.*[45]* On the evidence here the House is left in complete ignorance as to the political motives (if any) of the appellant. It would appear that he has sided with his father in a purely family dispute for reasons which may seem to him to be perfectly good. Whether they are religious grounds, or reasons of filial piety, or whatever reasons they are, they are certainly not shown to be political reasons. [Reference was also made to *Reg.* v. *Governor of Brixton Prison, Ex parte Kolczynski.*[46]*]

Buzzard in reply. The first limb of section 3 (1) of the Extradition Act, 1870, clearly refers to extradition crimes only, and therefore at any rate in that part of the subsection the offence under consideration (". . . if the offence in respect of which his surrender is demanded is one of a political character") must be

39 [1894] 2 Q.B. 415, 418, D.C.
40 [1941] 2 K.B. 169; [1941] 2 All E.R. 546, D.C.
41 (1866) L.R. 1 Q.B. 289, 320, 324.
42 [1953] 1 Q.B. 503; [1953] 2 W.L.R. 294; [1953] 1 All E.R. 346, D.C.
43 (1903) 20 T.L.R. 121, D.C.
44 [1891] 1 Q.B. 149, 153.
45 [1894] 2 Q.B. 415, 419.
46 [1955] 1 Q.B. 540; [1955] 2 W.L.R. 116; [1955] 1 All E.R. 31, D.C.

one of the extradition crimes and therefore cannot be an offence which on the face of it is in any sense political. It follows, therefore, that to make an offence in the first limb of section 3 (1) one of a political character, there must be some quality attaching to the particular crime additional to those qualities which constitute it an offence, and therefore, it must be an offence committed with a political motive.

Foster Q. C. in reply referred to *Reg.* v. *Prater*[47]; *In re Meunier*[48]*; *Rex* v. *Secretary of State for India, Ex parte Ezekiel*[49]*; *Reg.* v. *Governor of Brixton Prison, Ex parte Kolczynski.*[50]*

Their Lordships took time for consideration.

September 6. LORD REID. My Lords, on September 3, 1961, the Government of Israel requested the extradition of the appellant who is wanted in Israel for prosecution on three charges. These are child stealing in contravention of section 188 and perjury in contravention of section 117 of the Criminal Code Ordinance, 1936, and also a charge under section 259 in regard to which no separate point is taken. **[578]**

It is not in dispute that the parents of a boy, Yossele Schuchmacher, now 10 years old, being in some temporary difficulty, agreed some time in 1957 with the boy's grandparents that he should remain with them for about a year. He remained with them until September, 1959, when the parents asked for his return. This was refused because the grandfather feared that the boy would not receive a religious education in accordance with his views. In habeas corpus proceedings the Supreme Court on February 10, 1960, ordered the grandparents to hand over the boy by February 15. They did not do so and the grandfather was sent to prison.

The appellant is an uncle of the boy being a son of these grandparents. The allegation against him is that he took the boy to a settlement at Komemiyut in January, 1960, and arranged with a family called Kot that they should keep the boy for some time, giving false names for himself and the boy. They kept the boy for about three weeks and then the appellant took him away. If the Kots' evidence is to be accepted it shows that the accused knew that the parents desired the boy's return and was hiding him from them. The charge under section 188 is based on this. The appellant maintained that the Kots' evidence is false and that he never took the boy to the settlement.

The charge of perjury is in relation to evidence given by the appellant in the course of an application made to the High Court by the parents to obtain the return of the boy. The application was against both the grandparents and the appellant who was alleged to be making common cause with the grandparents and assisting them in their determination not to return the boy. The main evidence said to be perjured was a statement by the appellant that he had not seen the boy since Hanukka which ended on January 1, 1960. The case against the appellant was dismissed after he had given this evidence.

In consequence of the request for extradition the appellant was brought before the chief magistrate at Bow Street and after proceedings spread over two months he was committed on January 12, 1962. He then applied for a writ of habeas corpus. This application was refused by a Divisional Court which granted leave to appeal to this House.

A number of points have been argued before your Lordships. That of most general importance is whether the offences charged are of a political character, but I shall first deal as briefly as possible with the other points. The first is that the Israel (Extradition) Order, 1960 (S.I. 1960 No. 1660), does not apply **[579]** to Jerusalem because that part of Jerusalem in which the Israel Government exercises jurisdiction is not part of the "territory" of Israel. I need not consider whether this would be an answer to all the charges because in my view there is no substance in the point. It is true that the British Government does not

47 [1960] 2 Q.B. 464; [1960] 2 W.L.R. 343; [1960] 1 All E.R. 298, C.C.A.
48 [1894] 2 Q.B. 415, 418.
49 [1941] 2 K.B. 169.
50 [1955] 1 Q.B. 540.

recognise the sovereignty of Israel in Jerusalem but it does recognise that the Government of Israel exercises de facto authority in the part of the city which it occupies. In my judgment neither the Extradition Act, 1870, nor the Order to which I have referred is concerned with sovereignty; they are concerned with territory in which territorial jurisdiction is exercised. In addition to other reasons which have been given or which will be given by your Lordships I would refer to article 2 of the agreement between the British Government and the Government of Israel which is incorporated in the Order. This article draws no distinction between territories over which Her Majesty exercises sovereignty and Protectorates and other territories where Her Majesty is not sovereign but where her authority is exercised. There is no question of these latter being merely deemed to be "territories" for certain purposes. I find nothing in the Extradition Acts or in this Order to indicate that territory is used in any sense which would exclude from the "territory" of Israel that part of Jerusalem in regard to which the British Government recognises the de facto authority of the Government of Israel on the ground that that Government is not recognised as sovereign there.

The next point involves the question what is the proper function and jurisdiction of this House in an appeal of this kind. I understand that others of your Lordships intend to deal more fully with this question and I shall only state my views in outline. There is no appeal in the ordinary sense from the decision of a magistrate to commit. Such review as is competent can only take place in one or other of two ways. The accused can apply for a writ of habeas corpus, and, whether he does so or not, the Secretary of State can decide not to grant the request for extradition if in the exercise of his discretion he thinks that it is proper to take that course.

This House has no wider powers than the powers of a court. I do not find it necessary in this case to define precisely what those powers are. The court, and on appeal this House, can and must consider whether on the material before the magistrate a reasonable magistrate would have been entitled to commit the accused, but neither a court nor this House can retry the case so as to substitute its discretion for that of the magistrate. **[580]**

In the first place the court must see what is the offence charged. In this case no question arises on the definition of perjury, but there is a dispute as to the meaning of section 188 of the Code. The accused maintained that on its true construction that section does not apply to this case and that is a matter which we must determine. There is no question in this case of a translation because this section of the Code is in the English language. And there is no allegation that the law of Israel adopts any different method of construction from our own or that this section has received any authoritative interpretation in Israel. So in my view it must be construed in the same way as we would construe a section of a British statute. So construing it, I agree with your Lordships that it is wide enough to cover what the accused is alleged to have done in this case.

Next it is necessary to determine whether the material before the magistrate was adequate to justify committal. The main objection to it is that the Kots or at least two of the three were accomplices and that two of the Kots were in prison when their statements were taken. It is not in dispute that the proper test for the magistrate to apply was whether, if this evidence stood alone at the trial, a reasonable jury properly directed could accept it and find a verdict of guilty. Again, for reasons which will be given by your Lordships, I agree that the chief magistrate was entitled to commit on the material before him.

The accused sought to adduce further evidence before your Lordships in order to show that on the whole material now available it would be improper to commit him. In my judgment we are not entitled to look at such evidence and we have not done so. Owing to the restricted character of habeas corpus proceedings a court is not concerned with anything that comes to light after committal. This could easily lead to injustice if the accused had no other remedy: there may well be cases where new evidence throws quite a different light on the material originally before the magistrate. But that is a matter which the Secretary of State is entitled to consider when deciding whether to grant extradition.

Different considerations apply to the question whether the offences charged were of political character. Section 3 of the Act provides: "The following restrictions shall be observed with respect to the surrender of fugitive criminals: (1) A fugitive criminal shall not be surrendered if the offence in respect of which his surrender is demanded is one of a political character, or if he prove to the satisfaction of the police magistrate or the **[581]** court before whom he is brought on habeas corpus, or to the Secretary of State, that the requisition for his surrender has in fact been made with a view to try or punish him for an offence of a political character."

The interpretation of this subsection is not free from difficulty. Not only is the word "political" capable of more than one interpretation but the two parts of the subsection do not fit well together. I do not know how this came about but I would suspect that the last part may have been added by amendment without adequate consideration of the drafting. We must, I think, approach the interpretation of the subsection with two things in mind. In the first place, offences obviously of a political character are not within the scope of extradition at all: for example, there is no mention in the Schedule to the Act of 1870 or in article 3 of the Schedule to the Israel Order of treason, sedition, or any other offence of that kind. And, secondly, section 3 (2) of the Act requires that if extradition is granted the accused is not to be tried in the foreign country for offences other than the extradition crimes: so no foreign country could without a breach of faith use extradition as a means for bringing a refugee before its courts for trial on some other political charge. On this I agree with the views expressed by Lord Parker C.J. in the present case[51] and by Lord Goddard C.J. in *Reg.* v. *Governor of Brixton Prison, Ex parte Kolczynski*,[52]* and I cannot agree with Lord Russell of Killowen's view in *In re Arton*.[53]*

It appears to me that the purpose of the latter part of section 3 (1) is to emphasise the first part and also to provide a further opportunity of proving the political character of the offence. The purpose of the subsection as a whole is to enable an accused to show that an apparently non-political offence such as murder or arson was really of a political character, and he can try to do that by proving the circumstances in which it was committed. I have already stated my view that in the ordinary case a court cannot look beyond the material which was before the magistrate, but on this question section 3 (1) expressly permits the accused to "prove to the satisfaction of . . . the court before whom he is brought on habeas corpus . . . that the requisition for his **[582]** surrender has in fact been made with a view to try or punish him for an offence of a political character."

New material on this issue was tendered to your Lordships in this case and was admitted. Some of that material would also have been relevant on the other issues in this case if it had been before the magistrate, but we intimated when admitting it that we would only consider it in relation to the political issue. The subsection also permits the accused to "prove . . . to the Secretary of State" the political character of the offence. I cannot suppose that the Secretary of State was intended to be bound by the strict rules of evidence, nor can I hold that the word "prove," which is only used once in the subsection, means something different in relation to the Secretary of State from what it means in relation to the court or the magistrate. In fact some of the material which your Lordships have admitted could not normally have been received as evidence. No doubt such material may carry less weight than properly sworn statements, but it does not surprise me that the Parliament of 1870 intended that on this question of the political character of an offence committed by a refugee nothing of any value should be excluded from consideration.

On the political issue the view of the facts most favourable to the appellant appears to me to be this. In Israel politics and religion are and have long been closely intertwined and important political parties are based on religious views. In particular, religious education is a political issue. In this case the grandfather's

[51] [1963] 1 Q.B. 55, 81-83; [1962] 2 W.L.R. 976; [1962] 2 All E.R. 176, D.C.
[52] [1955] 1 Q.B. 540, 549; [1955] 2 W.L.R. 116; [1955] 1 All E.R. 31, D.C.
[53] [1896] 1 Q.B. 108, 113; 12 T.L.R 131, D.C.

conduct appears to have been actuated by his religious beliefs and, although this does not clearly appear, I am prepared to assume that this also applies to the appellant. The fate of this boy attracted much political attention. At the time of the appellant's alleged offence a well-attended political meeting addressed by a member of the Knesset approved of the boy being kept away from his parents. The Rabbi of Jerusalem stated that the grandfather was "in duty bound to prevent with all his strength that [the boy] should not come to apostasy and go in evil ways and whosoever can render him help in this matter is in duty bound to help him with all his strength." And then there were questions and debates in the Knesset about this case. It can therefore be said that these alleged offences were committed in a political context, and that the action of the grandfather and the appellant received considerable political support.

But, in my opinion, it does not follow that the offences were of a political character. In reading the Act of 1870 one is entitled **[583]** to look through mid-Victorian spectacles. Many people then regarded insurgents against continental governments as heroes intolerably provoked by tyranny who ought to have asylum here although they might have destroyed life and property in the course of their struggles. But, although such views may have given rise to section 3 (1) of the Act of 1870, I do not think that its scope can be limited to such cases. We cannot inquire whether a "fugitive criminal" was engaged in a good or a bad cause. A fugitive member of a gang who committed an offence in the course of an unsuccessful putsch is as much within the Act as the follower of a Garibaldi. But not every person who commits an offence in the course of a political struggle is entitled to protection. If a person takes advantage of his position as an insurgent to murder a man against whom he has a grudge I would not think that that could be called a political offence. So it appears to me that the motive and purpose of the accused in committing the offence must be relevant and may be decisive. It is one thing to commit an offence for the purpose of promoting a political cause and quite a different thing to commit the same offence for an ordinary criminal purpose.

Moreover, I do not think that the application of the section can be limited to cases of open insurrection. An underground resistance movement may be attempting to overthrow a government and it could hardly be that an offence committed the day before open disturbances broke out would be treated as non-political while a precisely similar offence committed two days later would be of a political character. And I do not see why the section should be limited to attempts to overthrow a government. The use of force, or it may be other means, to compel a sovereign to change his advisers, or to compel a government to change its policy may be just as political in character as the use of force to achieve a revolution. And I do not see why it should be necessary that the refugee's party should have been trying to achieve power in the State. It would be enough if they were trying to make the government concede some measure of freedom but not attempting to supplant it.

I do not get any assistance from the statements in some of the cases that there must be "disturbance" or "political disturbance." If this merely means that the political atmosphere must be disturbed that may be so, but it gets one nowhere. The political atmosphere was disturbed in Israel over religious education. But if it means that there must have been some disturbance of public order I would not agree that that is an essential element **[584]** in a political offence. It is suggested that that must have been in the minds of members of Parliament in 1870. But I feel that if it had been suggested to Mr. Gladstone, or any other member of the Liberal majority in 1870 that asylum should be denied to a refugee who had committed an offence, perhaps of a non-violent kind, as part of a campaign to induce or compel an autocratic government to grant a measure of civil or religious liberty, on the ground that there had been no disturbance of public order, he would have indignantly denied any such intention. And I do not find anything in the words of the Act to show that such a limitation was unwittingly inserted.

It appears to me that the provisions of section 3 of the Act of 1870 are clearly intended to give effect to the principle that there should in this country be asylum for political refugees, and I do not think that it is possible, or that the Act evinces any intention to define the circumstances in which an offence can properly be held to be of a political character.

With an expression so vague as "an offence of a political character" there must be many borderline cases, for example, actions against a turbulent group trying to seize power which the government is too weak to suppress. But the present case appears to me to be beyond any possible extension of that category. I am willing to assume that the accused did what he believed to be right, and that many people, and even a whole political party, agreed with him, but I cannot find any political character in the alleged offences. There is nothing to indicate that he acted as he did in order to force or even promote a change of government, or even a change of government policy, or to achieve a political objective of any kind. I do not say that every act done for such purposes would necessarily be of a political character, but without any such purpose it could only be in some exceptional case which I cannot foresee that the act could, in my view, be said to be of a political character.

There is one other aspect which I must mention although I do not think that it affects this case. It was and is still thought that some governments treat as political offences and punish more severely such acts which we would regard as ordinary crimes, if the guilty person is a political opponent of the government, or it may be for other reasons. The last part of section 3 (1)—"the requisition for his surrender has in fact been made with a view to try or punish him for an offence of a political character"—may refer to cases of that kind. But there is not the slightest **[585]** suggestion in this case that anything of that kind could apply to the Government or the courts of Israel.

For the reasons I have given I am of opinion that none of the offences with which the accused is charged has been shown to be of a political character. In my judgment this appeal should be dismissed.

VISCOUNT RADCLIFFE. My Lords, several points were argued before your Lordships on the hearing of this appeal. I do not think it necessary to deal with each of them separately, because, with one or two qualifications which I will notice, I agree with the way that they were dealt with in the judgment of the Lord Chief Justice in the Divisional Court.[54]* I have also had the advantage of reading in advance the opinion that will be delivered by my noble and learned friend, Lord Evershed, and I agree with the reasons that he gives for rejecting the evidence tendered in the supplementary petition except so far as it bears upon the issue of "political offence."

I think it clear that in habeas corpus proceedings which arise out of a commital order under the Extradition Act, 1870, the court does not rehear the case that was before the magistrate, nor does it hear an appeal from his order. Its function, apart from considering any issue raised as to the offence charged being a political one, is to see that the prisoner is lawfully detained by his gaoler. I think that the distinction was accurately drawn by Lord Russell of Killowen C.J. in *In re Galwey*,[55]* when he said: "The prisoner then, having been taken into custody under the warrant of the chief magistrate, was brought before him, and we should, after the order of committal, be entitled to review the magistrate's decision, not in the sense of entertaining an appeal from it, but in the sense of determining whether there was evidence enough to give him jurisdiction to make the order of committal. . . . It seems to me that the only ground on which this habeas corpus can be successfully maintained is that the committal order was made without jurisdiction and was illegal."

The issue whether the offence charged is an offence of a political character raises, I think, different considerations. Having regard to the wording of section 3 (1) of the Extradition Act, 1870, this issue must be regarded as introduced by way of a special condition peculiar to the Act, in the sense that it has nothing to do with **[586]** ordinary committal proceedings not under the Act: and it seems to be the evident intention of the statute that the issue should be con-

[54] [1963] 1 Q.B. 55.
[55] [1896] 1 Q.B. 230, 236; 12 T.L.R. 150.

sidered as a substantive matter at any stage by any authority, magistrate, court or Secretary of State, which has a duty to perform in relation to the extradition. If it is so regarded, it seems to me proper to consider on its merits any evidence that is available at the time when consideration is required. I should not treat this procedure so much as depending upon the court's duty to inquire into the magistrate's jurisdiction as upon the special conditions laid down by the Act for the carrying out of an extradition request. Despite what was said to the contrary in *Reg.* v. *Governor of Brixton Prison, Ex parte Kolczynski*,[56]* to treat the court's independent review of the "political offence" question as a review of the magistrate's jurisdiction to commit would raise just the difficulty of the court's right to hear further evidence that was not before him that we meet in dealing with the rest of the evidence tendered in the supplementary petition.

I agree also with what is said by my noble and learned friend on the subject of the sufficiency of the evidence before the magistrate to make a valid prima facie case supporting the charges of child stealing and perjury upon which extradition is sought, and I share his view that when the statute in question links "fraudulently" with "forcibly" as elements of the offence, "fraudulently" must involve the use of means of deceit just as "forcibly" involves the use of force.

That leaves me with some observations to make as to the argument that the extradition agreement between the United Kingdom and the State of Israel dated April 4, 1960, does not cover an offence committed in that part of the City of Jerusalem which is in Israel's occupation, and the argument that the offences charged are political offences or offences of a political character within the meaning of the Extradition Act, 1870.

The first of these two arguments is, in my opinion, insubstantial. In effect it amounts to saying that the words in article 1 of the agreement "offences . . . committed within the territory of the one Party" does not apply to offences committed within the Israeli-occupied part of Jerusalem, because the Government of the United Kingdom, though recognising the de facto authority of the Israeli Government in that case, does not recognise that it has sovereignty de jure. Territory, it is said, unless explicitly enlarged by some special definition, can only refer to an area over **[587]** which the contracting party concerned exercises a sovereignty which is acknowledged by the other party to the convention.

This is no more than a question of construing the word "territory" in this extradition agreement and I do not feel any doubt that it covers the area of Jerusalem over which Israel exercises de facto authority recognised by the United Kingdom, the other contracting party. Extradition is a function of the international regard for the enforcement of law and order and, if a State is recognised by another State as having de facto authority in an area, I think that it would require clear words of exception to interpret an extradition agreement as excluding on the one hand its obligation to hand over fugitive criminals found within that area and, on the other, its right to claim the surrender of such criminals in respect of offences committed there. The difference between de facto and de jure recognition is, after all, essentially a difference between a provisional and a final decision: it does not bear upon distinctions between the kinds of transactions in which the two States may engage. Both parties to the agreement must have known the Jerusalem situation at the time when it was made; there is no suggestion that the United Kingdom, while recognising Israeli authority de facto, acknowledges any sovereignty or any claim to sovereignty de jure over the area in any other international party; and I think that it is the inevitable conclusion that "territory" here includes whatever is under the State's effective jurisdiction. If, for instance, a British national were to suffer some outrage in the Israeli-occupied part of Jerusalem, the United Kingdom Government would properly address itself to the Government of Israel for investigation and, possibly, redress, because it would look to that Government as responsible for the maintenance of

[56] [1955] 1 Q.B. 540, 552.

law and order by virtue of its de facto authority. Extradition is, I think, based on similar considerations.

The remaining question is, what constitutes an "offence of a political character" for the purposes of the Act? I can clear the ground a little by saying that in my opinion the Act allows for no exception under this head unless it establishes the political nature of the very offence for which extradition is sought. In other words, neither the Secretary of State nor the court is entitled to inquire under section 3 (1) whether the requesting State is asking for extradition under one charge while really intending to try or punish the fugitive for another and different offence. The suggestion that there is this alternative ground of refusal, which was made by Lord Russell of Killowen C.J. in **[588]** *In re Arton*,[57]* has not been followed since and is due, in my view, to a misreading of the section. It has been pointed out that such a ground of refusal would amount to a finding that the requesting government did not intend to observe the conditions which, by virtue of section 3 (2), it must have already accepted as binding upon it, either by its municipal law or by the extradition treaty itself. That would be difficult and awkward enough: but I think that the final argument against this construction is that it is inconceivable, having regard to the way the legislature has tackled the question of what I may call "colourable extradition" by inserting the requirements of subsection (2), that it could have intended at the same time to guard against it by authorising the very difficult and embarrassing investigation of motive which, it is suggested, the second limb of subsection (1) allows for.

I do not think that it did. In my mind subsection (1) envisages two alternative way of identifying a political offence—one, a charge that on the face of it smacks of the "political," say caricaturing the Head of State or distributing subversive pamphlets, and the other, a charge which, ostensibly criminal in the ordinary sense, is nevertheless shown to be "political" in the context in which the actual offence occurred. It is said by way of objection to this reading that none of the extraditable offences listed in the First Schedule to the Act and introduced by section 19 and section 20 is "political" in the first sense and that therefore there would be no substance in the first suggested alternative. This objection is, I think, mistaken and arises from a misunderstanding as to the place and purpose of section 3 in the scheme of the Act. It is designed as an introductory section, describing both for internal and external readers the basic principles upon which extradition was to be allowed at all. It is not closely integrated with the sections that follow, whose function it is to provide procedure and machinery for regulating extradition in accordance with these conditions. The first limb of section 3 (1) therefore makes it plain to all concerned that extradition is not to cover political offences, and in fact section 7 gives the Secretary of State an overriding power, before there is any question of taking evidence before a magistrate, to refuse a request for extradition if he takes the view that the offence concerned is one of a political character. Consistently with this idea, the list of extraditable offences is drawn up, when the Act comes to them, so as to exclude offences that are on their face "political" and as such **[589]** are barred under the first limb. But the fact that the list is in this form does nothing, in my opinion, to show in what sense the opening words "offence of a political character" are used in section 3 (1), nor for that matter does the form of the list in itself afford any guarantee that other States, applying for extradition, will always confine the wording of their requests to exact compliance with the contents of the First Schedule.

What then is an offence of a political character? The courts, I am afraid, have been asking this question at intervals ever since it was first posed judicially in 1890 in *In re Castioni*,[58]* and no definition has yet emerged or by now is ever likely to. Indeed it has come to be regarded as something of an advantage that there is to be no definition. I am ready to agree in the advantage so long as it is recognised that the meaning of such words as "a political offence," while not to be confined within a precise definition, does nevertheless represent an idea

[57] [1896] 1 Q.B. 108, 114.
[58] [1891] 1 Q.B. 149; 7 T.L.R. 50, D.C.

which is capable of description and needs description if it is to form part of the apparatus of a judicial decision.

Generally speaking, the courts' reluctance to offer a definition has been due, I think, to the realisation that it is virtually impossible to find one that does not cover too wide a range. This is seen in the very full consideration that was given to the question in *In re Castioni*,[58]* particularly when Sir Charles Russell's argument in that case[59] is set against the subsequent observations of the three judges who decided it, Denman, Hawkins and Stephen JJ. It was recalled that during the debate of 1866 that preceded the Extradition Act John Stuart Mill, then a member of the House of Commons, had suggested as a definition "any offence committed in the course of or furthering of a civil war, insurrection or political commotion," while Stephen J. himself had offered the view in his History of the Criminal Law, Vol. 2, p. 71, that political offences comprised only those crimes that were "incidental to and formed a part of political disturbances."

The court was unanimous in holding Mill's definition to be altogether too wide. The offender must be at least politically motivated. Stephen J., despite his reverence for his late friend Mr. Mill, thought that in this instance Mill had made a mistake and attributed it to the philosopher being unaccustomed to use language with the degree of precision required of a parliamentary draftsman. Speaking as a war-weary veteran in that field he **[590]** observed[60] that in drafting Acts it is not enough to attain to a degree of precision which a person reading in good faith can understand: it is necessary to attain, if possible, such a degree of precision that a person reading in bad faith cannot misunderstand. Both he and Hawkins J. therefore adhered to the explanation that he had offered in his History, Hawkins J.[61] saying that he thought it as a definition "the most perfect to be found or capable of being given as to what is the meaning of the phrase which is made use of in the Extradition Act." This was high praise, but of course it still left a considerable area open to debate as to the significance of "political" in this setting and as to the nature of the conflict that amounts to a "disturbance." Moreover, Denman J. offered a reading of the words which, without affecting to be a definition, nevertheless seems to contemplate a rather larger ambit for "political offence." "I think," he said,[62] "that in order to bring the case within the words of the Act and to exclude extradition for such an act as murder . . . , it must at least be shown that the act is done in furtherance of, done with the intention of assistance, as a sort of overt act in the course of acting in a political matter, a political rising, or a dispute between two parties in the State as to which is to have the government in its hands. . . ." Of this at least it can be said that it does not fall into the error of confining the meaning of the statutory phrase within any rigid definition.

This idea of relating a political offence to a struggle between contending parties for control of the source of political power was adopted a year or two later by Cave J. when giving the judgment of the court in *In re Meunier*.[63]* Meunier was an anarchist and suffered the misfortune of his negative creed in that he was not protected from extradition to stand trial for a bomb outrage. "It appears to me," said Cave J.,[64] "that, in order to constitute an offence of a political character, there must be two or more parties in the State, each seeking to impose the Government of their own choice on the other, and that, if the offence is committed by one side or the other in pursuance of that object, it is a political offence, otherwise not."

There, in effect, the matter has rested. I do not think that anything that has been said since in other cases has thrown much additional light on the meaning of the crucial words. They came **[591]** up for consideration recently in *Reg.* v. *Governor of Brixton Prison, Ex parte Kolczynski*,[65]* but the decision seems to me only to show that the courts are unwilling to treat what was said in *In re Castioni*[66]* as laying down any exhaustive definition of the meaning of "political offence." Certainly, it would have been difficult to decide in favour of the

[59] Ibid. 153.
[60] [1891] 1 Q.B. 149, 167.
[61] Ibid. 166.
[62] Ibid. 156.
[63] [1894] 2 Q.B. 415, D.C.
[64] Ibid. 419.
[65] [1955] 1 Q.B. 540.
[66] [1891] 1 Q.B. 149.

fugitive in that case if it were always necessary to find a "disturbance" in being reflecting an uprising, insurrection or other struggle for State power. On the other hand, if, as I think, the idea of "political offence" is not altogether remote from that of "political asylum," it is easy to regard as a political offence an offence committed by someone in furtherance of his design to escape from a political régime which he has found intolerable. I have no criticism to make of the decision in *Reg.* v. *Governor of Brixton Prison, Ex parte Kolczynski,*[67]* but the grounds on which it was decided are expressed too generally to offer much useful guidance for other cases in the future.

In my opinion the idea that lies behind the phrase "offence of a political character" is that the fugitive is at odds with the State that applies for his extradition on some issue connected with the political control or government of the country. The analogy of "political" in this context is with "political" in such phrases as "political refugee," "political asylum" or "political prisoner." It does indicate, I think, that the requesting State is after him for reasons other than the enforcement of the criminal law in its ordinary, what I may call its common or international, aspect. It is this idea that the judges were seeking to express in the two early cases of *In re Castioni*[68]* and *In re Meunier*[69]* when they connected the political offence with an uprising, a disturbance, an insurrection, a civil war or struggle for power: and in my opinion it is still necessary to maintain the idea of that connection. It is not departed from by taking a liberal view as to what is meant by disturbance or these other words, provided that the idea of political opposition as between fugitive and requesting State is not lost sight of: but it would be lost sight of, I think, if one were to say that all offences were political offences, so long as they could be shown to have been committed for a political object or with a political motive or for the furtherance of some political cause or campaign. There may, for instance, be all sorts of contending political organisations or forces **[592]** in a country and members of them may commit all sorts of infractions of the criminal law in the belief that by so doing they will further their political ends: but if the central government stands apart and is concerned only to enforce the criminal law that has been violated by these contestants, I see no reason why fugitives should be protected by this country from its jurisdiction on the ground that they are political offenders.

In my opinion the offences charged against the appellant do not come within the conception of offences of a political character. If the charges are made good, what he has done is to involve himself in a family quarrel, taking the side of his father against that of his sister and her husband. Since, at this stage at any rate, he has offered no explanation of his actions, the inference is that the child-stealing and perjury alleged were committed in order to further the purposes of his father and the beliefs to which his father is committed. Those beliefs are, it seems, concerned with religious, educational, social principles, and they are, no doubt, matters of acute controversy in the State of Israel. More, parties, though not particularly political parties, divide upon these issues and they have political implications. This case has evidently become to some extent a political issue. But the evidence does not suggest that the appellant's offences, if committed, were committed as a demonstration against any policy of the Government of Israel itself or that he has been abetting those who oppose the Government. What he is said to have done is much more ascribable either to filial piety or to an independent wish to take his father's side in the quarrel. Indeed, from what I can learn from the evidence, which is unavoidably vague in a matter of this kind, the Government of Israel is not, either currently or generally, formed upon a straight division between the orthodox and the non-orthodox Jew and, as Mr. Adé Efrat testified in the magistrate's court, "the bringing up of children is not a matter of government policy. . . . Part of the opposition, and also part of the Government, consists of very orthodox Jewry." Nothing in the rest of the evidence contributed by Bishop Stewart, Mr. Eden, Mr. Marmorstein, and Mr. Kugler contradicts this general summary.

[67] [1955] 1 Q.B. 540.
[68] [1891] 1 Q.B. 149.
[69] [1894] 2 Q.B. 415.

For the reasons that I have given I would dismiss the appeal.

I should add that my noble and learned friend, Lord Jenkins, who is not able to be present today, has asked me to say that he concurs in the dismissal of the appeal. **[593]**

Lord Evershed. My Lords, the submission made, naturally and logically, first on the appellant's behalf was that the sector of the ancient city of Jerusalem which has been occupied as part of the State of Israel ought not properly to be regarded as within the "territory" of Israel within the meaning of article 1 of the First Schedule to the Israel (Extradition) Order, 1960. The submission was founded upon the language of the communication made by the British Foreign Office dated October 4, 1961, and recited in the judgment of the Lord Chief Justice. From this communication it appears that although His Majesty's Government accorded "de jure" recognition to the State of Israel on April 27, 1950, that recognition was so far qualified that His Majesty's Government did not recognise "the sovereignty of Israel over that part of Jerusalem which she occupies though, pending a final determination of the status of the area, they recognise that Israel exercises de facto authority in it." So it was suggested on the appellant's behalf that the relevant part of Jerusalem must be treated, for the purposes of the Order of 1960 and of the agreement therein recited between the Governments of this country and of Israel, as outside the "territory" of the latter. My Lords, upon this matter I am fully content to adopt the conclusion and the reasoning of the Lord Chief Justice.[70] It is not in doubt that ever since 1950 the State of Israel has exercised to the fullest extent jurisdiction for all practical purposes over this part of Jerusalem. Therein are situated Israel's seat of government and its legislature, as also its Supreme Court—in which the appellant in fact made the statements which are the foundation of the charge of perjury against him. I agree with the Lord Chief Justice that in the context of the Order and the agreement and of the Extradition Acts by virtue of which the Order was made the "territory" of any State must prima facie mean the area in which the jurisdiction of that State is practically and normally exercised; a view which, as the Lord Chief Justice observed, finds particular support in the language of sections 25 and 26 of the Extradition Act, 1870. It should also be noticed that although His Majesty's Government in 1950 felt unable to recognise the de jure sovereignty of Israel over the relevant part of Jerusalem there was and is no suggestion that such sovereignty resided or resides in some country other than Israel. Moreover, as the Lord Chief Justice also observed, a contrary conclusion would inevitably render the operation of the **[594]** agreement wholly one-sided and absurd if not, indeed, entirely ineffective.

The next question to be considered was that presented by the appellant's supplementary petition, namely, whether or to what extent it was competent or proper for your Lordships to look at certain further evidence which had come into the appellant's possession since the hearing before the Divisional Court. The purpose and effect of the additional evidence was, first, to discredit the evidence upon which the magistrate had reached his conclusion and, secondly, to supplement the evidence which was before the magistrate to the effect that the crimes of which the appellant has been charged are "of a political character" and therefore, by the terms of section 3 (1) of the Extradition Act, 1870, and likewise by the terms of article 6 of the agreement between the Governments of the United Kingdom and of Israel, such as to disqualify the magistrate from making any order for committal in respect thereof.

Your Lordships were informed that the evidence under the first head consisted of other statements made by those whose affirmations had been before the magistrate, tending to contradict them; and also evidence showing that the circumstances in which the affirmations were made were such as to discredit them. Upon this part of his case Mr. Foster urged before your Lordships that the Government of Israel, as the Requesting Party for the appellant's extradition, was in the same position as the Crown in any prosecution in this country; that

[70] [1963] 1 Q.B. 55, 74-76.

is to say, was bound to bring before the court any evidence or information in its possession favourable to the case of the accused. Although, therefore, it was not positively suggested that the Government of Israel had withheld or concealed the fresh evidence, nevertheless it was urged that upon the general principles applicable to a prosecution in this country such further evidence should be received by your Lordships.

Mr. Caplan, on behalf of the Government of Israel, did not oppose the reception of this part of the evidence by your Lordships provided that your Lordships read also certain further sworn statements prepared on the Government's behalf since the presentation of the supplemental petition. On behalf, however, of the Governor of Brixton Prison, Mr. Buzzard submitted that upon well-established principle and authority such further evidence could not be received by your Lordships. It is not in doubt that Mr. Buzzard was entitled to be heard upon this matter, the **[595]** Governor of the prison being a respondent to the appeal and having the appellant in his custody by the order of the magistrate.

In considering this question it cannot be in doubt that the jurisdiction and duties of your Lordships are by section 1 (4) of the Administration of Justice Act, 1960, the same as those of the Divisional Court, and I think it clear that the jurisdiction and functions of the Divisional Court in such a case as the present rest upon authority which has long been accepted. I am content to refer to the two cases of *Rex* v. *Governor of Holloway Prison, Ex parte Siletti*[71]* in 1902 and of *Rex* v. *Governor of Brixton Prison, Ex parte Perry*[72]* 22 years later. Both were cases of fugitive offenders under the Extradition Acts and in both the attempt was made, but rejected, to review the decision of the magistrate, upon an application for habeas corpus on the part of the person committed, by reference to fresh evidence produced since the date of the committal order. In the earlier case[73] Bigham J., after observing that the right to apply by way of habeas corpus was a common law right expressly made available to the committed person by the Extradition Acts, held that the right and competence of the court to have regard to such fresh evidence were limited to cases where such evidence went to the question of the magistrate's jurisdiction at the date of the committal order; by showing, for example, that the crime charged was outside the scope of the extradition agreement as being of a political character or otherwise not comprehended in the crimes enumerated in the agreement; or by showing that there was in truth no evidence at all to justify the magistrate's exercise of his discretionary jurisdiction to commit. In the same case Darling J. pointed out[74] that the principle applicable was the same as that applicable to a case of committal by justices for trial upon indictment in this country and that in neither case was the function of the Divisional Court that of an appellate court from the magistrate's decision or of a court hearing an application for a new trial. In the second case (that of *Ex parte Perry*[75]*) the reasoning of the court in *Ex parte Siletti*[76]* was affirmed, the judges expressing themselves as unwilling to accept certain obiter dicta inclining to a different view in the case of *In re Castioni*.[77]*

My Lords, I cannot doubt that the reasoning in *Ex parte* **[596]** *Siletti*[78]* and *Ex parte Perry*[79]* is well founded and should be accepted. As was observed by the Lord Chief Justice in the present case,[80] it must be assumed by the courts of this country that one who is extradited to Israel under the agreement between the Governments of the United Kingdom and Israel will be in Israel fairly and properly tried on the charges made against him. It follows, therefore, in my opinion, that the analogy is a true one between a committal by a magistrate in such a case as the present and a committal by justices for trial upon an indictment in this country and it cannot be suggested that in the latter case there is

[71] (1902) 20 Cox C.C. 353; 18 T.L.R. 771, D.C.
[72] [1924] 1 K.B. 455; 40 T.L.R. 181, D.C.
[73] 20 Cox C.C. 353, 357.
[74] Ibid. 358, 359.
[75] [1924] 1 K.B. 455.
[76] 20 Cox C.C. 353.
[77] [1891] 1 Q.B. 149.
[78] 20 Cox C.C. 353.
[79] [1924] 1 K.B. 455.
[80] [1963] 1 Q.B. 55, 82.

in the Divisional Court or in your Lordships' House any competence or duty to review the exercise by the magistrate of his powers if the proceedings before him were regular in form and practice and the subject-matter was one within the magistrate's jurisdiction. The principle applicable is of long standing and is the same and necessarily the same as that to be applied wherever final jurisdiction is conferred upon the magistrate's court—see particularly the judgment of Lord Denman C.J. in the case in 1841 of *Reg.* v. *Bolton*,[81] a case of an application for certiorari to quash an order of justices for delivery of a house to parish officers under the statute 59 Geo. 3, c. 12.

It may sometimes be a nice question whether the fresh evidence goes in truth to the magistrate's jurisdiction but your Lordships have been referred to no reported case in which fresh evidence has been received for the purpose merely of impeaching the magistrate's decision on the facts which were before him. It would therefore in my judgment be contrary to well-established principle for your Lordships to allow the receipt of such evidence in such a case as the present on the ground suggested by Mr. Foster. I add that in a case such as the present it is not to be forgotten that the man charged has the additional protection of the discretion of the Secretary of State under section 11 of the Extradition Act, 1870. Although, as I think, your Lordships have no competence to receive fresh evidence with a view to showing that the magistrate's decision might or should have been other than it was, it is no less clear that such fresh evidence may and should be weighed by the Secretary of State in whose power it is, if he thinks proper in the exercise of his discretion, to decline to order the extradition of the person charged.

I have so far confined myself to what I earlier called the first **[597]** head of the appellant's submission on the supplementary petition, that is, in regard to the fresh evidence submitted otherwise than in relation to the question whether the crimes with which he has been charged are of "a political character." It will, however, follow from what I have said that in so far as such fresh evidence is related to the alleged political character of the crimes charged, it goes not to the question of the magistrate's exercise of his discretionary powers and duties but to his jurisdiction. It follows that your Lordships are both competent and bound to receive such fresh evidence as tends to show that the crimes here charged were of a political character and therefore altogether outside the scope of the agreement between the respective Governments of the United Kingdom and Israel. To that extent, therefore, but to that extent only, I think your Lordships were entitled and bound to receive and consider the fresh evidence and rightly allowed the supplementary petition for such purpose.

Your Lordships have accordingly read, in addition to the evidence that was before the magistrate and the Divisional Court, the statement of a Mr. Kugler and other material, but have done so only upon the question whether the crimes here charged are of "a political character" as that phrase is used in the Extradition Act, 1870, and the United Kingdom and Israel extradition agreement. In the circumstances I find it convenient to express my view next upon that question.

It appears not at all to be in doubt that both the appellant and his father, the grandfather of the boy Yossele, are fervent adherents of what is called Jewish orthodoxy and that such adherence is the reason for the grandfather's sustained refusal to hand over the boy to his parents—notwithstanding the orders of the Israeli High Court of January 16 and February 10, 1960—on the ground that to do so would expose the boy to the evils of apostasy and of an education not proper for an orthodox Jew. It appears also from the evidence that the orthodox Jews—and the epithets "fanatical" and "bigoted" were used and adopted by Mr. Foster in respect of them—find themselves, by reason of their religious beliefs, generally opposed to the Mapai and other leading political parties in the State and, indeed, to all forms of "secular" government. It may, finally, be taken from Mr. Kugler's statement that the orthodox Jews are considerably organised in the promotion of their views and (more particularly for present purposes) were so organised in the steps taken by the boy's grandfather and those co-

[81] (1841) 1 Q.B. 66.

operating with him to save the boy from apostasy; and to that end, where necessary, a defiance **[598]** of the laws of the State was in the view of those persons justified by Divine command.

So it was contended by Mr. Foster that the religious fanaticism of the orthodox Jews was so necessarily and inevitably involved with "politics" (that is, in resistance to the government and the laws of the land) that the crimes here charged, being expressions of the religious tenets of the orthodox Jews, were, no less necessarily and inevitably, crimes of "a political character."

My Lords, I find myself, with the Lord Chief Justice, unable to accept the submission, even when fortified by the additional material which your Lordships have received. It is no doubt true that religious faith may at times involve defiance of the laws and of government. But in my judgment the exception with which we are concerned and which found expression in the Extradition Act, 1870, was not and cannot have been intended to have so wide and imprecise a scope. I agree with my noble and learned friends Lord Reid and Viscount Radcliffe in thinking that a proper construction of the formula calls for due regard to be had to the historical circumstances in which the Act of 1870 was passed and that the exception was intended for the protection of those who had sought political asylum in this country from the repressions of their own countries. There can be no question in the present case of the crimes with which the appellant is charged having been committed "in the course of or furthering of civil war, insurrection, or political commotion" the suggested definition of John Stuart Mill cited by Sir Charles Russell in his argument but regarded by all the judges as too wide in the case of *In re Castioni.*[82]* I do not myself attempt any definition. But it is at least clear from the evidence that the Government of Israel, so far from having attempted a forcible suppression of the orthodox Jews, has from time to time made concessions to their tenets. I am content, therefore, to say that the formula with which we are concerned cannot extend to cover the crimes here charged which, if committed, were, at the most, the expression and consequence of religious belief and could not be called "political" within the meaning of the Act and the agreement merely because adherence to or pursuit of such faith might at all times call for a disregard or defiance of civil law. If those alleged to have co-operated in the removal of the boy to the Komemiyut Settlement had committed a robbery, say, upon a bank in order to provide themselves with funds for the boy's maintenance, it **[599]** would in my opinion be no more proper or appropriate to treat the robbery as a crime of a "political character" than it would so to treat the crime with which the appellant has here been charged.

Upon the difference of view upon the language of section 3 (1) of the Extradition Act, 1870, between Lord Russell of Killowen C.J. in the case of *Arton* (*No. 1*)[83]* and Lord Goddard C.J. in the so-called *Polish Seamen's* case (*Reg.* v. *Governor of Brixton Prison, Ex parte Kolczynski*[84]*) I do not dissent from the opinions of my noble and learned friends Lord Reid and Viscount Radcliffe supporting the conclusion of the Lord Chief Justice. But, as it seems to me, the question upon which the divergence of view arose does not in truth call for determination in the present case because it has not been suggested in any event before us that the appellant, if extradited, to Israel, would there be "tried or punished" for any offences other than those with which he has now been charged.

There remains only the question whether upon the evidence before him there was justification for the magistrate's committal of the appellant upon the two charges of perjury and child stealing which, if they are not crimes of "a political character" are admittedly, as crimes, within the ambit of the extradition agreement between the United Kingdom and Israel.

Upon this question it is, I apprehend, necessary to have two things in mind; first, that your Lordships are concerned not with a conviction but with a committal; and, secondly, that the Divisional Court having affirmed the magistrate's order, your Lordships would be slow to express a different conclusion upon what are, essentially, matters of fact.

[82] [1891] 1 Q.B. 149.
[83] [1896] 1 Q.B. 108.
[84] [1955] 1 Q.B. 540.

I take first the alleged perjury. If the evidence of Shlomo Kot, Rachel Kot and Reuben Kot is true, it cannot be in doubt that the appellant was actively assisting his father in withholding the boy Yossele from his parents, and that some two or three weeks after a date which is accepted as being January 1, 1960, the appellant personally took the boy to the Komemiyut Settlement and saw him there afterwards on some two occasions before he was removed therefrom. But in an affidavit made before the High Court of Israel on February 25, 1960, the appellant swore: "I am not assisting or encouraging my parents or one of them in any decision whatsoever concerning . . . the boy." Further, according to the testimony of one Sergeant Tischler which was **[600]** before the magistrate the appellant, in the course of giving sworn evidence before the same High Court on May 12, 1960, stated that he had not seen the boy after January 1, 1960, though he is recorded in certain notes produced by him as later adding: "I do not remember whether I spoke to the child between" dates which covered (as I understand) the month of January and the first 10 days of February 1960.

I take the proper test to be the test which was accepted by the Lord Chief Justice, namely, that there must be before the magistrate such evidence that, if it be uncontradicted at the trial, a reasonably minded jury may convict upon it. Applying this test it cannot, as it seems to me, be seriously suggested that, upon the facts as I have stated them, there was not before the magistrate evidence upon which, in the proper exercise of his discretion, he could, on the charge of perjury, commit the appellant. I leave for consideration on the charge of child stealing the point made by Mr. Foster that the evidence of the Kots ought to have been rejected as being that of "accomplices"; for, with the Lord Chief Justice, I find some difficulty in seeing how the Kots could in any case be regarded as "accomplices" upon the perjury charge. And I am comforted upon this part of the case by the fact that, apart from its being a "political crime," Mr. Foster did not address much argument upon this charge before your Lordships. I only add that, like the Lord Chief Justice, I cannot regard the last alleged statement of the appellant according to the notes produced by the appellant, which I have already recited, as relevantly qualifying what he had, according to Sergeant Tischler's evidence, earlier stated.

I come finally to the child stealing charge. The offence is defined by section 188 of the Israeli Criminal Code Ordinance of 1936 in the following terms, so far as relevant: "Any person who, with intent to deprive any parent, guardian or other person who has the lawful care of charge of a child under the age of fourteen years, of the possession of such child:—(*a*) forcibly or fraudulently takes or entices away, or detains the child . . . is guilty of a felony." There follows a proviso: "It is a defence to a charge of any of the offences defined in this section to prove that the accused person claimed in good faith a right to the possession of the child."

The section raises difficulties of construction upon which Mr. Foster fastened. But it will be useful first to state what, if the evidence of the Kots be true, were the relevant facts. According to that evidence the appellant at some date about two or three **[601]** weeks after January 1, 1960, arrived with the boy at the Komemiyut Settlement and handed him over to Shlomo Kot. The appellant then stated that there was a dispute as to the upbringing of the boy between his father and mother which rendered it desirable that the boy should for a short period have asylum at the settlement. The appellant gave the boy's name as Israel Hazan. The appellant and the boy were identified by all three Kots by means of photographs.

So much for the evidence of the Kots. It is not in doubt that upon their arrival in Israel in 1957 the boy's parents, who were then without a home or occupation, handed the boy over, together with his sister, to the children's grandparents (the parents of the appellant and of the children's mother), but, having then substantially established themselves, demanded of the grandparents the return of the two children at some date in the latter part of 1959; whereupon the girl but not the boy was so returned. The parents then, in January, 1960, took proceedings in the Israeli High Court against the grandparents, obtaining an order nisi on January 16 calling upon the grandparents to show cause why they should not bring the boy into court so that he might be dealt with as the court should direct. The grandparents justified their refusal to deliver the boy to the court on the religious ground already mentioned. On February 10 the President of the High Court made the order nisi absolute, and in the course of his judgment stated that nothing had occurred which in the boy's interest deprived his father and mother of their natural right, as parents, to their own child. The grandparents maintained their refusal to comply with the orders of the court. Committal proceedings were accordingly instituted against the grandparents, the appellant being also joined as respondent on the ground that he was actively aiding and abetting his father in disregard of the court's order. The grandfather was committed to prison but no order was made against the appellant, having regard to the evidence then given by him to which I have already alluded. But it is, in my judgment, impossible in all the circumstances to resist the conclusion upon the whole of the evidence (including that of the Kots, if it be accepted) that the appellant was at least very well aware of the demands made for their son by his parents and of the parents' efforts to recover his possession.

But Mr. Foster submitted that the case nonetheless fell outside the scope and true interpretation of section 188 of the Criminal Code. It was Mr. Foster's contention that at all relevant dates the grandparents still had—or were at least entitled in good **[602]** faith to claim that they had—the right to "possession" of the child; at any rate that the boy's parents had not his "lawful care or charge," so that the appellant could not be said to have had the intent to deprive them of the boy's "possession" within the meaning of the section.

My Lords, the language of the section may present some difficulties of interpretation. It may not be clear whether the phrase "who has the lawful care or charge of a child under the age of fourteen years" qualifies the word "parent." There is at the least much to be said for the view that it does not. But even if it does, I do not doubt that in the months of January and February 1960 it was to the parents and not the grandparents that the "lawful care or charge"—that is, as I understand the phrase, the right according to law to the care and charge—of the boy belonged. In the absence of special circumstances I take it that by the law of Israel, as by the law of England, the parents of a child are regarded as prima facie entitled to his or her care and charge; and it is to be noted in this case that by the judgment of February 10, the High Court of Israel had stated that nothing in the present case had occurred to deprive the boy's parents of their ordinary and natural right.

It was pointed out in the course of the argument before your Lordships that the word "possession" may not be entirely apt as regards a child. But in the context of the section, including the proviso, I cannot doubt that by the phrase "to deprive any parent . . . of the possession of such child" is meant and intended "to deprive any parent of the right which he has at law to the custody of the child."

I therefore, for my part, entirely agree with the Divisional Court in thinking that upon the evidence, including that of the Kots (if accepted), there was ample justification for the magistrate's view that the appellant by his conduct had intended to deprive the boy's parents, who had at the relevant dates the lawful care or charge of him, of their "possession" of the boy, within the meaning of the section.

There remains the qualification implied by the adverb "fraudulently." I am unable to accept the view that the word means no more than "with intent to prejudice the parents' rights." In my opinion the word inevitably involves the use of deceit whether practised upon the child or upon any other person. In this respect the word must have, as it seems to me, the same significance as the phrase "by fraud" in section 56 of the (English) Offences against the Person Act, 1861, and should be **[603]** construed by your Lordships in the same sense (see *Reg.* v. *Bellis*[85]). But on the facts of the present case, if the evidence of the Kots is true, there can be no doubt of the appellant's deceit. He told the Kots that there was a dispute as regards the boy's upbringing between his father and mother—a statement which, if the evidence be accepted, he must have known

[85] (1883) 17 Cox C.C. 660; 9 T.L.R. 518.

to be quite untrue. It is difficult to resist the conclusion that the appellant made the statement in order to lead or "deceive" the Kots into a ready acceptance of the boy. Again, on the same evidence, the appellant gave to the boy, deliberately, a false name. The inference I think to be no less obvious.

My Lords, for the reasons which I have given I can feel no doubt that upon the evidence before the magistrate there was justification for his order for committal upon the charge of child stealing. There remains, however, the point most strongly pressed by Mr. Foster, namely, that the evidence of the Kots was so tainted as evidence of accomplices that it should not have been accepted. True it is that all those witnesses had been arrested upon charges in connection with the boy Yossele, and of them only Rachel had been released on bail when their affirmations were made. But they had not, at the date of their affirmations, been formally charged, still less had they been convicted—nor have they since been convicted. My Lords, I venture to recall what I earlier observed—that we are here concerned with a committal not a conviction; and I know of no rule which would disable a magistrate in such a case as the present from paying regard to the evidence of the Kots in the proper exercise of his jurisdiction. It follows, in my opinion, that there was before the magistrate evidence which, upon the application of the test already noticed, sufficed to justify his order, and that no adequate ground has been shown upon which your Lordships could reverse the conclusion of the Divisional Court in supporting that order. It remains for the Secretary of State to weigh independently all the matters to which Mr. Foster has so forcibly alluded and also (as I have earlier stated) to consider the fresh evidence which your Lordships have felt to be outside their powers to receive.

My Lords, I would dismiss this appeal.

Lord Hodson. My Lords, upon this appeal from the Divisional Court the appellant now detained in H.M. Prison at Brixton seeks a writ of habeas corpus. He is detained in pursuance of a warrant **[604]** of committal dated January 12, 1962, awaiting delivery to the State of Israel pursuant to the Extradition Acts, 1870 to 1935.

The charges on which he was committed were: (1) Perjury for that he on May 12, 1960, during proceedings in an application in the High Court of Justice of Israel knowingly gave false evidence touching a matter material in those proceedings contrary to section 117 of the Criminal Code Ordinance, 1936. (2) Child stealing (a) on a date between January 1 and February 15, 1960, with intent to deprive Alter and Ida Schuchmacher of their son Joseph [Yossele] (born in 1952) fraudulently detained him in the house of Shlomo Zalman Kot at Komemiyut, contrary to section 188 of the said ordinance. A further charge of wrongfully confining Joseph knowing that he was an abducted person is no longer material. The offences are extraditable under an agreement concluded on April 4, 1960, between H.M. Government in the United Kingdom and the Government of the State of Israel to which the Extradition Acts were made to apply by an Order in Council entitled "the Israel Extradition Order, 1960."

A preliminary point was taken that since the perjury is alleged to have been committed in Jerusalem, and the depositions in the case on all charges were taken in Jerusalem, this city not being part of the territory of Israel, the Extradition Acts have no application, the position being that Her Majesty's Government recognises that Israel exercises de facto (not de jure) authority in that part of the city which is occupied by the State of Israel. I agree with the learned Lord Chief Justice and with your Lordships that in its context the word "territory" where it appears includes territory over which H.M. Government recognises that Israel exercises de facto authority, and that so far as extradition is concerned as between Israel and the United Kingdom, no distinction is to be drawn between the conceptions de jure and de facto.

The facts giving rise to the charges may be summarised as follows:

Mr. and Mrs. Schuchmacher have two children, Zina now aged about 15 and Yosef or Yossele now aged about 10. About 1957 the parents left the two children in Jerusalem in charge of the mother's parents, Nachman and Miriam

Schtraks. This was a temporary measure due to the difficulties the parents had in making a living and having to change their home. In due course the daughter was returned but when, about September 1959, the mother asked for her son the grandfather, Nachman Schtraks, refused to return him, giving the reason that if he did so, Yossele would not be given the education proper to an orthodox Jew. It **[605]** was contended by the grandparents that it was in the interests of Yossele to remain with them, that he wished to do so, and that they feared lest the parents would emigrate and take him to Russia. On February 10, 1960, the grandparents were ordered to hand over Yossele to his parents by February 15. The whereabouts of Yossele were not disclosed and the order was not complied with. Contempt proceedings were brought by the parents against the grandparents and in those proceedings the appellant, Shalom Schtraks, son of the grandparents and uncle of Yossele, was joined as having encouraged the grandparents to withhold the boy in defiance of the order. In those proceedings the appellant gave evidence to the effect that he had not seen Yossele since January 1, 1960, and no order was made against him, but the grandfather was committed to be imprisoned until he had handed over the boy. On May 23, 1960, the appellant came to this country.

Meanwhile, the police in Israel made extensive searches and inquiries, and in the course of them, in August 1961, arrested three persons who lived at Komemiyut Settlement about 30 miles from Jerusalem. These were Shlomo Kot, Rachel Kot, his wife, and Reuben Kot, his brother. All three made affirmations to the effect that after January 1, 1960, a young man and a small boy whom they identified from photographs as the appellant and Yossele had come to the settlement.

The effect of their evidence is that the appellant was concealing Yossele and calling him by a false name at a time when, according to the appellant's sworn evidence, he had not seen Yossele at all.

Before considering the two charges in detail your Lordships were asked to receive further evidence which had come into the appellant's possession since the hearing before the Divisional Court. So far as this further evidence was tendered in order to contradict or discredit the evidence given before the magistrates, the evidence is clearly inadmissable. Proceedings by way of habeas corpus are not appeal proceedings, and counsel for the Governor of Brixton Prison rightly submitted that fresh evidence can only be received to show lack of jurisdiction in the magistrate ab initio, and in some cases to cure a technical defect in the proceedings with this exception, that under section 3 (1) of the Extradition Act, 1870, evidence is admissable to prove the political character of the crime, or to prove that the requisition for the surrender of the fugitive has in fact been made to try or punish him for an offence of a political character.

Proceeding by habeas corpus is analogous to that by certiorari **[606]** to remove a conviction, see Short and Mellor's Crown Practice (1908), p. 319. Affidavits are not admissable to controvert facts found by the judgment of a court of competent jurisdiction, though they may be received to show some extrinsic collateral matter essential to jurisdiction or to show total want or excess of jurisdiction. With regard to summary committals by justices it may very well be assumed that the same principles will be applied as on seeking to quash an order by certiorari, see Short and Mellor, p. 328. The truth or falsity of the charge does not determine the jurisdiction and the decision of the inferior court cannot be questioned, see the judgment of Lord Denman C.J. in *Reg.* v. *Bolton.*[86]

Committal under the Extradition Act is on the same footing as committal for trial by a magistrate in an ordinary case and, indeed, before 1848, habeas corpus would be used in ordinary cases coming before a magistrate.

In re Galwey[87]* is an example of an application for habeas corpus under the Extradition Act. There Lord Russell C.J. said[88]: "we should, after the order of committal, be entitled to review the magistrate's decision, not in the sense of entertaining an appeal from it, but in the sense of determining whether there was evidence enough to give him jurisdiction to make the order of committal: I

[86] 1 Q.B. 66, 71, 72, 73.
[87] [1896] 1 Q.B. 230.
[88] Ibid. 236.

mean evidence of the offence and of other necessary conditions for the application of the Act when the chief magistrate made the order of committal under which the prisoner is now in custody. It seems to me that the only ground on which this habeas corpus can be successfully maintained is that the committal order was made without jurisdiction and was illegal."

In *Rex* v. *Governor of Holloway Prison, Ex parte Siletti*,[89]* further evidence which might have affected the magistrate's decision was not admitted, and the sense in which the word "jurisdiction" is used was explained by Darling J.[90] Bigham J. said[91]: "the only question that this court can entertain is the question of jurisidction, and, applying that observation to this particular Act, all that the accused person may say is that the crime with which he was charged was not a crime within the meaning of the Extradition Act—that is to say, that it did not come within the class of offences contemplated, or that it **[607]** was an offence of a political character, and therefore was outside the Act altogether. He may also say that there was absolutely no evidence upon which the magistrate could exercise his discretion as to whether he would commit or not. These things he may say: but I am clearly of opinion there is one thing he cannot say namely, that there is evidence one way and the other, and that this court ought to enter into the consideration as to whether the magistrate has exercised his discretion as to it properly. That he cannot say."

The learned judge then went on to express his doubt as to some of the observations of Denman and Hawkins JJ. in the case of *In re Castioni*,[92]* which appeared to him, as they do to me, to be out of line with settled authority on this topic. These observations were obiter dicta and lend but slender support to the appellant's argument in this case.

Darling J. said in the course of his judgment[93]: "jurisdiction is not quite the right word to use. It is used by my brother Bigham, as I understand it, to cover a good deal more than is usually meant when we use the word jurisdiction in ordinary cases. It is used to cover want of jurisdiction in the magistrate—that is, want of that which would properly be called jurisdiction. It is also used to cover the case of there being no evidence against the accused at all . . . in such a case as that this court would go into the matter, and on ascertaining that there was no evidence, would make the rule absolute for a habeas corpus."

The appellant on this part of the case places reliance on a decision of the Privy Council (not strictly speaking of binding authority) in *Kossekechatko* v. *Attorney-General for Trinidad*,[94]* where on appeal to the Privy Council a piece of evidence was admitted in the prisoner's defence which had not been previously available. I do not know how this evidence came to be admitted. The case was argued on the footing that there was no evidence that the conviction of any of the appellants would have been possible under French law unless the crimes of which they had been convicted had in fact been committed in French territory. The appeal succeeded on this submission (which went to jurisdiction) being accepted, and in looking at an affidavit of a French lawyer, as they appear to have done, the Board of the Privy **[608]** Council did no more than remove a doubt which had already been resolved in favour of the prisoner.

The appellant also relies on certain cases wherein the Crown has been allowed to cure a technicality or fill a lacuna which, while it remained uncorrected or unfilled, would prima facie give the prisoner a right to the writ, although it would avail him little since he could be rearrested and the technicality corrected or the gap in the prosecution's case filled without difficulty. Examples of such cases are: *Rex* v. *Governor of Brixton Prison, Ex parte Percival*[95]*; *Rex* v. *Governor of Brixton Prison, Ex parte Servini*[96]* and *Reg.* v. *Governor of Brixton Prison, Ex parte Shuter*.[97]*

These decisions are, I think, justified on the basis that habeas corpus is not

[89] 20 Cox C.C. 353.
[90] Ibid. 358.
[91] Ibid. 357, 358.
[92] [1891] 1 Q.B. 149.
[93] 20 Cox C.C. 353, 358.
[94] [1932] A.C. 78; 48 T.L.R. 27, P.C.
[95] [1907] 1 K.B. 696; 23 T.L.R. 238, D.C.
[96] [1914] 1 K.B. 77; 30 T.L.R. 35, D.C.
[97] [1960] 2 Q.B. 89; [1959] 3 W.L.R. 603; [1959] 2 All E.R. 782, D.C.

granted on a mere technicality. In *Servini's* case[98]* Bailhache J., who doubted the propriety of refusing the writ, said: "I have no doubt that they" (the other members of the court) "are right in saying that the writ ought not necessarily to issue where the court is satisfied that although the applicant may not be quite regularly in custody yet substantially and on the merits he is properly in custody."

The appellant naturally contends that when he asks for further evidence in this case his application ought to be favourably considered, since the demands of justice will not be met if lacunae can be filled upon the application of the requesting government and not for the accused. I accept the logic of this argument but remain of the opinion that these cases do not justify any further inroad on the general rule that there cannot be in these cases a reconsideration of evidence "one way and the other."

I am of the opinion that fresh evidence as to the guilt of the accused cannot properly be received.

What I have said above applies to the criticisms which have been levelled at the character and position of the witnesses, the three Kots. The magistrate did not exceed his jurisdiction in receiving their evidence, even if the witnesses were in prison when they made their declarations, so that they may have had an inducement to give evidence against the appellant so as to secure their own release. Similarly, he did not exceed his jurisdiction whether or not any of them turn out to be accomplices, and for that reason witnesses whose evidence by our practice is not acceptable without a direction to the jury that they should not **[609]** convict unless they think the evidence of the accomplice is corroborated. This is not to say that a case can be withdrawn from a jury for want of corroboration, or that a magistrate has no discretion as to whether the evidence is or is not sufficient to justify a committal. See *In re Meunier.*[99]*

The appellant contends that even as the matter stands there was no evidence upon which he could be committed on either of the charges, that is to say, no evidence upon which, if uncontradicted at the trial, a reasonably-minded jury might commit. So far as perjury is concerned, I agree with what was said by the Lord Chief Justice in the Divisional Court.[1] There can be no question but that the alleged perjury was material to the issue being determined by the court when the evidence now said to be false was given. As to the supposed qualification of the untrue piece of evidence in that the appellant said: "I do not remember whether I spoke to the child between Hanukka and the trial," this is nothing to the point, for if his first statement that he had last seen the child before Hanukka was deliberately untrue, there is no reason to assume that his second statement was any the less deliberately untrue.

As to child stealing, I would refer to the words of section 188 of the Criminal Code Ordinance which reads:

"Any person who with intent to deprive any parent guardian or other person who has the lawful care or charge of a child under the age of fourteen years, of the possession of such child:—(*a*) forcibly or fraudulently takes or entices away, or detains the child; or (*b*) receives or harbours the child, knowing it to have been so taken or enticed away or detained, is guilty of a felony, and is liable to imprisonment for seven years.

"It is a defence to a charge of any of the offences contained in this section to prove that the accused person claimed in good faith a right to the possession of the child, or in the case of an illegitimate child is its mother or claimed to be its father."

If a defence is available to the appellant it does not arise at this stage of the proceedings, but it was said that in any event there was no force or fraud. There was no question of force but the word "fraudulently" is sufficiently satisfied by the evidence that the child was given a false name and concealed at the settlement at Komemiyut. It is unnecessary, and with all respect to the Lord Chief Justice, I think wrong to go further and say that the word "fraudulently" is equivalent to intending to prejudice **[610]** the parents' right to possession. The

98 [1914] 1 K.B. 77. 86.
99 [1894] 2 Q.B. 415.
1 [1963] 1 Q.B. 55, 79.

appellant relies strongly on the word "possession," saying that the child was not at any material time in the possession of his parents since he had been handed over to the grandparents, in whose possession he was, and against whom no offence was shown to have been committed. This contention is highly artificial and, to my mind, quite unacceptable. It is true that possession is not a very appropriate word to use in connection with a child or any other person not in a condition of slavery, but it is used in corresponding Acts of Parliament in this country such as the Offences against the Person Act, 1861, and the Children and Young Persons Act, 1933, and a sensible meaning must be given to it if possible. So far as parents are concerned, possession cannot be limited to manual or physical possession. It may well be that where a person has the lawful care or charge of a child, the words "care or charge" carry the same meaning, so that a person who fraudulently detains a child with intent to deprive such person of his possession in the physical sense is aimed at by the section as well as a parent whose possession will often, if not always, be interrupted in the ordinary course of the child's life. The child may be in the care or charge of a master or tutor, servant, relation or friend, but this does not prevent the persistence of the parents' possession in reality, call it constructive possession if you will. In this case the child was placed with the grandparents by the parents as a temporary measure, and no suggestion is made that the parents sought at any time to renounce their authority over the child. To speak of the parents as having a right to possession is at the present time perhaps misleading for, although they have a right to assert their claim to their child's company by self help, once the courts intervene as they did in this case the interests of the child are paramount, and all claims based on so-called rights give way to these interests. This was clearly in the mind of the President of the High Court in Israel who, in giving judgment on February 10, 1960, in the custody proceedings, stated that the answer of the grandparents to the claim of the parents contained nothing calculated to satisfy the court that the interest of the child requires the dismissal of the parents' claim. In my opinion, there is no flaw in the charge of child stealing from the parents since the possession of the parents was not brought to an end by the placing of their child with the grandparents.

Lastly, it was argued that the offence with which the appellant is charged is of a political character. Evidence was admitted before the House to supplement that given before the magistrate **[611]** in order to seek to show the political character of the offence with which the appellant is charged, at any rate so far as child stealing is concerned, it being contended that the matter has become a political issue in Israel and symbol of importance in the contest which is taking place between the secular Jews, who form the majority of the present government, and the orthodox Jews, who represent the idea of the theocratic state.

The grandparents are said to be orthodox Jews and so is the appellant, and they, it is said, are taking a stand against the seculars represented by the parents who contemplated emigrating to Russia with the child, and imperilling the right of the child to receive an orthodox religious education.

The appellant himself gave no evidence in support of this contention, he having stoutly denied that he was guilty of any offence. Child stealing is not on the face of it a political offence and, in my opinion, it does not become so because political passions have been roused in and out of the Parliament of Israel (Knesset) in connection with this particular incident. The additional evidence carried the matter no further than to show that these passions were strong and that members of the Knesset were concerned in them.

In *In re Castioni*[2]* it was pointed out in argument that Parliament, in using the words"of a political character," had probably intentionally used a vague expression, and that it seemed as if the legislature had purposely abstained from attempting to find an exhaustive definition, leaving it to the courts to decide in each case, as it were, whether the exceptions applied. The words of J. S. Mill were quoted as a suggested definition: "Any offence committed in the course of furthering civil war insurrection or political commotion." This seems to me to come near to the heart of the matter. Hawkins J.[3] adopted the definition used

[2] [1891] 1 Q.B. 149. [3] Ibid. 165.

by Stephen J. (also a member of the court) in his History of Criminal Law, Vol. 2, pp. 70 and 71: "I think, therefore, that the expression in the Extradition Act ought (unless some better interpretation of it can be suggested) to be interpreted to mean that fugitive criminals are not to be surrendered for extradition crimes if those crimes were incidental to and formed a part of political disturbances."[4] To the same effect is the judgment of Denman J. in the same case,[5] also cited by the Lord Chief Justice in the Divisional Court.[6] **[612]**

According to this test there must be either in existence or in contemplation a struggle between the State and the fugitive criminal. I prefer to adhere as closely as possible to the guidance which I find in the *Castioni* case,[7]* judgment in which was delivered in 1890, not long after the passing of the first Extradition Act. It may be that cases will arise as in the *Polish Seamen's* case, *Reg.* v. *Governor of Brixton Prison, Ex parte Kolczynski*,[8]* where special considerations have to be taken into account. In some modern States politics and justice may be inextricably mixed, and it is not always easy, for example, to say what amounts to a revolt against the Government. No special feature appears to exist in this case, and I find no substance in the contention that extradition should be refused because of the political character of the offences charged.

I would dismiss the appeal.

Appeal dismissed.

Solicitors: *Rubinstein, Nash & Co.; Herbert Oppenheimer, Nathan & Vandyk; Treasury Solicitor; Director of Public Prosecutions.*

EX PARTE SCHTRAKS

([1964] 1 Q.B. 191)

October 26, 1962: Queen's Bench Division: Lord Parker, C.J., Gorman, Salmon JJ.

Extradition—Habeas corpus—Successive applications—Refusal of application by Queen's Bench Divisional Court—Refusal by House of Lords to admit fresh evidence—Dismissal of appeal—Second application to Divisional Court—Fresh evidence sought to be adduced as discrediting witnesses—Contention that fresh evidence showing that committal order and decisions on first application obtained by fraud—Whether admissable—Fraud or collusion—Administration of Justice Act, 1960 (8 & 9 *Eliz.* 2, *c.* 65), *s.* 14 (2).
Habeas Corpus—Successive applications—Fresh evidence—Extradition—Fresh evidence to discredit evidence relied on and as to political character of offence—Administration of Justice Act, 1960, *s.* 14 (2).

On January 12, 1962, the applicant was committed to Brixton Prison to await return to Israel pursuant to an order made by the chief metropolitan magistrate under section 10 of the Extradition Act, 1870. The applicant applied to the Divisional Court for a writ of habeas corpus and the court dismissed that application. He then appealed to the House of Lords, seeking to adduce before the House further evidence in order to discredit the evidence on which the magistrate had made the order and to show that the offences with which he had been charged were of a political character. The House of Lords held the further evidence to be inadmissible and dismissed the appeal.

The applicant now made a second application to the Divisional Court for a writ of habeas corpus, in support of which he sought to rely on the same further evidence on the grounds that, under **[192]** section 14 (2) of the

[4] Ibid. 166.
[5] Ibid. 156.
[6] [1963] 1 Q.B. 55, 86.
[7] [1891] 1 Q.B. 149.
[8] [1955] 1 Q.B. 540.

Administration of Justice Act, 1960,[1] fresh evidence could be adduced on a second application, and that the nature of the fresh evidence was such as to show that the decisions on the first application had been obtained only by a suppression of material truths amounting to fraud:—

Held, (1) that the object of section 14 (2) of the Administration of Justice Act, 1960, was to make it clear that, there being a right of appeal under the Act in both civil and criminal applications for habeas corpus, there was no right to make successive applications before different judges or courts; that, while the subsection provided that a further application might be made if fresh evidence were adduced, it did not in extradition proceedings or proceedings under the Fugitive Offenders Act, 1881, permit evidence to be considered which was otherwise admissible; and that, since under the existing law fresh evidence might be admitted only to show lack of jurisdiction in the committing magistrate or that there was no evidence on which he might exercise his jurisdiction, the court was not entitled to receive the further evidence in so far as it went only to discredit the evidence of witnesses whose depositions were before the magistrate.

Reg. v. *Governor of Brixton Prison, Ex parte Schtraks** [1962] 3 W.L.R. 1013; (*sub nom. Schtraks* v. *Government of Israel*) [1962] 3 All E.R. 529, H.L.(E.) applied.

(2) That, assuming that the court was entitled to receive fresh evidence showing that an order had been obtained by the arresting power by fraud or collusion, the evidence which the applicant sought to adduce fell far short of establishing any such conduct. Accordingly, none of the further evidence was admissible and the application was misconceived.

Quaere, whether, if it were shown that a committal order had been obtained by fraud, as by concealing evidence or collusion with a witness, the court would have jurisdiction to interfere.

APPLICATION for a writ of habeas corpus ad subjiciendum.

The appellant, Schalom Schtraks, who, pursuant to an order made by the chief metropolitan magistrate on January 12, 1962, under section 10 of the Extradition Act, 1870, was detained in Brixton Prison to await return to Israel, applied to the Divisional Court for a writ of habeas corpus. The Divisional Court dismissed that application.[2] The applicant appealed to the House of Lords, **[193]** seeking on that appeal to adduce additional evidence in order (a) to discredit the evidence on which the magistrate had reached his conclusion, and (b) to supplement the evidence which was before the magistrate to the effect that the crimes charged were of "a political character" within the meaning of section 3 of the Act of 1870. The House of Lords* dismissed the appeal,[3] holding, inter alia, that the right and competence of the court to take cognisance of additional evidence was limited to cases where such evidence went to the question of the magistrate's jurisdiction at the date of the committal order.

The charges against the applicant were as follows: "1. Perjury for that he on May 12, 1960, during proceedings in an application No. 52/60 in the High Court of Justice of Israel knowingly gave false evidence touching a matter material in those proceedings contrary to section 117 of the Criminal Code Ordinance, 1936. 2. Child Stealing: (*a*) on a date between January 1 and February 15, 1960, with intent to deprive Alter and Ida Schuchmacher of their son Joseph [Yossele] (born in 1952) fraudulently detained him in the house of Shlomo Zalman Kot at Komemiyut, contrary to section 188 of the said Ordinance; (*b*) on a date between January 1 and February 15, 1960, wrongfully

[1] Administration of Justice Act, 1960, s. 14 (2): "Notwithstanding anything in any enactment or rule of law, where a criminal or civil application of habeas corpus has been made by or in respect of any person, no such application shall again be made by or in respect of that person on the same grounds, whether to the same court or judge or to any other court or judge, unless fresh evidence is adduced in support of the application: . ."

[2] *Reg.* v. *Governor of Brixton Prison, Ex parte Schtraks** [1963] 1 Q.B. 55; [1962] 2 W.L.R. 976; [1962] 2 All E.R. 176, D.C.

[3] [1962] 3 W.L.R. 1013; [1962] 3 All E.R. 529, H.L.(E.).

confined the said Joseph Schuchmacher in the said house knowing that he was an abducted person, contrary to section 259 of the said Ordinance." The evidence against him consisted, inter alia, of declarations made in Israel by Shlomo Kot, his wife Rachel Kot and his brother Reuben Kot, each of whom had been arrested by the police in Israel and subsequently released, Reuben never having been charged. The affirmations of each were to the effect, inter alia, that a boy had been brought to the Komemiyut Settlement by a young man and they identified the boy as the boy Yossele and the young man as the applicant from photographs.

The further facts and evidence are fully set out in the reports of the first application.[4]* After the decision of the Divisional Court was given the boy Yossele was found in New York.

The applicant now made a second application for a writ of habeas corpus in which he sought to adduce the same further evidence before the Divisional Court on the grounds (a) that, on the proper construction of section 14 (2) of the Administration of Justice Act, 1960, fresh evidence could be adduced on a second or subsequent application although it had not been admissible on **[194]** the first, and (b) that the nature of the fresh evidence which it was sought to adduce was such as to show that the decisions of the magistrate, the Divisional Court[4]* and the House of Lords[5]* on his first application had been obtained only by a suppression of material truths amounting to fraud, and that the grounds on which the court would interfere by way of habeas corpus with the decision of an inferior court being analogous to those which would apply in the case of a motion for certiorari, the court should now grant the writ.

Richard Du Cann for the applicant. On the proper construction of section 14 (2) of the Administration of Justice Act, 1960, it is clear that on a second or subsequent application for habeas corpus fresh evidence can be adduced, even though the court could not have received it on the first occasion. The evidence which the House of Lords[5]* refused to admit can now, therefore, be admitted. In considering whether it should be admitted, it should be examined to see whether it would have affected the decision of the magistrate. Its nature is, in fact, such as to show that the verdicts of the magistrate, the Divisional Court[6]* and the House of Lords were obtained only by a suppression of material truths. It is not merely a question (in the words of the Divisional Court) of the requisitioning government not coming with its tackle in order, but of deceit practised on the courts of this country. This has the same disqualifying effect as if perjury had been committed. Habeas corpus is a form of relief analogous to certiorari in so far as the grounds on which it will issue are concerned. Certiorari will issue where fraud (or bias) is disclosed, and here there is fraud as defined in the cases on certiorari.

J. H. Buzzard as amicus curiae. [*Reg.* v. *Ashford, Kent, Justices, Ex parte Richley* (*No. 2*)[7] and *Rex* v. *Recorder of Leicester*[8] were referred to.]

Lord Parker C.J. In these proceedings Mr. Du Cann moves for a writ of habeas corpus on behalf of the applicant, Shalom Schtraks, now detained in Her Majesty's prison at Brixton **[195]** pursuant to a warrant issued under the Extradition Act, 1870, by the Chief Magistrate at Bow Street.

The case, as is well known, has had a long history. The applicant's original application for the writ was refused by this court[9]*; he appealed to the House of Lords where it was again refused.[10]* Despite that, he now seeks to apply afresh in this court on the ground of new evidence. I must refer to the nature of that evidence in a moment, but it is only right to say, first, that everything that this court is asked to look at was available in the proceedings in the House of

[4] [1962] 1 Q.B. 55, D.C.; [1962] 3 W.L.R. 1013, H.L.(E.).
[5] [1962] 3 W.L.R. 1013.
[6] [1963] 1 Q.B. 55.
[7] [1956] 1 Q.B. 167; [1955] 3 W.L.R. 778; [1955] 3 All E.R. 604, C.A.
[8] [1947] K.B. 726; 63 T.L.R. 333; [1947] 1 All E.R. 928, D.C.
[9] [1963] 1 Q.B. 55; [1962] 2 W.L.R. 976; [1962] 2 All E.R. 176, D.C.
[10] [1962] 3 W.L.R. 1013; [1962] 3 All E.R. 529, H.L.(E.).

Lords but was not looked at; secondly, that all the evidence which we are asked to look at today has already been before the Home Secretary and considered by him before he ordered that the applicant be extradited.

Notwithstanding that, Mr. Du Cann, to whom the court is grateful for his argument, says that he is entitled to make this application, and he makes it on two grounds. He says in the first instance that he is entitled to do so under the express wording of section 14 (2) of the Administration of Justice Act, 1960, which provides that: "Notwithstanding anything in any enactment or rule of law, where a criminal or civil application for habeas corpus has been made by or in respect of any person, no such application shall again be made by or in respect of that person on the same grounds, whether to the same court or judge or to any other court or judge, unless fresh evidence is adduced in support of the application." That subsection, as everyone knows, was introduced into this Act in order to give legislative authority, if that were needed, to the various decisions in *In re Hastings*,[11] the intention being to make it quite clear that under this Act there should be an appeal both in civil and criminal applications for habeas corpus and that, there being an appeal, it was only right that there should not be an opportunity of going, as it was thought at one time one could go, from judge to judge and from court to court. The subsection went on to provide that if the evidence were different, then you could make another application.

In my judgment, however, this subsection does not permit a further application to be made when the only fresh evidence is **[196]** evidence tending to discredit the evidence already given before the magistrate, since habeas corpus proceedings are in no sense by way of appeal. I think that that is made plain by the House of Lords who, when this evidence was tendered to them, refused to look at it except insofar as it went to show that there were political motives behind the request. They emphasised that habeas corpus in extradition proceedings is not an appeal from the magistrate; that all the court has to do is to see that the prisoner is properly detained; and that no evidence can be admitted before the Divisional Court or the House of Lords except to show lack of jurisdiction in one or other of the ways suggested—either because the crime in question was not within the Act or because there was no evidence upon which the magistrate could exercise his jurisdiction to issue a warrant.

Accordingly, in so far as this new evidence that we are asked to look at went to discredit the evidence of witnesses whose depositions went before the magistrate. I am quite satisfied that we are not entitled to look at it and that, accordingly, the application is misconceived.

Mr. Du Cann, however, raises a second, more interesting, point, He says that, even granted that that is true, this evidence is directed not merely to discredit the evidence of witnesses whose evidence was before the magistrate, but to show—and he says it boldly—that the magistrate was deceived, and was imposed upon by the fraudulent conduct of the Government of Israel. He goes on to say that, if he could show that, that would be a ground for this court interfering, as undoubtedly this court can in cases of certiorari. Without deciding the matter, it seems to me that if he could show that, he might well bring himself within the principle that evidence can be given to show that there was no evidence upon which the magistrate could act. If he could show that this warrant had been secured by fraud, as the concealing of evidence or collusion with a witness, then it may well be that this court could interfere. At any rate, for the purposes of this application I will assume that that is so.

Accordingly, the question remains whether the new evidence which it is sought to adduce discloses evidence of that character. As I understand it, and I confess I have not looked in detail at all the evidence, it can be grouped under four heads. It is said in the first place that one at any rate of the three Kots, who alone identified this applicant, had failed to identify him from photo-

[11] *In re Hastings* [1958] 1 W.L.R. 372; [1958] 1 All E.R. 707, D.C.; *In re Hastings (No. 3)* [1959] 1 Q.B. 358; [1958] 3 W.L.R. 768; [1958] 3 All E.R. 625, D.C.; *In re Hastings (No. 4)* [1959] Ch. 368; [1959] 2 W.L.R. 454; [1959] 1 All E.R. 698, D.C.; [1959] 1 W.L.R. 807; [1959] 3 All E.R. 221, C.A.

graphs handed to him on a different occasion. It is said that, in those circumstances, the prosecution had concealed material **[197]** which ought to have been available to the defence. In other words, it is introduced not merely to discredit the Kots, but to say that there was suppression of the full truth by the prosecution.

A second head of evidence is to show that, as it is said, a bargain was struck between the prosecution and the three Kots, and I will assume that it can be shown that the three Kots, before they made the affirmations which were before the magistrate, were promised that what they said would not be used in charges against them. Thirdly, it appears that in the meanwhile three or, I think, four others had been prosecuted in Israel for this offence. Fourthly, it was said that the prosecution had suppressed the evidence of witnesses who contradicted the Kots. That is the nature of the evidence which it is sought to adduce.

In my judgment, even assuming that fraud of the nature to which I have referred would enable this court to hear the evidence and grant the writ of habeas corpus, I am quite satisfied that what is sought to be adduced in this case falls far short of such fraud as would justify this court in interfering. It may be that the practice of the prosecution in Israel differs from ours; it may be that we would not promise that evidence would not be used against the person who was giving it, and matters of that sort. But for my part I am quite satisfied that no sufficient evidence is to be found here of fraud which would justify this court in interfering.

I confess I am influenced to some extent by the fact that, as I have said, all this evidence was available before the House of Lords, and the applicant by his advisers deliberately and for good reason refrained from suggesting that this evidence disclosed any fraud which would justify the court in interfering. I would refuse this application.

GORMAN J. I agree. These are two passages in the report of *Reg.* v. *Governor of Brixton Prison, Ex parte Schtraks*[12]* to which I should like to call attention. Viscount Radcliffe said[13]: "I think it is clear that in habeas corpus proceedings which arose out of a committal order under the Extradition Act, 1870, the court does not rehear the case that was before the magistrate, nor does it hear an appeal from his order. Its function, apart from considering any issue raised as to the offence charged being **[198]** a political one, is to see that the prisoner is lawfully detained by his gaoler."

Lord Evershed said[14]: "In the earlier case"—referring to *Rex* v. *Governor of Holloway Prison, Ex parte Siletti*[15]*—Bigham J., after observing that the right to apply by way of habeas corpus was a common law right expressly made available to the committed person by the Extradition Acts, held that the right and competence of the court to have regard to such fresh evidence were limited to cases where such evidence went to the question of the magistrate's jurisdiction at the date of the committal order; by showing for example that the crime charged was outside the scope of the extradition agreement as being of a political character or otherwise not comprehended in the crimes enumerated in the agreement; or"—and this is the part I emphasise—"by showing that there was in truth no evidence at all to justify the magistrate's exercise of his discretionary jurisdiction to commit."

Those two passages to which I have referred determine the approach of this court to this case. Having regard to those, and in spite of the forcible submissions of Mr. Du Cann, I agree with my Lord.

SALMON J. I agree. Mr. Du Cann's first point, as I understand it, comes to this, that under section 14 (2) of the Administration of Justice Act, 1960, there is a prohibition, once an application for habeas corpus has been made, against making any further application unless fresh evidence is adduced in support of

[12] [1962] 3 W.L.R. 1013; [1962] 3 All E.R. 529.
[13] Ibid. 1027-8.
[14] [1962] 3 W.L.R. 1013, 1036.
[15] (1902) 20 Cox C.C. 353; 18 T.L.R. 771, D.C.

such further application. Mr. Du Cann says that this subsection entitles him to adduce fresh evidence to show that the magistrate ought never to have acted upon the evidence of those witnesses whose affirmations identified the applicant, and that, accordingly, a further application based on that fresh evidence can now be made.

I agree, however, that the subsection on which he relies clearly is not intended to alter the law, nor does it if one reads the words "unless fresh evidence is adduced" as meaning "unless relevant fresh evidence is adduced." The evidence which he seeks to introduce for the purpose of attacking the evidence called on **[199]** behalf of the requesting power before the magistrate is clearly inadmissible and therefore irrelevant evidence, as is shown by the decision of the House of Lords in the present case.

So far as Mr. Du Cann's second point is concerned, if it could be shown that a decision had been obtained from the magistrate by fraud or collusion on the part of the requesting power, it would be very difficult to persuade me that habeas corpus could not go. In this case, however, I agree that the evidence before us falls very far short of establishing any such conduct on the part of the requesting power. An attempt was made in the House of Lords to put forward the whole of this evidence on behalf of the applicant, but on other grounds; if it had then been thought that there was any warrant for suggesting that this evidence showed fraud or collusion on the part of the requesting power, it seems to me extravagantly unlikely that this point would not have been argued in the House of Lords. I agree that the application should be refused.

Application dismissed.

Solicitors: *Rubinstein, Nash & Co.*

6

SURRENDER UNDER THE FUGITIVE OFFENDERS ACTS

REGINA v. GOVERNOR OF BRIXTON PRISON. *Ex parte* CALDOUGH

([1961] 1 W.L.R. 464)

January 31, February 1, 1961: Queen's Bench Division: Lord Parker C.J. Winn, Widgery JJ.

Fugitive Offender—Evidence—Deposition—Sworn statements by witnesses—Refusal of Canadian magistrate to permit cross-examination by offender's counsel—Whether deposition admissible—"Deposition"—Fugitive Offenders Act, 1881 (44 & 45 *Vict. c.* 69), *ss.* 29, 39.

On October 3, 1960, a warrant was issued by a Canadian magistrate for the arrest of the applicant, a Canadian citizen, and on November 11 the applicant was arrested in London on a provisional warrant issued under section 4 of the Fugitive Offenders Act, 1881. On December 12 depositions consisting of statements made on oath by witnesses were taken before the Canadian magistrate. Immediately before taking the depositions, that magistrate, after hearing argument, refused to allow counsel for the applicant to cross-examine the witnesses or to take any part in the proceedings. **[465]** On January 10, 1961, on the warrant, duly endorsed, and on evidence consisting substantially of those depositions, the Chief Metropolitan Magistrate made an order under section 5 of the Act of 1881 committing the applicant to Brixton Prison to await return to Canada.

On an application for a writ of habeas corpus on the ground, inter alia, that having regard to sections 5 and 29 of the Fugitive Offenders Act, 1881,[1] and to section 453 of the Criminal Code of Canada, the depositions taken

[1] Fugitive Offenders Act, 1881, s. 5: "A fugitive when apprehended shall be brought before a magistrate, who . . . shall hear the case . . . and have the same jurisdiction and powers, as near as may be . . . as if the fugitive were charged with an offence committed within his jurisdiction.

"If the endorsed warrant for the apprehension of the fugitive is duly authenticated, and such evidence is produced as . . . according to the law ordinarily administered by the magistrate, raises a strong or probable presumption that the fugitive committed the offence . . . the magistrate shall commit the fugitive to prison to await his return, . . ."

S. 29: "A magistrate may take depositions for the purposes of this Act in the absence of a person accused of an offence in like manner as he might take the same if such person were present and accused of the offence before him.

"Depositions (whether taken in the absence of the fugitive or otherwise) and copies thereof, and official certificates of or judicial documents stating facts, may, if duly authenticated, be received in evidence in proceedings under this Act.

"Provided that nothing in this Act shall authorise the reception of any such depositions, copies, certificates, or documents in evidence against a person upon his trial for an offence."

S. 39: "In this Act, . . . the expression 'deposition' includes any affidavit, affirmation, or statement made upon oath as above defined."

before the Canadian magistrate were taken contrary to law and that, had they been excluded, there would have been insufficient evidence to justify the committal order: —

Held, (1) that since it had not been shown that the first paragraph of section 29 of the Fugitive Offenders Act, 1881, was part of the law of Canada, the Court could not consider whether what took place in Canada was proper under Canadian law and the provisions of both paragraphs of section 29 must be viewed as applying solely to this country.

(2) That the first and second paragraphs of section 29 were wholly independent provisions and therefore, in view of the definition of "deposition" in section 39, "depositions" admissible under the second paragraph were not limited to depositions taken under a procedure which complied with the provisions of the first paragraph, but all that the magistrate was concerned to see was that what was tendered as evidence consisted of depositions as so defined and that they were duly authenticated. The depositions taken in Canada, accordingly, were admissible and the application must be dismissed.

Rex v. *Secretary of State for India in Council, Ex parte Ezekiel** [1941] 2 K.B. 169; [1941] 2 All E.R. 546, D.C. applied.

APPLICATION for a writ of habeas corpus.

On October 3, 1960, the deputy police magistrate for Vancouver, British Columbia, issued a warrant for the arrest of the applicant, George Frederick Caldough, a Canadian citizen, on charges of conspiracy and committing certain overt acts in connection with the conspiracy. On November 11, 1960, the applicant was arrested in London on a provisional warrant issued **[466]** under section 4 of the Fugitive Offenders Act, 1881. On December 12, 1960, depositions consisting wholly or in part of statements made on oath by witnesses were taken before the deputy police magistrate for Vancouver. Immediately before taking the depositions the deputy police magistrate, after hearing argument, refused to allow counsel instructed on the applicant's behalf to cross-examine the witnesses or to take any part in the proceedings. On January 10, 1961, the metropolitan chief magistrate at Bow Street Magistrates' Court, on receipt of the warrant duly endorsed, and on evidence which consisted substantially of those depositions, made an order under section 5 of the Act of 1881 committing the applicant to Brixton Prison to await return to Canada.

The applicant applied for a writ of habeas corpus on the ground that the committal order made by the metropolitan chief magistrate was wrong in law, and was made without jurisdiction, in that (1) the counts charged in the warrant were lacking in precision and particularity, since counts 1 and 3 charged the applicant with others with conspiracy over a long period to commit the offences substantively charged in counts 2 and 4, and, in the circumstances, the metropolitan chief magistrate should not have found that, according to the law ordinarily administered by him, there was a strong or probable presumption that the applicant had committed those offences; and (2) having regard to sections 5 and 29 of the Fugitive Offenders Act, 1881, and to section 453 of the Criminal Code of Canada [c. 51 of the Statutes of Canada, 1953 to 1954] the depositions taken before the deputy police magistrate for Vancouver were taken contrary to law and were not admissible before the metropolitan chief magistrate and, had those depositions been excluded, there would have been no evidence to raise a strong or probable presumption that the applicant had committed the offences.

Further facts are stated in the judgment of Lord Parker C.J.

Christopher French for the applicant.

Victor Durand Q.C. and *J. Mathew* for the Attorney-General of British Columbia.

J. H. Buzzard for the Governor of Brixton Prison and the Home Secretary.

The following cases were referred to in argument: *In re Campbell*[2]; *Rex* v.

[2] [1935] N.Z.L.R. 352.

Secretary of State for India in Council, Ex parte Ezekiel[3]*; *Reg.* v. *Governor of Brixton Prison, Ex parte Shuter*[4]* and *Reg.* v. *Dawson.*[5]

LORD PARKER C.J. Mr. French moves for a writ of habeas **[467]** corpus on behalf of George Frederick Caldough now detained in Her Majesty's Prison at Brixton pursuant to an order of committal dated January 10, 1961, made by the metropolitan chief magistrate at Bow Street, pursuant to the Fugitive Offenders Act, 1881.

The applicant is a Canadian citizen in respect of whom a warrant was sent to this country by a justice of the peace for the Province of British Columbia, City of Vancouver. The applicant had in fact already been apprehended and detained in custody under a provisional warrant issued by the metropolitan chief magistrate under section 4 of the Act, but it was on the warrant received from Canada duly endorsed and certain alleged depositions that the metropolitan chief magistrate dealt with the case and committed him to Brixton Prison.

The jurisdiction of the magistrate is laid down by section 5 of the Fugitive Offenders Act, 1881, in these terms: "A fugitive when apprehended shall be brought before a magistrate, who (subject to the provisions of this Act) shall hear the case in the same manner and have the same jurisdiction and powers, as near as may be (including the power to remand and admit to bail), as if the fugitive were charged with an offence committed within his jurisdiction. If the endorsed warrant for the apprehension of the fugitive is duly authenticated, and such evidence is produced as (subject to the provisions of this Act) according to the law ordinarily administered by the magistrate, raises a strong or probable presumption that the fugitive committed the offence mentioned in the warrant, and that the offence is one to which this Part of this Act applies, the magistrate shall commit the fugitive to prison to await his return, and shall forthwith send a certificate of the committal and such report of the case as he may think fit, if in the United Kingdom to a Secretary of State, and if in a British possession to the Governor of that possession."

The evidence which may be adduced is dealt with by section 29 of the Act as follows: "A magistrate may take depositions for the purposes of this Act in the absence of a person accused of an offence in like manner as he might take the same if such person were present and accused of the offence before him.

"Depositions (whether taken in the absence of the fugitive or otherwise) and copies thereof, and official certificates of or judicial documents stating facts, may, if duly authenticated, be received in evidence in proceedings under this Act. Provided that nothing in this Act shall authorise the reception of any such depositions, copies, certificates, or documents in evidence against a person upon his trial for an offence." The section then goes on to deal with the proper method of authenticating the warrant and the depositions.

Finally, by section 39, the definition section, it is provided: "In this Act, unless the context otherwise requires, . . . the expression 'deposition' includes any affidavit, affirmation, or **[468]** statement made upon oath as above defined," and the words "above defined" refer to the preceding definition of "oath."

The warrant so received in this country charged the applicant, with others, on four counts. Counts 1 to 3 charged an extensive conspiracy between January 1, 1958, and March 31, 1960, "to commit an indictable offence, to wit, to make, circulate and publish statements, they knew to be false in material particulars with intent to induce persons to become shareholders" in certain companies; and in count 3 a similar conspiracy, "unlawfully by deceit, falsehood or other fraudulent means to defraud the public of property." Counts 2 and 4 alleged overt acts in connection with such conspiracy.

The first point taken on behalf of the applicant is that these charges were not such as, "according to the law ordinarily administered" by the magistrate, to quote the words of section 5, entitled him to commit. Thus, it is said that counts 1 and 3 alleged a conspiracy which is much too extensive and as such would not be allowed in this country; and in regard to counts 2 and 4 it is

[3] [1941] 2 K.B. 169; [1941] 2 All E.R. 546.
[4] [1960] 1 Q.B. 89; [1959] 3 W.L.R. 603; [1959] 2 All E.R. 782, D.C.
[5] [1960] 1 W.L.R. 163; [1960] 1 All E.R. 558, C.C.A.

pointed out that the allegations are unparticularised in a number of respects. It is, I think, sufficient to say in regard to this ground that I see nothing in the formulation of the charges which would entitle the magistrate, in effect, to disregard the warrant and the evidence and to decline to proceed in the matter.

The second point raised is of more substance. It goes to the admissibility of the evidence tendered before and received by the metropolitan chief magistrate. This, although I have not seen the depositions, I understand consisted in whole or in part of statements on oath made by witnesses before the deputy police magistrate for the City of Vancouver. It is said on behalf of the applicant that those depositions should not have been admitted, in which case there would have been no sufficient evidence to justify committal in the present case.

The facts giving rise to this contention are that the deputy police magistrate in Vancouver refused to allow counsel appearing for the applicant to cross-examine the witnesses, treating the taking of the evidence before him as in effect an ex parte proceeding. This, it is said, was contrary to the Act of 1881, or, at any rate, contrary to what was loosely called the principles of natural justice. Thus, section 453 of the Criminal Code, which appears in the Statutes of Canada for 1953-54, and which was in evidence before the metropolitan chief magistrate, lays down the position in regard to the taking of depositions when the accused is present and charged with an offence. It provides, so far as is material: "When the accused is before a justice holding a preliminary inquiry, the justice shall (*a*) take the evidence under oath, in the presence of the accused, of the witnesses called on the part of the prosecution and allow the accused or his counsel to cross-examine them." Section 29 of the Fugitive Offenders Act, 1881, however, by its first paragraph, provides that "A magistrate may take depositions for **[469]** the purposes of this Act in the absence of a person accused of an offence in like manner as he might take the same if such person were present and accused of the offence before him." Accordingly, it is argued that applying that provision to section 453 of the Canadian Criminal Code, there was nothing to exclude the right of the applicant not personally but by his counsel from cross-examining the witnesses.

Counsel for the applicant quite rightly drew our attention to a case in New Zealand, *In re Campbell*,[6] in which a similar point arose in connection with depositions taken in New South Wales, and in which the Chief Justice of New Zealand held that the proceedings in New South Wales were ex parte and that the fugitive had no right by his counsel to cross-examine the witnesses. Counsel for the applicant here submitted that that decision was wrong and that we ought not to follow it. Counsel for the Attorney-General of British Columbia on the other hand sought to support the decision, and contended that the purpose of the proceedings in the present case was the obtaining of a warrant. On examination, however, this proved to be quite untenable since the warrant had already been issued.

In my judgment, unless and until it is shown that the first paragraph of section 29 of the Act of 1881 is today part of the law of Canada, and no such evidence was adduced before the magistrate, it is impossible to embark on a consideration as to whether what took place in Canada was proper under Canadian law. The provisions of section 29, including the first paragraph, must therefore be viewed as applying solely to this country. Viewed in this way, the highest at which the point can be put is that depositions, duly authenticated, are not admissible unless such depositions have been taken under a procedure which, in the case of depositions taken in England, would have complied with the provisions of the first paragraph. The answer to that, however, is that the first and second paragraphs of section 29 are wholly independent provisions. Indeed, the word "such" before the word "depositions" in the second paragraph is significantly omitted. Moreover, it has already been held by this court in *Rex* v. *Secretary of State for India in Council, Ex parte Ezekiel*[7]* that the first two paragraphs of section 29 are wholly independent provisions, and by that decision this court is bound. Further, it is impossible to say that what occurred in Canada is contrary to

[6] [1935] N.Z.L.R. 352.
[7] [1941] 2 K.B. 169; [1941] 2 All E.R. 546.

natural justice once it is seen that affidavits are included in the definition of "depositions." It must also be remembered that the third paragraph of section 29 provides that none of this evidence shall be evidence against a person on his trial for the offence.

The truth of the matter, as I see it, is that all that the metropolitan chief magistrate at Bow Street is concerned to see **[470]** is that what is tendered as evidence consists of depositions as defined and that they are duly authenticated.

In my judgment, therefore, this application fails and must be refused.

WINN J. I agree, and for the reasons which my Lord has given. I would add only one point, and I am conscious that it may be only an alternative way of stating a point already made; it is this: When one appreciates that the expression "depositions" used in section 29 is made, by the force of the definition in section 39, to include any statement on oath, it seems that the construction of the section as a whole must be such as not to raise a conflict between the meaning of the word "depositions" in the first and second paragraphs in the light of that definition. I therefore find it impossible to accept the view urged on the court by Mr. French that "depositions" in the second paragraph means depositions taken in accordance with the normal procedure in an English magistrates' court.

WIDGERY J. I also agree.

Application dismissed.

Solicitors: *Rowley, Ashworth & Co.; Charles Russell & Co.; Director of Public Prosecutions.*

CALDOUGH v. GOVERNOR OF BRIXTON PRISON AND ANOTHER

([1961] 1 W.L.R. 738)

February 28, 1961: House of Lords: Viscount Simonds, Lords Tucker, Hodson.

PETITION for leave to appeal to the House of Lords from the decision of the Divisional Court of the Queen's Bench Division in *Reg.* v. *Governor of Brixton Prison, Ex parte Caldough*[1]* dismissing the petitioner's application for a writ of habeas corpus.

Christopher French for the petitioner.
J. Mathew for the Attorney-General of British Columbia.
J. H. Buzzard for the Governor of Brixton Prison.

The APPEAL COMMITTEE dismissed the petition.

Solicitors: *Rowley, Ashworth & Co.; Charles Russell & Co.; Director of Public Prosecutions.*

REGINA v. GOVERNOR OF BRIXTON PRISON EX PARTE NARANJAN SINGH

([1962] 1 Q.B. 211)

May 5, 1961: Queen's Bench Division: Lord Parker C.J., Salmon, Edmund Davies JJ.

Fugitive Offender—Court's jurisdiction to discharge—Delay—Charges of cheat-

[1] [1961] 1 W.L.R. 464; [1961] 1 All E.R. 606, D.C.

*ing—Arrest of offender ten years after offences committed—Offender living openly in England—Home and new life made in England—Whether "unjust and oppressive" to order return—***[212]** *Or "otherwise"—Whether power to discharge limited to cases where offence trivial or application for return made in bad faith—Fugitive Offenders Act,* 1881 (44 & 45 *Vict. c.* 69), *s.* 10.

On February 9, 1961, the chief metropolitan magistrate made an order under section 5 of the Fugitive Offenders Act, 1881, committing the applicant to Brixton Prison to await return to India on five charges of cheating under article 420 of the Indian Penal Code. The amount involved in the charges was 1,425 rupees, about £112. The alleged offences were committed in India about October, 1951. In April, 1952, the applicant came to this country where he obtained employment and lived openly under his own name. In 1956 he was joined by his wife, who had been living openly in India, and his child, and in the same year he obtained British nationality, surrendering his Indian passport. Meanwhile, depositions were taken in India, but they were not completed until the end of 1956 nor authenticated until 1958. On December 4, 1958, a warrant was issued which was authenticated in India on February 5, 1959, and indorsed in London by the chief metropolitan magistrate on March 3, 1960. The applicant was arrested in London on February 1, 1961. Despite the delays which had occurred in India, there was no suggestion that the Government of India was not sincere in its intention to prosecute.

On an application for a writ of habeas corpus and under section 10 of the Fugitive Offenders Act, 1881,[1] that the applicant be discharged on the ground that in view, inter alia, of the long delay shown by the Indian authorities, it would be unjust and oppressive to order his return to India, the point was taken that the discretion of the court to make an order in favour of an offender under section 10 of the Act was limited to cases where the offence was trivial or the application was not made "in good faith in the interests of justice or otherwise" not in good faith:—

Held, that, on its true construction, section 10 of the Act of 1881 gave the court a wide discretion to do what in all the circumstances was just, and that, in the circumstances, and since the applicant had made a home and a life for himself in this country, and would by reason of the delay inevitably experience difficulty in defending himself, the delay was of such a nature that it would be unjust and oppressive for him to be returned to India on the charges. The court, therefore, would exercise its discretion under the section and order his discharge.

APPLICATION for a writ of habeas corpus and under section 10 of the Fugitive Offenders Act, 1881. **[213]**

On February 9, 1961, the chief metropolitan magistrate at Bow Street made an order under section 5 of the Fugitive Offenders Act, 1881, committing the applicant, Naranjan Singh, to Brixton Prison to await return to India on five charges of cheating by dishonest inducement of the delivery of property under article 420 of the Indian Penal Code. The amount involved in the charges was 1,425 rupees, about £112. The alleged offences took place in about October, 1951, in the Province of Jullundur, in the Republic of India. In April, 1952, the applicant left India and came to this country where he obtained employment and lived openly under his own name. In 1956 he was joined by his wife and child, and in the same year he applied for, and obtained, British nationality. On February 1, 1961, he was arrested in London and brought before the chief metropolitan magistrate.

The applicant applied to the court, submitting that, in view of the small

[1] Fugitive Offenders Act, 1881, s. 10: "Where it is made to appear to a superior court that by reason of the trivial nature of the case, or by reason of the application for the return of a fugitive not being made in good faith in the interests of justice or otherwise, it would, having regard to . . . all the circumstances of the case, be unjust or oppressive or too severe a punishment to return the fugitive . . . such court may discharge the fugitive. . . ."

amount involved in the charges, the distance to the Republic of India and the long delay in ordering his return shown by the Indian authorities, and in all the circumstances of the case, it would be unjust and oppressive and too severe a punishment to order his return, and asking that in the premises, and by virtue of section 10 of the Fugitive Offenders Act, 1881, the court should issue a writ of habeas corpus that he might be brought before the court and discharged. The application was made ex parte on February 24, 1961, when it was adjourned until February 28 for notices to be served. On February 28, on the application of the Government of India, the hearing was adjourned for two months to enable evidence to be obtained from India.

The facts are more fully stated in the judgment of Lord Parker JC.

Brian Leary for the applicant. In view of the inordinate delay on the part of the Indian authorities this case clearly falls within section 10 of the Fugitive Offenders Act, 1881. That delay was in no way contributed to by the applicant, who has lived openly in this country and surrendered his passport to India House when he took British nationality. The charges are now 10 years old; they are complicated charges relating to the affairs of a company, and if the applicant were returned to India to stand his trial on them he would inevitably experience great difficulty in tracing the documents relating to the company and in finding witnesses, who must by this time be dispersed all over India. It would, indeed, be "unjust or oppressive" within **[214]** section 10 to return the applicant after 10 years to stand trial at which he could not be expected to defend himself adequately.

Mervyn Griffith-Jones for the Governor of Brixton Prison.

T. O. Kellock for the Government of India. It is conceded that the delay in this case is most unfortunate. But the court is asked to accept that, owing to the size of the country and the interplay between the local authority State Government and the Government of India, the preparation of a case such as this presents greater difficulty and necessarily takes a longer time in India than it would do in this country, and that the Indian Government has acted in good faith throughout.

Where the depositions show a prima facie case the court should only refuse to allow a fugitive to be returned if the offence is trivial or the application is not made in good faith. That appears as a matter of construction of section 10 of the Act of 1881. On a logical reading of the section, the words "or otherwise" are merely a qualification of the preceding words "the interests of justice." It is to be observed that there is no comma after the words "the interests of justice" as would be expected if the following words, "or otherwise," are not to be construed ejusdem generis. If the words "or otherwise" have a general meaning, there would be no necessity for the express references in the section to the "trivial nature of the case" and the application "not being made in good faith." There are, therefore, only two matters for this court to consider: first, if the offence is trivial, and, secondly, whether the application is made in good faith in "the interests of justice." If that reading of the section is right, delay on the part of the applying Power is only relevant in deciding whether it has acted in good faith, or, if the case is trivial, whether in "all the circumstances of the case" it would "be unjust or oppressive or too severe a punishment to return the fugitive."

In *Rex* v. *Governor of Brixton Prison, Ex parte Waite*[2] a submission was made that the section should be given a wider construction, but the court left that point open. In *In re Henderson*[3]* the court did appear to say that delay is not a reason for refusing to return a fugitive, but it is accepted that the point of construction was conceded. [Reference was also made to *Reg.* v. *Governor of Brixton Prison, Ex parte Campbell.*[4]*] **[215]**

In considering whether it would be harsh or oppressive to return a fugitive offender for trial, one consideration is whether it is worth doing so, e.g., whether he would merely receive a nominal sentence or be bound over: see *Reg.* v.

[2] (1921) *The Times*, February 22, D.C.
[3] [1950] 1 All E.R. 283, C.A.
[4] (1956) *The Times*, July 12, D.C.

Governor of Brixton Prison, Ex parte Green.[5]* It must be remembered, however, that other charges may in fact be laid against the fugitive at his trial. The purpose of this legislation is to return alleged criminals from one State of the Commonwealth to another, and only in the rare event of lack of good faith on the part of the applying State should his return be refused. Even if section 10 be given a wide construction, mere delay by the applying Power is insufficient ground for refusing to return the offender, because it is a matter which he may raise at his trial. Alternatively, if this court will take delay into consideration, it will only exercise its discretion to release the offender in rare and exceptional cases: see *Rex* v. *Governor of Brixton Prison, Ex parte McCheyne,*[6]* in particular *per* Lord Goddard C.J.[7] and Croom-Johnson J.,[8] and this is not such a case.

Mervyn Griffith-Jones was asked to assist the court on the point of construction. The words "or otherwise" give an open discretion to the court; unless so interpreted, the words are purposeless. The effect of section 10 is that the court may exercise its discretion to release the offender when to do otherwise would be "unjust"—a limited interpretation would mean that the court might release an offender when to do otherwise would be unjust only on the ground of the triviality of the offence or of bad faith on the part of the applying Power, but that, in all other cases, however unjust, it had no power to act. That would be a strange conclusion for the court to come to, since its only task is to see that no injustice is done. In his judgment in *In re Henderson*[9]* Tucker L.J.[10] clearly had the wider construction in mind, even though the matter had not been argued.

Leary was not called on to reply.

Lord Parker C.J. In these proceedings Mr. Leary moves on behalf of the applicant, Naranjan Singh, now detained in Her Majesty's Prison at Brixton, for an order of habeas corpus or, alternatively, for an order under section 10 of the Fugitive Offenders Act, 1881. The applicant was committed to Brixton **[216]** Prison by the chief magistrate on February 9, 1961, he having been satisfied on a warrant and depositions duly authenticated which had been sent over from India that a prima facie case had been made out against the applicant in respert of offences contrary to article 420 of the Indian Penal Code.

The alleged offences in this case were committed about October, 1951, and their nature was that the applicant was the managing director of a company, Public Pictures Ltd., that he got a number of people, up to 28, to deposit sums in rupees as a condition of being taken into employment, and that he in fact used that money without their authority in the purchase of shares in their names in the company, and thereafter dismissed them without paying them any salary. The offences in question are five in number, involving the equivalent in rupees of about £112.

In April, 1952, he came to this country. He says that he knew of no complaint having been made against him, but it is only right to say that it does appear from the depositions that a number of people alleged that they complained to him, and, indeed, some 30 of them did complain also to the Registrar of Joint Stock Companies, sending him a written petition on November 12, 1951. Having come to this country, the applicant obtained employment at Ealing, where he worked for a company for 2½ years, and in March, 1956, he was joined by his wife, whom he had left in India, accompanied by one child. After that they moved to West Bromwich, purchased a house on mortgage and he worked until September, 1960, in a rolled steel factory; the employers in that factory give the applicant a glowing reference, saying that they considered him to be one of the best coloured workers ever to be employed by the firm, and that they were sorry when he left of his own accord. In 1960 he left that job and came south to Southall, in Middlesex, where he obtained work with the British Overseas Airways Corporation. Meanwhile, in 1956, he had surrendered his Indian passport and had applied for and obtained British nationality.

[5] (1954) *The Times*, December 16, D.C.
[6] [1951] 1 T.L.R. 1155. D.C.
[7] Ibid. 1158.
[8] Ibid. 1159.
[9] [1950] 1 All E.R. 283.
[10] Ibid. 286.

This is the case of a man who, for whatever motive he left India in 1952, has a home and new life which he has made for himself in this country. He has a wife and now three children with him. That is the position from his point of view.

From the point of view of the Indian authorities, it appears that after the Registrar of Joint Stock Companies had drawn the attention of the police to the petition which he had received on November 12, 1951, certain steps were taken. It is only right to **[217]** say that, in my judgment, everything that was done, making all allowances for the difficulties involved in India, was dilatory in the extreme. At any rate, the applicant had left the country before anything was done, because the first record is a report from the Superintendent of Police on October 4, 1952. Thereafter, there was a long period of delay until the depositions were taken, apparently in the early part of 1956. It is said that there was difficulty in tracing the witnesses and their addresses, but it is difficult to believe that there was any really serious difficulty when, as I have said, there had been a written petition from these complainants to the Registrar of Joint Stock Companies. However, the depositions having been taken, they were not authenticated until 1958, and it was not until December 4 that a warrant was issued. On February 5, 1959, the signature on the warrant was authenticated, and then there was a delay of yet another year before the application was in fact made to the chief magistrate in London.

Finally, to complete the dates, there was then an adjournment for further authentication until the chief magistrate indorsed the warrant on March 3, 1960, and thereafter almost another year's delay before the applicant was arrested on February 1, 1961.

The Government of India have supplied the court with affidavits seeking to explain the delay, and I should like to say at once that I entirely accept that the work involved inevitably caused some delay, and that the Indian authorities are entirely sincere in the matter, and that they intend to prosecute. At the same time I feel that this was a very simple case and, making allowances for all the difficulties involved, it is almost inconceivable that if due diligence had been exercised the matter could not have been dealt with at a very much earlier stage. But, be that as it may, one thing is clear, and that is that the applicant, apart from the fact that he may have left India originally fearing some action, has done nothing but live perfectly openly under his own name in the circumstances which I have indicated. He is quite well known to the police under his proper name. His wife was living openly in India under her proper name before she came to this country in 1956. She was never questioned. She was never asked for photographs, and again, she has done nothing to conceal the whereabouts of her husband.

Pausing there, I feel that, if the discretion of this court is an unlimited discretion to do what in all the circumstances is just, it would in the particular circumstances of this case be unjust **[218]** and oppressive for this man at this very late date, having made his home here and having started a new life here, to be returned for trial in India on these charges. Having regard to the delay, one has only to envisage the difficulties he would be in in defending himself. While the courts there would no doubt take due account of the difficulties facing the applicant, it seems to me that the delay is of such a nature that this court can properly say that it would be unjust and oppressive for him to be forced to return.

However, Mr. Kellock, for the Government of India, has taken a point which has been, if I may put it, in the offing ever since 1881, but has never as yet been effectively taken, namely, that the powers of this court under section 10 are, on a true construction, very limited. The section reads thus: "Where it is made to appear to a superior court that by reason of the trivial nature of the case, or by reason of the application for the return of a fugitive not being made in good faith in the interests of justice or otherwise, it would, having regard to the distance, to the facilities for communication, and to all the circumstances of the case, be unjust or oppressive or too severe a punishment to return the fugitive either at all or until the expiration of a certain period, such court' may exercise its discretion in a certain way.

The rival interpretations of this section concern the meaning in the context of the words "or otherwise." The limited construction, and the one for which Mr. Kellock contends, is that the words "or otherwise" are merely descriptive of the application which is not made in good faith. In other words, he would read it as "Where it is made to appear that by reason of the application for the return of a fugitive not being made in good faith either because it is not being made in the interests of justice or otherwise not in good faith," and he points out that in so far as one is entitled to look at commas in an Act of Parliament, there is no comma, as one would otherwise expect, after the words "interests of justice." That is the limited construction. The wider construction is that one should read it as if there was a comma after the words "interests of justice," and that it would then mean that the court's discretion should be exercised in any other case where it would, having regard to the distance, etc., be unjust and oppressive.

As I have said, this point has been in the offing all these years, and there is no decision on it. What has happened, quite shortly, **[219]** in the past is that in *In re Waite,*[11] which is only reported in "The Times" newspaper, the Attorney-General had made a submission favouring what I may call the wide construction. The court made no decision upon it. In a case which followed, *Henderson* v. *The Secretary of State for Home Affairs,*[12]* the point was quite plainly before the court, but the intervening Government, which was again the Government of India, conceded for the purposes of that case that the wider construction was right, and the court proceeded on that wider construction, expressly saying that they were making no decision on that point of construction. Since then there have been several cases before this court; in particular, we were told that in *Reg.* v. *Governor of Brixton Prison, Ex parte Campbell,*[13]* which again is only reported in "The Times" newspaper, an order was made under section 10, and the court again appear to have come to the conclusion, without argument, that the wide construction was correct. I have not seen "The Times" newspaper report myself, but it is only right to say that it is not clear whether it was the triviality of the alleged offence which determined the decision or merely the matter of delay. At any rate, the court assumed that the wide construction was correct. The same was true in *Reg.* v. *Governor of Brixton Prison, Ex parte McCheyne,*[14]* in which the court went so far as to assume[15] that the wide construction had been decided in *Henderson's* case[16] to be correct. In fact, however, the court in *Henderson's* case[16] did expressly reserve the point.

The position, therefore, is that in every case which has so far come before this court, the wide construction has either been conceded by the intervening Government or has been accepted without argument by the court as the proper construction. I am quite satisfied that the wider construction is correct. In the first place—and this is approaching it on a broad basis—one would expect that the court would have a general discretion in all the circumstances of the case to do what is just. If the limited construction is correct, however, this court could only order the release of an applicant under the section on the ground of the triviality of the nature of the offence, or on the basis that the reason for the application for the return of the offender was made in bad faith. It seems to me extraordinary that the powers of this court should be so limited. At any rate it is a consideration to bear in mind if there is any ambiguity of construction. **[220]** Looking at it as a narrow point of construction, there are two matters which influence me. In the first instance, if the discretion can only be exercised in what I may call the trivial case or a case of bad faith, the words "having regard to the distance, to the facilities for communication, and to all the circumstances of the case," would seem to be quite inapt and meaningless. If the court is ordering release on the ground of bad faith, what do the other circumstances matter? What do the distances matter? What do the facilities for communication matter? And similarly, if it is the release of an applicant because of the trivial nature of the offence. Finally, and again as a point of construction, if the

[11] (1921) *The Times*, February 22.
[12] [1950] 1 All E.R. 283.
[13] (1956) *The Times,* July 12.
[14] [1951] 1 T.L.R. 1155.
[15] Ibid. 1158.
[16] [1950] 1 All E.R. 283.

limited construction is right, what is the need for the words "in the interests of justice or otherwise" as qualifying good faith? On the limited construction "or otherwise" is merely something being done not in good faith yet in the interests of justice. Again, and it is really the same point, one asks oneself: can one think of a case in which an application is not being made in good faith which is not also being made otherwise than in the interests of justice? It seems to me that as a matter of construction the position is plain, and that even if there can be said to be an ambiguity, the obvious purpose of this section would dictate that a wide construction should be given to it. Accordingly, holding as I do that under the section there is a wide discretion in the court, I would, in the circumstances of the present case, come to the conclusion that the applicant ought to be discharged absolutely.

SALMON J. I agree.

EDMUND DAVIES J. I also agree.

Application allowed with costs against the Government of India.

Solicitors: *Victor J. Lissack; Director of Public Prosecutions; T. L. Wilson & Co.*

IN RE ALLEN

(*The Times,* October 11, 1961)

October 10, 1961: Queen's Bench Division: Lord Parker C.J., Ashworth, Veale JJ.

Exiled Fugitive Must Return

The Divisional Court, refusing this motion by George Allen, of Coomer Road, Fulham, S.W. 6, for a writ of *habeas corpus* and refusing to make an order for his discharge from Brixton Prison under section 10 of the Fugitive Offenders' Act, 1881, held that a "fugitive" within the meaning of section 2 of the Fugitive Offenders' Act, 1881, was not merely a person who was fleeing justice but included a person who was accused of having committed an offence in a part of Her Majesty's Dominions and who had left that part.

Mr. Gerald Owen appeared for Allen.

The LORD CHIEF JUSTICE said that Allen was detained under an order made under section 5 of the Fugitive Offenders' Act, 1881, to await his return to Gibraltar on a warrant charging him with two counts of forgery. He had held the post of Secretary-Treasurer to the Gibraltar branch of the British Legion while he was serving in the Gibraltar police force. The allegations concerned two cheques which had been altered from £3 5s. to £23 5s. in one case and £73 5s. in the other. Lest it be thought that these were trivial matters, it must be pointed out that these two cheques were only sample evidence, and that it appeared from the documents that such alterations were made on a large scale.

It was said in argument that he was not a fugitive within section 2 of the Fugitive Offenders' Act, 1881. It appeared that while in the Gibraltar police force, he and his wife went by car to Spain on March 29, 1960, and it was said that they were discovered to be carrying contraband with the result that his contract with the Gibraltar police was terminated. Reference was made to the fact that the Governor of Gibraltar altered the original dismissal from service to termination of employment; and in the letter from the Gibraltar authorities making this change, it was said that neither the applicant nor his wife would be allowed to remain in Gibraltar and that they must make arrangements to leave. It was said, therefore, they did not flee from Gibraltar but merely carried out the Governor's request. However, a fugitive within section 2 of the Act, was not merely a person who was fleeing justice but included a person who was accused of having committed an offence in a part of her Majesty's dominions and who had left that part.

Relief was also sought under section 10 of the Fugitive Offenders' Act, 1881; but the Court could not see any valid ground for the exercise of its discretion under section 10, and the motion would be refused.

Solicitors: *Messrs. Martin, Boston & Co.*

IN RE ALLEN

(*The Times,* October 21, 1961)

October 20, 1961: Queen's Bench Division: Lord Parker C.J., Ashworth J.

Exiled Fugitive Refused Leave

The Divisional Court dismissed this application on behalf of Mr. George Allen, now detained in Brixton Prison under an order made under section 5 of the Fugitive Offenders' Act, 1881, to await his return to Gibraltar on a warrant charging him with two counts of forgery, for leave to appeal to the House of Lords from the declaration of the Divisional Court* (*The Times*, October 11) dismissing his application for a writ of *habeas corpus* or, alternatively, for relief under section 10 of the Act of 1881.

Mr. Gerald Owen appeared for the applicant; *Mr. Brian Leary* for the Government of Gibraltar.

Mr. Owen referred to the hearing of the application before the Divisional Court.

The LORD CHIEF JUSTICE. The real question was whether the Court should grant relief under section 10. So far as your application for *habeas corpus* is concerned, the question is whether this Court grants leave to go to the House of Lords. So far as relief under section 10 is concerned, is that a matter which we have to certify?

Counsel said that he thought not. He thought that the Court would not have to give a certificate of public importance under either of his applications. This could be a case where the House of Lords could indicate whether a person who had been exiled from a country was a fugitive within section 2 because "fugitive" was not defined in the Act, and also, both under section 2 and section 10, the special circumstances in which the Divisional Court could order the discharge of an offender.

The LORD CHIEF JUSTICE said that the Court refused leave.

Solicitors: *Messrs Martin, Boston & Co.; Messrs Charles Russell & Co.*

EX PARTE JAMES

(*The Times,* November 18, 1961)

November 17, 1961: Queen's Bench Division: Ashworth, Edmund Davies, Veale JJ.

Hire Purchase in Southern Rhodesia

The Court allowed this application by Mr. John Michael James for leave to apply for a writ of *habeas corpus.*

The Government of Southern Rhodesia had applied for Mr. James to be committed and returned to their country on the ground that he was guilty of fraud or false pretences in selling to another person a motor car which was the subject matter of a hire purchase agreement without disclosing to the buyer the existence of such hire purchase agreement. The Chief Magistrate committed Mr. James to Brixton Prison under section 5 of the Fugitive Offenders Act. 1881.

Mr. Harry Lester for Mr. James said that the evidence showed that the document which was alleged to be a hire purchase agreement did not contain the date of the payment or the subsequent instalments and that such date must have been inserted in the document after the applicant had appended his signature. Further, by reason of section 6 of the Hire Purchase Act of the Federation of Rhodesia and Nyasaland, No. 34 of 1956, the omission of the date had the effect of nullifying the hire purchase agreement altogether and substituting therefor a sale of the motor car by the "owner" to the "hirer". In these circumstances, the property in the motor car passed immediately to James when he appended his signature to the intended hire purchase agreement and he did not thereafter commit any offence by selling the motor car.

Mr. Justice ASHWORTH said that the Court would grant the application and that Mr. James would be admitted to bail.

His Lordship directed that the notice of motion should be served on the Governor of Brixton Prison and on the Government of Southern Rhodesia.

Solicitors: *Messrs Field, Roscoe & Co.*

IN RE JAMES

(*The Times*, November 29, 1961)

November 28, 1961: Queen's Bench Division: Lord Parker C.J., Ashworth, Widgery JJ.

Habeas Corpus Granted

The Divisional Court granted this application by John Michael James, formerly a police constable in Southern Rhodesia, for a writ of *habeas corpus* and ordered that he be released. The applicant had been committed to prison by the Bow Street Magistrate on November 16, 1961, under section 5 of the Fugitive Offenders Act, 1881, but was released on bail the following day pending his application to the Court* (*The Times*, November 18, 1961).

Mr. Harry Lester appeared for the applicant; *Mr. Brian Leary* for the Government of Southern Rhodesia; and *Mr. John Buzzard* for the Governor of Brixton Prison.

The LORD CHIEF JUSTICE said that in January the applicant entered into a hire purchase agreement for the purchase of a £300 motor car. In March, before coming to England, he sold the car to a fellow constable for £275. The applicant had decided not to go back to Rhodesia. Proceedings were started against him in Rhodesia charging him with fraud or theft by false pretences. The money still due under the hire purchase agreement had been paid in full on November 1.

It had been contended that the hire purchase agreement did not contain at the date of the applicant's signature the dates, or the mode of determining the dates on which the instalments were due and that by reason of this omission, the effect of section 6 of the Hire Purchase Act of the Federation of Rhodesia and Nyasaland, No. 34 of 1956, was to nullify the hire purchase agreement and substitute a sale of the motor car by the "owner" to the "hirer". It would be a complete answer to these charges if the property in the car had in fact passed to the applicant.

On the other hand, it had been argued that as the number of instalments and date of the final instalment had been inserted, the dates of the earlier payments could be spelled out of this agreement by inference from the date of the final instalment. However, the Act required other specific dates or a specific mode of determining the dates to be set out. It seemed that the object of the Act was that there should appear on the face of the document the date on which each instalment fell due.

It had also been contended that a pencil entry of the instalment dates in the copy of the agreement held by the Hire Purchase Finance Company provided some evidence that the pencil entry had been made before the agreement was signed and that the Court should not set itself the task of weighing evidence in proceedings under the Fugitive Offenders Act since this was a matter for the court of trial in Southern Rhodesia. But in order to justify committing the fugitive the magistrate must be satisfied that the evidence raised a strong or probable presumption that he had committed the offence. It could not be said that the magistrate was justified in this case in holding that a strong or probable presumption of the applicant's guilt arose. Accordingly, the writ of *habeas corpus* would issue and the applicant would be awarded costs against the Government of Southern Rhodesia.

Mr. Justice ASHWORTH and Mr. Justice WIDGERY agreed.

Solicitors: *Messrs Field, Roscoe & Co.; Messrs Charles Russell & Co.; Director of Public Prosecutions.*

REGINA v. GOVERNOR OF BRIXTON PRISON *EX PARTE* MOURAT MEHMET

([1962] 2 Q.B. 1)

December 8, 15, 1961: Queen's Bench Division: Lord Parker C.J., Slade, Widgery JJ.

Fugitive Offender—Habeas corpus—Jurisdiction—Evidence—Alleged offences under Cyprus Criminal Code—Committal to prison to await deportation to Cyprus—Whether evidence before magistrate disclosed strong or probable presumption of guilt—Power of court to look at evidence before magistrate—Fugitive Offenders Act, 1881 (44 & 45 Vict. *c.* 69), *ss.* 2, 5, 10.

Fugitive Offender—Warrant—Form of—"Stealing by clerk, fraudulent false accounting, etc. . . ."—Other charges investigated—Particulars to be attached to warrant.

The applicant, a former employee of a Turkish bank in Cyprus, was arrested on a warrant issued under section 2 of the Fugitive Offenders Act, 1881,[1] and brought before a magistrate who committed him to prison to await return to Cyprus to answer charges [2] under the Cyprus Criminal Code. The warrant charged him with "stealing by clerk, fraudulent false accounting, etc." and related to false entries in the ledger book of the bank, namely, a deposit slip of £2 on November 7, 1960, and a false withdrawal slip two days later whereby £400 was wrongfully withdrawn from a savings account of a bank customer. The magistrate investigated seven charges, including charges of forgery and

[1] Fugitive Offenders Act, 1881, s. 2: "Where a person accused of having committed an offence . . . in one part of Her Majesty's dominions has left that part, such person . . . if found in another part of Her Majesty's dominions, shall be liable to be apprehended and returned . . . to the part from which he is a fugitive. A fugitive may be so apprehended under an endorsed warrant . . ."

S. 5: "A fugitive when apprehended shall be brought before a magistrate, who . . . shall hear the case . . . If . . . such evidence is produced as . . . raises a strong or probable presumption that the fugitive committed the offence mentioned in the warrant, . . . the magistrate shall commit the fugitive to prison to await his return . . ."

S. 10: "Where it is made to appear to a superior court that . . . it would, having regard to . . . all the circumstances of the case, be unjust or oppressive . . . to return the fugitive . . . such court may discharge the fugitive . . ."

uttering false documents. The evidence was to the effect that the false deposit and withdrawal slips were in the handwriting of and initialled by the applicant; that the withdrawal slip had also been initialled by the assistant accountant and the cashier; and that if the proper procedure for withdrawal were followed it would be necessary for the customer to present the bank book at the bank. A copy of the bank ledger showed that on the day that the irregularities were discovered the chief accountant had made an entry therein relating to a refund of £398 arising out of irregularities by another bank clerk who had decamped on the day on which the £400 had been wrongfully withdrawn. The applicant was of good character:—

Held, that there was a power in the court to review the case as it appeared before the magistrate and to look at the facts there disclosed to see if they disclosed a strong or probable presumption of guilt which alone would justify the magistrate in making the committal order. On a proper analysis of the evidence, there was a strong element of doubt and no magistrate applying his mind to the question could come to the conclusion that such a strong or probable presumption had been made out and accordingly the applicant would be discharged.

Per Lord Parker C.J. It would be more satisfactory if in future the warrant contained on its face a reference to the charges with which it is sought to deal, and that those charges with proper particulars should be attached to the warrant.

ADJOURNED APPLICATION for a writ of habeas corpus.

The applicant, Mourat Mehmet, applied for a writ of habeas corpus ad subjiciendum directed to the Governor of Brixton Prison where he was detained pending his return in custody to the Republic of Cyprus pursuant to an order dated November 25, 1961, of the Chief Metropolitan Magistrate, Mr. R. H. Blundell, made under section 5 of the Fugitive Offenders Act, 1881.

The warrant under which the applicant had been arrested and brought before the magistrate was issued by the judge of the **[3]** District Court of Nicosia, Cyprus, and endorsed in the United Kingdom. It charged him with "stealing by clerk, fraudulent false accounting, etc." contrary to sections 268 and 313 (*b*) respectively of the Cyprus Criminal Code, Cap. 154, which offences are punishable by a maximum imprisonment of seven years each. When the case came before the magistrate seven charges against the applicant were investigated, including charges of forgery and of uttering false documents, only three of the charges being for stealing by a clerk, or fraudulent false accounting.

It was alleged before the chief magistrate that the applicant, whilst a clerk in the Turkish Ish Bank, A.S. of Nicosia, Cyprus, had on November 9, 1960, stolen the sum of £400 which had come into his possession on account of his employers; and that the means whereby he had done this involved two false entries in the ledger book of the bank, one on November 7, 1960, a false deposit of £2 in the account belonging to one Fatma Mehmed Haji Ibrahim, and the second, on November 9, a false withdrawal of £400 from the same account.

Mrs. Ibrahim gave evidence that she owned the account in question and that her savings bank book No. 5930 had never left her hands. On January 10, 1961, she went to the bank in order to close the account and the false entries in the ledger were then discovered. She had given no authority for the transactions. Her evidence was corroborated by the bank manager, who also said that the deposit and withdrawal slips had been made out and initialled by the applicant. Photostats of the ledger account and deposit and withdrawal slips were made exhibits in the case and it appeared that on discovery of the irregularities the chief accountant had made an entry in the ledger which when translated read: "Refund to the account, through the irregularities of Selchuk Mustafa . . . £398. The interest on £398 from last year's losses £2,028 mils." Selchuk Mustafa was another former clerk of the same bank who disappeared on the very day, November 9, 1960, when the money was alleged to have been taken by the applicant. The matter was adjourned until October 12, 1961, when further depositions were put in.

The assistant accountant who discovered the irregularities corroborated that the handwriting and initials on the deposit and withdrawal slips were those of the applicant and that he himself had initialled the withdrawal slip. The chief accountant gave evidence that he also had initialled the withdrawal slip and that the slip was made out in the handwriting of the applicant. The [4] cashier said that the withdrawal slip was in Mourat Mehmet's handwriting and initialled by him, and that he himself had initialled it, but that he did not remember the person to whom he had paid the money.

For the defence one Ruhi, another former employee of the same bank, gave evidence of the system of deposit and withdrawal and that evidence was uncontroverted. His evidence was to the effect that when a withdrawal was made, the customer must produce his or her book, the clerk then made out a withdrawal slip which was stamped and then signed by the customer. The clerk then checked the slip with the ledger and initialled it. The bank book and the slip were then taken by a messenger to the accountant who checked it again and initialled it. The slip then went to the cashier who checked to see that the slip was initialled by the accountant, and he then made an entry in his own book and called the customer to him, stamped the slip and initialled it and gave the customer his money. The cashier was the only person who received money from a customer or who paid it out to a customer. Money was never paid out to a clerk.

On that evidence the chief magistrate made the order committing the applicant to prison.

The applicant had remained at work at the bank in Cyprus until December 6, 1960, when he came to Great Britain. Selchuk Mustafa had disappeared and a warrant for his arrest under section 2 of the Fugitive Offenders Act, 1881, in respect of other defalcations from the same bank was issued on February 11, 1961.

The applicant applied for (1) a writ of habeas corpus on the ground that there was insufficient evidence to justify the magistrate in making the committal order; or (2) alternatively, relief under section 10 of the Fugitive Offenders Act, 1881.

R. D. L. Du Cann for the applicant. The form and contents of the warrant differ from the charges which were brought against the applicant before the magistrate, and no particulars of the offences are given on the warrant, which merely alleges "Stealing by clerk, fraudulent false accounting, etc.," contrary to sections 268 and 313 (*b*) of the Cyprus Criminal Code, Cap. 154. Neither the date of the offence of stealing nor the amount stolen are given, nor, in relation to the charge of false accounting, is it stated what documents were falsified. Before the magistrate the applicant was charged with seven offences, including forgery and uttering false documents, but only two of the offences charged are covered by the words of the warrant. The magistrate has jurisdiction to [5] commit only in respect of those charges which are set out in the warrant: see section 5 of the Fugitive Offenders Act, 1881. It is clear that the magistrate can commit only if the offences appear on the face of the warrant, and, therefore, the form of the present warrant is bad, certainly in respect of those charges not shown thereon, possibly on all seven charges.

The evidence before the magistrate shows that the withdrawal slip, though made out by the applicant, had been initialled by the cashier and by the chief accountant of the bank, and that the bank procedure is that the cashier never pays out money to another clerk of the bank, but only to the customer on presentation of the customer's savings bank book and after seeing that the withdrawal slip is duly initialled by the clerk. The evidence as to bank procedure given by Ruhi for the defence is uncontroverted and shows that a savings bank book must have been presented and passed from the clerk to the cashier, and, unless there was an accomplice, that destroys the case presented for the Government of Cyprus. The applicant's conduct in working out his month's notice and in writing to the bank manager after his arrival in England is not that of a fugitive. The evidence of the Ledger Book entry made by the chief accountant shows that the irregularities were at first attributed to Selchuk Mustafa, who absconded the very day when the withdrawal was made and who is a man against whom there is a warrant for his arrest on another charge of a similar fraudulent withdrawal of £1,600 from another account.

The question on these facts is whether this court can say that there is a strong or probable presumption of guilt against the applicant upon which he ought to stand his trial: see *Rex* v. *Governor of Brixton Prison, Ex parte Bidwell.*[2]* This court is entitled to look at the evidence before the magistrate to see if it is sufficient: see *In re James.*[3]* Here on the evidence before the magistrate it is impossible to say that the applicant was not deceived just as the cashier and the chief accountant were deceived. Here there was no fleeing, no sudden accession of wealth and no hiding in this country upon the part of the applicant; and, further, he is a man of good character. The method alleged in the case of Selchuk Mustafa is very similar to that alleged against the applicant.

[LORD PARKER C.J. Your case in a nutshell is "Why pick on me!"] **[6]**

John Bolland for the Government of Cyprus. It is agreed, in respect of the warrant, that only those charges recorded on its face can be sustained, but this in fact covers the first three charges.

[LORD PARKER C.J. The point is purely academic, since if the applicant is committed on any charge and sent to Cyprus the other matters can be raised when he gets there.]

As to the evidence against this applicant, it is clear that though at first the bank thought the irregularities were due to Selchuk Mustafa, later they became convinced that there were two dishonest clerks operating. The magistrate's duty is to hear the evidence on both sides and to resolve whether on that evidence there is a strong or probable presumption of guilt.

[LORD PARKER C.J. What evidence is there that it is more probable that the applicant committed the offence than that someone else did, perhaps Selchuk Mustafa?]

It is clearly shown that Selchuk Mustafa had nothing to do with the offence—there is a difference between the two systems.

If there was a book produced it must have been identical with the original—the number, the signature and the entries in it must have been the same. The inference is irresistible that someone in the bank must have forged it—unless he stole the original and returned it. If the first inference is correct, then some woman must have come along, able to sign the slip so identically that it passes on comparison with the specimen signature—it would require someone very clever indeed.

[LORD PARKER C.J. What do you suggest the applicant did? Do you say he had an accomplice or that he just forged the entries, or what?]

I concede that the case on the evidence presented to us was that there was no forged book. The bank's normal procedure cannot therefore have been followed properly. One is entitled on the evidence to say: "We don't know whether there was a forged book or a breakdown of bank procedure, but it was Mourat Mehmet who forged both slips—the payment in of £2 and the withdrawal of £400—and as the right customer has not got the money the only conclusion is that the applicant was guilty." It is not right to interfere with the magistrate's decision. The facts give rise to sufficient suspicion for this man to have to stand his trial.

John Buzzard for the Governor of Brixton Prison. I am inclined to agree with the applicant; but clearly there must have been someone operating inside the bank, who would have been **[7]** able to take impressions of the relevant signature. *In re James*[3] clearly settles the point, which had been left open in *Rex* v. *Governor of Brixton Prison, Ex parte Bidwell*[4]* and *Rex* v. *Vyner,*[5]* that this court has power to look at the evidence which was before the magistrate and to consider whether any magistrate, properly applying his mind to the question, could reasonably have come to the conclusion that a strong or probable presumption of guilt had been made out. This proposition is also supported by

[2] [1937] 1 K.B. 305; 53 T.L.R. 1; [1936] 1 All E.R. 31, D.C.
[3] *The Times,* Nov. 29, 1961, D.C.
[4] [1937] 1 K.B. 305.
[5] (1903) 68 J.P. 142, D.C.

In re Arton (*No. 1*),[6]* where it is said that this court is entitled and, indeed, bound to see whether such a prima facie case of guilt has been made out as would entitle the magistrate to commit. *Rex* v. *Governor of Brixton Prison, Ex parte Bidwell*[7]* was, of course, a case where an order nisi for a writ of habeas corpus was asked for and not relief under section 10 of the Fugitive Offenders Act, 1881. That case[7] and *Rex* v. *Vyner*[8]* are the only cases directly in point under the Fugitive Offenders Act, 1881, but there are many cases under the Extradition Act, 1870, s. 10, some deciding one way and some another, but in all of which it was agreed that this court could look at the depositions which were before the magistrate; and surely if it is entitled to do that it must be entitled here to see if the evidence is sufficient to justify the magistrate in coming to the conclusion that there was a strong or probable presumption of guilt—the only finding of fact which would give him jurisdiction to make the committal order. If this court looks at the evidence at all, it must look to see if it is sufficient; that is inescapable. In *In re James*[9]* it was not for this court to weigh the evidence provided that it was evidence that raised a strong or probable presumption of guilt. If there is such evidence the court will not interfere. In *In re Arton* (*No. 2*)[10]* Lord Russell C.J. said this court was not a court of appeal on questions of fact from the magistrate. It only has to see that he had such evidence before him as gave him authority to commit.

[SLADE J. In extradition cases it is quite different; you have only to show prima facie evidence, but here you have to show strong or probable presumption.]

Rex v. *Governor of Brixton Prison, Ex parte Bidwell*[11]* does, however, seem to equate the two phrases. **[8]**

[SLADE J. I should have thought strong or probable presumption of guilt was something more than mere prima facie guilt.]

As to the question whether the degree is the same, Swift J. in *Rex* v. *Governor of Brixton Prison, Ex parte Bidwell*[11]* seems to treat the phases as the same, but it was not necessary in that case to decide the point, so that his words are to that extent obiter. If one were considering the matter ab initio, one might well draw a distinction between the two phrases, but the principle must be the same.

As to the form of the warrant, where it is desired to incorporate certain charges the warrant should set out the particulars.

R. D. L. Du Cann in reply. The charges on the warrant are usually particularised on the back of the warrant.

LORD PARKER C.J. The applicant is detained pursuant to an order of the chief magistrate dated November 25, 1961, made under section 5 of the Act of 1881, committing him to Brixton Prison pending his return in custody to the Republic of Cyprus. The endorsed warrant was to this effect: "You are hereby commanded to apprehend Mourat Mehmet of Nicosia, Cyprus, but now suspected residing at No. 17, Goodge Street, London, W.7, or at No. 51, Dongola Road, Tottenham, United Kingdom, who has been charged of stealing by clerk, fraudulent false accounting, etc., contrary" to certain provisions of the Cyprus Criminal Code.

The first point to which our attention has been drawn in this case is the form of that warrant because it is to be observed that it does not give any particulars in the case of stealing by a clerk, as to whose clerk it is said he was or the amount of stealing or, in the case of the fraudulent false accounting, as to the amounts, etc. Finally, it ends with the word "etc.," to which no significance can be attached in the sense that anybody reading it can possibly see what he is

[6] [1896] 1 Q.B. 108; 12 T.L.R. 131, D.C.
[7] [1937] 1 K.B. 305.
[8] 68 J.P. 142.
[9] *The Times,* Nov. 29, 1961.
[10] [1896] 1 Q.B. 509; 12 T.L.R. 189, D.C.
[11] [1937] 1 K.B. 305.

being charged with. Nothing was attached to the warrant, but it does appear that the charges which were investigated by the chief magistrate were some seven in number, and included forgery and uttering false documents, and only three of which concerned stealing by a clerk and fraudulent false accounting. It is, I think, quite clear from section 5 of the Act of 1881 that the magistrate can only commit him in respect of charges referred to in the warrant and, accordingly, he could only strictly commit the applicant on those three charges of stealing by a clerk **[9]** and fraudulent false accounting. The matter is, of course, quite academic, because if he is committed and returned to Cyprus on one charge alone, the authorities, when he gets there, can charge all the rest. Nevertheless, for my part I think it would be far more satisfactory in the future if the warrant contained on its face a reference to the charges with which it is sought to deal and that those charges with proper particulars should be attached to the warrant.

[His Lordship stated the facts as substantially set out above and continued:] If the proper procedure had been followed in this case, there must have been some woman with a book which was a facsimile of the book of Mrs. Ibrahim, containing all the proper entries, and she would have had to forge Mrs. Ibrahim's signature. That is a possibility. The other possibility, and the suggestion here is that this was an inside job, is that it was the applicant who had obtained the money either by forging the book himself or by persuading the chief accountant and the cashier not to follow the procedure, and to act without a book at all.

For my part, I find the position very unsatisfactory. There may have been no book and a breakdown of procedure, in which case both the chief accountant and the cashier, who have given their evidence on depositions, did not do what they should have done, or it was a woman coming in with a forged book, I suppose the suggestion would be as an accomplice of this applicant, in which case she and her book had deceived the chief accountant and the cashier. Of course, it is equally possible that the person who enabled this woman to come with a forged book was somebody other than the applicant, some other clerk or, indeed, the chief accountant or the cashier of the bank, and for my part I cannot see why this applicant might not have been deceived just as it is said the cashier was deceived. I am still of the same opinion as I was in the course of the argument, when I suggested that the applicant's real case was: "Why pick on me?"

In that state of the evidence it is quite relevant, I think, to observe that the other man, Selchuk Mustafa, whose irregularities were said originally to have been the cause of this £400 going, in fact vanished the very evening of November 9, 1960, the day when the £400 was taken. I, personally, also take into consideration the fact that this applicant, so far from fleeing, stayed on until December 6, 1960, working out a month's notice which he had given and, finally, that he is a man of good character.

Taking all those matters into consideration, I find it very difficult to think, in so far as it rests with me, that a strong or **[10]** probable presumption has been made out that the offences referred to in the first three charges of the warrant have been committed. I appreciate, of course, although no point has been taken, that the question whether there is a strong or probable presumption is one for the magistrate. The matter has not been fully argued in this case, but Mr. Buzzard has quite rightly reminded us that there are a number of cases on the matter, and therefore it would perhaps be wrong for us to give a final ruling until a case emerges in which the matter is fully argued, but for my part I am quite clear that there is some power of review in this court. The matter was left open both in *Rex* v. *Vyner*,[12]* and also in *Rex* v. *Governor of Brixton Prison, Ex parte Bidwell.*[13]* But in a recent unreported case, *In re James*, [14]* this court has taken upon itself the right not only to look at the evidence which was before the magistrate, but to consider whether any magistrate, properly applying

[12] (1903) 68 J.P. 142, D.C.
[13] [1937] 1 K.B. 305; [1936] W.N. 275; 53 T.L.R. 1; [1936] 1 All E.R. 31, D.C.
[14] *The Times*, Nov. 29, 1961.

his mind to the question, could reasonably have come to the conclusion that a strong or probable presumption had been made out. Unless and until I am convinced by argument to the contrary, I would proceed on the basis upon which Mr. Buzzard has put the matter to us. He says: "Clearly this court can look to see what was the evidence before the magistrate, and if this court can do that, then surely it is looking to see and must look to see whether the evidence before the magistrate was such as to justify him in reaching the finding of fact which alone gave him jurisdiction to commit, namely, that a strong or probable presumption had been made out."

In the present case I have come clearly to the conclusion that on a proper analysis of this evidence, the matter was left in a high degree of doubt, and I do not think that any magistrate applying his mind to the question could come to the conclusion that a strong or probable presumption had been made out. In those circumstances, it seems to me that this applicant ought to be discharged.

SLADE J. I confess that, having heard all the evidence which was before the chief magistrate, my first impression was that there were materials upon which he was entitled to exercise his discretion in finding that there was a strong or probable presumption that the applicant had committed the offences forming [11]
charges 1, 2 and 3, that is to say, offences under sections 268 and 313 (*b*) of the Cyprus Criminal Code. I entirely agree, although this court is slow to differ from the exercise of discretion by the magistrate, that this court has jurisdiction to interfere and, having listened to the judgment of Lord Parker C.J., I have come to the conclusion that I, like the chief magistrate, was wrong, and therefore I agree with his judgment.

WIDGERY J. I also agree, and have no doubt whatever that the evidence before the magistrate could not be said to disclose a strong or probable presumption of guilt.

Writ of habeas corpus to issue, and order for discharge of applicant with costs against the Government of the Republic of Cyprus.

Solicitors: *Rubinstein, Nash & Co.; Geffen & Co.; Director of Public Prosecutions.*

ZACHARIA v. REPUBLIC OF CYPRUS AND ANOTHER ARESTIDOU v. SAME

([1963] A.C. 634)

November 21, 22, 1961: Queen's Bench Division: Lord Parker C.J., Ashworth, Widgery JJ.

March 13, 14, 15, 19, April 17, 1962: House of Lords: Viscount Simonds, Lords Reid, Radcliffe, Hodson, Devlin.

Fugitive Offender—Court's jurisdiction to discharge—Political offence—Whether court entitled to take cognisance of the political character of application for return of offender—Fugitive Offenders Act, 1881 (44 & 45 *Vict. c.* 69), *s.* 10.

Fugitive Offender—Habeas corpus—Jurisdiction—Whether court has jurisdiction under section 10 *on application only for habeas corpus—Nature of relief under section* 10*—Fugitive Offenders Act,* 1881, *ss.* 5, 10.

House of Lords—Leave to appeal—Criminal cause or matter—Habeas corpus—Proceedings under section 10 *of the Fugitive Offenders Act,* 1881*—Refusal of leave and no grant of certificate by Divisional Court that decision under Act of* 1881 *involved point of law of general public importance—Whether certificate* *necessary—Administration of Justice Act*, 1960 (8 & 9 *Eliz.* 2, *c.* 65), *ss.* 1 (2), 15 (3).

On September 13, 1961, at Bow Street Magistrates' Court an order was made under section 5 of the Fugitive Offenders Act, 1881, committing Z., a Cypriot, to Brixton Prison pending his return to Cyprus in respect of warrants upon which he had previously been arrested. The warrants alleged numerous offences including two murders. Z. thereupon applied to the Divisional Court of the Queen's Bench Division for a writ of habeas corpus ad subjiciendum and for relief under section 10 of the Fugitive Offenders Act, 1881.[1] **[635]**

Z. claimed relief under section 10 on three grounds: (i) that the murders for which his surrender was demanded were offences of a political character. The offences were not admitted, but it was stated that the allegations against him, if true, showed that the killings were done in the course of the fight for the independence of Cyprus made by the body called E.O.K.A. (ii) That the application for his return was not made in good faith in the interests of justice. (iii) That in all the circumstances of the case it would be unjust or oppressive to return him to stand trial, in particular, in view of the fact that there had been three attempts on his life between 1957 and January, 1961, when he came to live in England.

Z. had rendered services to the British Government as an informer against E.O.K.A. members before the independence of Cyprus was declared, and there was a real danger that in the event of his return (1) of his assassination, (2) that evidence would be fabricated against him.

The Divisional Court dismissed the application under both heads and refused leave to appeal. Subsequently leave was granted by the House of Lords.

On the hearing of the appeal the question arose whether the appeal under section 10 of the Act of 1881, being in a criminal cause or matter, could be entertained by the House of Lords notwithstanding that no certificate was asked for or given by the court below pursuant to section 1 (2) of the Administration of Justice Act, 1960,[2] that a point of law of general public

[1] Fugitive Offenders Act, 1881, s. 10: "Where it is made to appear to a superior court that by reason of the trivial nature of the case, or by reason of the application for the return of a fugitive not being made in good faith in the interests of justice or otherwise, it would, having regard to distance, to the facilities for communication, and to all the circumstances of the case, be unjust or oppressive or too severe a punishment to return the fugitive either at all or until the expiration of a certain period, such court may discharge the fugitive either absolutely or on bail, or order that he shall not be returned until after the expiration of the period named in the order, or may make such other order in the premises as to the court seems just."

Cyprus Act, 1960, s. 3 (1): "On and after the appointed day [August 16, 1960] any existing law which operates as law of, or of any part of, the United Kingdom, being a law applying in relation to Cyprus or persons or things in any way belonging thereto or connected therewith, shall, save as provided after the passing of this Act by the authority having power to amend or repeal that law or by the following provisions of this Act, continue to apply in like manner in relation to the Republic of Cyprus or persons or things in any way belonging thereto or connected therewith."

[2] Administration of Justice Act, 1960, s. 1: "(1) Subject to the provisions of this section, an appeal shall lie to the House of Lords, at the instance of the defendant or the prosecutor,—(*a*) from any decision of a Divisional Court of the Queen's Bench Division in a criminal cause or matter; . . . (2) No appeal shall lie under this section except with the leave of the court below or of the House of Lords; and such leave shall not be granted unless it is certified by the court below that a point of law of general public importance is involved in the decision and it appears to that court or to the House of Lords, as the case may be, that the point is one which ought to be considered by that House."

S. 15: "(1) Subject to the provisions of this section, an appeal shall lie in any proceedings upon application for habeas corpus, whether civil or criminal, against an order for the release of the person restrained as well as against the refusal of such order . . . (3) In relation to a decision of a Divisional Court on a criminal application for habeas corpus, section one of this Act shall have effect as if so much of subsection (2) as restricts the grant of leave to appeal were omitted."

importance was involved in the decision:—

Held, (1) (Viscount Simonds and Lord Hodson dissenting), that the House of Lords had jurisdiction to hear the appeal merely on leave granted, for the court's powers to grant relief under section 10 of the Fugitive Offenders Act. 1881, were an adjunct to its power to protect by habeas corpus, and that, accordingly, where, as here, an application for the writ was joined with proceedings under section 10, the provision of section 15 (3) of the Administration of Justice Act, 1960, that struck out the statutory restriction on the grant of [**636**] leave to appeal to both forms of proceedings (post, pp. 676, 685).

Per Lord Devlin. On an application only for habeas corpus a superior court can exercise its powers under section 10 (post, p. 685).

Quaere, whether in any event the House of Lords had not jurisdiction to entertain the appeal so long as its own order granting leave to appeal stood (post, p. 683).

Rex v. *Governor of Brixton Prison, Ex parte Savarkar** [1910] 2 K.B. 1056; 26 T.L.R. 561, C.A. considered.

(2) That a court acting under section 10 of the Act of 1881 was confined to the considerations of which it was there directed to take account; and that whether the alleged offences were of a political nature was irrelevant (post. pp. 661, 666, 680, 688).

been material to show that it was not made in good faith in the interests of *Ali Ahmed** [1952] 1 All E.R. 1060, 1063; [1952] 1 T.L.R. 964, D.C.

Dictum of Lord Goddard C.J. in *In re Government of India and Mubarak* disapproved.

Per Lord Hodson and Lord Devlin. If the application for the return of the fugitive had been made for purposes of political revenge, that would have justice (post, pp. 681, 688).

(3) (Lord Radcliffe dissenting) that there was no ground on which it would be proper to interfere with the exercise under section 10 of the discretion of the Divisional Court; and that, accordingly, the appeal must be dismissed.

Decision of the Divisional Court affirmed.

APPEALS from the Divisional Court (Lord Parker C.J., Ashworth and Widgery JJ.).

These were two appeals by leave of the House of Lords from the decision of the Divisional Court of the Queen's Bench Division dated November 22, 1961, refusing to order that writs of habeas corpus should issue for the release of the appellants, Antonis Zacharia and Euripides Arestidou from Brixton Prison, or to order their discharge pursuant to section 10 of the Fugitive Offenders Act, 1881.

The appellants, both of whom were Cypriots, had come to the United Kingdom from Cyprus at the beginning of 1961. Under the Cyprus Act, 1960, the island of Cyprus became an independent sovereign republic within the Commonwealth. On September 13, 1961, at Bow Street Magistrates' Court, orders were made under section 5 of the Fugitive Offenders Act, 1881, committing the appellants to Brixton Prison pending their return to Cyprus in respect of warrants upon which they had previously been arrested. These warrants had been duly indorsed under section 3 of the Act of 1881 and the appellants had been apprehended accordingly. There were four warrants relating to Zacharia and [**637**] they alleged numerous offences, namely, abduction, carrying a revolver or pistol contrary to the firearms law, assault, robbery with violence, demanding money with menaces, and two murders. Only one of the warrants related to Arestidou, who was described in the evidence as a friend and bodyguard of Zacharia, namely, warrant No. 2 which concerned the offences of robbery with violence and demanding money with menaces.

The appellants applied to the Divisional Court of the Queen's Bench Division for writs of habeas corpus ad subjiciendum and for relief under section 10 of the Fugitive Offenders Act, 1881.

Jeremy Hutchinson Q.C. and *J. C. Mathew* for the appellants.

Edward Clarke Q.C. and *John Bolland* for the Republic of Cyprus.
John Leonard for the Governor of Brixton Prison.

LORD PARKER C.J. In these proceedings Mr. Hutchinson moves on behalf of one Antonis Zacharia, now detained in Her Majesty's Prison at Brixton pursuant to an order of the Bow Street Magistrates' Court under section 5 of the Fugitive Offenders Act, 1881. The motion asks for a writ of habeas corpus or, alternatively, for relief under section 10 of that Act.

The matter arises in this way: The Fugitive Offenders Act not only applied to Cyprus prior to that country becoming a Republic on August 16, 1960, but under the new constitution the Act was continued in force in regard to the Republic rather than having a separate treaty and making the Extradition Act, 1870, apply.

The Cyprus authorities forwarded to this country four warrants asking for the applicant to be returned to Cyprus under the Act of 1881. The first warrant alleged three offences, first, of abducting one Mouyias, secondly, of carrying a revolver or pistol contrary to the firearms law, and thirdly, assaulting Mouyias and occasioning him actual bodily harm. The second warrant concerned an alleged robbery with violence of one Triantifillides, secondly, of demanding £250 from him by menaces, and thirdly, again of carrying a firearm contrary to the Firearms Act. The third warrant charged the applicant with the murder of one Papachakhas, and the fourth warrant again in respect of murder alleged that he murdered one Mouzomenos. Those warrants were supported before the magistrate by depositions, and in due course the magistrate found under section 5 of the Act that **[638]** thereby there was a strong or probable presumption that the fugitive committed the offences mentioned in the warrants.

In his application to this court the applicant's case, as appears from his affidavits, is quite shortly this: He says that between 1956 and 1960, when Cyprus was in a state of disturbance and the security forces were taking action against E.O.K.A., he became an agent of the security forces. He alleges that in doing so he became branded amongst the E.O.K.A. forces as a traitor to their cause, that as early as August 27, 1957, an attempt was made on his life by E.O.K.A. and that as the result of that incident he was provided with a gun and permit by the head of the C.I.D. Cyprus police. He further alleges that on several occasions he was charged or arrested for murder, the suggestion being that those charges were investigated by E.O.K.A., and that in fact the charges were either withdrawn or he was acquitted. In September, 1960, he says that leaflets were distributed appearing to emanate from "E.O.K.A. Fighters," in which leaflet he and others with him, referred to as "Zacharia and Co.," were branded traitors to the cause and the authors called in effect for his liquidation. Later, in November of 1960, when charged with the attempted murder of a Cypriot, an attempt was made on his life while he was in fact handcuffed to a police officer and was driving into the gates of the court, and that he only avoided death by leaping into the yard of the court, dragging the police officer with him. Not only that, but during that same trial while he was talking to a police officer outside the court another attempt was made to shoot him—he claims by a member of E.O.K.A.—but that the bullet missed him and killed the policeman who was standing beside him. As a result of this he says that he saw the Home Secretary and was afforded police protection by day and night, and that that continued until January 27, 1961, when, still under police protection, he was taken to Nicosia Airport and from there flown to this country. He further alleges that since he has been in this country his house in Cyprus has been partially destroyed by bomb attacks. He claims that if he is sent back to Cyprus he will be assassinated before he stands his trial or, if he is acquitted, after he has stood his trial. In a further affidavit he alleges that the Minister of Justice, who signed copies of the depositions in this case, is a well-known E.O.K.A. leader and that the investigating officer and the prosecuting officer are both members of E.O.K.A. The suggestion is that his recall to Cyprus is not made in good faith in the interests of justice but is made by representatives of **[639]** E.O.K.A. for purposes of revenge for the part he is alleged to have played in the disturbances.

On the other side there is a long affidavit from one Constantinides, Divisional Commander of Gendarmerie, Limassol. He paints quite a different picture. He says that the applicant in this case succeeded his father as the leader of a well-known gang who, for their own purposes and for money, had for long intimidated people in Cyprus. The affidavit concedes that he did at any rate purport to be an agent for the security forces and that he made use of his alleged connection with E.O.K.A. to kill persons out of revenge for the murder of his father and in the course of the general criminal activities of the gang. The affidavit states that it is thought that the applicant was involved in or responsible for a great number of murders; that it has been very difficult to collect the evidence; that in the cases that have been brought the evidence was not strong enough; and that quite apart from the offences alleged in these warrants there is yet another alleged case of murder in respect of which it is desired to prosecute the applicant. The affidavit further admits the distribution of the leaflets from "E.O.K.A. Fighters," but suggests that they were not true members of E.O.K.A. but were members of either a rival gang or people who desired to revenge themselves upon the applicant. Finally, the affidavit states that these proceedings are brought in good faith in the interests of justice to bring to book, to put it bluntly, a well-known thug; that it has been difficult to collect the evidence until peace has been restored to the country; but now this has been done and it is desired to bring this criminal to justice.

For my part, I find it impossible in this state of the evidence to say that this applicant, upon whom the onus lies, has satisfied me or has made it appear to me, to use the words in section 10, that the application has not been made in good faith in the interests of justice. It seems to me that when one is dealing with a friendly sovereign power and, indeed, a member of the British Commonwealth, that very strong evidence indeed would be required to justify this court in holding that such a government was not, in making such an application as this, acting in good faith and in the interests of justice. I further think that it would require very strong evidence to enable the court to hold that an applicant such as this applicant would not have a fair trial in the courts of that country. Quite apart from it being a friendly power and a member of the Commonwealth, it is well known that the police, the lawyers and the Bench in Cyprus **[640]** are at any rate modelled on the English model. I am quite unable to say in the present case that it has been made out to my satisfaction that this application is not made in good faith or in the interests of justice.

That, however, is not the end of the matter because there is little doubt that section 10 gives this court a very wide discretion. The section goes on to provide that the court may refuse to return such a fugitive if "otherwise, it would, having regard to the distance, to the facilities for communication and to all the circumstances of the case be unjust or oppressive or too severe a punishment to return the fugitive." Those words, "to all the circumstances of the case," coupled with the word "oppressive" seem to me to give this court a very wide discretion.

A number of points are conceded or, if not conceded are really clear. It seems to me, first, that this applicant did purport to assist the security forces during the disturbances in their efforts to suppress E.O.K.A. How far he did assist them is unknown, but the security forces clearly thought he was of assistance, and indeed, as I have said, he was issued with a gun and a permit. It is also clear, secondly, that persons claiming to be "E.O.K.A. Fighters," did distribute these leaflets naming the applicant as a traitor to their cause and calling for his extermination. Whether such persons were in fact E.O.K.A. representatives or merely persons bent on personal revenge, the fact does remain that they were out to have the applicant removed. Thirdly, whether by representatives of E.O.K.A. or by others prompted by a desire for personal revenge, no less than three attempts were made on his life, and two of them while he was in custody, and that after his departure some person caused his house to be partially destroyed. Fourthly, it is clear that the authorities in Cyprus clearly recognised that he was in need of protection; he was in fact given day and night protection after the third attempt on his life and until he was put on the aeroplane at Nicosia Airport on January 27. It is also clear, I think, that if he is returned to Cyprus the authorities may well bring further serious charges against him, particularly in the case of murder. Lastly, I should refer to the admitted fact that he has been, as I have said, charged with murder or attempted murder on several occasions in the past, and he has either been acquitted or the charges have been withdrawn.

Looking at those facts, which I think are clear, a number of points arise. In the first place, it seems probable that, owing to the way in which he is regarded by a number of people in Cyprus, [**641**] there is a real danger that evidence against him has been or will be fabricated. Secondly, that there is a very real danger of his being assassinated. So far as the first of those matters is concerned, as I have said there is no reason to think that so far as the courts are concerned in Cyprus that they will not give this man a fair trial, and that they can be trusted to look at the evidence with suspicion and see that it is properly tested. Indeed, Mr. Clarke, for the Government of Cyprus, has drawn our attention to the fact that the courts already have done that on the occasions when he has previously been before the courts.

As regards the second probability, namely, the real danger to his life, the position as it seems to me is this: In considering whether it would be oppressive to send this man back to stand trial, I should have thought that considerations as to the danger to his health and, a fortiori, the danger to his life, were matters which the court was entitled to take into consideration. It seems to me, however, that in every case the degree of danger to health or danger to life must be put against the degree of seriousness of the crime alleged. In other words, I can well conceive that this court might say that it was oppressive to send a man back to be tried on some comparatively small charge if the evidence was that he was almost certain to be killed. Here, the charges are of the most serious nature, two of them murder, and while there is a very real risk to his life, I do not myself feel able to say that purely for that reason it would be oppressive to send him back. After all, he will be in custody. True, in November of 1960, it availed him little to be in custody in the two attempts that were made on his life, but there is no reason to think that the police will not take even added precautions for the future. Certainly, they have shown every willingness to protect him, having protected him after the attempts on his life in November, 1960, until he left the country on January 27, 1961.

Those, as it seems to me, are the two main matters which arise for consideration once the court has held, as I do, that there is no question here of bad faith or of acting otherwise than in the interests of justice. Mr. Hutchinson, to whom the court is indebted for his very clear argument, has quite rightly emphasised that it is wrong to pick out one point rather than another and deal with that, and that one ought to look at all the circumstances and paricularly the whole background of the case. I have done that to the best of my ability, giving this case very anxious consideration, but I have come to the clear conclusion in the end that it is not a case in which the court should exercise the [**642**] very special powers given to them under section 10. I should add that it is comparatively rare for the court to exercise those powers, and for the very good reason that in dealing with the Government of a friendly power it would only be in an extreme case that the court would think it right to refuse their request to have their national returned to their country for an alleged offence committed in that country.

For those reasons, which I have endeavoured to state shortly, I have come to the conclusion, though I confess with some regret that there is no good reason why relief should be given under section 10 of the Act.

Another point was taken, namely, that in regard to warrant No. 2 alleging the robbery with violence of one Triantifillides and the offence of demanding £250 by menaces, no case appeared on the depositions which would justify the magistrate's holding that in the words of section 5 a strong or probable presumption of guilt had been made out. After going into the matter, it becomes, I think, clear that there was no sufficient evidence in regard to the first count, namely, that of robbery with violence. There was, however, in my judgment, evidence to support the charge of demanding £250 by menaces. That being so, there is enough to send the applicant back on that warrant. Whether or not in the circumstances the magistrate or this court says that the evidence does not support the first count does not seem to me to matter, because once the applicant is taken back to Cyprus it is for the Cyprus authorities to charge him, and whether they persist in that first count or whether they abandon it is for them to decide. Accordingly it does not seem to me that there is any ground for refusing his return in respect of that warrant No. 2.

There is another applicant to whom I have not yet referred, whose case has been dealt with at the same time. He is one Euripides Arestidou, who quite clearly was a friend, referred to as a bodyguard, of Antonis Zacharia. In so far as Zacharia was the leader of a gang, Arestidou was a member of that gang. He is only concerned with this warrant No. 2, to which I have referred. There is as I have said, sufficient evidence on the depositions to support one at any rate of the counts in that warrant and, accordingly, it cannot be said that the magistrate was wrong in committing him on that warrant. Everything that I have said in regard to Antonis Zacharia applies equally to this applicant, save this, that though he complains that he was before leaving the country and will be if he returns at danger and at risk of being assassinated, the case of anticipated violence against him is **[643]** nothing like so strong as in the case of Zacharia, and accordingly if there is no ground for exercising discretion in the case of Zacharia there certainly is not in the case of Arestidou. Accordingly, in my judgment, both these applications should be refused.

ASHWORTH J. I agree.

WIDGERY J. I also agree.

Hutchinson Q.C. I am instructed to ask for leave to appeal and it must be on a matter of law. On what your Lordship has said in your judgment the court could only consider the two matters you have enumerated once you have come to the conclusion that there was no bad faith, and that would appear to be a point of law.

LORD PARKER C.J. There is no question of certifying in regard to habeas corpus that there is a point of law of general public interest; that does not arise.

Hutchinson Q.C. I do not think I have anything more to say, save that I ask for leave to appeal on that and any other matters that arise.

LORD PARKER C.J. Mr. Clarke, do you want to say anything?

Clarke Q.C. In my submission, no; it is entirely a matter for your Lordships. All that your Lordships, as I understand it, have done is to refuse to exercise your discretion in a matter where your discretion is of the widest.

LORD PARKER C.J. I have a sort of feeling that if we had exercised our discretion the other way you might have desired to go higher.

Clarke Q.C. I have considered that, and may I say at once, though it is easy to be wise after the event, that I myself found great difficulty in asking to go to the House of Lords on a matter of discretion. In my submission, it would be equally difficult for both sides, whoever lost, to go to the House of Lords and argue a point on which your Lordships have exercised discretion, and I know of no case where leave has been granted or the House of Lords have considered that matter.

Hutchinson Q.C. That was why I mentioned the point, because obviously if it is a matter purely of your Lordships' exercising discretion then these considerations might apply, but it did **[644]** seem to me that there were obvious points of law that arose, though the court's decision is based on the exercise of discretion within section 10. Of course, the whole application involves the exercise of a final discretion, but as to how this court should exercise the discretion as, for instance, the court having come to a conclusion on one limb, is only able to consider certain other matters, would surely be a matter of law and be a matter whether your Lordships had exercised your discretion properly or not in law.

LORD PARKER C.J. Mr. Hutchinson, the court does not feel that it is in a position to give you leave, but of course under this procedure there is nothing to prevent you asking the Appeal Committee of the House of Lords for leave.

On December 19, 1961,* the House of Lords granted both appellants leave to appeal [See p. 642 below].

Jeremy Hutchinson Q.C. and *J. C. Mathew* for the appellants. The alleged offences were supposed to have been committed in Cyprus during the civil war which took place before Cyprus became a republic. The appellants are content in the main to argue these appeals on the facts as found by the Divisional Court. It is submitted: (1) On the facts as found the appellants had succeeded in making it appear that it would be "unjust and oppressive" to return them to Cyprus within the meaning of section 10 of the Fugitive Offenders Act, 1881. (2) The Divisional Court in exercising its discretion applied a wrong principle in (a) weighing the degree of danger to the appellants if they were returned against the gravity of the crimes alleged; (b) in placing too great a burden on the appellants in discharging the onus in relation to the words in section 10 "where it is made to appear." (3) The Divisional Court failed to take into account or consider the first appellant's contention that the two most serious offences, if committed, were of a political nature and character and that the reason for his return was to punish him for offences of a political character. (4) The appellants had succeeded in making it appear to the court that the application for their return was "not made in good faith in the interests of justice" within the meaning of section 10. (5) The Divisional Court was wrong in finding that in the second warrant relating to the offences of **[645]** robbery with violence and demanding money with menaces there was evidence amounting to a strong or probable presumption of guilt.

The appeal of Zacharia.

The appeal raises difficult questions of law in those cases where a Commonwealth country became an independent republic within the Commonwealth and the Fugitive Offenders Act, 1881, continues to apply. It is to be noted that there is no reciprocity in the application of the Act in view of a recent decision of a Cyprus court[3] that no citizen of Cyprus can be taken out of Cyprus on a demand of the Government of the United Kingdom under this Act. The Act applies to self-governing colonies and the Dominions. It is a domestic arrangement. The returnable offences are specified in section 9, but the net is cast far wider than under the Extradition Act, 1870. Further, the safeguards provided for fugitives under the Extradition Act, 1870, in particular, the political proviso, are not to be found in the Fugitive Offenders Act, 1881. It is by virtue of section 3 of the Cyprus Act, 1960, that the Act of 1881 is applicable here. In applying the Fugitive Offenders Act, 1881, to an independent republic within the Commonwealth the same principles should be applied as those applicable in the case of a British possession and not those applicable to an independent foreign state under the Extradition Act, 1870.

Section 10 of the Act of 1881 gives the court a wide discretion to do what in all the circumstances is just: *Reg.* v. *Governor of Brixton Prison, Ex parte Naranjan Singh.*[4]* [Reference was also made to *In re Henderson*[5]* and *Rex* v.

[3] See *The Times,* June 3, 1961, p. 8.
[4] [1962] 1 Q.B. 211; [1961] 2 W.L.R. 980; [1961] 2 All E.R. 565, D.C.
[5] [1950] 1 All E.R. 283, C.A.

Governor of Brixton Prison, Ex parte McCheyne.[6]*] To return Zacharia to Cyprus in the circumstances prevailing here would be "unjust or oppressive." If under section 10 there has to be weighed in the balance the oppression and the danger to the life of the fugitive on the one hand and the gravity of the offence on the other, then it is relevant to consider whether the evidence adduced on behalf of the application is reliable or likely to be reliable. It is said that Zacharia is a thug and that the alleged crimes were committed by him for reasons of personal revenge. But in the aftermath of every civil war allegations **[646]** are made that certain acts committed during it were done for reasons of that nature. There is nothing in the Act of 1881 to suggest that it is only in an extreme case that an English court would refuse an application to return an alleged offender. It is emphasised that it is wrong to balance the danger to the fugitive against the gravity of the alleged offence for if that were the criterion whenever the gravest crime, murder, was alleged it would be impossible to place anything on the other scale to balance it. There is no onus on the appellant to "make it appear"—to use the language of section 10—that it would be unjust or oppressive or too severe a punishment to return him. If the opening words of section 10 were "if the fugitive can prove to the satisfaction of a superior court . . ." then the onus on the fugitive would be to satisfy the court on the balance of probabilities.

As to the political nature of the alleged offences, the two alleged murders were of such a character and significance. In these circumstances the House should apply the same rules here as pertain under section 3 (1) of the Extradition Act, 1870, and the question of discretion would not arise: see *per* Lord Goddard C.J. in *In re Government of India and Mubarak Ali Ahmed.*[7]* On the question how the court should approach the problem whether the alleged offences are of a political character; see *Reg.* v. *Governor of Brixton Prison, Ex parte Kolczynski*,[8]* which goes as near as may be to imputing bad faith to the applicant government even in proceedings under the Extradition Act, 1870. See also *Reg.* v. *Governor of Brixton Prison, Ex parte Schtraks.*[9]* Where a political party as the result of a disturbance succeeds in overthrowing the government and itself takes office and thereupon applies for the return of a person who is alleged to have committed an offence during such disturbance, the offence should be considered one of a political character. Thus, here, if Zacharia with the connivance of the Cyprus police under British control killed a person as alleged, in the circumstances it cannot be denied that this disclosed an offence of a political character: see *In re Castioni.*[10]* It is a pure question of fact whether there was a disturbance, namely, a rebellion, and whether the act complained of was done as part of or in **[647]** furtherance of that disturbance. If it was, then on the principles of the Extradition Act, 1870, as propounded by Lord Goddard C.J. in the *Kolczynski* case,[11]* Zacharia must not be surrendered.

On the question whether the applications were made "in good faith in the interests of justice," it is to be observed that that is the phrase as it appears in section 10 of the Act of 1881 and that it should not be read as it is found in the judgment of Lord Parker C.J.[12] as though it were "in good faith and/or in the interests of justice." These applications were made by the Government of Cyprus, acting through the Attorney-General of Cyprus, who instructed a police officer to take steps to secure the issue of the warrants. It is only necessary to impeach the good faith of the inspector of police in Cyprus who applied for the warrants. Alternatively, what is impeached is the application itself, whoever it was made by. One can impeach the application either by showing that it was made from bad motives or by showing that although made from proper motives it was not truly made in the interests of justice.

[6] [1951] 1 T.L.R. 1155, D.C.
[7] [1952] 1 All E.R. 1060, 1063, D.C.
[8] [1955] 1 Q.B. 540; [1955] 2 W.L.R. 116; [1955] 1 All E.R. 31, D.C.
[9] [1962] 2 W.L.R. 976; [1962] 2 All E.R. 176, D.C.
[10] [1891] 1 Q.B. 149, 156, D.C.
[11] [1955] 1 Q.B. 540, 549, et seq.
[12] *Ante*, p. 639.

Having regard to (a) the fact that the Minister of Justice, the prosecuting officer and the investigating officer were all members of E.O.K.A.; (b) the statement of the Attorney-General of Cyprus, that attempts were made to assassinate Zacharia; (c) the fact that Zacharia was given police protection, and the police had knowledge 13 days before he left Cyprus of the details contained in an E.O.K.A. pamphlet concerning the alleged murder of Mouzomenos and (d) that Zacharia had four previous acquittals for murder, and the whole background of the case, in particular the affidavit in reply, there are grounds for querying whether the application was made in good faith in the interests of justice.

J. H. Buzzard for the Governor of Brixton Prison, intervened on a point of jurisdiction. The question arises whether the House has jurisdiction to entertain the appeals in so far as they relate to proceedings under section 10 of the Fugitive Offenders Act, 1881. It appears that they being appeals in a "criminal cause or matter" the grant of a certificate by the Divisional Court pursuant to section 1 (2) of the Administration of Justice Act, 1960, is a prerequisite to the hearing of the appeals by this House, and since this is a question of jurisdiction it cannot be waived. In so far as these appeals relate to the habeas corpus proceedings a certificate from the Divisional Court is not required: section 15 [**648**] of the Act of 1960. This House held in *De Demko* v. *Home Secretary*[13]* that an application for relief under section 10 of the Fugitive Offenders Act, 1881, lies to the Court of Appeal but not an application by way of habeas corpus. This shows that section 10 proceedings and habeas corpus proceedings are quite separate: see also *Rex* v. *Governor of Brixton Prison, Ex parte Savarkar.*[14]* The writ of habeas corpus goes if it is shown either that the committing magistrate had no jurisdiction or that the depositions do not disclose evidence from which a reasonable man could draw the conclusion that it was reasonable to suppose that the offence alleged had been committed. Section 10 is complete in itself; habeas corpus does not enter into it, for the section provides its own remedies.

It was thought right to raise this question as it is one of jurisdiction and because the situation here might well arise in other cases. The legislature in enacting the Administration of Justice Act, 1960, might well have thought that since a wide discretion is conferred on the Divisional Court under the provisions of section 10 of the Act of 1881 the exceptional provision that no certificate is necessary for an appeal in habeas corpus proceedings should not apply to appeals under section 10.

Edward Clarke Q.C. and *John Bolland* for the Republic of Cyprus. The respondents have always taken the view that this is a bad point. Once a case comes before the House on habeas corpus then the appeal is at large and section 10 is not excluded. This submission is reinforced by the fact that the Divisional Court[15] considered that no certificate was necessary when application was made for leave to appeal. In any event, in the present instance any defect could be remedied by an early application to the Divisional Court for a certificate. The Government of Cyprus would prefer the appeals to be decided on their merits and not on a technicality.

Hutchinson Q.C. Section 15 of the Administration of Justice Act, 1960, provides that "subject to the provisions of this section, an appeal shall lie in any proceedings upon application for habeas corpus . . ." and that in relation to a decision of a Divisional Court on a criminal application for habeas corpus there is no restriction on the right of appeal save that of obtaining leave to appeal.

The order of the Divisional Court shows that the application [**649**] in each case was *one* application and it was *the* application which was dismissed, and it was *the* application from which it was sought to appeal. The part of the application which is made under section 10 is made in proceedings upon application for habeas corpus; accordingly, proceedings under section 10 of the Fugitive Offenders Act, 1881, come within the ambit of section 15 of the Act of 1960.

13 [1959] A.C. 654; [1959] 2 W.L.R. 231; [1959] 1 All E.R. 341, H.L.
14 [1910] 2 K.B. 1056; 26 T.L.R. 561, C.A.
15 *Ante*, p. 643.

On the passing of the Fugitive Offenders Act, 1881, it must have been envisaged that the normal procedure would be, on an application to a superior court, for a writ of habeas corpus also to be laid before the superior court, who would thereupon consider the application as a whole and decide whether there was lack of jurisdiction in the magistrate or exercise the discretion vested in the court under section 10. It was said that the fact that the Court of Appeal has power to entertain an application under section 10 but not for habeas corpus is evidence of the distinctiveness of the two proceedings. But the extraordinary original jurisdiction of the Court of Appeal in proceedings under section 10 is purely fortuitous and quite artificial: see the *De Demko* case.[16]* In all modern cases relief under section 10 has been asked for in habeas corpus proceedings: see, for example, *Rex* v. *Governor of Brixton Prison, Ex parte McCheyne.*[17]* [Reference was made to *Reg.* v. *Governor of Brixton Prison, Ex parte Green*[18]* and *In re Clemetson.*[19]*]

Since the legislature has thought fit by the Act of 1960 to give a right of appeal without the prerequisite of obtaining a certificate in habeas corpus proceedings, the same principle should apply to appeals to this House under section 10 of the Act of 1881 where likewise the question of the liberty of the appellant is concerned.

For the purposes of section 15 (3) of the Act of 1960 the House is now considering *the* "decision of a Divisional Court on a criminal application for habeas corpus" and *the* decision involves consideration of section 10 of the Fugitive Offenders Act, 1881. Equally, when considering the ambit of section 1 of the Act of 1960 anything which arises out of the application to the Divisional Court arises in the course of a "criminal cause or matter." [Reference was also made to section 5 of the Administration of Justice Act, 1960.] **[650]**

Buzzard in reply on the question of jurisdiction. Subsection (1) of section 15 of the Administration of Justice Act, 1960, reinforces the contention that that section is confined to habeas corpus proceedings in the strict sense, for it only envisages circumstances where there has been an order for the release of the person restrained or a refusal to make such an order and is not apt to include an order made under section 10 which is wider in its terms: see the *Savarkar* case,[20]* where the question was left open whether on the dismissal by the Divisional Court of an application for a writ of habeas corpus proceedings under section 10 could not be taken under the original jurisdiction of the Court of Appeal. It follows that the dismissal of an application for the writ does not mean the ipso facto dismissal of an application under section 10.

It is conceded that in the authorities there are many examples of a confusion between the two remedies, but they are in fact different. Reliance is placed on *Ex parte Savarkar*[20]* as approved by this House in *De Demko* v. *Home Secretary.*[21]*

[Their Lordships conferred.]

VISCOUNT SIMONDS. Their Lordships are of the opinion that the preliminary point of jurisdiction is not well founded.

Hutchinson Q.C. continuing on the substantive appeals.

The appeal of Arestidou.

The only offence with which Arestidou is charged is that of demanding £250 with menaces. It would be oppressive and unjust to return him to Cyprus on this one charge since it is plain on the evidence that he would have to be kept in custody pending his trial in order to protect his life.

As to the meaning of the words in section 5 of the Act of 1881 "such evidence . . . as . . . raises a strong or probable presumption that the fugitive committed the offence mentioned in the warrant," it was held in *Rex* v. *Governor of Brixton*

[16] [1959] A.C. 654.
[17] [1951] 1 T.L.R. 1155, D.C.
[18] *The Times*, December 16, 1954, D.C.
[19] *The Times*, November 23, 1955, D.C.
[20] [1910] 2 K.B. 1056.
[21] [1959] A.C. 654.

Prison, Ex parte Bidwell[22]* that they meant such evidence as, if it remained uncontradicted at the trial, would entitle a reasonable jury to convict the alleged fugitive upon it. Contrast the language of section 25 of the Indictable Offences Act, 1848 (now section 7 of the Magistrates' Courts Act, 1952) relating to committals for trial in England, which is incorporated into section 10 of the Extradition Act, 1870, where the criterion for committal is twofold, namely, either the evidence must be sufficient in the **[651]** opinion of the magistrate to put the accused on trial, or raises a strong or probable presumption of guilt.

In *Reg.* v. *Governor of Brixton Prison, Ex parte Mourat Mehmet*[23]* Lord Parker C.J. said that the Divisional Court could look at the evidence before the magistrate and consider whether any magistrate, properly applying his mind to the question, could reasonably come to the conclusion that a strong or probable presumption of guilt had been made out. Anything which emerges in evidence before the superior court which might effect its discretion should be taken into consideration under section 10 of the Act of 1881, for nothing could be wider than the terms of that section.

There is here no evidence of a demand for money made with menaces; there was in fact originally a voluntary handing over of money by the complainant for protection. If, as is submitted, the observations of Swift J. in *Ex parte Bidwell*[24]* are correct, there is here no evidence on which a reasonable jury would convict this appellant.

On the question of reciprocity, it is to be observed that article 14 of the Constitution of the Republic of Cyprus, which came into force on August 10, 1960, provides that no citizen shall be banished or excluded from the republic in any circumstances. These alleged acts were done before the Constitution came into force and at a time when the appellants were British subjects residing in a British colony. [Reference was also made to Piggott on Extradition (1910), p. 299.]

Edward Clarke Q.C. The Government of Cyprus has a right of audience in these appeals merely because on the petitions the appeal was stated to be between the appellants and the Government of Cyprus. In strict law the requesting power has no right to appear before the magistrate. Further, on the fugitive's application to a superior court the matter would be headed "*Reg.* v. *Governor of Brixton Prison, Ex parte*" the fugitive, and the state concerned would not be a party.

It is to be remembered that the appellants have an additional safeguard in that after the legal process is complete the Secretary of State has power to review the whole matter: see section 6 of the Fugitive Offenders Act. 1881.

Reliance is placed on *In re Arton.*[25]* It is true that that was a decision under the Extradition Act, 1870, and that there are **[652]** important differences between that Act and the Fugitive Offenders Act, 1881, but the approach the courts should adopt towards an application by a friendly foreign state is relevant for present purposes where the application is by an independent republic within the Commonwealth.

There are important distinctions between the principles applicable to cases under the Extradition Act, 1870, and those applicable to cases under the Fugitive Offenders Act, 1881. The latter Act was enacted to deal with fugitives from one part of Her Majesty's dominions fleeing to another part of Her dominions, both parts being equally subject to the Crown. In the present century, with the rise of independent republics within the Commonwealth, like Cyprus and India, it is not possible for such countries to put into immediate operation a new code of law, and therefore the Acts proclaiming independence provide that all laws in operation prior to the date of independence shall continue in operation. The effect, so far as the Fugitive Offenders Act is concerned, is suddenly to translate it into a form of extradition statute between two independent countries.

[22] [1937] 1 K.B. 305; 53 T.L.R. 1; [1936] 3 All E.R. 1, D.C.
[23] [1962] 2 Q.B. 1; [1962] 2 W.L.R. 686; [1962] 1 All E.R. 463, D.C.
[24] [1937] 1 K.B. 305.
[25] [1896] 1 Q.B. 108, 113, 114, 115; 12 T.L.R. 131, D.C.

The important differences between the Extradition Act, 1870, and the Fugitive Offenders Act, 1881, are these: the Fugitive Offenders Act contains no provision exempting political offences from its operation, whereas the Extradition Act does; there is nothing in the Fugitive Offenders Act concerning reciprocity, in the Extradition Act there is; there is nothing in the Fugitive Offenders Act about the fugitive not being tried for any offence except that for which he is handed over, in the Extradition Act there is; in the Fugitive Offenders Act (section 10) there is a provision that the fugitive is not to be handed over where it is unjust or oppressive so to do, whereas in the Extradition Act there is no such provision.

The observations of Lord Goddard C.J. in *In re Government of India and Mubarak Ali Ahmed*[26]* are wrong in so far as he states that where the crime has a political character the court may take cognisance of it for the purposes of the Fugitive Offenders Act, 1881, in the manner prescribed under section 3 (1) of the Extradition Act, 1870. It is conceded that the court can consider the political character of the request for the return of the fugitive under the wide discretion conferred by section 10 of the Act of 1881, which provides that the court may discharge the fugitive where it is made to appear that the application is **[653]** not being made "in good faith in the interests of justice or otherwise." Here, the Divisional Court has exercised its discretion judicially and no error of law in the exercise of that discretion has been shown. In those circumstances the House would not interfere with the decision of the Divisional Court.

J. H. Buzzard. No concession is made relating to the power of the court to exempt under its general discretion the application of the Fugitive Offenders Act, 1881, to political offences. The Extradition Act, 1870, was intended to preserve the nineteenth-century principle of political asylum: see sections 3 (1), 7, 9, 24, proviso, First Schedule. Neither that Act nor any of its amending Acts includes political offences within its scope. Up to the early nineteenth century extradition was usually granted where the offence concerned was political, probably in order to prevent reprisals. For the history of political asylum, see Biron and Chalmers on Extradition (1903), pp. 7-11.

The purport of the Fugitive Offenders Act, 1881, is quite contrary to the scheme of the Extradition Act, 1870, for in section 9 of the former Act the first offence listed is treason, which is the political crime par excellence. Suppose the Republic of Cyprus sought the return of a person charged with treason, could it be said by the Divisional Court that although it is the first crime specified in section 9 nevertheless the court would exercise its discretion under section 10 and refuse the request? Such considerations are for Parliament and not for the courts. Whilst crimes of a political character do not come within the ambit of section 10, nevertheless if it appeared that a fugitive's surrender was required for purposes of political revenge that fact could be taken into consideration by the court under that section.

A request for surrender under the Extradition Act, 1870 (section 7), is made by a person of recognised diplomatic status; it is an act of state. In an application under the Fugitive Offenders Act, 1881 (section 3), on the other hand, the proceedings may be instituted by a private prosecutor. The present applications should be regarded as having been made by whoever was responsible for seeing that the warrants were issued. Assuming that it was the Attorney-General in Cyprus, then even though he acted in good faith, if he acts on information supplied, or depositions secured by his servants in bad faith, it ought to be open to the court to hold that the applications were made in bad **[654]** faith. The observations of Lord Russell C.J. in *In re Arton*[27]* on the question of good faith have no application to the Act of 1881. The Extradition Act, 1870, does not confer upon the court any discretion, and for the court to have imported a discretion in dealing with applications under that Act would have laid the Government of the United Kingdom open to the charge that it was evading its treaty obligations.

The appellants are not aliens but British subjects. If the Government of

[26] [1952] 1 All E.R. 1060, 1062, 1063.
[27] [1896] 1 Q.B. 108, 115.

Cyprus applied for the handing over of British police officers alleged to have counselled or procured the appellants to commit the murder referred to in the present proceedings, it may be that the courts would not be slow to find that there was bad faith in such applications as being brought for motives of political revenge, yet such motives are more likely to arise in a case such as the present, where the persons whose handing over is requested are said to be Cypriot traitors.

The reason for the insertion of the words "reasonable or probable presumption" in section 5 of the Fugitive Offenders Act, 1881, is that the section plainly envisages the return of fugitives for alleged summary offences and therefore it was thought inappropriate to equate proceedings under the Act of 1881 with committal proceedings before justices. Accordingly, the legislature sought by using those words to lay down a standard which could be applied throughout the Commonwealth. The statement in Piggott on Extradition, p. 300 is wrong.

Hutchinson Q.C. in reply. The statement of Lord Goddard C.J. in *In re Government of India and Mubarak Ali Ahmed*[28]* that in relation to political offences the principles of the Extradition Act, 1870, are applicable to the Fugitive Offenders Act, 1881, is right. In 1962 the question is one of great importance since there are now independent republics within the Commonwealth and the possibility arises of persons coming to the United Kingdom for political reasons.

As to the discretion conferred by section 10 of the Act of 1881, it is a relevant circumstance in considering whether these applications were made "in good faith in the interests of justice" that they were made by former members of E.O.K.A. On the evidence here it cannot be said that these words are satisfied.

It is true that under section 6 the Secretary of State is in a better position to deal with certain aspects of an application than is the court; nevertheless, certain duties are laid upon the court **[655]** under section 10 and those duties should be performed by the court and not left to the executive.

The question here is whether on the balance of probabilities it would be *oppressive* to return the applicants. To take the case of Zacharia, if there is evidence which shows that if he is returned attempts will be made on his life, and that if he is acquitted of the charges specified in the warrants further charges will be preferred against him, that would entitle the House to exercise its discretion under section 10.

At the conclusion of the argument their Lordships conferred.

VISCOUNT SIMONDS. Their Lordships will in due course report to the House that these appeals should in their opinion be dismissed. In view of the provisions of section 6 of the Fugitive Offenders Act, 1881, and the possibility of an application being made to the Home Secretary under that section, their Lordships think it right to add that the time of 15 days prescribed by that section will not run until the House itself has dealt with the Appellate Committee's report.

April 17. VISCOUNT SIMONDS. My Lords, your Lordships have to consider two appeals from orders of the Divisional Court of the Queen's Bench Division, the first entitled "In the matter of Antonis Zacharia and In the matter of an application for a writ of habeas corpus ad subjiciendum and for relief under section 10 of the Fugitive Offenders Act, 1881," the second similarly entitled with the substitution of the name of Euripides Arestidou for that of Antonis Zacharia. My reason for thus setting out the titles of the orders of the court will appear. Much that I have to say concerns both appeals, but I will for convenience deal in the first place with that of Zacharia.

On September 13, 1961, at Bow Street Magistrates' Court an order was made under section 5 of the Fugitive Offenders Act, 1881, committing Zacharia to Brixton Prison pending his return to Cyprus in respect of warrants upon which he had previously been arrested. These warrants, to which I will presently return,

[28] [1952] 1 All E.R. 1060, 1063.

had been duly indorsed under section 3 of the Act and Zacharia had been apprehended accordingly. Under section 5 it is the duty of the magistrate, before whom the fugitive when apprehended is brought, to hear the case in the same manner and exercise the same jurisdiction and powers as near as may be as if the fugitive **[656]** were charged with an offence committed within his jurisdiction. And, if the indorsed warrant for the apprehension of the fugitive is duly authenticated and such evidence is produced as, subject to the provisions of the Act, according to the law administered by the magistrate, raises a strong or probable presumption that the fugitive committed the offence mentioned in the warrant, and that the offence is one to which that part of the Act applies, it is his duty to commit the fugitive to prison and forthwith to send a certificate and such report of the case as he may think fit to the Secretary of State. It is further his duty when he commits the fugitive to inform him that he will not be surrendered until after the expiration of 15 days, and that he has a right to apply for a writ of habeas corpus or other like process.

I refer also to section 6, because it has a bearing on the observations I shall finally make. That section provides that upon the expiration of 14 days after a fugitive has been committed to prison to await his return or, if a writ of habeas corpus or other like process is issued with reference to such fugitive by a superior court, after the final decision of the court in that case the Secretary of State may, if he thinks it just, by warrant under his hand order that fugitive to be returned to the part of Her Majesty's dominions from which he is a fugitive with the necessary ancillary directions.

I pass over sections 7 and 8 of the Act and mention section 9 only to note that treason is specifically mentioned as an offence to which the Act applies, and that it beyond all question covers the several offences charged in the warrants upon which Zacharia was arrested.

It is section 10 with which your Lordships have been mainly concerned, and since it has been closely analysed by the learned counsel for the appellants, I must set it out in full. It provides as follows: "Where it is made to appear to a superior court, that by reason of the trivial nature of the case or by reason of the application for the return of the fugitive not being made in good faith in the interests of justice or otherwise, it would, having regard to the distance, to the facilities for communication and to all the circumstances of the case, be unjust or oppressive or too severe a punishment to return the fugitive either at all or until the expiration of a certain period, such court may discharge the fugitive either absolutely or on bail or order that he shall not be returned until after the expiration of the period named in the order or may make such other order as to the court seems just." **[657]**

The warrants to which I have referred alleged numerous offences by Zacharia, abduction, carrying a revolver or pistol contrary to the firearms law, assault, robbery with violence, demanding money with menaces, murder and again murder. They were supported by depositions upon which the magistrate came to the conclusion that they raised a strong or probable presumption that Zacharia had committed the offences named in the warrants. Some discussion took place before your Lordships as to the exact meaning and content of the words "strong or probable presumption." To me it appeared academic, for, unless the words mean nothing at all, I do not see how the magistrate could have failed to find in the depositions ample justification for the course which he took. He duly committed Zacharia to prison to await his return to Cyprus but, in further accordance with his duty, notified him of his right to apply for a writ of habeas corpus.

This right was in due course exercised by Zacharia and, in accordance with the modern practice, leave was sought of Plowman J. and granted by him that the Queen's Bench Division should in due course be moved on behalf of Zacharia that a writ of habeas corpus in the usual form should issue directed to the Cyprus Government representative in London and to the Governor of Her Majesty's Prison at Brixton.

The motion came before the Divisional Court consisting of the Lord Chief Justice of England, Ashworth and Widgery JJ. It was supported by numerous affidavits and exhibits, to which a number of affidavits were filed in answer by the Cyprus Government. It was dismissed by the court, the Lord Chief Justice delivering a long and careful judgment in which the other members of the court concurred. Leave to appeal was obtained from the Appeal Committee of this House and so the matter came before your Lordships.

It is now necessary to mention a matter which did not emerge until the hearing of the appeal had proceeded for some time. It then appeared that a serious question arose whether the appeal, being undoubtedly in a criminal cause or matter, could be entertained by this House unless a certificate had been given by the court below that a point of law of general public importance was involved in their decision. No such certificate had been asked for or obtained. Your Lordships proceeded to consider this as a preliminary point, and by a majority decided that it was not well founded. I feel constrained to express my own view that this is a **[658]** wrong decision and, I may add, my regret that it should have been reached.

Apart from the provisions of the Administration of Justice Act, 1960, the appeal would clearly have been incompetent. It is necessary then to consider the relevant sections of that Act. They are sections 1 and 15.

Section 1 (so far as relevant) provides that (1) an appeal shall lie to the House of Lords at the instance of the defendant or the prosecutor from any decision of the Divisional Court of the Queen's Bench Division in a criminal cause or matter; but (2) that no appeal shall lie under this section except with the leave of the court below or the House of Lords, and such leave shall not be granted unless it is certified by the court below that a point of law of general public importance is involved in the decision, and it appears to that court or to the House of Lords, as the case may be, that the point is one which ought to be considered by that House.

So far the matter is clear. No appeal lies in a criminal cause, including an application under section 10 of the Fugitive Offenders Act, 1881, without (inter alia) the proper certificate.

Section 15, however, which comes within a fasciculus of sections headed "contempt of court, habeas corpus, and certiorari," provides by subsection (1) that, subject to the provisions of that section, an appeal shall lie in any proceedings upon application for habeas corpus, whether civil or criminal, against an order for the release of the person restrained as well as against the refusal of such an order, and by subsection (3) that in relation to a decision of a Divisional Court on a criminal application for habeas corpus, section 1 of the Act should have effect as if so much of subsection (2) as restricted the grant of leave to appeal were omitted.

Here then is the question: "When an order is ex facie made upon an application for habeas corpus and for relief under section 10 of the Fugitive Offenders Act, 1881, is an appeal from that order to be regarded as an appeal in an application for habeas corpus within the meaning of section 15, when it is directed only to relief under the Act?"

Some guidance is to be obtained from authority. In *Rex* v. *Governor of Brixton Prison, Ex parte Savarkar*[29]* the distinction between an application for a writ of habeas corpus and an application for relief under section 10 of the Act of 1881 and between **[659]** the remedies which could be granted in regard to such applications respectively was clearly pointed out. The facts were somewhat complicated but are accurately stated in the headnote which I repeat. An order nisi for habeas corpus was obtained in the King's Bench Division on the application of a person in custody under the Fugitive Offenders Act, 1881, but was afterwards discharged. The affidavit upon which the order nisi was obtained stated (inter alia) matters material as ground for the exercise of the power given by section 10 of the Act, but the order nisi was simply in form for a habeas corpus and not in the alternative for relief under section 10. On the argument of the order nisi the matters referred to in the affidavit were discussed, and the court in giving judgment pronounced them as insufficient for the exercise of the power given by section 10. The order ultimately drawn up, however, was simply

[29] [1910] 2 K.B. 1056; 26 T.L.R. 561, C.A.

for a discharge of the order nisi for habeas corpus. An application was subsequently made to the Court of Appeal to exercise the powers given by section 10 as having original jurisdiction in that behalf under the Act concurrently with the High Court. A preliminary objection was taken to the hearing of the application on the ground that the matter had been previously adjudicated on by the King's Bench Division and was therefore res judicata. It was held unanimously by a strong court (Vaughan Williams, Fletcher Moulton and Buckley L.JJ.) that, inasmuch as the only matter adjudicated on by the order of the King's Bench Division as drawn up was that the order nisi for a habeas corpus should be discharged, the matter of the application to the Court of Appeal (that is for relief under the Act of 1881) was not res judicata. The point at issue is summed up most concisely by Fletcher Moulton L.J. in these words[30]: "In my opinion, the relief which the court is empowered to give under ss. 10 and 35 of the Fugitive Offenders Act, 1881, ought to be made the subject of a substantive application to the court. Such relief has in reality nothing to do with relief by habeas corpus; it can be obtained by an independent application to the court; and I think it was the intention of the statute that it should be so." Buckley L.J. puts it thus[31]: "The question which is raised upon the application for a habeas corpus is whether the fugitive is validly imprisoned or detained, and that which is raised under ss. 10 and 35 is whether, it having been found that he is lawfully detained, he ought or ought not to be deported." This view of the law has never so far as I am aware been challenged, though, as happened in **[660]** the case cited, it has sometimes been found convenient to raise and discuss upon a habeas corpus application matters that are relevant only to relief under the 1881 Act. But this should not obscure the fact that (as the title to the order shows) here are two different claims (1) that the fugitive is not lawfully detained, to which alone the remedy of a writ of habeas corpus is appropriate and (2) that relief should as a matter of discretion be granted by the court under the Act of 1881. It is only if the applicant fails on the first application that he needs to urge the second. And upon that application the relief that may be granted is far different from any that a court can grant upon a successful application or habeas corpus.

Is there then any reason why in section 15 of the Administration of Justice Act, 1960, the words "a criminal application for habeas corpus" should be extended to mean an application under the Fugitive Offenders Act, 1881, which has been joined with an application for a writ of habeas corpus? Where the fugitive has been found to be lawfully detained the writ of habeas corpus is spent. The hope remains to him that he may get relief under section 10 of the Act by judicial process or as a last resort under section 6 by executive favour. I see no reason for straining the language of section 15 of the Act of 1960. It is of course clear that that Act has opened the door wider than ever before to criminal appeals to this House. There remains under section 1 the substantial safeguard from frivolous application which subsection (2) affords. It is not provided in the case of criminal applications for habeas corpus under section 15, but I see no reason for giving to those words a wider meaning than they naturally bear. Nor, though Parliament has thought fit to give to the subject whose legal rights are involved, as they necessarily are in habeas corpus, an unqualified right to appeal, do I see any reason why he should be given a similar right where the relief that he claims is prima facie a matter of judicial discretion.

Your Lordships have, however, decided otherwise and the appeal has proceeded upon the footing that no certificate was necessary and it is upon that footing that I now examine it.

My Lords, I think that the only question of law that arises on this appeal is one that is not referred to in the judgment of the Lord Chief Justice. It is whether it is relevant to the consideration of relief under section 10 of the Fugitive Offenders Act to determine whether the offences with which the fugitive is charged are "political offences" within the meaning of the Extradition Act, 1870. That question arises in this way. By **[661]** the Cyprus Act, 1960, it was

[30] [1910] 2 K.B. 1056, 1075.
[31] Ibid. 1066, 1077.

provided by section 1 that on the day on which Her Majesty should by Order in Council declare that the Constitution of the Republic of Cyprus should come into force there should be established an independent sovereign Republic of Cyprus over which Her Majesty should have no sovereignty or jurisdiction. Section 3 provided that on or after that day any existing law which operated as law of, or any part of, the United Kingdom being a law applying in relation to Cyprus or persons or things in any way belonging thereto or connected therewith should (save as therein mentioned) continue to apply in like manner in relation to the Republic of Cyprus or persons or things in any way belonging thereto or connected therewith. It follows that the Fugitive Offenders Act, 1881, which before the establishment of the Republic of Cyprus applied to that island and its inhabitants, continued after the establishment and continues so to apply. But the Fugitive Offenders Act, unlike the Extradition Act, 1870, makes no exception of political offences. It would be strange if it did, since in the forefront of the offences for which a fugitive offender may be apprehended and returned to his own country is placed the offence of treason. I am therefore of opinion that it is irrelevant to consider whether the offences with which Zacharia has been charged could in another context be called "political offences," and I must respectfully dissent from a dictum of Lord Goddard in *In re Government of India and Mubarak Ali Ahmed*[32]* where a similar question arose upon the establishment of the Republic of India, that "in a proper case the court would apply the same rules with regard to applications under the Fugitive Offenders Act, 1881, as it does under section 3 (1) of the Extradition Act, 1870." It is proper that I should add that in any case I could not come to the conclusion that the offences with which Zacharia has been charged were political offences.

This question, which is undoubtedly of importance, having been disposed of, what remains? My Lords, the Divisional Court has exercised a discretionary jurisdiction under section 10 of the Act. Interference with such an exercise can only be justified if that court has clearly acted on some wrong principle, committed some error of law or failed to consider matters which demanded consideration. That is a principle upon which this House, sitting as a final Court of Appeal, has always acted and will, I hope, continue to act, not least in matters of criminal **[662]** jurisdiction which have traditionally been the province of the Court of King's Bench. I should therefore be content to say that I see no possible ground in this case for substituting my own view, if I had a different one, for that of the Divisional Court.

But the earnest and persuasive argument of Mr. Hutchinson leads me to make certain observations. In the first place he challenged the good faith of the application, denying that it was in the interests of justice and asserting that it was made for the purpose of revenge. I asked in vain whose good faith was impugned. It was said that various persons who played some part in the proceedings were or had been members of the organisation known as E.O.K.A. and therefore were suspect. But in effect your Lordships were asked to say that the whole background suggested a picture of the responsible authorities in Cyprus trying by these proceedings to punish a man who had been a traitor to a patriot cause. When such a contention is put forward I recall what was said by the first Lord Russell of Killowen in *In re Arton* (*No.* 1)[33]*: "I come now to the third, and last, ground upon which this rule has been moved—that the demand for extradition is not made in good faith and in the interests of justice. It has been pointed out by myself and my learned brothers during the argument that this is in itself a very grave and serious statement to put forward, and one which ought not to be put forward except upon very strong grounds; it conveys a reflection of the gravest kind, not only upon the motive and actions of the responsible Government, but also impliedly upon the judicial authorities of a neighbouring and friendly power. Is it open to us at all to consider such a suggestion? In my judgment, it is not, and I have already stated the grounds for my opinion." My Lords, I do not hesitate to apply these words to the present case. Whoever may in form be regarded as the applicant under section 10, the

[32] [1952] 1 All E.R. 1060, 1063; [1952] 1 T.L.R. 964, D.C.
[33] [1896] 1 Q.B. 108, 114, 115; 12 T.L.R. 131, D.C.

proceedings have been adopted by the Government of Cyprus who are a party appearing before the House. The charges made against Zacharia are supported by evidence which raises a strong or probable presumption that he has been guilty of very serious crimes. It has not been suggested that the courts of Cyprus will not try him fairly. He is, it is said, fearful lest evidence should be fabricated against him. But I do not doubt the competence of the court to discriminate between the false and the true. Why, then, should he not be tried? **[663]**

It is said that, even if he returns to Cyprus under police guard, he will be in danger of assassination by revengeful members of E.O.K.A. And it is true that attempts were made on his life before he left Cyprus in January 1961, and that his peril was then recognised by the Cyprus Government. It is said that for this reason it would be in the words of the section "unjust or oppressive" to send him back. How serious this danger will be, your Lordships are in no position to judge, but it is, I think, proper to assume that, forewarned of the danger, the Cyprus authorities will take the necessary precautions for his safety before and during his trial. If he is acquitted, he will be able to invoke the provisions of section 8 of the Act and procure his return free of cost to this country.

Some criticism was directed to the fact that the Cyprus authorities assisted Zacharia to leave Cyprus and, having done so, then commenced the proceedings which have culminated in this appeal. If there is any weight in this criticism, it bears upon the question of good faith with which I have already dealt. But I see no weight in it. It is a fair conclusion that the police authorities obtained after his assisted departure evidence that was not then available. On the other hand, it would be paradoxical to suppose that they would at any time have assisted him to escape from threatening danger if, as is now alleged, they are animated by a spirit of revenge and are not acting in good faith in the interests of justice.

I would for these reasons dismiss this appeal. I have only to add that, as I have already pointed out, the appellant can still have recourse to the Secretary of State. He may have access to information more reliable than that supplied by the conflicting affidavits upon which the court must come to a judicial decision.

There remains the appeal of Euripides Arestidou. The charge against him is less serious but it is within the scope of the Act. It was urged on his behalf that the depositions did not justify the magistrate in committing him, and your Lordships thought it right, while accepting the view that the magistrate's decision in these cases is not to be lightly disturbed, to scrutinise the evidence carefully. Having done so, your Lordships thought the matter so clear that it was not necessary to call on counsel for the respondents on this point.

In other respects I see no reason for distinguishing his case from that of Zacharia. His appeal also must be dismissed. **[664]**

LORD RADCLIFFE. My Lords, I have not found it easy to know what a court of law ought to do in dealing with these applications under the Fugitive Offenders Act, 1881. I do not think that their circumstances are at all usual or that there is any help to be got from what has been said by judges in the comparatively few reported cases under this Act or the Extradition Act, 1870.

There are, however, two matters upon which I do not feel any doubt. The first is that upon the appeal before us the only fairly debatable questions are those which relate to section 10 of the Act of 1881. It is true that under section 5 the magistrate before whom arrested persons are brought for committal to await return has to be satisfied on the evidence produced to him that it raises "a strong or probable presumption of guilt," and it was put to us on behalf of the appellants that no such presumption arose from the evidence adduced on the second warrant relating to the demanding of money by menaces from one Costas Triantifillides. Since the second warrant is the only one which concerns the appellant Arestidou, the point is material in his case: but I am satisfied that, as the evidence stands, it is impossible to say that there is not at any rate a probable presumption of guilt attaching to both appellants in respect of this charge.

The Divisional Court has already held that there was not sufficient evidence to support the probability on the first count covered by the second warrant, that of robbery with violence; but, even if that is kept out of the way, there is still enough to support the probability of guilt on the second count, that of demanding money with menaces. I do not think, therefore, that either of the appellants has any case to argue in this House as to the propriety of the magistrate's decision under section 5 of the Act. The whole appeal turns upon what should be the decision of a "superior court" exercising its powers and duties under section 10, having regard to the evidence that has been put before it as bearing upon that issue.

The second matter relates to the scope of the considerations of which the court is entitled to take account when it acts under section 10. It was urged before us that the evidence showed that the offences covered by the warrants were political offences or that the application made by the Republic of Cyprus for the return of the fugitives was made with a view of trying or punishing the appellants for offences of a political character. These considerations are avowedly borrowed from section 3 of the Extradition Act, 1870, and they are not referred to, expressly or by implication, in section 10 of the Act of 1881 which is the Act that we have to **[665]** apply. Is it permissible for the court exercising its jurisdiction under the Act to import them on its own authority and, having done so, to address itself to the possible political aspects of an application for the return of an offender? I know that it has been said that this importation is permissible (see *In re Government of India and Mubarak Ali Ahmed*[34]*) but I think that the point was there assumed rather than decided and in my opinion it is quite clear that a court acting under section 10 is confined to the considerations of which it is there directed to take account and has no authority to set up a separate category formed out of political considerations to which its attention is neither directed nor invited.

Apart from the fact that parts of the procedure and machinery employed are much the same, I can see no interconnection between the Extradition Act and the Fugitive Offenders Act. The former has as its basis some arrangement or treaty made between the Crown and a foreign power and Parliament has itself prescribed what are evidently regarded as fundamental restrictions upon the operation of any such extradition arrangements. The whole Act rests upon the importance of preserving in this country the right of political asylum as then recognised. Thus the first condition of section 3 forbids the surrender of a fugitive if his offence is of a political character or the extradition demand is found to be prompted by an intention to try him for a political offence: section 3 (2) forbids his being detained for trial, once extradited, upon any offence different from that for which he was surrendered: section 7 authorises the Secretary of State to refuse a requisition for surrender from the diplomatic representative of a foreign state if he considers the offence to be of a political character and on the same ground to discharge from custody a person so accused or convicted: section 9 directs the magistrate before whom the fugitive is brought to receive any evidence tendered as to the political aspect of the offence charged: and, lastly, the offence of treason is, perhaps noticeably, omitted from the list of extraditable crimes which is set out in the First Schedule.

The Fugitive Offenders Act, on the other hand, gives no indication that it is concerned with any right of political asylum. It is intended to apply as between the various portions of Her Majesty's Dominions and has no dependence upon the making of extradition treaties or arrangements. It does not require reciprocity because the Act is intended to apply by its own force to all the territories concerned and reciprocity is therefore assumed. **[666]** It operates without any of the restrictions that are a conspicuous feature of the Extradition Act. The crimes to which it is to apply are comprehensively described in section 9 and the only two which are identified by name are treason and piracy. The magistrate who hears an application for committal has no authority to consider whether the offence is of a political character; and the various considerations which are listed in section 10 as requiring the attention of a court to which application is made, though extensive and far-reaching, do not include any element that has any direct bearing upon those issues that are concerned with political asylum. For these reasons I conclude that the court, if it is to intervene at all, must find its

[34] [1952] 1 All E.R. 1060.

ground for action in one of the categories listed in section 10 and that "political offence" and "political character" are not among them. It can no more introduce these considerations into its decision under the Fugitive Offenders Act than a court acting under the Extradition Act could refuse an order on the ground that the application for surrender is not made "in good faith in the interests of justice" (see *In re Arton* (*No. 1*)).[35]*

Now section 10, as I have said, specifies a number of grounds for the intervention of a court where it is "made to appear" to it that certain circumstances exist. The only formula that could be relevant to the present case, as I see it, would be that "by reason of the application for the return of the fugitive not being made in good faith in the interests of justice or otherwise, it would, having regard to . . . all the circumstances of the case, be unjust or oppressive . . . to return the fugitive." The Divisional Court, from which the appeal reaches us, has stated its position very clearly in the judgment of the Lord Chief Justice, and I think that it is not unfair to summarise it as saying that, while there is a real danger that evidence against the appellant Zacharia will be fabricated, if he stands trial in Cyprus, and a very real danger of his being assassinated, it has not been made to appear that the application for return is not made in good faith in the interests of justice nor, weighing the danger to life against the gravity of the offences alleged, would it be oppressive to send him back "purely for that reason." As to the other appellant, Arestidou, the evidence of danger of assassination was much slighter in his case and, if Zacharia had to be sent back, so a fortiori must he go. The court stated that it reached its conclusion that it could not intervene with some regret and I am quite sure that if I came to **[667]** the same conclusion I should share that feeling, for the ascertainable facts of the case, to which I will come shortly, can only leave one with a sense of deep misgiving as to where the balance of justice lies.

It was argued, however, on behalf of the Republic of Cyprus that in refusing to act under section 10 the Divisional Court had exercised a discretionary power vested in it by the Act and that this exercise could not be interfered with on appeal unless vitiated by the adoption of some principle of law which was itself incorrect. For more than one reason I do not think that this argument should succeed. A court acting under section 10 may in one sense be exercising or refusing to exercise a discretion, but when its power to act is introduced by the words "where it is made to appear," I think that it is primarily a question of law in each case whether what does appear amounts to one or more of the specified circumstances. If it does, it is, I think, the court's duty to act, not its privilege to decide whether to act or not. "I hold that it is proved that the return of the fugitive would be unjust and oppressive and too severe a punishment, but nevertheless in the exercise of my discretion I shall take no action" is not in my opinion a maintainable attitude for a court faced with an application under this section.

Apart from this, however, there are other grounds which make it right to review the Divisional Court's decision. It is not, in my view, an adequate assessment of the evidence bearing on what is unjust or oppressive to allude only to the very real danger that Zacharia will be assassinated if he is taken back to Cyprus. There are several other circumstances of the case not alluded to at all in the Divisional Court judgment which have a direct bearing on the oppressive aspect of what is proposed to be done. I will mention them later, but I think that it is an error not to recognise that these factors too contribute weight to the critical balance.

Lastly, I am bound to say that in my opinion the judgment under appeal has erred in law in placing upon an applicant under section 10 an onus, or in putting him under the burden of a presumption for which neither the section nor the Act that contains it gives any authority. Briefly, it seems to have been the basis of the court's view that in considering applications made section 10 there must be imported some presumption in favour of the good faith and impartial desire for justice of a government that applies for the custody of a fugitive offender. "It seems to me that when one is dealing with a friendly sovereign power and,

[35] [1896] 1 Q.B. 108.

indeed, a member of the British Commonwealth, that very strong **[668]** evidence indeed would be required to justify this court in holding that such a government was not, in making such an application as this, acting in good faith and in the interests of justice," it is said at one point.[36] And again, more generally,[37] "it is comparatively rare for the court to exercise those powers, and for the very good reason that in dealing with the government of a friendly power it would only be in an extreme case that the court would think it right to refuse their request to have their national returned to their country for an alleged offence committed in that country."

I do not for one moment suppose that the learned Lord Chief Justice or his colleagues would ever be anything but scrupulous in weighing the balance of any case put before them in an application under section 10. I am quite sure that they would be. Nevertheless I think, with respect, that expressions such as those I have quoted are a bad guide to those who have to exercise this jurisdiction. To be specific, it is not a relevant consideration, nor does it give rise to any presumption, that an applicant for surrender is a friendly power or a member of the Commonwealth. The whole Fugitive Offenders Act was conceived as applicable to Her Majesty's Dominions only, just as the Extradition Act was conceived as relating only to those friendly powers with whom there had been made the appropriate extradition treaty. Yet, given the range within which the Act of 1881 can operate, Parliament has decreed in section 10 that if the facts show an application for surrender not to be made in good faith and in the interests of justice, the court must perform its duty and discharge the prisoner. This must depend on the evidence before it in each particular case: it must not be a matter that is aided or influenced by presumptions. In my opinion, the court has no right to demand a special standard of proof, such as "very strong evidence," or to decline to act except in "an extreme case" or on "comparatively rare" occasions either because the surrender is demanded by a Commonwealth government or by a friendly power, or because the good faith of such a demand is challenged on the application or because some imputation is sought to be made upon the judicial process to which the fugitive offender, if surrendered, will be subjected.

I do not doubt that in practice it will be very difficult for a fugitive offender to make good a case of this sort by any evidence that he can muster. Such cases are inherently difficult of **[669]** demonstration, and in that practical sense the occasions will probably be rare upon which a court will be entitled to intervene. But that, if anything, is a reason why it should address itself indifferently to the question what is "made to appear" by the evidence available without any preconceptions as to the probable result of its scrutiny. For these reasons I do not myself find it satisfactory to rely upon the observations of Lord Russell of Killowen C.J. in the case of *In re Arton* (*No. 1*)[38]* which were cited to us. While he was, if I may say so, clearly correct in ruling that the question whether a demand for extradition was made in good faith and in the interests of justice could not be entertained by the court under the Extradition Act, since it was not brought by the Act within the factors open to the court's review, the justification for that ruling lies in the frame and wording of that Act and not in the consideration that such a challenge involves a very grave and serious reflection upon the motive and actions of a responsible government. Certainly such allegations are very grave matters, but they are matters which the express wording of the Fugitive Offenders Act makes it permissible for an applicant to raise.

Having said this much I must add that, in my opinion, the evidence now before the court does not make it appear that the republic's application for return of the appellants is not made in good faith and in the interests of justice. There is no solid evidence to support the case. The most that can be said is that there is a curious inconsistency in the attitude of the government in first facilitating Zacharia's departure from the island and then seeking to reclaim him as a fugitive criminal; and that there is an uncontradicted statement by Zacharia that the Minister of Justice and the investigating and prosecuting officers in Cyprus, who are concerned with his case, are members of E.O.K.A., the terrorist

36 *Ante*, p. 639.
37 *Ante*, p. 642.
38 [1896] 1 Q.B. 108, 114, 115.

organisation against which he claims to have worked for the government forces during the disturbances which preceded the setting up of the independent republic. But there is nothing in those facts which is sufficient to support the case that the present government of Cyprus is actuated by other motives than a genuine desire to execute justice when it applies to have the appellants sent back to stand trial for the crimes that it believes itself able to prove against them.

There remains then the question whether for any other reasons, "otherwise," it would be unjust or oppressive to return the appellants and this, I think, constitutes the real difficulty of the case. **[670]** The difficulty lies partly in the fact that the court has to make up its mind on the basis of affidavit evidence only, that a great many of the statements made on one side are contradicted, often in the most vague and general terms, by statements made on the other, and that not a few of those statements, some of considerable possible importance, are expressed in a form which does not present even the elements of acceptable evidence upon which a court of law could act. This is particularly noticeable in the case of the affidavit of Costas Constantinides, the Divisional Commander of Gendarmerie at Limassol, which is put in as the main reply to the appellants' application. This deponent constantly founds his statements, which are serious indeed, upon such bases as "it is suspected that . . ." and "it appears that . . ."; and it is not reassuring to find that in paragraph 17 of this affidavit he treats the appellant Zacharia as equally implicated in a series of very grave charges, even though he knows that in respect of some of them Zacharia was arrested and discharged or had the charge withdrawn before he ever left Cyprus.

The other difficulty lies in the fact that the four warrants for the arrest of Zacharia relate to what can only be called terrible crimes for which, it is accepted, there has been shown a probability of guilt, and the offence charged against Arestidou is at any rate a serious one. No court could refuse to return such persons for trial unless it was satisfied that to do so came fairly within the admissible idea of what would be unjust or oppressive.

I have come to the conclusion that there is no other fitting description of an order for return than that it would be oppressive. Since any conclusion on this must depend on the total impression created by a number of separate factors, I will set out briefly such of them as I think can safely be extracted from the evidence before us, though I am aware and am sorry that the conclusion arrived at by others of your Lordships does not agree with mine.

(1) During the period of terrorist or insurrectionary activity against the then Government of Cyprus which preceded the setting up of the independent republic in 1960, Zacharia assisted the Special Branch of the Cyprus Police, providing them with information. There was an E.O.K.A. attempt to murder him in 1957, in which he was wounded and, after the incident, he was provided with a gun and permit by the then head of the Cyprus Police C.I.D.

(2) In the autumn of 1960 a leaflet was circulated in his neighbourhood, purporting to be composed by persons styling themselves "E.O.K.A. fighters," in which he was accused **[671]** of having "persecuted and tortured the heroes of E.O.K.A." and is referred to as a well-known traitor and criminal. The leaflet attributes to him, with the complicity of the Special Branch, the murder of Mouzomenos which is the subject of warrant No. 4 and it plainly announces the intention of the authors, whoever they may be, to exterminate Zacharia. Constantinides says in his affidavit (paragraph 22) that this leaflet, which he evidently knows of, cannot be an official E.O.K.A. proclamation and must be attributed to persons not connected with E.O.K.A. at all or not having its authority to make such announcements. According to him E.O.K.A. "as such" ceased to function or to have connection with any activities whatsoever after March, 1959.

(3) Shortly after distribution of the leaflet Zacharia says that four of his friends and associates (he is evidently some sort of gang leader) were murdered. He and his brother were arrested and charged with these murders, but the charges were subsequently withdrawn and he was discharged. While he was on remand his partner, Makrides, was murdered by E.O.K.A. Constantinides denies

that the murdered men were friends or associates of Zacharia.

(4) On November 22, 1960, Zacharia visited Archbishop Makarios to complain that his life was in danger from E.O.K.A. On returning to his home he was arrested and charged with the attempted murder of one Tryfonkafkari and, on the next day, while being driven into the court precincts handcuffed to a police officer, his assassination was attempted by five men armed with pistols. He escaped death by leaping into the yard of the court dragging the police officer with him. He was later discharged by the magistrate after preliminary hearings. Constantinides' affidavit does not accept the truth of this incident, but it is impossible to tell what it is that the deponent denies or what his knowledge of it amounts to.

(5) Zacharia's brother was sent for trial on the same charge and acquitted. During the course of the trial Zacharia was talking to a police officer outside the court when another attempt to kill him was made by a man whom he identifies as a member of E.O.K.A. called Panayotis. The bullet missed him but killed the policeman who was standing beside him, one Genethliou.

(6) After this attack Zacharia visited the Home Secretary, who advised him to stay at home and afforded him police protection by day and night. **[672]**

(7) In December two more of his associates suffered violent death.

(8) In the following month, January, 1961, Zacharia left Cyprus. The incidents accompanying his departure are of considerable importance to this case and I mention them in some detail. On January 25, he was taken under police protection from Limassol to Nicosia. On the next day he had his second interview with the Home Secretary in which he spoke of the murder of his friends. On January 27, he was taken to Nicosia airport still under police protection and the Captain of Gendarmerie who accompanied him has deposed at a trial in Nicosia, which took place in April of the same year, that in doing so he was acting on the instructions of the competent Ministry. Zacharia and his family then boarded an aeroplane and flew to England. On arrival he communicated with the Home Secretary in Cyprus, as he had been instructed to do, giving his London address.

(9) There can be no doubt that the authorities in Cyprus actually sent him out of the island with his family. They evidently regarded his life as in danger. This is shown somewhat strikingly by certain facts which came to light at the April trial already referred to in which one Rodosthenos, a member of the House of Representatives and stated by Zacharia to be of high rank in E.O.K.A., was prosecuted for illegal possession of arms. During the course of the trial Mr. Talarides, the Attorney-General, produced a letter, found, he said, in the accused's safe, in which a certain Mavros was instructed to murder Zacharia by a fixed date, otherwise he would himself be killed. The letter was signed "E.O.K.A. fighters." The Attorney-General said that he desired to prove through this letter and other facts such as certain killings referred to by him, that "not only Rodosthenos' life was not in danger but, on the contrary, a number of persons of A. Zacharia's group were murdered and for that reason Antonis Zacharia was obliged to leave Cyprus." I quote from a contemporary report in the daily newspaper "Ethniki," which is an exhibit in the case.

(10) There are only one or two more further relevant facts. Since Zacharia left Cyprus a bomb attack has been made on his house and all his possessions destroyed or ruined. Persons contemplating buying business assets of his have been threatened with death by E.O.K.A. agents. According to the deponent Constantinides the attribution of these threats to E.O.K.A. agents "appears to be unfounded." **[673]**

(11) When Archbishop Makarios and the Home Secretary visited London later in the year 1961, Zacharia states that he visited them both in order to discuss his difficulties in Cyprus caused by E.O.K.A.'s activities.

My Lords, the recital of these facts justifies a very brief summary of what they amount to. Here is a man who is the object of an implacable vendetta waged against his life by a number of persons in Cyprus and originating at any rate to some extent—one cannot say more—in the part that he took in assisting the police during the E.O.K.A. disturbances. There have been three attempts on his life already, two while he was in the custody or company of police officials. There are outstanding orders for his assassination and incitements to it. I cannot see that it can be safely assumed that, if he is sent back to Cyprus, these attempts will continue to be unsuccessful or that the conspirators will not find means of reaching him whatever form of protection is designed for him. Plainly, he will be in great danger of his life, and I do not think that it really matters under what precise authority his enemies are acting.

Four times already he has been arrested and charged with different murders. The charges have either been withdrawn or dismissed. I do not attach great importance to this circumstance, but it is perhaps permissible to reflect that there must be some limit to the number of occasions on which a man is arrested on one of the gravest of all charges without as yet having even been brought to trial.

Lastly, the reason that he is found in England, not in Cyprus, is that he left, with the connivance and protection of the government, because his life was in continual danger from his enemies. There is no definition of a fugitive offender in the Act of 1881, but it can hardly have been intended to apply to someone who is a fugitive not from prosecution for his offences but from a conspiracy to assassinate him. The same government that sent him out applies within a few months to have him sent back again. To send him back under those conditions presents itself to me as oppressive.

I do not think that the court has been furnished with any real explanation of this change of front. It is not possible to know what lies behind it and it is the more obscure because of the access that Zacharia apparently enjoyed both to Archbishop Makarios and to the Home Secretary. It is true that Constantinides says that the evidence supporting the present charges is, he believes, genuine evidence given only when the "atmosphere **[674]** of fear and terror of the criminal gang of Antonis Zacharia is removed," and no one can say that this may not well be true. There is some confirmation of it in the evidence filed in support of warrants 1 and 2. But what was the date when this atmosphere was dissipated? It needs a good deal more than that general statement, I think, to show how much that which is now charged against Zacharia was not known to the police authorities before the government sent him out of the country. After all, the evidence itself shows that the facts upon which the second warrant is based were communicated to the police 13 days before his departure and Constantinides seems from his affidavit to have known about the "E.O.K.A. fighters" leaflet, which deals in detail with Zacharia's alleged murder of Mouzomenos, since the end of September, 1960.

For these reasons I am of opinion that the Divisional Court should have intervened under section 10 of the 1881 Act and that the appeal of Zacharia ought to be allowed.

With regard to the second appellant Arestidou, it is difficult not to consider his case as in some sense a pendant to the other. It is necessary to remember, however, that, though the only warrant that touches him is the second, yet this involves a serious charge. There is no evidence that he left Cyprus under the same auspices as Zacharia, nor is there anything like the same direct evidence of a conspiracy against his life. Nevertheless he is put forward as a henchman of Zacharia and he is evidently one of his associates or gang. On the whole, if Zacharia were not to go back, I think that it would be unjust to send back his assistant.

I must now deal with the point as to jurisdiction raised during the course of the argument of this appeal. It is said that this House is not competent to hear an appeal under section 10 of the Fugitive Offenders Act unless the court below has certified that a point of law of general public importance is involved in the decision and either that court or this House has decided that the point is one which ought to be considered. The point is a short one of a technical nature which does not seem to have occurred to the Divisional Court when the question of an appeal to this House was raised: nor do I recall that it was present to anyone's mind when leave to appeal was granted by the Appeal Committee. In my opinion it is not a good point.

The issue depends upon the meaning of certain words which appear in section 15 of the Administration of Justice Act, 1960. That Act, as is well known, opened the House of Lords to an appeal (a) from any decision of a Divisional Court of the Queen's **[675]** Bench Division in a criminal cause or matter and (b) from any decision of the Court of Criminal Appeal on an appeal to that court; but the appeal so provided for in section 1 (1) was by section 1 (2) subjected to two conditions. One was that no appeal was to lie except with the leave of the court below or this House: the other imposed the requirement as to a point of law of general public importance being involved to which I have just alluded.

Section 15 of the Act contains certain special provisions about an appeal in habeas corpus proceedings. Subsection (3) declares that "In relation to a decision of a Divisional Court on a criminal application for habeas corpus, section 1 of this Act shall have effect as if so much of subsection (2) as restricts the grant of leave to appeal were omitted." Plainly, therefore, it was intended that, when the court has dealt with a criminal application for habeas corpus, nothing more should be needed to give the applicant his right of appeal to this House than its leave or the leave of the court below. The right was to be there, whether a point of law of any importance was thought to be involved or not.

Is there any reason for supposing that when an application for habeas corpus has been made in relation to detention and committal under the Fugitive Offenders Act and the powers or duties of the court under section 10 are invoked in connection with that application, there should be one régime for appeals in so far as they concern what may be called the strict habeas corpus considerations and another for appeals in so far as they concern considerations relative to section 10? I cannot myself think that section 15 was ever intended to enforce such a distinction nor can I see why a point of law of general public importance should be necessary to enable this House to act, if thought proper, under section 10 when it has not been made necessary in order to give it authority to deal with allied questions relating to habeas corpus.

It is no doubt true that the jurisdiction of a court to act under section 10 is not the same thing as its jurisdiction to act on habeas corpus. That is the point which is made very plain in the judgments of the Court of Appeal in *Rex* v. *Governor of Brixton Prison, Ex parte Savarkar*[39]* and I do not see how a study of the Fugitive Offenders Act could lead to any other conclusion. Theoretically at any rate, an application under section 10 could be made independently of a motion for a writ of habeas corpus; the considerations which the court must take into account are **[676]** those prescribed by the section and no others; and the relief which the court can give under the section is more flexible than that which is available on habeas corpus. But with all respect it seems to me highly unreal to say, as Fletcher-Moulton and Buckley L.JJ. did in that case, that these statutory rights have "nothing to do with habeas corpus." In reality they have a great deal to do with it. Both concern the power of the court to discharge a person who is detained under the Act. In practice, as I understand, the applications for discharge are made together and relief is asked for in the alternative, sometimes the writ of habeas corpus being asked for under section 10. A magistrate committing a fugitive under section 5 is directed to inform him that he has "a right to apply for a writ of habeas corpus or other like process" and I can hardly suppose that this provision was intended to mean that the magistrate was to refer specifically to habeas corpus but need not mention the wider jurisdiction of the court under section 10. In sum, I think that the court's powers under section 10 were from the first regarded as an adjunct to its power to protect by habeas corpus, and consequently, where, as here, an application for the writ is joined with proceedings under section 10, the provision of section 15 (3) of the Administration of Justice Act, 1960, that strikes out the section 1 (2) restriction on the grant of leave to appeal applies to both forms of proceedings.

In my opinion therefore this House had jurisdiction to hear the appeal merely on leave granted.

My noble and learned friend Lord Reid, who is unable to be present today, and was unable to complete the hearing of the appeal to this House, but was

[39] [1910] 2 K.B. 1056.

present at the decision taken by the committee with regard to this point of jurisdiction, has asked me to say that he has read what I have said on this point and agrees with it.

LORD HODSON. My Lords, both the appellants applied to the Divisional Court of the Queen's Bench Division, each seeking a writ of habeas corpus ad subjiciendum and praying for relief under section 10 of the Fugitive Offenders Act, 1881.

In each case the appellant was refused the act of habeas corpus and also relief under section 10 of the Fugitive Offenders Act.

In each case an application for leave to present a petition of appeal to this House was dismissed, but by an order of this House **[677]** of December 20, 1961, both appellants were granted leave to appeal.

Appeals to this House in criminal cases are governed by the Administration of Justice Act, 1960, which by section 1 (2) provides that no appeal shall lie under that section except with the leave of the court below or of the House of Lords, and that "such leave shall not be granted unless it is certified by the court below that a point of law of general public importance is involved in the decision and it appears to that court or to the House of Lords, as the case may be, that the point is one which ought to be considered by that House."

By section 15 (3) of the Act, in relation to a decision of a Divisional Court on a criminal application for habeas corpus the restrictions imposed by section 1 (2) have no application. Thus, so far as habeas corpus is concerned, there is no necessity for a certificate to be given as a prerequisite to an appeal, but the question remains whether there is jurisdiction to entertain an application under section 10 of the Fugitive Offenders Act without such a certificate. No certificate was sought in this case nor was the attention of the House drawn to the absence of a certificate when leave to appeal was given, but counsel on behalf of the Governor of Brixton Prison has now submitted that the appeal is incompetent except in so far as it relates to habeas corpus. In my opinion the submission is well founded.

It is true that an application under section 10 is often combined with an application for leave to issue a writ of habeas corpus, but the two are not the same, and I find myself unable to accept the view that, in truth, there is but one application before the House and not two or that, to put it another way, once the application for habeas corpus is before this House the way is open to the appellants to obtain relief under section 10. This section enables a superior court in the exercise of its discretion to ". . . discharge the fugitive either absolutely or on bail, or order that he shall not be returned until after the expiration of the period named in the order, or . . . make such other order in the premises as to the court seems just."

It seems to me, as it did to Fletcher Moulton L.J. in *Rex* v. *Governor of Brixton Prison, Ex parte Savarkar,*[40]* that the question of relief under section 10 has nothing in truth to do with the issue of the writ of habeas corpus, notwithstanding that it is convenient to hear applications for the writ and for the discretionary relief at the same time. The actual decision in *Savarkar's* **[678]** case,[41]* approved by your Lordships' House in *De Demko* v. *The Home Secretary,*[42]* was that inasmuch as the only matter adjudicated upon by the order of the King's Bench Division was "habeas corpus" the application which had been made by the same person under section 10 of the Fugitive Offenders Act was not res judicata. Stress was, however, laid on the feature of the case that the Act of 1881 gave to fugitive offenders statutory rights which had nothing to do with habeas corpus. The right to habeas corpus is absolute and the remedy provided by section 10 is discretionary and more extensive, and I am unable to accept the contention now put forward that the application for habeas corpus is all embracing, so that there is jurisdiction to hear the appeal against the discretionary order under the Act of 1881.

Since the majority of your Lordships are of a different opinion it is necessary to consider the appeal as a whole. So far as the application for habeas corpus is

[40] [1910] 2 K.B. 1056, 1075.
[41] [1910] 2 K.B. 1056.
[42] [1959] A.C. 654, 661; [1959] 2 W.L.R. 231; [1959] 1 All E.R. 341, H.L.

concerned, only the warrant No. 2 is in question alleging robbery with violence of one Triantafillides and the offence of demanding £250 by menaces. This warrant involves both applicants. The Divisional Court held that there was insufficient evidence of robbery with violence but that in the words of section 5 of the Act the evidence raised "a strong or probable presumption" against both fugitives that they had committed the second offence mentioned in the warrant. It was argued that there was insufficient evidence of any demand, of any intent to steal or of any menaces. So far from there being a demand for money or an intent to steal it was said the evidence was that Triantafillides was offering protection money and that, although a weapon was produced when the payment of money was discussed, it was not used as a threat.

I am unable to accept any of these submissions and arrive at the same conclusion as the Divisional Court.

On a plain reading of the evidence of the two witnesses for the prosecution, what happened at the material time was that money was being demanded from Triantafillides, first £500—a figure subsequently reduced to £250—under the threat of a weapon taken to be what Triantafillides called a ·45 pistol (sic) pointed out by Zacharia and drawn by Arestidou from his waist.

This must be evidence on which, if it be uncontradicted at the trial, a reasonably minded jury might convict, and so would raise **[679]** the necessary strong and probable presumption: *cf. Rex* v. *Governor of Brixton Prison, Ex parte Bidwell.*[43]*

The application under section 10 of the Act of 1881 is on a different footing, in that the Divisional Court has exercised its discretion against both applicants, and it must be shown that this discretion has been wrongly exercised before this House can interfere with the order made.

It has been urged on behalf of both applicants that (1) the court applied a wrong principle in weighing the danger to them if they are returned to Cyprus against the degree of gravity of the crimes alleged; (2) too great a burden has been placed upon the applicants, having regard to the words in section 10: "Where it is made to appear to a superior court . . ."; (3) the court failed to take into account the appellants' contention that the crimes with which they were charged were political, and that the application for the return of Zacharia had been made with a view to punishing him for offences of a political character; (4) the court failed to appreciate that the applications were not made in good faith in the interests of justice.

As to the first submission, I think the court was right upon the evidence before it in coming to the conclusion that in the case of Zacharia, and to a lesser degree in the case of Arestidou, there is a real danger of violence or assassination, seeing that both are marked men and have enemies in Cyprus who have declared in no uncertain language that they regard the applicants as traitors by reason of the services they rendered to the British Government as informers against E.O.K.A. members before the independence of Cyprus was declared. The court also recognised that even if, as will certainly be the case, the applicants are kept in custody while awaiting trial, this will not necessarily avail to protect them, as past experience has shown. The court also felt that presumably by reason of the hatred of their enemies there was a real danger of evidence being fabricated against them.

Nevertheless, taking all these things into account, having regard to the fact that in the case of Zacharia, at any rate, the charges against him were serious, in two cases charges of murder, and that the Cyprus authorities had shown in the past every willingness to protect him, and that in the case of Arestidou, though the charge was less serious, the risk of violence against him was also less, the court refused the application. **[680]**

I do not find anything to criticise in the way in which the court acted, nor do I understand upon what ground it was argued that the gravity of the charges should not be put in the balance against the danger to the appellants if they are returned, for the gravity of the charges must be material to the exercise of discretion under section 10.

[43] [1937] 1 K.B. 305; 53 T.L.R. 1; [1936] 3 All E.R. 1, D.C.

Similarly, with regard to the second ground, I do not accept that too great a burden was put upon the appellants to make it appear that it would be unjust or oppressive to return them. The evidence of the applicants was given upon affidavit, and their sworn statements are subject to correction which appeared manifestly necessary when the affidavit evidence in answer had been read. For example, the applicants put themselves forward as men of good character, but their records when disclosed showed that they had previous convictions, including convictions for violence, although neither had served sentences of imprisonment, so that their representations that they were men of good character were destroyed, without taking into account that they were alleged to be notorious as members of a gang of violent criminals of which Zacharia was the leader while Arestidou was his bodyguard.

As to the third submission based on the supposed political nature of some of the crimes alleged, this is based upon the proposition that under the Fugitive Offenders Act, as under the Extradition Act, 1870, crimes of a political nature are excluded. The reverse is the case and, indeed, crimes of a political nature are expressly included in paragraph 9 of the former Act, which refers to treason. This submission was based on a dictum of Lord Goddard C.J. in *In re Government of India and Mubarak Ali Ahmed*[44]* to the effect that in crimes of a political nature the rules of the Extradition Act should be applied to applications under the Fugitive Offenders Act, 1881, but with respect I do not think this dictum can be supported in view of the plain language of the Fugitive Offenders Act itself. The Extradition Act recognises the policy of giving political asylum in cases where application is made by foreign states for the return of political offenders. The Fugitive Offenders Act is by contrast a domestic Act to amend the law with respect to fugitive offenders in Her Majesty's Dominions which has been applied to Cyprus since the independence of Cyprus was established and concerns applications for the return of fugitive offenders whatever the nature of the offences charged against them. **[681]**

That is not to say that the court in exercising its discretion could not take into account evidence that application was being made for the return of a fugitive as an act of revenge whether actuated by political motives or not, but I see no reason why this application for return should not be treated as what on the face of it is, namely, an application by the Cyprus Government acting responsibly in the interests of justice. The past history of Zacharia, against whom several prosecutions have failed, shows that in his case no suggestion that he was unlikely to have a fair trial could properly be made, nor was any such suggestion made on behalf of either applicant.

Lastly, on behalf of Zacharia it was pointed out that he left Cyprus for this country on January 27, 1961, with the assistance of the Cyprus Government, although 14 days earlier the authorities had information as to the robbery which is the subject of one of the charges against him. It is said that, in these circumstances it would be unjust and oppressive to return him to Cyprus. The fact is that the other three charges, including the most serious, came to light after Zacharia had departed, the explanation given being that the witnesses against him were afraid to make any complaint until he had left the country. I see no reason in these circumstances to question the bona fides of the Home Secretary or of the Cyprus Government on this account.

I would dismiss the appeals.

LORD DEVLIN. My Lords, this is an appeal from an order made by the Divisional Court on November 22, 1961, whereby the court refused to order that a writ of habeas corpus should issue for the release of the appellant, now confined at Brixton Prison, or to order his discharge pursuant to the Fugitive Offenders Act, 1881, section 10.

The appellant [Zacharia] is a Cypriot who left Cyprus on January 27, 1961, and has since then been residing in this country. On April 15, 1961, criminal proceedings, including two charges of murder, were begun against him in the District Court of Limassol in Cyprus. Under the Cyprus Act, 1960, the island of Cyprus has been established as an independent sovereign republic. Under this

[44] [1952] 1 All E.R. 1060.

Act the Fugitive Offenders Act, 1881, which makes provision for the arrest in one part of Her Majesty's Dominions of a person who is accused of having committed an offence in another part, continues to apply. On August 17, 1961, the four warrants in this case were endorsed under section 3 of the Act by a magistrate at Bow Street and the appellant was **[682]** arrested and brought before him. Section 5 of the Act provides that if such evidence is produced before the magistrate as "raises a strong or probable presumption that the fugitive committed the offence mentioned in the warrant," the magistrate shall commit him to prison to await his return and shall inform him that "he has a right to apply for a writ of habeas corpus or other like process." On September 13, 1961, the magistrate committed the appellant to prison under this section.

On September 29, 1961, the appellant gave notice of motion for a writ of habeas corpus. Upon such a motion the court has by virtue of section 10 of the Act wider powers than it ordinarily exercises upon an application for the writ. Section 10 is as follows: "10. Where it is made to appear to a superior court that by reason of the trivial nature of the case, or by reason of the application for the return of a fugitive not being made in good faith in the interests of justice, or otherwise, it would, having regard to the distance, to the facilities for communication, and to all the circumstances of the case, be unjust or oppressive or too severe a punishment to return the fugitive either at all or until the expiration of a certain period, such court may discharge the fugitive, either absolutely or on bail, or order that he shall not be returned until after the expiration of the period named in the order, or may make such other order in the premises as to the court seems just."

The Divisional Court, as I have stated, refused the application. By the Administration of Justice Act, 1960, a right of appeal was for the first time given from a decision of a Divisional Court in a criminal cause or matter. The appeal lies only with the leave of the Divisional Court or of this House and section 1 (2) provides that such leave shall not be granted unless it is certified by the Divisional Court that a point of law of general public importance is involved. But it is specially provided by section 15 (3) that this latter restriction shall not apply in relation to a decision of the Divisional Court on a criminal application for habeas corpus. An application for leave to appeal was made to the Divisional Court. The Lord Chief Justice observed that no question of the certificate arose and the court was not asked to certify. The court refused to give leave.

An application for leave to appeal was then made to this House on December 20, 1961, and leave was given. It was not on the hearing of this petition suggested that a certificate by the Divisional Court was needed.

On the hearing of this appeal a preliminary point was taken **[683]** by the Governor of Brixton Prison, the second respondent, but not by the Republic of Cyprus. Mr. Buzzard on behalf of the Governor argued that the House had no jurisdiction to review the refusal by the Divisional Court to exercise its powers under section 10. His argument was based upon the assertion that there were brought before the Divisional Court two distinct applications—an application for a writ of habeas corpus pursuant to section 5 and an application for an order for discharge under section 10. He contended that an order refusing the latter application was not covered by section 15 (3) of the Act of 1960. Accordingly, he contended that in the absence of a certificate by the Divisional Court, the House had no jurisdiction to give leave to appeal from that order and therefore no jurisdiction now to entertain that appeal. Since the only effective grounds of appeal relate to section 15, there would be nothing left for the House to discuss.

This point was argued on the assumption that in the absence of a certificate the House not only would have no jurisdiction to grant leave but would now be without jurisdiction to hear this appeal. On reflection I doubt whether this assumption is correct. The jurisdiction of this House now to entertain this appeal is founded upon its own order of December 20, 1961. So long as that order stands, the House has jurisdiction. It may be that that order ought not to have been made because an essential condition for making it was not fulfilled, but that does not mean necessarily that the order, when it is made, can be disregarded as a nullity. That is so in the case of an inferior court when it exceeds its jurisdiction. But the House of Lords and all superior courts have power to determine the extent of their own jurisdiction and so their orders cannot be questioned for want of jurisdiction except on appeal, where there is a right of appeal, or by the court itself by virtue of its inherent power to set aside its own orders where the interests of justice so require. I am therefore disposed to think that Mr. Buzzard's point should have been taken by way of an application to the House to set aside its order of December 20, 1961, giving leave to appeal. It is unnecessary to consider whether the House would have entertained such an application at this stage. I do not seek to make any pronouncement on a matter that was not argued; but I am at the same time anxious that it should not hereafter be inferred from the manner in which the House deals with this point that the assumption on which it was made is well founded.

The construction of the Act of 1881 is not at all easy. The **[684]** question which the House has to determine depends upon the relationship between section 5, which provides for the fugitive making an application for the writ of habeas corpus, and section 10, which is described in the marginal note as "Powers of superior court to discharge fugitive when case frivolous or return unjust." Section 39 provides that the expression "superior court" includes the Court of Appeal. But for section 39, I should feel little doubt about the relationship between section 5 and 10. The natural construction of section 10 appears to me to be that it enlarges the powers of the court, so that upon the application for habeas corpus under section 5 the court can make orders of a class that it would not ordinarily have made and its orders can be based on grounds that would not ordinarily have been sufficient. But it appears that the only meaning that can be given to the reference in section 39 to the Court of Appeal is to treat it as being a superior court within section 10. Accordingly, the opening words of section 10 can be read as: "Where it is made to appear to the Court of Appeal." How can the matter reach the Court of Appeal? Is section 10 giving a right of appeal to the Court of Appeal from a decision of the High Court in a criminal matter? It would be very surprising to find that done without express words. But the only alternative would appear to be to treat the Court of Appeal as having original jurisdiction to grant relief under section 10. If that is so, there must be a process, presumably comprised within the term "like process" in section 5, whereby the Court of Appeal can be applied to directly.

The position is now governed by authority. In *Rex* v. *Governor of Brixton Prison, Ex parte Savarkar*[45]* the Court of Appeal, Vaughan Williams and Fletcher-Moulton L.JJ., with Buckley L.J., held that it had an original jurisdiction to grant relief under section 10. This decision was approved by the House in *De Demko* v. *Home Secretary*.[46]*

Accordingly it is not possible now to argue that the powers granted by section 10 can be exercised *only* on a habeas corpus application. That leaves two possible constructions of the Act. The first is that sections 5 and 10 are entirely dissociated and that the powers given by section 10 can be exercised only on a separate application made under section 10. If this construction is right Mr. Buzzard's contention succeeds. The other construction is that section 10 can be used in two ways. It does not follow from the fact there *can* be two applications that there **[685]** *must* be. On this argument the section can be used either to enlarge the powers of the court on a habeas corpus application or to permit an independent application to be made by any person who is prepared to concede that the exercise of the power under section 10 affords the only good ground for an order for his release. On this alternative construction Mr. Buzzard's point fails. It is only if the two things are entirely dissociated that the appellant can be prevented from relying upon section 10 in the habeas corpus proceedings that it is admitted are properly before the House.

The former construction is supported by the judgment of Fletcher-Moulton L.J. in *Rex* v. *Governor of Brixton Prison, Ex parte Savarkar*.[47]* The Court of

[45] [1910] 2 K.B. 1056.
[46] [1959] A.C. 654.
[47] [1910] 2 K.B. 1056.

Appeal in that case, having decided that it had original jurisdiction under section 10, had next to consider whether it was precluded from exercising its jurisdiction because the matter had already been heard and determined by a court of concurrent jurisdiction, namely, the Divisional Court. The court decided that it was not so precluded. Fletcher-Moulton L.J. held that section 10 could not be invoked by an application for habeas corpus but only by a separate application which was not before the Divisional Court. Vaughan Williams and Buckley L.JJ. did not go so far as that. They did not hold that the Divisional Court *could* not adjudicate under section 10 on an application for habeas corpus but that in the particular case before them it *had* not so adjudicated. They said for this purpose they could not look at the proceedings generally—the affidavits, the argument and the judicial utterance—but only at the formal order made which contained no reference to section 10. This point did not arise for consideration at all in *De Demko* v. *Home Secretary*.[48]*

My Lords, I cannot, with great respect, accept the reasoning of Fletcher-Moulton L.J. or the contention of Mr. Buzzard. The introductory words to section 10 lay down no special procedure. They do not insist upon any particular mode of application. It does not appear to me that the Act requires or even contemplates that two applications should invariably be made in the same matter, one by way of habeas corpus and the other by way of "a like process." If an application for habeas corpus only is before a superior court, it is natural to suppose that that court is intended to exercise the powers given by the Act which itself makes provision for the application; and in the absence of express words debarring the court from so doing, I hold that it can. **[686]**

That disposes of the preliminary point. But to avoid any misunderstanding in the future I should like to make it clear that my disagreement with the reasoning of Fletcher-Moulton L.J. does not necessarily involve an acceptance of the reasoning of Vaughan Williams and Buckley L.JJ. There are certainly difficulties about the application of the doctrine of res judicata to matters in which there are no proceedings and where the issues are not formally defined. It seems at first sight to be taking rather a narrow view of it to say that the effect of the order made cannot be determined in the light of the points argued. I express no opinion on this since it does not arise for consideration here. It has been the practice since then for the order of the Divisional Court to make it clear in terms, as was done in the present case, that relief under section 10 has been sought and refused. No doubt that practice will continue until Parliament removes from the Fugitive Offenders Act what everyone believes to be the unintended effect of section 39. I am concerned only to say that there is nothing in the judgments of Vaughan Williams and Buckley L.JJ. which says, either expressly or by implication, that on an application to the Divisional Court for habeas corpus only, the applicant would not be free to ask for relief under section 10 or the Divisional Court not free to adjudicate upon it; and that if any such thing had been said, I should have felt at liberty to disagree with it, for certainly that point was not considered in *De Demko* v. *Home Secretary*.[49]*

I turn now to the merits of the case. The appellant claims relief under section 10 on three grounds. First, he submits that the murders for which his surrender is demanded were offences of a political character. He does not admit that he committed them; but he says that the allegations against him, if true, show that the killings were done in the course of the fight for independence made by the body called E.O.K.A. He relies upon the principle expressed in *In re Castioni*[50]* in which it was held that homicide committed during an insurrection came within the restriction on the surrender of criminals provided by the Extradition Act, 1870, section 3. Secondly, he submits that the application for his return is not made in good faith in the interests of justice. Thirdly, he submits that in all the circumstances of the case it would be unjust or oppressive to return him to stand his trial. I do not think that he has made out any case on the second ground and I have nothing to add under this **[687]** head to what has already been said

[48] [1959] A.C. 654.
[49] [1959] A.C. 654.
[50] [1891] 1 Q.B. 149; 7 T.L.R. 50, D.C.

in the House. The first submission involves a point of law which requires a little consideration; and the second submission gives rise to a difficult question of fact, and also to matters of policy.

There cannot be cited in support of the first submission any provision in the Fugitive Offenders Act, such as there is in section 3 of the Extradition Act. In that Act, which gives effect to treaties negotiated with foreign countries, Parliament contemplates that there may be fugitives from oppression as well as fugitives from justice and excludes the former. In the Fugitive Offenders Act it is assumed that within the Commonwealth any fugitive on a criminal charge will be a fugitive from justice. I think it is assumed also that countries within the Commonwealth will have the same standards of freedom and justice and good order and will secure them by substantially the same safeguards. Mr. Hutchinson submits that this assumption is no longer true. He does not, I must say at once, impute any particular deficiencies to the Republic of Cyprus. His argument is the general one that with the rise of so many new and independent sovereign states within the Commonwealth, similarity of thought on fundamental questions is no longer to be expected: so it now becomes generally relevant to consider whether the offence for which the return of the fugitive is demanded is an offence of a political character. He submits that the wide discretion given to the court under section 10 should now be exercised in a way that treats the application for the return of the fugitive as if it were an application for extradition and subject to the same sort of restrictions. In this contention he is supported by a dictum of Lord Goddard C.J. in *In re Government of India and Mubarak Ali Ahmed*.[51]* The Lord Chief Justice said that in a proper case under the Fugitive Offenders Act the court would apply the rules in the Extradition Act.

In my opinion this argument is unsound. In the course of it it became clear that Mr. Hutchinson was not prepared to advance it without what appeared to me to be destructive qualifications. Treason is always an offence of a political character, yet it is expressly mentioned in section 9 of the Fugitive Offenders Act as one of the offences to which the Act applies. Mr. Hutchinson conceded that an application for the return of a fugitive on a charge of treason said to have been committed in one of the great dominions could not be refused simply on the ground that treason is a political offence. He conceded also that **[688]** neither in 1881 nor at the present day could it be intended that rebels in a colony could obtain immunity by taking refuge in Great Britain. He sought to argue that the position was different if the rebellion was successful but I think that to be quite illogical.

Alternatively, Mr. Hutchinson argued, if the court was not bound to exercise its discretion so as to refuse to return a political offender, the political nature of the offence was a factor to be taken into account. I cannot agree. The court could not exercise its discretion in that way without trespassing upon matters of policy. It does not exercise any discretion under the Extradition Act. Once it is established that the offence is of a political character, as, for example, homicide in the course of a rebellion, it does not matter whether the court approves or disapproves the political views of the offender or whether or not it sympathises with the desire to punish him. But it would inevitably involve itself in the merits of the individual case if it were to exercise its discretion so as to release some political offenders and not others.

I appreciate the force of the general considerations with which Mr. Hutchinson prefaced his submission. But if changing conditions within the Commonwealth are thought to require some modification of the law, it must be made by Parliament. I respectfully disagree with the dictum of Lord Goddard C.J. which I have cited.

To avoid misunderstanding on the facts of this particular case I must note that it was suggested that the return of the appellant was being demanded for the purposes of political revenge. If that suggestion had been made good (which in my opinion it was not), it would certainly have been material to show that the application was not being made in good faith in the interests of justice. But

[51] [1952] 1 All E.R. 1060.

that would not have been because it was for political revenge but because simply it was for revenge.

On the third point, I cannot add very much to what your Lordships have already said. I recognise that there are passages in the judgment of the Lord Chief Justice which, taken by themselves, are open to the criticism which my noble and learned friend Lord Radcliffe has directed against them. But looked at as a whole I can find no ground upon which I think it would be proper to interfere with the exercise of the discretion by the Divisional Court. Since, however, this matter is so grave, I think it right to say that on the material before the House I should not have been drawn to a different conclusion.

I do not attach overriding importance to the fact that the appellant has already been charged unsuccessfully three times with murder—one charge withdrawn, one lacking the evidence needed **[689]** for committal and one not proved beyond reasonable doubt. If in truth he has been for years a gangster who used his work for the security forces as a cover for his crimes—and this is the very point in issue—it is not surprising that he should be charged with many murders and that some should be difficult to prove. It is not suggested that he will not have a fair trial; three failures by the prosecution stand as an eloquent testimony to the contrary. Maybe these further charges are only concoctions made up by those who are seeking to use the law as a means of achieving their own wicked ends. A fair trial will bring that matter to the test. It cannot be determined by affidavits.

The decisive factor to my mind is the danger to the appellant's life from men who are resolved to defy the law and murder him if they can. But your Lordships must approach this third point from the footing that it has been established that, as matters stand, the appellant must be presumed at this stage of the proceedings to be probably guilty of two murders and that his return is requested in good faith so that he can stand his trial. It cannot be that a mere apprehension of harm should be allowed to secure his immunity from justice on charges such as that. On the other hand, if I thought that there was a near certainty or even a high probability that the legal process would itself be defeated by those who were determined that, guilty or not, the appellant should die, I should refuse to be a party to his return. How am I to assess the chances?

There is the matter that three attempts to assassinate him, one in 1957 during the troubles and two since the creation of the Republic, have been made. Whether the men who desire his death are moved to kill him because of the work he did for what was then the lawful government of Cyprus or because he is in truth a murderer whom they think might otherwise escape justice is not at all to the point. The one motive is as wrong as the other. The fact remains that for one reason or the other he is in danger of his life. It is the fact also that it cannot be said without question that while in custody and awaiting trial he is secure. There is evidence, which for this purpose I accept, that one attempt was made when he was actually in charge of the police on his way to court and another while he was awaiting trial and before he had police protection. But after these attempts he was given police protection, which kept him safe for two months, and under police protection he was put on the aeroplane which brought him to London. **[690]**

The whole question is whether on his return he will be safe from his enemies. I do not see how one can answer that without first inquiring what measures will be taken to protect him. I should also want to know what steps would be taken, if he is acquitted, to secure for him the benefits contemplated by section 8 of the Act and to ensure his safe return to this country. These are not matters that can be gone into on habeas corpus proceedings or under section 10. Oral evidence would on such an issue be no better than affidavit evidence. It is unreasonable to expect the competent authorities of a sovereign independent republic to submit to cross-examination on such matters in the court of another country; and if they were to state in public and on oath what precautions they intended to take, that in itself might defeat the object of their plans. These are matters which must be the subject of governmental and not of judicial investigation.

Section 6 of the Act provides that within 15 days after the court has decided, if it does, not to release the fugitive, the Secretary of State may, *if he thinks it just*, order the return of the fugitive. I have put these words in italics because they make it plain that the discretion given to the Secretary of State is as wide as that given to the court under section 10; the phrase corresponds to the words "unjust or oppressive or too severe a punishment" in that section. There is a concurrent jurisdiction conferred on the Secretary of State. I cannot suppose that it is intended that he should act as a second tribunal to consider only those matters which a superior court has already pronounced upon. It is plain to me that one reason at least why the provision is there is because there may be considerations of a political or administrative character which go to the justice of the fugitive's return and are better inquired into by the executive.

The evidence put before the Divisional Court and contained in the affidavits which your Lordships have read is insufficient to make it appear to me more probable than not that, if the appellant is returned, the competent authorities in Cyprus will fail to see that he is kept to stand a fair trial and safely returned if he is acquitted. It follows that in my judgment the appeal must be dismissed. The House is not shirking its responsibilities but is carrying out the intent of the Act if it declines to grant relief under section 10 except upon such proof as is acceptable in a court of law and if it leaves matters which of their nature are not susceptible of proof of that character to be considered by the executive. **[691]**.

In the case of Arestidou I agree that the appeal should be dismissed for the reasons given by my noble and learned friends Viscount Simonds and Lord Hodson.

Appeals dismissed.

Solicitors: *Sampson & Co.; Tuck & Mann; Geffen & Co.; Director of Public Prosecutions.*

EX PARTE ZACHARIA AND ARESTIDOU.

(*The Times*, December 20, 1961)

December 19, 1961: House of Lords: Viscount Simonds, Lords Reid, Radcliffe.

Cypriots' Petition Allowed.

The Appeal Committee, on this *ex parte* application by two Cypriots at present detained in Brixton Prison, granted them leave to appeal to the House of Lords against the refusal of the Divisional Court of the Queen's Bench Division* (The Lord Chief Justice, Mr. Justice Ashworth and Mr. Justice Widgery) on November 22, 1961 (*The Times*, November 23, 1961), to grant them relief under section 10 of the Fugitive Offenders Act, 1881, or to direct writs of *habeas corpus* to issue.

The petitioners, Antonis Zacharia, of Birchington Road, Hornsey, N.8, and Earipides Arestidou of Richmond Crescent, Caledonian Road, N.9, had been detained in Brixton following an order made on September 13, 1961, at the Bow Street Magistrates' Court, that they be committed to prison pending their return to Cyprus in respect of warrants on which they had been previously arrested on charges of a variety of offences, including, in the case of Zacharia, demanding money with menaces and murder.

Mr. Jeremy Hutchinson Q.C. and *Mr. John Mathew* appeared for the petitioners; *Mr. J. R. Cumming-Bruce* and *Mr. R. A. Barr* as *amici curiae*.

Mr. Hutchinson said that the Divisional Court had refused the applications for relief and for *habeas corpus* with regret but had also refused leave to appeal to their Lordships' House. The petitioners now appeal for leave on the grounds, first, that in the exercise of its discretion, the Divisional Court had failed to take into account the political aspect and character of the alleged offences and failed to apply the related provisions of section 3 of the Extradition Act, 1870, on which a suspected criminal should not be surrendered if the offence was of a political character. Secondly, that the application for return was not made "in good faith in the interests of justice" [section 10 of the Act of 1881].

VISCOUNT SIMONDS said that he thought there was authority that it was not for the court to discuss the good faith of a foreign government.

Counsel replied that "good faith" must mean something in section 10, and for the petitioner to succeed under that section, he did not have to impugn the motives of the Cyprus Government. It was merely a question of construing the words "in good faith in the interests of justice". The Lord Chief Justice had construed them as though they read "not being made in good faith and/or in the interests of justice", and had held that the onus lay on the petitioner to satisfy it that the Cyprus Government was neither acting in good faith nor in the interests of justice. A proper construction of those words only required the petitioner to establish that the demand for his return was in fact not in the interests of justice and therefore was not made in good faith. The words had to be read together.

Thirdly, the petitioner submitted that to return him to Cyprus would be, in all the circumstances, unjust and oppressive for the following reasons: From 1956 to 1960, he had acted as an agent of the Special Branch, Cyprus Police, under British control against the organization known as Eoka. In 1960 he had been branded as a traitor by Eoka and orders given for his assassination. Between 1957 and 1960, three attempts had been made on his life, two when he was in the custody of the police. In 1961, after he had arrived in this country, his home in Nicosia had been bombed; and on January 23, 1961, he left Cyprus under police escort at a time when the police knew of the alleged offences in the second warrant relating to demanding money by menaces.

He had since settled in this country with his wife and children on the advice of the Home Secretary in Cyprus and of Archbishop Makarios, who had been notified of his whereabouts. In these circumstances, he would not have a fair trial if returned, would be liable to be assassinated before his trial, or, if acquitted, he would be rearrested and charged with offences of a similar kind.

Fourthly, the petitioner submitted that the second warrant did not disclose a strong or probable presumption of guilt of the offence charged (demanding money with menaces).

VISCOUNT SIMONDS. I thought the law was that if there was any evidence, the superior court would not discuss whether the magistrate had sufficient evidence.

Counsel. Until Friday last (December 15), that point had been left open under the Fugitive Offenders Act, but on that day, in another case, of which the only report so far available is that in *The Times* newspaper (*In re Mourat Mehmet**, December 16) this very point was taken and the Divisional Court held that it was entitled to look at the evidence to see not only whether there was *some* evidence, but also whether, in their view, it amounted to a strong or probable presumption.

VISCOUNT SIMONDS. My knowledge is a little out of date.

Counsel referred their Lordships to the judgment of the Divisional Court* in the present case.

LORD REID asked counsel he put what seemed to his Lordship an important point accepted by the Divisional Court, namely, that if the petitioner Zacharia was sent back, there was the gravest risk of his being murdered either before or after his trial.

Counsel said that he put it, not on "good faith", but on "unjust and oppressive".

LORD REID. I notice that the Lord Chief Justice says: "Here the charges were of a serious nature and while there is a very real risk of his life, I do not feel myself able to say purely for that reason that it would be oppressive to send him back." I cannot think why. If there is a grave risk to his life, how can it fail to be oppressive to send him back? You would not be subjecting him to judicial process, but to murder by someone else. What is the evidence on that?

Council said that the evidence on the danger of his being assassinated, accepted by the Court consisted in a pamphlet, distributed in 1960 signed by

Eoka fighters which branded Zacharia as a traitor who was to be liquidated and Arestidou as his bodyguard. Other supporting evidence came from the trial of a deputy of the Cyprus Parliament in April, 1961, and showed that the petitioner was in danger of his life and had to fly to England because of Eoka threats. Further, three attempts had in fact been made on his life between 1957 and 1960.

Counsel made further submissions on the political nature of the alleged crimes.

On the case of the petitioner Arestidou, counsel said that although the complaint against him was much less grave, it was obvious from his association with Zacharia as his "bodyguard" that he too would be in grave danger of his life if he was returned to Cyprus.

When *Mr. Cumming-Bruce* rose to address the Committee, VISCOUNT SIMONDS said that under the present rules, the petitioner was not required to serve notice of leave to appeal on the opposite party. His Lordship thought that it should be considered very seriously whether the rule should not be altered so as to bring the opposite party before the Committee on a petition. He asked that the point should be taken up with the Attorney-General and the Lord Chancellor, for in every application concerning *habeas corpus*, the Committee wanted all the assistance it could have. It would not then require to trouble counsel on behalf of the Crown to attend as *amici curiae*.

Mr. Cumming-Bruce submitted that section 10 of the Fugitive Offenders Act did not impose any duty on the Court having found the fact that the return of the offender was likely for extraneous reasons to involve a real risk of death, to weigh that risk of death against the seriousness of the charges preferred against him and of which he might, in due course of law, be acquitted. There was here a question, fit for the consideration of the House of Lords, as to whether the Lord Chief Justice had applied the right test, having regard to his findings of fact and the gravity of the implications of those findings of fact. Further, it would be exceedingly valuable to have the views of their Lordships' House on the content and proper construction of the words "not being made in good faith in the interests of justice" in section 10 of the Act of 1881.

VISCOUNT SIMONDS, without having the Bar cleared, said that leave would be given to the petitioners to appeal.

Solicitors: *Messrs. Sampson & Co.; Messrs. Geffen & Co.*

R v. GOVERNOR OF BRIXTON PRISON, *EX PARTE* OTCHERE

((1962) 106 Sol. Jo. 856)

October 11, 1962: Queen's Bench Division: Lord Parker C.J., Gorman, Salmon JJ.

Fugitive Offenders—Affidavit—Need for authentication

Application for a writ of habeas corpus.

The Government of Ghana applied for the return of the applicant, a native of Ghana, under the Fugitive Offenders Act, 1881, the charge alleging that, in August, 1960, while in the employment of the Cocoa Marketing Board in Ghana, he stole the sum of £G422 6s. 8d., received by him in the course of his duties. A barrister in Ghana swore an affidavit which was not authenticated, to the effect that he had read the depositions and that the charge of stealing the sum of money in August, 1960, was an offence under the Ghana Criminal Code, 1960. The depositions disclosed a series of transactions between December, 1958, and January, 1960, that might amount to offences under the law of Ghana, but did not disclose such a transaction in August, 1960. On 3rd August, 1962, the metropolitan magistrate committed the applicant to prison pending his return to Ghana. The applicant applied for a writ of habeas corpus on the ground, *inter alia*, that the depositions did not disclose a transaction in August, 1960, that might amount to stealing under the law of Ghana.

LORD PARKER, C.J., said that in view of the fact that there was no evidence that the transactions between December, 1958 and January, 1960, disclosed by the depositions would amount to offences under the law of Ghana and that those transactions had inexplicably been placed together under a date eight months after the date of the last offence, it was open to the court to remit the matter to the magistrate for further evidence. That discretion would not, however, be exercised since the requisitioning country had made no attempt to put its tackle in order. The affidavit regarding the law of Ghana should have been authenticated in the way laid down by s. 29 of the Fugitive Offenders Act, 1881. That matter was put beyond a doubt by the fact that, in s. 39 of the 1881 Act, a deposition was defined as including an affidavit. Therefore, taking into account all the mistakes with which the present case was riddled, a writ of habeas corpus would be issued and the applicant discharged. Order accordingly.

GORMAN and SALMON, JJ., agreed.

APPEARANCES: *Neil Butter* (*Official Solicitor*); *John Baker* (*A. L. Bryden & Williams*); *J. H. Buzzard* and *John Leonard* (*Director of Public Prosecutions*).

REGINA v. GOVERNOR OF BRIXTON PRISON, *EX PARTE* SADRI

([1962] 1 W.L.R. 1304)

October 11, 1962: Queen's Bench Division: Lord Parker C.J., Gorman, Salmon JJ.

Fugitive Offender—Habeas corpus jurisdiciton—Evidence—Charge of falsification of document—No primary evidence of document—Order for committal—Primary evidence subsequently available—Affidavit stating offences punishable with imprisonment—No evidence that punishable on indictment or information with hard labour—Power of court to remit—Whether court power to receive evidence—Fugitive Offenders Act, 1881 (44 & 45 *Vict. c.* 69), *ss.* 5, 9.

On an application by the Government of the Colony of Aden for the return of the applicant under the Fugitive Offenders Act, 1881,[1] the endorsed warrant alleged three offences, falsification of a cash book, theft and conspiracy to commit a criminal breach of trust. Affidavit evidence referred in detail to the results of an examination of the cash book, but neither the book nor an authenticated copy of it or of the relevant entries was exhibited to the affidavit or produced in evidence. An affidavit by a lawyer practising in Aden referred to the appropriate sections of the penal code of Aden, which provided that each offence was punishable with imprisonment for a term exceeding 12 months, but there was no evidence that any of the offences were punishable on indictment or information by imprisonment with hard labour. Counsel

[1] Fugitive Offenders Act, 1881, s. 5: "A fugitive when apprehended shall be brought before a magistrate . . . If . . . such evidence is produced as . . . according to the law ordinarily administered by the magistrate, raises a strong or probable presumption that the fugitive committed the offence . . . and that the offence is one to which this Part of this Act applies, the magistrate shall commit the fugitive to prison to await his return. . . ."

S. 9: "This Part of this Act shall apply to the following offences, namely, . . . to every offence . . . which is for the time being punishable in the part of Her Majesty's dominions in which it was committed, either on indictment or information, by imprisonment with hard labour for a term of twelve months or more, or by any greater punishment; and for the purposes of this section, rigorous imprisonment, and any confinement in a prison combined with labour, by whatever name it is called, shall be deemed to be imprisonment with hard labour . . ."

for the requisitioning government informed the magistrate, who confirmed from the applicant, that he had seen the affidavits and had intimated to the police that he was not guilty and wished to return to Aden as soon as possible to prove his innocence. The cash book was not exhibited, but the magistrate was informed that photostat copies had been sent for and were expected to arrive in this country as soon as they could be prepared. The magistrate made an order committing the applicant to prison **[1305]** to await his return to the requisitioning country. Subsequently the cash book became available in this country.

On an application for a writ of habeas corpus on the grounds that there was no evidence that the alleged offences were punishable on indictment or information by imprisonment with hard labour as required by section 9 of the Fugitive Offenders Act, 1881,[1] and no evidence which raised a strong or probable presumption of guilt as required by section 5 of the Act [1] in which the court was asked to remit the case to the magistrate to examine the cash book and hear evidence as to the nature of the imprisonment, or to do so itself:—

Held, (1) that had the sole question been whether or not the offences were punishable on information or indictment with hard labour within the meaning of section 9, it would have been proper to remit the case to the magistrate to receive further evidence, or the evidence could be received in the Divisional Court.

Quaere whether, when evidence is given as to a term of imprisonment it should be inferred that it is imprisonment with "hard labour" within section 9.

Rex v. *Governor of Brixton Prison, Ex parte Percival** [1907] 1 K.B. 696; 23 T.L.R. 238, D.C. and *Reg.* v. *Governor of Brixton Prison, Ex parte Shuter** [1960] 2 Q.B. 89; [1959] 3 W.L.R. 603; [1959] 2 All E.R. 782, D.C., distinguished.

(2) But that, although a case might be remitted to a magistrate to hear further evidence on a question of jurisdiction or a technicality, a case should not be remitted to him to hear evidence of guilt when none had been tendered, nor should the Divisional Court receive such evidence itself; that since neither the cash book nor an authenticated copy was available before the magistrate, and the applicant himself could not waive essential evidence, there had been no evidence before the magistrate which raised a strong or probable presumption of guilt; and that, therefore, a writ of habeas corpus must issue.

Dictum of Lord Hodson in *Reg.* v. *Governor of Brixton Prison, Ex parte Schtraks** [1962] 3 W.L.R. 1013, 1047; [1962] 3 All E.R. 529, H.L.(E.) applied.

Per Lord Parker C.J. Although it is unnecessary for every exhibit to depositions taken in the foreign country or authenticated copies of every exhibit to be brought over to this country, when the exhibit in question is the very document which it is alleged was falsified, the requisitioning country should either produce the document or provide an authenticated copy of it or of the relevant extracts.

APPLICATION for writ of habeas corpus.

The applicant, Savak Sorabjee Sadri, applied for a writ of habeas corpus ad subjiciendum addressed to the Governor of **[1306]** Brixton Prison, where the applicant was detained to await his return to the Colony of Aden by virtue of a warrant of committal made on August 1, 1962, by the Bow Street magistrate (K. J. P. Barraclough) under the Fugitive Offenders Act, 1881.

The applicant was arrested on July 18, 1962, at Southampton, and brought before the magistrate on August 1, 1962. The warrant of arrest related falsification of accounts, theft and conspiracy, and was issued by the acting chief magistrate at Tawahi, Aden, on July 17, 1962. Attached to the warrant was a list of charges and four affidavits. The charges related to a period between September 25, 1961, and January 16, 1962, when the applicant was the chief accountant employed by a firm in Aden. The first count charged that he, being then a clerk employed by the firm, wilfully and with intent to defraud falsified the cash book belonging to the firm by deliberately making false calculations on various dates throughout that period, contrary to section 477A of the Aden Penal Code; the second count charged that he, intending to take dishonestly certain movable property, namely, the sum of 31,400 East African shillings in cash out of the possession of the firm without its consent, moved the property in order to such taking [sic] and thereby committed theft contrary to section 379 of the Code; and the third count charged that he and another named man agreed to do an illegal act, commit criminal breach of trust, and thereby were parties to a criminal conspiracy contrary to sections 120A and 408 of the Code. Two of the affidavits by partners, and a third from the successor to the applicant as accountant in the firm, deposed to an examination of three cash books, and with the results of the examination, in considerable detail, reference being made to pages in the books and certain figures on the pages, and alleged miscalculations and deliberately wrong addition of totals. The case against the applicant as appeared from the affidavits, was that he had, in conjunction with the cashier, devised a scheme whereby the payments side was deliberately inflated and that the cashier in charge of the cash register machine would work it in such a way as to produce a tally between the physical cash and the figure shown in the cash book, as a result of which there was a loss of 31,400 East African shillings. The fourth affidavit, from a lawyer practising in Aden, set out relevant sections of the Aden Penal Code providing the punishment for falsification of accounts to be "imprisonment for a term which may extend to seven years," for theft to be "imprisonment which may extend to three years," and for the criminal conspiracy to be "imprisonment which may extend to seven years." That affidavit did not state that those crimes were triable on indictment or information, or that the imprisonment was with hard labour.

The magistrate was informed by counsel for the requisitioning Government that the applicant had seen the affidavits and had intimated to the police officer that he was not guilty of the **[1307]** offences and that he wished to return as soon as possible to prove his innocence. The magistrate personally asked the applicant if he had had an opportunity of seeing the affidavits and whether he was in fact anxious to return to Aden to meet the charges. He replied in the affirmative on both inquiries. The magistrate was then informed by counsel that part of the evidence related to certain ledger accounts and cash books, which had not been exhibited to the affidavits, but that photostat copies of those documents had been sent for, and were expected to arrive in this country as soon as they could be prepared. The magistrate then considered the affidavits with counsel, and being satisfied that a prima facie case had been made out, and having regard to the representations previously made by the applicant, made the order.

The applicant applied for a writ of habeas corpus on the grounds that there was no evidence before the magistrate that any of the offences were punishable in the Colony of Aden on indictment or information, or by imprisonment with hard labour as required by section 9 of the Fugitive Offenders Act, 1881, and that the magistrate ought not to have relied upon the affidavits referring to the cash books which were not in any way exhibited to the affidavits or in the proceedings before him.

Neil Butter for the applicant.
John Mathew for the Government of the Colony of Aden.
J. H. Buzzard and *H. J. Leonard* for the Governor of Brixton Prison.

The following case, in addition to those referred to in the judgment, was cited in argument: *Rex* v. *Secretary of State for India, Ex parte Ezekiel.*[2]*

Lord Parker C.J. In these proceedings Mr. Butter moves for a writ of habeas corpus on behalf of the applicant, Savak Sorabjee Sadri, now detained in Her Majesty's prison at Brixton pursuant to a warrant of August 1, 1962, issued at Bow Street in pursuance of the provisions of the Fugitive Offenders Act, 1881. [His Lordship stated the facts set out above, read section 9 of the Fugitive

[2] [1941] 2 K.B. 169; [1941] 2 All E.R. 546, D.C.

Offenders Act, 1881, and continued:] Counsel for the applicant points out that the affidavit from the lawyer at Aden does not state that these three crimes are triable on indictment or information or that the terms of the imprisonment were terms of imprisonment with hard labour as that expression is used in section 9 of the Act of 1881. I am quite satisfied that, if that point stood alone, this would be a proper case in which to remit the matter to the magistrate to hear further evidence as to the nature of these offences or, alternatively, to receive evidence in this court. There is clear authority for permitting us to do that, **[1308]** in particular *Rex* v. *Governor of Brixton Prison, Ex parte Percival,*[3]* and the more recent case of *Reg.* v. *Governor of Brixton Prison, Ex parte Shuter.*[4]*

Before leaving that point, I should mention that Mr. Mathew who, I think, is concerned with quite a number of these cases representing requisitioning countries, in his anxiety to get all the assistance he can out of this court, has pointed to the difficulties nowadays of that expression, "imprisonment with hard labour," particularly having regard to the words which follow later defining hard labour as including "any confinement in prison combined with labour." He has really invited us to say that in every case where evidence is now given as to a term of imprisonment it should be inferred that that is imprisonment with hard labour within the meaning of the section. I would only say that I should hesitate very long before coming to that conclusion. There may be a number of cases where distinctions are capable of being drawn between what one might call simple imprisonment and imprisonment of a rigorous nature. However, it is unnecessary to come to any decision on that point, since in any event the affidavit is defective in not saying whether or not the offences are punishable on indictment or information.

The real difficulty in the present case concerns the second point raised by counsel for the applicant. The affidavits dealing with the discrepancies in the cash book do go into the matter in very considerable detail, but the book itself was not available at Bow Street, nor were any authenticated copies of it available, or of the extracts referred to in it.

Accordingly, on a strict view of the matter there was no evidence, or no admissible evidence, before the magistrates which, according to the law ordinarily administered by him, raised a strong or probable presumption that the applicant was guilty. The magistrate himself, as I understand it, clearly realised this, and he was told that the documents were on their way. Indeed, I understand his affidavit, which has been put in before us, to mean that in the ordinary way he would have adjourned for those documents to arrive. What had happened was this: apparently this applicant was shown the affidavits; he protested his innocence but said that he wished to return as soon as possible and prove that innocence; and, in those circumstances, rather than keep him in prison any longer over an adjournment, the magistrate made the order. Unfortunately, in my view, however meritorious that action was, I do not think it was an action which could properly be taken. I leave out the question entirely of the fact that this man may not fully have understood the affidavits, that he was unrepresented, that he would not understand the matters of secondary evidence and the objection he could take; but, quite **[1309]** apart from all that, it does not seem to me that any person in his circumstances can waive what is essential evidence before an order can be made.

In my judgment, in those circumstances, there was no evidence which could satisfy the magistrate, as he had to be satisfied, as to a strong or probable presumption of guilt under section 5 of the Act. This court, however, has been invited to send the case back to the magistrate to look at the documents which have now arrived in this country or, alternatively, this court is invited to look itself at the documents. For my part, I see very great difficulty in taking any such course. These proceedings are not by way of appeal; they are a matter of habeas corpus, and although in *Rex* v. *Governor of Brixton Prison, Ex parte*

[3] [1907] 1 K.B. 696; 23 T.L.R. 238, D.C.
[4] [1960] 2 Q.B. 89; [1959] 3 W.L.R. 603; [1959] 2 All E.R. 782, D.C.

Percival[5]* and *Reg* v. *Governor of Brixton Prison, Ex parte Shuter*[6]* the cases were remitted on the question of the jurisdiction of the magistrate based on the nature of the offences, there is no precedent whatsoever for sending a case book to the magistrate to hear evidence of guilt when no evidence of guilt has yet been tendered.

In *Reg.* v. *Governor of Brixton Prison, Ex parte Schtraks*[7]* it was the applicant who sought to adduce evidence which had not been adduced before the magistrate which pointed to his innocence, and their Lordships firmly refused the application. Lord Hodson said[8]: "The appellant also relies on certain cases wherein the Crown has been allowed to cure a technicality or fill a lacuna which, while it remained uncorrected or unfilled, would prima facie give the prisoner a right to the writ, although it would avail him little since he could be rearrested and the technicality corrected or the gap in the prosecution's case filled without difficulty. Examples of such cases are," and he refers to *Rex* v. *Governor of Brixton Prison, Ex parte Percival*[9]* and *Reg.* v. *Governor of Brixton Prison, Ex parte Shuter.*[10]* It is said that those words are quite general and that there is power to remit whenever the matter is a matter of curing a technicality. For my part, I do not think that this is a matter of pure technicality. In one sense it is, because it only means the production of authenticated copies of documents. Looked at in another way, it is far from technical because the strict view is that there was no evidence of guilt before the magistrate, and one cannot help seeing that Lord Hodson a few lines further down said[11]: "I am of the opinion that fresh evidence as to the guilt of the accused cannot properly be received."

I would not be a party to sending this case back. I do not think we have any power to do so, but in any event I would not do so. I think that requisitioning countries putting the machinery of the Fugitive Offenders Act, 1881, into force should come to **[1310]** this country properly armed with the necessary material. This court certainly does not wish to make difficulties, and I would like to make it plain that I should not have thought that it was necessary for every exhibit to depositions taken in the foreign country or authenticated copies of every exhibit to be brought over to this country, nor indeed all the exhibits in the case of a series of counts of a similar nature; but it does seem to me that when the exhibit in question is the very document, as here, which it is alleged was falsified, that at least the requisitioning country should either send over the document or provide an authenticated copy of it or of the relevant extracts.

It may be that this is a very lucky man, and it may be that further proceedings will be taken against him, but I think he is entitled to the writ and that it should go.

GORMAN J. I agree completely and do not desire to add anything.

SALMON J. I agree.

Application allowed with costs.

Solicitors: *Official Solicitor; Charles Russell & Co.; Director of Public Prosecutions.*

[5] [1907] 1 K.B. 696.
[6] [1960] 2 Q.B. 89.
[7] [1962] 3 W.L.R. 1013; [1962] 3 All E.R. 529, H.L.(E.).
[8] Ibid. 1047.
[9] [1907] 1 K.B. 696.
[10] [1960] 2 Q.B. 89.
[11] [1962] 3 W.L.R. 1013, 1047.

EX PARTE ORIMOLADE

(*The Times*, November 28, 1962.)

November 27, 1962: Queen's Bench Division: Ashworth, Salmon, Winn JJ.

Remedies Available for Detained Fugitives.

Their Lordships granted this *ex parte* application to issue a writ of *habeas corpus* on behalf of Samuel Orimolade, an alleged fugitive offender from Nigeria, at present detained in Her Majesty's Prison, Brixton, pursuant to an order of the Bow Street magistrate (Geraint Rees Esq.), made on October 30, 1962.

Section 10 of the Fugitive Offenders Act, 1881, entitles the Court to discharge a fugitive where it is made to appear to them "that by reason of the trivial nature of the case, or by reason of the application for the return of the fugitive not being made in good faith or in the interests of justice, or otherwise, it would be unjust or oppressive to return him".

Mr. Neil Butter appearing for the applicant, said that he made an application for relief under section 10 of the Fugitive Offenders Act, 1881.

Mr. Justice ASHWORTH said that it might assist counsel to know that the Court had read the papers and was minded to give leave. One point might require clarification, the nature of the relief sought.

Mr. Butter said that he was asking for relief under section 10. The affidavit was headed "by means of the issue of a writ of *habeas corpus ad subjiciendum* or otherwise". In the normal way two applications were made at the same time, an application for *habeas corpus* contending that the magistrate ought not to have made the order which he did and an application for relief under section 10 being in the nature of an alternative. In this case, having considered the papers, he (counsel) was satisfied that it would not be right to contend before this Court that the magistrate erred in making the order. In those circumstances, he (counsel) had wished to bring before their Lordships an application under section 10 alone. On considering the Rules of the Supreme Court, it became apparent that there was no rule of court which expressly or impliedly conferred jurisdiction on this Court under section 10 alone. R.S.C. O. 59 r.1 conferred jurisdiction in *habeas corpus* in certain other matters, but did not expressly or otherwise incorporate or include an application under section 10. In these circumstances, the proper course, it seemed, was to make what was in truth an application for relief under section 10, stating that that relief could be granted by the issue of a writ of *habeas corpus*.

In the ordinary way, if the application were to succeed under section 10, the Court would merely order the discharge of the applicant under that section; it had happened in the past that the court, taking that view, had ordered the applicant's discharge under section 10 by means of a writ of *habeas corpus*, although discharge under section 10 would seem to be more appropriate.

Mr. Justice ASHWORTH said that, *ex abundente cautela*, counsel had better apply for both. That was the view of the court. He ought to take leave to apply for the writ and for an order of discharge. That leave would be granted.

Counsel said that, as this was an application for *habeas corpus*, he asked for the motion to be adjourned for notice to be given to the appropriate representative of the Federation of Nigeria and the Governor of Brixton Prison.

Solicitor: *Official Solicitor*.

R. v. GOVERNOR OF BRIXTON PRISON AND ANOTHER; *EX PARTE* ORIMOLADE

((1963) 107 Sol. Jo. 37)

December 14, 1962: Queen's Bench Division: Lord Parker C.J., Salmon, Winn JJ.

Fugitive Offender—Delay in Proceedings—Whether Unreasonable or Oppressive

Application.

The applicant was committed to prison under the Fugitive Offenders Act, 1881, on a warrant of committal dated 30th October, 1962. The charges against him were six counts relating to offences alleged to have been committed in Nigeria in December, 1959, involving about £600 in money, and not reported to the police until April, 1960. In October, 1960, Nigeria became an independent State, and very great changes took place in personnel and organisation of Government departments and the Ministry of Justice. The depositions were taken in Lagos in November, 1960, and sent to this country in September, 1962. The applicant applied to the Divisional Court for relief under s. 10 of the 1881 Act on the ground that, in view of the delay in the proceedings, it would be unjust or oppressive for him to be sent back. It was conceded that the magistrates' committal could not be challenged by way of habeas corpus.

LORD PARKER, C.J., said that habeas corpus came into the matter only in so far as it might be necessary (he did not say it was) to secure the applicant's release if relief were given pursuant to s. 10 of the 1881 Act, which was in very wide words and had been given a very wide construction by the court. There had been very considerable delay. Cases on this did not help. Each case must depend upon its exact facts. While it could be said that any delay was of prejudice to an alleged offender, it had not been suggested that this applicant would be prejudiced in any particular respect. It had not been made clear that it would be unreasonable or oppressive to send him back.

SALMON and WINN, JJ., agreed. Application refused.

Appearances: *Neil Butter* (*Official Solicitor*); *John Buzzard* (*Director of Public Prosecutions*); *Brian Leary* (*Charles Russell & Co.*)

REGINA v. THE GOVERNOR OF BRIXTON PRISON *EX PARTE* ENAHORO.

(*The Times*, January 16, 1963)

January 15, 1963: Queen's Bench Division: Lord Parker C.J., Ashworth, Lyell JJ.

Habeas Corpus Refused.

The Court dismissed this application by Chief Anthony Eronsele Enahoro for an order of *habeas corpus* and for an order for relief under section 10 of the Fugitive Offenders Act, 1881.

Mr. Dingle Foot Q.C. and *Mr. Kenneth Potter* appeared for the applicant; *Mr. Jeremy Hutchinson Q.C.* and *Mr. J. C. Mathew* for the Nigerian Government; *Mr. John Buzzard for* the Governor of Brixton Prison.

The LORD CHIEF JUSTICE said that on November 27, 1962, a warrant was issued in Lagos for the arrest of the applicant on three undoubtedly serious charges. The first charge was treasonable felony and it was alleged that the applicant and three others "formed an intention to levy war against our Sovereign Lady, the Queen, within Nigeria in order by force or constraint to compel our Sovereign Lady the Queen to change her measures or counsel and manifested such intention. . . ." The overt acts alleged were that the applicant with others incited persons to take part in the levying of war against the Queen, and were concerned in the unlawful importation of arms, ammunition and explosives into Nigeria. The second charge, was conspiracy to commit a felony in that the applicant and others conspired to levy war against the Queen in order to intimidate or overawe the Governor-General. The third charge was a conspiracy to effect an unlawful purpose—namely, to contravene the Firearms Act and the regulations made thereunder.

The applicant moved for *habeas corpus* on the ground that the magistrate at Bow Street exceeded his jurisdiction in that his only power to commit was if the evidence raised a strong or probable presumption that the applicant had committed the offences and that the evidence before the magistrate was such that he could not take the view in law that a strong or probable presumption of guilt was made out.

It was sufficient to say that the evidence clearly disclosed a conspiracy on the part of persons in Nigeria, within the Action Group, to procure men to be trained in the use of arms and explosives in a neighbouring state, and to import arms and explosives into Nigeria and to use them for the overthrow of the Government. It seemed to his Lordship that the evidence raised a strong or probable presumption that the applicant was a party to that conspiracy. So far as the claim for a writ of *habeas corpus* was concerned, his Lordship was satisfied that the claim failed.

The second matter concerned relief under section 10 of the Fugitive Offenders Act, 1881, which only arose on the basis that there was a strong or probable presumption of guilt. In May, 1962, the Government of the Western Region purported to dismiss the Premier Chief Akintole, and to appoint Chief Adegbenro in his place. On May 25, two meetings of the Assembly broke up in disorder. The Court was told that the mace was smashed and the police used tear gas but as far as the Court knew there was no disturbance outside the House of Assembly. On May 29, the Federal Parliament enacted that a state of emergency existed in the Western Region; an administrator was appointed and all constitutional government in the area was abrogated. Chief Awolowo, the leader of the Action Group, Chief Adegbenro and other members of the Action Group were placed under restriction, including the applicant. The restriction on the applicant was lifted in August. A month later, he left for Ghana, where he was granted political asylum. By devious methods, devious routes and devious means, he succeeded in coming to this country.

It was submitted that this was a case where, on an examination of all the circumstances, it would appear that the application for the applicant's return was not being made in good faith or in the interests of justice, because it was an attempt to exterminate a political party, the Action Group. Unlike the Extradition Act, the Fugitive Offenders Act, 1881, was clearly dealing with political offences, including treason. The present case clearly dealt with a political offence, for it was a conspiracy to overthrow the constitutional government of Nigeria. Once one accepted that a strong or probable presumption of guilt of treason was made out, it was impossible to say that the application for the return of the fugitive was not being made in good faith albeit that it might result in the extermination of a political party.

In the present case, the Court was dealing with on the face of it with a political offence of a very serious character. Once a strong or probable presumption of guilt of that offence was made out, his Lordship found it impossible to say that the application for return was made in bad faith albeit that it would harass or exterminate a certain political faction.

As to whether it would be unjust or oppressive to return the applicant to Nigeria, it was said, first, that this Court should approach the matter on the basis that the emergency powers were of a sweeping nature and of a most drastic character. It was suggested that they were powers of doubtful validity and were used in an oppressive manner to harass the opposition, the Action Group. Another way it was put was that the Court should take cognizance of the suggestion that the emergency powers were out of all relation to what the emergency, if there was one, demanded. The difficulty his Lordship felt about that was that even if he acceded to it on the facts, all those drastic powers under the Emergency Powers Act were terminated on December 31, 1962. It was undoubtedly true that a state of emergency might again be declared and similar powers brought into force, but so far as the Court was concerned, those powers were no longer in force, and there were no grounds for the fear that the applicant might be detained without trial. The fact that the emergency was brought to an end on December 31, showed that the Nigerian Government were not allowing democratic government to be suspended any longer than necessary.

Finally, and this was the point that his Lordship thought was the main point in the case, was the point concerning the refusal to allow Queen's Counsel to enter Nigeria. His Lordship quite appreciated that this applicant might not want counsel from this country. Equally, the Court was not concerned with the powers under which Queen's Counsel was prevented from landing and appearing for Chief Awolowo. This Court was only concerned to see whether there was any danger that if the applicant desired counsel of his choice, he would be refused on the same grounds as Chief Awolowo. If his Lordship had felt there was a real danger of that, he would have hesitated before refusing this applicant some form of relief. Apart from the fact that the Court did not know whether the applicant wanted counsel from this country, Mr. Hutchinson had given an undertaking that if this applicant chose a counsel from England who, according to the law of Nigeria was entitled to appear in the Nigerian Court, the executive would not refuse counsel permission to land merely because he was going to represent the applicant. This being so, however oppressive the action in respect of Chief Awolowo might have been, and his Lordship was not saying it was because the Court did not have the full facts, he was satisfied that no oppressive action of that sort would be taken in the applicant's case.

Mr. Foot submitted in the alternative that it would be unjust and oppressive to return the applicant at the present moment. Chief Adegbenro, who had been detained under the emergency regulations, sought a declaration in the Supreme Court that the emergency regulations were unlawful and ultra vires and that his restriction was unlawful. He failed, and the Court was told that there was an appeal to the Privy Council. It was said that the applicant should not be returned until that position was resolved. It seemed to his Lordship that whether the emergency regulations were *ultra vires* or not was irrelevant, as the applicant was charged not with a breach of those regulations, but with treason under the common law. There was another action in which Chief Awolowo was claiming a declaration that he had unlawfully been deprived of counsel of his choice. There was an appeal to the Supreme Court pending, and it might be that there would be an appeal to the Privy Council. Once again, it was said that the applicant should not be returned until that was concluded, but, having regard to the undertaking given by Mr. Hutchinson, it mattered not what the result of that action was. Both the applications failed and had to be dismissed.

Mr. Justice Ashworth agreed but said that there might be cases where, in regard to a particular individual, although there was a strong or probable presumption that he was guilty, albeit in a case of treason, there might still be grounds for saying that an application by the requisitioning government was not made in good faith. His Lordship would hesitate to give illustrations but it did seem that there might be occasions where it would be an exercise of bad faith for a state to ask for a fugitive's return.

Mr. Justice Lyell agreed.

The court refused the applicant leave to appeal to the House of Lords and dismissed the application with costs.

Solicitors: *Messrs. Hatchett Jones & Co.; Messrs. E. F. Turner & Sons; The Treasury Solicitor.*

ENAHORO v. FEDERATION OF NIGERIA AND ANOTHER

(*The Times*, February 7, 1963)

February 6, 1963: House of Lords: Lords Reid, Morris of Borth-y-Gest, Pearce

Nigerian Chief Refused Leave to Appeal

The Appeal Committee refused this petition by Chief Anthony Eronsele Enahoro for leave to appeal from the refusal of the Divisional Court of the Queen's Bench Division* (the Lord Chief Justice, Mr. Justice Ashworth and Mr. Justice Lyell) on January 15, 1963 (*The Times*, January 16) of his application for an order of *habeas corpus* and for relief under section 10 of the Fugitive Offenders Act, 1881.

On November 10, 1962, a warrant was issued in Lagos, Nigeria, for the arrest of the petitioner, an opposition member of the Nigerian Federal Parliament, on three charges—treasonable felony, conspiracy to commit a felony, namely treason—and conspiracy to effect an unlawful purpose—namely to contravene the Firearms Acts and the Regulations made thereunder. At that time the petitioner was outside Nigeria. On December 13, 1962, Mr. K. J. P. Baraclough at Bow Street Magistrates' Court made an order under section 5 of the Act of 1881, committing the petitioner to Brixton Prison pending his return in custody to Nigeria.

Mr. Dingle Foot Q.C. and *Mr. Kenneth Potter* appeared for the plaintiff; *Mr. Jeremy Hutchinson Q.C.* and *Mr. John Mathew* for the Federation of Nigeria; *Mr. John Buzzard* for the Governor of Brixton Prison.

Mr. Foot said that the two questions arising on this application were, first, whether the evidence in the depositions taken in Lagos were such as to raise a strong presumption that the fugitive committed the acts mentioned in the warrant; and, secondly, if so, whether this was a case for the grant of relief under section 10 of the Act of 1881. It was important for both purposes to bear in mind the political background and recent history of Nigeria, beginning with the dismissal by the Governor of the Premier of Western Nigeria on May 21, 1962, proceeding to a declaration of emergency, followed by restriction on the movements of the leaders of the Action Group, and finally the trial of Chief Awolowo and the refusal to allow counsel from this country, a member of the Nigerian Bar, to land in Nigeria, on the ground that anyone connected with the trial would not be allowed to enter Nigeria, and the comments made by the trial judge when it was sought to bring that matter to his attention.

The petitioner had been a member of the Action Group from its inception, a vice-president from 1951 to 1959; he was a member of the West Region House of Assembly from 1954 to 1959, and Minister of Home Affairs of the West Region Government. Since 1959 he had been a member of the Federal Parliament. He was thus, undoubtedly at all times a prominent member of the governing party in the Western Region and of the opposition in the Federation Parliament. What was here alleged was that certain members of Action formed a conspiracy to overthrow by force the legitimate government of Nigeria. It appeared from the evidence that the conspiracy was limited to a small number of persons. But when it was investigated it attached to a large number of people so that even the most normal political activities might appear in a rather sinister light. It was important to bear that in mind in looking at the evidence. There was a good deal of evidence as to the existence of a conspiracy but very little to show that the petitioner was one of the conspirators or that he was engaged in anything except lawful political activities.

Counsel referred their Lordships in detail to the depositions and said that one of the remarkable features was that whenever one came up against anything really serious, such as the importation or distribution of arms or the overthrowing of the government, the petitioner was absent. That was a matter their

Lordships should take into account. All that the evidence showed was, first, that he became aware at some stage that persons had been undergoing military training in Ghana—but that was quite immaterial; secondly, that there had been a threat of death to someone for failure to carry out party duties—which did not link up at all with the alleged conspiracy; and thirdly, a consultation with Chief Awolowo, merely showing the petitioner wondering whether he should associate himself with some unknown persons who were planning a *coup d'état*. If the evidence was, as counsel submitted it was, equally consistent with the petitioner's guilt or innocence, it fell short of what was required.

On section 10, counsel submitted (1) that the application was not made in good faith in the interests of justice; (2) that it would be otherwise unjust or oppressive to return the fugitive; and (3) that in any case it would be unjust or oppressive to return him until certain appeals now pending had been disposed of.

Relying on the principles stated by their Lordships in relation to the Act of 1881 in *Zacharia* v. *Republic of Cyprus** (*The Times* April 17, 1962; [1962] 2 W.L.R. 1163) it should be observed that the Federal Government of Nigeria had over the last six or seven months used its powers to attack the opposition and in order to do so had completely abrogated the constitution of the Western Region. The genesis of that had been that on May 25 there had been two scenes of gross disorder in the Western Region House of Assembly—a state of affairs frequently occurring in our own House of Commons, though not in their Lordships' House. It was fantastic that such a pretext should lead to a state of emergency and to the use of powers of restriction on the opposition. Though the state of emergency was now at an end there was nothing to prevent the Federal Government taking similar powers whenever they found it convenient to do so. That was relevant to the question whether the application was made in good faith, for the whole of the state of emergency was directed at rendering impossible the position of the petitioner's political group. If he went back to stand his trial, he went back into the power of a government which had used these measures against an opposition party.

The case would be still stronger if two appeals now pending succeeded. The first was in an action brought by Chief Adegbenro for a declaration that the Emergency Powers Act and the measures taken under it were *ultra vires*. That was now the subject of an appeal to the Privy Council. There was also the action brought by Chief Awolowo for a declaration that by the exclusion of Mr. Gratiaen Q.C., he had been deprived of his constitutional right to be represented by a counsel of his choice. The appeal then pending was to the Federal Supreme Court. If those appeals were successful it would mean that not only had constitutional government been abrogated but that it had been done in defiance of the law. One could not tell what the results would be; but even if the petitioner ought to be returned it should not be carried out until after these appeals had been disposed of.

The Lord Chief Justice in his judgment had said that the action of the Federal Government in excluding Mr. Gratiaen had caused him considerable anxiety; and an assurance had been given to the Divisional Court by Mr. Hutchinson on behalf of the Nigerian Government that if the Chief Justice granted the necessary permission to counsel from outside Nigeria to appear, the Government would undertake that such counsel would not be refused entry on the ground *merely* that he was to take part in this trial. On that, counsel could only say that when somebody was excluded from Nigeria, no reasons were given.

Further, if the press report of what the trial judge had said when the matter of counsel's exclusion was raised at the trial of Chief Awolowo was correct—and it had not been challenged—that, too, was a material circumstance for if the petitioner went back to Nigeria, there was the possibility that he might be tried by that particular judge. A serious question arose as to whether the petitioner would receive a fair trial. For the reasons given, counsel submitted that the fugitive in this case should not be returned.

The Bar was cleared while their Lordships deliberated.

LORD REID when counsel returned, said that they wished to hear Mr. Hutchinson for the Federal Government, only on the allegation that there might not be a fair trial if the petitioner were returned.

Mr. Hutchinson said that the allegation was based on the refusal to allow Chief Awolowo to have the counsel of his choice.

LORD REID. And the allegation that the judge behaved in an unusual manner in dealing with Chief Awolowo's application.

Mr. Hutchinson said that so far as the refusal to allow Mr. Gratiaen to land was concerned, this was a treason trial which was being conducted in Nigeria on evidence that the persons concerned were trained in another country in the use of arms for the purpose of upsetting the lawfully elected Government. That was the background to the situation when counsel had arrived there. His entry had been refused under section 13 of the Immigration Act and though one was not in a position to go into the reasons for the refusal, it had been a lawful refusal. That act of refusal had been tested at once in the courts and the Minister's act had been upheld. Though perhaps the language of the trial judge as reported in the press, was not exactly judicial language as we know it in this country, the judge had been entitled to say that it was not a matter for him. Nothing in the affidavits suggested that the judiciary in Nigeria did not conduct trials in a perfectly fair way, and there was no reason to say that this petitioner would not get a fair trial, particularly having regard to the undertaking which he (counsel) had been able to get from the Attorney-General when the matter was raised in the Divisional Court.

LORD REID. But look at the last line of the undertaking. It is perfectly satisfactory up to the point where the Chief Justice gives authority for counsel to represent the accused. But the undertaking is only that authorised counsel will not be refused on the ground *merely* that he is to take part in this trial. If it had said that authorised counsel would be permitted to enter once the authority had been given by the Chief Justice, it would be wholly satisfactory. But how do we know that he won't be prevented from entering on some other ground altogether?

Mr. Hutchinson. I hope your Lordships will not be under any misapprehension about this. These words were suggested and agreed to at the hearing before the Divisional Court.

LORD REID. May I take it that the substance of the undertaking is this, that if the Chief Justice authorises the appearance at this trial of some named counsel, entry of that counsel to Nigeria will not be prohibited on any ground?

Mr. Hutchinson said that he could not give that undertaking without taking instructions. There might be some perfectly valid reason why the counsel chosen should not be allowed to enter.

LORD REID. Very well; "will be allowed to enter unless for some specified reason".

Mr. Hutchinson. I will take instructions.

LORD REID. It is very awkward, because Mr. Foot has stated quite properly that the Government are not in the habit of giving reasons and has accused the Government of bad faith. It would be most unsatisfactory if the Chief Justice authorised a certain counsel to appear and that gentleman arrived at the airport to be told: "you are not to be allowed to enter and we cannot tell you the reason". If the reason is specified it would be published—and I am not going to assume that the Government would act on an inappropriate reason. If they give a reason, everyone can see that they are being fair. What are we going to do about it?

Mr. Hutchinson, after taking instructions said that it was a difficult matter on which to give a decision immediately. It raised questions of principle.

LORD REID. But you have already given an undertaking and it appears to me to be rather ambiguous. It is undesirable to have an ambiguous undertaking. How far are you prepared to go?

Counsel. It would involve getting on to Nigeria on the telephone and getting approval for this suggested draft. A Government should not be expected to give its reasons under section 13 of the Immigration Act in general.

LORD MORRIS. There is affidavit evidence to show that when Mr. Gratiaen arrived the immigration officer did give the reason for not giving permission to land, and it was that he had orders to refuse entry to any lawyer arriving from England to represent Chief Awolowo. Was your undertaking meant fully to meet this point?

Counsel. That was the purpose of it. That was why the word "merely" was inserted.

LORD REID, after hearing Mr. Foot in reply, said their Lordships' decision was that the petition must be refused.

Mr. Hutchinson asked for costs.

LORD REID. It is not usual to apply for costs in these cases.

Their Lordships rose.

Solicitors: *Messrs. Hatchett Jones & Co.; Messrs E. F. Turner & Sons; Treasury Solicitor.*

REGINA v. GOVERNOR OF BRIXTON PRISON AND ANOTHER *EX PARTE* ENAHORO

([1963] 2 Q.B. 455)

April 25, 1963: Queen's Bench Division: Lord Parker C.J., Havers, Edmund Davies JJ.

Fugitive Offender—Warrant of Home Secretary—Delay in issue—Decision by Home Secretary to return fugitive—Consideration by House of Commons—". . . a Secretary of State . . . may, if he thinks it just" by warrant order the fugitive's return—Whether "may" mandatory—Whether Home Secretary entitled to delegate responsibility under section 6—Whether delegated to Parliament—Fugitive Offenders Act, 1881 (44 & 45 *Vict. c.* 69), *s.* 6.

Crown—Minister, determination by—Delegation of responsibility—Whether determination valid—Fugitive offender—Consideration by House of Commons as to return—Fugitive Offenders Act, 1881, *s.* 6.

The applicant was detained under a magistrate's order made on December 13, 1962, under section 5 of the Fugitive Offenders Act, 1881,[1] to await his return to Nigeria to answer charges there. After unsuccessful applications to the Divisional Court for an order of habeas corpus and for relief under section 10 of the Act of 1881, representations were made on the applicant's behalf to the Home Secretary, who, having considered them, decided on March 14, 1963, under section 6 of the Act of 1881, that it was just to order the applicant's return and announced his decision to the House of Commons. It then became clear to the Home Secretary that Parliament wished to debate his decision and on March 21 he gave an assurance that he would not order the applicant's return pending Parliament's decision. The debate took place on March 26 and was adjourned until April 10, when Parliament made its decision at 8 p.m. At 8.30 p.m. the Home Secretary received notice of the applicant's intention to make the present application to the court to order

[1] Fugitive Offenders Act, 1881, s. 6: "Upon the expiration of 15 days after a fugitive has been committed to prison to await his return, or if a writ of habeas corpus or other like process is issued with reference to such fugitive by a superior court, after the final decision of the court in the case . . . a Secretary of State . . . may, if he thinks it just, by warrant under his hand order that fugitive to be returned to the part of Her Majesty's Dominions from which he is a fugitive . . ."

S. 7: "If a fugitive who, in pursuance of this Part of this Act, has been committed to prison in any part of Her Majesty's dominions to await his return, is not conveyed out of that part within one month after such committal, a superior court . . . may, unless sufficient cause is shown to the contrary, order the fugitive to be discharged out of custody."

his discharge under section 7 of the Act of 1881 on the ground that there was no sufficient cause for his detention after March 14:—

Held, (1) That "may" in the phrase "a Secretary of State . . . may, if he thinks just," by warrant order the return of the fugitive, in section 6, was not mandatory and that once the Minister had decided that it was just, he was under no immediate duty to issue the warrant but had a discretion as to when it should issue.

(2) That assuming without deciding, that the Home Secretary had no power to delegate his responsibility under section 6, on the **[456]** facts, there was no ground for thinking that he had delegated to or shared with a majority of Parliament his statutory responsibility; accordingly, his reference of the matter to Parliament was reasonable in all the circumstances and therefore there were good grounds for detaining the applicant for more than 30 days and the application for release under section 7 would be dismissed.

*In re Shuter** [1960] 1 Q.B. 142; [1959] 3 W.L.R. 652; [1959] 3 All E.R. 481, D.C. considered.

APPLICATION for an order under section 7 of the Fugitive Offenders Act, 1881, and for a writ of habeas corpus.

By a notice of motion dated April 10, 1963, the applicant, Anthony Eronsele Enahoro, detained in Brixton prison, applied for an order under section 7 of the Fugitive Offenders Act, 1881, that he be discharged from custody. By a further notice of motion dated April 19, the applicant applied for a writ of habeas corpus.

By his affidavit dated April 11, 1963, the applicant stated that on December 13, 1962, at Bow Street Magistrates' Court an order was made under section 5 of the Act of 1881, committing him to Brixton prison pending his return in custody to Nigeria in respect of a warrant for his arrest issued in Nigeria on November 27, 1962, on charges of treasonable felony, conspiracy to commit a felony (namely, treason) and conspiracy to effect an unlawful purpose (namely, to contravene the Firearms Act and the regulations thereunder). On January 15, 1963, the Divisional Court of the Queen's Bench Division[2] dismissed applications made on the applicant's behalf for a writ of habeas corpus and for relief under section 10 of the Act of 1881. On February 6, the Appeal Committee of the House of Lords[3] refused the applicant's petition for leave to appeal to the House of Lords from the decision of the Divisional Court. On February 12, there was delivered to the Secretary of State for the Home Department, the Right Honourable Henry Brooke, M.P., on the applicant's behalf, a petition signed by himself requesting the Secretary of State to exercise his discretion under section 6 of the Act in his favour and not to order his return to Nigeria.

Notwithstanding that he was committed to prison on December 13, 1962, the applicant was still in custody in Brixton Prison, and notice of his intention to make the present application having been given to the Secretary of State for the Home Department, the applicant applied to the court for an order that he might be **[457]** discharged from custody under and in accordance with section 7 of the Act of 1881.

The applicant submitted, on the grounds hereinbefore appearing, that a writ of habeas corpus be issued to the Secretary of State for the Home Department and to the Governor of Brixton prison to have the applicant brought before the court.

By his affidavit the Home Secretary stated that, as Home Secretary, he was responsible for the exercise of the jurisdiction conferred by section 6 of the Fugitive Offenders Act, 1881, in the case of the applicant. On February 6, 1963, the Appeal Committee of the House of Lords had refused the petition of the applicant for leave to appeal to the House of Lords. It was then his duty by virtue of section 6 to consider whether it was just to order the return of the applicant to Nigeria. Immediately after the Appeal Committee gave its decision, the solicitors for the applicant notified the Home Office that they intended within seven days to make representations requesting that the applicant should be

[2] The Times, January 16, 1963. [3] The Times, February 7, 1963.

allowed to stay in the United Kingdom. On February 15 the applicant's solicitors handed in to the Home Office a letter enclosing a petition with annexures of wide scope and complexity for the Home Secretary's investigation and consideration. Members of Parliament submitted representations that it would not be just to order the return of the applicant to Nigeria. On February 14 the Home Secretary received a memorandum from the Member of Parliament in whose constituency the applicant had been arrested, with a request that he might be given further time to make representations. On March 5 a deputation of Members of Parliament brought to the Home Secretary's notice and asked him to consider grounds for holding that it would not be just to order the applicant's return. On March 6 and 11 further detailed factual material was submitted in support of the grounds put forward by that deputation.

The Home Secretary and his advisers were well aware of the importance of speed in arriving at his decision, and the provisions of section 7 of the Act of 1881 were present to his mind while he was considering the representations made in the applicant's petition. But the inquiries into the facts which he required to know in order to enable him to discharge his statutory duty were not completed until March 12. Two aspects of the case in particular protracted those inquiries. First, the applicant had submitted that there were serious grounds for apprehension that if he was tried he would not be allowed counsel of his choice. An undertaking had been given to the Divisional Court on behalf of **[458]** the Nigerian Government in that connection, but questions had been asked in the Appeal Committee of the House of Lords about the form and effect of that undertaking. The Home Secretary considered that in the interests of the applicant it was crucial that he should be left in no uncertainty about this. After an approach to the Nigerian Government through the British High Commissioner in Lagos the Home Secretary received on March 11 an assurance of a satisfactory character from the Prime Minister of Nigeria. Secondly, letters between the applicant's solicitors and the Home Office on facts complained of in the petition of the applicant culminated in a request by those solicitors that the Home Secretary should see the two gentlemen whose conversation had given rise to the misunderstanding. In order to prevent the risk of injustice to the applicant, the Home Secretary saw the two gentlemen together on March 12 and satisfied himself on the facts.

Paragraph 5 of the affidavit read: "On March 14 I was satisfied that I had properly investigated all the matters which had been raised for my consideration by or on behalf of the applicant and by Members of Parliament, and I decided under section 6 of the Fugitive Offenders Act, 1881, that it was just to order the return of the applicant to Nigeria." By paragraph 6: "I am answerable to Parliament for the discharge of my statutory duty under section 6. My decision did not accord with the representations urged upon me by a number of Members of Parliament of all parties, and the case raised problems concerning the discharge of that duty in relation to a person charged with political offences in the territory of an independent sovereign member of the Commonwealth. I considered that it was both my duty and in the interests of the applicant that I should report my decision to Parliament before ordering his return. A draft warrant ordering his return had already been prepared and was ready for my signature. Accordingly I made a statement announcing my decision to the House of Commons on March 14. It was clear to me that it was the wish of the House of Commons that the House should debate my decision before I ordered the return of the applicant. It was not possible for the House to debate my decision on that day but arrangements were made that the matter should be discussed in the course of a debate which was due to take place on March 21. I considered that it was right and consonant with the interests both of Parliament and of the applicant not to order the return of the applicant until this discussion had taken place. The discussion took place a week later on March 21 as arranged, **[459]** but on that occasion no question relating to my decision was before the House and consequently no decision of the House was possible upon it. At the conclusion of the discussion, as a result of representations made and of a statement that a motion relating to my decision would be tabled that night, I considered it right and consonant with the interests both of Parliament and the applicant to give an assurance to the House of Commons that there would be no order for the return of the applicant pending the decision of the House of Commons provided that the matter could be brought to an early conclusion. The debate took place in the House of Commons on March 26 and was adjourned. On April 10 the adjourned debate was resumed and concluded, and the House made its decision by a division about 8 p.m. I then felt for the first time free from the undertaking which I had given to the House of Commons on March 21 and I intended forthwith to issue my warrant ordering the return of the applicant." By pargraph 7: "Immediately after the end of the debate at about 8.30 p.m. the applicant's solicitors served the notice of the intention to make this application . . . I thereupon considered it my duty not to take any action to remove the applicant out of the jusisdiction until the termination of these proceedings, provided that the applicant prosecuted them with due diligence."

Dingle Foot Q.C., E. F. N. Gratiaen Q.C. and *Kenneth Potter* for the applicant. An adjournment is requested to obtain the leave of the House of Commons to cite passages from Hansard concerning proceedings in the House referred to in the Home Secretary's affidavit. The debates are relevant: first, to show that the decision to return the applicant to Nigeria was in part that of other members of the Cabinet and in part that of the House of Commons. If it be right that the decision should have been that of the Home Secretary alone acting under section 6, then whatever occurred after March 14, when the Home Secretary decided that it was just to issue the warrant, would not have been "sufficient cause" for the delay under section 7. Secondly, if the Home Secretary's statutory discretion under section 6 was not properly exercised, in as much as it was not his decision but that of some other persons, his decision would be invalid. Those points cannot be made good without reference to the proceedings in the House of Commons.

Sir John Hobson Q.C., A-G. and *J. R. Cumming-Bruce* for the Governor of Brixton Prison and the Home Secretary. The **[460]** adjournment is unnecessary because the evidence is irrelevant. What occurred before Parliament is no part of the Home Secretary's case in showing "sufficient cause" for the delay under section 7. The only question is whether it was reasonable for him not to order the applicant's return while Parliament was considering the matter.

[LORD PARKER C.J. The court feels that there is no sufficient cause at this stage to adjourn. If, as the case proceeds, the court thinks it necessary, it will listen to a further application.]

Dingle Foot Q.C. In re Shuter[4]* decides that the word "may" in section 7 of the Fugitive Offenders Act, 1881, is mandatory, from which it follows that, at the moment when the statutory month expires, the fugitive cannot be held for a single day in the absence of sufficient cause being shown to the contrary; the test may be what is reasonable in the circumstances. Unless reasonable cause is shown the fugitive is entitled to go free. Similarly with section 6; the word "may" is mandatory. It follows that, once the Home Secretary has decided that it is just that the fugitive should be returned, it is the Home Secretary's duty forthwith to sign, that is, issue the warrant. On the facts the Home Secretary came to his decision on March 14, and his duty was to sign the warrant then. Nothing that occurred later can amount to sufficient cause to the contrary, and the applicant is entitled to go free, the statutory month under section 7 having expired.

Section 6 places the duty of deciding on the Home Secretary as the Secretary of State seized of the matter. That duty cannot be delegated or surrendered or shared with any person (*Barnard* v. *National Dock Labour Board*[5]; *Vine* v. *National Dock Labour Board*[6]) even a Minister or with Parliament or the House of Commons. The necessary implication from the statements in the affidavit

[4] [1960] 1 Q.B. 142; [1959] 3 W.L.R. 652; [1959] 3 All E.R. 481, D.C.
[5] [1953] 2 Q.B. 18; [1953] 2 W.L.R. 995; [1953] 1 All E.R. 1113, C.A.
[6] [1957] A.C. 488; [1957] 2 W.L.R. 106; [1956] 3 All E.R. 939, H.L.(E.).

of the Home Secretary is that he was either surrendering to or sharing with some Minister, the House of Commons or Parliament his statutory duty, that is, the final decision in this case. Accordingly, that cannot amount to sufficient cause within section 7.

Sir John Hobson Q.C., A.-G. The correctness of the decision on section 7 in *In re Shuter*[7]* is not disputed, but the position **[461]** under section 6 is quite different. Under section 6 the Home Secretary has a complete discretion: *per* Lord Devlin in *Zacharia* v. *Republic of Cyprus.*[8]* First, he has to decide whether or not he thinks it just to order the fugitive's return. If he does think it just, he still has a discretion whether and when to issue the warrant, subject only to the fugitive's rights under section 7.

By March 14, the Home Secretary had decided that it was just to order the applicant's return, but he had not then decided whether to issue his warrant. He was in no way delegating or sharing his functions with Parliament by declining to issue his warrant until Parliament had concluded its discussions on the matter. The matter was referred to Parliament for two reasons. First, the House of Commons is one of the guardians of the liberty of the subject and ought to have the benefit of pronouncing on the matter, and secondly, it was in the interests of the applicant himself, because if Parliament condemned the Home Secretary's action, he would have to resign. Thus it was not the Home Secretary who was going to change his view if Parliament disagreed with him; a new Home Secretary would have to take a fresh decision.

An alternative way of putting the matter is this: having decided that it is just to issue the warrant, the Home Secretary is still entitled to decide whether to issue it or not, and he is entitled to listen to and take advice throughout that stage and to consider anything said to him up to the moment he issues the warrant.

[LORD PARKER C.J. Why were you at such pains to draw a distinction between the two steps; suppose the Home Secretary decided that it was just to issue the warrant but felt that he could be persuaded to come to a contrary conclusion and therefore sought the views of Parliament on the matter. As a result of those views he might come to the conclusion that it was unjust to issue the warrant. He would then be taking the views of the House on the justice of the matter and not on whether he should issue the warrant.]

Yes, the Home Secretary could do that. The matter can be put in two ways. Either the Home Secretary must consider that it is just to issue the warrant, and then decide when to issue it, or alternatively, even though he has decided at one stage that it is just he is entitled to reopen his decision, and reconsider the matter. His decision is not irrevocable; it can be altered at **[462]** any time up to the issue of his warrant. He can listen to anything that is said about the matter, including the views expressed in Parliament. It is inherent that in carrying out his duties the Home Secretary must act in accordance with the wishes of Parliament. If that were not so, once he has decided it is just he should issue his warrant forthwith and only report to Parliament after the fugitive has been returned to his own country.

[LORD PARKER C.J. It is suggested that Ministers other than the Home Secretary gave certain assurances in Parliament. If that were right what would the position be?]

Under section 7 the only question to be decided is whether it was reasonable or not to hold the applicant in custody, and in considering that, the Home Secretary's discretion under section 6 whether exercised properly or not, is irrelevant, as the applicant is still held on the original warrant of the Bow Street magistrate. The only evidence that could be put in at this stage would be in rebuttal of the Home Secretary's evidence in order to show that it was unreasonable to detain the fugitive.

The Home Secretary was not sharing or delegating his functions by reporting to Parliament. He merely postponed his decision until Parliament had had an opportunity of discussing the matter. For the Home Secretary to do that is just

[7] [1960] 1 Q.B. 142.
[8] [1962] 2 W.L.R. 1163, 1202; [1962] 2 All E.R. 438, H.L.(E.).

cause for delay, is reasonable and is in the interests of the applicant. The courts will not inquire whether Parliament acted in a reasonable way, but the evidence shows that Parliament dealt with the case exceedingly promptly. It is relevant for the court to consider that the applicant took no action while Parliament was considering the matter. It was only when their decision was unfavourable that he took the present proceedings.

Dingle Foot Q.C. in reply. It is agreed that the courts will not inquire whether Parliament has acted reasonably. The court is not being invited to inquire into the conduct of the House of Commons but that of the Home Secretary. Even if it be true that the applicant waited to see how he would fare in Parliament, he is still entitled to seek his remedy at law. The submission concerning the sharing or delegation of the Home Secretary's functions arose directly out of the proceedings before Parliament and could not have been taken sooner.

LORD PARKER C.J. stated the facts, read section 7 of the Fugitive Offenders Act, 1881, and continued: So far as is known, there has only been one case under section 7 of the Act, which is **[463]** *In re Shuter.*[9]* The only materiality for this purpose of that decision is as to the meaning of the words, "may, unless sufficient cause is shown to the contrary, order the fugitive to be discharged out of custody." In the first place, the court came to a decision that the word "may" should be interpreted as mandatory, so that in the absence of sufficient cause being shown to the contrary, there was no further discretion; the fugitive had to be discharged.

The second matter which is important is that it had been argued in that case that sufficient cause to the contrary must relate to something outside the control of the relevant authorities, as some strong and compelling reason such as the serious illness of the fugitive. The court, however, took the view that that interpretation was too narrow, and that the words "unless sufficient cause is shown to the contrary" brought matters of reasonableness under consideration. In giving judgment in that case, I said[10]: "Accordingly, it seems to me that when one is construing the words in section 7, 'unless sufficient cause is shown to the contrary,' one is entitled to take into account questions such as reasonableness in all the circumstances. Once one gets as far as that as a matter of construction, it seems to me quite plain that on the facts disclosed in Mr. Rushford's affidavit, no one could say that he was not acting perfectly reasonably in making the arrangements he did. One cannot shut one's eyes to the fact that this is only a matter of a day or two's delay and that the alleged offences are serious offences. There is also the fact that the applicant's solicitor was informed of the arrangements and took no objection. Of course that latter observation is always subject to the comment that he might well not have had section 7 in mind, but when one is thinking of this matter in terms of reasonableness, it is some evidence that what was being done was perfectly reasonable, and that this man was not being detained for an unreasonable time."

Approaching the matter in that way, it would seem that the true effect of section 7 is that when a fugitive is found to have been detained for more than 30 days from the time of his committal, it is for the Secretary of State to account for the delay, and that unless he satisfies the court that the detention in all the **[464]** circumstances for the period exceeding 30 days is reasonable, then this court should discharge the fugitive.

It is only right to say that no complaint is made of any detention up to and including March 14. Everything that had been done up to that stage had certainly been in the interests of the applicant, and to ensure that he would suffer no injustice if he was sent back to Nigeria. It is in respect of the period subsequent to that date that complaint is made. It is said that no sufficient cause has been shown for that further detention.

[His Lordship read paragraphs 5 and 6, referred to paragraph 7 of the Home Secretary's affidavit, and continued:] I confess that for my part were it not for

[9] [1960] 1 Q.B. 142; [1959] 3 W.L.R. 652; [1959] 3 All E.R. 481, D.C.
[10] [1960] 1 Q.B. 142, 148.

the very able and ingenious argument of Mr. Dingle Foot, I should consider this a thoroughly impudent application. Everything, as it seems to me, that has been done from the date of his committal until today has been as much in the interests of the applicant as could be. Every possible step has been taken to see that it would be just that he should be sent back, and if one may use the expression, everybody seems to have leant over backwards in his favour. However, if he has a legal right to be discharged now, he is, whatever I might think of the nature of the application, of course fully entitled to be discharged.

The way in which the matter is put is this. It is said that under section 6 it is the duty of the Home Secretary, once he has come to a decision that it is just that the fugitive should be returned, forthwith to issue a warrant for that purpose. Section 6 provides that: "Upon the expiration of 15 days after a fugitive has been committed to prison to await his return, or if a writ of habeas corpus or other like process is issued with reference to such fugitive by a superior court, after the final decision of the court in the case . . . a Secretary of State . . . may, if he thinks it just, by warrant under his hand order that fugitive to be returned to the part of Her Majesty's Dominions from which he is a fugitive"; that, I think, is all that is relevant for this purpose.

The argument as I understand it runs thus: that "may, if he thinks it just," by warrant order the fugitive's return, is mandatory in the same way as "may" is mandatory under section 7, and that accordingly once the Home Secretary has decided that it is just that the fugitive should be returned, he must by warrant under his hand order the return. If that be right, so runs the argument, then on March 14 when the Home Secretary decided that it was just to order the return, he should have signed the **[465]** warrant. Observe again on the merits that if he had, the fugitive would presumably be back in Nigeria. But be that as it may, it is said that anything that happened after March 14, that is after the Home Secretary had decided it was just that he should be returned, cannot amount to any sufficient cause to the contrary within section 7.

For my part, I am quite satisfied that that argument ultimately depends on whether it is right to treat the word "may" in section 6 as mandatory. *Shuter's* case[11]* to which I have referred, is a decision of this court that in connection with section 7 "may" is mandatory. But I am quite satisfied that in section 6 it cannot be read in that sense.

Section 7, as I have already said, is dealing with the liberty of the subject, and the prevention of his being detained for an unduly long period. After 30 days he must be discharged unless sufficient cause is shown. Section 6, on the other hand, so far as time is concerned, is not saying that something must happen after a certain time, but is saying that something shall not happen before a certain time has expired, namely, the person is to be allowed 15 days after a committal or the termination of habeas corpus proceedings before the Secretary of State can take any steps, and I can see no reason for giving "may" a mandatory meaning in that connection. He must, of course, first be satisfied that it is just, and if he is not satisfied that it is just, then no question of a warrant being signed arises.

If, on the other hand, he is satisfied that it is just, it is still a matter of discretion for him as to when he should issue the warrant. If he does delay, if he leaves the prisoner in custody without either releasing him or signing a warrant for his return, then section 7 comes into operation for the protection of the fugitive. If that be right, then one has to look to see what happened after March 14 to see whether what took place then amounts to a sufficient cause to the contrary under section 7.

With regard to that, Mr. Dingle Foot urges that the true effect of paragraph 6 of the Home Secretary's affidavit is that the Home Secretary was either surrendering to Parliament or sharing with Parliament what under section 6 of the Act was his statutory responsibility. He said that action by the Home Secretary in a manner which the law does not permit could not on any view disclose sufficient cause to the contrary within section 7.

It is well settled that certainly no person made responsible for **[466]** a judicial

[11] [1960] 1 Q.B. 142.

decision can delegate his responsibility. Equally in certain cases of administrative decisions there is no power to delegate and I would assume, without deciding it, that here the Home Secretary, albeit the decision whether to sign the warrant may be treated as an administrative decision, has no power to delegate that responsibility. Assuming that, however, I can see no ground, accepting literally everything that is said in paragraph 6 of the Home Secretary's affidavit, for thinking that he has delegated to a majority of the House of Parliament or shared with the majority of the House of Parliament what is his statutory responsibility.

The matter can be considered really in two ways. One can consider his duties under section 6 of the Act as twofold: first, to ascertain whether it is just that the fugitive should be returned, and secondly, whether in the exercise of his discretion he should sign a warrant, and if so, when. Approached in this way it could be said, and indeed has been said by the Attorney-General, that all that he was inviting Parliament to express a view on was as to the signing of the warrant. For my part, I think that that is the wrong approach. I think, to be realistic, he was inviting Parliament to express a view as to whether his decision that it was just was the view also of the majority of the House. But even so, I can see no reason why he should not. Granted that it is his duty to decide, granted that he has decided, not expressed as a preliminary or provisional opinion, but has decided that it is just, there is no reason why he should not invite the expression of further opinion, and, if influenced by it, change his mind. Looked at in that way, I cannot see that by inviting Parliament or by allowing Parliament to express an opinion on his decision, he was in any way surrendering or sharing with Parliament what was his statutory responsibility.

Accordingly, as it seems to me, and as I said at first, everything that has been done in this case has been so far as possible to assist this fugitive, the Home Secretary has shown sufficient cause to the contrary within section 7 of the Act.

Finally there is a further point upon which this court has been asked to adjourn the case, in order that the permission of Parliament should be obtained for this court to consider what was said in the debate in question. As I understand it, Mr. Dingle Foot would seek, from reading passages in Hansard, to show that in the course of the debate other Ministers may have intervened, that other Ministers, that is Ministers other than the Home Secretary, may have expressed a view which was for the Home **[467]** Secretary to express or have given an assurance which only the Home Secretary could properly give, and that in some way the Home Secretary had surrendered or shared with that Minister or Ministers what was his responsibility, in other words, there has been some wrongful delegation. The court has refused to adjourn to look into that matter because, and this is my own opinion, it seems to me that at the end of the day, even if all that were shown, it is completely irrelevant to the application under section 7.

It is, however, said to be relevant to the application for a writ of habeas corpus, and that, the second application before the court, I have not dealt with. So far as the habeas corpus application is concerned, it was put in, as I have said, on April 19, some nine days after the other motion and, it seems to me, as a pure adjunct. It asks for the writ of habeas corpus, and it states as grounds the grounds set forth in the affidavit of the applicant and of his solicitor which are the affidavits in support of the application I have already considered under section 7. No further ground is advanced for a writ of habeas corpus. I find it very difficult to see how there could be. This matter of habeas corpus has already been before the court.[12] It has been shown that the fugitive is held under a valid warrant, and nothing that has been advanced in these proceedings seems to me capable of challenging the warrant under which he is held. I cannot see that an application for habeas corpus could succeed in the present case, certainly not on the matters advanced in connection with the section 7 application.

Accordingly, as it seems to me, it would be idle to adjourn this case. Even if Mr. Dingle Foot is right in what he suggests might be found if we looked at

[12] *The Times*, January 16, 1963.

Hansard, yet I am quite satisfied that it would be wholly irrelevant in these applications. Accordingly, I have come to the opinion that both applications fail and should be refused.

HAVERS J. I agree with the judgment given by my Lord and with the reasons which he has given for it. I am satisfied by the affidavit of the Secretary of State that sufficient cause has been shown to the contrary within the meaning of section 7 of the Fugitive Offenders Act, 1881. I agree that both these applications should be dismissed.

EDMUND DAVIES J. I agree. I would only add that, speaking for myself, I find difficulty in conceiving of how a clearer or more **[468]** sufficient cause could be shown within section 7 of the Act of 1881 than where the lapse of more than a month since committal is overwhelmingly, if not indeed entirely, attributable to (a) the representations of the supporters of the fugitive himself and his advisers and other well intentioned parties to prevent or delay his return; and (b) the unimpeached and unimpeachable desire of the Home Secretary to give due, proper and reasonably prompt consideration to those representations. That is clearly what had happened in the present case.

It follows that in my judgment, like that of Lord Parker C.J. and Havers J., the relief now sought under section 7 should and indeed must be refused.

Dingle Foot Q.C., for the applicant, asked for leave to appeal to the House of Lords, and for a certificate under section 1 of the Administration of Justice Act, 1960.

LORD PARKER C.J. So far as it is necessary, that is to say in respect of the section 7 application, we will give a certificate that a point of law of general public importance is involved. If their Lordships desire to know what the court had in mind, it would be solely the question as to the true interpretation of the word "may" in section 6 in connection with your argument, and no more. On the other hand, both in that application and in the application for habeas corpus, the application is refused; in other words, you would have to go to the Appeal Committee on both.

Applications dismissed.
Certificate granted that a point of general public importance involved in the first application.
Leave to appeal refused in respect of both applications.

May 7. The Appeal Committee of the House of Lords[13] refused leave to appeal.

Solicitors: *Hatchett Jones & Co.; Treasury Solicitor.*

REGINA v. GOVERNOR OF BRIXTON PRISON AND ANOTHER *EX PARTE* ENAHORO.

(*The Times*, May 8, 1963.)

May 7, 1963: House of Lords: Lords Reid, Morris of Borth-y-Gest, Hodson.

Chief Refused Leave to Appeal

The Appeal Committee refused this petition by Chief Anthony Eronsele

[13] *The Times,* May 8, 1963.

Enahoro for leave to appeal from the dismissal by the Divisional Court of the Queen's Bench Division* (the Lord Chief Justice, Mr. Justice Havers and Mr. Justice Edmund Davies) on April 25, 1963 (*The Times*, April 26) of his application for relief under section 7 of the Fugitive Offenders Act, 1881, and for an order of *habeas corpus*. In previous proceedings by the applicant the Divisional Court had refused applications for *habeas corpus* and relief under section 10 of the Act of 1881* (*The Times*, January 16, 1963); and the Appeal Committee refused a petition for leave to appeal against that decision on February 6, 1963* (*The Times*, February 7.).

The Fugitive Offenders Act, 1881, provides by section 6: "Upon the expiration of 15 days after a fugitive has been committed to prison to await his return, or if a writ of *habeas corpus* or other like process is issued with reference to such a fugitive by a superior court, after the final decision of the court in the case. . . . a Secretary of State. . . . may, if he thinks it just, by warrant under his hand order that fugitive to be returned to the part of her Majesty's dominions from which he is a fugitive. . . ."

By section 7: "If a fugitive who, in pursuance of this Part of this Act has been committed to prison in any part of her Majesty's dominions to await his return, is not conveyed out of that part within one month after such committal, a superior court, upon application by or on behalf of the fugitive, and upon proof that reasonable notice of the intention to make such application has been given . . . to a Secretary of State . . . may, unless sufficient cause is shown to the contrary, order the fugitive to be discharged out of custody".

Mr. Dingle Foot Q.C., Mr. Kenneth Potter and *Miss Diana Phillips* appeared for the applicant; the *Attorney-General* (*Sir John Hobson Q.C.*) and *Mr. J. R. Cumming-Bruce* for the Home Secretary and the Governor of Brixton Prison.

When the Committee sat, Lord Reid told Mr. Foot that their Lordships had read the petition and also looked at Hansard, so that they had a pretty good notion of what had taken place in another place. He asked the Attorney-General whether there was any objection to Hansard being considered in these proceedings.

The *Attorney-General* said that he had no objection to Hansard in respect of admissibility as a document which could be looked at, but would submit that it was irrelevant.

Mr. Foot said that the Attorney-General had never objected to references to Hansard. It had simply been a question of the privileges of the House of Commons.

LORD REID. I understand that difficulty has been got over.

Mr. Foot for the petitioner, said that the point of law of general public importance, as certified by the Divisional Court, was the interpretation of the word "may" in section 7 of the Fugitive Offenders Act, 1881. In *In re Shuter** ([1960] 1 Q.B. 142) it had been held that the word "may" in section 7 of the Act was mandatory and, unless "sufficient cause" was shown to the court, the court was, after the expiry of one month bound to order the fugitive to be discharged from custody. Precisely the same construction, he submitted should be applied to "may" in section 6. It was also mandatory and once the Secretary of State had exercised his discretion and made up his mind that it was "just" to return the fugitive, it was mandatory for him to sign the warrant for his return. There was no room here for the double discretion which the Divisional Court had found in the Statute, namely, that the Secretary of State had a discretion first to decide whether he thought it just to return the fugitive, and then a further discretion as to whether or not he would sign the warrant. Once he had made up his mind, all that was left for him to do was the purely administrative act of signing the warrant.

LORD REID said that under section 7 the discretion was that of the court, and one would not infer so strange a discretion in a judicial body as to order a man to be kept without "sufficient cause". But the "may" in section 6 was the discretion of the Secretary of State.

Counsel said that the effect of *Shuter's Case* was that one could not hold the fugitive for a day longer than one had sufficient cause to do so. Every day had to be accounted for, and once the month had expired the man was entitled to go free.

LORD MORRIS asked whether the month in this case dated from December 1962. Section 7, he pointed out, did not repeat the words in section 6 about an application for *habeas corpus*. His Lordship supposed that time taken up for such an application would be reasonably employed.

Counsel said that the time taken up for an application for *habeas corpus* or for relief under section 10 or both would certainly furnish "sufficient cause"; but in this case those proceedings terminated on February 6, 1963. Under section 6, the Secretary of State could act after 15 days after the fugitive had been committed to prison; and he acted when he had made up his mind that it was "just" to order the return. Counsel conceded that one could not draw an analogy between the position of the Court under section 7 and the Secretary of State under section 6; but having regard to the purpose of section 6 and the whole structure of the Act, "may" in that section should be interpreted as mandatory.

LORD REID. Do you say that you must always show a point of time when in his own mind the Secretary of State has considered it "just"? Sometimes that is ascertainable; sometimes it is not.

Counsel. It is always capable of ascertainment so far as he himself is concerned. He must know when he has made up his mind.

LORD REID. I hope so. But it does not apply to everybody.

Counsel said that one must assume that a Secretary of State discharging a statutory duty knew when he had discharged it. In this case, the Home Secretary has no doubt that by March 14, 1963, he had made up his mind. He had said so in his affidavit and in Parliament on March 14.

LORD REID. But suppose the day after he makes his decision some completely new fact or some change in the situation comes to his knowledge, do you say that he has irrevocably committed himself to send the man back?

Counsel replied that what the Secretary of State could not do was simply to keep the man while he gave the matter further thought.

LORD REID. Then you say that on the facts and the evidence in this case you can show that the Secretary of State has made up his mind finally that it was "just" not reserving to himself any *locus poenitentiae*; that that is an end of the matter; and that he is then bound by the statute to sign the warrant? Yes.

LORD REID. Has he to act in a quasi-justical way and take into account only the question of "just", or may he take into consideration other factors which would not normally enter into judicial consideration?

Counsel. It is a quasi-judicial discretion and cannot take into account quite extraneous considerations. For instance, if it was represented to him that it was politically expedient that this man should be returned, that should not be a matter for the Secretary of State, for that would give him a much wider discretion than the Act gives him. If, as in this case, questions are being asked in Parliament and the matter is being widely canvassed in the press, some of his colleagues in the Government might take the view that politics were involved. But no consideration of that sort can or should affect the mind of the Secretary of State once he has arrived at a decision. Moreover, he has a statutory duty to discharge and he cannot delegate or share that duty.

LORD REID. If he does not like the opinions of his colleagues, his duty is to resign.

Counsel. The opinions of his colleagues do not come into this at all.

LORD REID. I am not sure. If "just" means quasi-judicial, he must make up his own mind; but if it means something wider, he is entitled to consider other people and other aspects.

Counsel said that if he thought it "just" that the fugitive should be returned and the majority of the Cabinet did not agree with him, the Home Secretary could not be influenced by that at all. This was a statutory duty imposed on him alone. It was the sort of issue which arose in the *Campbell Case* when it was alleged that the decision of the Minister concerned had not been his own but had been taken on political grounds by somebody else. When one looked at the affidavit of the Secretary of State in this case and at the passages in Hansard which their Lordships had already studied, it did appear that there was here a surrender of this function, or at any rate a sharing of it with the House of Commons or other Ministers. If that could be made good, it meant that there could not possibly be a "sufficient cause" under section 7.

LORD REID. I am not sure that surrender or sharing is right. You say he had made up his mind on March 14 and then wrongly consulted others and in particular the House of Commons, and at the end of the day they backed him up. If they had not done so, I suppose he would have resigned. But that is not a sharing. It may be an illegitimate postponing or illegitimate consultation with someone else with a view to a possible change of the decision; but the decision is his; and you are founding your submission on the fact that he decided on March 14, and that is the essential date.

Counsel said that if, as the Home Secretary had said, he finally arrived at this decision on the 14th then, unless he could show "sufficient cause", the fugitive must either be released or sent back. There was no escape from that and this proceeding of Parliamentary debate, salutory though it might be, was not in itself "sufficient cause" within section 7. The interests of Parliament had nothing to do with the Home Secretary's responsibility under section 6. It was a wholly extraneous matter. The affidavit alone showed that what the Secretary of State did was to subject himself in this matter to the House and the inference to be drawn was that if the House had decided the other way the fugitive would not have been returned. If that was right, it meant that the Secretary of State had recalled his decision of the 14th and was allowing the House of Commons to discharge the responsibility which the Act laid upon him alone. Even on the affidavit the matter was tolerably clear; but Hansard made it very much clearer.

Counsel referred their Lordships to speeches reported in Hansard for March 14, 21 and 27.

LORD REID. We are using the Hansards in order to discover the state of mind of the Home Secretary and what happened. I do not think we can consider other views.

Counsel said that the reports showed that other people were assisting the Home Secretary to take a decision. It showed an undertaking given on behalf of the Prime Minister and the Government.

LORD REID. That is all on the footing that the decision is of a judicial character and that any factor which cannot be brought within the four corners of the word "just" is excluded by section 6, so that anything like a debate which would interfere is wrong. But I think we ought to keep off what other people said—at least people who are not members of the Cabinet.

Mr. Foot said that the Prime Minister had said in the debate that he would give an undertaking that until he was satisfied on specified points, they would not return this man.

LORD REID. I am very reluctant to discuss the proceedings in another place in detail. I am not sure that we are entitled to do that.

Counsel said that there could be no objection to their Lordships looking at what happened, for even if a question of privilege were involved that privilege had been waived by the House of Commons. The conclusions were to be drawn from this material. First, that there was a usurpation by other Ministers of the function of the Secretary of State; and, secondly, that there had been a surrender of his statutory responsibility to the House of Commons. Even if their Lordships were not with him on the construction of "may" in section 6, what had been disclosed in the affidavit of the Home Secretary, supported by Hansard, was not enough to show "sufficient cause" within section 7.

LORD REID told the Attorney-General that they wished to hear him only on the point that the intervention of the Government and the House of Commons had in some way invalidated the Home Secretary's final decision.

The Attorney-General said that if section 6 gave the Home Secretary the widest possible discretion not only to change his mind but also to do whatever he considered "just" in its broadest sense and not confined to the narrow matters of legality, which only the Courts could consider, under section 10—then the section meant that at the moment when the Secretary of State signed the warrant he must consider it "just"; what happened in the House of Commons was irrelevant to the proceedings under section 7. The references to the debates were merely an attempt on behalf of the petitioner to try to show that those events would invalidate the Home Secretary's act if and when in the future he came to sign the warrant.

But if it was right for the Home Secretary to keep his mind open and he had the capacity finally to make up his mind, he could not be disqualified merely because other Ministers might have said something on these matters in debates in the House, provided that at the end of the day, it was his decision, and that at that moment he considered it just to make that decision. There was nothing in the evidence to show that the Home Secretary had in any way surrendered his own right and duty to make a decision. On March 14, he had quite plainly asserted it was his responsibility, and at the end, on April 10, he was still asserting that it was his personal responsibility and he told the House of Commons that that was so.

After hearing Mr. Foot in reply, their Lordships ordered that the Bar be cleared. When Counsel returned, LORD REID said that their Lordships did not grant leave to appeal.

Mr. Foot asked for leave for the petitioner to see friends living in this country before he left this place.

LORD REID. Why do you have to ask for leave? What have we to do with the Governor of Brixton Prison? (To the Attorney-General) Do we require leave to your client to allow someone to see this gentleman?

The Attorney-General said that the prison regulations were quite plain, but he was prepared to give an undertaking that reasonable facilities would be given for an immediate visit by those who desired to see the petitioner.

Solicitors: *Messrs. Hatchett Jones & Co.; Treasury Solicitor.*

EX PARTE ENAHORO

(*The Times*, May 10, 1963)

May 9, 1963: Queen's Bench Division: Lord Parker C.J., Havers, Edmund Davies JJ.

Chief's New Plea Rejected

The Divisional Court dismissed this application by Chief Anthony Eronsele Enahoro for a writ of *habeas corpus*. The applicant made the application in person on the ground that he wished to adduce fresh evidence to show that the evidence before the magistrate at his committal at Bow Street was false and improperly obtained. A previous application for a writ of *habeas corpus* on the ground that there was no evidence before the magistrate had been refused by the Divisional Court on January 15* (*The Times*, January 16, 1963).

The LORD CHIEF JUSTICE said that he understood that the applicant was applying for leave to move for a writ of *habeas corpus*, but that it was the practice of the Court not to hear such an application by an applicant in person. If the Court heard Mr. Enahoro they would have to hear every prisoner.

HIS LORDSHIP asked the applicant if he wished to instruct counsel.

The applicant said that he would like to do so.

The LORD CHIEF JUSTICE said that the Court sometimes asked the Official Solicitor to instruct counsel to make the application. If the applicant found it too difficult to do so himself the Court would ask the Official Solicitor to look into the matter.

The applicant agreed to that course.

HIS LORDSHIP said that the Court would adjourn the matter until 2 p.m. In the meantime, the Court would get in touch with the Official Solicitor, who would instruct counsel to appear.

The applicant asked if this was the proper place to ask for legal aid.

The LORD CHIEF JUSTICE said that this was not the proper place, but the Court would ask the Official Solicitor to look into it.

When the hearing was resumed, the Court gave the applicant permission to present his case in person.

The applicant, standing in the well of the Court, said: "I am deeply grateful to you for allowing me to address the Court personally. I have always had faith in British justice, otherwise I would not be coming before you for the third time. I am a layman, and it is not a platform to which I am accustomed, but I am fighting for my life and that is why I have the temerity to plead my own case before you".

The applicant said that the application was based on fresh evidence which had come to light since the other proceedings terminated. He read an affidavit by Abraham Aderibigbe Adesanya, a member of the Nigerian Bar and a member of the House of Assembly of Western Nigeria, who acted for the applicant in Nigeria and who was one of the defence counsel in the treason trial which was now proceeding in Lagos, and he represented Chief Ekwejunor-Eitche.

The affidavit stated that the evidence for the defence had been completed in the treason trial and the Court was now engaged in hearing counsel's speeches for the 24 accused. The deponent had been present in Lagos throughout the trial except on five occasions when he visited London, namely November 29 and December 12, 1962; January 13, February 17 and April 19, 1963. The deponent had studied and was familiar with the evidence taken on deposition in Lagos in support of the proceedings under the Fugitive Offenders Act, 1881, for the return of the applicant to Nigeria, for alleged treasonable felony and conspiracy to commit treason. Each of the four deponents gave evidence at the Lagos treason trial. He referred to a transcript of the evidence in that trial which showed that one of the deponents, Anthony Oboh, was charged in September, 1962, with unlawful importation and possession of firearms and that there had been up to January 10, 1963, five or six adjournments of the case against him on the alleged charges. Another deponent, Henry Olearie, was also charged in September, 1962, with the same firearms offences alleged against Oboh.

It was common knowledge in Lagos that the charges against Oboh and Olearie had been kept but not prosecuted by way of numerous adjournments throughout the time that they had been giving evidence for the prosecution and had still not been prosecuted or withdrawn. Oboh and Olearie had given evidence against him. It was within the present deponent's knowledge that the cases against these two deponents had still not been heard nearly eight months since their arrest.

The applicant said that further affidavits were being obtained to support that affidavit. Evidence was also being prepared to show that the Nigerian Government would prefer further charges against the applicant which carried the death penalty. Those affidavits would be in this country within ten days. Having only known that he would appear in person within the last few hours, the applicant asked for an adjournment for ten days to allow him to prepare his case and to allow time for the other evidence to arrive.

"Ten days for a citizen fighting for his very life cannot be too much to ask for. Before I pass out of the jurisdiction of this court to what may well be my death, I am sure that this court will want to be satisfied beyond all doubt in the light of the fresh evidence available that it is just to return me."

The LORD CHIEF JUSTICE asked the applicant what inference he wished the Court to draw from the affidavit he had just read. The suggestion is that they [the two deponents] are being kept in suspense in order to make certain that they give the proper evidence against you.

The applicant. Yes.

The LORD CHIEF JUSTICE asked why, if the last adjournment was in January, 1963, the Court had not heard of the matter before.

The applicant said that he had only just become aware of it.

The LORD CHIEF JUSTICE. But your legal adviser knew.

The applicant said that he was in Court.

The LORD CHIEF JUSTICE said that the Court could not hear him, but the applicant could ask him about it.

After consultation, the applicant said that until the evidence was concluded in the treason trial it was not known that the deponents were not going to be tried.

The applicant said that the further affidavits would corroborate the affidavit he had read, and would contain further evidence, which included allegations to witnesses.

The LORD CHIEF JUSTICE said that in these proceedings Mr. Enahoro moved for a writ of *habeas corpus*. This was not the first application which he had made but pursuant to section 14(2) of the Administration of Justice Act, 1960, he was entitled to make another application if his grounds were different and if his evidence was different.

On the previous occasion, the applicant moved by counsel on the ground that there was no evidence before the magistrate that could justify his committal. He now sought to adduce fresh evidence to show that the evidence before the magistrate at Bow Street was false and improperly obtained by the Government of Nigeria.

It was now well-known that this Court would not listen to fresh evidence on matters on which the magistrate had made up his mind whether to commit a person or not. The highest it had gone was in *ex parte Schtraks** [1962] 3 W.L.R. 1435. In that case, the evidence of certain deponents which was put in before the magistrate was later attacked. It was said that the Israeli Government had made a bargain with the witnesses not to prosecute them if they gave certain evidence. His Lordship said in that case [1962] 3 W.L.R. 1435, 1439: "Mr. Du Cann, however, raises a second, more interesting point. He says that, even granted that that is true, this evidence is directed not merely to discredit the evidence of witnesses whose evidence was before the magistrate, but to show—and he says it boldly—that the magistrate was deceived, and was imposed upon by the fraudulent conduct of the Government of Israel. He goes on to say that, that would be a ground for this Court interfering, as undoubtedly this Court can, in cases of *certiorari*. Without deciding the matter, it seems to me that if he could show that, he might bring himself within the principle that evidence can be given to show that there was no evidence upon which the magistrate could act. If he could show that this warrant had been secured by fraud, as the concealing of evidence or collusion with a witness, then it may well be that this Court could interfere".

That, his Lordship thought, was the highest it had been put. For his part, without deciding it, his Lordship would assume that the Court could interfere if it could be shown that the magistrate was imposed upon and a fraud perpetrated on him.

Mr. Enahoro had adduced an affidavit from his legal adviser in Nigeria pointing to the fact that certain of those whose depositions were put in before the magistrate had been in custody for 8 months and that they had not been prosecuted nor had the cases against them been withdrawn. It was said that it should be inferred that the witnesses were being kept in suspense to ensure that they gave evidence against the applicant.

It was also said that there were affidavits on the way from Nigeria containing evidence to show that other charges would be preferred against the applicant and he asked for an adjournment so that he might prepare his argument and have the further evidence before Court. Before granting an adjournment, the Court had to know why it was needed and whether it would be of any avail. As far as this Court was concerned, the Nigerian Government were fully entitled to prefer what charges they liked. This was not a case under the Extradition Act where the Court only granted extradition for the purposes of the charges actually preferred. The fact that in the present case other charges were being preferred did not affect the matter.

The Court had to consider whether there was any conceivable evidence from which they could draw the inference that the magistrate's order was obtained by fraud. His Lordship was unable to say that because witnesses were kept in prison and their cases were adjourned that that was to ensure that they gave evidence in a particular way. In *ex parte Schtraks** it was suggested that a bargain had actually been made with the witnesses and the Court held that that fell far short of what was necessary.

HIS LORDSHIP would refuse the adjournment and the application for a writ of *habeas corpus* on the ground that neither in the affidavits before the Court nor in those that were on the way was there any evidence which would enable the Court to interfere.

It was not the practice of this Court to hear applications for writs of *habeas corpus* by an applicant in person. Nevertheless the Court had thought it right in the present case and to avoid delay, that nothing should be done to prevent Mr. Enahoro from putting the matter in the way in which he wanted to do so, and, for that reason, they had heard the applicant in person.

Mr. Justice HAVERS agreed.

Mr. Justice EDMUND DAVIES, agreeing, said that he adopted the words of Mr. Justice Salmon in *ex parte Schtraks** (supra, at p. 1441): "if it could be shown that a decision had been obtained from the magistrate by fraud or collusion on the part of the requesting Power, it would be very difficult to pursuade me that *habeas corpus* could not go". The evidence in the affidavits fell far short of the fraud alleged. The matter of fresh charges was no concern of the Court. Whether the executive would think it a matter for them, was again no concern of this Court.

Leave to appeal to the House of Lords refused.

ENAHORO v. GOVERNOR OF BRIXTON PRISON AND THE SECRETARY OF STATE FOR HOME AFFAIRS

(*The Times*, May 16, 1963)

May 15, 1963: House of Lords: Viscount Simonds, Lords Morris of Borth-y-Gest, Hodson.

Chief's Petition Fails

The Appeal Committee refused this application by Chief Anthony Eronsele Enahoro for leave to appeal from the dismissal by the Divisional Court of the Queen's Bench* (the Lord Chief Justice, Mr. Justice Havers and Mr. Justice Edmund Davies) on May 9, 1963 (*The Times*, May 10) of his application, *ex parte*, for a writ of *habeas corpus* on the ground that he wished to adduce fresh evidence to show that the evidence before the magistrate at Bow Street on his committal was false and improperly obtained.

The petitioner appeared in person; *the Attorney-General* (*Sir John Hobson, Q.C.*) and *Mr. J. R. Cumming-Bruce* for the Home Secretary and the Governor of Brixton Prison.

When the Appeal Committee sat, Lord Simonds asked the petitioner his reason for seeking the indulgence of their Lordships' House to present his petition in person. It was a rule of their Lordships' House not to hear applicants for *habeas corpus* in person.

The petitioner said that he had had an ultimatum from the Home Secretary that he must lodge his petition by 2.20 p.m. on Monday and that if that was not done, the Home Secretary would regard himself as absolved from his undertaking not to order the petitioner's deportation. He had thus had four days only—only two of which were working days—and the Divisional Court's judgment had only been made available to him on Monday. It was not possible to instruct counsel in this very, very complicated action in the time available and, with due respect, he was not satisfied that any counsel could familiarize himself with the case in the time available, so he preferred to put the case himself, if their Lordships would grant that indulgence. He knew that it was contrary to the decided cases.

LORD SIMONDS said that the petitioner underestimated the ability of counsel to get up a case; but as the Lord Chief Justice had shown himself indulgent in the Divisional Court, their Lordships would be prepared, on that ground alone, to give a similar indulgence. But it must not be taken as a precedent in any other case, for it was a very dangerous one.

The petitioner then asked whether he might have an adjournment. The Home Secretary's ultimatum of four days in which to lodge the petition had been given although under the rules of their Lordship's House he was entitled to 14 days as of right to lodge the petition. He had been driven in this case—in which the liberty and very life of the subject was at stake—to act at breakneck speed. The Home Secretary knew quite well that further evidence on which he intended to rely in his petition was being obtained in Nigeria and that his legal adviser had flown to Lagos to expedite the extraction of that evidence. Part of his case would be that the Magistrate at Bow Street had been deceived because of the fraudulent presentation to the Court of perjured evidence obtained in some cases by brutalities, threats and intimidation, and in others by promises. The evidence expected from Nigeria would prove that that was correct, and if the Home Secretary had not compelled him to act so hastily, that evidence would have been available for their Lordships' hearing of the petition.

LORD SIMONDS said that the point that he was entitled as of right to 14 days was a bad one. All that was laid down was that a petition must be presented within 14 days and if that was done, it came on for hearing by whatever method was convenient to the House. On the other point, that further evidence might be available, he asked the petitioner to indicate the nature of the evidence to see whether it supplemented or went beyond the evidence already before their Lordships. If it was of the same character as that which they had already had, it might not carry the petitioner much further.

The petitioner. May I put a question to your Lordships?

LORD SIMONDS. Certainly, by all means.

The petitioner asked whether if one or two or three of the deponents at the Bow Street proceedings were in a position at this moment to swear that their depositions which were before the magistrate were false in the particulars which related to himself, would that not be the sort of evidence to wait for?

LORD SIMONDS. I don't think I will answer that, Mr. Enahoro. It would depend on the nature of the evidence.

The petitioner referred their Lordships to *ex parte Schtraks* ([1962] 3 W.L.R. 1435)* ("the second Schtraks Case") and a citation from Lord Evershed that the right and competence of the Court to have regard to fresh evidence were limited to certain cases, including the case where it was shown "that there was in truth no evidence at all to justify the magistrate's exercise of his discretionary jurisdiction to commit." He submitted that if he could show that the decision in this case had been obtained from the magistrate by the requsitioning power by fraud or collusion it would be very difficult to say that *habeas corpus* should not go.

The depositions made three allegations against him, first, that there was a conspiracy and, secondly, that he was a party to it. The second allegation rested entirely on the third allegation, namely that on certain dates and at certain times, he had made certain statements or taken certain actions or was present at certain places. If the evidence now available and the fresh evidence expected showed, from evidence of the deponents given on oath in the course of the "treason trial" in Nigeria of persons standing trial on these same charges, that these same deponents had said that he, the petitioner, had not been where the deponent said he was, that he did not make the statements which they claimed in their depositions he had made, and that they now said that he was not in the places where the depositions alleged he had been, there could not in the words of Lord Evershed, have been "sufficient evidence before the magistrate to justify his exercise of his discretionary jurisdiction to commit."

LORD SIMONDS asked when the statements conflicting with the depositions had been made.

The petitioner said that it was in the course of the trial which was still proceeding; but the transcripts, which were not dated, had only just arrived.

LORD SIMONDS asked the Attorney-General whether he opposed an adjournment.

The Attorney-General said that he did, on the ground that the complaint made was already in substance before their Lordships and the additional evidence desired to be brought for which an adjournment was required, was in substance only an elaboration of that already before the Committee. Moreover, the evidence so far as it controverted or contradicted the deponents' evidence, had been put before the magistrate at Bow Street. Part of the fresh evidence was given by two of the deponents at the treason trial at Lagos on January 2 and 8, 1963.

After the Bar had been cleared, Lord Simonds told the petitioner that this was not a proper case for an adjournment. Although their Lordships would have been willing to grant one if they had considered the petitioner was not in a position to argue his case, they were satisfied that he would not be at any disadvantage. He should, therefore, deal with the substance of the case.

The petitioner said that he understood that he was not expected in this hearing to argue his case exhaustively.

LORD SIMONDS. No. What you must show is a *prima facie* case for thinking that the Divisional Court came to a wrong decision when they held that they should not in their discretion interfere with the magistrate.

The petitioner said that he was well aware that this was not a case where he must satisfy their Lordships by controverting the evidence in the depositions with belated last minute evidence from other witnesses; but it was a case of deponents themselves giving evidence at the trial in Lagos controverting their own evidence in the depositions before the magistrate. With regard to the two principal deponents, Olearie and Oboh, it was clear that they both stood charged with serious offences and had been awaiting trial for many months. Two months' delay might be excusable, even four might be understood, but six months' got a bit suspicious, while eight months' was, he submitted, somewhat sinister, and he suggested that it was because those persons were required to give evidence against him.

The petitioner referred their Lordships to the evidence at the Lagos trial when a witness was reported as saying "I made a false declaration to the police. It is usual to do that."

LORD SIMONDS. Yes, I remember that.

The petitioner referred their Lordships to affidavits in evidence and said that the picture which emerged was one of two frightened deponents who had serious charges hanging over their heads, one deponent who was looking for "a new cow to milk" and one deponent longing to return to his own house and wishing to make peace with the government party, having failed to obtain money from the Action Group. Those four deponents were then passed through the tender hands of two interrogators and were subjected to interrogation in the manner described in other evidence; and then two months later they had made the depositions against him (the petitioner). It was his case that these four deponents perjured themselves and thereby caused a fraud to be perpetrated on the magistrate. Their Lordships should, he submitted, apply one of two tests: (1) they should look at the depositions as they would have stood before the magistrate had the passages therein contained and not controverted not appeared in the depositions; or (2) they should look at the depositions as they would have appeared had the controverting evidence been substituted for the controverted passages.

After applying those tests to the depositions and the transcripts before their Lordships in detail, the petitioner said that the discrepancies, the differences and the contradictions between the evidence in the depositions and the evidence at the Lagos trial went far beyond mere contradiction because the effect of the contraverting evidence was so to rewrite the depositions that, whichever of the two tests were applied, there was practically nothing left in the depositions to show even a *prima facie* strong and probable presumption of guilt on his part, and, therefore, the magistrate would not have made the order of committal. The evidence at the Lagos trial had been presented by the prosecution and accepted by the prosecution, and yet it completely controverted the evidence presented before the magistrate.

He submitted that fraud had been committed. If he (the petitioner) had had the opportunity to present to the magistrate the evidence taken at the trial in Lagos he was confident that the order would not have been made. These depositions had one purpose and one purpose only, to secure his return to Nigeria. Even if there had to be collusion and witnesses locked up together for three weeks and maltreated and starved, what did it matter as long as these depositions could get "this man" back to Nigeria? His return was not sought in the interests of justice. It was part of the calculated plan of the Nigerian Government to crush the Parliamentary opposition in Nigeria. Ever since these proceedings began, members of the Opposition Party had had their passports impounded, private property had been confiscated, members of the opposition party were being constantly harassed. The Government party had intimated that if he were not returned, they would withdraw from the Commonwealth—as if they were doing anyone a special service by being in the Commonwealth! Threats had been made by the Government Party to break off diplomatic relations with Her Majesty's Government in the United Kingdom if he were not returned. This was supposed to be in the interests of justice. He begged their Lordships for leave to appeal to their House.

The Attorney-General said that this was an appeal from the refusal of a motion made *ex parte* in the Divisional Court and to that extent, those for whom he appeared were prospective parties only, in the event of leave being given.

The petitioner had made many points, particularly with regard to the threats and inducements which might have been held out to those whose depositions were taken before the magistrate and had pointed to what he said were inconsistencies between the evidence given before the magistrate and that in the subsequent proceedings on oath in Nigeria. That might be a powerful argument which would enable him, in the course of his trial in Nigeria, should he be returned, to assert that he ought not to be convicted. They were, if they could be established, exactly the sort of allegations that would tell most favourably on his trial in Nigeria. That was the place where they ought to be investigated. They were not submissions in the form that there was no evidence against him before the committing magistrate, nor such as would be made at the conclusion of the prosecution case against him. They were, in form and content, the sort of arguments to be addressed to the Court at the conclusion of all the evidence.

That showed that the substance of this application was an attempt to get a preliminary trial in this country of the issues which ought to be tried on the indictment in Nigeria. The petitioner was right when he submitted that he had to show on the material he had placed before their Lordships that the Nigerian Government, as the demanding Government, had knowingly put evidence before the Bow Street magistrate which amounted to a fraud, and that anything less than that was insufficient for the purpose of challenging or reversing or bringing in question the committal order of the magistrate.

The petitioner had, fairly enough, asked their Lordships to read the depositions as though a large part of the evidence given before the magistrate had not been given or, alternatively, as though it was amended. That was exactly what neither the Divisional Court on a subsequent application for *habeas corpus* nor their Lordships' House would allow, as had been stated in the first *Schtraks Case** in their Lordships' House (*Schtraks* v. *Government of Israel and Others** [1962] 3 W.L.R. 1013).

LORD SIMONDS said that the petitioner's case was that looking at all the circumstances as they were now known, it was a case where a fraud had been perpetrated. He regarded what he called perjury as equivalent to a fraud.

The Attorney-General said that the applicant put his case on two footings:

first, that there had been threats and inducements, and, secondly, that there were inconsistencies, which showed that the witnesses had perjured themselves. On the first head, the only evidence of pressure in the voluminous transcripts of the trial, was that of one witness, Oboh, and he had said that he was not moved by the threat.

LORD SIMONDS. We are not asked to infer that there must have been threats because the interrogator was Mr. Coulman.

Counsel said that most of the evidence on threats was hearsay. As to these four deponents, he should tell their Lordships that both Mr. Olearie and Mr. Oboh had been on bail since January and had not been kept in custody as some of the affidavits seemed to suggest.

As to the inconsistencies, they did not begin to show that the depositions were fraudulent. They were capable of explanation by a witness under cross-examination. If inconsistencies were an indication that this case put forward by the Nigerian Government was founded in fraud and intended to deceive the magistrate, it came back to the extent to which the depositions put in before the magistrate were the result of a plot to produce a fresh case, against the accused. The principles stated in the first *Schtraks Case** (namely, that the Court did not rehear the case that was before the magistrate), applied here.

The petitioner, replying, said that he had been surprised to hear Mr. Attorney stating that Mr. Olearie and Mr. Oboh had been put out on bail for there was no evidence to that effect. If he had known that it was open for him to give such evidence, these proceedings would not have been so protracted.

After further submissions in reply by the petitioner, the Bar was ordered to be cleared.

When counsel and the parties returned, LORD SIMONDS said: Their Lordships are of opinion that the petitioner has not made out a *prima facie* case that the Divisional Court came to a wrong conclusion and failed properly to apply the principles laid down in the first *Schtraks Case** (*supra*) and the petition is refused. I should like to add this, that no one could have argued the case more candidly and with a more real knowledge of the relevant facts than the petitioner.

The petitioner then asked whether he might have permission to see friends before he left.

LORD SIMONDS said that it did not lie with their Lordships at all. It was a matter for the Governor of Brixton Prison.

The Attorney-General said that on the last occasion, he had given an undertaking that facilities would be given for the petitioner to see his friends. On this occasion, he had no authority to give such an undertaking.

LORD SIMONDS (to the petitioner). You must apply to the Governor.

Solicitor: *Treasury Solicitor.*

7

SURRENDER UNDER BACKED WARRANT

REGINA v. METROPOLITAN POLICE COMMISSIONER *EX PARTE* HAMMOND

([1964] 2 Q.B. 385)

February 11, 18, 1964: Queen's Bench Division: Finnemore, Paull, Widgery JJ.

Fugitive Offender—Ireland, Republic of—Warrant issued by justice in Ireland—Person named in warrant Englishman—Endorsed in Eire for execution in England—Endorsement by deputy commissioner of Garda Siochana—Automatic endorsement of English magistrate on production of warrant and proof of signature of issuing justice—Whether discretion in magistrate—Whether proof of compliance with statutory requirements and prima facie case necessary—Whether signature by deputy commissioner of Garda Siochana sufficient—Indictable Offences Act, 1848 (11 & 12 *Vict. c.* 42), *s.* 12—*Petty Sessions* (*Ireland*) *Act,* 1851 (14 & 15 *Vict. c.* 93), *s.* 27 (3)—*Irish Free State* (*Consequential Provisions*) *Act,* 1922, (13 *Geo.* 5, *c.* 2), *s.* 6—*Irish Free State* (*Consequential Adaptation of Enactments*) *Order,* 1923 (*S.R. & O.*, 1923, *No.* 405), *art.* 8—*Magistrates' Courts Act,* 1952 (15 & 16 *Geo.* 6 & 1 *Eliz.* 2, *c.* 55), *Sch.* 5.

A warrant was issued by a justice of a district court in Eire for the arrest of the applicant, an Englishman, charged with an indictable misdemeanour in Eire contrary to a statute which had been superseded in England before the warrant was issued. The warrant was endorsed in Eire by a deputy commissioner of the Garda Siochana for execution in England, and was accompanied by proof of the signature of the issuing justice in the form provided by the Petty Sessions (Ireland) Act, 1851. An English magistrate, having before him nothing but the warrant and proof of signature, automatically endorsed the warrant for execution and the applicant was arrested by the metropolitan police. He applied for, and was granted, a writ of habeas corpus directed to the respondent, the Commissioner of Metropolitan Police, and, on the return to the writ, contended that the arrest was unlawful since the English magistrate had a discretion, which he had not exercised, under section 12 of the Indictable Offences Act, 1848,[1] as amended, or **[386]** section 27 (3) of the Petty Sessions

[1] Indictable Offences Act, 1848 (as amended by Magistrates' Courts Act, 1952, Sch. 5), s. 12: ". . . if any person against whom a warrant shall be issued in any county or place in Ireland, by any justice of the peace . . . for any crime or offence against the laws of that part of the United Kingdom, shall escape, go into, reside, or be, or be supposed or suspected to be, in any county . . . in that part of the United Kingdom called England or Wales, it shall and may be lawful for any justice of the peace in and for the county . . . into which such person shall escape or go, or where he shall reside or be, or be supposed or suspected to be, to make an indorsement on the warrant, signed with his name, authorising the execution of the warrant . . . which warrant so indorsed shall be a sufficient authority to the person . . . bringing such warrant . . . and also to all constables . . . of the county . . . where such warrant shall be indorsed, to execute the said warrant . . . and to convey him before the justice . . . who granted the same . . ."

(Ireland) Act, 1851,[2] whether or not to endorse the warrant, and also to invite the applicant to appear and give reasons why the warrant should not be endorsed. On the respondent contending that the English magistrate had no jurisdiction to inquire into the facts or to do other than endorse the warrant:

Held (Widgery J. dissenting), that a magistrate had a discretion whether or not to endorse a warrant issued by a justice in Eire, and was not bound to endorse it by the provisions of either the Indictable Offences Act, 1848, as amended, or the Petty Sessions (Ireland) Act, 1851 (post, pp. 398, 399). Accordingly, since the magistrate had automatically endorsed the warrant upon proof of the signature of the issuing justice, and had not exercised his discretion, the endorsement was invalid, the applicant's arrest was unlawful, the writ of habeas corpus should be filed, and the applicant discharged from custody.

Held, further, that the provisions of section 27 (3) of the Petty Sessions (Ireland) Act, 1851, had not been complied with since the warrant was endorsed in Eire by a deputy commissioner of the Garda Siochana, and there was no provision in English law for such endorsement (post, pp. 396-397).

Rex v. *Commissioner of Metropolitan Police, Ex parte Nalder** [1948] 1 K.B. 215; 63 T.L.R. 591; [1947] 2 All E.R. 611, D.C. explained.

Per Paull and Finnemore JJ. In exercising his discretion whether or not to endorse a warrant issued in Eire a magistrate should take steps to satisfy himself that the warrant complies strictly with the technicalities of the provisions of the Indictable Offences Act, 1848, or the Petty Sessions (Ireland) Act, 1851; and that facts are proved showing prima facie that an offence was committed in Eire, and that an element of escape exists, in that the person named in the warrant came to England after committing the offence in Eire There is no rule that the magistrate must give the person named in the warrant an opportunity to make representations, but it is most advisable that that be done (post, pp. 398, 399).

Per Finnemore J. The court has an inherent power and a duty to make sure that, at all events, a prima facie case has been made out (post, p. 400).

APPLICATION for writ of habeas corpus ad subjiciendum.

On December 23, 1963, the following warrant was issued at Dublin in Eire: "The district court. Warrant to arrest. The **[387]** Attorney-General at the suit of Superintendent Patrick Mullaney, Garda Siochana, Howth, complainant *v.* Peter David Hammond." [the applicant] "defendant. District court area of Howth. District No. 10. Whereas a complaint has been made on oath and in writing that" the applicant, "being a person over the age of 17 years, and having the custody of two children, Kimberley Hammond and Joan Hammond, both under the age of 17 years, did, within the six months preceding December 16, 1963, at No. 14, Railway Avenue, Sutton, County Dublin, in the said court area and district, wilfully neglect said children in such a manner likely to cause them unnecessary suffering or injury to their health, contrary to section 12 of the Children Act, 1908, as amended by section 4 of the Children (Amendment) Act, 1957. This is to command you to whom this warrant is addressed to arrest" the applicant, "of Maida Car Hire, 1, Fernhead Road, London, W.9, and to bring him without any delay before me or another justice or some peace commissioner to be dealt with according to law. Donnchadg Ua Donnchadha, justice of the district court. To the superintendent of the Garda Siochana at Howth and his assistants." The warrant was attached to a form headed "Petty Sessions Act, 1851, 14 & 15 Vict. c. 93," and the signature of Donnchadg Ua Donnchadha on the warrant was verified on oath on the form by a sergeant of the Garda Siochana on January 22, 1964. On January 28, 1964, the superinten-

[2] Petty Sessions (Ireland) Act, 1851, s. 27: "(3) . . . Whenever it shall appear" [that the person named on the warrant is] "to be found in some place in England . . . it shall be lawful for the . . . inspector general, or for either of the . . . deputy inspectors general . . . to indorse the warrant . . . and it shall thereupon be lawful for any justice . . . having power to issue any warrant . . . in" [England] . . . "upon proof on oath of the handwriting either of the inspector or deputy inspector general or of the justice by whom the warrant shall have been issued, to indorse the same."

dent of the Garda Siochana, by endorsement on the warrant, certified that he had reason to believe that the person against whom the warrant was issued was to be found at the address stated in England. On January 30, 1964, the deputy commissioner of the Garda Siochana endorsed the warrant for execution in the London metropolitan police district, London, in England, and forwarded it and the attachment to the Metropolitan Police Commissioner, New Scotland Yard.

On February 7, 1964, a station police sergeant of the metropolitan police brought the warrant and attachment before the Marylebone magistrate, Walter Frampton, who endorsed the warrant in the following terms: "Whereas proof upon oath hath this day been given to me, one of the magistrates of the magistrates' courts of the metropolis sitting at the Marylebone magistrates' court and within the metropolitan police district, the name of Donnchadg Ua Donnchadha to the within warrant subscribed, is of the handwriting of the district justice within mentioned; I do therefore hereby authorise the station police **[388]** sergeant who bringeth me this warrant and all other persons to whom this warrant was originally directed, or by whom it may lawfully be executed, and also all constables of the metropolitan police force, to execute the same within the said metropolitan police district." At 3 p.m. on February 7, 1964, the applicant was arrested and taken to Harrow Road police station where he was kept in custody.

On February 8, 1964, the applicant applied for a writ of habeas corpus, and deposed as follows: "I was married on November 19, 1955, at a church in Scottow, Norfolk, to Sheila Anne Hammond, who, I believe, resides now at 14, Railway Avenue, which is the home of her parents; Kimberley Anne, born on September 25, 1957, is a child of my marriage, but I have never admitted, and dispute, paternity of Joan, born on March 17, 1960; I believe the children are living with my wife; I ceased to cohabit with my wife at the end of 1959, when she left with the child from our house in Rochester, Kent, to return to Eire to her parents; there have been no proceedings in any court concerning my marriage or the children or either of them; I intend to bring divorce proceedings against my wife on the ground of adultery; until approximately February, 1961, my wife was receiving my navy allowance of £6 a week, but that ceased in that month; at the end of the year 1960 my wife received my gratuity of £90 on my discharge from the navy on medical grounds; I have written to my wife but received no reply, and sent £15 in 1963 to her; I was last in Eire in March, 1960, when I saw my wife and tried to effect a reconciliation; at this time my wife told me that Kimberley was very well; I have received no letters, complaints or requests from my wife or any one for money for the children and thought that my wife was caring for them from her earnings from employment; no particulars of the offence alleged against me appear on the warrant, and I am unable to know the nature of the complaint made against me." There was no challenge to the facts so deposed to. On February 8, 1964, Streatfeild J., in chambers, ordered that a writ of habeas corpus issue, directed to the Metropolitan Police Commissioner, to have the body of the applicant before the court. On February 10, 1964, the writ was issued. The return to the writ was made by Joseph Simpson, Metropolitan Police Commissioner.

Thomas Kellock for the applicant. The magistrate was wrong to endorse the warrant. Although the complaint is stated, the **[389]** terms are wide and vague, and the cause of complaint is not stated, since the particulars required under section 11 of the Petty Sessions (Ireland) Act, 1851, are not set out. If the magistrate purported to exercise jurisdiction under that Act, he was wrong so to do. Further, the magistrate has a discretion, which he did not exercise, whether or not to endorse such a warrant exercising jurisdiction under that Act or the Indictable Offences Act, 1848, and should not endorse a warrant without giving an opportunity to the applicant to be heard and unless the magistrate is satisfied that the particulars required under English law appear on the face of the warrant, that other remedies have been sought or exhausted, and that there is some suggestion that the applicant has disappeared from Eire. This court has jurisdiction to inquire into the facts, and has a discretion, which on the facts should be exercised in favour of the applicant's release from custody.

H. J. Leonard for the respondent commissioner of police. The warrant was issued in respect of an alleged criminal offence and was sufficiently particularised. [Reference was made to *Rex* v. *Connor*.[3]] The magistrate was right to endorse the warrant. No procedure exists whereby he can inquire into the merits. He has no discretion, and must automatically endorse the warrant provided the procedural provisions are properly observed. The procedure laid down by the Petty Sessions (Ireland) Act, 1851, is still available: *Rex* v. *Police Commissioner, Ex parte Nalder*.[4]* The court has no jurisdiction to inquire into the facts, and the applicant was not before him.

Kellock replied.

February 11. FINNEMORE J. This is a point of some difficulty. The court will take time to consider the matter. In the meantime the applicant will be released on bail.

Cur. adv. vult.

February 18. FINNEMORE J. Paull J. will give the first judgment.

PAULL J. read the following judgment. By a writ of habeas corpus granted on February 10, 1964, Peter David Hammond, the applicant, has been brought before this court. He was arrested on February 7, 1964, on a warrant issued by one **[390]** Donnchadg Ua Donnachadha, a justice of the district court area of Howth in County Dublin, Eire. This warrant is endorsed for execution in the London metropolitan police district by the deputy commissioner of the Garda Siochana. One of the magistrates of the magistrates' courts of the metropolis of London, Walter Frampton, having before him nothing except the warrant and evidence on oath that the signature Donnchadg Ua Donnchadha is the signature of the district justice, endorsed the warrant authorising the execution of the warrant by, inter alios, any constable of the metropolitan police force. As a result police constable Alan Lonsborough arrested the applicant and conveyed him to Harrow Road Police Station where he has been kept in custody, except for the period during which he was on bail granted by this court.

The warrant is in the following terms: "Whereas a complaint has been made on oath and in writing that the defendant, Peter David Hammond, being a person over the age of 17 years, and having the custody of two children, Kimberley Hammond and Joan Hammond, both under the age of 17 years, did, within the six months preceding December 16, 1963, at No. 14, Railway Avenue, Sutton, County Dublin, in the said court area and district, wilfully neglect the said children in such a manner likely to cause them unnecessary suffering or injury to their health, contrary to section 12 of the Children Act, 1908, as amended by section 4 of the Children (Amendment) Act, 1957. This is to command you to whom this warrant is addressed to arrest the said Peter David Hammond, of Maida Car Hire, 1, Fernhead Road, London, W.9, and to bring him without any delay before me or another justice or some peace commissioner to be dealt with according to law."

By section 12 of the Children Act, 1908, it is enacted that if any person who has the custody, charge or care of any child neglects him in a manner likely to cause him unnecessary suffering or injury to his health that person shall be guilty of a misdemeanour. The offence is made an indictable one. Since Eire is now a wholly independent country I presume, although it has not been proved before us, that Eire has in some way made this Act part of the law of Eire. No English Act could have that effect. In England this Act has now been superseded and is no longer the law. Section 4 of the Children (Amendment) Act, 1957, passed by the legislature of Eire, amends section 12 of the Children Act, 1908. Counsel for the respondent submitted that **[391]** it was no

[3] [1908] 2 K.B. 26; 24 T.L.R. 483.
[4] [1948] 1 K.B. 215; 63 T.L.R. 591.

concern of ours what that amendment enacts. In fact, it increases from 16 to 17 the necessary age of the person who may be punished, and is, therefore, immaterial in this case.

Prima facie the Children Act, 1908, which is now solely an Act of Eire, does not govern a citizen of this country who does not reside, and has not resided, in Eire at any material time—although it may, in certain circumstances, possibly do so, for instance, if the citizen has resided in Eire before the material time and comes to this country to escape his marital responsibilities. In England the word "neglect," in relation to children, means the absence of such reasonable care as an ordinary parent would use for the care and protection of his child: see *Reg.* v. *Senior*.[5] Whether, since Eire became a separate state, there has been any other definition in that country of the word "neglect" I do not know. None has been suggested to us.

By section 12 of the Indictable Offences Act, 1848, as amended by the Magistrates' Courts Act, 1952, ". . . if any person against whom a warrant shall be issued in any county or place in Ireland, by any justice of the peace . . . for any crime or offence against the laws of that part of the United Kingdom, shall escape, go into, reside, or be, or be supposed or suspected to be, in any county . . . in that part of the United Kingdom called England or Wales, it shall and may be lawful for any justice of the peace in and for the county . . . into which such person shall escape or go, or where he shall reside, or be, or be supposed or suspected to be, to make an indorsement on the warrant, signed with his name, authorising the execution of the warrant . . . which warrant so endorsed shall be a sufficient authority to the person . . . bringing such warrant . . . and also to all constables . . . of the county . . . where such warrant shall be so endorsed, to execute the said warrant . . and to convey him before the justice . . . who granted the same . . ." The justice who granted the warrant is, of course, the justice in Ireland.

By article 8 of the Irish Free State (Consequential Adaptation of Enactment) Order, 1923 (S.R. & O. 1923, No. 405), made under the Irish Free State (Consequential Provisions) Act, 1922, s. 6, it is provided that the provisions of any enactments which are applicable to the endorsement and execution in England of warrants issued by justices in Ireland shall apply to warrants issued by justices in the Irish Free State; that is Eire. **[392]**

[His Lordship stated the facts deposed to by the applicant set out above and continued:] Mr. Leonard, for the respondent metropolitan police commissioner, has submitted to us that we have no jurisdiction to inquire into the facts of this matter or make any order which would result in the applicant being released. His contention is that, once a warrant has been issued by a justice of the peace of Ireland and his signature is authenticated, there is no power in a magistrate in this country to do other than endorse the warrant no matter what the facts may be. There need be no evidence showing a prima facie case against the man to be arrested. The man in question may be proved not to have lived in Eire, never to have committed any offence in Eire, and indeed never to have been in Eire. Even if all three of these matters are proved conclusively the magistrate in England must still endorse the warrant and, moreover, endorse it without giving to the man any opportunity of proving to him such facts. It is to be noted that there is no protection against the man being charged with quite another offence once he is in Eire, and there is no provision for his being returned to this country at any time in any circumstances.

Mr. Kellock, for the applicant, has submitted that the minimum required to be proved before a magistrate here endorses a warrant is that the man to be arrested must at least be told the particulars of the offence alleged, namely, in this case, how it is alleged that the applicant has neglected the children who are alleged to be in his custody in a manner likely to cause them unnecessary suffering. Mr. Kellock has also submitted that the magistrate has a discretion whether he endorses the warrant, and that he ought, or at least has a discretion, to invite the man to appear before him in order to give any reasons why the warrant should not be endorsed.

[5] [1899] 1 Q.B. 283, 291.

The matter is of some importance. In this case it is difficult to see how a man who has not been in Eire at all since 1960, and then only to try and persuade his wife to return to this country with the children, and has not since then received any letters from his wife or from the children, not even an acknowledgment of money which he has sent, can commit an offence in Eire under what is now purely a statute of Eire and which by its nature provides against offences committed in Eire. If the wife of a Frenchman who has never been to England chooses to bring the children of the marriage, or the alleged children of the marriage, to this country, it is difficult to see how the Frenchman commits a breach of any law of this country so long as he remains in **[393]** France by not communicating with her or them when he has received no communication from her or them. Even if his wife writes and demands money one would have thought that he is entitled to say "I am not governed by the law of England as to these matters." The immediate danger of the procedure adopted in this case is that once the applicant is taken to Eire then, even if these proceedings fail, proceedings may be brought based upon his failure to support his children while he is, however unwillingly, in Eire.

With these considerations in mind, I turn to the provisions of the Indictable Offences Act, 1848, passed at a time when, of course, the Queen's writ ran in what is now Eire and when, therefore, full protection could be afforded to anyone taken to any part of Ireland.

In my judgment section 12 of the Indictable Offences Act, 1848, does not impose upon a magistrate in this country an imperative duty to endorse any warrant, it merely gives a right to endorse the warrant. There is no provision for the proof of anything. The words are not "a justice of the peace shall endorse"; the words are "It shall and may be lawful . . . to make an endorsement."

The words "it shall be lawful" have been considered in a number of cases. As Crompton J. said in *Castelli* v. *Groom*[6]: "The words 'it shall be lawful' in a statute are obligatory or not according to the subject-matter." In that case the words were used in connection with the superior courts issuing commissions to examine witnesses abroad and it was held that the court was not bound to issue such a commission simply on proof that persons whose evidence was required were abroad, but that it was in the discretion of the court to determine on the special circumstances of each case whether it was advisable in the interests of justice to issue it or not. This interpretation is the one adopted generally in cases where the act to be done requires judicial consideration before it is done, although of course if the refusal is based on no, or no proper, grounds a superior court can compel the doing of the act. In *Julius* v. *Bishop of Oxford*[7] the words "it shall be lawful" were very fully discussed. It was there held, reversing the lower court, that the words "it shall be lawful" in relation to a bishop issuing a commission of inquiry merely made legal or possible that which there would otherwise be no authority to do. All their Lordships held that **[394]** the words "it shall be lawful" are in themselves merely permissive or enabling. Each of them held that in some circumstances a duty was also to be implied. Perhaps those circumstances can best be summed up in the words of Lord Penzance,[8] where he said that the effect of the cases in which the exercise of the power conferred was held to be obligatory was that although the statutes concerned had in terms only conferred a power the circumstances were such as to create a duty and to show that the exercise of any discretion by the person empowered could not have been intended.

Here the provisions of section 12 of the Indictable Offences Act, 1848, indicate to me that the section is primarily aimed at those who, having committed a crime in the one country, go to the other country in order to escape the consequences which may follow. The right is given in those circumstances. The words are "into which such person shall escape or go" and then, to make sure

[6] (1852) 18 Q.B. 490, 495.
[7] (1880) 5 App. Cas. 214, H.L.(E.).
[8] 5 App. Cas. 214, 231, 232.

that the object aimed at is not defeated by some such argument that it has not been proved that the person "escaped" or "went" because of the crime, the words "or where he shall reside or be or be supposed or suspected to be" are added. If that be so then clearly the duty cannot arise until it has been shown that something in the nature of an escape has taken place.

It is interesting to note that the marginal note to section 12 of the Indictable Offences Act, 1848, reads: "English warrants may be backed in Ireland, and vice versa." Now it has been said that the marginal notes must be disregarded (see Slade J. in *Longdon-Griffiths* v. *Smith*[9]) on the ground that they are not to be taken as parts of the statute (see *Claydon* v. *Green*,[10] *per* Bovill C.J.[11] and Willes J.,[12] as well as other cases). This rule, however, has not always been observed: see, for instance, *Nicholson* v. *Fields*,[13] *Sheffield Waterworks Co.* v. *Bennett*,[14] and *Bushell* v. *Hammond*,[15] where Henn Collins M.R. said[16] "some help will be derived from the side-note (though of course it is not part of the statute), which shews that the section is dealing with . . ." and then mentions certain matters. This marginal note to section 12 of the Indictable Offences Act, 1848, if it can be taken into consideration, **[395]** certainly shows (1) that the contemplation was that the backing should be used in the event of the parties "escaping"; and (2) that it is discretionary whether the warrant is or is not backed. I see no indication that the exercise of a discretion could not have been intended.

Presumably, this warrant was issued under the provisions of the Petty Sessions (Ireland) Act, 1851. I say presumably since I have no knowledge of any statute passed in Eire since 1923 which repeals or varies that Act.

The first question which arises here is whether the warrant issued complied with the provisions of the Petty Sessions (Ireland) Act, 1851. This is, primarily, not a question for us but for the courts of Eire. Dealing with the matter as though it came under the principles of English law one starts with the fact that by section 11 of that Act it is provided that "In all cases of indictable crimes and offences (where an information that any person has committed the same shall have been taken in writing and on oath) the justice shall issue a warrant to arrest and bring such person before him, . . . or, if he shall think that the ends of justice would be thereby sufficiently answered, it shall be lawful for him, instead of issuing such warrant, to issue a summons in the first instance to such person." Prima facie, therefore, the justice in this case was entitled to issue a warrant in respect of any person who had committed, or was suspected of having committed, an offence within his jurisdiction, which is limited by the bounds of his county, for by section 7 (1) of the Act " a justice for any county may act . . . in all matters arising within such county." The county by section 1 (1) may be divided into districts, but that does not prevent the justice of a district from dealing with matters within the county, but the justice has no jurisdiction to issue a warrant unless the crime has been committed in his county. We do not know what statement was made in writing and on oath to the justice, but it is difficult to see, under the law of England, how the condition as to jurisdiction could have been alleged to have been fulfilled had the facts deposed to before us been before the magistrate and uncontradicted. Assuming that that condition was fulfilled, section 11 provides that the warrant "shall state shortly the cause of complaint." One of the points taken by Mr. Kellock is that this warrant does not state the cause of complaint. He submitted that the warrant states the complaint, namely, a wilful neglect under the Children Act, 1908, but, in order to state the cause of complaint, it would be necessary to state shortly the **[396]** facts upon which it was alleged that the applicant had wilfully neglected his children. In the civil case of *Read* v.

[9] [1951] 1 K.B. 295; 66 T.L.R. (Pt. 2) 627; [1950] 2 All E.R. 662, 672.
[10] (1868) L.R. 3 C.P. 511.
[11] Ibid. 519.
[12] Ibid. 522.
[13] (1862) 31 L.J.N.S. Ex. 233, 237.
[14] (1872) L.R. 7 Ex. 409, 421.
[15] [1904] 2 K.B. 563; 20 T.L.R. 413, C.A.
[16] [1904] 2 K.B. 563, 567.

Brown,[17] where the question arose as to what constituted a cause of action, Lord Esher M.R. said[18]: "What is the real meaning of the phrase 'a cause of action arising in the City'? It has been defined in *Cooke* v. *Gill*[19] to be this: every fact which it would be necessary for the plaintiff to prove, if traversed, in order to support his right to the judgment of the court. It does not comprise every piece of evidence which is necessary to prove each fact, but every fact which is necessary to be proved." Mr. Kellock contends that, since it is necessary to state not only the complaint but the cause of complaint, it is at least necessary, by the law of England, in a case such as this where the person affected by the warrant may know nothing of the facts which are alleged to constitute the offence charged, that the warrant should go as far as shortly stating how it is alleged that a man who at all material times was in England is alleged to have caused in Eire unnecessary suffering or injury to his children's health by failing to take the reasonable care of an ordinary parent. Since the law which governs this matter is the law of Eire, I do not feel, in the absence of proof to the contrary, that one ought to do other than assume that, so far as the law of Eire is concerned, the warrant is good.

Somewhat curiously the Petty Sessions (Ireland) Act, 1851, which is expressed to apply only to Ireland except for the provisions respecting the backing and execution of warrants and the taking of examinations, also makes provisions for the backing of warrante in England. By section 27 (3) of that Act, "whenever it shall appear" to the sub-inspector of constabulary to whom the warrant has been addressed that the person who is named on the warrant is "to be found in some place in England . . . it shall be lawful for the . . . inspector general, or for either of the . . . deputy inspectors general, to endorse the warrant . . . and it shall thereupon be lawful for any justice . . . having power to issue any warrant in England upon proof on oath of the handwriting either of the inspector or deputy inspector general or of the justice by whom the warrant shall have been issued, to endorse the same."

Since proof of handwriting was the only fact proved before the magistrate, presumably he purported to act under the Petty **[397]** Sessions (Ireland) Act, 1851. If so, the proceedings in this case, in my judgment, do not come within the provisions of the Petty Sessions (Ireland) Act, 1851, so far as this procedure for indorsing the warrant is concerned. It is true that the signature of the Eire justice was proved, but I can find no provision in English law substituting the deputy-commissioner of the Garda Siochana for the deputy inspector general. It is not one of the provisions of paragraph 8 of the Irish Free State (Consequential Adaptation of Enactments) Order, 1923 (S.R. & O. 1923, No. 405). Where the liberty of the subject is concerned the formalities must be strictly observed. One cannot assume against the subject, and any legislation must be strictly complied with.

Even assuming that the proceedings for endorsement in this case did come within the Petty Sessions (Ireland) Act, 1851, it is to be noted that section 27 (3) also uses the words "it shall be lawful" and in this respect does not differ from the wording of the Indictable Offences Act, 1848, except that the words "and may be" are omitted. Indeed, apart from the matters already referred to, the only relevant difference between the provisions of the Indictable Offences Act, 1848, and the Petty Sessions (Ireland) Act, 1851, is that the words "escape or go into reside or be or be supposed or suspected to be" are changed into the words "is to be found." I am inclined to think that these latter words in their context have the same connotation as the words in the Indictable Offences Act, 1848, the underlying intention being clearly that the person concerned has committed a crime within the jurisdiction of the justice in Ireland and then disappeared into England. It is almost inconceivable that Parliament within three years of the passing of the Act of 1848 should, without repealing in any way the provisions of that Act, bring a quite different concept into existence.

It is to be noted in the Petty Sessions (Ireland) Act, 1851, the same words

[17] (1888) 22 Q.B.D. 128; 5 T.L.R. 97, C.A.
[18] 22 Q.B.D. 128, 131.
[19] (1873) L.R. 8 C.P. 107.

"it shall be lawful" are used in respect of the functions of both the inspector general and the English magistrate. If, therefore, the contention of the respondent is correct, and is the law of Eire, any member of the police force in Eire who can persuade any justice of his county to sign a warrant on any charge, possibly trumped up and with an ulterior motive, can ensure that an English citizen shall be taken out of the protection of the English courts, without any knowledge of anything until his arrest, and without any opportunity of protesting against his arrest and extradition, for the inspector general or the deputy inspector general would have no other duty than an English **[398]** magistrate has. I find it difficult to think that that is the law of England under either the Indictable Offences Act, 1848, or the Petty Sessions (Ireland) Act, 1851.

In *Rex* v. *Commissioner of Metropolitan Police, Ex parte Nalder*[20]* the question arose whether a warrant issued by a justice of the district court of Eire for an indictable misdemeanour could be used to arrest an Englishman in England under the procedure laid down by the Petty Sessions (Ireland) Act, 1851, the argument in that case being that the proper course to take in this country in the case of an Englishman whose arrest and extradition were desired was to use the provisions of the Fugitive Offenders Act, 1881. This court held in that case that there was nothing to prevent the provisions of the Petty Sessions (Ireland) Act, 1851, being used, and if it was used then a warrant could be endorsed under the provisions of that Act. It is to be noted, however, that in that case it was assumed that if the procedure was available the case fell within that procedure.

The conclusion I have come to is that the proceedings in this country to be valid must have been under the Indictable Offences Act, 1848, since the provisions of the Petty Sessions (Ireland) Act, 1851, were not strictly complied with, but that whether that is so or not there was nothing to compel the magistrate to append his signature to the endorsement under either Act merely upon the presentation of the warrant and proof of signature and that he had a discretion whether he would do so or not.

Normally, where it is necessary for a magistrate to exercise a discretion and to assure himself that prima facie the technicalities have been observed, that there is a prima facie case of an offence having been committed in Eire, and that there has been shown to be, prima facie, an element of escape, the court will assume, subject to evidence to the contrary, that the magistrate has so acted before endorsing the warrant. In this case, however, the whole argument of the respondent has rested on the assumption that the magistrate has done no such thing and was not entitled to do any such thing. So far as I understand it from the argument of Mr. Leonard, magistrates automatically endorse on being satisfied that the purported signature of the Irish magistrate is in fact his signature. The word "therefore," in the endorsement, certainly supports this view. I do not feel, therefore, that I am doing any injustice by assuming that my understanding on this is correct. In my judgment on that basis the endorsement is not **[399]** valid even if purported to be made under the Indictable Offences Act,1848, and is not valid under the Petty Sessions (Ireland) Act, 1851.

How a magistrate chooses to be satisfied is for him. I would lay down no rule that he must give the person named in the warrant an opportunity to make representations, although it seems to me that it is most advisable that he should do so. I can only say that the magistrate should take such steps as he thinks proper to satisfy himself (1) that the warrant satisfies strictly the technicalities of the provisions of the Indictable Offences Act, 1848, or the Petty Sessions (Ireland) Act, 1851; (2) that there are facts proved that show that prima facie an offence has been committed in Eire; and (3) that there are facts proved showing that there is prima facie an element of escape (possibly in a case of this sort this could be done by showing that the man has deliberately left a wife and children in Eire without support and come to England).

It must, as I have already indicated, always be borne in mind that the effect of an endorsement in the case of a British citizen is that the citizen is taken by force out of his own country and beyond the confines of where he may

[20] [1948] 1 K.B. 251; 63 T.L.R. 591; [1947] 2 All E.R. 611, D.C.

appeal to the courts of his own country. In my judgment the proper order to make in this case is that the applicant be released from custody.

FINNEMORE J. I find myself fully in agreement with the detailed judgment which has just been delivered, and I do not propose to add more than a few general observations for my own part.

I agree entirely with the general principle that escape in some form or another is really the basis of this procedure. Whatever name we use—and I do not use this in the technical sense—it is really a procedure between England and Eire for enabling the one country or the other to get back fugitive offenders. A person commits a crime in this country or in Eire; he goes away to the other country and then a warrant is issued in the country where the offence is alleged to have taken place and taken to the other country to which he has gone. On the warrant being backed by a magistrate there, the man is brought back to be tried in the country where he committed the offence.

Three things are essential in this case: (1) an offence must be committed in Eire, (2) by someone who was resident there, and (3) who then escaped or came to this country. It seems to me that those conditions are not fulfilled in this case. The **[400]** applicant married his wife in this country, he has always lived in this country; he lived in this country with his wife and child until she decided to leave him to go back to live with her parents in Eire; he remained in this country; he has never lived in Eire at all. He made a visit there in 1960 in order to get his wife to come back, but she did not come back; he then returned to this country, where he has lived and earned his living since. He has never resided in Eire in or near the material time, that being six months before December 16, 1963, the period when the neglect of children is alleged.

It seems to me, in those circumstances, that there is no basis at all for the exercise of this procedure, whichever Act happens to apply, because the applicant was never in Eire. It seems to me that he never committed any offence in Eire and he certainly never escaped from Eire or came from Eire, where he never at any time lived.

The argument of counsel for the respondent is that that may or may not be so; the magistrate has no power whatever to go into any of those points, nor has this court. What I would like to say, speaking for myself, is that I agree with what Paull J. has said in regard to the responsibility on the shoulders of the magistrate. I also want to add that, whether the magistrate can or cannot do more than back the warrant once he is satisfied it has been signed by the proper person in Ireland, I take the view strongly that this court has an inherent power and a duty to make sure that, at all events, a prima facie case has been made out. This court has a duty, in many ways an overriding duty, to see that no subject of the Queen in this country is taken away overseas to another country out of the jurisdiction of these courts and away from the protection of the Queen's laws unless this court is satisfied there is at least a prima facie case for such a procedure.

I think that this court has both the power and the duty to inquire into this matter. If we have not, it means that we are handing over the liberty of a subject in this country to another land altogether. Nothing that is said in this court implies the slightest disrespect to Eire or its courts. This is a reciprocal procedure; it applies to both countries in just the same way.

I am bound to say for myself that it seems a somewhat alarming position that a wife in this country with a home and husband in this country can go away with the children overseas beyond the jurisdiction of this country, and can then say, "My **[401]** husband, whom I have left in England, has committed an offence in this new country because he is not supporting the children in this country." If, of course, under statutes passed by Parliament we are bound to take that view then, whatever we may think about it, so be it. I do not think there is any Act that binds this court to shut its eyes to the evidence, to act as though that affidavit which has been filed had never been sworn at all. I think this court has both the power and the duty to inquire into this matter, and as soon as we inquire into it on the only evidence we have, in my opinion, the whole basis for this procedure fails, and I am therefore agreed that this man should be released.

WIDGERY J. read the following judgment. I have reached the opposite conclusion, and I do so with diffidence. I associate myself with all which has been said about the unsatisfactory nature of the procedure used in this case and about its potential as a source of injustice.

We have no evidence before us except the affidavit of the applicant, but if what he says is correct, he is an Englishman living a perfectly virtuous life in England who has been torn from his home and his work without warning and is about to be conveyed in custody to Eire without any inquiry in this country as to the existence of a prima facie case against him in Eire. If it is lawful for the authorities in Eire to do this, it is equally lawful for the English police to arrest an Irishman in Eire upon an English warrant and with a similar lack of safeguards, and I cannot think that the existence of such a right can be regarded as healthy in either of the two countries concerned. However, the position is regulated by statute, and if Parliament has decreed that what has been done may be done it is not open to this court, in my judgment, to declare that the applicant's detention is unlawful.

The Petty Sessions (Ireland) Act, 1851, was held to be still in force in *Rex* v. *Commissioner of Metropolitan Police, Ex parte Nalder*[21]* (to which Paull J. has referred) and it contains provisions for the backing of warrants issued in Ireland so as to authorise the execution of such warrants in England. It is an Act passed by the Queen in Parliament at Westminster and, by section 47, its application is not confined to Ireland so far as its provisions for the backing and execution of warrants are **[402]** concerned. I find it difficult to understand why these powers were conferred, and have been allowed to survive, when substantially similar powers existed under the Indictable Offences Act, 1848, but that they do not survive appears to be clear and I think that they were the powers which were invoked by the Irish authorities in the present case as the forms used are, in the main, those prescribed by the Act of 1851. It follows, in my judgment, that if the action taken in the present case was authorised by the Petty Sessions (Ireland) Act, 1851, it cannot be said to be contrary to law even if it does not comply with the Indictable Offences Act, 1848, as to which I express no opinion.

Sections 10 and 11 of the Petty Sessions (Ireland) Act, 1851, authorise any justice in Ireland to issue a warrant on information that any person has committed or is suspected of having committed an offence, inter alia, within the jurisdiction of such justice. Section 11 provides that such warrant shall "state shortly the cause of complaint"; and by section 25 (2) the warrant is to be addressed for execution to the sub-inspector or head constable of constabulary of the petty sessions district concerned. Section 26 (1) then proceeds to enact that, if the person against whom the warrant has been issued "shall be to be found" in the place for which such sub-inspector shall act, that officer shall execute the warrant, whereas by section 26 (3), if such person is "not to be found in the county" to which such sub-inspector shall belong, the latter shall transmit the warrant to the inspector general of constabulary for backing. Section 27 (3) provides that when the warrant has been received by the inspector general and it shall appear that the person against whom it has been issued is "to be found in some place in England . . . it shall be lawful for the said inspector general . . . to endorse the warrant . . . and it shall thereupon be lawful for any justice . . . in any of the said places" (for example, in England) "upon proof on oath of the handwriting . . . of the justice by whom the warrant shall have been issued to endorse the same . . . authorising its execution within the jurisdiction of the said justice." Section 31 authorises the person executing a warrant which has been endorsed in this manner to arrest the person against whom the warrant was issued and convey him before the justice by whom it was issued.

It appears to me that this procedure has been followed in the present case. Objection was taken before us that the warrant did not "state shortly the cause

[21] [1948] 1 K.B. 215

of complaint" as required by section 11, but the warrant has been read by Paull J., and it **[403]** will have been observed that it states the place and date of the alleged offence, the nature of the offence, the names of the children concerned and the title of the statute creating the offence. Indeed it contains all the information which would appear in an indictment for a similar offence in this country, and I cannot believe that more is required, especially when it is remembered that section 11 applies to all warrants issued in Ireland and not merely to those which may be executed elsewhere.

I do not find it necessary to decide whether the Indictable Offences Act, 1848, is concerned primarily with the backing of Irish warrants when issued against persons who are fugitives from Ireland because there is nothing in the Petty Sessions (Ireland) Act, 1851, to suggest that the terms of that Act are so limited. Section 27 merely requires that the person against whom the warrant is issued is "to be found" in England and this same phrase is used in section 26 when dealing with suspects who are still in the county in which the crime was committed and who cannot be considered as escapers or fugitives.

Finally, I consider that, for all practical purposes, Mr. Leonard is right when he submits that the magistrate backing a warrant in England has no power to go behind the warrant, and is bound to back it if it is good on its face and the signature of the justice is duly authenticated. The words "it shall be lawful" are not mandatory in themselves, but it is well established that when a power is given in those terms there may be a duty cast upon the donee to exercise that power. In *Julius* v. *Bishop of Oxford,*[22] to which reference has already been made, Lord Blackburn said[23]: "I do not think the words 'it shall be lawful' are in themselves ambiguous at all. They are apt words to express that a power is given; and as, prima facie, the donee of a power may either exercise it or leave it unused, it is not inaccurate to say that, prima facie, they are equivalent to saying that the donee may do it; but if the object for which the power is conferred is for the purpose of enforcing a right, there may be a duty cast on the donee of the power, to exercise it for the benefit of those who have the right, when required on their behalf. When there is such a duty, it is not inaccurate to say that the words conferring the power are equivalent to saying that the donee must exercise it." In my judgment the power conferred on an English magistrate to back an Irish warrant is a power which he is under a duty to exercise **[404]** if the warrant is in order and duly authenticated. If Parliament had contemplated that the magistrate should go into the merits or consider whether a prima facie case existed it would have provided some machinery for this purpose, but there is no provision for the person tendering the warrant to submit evidence on the merits nor for the magistrate to hold any kind of hearing before backing the warrant. In any case one must, I think, construe these Acts in the light of the circumstances prevailing when they were enacted. In the mid-19th century it may have been thought that warrants issued in Ireland should be enforced in England as readily as warrants issued, for example, in Wales or in the Isle of Man; and if, as I venture to think, the situation has now radically changed it is for Parliament and not for the courts to alter the law. Accordingly, I would dismiss the application.

Writ of habeas corpus ad subjiciendum filed.
Applicant discharged out of custody.
Order for costs against the respondent.
Leave to appeal refused.

March 19. The Appeal Committee of the House of Lords (Lord Reid, Lord Guest and Lord Upjohn) gave leave to the Metropolitan Police Commissioner to appeal.

Solicitors: *Howard, Kennedy & Co.; Solicitors, Metropolitan Police.*

[22] 5 App. Cas. 214.
[23] Ibid. 241

METROPOLITAN POLICE COMMISSIONER v. HAMMOND

[Appeal in *Reg.* v. *Metropolitan Police Commissioner. Ex parte* Hammond]

([1965] A.C. 810)

April 21, 22, June 4, 1964: House of Lords: Lords Reid, Morris of Borth-y-Gest, Hodson, Pearce, Donovan.

Fugitive Offender—Ireland, Republic of—Warrant issued by justice in Ireland —Person named in warrant Englishman—Endorsed in Ireland for execution in England—Endorsement by deputy commissioner of Garda Siochana—Automatic endorsement by English magistrate on production of warrant and proof of signature of issuing justice—Whether discretion in magistrate—Whether proof of compliance with statutory requirements and prima facie necessary—Whether signature by deputy commissioner of Garda Siochana sufficient—Indictable Offences Act, 1848 (11 & 12 *Vict. c.* 42), *s.* 12—*Petty Sessions* (*Ireland*) *Act,* 1851 (14 & 15 *Vict. c.* 93), *s.* 27 (3)—*Irish Free State* (*Consequential Provisions*) *Act,* 1922 (13 *Geo.* 5, *c.* 2), *s.* 6—*Irish Free State* (*Consequential Adaptation of Enactments*) *Order,* 1923 (*S.R. & O.*, 1923, *No.* 405), *art.* 8—*Magistrates' Courts Act,* 1952 (15 & 16 *Geo.* 6 & 1 *Eliz.* 2, *c.* 55), *Sch.* 5.

A warrant was issued by a justice of a district court in the Republic of Ireland for the arrest of the respondent, an Englishman, charged with an indictable misdemeanour in Ireland contrary to a statute which had been superseded in England before the warrant was issued. The warrant was endorsed in Ireland by a deputy commissioner of the Garda Siochana for execution in England, and was **[811]** accompanied by proof of the signature of the issuing justice in the form provided by the Petty Sessions (Ireland) Act, 1851. An English magistrate, having before him nothing but the warrant and proof of signature, automatically endorsed the warrant for execution and the respondent was arrested by the metropolitan police. He applied for, and was granted, a writ of habeas corpus directed to the Commissioner of Metropolitan Police, and, on the return to the writ, contended that the arrest was unlawful since the English magistrate had a discretion, which he had not exercised, under section 12 of the Indictable Offences Act, 1848,[1] as amended, or section 27 (3) of the Petty Sessions (Ireland) Act, 1851,[2] whether or not to endorse the warrant, and also to invite the respondent to appear and give reasons why the warrant should not be endorsed. For the Commissioner it

[1] Indictable Offences Act, 1848 (as amended by Magistrates' Courts Act, 1952, Sch. 5), s. 12: ". . . if any person against whom a warrant shall be issued in any county or place in Ireland, by any justice of the peace . . . for any crime or offence against the laws of that part of the United Kingdom, shall escape, go into, reside or be, or be supposed or suspected to be, in any county . . . in that part of the United Kingdom called England and Wales, it shall and may be lawful for any justice of the peace in and for the county . . . into which such person shall escape or go, or where he shall reside or be, or be supposed or suspected to be, to make an indorsement (K) on the warrant, signed with his name, authorising the execution of the warrant . . . which warrant so indorsed shall be a sufficient authority to the person . . . bringing such warrant . . . and also to all constables . . . of the county . . . where such warrant shall be so indorsed, to execute the said warrant . . . and to convey him before the justice . . . who granted the same . . ."

[2] Petty Sessions (Ireland) Act, 1851, s. 27: ". . . (3) . . . Whenever it shall appear" [that the person named on the warrant is] "to be found in some place in England . . . it shall be lawful for the . . . inspector general, or for either of the . . . deputy inspectors general . . . to indorse the warrant . . . and it shall thereupon be lawful for any justice . . . having power to issue any warrant . . . in" [England] . . . "upon proof on oath of the handwriting either of the inspector or deputy inspector general . . . or of the justice by whom the warrant shall have been issued, to indorse the same . . ."

was contended that the English magistrate had no jurisdiction to inquire into the facts or to do other than endorse the warrant. The Divisional Court ordered the respondent's discharge from custody.

On appeal to the House of Lords:—

Held, (1) that notwithstanding section 12 of the Act of 1848 (as amended), the provisions of section 27 (3) of the Act of 1851 must be complied with (post, pp. 830, 833, 839).

(2) That, accordingly, the arrest of the respondent could not be ordered in the absence of the endorsement of the warrant by the inspector general, notwithstanding that that office had disappeared with the Royal Irish Constabulary in 1922, since there was no provision in English law for indorsement in Ireland by a deputy commissioner of the Garda Siochana (post, pp. 832, 839). Accordingly, the respondent was entitled to his discharge from custody. **[812]**

Per curiam. A magistrate in England has no power under these provisions to inquire whether a prima facie case is made out against the alleged offender (post, pp. 837, 838), in contrast to the procedure provided by the Fugitive Offenders Act, 1881 (post, pp. 827, 838).

Decision of the Divisional Court* [1964] 2 Q.B. 385; [1964] 2 W.L.R. 777; [1964] 1 All E.R. 821, D.C. affirmed.

APPEAL from the Divisional Court of the Queen's Bench Division (Finnemore, Paull and Widgery JJ.).

On December 23, 1963, the following warrant was issued at Dublin in the Republic of Ireland: "The district court. Warrant to arrest. The Attorney-General at the suit of Superintendent Patrick Mullaney, Garda Siochana, Howth, complainant *v.* Peter David Hammond," [the respondent], "defendant. District court area of Howth. District No. 10. Whereas a complaint has been made on oath and in writing that" the respondent, "being a person over the age of 17 years, and having the custody of two children, Kimberley Hammond and Joan Hammond, both under the age of 17 years, did, within the six months preceding December 16, 1963, at No. 14, Railway Avenue, Sutton, County Dublin, in the said court area and district, wilfully neglect said children in such a manner likely to cause them unnecessary suffering or injury to their health, contrary to section 12 of the Children Act, 1908, as amended by section 4 of the Children (Amendment) Act, 1957. This is to command you to whom this warrant is addressed to arrest" the respondent, "of Maida Car Hire, 1, Fernhead Road, London, W.9, and to bring him without any delay before me or another justice or some peace commissioner to be dealt with according to law. Donnchadg Ua Donnchadha, justice of the district court. To the superintendent of the Garda Siochana at Howth and his assistants." The warrant was attached to a form headed "Petty Sessions Act, 1851, 14 & 15 Vict. c. 93," and the signature of Donnchadg Ua Donnchadha on the warrant was verified on oath on the form by a sergeant of the Garda Siochana on January 22, 1964. On January 28, 1964, the superintendent of the Garda Siochana, by endorsement on the warrant, certified that he had reason to believe that the person against whom the warrant was issued was to be found at the address stated in England. On January 30, 1964, the deputy commissioner of the Garda Siochana endorsed the warrant for execution in the London metropolitan police district, London, in England, and forwarded **[813]** it and the attachment to the Metropolitan Police Commissioner, New Scotland Yard.

On February 7, 1964, a station police sergeant of the metropolitan police brought the warrant and attachment before the Marylebone magistrate, Walter Frampton, who endorsed the warrant in the following terms: "Whereas proof upon oath hath this day been given to me, one of the magistrates of the magistrates' courts of the metropolis sitting at the Marylebone magistrates' court and within the metropolitan police district that the name of Donnchadg Ua Donnchadha to the within warrant subscribed, is of the handwriting of the district justice within mentioned; I do therefore hereby authorise the station police sergeant who bringeth me this warrant and all other persons to whom this warrant was originally directed, or by whom it may lawfully be executed, and also all constables of the metropolitan police force, to execute the same within the said metropolitan police district." At 3 p.m. on February 7, 1964, the respondent was arrested and taken to Harrow Road police station, where he was kept in custody.

On February 8, 1964, the respondent applied for a writ of habeas corpus, and deposed as follows: "I was married on November 19, 1955, at a church in Scottow, Norfolk, to Sheila Anne Hammond, who, I believe, resides now at 14, Railway Avenue, which is the home of her parents; Kimberley Anne, born on September 25, 1957, is a child of my marriage, but I have never admitted, and dispute, paternity of Joan, born on March 17, 1960; I believe the children are living with my wife; I ceased to cohabit with my wife at the end of 1959, when she left with the child from our house in Rochester, Kent, to return to Eire to her parents; there have been no proceedings in any court concerning my marriage or the children or either of them; I intend to bring divorce proceedings against my wife on the ground of adultery; until approximately February, 1961, my wife was receiving my navy allowance of £6 a week, but that ceased in that month; at the end of the year 1960 my wife received my gratuity of £90 on my discharge from the navy on medical grounds; I have written to my wife but received no reply, and sent £15 in 1963 to her; I was last in Eire in March, 1960, when I saw my wife and tried to effect a reconciliation; at this time my wife told me that Kimberley was very well; I have received no letters, complaints or requests from my wife or any one for money for the children and thought that my wife was caring for them from her earnings from employment; **[814]** no particulars of the offence alleged against me appear on the warrant, and I am unable to know the nature of the complaint made against me." There was no challenge to the facts so deposed to. On February 8, 1964, Streatfeild J., in chambers, ordered that a writ of habeas corpus issue, directed to the Metropolitan Police Commissioner, to have the body of the respondent before the Court. On February 10, 1964, the writ was issued. The return to the writ was made by the appellant, Joseph Simpson, Metropolitan Police Commissioner.

On February 18, 1964, a Divisional Court, by a majority (Finnemore and Paull JJ., Widgery J. dissenting), ordered that the respondent be forthwith discharged.

An application for leave to appeal was refused.

On March 19, 1964, the Appeal Committee of the House of Lords granted the appellant leave to appeal.

H. A. P. Fisher Q.C. and *H. J. Leonard* for the appellant. This appeal raises the question of the mutual backing of warrants between England and the Republic of Ireland. The system of backing warrants is the only procedure in either country by which a person accused can be returned. Neither the Fugitive Offenders Act, 1881, nor the Extradition Act, 1870, applies to the Republic.

Backing procedure rests on the Indictable Offences Act, 1848, an English statute, and the Petty Sessions (Ireland) Act, 1851, an Irish Act, which, save in respect of the backing provisions contained therein, does not apply to England.

Originally, magistrates in England only had local jurisdiction and a warrant was only maintainable in the jurisdiction of the issuing magistrate. There grew up administratively a practice, where the accused had left the jurisdiction of the issuing magistrate and gone to another part of England, for a justice, who had jurisdiction over the territory where the accused was known to be, to back or indorse the warrant so that it could be executed there. From the reign of King George II the position as between counties in England was governed by statute and subsequently the same statutory procedure was adopted as between England and Scotland and Scotland and Ireland. Backing is a purely administrative act and the magistrate was not called upon to follow any form of judicial inquiry. Where Parliament intends that a judicial inquiry shall take place before a warrant is backed, it expressly so provides: see, for example, the Extradition Act 1870, and the Fugitive Offenders Act, 1881 **[815]** For the pre-statutory position regarding the backing of warrants, see Blackstone's Commentaries on the Laws of England, 8th ed. (1778), Vol. 4, pp. 291, 292.

The first English statute to authorise the practice of backing warrants as between counties was 23 Geo. 2, c. 26 (1750), s. 11. This was limited to escapes, that is, where the offender had physically gone out of the county where it was desired to charge him into another county. The words "shall and may be lawful" in that section also occur in section 11 of the Act of 1848, and therefore the pre-1848 authorities on those words are applicable in considering that Act. The preamble to 24 Geo. 2, c. 55 (1751), recites the substantive part of 23 Geo. 2, c. 26, s. 11, and the statute thereupon authorises the backing of warrants in respect of offenders who "escape, go into, reside or be in any other county . . ." out of the jurisdiction of the magistrate granting the warrant. Sections 2 and 3 make it plain that the indorsing magistrate is not liable in respect of his action in indorsing the warrant and therefore shows that his act is a purely ministerial act: see *Clark* v. *Woods.*[3] Section 4 repeals section 11 of the Act of 1750.

13 Geo. 3, c. 31 (1773), applies the backing proceeding between England and Scotland and vice versa in respect of offenders who from one kingdom "escape, go into, reside or be in" the other. 44 Geo. 3, c. 92 (1804), is the first of these statutes which relates to Ireland. Section 1 brought into force in respect of counties in Ireland the same procedure as had previously been enacted in relation to counties in England. By section 2 magistrates who endorsed warrants were made not liable to actions in respect thereof. Sections 3 and 4 made provision respectively for offenders escaping from Ireland into Great Britain to be apprehended and conveyed to Ireland and for offenders escaping from Great Britain into Ireland to be apprehended and conveyed back in like manner.

45 Geo. 3, c. 92 (1805), which amended 13 Geo. 3, c. 31, and 44 Geo. 3, c. 92, by section 1 introduced a provision for admitting persons to bail if the offence was bailable by law. By section 6, where a warrant was to be acted upon in any part of the United Kingdom, apart from that in which it was originally issued, proof was required that the signature of the issuing magistrate was genuine. 54 Geo. 3, c. 186 (1814), applied 13 Geo. 3, c. 31, generally as between England, Scotland and Ireland: see sections 1 and 2. **[816]**

The above was the statutory position until the enactment of the Indictable Offences Act, 1848, section 34 of which repealed the previous Acts except 24 Geo. 2, c. 55, which was repealed by the Statute Law Revision Act, 1867. Section 11 of the Act of 1848 prescribes the procedure to be followed in backing warrants and it expressly provides that the endorsing magistrate need only be satisfied of the genuineness of the handwriting of the magistrate issuing the warrant before endorsing it. The form of the warrant is set out in Form K of the Schedule to the Act. The section has a wider ambit than the earlier enactments, for it relates to offenders who shall "escape, go into, reside or be, or be supposed or suspected to be, in any place in England or Wales out of the jurisdiction" of the issuing magistrate.

Section 12 provides, inter alia, for the backing of Irish warrants in England, and a warrant endorsed in England by a magistrate as prescribed by section 11 is sufficient authority to the persons whose duty it is to execute it (however bad the warrant may be), provided the endorsing magistrate is satisfied of the authenticity of the signature of the issuing magistrate. Any question of invalidity is for the Irish courts to decide. The words in section 12 "it shall and may be lawful" show that it is a ministerial duty that a magistrate carries out in endorsing a warrant. The Act of 1848 shows that the procedure of backing was to make more effective the process of bringing the person charged to the place where the issuing magistrate sits. The place of endorsement is not the place where the validity of the warrant or the strength of the charges preferred against the offender named in the warrant should be investigated.

In 1922 the Irish Free State came into existence. By paragraph 8 (1) (*a*) of the Irish Free State (Consequential Adaptation of Enactments) Order, 1923 (S.R. & O. 1923, No. 450), made pursuant to section 6 of the Irish Free State (Con-

[3] (1848) 2 Ex. 395.

sequential Provisions) Act, 1922 (Session 2), it was provided that the provisions of any enactments applicable to the endorsement and execution in England of warrants issued by justices' courts or judges of courts in Ireland should apply to warrants issued by justices' courts or judges of courts in the Irish Free State. Section 49 and the Third Schedule of the Criminal Justice Act, 1925, repealed section 11 of the Indictable Offences Act, 1848, except so far as it was applied by any other provision of the Act or by any other enactment.

In 1949 the Irish Free State, then known as Eire, became a republic. By section 3 (1) (*a*) (iii) of the Ireland Act, 1949, it **[817]** was provided that the operation of Orders in Council "made under sections 5 and 6 of the Irish Free State (Consequential Provisions) Act, 1922 (Session 2) is not affected by the fact that the Republic of Ireland is not part of His Majesty's dominions."

Section 132 and the Sixth Schedule of the Magistrates' Courts Act, 1952, repealed for all purposes section 11 of the Act of 1848, for it repeals the whole of that Act save sections 12 to 15, sections 30 to 32 and Form K. Section 12 itself was slightly amended by section 131 and the Fifth Schedule of the Act. It will be seen, therefore, that section 12 of the Act of 1848 is still in force as a self-contained provision and that the legislature has preserved it and went to the trouble of amending it in 1952 despite the changed status of Ireland. It is submitted that the provisions of section 12 are applicable to the present warrant. It may be that there is no longer a statutory requirement, which was fulfilled here, for the endorsing magistrate to be satisfied *on oath* of the genuineness of the signature of the issuing magistrate, but see Form K, which is preserved by the Act of 1952.

It is submitted, however, that the endorsing magistrate has only to satisfy himself that the warrant is a warrant and, if he is so satisfied and thereupon endorses it, that constitutes a sufficient return to an application for a writ of habeas corpus. This contention is reinforced by an examination of the language of section 39 of the Criminal Justice (Scotland) Act, 1963, for in relation to the execution of Scottish warrants in England and vice versa it provides that a warrant may be executed by virtue of this section whether or not it has been endorsed under section 14 or section 15 of the Indictable Offences Act, 1848, which shows that Parliament cannot have considered that backing constituted anything in the nature of a judicial inquiry but rather that it is considered as an alternative to service.

If the above argument be rejected then the appellant relies on the Petty Sessions (Ireland) Act, 1851. This is a consolidating Act. It would be surprising if it altered English law, since it relates to Irish provisions: see the long title. Section 47 provides that the Act shall extend and be construed to extend to Ireland only, save as regards the provisions concerning the backing and execution of warrants.

Sections 10 and 11 authorise any justice in Ireland to issue a warrant on information that any person has committed or is suspected of having committed an offence, inter alia, within the **[818]** jurisdiction of such justice. By section 25 (2) the warrant is to be addressed for execution to the sub-inspector or head constable of constabulary of the petty sessions district concerned. Section 26 (3) provides that if the offender is "not to be found in the county" to which such sub-inspector shall belong this officer shall transmit the warrant to the inspector general of constabulary for backing. Section 27 (3) provides that when the warrant has been received by the inspector general and it shall appear that the person against whom it has been issued is "to be found in some place in England . . . it shall be lawful for the said inspector general . . . to endorse the warrant . . . and it shall thereupon be lawful for any justice . . . in any of the said places" (which include England) "upon proof on oath of the handwriting either of the inspector general by whom the same shall have been endorsed or of the justice by whom the warrant shall have been issued to endorse the same . . ." The terms of the subsection are quite general and it is not limited to offenders who "escape." Sections 31 and 39 show that the legislature is not laying down a mandatory procedure but is prescribing the steps necessary to authorise an arrest and detention.

The Act of 1851 cannot be taken to repeal by implication section 12 of the Act of 1848, for in 1952 Parliament amended section 12, showing that Parliament treated the section as still being in force. An earlier statute is repealed by a later statute if it is inconsistent with it, but the courts will lean against an implied repeal. Where there are two affirmative enactments they will be construed side by side and the courts will not consider the earlier of the two Acts as repealed by the later. The repealing provision of the Act of 1851, section 47, is expressly related to statutes relating to Ireland and it does not refer to the Act of 1848. This is a strong indication against any implied repeal of the Act of 1848. There is no inconsistency between the two Acts in relation to the powers and duties of English magistrates. On repeal by implication, see Maxwell on the Interpretation of Statutes, 11th ed., p. 156 et seq.

Section 27 (3) of the Act of 1851 gives an option, since the warrant may be lawfully executed in England if the English magistrate is satisfied on oath of the handwriting either of the inspector general who endorsed it or of the justice who issued it. If the latter option is taken then the backing of the warrant by the inspector general is idle and this supports the contention that in passing the Act of 1851 the legislature was mindful that the **[819]** Act of 1848 was still operative and therefore provision was made for alternative procedures.

The majority of the Divisional Court held (1), that before endorsing the warrant the English magistrate ought to have satisfied himself that there was a prima facie case against the respondent that he had committed an offence in Ireland. (2) That the statutes only apply where there is an element of escape and that before making his endorsement the magistrate must satisfy himself that such an element exists. (3) That the procedure required to be followed had not been followed.

(1) It is conceded that the magistrate did not conduct an inquiry in this case. His function is ministerial and once he is satisfied of the authenticity of the warrant he is bound to endorse it: see *Clark* v. *Woods*[4]; *Murphy* v. *Brooks.*[5] The proceedings before the magistrate are ex parte and it is not considered necessary to have a hearing inter partes.

The Fugitive Offenders Act, 1881, prescribes an entirely different procedure from the present: see Part I, sections 2, 3, 5, 6 and 10. Part II is more akin to the backing procedure: see sections 12, 13 and 19. The Extradition Act, 1870, is also entirely distinct and there the Act only applies if a treaty has been made with the extraditing power.

(2) Paull J.[6] placed reliance on the sidenote to section 12 of the Act of 1848 as showing that the section is concerned with offenders who escape from one country to the other. But sidenotes cannot be used as an aid to construction: see *per* Lord Reid in *Chandler* v. *Director of Public Prosecutions.*[7] This very question of escape was expressly raised in relation to the Act of 1804 (44 Geo. 3, c. 92) in the case of the *Hon. Mr. Justice Johnson*[8] where it was contended on behalf of the applicant that the scope of that Act was limited to persons who had been corporally present in the jurisdiction of the country seeking the warrant, but this argument was rejected in all three Irish courts. The judgment of Daly J.[9] in the Court of King's Bench in Ireland is adopted as part of this argument. There is nothing in that judgment relating to the construction of the preamble to the Act of 1804, namely, that where the enacting words are unambiguous they cannot be cut down by the preamble, which is contrary to what was held in *Attorney-General* v. *Prince Ernest Augustus of* **[820]** *Hanover*[10]* concerning the assistance to be obtained from the preamble to a statute.

Under the Extradition Act, 1870, a person can be extradited for committing a crime in another country even although he has never been physically present

[4] 2 Ex. 395.
[5] 1935 S.C. (Court of Justiciary) 11.
[6] [1964] 2 Q.B. 385, 394.
[7] [1964] A.C. 763, 789; [1962] 3 W.L.R. 694; [1962] 3 All E.R. 142, H.L.
[8] (1805) 29 St.Tr. 81.
[9] Ibid. 180 et seq.
[10] [1957] A.C. 436; [1957] 2 W.L.R. 1; [1957] 1 All E.R. 49, H.L.

in that country: *Reg.* v. *Nillins*[11]* which was approved in *Rex* v. *Godfrey*.[12]* On these authorities it is plain that Finnemore J.'s view[13] that the basis of the present procedure is one for the return of fugitive offenders, and, therefore, that there must be an element of escape before the procedure can be put into operation, is wrong even in relation to an alleged crime of omission.

(3) If the House holds that the Act of 1848 is to be operated as limited by the Act of 1851 the question arises whether the procedure laid down by the latter Act was followed. It is submitted that under section 27 (3) of the Act of 1851 the inspector general's duty is equally ministerial with that of the justice. It would be very strange if the inspector general had a discretion in a matter initiated by a judicial process. The Petty Sessions (Ireland) Act, 1867, amended the Act of 1851 by providing that in the absence of the inspector general and deputy inspector general warrants may be backed by any one of the assistant inspectors general. A further extension of powers was given by section 6 of the Constabulary (Ireland) Act, 1882.

In 1922 the Royal Irish Constabulary was disbanded: the Constabulary (Ireland) Act, 1922, s. 1, by S.R. & O. 1922, No. 1441, the date of disbandment was fixed at August 31, 1922, and thereafter there was no longer an inspector general, deputy inspector general or assistant inspector general and, accordingly, the procedure prescribed by the Act of 1851 could not be followed. But see paragraph 8 of the Irish Free State (Consequential Adoption of Enactments) Order, 1923 (S.R. & O. 1923, No. 405), which was confirmed by the Ireland Act, 1949.

It may be said that the Order of 1923 was in this connection a dead letter from the start. This conclusion can be circumvented by holding (a) that the Act of 1848 was always a separate procedure and that when the Act of 1851 could no longer be operated the Act of 1848 came into operation again, or (b) that the provision in the Act of 1851 that a warrant was to travel to the English magistrate via the inspector general was a matter of local machinery in Ireland and that if the appropriate legislative **[821]** authority in Ireland substituted a different form of machinery that that was sufficient for an English magistrate proceeding under the Act of 1851.

The present police force in Ireland is governed by the Irish Free State Constitution Act, 1922, and the Garda Siochana Act, 1924 (No. 25 of 1924): see sections 2, 3 (1), 19 and Schedule 1 of the latter Act. The Courts of Justice Act, 1924 (No. 10 of 1924) provided by sections 90, 91 and 92 for the making of rules for the District Court. Rule 41 of the District Court Rules, 1926, prescribed the procedure to be followed when a warrant was addressed to a superintendent or inspector of the Garda Siochana for execution, and when the offender could not be found within the state but might be found within another state under whose laws the warrant was capable of being executed. The matter is now governed by the District Court Rules, 1948, rr. 1 (3) and 74, under which a superintendent or inspector is to certify according to a prescribed form and is to certify that he believes the signature to the warrant to be genuine, and the warrant is then to be transmitted to the "Commissioner of the Garda Siochana" who in turn (or a deputy commissioner, or, in their absence, an assistant commissioner), is to endorse the warrant according to a prescribed form, for execution in such other state. The prescribed forms are in substantially the same form except in regard to the persons who are to sign them, as the forms prescribed by the Act of 1851 (Forms Gb and Gc).

The Act of 1851 only applies to England in so far as it is necessary for the purpose of backing warrants. It cannot be a matter of English law how the warrant is dealt with in Ireland—the local Irish machinery is part of Irish law, and this was properly amended by the Irish statutes on the advent of the Irish Free State which substituted new ranks for the old Irish constabulary. Finally, there is a well-known distinction between mandatory and directory provisions in statutes. A consideration of the subject-matter of section 27 of the Act of 1851 shows that it is a directory and not a mandatory provision. Here, the

[11] (1884) 53 L.J.(M.C.) 157.
[12] [1923] 1 K.B. 24; 39 T.L.R. 5, D.C. [13] [1964] 2 Q.B. 385, 399.

duty is given to the magistrate and if he is satisfied that there has been compliance with the provisions of the Act that is sufficient for present purposes: *The King* v. *Commissioner of Metropolitan Police, Ex parte Nalder.*[14]* [Reference was also made to *The State* (*Dowling*) v. *Brennan and Kingston.*[15]] **[822]**

Dick Taverne for the respondent. There are two submissions: (1) the Act of 1851 as it stands cannot be applied in England without amending legislation, and the Act of 1851 is the relevant Act since it modifies the operation of the Act of 1848. (2) The endorsing magistrate has a limited discretion.

(1) When the Act of 1851 was passed a new safeguard was provided and unless the 1851 procedure is substituted for the 1848 procedure the additional provisions would be quite otiose. An additional safeguard was that the inspector general or his deputy had a discretion in respect of the signing of the warrant. Under section 27 (3) the inspector general was required to be satisfied that the person named in the warrant was abroad. A warrant is to be endorsed either by the inspector general or by one of his two deputies: section 27 (3). If the appellant be right, a different officer could be substituted by Irish legislation, with quite different powers and possibly subject to no control, which might affect a person in England. It is unthinkable that the Irish Parliament could legislate for England. It is submitted that the Irish provisions relating to commissioners *do* alter the law. Under rule 74 (3) of the District Court Rules, 1948, no discretion is given to the officer concerned with this particular task; the words "shall be endorsed" leave no right of discretion.

The difficulties mentioned in *The State* (*Dowling*) v. *Brennan and Kingston*[16] apply even more cogently to the position of an English magistrate who is requested to endorse a warrant, for he does not know the Irish law, and there is no English provision comparable to section 11 of the Adaptation of Enactments Act, 1922 (No. 2 of 1922) and therefore the appellant is in an even more difficult position than was the respondent in that case.[17]

In paragraph 8 of the Irish Free State (Consequential Adaptation of Enactments) Order, 1923, provision is made that references to Ireland shall be read as references to the Irish Free State, but nowhere in that order is there a provision that the commissioner is to be substituted where there are references to the inspector general. The Act of 1851 has not been repealed but at the present time its provisions cannot be complied with. Further, the Fugitive Offenders Act, 1881, has no application to the present case.

(2) Under the Act of 1848 magistrates were given a limited discretion In earlier statutes there is a significant difference **[823]** in language between those provisions relating to the backing of warrants as between counties and those relating to backing as between different parts of the United Kingdom. Thus 24 Geo. 2, c. 55 (1751) states that the endorsing magistrate or magistrates "*is and are hereby required*, upon proof being made upon oath, of the handwriting" of the issuing magistrate to endorse the same. It is quite plain that under that Act the endorsing magistrate is performing a purely ministerial act for all that he has to be satisfied of is the handwriting of the magistrate granting the warrant. It was that statute which was construed in *Clark* v. *Woods*[18] and, accordingly, the authority of that decision is limited to between-counties procedure.

13 Geo. 3, c. 31 (1773) relates to Scotland. The preamble makes it plain that it concerns persons who escape from one jurisdiction to the other. This Act provides that *"it shall and may be lawful"* for a magistrate to back a warrant in the prescribed circumstances. There is no provision of the magistrate being *required* to endorse it. Further, there is no provision akin to section 2 of 24 Geo. 2, c. 55, that the endorsing magistrate shall not be liable to an action for trespass or false imprisonment.

44 Geo. 3, c. 92 (1804) concerns Ireland. Section 1 relates to backing as between counties in Ireland. The endorsing magistrate or magistrates "is and

[14] [1948] 1 K.B. 251, 255; 63 T.L.R. 591; [1947] 2 All E.R. 611, D.C.
[15] [1937] I.R. 483.
[16] [1937] I.R. 483, 502, 505.
[17] [1937] I.R. 483
[18] 2 Ex. 395.

are hereby required" to endorse the same on proof upon oath of the handwriting of the issuing magistrate. Section 2 provides that the magistrate endorsing the warrant shall not be liable to an action for trespass or false imprisonment, and plainly this provision only refers to warrants covered by section 1 where the endorsing magistrate performs a purely ministerial act. There is a significant change of language in section 3 which relates to the backing of warrants in England: "it shall and may be lawful." This is discretionary and there is no provision exempting the endorsing magistrate from actions.

In the Act of 1848 there is again a contrast in the language used in the different sections of the Act. Thus, section 3, which relates to the issuing of warrants to apprehend a party against whom an indictment is found, states that the magistrate or magistrates "he and they are hereby required" to issue his or their warrant to apprehend the person indicated. In section 11, however, which relates to the backing of warrants as between counties in England the phrase used is, "it shall and may be lawful," which is discretionary. The same phrase occurs in section 12, which is the relevant section. The words in section 12 **[824]** "in the manner hereinbefore mentioned" do not relate solely to the proof of the signature of the issuing magistrate. Reliance is placed on the form that the amendment of section 12 took in the Fifth Schedule to the Magistrates' Courts Act, 1925.

[Reference was made to section 16 of and Form K in the Schedule to the Indictable Offences Act, 1848.]

In the scheme of this series of Acts section 12 of the Act of 1848 would seem to presuppose the person named in the warrant residing in England after his departure from the place where the offence was alleged to have been committed. In other words, it presupposes that at some time the person charged was residing in Ireland. For the purposes of the section an actual escape is not necessary, but the person charged must have been physically present in Ireland and thereafter there occurred his departure for England. If that be so then the requirements of section 12 have not been complied with here. The warrant must show on its face that the person named therein was physically present in Ireland at the time when the offence was alleged to have been committed.

Under section 12 the English magistrate has a discretion whether or not to endorse the warrant. Here, the magistrate did not exercise that discretion and, accordingly, habeas corpus lies. Further, section 11 of the Act of 1851 requires the warrant to "state shortly the cause of complaint." There was here a lack of particularity. The magistrate was under a duty to ascertain whether the warrant sufficiently showed that during the specified period the respondent was in Ireland wilfully neglecting his children as alleged.

Fisher Q.C. in reply. As to discretion, under the Act of 1848 any difference in backing procedure between warrants relating to different counties and those relating to different countries has gone: see sections 11, 12, 13, 14 and 15. There is no difference in the language in these sections on the question relevant here. In all cases a warrant is to be backed in the manner prescribed in Form K, which only requires the endorsing magistrate to be satisfied on oath of the handwriting of the issuing justice. For what appears to be the granting of a real discretion by this Act, see the opening words of section 16, which is a provision empowering magistrates to summon witnesses to attend and give evidence.

There is no method by which a magistrate can satisfy himself of matters apart from those questions which arise on the face of the warrant. In view of the terms of section 12 and Form K **[825]** there are no circumstances in which an endorsing magistrate could bring the person charged before him.

As to escape, this argument is completely answered by the *Johnson* case[19] which relied on the argument that plain enacting words are not cut down by the preamble—a principle of construction approved by this House in the *Prince of Hanover* case.[20]* It is to be remembered that the *Johnson* case[21] was a decision on the pre-1848 statutes relied on by the respondent here. Further, in

19 29 St.Tr. 81.
20 [1957] A.C. 436.
21 29 St.Tr. 81.

relation to the Act of 1851, sections 26 and 27 relate to goods as well as to persons and, therefore, those provisions cannot be limited to cases involving an element of escape.

As to whether the cause of complaint is sufficiently set out in the warrant, the judgment of Widgery J.[22] is adopted.

Their Lordships took time for consideration.

1964. June 4. Lord Reid. My Lords, in this case a warrant to arrest the respondent was granted on December 23, 1963, by the district judge at Howth in County Dublin. That warrant was forwarded to the appellant with two endorsements. The first was a certificate by a superintendent of the Garda Siochana that he had reason to believe that the respondent was to be found at 1, Fernhead Road, London, W.9, and that he believed the signature of the district judge to be genuine. The second was signed by a deputy commissioner of the Garda Siochana and stated "I hereby endorse the within warrant for execution in the London Metropolitan Police District London England." The warrant so endorsed was presented to a magistrate in the Marylebone Magistrates Court on February 7, 1964, and he thereupon authorised the arrest of the respondent. The respondent was arrested the same day and he would forthwith have been taken in custody to the Republic of Ireland but for the issue of a writ of habeas corpus at the instance of his solicitors. On February 18, 1964, a Divisional Court by a majority (Finnemore and Paull JJ. Widgery J. dissenting) ordered that the respondent be forthwith discharged.

An application by the appellant for leave to appeal was granted by this House. Assurances have been given by the authorities in the Republic of Ireland that in the event of this appeal succeeding no further warrant in this matter would be forwarded for execution here, so the respondent has no substantial personal interest. But the appeal raises a very important general **[826]** question. It appears that the procedure followed in this case has been regularly followed for many years and we were informed that under it on the average nearly a hundred persons per annum have been sent in custody from this country to the Republic of Ireland.

The question for your Lordships' decision does not depend on the facts of this case, but they give a useful illustration of the problem. We have an affidavit of the respondent sworn the day after he was arrested, and we have the terms of the warrant. The warrant states that a complaint had been made on oath that the respondent, having the custody of two children, did at an address in County Dublin "wilfully neglect said children in such a manner likely to cause them unnecessary suffering or injury to their health." The facts as stated by the respondent are that he was married in this country in 1955, that he works in London, that his wife left him at the end of 1959 and returned to her parents in Ireland, and that he admits paternity of one of the children but disputes paternity of the other, and intends to bring divorce proceedings. He says that he was last in Ireland in March, 1960, when he tried to effect a reconcilation, that he has sent money on various occasions since that time, that he has written to his wife but received no reply, that he has never received from her any letters, complaints or requests for money and that he was unaware of any proceedings in any court.

We do not know that this story is true and probably the facts put before the district judge at Howth were different. But the appellant argues that, even if the respondent's story is accurate in every detail, the law allowed him no opportunity of putting his case to anyone in this country and no opportunity of applying for bail, the magistrate in this country has no right to make any inquiry or to grant bail but must back any warrant sent from the Republic of Ireland by an appropriate officer of the Garda Siochana, at least unless it is plainly bad on its face; and the police must forthwith arrest any person named in the warrant and send him in custody to the Republic of Ireland. Plainly it is of the utmost importance that there should be an authoritative decision whether this really is

[22] [1964] 2 Q.B. 385, 402, 403.

the law because cases of great hardship can easily arise if it is. I wish to make it quite clear that I do not doubt for a moment that justice would be done in the court of the Republic if the accused is able to bring his witnesses from England and pay for his defence. I do not know whether legal aid is available in the Republic. But it is a serious matter if, in a case of this kind, a person can be sent under arrest **[827]** out of Her Majesty's dominions without any warning or any opportunity of preparing or stating his defence or of applying for bail or of representing the hardship which that will involve for him.

Normally persons resident in this country who are accused of an offence in a foreign country are dealt with under the Extradition Act, 1870, which contains elaborate safeguards. And if they are accused of an offence in another part of Her Majesty's dominions they are dealt with under the Fugitive Offenders Act, 1881, which contains very considerable safeguards. Even under the modified scheme for contiguous groups of British possessions under Part II of the Act of 1881 the accused must be brought before a magistrate in the place where he is arrested, and section 19 allows the court to take into account the trivial nature of the case or whether it would be unjust or oppressive to put the warrant into operation immediately or at all. I realise that the Republic of Ireland has always been treated as a special case, and it is quite clear that neither the Extradition Act nor the Fugitive Offenders Act can be applied as they stand to cases like the present. So it would seem that if your Lordships agree that the present appeal must be dismissed it will be necessary to give urgent consideration to the whole matter of sending accused persons from this country to the Republic of Ireland, and in particular to the case of British subjects who have never resided in that part of Ireland or caused anything to be done there.

I have had an opportunity of reading the speech prepared by my noble and learned friend Lord Morris of Borth-y-Gest and I agree that this appeal must be dismissed with costs to the respondent.

LORD MORRIS OF BORTH-Y-GEST. My Lords, the system under which a warrant to arrest issued by a justice in one jurisdiction could be backed by a justice in another jurisdiction within which an alleged offender was said to be, has doubtless been necessary in the interests of justice. It has, therefore, been a desirable system. In earlier times a warrant issued by a justice of the peace in England could only be executed within the area of his local jurisdiction. If, however, after a county justice in one county in England had issued a warrant to arrest an alleged offender such person had been able with impunity to avoid arrest by going to or being in another county, the law would have been mocked and frustrated. Various legislative enactments were therefore introduced which provided for the indorsement of warrants so that they could be acted upon within the area of **[828]** and by virtue of the authority of the indorsing justice. It is not necessary for present purposes to trace the history of these enactments nor the steps by which the system became applicable, not only as between and in reference to places in England and Wales but also as between England and Wales and Scotland, Ireland, the Isle of Man and the Channel Islands. Prior to 1848 there were such statutes as 23 Geo. 2, c. 26, 24 Geo. 2, c. 55, 13 Geo. 3, c. 31, 44 Geo. 3, c. 92, 45 Geo. 3, c. 92 and 54 Geo. 3, c. 186. In 1848 the Indictable Offences Act (11 & 12 Vict. c. 42) was passed. It was an "Act to facilitate the performance of the Duties of Justices of the Peace out of Sessions within *England* and *Wales* with respect to Persons charged with indictable Offences." It was primarily an English Act and nothing in the Act was to be deemed or taken to extend to Scotland or Ireland or the Isles of Man, Jersey or Guernsey save and except the provisions in respect of the backing of warrants (see section 32). Those provisions were contained in sections 12, 13, 14 and 15.

Three years later (in 1851) the Petty Sessions (Ireland) Act (14 & 15 Vict. c. 93) was passed. That was primarily an Irish Act. It was provided (see section 47) that save and except the several provisions respecting the backing and execution of warrants and the taking of examinations it only applied to Ireland.

By section 12 of the Act of 1848 there were mutual provisions for the backing of warrants as between England and Wales on the one hand and Ireland on the other. It was provided that if a warrant should be issued in England or Wales by any justice of the peace or by any judge of Her Majesty's Court of Queen's Bench or justice of oyer and terminer or gaol delivery for any indictable offence "against the laws of that Part of the United Kingdom," and if the person against whom the warrant was issued should "escape, go into, reside, or be, or be supposed or suspected to be" in Ireland, then it should be lawful for any justice of the peace in or for the county or place into which such person should "escape or go, or where he shall reside or be, or be supposed or suspected to be" to indorse the warrant. The endorsement was according to a form known as Form K. The warrant so endorsed was authority to arrest. The arrested person was then to be conveyed before the justice who granted the warrant, or before some other justice in the same county or place. In the same section there were corresponding provisions to deal with the cases of persons against whom a warrant was issued in Ireland (by any justice of the peace or by any judge of Her Majesty's Court of Queen's Bench there) if such person should "escape **[829]** go into, reside, or be, or be supposed or suspected to be" in England or Wales.

The Act of 1851 introduced certain changes. Section 25 dealt with the question of the persons to whom warrants should be addressed. In proceedings as to offences punishable either by indictment or upon summary conviction warrants issued in any petty sessions district were to be addressed to the sub-inspector or head constable of constabulary acting for the place where the petty sessions for such district were held. Then if (see section 26) the person against whom the warrant was issued could not be found in the county to which the sub-inspector or head constable belonged but was to be found elsewhere out of the county, the sub-inspector or head constable was required to certify on the warrant in a prescribed form (Form G b) and to transmit the warrant to the inspector general of the constabulary force to be backed by him. Then by section 27 the manner of backing by the inspector general for execution elsewhere was prescribed. By section 27 (3) it is provided that whenever it shall appear that the person is "to be found in some place in *England* or *Scotland*, or in the *Isles of Man, Guernsey, Jersey, Alderney* or *Sark*, it shall be lawful for the said inspector general, or for either of the said deputy inspectors general, in like manner as before, to indorse the warrant, according to Form (G c), and it shall thereupon be lawful for any justice or officer having power to issue any warrant, or process in the nature of a warrant, for the arrest of offenders in any of the said Places, upon proof on oath of the handwriting either of the inspector or deputy inspector general by whom the same shall have been indorsed or of the justice by whom the warrant shall have been issued, to indorse the same according to the Form (G c), authorising its execution within the jurisdiction of the said justice or officer by the person bringing the same, or by any constable or other peace officer of the county or place where it shall be so indorsed." Section 31 gave authority to execute warrants so endorsed.

It will be seen that though these provisions (contained in sections 25, 26 and 27 of the Act of 1851) introduced the requirement that in certain cases (including the case where the wanted person was in England) warrants could be backed by the inspector general (or one of the deputies), there was no repeal of section 12 of the Act of 1848. Indeed, that section, as I will later mention, remains in force. It does not, however, seem reasonable to suppose that after the passing of the Act of 1851 the procedure **[830]** for the backing of warrants by the inspector general (or one of the deputies) could have been ignored or neglected. The procedure amounted to a safeguard which ensured that statutory conditions were being observed. I consider, therefore, that the position was that regard could not after 1851 have been paid solely to the terms of the Act of 1848 and that the requirements of the Act of 1851 had to be satisfied. When section 27 (3) provided, as recited above, that it should "thereupon be lawful" for the English justice to back a warrant so that an arrest could be made, the word "thereupon" denoted the prior backing by the inspector general or one of the deputies. I cannot, therefore, regard section 12 of the Act of 1848 as being a self-contained provision which could be operated in disregard, after 1851, of the provisions of the Act of 1851.

By the year 1867 the number of deputy inspectors general of constabulary had been reduced to one, but there were three assistant inspectors general, and an Act of 1867 (30 & 31 Vict. c. 19) amended the Act of 1851 so as to give power to one of such assistant inspectors general, in the absence of the inspector general and deputy inspector general, to back warrants and to transmit them for execution in the same way as the latter were authorised to do. By section 6 of the Constabulary (Ireland) Amendment Act, 1882 (45 & 46 Vict. c. 63) it was provided that any acts which might be done by the deputy inspector general (acting instead of the inspector general) might be done by any other officer of the force, not being below the rank of assistant inspector general, who was authorised by writing under the hand of the Lord Lieutenant.

In 1922 came the Act to provide for the Constitution of the Irish Free State (13 Geo. 5 (Session 2), c. 1). By article 73 of the Constitution of the Irish Free State it was provided that subject to the Constitution and to the extent to which they were not inconsistent therewith, the laws in force in the Irish Free State at the time of the coming into operation of the Constitution should continue to be of full force and effect until the same or any of them should have been repealed or amended by the Parliament of the Irish Free State. Thereafter, by section 6 of the Irish Free State (Consequential Provisions) Act, 1922, it was provided that by Orders in Council there could be made such adaptations of any enactment so far as they related to any of the Dominions other than the Irish Free State as were necessary or proper as a consequence of the establishment of the Irish Free State. By the Irish Free State (Consequential Adaptation of Enactments) **[831]** Order, 1923 (S.R. & O. 1923, No. 405) it was provided (inter alia) (see paragraph 8 (1) (*a*)) that the provisions of any enactments applicable to the endorsement and execution in England of warrants issued by justices' courts or judges of courts in Ireland should apply to warrants issued by justices' courts or judges of courts in the Irish Free State. The effect of that provision was to substitute "Irish Free State" for "Ireland," but the procedural requirements of the Act of 1851 remained unaffected.

After the disbandment of the Royal Irish Constabulary there was legislation in the Irish Free State to make permanent provision for the maintenance and regulation of the force of police called the Garda Siochana. At a later date the rule-making authority established under legislation in the Irish Free State made rules which governed the procedure to be followed when a warrant was addressed to a superintendent or inspector of the Garda Siochana for execution, and when the person against whom the warrant was issued could not be found within the State but might be found within another State under whose laws the warrant was capable of being executed. Under the District Court Rules of the Irish Free State of 1948 a superintendent or inspector is to certify according to a prescribed form and is to certify that he believes the signature to the warrant to be genuine and he is to transmit the warrant to "the Commissioner of the Garda Siochana" who in turn (or a deputy commissioner or, in their absence, an assistant commissioner) is to endorse the warrant, according to a prescribed form, for execution in such other State. The prescribed forms (Forms 15 and 16) seem substantially to correspond save in regard to the persons who are to sign them, with the forms prescribed by the Act of 1851 (Forms G b and G c).

Though the legislative provisions made in the Irish Free State to which I have referred were brought to our attention, and though the endorsements which in this case were made upon the warrant to arrest would appear to have been made by the persons referred to in the Irish Free State District Court Rules and would appear to have been made in accordance with the prescribed forms, it is to be observed that the only authority which an English justice can possess is that which is given to him by the provisions of the English Acts to which I have referred. It is to be remembered also that in practice a justice in England would not have knowledge of Irish enactments and would not have the opportunity to consider whether endorsements were in fact made by those who are designated by Irish enactments as being the proper **[832]** persons to make them, and would not know what person or persons should now be substituted for the inspector general or his deputy. Quite apart, however, from this consideration, if the authority which is by statute granted to an English justice for authorising an arrest is made conditional upon his having presented to him a warrant to arrest which has been backed by a specified person, he cannot act unless a warrant is produced to him which is so backed. It cannot avail to say that the warrant has been backed by someone else nor to say that the substitute should be deemed to be the equivalent of or the successor of the specified person. In a matter of such consequence as authorising an arrest pursuant to statutory power no statutory prerequisite can be ignored. If the statute provides that an arrest can be ordered by endorsing a warrant which has the prior endorsement of a designated officer of the Royal Irish Constabulary, and if such prior endorsement does not exist and cannot be forthcoming, then arrest cannot be ordered.

By the Ireland Act, 1949 (12 & 13 Geo. 6, c. 41), it was recognised and declared that the part of Ireland theretofore known as Eire (in any later Act to be referred to as the Republic of Ireland) ceased as from April 18, 1949, to be part of His Majesty's dominions, but it was declared that the Republic of Ireland is not a foreign country.

The Act of 1848 has been affected in important respects by recent Acts. The Criminal Justice Act, 1925 (15 & 16 Geo. 5, c. 86), repealed section 11 (which dealt with the backing by a justice of the peace in one county of England or Wales of a warrant issued by a justice of the peace in another county) except so far as that section was applied by any other provision of the Act or by any other enactment. Section 31 (3) effected the ending of the necessity for backing as between counties in England and Wales. (As between England and Scotland, see now the Criminal Justice (Scotland) Act, 1963 (11 & 12 Eliz. 2, c. 39).) By the Magistrates' Courts Act, 1952 (15 & 16 Geo. 6 & 1 Eliz. 2, c. 55), the whole of the Indictable Offences Act, 1848, was repealed except sections 12 to 15 and 30 to 32 and Form K: certain words in section 30 were also repealed. A consequential amendment was also made to section 12. For the words "indorse (K) such warrant in manner hereinbefore mentioned" there were substituted the words "make an indorsement (K) on the warrant, signed with his name, authorising the execution of the warrant within the jurisdiction of the justice making the indorsement." **[833]**

The position is, therefore, that since 1848 the provisions of section 12 of the Act of 1848 have remained in force (subject to the amendment made in 1952) and (subject to that amendment) still remain in force. So also the relevant provisions of the Act of 1851 (notably sections 25, 26 and 27) have remained and still remain in force. It was submitted on behalf of the appellant that the effectiveness of the backing by the magistrate in London could be supported by having regard solely to section 12 of the Act of 1848 and by depending upon that section. That, however, would involve disregarding the provisions of the Act of 1851 which continue to possess legislative validity. Those provisions (requiring the backing of the inspector general) gave an extra safeguard to ensure that all was in order. They could not have been ignored in the years after 1851. The mere passing of time does not warrant their being ignored now. It was further submitted that matters might proceed on the basis that section 27 of the Act of 1851 prescribed certain local machinery and that there had been legislative changes effected in the Republic of Ireland in regard to such local machinery and to those parts of the procedure which are to be followed in the Republic of Ireland, and that the English magistrate should be content to recognise that changes have been made. Apart from the practical difficulties of ascertaining what changes may have been made in the Republic of Ireland, that would again involve a disregard of the provisions of the Act of 1851 which gave authority to the English magistrate to act. It would mean that the English magistrate was being invited to treat the Act of 1851 as though it had been amended. He clearly could not proceed on such a basis. It was additionally submitted that if in present circumstances the provisions of the Act of 1851 have become of no avail because they cannot be operated without amending legislation, regard might be paid in England solely to the provisions of section 12 of the Act of 1848. This is but another way of submitting that the Act of 1851 should be quietly ignored. The submission cannot be accepted. As a result, I consider that the respondent was entitled to succeed on his application for a writ of habeas corpus on the ground that the statutory prerequisites for the backing by the magistrate in London were not satisfied.

It can truly be said that as section 12 of the Act of 1848 remains in force (subject to the minor amendments effected as recently as 1952) and as sections 25, 26 and 27 (inter alia) of the Act of 1851 remain in force, there is a recognition both in this country and in the Republic of Ireland of a continuing confidence **[834]** in each other's institutions. Indeed, I have no doubt that, though the system of backing warrants began when there was a common legislature for the two countries, some appropriate machinery for the backing of warrants is still desirable in the interests of justice in both countries. This circumstance, however, does not (and particularly in matters affecting the liberty of the subject) justify proceeding other than strictly. If amending legislation is thought to be desirable the features of the present case point to the necessity of devising some procedure to deal with the sort of situation which confronted the respondent. He has sworn an affidavit in which he states that he ceased to cohabit with his wife at the end of 1959. There was then one child of the marriage. He says that his wife then left their home in England and returned to her parents in the Republic of Ireland where another child was born (in March, 1960) whose paternity he does not admit. He states that he intends to bring divorce proceedings against his wife on the ground of her adultery. He says that he was last in the Republic of Ireland in March, 1960, and that he then saw his wife and tried to effect a reconciliation; that until approximately February, 1961, she received his navy allowance of £6 per week and at the end of 1960 received his gratuity of £90 on his discharge from the navy on medical grounds; that he had written to his wife but had received no reply; that he had sent her £15 in 1963 but had received no letters or complaints or requests for money either from her or from anyone else and that he thought that she was caring for the children from her earnings from employment.

If these facts are correct it is startling to think the next episode should be the arrest of the respondent in London without any prior awareness on his part of the issue of a warrant for his arrest in the Republic of Ireland or any knowledge of a suggestion that he had committed in Dublin the offence of wilfully neglecting the two children in a manner likely to cause them unnecessary suffering or injury to their health. Equally startling, if the facts sworn to by the respondent be true, is it to contemplate that without being heard in England and without any opportunity to make any representations to anyone, unless upon application for a writ of habeas corpus and without inquiry by the magistrate and without his necessarily possessing knowledge of the circumstances under which a warrant to arrest could be issued in the Republic of Ireland or as to the jurisdiction of a particular court there, the respondent would be detained by the police in London to await escort from the Garda Siochana and would then be taken in **[835]** custody to Dublin. He would doubtless there be treated fairly and in accordance with law, but even so it seems open to question whether, if the respondent's affidavit is correct, a system would be satisfactory which would in the circumstances of the present case inevitably bring about an arrest which would be followed by inevitable removal in custody across the Irish Sea. The submission of the appellant was that the magistrate in London had no other course open to him than to order the respondent's arrest and that thereafter no consequence could follow other than that the London police should detain and that the Garda Siochana should transport him.

The respondent submitted that no particulars of the offence alleged against him appeared on the warrant issued on December 23, 1963, by the justice of the District Court in the area of Howth and that he was unable to know the nature of the complaint made against him. Reference was made to the requirement of section 11 of the Act of 1851 that a warrant shall state shortly the cause of complaint. I do not think that it was on this ground that the respondent was entitled to succeed on his application for a writ of habeas corpus. The warrant does sufficiently state what was the cause of complaint. Nor do I think that the respondent's entitlement to succeed was on the suggested ground that the procedure of backing warrants only applies where there has been an evasion of arrest amounting in effect to an escape. It was said that the magistrate should not only have considered whether the warrant sufficiently described the alleged offence or sufficiently set out that it had been committed in the Republic of Ireland but that he should have considered whether the respondent had been in the Republic of Ireland. It was submitted that a warrant could only be backed in a case where there had been a physical presence in the one country followed by a departure to the other even though such departure would not in the strictest sense be regarded as an escape. I am unable to take this view. If an offence is alleged to have been committed (and it may be recognised that in some circumstances an offence may be committed in a place without physical presence there) a warrant could under the Acts of 1848 and 1851 be backed, if the alleged offender is in England, without considering whether or not he had sought to evade arrest or had made any journey to evade arrest. The language of section 12 of the Act of 1848 is very wide. It covers persons who escape or go into England: so also does it cover persons who reside in England or who are or are supposed or suspected to be in England. The language of section 27 of **[836]** the Act of 1851 is equally wide; it covers persons who are to be found in England.

It would appear from a consideration of the documents in the present case that matters proceeded in the Republic of Ireland on the basis that the Act of 1851 was being followed but subject to the amendments to that Act which have been made in the Republic of Ireland. The warrant to arrest was addressed to the Superintendent of the Garda Siochana at Howth. The endorsement that he made on the warrant appears to have been made in compliance with rule 74 (3) of the District Court Rules, where it is provided that in the stated events the superintendent "shall certify" and "shall forthwith transmit the warrant to the Commissioner of the Garda Siochana." The endorsement was in the form prescribed (Form 15). The next endorsement (as prescribed by Form 16) appears to have been signed by a deputy commissioner of the Garda Siochana. The wording of rule 74 (3) shows that after transmission of an endorsed warrant to the commissioner "the warrant shall be indorsed (Form 16) by the Commissioner" . . . (or by certain others as specified) . . . for execution in such other State." This wording is to be compared with the wording in section 27 of the Act of 1851. It had in that Act first been provided by section 26 (3) that if a person against whom a warrant had been issued was not to be found in the county but was to be found elsewhere out of the county "the said sub-inspector or head constable shall, as before, certify on the warrant, according to the Form (G b), and forthwith transmit the same to the Inspector General of the Constabulary Force, to be backed as herein-after mentioned." In contrast to that language, when section 27 laid down the manner in which a warrant was to be backed for execution elsewhere, it was provided by subsection (3) that if the person was to be found in England (or in Scotland or in the Isle of Man, Guernsey, Jersey, Alderney or Sark) "It shall be lawful for the said Inspector General, or . . . in like manner as before, to indorse the warrant, according to Form (G c) . . ." The contrast in the Act between the word "shall" when transmitting to the inspector general and the words "it shall be lawful" in reference to an endorsement to be made by him may suggest that the inspector general had a measure of discretion which was something that went beyond being satisfied that the warrant and its endorsement were genuine. If this were so then it is to be noted that the words that follow in subsection (3) are that "it shall thereupon be lawful for any justice . . . having power to issue **[837]** any warrant . . . for the arrest of offenders in any of the said places, upon proof on oath of the handwriting either of the inspector or . . . or of the justice by whom the warrant shall have been issued to indorse the same, according to the Form (G c). . . ." The use again of the words "shall thereupon be lawful" in contrast to the earlier use of the word "shall" may likewise suggest that there is some measure of discretion in the English (or other) justice. It is to be observed, however, that no procedure is established under which a magistrate in England can inquire into the alleged offence or can inquire as to the circumstances under which the person against whom the warrant was issued has come to be within the jurisdiction of the English magistrate. The magistrate must in accordance with the section be satisfied by proof upon oath in regard to handwriting, but he has no opportunity to inquire whether a prima facie case is made out against the alleged offender. It may be, therefore, that the duties of the magistrate are no more than ministerial (compare *Murphy* v. *Brooks*[23]). It is, however, unnecessary to explore further this aspect of the matter or to express a final opinion in regard to it. For the reasons which I have earlier set out I consider that the writ of habeas corpus was properly granted and I would dismiss the appeal.

LORD HODSON. My Lords, the decision in this appeal depends on a very short point which, though technical, is decisive in favour of the respondent if well founded, since where the liberty of the subject is concerned the formalities required must be strictly observed.

The warrant for the arrest of the respondent was signed by a justice of the District Court of Howth and was indorsed by the deputy commissioner of the Garda Siochana upon a certificate signed by a superintendent of the Garda Siochana that the person against whom the warrant was issued is to be found at Maida Car Hire, 1 Fernhead Road, London, W.9., England.

Upon proof upon oath of the signature of the Howth justice, one of the Metropolitan magistrates authorised the execution of the warrant within the Metropolitan Police District.

There can be no doubt that in so doing the magistrate was performing a merely ministerial act, and was not acting judicially in the sense that he was performing a duty to ascertain whether there was a prima facie case for the arrest of the respondent. **[838]** There is nothing in any of the statutes which deals with the backing of warrants as between countries and as between the component parts of the United Kingdom to support the contention that the power conferred on an English magistrate through an Irish warrant is other than a power which he is under a duty to exercise if the warrant is in order and duly authenticated. This procedure, which is essentially domestic in character, is in marked contrast to that provided by the Fugitive Offenders Act, 1881, which though also of a semi-domestic character takes into account the hardship which would be involved in executing warrants in this country issued in a distant part of the world without any check on the process in this country.

The short point which is, I think, fatal to the contention of the Commissioner of Police is to be found by reference to section 27 (3) of the Petty Sessions (Ireland) Act, 1851, which applies only to Ireland except for the provision for the backing and execution of warrants and the taking of examinations. This sub-section provides "whenever it shall appear [to the sub-inspector of Constabulary to whom the warrant has been addressed that the person named on the warrant is] to be found in some place in England . . . it shall be lawful for the inspector general, or either of the deputy inspectors general, . . . to indorse the warrant . . . and it shall thereupon be lawful for any justice . . . having power to issue any warrant, . . . in England upon proof on oath of the handwriting of the inspector general or deputy inspector general . . . or of the justice by whom the warrant shall have been issued to indorse the same."

It is true that proof on oath of the handwriting of the inspector general or deputy inspector general and of the justice by whom the warrant was issued are stated as alternatives, but it is not possible to regard the backing by the inspector general or his deputy as an idle formality although the signature need not be verified. The requirement of endorsement by this officer must have been inserted in the Act of 1851 as a safeguard, and in the absence of subsequent amending legislation it cannot be ignored. The Indictable Offences Act, 1848 (11 & 12 Vict. c. 42), which also provides for the backing of warrants is an English Act, and,

[23] 1935 S.C. (Court of Justiciary) 11.

so far as the backing of warrants is concerned, has not been repealed, contains no corresponding requirements of the intervention of the inspector general. The Magistrates' Courts Act of 1952, which repealed the greater part of the 1848 Act, preserved sections 12 to 15 and sections 30 to 32, both inclusive, and also Form 1c (the form of endorsement or backing a warrant). Hence **[839]** it was argued for the Commissioner of Police that the procedure adopted in this case was valid, being in compliance with the unrepealed provisions of the Act of 1848 which could be operated as an alternative to the Act of 1851.

I do not think this contention can be accepted and that it is possible to ignore the mandatory provision for endorsement by the inspector general contained in section 27 of the Act of 1851 (14 & 15 Vict. c. 93), which had to be transmitted to him for backing as provided by the preceding section 26 of the same Act.

Although there have been amending Acts, to which I need not refer, extending the number of those who could endorse a warrant as alternates of the inspector general, there has been no legislation which amends the 1848 and 1851 Acts so as to enable the deputy commissioner or other officer of the Garda Siochana to endorse the warrant. The Royal Irish Constabulary ceased to exist in 1922 and the office of inspector general disappeared. There has been no substitution of any other officers for the inspector general and his alternates, and it may have been thought that none was necessary, for a Statutory Rule and Order 405 of 1923, to which your Lordships' attention was drawn, provides for the procedure of backing of warrants as if no substitution were necessary. It does not, however, by its terms have the effect of making such parts of the 1848 Act as have not been repealed take effect as if the 1851 Act had never been passed. The latter Act provided machinery which no longer exists and the appropriate legislative authority, the Government of Eire, has put in its place a different form of machinery, but one which in my opinion cannot be operated without the appropriate legislation being passed in this country.

The inspector general and his alternates are in my view personae designatae to whom authority was given, and this designation has never been effectively displaced. I would dismiss the appeal.

LORD PEARCE. My Lords, for the reasons set out in the opinion of my noble and learned friend, Lord Morris of Borth-y-Gest, I agree that this appeal should be dismissed. I also agree with the observations of my noble and learned friend Lord Reid.

LORD DONOVAN. My Lords, I have had the advantage of reading the opinion prepared by my noble and learned friend, **[840]** Lord Morris of Borth-y-Gest. I agree with it, and do not desire to add anything to it.

Appeal dismissed.

Solicitors: *J. S. Williams; Howard, Kennedy & Co.*

THE STATE (AT THE PROSECUTION OF JOSEPH H. GRIFFIN) v. SERGEANT SAMUEL J. BELL, GARDA SIOCHÁNA, AND IN THE MATTER OF THE COURTS OF JUSTICE ACTS, 1924 TO 1959, AND IN THE MATTER OF THE CONSTITUTION

([1962] I.R. 355)

June 12, 1961: Republic of Ireland, High Court: Davitt P.

July 18, 19, December 3, 20, 1962: Republic of Ireland, Supreme Court: O'Dálaigh C.J., Lavery, Kingsmill Moore, Haugh, Walsh JJ.

Jurisdiction—Habeas corpus—*Irish citizen—Charges of alleged offences committed in London contrary to the Bankruptcy Act,* 1914—*Offences under an English statute which was never applicable in Ireland—English warrants endorsed for execution in Ireland by a Deputy Commissioner of Garda Siochána —Arrest—Evidence adduced verifying authenticity of warrants—Sufficiency of evidence—Whether acts alleged in warrants constitute offences in English law— Petty Sessions* (*Ir.*) *Act,* 1851 (14 & 15 *Vict., c.* 93), *s.* 29.

On the 6th December, 1960, the prosecutor was taken into custody by a member of the Garda Siochána on foot of two warrants signed by a Justice of the Peace for the Borough of Kingston-upon-Thames, London, and duly endorsed for execution in Ireland by a Deputy Commissioner of the Garda Siochána. The prosecutor was brought to, and detained in, the Bridewell, in Dublin, for the purpose of being handed over to the British police authorities. The warrants contained recitals that informations on oath had been laid against the prosecutor alleging offences under ss. 154 and 156 of the Bankruptcy Act, 1914, as amended, an English statute which had never applied in Ireland. The prosecutor obtained in the High Court a conditional order of *habeas corpus ad subjiciendum,* directed to the Station Sergeant at the Bridewell, and on the application to make absolute the conditional order the cause shown was allowed and the conditional order discharged. Against this order the prosecutor appealed to the Supreme Court on the ground, *inter alia,* that there was no evidence that the acts alleged in the warrants constituted a crime or offence under English law.

Held by the Supreme Court (reversing the order of the High Court) that the cause shown should be disallowed and the conditional order of *habeas corpus* made absolute.

Per Walsh J. (delivering the judgment of the Court): "In this case there is no evidence that the matters complained against the applicant in the warrants are offences or crimes under English law and, in my view, it is no answer for the respondents to say that the applicant has not adduced evidence to prove that these matters do not constitute crimes or offences. Sect. 29 of the Petty Sessions (Ir.) Act, 1851, authorises the 'backing' of a warrant only when it is for a crime or an offence in the country in which the warrant is issued. To assume that a crime or offence has been properly charged in a foreign country would be to be satisfied as to a fact in respect of which there has been no evidence.

"Adopting the view expressed by Gavan Duffy J. in *The State* (*Dowling*) v. *Brennan and Kingston* [1937] I. R. 483, at p. 509, I am of the opinion that the appropriate authority in Ireland should decline to affix his indorsement to such a warrant until he is satisfied on proper evidence that the warrant was issued for a crime or an offence according to the law for the time being in force in the country in which the warrant originates."

HABEAS CORPUS.

On the 28th November, 1960, two warrants were issued and signed by a

Justice of the Peace for the Borough of Kingston-upon-Thames for the arrest of Joseph Harold Griffin, the prosecutor. One warrant (referred to as warrant "B,") charged that on the 22nd February, 1958, the 14th April, 1958, the 30th May, 1958, and on a day in June of 1958, in **[356]** the said Borough, the County of London and the County of Surrey, respectively, within twelve months next before the presentation of a bankruptcy petition against him the prosecutor obtained by fraud property to the value of £803 2s. 1d., £432 14s. 7d., £24 11s. 2d. and £76 3s. 0d. upon credit and for which he had not paid, contrary to s. 154, sub-ss. 1 and 13, of the Bankruptcy Act, 1914, as amended. The other warrant (referred to as warrant "A") charged that the prosecutor was adjudged a bankrupt on the 30th October, 1958, and, on a day in March, 1958, in the County of Surrey obtained credit for rent to the extent of £204 15s. 0d. under false pretences or by means of other fraud, and that, on another day in March, 1958, in the same county obtained credit for rent to the extent of £160 under false pretences or by means of other fraud contrary to s. 156 (*a*) of the said Act. The said warrants were sent by post to Patrick J. Carroll, a Deputy Commissioner of the Garda Siochána, and were endorsed by him on the 2nd December, 1960, for execution in the City and County of Dublin. On the 6th December, 1960, the warrants were issued for execution by Michael J. Wymes, a Superintendent of the Garda Siochána. The prosecutor was arrested on the warrants by a member of the Garda Siochána on the 6th December, 1960, in Dublin and was brought to, and detained in, the Bridewell in Dublin for the purpose of being handed over to the British police authorities for conveyance to London to answer the said charges. On the 6th December, 1960, a conditional order of *habeas corpus ad subjiciendum* was granted to the prosecutor by Mr. Justice Walsh, directed to Sergeant Samuel J. Bell, Garda Siochána, of the Bridewell Garda Station in the City of Dublin. On the hearing of the application to the High Court (Davitt P.) to make absolute the conditional order evidence was adduced in support of the cause shown verifying the authenticity of the warrant. There were also evidence on affidavit from a British barrister-at-law of Gray's Inn, London, deposing that under the law of England a Justice of the Peace (before whom the affidavit of authentication of the warrant was sworn) is empowered to take affidavits of that nature and to administer oaths to a police officer in the form used for the purpose of proving the signature of the Justice of the Peace to a warrant for the arrest of a person alleged to have committed an offence. The affidavit of authentication of the signature of the Justice of the Peace on the warrants was sworn by a Detective Inspector.

Seán MacBride, Senior Counsel, and *Rex Mackey* for the prosecutor. **[357]**
Colm Condon, Senior Counsel, and *J. B. Cassidy,* for the Attorney General and Sergeant Bell.

The arguments were substantially the same as those in the Supreme Court, reported *post.*

DAVITT P.:—
I am unable to distinguish this case from this Court's decision in *Hully's Case** (unreported) and, accordingly, I will discharge the conditional order.

From this judgment and order the prosecutor appealed to the Supreme Court on the ground, *inter alia,* that there was no evidence that the acts alleged in the warrants constituted a crime under English law. In view of the fundamental importance of this ground the Supreme Court did not consider it necessary to hear argument on any of the other grounds of appeal raised until a decision had been given on this ground, the Court being of opinion that if this ground of appeal was resolved in favour of the prosecutor it would entitle him to the order sought.

Seán MacBride, Senior Counsel, T. J. Conolly, Senior Counsel (with them *Rex Mackey* and *S. Sorahan*) for the appellant:—

The offences alleged in the warrants are offences under the Bankruptcy Act, 1914, an English statute which does not apply, and never has applied in this country: consequently, it is submitted, the statute will have to be proved as foreign law.

It is also submitted that the warrants are defective. The warrant, described as warrant "A," is defective on its face, as s. 150 (*a*) of the Bankruptcy Act, 1914, only applies to a person "who has been adjudged a bankrupt." This warrant shows on its face that the offences were alleged to have been committed "on a day in March 1958," whereas the warrant alleges that the applicant was adjudged a bankrupt on the 30th October, 1958.

Furthermore, the warrants are defective in that neither of the warrants avers that the applicant committed any offence against Irish law and there is no evidence that the acts alleged in the warrants constitute a "crime or offence" under English law. Neither warrant is endorsed with the G b. or the G c. certificate prescribed by the Petty Sessions (Ir.) Act, 1851. [They referred to the judgment of O Dálaigh J. (as he then was) in *The State (Hully)* v. *Superintendent Hynes** **[358]** (unreported)]. There is no evidence that the warrants or either of them were presented for backing by the person who brought them from England. On the contrary, the evidence is that they were forwarded by post to the Deputy Commissioner of the Garda Siochána.

It is also submitted that the backing of the warrants by Deputy Commissioner Carroll constitutes an exercise of judicial power, or the exercise of limited functions and powers of a judicial nature, in a criminal matter: that the execution of the warrants by a magistrate in England and the backing thereof by a Deputy Commissioner of the Garda Siochána jointly constitute an exercise of limited functions and powers of a judicial nature in a criminal matter. [They also referred to *O'Boyle & Rodgers* v. *Attorney-General & O'Duffy*[1]; *The State (Kennedy)* v. *Little*[2]*; *The State (Dowling)* v. *Brennan and Kingston*[3]; *The State (Dowling)* v. *Kingston (No. 2)*[4]; *The State (Burke)* v. *Lennon and the Attorney-General*[5]; *The State (Duggan)* v. *Tapley*[6]*; *In re O Laighléis*[7]*; *In re Solicitors Act,* 1954[8], *The State (Hully)* v. *Superintendent Hynes* (unreported); *In re Bellencontre*[9]*; *Rex* v. *Governor of Brixton Prison. Ex parte Sarno*[10]*; *The King* v. *Commissioner of Metropolitan Police. Ex parte Nalder*[11]*; 44 Geo. III, c. 92; Indictable Offences (Ir.) Act, 1849 (12 & 13 Vict., c. 69); British Law Ascertainment Act, 1859 (22 & 23 Vict., c. 63); Foreign Law Ascertainment Act, 1861 (24 & 25 Vict., c. 11)].

R. N. Cooke, Senior Counsel (with him *Colm Condon, Senior Counsel,* and *J. B. Cassidy*), for the Attorney General and Sergeant Bell:—

The warrants have been shown to be authentic and, it is submitted, once the authenticity of the warrants has been established there is a presumption that they are in every way regular and their validity should not be questioned. Furthermore, in such circumstances there is no duty upon the Court to enquire whether the warrants disclose an offence under the law of the country in which they originate.

[1] [1929] I. R. 558.
[2] [1931] I. R. 39.
[3] [1937] I. R. 483.
[4] [1937] I. R. 699.
[5] [1940] I. R. 136.
[6] [1952] I. R. 62.
[7] [1960] I. R. 93.
[8] [1960] I. R. 239.
[9] [1891] 2 Q. B. 122.
[10] [1916] 2 K. B. 742.
[11] [1948] 1 K. B. 251.

If it is sought to show that the warrants do not disclose crimes or offences under the law of England, it is submitted that the onus of proving this is upon the person seeking the order of *habeas corpus*: *The State* (*Dowling*) v. *Brennan and Kingston*[12] **[359]**

Seán MacBride, Senior Counsel, in reply.

On the conclusion of the arguments the Chief Justice stated that the judgment of the Court on the question as to whether evidence that the warrant in question was issued for a crime or offence according to the law for the time being in force in the country in which the warrant originated must be adduced would be reserved and that the other matters raised in the appeal would be adjourned.

Cur adv. vult.

O DÁLAIGH C.J.:—

The judgment of the Court will be delivered by Mr. Justice Walsh.

WALSH J:—

In these proceedings an order of *habeas corpus* is sought on behalf of Joseph Harold Griffin who was arrested in Dublin on the 6th December, 1960, by Detective Sergeant John Martin and was then lodged in custody in the Bridewell, Dublin. The arrest was effected on foot of two warrants, each dated the 28th November, 1960, and signed by one H. S. Saunders, a Justice of the Peace for the Borough of Kingston-upon-Thames, London, which had been sent by post to Deputy Commissioner of the Garda Siochána, Patrick J. Carroll, for execution in the Dublin Metropolitan District. On the 2nd December, 1960, the said Deputy Commissioner endorsed each of the warrants for execution in the Dublin Metropolitan District. One of the warrants, namely, warrant "A", contains recitals to the effect that information on oath had been laid against the applicant in respect of matters alleged to amount to offences under s. 156 (*a*) of the Bankruptcy Act, 1914, an English statute. Warrant "B" recites that informations on oath had been laid in respect of four matters alleged to constitute offences under s. 154, sub-s. 13, of the Bankruptcy Act, 1914, as amended. The matters referred to in warrant "A" are alleged to have occurred in March, 1958, and the matters referred to in warrant "B" are alleged to have taken place respectively in February, May, April and June, 1958. The applicant was released on bail by order of the High Court on the 7th December, 1960, and has been on the said bail ever since. He had previously been granted a conditional order of *habeas corpus* in the High Court on the 6th December, 1960. Upon cause having been shown, the learned President of the High Court, on the 12th June, 1961, allowed the cause shown against making the conditional order absolute and discharged the conditional order. The proceedings in this **[360]** Court are by way of appeal against that order of the learned President of the High Court.

For the purpose of this decision it is unnecessary to set out the various grounds upon which it was sought to have the conditional order made absolute or the grounds upon which this appeal is based, save one ground only, namely, that there is no evidence that the acts alleged in the warrants constituted a crime or offence under English law. In view of the fundamental importance of this ground the Court did not consider it necessary to hear counsel on any of the other matters raised until a decision had been given on this particular ground because if it is resolved in favour of the applicant it will entitle him to an order for *habeas corpus* and to his release. Of the many cases which have been heard in our Courts arising out of the "backing" of English warrants in this country pursuant to the provision of s. 29 of the Petty Sessions (Ireland) Act, 1851, this point, so far as I am aware, has been raised only once before, namely, in the case of *The State* (*Dowling*) v. *Brennan and Kingston,* decided by the High Court.[13] But in that case the decision turned on a different point.

Sect. 29 of the Petty Sessions Act, 1851, provides that "Whenever any person

[12] [1937] I. R. 483, at pp. 495, 497.
[13] [1937] I. R. 483.

against whom any warrant shall be issued by any Justice or other such officer as aforesaid in England . . . for any crime or offence, shall reside or be, or be suspected to reside or be, in any place in Ireland, it shall be lawful . . . to endorse the same in like manner and upon like proof as aforesaid, authorising the execution of the same within his jurisdiction." It is therefore clear beyond doubt that the warrant would not be good unless it were "for any crime or offence" in England. In the present application there is evidence, in support of the cause shown, verifying the authenticity of the warrant and an affidavit from an English barrister-at-law of Gray's Inn, London, deposing that under the law of England a Justice of the Peace (before whom the affidavit of authentication of the warrant was sworn) is empowered to take affidavits of that nature and to administer oaths to a police officer in that form for the purpose of proving the signature of the Justice of the Peace to a warrant for the arrest of a person alleged to have committed an offence. The affidavit of authentication of the signature of the Justice of the Peace on the warrants was sworn by Detective Inspector Albert Overall. As there has been no rebuttal of this evidence I am of opinion that the English law on this particular subject has been sufficiently proved to the satisfaction of this Court and that the authenticity of the warrant has been established. **[361]** That, however, does not dispose of the matter. The other question of English law which arises is the question of whether the subject-matters of the information referred to in the warrants constitute offences in English law. The statutes alleged to have been infringed are English statutes which do not apply, and never have applied, to Ireland. I wish to observe at this stage, however, that even if these statutes were ones which had applied to Ireland and were still in force in this country, the opinion which I am about to give would not be modified.

Prior to the establishment of Saorstát Éireann a person arrested in Ireland on foot of a "backed" English warrant could be surrendered merely on proof of the authenticity of the English warrant. At that time all the Courts in Ireland had judicial notice of every statute of the Parliament of the then United Kingdom of Great Britain and Ireland. Since the establishment of Saorstát Éireann, however, the law of any state other than this State must be proved in the Courts of this country by the testimony of witnesses of competent skill, and foreign written law cannot be proved by the production of the written law itself, or even of an authenticated copy of it, but only by some skilled witness who describes the law. In *O'Callaghan* v. *O'Sullivan*[14], it was decided by the Supreme Court that ". . . all law is foreign to these Courts other than the laws which these Courts have been set up under the Constitution of Saorstát Éireann to administer and enforce, that is to say, other than the laws given force and validity by Article 73 of the Constitution and the enactments of the Oireachtas made after the coming into operation of the Constitution. No other laws are known to us judicially; nor can we take judicial notice of any other laws, unless they are proved to us as facts." The witness to prove a foreign law must be a person *peritus virtute officii* or *virtute professionis.* In my view, this is equally applicable in the case of statutes of the Parliament of the former United Kingdom still in force in this country and in Great Britain, for example, the Forgery Act, 1913, or the Larceny Act, 1916, because who is to know that it has not been recently amended in England or that the printer's copy of the statute tendered is in fact the latest version of the foreign law in question: see also the observations of Parker L.J. in *Regina* v. *Governor of Brixton Prison. Ex parte Shuter.*[15]*

Each of the warrants in this case, in as much as it recites the allegations which are said to constitute offences in England, contains a statement of the law in England. The proof **[362]** of the authenticity of the warrants is not proof of the correctness of statements of law which they contain and in the absence of the appropriate evidence on this subject this Court is in the position of having to examine these warrants without knowing whether or not they have been issued in respect of a crime or an offence in England.

[14] [1925] 1 I. R. 90, at p. 109.
[15] [1959] 3 W. L. R. 603, at p. 609.

The submission made on behalf of the Attorney General is that once the warrants have been shown to be authentic there is a presumption that they are in every way regular and that if it is sought to show that they do not disclose offences or crimes under the law of England the onus of showing that is upon the person seeking the order of *habeas corpus.* In support of this submission Mr. Cooke cited the observations of the learned judges who constituted the majority in the High Court in giving the decision in *The State* (*Dowling*) v. *Brennan and Kingston.*[16] These observations, which appear at pp. 495 and 497 of the report, are to the effect that once the authenticity of the warrant has been established its validity cannot be questioned in Court and that there is no duty upon the Court to enquire whether the warrant discloses an offence under the law of the country from which it emanates. For my part, I cannot accept that it is sufficient for a gaoler in this country who has custody of a person arrested on foot of a foreign warrant, indorsed for execution in this country pursuant to s. 29 of the Petty Sessions (Ireland) Act, 1851, simply to lay down the warrant with proof of its authenticity and no more. Authenticity is not proof of validity. It is clear from the report of the case that the observations just referred to were merely *obiter* and that in fact the Court did not think it necessary for the purpose of its decision, which as I have already said turned upon a completely different point, to accept the offer of counsel for the complainant, the Inspector of the Poor of Glasgow, to hear what evidence he had to offer on the validity of the warrant under Scottish law.

Article 40, sub-article 4, 2°, of the Constitution makes it mandatory upon the Court to order the release of a person who has complained that he is being unlawfully detained unless the party detaining the complainant satisfies the Court that the detention is in accordance with the law. I respectfully agree with the view expressed by Mr. Justice Kingsmill Moore in his judgment in *The State* (*Hully*) v. *Superintendent Hynes* (unreported) that the effect of the wording of this portion of the Constitution is to throw upon the person showing cause the onus of justifying the detention in all respects to the satisfaction of the Court. In *The State* (*Hughes*) **[363]** v. *Lennon and Others,*[17] the same view was expressed by Mr. Justice O'Byrne with reference to Article 6 of the Constitution of Saorstát Éireann which corresponded to Article 40, 4, 2°, of the present Constitution.

In this case there is no evidence that the matters complained against the applicant in the warrants are offences or crimes under English law and, in my view, it is no answer for the respondents to say that the applicant has not adduced evidence to prove that these matters do not constitute crimes or offences. Sect. 29 of the Petty Sessions (Ireland) Act, 1851, authorises the "backing" of a warrant only when it is for a crime or an offence in the country in which the warrant is issued. To assume that a crime or offence has been properly charged in a foreign country would be to be satisfied as to a fact in respect of which there has been no evidence.

Adopting the view expressed by Gavan Duffy J. (as he was then) in *The State* (*Dowling*) v. *Brennan and Kingston,*[18] I am of the opinion that the appropriate authority in Ireland should decline to affix his indorsement to such a warrant until he is satisfied on proper evidence that the warrant was issued for a crime or an offence according to the law for the time being in force in the country in which the warrant originates.

If a person is arrested here on a "backed" English warrant he may, if he wishes, decide not to contest his custody but allow himself to be surrendered to the English police. If, on the other hand, he does challenge the validity of the warrant in the High Court, his release must be ordered unless the person showing cause satifies the Court, *inter alia,* that the matter in respect of which the warrant has been issued is a crime or offence under English law.

As evidence was tendered here on behalf of the person showing cause as to matters of English law concerning the function of a Justice in England

16 [1937] I. R. 483.
17 [1935] I. R. 128, at p. 162.
18 [1937] I. R. 483, at p. 509

in administering an oath for the purpose of an affidavit, it does not appear to me that there would have been any particular difficulty in also tendering evidence upon the question of the alleged crime or offence. When offered an opportunity to do so, counsel for the Attorney General did not wish to avail himself of it, due no doubt to the desire to see a settled practice established in these matters which so directly concern the liberty of the citizen. In my view, the applicant's appeal should be allowed, the cause shown disallowed, and the conditional order should be made absolute.

Solicitor for the applicant: *Edward Daly.*

Solicitor for the respondents: *The Chief State Solicitor.*

THE STATE (AT THE PROSECUTION OF PHILIP ANTHONY QUINN) v. DETECTIVE INSPECTOR MATTHEW G. RYAN AND DEPUTY COMMISSIONER W. P. QUINN AND IN THE MATTER OF THE HABEAS CORPUS ACT, 1782, AND IN THE MATTER OF THE COURTS (SUPPLEMENTAL PROVISIONS) ACT, 1961 AND 1962, AND IN THE MATTER OF THE COURTS OF JUSTICE ACTS, 1924-1961, AND IN THE MATTER OF THE PETTY SESSIONS (IRELAND) ACT, 1851, AND IN THE MATTER OF THE CONSTITUTION.

([1965] I.R. 70)

Republic of Ireland:
July 15, 1963: High Court: Teevan J.
July 16, 1963: Supreme Court: O Dálaigh C.J., Lavery, Kingsmill, Moore, Haugh, Walsh JJ.
July 23, 24, 25, 29, November 18, 1963: High Court: Davitt P., McLoughlin, Teevan JJ.
June 22, 23, 24, 25, July 13, 14, 15, 31, November 16, December 4, 1964: Supreme Court: O Dálaigh C.J., Lavery, Kingsmill, Moore, Haugh, Walsh JJ.

Constitution of Ireland—Statute—Validity—Repugnancy to provisions of the Constitution—Habeas corpus—*Prosecutor arrested on English warrant—Warrant held to be bad—Prosecutor released on order of High Court—Prosecutor re-arrested on fresh warrant and removed forthwith from the jurisdiction—Denial of right of access to the Courts—Denial of opportunity to question validity of warrant—Provisions of Petty Sessions (Ir.) Act,* 1851, *s.* 29, *and consequential provisions repugnant to the Constitution and invalid—Constitution of Ireland, Articles* 40 *and* 50—*Petty Sessions (Ir.) Act,* 1851 (14 & 15 *Vict., c.* 93), *ss* 26 *and* 29.
Contempt of Court—Conduct of police officers—British warrant backed in Ireland—Arrest of accused in Ireland—Irish police officers conspiring with British police officers to remove accused from jurisdiction—Denial of opportunity to question validity of warrant—Violation of provisions of the Constitution.

Sect. 29 of the Petty Sessions (Ireland) Act, 1851, which authorises the backing of British warrants in Ireland and the immediate removal from the jurisdiction of the Irish Courts of a person who has been arrested and detained under such a warrant, is repugnant to the provisions of the Constitution and is void and ineffective.

So *held* by the Supreme Court (O Dálaigh C.J., Lavery, Kingsmill Moore, Haugh and Walsh JJ.).

Held further by the Supreme Court that it is contempt of Court for police officers to arrange to remove a prisoner out of the jurisdiction of the Irish Courts on an English warrant with such speed that he has no opportunity to apply to the Courts to question the validity of such warrant or to apply to the Court for an order of *habeas corpus.*

NOTICE OF MOTION.

The prosecutor, Philip Anthony Quinn, was arrested in Dublin on a British warrant. He was an Irish citizen. It was found that there was a defect in the British warrant and accordingly a fresh warrant was applied for in England and was transmitted to Dublin to British police officers already there for the execution of the first warrant. Prior to the transmission of the second warrant the prosecutor had commenced *habeas corpus* proceedings, questioning the validity of the first warrant, and the second warrant was received in Dublin while he was in custody pending the outcome of the proceedings on the first warrant. The arrest on foot of the first warrant took place on the 6th July, 1963, and on the 7th July the President of the High Court granted a conditional order of *habeas corpus* **[71]** upon the ground that the person named in that warrant was not the prosecutor. On the 12th July the new warrant was issued in London and on the following day Inspector Ryan, the first-named respondent herein, was advised that the earlier warrant was bad. The new warrant was received by Inspector Ryan on the morning of the 15th July, 1963, backed for execution by Deputy Commissioner Quinn. At 11 a.m. on that morning counsel for Inspector Ryan applied *ex parte* to the President of the High Court to discharge the prosecutor. The President refused to do this and directed that the prosecutor and his counsel should be present in Court. Accordingly, at 11.15 a.m. the prosecutor was brought to the President's Court and counsel for Inspector Ryan renewed his application in the presence of junior counsel for the prosecutor and the prosecutor was ordered to be released. The prosecutor then left Court in company with his counsel, but, being apprehensive that he might be re-arrested, he made an arrangement to meet his counsel who had an engagement in another Court. He parted company with his counsel at approximately 11.20 or 11.25 a.m. He was re-arrested at 11.30 a.m., either in the west courtyard of the Four Courts or in Chancery Street, the exact location not being made clear in evidence as there was a conflict of testimony between the police and the prosecutor. He was taken immediately to Carrickarnon, on the border between the State and Northern Ireland, in a Garda car and transferred there on the Northern side of the Border to a Royal Ulster Constabulary car and he was subsequently taken to England.

Further details and facts appear from the judgments.

On the 15th July, 1963, the prosecutor applied to Mr. Justice Teevan for a conditional order of *habeas corpus.* At the hearing he was represented by Mr. P. A. O. Síocháin S.C. and Mr. L. Meagher. Mr. Justice Teevan, refusing the order sought, delivered the following judgment:—

TEEVAN J.:—

I must refuse this order. I am not satisfied that counsel or solicitor have instructions to make it at all, but the main ground is that they cannot tell me whether Philip Anthony Quinn, the supposed applicant, is at large or in the custody of any person against his will, and the suspicions of Mr. Concannon and Mr. Meagher were not borne out by anything they learned at the Bridewell, save perhaps the statement made or the allegation made by the police officer, whose name Mr. Concannon does not know, that he believed there was a warrant extant for his, for Mr. Quinn's, apprehension; but **[72]** there is no evidence before me that he was arrested on that or any warrant or arrested at all and particularly as we know there was, or had been, a warrant—an English warrant—that had led to the previous order being granted by the President. The police officer may have been speaking about that one, or may have been speaking about the earlier incidents. However, the ground is that I have no one to whom I can direct the order of this Court for the release of Mr. Quinn *if*—but it's a very big "if"—Mr. Quinn is in anyone's custody at all, or held by any person against his will. He indicated a desire to go to Clery's, he was left for 15 or 20 minutes standing outside Court No. 6. He may very well have gone off, particularly if he saw the police officers—who he presumed were waiting for him—disappear, go off outside. He may have been arrested outside. I don't know where—*if* he was arrested, I say, and I underline the "if" —he may have been arrested on all these grounds. I can see no grounds for the Court's intervention and I decline the application.

From the above judgment the prosecutor appealed to the Supreme Court which heard evidence from the prosecutor's solicitor, Mr. J. P. MacD. Concannon, on the 16th July, 1963. At 4.30 p.m. the Chief Justice delivered the judgment of the Supreme Court which was as follows:—

O DÁLAIGH C.J.:—

This is an appeal from an order of Mr. Justice Teevan, refusing a conditional order of *habeas corpus.*

The application is made in respect of the body of Philip Anthony Quinn, an Irish citizen, whose home is stated to be in Clonakilty, County Cork, and whose last residence was in England.

The prosecutor was arrested in Dublin on the 6th July on an English warrant alleging the offence of larceny in England. His arrest on the 6th July was after discharge from Mountjoy Prison where he had been serving a sentence of imprisonment.

On leaving Mountjoy Prison a Garda officer spoke to him about a warrant for committal to Limerick Prison for two weeks for default in payment of a fine. The Garda officer said nothing about arresting the prosecutor, but, accompanied by two other men, walked with him to the North Circular Road. There he was ordered into a motor car and then told that there was an English warrant for his arrest. The warrant was read out to him and he was brought to the Bridewell and lodged there. **[73]**

When in the Bridewell the prosecutor communicated with his solicitor, Mr. Concannon, and as a result an application was made on the following day, Sunday, the 7th July, to the President of the High Court for a conditional order of *habeas corpus.* The President made a conditional order, directed to Inspector Matthew G. Ryan and the gaoler at the Bridewell. The conditional order was duly served and the prosecutor's advisers then issued a motion seeking bail.

Yesterday morning Mr. Donnelly, counsel for the respondents, invited Mr. Meagher, junior counsel for the prosecutor, to accompany him to the President's Court for the purpose of informing the Court that the respondents were consenting to the conditional order being made absolute. The order was made absolute and the prosecutor, who was in Court in the custody of Sergeant Bell of the Bridewell, was thereupon by direction of the President discharged.

The prosecutor left the President's Court, accompanied by his junior counsel, and both went as far as Court No. 6 where Mr. Meagher had other business to attend to. Mr. Meagher understood that the prosecutor would wait outside the Court until counsel had completed his business. When counsel came from Court some 15 minutes later the prosecutor was not there. The prosecutor and counsel had been followed from the President's Court to the precincts of Court 6 by a number of police officers.

Inquiries by the prosecutor's solicitor have failed to bring to light the whereabouts of the prosecutor. Mr. Concannon had been informed that the prosecutor is not in Limerick Prison. Mr. Concannon was also informed in a telephone conversation with the duty officer at Garda Headquarters that Deputy Commissioner Carroll said that the prosecutor was not now in custody anywhere in the Dublin Metropolitan District. It is alleged he was taken into custody on foot of an English warrant and is unlawfully detained by Irish police officers. The prosecutor's solicitor was informed by Detective Sergeant Friel that the prosecutor had been arrested on another warrant but he learned nothing further from him as to the whereabouts of the prosecutor. The prosecutor's solicitor said in the High Court that he believed the prosecutor is in custody within the jurisdiction.

If such a warrant exists the prosecutor is entitled to have its validity examined before he is sent out of the jurisdiction.

Mr. Justice Teevan refused a conditional order because he considered that the solicitor for the prosecutor had not his client's authority to make an application for a conditional order of *habeas corpus* and because it was not shown that he was in custody. It might be, the Judge thought, that the [74] prosecutor had vanished of his own volition. This is possible, but the probabilities on the information available to this Court are otherwise: they point to an arrest.

As to the authority of the prosecutor's solicitor the Court is of opinion in the circumstances of this case that there is sufficient shown to entitle the solicitor to maintain this application. The indications are that the prosecutor was prevented from consulting with his legal advisers and the Court cannot permit an Article of the Constitution to be set at nought with impunity.

The Court will, therefore, in the terms of Article 40, 4, 2°, of the Constitution order Mr. D. Costigan, the Commissioner of the Garda Siochana, Detective Inspector Matthew Ryan and Sergeant Samuel J. Bell to produce the body of the prosecutor in the High Court at 11 o'clock in the forenoon on Friday next, the 19th July, and to certify in writing the grounds of his detention. The High Court will proceed as in the said Article provided.

In pursuance of the above order application was then made on behalf of the prosecutor to the High Court.

Seán MacBride S.C., P. A. O. Siocháin S.C. and *L. Meagher* for the prosecutor.

R. McGonigal S.C., Niall McCarthy S.C. and *T. F. Donnelly* for the respondents.

The arguments were similar to those in the Supreme Court, reported *post.*

The Court issued the following direction:—

"The Court wishes to have the following information:

"1, On Monday, 15th July, when counsel for the Attorney General in the President's Court consented to have the conditional order, granted on the 7th July, made absolute, was the Attorney General aware (*a*) actually, or (*b*) constructively through counsel for the respondents or otherwise, that a new English warrant for the arrest of the prosecutor had been endorsed for execution by Deputy Commissioner Quinn, or that it was the intention of certain members of the Garda Siochana to re-arrest the prosecutor on his release?

"2. Were the members of the Garda Siochana who were present in the President's Court on the occasion in question, or any of them, aware of the intention to re-arrest the prosecutor on his release? [75]

"3. What are the names of all the members of the Garda Siochana concerned with the re-arrest of the prosecutor?

"The respondents are required to have available for the Court on Tuesday, 23rd July next, on the adjourned hearing of this matter, the following documents:—

"(*a*) Garda patrol car log book relating to the car in which the prosecutor was conveyed to Carrickarnon on Monday, 15th July;

"(*b*) Copy of all written instructions given to members of the Garda Siochana relating to the re-arrest of the prosecutor;

"(*c*) Copy of all correspondence between members of the Garda Siochana and of the English police relating to the re-arrest of the prosecutor.

"Mr. Commissioner Costigan, Sergeant Samuel J. Bell and Detective Inspector Matthew G. Ryan of the Garda Siochana are required to attend for cross-examination on their affidavits on the adjourned hearing of this matter on Tuesday, 23rd July.

"The information required at 2 and 3 above should be made available to the prosecutor's solicitor as soon as possible."

Cur. adv. vult.

DAVITT P.:—

The facts of this matter appear to me to be as follows:—

In February last the prosecutor, Philip Anthony Quinn, was convicted in the Dublin District Court of attempted larceny and was sentenced to six months' imprisonment. He duly served this sentence and was released on the 6th July. He was at once re-arrested on foot of an English warrant which charged one, Patrick Anthony Quinn, with the larceny, on the 22nd August, 1962, of certain property belonging to Dansette Products Ltd., valued at £3,000. On the following day, the 7th July, his counsel, Mr. O Síocháin S.C., with whom was Mr. Laurence Meagher, instructed by Mr. Concannon, applied to me for a conditional order of *habeas corpus*. This was granted on the ground that the person named in the warrant was not the prosecutor. The order was directed to Detective Inspector Matthew G. Ryan and to the gaoler of the Bridewell Garda Station, Dublin, who was in fact Sergeant Samuel Bell; it was made on the 7th July, so that the respondents had, under the provisions of Or. 84, r. 46, at least until the 17th July to show cause for the detention of the prosecutor in custody.

On the morning of the 15th July the respondent, Inspector Ryan, received from one, Detective Constable Alan Johns, of the London Metropolitan Police, another English warrant **[76]** charging the prosecutor in his proper name, Philip Anthony Quinn, with the same offence as had been charged in the previous warrant. With this warrant in his possession Inspector Ryan proceeded to my Court and was there present when, shortly after eleven o'clock, his counsel, Mr. Donnelly, instructed by the Chief State Solicitor, made an application to me. Mr. Donnelly stated that he appeared so instructed for the respondents in the *habeas corpus* matter; that they were satisfied that the warrant under which the prosecutor had been arrested was not valid; and that they were prepared to release him from custody. He asked me in the circumstances to discharge the conditional order. I said that the proper course was to make the conditional order absolute, and that the prosecutor's counsel should be informed. I asked where the prosecutor was, and was told he was in the Bridewell. I directed that he should be brought before me so that I could order his discharge from custody. Some time later Mr. Donnelly and Mr. Meagher attended in my Court. The prosecutor was present, attended by Inspector Ryan and Sergeant Bell. Mr. Donnelly said that he was now instructed to consent to having the conditional order made absolute with costs to the prosecutor. I made the order as requested and directed that the prosecutor be released from custody forthwith.

It is now quite clear that while his counsel was making these applications to me the respondent, Inspector Ryan, was sitting in Court with the fresh English warrant in his possession, intending to execute it at the first suitable opportunity by arresting the prosecutor and delivering him into the custody of Detective Constable Johns for conveyance out of the jurisdiction. Nobody concerned, however, saw fit to disclose to the Court the existence of the fresh warrant or any such intention on the part of the Garda authorities.

Having made the order for the discharge of the prosecutor from custody, I told him that he was free and he left the Court in the company of his junior counsel, Mr. Meagher. He was arrested shortly afterwards by Inspector Ryan and handed over to the custody of Constable Johns who was accompanied by Constable Perry, also of the London Metropolitan Police. The party of four were then driven in a Garda patrol car to the Northern Ireland border. From there the prosecutor was taken, in company with Constables Johns and Perry, to Belfast in a Northern Ireland police car, whence he was eventually conveyed to London.

The circumstances of the prosecutor's arrest are the subject of some conflicting evidence which has to be dealt with. According to his affidavit he walked, on leaving my Court, in **[77]** company with Mr. Meagher to the door of Court 6 where Mr. Meagher had some business to attend to. They parted there and the prosecutor left the building by a back door leading into the yard where cars are parked. He was immediately arrested by Inspector Ryan who told him that he was arresting him on a British warrant. The warrant was not read to him, but he does not say that he asked to see it or have it read. He told Inspector

Ryan that he wished to see his solicitor, whereupon Constable Johns, who was standing near, remarked that he could see a solicitor when he got to London. He was taken to a car which was standing in the yard, and, in company with Inspector Ryan and Constables Johns and Perry, was driven by a Garda driver to the Northern Ireland border after short stops at Whitehall Garda Station and Drogheda.

Inspector Ryan's account of the transaction is somewhat different. In his affidavit he says that he arrested the prosecutor in Chancery Street immediately outside the Bridewell Garda Station. He brought him into the hallway of the station where he handed him over, together with the warrant, to Constables Johns and Perry and obtained from Constable Johns a receipt which he exhibits. He accompanied the prosecutor and Constables Johns and Perry to the Northern Ireland border and saw them cross into Northern Ireland. It was then about 1.10 p.m. on the 15th July and he has not seen the prosecutor since. At no time did the prosecutor ask him, or anyone in his presence or to his knowledge, for sight of the warrant or express any desire to question its validity or make any request to see a solicitor or counsel.

Under cross-examination Inspector Ryan said that the party stopped at Whitehall Garda Station, where he and Constable Johns went in, and he made a telephone call. It was here that he got the receipt from Constable Johns. When his attention was directed to the fact that there was a discrepancy between his affidavit and his oral evidence on this point he said that he considered that what happened at the Bridewell and at Whitehall Garda Station was all part of the same transaction. He said that he read the warrant to the prosecutor when he arrested him. When his attention was directed to the fact that he had made no reference to this in his affidavit, he said that in making his affidavit he was acting under the instructions of his legal advisers.

I regret to say that I find it very difficult to reconcile the Inspector's oral evidence with his affidavit. If, as he implies and all the probabilities suggest, the drafting of his affidavit was carefully considered, it is very difficult to construe it otherwise than as implying that the warrant was not shown to the prosecutor because he did not ask to see it. If it had in **[78]** fact been read to him there would be little purpose in making a point of the fact that he had not asked to see it. In the circumstances I have the gravest doubts as to whether the warrant was in fact read to the prosecutor. This may not in itself be of any great importance, since the prosecutor does not say that he asked to see the warrant or to have it read to him; but it does have the effect of shaking my confidence in the accuracy of the Inspector's account of the circumstances of the arrest. This is of importance when I come to consider whether the prosecutor asked to be allowed to see his solicitor and was prevented from doing so. He says that he did ask; Inspector Ryan says that he did not. It seems to me that it would be really quite extraordinary in the circumstances of this case if the prosecutor had not asked to see his solicitor. Only a few minutes earlier he had been restored to freedom as the result of proceedings initiated by his solicitor. Finding himself again in custody it would, I think, be strange indeed if he did not hope that his solicitor could again do something helpful and if he did not say that he wanted to see him. I find little difficulty in believing him when he says that he did ask to see his solicitor. When Mr. Meagher parted from the prosecutor outside Court 6 he expected to see him again when his business in that Court was finished. When he failed to do so inquiries as to his whereabouts were instituted. His solicitor, Mr. Concannon, made inquiries of several officers and members of the Garda Siochana, and at Dublin Airport, but without success. Eventually, inquiries made by telephone of the duty officer at Garda Headquarters yielded the information, some time after nine o'clock that evening, that the prosecutor was not then in custody anywhere in the Dublin Metropolitan Division, and that any queries which Mr. Concannon desired to put in writing would be dealt with early the following morning by Deputy Commissioner Carroll. Inquiries made the following afternoon of the Governor of Limerick Prison yielded the information that the prosecutor was not held in custody there. Meanwhile the prosecutor's counsel had applied unsuccessfully to Mr. Justice Teevan for a conditional order of *habeas corpus*. On Tuesday, the 16th July, they applied to the Supreme Court by way of appeal from such refusal and obtained an order which was made pursuant to Article 40, 4, 2° of the Constitution and directed to Mr. Commissioner Costigan, Inspector Ryan and Sergeant Bell, requiring them to produce the body of the prosecutor before this Court on Friday, the 19th July, and to certify in writing the grounds of his detention. The order directed this Court to proceed as provided in the said Article.

On Friday, the 19th July, I sat alone to deal with the matter. **[79]** Order 84, Rule 6, requires that the return to an order of *habeas corpus,* when the body is not produced, shall be by affidavit, to be made by the party to whom the order is directed, which shall contain such full answer to the allegation that the person is detained as the circumstances may require. In accordance with this Rule each of the respondents made an affidavit. Each affidavit was sworn on that date. Mr. Commissioner Costigan said that he had been informed that I had made the conditional order of *habeas corpus,* but did not become aware until some time after 1 p.m. on the 15th July that I had made it absolute. He said that he never at any time had the prosecutor in his custody nor was the prosecutor, to the best of his knowledge, information and belief, then detained by any member or members of Garda Siochana. Sergeant Bell said that he had conveyed the prosecutor to my Court on the morning of the 15th July; that when his discharge was ordered he had returned to the Bridewell; and that he had not seen him since. I have already summarised the contents of Inspector Ryan's affidavit. This was all the evidence tendered and a copy of the second warrant was not exhibited. I expressed the view that the affidavits did not constitute a good return to the Supreme Court order as a copy of the second warrant had not been exhibited. A photostatic copy was in Court and counsel for the respondents undertook to have it duly exhibited, which has been done. Counsel for the prosecutor asked that the respondents should be required to attend for cross-examination upon their affidavits, and I so directed. I also requested counsel for the respondents to see that certain information should be made available to the Court and to counsel for the prosecutor and that certain documents should be made available for production in Court, if so ordered, upon the resumed hearing. I came to the conclusion that this was a matter which should be dealt with by a Court of three judges and I directed accordingly.

Such, briefly, is the history of the matter up to the point when it came before the Court as at present constituted. Its salient features appear to me to be as follows: the respondent, Inspector Ryan, arrested the prosecutor on the 6th July on foot of an English warrant which, as his counsel subsequently admitted, was invalid. He was detained in custody under this invalid warrant until the 15th July while the London police were procuring the issue of a second warrant. This warrant reached the hands of Inspector Ryan on the 15th July. He had then until the 17th July at least to show cause, in compliance with the conditional order of the 7th July, for the prosecutor's detention. The prosecutor could have been taken into custody under this second warrant which could **[80]** then have been exhibited in the affidavit showing cause. If this course had been adopted the matter could have been brought before the Court and the question whether he was being lawfully detained in custody under the second warrant could have been argued and decided. This, it seems to me, would have been in the circumstances the proper and straightforward course to adopt. It was not, however, adopted. The existence of the second warrant was never disclosed to the Court; and the prosecutor was, upon his release pursuant to my direction, almost immediately re-arrested and hurried out of the jurisdiction without being allowed any opportunity of consulting his legal advisers. This did not, of course, happen just fortuitously. It happened as the result of a decision taken by somebody. It had the effect, whether designed or not, of preventing the prosecutor from exercising, before he was conveyed out of the jurisdiction, his right under Article 40 of the Constitution of resort to the High Court for the purpose of testing the legality of his arrest under the second warrant.

I have already summarised the contents of the respondents' affidavits made by way of return to the order of the Supreme Court. They show, in the case of the Commissioner and Sergeant Bell, that neither had the prosecutor in his custody at any time material in these proceedings; and each of their returns is in my view good. In the case of Inspector Ryan the position is different. His return shows that he had the prosecutor in his custody on the day before the order was made; that on the same day he handed over custody to the London police officers; and that when the order was made the prosecutor had already been taken out of the jurisdiction. His counsel now submit that this is a good return, and that as far as these proceedings are concerned it is quite immaterial whether the prosecutor's arrest under the second warrant and his transfer to the custody of the London officers for conveyance out of the jurisdiction was or was not illegal. I propose, in the first instance, to examine this submission in the light of cases decided in relation to the common law writ of *habeas corpus,* and apart from the provisions of Article 40 of the Constitution.

Counsel's submission in so far as it rested on authority was based upon the opinions expressed in the House of Lords in *Barnardo* v. *Ford*[1] on appeal from the decision of the English Court of Appeal, reported in *Gossage's Case*[2]. In order properly to appreciate these opinions it is necessary to refer to *Reg.* v. *Barnardo* (*Tye's Case*).[3] In that case the English Court of Appeal expressed approval of a decision of the Irish **[81]** Court of Queen's Bench in *In re Matthews.*[4] I propose to examine these cases in some detail.

In re Matthews[4] was concerned with the custody of a child, and the essential facts were as follows. A certain Miss Aylward, who had received the child lawfully into her custody, gave it to a Nurse Kenny to look after. The child's mother demanded the return of the child from Miss Aylward and was refused. A writ of *habeas corpus* having issued, Miss Aylward stated in her return that she had not at the time the writ was issued nor at any time thereafter the body of the child in her custody or control, nor had she any means of procuring her so as to produce her in Court; that some person unknown to her and without her sanction had by means of a forged order purporting to have been signed by her, obtained possession of the child from Nurse Kenny; that she had not since had the child in her custody or control, nor had she any means of knowing where or in whose custody the child was; and that by reason of these facts she could not produce the child in Court. The Court, consisting of Lefroy L.C.J., O'Brien and Hayes JJ., held that this was not a good return. Hayes J. said, at p. 245, that they had to pronounce their judgment upon the return and say whether it was sufficient in law, and if so, whether it was true in fact. He said that it was unnecessary to enter upon an inquiry as to its truth as he was satisfied that the primary question as to its sufficiency in law had to be decided against Miss Aylward. He held (at p. 250) that Miss Aylward had taken the child and held it subject to the mother's right to claim its return; that she had not rid herself of this responsibility by giving the child to Nurse Kenny; and that the child still continued, in the contemplation of the law, to be in her custody, possession and power; and that by her wrongful refusal to return the child to her mother she had made herself responsible for what had subsequently taken place. He said (at p. 252):—"When the Court can collect from the writ and return that the party has been in illegal custody, at a period antecedent to the issuing of the writ, it will not rest satisfied with the stereotyped form that, at the issuing of the writ, or at any time since, the party has not been in his possession, custody or power; but will insist on the person to whom the writ is directed producing the party, or showing that he has lawfully discharged himself of such custody . . ." O'Brien J. considered that the return was good, and dissented. Lefroy L.C.J. said (at p. 264) that he was of opinion that the return was insufficient in point of law, and also unsatisfactory and evasive in point of fact Most of his judgment appears to be concerned with the facts as **[82]** disclosed in the return, and their evasive nature, and he does not make it very clear why he considered it insufficient in point of law.

[1] [1892] A.C. 326.
[2] 24 Q. B. D. 283.
[3] 23 Q. B. D. 305.
[4] 12 Ir. C. L. R. 233.

In Reg. v. *Barnardo* (*Tye's Case*)[5] the facts were somewhat similar. The widowed mother of a child gave it into the custody of Dr. Barnado under an agreement whereby he was authorised to place it in one of his Homes, and afterwards in a situation in the United Kingdom or one of the colonies. Having remarried, she requested the return of her child. Within a few days of this request Barnardo gave the child to a Madame Rômand with the intention that she should take it out of the jurisdiction and ultimately to Canada. It was taken out of the jurisdiction. A writ of *habeas corpus* issued and in his return to the writ Barnardo stated that before the issue of the writ he had, under the terms of his agreement with the child's mother, given the child to Madame Rômand; that she refused to give it up; and that it was no longer in his control. The Queen's Bench Divisional Court held this return to be insufficient and made an order for Barnardo's attachment. An appeal against this order was refused by the Court of Appeal, consisting of Lord Esher M.R., Cotton and Lindley L.JJ. The Court took the same view of the law as was taken by the Irish Court of Queen's Bench in *In re Matthews.*[6] They held that from the time the mother had unsuccessfully requested the return of her child it was illegally in the custody of Barnardo; and that it was no valid return for him to say that he had handed it over to someone else and could not procure its production in Court. Lindley L.J. said (at p. 315):—"As matter of law I think that it is no valid excuse for not producing a child or other person in obedience to a writ of *habeas corpus,* to state inability to obey, if such inability is the result of the previous illegal conduct of the person to whom the writ is addressed. Here the defendant's inability arises from his having illegally sent the child abroad against the will of the lawful guardian; and that he did this before any legal proceedings against him were commenced is immaterial. Persons who illegally put a child out of their power do so at their peril, and, if they are ordered to produce the child, no excuse founded on their own inability to comply with the order will be held a sufficient answer to the writ." The essential facts in *Reg.* v. *Barnardo* (*Gossage's Case*)[7] were as follows: a widow, Mrs. Gossage, gave her boy, aged twelve, into the custody of a man who deserted him and left him destitute. He was brought to one of Barnardo's Homes, and the usual form of agreement was sent to the mother to be **[83]** completed; but she did not sign or return it. She subsequently authorised a Mr. Newdigate to write to Barnardo saying that she wished to have the boy transferred to a Catholic institution, and inquiring when it would be convenient to collect him. Within a few days of the receipt of this letter the boy was handed over to a Mr. Norton, a resident in Canada, for adoption. Subsequently, demands on behalf of the mother for the return of the boy were refused. She obtained a conditional order of *habeas corpus* from the Queen's Bench Division which was later made absolute; and against this decision Barnardo appealed. The Court of Appeal, consisting of Lord Esher M.R. and Fry L.J. refused the appeal. Lord Esher re-stated the law as applied in *Tye's Case,*[8] but implied that it had in that case been somewhat too broadly stated. He said that if it could be shown that a person who had a child unlawfully in his custody had parted with all control of it so that it was absolutely impossible for him to secure its production in Court he would agree that a writ of *habeas corpus* should not issue merely for the purpose of punishing a past illegality; but no such impossibility had been shown in *Tye's Case*[8] nor in the case under consideration. He approved of the decision in *In re Matthews*[9] and quoted with approval the passage from the judgment of Hayes J. which I have quoted. Fry L.J. said that he differed from *Tye's Case*[8] if it meant that a writ should issue even if it were impossible to comply with it; as a person could not be in contempt for not doing the impossible. He said (at p. 299):—"I think that, where a child has been illegally handed over shortly before the issue of the writ, under circumstances of great suspicion, and which give reason to believe that it was done for the purpose of avoiding the exigence of a writ about to be issued, an exception arises to the

[5] 23 Q. B. D. 305.
[6] 12 Ir. C. L. R. 233.
[7] 24 Q. B. D. 283.
[8] 23 Q. B. D. 305.
[9] 12 Ir. C. L. R. 233.

general principle I have mentioned." He continued, at p. 300:—"If there be reason to believe that an illegal act has been done in order to defeat the anticipated process of the Court, and that on the issue of the writ, the person will ultimately be produced, then, in my opinion, the writ ought to go. In the present case the circumstances do, in my opinion, afford strong grounds for inferring that that is the real nature of the case." Having reviewed the evidence, he concluded by saying:—"I think, therefore, that the true conclusion upon the materials before us is that the child was made over in order to evade process, and that if the process goes it is highly probable that the appellant may yet be able to produce the child. For these reasons I concur in dismissing the appeal." **[84]**

Barnardo appealed to the House of Lords[10] and his appeal was dismissed. Lord Halsbury L.C. considered that it should be dismissed on the ground that the applicant had a right to have a return made to the writ so that on the return further questions of evidence might be raised. He said that he could not agree with the view that if a Court is satisfied that illegal detention has ceased before application for the writ had been made, nevertheless the writ might issue in order to vindicate the authority of the Court against a person who has once, though not at the time of the issue of the writ, unlawfully detained another or wrongfully parted with the custody of another. He said, however, that where a counterfeited release had taken place, and a pretended ignorance of the place of custody or of the identity of the custodian is insisted on, a Court might and ought to examine into the facts by a writ of *habeas corpus,* because the detention is in fact being continued by someone who is really the agent of the original wrong-doer to continue and persist in the unlawful detention. Lord Watson concurred, but went on to examine the nature of the writ of *habeas corpus* and expressed doubts as to whether the law as laid down by Lindley L.J. in *Tye's Case*[11] in the passage which I have quoted, and adopted and repeated by Lord Esher in the case under consideration, was sound. He said that where it was shown to the satisfaction of the Court that the person charged with unlawfully detaining a child or adult had *de facto* ceased to have any custody or control he was of opinion that the writ should not issue. He went on to say (at p. 335):—"A man who parts with the custody of a child after he is served with the process of the Court, or who evades service in order that he may get rid of such custody, commits a plain contempt, for which he is answerable to the Court. Even in that case I doubt whether it is competent, and I do not doubt that it is inexpedient, to enforce the writ *de plano.* The case ought to be dealt with, in such circumstances, as one of contempt; and the Court has power to pronounce an order which will compel the *quondam* custodian to choose between placing himself in a position which will make him liable to the writ and bearing the consequences of his contumacy. I think it right to add that, in my opinion, no contempt is committed by a person who, lawfully or unlawfully, absolutely gives up the custody and control of a child from the mere apprehension that by retaining it he may become liable to a writ of *habeas corpus,* and without any notice that such a proceeding will be taken." He concluded by saying that he willingly deferred to those of his colleagues who were of opinion that the case might be more conveniently **[85]** disposed of after a return had been made to the writ; but that if there had been no other reason for sustaining the decision appealed from he would have had no hesitation in reversing it. Lord Herschell said that if in order to support the decision appealed from it were necessary to give his adhesion to the law laid down in *Tye's Case*[12] he would hesitate much before doing so. Having regard to the nature of the writ of *habeas corpus* he could not, as then advised, feel satisfied that it was not a good return to the writ that the person to whom it related was not at the time it was issued in the custody, power or control of the person on whom it had been served. The doctrine that he must show that before the writ had been issued, or before he had received notice of the application for its issue, he had not wrongfully parted with custody of the person named in the writ was novel, and appeared to him to involve great

[10] [1892] A. C. 326.
[11] 23 Q. B. D. 315.
[12] 23 Q. B. D. 305.

difficulty. The question remained, however, whether, even assuming that the decision in *Tye's Case*[12] was not well founded, the appellant was entitled to have the order appealed from discharged. If it had been an admitted fact that before notice of the application for the writ the appellant had ceased to have the custody of, or any control over, the boy alleged to be detained, that might have been grounds for reversing the order made by the Queen's Bench Division. It was, however, impossible to read the judgment of the Lord Chief Justice without seeing that he did entertain a doubt as to whether that were so, and he was not prepared upon the affidavits to accept as conclusive the statements of the appellant. The proper time to try the question was when the appellant had returned to the writ that he was not detaining the child, and that it had not been in his custody, power or control when the writ was issued. Lords Macnaghten and Hannen agreed with Lord Herschell. Lord Morris concurred in the judgment which had been moved, but desired to say that in doing so he adopted the reasons assigned and the views given of the law, both in the Queen's Bench Division and in the Court of Appeal, as the foundation of his concurrence.

I have examined these cases, I am afraid, at too great length, in order to emphasise certain matters that appear to me to be quite clear. The basis of the decisions in *In re Matthews*[13] and in *Tye's Case*[12] was that, where shortly before a writ of *habeas corpus* was issued the person to whom it was directed had the body of the person named in the writ in illegal custody, it was not a good return to the writ to state that before its issue he had handed over custody to someone else, and therefore could not produce the body in obedience **[86]** to the writ because he no longer had it in his custody, power or control, unless the person to whom he had handed over custody had himself a legal right to such custody. It appears to me that this clearly was the principle on which these cases were decided. It would appear, however, that in each case the Court entertained the suspicion that the person to whom the writ was directed had not in reality surrendered all control over the body of the person named in the writ; and that he might, under pressure of the writ and its sanction of punishment for contempt, eventually secure production of the body. While this appears to be so, the legal principle on which the cases were decided is as I have stated. In *Gossage's Case*[14] the Court of Appeal considered that this principle was too broadly stated in *Tye's Case*[15]; and Lord Esher qualified it by implying that if the person to whom the writ was directed could show that it was really and absolutely impossible to produce the body in obedience to the writ, this might be a good return, but stated that no such impossibility had been shown in either case. On the appeal in *Gossage's Case*[14] the House of Lords decided nothing other than that the writ should issue because there was room for doubt on the evidence as to whether Barnardo had really parted with all control over the child, and the applicant was therefore entitled to have a return made so that this question could be further examined. They affirmed the decisions of the Queen's Bench Division and the Court of Appeal, and they did not over-rule *Tye's Case*[15]. The majority clearly disapproved of the principle so broadly stated in *Tye's Case*[15]; but it is worthy of note that Lord Watson and Lord Herschell, with whom Lords Macnaghten and Hannen agreed, did so, initially at least, by way only of doubt as to its soundness. Moreover, none of the Lords adverted to the modification of the principle implied by Lord Esher in *Gossage's Case*[14]; so modified, the principle would not appear to conflict very materially with the view taken by the Lords. If on the return Barnardo was unable to satisfy the Court that it was really impossible for him to procure the production of the child, and there was still room for a reasonable belief that he could, if he did make every reasonable effort, secure its production, what would have been the reaction of the Lords to such a situation? I take the view that the majority of the Lords did not clearly disapprove of the principle in *Tye's Case*[15] in its modified form; and that, in any event, the opinions expressed, while entitled to the greatest respect, were not necessary to the decision of the appeal and were, therefore, strictly *obiter* and are not binding on anybody. It is true that in *Rex*

[13] 12 Ir. C. L. R. 233.
[14] 24 Q. B. D. 283.
[15] 23 Q. B. D. 305.

v. [**87**] *Secretary of State for Home Affairs.* Ex parte *O'Brien*[16] Scrutton L.J. said (at p. 391):—"Now it has been laid down by the House of Lords in Barnardo v. Ford[17] that if the Court is satisfied that the body whose production is asked is not in the custody, power or control of the person to whom it is sought to address the writ, a writ of *habeas corpus* is not the proper remedy, though there was an original illegal taking and detention." With all respect it seems to me that it is overstating matters somewhat to say that this was "laid down" by the House of Lords. The other members of the Court, Bankes and Atkin L.JJ., both referred to *Barnardo* v. *Ford*[17] without claiming that it laid down any such proposition. They accepted it as deciding what I have stated it did decide. In *Ex parte Mwenya*[18]* Lord Parker, at p. 279, referred to *Barnardo* v. *Ford*[17] and *O'Brien's Case*[19] as authorities for the proposition that the writ will issue not only to the actual gaoler but to a person who has power or control over the body.

It seems to me that the submission made by counsel for the respondents that the return made in the present case is good, and that it is immaterial whether the prosecutor was illegally arrested and illegally handed over to the custody of the London police officers for conveyance out of the jurisdiction, is not, so far as the cases mentioned in argument are concerned, supported by authority in the strict sense; but that on the contrary such authority is against the acceptance of the submission. If what I may call the modified rule in *Tye's Case*[20] were the proper principle to apply in this case, then the return made by Inspector Ryan would have to be considered as insufficient since, in effect, it merely states that the prosecutor is no longer in his custody.

The question arises: Is that rule the proper principle to apply? In *Exham* v. *Beamish*[21] Gavan Duffy J. (as he then was) considered what effect should be given to judicial decisions of the period preceding the enactment of the Saorstát Eireann Constitution of 1922, under the provisions of Article 73 of that Constitution and Article 50 of the present Constitution. At page 348 he said:—"In my opinion, judicial decisions in Ireland before the Treaty, and English decisions which were followed here, are binding upon this Court only when they represent a law so well settled or pronounced by so weighty a juristic authority that they may fairly be regarded, in a system built up upon the principle of *stare decisis*, as having become established as part of the [**88**] law of the land before the Treaty; and to bind, they must, of course, not be inconsistent with the Constitution." If this matter had to be decided according to common law and apart from the provisions of Article 40 of the Constitution, then, having regard to all the circumstances, including the opinions expressed in the House of Lords in *Barnardo* v. *Ford*[22], I would feel unable to say that what I have called the modified rule in *Tye's Case*[23], resulting from the decisions in *In re Matthews*[24] and in *Tye's Case*[23] and *Gossage's Case*[25], represents a principle so well settled, or pronounced by so weighty a juristic authority, that it became part of the law under the combined operation of Article 73 of the Constitution of 1922 and Article 50 of the present Constitution. I would take the view that this Court was free to accept, reject, modify or ignore that principle as we see fit.

For my part, I would prefer to accept it. I concede that the purpose of the writ of *habeas corpus* was not merely punitive; though it must be realised that had it not been for the power of the Courts to punish for the contempt of disobedience to the writ it would have been a singularly useless device for protecting the subject against unlawful deprivation of liberty. I agree that it would have been absurd to have issued the writ where it was perfectly clear to the Court that it could not possibly be obeyed. I am of opinion, however, that where the writ had issued, and the only return made showed that the person to whom the writ had been directed had had the person named therein unlawfully in his custody immediately before the issue of the writ and had before its issue handed over

16 [1923] 2 K. B. 361.
17 [1892] A. C. 326.
18 [1960] 1 Q. B. 241.
19 [1923] 2 K. B. 361; [1923] A. C. 603.
20 23 Q. B. D. 305.
21 [1939] I. R. 336.
22 [1892] A. C. 326.
23 23 Q. B. D. 305.
24 12 Ir. C. L. R. 233.
25 24 Q. B. D. 283.

custody to someone who was not legally entitled to it, that would not be a sufficient return unless he also showed a real and absolute impossibility of producing, or procuring the production of, the body of the person named in the writ. Until such impossibility had been shown there would always be room for doubt whether the person to whom the writ had been directed had really parted with all control over the custody of the person named in the writ.

In the result, I take the view that, considered in the light of these cases decided in relation to the common law writ of *habeas corpus* and apart from Article 40 of the Constitution, the submission of counsel for Inspector Ryan on this aspect of the case ought not to be accepted. If Inspector Ryan's return would not have been sufficient if made to a writ of *habeas corpus* then, it seems to me, *a fortiori* it cannot be a good return to an order issued under the provisions of Article 40, 4, 2°. If these provisions had to be considered alone and **[89]** isolated from the other provisions of the Article it might reasonably be argued that they did no more than re-state some of the provisions of the common law in regard to *habeas corpus*. They occur, however, in an article dealing with personal rights which, in turn, is contained in a section of the Constitution which deals with fundamental rights. Paragraph 3 provides, in sub-para. 1°:—"The State guarantees in its laws to respect, and, as far as practicable, by its laws to defend and vindicate the personal rights of the citizens." In sub-para. 2° it provides:—"The State shall, in particular, by its laws protect as best it may from unjust attack and, in the case of injustice done, vindicate the life, person, good name, and property rights of every citizen." These guarantees are given on behalf of the State and apply to all its organs. They apply not merely to the Legislature but also to the Executive and the Judiciary. Not merely are the appropriate laws as enacted to comply with the requirements of these guarantees, but they are, so far as their nature permits, to be interpreted by the Courts and administered and enforced by the Executive with a similar regard to the requirements of the Constitutional guarantees. Paragraph 4, in sub-para. 1°, provides that no citizen shall be deprived of his liberty save in accordance with law; and in sub-para. 2° provides in broad outline the means of protecting the citizen's constitutional right. The obligation is laid upon the High Court of making inquiry into any complaint that a person is being unlawfully detained in custody. On such inquiry being made it may require production of the person alleged to be unlawfully detained and a return in writing of the grounds of detention. When the person is produced the Court must order his release unless satisfied that his detention is in accordance with law. There is no provision as to what is to be done if the person is not produced and the return of the grounds of detention is not satisfactory. It would, however, be strange indeed if the Court had no power to deal adequately with such a situation. Suppose the return made by the person to whom an order of *habeas corpus* was directed were, in effect, "I took the person named in the order unlawfully into custody; but before he could apply for *habeas corpus*, I handed him over to someone else for conveyance out of the jurisdiction; he is now outside the jurisdiction and there is nothing that I, or the Court, can do about it." It may not be easy to evaluate precisely the constitutional guarantees solemnly set forth in the earlier paragraphs of Article 40; but, unless they are mere platitudes, it would be a strange anti-climax if this Court, faced with such a return, had not at least the same power of dealing with the situation as a Court would have had if the same return had **[90]** been made to a writ of *habeas corpus*. If in truth the prosecutor has been unlawfully arrested and unlawfully handed over to the London police officers, so that he could be unlawfully taken out of the jurisdiction, and all this has been done in such a way as to deprive him of any opportunity to exercise his right under Article 40 of the Constitution to apply for an order of *habeas corpus*, then a gross injustice has been done. Can this Court on whom Article 40, 4, 2°, of the Constitution places the duty of inquiring into any complaint of unlawful detention accept such a return as satisfactory? It has the obligation in the case of injustice done to vindicate the prosecutor's personal right not to be deprived of liberty save in accordance with law. It may be that it is in fact quite impossible for Inspector Ryan to secure the return of the prosecutor to this jurisdiction so that he may be produced in Court in obedience to the order of the Supreme Court; but what is in issue in these proceedings at this stage is the sufficiency of Inspector Ryan's return; and no such impossibility is stated therein. If injustice has been done to the prosecutor he is entitled to vindication; he is, I think, entitled to have it determined by this Court in these proceedings, and declared, that his claim that he was unlawfully deprived of his liberty was justified. The question whether or not it is absolutely impossible for Inspector Ryan to comply with the order of the Supreme Court may have to be considered at a later stage. I take the view that his return is not sufficient in law unless the arrest of the prosecutor and his transfer to the custody of the London police officers for conveyance out of the jurisdiction were made in accordance with law.

The question whether the prosecutor was lawfully arrested and conveyed out of the jurisdiction depends, *inter alia,* upon the validity of the warrant upon foot of which he was arrested; and upon whether it was lawfully indorsed for execution by Deputy Commissioner Quinn for execution here. It is therefore necessary to examine the warrant and its endorsements. It bears an imprint of the Royal Arms of the United Kingdom and is headed, "Ealing Court in the County of Middlesex. Petty Sessions Division of Brentford." It is addressed to each and all the constables of the Metropolitan Police Force. It recites that an information on oath has been laid before the issuing Justice by Detective Constable Alan Johns of the Metropolitan Police, stationed at Wembley Police Station, that Philip Anthony Quinn, thereinafter styled the defendant, had on the 22nd August, 1962, at a named place in the said county stolen certain goods of the property of Dansette Products Ltd., by whom he was employed as a servant, **[91]** contrary to s. 17, sub-s. 1, of the Larceny Act, 1916. It commands those to whom it is addressed to bring the defendant before the Magistrates Court sitting at Ealing forthwith to answer to the information. It is dated the 12th July, 1963; bears the signature, "Robert Bailey, Justice of the Peace for the County first above mentioned," and bears a seal in the form of a crown. It has several endorsements. The first purports to be signed by Detective Constable Alan Johns and to certify that he has reason to believe that Phillip Anthony Quinn is to be found in Dublin. It is dated the 12th July, 1963. I shall refer to it as "the Gb endorsement." The next endorsement is dated the 15th July and purports to be signed by Deputy Commissioner Quinn. It is as follows:—"Proof upon oath having this day been produced before me that the signature 'Robert Bailey' to this warrant is in the handwriting of the Justice of the Peace within mentioned, I hereby endorse this warrant for execution in the City and County of Dublin." The endorsement directs the warrant to "The Superintendent, Garda Siochana, 'D' District, Bridewell Station, Dublin." The next endorsement is dated the 15th July and purports to be signed by Thomas F. Shaughnessy, Inspector (acting Superintendent), Garda Siochana, "D" District. It addresses the warrant for legal execution to Inspector Ryan and certain other named members of the Garda jointly or severally. There are two final endorsements purporting to be signed by Inspector Ryan and Constable Johns to the effect, respectively, that each has executed the warrant by arresting the prosecutor—Inspector Ryan at 11 a.m. and Constable Johns at 11.30 a.m. on the 15th July.

Counsel for the prosecutor have made several submissions as to the validity of the warrant and its endorsements. Similar submissions were made in the case of *The State* (*Potter*) v. *Ryan and Others* (unreported), in which judgment has just been delivered, and have been rejected.

Counsel's first submission, as I understand it, was that if the prosecutor could not have been legally arrested on foot of the warrant in England he could not be legally arrested on foot of it here; that the matter of the validity of the warrant *qua* England was a matter of English law which has to be proved as a matter of fact by expert evidence, and this had not been done. Involved in this submission were the considerations (*a*) whether a Justice of the Peace in England has any legal authority to issue a warrant for the arrest of a person against whom an information has been sworn, charging him with a criminal

[25] 24 Q. B. D. 283.

offence; (*b*) whether the offence charged against the prosecutor was an offence against English law; and (*c*) whether the warrant was an instrument capable of legally **[92]** authorising those to whom it is addressed lawfully to arrest the prosecutor. For the reasons stated in my judgment in *Hully's Case* (unreported) and *Potter's Case* (unreported) I am of opinion that the presumption of the identity of laws affords a complete answer to counsel's first submission.

Counsel's next submission was that the warrant could not be validly endorsed for execution here because the Gb endorsement was not according to the Form Gb in the Schedule to the Petty Sessions Act. It is not, in fact, strictly in accordance with the Form. It certifies only that Constable Johns has reason to believe that the prosecutor is in Dublin, and does not certify the genuineness of the Justice's signature. In a case coming within the provisions of s. 29 of the Act the Justice's signature has to be verified on oath; and a Gb certificate to this effect is both insufficient and unnecessary. The departure from this form in this case is therefore of no significance.

Counsel's next submission was that the Deputy Commissioner had no power to endorse the warrant for execution by anybody other than the "person bringing such warrant" and that he could not lawfully authorise any member of the Gardai to execute it. Sect. 31 of the Act authorises the execution of a properly endorsed warrant by "the person bringing the warrant" and also by all constables and peace officers of the country or place where the warrant is endorsed. The warrant in this case being endorsed in Dublin could be lawfully executed by any Garda stationed in Dublin. The Deputy Commissioner could properly address the warrant by endorsement to the Superintendent, "D" District, Bridewell Station, Dublin; and his Gb endorsement, though not strictly in accordance with the Form Gb in the Schedule, is, for the reasons stated later, perfectly in order. Counsel's submission cannot, in my opinion, be accepted.

Counsel's next submission, if I understood it correctly, was that if Inspector Ryan had authority to execute the warrant he could do so only by himself conveying the prosecutor before the issuing Justice in England; and, alternatively, that if Constable Johns had authority to execute the warrant he could do so only by himself arresting the prosecutor in the first instance, and that taking over custody from Inspector Ryan was not an arrest. For the reasons stated in *Potter's Case* (unreported) I am of opinion that the person named in a properly endorsed English warrant can be lawfully arrested on foot thereof by any Garda of the county or place where the warrant has been endorsed, who can then lawfully hand over custody to the English police officer empowered to execute it, such as any of the constables to whom it was **[93]** originally addressed for execution. He must, however, deliver the warrant to the English police officer at the same time as he hands over custody of the person; and the officer then becomes, so to speak, the holder of the warrant in due course and the "person bringing such warrant" within the meaning of the expression as used in s. 31 of the Act. The act of Constable Johns in taking over custody of the prosecutor from Inspector Ryan was an arrest: see *In re O Laighléis*[26]*. In my opinion counsel's submission is not well founded and should be rejected. Constable Johns, as a member of the London Metropolitan Police Force, to all constables of which the warrant was originally addressed, could lawfully execute the warrant by taking over the custody of the prosecutor from Inspector Ryan.

Counsel's next submission was that the Deputy Commissioner's Gc endorsement was bad because it is not in accordance with the Form Gc in the Schedule, since it contains no recital that the whereabouts of the prosecutor had been certified to him. An exactly similar submission was made to this Court in *Potter's Case* (unreported), and was rejected for the reasons stated. There is no necessity, in my opinion, for such a recital where the warrant contains on one of its faces a proper Gb endorsement.

Counsel's final submission was that Inspector Shaughnessy had no authority to direct execution of the warrant by Inspector Ryan and the other members of the Garda Siochana named in his endorsement. The fact that the Deputy Commissioner by his endorsement addressed the warrant to the Superintendent,

[26] [1960] I. R. 93.

"D" District, did not preclude its execution by members of the Garda other than the Superintendent. It did not mean that the Superintendent, or his acting deputy, Inspector Shaughnessy, must execute it personally. I can see no reason why he should not direct some of his subordinates to execute it.

I am unable to accept any of these submissions made by counsel for the prosecutor and am satisfied to accept Inspector Ryan's return to the order of the Supreme Court as good and sufficient in law.

McLoughlin J.:—

This matter comes before this Court as the result of an order of the Supreme Court, dated Tuesday, the 16th July, 1963. The operative part of that order reads:—"The Court doth order in accordance with Article 40, 4, 2°, of the Constitution that Daniel Costigan, Commissioner of the Garda Siochana, Detective Inspector Matthew Ryan and Garda **[94]** Samuel J. Bell do produce before the High Court (President's Court) at 11 o'clock in the forenoon of Friday, the 19th day of July, 1963, the body of the prosecutor Philip Anthony Quinn and do certify in writing the grounds of his detention and that the High Court do proceed as in the said Article provided." On that date, counsel appearing for the prosecutor and for the respondents, the President adjourned the hearing of the matter to a full Court of three Judges and the matter was heard before us on the 23rd, 24th, 25th, 26th and 29th July. The facts upon which the order of the Supreme Court was made are fully set out in the judgment of the Court, delivered by the Chief Justice, and I do not find it necessary to repeat them at this stage. I am satisfied, however, and I think it is clear from the judgment of the Chief Justice, the order of the Supreme Court was made on the assumption that the prosecutor then was, or might well be supposed to be, in the custody of some members of the Civic Guards and within the jurisdiction of the Court. The application to the Supreme Court was an appeal *ex parte* from the refusal of an application for an order of *habeas corpus* made to Mr. Justice Teevan, also *ex parte*. It now transpires that the prosecutor had been arrested on the previous day, the 15th July, some time in the forenoon by Detective Inspector Matthew Ryan in company with two English police officers, driven from the vicinity of the Bridewell Garda Station in Dublin to the Border at Carrickarnon and there handed over to the custody of those English police officers and taken in a car of the Royal Ulster Constabulary and brought *via* Belfast to England and London. The prosecutor, in an affidavit sworn by him on the 20th July at Brixton Prison in the County of London and read by leave of the Court, states that some time on the morning of the 16th July he was remanded by the magistrate at Ealing in custody to Brixton Prison on a charge that he stole £3,000 worth of transistor radios and other articles from Dansette Products Ltd., Brent Crescent, London. A photocopy of the warrant upon which the prosecutor was arrested in Dublin and handed over to the English police authorities has been given in evidence before us. It is dated the 12th July, 1963, headed "Ealing Court in the County of Middlesex, Petty Sessions Division of Brentford," and it is addressed to each and all the Constables of the Metropolitan Police Force, and recites:—"An information on oath this day laid before me the undersigned Justice of the Peace by Alan Johns, Detective Constable of the Metropolitan Police, stationed at Wembley Police Station, X-Division, that Philip Anthony Quinn of 155 Mortimer Road, Harlesden, N.W.10. on 22nd day of August, 1962, at" etc., and therein sets out a **[95]** charge of stealing of certain transistor radio sets alleged to be contrary to s. 17, sub-s. 1, of the Larceny Act, 1916, and continues:—"You are hereby commanded to bring the defendant before the Magistrates Court sitting at Ealing forthwith to answer to the said information." The warrant bears several endorsements: see the judgment herein of the President. Attached to the photo-copy warrant were the following photo-copy documents:—1, an affidavit of Detective Constable Alan Johns swearing to the signature and seal of the issuing Justice; 2, an affidavit of a senior legal assistant in the office of the Commissioner of Police swearing to the charge set out in the warrant constituting a criminal offence under the law of England.

Each of the three persons directed by the Supreme Court to make a return to the order of the Supreme Court has done so by filing affidavits, all dated the 19th July. Mr. Daniel Costigan, the Commissioner of the Garda Siochana, says in his affidavit that he was not aware of the arrest or of the warrant for the arrest of the prosecutor until some time after 1 p.m. on Monday, the 15th July, and that he had not the prosecutor in his custody, nor was he then detained to the best of his knowledge, information and belief by any member or members of the Garda Siochana. Sergeant Bell of the Bridewell Garda Station said that since the making of the order absolute—it was made by the President of the High Court on the morning of the 15th July, 1963—he had not, nor had he then, the prosecutor in his custody. Detective Inspector Matthew Ryan, in his affidavit, detailed the arresting of the prosecutor at approximately 11.30 a.m. on the 15th July, 1963, upon a British warrant duly endorsed for execution in Ireland by Deputy Commissioner W. P. Quinn, and the handing over of the prosecutor, in the hallway of the Bridewell, to detective constables of the London Metropolitan Police. He further detailed the journey by a Garda car to the Border at Carrickarnon and he says that, since he observed the prosecutor crossing the Border at 1.10 p.m. in the custody of the English police constable, he had not since that time had him in his custody. These three persons were cross-examined on their affidavits. Of the evidence given by them I find it only necessary to quote the following:—

Evidence of Commissioner Daniel Costigan:—"I cannot say how the warrant arrived in this case. I can't say if it was addressed to Detective Commissioner Quinn. Normally I back warrants only in the absence of the Deputy Commissioner, and I don't see these communications normally. Since 1 p.m. on the 15th July last I have had no control over **[96]** the prosecutor and no means of getting him back and I have made no endeavour to get him back."

Evidence of Detective Inspector Matthew Ryan:—"I got the warrant, that is, the second warrant, from Detective Commissioner Quinn at 10 a.m. on the morning of the 15th July at the Depot, Phoenix Park. I was present in Court and had the warrant in my possession when the order was made by the President, Judge Davitt, on the morning of the 15th July. After the prosecutor was discharged by the President of the High Court I followed him when he went with his counsel to the ground floor of the building near Court No. 6. The prosecutor left his counsel there and went down the corridor towards the District Court and emerged from the building at the door leading into the District Courts and into the yard, where all the cars are parked. I went out of the yard ahead of him, and when he left the yard I beckoned him over to where I was standing outside the main entrance to the Bridewell Garda Station. I said to him:—'I am Detective Inspector Ryan, I have an English warrant for your arrest,' and I read it over to him. I said, 'Do you understand?' and he said, 'Yes.' I then told him I was handing him over into the custody of the two British policemen who were standing nearby. He did not at any stage say he wanted to see a solicitor. I knew at the time that I went into the Court with the second warrant that the prosecutor would be discharged on the first warrant and I then had the intention of re-arresting him on the second. I endorsed the warrant at Whitehall Garda Station, on the way up to the Border."

In the circumstances which have come to light since the order was made by the Supreme Court I do not know what this Court is being asked to do. What order should be made by this Court in the new circumstances? The case for the prosecutor has been argued by Mr. MacBride and by Mr. O Síocháin, but although they have raised numerous points with regard to the validity of the warrant, with regard to the constitutionality of the procedure for the execution of British warrants in this country, under the Petty Sessions Act of 1851, and as to what might be described as the sudden and expeditious nature of the arrest of the prosecutor under the second warrant, I do not think any effective order can properly be made by this Court. At the end of his argument, Mr. O Síocháin did ask that the Commissioner, Detective Inspector Ryan, Sergeant Bell and Deputy Commissioner Quinn should be attached for contempt of Court. The only contempt alleged against anyone was the failure by Commissioner Costigan to take any steps to secure the return of **[97]** Quinn from his present custody in England. On this basis I see no reason why this Court should accept the burden of contention that has not even been fully argued as to the validity of the warrant, the lawfulness of the arrest, the constitutionality of the Petty Sessions Act, or the authority of persons in this country to back English warrants for execution in this country, but I do propose to say something on the contention that this Court should attach the persons I have mentioned for contempt of Court. On this branch of the case some authorities were referred to which it may be necessary for me to deal with, but, before doing so, I wish to make some remarks upon what I conceive to be the nature of the right of personal liberty and the right of persons to resort to the Court where liberty has been taken away not in accordance with law.

The right to personal liberty goes back a long way in the history of the law. Formerly it was said to have been enshrined in the Charter of Magna Carta, and received further statutory recognition in the Habeas Corpus Act of 1849, and had a prominent place in the Constitution of Saorstát Eireann, 1922, and of course, now in our constitution of 1937. Prior to the establishment of this State the way in which a person sought to enforce his right to liberty in the Courts was governed by procedure then in force. In order to understand the applicability of some of the cases to which we have been referred, it is necessary to state shortly what this special procedure was. A writ of *habeas corpus* being what is called, or described as, a King's writ or prerogative writ, did not issue at the instance of the party; a party aggrieved had to apply for the issue of the writ and get an order from the Court for its issue. The procedure was to apply to the Court for leave to issue the writ; that application was made *ex parte* and might be granted or a conditional order might be granted, directed to the party against whom it was intended to issue the writ, to show cause why it should not be issued; depending upon the cause shown the writ then might not be issued or might be directed to issue. If the writ was directed to issue, the party against whom it was directed was entitled then to make return to the writ. To what extent that procedure is now extant is a matter of some doubt, but, in any event, I do not think it matters in the circumstances of this case. It would appear to me at all events that the order of the Supreme Court is in the nature of a writ of *habeas corpus*, actually issued, and the return made to that writ by the person against whom it was directed is a return of "I do not detain and have not had under my detention or in my custody the body of the person in respect of whom complaint is made **[98]** that he is being unlawfully detained and I did not have such body in my custody or under my control at the time at which the order was made." There is no doubt that a return of a writ may be deemed insufficient and that a return which amounts to a disobedience of the order of the Court may be punished by attachment, but I am not aware of any case in which an order for attachment was made in a case where the act complained of or done by the party sought to be attached was an act done in purported exercise of a public duty before any application was made for the issue of a writ of *habeas corpus*.

In this matter it should be realised that it is a matter which was directed to be heard by this Court under Article 40, 4, 2°, of the Constitution. There is no motion in these proceedings asking for relief by way of attachment; there is no disobedience by any of the parties of any order of the Court; also, there is no appearance for one of the persons sought to be attached. Furthermore, the acts alleged to be contempt are acts which were done by executive officers in the ordinary execution of normal duty. I was not clear whether this Court is being asked to exercise its jurisdiction to attach at the instance of a party or its jurisdiction to commit of its own motion in exercise of its inherent power to punish for disobedience to a peremptory order. In this connection, see the case of *In re Earle*[27] and the judgment of FitzGibbon J. therein, at page 501. In order to examine whether there is anything in the contempt alleged, I find it necessary to refer back for a moment to the earlier history of this case. On foot of the first warrant upon which the prosecutor was arrested and later discharged,

[27] [1938] I. R. 485.

the application to the Court for a conditional order was based upon several grounds. The principal ground seems to have been that the prosecutor was not the person referred to in the warrant, the name therein being Patrick Anthony Quinn, not Philip Anthony Quinn. As this conditional order was made absolute on consent it is not possible to state if, on that application, any of the other grounds would have been held to be good if cause had been shown. It was only to be expected, I would think, that a second warrant would issue in which the prosecutor would be properly described and that on his discharge on foot of the first warrant he would promptly be re-arrested on the second warrant. I think it is quite clear from the prosecutor's own affidavit that he expected this to happen on his release on the first warrant, and so it happened. Unless Detective Inspector Ryan should reasonably have assumed that the second warrant, properly describing the prosecutor, could be held **[99]** to be bad on some other ground, for example, the constitutionality of the procedure under the Petty Sessions Act or the incompetence of Deputy Commissioner Quinn to back the warrant or for some other such reason, his ordinary course of duty was to do what he was directed by his superior to do and execute the warrant by arresting the prosecutor and handing him over to the British constables who were the persons responsible for bringing the prosecutor before the English magistrate, who issued the warrant.

For myself, I cannot see how there was any contempt of Court on the part of anybody concerned in the execution of the warrant or any disobedience to any order of the Court.

The issue of a second warrant to rectify a fault in a first warrant is no new thing. It happened in similar circumstances as far back as the year 1937 in the two *Kingston Cases.*[28] I do not think it is any function of mine as a Judge, to advise either the Legislature or the Executive as to how they should carry out their functions. I suppose I am entitled to express the view that the procedure of executing English warrants would be better carried out by means of an extradition treaty rather than by the adoption of the procedure under the Petty Sessions Act. I suppose I am also entitled to express the view that as long as this procedure is the only procedure available for the purpose, it should be carried out subject to certain safeguards—that the person arrested be told that he may seek legal advice if he wishes to challenge the legality of the arrest in accordance with his constitutional rights, and that he be given an opportunity to do so before being taken out of the jurisdiction of these Courts.

I am perfectly satisfied that this Court has no jurisdiction in the circumstances of the case, as I find them, to order the committal of the persons named as respondents or any other person, because I hold, for reasons I shall later state, that the return made by the respondents to the order of the Supreme Court is a good and sufficient return. There are authoritative cases which illustrate the circumstances under which the remedy of attachment is called in aid for the enforcement of *habeas corpus*—the *Barnardo Cases* and the *Matthews Case*[29] referred to during the course of the argument, and the Irish case, *In re Earle,*[30] which was not referred to. The circumstances alleged to constitute contempt of Court in this case fall far short of the circumstances alleging the contempt in these cases, the facts of which are set out in the judgment of the learned President and which I need not repeat. For the facts in the *Earle Case,* I refer to the report[30]. **[100]**

Although, as I have already said, it is desirable that a person arrested on a foreign warrant in this country should be given an opportunity to exercise his constitutional right to challenge the validity of his arrest before being taken out of the country, I do not agree with the view expressed by the President in his judgment that the proper procedure to have been adopted in this case was for the prosecutor to have been arrested on the second warrant before he had been discharged on the first one, in order to have the validity of the fresh warrant challenged in the proceedings relating to the first warrant. Such a procedure was not adopted in the *Kingston Cases,*[31] I have never heard of such a pro-

[28] [1937] I. R. 483; 717.
[29] 12 Ir. C. L. R. 233.
[30] [1938] I. R. 485.
[31] [1937] I. R. 483; 717.

cedure being adopted before, and I can imagine many technical objections being taken to such a procedure. Furthermore, I think it is wrong to construe the return made by Detective Inspector Ryan in this case as the prosecutor contends it should be construed, simply:—"I have not had the prosecutor in my custody since before the making of the Supreme Court order. I did have custody of him, but I parted with the custody to another to avoid the making of an effective order." The way I read the return is this:—"I did have custody of the prosecutor, having arrested him in pursuance of a foreign warrant, apparently valid for execution in this country, authorising me to hand over such custody to an English police officer to be tried for a criminal offence in England. I cannot produce the warrant because, as I was bound to do, I handed it back to the English police officer when handing over custody of the prosecutor to him. I had no reason to suppose that the warrant, as endorsed by Deputy Commissioner Quinn, was not a valid warrant authorising me so to act."

This interpretation of the return does not preclude the Court from enquiring into the validity of the warrant and, accordingly, before the case came to be argued before the Court as now constituted, the President required to have produced a copy of the warrant. To comply with this direction there was handed to the members of this Court what purported to be photo-copies of the warrant to which were attached photo-copies of two affidavits, one being by Detective Alan Johns, dated the 13th July, 1963, exhibiting by reference the warrant and testifying to the signature and seal of the issuing Justice of the Peace; the other, of the same date, by an English solicitor, exhibiting the warrant as being attached thereto and certifying the offence mentioned in the warrant to be a criminal offence under English law.

Assuming that the photo-copies are what they purport to be, namely, photographs of an original warrant and of **[101]** affidavits, relating to it, Mr. O Síocháin made several submissions as to the validity of the warrant and as to the authority of a member of the Garda Siochana to execute it in the City of Dublin by arresting the prosecutor and handing him over in custody to Detective Constable Johns to be brought before the Justice of the Peace who issued the warrant to answer the information laid in the warrant. The warrant with its endorsements and the affidavits are identical in terms with the like documents in *Potter's Case* (unreported), which was fully argued before this Court, and the submission made in both cases cover the same ground. In accordance with our decision in the *Potter Case* (unreported), the submission made by Mr. O Síocháin must be rejected.

Most of the burden of arguing this case on behalf of the prosecutor was undertaken by Mr O Síocháin, and although he submitted that the three respondents and Deputy Commissioner Quinn should be committed for contempt, he stated the contempt to be the failure of these four persons to take any steps to secure the return of the prosecutor from England. To show the weakness of his challenge to the actual return made by the respondents I quote some passages from a written submission, which he handed into Court on the morning of the 24th July:—"As an absolute order of *habeas corpus* granted by the Supreme Court has not been complied with by the respondents the arguments regarding the validity of the warrant do not arise, it is possible that, in the circumstances of this case, the British authorities, out of respect for the order of the Supreme Court, would return the body of the prosecutor to Ireland if so requested by the Irish Government—the Court might consider indicating that it would welcome any effort that might be made by the Government to secure the return to Ireland of the prosecutor—that if the transfer of the prosecutor out of the jurisdiction was done through error or inadvertence then we feel certain that the Attorney General, and the Government here would co-operate with the Courts in endeavouring to secure this; without prejudice to these submissions, we are prepared to argue that the warrant is invalid if the Court so desires."

What this Court has to determine is the sufficiency of the return made by the respondents to the order made by the Supreme Court to produce the body of the prosecutor. The return indicates why they are unable to comply with the order, and, in my opinion, on the evidence given and for the reasons which I have stated, it is a good and sufficient return.

TEEVAN J.:—

I would accept Mr. McGonigal's submission. Even within [**102**] the authority of the *Matthews Case,*[32] I am of opinion that the return and plea of jurisdiction for the non-production of the body of the prosecutor, made by Inspector Ryan, in his affidavit of the 19th July, 1963, was good and sufficient return in law. (It has now been held good and sufficient in fact as well). I respectfully differ from the opinion of the learned President, that before pronouncing the return good the Court must examine and enquire into the validity of the warrant and its endorsements. The return shows that prior to the order of *habeas corpus,* Inspector Ryan's custody of the prosecutor had not alone ceased but had passed out of the respondent's power and control, so as to make it impossible for him to produce the body.

Leaving out of account the cause shown by the respondent in the *Matthews Case*[32] against the conditional order (without overlooking, however, its significance and importance to the particular case) and coming to the return to the writ, it seems to me that the return was held bad in law because of an insufficiency apparent in the return itself. At page 247, Hayes J. says:—"Taking the whole return together, as, I think, we are entitled and bound to do, and looking at the four corners of the writ and return, and giving to the return such a construction as we would give to a special plea of justification, it appears to me to convey that, previous to and on the 8th July, 1858, this child was in the actual custody and possession of Miss Aylward, and, being so in her possession, it was handed over by that lady, *of her own authority,* to Elizabeth Kenny; and that, while so in the possession of this Elizabeth Kenny (the nurse selected by Miss Aylward), the child was taken and removed from her custody and possession by some person unknown, without the sanction or authority of Miss Aylward; since which time Miss Aylward is unable to give any further account of the child, and, therefore, does not produce it. I hold this to be an insufficient answer to the writ. It does not traverse the suggestion of the writ, that Miss Aylward took the child, but, in fact, admits the taking by her. Neither does it show any sufficient legal excuse or justification for not obeying the writ, by producing the child in Court."

Coming to the conclusion of his judgment, Hayes J. gives in form, to my mind, the principle on which the foregoing rested. He says (at pp. 252 and 253):—"When the Court can collect from the writ *and return* that the party has been in illegal custody, at a period antecedent to the issuing of the writ, it will not rest satisfied with the stereotyped form that, at the issuing of the writ, or at any time since, the party has not been in his possession, custody or power; but will insist [**103**] on the person to whom the writ is directed producing the party, or showing that he has lawfully discharged himself of such custody." Then, having referred to the case of *Rex* v. *Wright*[33] he concludes in these words:—"Upon the whole of this case, I am of opinion that it sufficiently appears, from a perusal of the writ and return, that, at a period antecedent to the issuing of the writ, Miss Aylward had the child in her custody; and that a responsibility thereby attached to her, which, not being divested by any of the matters set forth in the return, still continues; and that the child not having been produced in obedience to the writ, an attachment ought to be awarded against her."

The return made by Miss Aylward is cited in full in the report and supplies the facts upon which the return was held insufficient in law, although, as the President has shown, Lefroy C.J. seemed to treat it rather as a return insufficient in fact.

In his affidavit of return Inspector Ryan says:—"At approximately 11.30 a.m. on the 15th day of July, 1963, I arrested the said Philip Anthony Quinn, on foot of a British warrant duly endorsed for execution in Ireland by Deputy Commissioner Quinn. The said arrest was carried out in Chancery Street immediately outside the Bridewell Station.

[32] 12 Ir. C. L. R. 233. [33] 2 Str. 915.

"Having arrested the said Philip Anthony Quinn I brought him into the hallway of the Bridewell and handed him over to Detective Constable Alan Johns and Police Constable Perry, both members of the London Metropolitan Police. At the same time, I handed Detective Constable Alan Johns the said original warrant and received from him a receipt"—and he exhibited this receipt.

He then goes on to state that he accompanied the two British police officers and the prosecutor to the Border and saw all three of them cross into Northern Ireland, at 1.10 p.m. on the 15th July, 1963, that is, prior to the application made to me for a conditional order.

There is nothing in that return (or elsewhere) to suggest that the parting with the custody by Inspector Ryan was equivocal, or for the purpose of evading or forestalling the process of the Court. There was nothing to show (as there was in the return in the *Matthews Case*[34]) that at any stage the custody had ceased to be legal, or, for that matter (although the submission I am dealing with is independent of it), that it had been illegal at any stage. Inspector Ryan offers that the warrant was duly endorsed by the Deputy Commissioner for execution in Ireland, which should be taken to mean in accordance with the law as it then stood. So far as I recall, **[104]** counsel for the prosecutor did not challenge the factual substance of the return. It was, of course, put in issue when the President directed the respondents to produce and verify the warrant. I mean the facts pleaded were not thereafter challenged.

I desire to draw attention to what I consider to be a vital distinction between the *Matthews Case*[35] and *Barnardo Cases* and cases like the present. The former cases were concerned with subjects taking or keeping custody of other subjects after such custody had become plainly illegal and with the added probability of designed evasion of legal process. The law never provided immunities for the like. With police and other peace officers making arrests on warrants the case is different. The law provides immunity where action is taken on warrants good on their face. Police officers are obliged to execute warrants entrusted to them, and are answerable for failure to do so; they have no choice or discretion in the matter.

I agree that the principle cannot be variously stated, but I do not think that the distinction I refer to calls for any variation of, or exception from, principle, in favour of police officers.

In the *Matthews Case*[35] "the child still continued, in contemplation of law, to be in the custody, possession and power of Miss Aylward": per Hayes J., at page 250. Later, at the same page, Hayes J. (referring to the abduction alleged to justify non-production of the body) says:—"But is Miss Aylward to found a legal excuse upon a misfortune which resulted from her own misconduct and neglect?" and Miss Aylward's attitude and inactivity in regard to the alleged abduction "tends to raise in the mind a strong suspicion of secret management and connivance ..."

In handing over custody of the present prosecutor, Inspector Ryan was fulfilling a duty. I refer now solely to the act of handing over. The purpose of the arrest was to hand over the prisoner to the British authorities. Even if other things on the occasion remain, or are later to be found censurable, the act of handing over, of parting with the custody, was the performance of a legal duty as police officer, and I am discussing the legal interpretation of the return, the main pleas of which are cessation of custody before process and justification for non-production.

In *Gossage's Case,*[36] Lord Esher, referring to the decision in *Tye's Case*[37] to which he was a party, said (at p. 294):—"It was not necessary there to determine whether, if it could be shown that it was absolutely impossible in the nature of **[105]** things that he should produce the child, as for instance if it had since died, then a writ of *habeas corpus* ought to go merely for the purpose of punishing him, nor is it necessary to determine that question now. I have very little

[34] 12 Ir. C. L. R. 233.
[35] 12 Ir. C. L. R. 233.
[36] 24 Q. B. D. 283.
[37] 24 Q. B. D. 305.

hesitation, however, in saying that, if the case could be brought up to that pitch, and if it could be shown that, however wrong the conduct of the person proceeded against had been, it had become absolutely impossible for him to produce the child, then the writ of *habeas corpus* ought not to go merely for the purpose of punishing a past illegality. *In that case we did not think that any such absolute impossibility was made out.* We intended to decide not, I think, that, if the production of the child was absolutely impossible, a writ of *habeas corpus* ought to go, but that, unless such absolute impossibility was clearly shown, it was no excuse for the defendant to show that he had illegally parted with the possession of the child under such circumstances that it would be extremely difficult or almost impossible for him to produce the child, seeing that such difficulty was the result of his own illegal act."

The issue in *Gossage's Case*[38] was whether the writ should go. Here we are concerned with the return. Even Fry L.J., who considered that a writ should not issue if it should appear to the Court to demand the impossible, said (at p. 299):—"Matters to which I will further refer create in my mind a great suspicion as to the circumstances under which the child was made over. I think that, where a child has been illegally handed over shortly before the issue of the writ, under circumstances of great suspicion, and which give reason to believe that it was done for the purpose of avoiding the exigence of a writ about to be issued, an exception arises to the general principles I have mentioned." At page 300, he says:—"If there be reason to believe that an illegal act has been done in order to defeat the anticipated process of the Court, and that on the issue of the writ, the person will ultimately be produced, then, in my opinion, the writ ought to go. In the present case the circumstances do, in my opinion, afford strong grounds for inferring that that is the real nature of the case." His judgment concludes with the words, "I think, therefore, that the true conclusion upon the materials before us is that the child was made over in order to evade process, and that if the process goes it is *highly probable that the appellant may yet be able to produce the child . . .*"

I see a great distinction between cases such as those and the case of a policeman who, acting in pursuance of a warrant duly backed for execution here, effects an arrest, and who in pursuance of his duty has, before process, parted with his **[106]** custody to the authorities of the place of issue. That apart, however, the probability which existed in the cases referred to, that, under the pressure of the Court process, the defendant might secure the return of the person formerly held by him—in other words, that the pleaded impossibility was only a seeming impossibility—is out of such cases as the present. It would be absolutely impossible for Inspector Ryan to resume custody or otherwise secure production in Court of the prosecutor. The facts averred to in his affidavit reveal that impossibility.

Furthermore, that impossibility appears to be recognised as such by the prosecutor's counsel in that, in their written submission, they requested this Court to use its endeavours towards procuring governmental intervention with the British authorities for the return of the prosecutor. As I read this submission it implies the concession that Inspector Ryan is powerless to produce, or to arrange for the production of, the prosecutor. This is not a case where the facts throw doubt on whether the respondent has truly ceased to have control over the prosecutor.

The Court has, however, enquired into the arrest made by the respondent, Inspector Ryan, and into the validity of the warrant and its endorsements, and I agree with the judgment of the learned President, and with his conclusion, that the arrest and detention of the prosecutor, until he was handed over, were in accordance with law.

From the above decision the prosecutor appealed to the Supreme Court. The grounds of the appeal were as follows:—

[38] 24 Q. B. D. 283.
[39] [1952] I. R. 62.

"The High Court was wrong in law and in fact 1, in holding that the prosecutor was in lawful custody when arrested on the 15th day of July, 1963, for the purpose of being handed over to the police of another State to be removed out of the jurisdiction;

"2, In holding that the warrant on which the prosecutor was arrested was lawfully and validly executed by the arrest of the prosecutor by Detective Constable Alan Johns of 'X' Divison of London Metropolitan Police at Bridewell Garda Siochana Station, in the City of Dublin, at 11.30 a.m. on the 15th day of July, 1963, as per return of execution shown on copy of said warrant exhibited by Detective Inspector Matthew G. Ryan in his affidavit of the 19th July, 1963;

"3, In holding that the provisions of s. 29 of the Petty Sessions (Ireland) Act, 1851, relating to the backing of **[107]** warrants by the Inspector General and the Deputy Inspector General of the Royal Irish Constabulary, are part of the law of Ireland by virtue of the Constitution of Saorstát Eireann and of An Bunreacht;

"4, In holding that s. 29 of the Petty Sessions (Ireland) Act, 1851, which relates to the backing of warrants by the Inspector General and the Deputy Inspector General of the Royal Irish Constabulary was in force on the 6th day of December, 1962;

"5, In holding that the Adaptation Order was effective and made with statutory authority;

"6, In holding that the jurisdiction of the Inspector General and Deputy Inspector General of the Royal Irish Constabulary in backing warrants under s. 29 of the Petty Sessions (Ireland) Act, 1851, was *qua* Justice and not *qua* police officer;

"7, In holding that the requirement that the person backing the warrant should certify on the Form Gc to render the certificate effective had been complied with;

"8, In holding that the jurisdiction of the Inspector General and the Deputy Inspector General of the Royal Irish Constabulary to back warrants under s. 29 of the Petty Sessions (Ireland) Act, 1851, was *qua* Justice and not *qua* police officer as transferred to the District Court;

"9, In holding that the endorsement on the warrant by Deputy Commissioner W. P. Quinn was sufficient to justify the arrest despite the failure of the Deputy Commissioner to certify as required by Form Gc;

"10, In holding that the Adaptation Order could adapt or modify s. 29 of the Petty Sessions (Ireland) Act, 1851, so as to render the backing of a warrant effective in an area in which the Inspector General and the Deputy Inspector General never had jurisdiction, namely, the Dublin Metropolitan Police Area;

"11, In holding that to justify detention proof was not necessary or required (*i*) that the person issuing the warrant had jurisdiction to do so;

"(*ii*) That the offence charged in the warrant was at the time of arrest an offence against English law;

"(*iii*) That the warrant was effective in the area outside which it was issued and that it was a good warrant;

"(*iv*) That Detective Constable Alan Johns had jurisdiction to execute the warrant outside the area and jurisdiction in which it was issued; **[108]**

"12, In holding that the arrest and the detention of the prosecutor was good in law;

"13, In holding that the person issuing the warrant had jurisdiction to do so, that the offence charged was at the time of detention an offence against English law, and that the warrant was effective outside the area in which it was issued and was good despite the fact that, at the date and time when the warrant was issued, a warrant to like effect and purpose was already in existence and on which the prosecutor was arrested and held in custody, and that Detective Constable Alan Johns had jurisdiction to execute the warrant outside the area in which it was issued;

"14, In holding that Detective Inspector Matthew G. Ryan who arrested the prosecutor was entitled to release him to Detective Constable Alan Johns and that the said Detective Inspector Ryan was not bound to bring the prosecutor before the Justice who issued the warrant or any Justice;

"15, In holding that the provisions of s. 31 of the Petty Sessions (Ireland) Act, 1851, have not been affected by the provisions of the District Justices (Temporary Provisions) Act, 1923, s. 4, sub-ss. 3 and 4; the Courts of Justice Act, 1924, s. 89, sub-s. 4, and similar statutes of criminal jurisdiction and the Criminal Justice Act, 1951, s. 15, which provides that any person charged with an offence shall on arrest be brought before a Justice of the District Court having jurisdiction to deal with it, to be dealt with according to law;

"16, In holding that the provisions of s. 31 of the Petty Sessions (Ireland) Act, 1851, which provides for the bringing of the person arrested on a 'backed' English warrant before the Justice who had issued same have not been impliedly repealed by the effect of each, and the combined effect of all, the following statutes:—(*a*) District Justices (Temporary Provisions) Act, 1923, s. 4, sub-ss. 3 and 4; (*b*) Courts of Justice Act, 1924, s. 89, sub-s. 4; (*c*) Courts of Justice Act, 1928, s. 19; (*d*) Criminal Justice Act, 1951, s. 15;

"17, In holding that where a warrant is addressed to each and all of the constables of the Metropolitan Police Force it is effective outside the area of the jurisdiction of the Justice issuing same and of the County in which same was issued;

"18, In holding that the power to back a warrant which was executable in the Dublin Metropolitan Area in 1922 only by Justices can by reason of the Adaptation Order now be exercised by persons other than District Justices; **[109]**

"19, In holding that the provisions of s. 29 of the Petty Sessions Metropolitan Area on an endorsement by the Deputy Commissioner and An Garda Siochana" [*sic*];

"20, In holding that where it appears the person named in the warrant was to be found in the police district of the Dublin Metropolis there was jurisdiction to address the warrant to persons other than the Commissioner of Police for the Metropolis.

"21, In holding that the magistrate who signed the warrant was a Justice of the Peace and that it was established on the warrant itself to that effect without proof;

"22, In holding that it was not essential that the warrant itself should show that the person signing it was a Justice of the Peace;

"23, In holding that the warrant for the taking of the prosecutor from the jurisdiction authorised his taking into the jurisdiction of Northern Ireland;

"24, In holding that the warrant authorised the taking of the prosecutor by Detective Constable Alan Johns after execution by arrest by him of the prosecutor through the Counties of Dublin, Meath and Louth, into the County of Armagh;

"25, In holding that the Petty Sessions (Ireland) Act, 1851, authorised the removal of the prosecutor from the jurisdiction to that part of Ireland which on the 7th day of December, 1921, opted to exercise jurisdiction independent of the Courts in this country;

"26, In holding that the arrest and handing over of the prosecutor for arrest to a member of a foreign police force and forcible deportation from out of the jurisdiction of the Court was not *ultra vires* An Bunreacht;

"27, In not holding that the action of Detective Constable Alan Johns of the London Metropolitan Police Force was a usurpation of powers conferred by statute to be exercisable by members of the Garda Siochana only;

"28, In holding that the arrest of the prosecutor on a second warrant and within the precincts of the Court was not a contempt of Court."

P. A. O Sícháin S.C. and *D. E. Bell S.C.* (with them *L. Meagher*) for the appellant (prosecutor):—

The appellant has been deprived of his constitutional right to apply to the High Court to question the validity of the warrant under which he was arrested and to obtain an order of *habeas corpus* He had been removed from the jurisdiction **[110]** before he was given any opportunity of applying to the Court;

that is a clear breach of the provisions of the Constitution and brings the respondent into contempt of Court.

By reason of the action of Inspector Ryan and his colleagues and subordinates the personal rights guaranteed to the citizen by the Constitution, and in particular the personal right of personal liberty guaranteed by Article 40, 4°, 1, has been flouted. It is true that the provisions of the Petty Sessions (Ireland) Act, 1851, provide for the instant removal of a person arrested out of the jurisdiction of the Irish Courts; but, that being so, those provisions are repugnant to the provisions of the Constitution which guarantee the right of personal liberty and which guarantee the right to any such person to invoke the jurisdiction of the High Court; such provisions are contrary to and repugnant to the Constitution, which overrides all legislation.

The case of *The State* (*Duggan*) v. *Tapley*[39]* is distinguishable from the present case in that, although it was there held that s. 29 was not repugnant to the Constitution, it was so held on the ground that Article 29 of the Constitution did not make international law a part of the domestic law of this State and that decision did not compare or set up s. 29 in opposition to Article 40 of the Constitution. All that was decided in that case was that there was no generally recognised principle in international law which forbade surrender in accordance with s. 29 of the Petty Sessions (Ireland) Act, 1851. That case decided that international law did not make it necessary that there should always be a judicial enquiry before an order of extradition was granted. In the *State* (*Dowling*) v. *Kingston* (*No.* 2)[40] the prosecutor—as in *Tapley's Case*[39] was exercising his right to apply to the Courts while he was present within the jurisdiction. Accordingly, the question of a conflict between s. 29 of the Act of 1851 and Article 40 of the Constitution never arose at all. In *Dowling's Case*[40] the relevant provision was Article 6 of the Constitution of Saorstát Eireann, but it is in much the same terms as Article 40 of the present Constitution.

What the police have done in the present case is a violation of the prosecutor's right of personal liberty and is unlawful and accordingly the respondents are in contempt of Court.

Niall McCarthy S.C. and *Seán Butler S.C.* (with them *T. F. Donnelly*) for the respondents:—

There is no doubt that an arrested person has a right to question the validity of his arrest in the Court, but the Petty Sessions (Ireland) Act operates immediately unless that person **[111]** states that he wants to apply to the Court. The Act contains no express prohibition of immediate removal from the jurisdiction. The evidence shows that the prosecutor in this case did not make any enquiry or request to apply to the Court upon his arrest. Such a person has a right if he makes a request to have the legality of his arrest determined by the Court. If any person by whatever means deprives or endeavours to limit that right, he is acting wrongfully and acting contrary to Article 40 of the Constitution. Sect. 29 of the Act of 1851 authorises the instant removal of the prosecutor out of the jurisdiction unless he requests otherwise. That section, at the date of the happenings in this case, was part of the law of the State and as such was binding upon the police officers and they acted in accordance therewith and, therefore, lawfully.

The relevant sections (ss. 29, 30 and 31) of the Petty Sessions (Ireland) Act, 1851, have already been held not to be repugnant or inconsistent with the Constitution of Saorstát Eireann in *The State* (*Dowling*) v. *Kingston* (*No.* 2)[41]* and also not inconsistent with the provisions of the present Constitution in *The State* (*Duggan*) v. *Tapley*.[42]* Those decisions are decisions of the Supreme Court and so are binding upon the Court. Therefore, the respondents, having acted in accordance with the law the validity of which has been decided, were acting perfectly lawfully and have not committed any breach of the Constitution or any wrong against the prosecutor.

[40] [1937] I. R. 699.
[41] [1937] I. R. 699.
[42] [1952] I. R. 62.

Furthermore, the provisions of ss. 29, 30 and 31 are not inconsistent with the Constitution because there is no command in those sections that a prisoner is to be instantly removed out of the jurisdiction. It is quite possible that those provisions may be operated in a manner completely consistent with the provisions of Article 40, 4, of the Constitution. If the sections made it mandatory immediately upon an arrest that the arrested person was to be removed out of the jurisdiction, then the situation might be different. However, as the sections do not do so, they are not inconsistent with the Constitution as they are capable of being operated in a manner consistent and consonant with the provisions of the Constitution.

The Court adjourned on 25th June, so that notice might be served on the Attorney General in relation to the constitutionality or otherwise of the relevant sections of the Petty Sessions (Ireland) Act, 1851, and the hearing was resumed on the 13th July, 1964. **[112]**

Eoin Ryan S.C. (with him *D. P. Sheridan*) for the Attorney General:—

The Petty Sessions (Ireland) Act, authorises the immediate removal of a prisoner from the jurisdiction without any opportunity of having recourse to the Courts, even though that may be deliberately contrived. It allows of his being "whisked" away. The constitutionality of the relevant sections has been already decided by this Court and the position is entirely covered by the two decisions of this Court, *The State (Dowling)* v. *Kingston* (No. 2)[43] and *The State (Duggan)* v. *Tapley*.[44]* Those cases have established beyond argument the validity of the procedure followed in the present case. [He also referred to *Attorney General and the Minister for Posts and Telegraphs* v. *Coras Iompair Eireann*[45]; *Morelle Ltd.* v. *Wakeling*[46]].

P. A. O. Síocháin S.C. in reply.

Cur. adv. vult.

Ó DÁLAIGH C.J.:—

The appellant in these proceedings is Philip Anthony Quinn, an Irish citizen.

The proceedings arise out of Quinn's disappearance on Monday, the 15th July, 1963, at about 11.30 a.m.

At 11.15 a.m. on the 15th July, 1963, the President of the High Court made absolute a conditional order of *habeas corpus* and ordered Quinn's release. Quinn was in the President's Court in the custody of Detective Inspector Matthew G. Ryan when his release was ordered.

He walked with his junior counsel as far as Court No. 6. Counsel had business in that Court, and he agreed to meet Quinn outside Court No. 6 in a short while. When counsel came out from Court No. 6 Quinn was nowhere to be seen.

Counsel (it would appear) got into communication with Quinn's solicitor, Mr. Concannon, who began enquiries without delay by going to the Bridewell Garda Station. He asked for Detective Inspector Ryan and he was told he was on holidays. He there interviewed an inspector and three sergeants. The inspector and two of the sergeants had no information to impart. The third sergeant, Detective Sergeant Friel, said he understood a warrant had been issued for Quinn's arrest but that he did not know the name of the Irish officer who had the warrant. A garda, whom Mr. Concannon was unable to identify, said that Quinn had gone to the Airport. Mr. Concannon went to the Airport and there searched in vain **[113]** for his client. He returned to the Four Courts and made a further search without avail.

In these circumstances Mr. Concannon instructed counsel to apply to Mr. Justice Teevan for a conditional order of *habeas corpus* to be directed to Detective Inspector Ryan and to the jailer of the Bridewell Garda Station. The application was made at 3.45 p.m. Mr. Justice Teevan refused it.

Later that afternoon Mr. Concannon renewed his enquiries at the head-

43 [1937] I. R. 699.
44 [1952] I. R. 62.
45 90 I. L. T. R. 139.
46 [1955] 2 Q. B. 377; [1955] 1 All E. R. 708.

quarters of the Metropolitan Division of the Garda Siochana in Dublin Castle. He obtained no information. Next he communicated by telephone with Garda Headquarters in Phoenix Park and formulated a number of questions for the attention of the Assistant Commissioner. He again telephoned Garda Headquarters that evening at about 9 p.m. when he was given the following message:—"Inform Mr. Concannon that Philip Anthony Quinn is not now in custody anywhere in the Dublin Metropolitan Division. Deputy Commissioner Carroll is not prepared to deal with this matter over the telephone but if Mr. Concannon wants to put any queries in writing he would deal with them the first thing in the morning."

Having thus failed to obtain from the Garda authorities information as to his client's whereabouts Mr. Concannon instructed counsel on the following morning, the 16th July, 1963, to renew in this Court an application for a conditional order of *habeas corpus* by way of appeal from the refusal of Mr. Justice Teevan.

This Court on that application made an order in the terms of Article 40, 4, of the Constitution directed to the Commissioner of the Garda Siochana, Detective Inspector Ryan and the jailer of the Bridewell Garda Station to produce the body of Philip Anthony Quinn in the High Court at 11 o'clock on the forenoon of Friday, the 19th July, 1963, and to certify in writing to that Court the grounds of detention. The order was directed to the Commissioner of the Garda Siochana in view of the evasive attitude of the Garda authorities to the proper inquiries of Quinn's solicitor.

All three respondents filed affidavits by way of return to this Court's order, and a Divisional Court of the High Court, presided over by the President, by order dated the 18th November, 1963, held that the respondents' return was good and sufficient and ordered the prosecutor to pay the respondents' costs.

The prosecutor has appealed.

The respondents were cross-examined in the High Court on their affidavits.

The prosecutor's account of his arrest and that given by **[114]** Detective Inspector Ryan differ in a number of respects: (*i*) the prosecutor says he was arrested in the west courtyard of the Four Courts; Inspector Ryan says he made the arrest in Chancery Street, the public street adjoining this courtyard.

(*ii*) The prosecutor says that the warrant was neither shown nor read to him; the Inspector says he read the warrant over to the prosecutor, asked him did he understand it and cautioned him, using the usual form of caution.

(*iii*) The prosecutor says he told Inspector Ryan he wished to see his solicitor and that he was answered by Detective Constable Johns, who said:—"You can see a solicitor when you get to London"; Inspector Ryan says the prosecutor did not on arrest or at any other time say he wanted to see his solicitor.

(*iv*) The prosecutor says he was put into a motor car and driven first to a Garda Station (which is identified as Whitehall Garda Station) and then to the Northern Ireland boundary post at Carrickarnon; Inspector Ryan says there was an initial visit to the Bridewell Garda Station.

The President of the High Court accepted the prosecutor's account; his two colleagues do not appear to have addressed themselves specifically to the important differences in the two accounts. The President called attention to the fact that Inspector Ryan in his affidavit said expressly that the prosecutor did not ask him or anyone else in his presence and to his knowledge for sight of the warrant, while on cross-examination the Inspector said he read the warrant over to the prosecutor and asked him did he understand it. When the President asked the Inspector how he came to leave out of his affidavit that he read over the warrant to the prosecutor the Inspector answered:—"Well, I was in the hands of my legal advisers."

I do not propose to rest my opinion upon any matter where the account of the prosecutor and the account of Inspector Ryan are at variance; I do not find it necessary to do so.

The following facts are clearly established: I set them out in a chronological table:—

Saturday, 6th July, 1963.	The prosecutor was arrested in Dublin on an earlier warrant and lodged in the Bridewell Garda Station.
Sunday, 7th July, 1963.	The President granted a conditional order of *habeas corpus* upon the ground that the person **[115]** named in the warrant was not the prosecutor. The order was directed to Detective Inspector Ryan and the jailer of the Bridewell Garda Station.
Friday, 12th July, 1963.	A new warrant—the warrant in question in these proceedings—was issued in London in respect of Philip Anthony Quinn, which is the prosecutor's correct name.
Saturday, 13th July, 1963.	Inspector Ryan was advised that afternoon that the earlier warrant was bad.
Monday, 15th July, 1963. 10 a.m.	Inspector Ryan was handed the new warrant by Sergeant Dunne at Garda Headquarters where the office of Deputy Commissioner Quinn is situated. The warrant had already been backed for execution by Deputy Commissioner Quinn.
10.30 a.m.	Sergeant Bell entered the prosecutor's cell in the Bridewell and told the prosecutor to pack all his belongings and to be ready to leave at a moment's notice. The prosecutor packed his belongings as directed.
10.30 a.m.	A conference attended by Commissioner Costigan and Deputy Commissioner Quinn began in Garda Headquarters and finished at 12.30. In the course of this conference Deputy Commissioner Quinn informed the Commissioner that arrangements had been made for the conveyance of a prisoner to Great Britain *via* the Border. The Commissioner did not then realise that the prisoner referred to was Philip Anthony Quinn.
10.45 a.m.	Inspector Ryan arrived at the Four Courts accompanied by **[116]** Detective Constable Johns of the London Metropolitan Police Force.
11 a.m.	Counsel for Inspector Ryan applied *ex parte* to the President of the High Court to discharge the prosecutor. President directed that the prosecutor and his counsel should be present in Court.
11.15 a.m.	The prosecutor is brought to the President's Court and counsel for Inspector Ryan renews his application in the presence of junior counsel for the prosecutor. The prosecutor is ordered to be released.
11.20/25 a.m.	Prosecutor parts company with his counsel outside Court No. 6 and arranges to meet him there after counsel has attended to some business in that Court. He is apprehensive that he may be arrested.
11.30 a.m.	The prosecutor is re-arrested, either in the west courtyard of the Four Courts or in Chancery Street, and is handed over into the custody of Detective Constable Johns and Constable Perry. A Garda car is in attendance close by; after a brief

	delay the prosecutor is put into the back of the car and Inspector Ryan sits into the car beside the driver. A short stop is made at Whitehall Garda Station when Inspector Ryan made a telephone call on official business.
12.30—1 p.m.	At lunch, following upon the termination of the Garda Commissioner's conference at 12.30 p.m., the Commissioner for the first time realised that the prisoner referred to by Deputy **[117]** Commissioner Quinn was Philip Anthony Quinn. Deputy Commissioner then told the Commissioner (in the words of the Commissioner) the full story of the making absolute of the order, of the re-arrest of the prosecutor and of his conveyance (*sic*), and of the arrangements that had been made for his conveyance to the Border.
1.10 p.m.	The Garda car crosses the Border at Carrickarnon and the prosecutor is taken to Belfast.
9.10 p.m.	The prosecutor is taken on board the Heysham boat for England by Detective Constable Johns and Constable Perry and in their custody.

It should be added that no notification was given to the prosecutor's solicitor of the respondents' intention to apply to the President to discharge the prosecutor, nor was the President informed when the application was made to him that it was proposed to re-arrest the prosecutor immediately and that police officers were then sitting in Court with a new warrant ready to execute this purpose.

From this survey of the evidence it becomes clear that a plan was laid by the police, Irish and British, to remove the prosecutor after his arrest on the new warrant from the area of jurisdiction of our Courts with such dispatch that he would have no opportunity whatever of questioning the validity of the warrant. It is also clear that the applicant's solicitor was refused information (and in one instance supplied with misinformation) as to his client's whereabouts while his client was still within the jurisdiction, and that this refusal was persisted in while the prosecutor was still in Northern Ireland.

It should be pointed out that in zeal for celerity of action the plan provided for sending the prosecutor into Northern Ireland where on no view of the law he was authorised to be sent. The authority of the warrant (if authority it had) was to transmit him to Britain. To have done this would, however, have involved delay in Dublin while the departure of aeroplane or ship was awaited. But any delay within the jurisdiction might have afforded the prosecutor's solicitor an opportunity to challenge the validity of the new warrant in **[118]** the Courts and this would have set at nought the whole purpose of this plan.

In plain language the purpose of the police plan was to eliminate the Courts and to defeat the rule of law as a factor in Government.

Two main questions have arisen on the argument of this appeal. The first concerns the construction of the Petty Sessions (Ireland) Act, 1851, and the second, arising out of the first, concerns the question of the constitutionality of the Act.

The question of construction is this: whether, when a person has been arrested under a British warrant which has been backed for execution under the provisions of s. 29 of the Act, the Act purports to authorise the immediate removal of the prisoner out of the jurisdiction without his being afforded a reasonable opportunity of applying to the Courts to question the validity of such warrant? If this is the correct construction of the Act, then, there arises the second question, whether or not the Act in so authorising is consistent with the Constitution? Article 50 of the Constitution continues in force the laws in force in Saorstát Eireann, subject however to the Constitution and to the extent to which they were not inconsistent therewith.

The submission made on behalf of the Attorney General (who is a notice party only) was both forceful and unequivocal. As to the construction of the Act, it was that the Act authorises a prisoner's immediate removal without opportunity of having recourse to the Courts, even though this is deliberately contrived: it allows (as it was said) of his being "whisked" away. As to constitutionality, the submission was that the judgment of the Supreme Court in *The State (Dowling)* v. *Kingston (No.* 2)[47] and *The State (Duggan)* v. *Tapley*[48]* had established, beyond recall, the validity of this procedure.

The position taken up on behalf of the respondents was more equivocal. The Attorney General's submission, it was said, was "supported" and, then, "qualified." The qualification was this: an arrested person has a right to question the validity of his arrest in the Courts, but the Act operates immediately unless the prisoner says he wants to apply to the Courts. The Act, it was said, contains no express prohibition of immediate removal.

In my opinion the Attorney General's first submission is well founded. The Petty Sessions (Ireland) Act, 1851, does purport to authorise removal from the jurisdiction *instanter* without any opportunity, reasonable or otherwise, to invoke the Courts. There can be little doubt that this was the purpose **[119]** of the Act when it was enacted. Ireland was then part of the entity known as the United Kingdom of Great Britain and Ireland and was in enjoyment of the benefits of the Act of Union. One of these benefits was the free interchange of alleged offenders subject to the formality of local backing of warrants.

However unreal, the theory was that an Irishman, as a subject of the Queen, should have been as happy, safe and as much at home in Britain as in Ireland. The backing provisions of s. 29 of the Act are the counterpart of the provisions of s. 27, para. 3, for the backing of Irish warrants into Britain; and both sets of provisions are a mere extension of the inter-district and inter-county backing provisions of sect. 26. The whole pattern (understandably in what was a homogeneous political system) is a pattern of domestic dealing; and no question could arise of an arrested person not being in a position to invoke the Courts: the Queen's Courts were as much, if not more so, in Britain as in Ireland.

There is, in my opinion, no room here for the doctrine advanced in argument by counsel for the respondent police officers that the Act should be construed to accord with the Constitution. A basis can be found for such an approach in construing an Act of the Oireachtas; it is entirely lacking in the case of a statute of the British Parliament.

I now turn to an examination of the constitutionality of the provisions of the Petty Sessions (Ireland) Act, 1851, touching the backing of British warrants for execution in Ireland.

As I have already said, counsel for the Attorney General relied upon two cases as establishing the constitutionality of s. 29 having regard to the provisions of the Constitution of Ireland.

First, as to *Dowling's Case* (*No.* 2)[49]: (i) This is a decision based on the terms of Article 6 of the Constitution of the Irish Free State. (ii) It is a decision of the Supreme Court of the Irish Free State. (iii) The *ratio* of the decisions is an affirmation of *The State* (*Kennedy*) v. *Little*,[50]* in which the Court rejected an attack upon the constitutionality of the Fugitive Offenders Act, 1881. This Act does not permit of an arrested person being removed from the jurisdiction *instanter*; on the contrary, it requires that he must be brought before a magistrate before removal.

Chief Justice Sullivan, at p. 731, says:—"The same argument that Mr. Ryan addressed to us in this case was advanced on behalf of the prosecutor in *The State* (*Kennedy*) v. *Little*[50] in support of the contention that the Fugitive Offenders Act, 1881, was inconsistent with the Constitution, but it was **[120]** rejected by the High Court—Johnston, Hanna, and O'Byrne JJ.—and the deci-

[47] [1937] I. R. 699.
[48] [1952] I. R. 62.
[49] [1937] I. R. 699.
[50] [1931] I. R. 39.

sion of the High Court was affirmed by this Court on appeal. I am of opinion that s. 29 is not inconsistent with the Constitution, and it, therefore, continued to be of full force and effect after the Constitution had come into operation."

Mr. Justice FitzGibbon, at p. 746, took the same ground:—"Upon the other main question, the alleged inconsistency between the provisions of the Petty Sessions (Ireland) Act, 1851, s. 29, and the Constitution, I am of opinion that it is covered by the decision of this Court in *The State* (*Kennedy*) v. *Little*[51]*."

Mr. Justice Meredith, at p. 758, also saw no distinction between the Fugitive Offenders Act and the Petty Sessions Act provisions, and he accepts *The State* (*Kennedy*) v. *Little*[51]* as ruling the case (pp. 758-9).

Mr. Justice Geoghegan is to the same effect: see page 759.

Mr. Justice Murnaghan agreed with the Chief Justice and Mr. Justice FitzGibbon on the question of the constitutionality of the statute (p. 752).

Counsel referred the Court to a passage in the report of Dowling's first application: *The State* (*Dowling*) v. *Brennan*.[52] There Gavan Duffy J. (as he then was) in the course of the argument said to counsel for the Attorney General:—"Under this procedure a man could be arrested and removed from this country without any opportunity of appearing before a Court here. Under the Fugitive Offenders Act, 1881, were there not safeguards?"

This seems to be an advertence by Mr. Justice Gavan Duffy to the point raised in this case, but the point was not taken by counsel nor was it considered by the Court. In fact Dowling in that application and in his second application was exercising the right which the prosecutor here complains he was not permitted to exercise, i.e., an opportunity to question the validity of the warrant on foot of which he was arrested.

It requires to be said that a point not argued is a point not decided; and this doctrine goes for constitutional cases (other than Bills referred under Article 26 of the Constitution and then by reason only of a specific provision) as well as for non-constitutional cases.

The second of the two cases relied upon, *Tapley's Case*,[53]* was a decision under the Constitution of Ireland. The argument presented on behalf of the prosecutor was that *Dowling's Case* (*No.* 2)[54] was to be distinguished by reason of the provisions of Article 29 of the Constitution, which deals with **[121]** "international relations." Gavan Duffy P. in the course of his judgment in the Divisional Court said, at p. 64:—"I fail to discern in the present case anything in law (except Article 29 of the Constitution) to distinguish it in principle from the case of *The State* (*Dowling*) v. *Kingston* (*No.* 2)[55] . . . I shall therefore confine myself in the main to an examination of Article 29, governing our international relations." Haugh and Kingsmill Moore JJ. concurred.

Chief Justice Maguire delivered the judgment of the Supreme Court. He said, at p. 75:—"Apart from Article 29 of the Constitution, upon which the main reliance was placed, Mr. Ryan contended that the section was inconsistent with Articles 1, 5, 6 and 9 of the Constitution.

"The Court agrees with the President of the High Court that there is nothing in the Constitution, save Article 29, to distinguish the present position from that existing in *The State* (*Dowling*) v. *Kingston*.[55]

"The question whether Article 29 of the Constitution has altered the position has been fully argued and is, in fact, as the learned President has said, the main question to be examined."

This brief examination is enough to dispose of the cases of *Dowling* (*No.* 2)[55] and *Tapley*.[56]* It should be added that Tapley, like Dowling, had an opportunity of challenging the validity of the warrant under which it was proposed to send him out of the jurisdiction.

The Court had no argument advanced to it in support of the constitutionality of s. 29 of the Petty Sessions (Ireland) Act, 1851, by counsel for the Attorney

[51] [1931] I. R. 39.
[52] 71 I. L. T. R. 131, at p. 134.
[53] [1952] I. R. 62.
[54] [1937] I. R. 699.
[55] [1937] I. R. 699.
[56] [1952] I. R. 62.

General other than the argument based on the *Dowling* (*No.* 2)[55] and *Tapley*[56]* cases.

Counsel for the respondent police officers did, however, say there was a constitutional right of resort to the Courts but only if one specifically asked for it. This matter has been fully examined by Mr. Justice Walsh in the judgment he is about to deliver. I agree with that judgment and the conclusion he reaches that the Petty Sessions (Ireland) Act, 1851, s. 29, and the consequential provisions are repugnant to the Constitution and invalid.

The claim made on behalf of the police to be entitled to arrest a citizen and forthwith to bundle him out of the jurisdiction before he has an opportunity of considering his rights is the negation of law and a denial of justice.

It remains now to consider what is the effect of s. 29 of the Petty Sessions (Ireland) Act, 1851, being held to be repugnant to the Constitution. **[122]**

On behalf of Inspector Ryan it has been submitted that the return he makes to the order of this Court is good and sufficient: that he no longer has custody of the prosecutor.

The action which Inspector Ryan took with regard to the prosecutor was taken in disregard of the prosecutor's constitutional rights, and the return he makes to the order of this Court is in effect this: that he should not be held answerable by this Court because he has succeeded by reason of careful planning and the celerity of his action in preventing the prosecutor from obtaining effective relief in the Courts.

It was not the intention of the Constitution in guaranteeing the fundamental rights of the citizen that these rights should be set at nought or circumvented. The intention was that rights of substance were being assured to the individual and that the Courts were the custodians of these rights. As a necessary corollary it follows that no one can with impunity set these rights at nought or circumvent them, and that the Courts' powers in this regard are as ample as the defence of the Constitution requires. Anyone who sets himself such a course is guilty of contempt of the Courts and is punishable accordingly.

The proper order to be made in respect of Detective Inspector Matthew G. Ryan is that he be served with notice to show cause why he should not be held to be guilty of contempt of the Courts and dealt with accordingly.

As the Long Vacation intervenes he will have until the opening day of the Michaelmas Term to file such further affidavits as he may be advised. The matter will be listed again in this Court on Monday, 2nd November, at 11 o'clock in the forenoon.

It is not shown that the other respondents were concerned in the planning or execution of the police action taken in regard to the prosecutor; their returns may therefore be deemed good and sufficient. There is, however, evidence that others played an active role in either the planning or execution of the police action taken in regard to the prosecutor.

The evidence at present before the Court points to Deputy Commissioner Quinn as a person who was foremost in the planning of the police action and points to the two British policemen, Detective Constable Johns and Constable Perry, as persons who engaged in both the planning and execution of the police action, all with the same general purpose of depriving the prosecutor of a reasonable opportunity of exercising his constitutional right of applying to the Courts to question the validity of the warrant under which he was arrested. **[123]**

Orders will therefore issue in respect of Deputy Commissioner Quinn and Detective Constable Johns and Constable Perry in the same terms as the order made in respect of Detective Inspector Ryan, with the same concessions with regard to the time for showing of cause and listing as is proposed in the case of Detective Inspector Ryan.

Notice of the Court's orders in respect of Detective Constable Johns and Constable Perry will be sent to them by registered post, c/o The Commissioner of London Metropolitan Police.

LAVERY J.:—

I agree with the judgment of the Chief Justice and with the order he proposes. I have read the judgment which Mr. Justice Walsh will deliver and I also agree with it.

KINGSMILL MOORE J.:—

In my opinion the terms of ss. 29, 30, 31 of the Petty Sessions Act, 1851, purport to authorise the removal from Ireland, under a British warrant, properly endorsed, of the person named in such warrant; and to authorise the removal with such speed and in such circumstances as are calculated to defeat his constitutional right to apply to the High Court under Article 40, 4, of the Constitution. To this extent these sections are in conflict with the provisions of the Constitution and must be considered invalid and no longer part of the law of Ireland.

The judgments in *The State* (*Dowling*) v. *Kingston* (*No.* 2)[57]* and *The State* (*Duggan*) v. *Tapley*[58]* are not based on, nor do they advert to, the above consideration and even if it was touched on in the arguments (which seems doubtful) it was certainly not pressed or fully argued. These judgments therefore cannot be regarded as having decided the point.

I agree with the Chief Justice and Mr. Justice Walsh that the facts proved in this case point to a deliberate and concerted attempt to remove the prosecutor from the jurisdiction in such a manner and with such celerity as would render it difficult, if not impossible, to exercise his constitutional right of applying to the Courts; and I agree with the action proposed by the Chief Justice.

HAUGH J.:—

I agree with the judgments which have just been delivered and with the judgment about to be delivered. **[124]**

WALSH J.:—

Among the personal rights guaranteed by the Constitution is the right not to be deprived of personal liberty save in accordance with law: Article 40, section 4, sub-section 1. At sub-section 2 it is provided that upon complaint being made by any person to the High Court (and, therefore, on appeal to this Court) that he is being unlawfully detained his release must be ordered unless the Court is satisfied that he is being detained in accordance with the law. At section 3 the State guarantees in its laws to respect and, as far as practicable, by its laws to defend and vindicate the personal rights of the citizen and in particular by its laws to protect as best it may from unjust attack, and in the case of injustice done, vindicate the right, person, good name, and property rights of every citizen. At section 4, sub-section 3, of Article 40 the Constitution recognises the possibility of a person's detention being in accordance with a law but such law being invalid having regard to the provisions of the Constitution.

It is quite clear that a right to apply to the High Court or any Judge thereof is conferred on every person who wishes to challenge the legality of his detention. It must follow that any law which makes it possible to frustrate that right must necessarily be invalid having regard to that provision of the Constitution. One very effective method of frustrating this right of access to the High Court would be to make it physically impossible for the person detained to apply to the Court by removing him out of the jurisdiction before he would have had an opportunity of doing so. Any law authorising the removal of a detained person out of the jurisdiction must, to avoid the taint of unconstitutionality, permit the detained person to remain or to be kept within the jurisdiction for such a length of time as would afford him a reasonable opportunity to consider and, if he so desired, to exercise his constitutional right to apply to the High Court for the purpose of questioning the validity of his detention.

In the present case the prosecutor had been removed to a place outside the jurisdiction, namely, across the Border, within two hours of his arrest in the

[57] [1937] I. R. 699. [58] [1952] I. R. 62.

immediate vicinity of these Courts. It was submitted on his behalf, and indeed agreed to and urged on behalf of the Attorney General and the respondents, that under the provisions of ss. 29, 30 and 31 of the Petty Sessions (Ireland) Act, 1851, a person arrested within the jurisdiction upon a warrant issued in any of those places outside the jurisdiction which are set out in s. 29, may be removed *instanter* out of this jurisdiction. It was further submitted on behalf of the Attorney General and the respondents that a person arrested under those statutory provisions **[125]** could exercise his Constitutional right to invoke the High Court only if he were fortunate enough to gain access to the Court before his removal from the jurisdiction and that the existence of such a constitutional right did not in any way act as a bar or a stay upon the execution of the powers conferred upon the Gardai or other police officers by the sections referred to.

Acts of the Oireachtas enjoy the presumption of being not repugnant to the Constitution in force at the date of their enactment unless such repugnancy be clearly shown. Acts of the Parliament of the former United Kingdom of Great Britain and Ireland, of which the Petty Sessions Act, 1851, is one, enjoy no such privileged position. By virtue of Article 50 of the Constitution the Petty Sessions Act, 1851, continued to be in force after the coming into operation of the Constitution only to the extent to which its provisions were not inconsistent therewith. Article 50, is, of course, not confined to statutes of the former United Kingdom but refers to all laws in force in Saorstát Eireann immediately prior to the coming into operation of the present Constitution. Article 73 of the Constiution of Saorstát Eireann provided that subject to that Constitution and to the extent to which they were not inconsistent therewith the laws in force in Saorstát Eireann at the date of the coming into operation of that Constitution should continue to be of full force and effect until either repealed or amended by the Oireachtas. Thus the provisions of the Petty Sessions Act, 1851, never enjoyed under either Constitution a presumption of constitutionality.

It has been urged upon this Court on behalf of the Attorney General and on behalf of the respondents that these sections have already been held to be not inconsistent with the Constitution of Saorstát Eireann in *The State* (*Dowling*) v. *Kingston* (*No.* 2)[59] and not inconsistent with the provisions of the present Constitution in *The State* (*Duggan*) v. *Tapley*[60]*. It has been further urged that these decisions are binding upon this Court. It is unnecessary in this case to explore the consequences of the fact that this Court is not the Court which decided either of those cases; this Court was established in 1961. It is also unnecessary to express any final view upon the constitutionality of subjecting this Court (as distinct from all other Courts set up under the Constitution) to the rule of *stare decisis*. Neither is it necessary to discuss in detail the question of whether in the case of a Court of final appeal *stare decisis* can ever be anything more than judicial policy, albeit strong judicial policy. However, in view of the implications in the submissions advanced in this Court on behalf **[126]** of the Attorney General and of the respondents it must be clearly stated, though one would have hoped it should not have been necessary to do so, that this Court is the creation of the Constitution and is not in any sense the successor in Ireland of the House of Lords. The jurisdiction formerly enjoyed by the House of Lords in Ireland is but part of the much wider jurisdiction which has been conferred upon this Court by the Constitution. I reject the submission that because upon the foundation of the State our Courts took over an English legal system and the common law that the Courts must be deemed to have adopted and should now adopt an approach to Constitutional questions conditioned by English judicial methods and English legal training which despite their undoubted excellence were not fashioned for interpreting written constitutions or reviving the constitutionality of legislation. In this State one would have expected that if the approach of any Court of final appeal of another State was to have been held up as an example for this Court to follow it would more appropriately have been the Supreme Court of the United States rather than the House of Lords. In this context it is not out of place to recall that in delivering the judgment of the Supreme Court in *In the Matter of Tilson*

[59] [1937] I. R. 699. [60] [1952] I. R. 62.

Infants[61] Mr. Justice Murnaghan stated, at p. 32:—"It is not a proper method of construing a new constitution of a modern state to make an approach in the light of legal survivals of an earlier law."

So far as the provisions of the Constitution itself bear upon the place of *stare decisis* in constitutional cases the provisions of section 3, sub-section 3, of Article 34, which is an amendment to the Constitution as enacted by the People, appear to me to clearly indicate that it is only in the case of a law or a provision of a law, the Bill for which had been referred to the Supreme Court by the President under Article 26 of the Constitution, that there is no longer jurisdiction in any Court to question the constitutional validity of that law or that provision of that law. It has been submitted on behalf of the Attorney General and the respondents that this amendment to the Constitution was designed only to meet a possible argument that because it was a Bill which *had been* approved by the Court that the law when enacted would be open to challenge again once it was signed by the President and that it was to be inferred from this provision that the Constitution impliedly imposed the rule of *stare decisis* in respect of constitutional cases. In my view this contention is quite unsustainable and it would be strange indeed if the Constitution in making such an express provision for Bills only **[127]** would leave unexpressed but to be inferred a provision in similar terms applicable to Acts. To my mind the absence of such an express provision is an indication that the People in enacting this Constitution and the Oireachtas in amending it within the period limited by the transitory provisions of the Constitution, which have since expired, had no intention of creating by inference only a situation in which a decision of this Court upon the interpretation of the Constitution could be altered only by way of a national referendum for the purpose of amending the Constitution. Far from being daunted by this formidable but inescapable conclusion arising from their submissions counsel for the Attorney General and for the respondents urged that this was the position envisaged by the Constitution. Having regard to the express provision of the Constitution I have no hesitation in rejecting the submissions which lead to such a conclusion. This is not to say, however, that the Court would depart from an earlier decision for any but the most compelling reasons. The advantages of *stare decisis* are many and obvious so long as it is remembered that it is a policy and not a binding, unalterable rule.

Acts of the Oireachtas are, as I have already stated, presumed to be valid and not repugnant to the Constitution under which they were enacted. If, therefore, an Act or a section of an Act is unsuccessfully challenged as to its validity, the rejection of that challenge is not what gives validity to the Act. The Act continued to enjoy its original presumption of validity. A challenge to an Act based on a particular ground or upon several particular grounds does not ordinarily, if ever, involve an examination of every possible ground of invalidity and the decision of a Court in rejecting the challenge is a decision that the presumption of validity has not been displaced by any of the grounds advanced in support of the challenge. In contrast, the Constitution expressly provides in the case of Bills referred to the Supreme Court that by the operation of Article 26 and Article 34, section 3, sub-section 3, of the Constitution a decision of this Court concludes all points in respect of the Bill or a provision of the Bill, as the case may be, which is referred to it. In such case this Court gives an advisory opinon upon a reference unlimited as to grounds with the consequence that if in the opinion of this Court the Bill or the specified provision thereof is not in any respect repugnant to the Constitution or to any provision thereof, the President shall sign the Bill. One can therefore readily appreciate that the reason for such an express provision in the Constitution was to avoid the anomaly of a judicial review of legislation which only became law upon the advice of this Court after an unrestricted examination of **[128]** the measure which thus acquired validity from the judgment of this Court.

It remains to consider what was decided in the cases relied upon by the Attorney General and the respondents. In *The State* (*Duggan*) v. *Tapley*[62]* s. 29 of the Petty Sessions (Ireland) Act, 1851, was challenged on the grounds of an

[61] [1951] I. R. 1. [62] [1952] I. R. 62.

alleged repugnancy to Article 29 of the Constitution. It was submitted that Article 29 made international law a part of domestic law of this State and that the provisions of s. 29 of the Act of 1851 were not in accord with the generally recognised principles of international law. It was submitted that the usual safeguards contained in extradition treaties were missing from s. 29 in that, among other things, there was no provision made for any judicial enquiry prior to the surrender of the prisoner and that, further, international law required reciprocity as a necessary condition for the existence of a valid extradition law and that therefore s. 29 of the Act of 1851 could only exist if there was a similar legislation in Great Britain. The Supreme Court decided that there was no generally recognised principle in international law which forbade surrender in accordance with s. 29 of the Petty Sessions Act, 1851, or which required reciprocal legislation in Great Britain or in any other state to which a prisoner might be surrendered under provisions similar to or identical with the provisions of s. 29 of the Act of 1851. It has been urged in this Court on behalf of the Attorney General and of the respondents that because the lack of a safeguard providing for a judicial enquiry before surrender was adverted to in the course of that case the Court must be taken to have decided that the provisions of s. 29 of the Act of 1851 were not inconsistent with the provisions of Article 40 of the Constitution. In my view no such inference can be drawn from the case and the only inference with regard to judicial enquiry which can be drawn from the case is that the Court was satisfied that international law did not require that extradition should always be preceded by a judicial enquiry. The question of the inconsistency of s. 29 with Article 40 of the Constitution was not raised or adverted to at all. That is perhaps not surprising when one recalls that the prosecutor in that case, unlike the prosecutor in the present case, was in fact exercising the constitutional right conferred on him by Article 40, section 4, while being present within the jurisdiction with the consequent right to be released if his gaolers could not satisfy the Court that he was being detained in accordance with law. A similar position was enjoyed by the prosecutor in *The State* (*Dowling*) v. *Kingston* (*No.* 2)[63]. If his gaolers had not **[129]** succeeded in justifying his detention he also would have obtained his release (as he had in his first case, reported in the same volume, at p. 483) under Article 6 of the Constitution of Saorstát Eireann which corresponded to section 4 of Article 40 of the present Constitution. It is to be noted in passing that Article 6 did not contain any provision similar to the provision of section 3 of Article 40 of the present Constitution. In that case s. 29 of the Act 1851 was challenged as being inconsistent with the Constitution of Saorstát Eireann in that it would authorise the arrest of a citizen in Saorstát Eireann on a warrant issued by the Court of another country and was therefore incompatible with the sovereignty of Saorstát Eireann over its citizens. In that case the Supreme Court rejected the argument that the existence of legislation similar to or the same as s. 29 was unconstitutional for being incompatible with the sovereignty of the State and it held that the existence of such legislation was not inconsistent with the sovereignty of the State. Reliance has been placed upon observations of Mr. Justice Meredith, in the course of his judgment, in which it is sought to show that he held that the existence of s. 29 was not inconsistent with Article 6 of the Constitution of Saorstát Eireann. When one examines his words it is clear that what he was dealing with was the question of whether an international agreement for extradition or a provision such as s. 29 was inconsistent with any Article of the Constitution, and in particular with Article 6, but only in the context of whether extradition as such or the delivery of a prisoner to another jurisdiction by virtue of a statutory provision such as s. 29 was inconsistent with the Constitution and, in particular, Article 6 thereof. This is made clear when he points out, at p. 756, that to comply with the submissions being advanced on behalf of the prosecutor, Article 6 should have had added to it the words (I quote), "and no person shall be removed out of Saorstát Eireann for the purpose of giving jurisdiction to the Courts of any other State."

[63] [1937] I. R. 699.

He does not for a moment suggest that the right conferred by Article 6 to apply to the Court for the purpose of testing the validity of a detention could lawfully be encroached upon or set at naught by s. 29 or any other statutory provision and at no stage was his mind directed towards the impact of s. 29 upon the exercise of that right of application to the High Court.

In my view, therefore, these two decisions do not bear out the claim made for them by counsel for the Attorney General and for the respondents, namely, that these cases have already decided the point at issue in this case.

Lastly, I turn to the submission made on behalf of the **[130]** respondents, though not on behalf of the Attorney General, namely, that because the Garda or other police officers when operating ss. 29, 30 and 31 of the Act of 1851 might choose not to remove a prisoner *instanter* from the jurisdiction that these provisions are not inconsistent with the Constitution in that they may thus be operated in a manner not inconsistent with the provisions of Article 40, section 4, of the Constitution. It is at the same time contended, and in my view correctly so, that the sections of the Petty Sessions Act, 1851, do authorise the instant removal of a prisoner from the jurisdiction. If that were to be the position Article 40, section 4, would be of no value so far as those arrested here on English warrants are concerned and to sanction such a view would be to affirm by decision of this Court, which is bound to uphold the Constitution, a manifest neglect, if not an open defiance, of the provisions of the Constitution intended for the protection of persons deprived of personal liberty. No Court charged with the duty of upholding the Constitution could permit the provisions of it to be revoked or suspended at the choice of members of the Garda or other police forces in the name of law enforcement.

The true test is to discover what is *intra vires* the statute. At the time the statute was passed and at all times up to the enactment and coming into force of the Constitution of Soarstát Eireann a prisoner could under these sections be instantly removed from this jurisdiction to the jurisdiction from whence the warrant came. If an act is *intra vires* a statute but at the same time inconsistent with the Constitution it is clear that the statute cannot stand. In the exercise of powers conferred by an Act of the Oireachtas any act inconsistent with the provisions of the Constitution is probably *ultra vires* the statute unless expressly authorised by the statute or authorised by necessary implication because it may be presumed until the contrary be clearly shown that the Oireachtas did not intend to give legislative authority for acts inconsistent with the Constitution to which the Oireachtas itself is subject. In my view the provisions of s. 29, s. 30 (so far as it deals with warrants issued outside the jurisdiction) and s. 31 were inconsistent with the provisions of Article 6 of the Constitution of Saorstát Eireann and are inconsistent with the provisions of Article 40 of the Constitution of Ireland, sub-Articles 3 and 4, in that the instant removal of a person arrested authorised by those sections is inconsistent with the provisions of Article 40, section 4, of the Constitution. For that reason I am of opinion that s. 29, s. 30 (so far as it referred to warrants issued outside the jurisdiction) and s. 31 of the Act of 1851, were, by virtue of Article 78 of the Constitution of Saorstát Eireann, not carried over; but even **[131]** if they were carried over, they ceased to have full force and effect since the coming into operation of the Constitution by virtue of Article 50 thereof. The similar provisions of the Indictable Offences (Ireland) Act, 1849, to the extent (if any) to which they had not been repealed prior to 1922 are also inconsistent with the Constitution for the reasons already given in reference to the Petty Sessions Act, 1851.

I also agree with the judgment which has been delivered by the Chief Justice and with the order he proposes.

The case was re-listed for hearing on the 16th November, 1964.

Niall McCarthy S.C., Seán Butler S.C. and *T. F. Donnelly* for Detective Inspector Ryan and Deputy Commissioner W. P Quinn.

G. A. Clarke S.C. and *R. P. Barr* for Detective Sergeant Johns and Detective Constable Parry of the British Police.

Affidavits were opened to the Court on behalf of the police officers and apologies were tendered on behalf of Detective Inspector Ryan and Deputy Commissioner W P. Quinn.

Mr. Clarke stated that his clients would not tender an apology to the Court unless and until they had been found in contempt.

Cur. adv. vult.

O DALAIGH C.J.:—

The judgment which I am about to read is the judgment of the majority of the Court, consisting of Mr. Justice Lavery, Mr. Justice Kingsmill Moore, Mr. Justice Walsh and myself, and it is the judgment of the Court in this matter.

The four persons now before the Court are here to show cause why they should not be held to be guilty of contempt of the Courts and punished accordingly.

Only one of these persons, Detective Inspector Matthew G. Ryan of the Garda Siochana, was a party to the original proceedings in this matter. Inspector Ryan's return to this Court's order of *habeas corpus* was adjudged bad and insufficient. As a result of Inspector Ryan's actions the prosecutor, Philip Anthony Quinn, was in fact deprived of his constitutional right to apply to the Courts to test the legality of the warrant for his arrest and deportation (the warrant may be so shortly described) and, as it has been now established, was unlawfully arrested and deported to England.

It first came to the notice of this Court in the proceedings to which the order granted on the 16th July, 1964, was made **[132]** absolute that the other three persons now before the Court were associated in different ways with the prosecutor's arrest and deportation: Detective Constable Johns and Police Constable Perry, both officers of the London Metropolitan Police, were the English policemen who took over custody of the prosecutor from Inspector Ryan, and, accompanied by him, brought the prosecutor out of the jurisdiction; and it appeared that Inspector Ryan, in carrying out the prosecutor's arrest and assisting in his deportation, was in communication, either directly or indirectly, with the fourth person now before the Court, Deputy Commissioner William P. Quinn, of the Garda Siochána, who backed the warrant for execution.

All four have filed affidavits showing cause; and on request they were granted leave to file, and have filed, supplementary affidavits.

What is said in the affidavits is in effect this: the decision to take the prosecutor out of the jurisdiction with the dispatch which was employed was not designed to defeat the Courts. The English officers were unable to obtain suitable accommodation on the Dun Laoire-Holyhead boat, and in these circumstances they decided to travel *via* Northern Ireland on the Belfast-Heysham boat. One of the English officers also says that he disclosed to a barrister (whom he purports to identify as the counsel who appeared for the prosecutor) that it was the intention of the English police to re-arrest the prosecutor. What is not explained is why notice was not given to the prosecutor's solicitor of the application to the President of the High Court to procure the discharge of the prosecutor by consenting to the making absolute of the original conditional order of *habeas corpus*. Nor, indeed, is any explanation furnished of a number of other features of the case, viz., why the President was not informed that it was the intention to re-arrest the prosecutor on a fresh warrant immediately he left the Court; why it was necessary to have directed the prosecutor, who was in custody in the Bridewell, to pack his bag before going to the High Court and to be ready to leave at a moment's notice; why it was necessary to have a police car standing ready in the vicinity of the Four Courts; why the formal receipt of the transfer of the custody of the prisoner was executed not at the Bridewell but at another Garda Barracks in the course of the journey northwards.

None of these features has been explained. They are not the marks of a police transaction carried out in the ordinary way; rather do they indicate a desire to have the prosecutor **[133]** out of the jurisdiction before he or his legal advisers could move to question the legality of what was afoot.

The Court does not overlook that the prosecutor's evidence is that on arrest he asked to see his solicitor and was told he could see one in London. But this is denied, both by Inspector Ryan and the English police officers. The President of the High Court, having heard Inspector Ryan's evidence on this point, did not accept his denial. However, in the absence of the prosecutor, due to the action of Inspector Ryan and of the English officers, Johns and Perry, and having regard to the fact that the English officers were not before the High Court, the Court is not now in a satisfactory position to resolve this conflict of testimony.

The effect of the actions of the respondents here has been that the jurisdiction and authority conferred on the Courts by the Constitution has been interfered with in that the right of recourse to these Courts guaranteed to Philip Anthony Quinn was impaired and in the result defeated. To that extent the contempt, if there be contempt, has been completed. As was pointed out in my judgment, which was the judgment of the Court on this point, given in the *habeas corpus* matter on the 31st July, the Court's powers to deal with such a situation are as ample as the defence of the Constitution requires. This special contempt is one which the Courts themselves take notice of, and is a criminal contempt.

It has been urged that a contempt must be brought home to a person called upon to show cause with the same certainty as is required in the case of a criminal offence. The Court accepts this as a correct statement of the degree of certainty which is required, namely, that it should be established beyond reasonable doubt. It has also been urged that prior to the decision of this Court in this case it was a matter of bona fide belief that instant deportation was lawful by virtue of the provisions of the Petty Sessions (Ireland) Act, 1851. Moreover, regret has now been expressed by the Irish officers concerned, somewhat belatedly, to the Court for what was done.

The Court accepts it that the Petty Sessions (Ireland) Act purported to authorise instant deportation, but it cannot accept the view that in a State whose Constitution guarantees personal rights it is enough to look to statute only as the warrant for one's actions.

The statute in question here is a statute of the former United Kingdom Parliament and all such statutes have been kept in force only in so far as they are not inconsistent with the Constitution. It is therefore no answer in law to call in aid such a statute and ignore the Constitution. Moreover, so far **[134]** as reported cases go, the Court has not had its attention called to any instance where the Act was operated as it was in the case now before the Court. Nor was it so operated here on the occasion of the prosecutor's first arrest.

The Court does not accept it that the prosecutor's immediate removal to Northern Ireland was effected merely in compliance with the request of the British police. The action of both police groups immediately upon the re-arrest of the prosecutor bears all the marks of a detention to avoid any further "Court delays" by presenting the Courts with a *fait accompli.* It is unnecessary to recall the submissions made here in the *habeas corpus* proceedings on behalf of Inspector Ryan, that the Courts were now powerless. This Court is satisfied beyond reasonable doubt that it was the intention of the members concerned of both the Irish and British police that the prosecutor should be removed from the jurisdiction at once to prevent all further "Court delays" and that nothing more should be heard of his whereabouts until he was thought to be beyond the reach of the Irish Courts. As this intention ripened rapidly into an accomplished fact the authority of the Courts was unlawfully interfered with, and the officers concerned had completed an act of contempt. A belief, or hope, on the part of the officers concerned that their acts would not bring them into conflict with the Courts is no answer, nor is an inadequate appreciation of the reality of the right of personal liberty guaranteed by the Constitution.

However, the reliance upon the provisions of the Petty Sessions (Ireland) Act is undoubtedly a mitigating factor, and the Court while holding that the officers concerned were in contempt accepts their statements that they believed that what they did was authorised by law. It should nevertheless be made clear that the issue before the Court would have been precisely the same if the constitutionality of the Act had been upheld and the warrant pronounced valid.

The Irish police officers now concerned in this matter have had an opportunity of expressing regret for their conduct. The affidavits first filed offered no expression of regret. These Irish officers, employing a common formula, said they greatly regretted that a situation should have arisen in which this Court should have thought they might have had any intention of being disrespectful to the Courts or of impeding in any way their functioning. Whatever this may mean, it is not an expression of regret for violating the prosecutor's constitutional rights, or of having impeded the functioning of the Courts.

In the supplementary affidavits which were later filed there **[135]** is a recognition of the importance of the personal rights guaranteed under the Constitution, but it is regrettable that police officers should so grudgingly concede constitutional rights once these rights were clearly enunciated by this Court.

However, the Court is satisfied that the Irish officers now have a full appreciation of the seriousness of what happened and sincerely regret their actions.

The Court has given full consideration to the question of the penalties it should impose in their case. In view of the expressions of regret which have now been conveyed to the Court and in the knowledge that there cannot be a recurrence of the conduct in question the Court now sees its way to forego the imposition of penalty in their case.

The English police officers in their affidavits and through their counsel accept full responsibility for everything done following the re-arrest of the prosecutor on the 15th July. These affidavits do not disclose any appreciation or even knowledge on the part of these officers of the constitutional guarantees of personal liberty which operate in this State. It seems an extraordinary state of affairs that English police officers sent to another country to execute a warrant of arrest should be so uninformed of the rights of the person to be arrested as to find themselves unwittingly in collision with the authority of the Courts of that country. Notwithstanding that this deficiency was made good by the service on them of the judgments of this Court in the *habeas corpus* proceedings before they swore and filed their affidavits, these affidavits speak of "doing their duty" and contain no expression of regret. In this Court their counsel maintained that no regret would be expressed unless and until they were found to have been in contempt. They have now been so found. If regret is now to be expressed the Court in considering the question of penalties must consider what weight (if any) is to be given to such expressions of regret.

There is one other matter which the Court cannot permit to pass without comment.

It is unnecessary to repeat here the story of the manner in which the enquiries of the applicant's solicitor were received at the Bridewell Garda Station, at the Dublin Metropolitan Garda Headquarters and at Garda Headquarters at Phoenix Park. At no stage in these proceedings was the Court furnished with any explanation of the Garda conduct in this regard. It is conduct which merits unqualified condemnation. Deputy Commissioner Quinn and Inspector Ryan have disassociated themselves from it and have disclaimed all knowledge of it, and they do not attempt to justify it. The Court accepts this, but draws attention to the matter in the hope that suitable **[136]** action will be taken by the appropriate authorities and that whatever is necessary will be done to ensure that there can never be a repetition of such conduct. It is quite intolerable that the legal advisers of a person in custody should be obstructed or misled in their efforts to ascertain the whereabout of their client.

Mr. G. A. Clarke then tendered to the Court apologies on behalf of the British police officers.

O DÁLAIGH C.J.: —

The respondents, Detective Constable Johns and Police Constable Perry, have been found guilty of contempt of the Courts.

In the absence of an unqualified apology the Court would have found it necessary to impose an exemplary penalty upon them in vindication of the Constitution.

Such an apology has now been made to the Court, and on this account the respondents, Johns and Perry, are discharged without penalty.

HAUGH J.:—

The arrest and deportation of Philip Anthony Quinn on the 15th July, 1963, in circumstances now well known, resulted in extensive hearings before the High Court and this Court.

An unsuccessful application for an order of *habeas corpus* was made to Mr. Justice Teevan on that morning. On the following day this Court made an order in the matter of an absolute order of *habeas corpus* and directed service on Mr. Commissioner Costigan, Detective Inspector Ryan, and Sergeant Bell of the Bridewell Garda Station. Cause was shown by these three officers, and the matter then came before the President of the High Court later in that month. It is both obvious and understandable that the President was gravely concerned and disturbed by the events that had occurred, before, during, and after his Court had sat, on that Monday morning. In a prepared statement he said he wished to have information on a number of matters, one of which was as follows (I quote):—"On Monday, 15th July, when counsel for the Attorney General in the President's Court consented to have the conditional order granted on the 7th July made absolute, was the Attorney General aware (*a*) actually, or (*b*) constructively through counsel for the respondents or otherwise, that a new English warrant for the arrest of the prosecutor had been endorsed for execution by Deputy Commissioner Quinn, or that it was the intention of certain **[137]** members of the Garda Siochána to re-arrest the prosecutor on his release?"

Counsel appearing on behalf of the Attorney General later stated that the Attorney General believed he should not have been asked such question, but he was prepared in the circumstances set out by counsel to answer as to his own actual knowledge; I quote from counsel's remarks:—"He instructs me to state that when the matter was before the President of the High Court on the morning of the 15th July, he was not aware that a second warrant had been issued, or endorsed for execution, or that it was the intention of any member of An Garda Siochána to re-arrest the prisoner on his release." As regards his constructive knowledge, his counsel stated:—"As to counsel, and the staff of the Chief State Solicitor's Office, they acted as legal advisers to the members of An Garda Siochána concerned as well as for the Attorney General, and matters might well have come to their knowledge in that capacity of which the Attorney General would be ignorant. Whether or not such is the position in the present case the Attorney General submits should not be considered or discussed in this Court, and in so far as the persons concerned were acting for him, he insists on his right to claim privilege in respect of any communications made to them." Such was the position, as regards the Attorney General's actual personal knowledge and the knowledge (if any) of Mr. Thomas Donnelly, junior counsel, and his instructing solicitor when the matter came before the High Court.

The President further directed that Commissioner Costigan, Inspector Ryan and Sergeant Bell should attend for cross-examination on their affidavits at the adjourned hearing, fixed for the 23rd July.

The Court sat on that date and, because of the seriousness of the whole matter, by direction of the President the Court consisted of three Judges—the President, Mr. Justice Davitt, Mr. Justice McLoughlin and Mr. Justice Teevan. It sat on the 23rd, 24th, 25th and 29th July, and duly reserved its decision. The Long Vacation intervened and three written judgments were delivered on the 18th November following. All of the Judges allowed the cause shown and directed that the prosecutor, Philip Anthony Quinn, should pay all costs.

Appeal was taken against that order, which, as regards *habeas corpus* only, was heard on the 22nd, 23rd, 24th, 25th and 26th June of this year. As this Court was of opinion that the record disclosed *prima facie* evidence of contempt of the Courts by the four persons now before it, it formulated a **[138]** charge and directed their attendance. They were allowed up to the 5th October, 1964, to file affidavits to show cause.

All four have filed such affidavits and this Court sat on the 2nd November and subsequent dates to hear argument advanced by counsel only for these parties.

A person accused of acting in contempt of the Courts faces a serious charge of a criminal nature, deserving of heavy punishment on conviction. In my view all the legal principles that attend criminal trials exist in an inquiry investigating charges of contempt, a matter I have endeavoured to keep in mind, as the Court is the accuser, and is a Court of first instance in the contempt matter, and from its order there is no appeal.

The case against all four, and each of them, must be proved beyond all reasonable doubt—that is, I must be satisfied that guilt has been established, on the basis that all the evidence is consistent only with guilt and is inconsistent with innocence. The evidence before us consists of a transcript of what was said by Commissioner Costigan and Inspector Ryan to the High Court on the 23rd July, their affidavits and many other affidavits sworn at varying intervals, including one from the prosecutor, sworn at Brixton Prison, London.

This Court has not had the opportunity of observing the demeanour of these persons and is without the benefit of cross-examination.

If such lack is in fact a disadvantage, such disadvantage should not weigh against the four now accused.

The evidence as presented raises at least one serious conflict of fact. The prosecutor has sworn that at the time of his arrest and when he had been handcuffed to Constable Johns he said to Inspector Ryan:—"I wish to see my solicitor," and Constable Johns then said:—"You can see a solicitor when you get to London." This conversation has been denied on oath by the three police officers who were then within earshot. I must take the evidence as I find it, and not seeing or hearing the four concerned, both on examination and under cross-examination, I am quite unable to resolve this conflict of testimony, and as it is a very relevant and important matter, it is one that should be proved beyond all reasonable doubt if it is to be used against Inspector Ryan and Constables Johns and Perry. If evidence in a criminal matter can equally be resolved in a favourable or unfavourable way to an accused person it is usual for a judge to tell a jury that, if in doubt, the one that is more favourable should outweigh the other. In this matter I can come to no conclusion and leave the matter undecided in my mind.

To fulfil the requirements of the criminal law, as I view **[139]** them, I keep in mind the nature of the elements necessary to support a charge of acting in contempt of the Courts. The words used in the order of this Court made on the 31st July last clearly inform the four persons charged of what they were being accused. Each one of them was told:—". . . by reason of the active role you took in the planning and execution of the police action taken with regard to the above-named prosecutor on the 15th July, 1963, with the general purpose of depriving him of a reasonable opportunity of exercising his constitutional right of applying to the Courts to question the validity of the warrant under which he was arrested."

To me it seems, at least, arguable, that if a person acts so as to deprive another of a particular constitutional right, that person must have a knowledge and appreciation of the existence of such right and that such right is paramount to the right to arrest and remove under what is believed to be a good warrant.

To that degree *mens rea* must be proved. I would like to have established beyond doubt an intention or general purpose on the part of the police concerned to deprive the prosecutor of his known constitutional right—a right which they knew, or ought to have known, existed and was one paramount or superior to the rights of any police officer to arrest and immediately deport the prosecutor under an English warrant believed to be valid.

In July, 1963, was there room for the view that it was lawful to arrest and immediately remove from the jurisdiction a man properly named and wanted on an English warrant believed to be good? In my view there was room for a bona fide belief that such could be done. In the main the police officers concerned have sworn that they so believed. In fact, no judgment on the particular issue was ever pronounced until July of this year. In the course of his judgment (the other members of the Court assenting) the Chief Justice stated:— "In my opinion the Attorney General's ... submission is well founded. The Petty Sessions (Ireland) Act, 1851, does purport to authorise removal from the jurisdiction *instanter* without any opportunity, reasonable or otherwise, to invoke the Courts." It might with reason be urged that this judgment should not now have a retrospective effect.

In short, in my view, in July, 1963, there was room for a wrong, but bona fide belief, on the part of the police and those (if any) advising them, that such action was at least within the letter of the law if not within its spirit.

As regards the events that happened before and after the hearing before Mr. Justice Davitt on the 15th July, 1963, it now transpires that Deputy Commissioner Quinn sought **[140]** advice from the Chief State Solicitor late on Sunday, the 14th July, after he had known of the second warrant on that afternoon. He wished to know whether the new warrant was in order and he was advised that this warrant was in order. As regards what was done by the instructing solicitor from the Chief State Solicitor's Office, and by counsel whom he instructed before the President of the High Court on the Monday, this much now seems to emerge: the control of what should be said and done in that Court lay exclusively on counsel and on his instructing solicitor, subject, however, to the extent of the actual knowledge of counsel and the solicitor. I know nothing of the nature and extent of such knowledge (I have already referred to the Attorney General's statement on this matter) but I do know and believe that Mr. Quinn on the previous night disclosed the existence of the second warrant to the Chief State Solicitor and sought advice as to its effectiveness.

In my view Inspector Ryan and the two London police officers (if, and only if, all the facts were known to counsel) were in no position to control the procedure that was to be followed before the President on that morning. In these circumstances the construction most favourable to the four accused is, in my opinion, the one that should be drawn, and I so do as regards what happened in Court on that Monday morning.

Another matter, to which I have given careful and anxious consideration, and which affects me considerably is as follows: this whole matter was litigated at great length before three Judges of the High Court, all lawyers of long experience. The hearing lasted many days. Judgment was reserved for many months and three judgments were delivered on the 18th November. That the issue of "contempt" was discussed in some form before the High Court appears from the judgment of Mr. Justice McLoughlin alone. I will quote from it later.

The President, who, one might well feel, was the Judge who did feel personally affronted by what took place in his Court on Monday, the 15th July, made no use of the words "contempt of the Courts" throughout his whole judgment.

Mr. Justice McLoughlin did say:—"Mr. O Síorcháin did ask that the Commissioner, Detective Inspector Ryan, Sergeant Bell and Deputy Commissioner Quinn should be attached for contempt of Court. The only contempt alleged against anyone was the failure by Commissioner Costigan to take any steps to secure the return of Quinn from his present custody in England"; and later, "For myself, I cannot see how there was any contempt of Court on the part of anybody **[141]** concerned in the execution of the warrant or any disobedience to any order of the Court."

It seems clear that the nature of the contempt in the mind of this Judge was completely different to the nature of the contempt attributed to the four men now accused.

Mr. Justice Teevan did not deal with any form of contempt in his judgment.

I have posed to myself this question: if the High Court after a lengthy hearing failed, as far as I can see it, to detect any contempt of the nature now alleged against the four men now charged, in as much as they did not advert to it in some practical way during, or at the conclusion of, the hearing, can I, in a criminal charge of this serious nature, now say that it has been proved beyond reasonable doubt that these accused were possessed of a common guilty mind?

For myself, I cannot, and would accordingly hold that the cause shown should be allowed in all four cases.

Solicitor for the prosecutor: *James P. McD. Concannon.*

Solicitors for the respondents, Inspector Matthew G. Ryan and Deputy Commissioner W. P. Quinn and for the Attorney General: *The Chief State Solicitor.*

Solicitors for the British police officers: *James J. O'Connor & Son.*

E.

COMMONWEALTH IMMIGRANTS

1

ADMISSION

JACK ERIC THORNTON v. THE POLICE

([1962] A.C. 339)

March 26, 1962: Judicial Committee of the Privy Council (on appeal from the Supreme Court of Fiji, Appellate Jurisdiction): Viscount Simonds, Lord Morton of Henryton, Rt. Hon. L. M. D. De Silva.

Nationality—Colonial immigration ordinance—Validity—Regulation of entry into and residence in colony—Not repugnant to Imperial Act extending to colony and conferring citizenship of "United Kingdom and Colonies"—Colonial Laws Validity Act, 1865 (28 & 29 *Vict. c.* 63), *s.* 2—*British Nationality Act,* 1948 (11 & 12 *Geo.* 6, *c.* 56), *s.* 12—*Immigration Ordinance* (*Fiji*), *No.* 33 *of* 1947, *s.* 8.
Colony—Ordinance—Validity—Immigration ordinance—Colonial Laws Validity Act, 1865, *s.* 2—*British Nationality Act,* 1948, *s.* 12—*Immigration Ordinance* (*Fiji*), *No.* 33 *of* 1947, *s.* 8.

The Colonial Laws Validity Act, 1865, provides by section 2: "Any colonial law which is . . . in any respect repugnant to the provisions of any Act of Parliament extending to the Colony to which such law may relate . . . shall be read subject to such Act . . . and shall, to the extent of such repugnancy, but not otherwise, be and remain absolutely void and inoperative."

By section 12 (1) of the British Nationality Act, 1948: "A person who was a British subject immediately before the date of the commencement of this Act shall on that date become a citizen of the United Kingdom and Colonies. . . ."

By section 8 of the Immigration Ordinance, 1947, of Fiji: "(2) The Principal Immigration Officer may issue a permit to any **[340]** person entitling him to enter and reside or remain in the Colony . . . (5) If a person who has entered the Colony . . . (c) Fails to leave the Colony within four months of his arrival, it shall be lawful for the Principal Immigration Officer . . . to order such person forthwith to leave the Colony" and if he fails to do so is guilty of an offence.

There is not, within the meaning of the Colonial Laws Validity Act, 1865, any repugnancy between the Immigration Ordinance, 1947, of Fiji, and the British Nationality Act, 1948, which extends to the colony. Accordingly, the petitioner, a British-born subject, who had been issued with a permit to enter the colony and had subsequently refused to leave when ordered to do so on the expiration of the period for which the permit had been granted, had been rightly convicted of an offence pursuant to the provisions of the Immigration Ordinance.

Dictum of Lord Watson, delivering the judgment of the Board in *Montréal Cité* v. *St. Sulpice de Montréal* (*Ecclesiastiques du Séminaire*) (1889) 14 App. Cas. 660, 662, P.C. applied.

PETITION.

By this petition Jack Eric Thornton, a journalist, sought special leave to appeal from a judgment of the Supreme Court of Fiji, Appellate Jurisdiction (Hammett J.) (October 18, 1957), dismissing his appeal from a decision of the Magistrates' Court of the First Class, sitting at Suva, dated March 11, 1957, whereby he was convicted of the offence of failing to leave the colony when ordered by the Principal Immigration Officer, contrary to sections 8 (5) and 9 (2) of the Immigration Ordinance, 1947, and fined £30, or in default two months' imprisonment, and it was recommended that he be deported. The petitioner paid the fine.

S. N. Bernstein for the petitioner. The grounds on which the petitioner is seeking to appeal are that, being a citizen of the United Kingdom and Colonies, as enacted and provided by the British Nationality Act, 1948, he is a citizen of the colony of Fiji and, therefore, entitled freely and without restriction at all times and whenever and as often as he should choose to enter, remain in, leave and re-enter the colony; and that the provisions of the Ordinance under which he was purportedly convicted sentenced and deported are absolutely void and inoperative under and as provided by the Colonial Laws Validity Act, 1865, inasmuch as those provisions of the Ordinance of 1947 are repugnant to the Act of 1948, which is an Act of Parliament extending to the colony to which the provisions of the Ordinance relate.

The petitioner, who was born in England, was convicted **[341]** because, having entered Fiji under a permit and stayed for the period for which it was granted, he refused to leave when ordered to do so. It had nothing to do with him being unreliable or anything of that kind. The British Nationality and Status of Aliens Act, 1914, by providing in section 1 (1) (*a*) that any person born within the Dominions and owing allegiance to the Crown should be deemed to be a British subject, put into statutory form the common law conception of citizenship.

[Counsel referred to the terms of section 12 (1) of the British Nationality Act, 1948, and section 8 of the Immigration Ordinance, 1947, and continued:] What the Immigration Ordinance purports to do is to deprive the petitioner of a right which he has. Under the Act of 1948 he has one single nationality of the United Kingdom and the colonies, and in consequence of that nationality he is entitled as of right as a national to enter the territory of Fiji without any restriction.

There is repugnancy between the Ordinance of 1947 and the British Nationality Act of 1948 which extends to the colony. The power of a colonial legislature is subject to the overriding power of the Imperial Parliament, which is enforced by means of the Colonial Laws Validity Act, 1865, whereby any provision in a colonial Ordinance repugnant to a United Kingdom Act is rendered void and inoperative to the extent of the repugnancy. [Reference was made to *Reg.* v. *Marais, Ex parte Marais,*[1] *Attorney-General for Queensland* v. *Attorney-General for the Commonwealth*[2] and *Rex* v. *Soon Gim An.*[3]] The petitioner has a right which has been contradicted by the whole of this Immigration Ordinance. The point now in issue was raised in *Musson* v. *Rodriguez*[4]* but was not decided. [Reference was also made to Oppenheim's International Law, 8th ed., vol. I, pp. 640, 642, 644-646.] The petitioner had a right to enter and remain in Fiji as a national.

H. A. P. Fisher Q.C. and D. A. Grant for the respondents. The only ground submitted for the petitioner was that the Immigration Ordinance is repugnant to the British Nationality Act, 1948. It is not sought to contend that the Act of 1948 does not apply by necessary intendment to Fiji, but on the question whether there is any inconsistency Mr. Bernstein has not pointed to any express provision in the Act of 1948 with which the **[342]** Immigration Ordinance is inconsistent. The Act of 1948 lays down what classes of persons possess the status of British subjects and what classes of persons possess the status of

[1] [1902] A.C. 51, 53-54; 17 T.L.R. 704, P.C.
[2] (1915) 20 C.L.R. 148, 166.
[3] [1941] 3 D.L.R. 125, 128.
[4] [1953] A.C. 530; [1953] 3 W.L.R. 212, P.C.

citizens of the United Kingdom and the colonies. In 1914 there was a single status of British subject which applied throughout the Empire. The only change which the Act of 1948 made is that instead of having a single status of British subject there is now a nationality citizenship of the United Kingdom and the colonies. The ordinance here is common form which applies throughout the Commonwealth. There is nothing inconsistent with status in saying that a British subject shall not be permitted to enter the territory. There is nothing in the Act of 1948 which states what rights a citizen of the United Kingdom and the colonies has; one looks to the legislation of the different colonies and so far as it is inconsistent with the Act of 1948, section 3 of the Colonial Laws Validity Act, 1865, says that that inconsistency is not to render it void. [Reference was made to *Reg.* v. *Marais, Ex parte Marais.*[5]] The point which it is sought to make is correctly put by Hammett J. in his judgment: "It is submitted that all citizens of the United Kingdom and colonies have, by virtue of the British Nationality Act, 1948, the free and unfettered right to enter and to reside in any place in the United Kingdom and colonies. I have examined the British Nationality Act, 1948, with some care and I can find no provisions in it to this effect. This statute merely governs the status of persons and does not lay down what rights of movement or residence are granted by or attach to that status. . . . I know of no provision in the British Nationality Act, 1948, which precludes either the United Kingdom or any of the colonies from enacting such legislation they chose to regulate and control the entry into their territory or residence therein of persons whatever their status may be. I cannot accept the contention that the parts of the Immigration Ordinance, 1947, referred to are repugnant to the British Nationality Act, 1948."

Leave to appeal should not be granted in the circumstances of this case: see per Lord Watson, delivering the judgment of the Board in *Montréal Cité* v. *St. Sulpice de Montréal* (*Ecclesiastiques du Séminaire*).[6]

Bernstein in reply referred to *Ex parte Weber.*[7]* There is repugnance between this Ordinance of 1947 and the Act of 1948. **[343]**

VISCOUNT SIMONDS. Their Lordships, having listened to a full argument on behalf of the petitioner, are satisfied that there is no valid ground for saying that there is, within the meaning of the Colonial Laws Validity Act, 1865, any repugnancy between the Immigration Ordinance of Fiji, which was enacted in 1947, and the British Nationality Act, 1948.

This is a case to which, in their Lordships' opinion, the words used by Lord Watson in delivering the opinion of the Board in the *City of Montreal* case[8] are exactly applicable. He said: "A case may be of a substantial character, may involve matter of great public interest, and may raise an important question of law, and yet the judgment from which leave to appeal is sought may appear to be plainly right, or at least to be unattended with sufficient doubt to justify their Lordships in advising Her Majesty to grant leave to appeal." Their Lordships will, accordingly, humbly advise Her Majesty that this petition must be refused.

Solicitors: *Ernest Randall & Rose; Charles Russell & Co.*

5 [1902] A.C. 51.
6 (1889) 14 App.Cas. 660, 662, P.C.
7 [1916] 1 A.C. 421, 426; 32 T.L.R. 312, H.L.
8 14 App.Cas. 660, 662.

2

DEPORTATION

YAGER v. MUSA

(*The Times*, January 31, 1962)

January 30, 1962: Queen's Bench Division: Paull J.

Problem Man from Sierra Leone

His Lordship, on this motion by the plaintiff, Mr. Max Yager, of Poynter's Close, Totteridge, ordered that Brima Musa, formerly of Sierra Leone and now in Pentonville Prison, be committed to prison for failing to obey an injunction of September 29, 1959, restraining him from causing a nuisance or annoyance to the plaintiff or his family.

Mr. Alan Lipfriend for the plaintiff; the defendant appeared in person.

Mr. Lipfriend said that last week Musa had appeared in a magistrates' court in a charge of obstructing the police. He was remanded in custody for seven days for a medical report.

The present application arose from a most distressing matter which had extended over nearly two and a half years. During that period, the defendant had appeared before eight judges of the High Court and had been committed to prison on three occasions. On each occasion on which he had been warned, he had undertaken not to molest the plaintiff and his family and presumably had made similar undertakings when he had been released from prison.

His last committal was by Mr. Justice Ashworth in December, 1960. He applied to Mr. Justice Howard in March to be released. The matter was adjourned for three months, and, when Musa appealed, the Court of Appeal ordered his release on August 7, 1961 ([1961] 2 Q.B. 214). Lord Justice Devlin then said that in 1958, Musa obtained employment with Mr. Yager and formed an obsession for Mr. Yager's daughter which was wholly unreciprocated and in no way encouraged by her; he began to pursue her and to make a nuisance of himself not only to her but also to Mr. Yager and his family.

Musa had formed the attachment for Mr. Yager's elder daughter, Millicent, who had since married and moved to another address.

In an affidavit, the plaintiff's wife, Mrs. Doris Yager, stated that on January 17, Musa telephoned and asked to speak to the elder daughter. On January 20, he came to the house, ringing the bell and shouting "Open the door". She 'phoned the police, who forcibly removed him to a police car. Musa had sent five Christmas cards addressed to members of the family.

Mr. Yager did not know what to do, counsel continued. He did not want to harm this man, but he was entitled to some protection from the Court.

HIS LORDSHIP to Musa. You will have to stay in prison at the moment. We cannot have you keeping on going to the Yagers' house and interfering with them and writing them letters. Supposing I commit you to prison and communicate with the authorities to see if there is any chance of putting you on board a ship going to Sierra Leone, will you go on board the ship and stay?

The defendant. Yes.

HIS LORDSHIP asked a representative who was present in Court of the Official Solicitor whether there was any machinery by which Musa could be sent back to Sierra Leone with his consent.

The representative replied that it would mean communicating with the Commonwealth Relations Office. This question had cropped up previously. It had always been understood that because he was a British subject he could not be deported.

HIS LORDSHIP. He cannot be deported in the sense of being sent against his will. If this man can be put on board a ship voluntarily it may well save considerable trouble. Take some steps in the next week or so to see if something can be done.

Solicitor: *Messrs. Offenbach & Co.*

R v. RILEY

([1962] Crim. L.R. 712)

June 4, 1962: Court of Criminal Appeal: Lord Parker C.J., Streetfield, Lawton JJ.

Facts and charge: R. (male) was bound over to come up for judgment if called upon; it being made a condition of the order he should return to Ireland and not re-enter England for three years. He was found in England two and a half years later. *Previous convictions*: in 1959 convicted of loitering with intent; committed for sentence as an incorrigible rogue. *Special circumstances*: apparently of good behaviour for two and a half years, but warned if he returned to England within three years he would almost certainly be imprisoned for twelve months. *Court order*: if people bound over in this way (as now frequently happened to those from Eire) disobeyed the order in any manner, they would receive the sentence that would otherwise have been imposed. Appeal dismissed and sentence of twelve months upheld as being right in principle.

R v. ABRAHAMS

([1963] Crim. L.R. 129)

October 22, 1962: Court of Criminal Appeal: Winn, Fenton Atkinson, Thompson JJ.

Age: forty (male). *Facts*: convicted of wounding with intent to do grievous bodily harm. *Previous convictions*: one for living on immoral earnings. *Special considerations*: a coloured man from South Africa married to a white woman; several children; could not live with his wife in South Africa because of legislation there. *Decision*: recommendation for deportation quashed.

R v. RYAN

([1963] Crim. L.R. 129)

November 2, 1962: Court of Criminal Appeal: Ashworth, Fenton Atkinson, Thompson JJ.

Age: twenty-three (male). *Facts*: stole a jacket from a public-house and money that was in a pocket of the jacket. *Previous convictions*: four for dishonesty since coming to England at the age of seventeen; probation, borstal and prison. *Special considerations*: all his near relations, apart from his mother who was still in Ireland, were in England. *Decision*: a proper case for a recommendation for deportation.

R v. CHOUDHURY

([1963] Crim. L.R. 129)

November 22, 1962: Court of Criminal Appeal: Ashworth, Salmon, Winn JJ.

Age: thirty-six (male). *Facts*: a native of Pakistan. Had lived in England for a number of years. He was convicted of causing grievous bodily harm to the woman with whom he lived. *Previous convictions*: none. *Special considerations*: had a clean record and had worked hard and lived honestly since he came to England. *Decision*: three years' imprisonment not wrong in principle; but recommendation for deportation not justified.

R v. DOCHERTY

((1962) 106 Sol. Jo. 1054)

December 11, 1962: Court of Criminal Appeal: Lord Parker C.J., Salmon, Winn JJ.

Deportation: Recommendation for Deportation not made in Open Court

Appeal against deportation order.

The defendant, an Irishman, came to England in 1961 to earn money to support his family, and for fourteen months he earned from £15 to £20 a week. In April, 1962, he became unemployed and then committed offences of housebreaking and larceny. In June he was bound over to go to Ireland and not return for five years. In fact, he did not go to Ireland and in August was convicted of receiving and sentenced to nine months' imprisonment. Nothing was said about a recommendation for deportation but an endorsement to that effect appeared on the indictment. The defendant appealed.

LORD PARKER, C.J., said that a recommendation for deportation under the Commonwealth Immigration Act, 1962, should be made in open court in the presence of the defendant, when reasons could be given. Had the court been in doubt, the case would have been adjourned to find out how the entry on the indictment came to be made, when nothing had been said in open court; but the court had come to the conclusion that on the facts this was not a proper case for deportation and the order should be quashed. Appeal allowed.

APPEARANCES: *J. N. Watkins* (*Registrar, Court of Criminal Appeal*).

REGINA v. EDGEHILL

([1963] 1 Q.B. 593)

December 11, 1962: Court of Criminal Appeal: Lord Parker C.J., Salmon, Winn JJ.

Commonwealth Immigrant—Deportation order—Requirements for making recommendation—"Ordinarily" and "continuously" resident for five years—Detention for six months to be excluded—Short visit abroad—Detention by

foreign court—Whether "any court"—Duty of sentencing court to inquire into eligibility for deportation—Whether deportation order part of punishment—Whether a sentence—Right of appeal—Commonwealth Immigrants Act, 1962 (10 & 11 *Eliz.* 2, *c.* 21), *ss.* 7 (2), 8 (1), (3), (4).
Residence—Commonwealth immigrant—"Ordinarily" and "continuously" resident—Short visit abroad during five-year period—Detention by foreign court—Commonwealth Immigrants Act, 1962, *s.* 7 (2).

In July, 1962, the defendant, having pleaded guilty at a magistrates' court to being a suspected person loitering with intent, was committed to London Sessions for sentence. The deputy-chairman sentenced him to 12 months' imprisonment and said: "I agree with your recommendation for deportation" and made an order recommending deportation. The defendant appealed against the recommendation for deportation under section 8 (4) of the Commonwealth Immigrants Act, 1962,[1] on the ground that, having been resident in this country for five years, he was not liable to deportation by virtue of the provisions of section 7 (2). At the hearing of the appeal the defendant gave evidence that he came to England from Jamaica in June, 1957; that at all material times he had lived **[594]** here with a woman by whom he had a child; that on May 16, 1959, he went to Belgium for a fortnight's holiday but was sentenced to detention by the Belgian authorities who, on October 14, 1959, deported him to this country where he had continued to reside. On the question whether an order recommending deportation could be made:—

Held, (1) that a defendant was entitled and ought to be invited to give evidence regarding his ineligibility for deportation under section 7 (2); he had to prove that not only was he ordinarily resident in this country at the date of his conviction, which was a question of fact, but that he had been continuously resident in that sense for a period of at least five years ending with the date of his conviction.

Stransky v. *Stransky* [1954] P. 428; [1954] 3 W.L.R. 123; [1954] 2 All E.R. 536, applied.

(2) That the sentencing court was the appropriate court to inquire into the defendant's eligibility for a recommendation for deportation; and that, the deputy-chairman, having failed to make the necessary inquiries and the defendant having satisfied the Court of Criminal Appeal that he had been ordinarily resident in this country at the date of his conviction and had, for five years before that date, been continuously so resident, the deputy-chairman had no power to make the recommendation for deportation which would therefore be quashed.

(3) That the proviso to section 7 (2) indicated a period of actual detention for six months or more, pursuant to an order of "any court" (meaning a

[1] Commonwealth Immigrants Act, 1962, s. 7: "(2) No recommendation under this section (in this Part of this Act referred to as a recommendation for deportation) shall be made upon the conviction of an offender who satisfies the court—(*a*) that he is or was ordinarily resident in the United Kingdom on the date of his conviction; and (*b*) that he has been continuously so resident for a period of at least five years ending with that date: Provided that for the purpose of calculating the period for which any person has been so resident (but not of determining whether he has been continuously so resident) no account shall be taken of any continuous period of six months or more during which he has been detained under a sentence or order passed or made by any court on a conviction of an offence."

S. 8: "(1) No recommendation for deportation shall be made in respect of an offender unless a notice has been given to him at least seven days before the recommendation is made. . . . (3) Where a person convicted of an offence by any court is committed for sentence to another court, any power to make a recommendation for deportation in respect of him shall be exercisable by the court to which he is committed and not by the court by which he is convicted. (4) For the purposes of any enactment relating to appeals in criminal cases, a recommendation for deportation shall be treated as an order made on conviction . . . and the validity of such a recommendation shall not be called in question except on an appeal against the recommendation or against the conviction upon which it is made."

court having jurisdiction under the Act), should be excluded in calculating the period of residence; accordingly, the sentence of the Belgian court was not a sentence of "any court" within section 7 (2) and in any event the period of actual detention being less than six months, the Belgian proceedings and detention were irrelevant to the calculation of the defendant's period of residence in this country.

Per curiam. (1) A recommendation for deportation is not part of the punishment for an offence; a court should first sentence the defendant according to the merits of his case and then consider the recommendation for deportation separately; accordingly, an appeal can be brought against a recommendation for deportation alone without including an appeal against sentence: section 8 (4).

(2) As no recommendation can be made without a notice under section 8 (1) being served on the defendant, the acknowledgment of such notice should be attached to the papers in the case.

APPEAL against recommendation for deportation.

The defendant, Frank Lloyd Edgehill, on July 21, 1962, pleaded guilty at Marlborough Street Magistrates' Court (Mr. L. A. Gladwell) to being a suspected person loitering with intent, and on his previous convictions being proved was committed to London Sessions for sentence as an incorrigible rogue. On the same day, he was served with a notice under section 8 (1) **[595]** of the Commonwealth Immigrants Act, 1962, that a recommendation for deportation might be made. On August 3 the deputy-chairman (Mr. Henry Elam) at London Sessions sentenced the defendant to 12 months' imprisonment as an incorrigible rogue and then said: "I agree with your recommendation for deportation." An order recommending deportation was accordingly made.

The defendant appealed against the recommendation for deportation.

The facts are more fully set out in the judgment of the court.

John Murchie for the defendant. The defendant has not served six months' imprisonment anywhere and as he has been in this country for five years he is not liable for deportation unless between May and October, 1959, he became resident in Belgium. The recommendation for deportation was made under a new Act, the Commonwealth Immigrants Act, 1962, in respect of a defendant who was not represented and who was not asked if he had anything to say about the making of a recommendation for deportation. It is conceded that the notice which was served on the defendant under section 8 (1) on July 21, 1962, more than seven days before the hearing at London Sessions, was clearly good. Although the deputy-chairman might have thought that he was agreeing with a recommendation made by the magistrate, in fact the magistrate did not make any recommendation and, not being a sentencing court, had no power to do so: section 8 (3).

The defendant did not come within any of the exceptions in section 6. He came to this country in June, 1957, when he was 17¾ years of age. As he was not represented and was not asked if he wished to give evidence, there is little evidence before the court to show that he is ordinarily resident here within section 7 (2) (*a*). But if he had given evidence he would have said that he has a common law wife, a child and a television set in this country. The onus must lie on the defendant to show, on the balance of probabilities, that he is resident here. For the meaning of "ordinarily resident" in section 7 (2) (*a*) the same principles should be applied as in construing those words in section 18 (1) (*b*) of the Matrimonial Causes Act, 1950: see *Hopkins* v. *Hopkins*[2] and *Stransky* v. *Stransky*.[3] "Continuously so resident" in section 7 (2) (b) means "continuously **[596]** ordinarily resident" over a period, so that a temporary absence would not count. Had the Belgian government been asked they would certainly have said that the defendant was not ordinarily resident in Belgium. If the defendant

[2] [1951] P. 116; 66 T.L.R. (Pt. 2) 896; [1950] 2 All E.R. 1035.
[3] [1954] P. 428; [1954] 3 W.L.R. 123; [1954] 2 All E.R. 536.

was not continuously resident here by reason of his five months' stay in Belgium, then no Commonwealth citizen would be able to go on a prolonged holiday or return home temporarily for family or business reasons without losing the protection afforded to him by section 7 (2).

The proviso to section 7 (2) contemplated a sentence of a court superior to a magistrates' court, since it specified that six months' actual detention had to be served and not a six months' sentence which with remission would be less than six months' actual detention.

[LORD PARKER C.J. Are you applying for leave to call the defendant as a witness?]

Yes.

[LORD PARKER C.J. Do you object Mr. Howard?]

No.

[The defendant gave evidence which is summarised in the judgment of Lord Parker C.J.[4]]

Murchie. The court now has material to consider whether the defendant has satisfied you that, on the balance of probabilities, he is ordinarily resident here.

[Counsel was stopped.]

William McLaren Howard for the Crown. It would not be right to address the court on the evidence. Looking at the Act as a whole, "any court" in the proviso to section 7 (2), does not mean any court in the world but any court which has jurisdiction under this Act.

Section 8 (3) clearly shows that where a magistrate commits a defendant for sentence to another court, the magistrate has no power to make a recommendation for deportation. It is only the court sentencing the defendant which has that power.

"Ordinarily resident" in section 7 (2) (*a*) should be construed in accordance with the principles set out in *Stransky* v. *Stransky.*[5] It is a matter of fact for the court, but it should be remembered that a person can be ordinarily resident in more than one place at the same time. **[597]**

LORD PARKER C.J. giving the judgment of the court. Before dealing with the facts of this case in any detail it is convenient, since this is the first or one of the first appeals that has come before this court against a recommendation for deportation, if the court makes one or two comments on the Commonwealth Immigrants Act, 1962, itself and the working of the Act. In doing so the court appreciates that they may not have heard full argument on a number of points but, as this case itself shows, there are always teething troubles on the introduction of a new Act, and it may be convenient if this court expresses its view, as at present advised, on how the Act should work.

In the first place, it is to be observed that section 8 (4) provides for an appeal to this court against a recommendation for deportation. As at present advised, this court is of the clear opinion that an appeal can be brought against that recommendation alone and not against the sentence generally. The court is satisfied in regard to that because they do not feel that the intention of the Act is that recommendation for deportation should, as it were, be part of the punishment in the sense that a court is justified in saying: "We will give a reduced sentence because we are making a recommendation for deportation." In that connection our attention has been drawn to one or two cases which clearly show that some courts take a different view. In particular, there have been cases in which chairmen have postponed sentence, in other words, have not at the time sentenced a man to imprisonment at all but have postponed it pending the outcome of the recommendation for deportation. In other words, some courts take the view that if the Home Secretary—with whom the ultimate decision rests—implements the recommendation and deports, the case does not call for a sentence at all, or only a nominal sentence. This court is quite satisfied that that is the wrong approach. Courts should deal with the offence on its merits and sentence the defendant to the penalty or sentence which he deserves, and, having done that, should deal with the recommendation for deportation quite separately.

[4] *Post,* p. 600. [5] [1954] P. 428.

The next matter to be observed is that no recommendation can be made unless a notice is given under section 8 (1). So far as the present case is concerned, there is no dispute but that a proper notice was given within the time permitted, but in case any dispute should arise in other cases, the court thinks that the proper course would be for the acknowledgment of such a notice to be attached to the papers in the case so that any court on appeal can see that the condition precedent has been complied with. **[598]**

The next matter to observe is in regard to residence. Section 7 (2) provides: "No recommendation under this section (in this Part of this Act referred to as a recommendation for deportation) shall be made upon the conviction of an offender who satisfies the court—(*a*) that he is or was ordinarily resident in the United Kingdom on the date of his conviction; and (*b*) that he has been continuously so resident for a period of at least five years ending with that date." Pausing there, that is a matter as to which the court must be satisfied, and of course the defendant is entitled and should be allowed and invited to give evidence on that matter. After all, the facts are peculiarly within his knowledge, and he should be invited to give evidence in regard to them.

The proviso to subsection (2) goes on in these words: "Provided that for the purpose of calculating the period for which any person has been so resident (but not of determining whether he has been continuously so resident) no account shall be taken of any continuous period of six months or more during which he has been detained under a sentence or order passed or made by any court on a conviction of an offence." In other words, any period of actual detention, not the period of the sentence but the period of the sentence which is actually served, if and only if it is six months or more will be excluded from the period in which he has been in this country for the purposes of seeing whether or not he is within the five-year limit.

Further, the sentence or order to which reference is made is by any court, and "any court" in the context of this Act must clearly, as it seems to this court, be a court which would have jurisdiction under the Act; in other words, one of the courts of this country and not a court of any foreign country.

Finally, reference has been made in the present case to the meaning of the expression that he "has been continuously so resident for a period of at least five years ending with that date." It seems to this court that the words "continuously so resident" refer back to the earlier provision which says that he must be ordinarily resident at the date of his conviction; in other words, he must not only be ordinarily resident at the date of his conviction but also have been continuously resident in that sense for a period of at least five years ending with that date.

The expression "ordinarily resident" appears in a number of Acts, including the Matrimonial Causes Act, 1950, the Adoption Act, 1959, and the Income Tax Acts, and the matter is conveniently and recently dealt with in *Stransky* v. *Stransky*.[6] That **[599]** was a case under the Matrimonial Causes Act, 1950, and Karminski J. went into the matter in some detail, referring to the other Acts, and said[7]: "Clearly, mere temporary absences from England, such as a holiday abroad, would not make a gap in the period of ordinary residence." It will be a matter no doubt of fact and degree in every case, and all that the court would like to say is that the principles enunciated in the Income Tax cases and *Stransky* v. *Stransky*[8] would seem to apply to section 7 (2) of the Act now under consideration.

Finally, it is to be observed in this connection that section 8 (3) provides: "Where a person convicted of an offence by any court is committed for sentence to another court, any power to make a recommendation for deportation in respect of him shall be exercisable by the court to which he is committed and not by the court by which he is convicted."

Coming, then, to the facts of this case, it is clear that the court in dealing with this matter had not the provisions of the Act fully in mind. The deputy-

[6] [1954] P. 428; [1954] 3 W.L.R. 123; [1954] 2 All E.R. 536.
[7] [1954] P. 428, 437.
[8] [1954] P. 428.

chairman sentenced the defendant on committal to him to 12 months' imprisonment. In doing so he said: "The law always frowns upon pickpockets whether they are expert or otherwise. You must go to prison for 12 months and I agree with your recommendation for deportation." Unfortunately, the deputy-chairman did not appreciate that it was for him and for him alone under section 8 (3) to go into the matter to see whether the defendant qualifed for a recommendation and, if so, whether it was a proper case in which to make the recommendation. He conceived that he was agreeing with someone else, and that no doubt arose because unfortunately counsel outlining the facts at London Sessions said: "He is recommended for deportation," which might well have conveyed to the deputy-chairman that it was the magistrate at Marlborough Street who had recommended him for deportation. In fact the magistrate had not done so and, by reason of section 8 (3), had no power to do so. It may be for that reason the deputy-chairman never went into the facts of the case at all. The defendant was unrepresented; he did not give evidence. He was not invited to deal with any matters of qualification for a recommendation, that is to say, as to his residence, but he was merely asked: "Would you like to say something?", and the defendant said: "So far I have not had a chance of probation and last year my **[600]** father died," from which answer it is quite clear that the defendant's mind had not been brought to bear on the vital questions which had to be considered before a recommendation for deportation was made.

It may well be that in cases where a recommendation for deportation is made, legal aid should be granted. The court is not laying that down as an absolute direction, but it would seem to be only right in considering the provisions of this Act and how the Act applies to the particular case that a Commonwealth citizen, who may be liable to have a deportation order made, should have the assistance of legal advice, and the court thinks it clearly advisable that in these cases he should be granted legal aid.

That being the position in the present case, this court has thought it right on the invitation of the defendant's counsel to allow him to give evidence, which ought, of course, to have been given at London Sessions. From that evidence it appears that he came in June of 1957. He began to associate with a woman, and a child was born, and at all material times he lived at an address, 24 Prince's Square, W.2, with that woman and with that child. It appears that on May 16, 1959, according to his evidence, he went with two friends to Belgium. He says he went there for 14 days' holiday. This man, who really has no merit at all, is a professional pickpocket, and the court may well suspect that he went to Brussels in the course of his profession, if one may call it his profession, and that if business were good he would have stayed there. But the evidence as it is presented to the court is that he went for a 14-day holiday. He says, and there is nothing to controvert it, that he bought a return ticket. When he was in Belgium, however, he and his friends were up before the courts and they were sentenced to detention, and finally, on October 14, 1959, the Belgian authorities deported him to this country, where he has continued to reside.

Those are the facts as they emerged, and there is nothing to contradict them whatever our suspicions may be. On those facts it is clear, first, that the Belgian court is not "any court" for the purposes of section 7 (2). In any event, he did not serve six months or more. Further, on the evidence it seems to this court that he was not only ordinarily resident in this country when he was convicted but that he has been continuously so resident for five years since his arrival in this country. **[601]** That being so, he does not qualify for a recommendation for deportation, and however much this court thinks that he is a man who should be deported, there is no power under this Act to do so. Accordingly, this court allows the appeal and sets aside the recommendation for deportation.

Mr. Murchie did indicate in opening this appeal that the defendant did not realise that he had any right of appeal. I do not know whether that is really so or not, but if it is so, it is only because it was in the early stages, because this court is informed that in every prison now there are ample notices showing that a man has a right of appeal against any recommendation for deportation. I only say that to make it clear that, whatever might have been the position in earlier cases, provision has been made for those notices to be posted.

Appeal allowed. Deportation order quashed.

Solicitors: *Alban Gould, Baker & Co.; The Solicitor, Metropolitan Police.*

REGINA v. BARRETT

(*The Times*, January 16, 1963)

January 15, 1963: Court of Criminal Appeal: Lord Parker C.J., Ashworth, Lyell JJ.

Application Refused

The Court refused this application by James Barrett, aged 27 years, now detained in H.M. Prison, Bedford, for leave to appeal against the recommendation of the assistant Recorder of the Birmingham Quarter Sessions (T. R. Fitzwalter Butler Esq) that he should be deported. The applicant had pleaded guilty to housebreaking with intent to commit a felony and was sentenced to two years' imprisonment and recommended for deportation.

MR. JUSTICE ASHWORTH, giving the judgment of the Court said that the applicant had been passing to and fro between this country and Eire since 1954 and most of the time he had spent in prison. In 1962, he was released from prison in England and went to Eire. In May, 1962, he was sent to prison in Eire and released in October. He came to England and on November 5, 1962, he was sentenced for this offence of housebreaking.

This was manifestly a case for a recommendation for deportation and the only criticism that could be made was that the assistant Recorder had expressed the view that because of the recommendation he could pass a lower sentence. This approach was not correct and an offender ought to be treated on the merits without the recommendation for deportation being taken into consideration.

R. v. GREEN

([1963] Crim. L.R. 212)

January 15, 1963: Court of Criminal Appeal: Lord Parker C.J., Ashworth, Lyell JJ.

Age: twenty-three (male); came to England in March, 1961; done little or no work since. *Facts*: convicted of living on the earnings of prostitution. *Previous convictions*: one, for an identical offence in January, 1962. *Decision*: precisely the sort of case for a recommendation for deportation.

R. v. McGRATH

([1963] Crim. L.R. 212)

January 15, 1963: Court of Criminal Appeal: Lord Parker C.J., Ashworth, Lyell JJ.

Age: nineteen (male). *Facts*: pleaded guilty to burglary and larceny of

£2,500; left door of public house where he worked unlocked so that his elder brother could gain access. *Previous convictions*: none. *Special considerations*: was of previous good character; tempted by his elder brother; came to England in July, 1961, and had worked well. *Decision*: not a case for a recommendation for deportation.

REGINA v. RAPIER

(*The Times*, January 16, 1963)

January 15, 1963: Court of Criminal Appeal: Lord Parker C.J., Ashworth, Lyell JJ.

The Court set aside a recommendation for the deportation of the appellant, Franklyn Rapier, aged 19, a native of Grenada, made by Mr. Justice Thesiger at Glamorgan Assizes on October 12, 1962.

Mr. Peter Perrin appeared for the appellant.

The Lord Chief Justice, giving the judgment of the Court said that the appellant was sentenced to nine months' imprisonment for larceny and assault, occasioning actual bodily harm, and was recommended for deportation under the Commonwealth Immigration Act, 1962. Although the offence was a serious one, it was not as serious as some that came before this Court. On September 28, 1962, in the course of a fight, the appellant used a bottle to hit a man, and, later, the man's jacket was found in the appellant's possession.

The appellant came to this country in June, 1961 and committed an offence in May, 1962, when he broke the window of a bank. When recommending the appellant for deportation, the Judge said that the appellant had repeated this offence of May, 1962, and that, as he was of limited intelligence and could not speak English, he was not suited to living here and a recommendation would be made for his deportation.

The Judge stated that the appellant had repeated his previous offence, although the two offences were different. Moreover, the facts that the appellant was of limited intelligence and could not speak English, were not adequate reasons for making a deportation order. Such a recommendation was limited to bad behaviour. The offence, though serious, was not sufficient to justify the recommendation for the deportation of a young man of 19 who had come to England in June, 1961, and had not yet had time to settle down. The recommendation for deportation would, accordingly, be set aside.

Solicitor: *Registrar, Court of Criminal Appeal.*

REGINA v. REID

(*The Times*, January 16, 1963)

January 15, 1963: Court of Criminal Appeal: Lord Parker C.J., Ashworth, Lyell JJ.

Deportation Recommendation Set Aside

The Court set aside a recommendation for the deportation of the appellant, Vincent Albert Reid, a Jamaican, aged 27, made by the Chairman (R. E. Seaton Esq.) at London Sessions on September 27, 1962.

Mr. Patrick McEnery appeared for the appellant; *Mr. William Howard* for the Crown.

The LORD CHIEF JUSTICE, giving the judgment of the Court, said that the appellant was sentenced to a total of 21 months' imprisonment for larceny and receiving, and a recommendation was made for a deportation order under the Commonwealth Immigration Act, 1962. The appellant came to England in 1948 at the age of 13. After leaving school, he worked for the Post Office and then served with the Royal Air Force until 1957, when he was discharged with the rank of corporal and very good character. The appellant then worked for B.O.A.C. and his troubles began at the age of 23 when he was fined for stealing.

In October, 1959, the appellant visited France and, within five days, he was arrested for an offence concerning travellers' cheques. He was convicted in February, 1960, and was released in October, 1960, when he returned to this country. He then spent one year in hospital where he was treated for tuberculosis which he was said to have contracted in a French prison. In November, 1961, for two offences he was sentenced to three months' and 14 days' imprisonment. He was released in January, 1962 and in August was sentenced to three months for possessing housebreaking instruments.

The two questions that arose in the present case were first, whether on the merits, the appellant should have been recommended for deportation and secondly, whether he qualified for deportation by reason of the year that he spent in France. On the merits, each member of the Court had come to the conclusion that he should not have received deportation in the present case because the appellant had, in general, been in this country since the age of 13, and had had a long period of service in the Royal Air Force from which he was discharged with a very good character. Accordingly, the question of the appellant's eligibility for deportation did not arise. The Court would allow the appeal and set aside the recommendation for a deportation order.

Solicitors: *Registrar, Court of Criminal Appeal; Solicitor, Metropolitan Police.*

REGINA v. WILSON

(*The Times*, January 16, 1963)

January 15, 1963: Court of Criminal Appeal: Lord Parker C.J., Ashworth, Lyell JJ.

The Court set aside a recommendation for an order of deportation of the applicant, Edward Wilson, aged 22, a native of Georgetown, British Guiana, made by the Recorder (Judge Neville Laski) at the Liverpool Crown Court on October 12, 1962.

MR. JUSTICE ASHWORTH, giving the judgment of the Court, said that the applicant had been convicted of wounding with intent and sentenced to 18 months' imprisonment and recommended for deportation. The offence occurred when a girl, whom the applicant was courting, was struck by a man with whom she was then dancing. It was said that, after a fracas, the applicant followed the man out and struck him with a bottle. The man sustained severe cuts on the hands when shielding his face. The jury found the applicant Guilty of wounding but added that he had acted under provocation. It was clear that the Recorder did not see the reason for the jury's rider. The Court felt that there was material on which the jury could have believed that there had been provocation.

The Recorder stated that, but for the jury's rider, he would have sentenced the applicant to three years' imprisonment, and that the Home Secretary would take the rider into account. The Court would take that rider into account in the present case although there were no grounds for an appeal against conviction, since the summing-up was both careful and correct, yet the application for leave to appeal would be treated as the hearing of the appeal and the recommendation for deportation would be set aside.

R. v. SINGH

([1963] Crim. L.R. 297)

January 25, 1963: Court of Criminal Appeal, Ashworth, Winn, Lyell JJ.

Age: 40 (male). *Facts*: convicted of wounding with intent and sentenced to 3 years' imprisonment. *Previous history*: came to England in 1960; no previous convictions. *Decision*: not a case for a recommendation for deportation.

R. v. BLACK

((1963) 107 Sol. Jo. 137)

February 6, 1963: Court of Criminal Appeal, Ashworth, Winn, Lyell JJ.

Commonwealth Immigrant: Deportation: Information as to Length of Residence

Appeal against sentence.

The appellant, an Irishman aged thirty-one, had been in this country for about eight years. In 1957 he had been conditionally discharged, under a different name, for twelve months for being a suspected person loitering; in February, 1959, he had been sentenced to twenty-one months' imprisonment for causing grievous bodily harm with intent, and in February, 1962, to two months for being a suspected person loitering. He was released from prison on 1st April, 1962. On 25th September, 1962, after a notice under the Commonwealth Immigrants Act, 1962, had been served on him, he pleaded guilty to shop breaking and larceny on 20th September, 1962, and was committed to London sessions for sentence. He was unrepresented and, when the chairman asked him what he wanted to say, said that there was nothing to say. His mind was not directed to the question of the length of his residence in this country. He was sentenced to twelve months' imprisonment, and also to recommendation for deportation. He appealed against the recommendation.

ASHWORTH, J., said that, although the language as recorded in the transcript was not the same, the effect was similar to *R.* v. *Edgehill** [1963] 2 W.L.R. 170. It was a matter for serious consideration whether, when an accused man was unrepresented and the prosecution knew that the question of continuous residence for five years was a live issue, the prosecution should not, of their own motion, having full regard to where the onus of proof was, see that the court was informed of all the relevant facts. Apart from that, it was not right to make a recommendation for deportation on the material of the appellant's record. On those two grounds the appeal would be allowed, and the recommendation set aside. Appeal allowed.

APPEARANCES: *Petre Crowder* (*R. W. Platt*); *Michael Worsley* (*Solicitor, Metropolitan Police*).

R. v. BROOMFIELD

([1963] Crim. L.R. 297)

February 7, 1963: Court of Criminal Appeal: Ashworth, Winn, Lyell JJ.

Age: 32 (male). *Facts*: pleaded guilty to assault occasioning actual bodily harm and convicted of robbery with violence; sentenced to 3 years' imprisonment and recommended for deportation. *Previous history*: came to England in 1958; convicted in 1960 of possessing Indian hemp and in 1961 of assaulting a police officer. *Decision*: was obviously of bad character; a proper case for a recommendation for deportation.

REGINA v. AIRDROOS

(*The Times*, February 20, 1963)

February 19, 1963: Court of Criminal Appeal: Finnemore, Hinchcliffe, Marshall JJ.

Commonwealth Citizen to be deported

The Court dismissed an application by Sayed Airdroos for leave to appeal against a recommendation for deportation made against him at Oxford Quarter Sessions on December 3, 1962, he having pleaded Guilty to driving while disqualified, taking and driving a motor car without the consent of the owner, store-breaking and larceny, attempted shop-breaking with intent to commit a felony, and attempted larceny. In addition to being recommended for deportation, he had been sentenced to concurrent sentences amounting in all to nine months' imprisonment.

MR. JUSTICE HINCHCLIFFE, giving the judgment of the Court, said that the point which was raised by the applicant was that the Commonwealth Immigrants Act, 1962, did not apply to him, being a citizen of the Crown Colony of Aden, so that he was not eligible for deportation. This matter had been fully argued at Quarter Sessions, who had held that the Act applied to the applicant. The Court of Criminal Appeal agreed. Having been born in a Crown Colony, the applicant was a Commonwealth citizen and clearly fulfilled the conditions laid down in the Act. There was no point of substance in the matters which he had raised, and it was quite clear, having regard to his record of five previous convictions from 1960 to 1962, that he had properly been recommended for deportation.

R. v. DALY

([1963] Crim. L.R. 445)

March 4, 1963: Court of Criminal Appeal: Lord Parker C.J., Ashworth, Winn JJ.

Age: twenty (male). *Facts*: pleaded guilty to shop-breaking and larceny; six similar offences taken into consideration. *Previous history*: continuously in trouble since the age of eleven. Came to England in August 1959; the following month sent to borstal for twenty-nine offences of housebreaking. Went to Ireland on licence in 1960; did not return until 1962 when he committed the present offences. *Special considerations*: said he wanted to marry a girl in England; but his family lived in Ireland. *Decision*: having regard to the number of offences he had committed it was a proper case for a recommendation for deportation.

REGINA v. KILMARTIN

(*The Times*, March 12, 1963)

March 11, 1963: Court of Criminal Appeal: Lord Parker C.J., Ashworth, Winn JJ.

Irishman not to be Deported

The Court granted this application by James Kilmartin, aged 21, at present detained in H.M. Prison, Maidstone, for leave to appeal against sentence of three years' imprisonment and recommendation for deportation passed on him at Lewes Assizes (Mr. Justice Melford Stevenson) on December 10, 1962, when he pleaded Guilty to a charge of wounding with intent.

Their Lordships, treating the hearing of the application as that of the appeal, reduced the sentence to one of two years' imprisonment and made no recommendation for deportation.

Mr. Felix Waley appeared for Kilmartin.

The LORD CHIEF JUSTICE said that Kilmartin came from Ireland, had no previous convictions and an excellent work record, and the police acknowledged that he was, in the ordinary way, a quiet man. What happened in the present case, was not in character.

It appeared that he was involved in a fight outside a public house, when he picked up an empty milk bottle and smashed it and drove it, with what must have been considerable force into the back of an 18-year-old student. The glass went right through his jacket, and caused a laceration 1½ inches deep, between the spine and shoulder blade.

It was only fair, however, to say that, earlier in the evening on which this occurred he had been hit with the fist of this student, and that a girl with the student had attacked Kilmartin in the face with a stilletto heel, which was known to be a very dangerous weapon. Outside the public house, Kilmartin saw this same girl, armed with the stilletto heel and also with a glass in her hand. True, the glass was not broken, but there she was with it. Kilmartin had been drinking in the interval, and, seeing the girl armed in that way, he undoubtedly lost his temper.

The judge clearly looked upon it as a serious case, as indeed it was; but he treated it as a case of premeditation. The only premeditation involved was the time that elapsed in breaking the milk bottle. When one compared this case with the many other glass cases which, unfortunately, came before this Court, this was certainly not a case of real premeditation. On the whole, the Court felt that for a man of this character, three years was an excessive sentence, even when one recognized the need for a deterrent sentence in the case of these attacks with broken bottles.

The matter of deportation was not gone into, save that the police stated that the necessary notice had been served under section 8 of the Commonwealth Immigrants Act, 1962; no further reference appeared to have been made to deportation.

Having regard to this man's character and the fact that, as this Court viewed it, he was gravely provoked, the Court hardly thought that this was a case for deportation. He was a young man, earning £20 a week, living apparently with his uncle who looked after him, and sent £8 a week to his parents in Ireland.

The sentence should be reduced to one of two years' imprisonment, and there should be no recommendation for deportation.

Solicitors: Messrs. *Lightfoot Marchbanks,* Sutton.

R. v. HAYLES

([1963] Crim. L.R. 446)

March 12, 1963: Court of Criminal Appeal: Lord Parker C.J., Ashworth, Lyell JJ.

Age: twenty-seven (male). *Facts*: robbery with aggravation and unlawful wounding. He robbed a man of his wallet and used a knife to effect his escape. *Previous history*: came to England in 1959; worked for short periods only; three previous convictions including one for malicious wounding (with a knife), and one for carrying an offensive weapon (also a knife). *Decision*: a proper case for a recommendation for deportation. The court did not endorse the following observation by the trial judge: "I shall make a recommendation for deportation and that may mean that, instead of serving your sentence, you may just be sent out of this country. In my opinion that is the proper thing to do."

R. v. LESMOND

([1963] Crim. L.R. 376)

March 13, 1963: Court of Criminal Appeal: Lord Parker C.J., Ashworth, Winn JJ.

Age: twenty (male). *Facts*: pleaded guilty to stealing a motor-car from the street. He had an obsession for motor-cars. *Previous history*: came to England in April 1960; had not worked regularly since November 1960; six previous convictions for dishonesty and motoring offences. *Special considerations*: said he wished to return to West Indies, but of his own accord. *Decision*: a proper case for a recommendation for deportation. The court did not endorse the following observations of the trial judge: "I do not see why we should pay the expense of putting you in a borstal institution. Therefore the sentence will be one of imprisonment for nine months. There will be a recommendation for deportation and, if the authorities like to deport you before the nine months are up, they are welcome to do so, and the sooner they do it the better."

R. v. TULSIE

([1963] Crim. L.R. 376)

March 18, 1963: Court of Criminal Appeal: Lord Parker C.J., Ashworth, Winn JJ.

Age: twenty (male). *Facts*: pleaded guilty to burglary, attempted burglary and housebreaking and asked for fourteen similar offences to be taken into consideration. The offences were committed from July to October 1962. *Previous history*: came to England in 1960; one previous conviction in September 1962 for burglary—put on probation. *Special considerations*: committed twelve of the offences after being put on probation, seven within a week thereof; his youth; mother lived in England, but he did not live with her or support her. *Decision*: he had committed eighteen serious offences and there was therefore no error in principle in recommending him for deportation.

R. v. DUBHIR

([1963] Crim. L.R. 445)

March 22, 1963: Court of Criminal Appeal: Winn, Mocatta, Roskill JJ.

Age: twenty (male). *Facts*: pleaded guilty to malicious wounding of a fellow borstal detainee but after provocation. Six months' imprisonment and recommended for deportation. *Previous history*: came to England in 1958. Five previous convictions: three for dishonesty, one for importuning, one for [**446**] disorderly behaviour. *Special considerations*: he said that he had no ties with his native country and had a half-brother in England; Prison Commissioners reported unfavourably on his behaviour at borstal. *Decision*: a proper case for a recommendation.

R. v. MULROY

((1963) 107 Sol. Jo. 274)

March 25, 1963: Court of Criminal Appeal: Lord Parker C.J., Ashworth, Winn JJ.

Commonwealth Immigrant: Father born in United Kingdom: Deportation Recommended: Importance of Legal Representation.

Appeal against recommendation for deportation.

After pleading guilty to larceny from a bank the appellant was committed to quarter sessions for sentence. He was twenty-three, of no fixed abode, had no previous conviction, and had been born in Eire, his father having been born in Cornwall. Notice under s. 8 of the Commonwealth Immigrants Act, 1962, was served. He was not legally represented at quarter sessions, the proceedings were concerned mainly with the larceny, the question of eligibility for deportation was not discussed, the notice was referred to at a late stage and he did not address the court. He was sentenced to twelve months' imprisonment with a recommendation for deportation. He appealed against the recommendation, contending that he was a person whose father was born in the United Kingdom and he was, therefore, within the provisions of s. 6 (2) (*a*) of the 1962 Act, a person who could not be deported. On appeal, after police inquiries had been made, the Crown conceded that the father had been born in Cornwall.

LORD PARKER, C.J., said that, as his father had been born in Cornwall, the appellant did not qualify for deportation and the recommendation must be set aside. This case showed again the importance of persons who qualified for recommendation for deportation being legally represented. No doubt, the notice under s. 8 of the 1962 Act set out the qualifying conditions, but the persons concerned could not be expected, in every case, to read them, much less to understand them. Appeal allowed.

APPEARANCES: *M. D. L. Worsley* (*Registrar, Court of Criminal Appeal*); *Cyril Salmon* (*Solicitor, Metropolitan Police*).

R. v. PRINGLE

([1963] Crim. L.R. 446)

March 25, 1963: Court of Criminal Appeal: Lord Parker C.J., Ashworth, Winn JJ.

Age: thirty-four (male). *Facts*: convicted of wounding with intent; sentenced to four years' imprisonment and recommended for deportation. *Previous history*: came to England in 1960 and worked until February 1962; no previous convictions. *Special considerations*: his wife and child were in Jamaica and he had no ties with England; the offence was serious. *Decision*: recommendation upheld.

REGINA v. WEEKES

(*The Times*, March 26, 1963)

March 25, 1963: Court of Criminal Appeal: Lord Parker C.J., Ashworth, Winn JJ.

The Court allowed this appeal against a recommendation for deportation made against Frank Michael Weekes, of H.M. Prison, Wandsworth. The recommendation was made when the defendant was convicted at County of London Sessions on December 19, 1962, of malicious wounding, for which he was also sentenced to 15 months' imprisonment.

Mr. Dennis Kelly appeared for the defendant.

The LORD CHIEF JUSTICE said that the defendant came to England in August, 1956 and had, therefore, been in England about six years and four months at the time of the trial.

The Deputy Chairman had asked whether the defendant had been in this country too long for deportation under the Commonwealth Immigrants Act, 1962 and had been told that he had served over two years in prison.

In fact, by section 7 (2) of that Act, only periods of six months or more spent in prison were to be deducted when computing the five years' residence which gave immunity from deportation. The defendant had served one period of imprisonment of about 12 months and another period of six months. However, part of the latter period had been spent on remand, before the sentence was imposed; consequently, that sentence could not be taken into account.

Accordingly, the period of twelve months in prison was the only one relevant to deportation, for which purposes the defendant had been in this country five years and four months, and the recommendation must be quashed.

Police and counsel must remember that it was only periods of imprisonment after sentence that could be regarded when considering eligibility for deportation.

Solicitor: *The Registrar, Court of Criminal Appeal*

R. v. CRAIG

([1963] Crim. L.R. 445)

March 29, 1963: Court of Criminal Appeal: Lord Parker C.J., Ashworth, Winn JJ.

Age: twenty-two (male). *Facts*: pleaded guilty to house-breaking and larceny; three other offences taken into consideration; twelve months' imprisonment and recommended for deportation. *Previous history*: eight previous convictions for dishonesty; came to England in 1958, 1961 and 1962 and each time committed an offence of dishonesty. *Special considerations*: wife and child in England; but his father wanted him to return to Ireland where work was available. *Decision*: a proper case for a recommendation.

REGINA v. STEWART

(*The Times*, April 9, 1963)

April 8, 1963: Court of Criminal Appeal: Edmund Davies, Winn, Nield JJ.

The Court allowed this appeal by Dorril Stewart, at present detained in H.M. Prison, Pentonville, against a sentence of recommendation for deportation. He had been convicted by the Watford Justices on two charges of obtaining money by false pretences and had been committed to Sessions for sentence. At Hertfordshire Quarter Sessions (Chairman: Sir Henry Wynn Parry) he was sentenced to three years' concurrent imprisonment on each count and was recommended for deportation. On March 13, 1963, the Court had dismissed his appeal against the sentences of imprisonment, but had adjourned the appeal against deportation. Stewart had come to this country from Jamaica.

Mr. *M. D. L. Worsley* appeared for Stewart.

MR. JUSTICE EDMUND DAVIES, giving the judgment of the Court, said that if Stewart was deported, his wife and five-year-old child would become virtually destitute. His wife's mother was a very sick woman and his wife had to stay in England to look after her. Also the child would be deprived of the father's attention. At the moment, the appellant and his wife were living apart, but this might be a purely temporary arrangement. Having regard to all the circumstances, a deportation order was not justified.

Solicitor: *Messrs. Lincoln and Lincoln.*

REGINA v. NEMBHARD

(*The Times*, April 24, 1963)

April 23, 1963: Court of Criminal Appeal: Lord Parker C.J., Havers, Edmund Davies JJ.

Power to Order Deportation

The Court of Criminal Appeal dismissing an appeal by Terence Nembhard, a West Indian, aged 20, against a sentence of Borstal training imposed at London Sessions (Chairman: Mr. R. E. Seaton) for offences of burglary and larceny, taking and driving away a motor car and driving while disqualified, to which the appellant had pleaded Guilty, considered whether the Court had power to make a recommendation for deportation under the Commonwealth Immigrants Act, 1962, on an appeal against sentence.

The LORD CHIEF JUSTICE, giving the judgment of the Court, said that it was clear that Borstal training was the appropriate sentence. Although the matter had not been fully argued, the Court, as at present advised, did not think it had power to make a recommendation for deportation on an appeal against sentence. It was clear from section 8 (4) of the Act of 1962 that sentence and a recommendation for deportation were two separate matters, and as the appeal was against sentence only, there was no power to consider a recommendation for deportation.

Even if the Court did have such a power, it would not feel that this was a proper case in which to exercise it. Cases in which the appropriate sentence was Borstal training, which at the same time were appropriate for a recommendation for deportation, must be comparatively rare.

R. v. OKENARHE

([1963] Crim. L.R. 526)

May 14, 1963: Court of Criminal Appeal: Edmund Davies, Marshall, Phillimore JJ.

Age: twenty-seven (male). *Facts*: convicted on three counts of larceny of a postal packet and three of causing a cheque to be delivered by means of a forged instrument; had by this means obtained over £2,500. *Previous history*: came to England in 1960; no previous convictions. *Decision*: nothing wrong in principle with sentence of three years' imprisonment and recommendation for deportation.

R. v. HENRIQUES

([1963] Crim. L.R. 525)

May 15, 1963: Court of Criminal Appeal: Lord Parker C.J., Havers, Edmund Davies JJ.

Age: eighteen (male). *Facts*: pleaded guilty to wounding with intent, attempted rape, housebreaking and larceny, burglary and larceny, larceny and possessing housebreaking implements by night. *Previous history*: came to England in 1962; no previous convictions. *Decision*: having regard to the serious nature of the charges, a proper case for a recommendation for deportation. (He did not appeal against sentence of 4 years' imprisonment.)

REGINA v. ALLAN AND OTHERS

([1965] 1 Q.B. 130)

June 11, 12, 13, 18, 1963: Court of Criminal Appeal: Edmund Davies, Marshall, Lawton JJ.

Crime—Affray—Principal in the second degree—When jury may properly convict—Whether encouragement a requirement before an accused person can be convicted.

Crime—Aiding and abetting—Encouraging unlawful act—Minimal requirement to constitute principal in second degree—Affray.

Three men pleaded not guilty before a judge and jury on a charge of making an affray. In the course of his summing-up the trial judge handed to the jury copies of his direction on the law of affray. Paragraph 4 of the direction read as follows: "Every person is, however, a party [to an affray] and guilty who: (i) agrees that such a fight should take place and, in pursuance of that agreement, is later present at it; *or* (ii) without such agreement unlawfully joins in such a fight, or, being present, chose to remain present, either (a) knowing that his continued **[131]** presence encouraged the fight, *or* (b) intending to join in the fight if his help was needed by his side."

All three defendants were found guilty and were sentenced to various terms of imprisonment. On appeal against convictions and sentences by the first two defendants and against conviction only by the third: —

Held, allowing the appeals, that the judge had misdirected the jury as part of his direction was tantamount to telling the jury that they were duty bound to convict an accused who was proved to have been present and witnessing an affray if it was also proved that he nursed an intention to join in if help was needed by the side he favoured, and this notwithstanding that he did nothing by words or deeds to evince his intention and outwardly played the role of a purely passive spectator, whereas the law was that before a jury could properly convict an accused person of being a principal in the second degree to an affray, they must be convinced by the evidence that, at the very least, he by some means or other encouraged the participants; to hold otherwise would be, in effect, to convict a man on his thoughts, unaccompanied by any physical act other than the fact of his mere presence.

Dicta of Cave J. and Lopes J. in *Regina* v. *Coney* (1882) 8 Q.B.D. 534, 539, 552 applied.

Per curiam. Encouragement in one form or another is a minimal requirement before an accused person may properly be regarded as a principal in the second degree to any crime (post, p. 138).

Dictum of Devlin J. in *National Coal Board* v. *Gamble* [1959 1 Q.B. 11, 24; [1958] 3 W.L.R. 434; [1958] 3 All E.R. 203, D.C. explained.

APPEALS against conviction and sentence.

George Donald Allan, James Joseph Boyle, Albert Ballantyne, Michael Mooney and others appeared at Lincoln Assizes on January 30, 1963, before Thesiger J. and a jury on an indictment charging that on September 8, 1962, they unlawfully fought and made an affray in certain highways in Scunthorpe.

Allan, Boyle and Ballantyne pleaded not guilty; Mooney pleaded guilty to the charge.

The following facts are taken from the judgment. On September 8, 1962, a fight with knives took place between a number of Somalis and white men in the vicinity of the Oswald Hotel in Scunthorpe. During the evening a Somali named Yusef was stabbed to death in Allanby Street. The fight appeared to have lasted 15 minutes; a large number of people had collected in Frances Street, West Street and Allanby Street, where the principal fighting occurred, and during its course Allan, Ballantyne and Mooney received knife wounds.

The Court of Criminal Appeal had on June 12, 1963, dismissed **[132]** the appeal of John Gow against his conviction for non-capital murder in respect of Yusef.

At the trial the judge in the course of his summing-up directed the jury on the law of affray. He had caused to be typed copies of his direction which were handed to the jury. The direction was in the following terms:

"1. An affray is a fight between two or more people in a public street that is likely to terrify passers-by or residents.

"2. Every person who is a party to an affray is guilty of an offence.

"3. Mere presence at the fight does not make a person a party to it, even if he does nothing to stop it; nor is he a party to it if he tries to stop the fight and restore the Queen's peace, or if he tries to defend someone from being hurt, because it is lawful to intervene for this purpose.

"4. Every person is, however, a party and guilty who: (i) agrees that such a fight should take place and, in pursuance of that agreement, is later present at it; *or* (ii) without such agreement unlawfully joins in such a fight, or, being present, chose to remain present, either (a) knowing that his continued presence encouraged the fight, *or* (b) intending to join in the fight if his help was needed by his side."

All four defendants were found guilty on February 11, 1963. Allan and Boyle were sentenced to four years' imprisonment, Ballantyne to three years' and Mooney, in addition to three years' imprisonment, was recommended to be deported to Ireland at the end of his sentence.

Allan and Boyle appealed against their convictions and sentences, Ballantyne against conviction only, and Mooney against the order recommending deportation.

Anthony Cripps Q.C. and *Alan de Piro* for Allan and Ballantyne. Allan's ground of appeal is that the evidence did not warrant his conviction. His defence was that he was a drunken bystander and was almost incapable of participating in the affray through the influence of drink. It was not challenged that by reason of drink he was unable to give a coherent account of what had happened. Ballantyne appeals on the ground that his defence was not sufficiently put in the trial judge's summing-up.

Geoffrey Lane Q.C. and *R. D. Lymbery* for Boyle and Mooney. The legal point that calls for determination is the correctness or otherwise of the trial judge's direction regarding the proof necessary to convict a person of making an affray. The **[133]** effect of paragraph (ii) (b) of that direction is that the jury were instructed to convict any accused man who was proved to have been present and witnessing the affray, if it was also proved that he nursed an intention to join in in the event of help being needed by the side he favoured. This notwithstanding that he did nothing by words or deeds to evince his intention, and notwithstanding he outwardly played the role of a purely passive spectator. If that direction was correct, then where A and B behave themselves to all outward appearances in an exactly similar manner, but it is proved that A had the intention to participate if needs be, whereas B had no such intention, it must result in A being convicted as a principal in the second degree to the affray, whereas B would be acquitted. To do that would be to convict A on his thoughts, even though they found no reflection in his actions.

One who actually participates in an affray is guilty of being a principal in the first degree. One who aids, abets, counsels or procures but is absent at the time of the affray is clearly guilty of being an accessory before the fact. A principal in the second degree is one who is present and participating in an affray without actually fighting. There must at least be some encouragement. Mere presence is not encouragement. Mere intention to encourage or an intention to fight is not enough. The essentials in the case of a principal in the second degree are mens rea, i.e. an intention to provide assistance or encouragement, and an actus reus, i.e. the actual provision of encouragement or assistance. In the absence of either of those two essentials, a person is not guilty as a principal in the second degree. The real question for the jury was: Has the prosecution proved mens rea and actus reus beyond all reasonable doubt? What the trial judge was directing the jury amounted to evidence of guilt as a matter of law was merely evidence from which such guilt might or might not be inferred by the jury. [Reference was made to *Regina* v. *Coney*[1] and *Rex* v. *Murphy*.[2]]

J. A. Grieves Q.C. and *E. F. Jowitt* for the Crown. The direction of the trial judge was correct in law and in the given circumstances a jury doing its duty was bound to convict A of aiding and abetting an affray even though he uttered no word of encouragement and acted throughout in exactly the same manner as all the other spectators of what was happening. A principal in the second degree

[1] (1882) 8 Q.B.D. 534.
[2] (1883) 6 C. & P. 103.

is a person who is present aiding and abetting an affray [Reference was made to *Regina* v. *Young*[3] (cited in [**134**] *Regina* v. *Coney*[4]) and *Wilcox* v. *Jeffery*.[5]*] A person who arrives when a fight is in progress and chooses to remain at the spot whilst the fight continues is committing an overt act. There must be some evidence of the purpose for which he continues to remain there. The decision in earlier cases was that while the courts were troubled by elements of the evidence, there was no clear distinction between intention and overt act. This case involves fundamental principles of criminal law. As to the meaning of "countenance," see Shorter Oxford English Dictionary (2nd ed.), p. 405.

Alan de Piro replied.

Geoffrey Lane Q.C. in reply. *Regina* v. *Young*,[6] cited in *Regina* v. *Coney*,[7] is misleading.

Cur. adv. vult.

1963. June 18. EDMUND DAVIES J. read the judgment of the court. After a trial lasting nine days at the Lincoln Assizes in February last, the appellants Allan, Boyle and Ballantyne were convicted of making an affray, the appellant Mooney having pleaded guilty on the second day of the trial. Allan and Boyle now appealed against conviction and their sentences of four years' imprisonment, Ballantyne against conviction only. Mooney appeals only against the recommendation that he be deported to his native Ireland. Having regard to the decision this court has arrived at on the point of law relied on by the first three appellants, the facts need not be gone into in very great detail.

[His Lordship reviewed the facts and continued:] Despite the submissions of defence counsel, the court has come to the conclusion that in the case of each of the appellants there was sufficient evidence to justify the jury coming to the conclusion, on a proper direction, that they had all unlawfully fought and made an affray. The case against Allan was a good deal less strong than that against the other appellants, but, even so, we should not have interfered with his conviction had the jury been properly directed.

The legal point that calls for determination is as to the judge's direction regarding the proof necessary before an accused person may properly be convicted of making an affray, but the criticism made upon it involves consideration of matters which have an importance which reaches beyond the confines of the law as to [**135**] affrays. The judge had caused to be typed out copies of his direction which were handed to the jury and, one may take it, this was carefully studied by them and operated to guide their deliberations, as it was intended to do.

[His Lordship stated the terms of the direction as set out above and continued:] No criticism has been, or properly could be, levelled against paragraphs 1, 2, 3, and 4 (i) of that direction, nor as to the direction in paragraph 4 (ii) that a person unlawfully joining in an affray is guilty, notwithstanding the absence of prior agreement. Paragraph 4 (ii) (a) is, however, attacked as containing what counsel described as "a concealed dichotomy." This highly alarming concept fortunately does not call for comment and we can turn forthwith to consider the more telling attack made upon paragraph 4 (ii) (b). In effect, it amounts to this: that the judge thereby directed the jury that they were duty bound to convict an accused who was proved to have been present and witnessing an affray if it was also proved that he nursed an intention to join in if help was needed by the side he favoured and this notwithstanding that he did nothing by words or deeds to evince his intention and outwardly played the role of a purely passive spectator. It was said that, if that direction is right, where A and B behave themselves to all outward appearances in an exactly similar manner, but it be proved that A had the intention to participate if needs

[3] (1883) 8 C. & P. 644.
[4] (1882) 8 Q.B.D. 534.
[5] [1951] 1 T.L.R. 706; [1951] 1 All E.R. 464, D.C.
[6] 8 C. & P. 644.
[7] 8 Q.B.D. 652.

be, whereas B had no such intention, then A must be convicted of being a principal in the second degree to the affray, whereas B should be acquitted. To do that, it is objected, would be to convict A on his thoughts, even though they found no reflection in his actions. For the Crown, on the other hand, it is contended that the direction was unimpeachable, and that in the given circumstances a jury doing its duty would be bound to convict A of aiding and abetting in an affray even though he uttered no word of encouragement and acted throughout in exactly the same manner as all the other spectators of what was happening.

The locus classicus on this branch of the law is the majority decision of the Court of Crown Cases Reserved in *Regina* v. *Coney*,[8] whereby the conviction of mere spectators of a prize-fight as being aiders and abettors in the fight was quashed. Before proceedings to quote from Hale (1 Hale P.C. 439) and from Foster's Crown Law (1792), p. 104, Cave J. said[9]: "Now it is a general rule in the case of principals in the second degree that there must be participation in the act, and that, although **[136]** a man is present whilst a felony is being committed, if he takes no part in it, and does not act in concert with those who commit it, he will not be a principal in the second degree merely because he does not endeavour to prevent the felony, or apprehend the felon." The opening words of the trial judge in paragraph 3 of his direction accurately adopted this passage, but the difficulty arises, as we have said, in relation to the following paragraph (para. No. 4). In *Rex* v. *Murphy*[10] Littledale J. directed the jury as follows: "I am of opinion that persons who are at a fight, in consequence of which death ensues, are all guilty of manslaughter if they encouraged it by their presence, I mean, if they remained present during the fight. I say that if they were not casually passing by, but stayed at the place, they encouraged it by their presence, although they did not say or do anything.... If the death occurred from the fight itself, all persons encouraging it by their presence are guilty of manslaughter." Commenting on this direction, Cave J. had this to say in *Regina* v. *Coney*[11]: "This summing-up unfortunately appears to me capable of being understood in two different ways. It may mean either that mere presence unexplained is evidence of encouragement, and so of guilt, or that mere presence unexplained is conclusive proof of encouragement, and so of guilt. If the former is the correct meaning, I concur in the law so laid down; if the latter, I am unable to do so. It appears to me that the passage tending to convey the latter view is that which was read by the chairman in this case to the jury, and I cannot help thinking that the chairman believed himself, and meant to direct the jury, and at any rate I feel satisfied that the jury understood him to mean, that mere presence unexplained was conclusive proof of encouragement, and so of guilt; and it is on this ground I hold that this conviction ought not to stand."

With this judgment that great master of the criminal law, Stephen J., expressed his agreement.[12] The basis of the majority decision was neatly expressed in the short judgment of Lopes J., which contains this passage[13]: "I cannot hold, as a proposition of law, that the mere looking on is ipso facto a participation in or encouragement of a prize-fight. I think there must be more than that to justify a conviction of an assault. If, for instance, it was proved that a person went to a prize-fight, knowing it was to take place, and remained there for some time looking **[137]** on, I think that would be evidence from which a jury might infer that such person encouraged, and intended to encourage the fight by his presence."

Finally, Hawkins J. had this to say[14]: "In my opinion, to constitute an aider and abettor some active steps must be taken by word, or action, with the intent to instigate the principal, or principals . . . Non-interference to prevent a crime is not itself a crime. But the fact that a person was voluntarily and purposely present witnessing the commission of a crime, and offered no opposition to it,

[8] (1882) 8 Q.B.D. 534.
[9] Ibid. 539.
[10] (1833) 6 C. & P. 103, 104.
[11] (1882) 8 Q.B.D. 534, 543.
[12] Ibid. 548.
[13] Ibid. 552.
[14] (1882) 8 Q.B.D. 534, 557, 558.

though he might reasonably be expected to prevent and had the power so to do, or at least to express his dissent, might under some circumstances offer cogent evidence upon which a jury would be justified in finding that he wilfully encouraged and so aided and abetted. But it would be purely a question for the jury whether he did so or not."

Applying these passages to the direction in the present case, we have come to the conclusion that, in effect, the trial judge here dealt with facts which, at most, might provide some evidence of encouragement as amounting to conclusive proof of guilt. The jury were in terms told that a man who chooses to remain at a fight, nursing the secret intention to help if the need arose, but doing nothing to evince that intention, *must* in law be held to be principal in the second degree and that, on these facts being proved, the jury would have no alternative but to convict him. In our judgment that was a misdirection. As Cave J. said in *Regina* v. *Coney*[15]: "Where presence is prima facie not accidental it is evidence, but not more than evidence, for the jury," and it remains no more than evidence for the jury even when one adds to presence at an affray a secret intention to help.

No authority in support of the direction given in the present case has been cited to us. The passage in *Regina* v. *Young*[16] cited in *Regina* v. *Coney*[17] is incomplete, and reference to the report itself makes clear that Vaughan J. was there dealing with presence at a fight as the result of a previous arrangement. The only other case cited by the Crown, *Wilcox* v. *Jeffery*,[18*] turned on special facts very different from the present and is one from which we think no general principle can be deduced. In the present case, the trial judge dealt with matters of evidence from which encouragement (and, therefore, guilty participation) might **[138]** be inferred if—but only if—the jury thought fit to do so as necessarily amounting in law to proof that guilt was established. In our judgment this amounted to a misdirection, and one, unfortunately, of a basic kind.

This court considers that there is a further ground for criticism of the directions to the jury. By the third direction they were rightly told that proof of mere presence at an affray is not sufficient ipso facto to establish guilt as a principal in the second degree. So far, so good. By paragraph 4 (ii) (a) of the directions the element of encouragement was dealt with. But, owing to the somewhat complex grammatical construction of that paragraph and the use of the disjunctive between parts (a) and (b) thereof, when they came to deal with paragraph 4 (ii) (b) the jury may well have been led into thinking that the element of encouragement was a matter with which they need not then concern themselves at all. So to think would be wrong. In our judgment, before a jury can properly convict an accused person of being a principal in the second degree to an affray, they must be convinced by the evidence that, at the very least, he by some means or other encouraged the participants. To hold otherwise would be, in effect, as the appellants' counsel rightly expressed it, to convict a man on his thoughts, unaccompanied by any physical act other than the fact of his mere presence.

Indeed, in our judgment, encouragement in one form or another is a minimal requirement before an accused person may properly be regarded as a principal in the second degree to any crime. It is true that in *National Coal Board* v. *Gamble*,[19] Devlin J., referring to *Regina* v. *Coney*,[20] said: "It would be wrong to conclude . . . that proof of encouragement is necessary to every form of aiding and abetting." But when the facts of that case are examined, it does not, in our judgment, affect the validity of the proposition we have stated, for there the accused had intentionally supplied an article essential to the perpetration of the crime charged, and this Devlin J. described[21] as an a fortiori case to that of voluntary presence. In that case there was what was judicially described as

[15] Ibid. 540.
[16] (1838) 8 C. & P. 644, 652.
[17] (1882) 8 Q.B.D. 534, 541.
[18] [1951] 1 T.L.R. 706; [1951] 1 All E.R. 464, D.C.
[19] [1959] 1 Q.B. 11, 24; [1958] 3 W.L.R. 434, 443; [1958] 3 All E.R. 203, 209, D.C.
[20] (1882) 8 Q.B.D. 584.
[21] [1959] 1 Q.B. 11, 24.

"proof of intent to aid," which may properly be regarded as but one of the numerous possible manifestations of encouragement.

In the light of these criticisms, we have considered whether, in the circumstances, it would be proper to apply the proviso to **[139]** section 4 (1) of the Criminal Appeal Act, 1907. But counsel for the Crown, with characteristic candour, intimated that, should we hold (contrary to his submissions) that what was here said to the jury amounted to a misdirection in the respects already indicated, he felt unable to invite this court to say that it was clear that no substantial miscarriage of justice had flown therefrom. We think that the attitude of counsel for the Crown is right. For the proviso to operate where there has been a wrong direction on the law, ". . . the Crown have to show that, on a right direction, the jury must have come to the same conclusion" (*per* Channell J. in *Rex* v. *Cohen and Bateman*[22]) and that the Crown concede they cannot here show. This was in many respects a complex and difficult case, as well as a long one. The witnesses were numerous, there was not unimportant discrepancies even on the prosecution side as to the parts alleged to have been played by the various accused, and in their two-hour deliberations the jury must often have turned to the typed legal directions as to a sheet-anchor. Profitless though it is to conjecture how their minds worked, it is by no means fanciful to entertain the suspicion that their thought-process may well have been: "The accused were present at the scene of the affray and chose to remain there, and we are satisfied that they intended to intervene if they thought the Somalis were getting the better of the whites; the judge has said that on those facts we *must* hold that they were parties to the affray; we, therefore, find them guilty."

For these reasons, in our judgment the misdirection was one in respect of which the proviso cannot properly be invoked. It follows that the appeals of Allan, Boyle and Ballantyne succeed, their convictions are quashed and they are discharged.

There remains the appeal of Mooney against the recommendation that he be deported. He is 24, was convicted three times in Eire as a juvenile, and came here in August, 1958. He was fined £5 for larceny in January, 1959, £5 for wilful damage in October of that year, and £15 in November, 1960, for receiving stolen money, but has no previous convictions for violence to the person. His work-record, whilst not of the best, cannot be described as a bad one, as these things go. He had taken drink and himself received a serious stomach wound. It was established that, at some risk to himself, he intervened to prevent one of the Somalis from being kicked. He comes from a poor part of Ireland, would have difficulty in finding re-employment there, **[140]** and is engaged to an English girl. We would not be prepared to interfere with the sentence of three years' imprisonment passed upon him, nor has he sought this, but, in the light of all the circumstances, we do not think that his participation in this affray justifies his being deported. We accordingly allow his appeal by removing the recommendation to that end made by the trial judge.

Appeals allowed.

Solicitors: *Registrar, Court of Criminal Appeal; Director of Public Prosecutions.*

[22] (1909) 2 Cr.App.R. 197, 207, C.C.A.

R. v. WALKER

([1963] Crim. L.R. 582)

June 14, 1963: Court of Criminal Appeal: Havers, Melford Stevenson, Roskill JJ.

Age: thirty-one (male). *Facts*: convicted of living on immoral earnings. *Previous history*: came to England in 1960; convictions for carrying offensive weapon, burglary and living on immoral earnings. *Decision*: a clear case for a recommendation.

R v. FLYNN

([1963] Crim. L.R. 647)

July 1, 1963: Court of Criminal Appeal: Lord Parker C.J., Widgery, John Stephenson JJ.

Sentence and recommendation for deportation—procedure

For the appellant: *Miss J. Southworth* (instructed by the Registrar, Court of Criminal Appeal). The Crown was not represented.

F. pleaded guilty to receiving and was sentenced to borstal training. He was nineteen and came to England in 1959. He had **[648]** two convictions for dishonesty and one for possessing drugs. He was also recommended for deportation. The judge purported to give him a certificate to appeal being uncertain whether he had correctly interpreted *R.* v. *Edgehill** [1963] 1 Q.B. 593; [1963] Crim. L.R. 92 and *R.* v. *Nembhard**, [1963] Crim. L.R. 447.

Held, (1) the proper approach is first to consider what is the appropriate sentence, and then to consider whether it is a case for a recommendation: *R.* v. *Edgehill.** This approach is necessary because it is not known at that stage whether the defendant will be deported or not. Where the appropriate sentence is Borstal only rarely will it also be a case for a recommendation: the reasons being that the Home Secretary is loth to deport youthful offenders except in extreme circumstances, and the crime though serious may not be the type of crime for which a young person would be deported since that type of crime might well attract imprisonment rather than Borstal: explaining *R.* v. *Nembhard**. In the present case there was some ground for making the recommendation since F. had not settled down and had committed four offences and it would be allowed to stand. (2) There is no power to give a certificate to appeal against sentence.

R v. ROMANO

[1963] Crim.L.R. 638

July 15, 1963: Court of Criminal Appeal: Lord Parker C.J., Widgery, John Stephenson JJ.

Deportation of person with dual nationality precluded

For the appellant: *M. D. L. Worsley* (instructed by Lincoln & Lincoln)

For the Crown: *R. Frisby* (instructed by the Metropolitan Police Solicitor).

R. was convicted of larceny and thirteen cases of fraud. He had a bad record and was sentenced to three years' imprisonment and recommended for deportation. He had come to England in 1959. The Home Secretary had indicated in the past that he felt precluded from deporting Cypriots ordinarily resident in England prior to August, 1960. This was because of the terms of the Treaty with Cyprus and the British Nationality (Cyprus) Order, 1960, which gave such persons dual citizenship, and of the Declaration of Human Rights which gives everyone the right to return to his own country.

Held, in the circumstances it would be idle to allow the recommendation to go forward and it would be quashed.

REGINA v. LENNON

(*The Times*, June 19, 1963)

June 18, 1963: Court of Criminal Appeal: Edmund Davies, Marshall, Lawton JJ.

An International Criminal

The Court dismissed this appeal by Percy Frederic Lennon, an Australian, aged 44 against a sentence of seven years' imprisonment imposed at the Central Criminal Court by the Commissioner, Sir Ernest Goodman Roberts, Q.C., for forging a valuable security. The Court made a recommendation for deportation to take effect after the appellant had served his sentence.

MR. JUSTICE EDMUND DAVIES said that the appellant was rightly described by the Commissioner as an international criminal who had been preying on the public. The appellant was convicted on an indictment charging him with forging a valuable security. He then pleaded guilty to another indictment charging him with making a false statement to obtain a passport. He was sentenced to seven years' imprisonment on the first indictment and to two years concurrent on the second one. The appellant complained that the sentence was too severe and referred to the fact that charges against him were outstanding in France, Italy and Australia. The appellant asked for leniency and for an order that he might be deported to Australia.

The appellant came to this country and was arrested after six days. He had requested deportation but the Commissioner had refused to make the order, saying "I certainly do not propose to recommend you for deportation, when you might be sent to Australia and not receive what is due to you for your criminal actions".

The Court took the not surprising view that the sooner the appellant was out of the country, the better it would be for the citizens of this country.

The appellant got a photographic negative made of a signature, "J. M. Carruthers", then a large number of travellers' cheques were made with that signature. Three hundred and thirty one cheques with a face value exceeding £9,000 were found on the appellant.

The appellant had an extremely bad record. He had 20 convictions in various parts of the world of all kinds of crime. In 1960, he was sentenced to four terms of nine months' imprisonment consecutive, for stealing a motor car and for three cases of making untrue statements to obtain passports. He was released in August, 1962.

The appellant said that the present sentences were excessive. This Court thought that they were not a day too long. The appellant also renewed his application that a recommendation should be made for him to be deported at the end of his sentence. That appeared to be a highly desirable course. While dismissing the appeal against sentence, the Court recommended the appellant for deportation to Australia in due course.

R. v. FRANCIS AND LEWIS

([1963] Crim.L.R. 790)

August 21, 1963: Court of Criminal Appeal: Sachs, Elwes, Nield JJ.

Age: twenty-one (male). *Facts*: arrested in café in possession of Indian hemp. *Previous history*: both came to England in 1960; F. had no convictions; L. had convictions for forgery, larceny, assaulting the police and possessing Indian hemp. *Decision*: sentences of twelve and eighteen months' imprisonment upheld; recommendation for deportation quashed in case of F. upheld in case of L.

REGINA v. HOLDEN

(*The Times*, August 22, 1963)

August 21, 1963: Court of Criminal Appeal: Sachs, Elwes, Nield JJ.

Deportation Recommendation Set Aside

The Court allowed this appeal by John Gordon Holden, aged 17, a native of the Republic of Ireland, at present in Hollesley Bay borstal institution, against sentence under the Commonwealth Immigrants Act, 1962, of recommendation for deportation passed on him on May 28, 1963, at Bristol City Sessions (Recorder: N. R. Fox-Andrews, Esq., Q.C.), where he had been committed for sentence from Bristol City Magistrates' Court, after pleading Guilty to stealing a cine-camera and case, exposure meter, flash gun and tape recorder, together valued at £171 from a parked car on March 29. He has been sentenced also to undergo a period of borstal training; he did not appeal against that sentence.

Mr. Giles Harwood appeared for the appellant.

MR. JUSTICE SACHS said that the appellant had been unemployed and sleeping rough and, at the time of the offence was on probation for stealing a bicycle. His conduct during probation had not been satisfactory, and he had been fined £5 for an assault occasioning actual bodily harm. In the circumstances, the sentence of borstal training was very proper. Having regard, however, to the age of the appellant and the categories of offences which were for consideration by the Recorder, this Court was of opinion that the order for recommendation for deportation was not warranted.

It was to be seen from the notice of appeal that the appellant stated that this borstal training would do him good and teach him a trade. The Court hoped that his statement as to his attitude to borstal training was correct, and that he would, now that the recommendation for deportation had been set aside, take this opportunity to become a useful citizen.

Solicitor: *Registrar, Court of Criminal Appeal.*

REGINA v. BROOKS
REGINA v. WALDRON

(*The Times*, October 4, 1963)

October 3, 1963: Court of Criminal Appeal: Lord Parker C.J., Ashworth, Hinchcliffe JJ.

Recommendations for Deportation Upheld

Their Lordships dismissed this appeal by Swinton Rowland Brooks, aged 23 years, now detained in prison, and refused leave to appeal to John Francis Waldron, aged 36, also detained in prison, against the recommendations for their deportation. They were both convicted at the Central Criminal Court of robbery with violence and the appellant Waldron with assault causing actual bodily harm. Judge Maude sentenced the appellant Waldron to a total term of 18 months and the appellant Brooks to 12 months' imprisonment.

Mr. C. A. Hart-Leverton appeared for the appellant Brooks; the appellant Waldron was neither present nor represented.

The Lord Chief Justice giving the judgment of the Court said that the appellants had entered a tailor's shop kept by an elderly couple, Mr. and Mrs. Sobell. While Mr. Sobell was wrapping up articles that the appellants had chosen, he was knocked down and gagged. Then his wife was knocked down and the appellants went through Mr. Sobell's pockets and then robbed him of some clothes and £112.

Mr. Sobell received some bruises but his wife was not only bruised, but received a black eye, cuts on her tongue and in her mouth and a broken nose.

The appellant Waldron had entered the Country as a stowaway, unmarried, with two children in the West Indies. The Court was clearly of the opinion that the recommendation for deportation was fully justified not only because of the seriousness of the crime, but also because he had no real family connections in this country. At the Central Criminal Court, he had said that he would like to go back to his country and, when told that he would be recommended for deportation, he said that he would be thankful.

The appellant Brooks was born in Jamaica and, like Waldron, had no previous convictions. He had come to this country in 1961 and was employed as a welder. Both his parents were dead and his only living relative was an aunt living in London. The Court had given anxious consideration to his case; it was not for the Court to say whether he should be deported, but whether the recommendation for deportation was right in principle. Having regard to the very serious nature of the case it was impossible to say that there had been an error of principle.

Solicitor: *Registrar, Court of Criminal Appeal.*

R. v. SINGH

((1963) 107 Sol. Jo. 833)

October 14, 1963: Queen's Bench Division: Lord Parker C.J., Ashworth, Hinchcliffe JJ.

Commonwealth Immigrant—Deportation—Sentence

Appeal against recommendation for deportation.

The defendant, a native of India, pleaded guilty at Stafford Assizes to rape of a girl under four years of age living with her parents in the same house as he and his father. The father had lived in England for about seven years, the appellant for about one year. His family circumstances were not investigated at the court, and he was believed to be seventeen years old. In fact, he had no relatives in India, and his father, with whom he lived, was his only relative. The defendant was less than seventeen years old. The trial judge sentenced him to eighteen months' imprisonment and to recommendation for deportation, saying: "Of course, I understand that, under the [Commonwealth Immigrants] Act [1962], the Home Secretary acts on the recommendation and does not have to wait until the expiration of the sentence." The defendant appealed against the recommendation for deportation only.

Lord Parker, C.J., said that the offence was horrible but, in view of the family circumstances, it was very doubtful whether any recommendation for deportation would be implemented, and because of them the court would have been minded to set it aside. However, under s. 7 (1) of the 1962 Act the defendant was not eligible for recommendation for deportation not being seventeen years old, and it would have to be set aside. Further, it was well known that the Home Secretary did not have to act on the recommendation; it was perfectly open to him not to act. While the Home Secretary could, at any time, if he was minded to deport, do so before the sentence expired the court understood that at the moment at any rate as a matter of policy the Home Secretary would not implement any recommendation until the sentence imposed for the offence had been served. For those reasons the court must sentence a defendant regardless of whether he was to be deported, in other words, it must give him the sentence which he deserved. Appeal allowed.

Appearances: *Malcolm Ward* (*Registrar, Court of Criminal Appeal*).

R v. MOSELEY

([1964] Crim.L.R. 67)

October 28, 1963: Court of Criminal Appeal: Lord Parker C.J., Ashworth, Hinchcliffe JJ.

Age: twenty-one (male). *Facts*: convicted of robbery with violence; he and another man attacked a seaman and took his money. *Previous history*: came to England in 1961. Worked for a time and was then convicted of embezzlement. Thereafter lived on national assistance and immoral earnings. *Decision*: having regard to the nature of the offence and his record, a proper case for deportation.

REGINA v. SWEENEY

(*The Times*, November 12, 1963)

November 11, 1963: Court of Criminal Appeal: Edmund Davies, MacKenna, Thompson JJ.

The Court refused this application by Richard Thomas Sweeney, aged 27, a native of Ireland for leave to appeal against sentences totalling a fine and a two years' imprisonment for assault occasioning actual bodily harm, malicious damage and causing grievous bodily harm, imposed on him by Middlesex Sessions, who also made a recommendation for deportation.

The Commonwealth Immigrants Act provides by section 7(2): "no recommendation [for deportation] . . . shall be made upon the conviction of an offender who satisfies the Court (a) that he is or was ordinarily resident in the United Kingdom on the date of his conviction; and (b) that he has been continuously so resident for a period of at least five years ending with that date".

MR. JUSTICE EDMUND DAVIES, giving the judgment of the Court and treating the application as embracing leave to appeal against the recommendation for deportation, said that the Court had wrongly treated the terminal date for calculating the period of five years' residence as being June 13, 1963, when the defendant pleaded guilty at the magistrates' court. The true terminal date was July 4, 1963, when the defendant first appeared before Middlesex Sessions for sentence. If, by the time the defendant appeared for sentence, the five years had elapsed, no recommendation for deportation could be made and the court could not exercise its power to adjourn for serving the necessary seven day notice.

The present case presented no practical difficulties because, even on the true terminal date, the defendant had not been ordinarily resident in this country for five years. The sentence and recommendation were fully merited and the application would be refused.

REGINA v. JACOBS

(*The Times*, November 16, 1963)

November 15, 1963: Court of Criminal Appeal: Edmund Davies, Thesiger, Megaw JJ.

Recommendation for Deportation

Their Lordships refused this application of Wilfred Jacobs, aged 31 years, now detained in prison for leave to appeal against a recommendation for his deportation. The applicant was convicted, on July 31, 1963, at the Manchester Crown Court of assaulting a police officer and was sentenced by Mr. Commissioner J. F. Marnan Q.C. to nine months' imprisonment and was recommended for deportation.

The applicant was neither represented nor present.

MR. JUSTICE EDMUND DAVIES, giving the judgment of the Court, said that the applicant was a South African who came to this country in 1952. In the grounds for his application he stated that if he was deported to South Africa life would not be worth living because of the colour bar.

At 12.30 a.m., a police sergeant went to a cafe to investigate a robbery by Abdie. The applicant was in the cafe with Abdie and another man, Gilbert. While the sergeant was taking Abdie to the police station, the appellant threw a piece of concrete, hitting the sergeant on the back. The applicant, then with

Gilbert threw stones at the sergeant. Byestanders came to the aid of the sergeant and the sergeant had to have medical attention.

The applicant had seven previous convictions of which two were for assault, two for living on immoral earnings and three for larceny. There were also some convictions for drunkenness. The Secretary of State had reported that the applicant was unfit for corrective training and the Home Office had stated that he was eligible for deportation. The recommendation for deportation was not wrong in principle and the application was refused.

REGINA v. SULLIVAN

(*The Times*, November 23, 1963.)

November 22, 1963: Court of Criminal Appeal: Winn, Fenton Atkinson, Roskill JJ.

MR. JUSTICE WINN, considering an application for leave to appeal against a recommendation for deportation, drew attention to the statement by the Lord Chief Justice in *Regina v. Edgehill* ([1963] 1 Q.B. 593*; *The Times*, December 12, 1962), concerning the desirability of granting legal aid in cases where recommendations for deportation were made. That had not yet been carried into effect in all cases.

His Lordship emphasised that legal aid should always be granted in respect of a person who was liable to deportation and in respect of whom it was anticipated that there would be such a recommendation.

R v. ANDERSON

([1964] Crim.L.R. 554)

April 2, 1964: Court of Criminal Appeal: Lord Parker C.J., Phillimore, Winn JJ.

Age: twenty-eight (male). *Facts*: pleaded guilty to two counts of burglary and larceny—asked for eight other offences to be taken into account—sentenced to three years' imprisonment. *Previous convictions*: after coming to England from the West Indies in 1955, had had five previous convictions for dishonesty—sentences up to three years. Not settled in any one job. *Decision*: recommendation for deportation upheld.

R v. BLAIR

([1964] Crim.L.R. 530)

April 21, 1964: Court of Criminal Appeal: Lord Parker C.J., Phillimore, Winn JJ.

For the appellant: *A. H. M. Evans* (instructed by the Registrar, Court of Criminal Appeal). For the Crown: *D. Williams* (instructed by the Prosecuting Solicitor, Cardiff).

B. was convicted on two counts of burglary and larceny and asked for six other offences to be taken into consideration and was sentenced to twelve months' imprisonment. He had had four previous convictions for dishonesty and violence. He came to England from the West Indies in 1955, intending, he said, to settle permanently and had remained here ever since except for one period of six months in 1959-60 when he had gone to the West Indies to marry and another period of six months in 1963 when he had been on holiday in Europe. He asserted that he was not eligible for deportation on the ground that he had been continuously and ordinarily resident in England for five years prior to conviction. The trial judge held that the two absences were breaks in his residence and made a recommendation for deportation.

Held, the court was unable to say that the judge had erred in law in coming to that conclusion or that there was anything in the facts which prevented him from doing so. As had been said in *R.* v. *Edgehill** [1963] Crim.L.R. 92; 47 Cr.App.R. 41, it is a matter of fact and degree in every case. The recommendation was merited and the appeal against it would be dismissed.

R v. DUNNE

([1964] Crim. L.R.554)

April 27, 1964: Court of Criminal Appeal: Paull, Fenton Atkinson, John Stephenson JJ.

Age: nineteen (male). *Facts*: pleaded guilty to larceny of property worth £66: sentenced to borstal training. *Previous convictions*: three convictions in Ireland for dishonesty; came to England in 1958; five further convictions for dishonesty. *Decision*: recommendation for deportation upheld.

R v. STORER

([1964] Crim.L.R. 729)

July 31, 1964: Court of Criminal Appeal: Hinchcliffe, Marshall, Phillimore JJ.

Age: twenty-two (male). *Facts*: pleaded guilty to house-breaking and larceny. *Previous convictions*: none. *Special considerations*: a native of Ceylon, at the time of the offence he was homeless and penniless. *Decision*: six months' imprisonment and recommendation for deportation varied to three years' probation.

R v. JACKSON

((1964) 108 Sol. Jo. 881)

October 26, 1964: Court of Criminal Appeal: Hinchcliffe, Marshall, Lyell JJ.

Commonwealth Immigrant—Deportation—English Residence for five years—Onus of Proof on Immigrant.

Application for leave to appeal against recommendation for deportation.

After the defendant, a Jamaican, aged twenty-one, using the name *A*, had been convicted, it was said that he had arrived in England in January, 1960; he did not challenge the statement, and the court did not recommend him for deportation. Some time later he was charged, under name ***B***, with robbery, and a form was served on him under the Commonwealth Immigrants Act, 1962; he deliberately lied, saying that he could not read or write, and signed the acknowledgment of service of the form with a mark "X," but, in fact, he was educated and had good handwriting. The evidence was that he had been living rough for some time before his arrest, and he was convicted on 4th February, 1964, of robbery; the police officer dealing with his antecedents and the facts in connection with recommendation for deportation stated that the defendant had arrived in England in January, 1960; that statement was not challenged although the defendant was expressly asked whether he had any observation to make, and he declined to give or call evidence. He was sentenced to eighteen months' imprisonment, and an order was made recommending him for deportation. He gave notice of application for leave to appeal against the recommendation, claiming, *inter alia*, that he had, in fact, arrived in England in January 1959, and therefore had been resident for five years, and was, under s. 7 of the Act, exempt from the order; that his passport could not be produced because it had been stolen from his address when he was arrested; and that his name was, in fact, *C*. Extensive inquiries set on foot by the registrar of the Court of Criminal Appeal, through the police, Labour Exchange and Ministry of Pensions and National Insurance failed to support the claim of arrival in England in January, 1959, and his first verified employment was in March, 1960.

MARSHALL, J., said that, under s. 7 of the 1962 Act, the burden of proving that the defendant had been in England for the requisite five years was on him. His first verified employment tied in with arrival in January, 1960, better than twelve months earlier. He was shown to be wholly unreliable in what he said, and, in the circumstances, his own word, unsupported by the registrar's inquiries or the passport, could not be accepted. He had failed completely to make out a case for reviewing the order on the ground that he had been in England for five years, and the application should be refused. Application refused.

R v. SABRI

((1964) 108 Sol. Jo. 922)

November 9, 1964: Court of Criminal Appeal: Lord Parker C.J., Ashworth, Milmo JJ.

Commonwealth Immigrant—Deportation Recommendation—Effect of dual Nationality.

Appeal against recommendation for deportation.

The defendant, a Cypriot, who had been resident in this country before 16th August, 1960, pleaded guilty to a charge of burglary at the Central Criminal Court on 16th September, 1964. On 18th September, 1964, he was sentenced to eighteen months' imprisonment and was recommended for deportation. He appealed against the recommendation for deportation only, contending that, since he had lived in this country for four years and nine months, after a further three months he would have been exempt from deportation, but for the conviction.

LORD PARKER, C.J., said that the defendant had been ordinarily resident in the United Kingdom on and before 16th August, 1960, the date on which Cyprus became independent. Under the terms of the British Nationality (Cyprus) Order, 1960, he remained a citizen of the United Kingdom and Colonies. Although that did not legally exempt him from the deportation provisions of the Commonwealth Immigrants Act, 1962, the Home Secretary had stated that in such a case of dual nationality he would not implement a recommendation for deportation. In *R. v. Romano** (unreported, 15th July, 1963), the Court of Criminal Appeal said "this court feels that it would be idle, however much this man deserves the recommendation, to allow it to go forward to the Home Secretary when the inevitable result will be that it will not be implemented." Appeal allowed.

R v. KARAGHLI

((1965) 109 Sol. Jo. 92)

January 18, 1965: Court of Criminal Appeal: Glyn-Jones, Megaw, Lyell JJ.

Commonwealth Immigrant—Deportation —Recommendation—Allegations of Happenings Overseas—Inability of Court to Investigate

Application for leave to appeal against recommendation for deportation.

The defendant, aged twenty-six, a Cypriot without previous convictions, who entered England in February, 1964, was convicted of having in his possession 24,405 grains of Indian hemp without being duly authorised, and was sentenced to twelve months' imprisonment and, his counsel agreeing that it was in his best interests for him to go back to Cyprus, a recommendation for deportation was made. The defendant applied for leave to appeal against sentence of recommendation for deportation only, stating in his application that he, a citizen of the Republic of Cyprus, came to England when he did because of the communal troubles in Cyprus, that in January, 1964, his village had been attacked by Greek Cypriots, his family killed and house and property burned, so that it was impossible for him to live in Cyprus, and that, therefore, he would like to stay and live for ever in England.

MEGAW, J., said that it was not possible for the court to investigate the truth or otherwise of what the defendant said about the circumstances in which he came to leave Cyprus. It was, however, open to the Secretary of State, if he thought fit, to investigate those matters in so far as he regarded them as being relevant to his decision on the court's recommendation. There was no reason for saying that the recommendation for deportation was anything other than right. Application refused.

FERNANDES AND ANOTHER v. FERNANDES

((1965) 109 Sol. Jo. 92)

January 19, 1965: Queen's Bench Division: Marshall J.

Contempt of Court—Commonwealth Immigrant—Repatriation—Imprisonment —Release Ordered 'on Boarding' Aircraft

Application.

The applicant, a native of the Seychelles, who had been imprisoned for his contempt in being in breach of an undertaking to obey the terms of an interlocutory injunction ordering him, *inter alia*, not to molest his former wife, a cook, and her employer who had paid for her passage from the Seychelles, purged his contempt and was released. On a further application to commit him for a renewed breach of the order, he expressed his willingness to be repatriated, the wife and her employer stated that they were prepared to meet the expense of the passage, and an order was made committing the applicant to prison, but giving him liberty to apply for release when arrangements had been made for him to board an aeroplane for conveyance to Mombasa where he was to board a ship to convey him to the Seychelles. Arrangements were made, and, four days before the scheduled flight, the applicant applied to the court for his release, apologising for his contempt. Counsel put before the court a suggested order in the terms that '. . . upon [*the applicant*] boarding an aircraft, flight number [—] scheduled to depart at [—] p.m. or such other time as may be arranged for the said flight from London Airport on [—] for Nairobi *en route* for the Seychelles he be discharged and released from the custody of' the prison governor in respect of the committal for contempt. The application was unopposed.

MARSHALL, J., said that he would make the order in the terms suggested. That was obviously the best solution. Application granted.

APPEARANCES: *B. Holroyd Pearce* (*Official Solicitor*); *John Davies* (*Simmons & Simmons*).

REGINA v. ASSA SINGH

([1965] 2 Q.B. 312)

February 23, 1965: Court of Criminal Appeal: Lord Parker C.J., Marshall, Widgery JJ.

Commonwealth Immigrant—Deportation order—Whether part of sentence—Life imprisonment sentence fixed by law—Whether recommendation precluded —Whether appropriate—Whether "order ... made on conviction"—Jurisdiction of Court of Criminal Appeal—Criminal Appeal Act, 1907 (7 *Edw.* 7, *c.* 23), *s.* 21—*Commonwealth Immigrants Act,* 1962 (10 & 11 *Eliz.* 2, *c.* 21), *ss.* 7 (1) (3), 8 (4). **[313]**

Crime—Sentence—Life sentence—Possibility of release on licence or remission not taken into account—Deportation order inappropriate.

Crime—Court of Criminal Appeal—Jurisdiction—Deportation order—"Order made on conviction"—Criminal Appeal Act, 1907, *s.* 21—*Commonwealth Immigrants Act,* 1962, *s.* 8 (4).

By section 7 (1) of the Commonwealth Immigrants Act, 1962: "Subject to the provisions of this section, where a Commonwealth citizen to whom section 6 of this Act applies, and who has attained the age of 17 years, is convicted of an offence punishable with imprisonment, the court by or before which he is convicted, or any court to which his case is brought by way of appeal against conviction or sentence, may recommend that a deportation order be made in respect of him . . . (3) In this section 'offence punishable with imprisonment' includes an offence which would be so punishable apart from any enactment restricting the imprisonment of young offenders or of first offenders; . . ."

By section 8 (4): "For the purposes of any enactment relating to appeals in criminal cases, a recommendation for deportation shall be treated as an order made on conviction . . .; and the validity of such a recommendation shall not be called in question except on an appeal against the recommendation or against the conviction upon which it is made."

The appellant, a native of India born in Hong Kong, who had come to this country in 1962, was convicted on July 6, 1964, of the non-capital murder of his wife; he was sentenced to life imprisonment and a recommendation that a deportation order be made in respect of him was made. On appeal against the recommendation for deportation on the grounds, inter alia, (1) that a recommendation for deportation being an order made on conviction by virtue of section 8 (4) of the Commonwealth Immigrants Act, 1962, could not be added to a sentence of life imprisonment fixed by law by section 9 (1) of the Homicide Act, 1957, since by section 21 of the Criminal Appeal Act, 1907,[1] "sentence includes any order of the court made on conviction" and,

[1] Criminal Appeal Act, 1907, s. 21: "In this Act, unless the context otherwise requires . . . The expression 'sentence' includes any order of the court made on conviction with reference to the person convicted . . ."

(2) that, as a matter of practice it was not appropriate to make a recommendation for deportation in the case of a sentence of imprisonment for life:—

Held, (1) that a recommendation for deportation under section 7 (1) of the Commonwealth Immigrants Act, 1962, which did not become an order until implemented by the Home Secretary, was not part of a sentence, the effect of the provision in section 8 (4) that it was to be treated as an order made on conviction for the purposes of any enactment relating to appeals in criminal cases being to bring it within the ambit of section 21 of the Criminal Appeal Act, 1907, thereby giving the Court of Criminal Appeal jurisdiction: the recommendation for deportation in respect of the appellant, therefore, was not a sentence added to a sentence fixed by law. **[314]**

(2) But that, although the trial judge had power to make the recommendation for deportation, it was inappropriate in a case where a life sentence was imposed, for such a sentence was a sentence for life, and any release on licence or remission resulting in release was a matter for the Home Secretary; that the courts in sentencing never had taken the possibility of release or remission into account; and that the court, in recommending for deportation, should adhere to its practice of refusing to take into consideration the possibility of release; and that, accordingly, the recommendation for deportation would be quashed.

APPEAL against recommendation for deportation.

The appellant, Assa Singh, a native of India born in Hong Kong, came to this country in 1962. On July 6, 1964, he was convicted at Kent Assizes of the non-capital murder of his wife, and Melford Stevenson J. sentenced him to life imprisonment and recommended that a deportation order be made in respect of him under section 7 (1) of the Commonwealth Immigrants Act, 1962. On January 12, 1962, the Court of Criminal Appeal (Lord Parker C.J., Marshall and Widgery JJ.) refused leave to appeal against conviction but granted leave to appeal against the recommendation for deportation directing that, since the recommendation raised matters of practice and of law which required further investigation, the prosecution should be prepared to argue the legal points raised in the grounds of appeal in regard to the recommendation and also whether it was good practice to make such a recommendation in the case of a sentence of imprisonment for life.

On appeal, it was contended for the appellant that the recommendation was not permissible in law on three grounds: (1) that no sufficient notice had been served for the purposes of section 8 (1) (*a*) and (*b*) of the Commonwealth Immigrants Act, 1962; (2) that he was an exempted person under section 6 (2) (*b*) (iii) of the Act of 1962, and was further exempted because he was not a Commonwealth citizen but was a citizen of the United Kingdom and Colonies; (3) that by section 8 (4) of the Act of 1962 the recommendation was an order made on conviction and as part of the sentence, was not permissible under section 9 (1) of the Homicide Act, 1957, since, by section 21 of the Criminal Appeal Act, 1907, "sentence includes any order made on conviction"; and (4) that, as a matter of practice and procedure, it was not appropriate to make such a recommendation in a case of a sentence of life imprisonment.

M. George Polson Q.C. and *J. A. Kirpal* for the appellant. By section 9 (1) of the Homicide Act, 1957, the sentence for **[315]** non-capital murder is fixed as imprisonment for life and there is no discretion in the court to add to or subtract from that sentence. By section 8 (4) of the Commonwealth Immigrants Act, 1962, a recommendation for deportation is an order made on conviction and the effect of making such a recommendation is to make it part of the sentence. That cannot, in law, be done in the case of a sentence fixed by law. By section 21 of the Criminal Appeal Act, 1907, "'sentence' includes any order of the court made on conviction." This makes a recommendation for deportation part of the sentence for the purposes of appeal, but section 21 does not apply to a sentence fixed by law. The appellant relies on section 8 (4) of the Commonwealth

Immigrants Act, 1962, that a recommendation for deportation is part of the sentence for the purposes of appeal. With regard to the second part of section 8 (4) of the Act of 1962, which mentions validity, there is a distinction between validity and propriety. [Reference was made to *Reg.* v. *Edgehill.*[2]*] The propriety of a recommendation for deportation is attacked by appeal against sentence. Adding a recommendation for deportation to a sentence fixed by law is invalid. The Homicide Act, 1957, cannot be amended save by express reference in an amending statute. A recommendation for deportation is part of the sentence in the court of trial and the definition is in the Commonwealth Immigrants Act, 1962.

It is not good practice to make a recommendation for deportation in the case of a sentence of imprisonment for life because the court will not make such a recommendation where that order cannot be put into effect. The court should not have regard to anything but the fact that a life sentence is a sentence of imprisonment for life. [Reference was made to *Reg.* v. *Blake.*[3]] The court has said in a number of cases when considering sentence that it will not have regard to remissions or to what the Home Secretary might do in the exercise of the Royal Prerogative. [Reference was made to *Rex* v. *Goldfarb*[4]* and *Reg.* v. *Tarlochan Singh.*[5]*] Both in law and as a matter of practice, this order should not have been made.

Sir David Renton Q.C. and *John Gower* for the Crown. The two questions are whether it is permissible in law for a judge **[316]** who has passed a life sentence to make a recommendation for deportation and whether it is good practice to do so. On the first, are a sentence of life imprisonment and such a recommendation consistent with each other bearing in mind that a man so sentenced may be in prison for the rest of his natural life or only for a few years? The operative words are in section 7 (1) of the Commonwealth Immigrants Act, 1962, "an offence punishable with imprisonment" and mean any kind of imprisonment. If Parliament had intended that "imprisonment" should be qualified, for instance to exclude life imprisonment, it would have said so. It is proper to bear in mind the Home Secretary's powers of release on licence under section 27 of the Prison Act, 1952, and under the royal prerogative. With regard to Home Office procedure under the Aliens Order, 1953, and the Commonwealth Immigrants Act, 1962, the position appears to be that if the Home Secretary had the opportunity of making a deportation order on a person serving a life sentence, he would release that person on licence under section 27 of the Prison Act, 1952. Under section 27 he may attach conditions when releasing a prisoner on licence. In a case of life imprisonment the Home Secretary could, if a recommendation for deportation were made, release the prisoner on licence on condition that he did not return to this country. There would be advantages to the prisoner and to the public if the Home Secretary were armed with a recommendation to deport because, unlike the position under the Aliens Order, he cannot act without such a recommendation. Both the power to deport and to release on licence are statutory provisions but the Home Secretary would have flexibility only if he had a recommendation for deportation. There would be no inconsistency because many prisoners are released from life imprisonment after serving about 10 years. A recommendation for deportation is not an order because only the Home Secretary can make the order. The words in section 8 (4) of the Commonwealth Immigrants Act, 1962, "a recommendation for deportation shall be treated as an order made on conviction" are merely used to give jurisdiction to this court under sections 3 and 21 of the Criminal Appeal Act, 1907, on a matter which is not a sentence. The legal position can be summarised in three points: (i) section 7 (1) of the Act of 1962 applies to life imprisonment as much as to any term of imprisonment; (ii) there is no inconsistency in a sentence of life imprisonment coupled with a recommendation for deportation; **[317]** (iii) a recommendation for

[2] [1963] 1 Q.B. 593; [1963] 2 W.L.R. 170; [1963] 1 All E.R. 181, C.C.A.
[3] [1962] 2 Q.B. 377; [1961] 3 W.L.R. 744; [1961] 3 All E.R. 125, C.C.A.
[4] (1936) 52 T.L.R. 254; [1936] 1 All E.R. 169; 25 Cr.App.R. 161.
[5] [1963] Crim.L.R. 844, C.C.A.

deportation is not a sentence so no technical difficulty arises.

On the second question, it is not bad practice to make a recommendation for deportation, in suitable cases, after passing a sentence of life imprisonment. This is the first case of its kind which has come to the attention of the Home Office and the first time such a case has come before this court. With regard to Home Office practice, it is rare that a prisoner remains in custody for the rest of his natural life but no view can be expressed as to when he will be released until the prison authorities have made the usual and necessary observations. The normal practice is not to fix a date until nearly a year in advance but there is no hard and fast rule. The system of review in such cases enables those advising the Home Secretary to give some idea of the release date but not more than one year in advance. The Home Secretary sees no objection in principle to acting on a recommendation for deportation of a person serving a life sentence. Of recorded cases of aliens deported while serving life sentences each has been decided on its merits. A deportation order would coincide with the date on which a prisoner was released on licence. It is not a good thing to keep murderers in this country who cannot settle here and a prisoner released on licence is a potential charge on public funds. In these circumstances deportation could be in the public interest. It could also sometimes be in the interest of the prisoner by giving him a free passage back to his own country to start life afresh.

Polson Q.C. replied.

LORD PARKER C.J. gave the following judgment of the court. The appellant was convicted at Kent Assizes of the murder of his wife and was sentenced to life imprisonment. In sentencing him the judge recommended him for deportation. He applied to this court for leave to appeal both against his conviction and against that recommendation for deportation. The matter came before the court on January 12 last when the court refused him leave to appeal against conviction, but granted leave to appeal against the recommendation for deportation. It was clear to the court then that important issues were involved, and the court asked for the assistance of prosecuting counsel. As a result we had the advantage of hearing the submissions of Sir David Renton, not to oppose the appeal, but more in the nature of amicus.

The appellant, aged 39, is a native of India, born in Hong Kong. He came to this country in 1962 and was then the holder **[318]** of a British passport. Mr. Polson on his behalf has taken in effect four points. The first he only advanced because it is in the grounds of appeal, and he acknowledges frankly that he attaches no weight to it. That is that the notice in this case was in effect bad in form. The court finds it quite unnecessary to go into that matter; it seems to the court that the form is perfectly in order and that no point can be made under that head.

The second ground of appeal is that while the appellant was undoubtedly a Commonwealth immigrant, yet under section 6 (2) (*b*) (iii) of the Commonwealth Immigrants Act, 1962, he was exempt. That subsection provides so far as it is material: "This section applies to any Commonwealth citizen not being— . . . (*b*) a citizen of the United Kingdom and Colonies who became such— . . . (iii) by being registered under Part II of the British Nationality Act, 1948, either in the United Kingdom or in any country mentioned in subsection (3) of section 1 of that Act as originally enacted or as amended by any subsequent enactment."

Subsection (4) provides that: "If any question arises whether a person is a Commonwealth citizen to whom this section applies, it shall lie on him to prove that he is not such a citizen." There appears to be some doubt as to whether in fact the appellant is eligible for registration, but be that as it may, Mr. Polson has frankly said that he, and the burden is on him, is unable to say one way or another whether the appellant was registered. Accordingly, the appeal under that head also fails.

The third and fourth grounds raise more important questions both of law and of practice. So far as the law is concerned, Mr. Polson submits that having regard to the fact that section 9 (1) of the Homicide Act, 1957, provides that the sentence shall in such a case as this be one of imprisonment for life, it is impossible to add to that sentence. It is to be observed that that argument presupposes that the recommendation for deportation is a sentence which is being added to the only sentence fixed by law, life imprisonment.

In this connection he refers to section 8 (4) of the Commonwealth Immigrants Act, 1962, under which it is provided that "For the purposes of any enactment relating to appeals in criminal cases, a recommendation for deportation shall be treated as an order made on conviction" and "the validity of such a recommendation shall not be called in question except on an appeal against the recommendation or against the conviction upon which it is made." Mr. Polson argues that, being an **[319]** order made on conviction, the recommendation for deportation is part of the sentence. In that connection he also refers to the definition in section 21 of the Criminal Appeal Act, 1907, under which "the expression 'sentence' includes any order of the court made on conviction with reference to the person convicted."

In the opinion of this court, that argument fails, since a recommendation for deportation is no part of the sentence, certainly in the court of trial. To begin with, it is not an order. Section 8 (4) recognises that fact by saying specifically that "a recommendation for deportation shall be treated as an order." It is in effect merely a recommendation and any order that results, the deportation order, is of course a matter for the Home Secretary.

Secondly, it is to be observed that section 8 (4) is specifically providing that the recommendation is to be treated as an "order for the purposes of any enactment relating to appeals in criminal cases." That clearly in the opinion of this court is to bring a recommendation for deportation within the ambit of section 21 of the Criminal Appeal Act, 1907, thereby giving this court jurisdiction to deal with something which, though passed at the time of the conviction, did not rank otherwise as a sentence. This court is quite satisfied that this is not a case of adding a sentence to a sentence fixed by law.

Before leaving that point, it is to be observed that section 7 (1) of the Act of 1962, which is giving the court power to recommend for deportation, in no way qualifies that power by excluding a sentence of imprisonment which is fixed by law. Subsection (1) provides that: "Subject to the provisions of this section, where a commonwealth citizen to whom section 6 of this Act applies, and who has attained the age of 17 years, is convicted of an offence punishable with imprisonment." There is no qualification whatsoever of those words, and indeed subsection (3) of the same section provides that an "'offence punishable with imprisonment' includes an offence which would be so punishable apart from any enactment restricting the imprisonment of young offenders or of first offenders." No attempt is made to exclude from the definition a life sentence.

The last point is the one which has chiefly concerned this court. That point relates not to the legal power of the court to recommend deportation in the case of a sentence of imprisonment for life, but whether it is appropriate, according to the recognised practice of the court, to make such a recommendation. This court has come to the conclusion that it is not appropriate. In saying that, the court has in mind that "life sentence" means a **[320]** sentence for life, and that any release on licence or remission as a result of which a prisoner is released is a matter entirely for the Home Secretary, either under the Royal Prerogative or under section 27 of the Prison Act, 1952. It is the practice of this court to treat matters of release on licence or remission as matters for the Home Secretary alone, and in particular this court has never in sentencing a man taken into consideration that he may be released for good conduct, and for that reason increased the sentence.

That is all that is really necessary to say; it may be that the Home Secretary has power if he chooses to exercise it in releasing a prisoner under section 27, to make it a condition that he leave and stay out of the country, but it has been agreed that it would be easier for him to act if he did have a recommendation of the court.

The court, however, feels that they should adhere to their present practice and should refuse to take into consideration in recommending for deportation that the man may be released before he has served his sentence. In those circumstances, this appeal is allowed and the recommendation for deportation is quashed.

Order accordingly.
Certificate under section 1 (2) *of the Administration of Justice Act,* 1960, *refused.*

Solicitors: *Nehra, Emerson, Naylor & Co., Wembley; Director of Public Prosecutions.*

REGINA v. AHERNE

(*The Times*, July 3, 1965.)

July 2, 1965: Court of Criminal Appeal: Lord Parker C.J., Ashworth, Waller JJ.

No Opportunity to Explain

The Court granted this application by John Paul Aherne, aged 19, now detained in prison, for leave to appeal against a recommendation for deportation and allowed the appeal. On April 22, 1965, at the Inner London Sessions, he pleaded Guilty to a charge of burglary and was sentenced by the chairman (Mr. R. E. Seaton) to six months' imprisonment and recommended for deportation.

THE LORD CHIEF JUSTICE, delivering the judgment of the Court, said that one night the applicant and another set out with a butter knife and two sacks to break into a Chinese shop. They made a mistake and entered a dairy, but afterwards used the butter knife to enter into the Chinese shop, where they were caught.

The applicant was a native of Ireland and had one previous conviction for possessing drinamyl. Before sentence, the case was adjourned so that notices could be served under the Commonwealth Immigrants Act, 1962, and the applicant and his accomplice were afterwards recommended for deportation.

This was yet another case of a man being recommended for deportation who had not had legal aid and, more important, had never had the opportunity to deal with the matter before the order was made. When the two accused returned to court, a detective-sergeant gave evidence of having served them with the notices. They were asked if they had any questions to ask that officer concerning the service of the notices; they said "No". They were never given an opportunity to deal with their family circumstances.

In the ordinary way the Court would have given legal aid so that the circumstances might be gone into but the Court thought that it was just not worth while. The applicant had only one previous conviction and the order for recommendation for deportation would be quashed.

REGINA v. LYNCH

([1966] 1 W.L.R. 92)

November 8, 1965: Court of Criminal Appeal: Lord Parker C.J., Ashworth, Widgery JJ.

Commonwealth Immigrant—Deportation order—Appeal from—Order made by quarter sessions on committal for sentence—Right of appeal only where a right of appeal against sentence—Commonwealth Immigrants Act, 1962 (10 & 11 *Eliz.* 2, *c.* 21), *s.* 8 (4).[1]
Crime—Court of Criminal Appeal—Jurisdiction—Deportation order—Order made by quarter sessions on committal for sentence—Right of appeal from quarter sessions only where right of appeal against "sentence"—Commonwealth Immigrants Act, 1962, *s.* 8 (4).

The applicant, an Irishman, pleaded guilty at a magistrates' court to charges of attempted larceny, larceny and being in possession of an offensive weapon and was committed to quarter sessions for sentence. Quarter sessions imposed concurrent sentences of three months' imprisonment and made a recommendation for deportation.

On application for leave to appeal against that recommendation:—

Held, that a recommendation for deportation being, by section 8 (4) of the Commonwealth Immigrants Act, 1962, a "sentence," when there had been a committal to quarter sessions for sentence, there was a right of appeal to the Court of Criminal Appeal only in cases where the committal was made under section 28 or section 29 of the Magistrates' Courts Act, 1952, and, this not being such a case, the application was misconceived.

Application for leave to appeal against sentence.

The applicant, Joseph Francis Lynch, whose home was in Ireland, pleaded guilty at West London Magistrates' Court on September 16, 1965, to attempted larceny, two charges of larceny, and to having an offensive weapon in a public place. He was committed to Inner London Sessions for sentence and was sentenced by the chairman to concurrent terms of three months' imprisonment [93] and a recommendation for deportation was made. He applied for leave to appeal against the recommendation for deportation.

The applicant did not appear and was not represented.

LORD PARKER C.J., giving the judgment of the court, stated the facts set out above and continued: This application raises a somewhat curious state of affairs in regard to appeals against recommendations for deportation. So far as sentence is concerned, an appeal to this court from quarter sessions to which a convicted person has been committed for sentence lies only in certain cases. The first is where a person has been committed under section 28 of the Magistrates' Courts Act, 1952 [committal by a magistrates' court to quarter sessions with a view to a Borstal sentence], and has been sentenced to Borstal; the second is where a person has been committed under section 29 of the act [committal for sentence for an indictable offence tried summarily] and had passed upon him by quarter sessions a sentence which a magistrates' court would not have had the power to pass. In those two cases, and only in those two cases, is there a right to appeal to this court.

[1] Commonwealth Immigrants Act, 1962, s. 8 (4): "For the purposes of any enactment relating to appeals in criminal cases, a recommendation for deportation shall be treated as an order made on conviction . . . and the validity of such a recommendation shall not be called in question except on an appeal against the recommendation or against the conviction upon which it is made."

So far as deportation is concerned, section 8 (4) of the Commonwealth Immigrants Act, 1962, provides that a recommendation for deportation shall be treated as an order made on conviction, in other words, the recommendation for deportation is brought within the definition of "sentence" given in section 21 of the Criminal Appeal Act, 1907. The position still remains, however, that unless there is a right of appeal to this court from quarter sessions in regard to sentence, there can be no appeal in regard to the recommendation for deportation which is made part of the sentence. This is clearly a case where this court has no jurisdiction, and where the application is misconceived and must be dismissed.

The court, however, feels that this is a case where some special order should be made. No doubt the applicant thought that he had a right to appeal, and it would be quite wrong in those circumstances that he should lose time. Accordingly, an order will be made in this case that he should lose no time.

Application dismissed.

5

DIPLOMATIC AND CONSULAR AGENTS

A.

PERMANENT DIPLOMATIC AGENTS

2

SUBORDINATE DIPLOMATIC AGENTS

REGINA v. MADAN

[1961] 2 Q.B. 1

January 30, 1961: Court of Criminal Appeal: Lord Parker C.J., Winn, Nield JJ.

Conflict of Laws—Sovereign immunity—Diplomatic immunity—Waiver—Crime—Clerk employed by Indian High Commissioner—Purported waiver by defendant at committal proceedings—Fact of immunity not known to court of trial until after conviction—Waiver by High Commissioner three months after trial—Whether conviction valid—Diplomatic Immunities (Commonwealth Countries and Republic of Ireland) Act, 1952 (15 & 16 *Geo.* 6 & 1 *Eliz.* 2, *c.* 18), *s.* 1 (5).

Criminal proceedings brought against a person entitled to diplomatic immunity under the Diplomatic Immunities (Commonwealth Countries and Republic of Ireland) Act, 1952,[1] whether the chief **[2]** representative of a State or a member of his staff, in a case of mala prohibita, are proceedings without jurisdiction and null and void unless and until there is a valid waiver which must, under section 1 (5) of the Act, be made by the chief representative of the State in question or by his agent acting on his behalf.

Rex v. *A.B.** [1941] 1 K.B. 454; sub nom. *Rex* v. *Kent*, 57 T.L.R. 307, C.C.A. applied.

A clerk on the staff of the High Commissioner for India, who was entitled to diplomatic immunity under section 1 of the Diplomatic Immunities (Commonwealth Countries and Republiic of Ireland) Act, 1952, was charged with obtaining a railway season ticket and attempting to obtain a sum of money by false pretences. He purported to waive his immunity at the committal proceedings and his position under the Act was not known to the court of

[1] Diplomatic Immunities (Commonwealth Countries and Republic of Ireland) Act, 1952, s. 1: "(1) Subject to the provisions of this section—(*a*) a person for the time being recognised by Her Majesty's Government in the United Kingdom as the chief representative in the United Kingdom of any country to which this section applies, whether he is known by the title of High Commissioner for that country or by any other title, (in this section referred to as 'a chief representative'), shall be entitled to the like immunity from suit and legal process, and the like inviolability of residence, . . . as are accorded to the envoy of a foreign sovereign Power accredited to Her Majesty; (*b*) such members of the official staff of a chief representative as are performing duties substantially corresponding to those performed by members of the official staff of an envoy of a foreign sovereign Power shall be entitled to the like immunity from suit and legal process as is accorded to members of the official staff of such an envoy; . . . (4) The Secretary of State shall compile a list of the persons appearing to him to be entitled to immunity from suit and legal process under subsection (1) of this section, . . . (5) Notwithstanding anything in the preceding provisions of this section—(*a*) a chief representative may waive any immunity conferred by or under this section on himself or on a member of his staff, . . . or on a person in the service of the Government of the country which he represents; (*b*) a State representative may waive any immunity conferred under this section on himself or on a member of his staff. (6) The countries to which this section applies are . . . India . . ."

trial until after the jury had convicted him, when it was said that he must have waived the immunity, and that it was too late to raise it then. Three months later the High Commissioner waived the immunity. On appeal against conviction:—

Held, that the appellant's purported waiver was ineffective, and that, as the waiver made by the High Commissioner did not purport to be retrospective, the appellant had been subjected to proceedings without jurisdiction and the convictions must be quashed.

APPEAL AGAINST CONVICTION.

The appellant, Kanya Lal Madan, aged 34, a native of India employed as a clerk in the Passport Division of the office of the High Commissioner for India, was convicted at County of London Sessions on August 9, 1960, of (1) obtaining from the London Transport Executive on March 3, 1960, with intent to defraud a duplicate three-monthly railway season ticket, falsely pretending that a ticket issued to him a few days previously was lost, and (2) with intent to defraud, attempting to obtain from the London Transport Executive the sum of 8s. 9d. He was sentenced by [3] the deputy-chairman (F. H. Cassels, Esq.) to four months' imprisonment on each count, to run concurrently.

The case for the prosecution was that on March 3, 1960, the appellant, having purchased a three-monthly railway season ticket for a journey between Baker Street and Clapham South on February 28, 1960, applied for and later obtained a duplicate from the London Transport Executive on the ground that he had lost the previous one on February 29, when he had in fact given the original ticket to a friend who had been living in the same house as he was. The appellant continued to use the duplicate ticket himself. The 8s. 9d. he was alleged to have obtained by false pretences represented reimbursement of fares he had paid until the duplicate ticket was issued. Although unknown to the court which tried him, the appellant was at all times entitled to diplomatic immunity as a member of the staff of the High Commissioner for India, his name being on the list kept by the Secretary of State under section 1 (4) of the Diplomatic Immunities (Commonwealth Countries and Republic of Ireland) Act, 1952. That matter came to light in the following circumstances: It appeared for the first time in the committal proceedings when one of the police witnesses in cross-examination stated that he had ascertained that the appellant was on the High Commissioner for India's staff. A solicitor then appearing for the appellant purported to waive the immunity. The appellant's position on the High Commissioner's staff again emerged when he gave evidence at the trial but nothing more was thought of the matter until after he had been convicted of the two offences with which he was charged, when the probation officer was called and questioned as to what steps the High Commissioner's Office was likely to take. After an adjournment, during which the probation officer got in touch with the High Commissioner's Office, the probation officer informed the deputy-chairman that a representative of the High Commissioner's Office was under the impression that the appellant was entitled to diplomatic immunity. The deputy-chairman then said that so far as that was concerned the defendant must at some time, if he ever thought of it, have waived it. He added: "It is a bit late to claim it now." Counsel for the prosecution told the deputy-chairman that he thought the appellant was entitled to diplomatic immunity but had expressly waived it before the magistrate either by himself or by his solicitor. On November 21, 1960, the Deputy High Commissioner for India wrote to the Commonwealth Relations Office in the following [4] terms: "The High Commissioner desires me to say that Mr. Madan is and was entitled to diplomatic immunity in accordance with the Diplomatic Immunities (Commonwealth Countries and Republic of Ireland) Act, 1952. I am further directed to say that in order not to impede the course of justice and as a very special case, the High Commissioner is prepared to waive the immunity in the present instance without any prejudice to the interests of this High Commission and on the clear understanding that it will not be treated as a precedent in the future."

The appellant appealed against his conviction by leave of the single judge, on the ground, inter alia, that the deputy-chairman was wrong in law in holding that he, by appearing before the court, had waived the diplomatic immunity to which he was entitled.

Christmas Humphreys Q.C. and *J. A. Kirpal* for the appellant. On the facts at all material times the appellant was entitled to diplomatic immunity by virtue of section 1 (1) (*b*) of the Diplomatic Immunities (Commonwealth Countries and Republic of Ireland) Act, 1952. Any attempt made by him to waive that immunity is irrelevant because, on the authorities, the only person who could make an effective waiver was the High Commissioner for India. As no waiver had been made by the High Commissioner until after the date of the trial and conviction, all the proceedings, at least from the date of committal, were for all purposes null and void.

On the question of waiver, the authorities show that the immunity of a diplomatic agent can only be waived with the sanction of the sovereign or the chief diplomatic representative of the country concerned: *In re Republic of Bolivia Exploration Syndicate Ltd.*[2]* and *Dickinson* v. *Del Solar.*[3]* *Taylor* v. *Best,*[4]* which was referred to in *In re Republic of Bolivia Exploration Syndicate Ltd.,*[5]* has been so derogated from as to be of doubtful value. All the cases referred to were decided under the Diplomatic Privileges Act, 1708, which was merely declaratory of the common law. The Act of 1952 overrules the Act of 1708 but there is no case under the later Act which derogates in any way from the principles laid down in the cases decided under the Act [5] of 1708. [Reference was made to *High Commissioner for India* v. *Ghosh.*[6]*] The appellant, as a servant of the chief diplomatic representative, has proved that he was entitled at all times during the proceedings to immunity under the Act of 1952. Therefore he was immune from criminal process until his immunity was waived by his superior. As there was no such waiver until after conviction his immunity remained and the appeal should be allowed.

Sir Reginald Manningham-Buller Q.C., A.-G. and *J. R. Cumming-Bruce* as amici curiae. The conviction cannot be supported. It is common ground that under the Act of 1952 the appellant was at all material times entitled to diplomatic immunity because he was on the list which the Secretary of State has to maintain under section 1 (4) of the Act. Therefore he is entitled to immunity from suit and legal process. It was not in his power to waive that immunity even if he purported so to do through his solicitor at the magistrate's court. Immunity can only be waived by the chief representative of the country concerned: section 1 (5) of the Diplomatic Immunities (Commonwealth Countries and Republic of Ireland) Act, 1952; *Dickinson* v. *Del Solar*[7]* and *Baccus S.R.L.* v. *Servicio Nacional del Trigo,*[8]* in which the principle as laid down in *In re Republic of Bolivia Exploration Syndicate Ltd.*[9]* was stated by Jenkins L.J.[10] Singleton L.J., who dissented on the facts, did not dissent on the principle. In the present case, therefore, an effective waiver could only be made by the High Commissioner for India and there was in fact no waiver until November 21, 1960, which was a long time after the trial and a very long time after the appellant's appearance before the examining magistrate.

The cases cited refer to civil actions, and the question arises as to the extent of diplomatic immunity in relation to criminal prosecutions. In *Rex* v. *A.B.*[11]* Lord Caldecote C.J.[12] expressly left that question open. The position is

[2] [1914] 1 Ch. 139; 30 T.L.R. 78.
[3] [1930] 1 K.B. 376; 45 T.L.R. 637.
[4] (1854) 14 C.B. 487.
[5] [1914] 1 Ch. 139.
[6] [1960] 1 Q.B. 134; [1959] 3 W.L.R. 811; [1959] 3 All E.R. 659. C.A.
[7] [1930] 1 K.B. 376.
[8] [1957] 1 Q.B. 438; [1956] 3 W.L.R. 948; [1956] 3 All E.A. 715, C.A.
[9] [1914] 1 Ch. 139.
[10] [1957] 1 Q.B. 438, 470.
[11] [1941] 1 K.B. 454; sub. nom *Rex* v. *Kent*, 57 T.L.R. 307, C.C.A.
[12] [1941] 1 K.B. 454, 457.

accurately stated in Halsbury's Laws of England, 3rd ed., vol. 7, p. 268, para. 573, where it is said that a public minister "is exempt from the criminal jurisdiction of the State in which he resides, and is **[6]** not subject to interference or arrest except, possibly, in the one instance of his engaging in acts contrary to its safety and welfare." The proposition in footnote (*q*) to the effect that a distinction may be drawn between the degree of immunity enjoyed by an ambassador or High Commissioner and those who come under his cloak and are covered by his immunity is not supported by the authorities there cited. There are authorities which draw a distinction between offences mala in se and offences mala prohibita, but they are not of assistance because clearly here the offence would come within mala prohibita. So far as mala prohibita are concerned, the English courts have no jurisdiction to try a person on a criminal charge of that character if he is entitled to diplomatic immunity. Immunity does not depend on whether a claim for it is put forward or not: *In re Suarez.*[13]* Ignorance of the fact that an accused is entitled to it cannot give the court jurisdiction to try him. Therefore in this case the examining magistrate had no jurisdiction to inquire into the matter: *Rex* v. *Gee.*[14] There having been no waiver, it followed that the committal was bad. All the proceedings prior to the waiver of November 21, 1960, were proceedings without jurisdiction and so were a nullity. The court could order a venire de novo: see *Crane* v. *Director of Public Prosecutions,*[15] but as amicus curiae it is not for me to advise the court to take that course. [Reference was made to *Mighell* v. *Johore* (*Sultan of*)[16]* and Oppenheim's International Law, 7th ed., vol. 1, pp. 707-710.]

Ian Kennedy for the prosecutor. In view of the advice tendered, the prosecutor will not seek to support the conviction. Having regard to the appellant's position under the Act of 1952, the proceedings would be bad but the information would not itself be bad, so the question which arose was whether to apply for a new summons or for a voluntary bill, but unless the court takes a different view the matter will not be proceeded with.

Humphreys Q.C. in reply. On the question of retrospective waiver the Attorney-General's argument as to the law is adopted. As to the facts, the letter of November 21, 1960, stated in terms that the appellant "was" and "is" entitled to diplomatic immunity, so that his position prior to that date was clear. Up to the moment of the letter from the Deputy High Commissioner he was always entitled to diplomatic immunity. **[7]**

Lord Parker C.J. stated the facts and continued: the appellant asserts that the waiver could only operate from November 21, 1960, in that it must be a waiver by the High Commissioner and not by himself or by his solicitor, and that, in those circumstances, both the committing magistrate and the court of trial had no jurisdiction to deal with him at all; in other words, that all the proceedings prior to November 21 last were a complete nullity, and it would follow that he has not been properly convicted.

Certain things are, we think, clear. In the first place, it is not for someone who is entitled to diplomatic immunity to claim it in the courts. It is unnecessary to refer to the authorities, but we think it is clear that proceedings brought against somebody, certainly civil proceedings brought against somebody entitled to diplomatic immunity, are, in fact, proceedings without jurisdiction and null and void, unless and until there is a valid waiver which, as it were, would bring the proceedings to life and give jurisdiction to the court. Moreover, it is clear that that waiver must be a waiver by a person with full knowledge of his rights, and a waiver by or on behalf of the chief representative of the State in question. In other words, it is not the person entitled to a privilege who may waive it, unless, of course, he does so as agent for or on behalf of the representative of the country concerned; it must be the waiver of the representative of the State. That that is clear can, we think, be seen from the Diplomatic Immunities

[13] [1918] 1 Ch. 176; 34 T.L.R. 127, C.A.
[14] [1936] 2 K.B. 442; 52 T.L.R. 473; [1936] 2 All E.R. 89, C.C.A
[15] [1921] 2 A.C. 299, H.L.
[16] [1894] 1 Q.B. 149; 10 T.L.R. 115, C.A.

(Commonwealth Countries and Republic of Ireland) Act, 1952, itself. [His Lordship read section 1 (5) and continued:]

Quite apart from section 1 (5), the law, as we understand it, has always been that the privilege can only be waived by the accredited diplomatic agent. It is sufficient, perhaps, in this connection to refer to *Rex* v. *A.B.*,[17]* where Lord Caldecote C.J. said[18]: "The first thing to be said is that the privilege claimed by the appellant is a privilege which is derived from, and in law is the privilege of, the ambassador and ultimately of the State which sends the ambassador. It was a privilege which was originally based on the comity of nations, before it was declared by 7 Anne, c. 12, in 1708. Lord Buckmaster, in the case of *Engelke* v. *Musmann*,[19]* said: 'My Lords, the privilege affording ambassadors and other accredited representatives of **[8]** foreign countries immunity from all writs and processes is an ancient doctrine of the common law declared in terms by the Statute 7 Anne, c. 12'; and the statement that I have made that the privilege is the privilege of the ambassador was stated by Lord Hewart C.J. in his judgment in *Dickinson* v. *Del Solar*[20]*: 'The privilege is the privilege of the Sovereign by whom the diplomatic agent is accredited, and it may be waived with the sanction of the Sovereign or of the official superior of the agent.' "

Lord Caldecote C.J. in his judgment in *Rex* v. *A.B.*[21]* further referred to *Marshall* v. *Critico*,[22]* where Lord Ellenborough said: "This is not a privilege of the person, but of the State which he represents." Accordingly, in the judgment of this court, it matters not that the appellant may have expressly through his solicitor waived his diplomatic immunity. That is the general position as the court understands it in regard to civil proceedings.

So far as criminal proceedings are concerned, there is no express authority on the matter. Indeed, in *Rex v. A.B.*[23] Lord Caldecote C.J. expressly kept the question open in these terms: "I find it unnecessary to decide whether or not the diplomatic privilege of the character discussed before us can be claimed by a member of a diplomatic staff in connection with a criminal charge."

The matter is dealt with in Halsbury's Laws of England, 3rd ed., vol. 7, p. 269, where it is stated in these terms: "He [the representative of the State concerned] is exempt from the criminal jurisdiction of the State in which he resides, and is not subject to interference or arrest except, possibly, in the one instance of his engaging in acts contrary to its safety and welfare." In a long note (*q*) dealing with that passage the rival theories on the matter are set out, and the note ends in these terms: "There is no modern English authority on the subject, but judicial statements suggest that the courts do not regard the immunity to be complete in point of law, at any rate as regards persons other than the public minister himself, whatever may be the position in practice having regard to amity in foreign relations."

The Attorney-General, to whom the court is indebted for his argument in this case, informs the court that he has been through the various cases and passages dealt with in that note, and that **[9]** he can find no passage whatsoever which supports the proposition that any distinction is to be drawn between the privilege of the representative of the State himself and the privilege of those on his staff. When one is dealing with something, as in this case, which is mala prohibita, this court takes the view that there is no distinction to be drawn between the principles of law applicable in the case of civil proceedings and criminal charges. It would follow, therefore, that in the present case the appellant was subject to proceedings carried on without jurisdiction in that all the time he was entitled to diplomatic immunity. The sole question is whether the effect of the letter of the Deputy High Commissioner of November 21 last

[17] [1941] 1 K.B. 454; sub nom. *Rex* v. *Kent*, 57 T.L.R. 307, C.C.A.
[18] [1941] 1 K.B. 454, 457.
[19] [1928] A.C. 433, 440; 44 T.L.R. 731, H.L.
[20] [1930] 1 K.B. 376, 380; 45 T.L.R. 637.
[21] [1941] 1 K.B. 454, 458.
[22] (1808) 9 East 447.
[23] [1941] 1 K.B. 454, 457.

waiving the immunity can be said to operate in any way retrospectively. It is enough for our decision in the present case to say that on its face it does not purport to do so. What the true position would be if it had purported to be retrospective it is unnecessary for us to say. It is sufficient that in the present case it does not on any view purport to be retrospective.

In these circumstances, this court has no option but to quash both convictions. It makes no further order.

Appeal allowed.

Solicitors: *Percy Short & Cuthbert; M. H. B. Gilmour, Solicitor, British Transport Commission; Treasury Solicitor.*

GHOSH v. D'ROZARIO

([1963] 1 Q.B. 106)

April 11, 12, 1962: Court of Appeal: Holroyd-Pearce, Davies L.JJ., Wilberforce J.

Conflict of Laws—Sovereign immunity—Diplomatic immunity—Time of immunity—Claim against member of staff of High Commissioner's staff—Diplomatic status arising after issue of writ—Whether action should be stayed—Whether continuance would infringe immunity—Diplomatic Privileges Act, 1708 (7 *Anne, c.* 12), *ss.* 1, 3, 4, 6[1]*—Diplomatic Immunities* (*Commonwealth Countries and Republic of Ireland*) *Act,* 1952 (15 & 16 *Geo.* 6 & 1 *Eliz.* 2, *c.* 18), *S.*1. **[107]**

In 1959 the plaintiff, an Indian doctor living in the United Kingdom and connected professionally with an Indian Government hostel in London, issued a writ against the defendant, another Indian, alleging that in 1956 he had uttered slanders of and concerning the plaintiff in the way of his profession in connection with the hostel. From 1951 until November, 1957 the defendant had been a counsellor for education on the official staff of the High Com-

[1] Diplomatic Privileges Act, 1708, s. 3: "And to prevent the like insolences for the future, be it further declared . . . that all writs and processes that shall at any time hereafter be sued forth or prosecuted, whereby the person of any ambassador, or other publick minister of any foreign prince or State, authorized and received as such by Her Majesty, her heirs or successors, or the domestick, or domestick servant of any such ambassador, or other publick minister, may be arrested or imprisoned, or his or their goods, or chattels may be distrained, seized, or attached, shall be deemed and adjudged to be utterly null and void to all intents, constructions, and purposes whatsoever."

S. 4: "And be it further enacted . . . that in case any person or persons shall presume to sue forth or prosecute any such writ or process, such person and persons, and all attornies and solicitors prosecuting and soliciting in such case, and all officers executing any such writ or process, being thereof convicted, by the concession of the party, or by the oath of one or more credible witness or witnesses, before the Lord Chancellor, or Lord Keeper of the Great Seal of Great Britain, the Chief Justice of the Court of Queen's Bench, the Chief Justice of the Court of Common Pleas for the time being, or any two of them, shall be deemed violators of the Laws of Nations, and disturbers of the publick repose and shall suffer such pains, penalties and corporal punishment, as the said Lord Chancellor, Lord Keeper, and the said Chief Justices, or any two of them shall judge fit to be imposed and inflicted."

S. 6: "And be it further enacted . . . that this Act shall be taken and allowed in all Courts within this Kingdom as a publick Act; and that all judges and justices shall take notice of it without special pleading; and all sheriffs, bailiffs, and other officers and ministers of justice, concerned in the execution of process, are hereby required to have regard to this Act, as they will answer the contrary at their peril."

missioner for India in this country and during that time had been on the diplomatic list. After November, 1957, the defendant went to India returning temporarily to this country in 1959, when, his name being no longer on the diplomatic list, the writ was served on him. A second writ was issued and served on him in respect of a further alleged slander uttered when the first writ was served. The defendant entered an appearance to the first writ and the two actions were later consolidated, pleadings were delivered and various orders made on the summons for directions. The defendant again returned to India but in July, 1960, came back and from July 12, served as scientific adviser to the High Commissioner. On July 19, he issued a summons to stay further proceedings claiming diplomatic immunity. Certificates issued in July, 1960, and again in January, 1962, showed that once again his name appeared in the diplomatic list. On January 29, 1962, the Master ordered a stay of proceedings and his order was upheld by Thompson J. On appeal by the plaintiff in which it was contended that once an action had begun and was pursuing its normal course, the court should not allow a defendant the protection of diplomatic immunity:—

Held, that so far as the merits were concerned, it made no difference whether the facts which were the basis of the protection afforded by diplomatic immunity occurred before the writ was issued or while the action was in existence; and that the general principles **[108]** that conferred diplomatic immunity against the initiation of legal proceedings conferred an equal immunity against the continuation of pre-existing and hitherto properly constituted proceedings; and that, therefore, the action against the defendant should be stayed.

Dictum of Lord Campbell C.J. in *Magdalena Steam Navigation Co.* v. *Martin** (1859) 2 E. & E. 94 at p. 111; and dictum of Lord Phillimore in *Engelke* v. *Musmann** [1928] A.C. 433 at p. 454; 44 T.L.R. 731, H.L. considered.

Decision of Thompson J. affirmed.

APPEAL from Thompson J. in chambers.

The plaintiff, Satya Ranjan Ghosh, was an Indian doctor living and practising in the United Kingdom and connected with an Indian Government hostel for Indian students. The defendant, Doctor A. N. D'Rozario, who was also an Indian, was from 1951 until November, 1957, a counsellor for education on the official staff of the High Commissioner for India in this country. During that period his name was on the diplomatic list prepared pursuant to section 1 (4) of the Diplomatic Immunities (Commonwealth Countries and Republic of Ireland) Act, 1952. In 1956 the defendant, it was alleged, uttered slanders of and concerning the plaintiff in the way of his profession in connection with the hostel. After November, 1957, the defendant returned to India and there continued his educational work for the Government, but, in the summer of 1959, he came temporarily to this country and his name being then no longer on the diplomatic list a writ was issued and served on him by the plaintiff's solicitors claiming damages for the alleged slanders uttered in 1956. When the writ was served the defendant, it was alleged, uttered a further slander, and a second writ was immediately issued and served in respect of that further slander.

On July 24, 1959, the defendant entered a conditional appearance to the first writ without prejudice to an application to set it aside on the ground that the defendant was entitled to diplomatic immunity. The defendant believed that the immunity which he possessed in 1956 would protect him against liability for the alleged slanders uttered in that year, although he had since lost that immunity. He found, however, that he was not so protected and his appearance was then made unconditional. During the autumn of 1959 defences in both actions were delivered and requests made for particulars of both statements of claim, and on January 29, 1960, the actions were consolidated pursuant to the order of Master Diamond and at the same time various other **[109]** appropriate orders were made on the summons for directions. In February, 1960, the defendant, who had by then returned to India, asked that his evidence should be taken on commission in that country and supported his application by an affidavit sworn at New Delhi on February 10, 1960, in which he deposed, inter alia, that he was joint secretary in the Ministry of Scientific Research and Cultural Affairs to the Government of India, that he did not expect to visit the United Kingdom either on behalf of the Government of India or personally during the next two years; and that the duties of his office were extremely heavy and would not permit him to go to the United Kingdom. However, in July, 1960, he did come to this country, and from July 12, 1960, he served as scientific adviser on the staff of the High Commissioner for India. On July 19, 1960, a summons was issued to stay the consolidated actions on the ground of his diplomatic immunity, and on July 22, 1960, a certificate was issued by the Commonwealth Relations Officer showing that his name would be included in the diplomatic list to be published in the following August under section 1 (4) of the Diplomatic Immunities (Commonwealth Countries and Republic of Ireland) Act, 1952. For over a year the summons remained in abeyance, but on January 23, 1962, a further certificate was issued by the Commonwealth Relations Office showing that he was still on the diplomatic list and that he performed functions substantially corresponding to those performed by members of the official staff of an envoy of a foreign power. On January 29, 1962, Master Grundy ordered that all further proceedings be stayed and on February 8 Thompson J. upheld the master's order.

The plaintiff appealed on the grounds (1) that the orders of the master and Thompson J. were wrong in law; (2) that both the acquisition of diplomatic status and the claim to immunity from further proceedings on the ground of diplomatic immunity lacked bona fides on the part of the defendant; (3) that the diplomatic status was acquired and the claim to immunity put forward after the defendant had taken numerous steps in the action; and (4) that the defendant was not entitled to have the action stayed on the ground of diplomatic immunity.

Edward Gardner Q.C. and *Ralph Millner* for the plaintiff. This appeal raises the novel issue, untouched by authority, whether diplomatic immunity extends to protect the holder from an action commenced before he became entitled to claim the privilege. Here, the claim to diplomatic immunity arises from **[110]** the fact that the defendant is on the staff of the High Commissioner for India, having been appointed in July, 1960, to an office which he still holds. The two actions were, however, commenced before that date and the defendant took numerous steps in them before he acquired the immunity behind which he now seeks to shelter—defences were delivered, requests made for particulars of both statements of claim, the actions were consolidated and the defendant submitted to the summons for directions when other appropriate orders were made. He also asked that his evidence should be taken on commission in India.

Dealing first with the second ground of appeal, namely, that both the acquisition and the claim to immunity from further proceedings lacked bona fides, diplomatic immunity is accorded for the benefit of the State in whose service the person claiming the immunity is employed; it is not a benefit for the advantage of the person as an individual, and the circumstances here do show an abuse of immunity on the part of the defendant. Immunity may be waived in cases such as this by the chief representative, but the question of waiver does not arise here.

This case is unusual because when the action was begun the defendant was not protected by diplomatic immunity, but became so during the pendency of the proceedings. When the action was begun there was jurisdiction and the defendant submitted to it, and immunity was only claimed after the numerous steps already referred to had been taken in the action. In law jurisdiction is absolute at the time of the issue of the writ, immunity cannot be claimed at a later stage. There is great hardship on the plaintiff here in that numerous stages of the action have been proceeded with.

On this second ground of appeal—as to lack of bona fides—the plaintiff is faced with obvious difficulties; he has no direct evidence; the best he can do is to point to the admissions in the defendant's affidavit and the fact that he there says that he is holding a post in Delhi and does not expect to visit England and yet he is found in this country shortly afterwards.

The other grounds of appeal are: (1) The orders of the master and of Thompson J. were wrong in law. (3) The diplomatic status was acquired and the claim to immunity put forward after the defendant had taken numerous steps in the action. (4) The defendant was not entitled to have the action stayed on the ground of diplomatic immunity.

The reasons for the passing of the Diplomatic Privileges Act of 1708 are given in the preamble to the Act: see *per* Lord **[111]** Mansfield C.J. in *Triquet* v. *Bath*.[2]* As has frequently been pointed out, section 3 of that Act was declaratory of the common law and must be construed according to the common law and in accordance with the Law of Nations. In 1952 the Diplomatic Immunities (Commonwealth Countries and Republic of Ireland) Act, 1952, was passed to confer immunity on the representatives of Commonwealth countries. The purpose of the Act was to ensure that High Commissioners who were not ambassadors received the same immunity. Section 1 (1) (*b*) confers the like immunity on such members of the official staff of a chief representative as are performing duties substantially corresponding to those of an envoy of a foreign sovereign. It is the usual diplomatic practice for the immunity to be waived where such a person is involved in what is really a personal action. [Reference was made to Command Paper 8460 published on July 13, 1951, which deals generally with the law and practice of diplomatic immunity.]

The main point here is that the court's jurisdiction has been established once the writ has been validly issued, and it would be wrong in these circumstances to allow diplomatic immunity now to extinguish that jurisdiction. There is no authority on this point, but see *per* Lord Denning in *Rahimtoola* v. *The Nizam of Hyderabad*[3]* to the effect that diplomatic immunity does not apply where the foreign government is concerned in operations of a commercial nature which have no element of government or sovereignty about them.

[Holroyd Pearce L.J. Why should the nature of a dispute affect the principle of immunity?]

Where the action is against a member of the staff personally, one is entitled to look at the nature of the dispute. There might be difficulties with this argument if the action were against the ambassador himself.

[Davies L.J. Are you saying that where an action for goods sold and delivered is brought against X, but before the action is tried X is approved as Ambassador to the Court of St. James, the plaintiff is entitled to proceed with the action?]

Yes. Jurisdiction was established when the writ was issued, and the subsequent acquisition of diplomatic immunity should have no effect upon the jurisdiction. Any extension of the principles of diplomatic immunity which merely affords an interference **[112]** with the course of justice without satisfying any of the law's intentions with regard to diplomatic immunity should not be accepted. In the present case, in the absence of authority, the court should not extend the principle and say that the defendant is immune, especially since in this case there is no question of molestation or interference with the person or his property. The object of the law in allowing a defendant immunity is not to permit him to escape from all the duties and responsibilities of private life, but to prevent offence to the ambassador's dignity or interference with his duties—it cannot prevent personal inconvenience to members of a chief representative's staff.

T. O. Kellock for the defendant. Mr. Gardner accepts that no writ could be issued at the present time; the only question is whether or not the fact that the defendant acquired diplomatic status after the issue of the writ permits the action going further.

This is not a personal action; the alleged slander was spoken by the defendant whilst he was a diplomat and was made relative to his job at that time—it concerned the hostel, which was in some manner under his control. But assuming, as was suggested for the plaintiff, that it was a personal action, it is disputed

[2] (1764) 3 Burr. 1478, 1480.

[3] [1958] A.C. 379, 422; [1957] 3 W.L.R. 884; [1957] 3 All E.R. 441, H.L.

that the two factors taken together, namely, that it was a personal action, and that the immunity was only acquired after the issue of the writ, could have the effect for which the plaintiff contends.

The object of diplomatic immunity is to obtain immunity from the vexation of litigation with its impediment to the discharge of the diplomat's functions or those of his domestic servant: see *Engelke* v. *Musmann*[4]* *per* Lord Phillimore and Lord Campbell C.J. in *Magdalena Steam Navigation Co.* v. *Martin.*[5]*

Under the Act of 1708 it is not only the suing forth of writs and processes that is null and void but their prosecution; thus it is not just the initial step in an action but all steps thereafter. It is freedom from jurisdiction while the office is held that is intended. The privilege is not that of the person concerned but of the State by whom he is employed. If argument for the plaintiff is correct that once a writ is issued it can proceed irrespective of immunity, a government in deciding whom to appoint to the office might not know that a writ had been issued against him if it had not been served upon him.

[HAROLD PEARCE L.J. I think the proposition was rather **[113]** that where the jurisdiction has once been accepted it could not be ousted.]

In *Reg.* v. *Madan*,[6]* where a man was charged with obtaining a railway ticket by fraud and convicted and sentenced to imprisonment, a certificate was subsequently issued showing that at the relevant time he had been a member of the High Commissioner's staff. The High Commissioner did in fact waive the immunity, but that was after the trial, and the High Commissioner's letter waiving immunity was never expressed to be retrospective, and the man was accordingly held to be immune at the time of the proceedings and the conviction was quashed. The Chief Justice in that case cited *Rex* v. *A.B.*[7]* which shows that the privilege is not that of the person but of the State that employs him.

[HOLROYD PEARCE L.J. It is fully established that the person himself cannot waive the immunity. There is a reference to *United States of America and the Republic of France* v. *Dollfuss Mieg et Cie S.A. and the Bank of England.*[8]*]

Dickinson v. *Del Solar*[9]* shows that diplomatic immunity does not confer immunity from liability but only exemption from the local jurisdiction.

Gardner Q.C. in reply. The authorities cited do not help much in deciding this point of law; each of the cases referred to dealt solely with immunity existing at the time the action began, and does not cover the present case. Here no immunity existed at the time when the action was begun. There is no authority for the proposition that once the jurisdiction has been established diplomatic immunity can override it. Once the jurisdiction is established there is nothing to oust it.

HOLROYD PEARCE L.J. The plaintiff appeals against an order of Thompson J. in chambers confirming the master's order that all proceedings in two consolidated actions for slander be stayed on the ground of the defendant's diplomatic immunity which arose while the action was pending.

[His Lordship stated the facts and, having observed that the defendant's immunity in 1956 did not protect him against liability for the slanders uttered in that year (*Dickinson* v. *Del Solar*[10]*), **[114]** and his appearance became unconditional, continued:] Mr. Gardner, for the plaintiff, contends that when an action is actually in existence and pursuing its normal course, the hardship on a plaintiff and the unmeritorious evasion by a defendant create a special situation in which the court should not allow to a defendant the normal protection of diplomatic immunity. I cannot accept this contention. There is always a hardship on any plaintiff who cannot obtain redress from a defendant who is protected by diplomatic immunity. I see no difference, so far as merits are concerned, whether the facts which are the basis of that protection occur before

[4] [1928] A.C. 433, 454; 44 T.L.R. 731, H.L.
[5] (1859) 2 E. & E. 94.
[6] [1961] 2 Q.B. 1; [1961] 2 W.L.R. 231; [1961] 1 All E.R. 588, C.C.A.
[7] [1941] 1 K.B. 454; 57 T.L.R. 307, C.C.A.
[8] [1952]A.C. 582; [1952] 1 T.L.R. 541; [1952] 1 All E.R. 572, H.L.
[9] [1930] 1 K.B. 376; 45 T.L.R. 637.
[10] [1930] 1 K.B. 376; 45 T.L.R. 637.

the writ is served, or while the action is in existence. Nor can I accept the suggestion that there is here shown to be a lack of bona fides on the defendant's part. There is nothing in the evidence to show that he engineered his transfer to this country so that he might enjoy an immunity which he could not have while he was serving his Government in India. Therefore the particular merits do not help the plaintiff, however much he may be entitled to sympathy. Mr. Gardner further contends that this is a purely personal action and as such is unaffected by diplomatic immunity. He cannot refer us to any decided case which supports this proposition. He seeks support from a dictum of Lord Denning in *Rahimtoola* v. *Nizam of Hyderabad*[11]* as tending to show that diplomatic immunity does not apply in cases of a commercial nature which have no element of government or sovereignty about them. I doubt, however, whether this action can be said to be wholly personal since the slander arose out of, and was linked to, the defendant's duty in respect to the hostel. Moreover, the dictum of Lord Denning is obiter,[12] and not, I respectfully think, wholly in accord with the opinions of the other noble Lords.

The Report on Diplomatic Immunity[13] throws some light on the practical aspects of the immunity. The State of a potential defendant will usually, in practice, waive its immunity or make arbitration arrangements wherever it seems to be proper in the interest of individual justice, and can be done without detriment to the State concerned. If it declines to do so, the Foreign Office or the Commonwealth Relations Office, in the interests of the subjects of this country, may refuse to continue to accept the offending potential defendant as possessing diplomatic status. **[115]**

The real point in the case is whether, as a matter of principle, a defendant's diplomatic immunity which comes into existence after an action has been started, and while it is pending, necessitates a stay of those proceedings. It is conceded that had the defendant's diplomatic immunity existed when the writ was issued, the proceedings would not be maintainable. It is conceded further that the steps taken by the defendant earlier in the action when he had no diplomatic immunity cannot constitute any waiver or voluntary acceptance of jurisdiction by the defendant, for he had then no right of immunity which he could waive and, having been duly served, he was bound to submit to the jurisdiction. It is argued, however, that once this court has taken jurisdiction between the litigants, it will not relax its grasp even though facts occur thereafter which would create diplomatic immunity.

In 1708 the Diplomatic Privileges Act (7 Anne, c. 12) was passed with the following preamble: "Whereas several turbulent and disorderly persons having in a most outrageous manner insulted the person of his excellency Andrew Artemonowitz Mattueof, ambassador extraordinary of his Czarist Majesty, Emperor of Great Russia, Her Majesty's good friend and ally, by arresting him, and taking him by violence out of his coach in the publick street, and detaining him in custody for several hours, in contempt of the protection granted by Her Majesty, contrary to the law of nations, and in prejudice of the rights and privileges which ambassadors and other publick ministers, authorised and received as such, have at all times been thereby possessed of, and ought to be kept sacred and inviolable." Section 3 reads: "And to prevent the like insolences for the future, be if further declared by the authority aforesaid, That all writs and processes that shall at any time hereafter be sued forth or prosecuted, whereby the person of any ambassador, or other publick minister of any foreign prince or state, authorised and received as such by Her Majesty, her heirs or successors, or the domestick, or domestick servant of any such ambassador, or other publick minister, may be arrested or imprisoned, or his or their goods or chattels may be distrained, seized, or attached, shall be deemed and adjudged to be utterly null and void to all intents, constructions, and purposes whatsoever."

Section 4 sets out pains and penalties against any person who shall presume

[11] [1958] A.C. 379; [1957] 3 W.L.R. 884; [1957] 3 All E.R. 441, H.L.
[12] [1958] A.C. 379, 417, 418.
[13] (1952) Command Paper, 8460.

to sue for or prosecute any such writ or process and deems them violaters of the law of nations and disturbers of the public repose. By section 6 servants of ambassadors shall **[116]** not be privileged unless registered in the office of a secretary of state and duly published as such. Lord Mansfield C.J. said in *Triquet* v. *Bath*[14]*: "This privilege of foreign ministers and their domestic servants depends upon the law of nations. The Act of Parliament of 7 Anne, c. 12, is declaratory of it."

The Diplomatic Immunities (Commonwealth Countries and Republic of Ireland) Act, 1952, s. 1 (1) (*b*), provides: "such members of the official staff of a chief representative as are performing duties substantially corresponding to those performed by members of the official staff of an envoy of a foreign Sovereign or . . . Power shall be entitled to the like immunity from suit and legal process as is accorded to members of the official staff of such an envoy." Section 1 (3) provides that a certificate of the Secretary of State shall be conclusive; and section 1 (5) provides that a chief representative and a state representative may waive any immunity. The immunity is derived from the rules of international law and from the legal maxim par in parem non habet imperium; see Dicey's Conflict of Laws, 7th ed., p. 132. This rule of international law has been "engrafted into our domestic law": *per* Lord Atkin in *Compania Naviera Vascongado* v. *S.S. Cristina.*[15]*

In *Magdalena Steam Navigation Co.* v. *Martin*[16]* it was held that the accredited public minister of a foreign state cannot be sued in a civil action even though the action arose out of commercial transactions by him here, and although neither his person nor his goods be touched by the suit. Lord Campbell C.J., in delivering the judgment of the court, said[17]: "The great principle is to be found in *Grotius de Jure Belli et Pacis*, lib. 2, c. 18, s. 9, 'Omnis coactio abesse a legato debet.' He is to be left at liberty to devote himself body and soul to the business of his embassy. He does not owe even a temporary allegiance to the Sovereign to whom he is accredited, and he has at least as great privileges from suits as the Sovereign whom he represents. He is not supposed even to live within the territory of the Sovereign to whom he is accredited, and, if he has done nothing to forfeit or to waive his privilege, he is for all juridical purposes supposed still to be in his own country. For these reasons, the rule laid down by all jurists of authority who have written upon the subject is, that an ambassador is exempt from **[117]** the jurisdiction of the courts of the country in which he resides as ambassador."

In *Engelke* v. *Musmann*[18]* Lord Phillimore said[19]: "The object to be attained is immunity from the vexation of litigation with its impediments to the discharge of the functions of the domestic or domestic servant, as illustrated in the case which I have already quoted of the *Magdalena Steam Navigation Co.* v. *Martin.*[20]*

Diplomatic immunity is likely to create individual hardship. But this hardship must bow to a general overriding principle of comity between conflicting jurisdictions. An ambassador must live in a foreign land, and if he could be summoned before the tribunals of that foreign land, or coerced by its legal process, it would be an affront to his sovereign, and an interference with his work. For the same reasons it is necessary that the embassy staff as well as the ambassador should be immune. The immunity belongs to the State, and not to its representatives individually. There is no difference in principle between the ambassador and the humbler members of his staff providing that they are properly accredited, and on the necessary list. The Statute of 1708, by using the word "prosecute," may well have intended to prevent the continuation of any pre-existing action that arose before the defendant had immunity. But I prefer to decide the matter

14 (1764) 3 Burrows, 1478, 1480.
15 [1938] A.C. 485, 490; 54 T.L.R. 512; [1938] 1 All E.R. 719, H.L.
16 (1859) 2 E. & E. 94.
17 2 E. & E. 94, 111.
18 [1928] A.C. 433; 44 T.L.R. 731, H.L.
19 [1928] A.C. 433, 454.
20 2 E. & E. 94.

on a broader ground. It would be no less an affront and an interference to subject an ambassador to actions that were in existence before he acquired his diplomatic status and immunity than it would be to allow a writ to be served on him. Moreover, if a pre-existing action were allowed to proceed against an ambassador, it would create undesirable practical difficulties. The court could not order him or impose any sanction on his conduct. He could with impunity be a most unruly litigant. The mischief which the general rule is intended to avoid at the cost of some individual hardship would inevitably arise. In my judgment the general principles that confer diplomatic immunity against the initiation of proceedings confer an equal immunity against the continuation of pre-existing and hitherto properly constituted proceedings. I would, therefore, dismiss the appeal.

DAVIES L.J. I agree. Of the principles which underlie the law of diplomatic immunity, that which perhaps applies most closely to the facts of this case—that is, to the question of the **[118]** continuation of legal proceedings as opposed to their institution—is that a person entitled to such immunity is to be permitted to perform his duties as a diplomat or other accredited person without interference from the courts of this country. If this action were allowed to proceed, the defendant would be under the necessity of instructing solicitors and counsel and of attending court to give evidence. To expose him to this possibility would be contrary to the law as laid down in the authorities referred to by Holroyd Pearce L.J. But the matter does not rest there. It may be that, at the stage which the action has reached, there would probably be no occasion for the court to make any order on the defendant before trial, although one can never be sure that some interlocutory order might not be necessary. At the end of it all, however, if the plaintiff were successful, the result would be a judgment against the defendant for damages and, no doubt, an order for the payment of costs. Mr. Gardner does not shrink from the proposition that his argument would apply equally if, in the circumstances of this case, the defendant had been appointed to be not a member of the High Commissioner's staff but the High Commissioner himself or (if of a different nationality) an ambassador. The proposition that the court could give a judgment for damages and make an order for the payment of costs—quite apart from any question of execution—against a High Commissioner or an ambassador contains, in my view, its own refutation.

It is, in some sense, an unfortunate case. I suppose that most of these cases are. But we know nothing at all about the merits of the action. Still less is it any part of our province to consider whether the Indian Government acted wisely or diplomatically in re-appointing to a diplomatic post in this country one who at the time of that re-appointment was a defendant in an action validly instituted and properly carried on and pending in the courts here. However, the action is not at an end, but merely stayed; should the defendant at any time cease to enjoy diplomatic immunity, it will be able to proceed.

WILBERFORCE J. I agree, and I will only add a few words on what Holroyd Pearce L.J. has described as the real point of principle in this case. There is no doubt that the defendant now holds an appointment under the High Commissioner for India of such a character as would make it impossible for a writ effectively to be served on him unless the High Commissioner were to waive the immunity which the latter possesses. The question is whether **[119]** the position is altered in law by reason of the fact that the defendant, before the appointment was assumed, had been validly served with the writ, had not taken steps to set it aside, and had submitted to the jurisdiction of this court.

In order to maintain a proposition of this nature, the plaintiff must in effect contend that the High Commissioner, to whom this privilege belongs, was, at the date when the defendant assumed his appointment, and is at the present time, bound by the submission to the jurisdiction of the defendant, made at a time when the defendant himself had no immunity, and when the High Commissioner had no interest in the defendant's immunity, and no means of asserting it. This, if accepted, involves the consequences that the High Commissioner, although he does not waive the immunity of his officer, must accept a position in which that officer absents himself from his duties in order to defend himself against a claim which, if established, or left to go by default, may present him in an unfavourable light to the public of this country. It seems to me impossible to say—however much it be assumed that the court would adapt its procedure to suit the convenience of the High Commissioner—that to place him in this situation might not both interfere with the proper functioning of his organisation, and affect his dignity as the representative of a sovereign State. It may be answered to this that the High Commissioner was under no obligation to employ the defendant and so, if I may adopt a catch phrase, "to employ a law suit." But so to contend involves a limitation on the freedom of a representative of a foreign State to choose his officials which, though perhaps possible by diplomatic representation, should not be imposed by the court.

To distinguish this from the normal case, where immunity from process is claimed for the member of the staff of an ambassador or a high commissioner, on the ground that the critical act is the issue of the writ containing the sovereign's formal command, to my mind would be an unduly technical approach, and one inconsistent with the principles underlying claims to immunity which are general principles of public policy, requiring that the effectiveness and dignity of the representatives of foreign States should not be impaired. It would be as contrary to those principles to let this action go on, as it would to permit an action commenced against a private individual to continue against him after he had been appointed and accepted as an **[120]** ambassador in this country. For these reasons, as well as those given by my Lord, although regretting the hardship which this involves for the plaintiff, I agree that the action should be stayed.

Appeal dismissed with costs.
Leave to appeal refused.

Solicitors: *Cree, Godfrey & Wood; T. L. Wilson & Co.*

GHOSH v. D'ROZARIO

([1962] 1 W.L.R. 1083)

June 7, 1962: House of Lords: Lords Hodson, Cohen, Guest.

PETITION for leave to appeal to the House of Lords from the decision of the Court of Appeal in *Ghosh* v. *D'Rozario*.[1]*

The APPEAL COMMITTEE dismissed the petition.

EMPSON v. SMITH

([1966] 1 Q.B. 426)

May 18, 26, 1965: Court of Appeal: Sellers, Danckwerts, Diplock L.JJ.

Conflict of Laws—Sovereign immunity—Diplomatic immunity—Act of 1964—*Waiver—Technical and Administrative officer—Tenancy agreement with officer employed by diplomatic mission—Alleged breach of agreement—Action for damages stayed on production of certificate that tenant a member of mission*

[1] [1962] 3 W.L.R. 405; [1962] 2 All E.R. 640, C.A.

staff—Act modifying privilege of technical and administrative officers—Act passed while action subsisting—Effect—Diplomatic Immunity (Commonwealth Countries and Republic of Ireland) Act, 1952 (15 *&* 16 *Geo.* 6 *&* 1 *Eliz.* 2, *c.* 18), *s.* 1 (3), *Diplomatic Privileges Act,* 1964 (*c.* 81), *s.* 4, *sch.* I, *arts.* 31, 37.
Practice—Revival of proceedings—Change of law—Action stayed on ground of diplomatic immunity—Change in law possibly depriving defendant of immunity —Whether action still subsising—Whether action to be tried—Diplomatic Privileges Act, 1964, *s.* 4, *sch.* I, *arts,* 31, 37. **[427]**
Statute—Retroactive effect—Diplomatic immunity—Act limiting immunity to acts done in course of duty—Whether procedural—Effect on subsisting action stayed on ground of immunity—Diplomatic Privileges Act, 1964, *art.* 37.

On October 17, 1961, the plaintiff let her house in London for one year certain less one day to the defendant, an administrative officer in the employ of the High Commissioner for Canada in the United Kingdom. A special clause in the tenancy agreement provided, inter alia, that in the event of the tenant being officially ordered by his Government to duty outside London and the landlord being duly notified in writing by the tenant, the agreement should cease and terminate three calendar months after the date of the delivery of such notice to the landlord. In December, 1961, the defendant, who alleged that he had been officially ordered to Europe for duty, gave notice to the plaintiff to terminate the tenancy agreement and left the premises in March, 1962. In March, 1963, the plaintiff began proceedings in the county court for damages for breach of the tenancy agreement. The defendant did not enter an appearance, but a certificate was issued by the Ministry of Commonwealth Relations under section 1 (3) of the Diplomatic Immunities (Commonwealth Countries and Republic of Ireland) Act, 1952,[1] certifying that he was a member of the official staff of the High Commissioner. On the basis of that certificate the registrar, on March 26, 1963, stayed the action. On July 31, 1964, the Diplomatic Privileges Act, 1964, article 37 (2) of which provided that the immunity of members of the administrative and technical staff of a mission from the civil and administrative jurisdiction should not extend to acts performed outside the course of their duties, was passed and on August 31 the plaintiff applied for removal of the stay, her application being adjourned. On October 1, 1964, the Diplomatic Privileges Act, 1964, came into force. On November 4, the defendant applied for an order dismissing the action on the ground that it was a nullity. On December 15 both applications were heard together and a certificate, issued under section 4 of the Act of 1964,[2] certifying that the defendant was a member of the **[428]**

[1] Diplomatic Immunities (Commonwealth Countries and Republic of Ireland) Act, 1952, s. 1 (1): "Subject to the provisions of this section . . . (*b*) such members of the official staff of a chief representative as are performing duties substantially corresponding to those performed by members of the official staff of an envoy of a foreign sovereign Power shall be entitled to the like immunity from suit and legal process as is accorded to members of the official staff of such an envoy; . . . (3) If in any proceedings any question arises whether or not any person is entitled to immunity from suit and legal process under any provision of this section or of any Order in Council made thereunder, a certificate issued by or under the authority of the Secretary of State stating any fact relevant to that question shall be conclusive evidence of that fact."

[2] Diplomatic Privileges Act, 1964, s. 2 (1): "Subject to section 3 of this Act, the articles set out in Schedule 1 to this Act (being articles of the Vienna Convention on Diplomatic Relations signed in 1961) shall have the force of law in the United Kingdom. . . ."

S. 4: "If in any proceedings any question arises whether or not any person is entitled to any privilege or immunity under this Act a certificate issued by or under the authority of the Secretary of State stating any fact relating to that question shall be conclusive evidence of that fact."

Sch. I, art. 31: "A diplomatic agent shall enjoy immunity from the criminal jurisdiction of the receiving State. He shall also enjoy immunity from its civil and administrative jurisdiction, except in the case of: (*a*) a real action relating to private administrative staff of the High Commissioner, was before the judge. The judge struck out the action on the ground that the proceedings were a nullity at the time they were begun and were not affected by the Act of 1964. On appeal by the plaintiff:—

Held, (1) that, as the law stood at the time that the proceedings were begun, the defendant was covered by diplomatic immunity, and the proceedings could not be lawfully maintained while that immunity remained; but that the action subsisted until struck out by the judge and the stay imposed by the registrar could have been removed and the action allowed to proceed if the immunity had been lost either by a valid waiver or, in respect of acts done by the defendant in his personal capacity, by the cessation of his diplomatic employment; that a change in the law similarly permitted the action to proceed, if not barred by the Limitation Act, 1939, if it removed the immunity previously enjoyed, which was probably the case here (post, pp. 432-433, 434, 437, 439, 440).

Reg. v. *Madan** [1961] 2 Q.B. 1; [1961] 2 W.L.R. 231; [1961] 1 All E.R. 588, C.C.A.; *Zoernsch* v. *Waldock** [1964] 1 W.L.R. 675; [1964] 2 All E.R. 256, C.A. and *Dickinson* v. *Del Solar** [1930] 1 K.B. 376; 45 T.L.R. 637, applied.

(2) That, since the defendant had not applied to have the action dismissed on the grounds that it was a nullity before the Act of 1964 came into force, he could not now do so, since under the new Act immunity from civil suit of administrative and technical officers had been curtailed, and the defendant's immunity depended on whether the acts done by him in relation to the tenancy were within or outside the course of his duty. Accordingly, the plaintiff was entitled to have her action tried and that issue determined (post, pp. 432-433, 435, 437-438).

Per Diplock L.J. Statutes relating to diplomatic immunity from civil suit are procedural statutes, and the Diplomatic Privileges Act, 1964, is applicable to suits brought after the date on **[429]** which it came into force in respect of acts done before that date. If, therefore, the plaintiff had issued her plaint after October 1, 1964, instead of before, the action could not have been dismissed upon the ground of diplomatic immunity unless and until the court had determined the issue, whether or not the defendant's acts alleged by the plaintiff to constitute her cause of action against him were acts performed outside the course of his duties (post, p. 438). The reference by Lord Parker C.J. in *Reg.* v. *Madan** ([1961] 2 Q.B. 1, 7) to the proceedings being "null and void unless and until there is a valid waiver which, as it were, would bring the proceedings to life and give jurisdiction to the court" should not be read as meaning that *only* waiver can bring the proceedings to life. The removal of the procedural bar from any other cause will have the same effect (post, p. 439).

Decision of Deputy Judge Granville Slack reversed.

APPEAL from Deputy Judge Granville Slack, sitting at Willesden County Court.

The following statement of facts is taken substantially from the judgment of Danckwerts L.J. On October 17, 1961, the plaintiff, Mrs. Agnes Mary Stella Empson, by a tenancy agreement, let a house, No. 32, The Vale, Golders Green, London, furnished, to the defendant, Clarence Burton Smith, for a term of one

---

immovable property situated in the territory of the receiving State, unless he holds it on behalf of the sending State for the purposes of the mission; (*b*) an action relating to succession in which the diplomatic agent is involved as executor, administrator, heir or legatee as a private person and not on behalf of the sending State; (*c*) an action relating to any professional or commercial activity exercised by the diplomatic agent in the receiving State outside his official functions."

Art. 37 (2): "Members of the administrative and technical staff of the mission, . . . shall, if they are not nationals of or permanently resident in the receiving State, enjoy the privileges and immunities specified in arts. 29 to 35, except that the immunity from civil and administrative jurisdiction of the receiving State specified in para. 1 of art. 31 shall not extend to acts performed outside the course of their duties. . . ."

year certain from October 17, 1961, less one day, at a rental of 19 guineas a week. As the defendant was an administrative officer in the employment of the High Commissioner for Canada in the United Kingdom, a special clause was incorporated in the tenancy agreement, which provided as follows: "In the event of the tenant being officially ordered by his Government to duty outside the Metropolitan area of London or is ordered to return to Canada or leaves the service of his Government for any reason and the landlord is duly notified thereof in writing by the tenant then in that event this agreement shall cease and terminate three calendar months after the date of delivery of such notice to the landlord...."

On December 4, 1961, the defendant told the plaintiff, what he subsequently swore by affidavit, that he had been officially ordered to proceed for a tour of duty on the Continent of Europe and gave a notice dated December 12, 1961, to determine the tenancy agreement. He left the premises on or about March 13, 1962.

On March 22, 1963, the plaintiff began proceedings in the Willesden County Court in which she claimed damages for breach of the tenancy agreement. A letter dated April 19, 1963, from **[430]** the Ministry of Commonwealth Relations, was sent to the registrar of the Willesden County Court enclosing a certificate issued under section 1 (3) of the Diplomatic Immunities (Commonwealth Countries and Republic of Ireland) Act, 1952. That certificate was in the following terms: "By direction of Her Majesty's Principal Secretary of State for Commonwealth Relations, it is hereby certified under subsection (3) of section 1 of the Diplomatic Immunities (Commonwealth Countries and Republic of Ireland) Act, 1952, that Mr. C. B. Smith became in September, 1961, a member of the official staff of the High Commissioner recognised by Her Majesty's Government in the United Kingdom as the chief representative in the United Kingdom of Canada, and he is still a member of the official staff of the High Commissioner and as such member he performs functions corresponding to those performed by members of the official staff of an envoy of a foreign sovereign Power."

The matter came before the registrar on April 26, 1963. The plaintiff's solicitor was present. The defendant did not appear but the registrar ordered the action to be stayed.

On July 31, 1964, the Diplomatic Privileges Act, 1964, was passed. It came into force on October 1, 1964.

On August 31, 1964, the plaintiff applied to Willesden County Court for the removal of the stay imposed by the registrar, and for the case to be restored. After several adjournments before Judge Leon on October 22, 1964, and before Judge Edgedale on November 10, 1964, the plaintiff's application came before Deputy Judge Granville Slack on December 15, 1964. On that date there was also an application by the defendant, dated November 4, 1964, for an order that the action be dismissed on the ground that the proceedings were a nullity. The deputy judge ordered that the plaintiff's application to remove the stay and restore the action be dismissed, and that the action be struck out, and that the plaintiff should pay the defendant's costs on scale 4 on both applications.

The plaintiff appealed on the ground that the deputy judge misdirected himself in law in considering the effect of the Diplomatic Privileges Act, 1964, to proceedings begun and not determined before the commencement of that Act.

The plaintiff in person. The registrar who stayed the action on April 26, 1964, said that application for a removal of the stay could be made if there was a change in the law. The application made after the Diplomatic Privileges Act, 1964, was passed was not **[431]** dismissed but only adjourned. By the time it came before deputy judge Granville Slack on December 15, 1964, the Diplomatic Privileges Act, 1964, had come into force. That Act affected the position of members of administrative and technical staffs of diplomatic missions and might have affected the position of the defendant. The judge was wrong in striking out the action. I am entitled to have it tried.

David Sullivan for the defendant. The deputy county court judge was right in striking out the action. Reliance is placed on the words of Lord Parker C.J. in *Reg.* v. *Madan*[3]* that civil proceedings brought against somebody entitled to diplomatic immunity are, in fact proceedings without jurisdiction and null and void. Support for this is found in the Diplomatic Privileges Act, 1708, s. 3, which makes proceedings against an ambassador or his servants "utterly null and void to all intents, constructions, and purposes whatsoever." That Act, which was passed as a result of the arrest of the Russian ambassador (see *Triquet* v. *Bath*[4]*) did no more than declare the common law, of which the law of nations is part: see *In re Suarez.*[5]*

The privilege of an ambassador's suite is the same as that declared in relation to an ambassador himself and his servants. The defendant has always been a member of the High Commissioner's suite and he remains so, although he now falls into a different category. Unless there was a waiver by the High Commissioner which, in the words of Lord Parker C.J. in *Reg.* v. *Madan*[6]* would "bring the proceedings to life and give jurisdiction to the court" these proceedings were without jurisdiction. The stay on April 26 was a de facto recognition of this but probably the right course at that time would have been to strike out the plaintiff's claim.

The privilege is the privilege of the High Commissioner and not that of the defendant who has no right to waive it. In *Dickinson* v. *del Solar*[7]* there was waiver and Lord Hewart C.J.'s words[8] must be construed in the light of it. The plaintiff's action here was without jurisdiction, whatever the position might be as regards another action in the light of the Diplomatic Privileges Act, 1964. **[432]**

If these submissions are wrong, the facts relating to the privilege of the defendant as a member of the administrative and technical staff of the High Commissioner will have to be tried.

Cur. adv. vult.

May 26. The following judgments were read.

SELLERS L.J. I doubt the wisdom of this appeal, for success means that the plaintiff's case will be heard and the claim seems to present difficulties for her. It depends solely on whether the defendant can establish, if he is called upon to defend, what he has sworn by affidavit, namely that when he gave notice to terminate the tenancy he had been officially ordered by his Government to duty outside the Metropolitan area of London. The plaintiff conducted her own appeal and, although discouraged by the court, she pressed for a decision in her favour in respect of the claim for diplomatic immunity from being sued in our courts made by or on behalf of the defendant.

As I am in entire agreement with the judgments prepared by both my brethren dealing fully with this issue I will not retrace all the ground.

The plaintiff is entitled to succeed to the extent of having the matter heard by the county court first to consider whether the stay should be removed on the ground that the defendant has not been entitled to diplomatic immunity in respect of his liability under his tenancy agreement with the plaintiff since the Diplomatic Privileges Act, 1964, came into force on October 1, 1964, and second, if that is so, to hear the claim on its merits.

The action was originally stayed on April 26, 1963. The stay remained after applications by the plaintiff for its removal before Judge Leon on October 22, 1964, and Judge Edgedale on November 10, 1964, and the action subsisted, though stayed, until December 15, 1964, when it was struck out by the order from which this appeal now comes.

[3] [1961] 2 Q.B. 1, 7; [1961] 2 W.L.R. 231; [1961] 1 All E.R. 588, C.C.A.
[4] (1764) 3 Burr. 1478.
[5] [1918] 1 Ch. 176; 34 T.L.R. 127, C.A.
[6] [1961] 2 Q.B. 1, 7.
[7] [1930] 1 K.B. 376; 45 T.L.R. 637.
[8] [1930] 1 K.B. 376, 380.

At any time while the action remained subsisting if the immunity claimed had been waived the stay could have been lifted and the action allowed to proceed to trial. A waiver in such circumstances follows and does not precede the writ or summons. Removal from the diplomatic employment occasioning the immunity would likewise remove the immunity in respect of acts done in a personal capacity and a subsisting action could proceed. A change in the law, as here, similarly in my view **[433]** permits the action to proceed if it removes the immunity previously granted. It would be idle to require a fresh writ or summons when a sufficient one is before the court. The defendant did not previously apply to have the action struck out as a nullity. He is too late now if, as seems probable, he is no longer entitled to immunity in respect of this present claim before the court.

I would allow the appeal accordingly.

DANCKWERTS L.J. stated the facts as set out above, and continued:

The relevant statutes at the date when the proceedings were begun were the Diplomatic Privileges Act, 1708 (7 Anne, c. 12), and the Diplomatic Immunities (Commonwealth Countries and Republic of Ireland) Act, 1952. The Act of Anne, which was passed as the result of the arrest of the Russian Ambassador in his coach and his detention in custody for several hours, is regarded as declaratory of the existing position at common law. Section 3 declares as follows: "All processes against any publick Minister, or any of his servants, to be adjudged void for the time to come. And to prevent the like insolences for the future, be it further declared by the authority aforesaid, that all writs and processes that shall at any time hereafter be sued forth or prosecuted, whereby the person of any ambassador, or other publick minister of any foreign prince or state, authorised and received as such by Her Majesty, her heirs or successors, or the domestick, or domestick servant of any such ambassador, or other publick minister, may be arrested or imprisoned, or his or their goods or chattels may be distrained, seized, or attached, shall be deemed and adjudged to be utterly null and void to all intents, constructions, and purposes whatsoever."

The Act of 1952 provides, by section 1 (1): "Subject to the provisions of this section" (then omitting (*a*)) "(*b*) such members of the official staff of a chief representative as are performing duties substantially corresponding to those performed by members of the official staff of an envoy of a foreign sovereign Power shall be entitled to the like immunity from suit and legal process as is accorded to members of the official staff of such an envoy"; subsection (3) provides that: "If in any proceedings any question arises whether or not any person is entitled to immunity from suit and legal process under any provision of this section or of any Order in Council made thereunder, a certificate issued by or under the authority of the **[434]** Secretary of State stating any fact relevant to that question shall be conclusive evidence of that fact."

That last subsection is, of course, the basis of the certificate which was given in the present case.

Since the beginning of the action, however, on October 1, 1964, the Diplomatic Privileges Act, 1964, came into force, and this Act draws a distinction between the immunity which is given to a "diplomatic agent" and the "members of the administrative and technical staff" of a mission. Schedule 1, Article 31 provides: "1. A diplomatic agent shall enjoy immunity from the criminal jurisdiction of the receiving State. He shall also enjoy immunity from its civil and administrative jurisdiction, except in the case of: (*a*) a real action relating to private immovable property situated in the territory of the receiving State, unless he holds it on behalf of the sending State for the purposes of the mission." Article 37 provides, inter alia: 2. members of the administrative and technical staff of the mission . . . shall, if they are not nationals of or permanently resident in the receiving State, enjoy the privileges and immunities specified in articles 29 to 35, except that the immunity from civil and administrative jurisdiction of the receiving State specified in paragraph 1 of article 31 shall not extend to acts performed outside the course of their duties."

A further certificate has been given by the Secretary of State as follows: "By the direction of Her Majesty's Principal Secretary of State for Commonwealth Relations it is hereby certified under section 4 of the Diplomatic Privileges Act, 1964, that Mr. C. B. Smith was on [October 1] a member of the administrative and technical staff of the diplomatic mission of Canada in the United Kingdom, that he has since that date continued to be a member of the said administrative and technical staff and he is now such a member."

Consequently, it appears that the position of the defendant may have been altered before December 15, 1964.

If the defendant was covered at a material time by diplomatic immunity, proceedings could not lawfully be maintained. The position is stated by Lord Parker C.J. giving the judgment of the court in *Reg.* v. *Madan*[9]*: "Certain things are, we think, clear. In the first place, it is not for someone who is entitled to **[435]** diplomatic immunity to claim it in the courts. It is unnecessary to refer to the authorities, but we think it is clear that proceedings brought against somebody, certainly civil proceedings brought against somebody, entitled to diplomatic immunity are, in fact, proceedings without jurisdiction and null and void, unless and until there is a valid waiver which, as it were, would bring the proceedings to life and give jurisdiction to the court. Moreover, it is clear that that waiver must be a waiver by a person with full knowledge of his rights and a waiver by or on behalf of the chief representative of the state in question. In other words, it is not the person entitled to a privilege who may waive it, unless, of course, he does so as an agent for or on behalf of the representative of the country concerned; it must be a waiver of the representative of the state."

There has, of course, been no waiver in the present case, but diplomatic immunity may be lost by change of circumstances. Apart from waiver, it may be lost in respect of a private debt of the agent, by the cessation of his diplomatic employment and status: see *Zoernsch* v. *Waldock*.[10]*

The result may then be that stated by Lord Hewart C.J. in *Dickinson* v. *Del Solar*[11]*: "Diplomatic agents are not, in virtue of their privileges as such, immune from legal liability for any wrongful acts. The accurate statement is that they are not liable to be sued in the English courts unless they submit to the jurisdiction."

The result is that if the immunity ceases, the cause of action, if not barred by the Limitation Act, 1939, will remain.

Consequently, when the Order of December 15, 1964, was made, the defendant's diplomatic immunity from legal process in England had ceased, and the plaintiff was entitled to have her action tried.

Some logical difficulties have been suggested in regard to the survival of an action which is described as having been a nullity, but, in my opinion, in the circumstances these do not form a useful mental exercise. I would allow the appeal, but if the plaintiff goes on with her action she will have to meet the difficulty presented against her success by the special clause in the tenancy agreement. **[436]**

DIPLOCK L.J. The plaintiff owns a house in Golders Green. By a tenancy agreement of October 17, 1961, she let it to the defendant, who was then and still is a member of the administrative and technical staff of the High Commissioner for Canada in the United Kingdom. In March, 1962, he vacated the premises in circumstances which the plaintiff thinks entitled her in law to recover damages from him. Whether she is right in thinking this is neither here nor there so far as this appeal is concerned. Neither her claim nor the defendant's answer to it has yet been investigated. She started proceedings against the defendant in the Willesden county court on March 22, 1963, claiming damages for breach of tenancy agreement. He entered no appearance and until a much later stage took no part in the proceedings. On April 19, 1963, the Commonwealth Relations Office forwarded to the registrar of the county court a certificate under section

[9] [1961] 2 Q.B. 1, 7; [1961] 2 W.L.R. 231; [1961] 1 All E.R. 588, C.C.A.
[10] [1964] 1 W.L.R. 675; [1964] 2 All E.R. 256, C.A.
[11] [1930] 1 K.B. 376, 380; 45 T.L.R. 637.

1 (3) of the Diplomatic Immunities (Commonwealth Countries and Republic of Ireland) Act, 1952, certifying that the defendant was a member of the official staff of the High Commissioner for Canada. Such a certificate was at that date conclusive evidence that the defendant was entitled to the same diplomatic immunity as that accorded at common law and under the Diplomatic Immunities Act, 1708, to members of the official staff of an envoy of a foreign sovereign power. On April 26, 1963, after a hearing at which the defendant did not appear but the plaintiff was represented by a solicitor, the registrar ordered that the action be stayed. It was not dismissed nor was the plaint set aside.

And so the matter rested until August 31, 1964, when the plaintiff, probably under the impression that the Diplomatic Privileges Act, 1964, which was passed on July 31, 1964, had come into force, applied for the stay to be removed. A series of adjournments followed and the application was not heard until December 15, 1964. In the meantime the defendant had at last taken a step in the proceedings. On November 4, 1964, he made an application for an order dismissing the action on the grounds that the proceedings were a nullity. This I apprehend would be equivalent to an application in the High Court under R.S.C., Ord 12, r. 9, to set aside a writ before entering appearance. This application was heard on December 15, 1964, at the same time as the plaintiff's application for removal of the stay.

By that date the Diplomatic Privileges Act, 1964, had come into force on October 1, 1964. That Act makes radical amendments in the previously existing law on diplomatic privileges and immunity and in particular draws a distinction between the **[437]** immunities enjoyed by "members of the diplomatic staff and members of the administrative and technical staff" of a mission. Section 4 of that Act provides that a certificate issued by or under the authority of the Secretary of State shall be conclusive evidence of any fact relevant to any person's entitlement to any privilege or immunity. A further certificate dated October 20, 1964, was issued under that Act certifying that the defendant was on October 1 and has continued to be a member of the administrative and technical staff of the Diplomatic Mission of Canada in the United Kingdom.

When the action was commenced in March, 1963, the defendant was entitled under section 1 (1) (*a*) of the Act of 1952 "to the like immunity from suit and legal process as is accorded to members of the official staff of an envoy of a foreign sovereign power." He was thus entitled so long as he remained en poste to complete immunity from civil suit in the United Kingdom, both as respects acts done in his official capacity on behalf of his government and as respects acts done in his private capacity. This immunity he could, however, lose at that date in one of two ways: first, as respects acts done in either capacity if his immunity were waived by the head of his mission on behalf of the Government of Canada (see Act of 1952, s. 1 (5) (*a*)) *Taylor* v. *Best*[12]*; *In re Suarez*[13]* or secondly, but only as respects acts done in his personal capacity if he should cease to be en poste and a sufficient time had elapsed thereafter for him to wind up his affairs: *Magdalena Steam Navigation Co.* v. *Martin*[14]*; *Musurus Bey* v. *Gadban*[15]*; *Zoernsch* v. *Waldock.*[16]*

If the defendant had applied before the passing of the Diplomatic Privileges Act, 1964, to have the plaintiff's action dismissed there would have been no answer to his application. But he delayed until November, 1964. By that date his right to immunity from civil suit had been curtailed by that Act which applies to the United Kingdom the provisions of the Vienna Convention on Diplomatic Relations, 1961, contained in the schedule to the Act. By the combined effect of articles 31 and 37 of the Convention as a member of the administrative and technical staff of the mission his immunity from the civil jurisdiction of the courts of the United Kingdom does not extend to acts performed outside the course of his duties. Whether he is entitled to immunity in **[438]** any particular

[12] (1854) 14 C.B. 487.
[13] [1918] 1 Ch. 176; 34 T.L.R. 127, C.A.
[14] (1859) 2 E. & E. 94.
[15] [1894] 2 Q.B. 352; 10 T.L.R. 493, C.A.
[16] [1964] 1 W.L.R. 675.

suit no longer depends solely upon his status but also upon the subject-matter of the suit.

It is elementary law that diplomatic immunity is not immunity from legal liability but immunity from suit. If authority is needed for this it is to be found in *Dickinson* v. *Del Solar*,[17*] which has been cited by my brother Danckwerts L.J. Statutes relating to diplomatic immunity from civil suit are procedural statutes. The Diplomatic Privileges Act, 1964, is in my view clearly applicable to suits brought after the date on which that statute came into force in respect of acts done before that date. If, therefore, the plaintiff had issued her plaint after October 1, 1964, instead of before, the action could not have been dismissed upon the ground of diplomatic privilege unless and until the court had determined the issue: whether or not the defendant's acts alleged by the plaintiff to constitute her cause of action against him were acts performed outside the course of his duties. It is, to say the least, arguable that acts done by the defendant in relation to his tenancy of his private residence in London were performed by him outside the course of his duties. But this issue is one which can be decided only upon evidence. It has not yet been considered, for the deputy county court judge found it unnecessary to go into it. He dismissed the plaintiff's action upon other grounds. He took the view that "the proceedings were a nullity at the time they were commenced, they are not affected by the 1964 Act which came into operation subsequently."

The deputy county court judge did not refer to section 3 of the Diplomatic Privileges Act, 1708, but counsel for the defendant has in this court relied strongly upon it in support of the proposition that Mrs. Empson's plaint was void ab initio. The Act of Anne, whose history is entertainingly related by Lord Mansfield in *Triquet* v. *Bath*,[18*] has been repeatedly held to be declaratory of the common law, and must therefore be construed according to the common law of which the law of nations must be deemed a part: *In re Suarez*,[19*] *per* Swinfen Eady L.J.[20] It is unnecessary to determine whether a plaint in a county court fell within the express provisions of section 3 of the Act of Anne or whether that section applies to a person in a situation of the defendant, for it was decided in *In re Suarez*[21*] that notwithstanding that Act a writ issued in the High Court against an ambassador was not void ab initio. If it were it would, indeed, be impossible for **[439]** the privilege ever to be waived for, as was decided in *Kahan* v. *Pakistan Federation*,[22*] there can be no effective waiver until the court is actually seised of the proceedings. The waiver is an undertaking given not to the other party to the proceedings but to the court itself. It can effectively be given only after the proceedings have commenced. *Kahan's* case[22*] was one of state immunity, but it is well settled that diplomatic immunity is governed by the same principles for it is claimed by the head of the mission on behalf of his state.

It follows therefore that until steps were taken to set it aside or to dismiss the action the plaintiff's plaint was no nullity: it was a valid plaint. If the defendant had, with the permission of his High Commissioner, appeared to it before October 1, 1964, the procedural bar to the hearing would have been removed. So, too, if the defendant had ceased to be en poste while the plaint was still outstanding the action could then have proceeded against him. I can see no reason in logic or the law of nations why the position should be any different when the procedural bar has been removed by Act of Parliament—particularly when that Act of Parliament gives statutory effect to an international convention, by which sovereign states have mutually waived in part immunities for members of the staff of their foreign missions to which they were formerly entitled by the law of nations.

In holding, in my view, incorrectly, that the proceedings were a nullity at

[17] [1930] 1 K.B. 376, 380.
[18] (1764) 3 Burr. 1478, 1480.
[19] [1918] 1 Ch. 176.
[20] Ibid. 192.
[21] [1918] 1 Ch. 176.
[22] [1951] 2 K.B. 1003; [1951] 2 T.L.R. 697, C.A.

the time they were commenced, the deputy county court judge founded himself upon a passage in the judgment of Lord Parker C.J. in *Reg.* v. *Madan*[23]* in which he referred to the proceedings being "null and void unless and until there is a valid waiver which, as it were, would bring the proceedings to life and give jurisdiction to the court." Lord Parker was clearly not using the words "null and void" in a precise sense for what is null and void is not a phoenix, there are no ashes from which it can be brought to life. In that case he was concerned only with waiver as removing the procedural bar of diplomatic immunity. His words should not be read that *only* waiver can, as it were, bring the proceedings to life. The removal of the procedural bar from any other cause will have the same effect.

I am therefore of opinion that the deputy county court judge was wrong in dismissing the action as he did. The applications by the plaintiffs for removal of the stay and by the defendant for dismissal of the action must go back to the county court for **[440]** determination of the issue whether the acts of which the plaintiff complains were performed by the defendant outside the course of his duties. Upon this issue evidence will be required. If on that evidence it is not determined that the acts complained of were performed outside the course of his duties he is entitled to have the action dismissed. If, on the other hand, it is determined that the acts complained of were performed outside the course of his duties the plaintiff is entitled to have the stay removed and to proceed to trial.

Appeal allowed with costs.
Leave to appeal refused.

Solicitors: *Reid, Sharman & Co.*

[23] [1961] 2 Q.B. 1, 7.

D.

INTERNATIONAL ORGANISATIONS

ZOERNSCH v. WALDOCK AND ANOTHER

([1964] 1 W.L.R. 675)

March 19, 20, 24, 1964: Court of Appeal: Willmer, Danckwerts, Diplock L.JJ.

Conflict of laws—Diplomatic immunity—International organisation—Plaintiff's petition to European Commission of Human Rights rejected—Action against president and secretary of commission—Retirement of president prior to action—Whether both defendants entitled to immunity from legal process—Whether commission "organ" of council—"Words . . . and acts done . . . in official capacity"—International Organisations (Immunities and Privileges) Act, 1950 (14 *Geo.* 6, *c.* 14), *ss.* 1, 2—*Council of Europe* (*Immunities and Privileges*) *Order*, 1960 (*S.I.* 1960, *No.* 442), *arts.* 11, 12.

The plaintiff petitioned the European Commission of Human Rights, set up under the Convention for the Protection of Human Rights and Fundamental Freedoms, dated November 4, 1950, alleging a violation of the convention by the Federal Republic of Germany. By decisions dated May 31 and December 14, 1961, the commission rejected the petition. The plaintiff then issued a writ against the first and second defendants, who were the president of the commission and the secretary, respectively, at the time of the rejection of the petition, alleging negligence and corruption. The first defendant ceased to be a member of the commission in January, 1962. The defendants entered a conditional appearance contending that the court had no jurisdiction because of the immunity granted to them by the International Organisations (Immunities and Privileges) Act, 1950,[1] and the Council of Europe (Immunities and **[676]** Privileges) Order, 1960,[2] made thereunder.

[1] International Organisations (Immunities and Privileges) Act, 1950, s. 1 (2): "His Majesty may by Order in Council—(*a*) provide that any organisation to which this section applies . . . shall, to such extent as may be specified in the Order, have the immunities and privileges set out in Part I of the Schedule to this Act . . .; (*b*) confer upon—(i) any persons who are representatives (whether of governments or not) on any organ of the organisation or are members of any committee of the organisation or of an organ thereof; . . . to such extent as may be specified in the Order, the immunities and privileges set out in Part II of the Schedule to this Act; (*c*) confer upon such other classes of officers and servants of the organisation . . . to such extent as may be so specified, the immunities and privileges set out in Part III of the Schedule to this Act . . ."

S. 2: "(1) Where immunities and privileges are conferred on any persons by an Order in Council made under [section 1 (2)], the Secretary of State—(*a*) shall compile a list of the persons entitled to immunities and privileges conferred under paragraph (*b*) of that subsection, and may compile a list of the persons entitled to immunities and privileges conferred under paragraph (*c*) of that subsection; . . . (2) Every list or notice published under the foregoing subsection shall state the date from which the list or amendment takes or took effect; and the fact that any person is or was included . . . among the persons entitled to the immunities and privileges in question may, if a list of those persons has been so published, be conclusively proved by producing the Gazette containing the list . . . and by showing that the name of that person is or was at that time included or not included in the said list."

[2] Council of Europe Immunities and Privileges) Order, 1960, art. 11: "Except in so far as in any particular case any privilege or immunity is waived by the Secretary-General, all permanent and temporary members of the staff of the council shall enjoy:—(*a*) immunity from legal process in respect of words spoken or written and all acts done by them in their official capacity and within the limits of their authority . . ."

Art. 12 (1): "Except in so far as in any particular case any privilege or immunity is waived by the European Commission of Human Rights, members of the commission shall enjoy:—(*a*) in respect of words spoken or written and all acts done by them in their official capacity, the like immunity from legal process as is accorded to an envoy of a foreign sovereign power accredited to Her Majesty; . . ."

The commission had not waived the first defendant's immunity nor had the Secretary-General of the Council of Europe waived the immunity which the second defendant claimed as a member of the staff of the council. The first defendant's name was at all material times included in the Secretary of State for Foreign Affair's list of persons entitled to the immunities and privileges conferred by section 1 (2) (*b*) of the Act of 1950. The second defendant's employment as a member of the staff of the council and secretary of the commission was proved by a certificate of the Secretary-General of the Council. Master Jacob held that the immunity attached to both defendants and ordered the writ to be set aside. Thompson J. affirmed that decision. On the plaintiff's appeal.

Held, (1) that whether the commission was an "organ" of the council within the meaning of section 1 (2) (*b*) of the Act of 1950 was a question of fact to be resolved by considering the convention and the Statute of Europe; that, on such a consideration, the commission was so related to and bound up with the council that it could properly be described as an "organ" of the council; and that, accordingly, the immunities granted by articles 11 and 12 of the Order in Council of 1960, to which the defendants were prima facie entitled, were intra vires the powers conferred by section 1 (2) (*b*) and (*c*) of the Act of 1950 (post, pp. 682, 683, 687, 690).

(2) That the fact that the first defendant's name still appeared on the Secretary of State's list (although he had ceased to be a member of the commission) was conclusive proof by section 2 (2) of the Act of 1950, that he was entitled to the immunities prescribed by section 1 (2) (*b*) (post, pp. 683, 688, 691); but that, in any event, the first defendant would be entitled to immunity, although no longer a member of the commission, since the immunity under article 12 of the Order in Council of 1960, on the construction of the article, depended on the quality of the words spoken or the acts done and not on the time when the suit was brought, and was the like immunity as was accorded to an envoy while he was an envoy (post, pp. 683, 684): although an envoy when he ceased to be an envoy lost his immunity in respect of acts done in his private capacity he could not be sued in respect of acts performed in his official capacity because that would involve impleading a foreign sovereign (post, pp. 684, 689, 692).

Rahimtoola v. *Nizam of Hyderabad** [1958] A.C. 379; [1957] 3 W.L.R. 884; [1957] 3 All E.R. 441, H.L. applied.

(3) That the compilation of the Secretary of State's list was **[677]** only mandatory in the case of persons (like the first defendant) who came within section 1 (2) (*b*); in the case of others, such as the second defendant, it was permissive and, accordingly, the second defendant was entitled to the immunity conferred on him by article 11 of the Order in Council, although his name did not appear on the list (post, p. 685).

(4) That the commission owed no duty to individual members of the public and therefore even if the plaintiff's complaints were, as he alleged, restricted to omissions, that would not furnish the plaintiff with any cause of action, in the absence of some duty to act owed by the defendants to the plaintiffs (post, p. 685).

Decision of Thompson J. affirmed.

APPEAL from Thompson J.

The plaintiff, Dr. Jur. Carl-Theo Zoernsch, believing himself to be the victim at the hands of the Federal Republic of Germany of a violation of the right to liberty and security of the person as set forth in article 5 of the Convention for the Protection of Human Rights and Fundamental Freedoms, dated November 4, 1950, presented a petition against the Federal Republic of Germany before the European Commission of Human Rights, set up under the convention. The commission rejected the petition by decisions dated May 31 and December 14, 1961. The plaintiff sought to bring an action against the then president of the commission, Sir Claud Humphrey Waldock, the first defendant, and the secretary, A. B. MacNulty, the second defendant, arising out of the rejection of his petition. In the endorsement to his writ he alleged negligence and corruption against both defendants. The first defendant had ceased to be a member of the commission in January, 1962, but the second defendant still retained his office. The defendants entered a conditional appearance and by summons sought to set aside the writ on the ground that the court had no jurisdiction to entertain the claim because of immunity granted by the International Organisations (Immunities and Privileges) Act, 1950, and the Council of Europe (Immunities and Privileges) Order, 1960, made thereunder.

It was proved that the commission had not waived the immunity from legal process which the first defendant claimed, nor had the Secretary-General of the Council of Europe waived the immunity which the second defendant claimed as a member of the staff of the council. The first defendant's name was at all material times included in the list compiled by the Secretary of State under section 2 (1) (*a*) of the Act of 1950, of persons entitled to immunities and privileges conferred by section 1 (2) (*b*) of the Act of 1950. The second defendant's employment as a member of the staff of the council and secretary of the commission was proved by a certificate of the Secretary-General of the council.

By an order dated November 5, 1963, Master Jacob held that immunity attached to both defendants and he ordered that the writ of summons be set aside and the action be dismissed with **[678]** costs. Thompson J., by an order dated November 20, 1963, affirmed that order.

The plaintiff appealed.

The facts and relevant statutory provisions are more fully set out in the judgment of Willmer L.J.

The plaintiff in person.

M. E. Bathurst for the defendants.

Sir John Hobson Q.C., A.-G., and *J. R. Cumming-Bruce* as amici curiae.

The following cases, in addition to those referred to in the judgments, were cited in argument: *Reg.* v. *Wilson*[3]*; *Reg.* v. *Governor of Brixton Prison, Ex parte Caborn-Waterfield*[4]*; *Hogg* v. *Toye & Co.*[5]; *In re Suarez*[6]*; *Engelke* v. *Musmann*[7]*; and *Dickinson* v. *Del Solar.*[8]*

Cur. adv. vult.

March 24. The following judgments were read.

WILLMER L.J. This is an appeal from an order made by Thompson J. on November 20, 1963, affirming an order made by Master Jacob on November 5, 1963, whereby he ordered that the writ of summons be set aside and that the action be dismissed with costs. The first defendant was from 1954 until January 1962 a member and president of the European Commission of Human Rights (hereinafter referred to as "the commission"). The second defendant has been since July 1954 a permanent member of the staff of the Council of Europe (hereinafter referred to as "the council"), and since January 1960 has served as secretary of the commission.

The plaintiff complains that he was a victim of injustice at the hands of the courts of the Federal Republic of Germany, in that he was denied a fair trial in violation of one of the rights set forth in the Convention for the Protection of Human Rights and Fundamental Freedoms, to which the Federal Republic is a party. In pursuance of what he conceived to be his rights under the convention he instituted proceedings before the commission by way of petition against the Federal Republic, but by two decisions, dated respectively May 31 and December 14, 1961, his petition was rejected by the commission. He com-

[3] (1877) 3 Q.B.D. 42, D.C.
[4] [1960] 2 Q.B. 498; [1960] 2 W.L.R. 792; [1960] 2 All E.R. 178, D.C.
[5] [1935] Ch. 497; 51 T.L.R. 301, C.A.
[6] [1918] 1 Ch. 176; 34 T.L.R. 127, C.A.
[7] [1928] A.C. 433; 44 T.L.R. 731, H.L.
[8] [1930] 1 K.B. 376; 45 T.L.R. 637.

plains that the failure of his petition was due to the fact that the second defendant, as secretary, acting on the instructions of the first defendant, failed to present it properly to the commission. **[679]**

In these circumstances the plaintiff on July 15, 1963, issued the writ in the present action indorsed with a claim in the following terms: "The plaintiff's claim is for damage arising from negligence and corruption in running the business as president (1st defendant) and chairman of the secretariat (2nd defendant) of the Commission of Human Rights of the Council of Europe in Strasbourg." The defendants entered a conditional appearance, and applied to set aside the writ as null and void on the ground that the court has no jurisdiction to adjudicate upon the claim indorsed thereon by reason of the immunity from legal process enjoyed by the defendants and each of them.

The defendants' application was based on the provisions of the International Organisations (Immunities and Privileges) Act, 1950, and the Council of Europe (Immunities and Privileges) Order, 1960 (S.I. 1960 No. 442), made thereunder. The material provisions of the Act of 1950 are as follows: section 1: "(1) This section shall apply to any organisation declared by Order in Council to be an organisation of which the United Kingdom or His Majesty's Government therein and one or more foreign sovereign powers or the government or governments thereof are members. (2) His Majesty may by Order in Council—(*a*) provide that any organisation to which this section applies (hereinafter referred to as 'the organisation') shall, to such extent as may be specified in the order, have the immunities and privileges set out in Part I of the Schedule to this Act, and shall also have the legal capacities of a body corporate; (*b*) confer upon—(i) any persons who are representatives (whether of governments or not) on any organ of the organisation or are members of any committee of the organisation or of an organ thereof; (ii) such number of officers of the organisation as may be specified in the order, being the holders of such high offices in the organisation as may be so specified; and (iii) such persons employed on missions on behalf of the organisation as may be so specified; to such extent as may be specified in the order, the immunities and privileges set out in Part II of the Schedule to this Act; (*c*) confer upon such other classes of officers and servants of the organisation as may be specified in the order, to such extent as may be so specified, the immunities and privileges set out in Part III of the Schedule to this Act; and Part IV of the Schedule to this Act shall have effect for the purpose of extending to the staffs of such representatives and members as are mentioned in sub-paragraph (i) of paragraph (*b*) of this subsection and to the families of officers of the organisation any immunities and privileges conferred on the representatives, members or officers under that paragraph, except in so far as the operation of the said Part IV is excluded by the order conferring the immunities and privileges: Provided that the Order in Council shall be so framed as to secure that there are not conferred on any person any immunities or **[680]** privileges greater in extent than those which, at the time of the making of the order, are required to be conferred on that person in order to give effect to any international agreement in that behalf and that no immunity or privilege is conferred upon any person as the representative of His Majesty's Government in the United Kingdom or as a member of the staff of such a representative."

Section 2 (i): "(1) Where immunities and privileges are conferred on any persons by an Order in Council made under subsection (2) of the foregoing section, the Secretary of State—(*a*) shall compile a list of the persons entitled to immunities and privileges conferred under paragraph (*b*) of that subsection, and may compile a list of the persons entitled to immunities and privileges conferred under paragraph (*c*) of that subsection; (*b*) shall cause any list compiled under this subsection to be published in the London, Edinburgh and Belfast Gazettes; and (*c*) whenever any person ceases or begins to be entitled to the immunities and privileges to which any such list relates, shall amend the list and cause a notice of the amendment or, if he thinks fit, an amended list, to be published as aforesaid. (2) Every list or notice published under the foregoing subsection shall state the date from which the list or amendment takes or took effect; and the fact that any person is or was included or not included at any time among the persons entitled to the immunities and privileges in question may, if a list of those persons has been so published, be conclusively proved by producing the Gazette containing the list or, as the case may be, the last list taking effect before that time, together with the Gazetes (if any) containing notices of the amendments taking effect before that time, and by showing that the name of that person is or was at that time included or not included in the said list."

Part II of the Schedule, which provides for "Immunities and privileges of representatives, members of committees, high officers and persons on missions," confers upon them, by paragraph 7: "The like immunity from suit and legal process as is accorded to an envoy of a foreign sovereign power accredited to His Majesty." Part III of the Schedule, which deals with Immunities and privileges of other officers and servants," confers upon them, by paragraph 10: "Immunity from suit and legal process in respect of things done or omitted to be done in the course of the performance of official duties."

Part I of the Order in Council, the Council of Europe (Immunities and Privileges) Order, 1960, provides by article 1: "The Council of Europe (hereinafter referred to as the council) is an organisation of which Her Majesty's Government in the United Kingdom and the Governments of foreign sovereign powers are members." **[681]**

Part II deals with the privileges and immunities of the permanent representatives of the members of the council, representatives of members of the council or the committee of Ministers, and representatives to the consultative assembly. Part III, by article 10, provides for the privileges and immunities of the Secretary-General and the Deputy Secretary-General of the council. Article 11, which deals with other officers of the council, provides: "Except in so far as in any particular case any privilege or immunity is waived by the Secretary-General, all permanent and temporary members of the staff of the council shall enjoy:—(a) Immunity from legal process in respect of words spoken written and acts done by them in their official capacity and within the limits of their authority . . ."

Part IV, which is headed "European Commission of Human Rights," provides by article 12: "(1) Except in so far as in any particular case any privilege or immunity is waived by the European Commission of Human Rights, members of the commission shall enjoy:—(*a*) In respect of words spoken or written and all acts done by them in their official capacity, the like immunity from legal process as is accorded to an envoy of a foreign sovereign power accredited to Her Majesty; . . ."

On behalf of the first defendant it is contended that he is entitled to the immunity prescribed for members of the commission by article 12 of the Order in Council, which is within the powers conferred by section 1 (2) (*b*) and Part II of the Schedule to the Act of 1950. The second defendant claims the immunity prescribed for members of the staff of the council by article 11 of the Order in Council, which is said to be within the powers conferred by section 1 (2) (*c*) and Part III of the Schedule to the Act. It is proved and not denied that the commission has not waived the immunity from legal process which the first defendant claims to enjoy: nor has the Secretary-General of the council waived the immunity which the second defendant claims to enjoy as a member of the staff of the council. It has further been proved, by the production of the relevant copy of the London Gazette, that the first defendant's name is included, and has been included since July, 1958, in the list compiled by the Secretary of State for Foreign Affairs of the persons entitled to immunities and privileges conferred under section 1 (2) (*b*) of the Act. The name of the second defendant, on the other hand, is not included in any such list; but his employment as a member of the staff of the council and as secretary of the commission is proved by a certificate furnished by the Secretary-General of the council.

The plaintiff, who has conducted his case in person, has put forward, in the course of an ingenious and good-tempered argument, a number of points in his attempt to show that the defendants are not entitled to the immunities claimed on their behalf. On the other side we have had a full argument from Mr. Bathurst, who has appeared for both defendants. We have **[682]** also had the advantage of hearing an argument from the Attorney-General, who has attended as amicus curiae and has been of great assistance. Having carefully considered the various arguments presented to us, I have formed the opinion that Master Jacob and the judge came to the right conclusion, and I am satisfied that there is no ground on which we should be justified in interfering. I will endeavour to summarise as briefly as possible the various submissions put forward by the plaintiff and the reasons why I do not feel able to accept them.

(1) It has been contended that the commission is not an "organ" of the council. If this contention were well founded, we should have to hold that article 12 of the Order in Council is ultra vires; for unless the commission is an organ of the council, there would be no power under section 1 (2) (*b*) of the Act to confer, by Order in Council, any immunities or privileges on its members. This would be fatal to the first defendant's claim to immunity, though it would not, I think, affect that of the second defendant, whose claim to immunity rests on article 11 of the Order in Council.

Whether or not the commission is an organ of the council seems to me to be a question of fact, to be resolved by a consideration of the provisions of the convention of November 4, 1950, whereby it was set up. Reliance is placed by the plaintiff on the fact that the convention was made by the signatory governments as such, albeit they were described as being members of the council. It follows that the commission was set up by agreement between the signatory governments, and not by the council. This, it is said, shows that the commission cannot be an organ of the council. I can see no substance in this contention. I do not think that the fact of the commission being imposed on the council by the signatory governments rather than being set up by the council itself is in any way decisive. It may still be an organ of the council even if imposed from without. It is not without significance that the plaintiff himself described the commission in the indorsement of the writ as "the Commission of Human Rights *of* the Council of Europe."

I think it is important to look first at the statute of the Council of Europe, article 1 of which makes it clear that one of the principal aims sought to be achieved was the maintenance and further realisation of human rights and fundamental freedoms. To this aim the members of the council pledged themselves by article 3 of the statute of the Council of Europe. This aim is specifically referred to in the recitals to the convention for the Protection of Human Rights and Fundamental Freedoms. I do not think it is necessary to refer in detail to all the articles of the convention through which the Attorney-General took us in the course of his helpful argument. Suffice it to say that they reveal a very close nexus between the commission and the council. The following articles of the convention seem to me to be of special significance: Article 21, which provides that the members of the **[683]** commission shall be elected by the committee of ministers; articles 24 and 25, which provide that references to the commission, whether by one of the high contracting parties or by an individual, shall be made through the Secretary-General of the council; articles 30 and 31, which provide that reports by the commission or a sub-commission shall be transmitted to the committee of ministers or the Secretary-General of the council; article 35, which provides that meetings of the commission shall be convened by the Secretary-General of the council; article 37, which provides that the secretariat of the commission shall be provided by the Secretary-General of the council; article 58, which provides that the expenses of the commission shall be borne by the council.

These and other provisions of the convention seem to me to show that the commission is so related to, and so bound up with, the council that it cannot properly be described as anything other than an organ of the council.

(2) The plaintiff next submitted that, whatever the immunity to which the first defendant was entitled while he was a member of the commission, it cannot be regarded as having survived after January, 1962, when he ceased to be a member. As to this, I am of opinion that section 2 (2) of the Act of 1950 is conclusive against the plaintiff's submission, having regard to the fact that the first defendant's name still appears in the list published by the Secretary of State of those entitled to the immunities prescribed by section 1 (2) (*b*). I

can see no answer to this point. I confess that it would not be an attractive ground for refusing jurisdiction if it were shown that, apart from it, the first defendant would otherwise have lost the immunity which he enjoyed while a member of the commission. In fairness to the plaintiff, therefore, I think it right to say that quite apart from the provisions of section 2 (2) of the Act I am satisfied that the first defendant would in any case be entitled to the immunity claimed on his behalf. I have reached that conclusion for several reasons.

(a) The immunity claimed is no greater than that authorised by the proviso to section 1 (2) of the Act. In this connection reference should be made to the Second Protocol to the General Agreement on Privileges and Immunities of the Council of Europe signed at Paris on September 2, 1949. This protocol was dated December 15, 1956, and article 3 provides as follows: "In order to secure for the members of the commission complete freedom of speech and complete independence in the discharge of their duties, the immunity from legal process in respect of words spoken or written and all acts done by them in discharging their duties shall continue to be accorded, notwithstanding that the persons concerned are no longer engaged in the discharge of such duties."

(b) The immunity attaches, under article 12 of the Order in Council, "in respect of words spoken or written and all acts done by" the members of the commission "in their official **[684]** capacity." I construe this as meaning that the immunity depends on the quality of the words spoken or the acts done, and not on the time when suit is brought. Once attached, it is not lost by the mere fact of the first defendant ceasing to be a member of the commission.

(c) The immunity conferred is "the like immunity from legal process as is accorded to an envoy of a foreign sovereign power." It is argued by the plaintiff that since an envoy loses his immunity when he ceases to be an envoy, so also a member of the commission loses his immunity when he ceases to be a member. I think that this contention is based on a misconstruction of the words used. The immunity conferred is the like immunity as is accorded to an envoy while he is an envoy. If this is right, the fact of the first defendant having ceased to be a member of the commission is not of any necessary relevance.

(d) While it is true, as has been held in a number of the cases that have been referred to, that an envoy when he ceases to be an envoy loses his immunity in respect of acts done in his private capacity, I do not think that this is by any means the case in relation to acts done by him in his official capacity. In so far as he acts in an official capacity, his acts are the acts of the foreign sovereign whom he represents. I do not accept that an envoy, after he has ceased to be an envoy, can be sued in respect of acts performed in his official capacity. For this would involve impleading the foreign sovereign, in the sense in which "impleading" was defined by Viscount Simon in *Sultan of Johore* v. *Abubakar Tunku Aris Bendahar*,[9]* quoting the words of Brett L.J. in *The Parlement Belge*[10]* as follows: "Either is affected in his interests by the judgment of a court which is bound to give him the means of knowing that it is about to proceed to affect those interests and that it is bound to hear him if he objects. That is, in our opinion, an impleading." That this is so is, I think, clearly shown by the decision of the House of Lords in *Rahimtoola* v. *Nizam of Hyderabad*,[11]* where the appellant, after he had ceased to hold office as High Commissioner for Pakistan, was nevertheless held entitled to immunity in respect of an act done by him in his official capacity during his tenure of office. Viscount Simonds said[12]: "No doubt, if a defendant, by whatever name he is called, can be identified with the Sovereign State, his task is easy: he need prove no more in order to stay the action against him. But, as soon as it is proved that quoad the subject-matter of the action the defendant is the agent of a Sovereign State, that, in other words, the interests or property of the State are to be the subject of adjudication, the same result is reached."

For these reasons, I am unable to accept the view that the **[685]** first defen-

[9] [1952] A.C. 318, 343; [1952] 1 T.L.R. 1106; [1952] 1 All E.R. 1261, P.C.
[10] (1880) 5 P.D. 197, 219, C.A.
[11] [1958] A.C. 379; [1957] 3 W.L.R. 884; [1957] 3 All E.R. 441, H.L.
[12] [1958] A.C. 379, 393-4.

dant, upon ceasing to hold office, lost such immunity as he previously enjoyed.

(3) Whatever may be the position with regard to the first defendant, the plaintiff as against the second defendant relies on the fact that his name is not included in any list compiled by the Secretary of State for Foreign Affairs under section 2 of the Act. As appears from section 2 (1) (*a*), the compilation of such a list is mandatory only in the case of persons falling within section 1 (2) (*b*); in the case of others, such as the second defendant, the compilation of a list is merely permissive. I do not think, therefore, that anything is to be inferred from the fact of the second defendant's name not being included in any such list of names. In fact, it is proved by a certificate from the Secretary-General of the council that the second defendant is a permanent member of the staff of the council, and that he holds the office of secretary of the commission. It is also proved that what he said or did as secretary of the commission he said or did in his official capacity as a permanent member of the staff of the council.

(4) The plaintiff took the further point that his complaint against the two defendants is in respect of omissions rather than positive conduct on their part. He therefore submitted that they are not covered by the immunity conferred by the Order in Council "in respect of words spoken or written and all acts done." There are in my judgment two answers to this submission. (a) The indorsement on the writ does not in fact confine the plaintiff's complaints to omissions on the part of the defendants; on the contrary, it is clear that positive misbehaviour is alleged. (b) An omission on the part of one or other of the defendants would not furnish the plaintiff with any cause of action in the absence of some duty to act owed by the defendants to the plaintiff. No such duty is alleged, nor in my judgment could it be. Article 25 of the convention makes it abundantly clear that no duty is owed by the commission towards an individual member of the public desiring to present a petition.

(5) Lastly, I must not omit to refer to the suggestion put forward by the plaintiff that there is something disreputable in the defendants' claim to immunity from legal process. This, it is said, is all the more so in the case of the present defendants, who by reason of the positions they hold or held might reasonably be expected to be persons dedicated to the protection of human rights and fundamental freedoms. In such circumstances it is submitted that to shelter behind immunity from legal process and refuse to face trial of the charges raised by the plaintiff constitutes conduct that is contra bonos mores. In my judgment this comment on the morality of the course taken by the two defendants is entirely misconceived. It is clear from the terms of both article 11 and article 12 of the Order in Council that the immunities conferred are to apply except in so far as they may be waived in the one case by the Secretary-General of the council, and in the other case by the commission itself. In other words, **[686]** the immunity is not that of the defendants to waive. In the present case it is proved that the Secretary-General has decided not to waive the immunity enjoyed by the second defendant, and that in the case of the first defendant the commission has unanimously resolved that his immunity shall not be waived. In view of the comments made by the plaintiff, it is only fair to the two defendants that this situation should be made abundantly clear.

In all the circumstances, I do not find it possible to say that the plaintiff has shown any good ground for interfering with the order made by Master Jacob and affirmed by the judge. I would accordingly dismiss the appeal.

Danckwerts L.J. This is an action which has been brought by Dr. Jur. Carl-Theo Zoernsch against Sir Claud Humphrey Waldock and A. B. MacNulty. The indorsement on the writ (which is dated July 15, 1963) is as follows: "The plaintiff's claim is for damage arising from negligence and corruption in running the business as president (1st defendant) and chairman of the secretariat (2nd defendant) of the Commission of Human Rights of the Council of Europe in Strasbourg."

It is not necessary to go into the facts further, because it is plain from that endorsement that the plaintiff's claim is against the two defendants for damages in respect of acts done by them in the course of their official duties as holders of the offices mentioned in the writ.

Sir Claud Humphrey Waldock was a member and president of the European Commission from 1954 until January, 1962, when he ceased to hold those positions, but his name still appears on the list of persons entitled to immunities and privileges prepared by Her Majesty's Principal Secretary of State for Foreign Affairs pursuant to the International Organisations (Immunities and Privileges) Act, 1950, as appears from a copy of the London Gazette of August 13, 1963.

A. B. MacNulty was appointed to be a permanent member of the staff of the Council of Europe, and as such he was appointed to be, and still is, the secretary of the European Commission of Human Rights. His position is verified by a certificate of the secretary-general of the Council of Europe.

On November 5, 1963, an order was made by Master Jacob setting aside the writ, and on November 20, 1963, an appeal from that order was dismissed by Thompson J. with costs.

The point on this appeal is whether the two defendants possess immunities which protect them from proceedings in respect of acts done in the course of their official duties, so that this action is not maintainable.

The relevant statute upon which the question must depend is the International Organisations (Immunities and Privileges) Act, 1950, which is a consolidating Act.

[His Lordship read sections 1 and 2 of the Act of 1950 and **[687]** continued:] Section 3 of the Act provides for immunities and privileges for judges and suitors to the International Court of Justice. I only mention this section because it was used in argument, but, in my view, it has no materiality in the present case.

The kind of immunity provided for is contained in the Schedule to the Act, and the relevant provisions are:

"Part II. Immunities and privileges of representatives, members of committees, high officers and persons on missions. 7. The like immunity from suit and legal process as is accorded to an envoy of a foreign sovereign power accredited to His Majesty. 8. The like inviolability of residence as is accorded to such an envoy. 9. The like exemption or relief from taxes as is accorded to such an envoy.

"Part III. Immunities and privileges of other officers and servants. 10. Immunity from suit and legal process in respect of things done or omitted to be done in the course of the performance of official duties."

In pursuance of the provisions of that Act, Orders in Council were made. The relevant order, for the purposes of this case, is the Council of Europe (Immunities and Privileges) Order, 1960 (No. 442 of 1960).

[His Lordship read articles 1, 10, 11, and 12 and continued:] The first question (which affects Sir Claud Humphrey Waldock, but not Mr. MacNulty) is whether the European Commission of Human Rights is an "organ" of the organisation known as the Council of Europe. I have no doubt whatever that it is. An organ has been defined in dictionaries as a body of persons by which some purpose is carried out or functions performed. The relations between the Council of Europe and the European Commission of Human Rights, as shown by the documents before us, make it clear that the latter body carries on certain purposes and functions of the Council of Europe for which the commission was formed. Sir Claud Humphrey Waldock is, therefore, a member of such an organ and was and is entitled to the immunities and privileges which are relevant to his position. MacNulty comes under different provisions and was and is entitled to the immunities and privileges which are relevant to his position as set out in the statute and the Order in Council.

The real question to which most of the arguments were directed was the nature of the immunities so conferred.

In the case of the members of the commission, the immunity conferred is in respect of words spoken or written and all acts done by them in their official capacity, the like immunity from legal process "as is accorded to an envoy of a foreign sovereign power accredited to Her Majesty." In the case of all permanent and temporary members of the staff of the council, the immunity is expressed in somewhat different terms: "Immunity from legal process in respect of words spoken or written and all **[688]** acts done by them in their official capacity and within the limits of their authority."

The principal argument for the appellant was that as Sir Claud Humphrey Waldock had ceased to hold office since January, 1962, he no longer enjoyed any immunity from legal proceedings, because the immunity of an envoy only operates during the period for which he enjoys that office and such reasonable time after his recall as will enable him to make the necessary arrangements for his departure: see Halsbury's Laws of England, 3rd ed. (1954), p. 270, paragraph 574, and cases there referred to.

A short answer which would be fatal to the writ in the present action as regards Sir Claud Humphrey Waldock, is that as long as his name remains on the list prepared by the Secretary of State that is conclusive that his immunity is still in operation by virtue of the provisions of section 2 (2) of the Act of 1950. But that might only be temporary protection.

If the immunity of either of the defendants comes to an end after they leave office in respect of acts done in the course of their official duties, the protection would be frail and unsatisfactory, and it might well be difficult to get persons to serve in such circumstances.

We have had the advantage of an argument by the Attorney-General as amicus curiae. Mr. Bathurst delivered to us a careful and elaborate argument to show that the conventions and other documents indicate an intention to require a more complete protection than such temporary immunity as had been suggested as being appropriate. He contended that the statutes and orders made in this country must accordingly be interpreted in the light of those requirements, and that Parliament must be taken to have fulfilled the obligations which were expected of them and which they must have had in mind. I can see difficulties in this line of approach. But I do not propose to express any opinion upon this aspect of the case, because, in my view, there is a much more satisfactory basis for the defendants' claim to immunity (which indeed was Mr. Bathurst's alternative argument).

The cases relied on by the appellant and cited as authority for the termination of an envoy's immunity after vacating office, are all cases concerned with the private debts and obligations of ambassadors and the like, which they have incurred for their own private purpose, while holding office, but were not incurred for the purpose of or in the course of their official duties. In the case of acts done in the course of their official duties, no legal proceedings can be taken against envoys, even after they have ceased to hold office. The reason for this situation is that the envoy is the representative of the foreign sovereign whom he represents, and so it is the immunity of the sovereign which is involved, and not that of the envoy as a private person.

Support for this principle is to be found in the House of **[689]** Lords' decision in *Rahimtoola* v. *Nizam of Hyderabad.*[13]* The immunity of a sovereign state from legal proceedings has long been recognised as a principle of international law. For this reason, neither of the defendants is amenable to the legal proceedings of this court. They are protected in respect of acts done by them in the course of their official duties and will continue to be so protected by an indemnity similar to that enjoyed by an envoy in respect of acts done by him in the course of his official duties.

Consequently the present action is not maintainable. The appeal cannot succeed and must be dismissed.

DIPLOCK L.J. The question before us is as to the writ issued by the plaintiff on July 15, 1963, against Sir Humphrey Waldock and Mr. MacNulty claiming relief "for damage arising from negligence and corruption in running the business as president (1st defendant) and chairman of the secretariat (2nd defendant) of the Commission of Human Rights of the Council of Europe." Although the plaintiff has referred freely to a document which he described as a statement

[13] [1958] A.C. 379.

of claim, the real issue is whether the court would have jurisdiction to grant to the plaintiff the relief sought by the endorsement on his writ, whatever the facts were on which he relied in support of his claim to that relief. For this reason the plaintiff, who has appeared in person, has been given the opportunity, of which he has taken full advantage, of telling the court just what it is he would seek to prove if his action were allowed to proceed irrespective of whether such allegations are contained in the statement of claim.

As appears from the indorsement on the writ, the duty which the plaintiff alleges was owed to him by the defendants, and of which he alleges they were in breach, is alleged to be owed to him by them in their official capacities as President and Chairman of the Secretariat respectively, of the Commission of Human Rights, and not otherwise. Indeed, if I understand him correctly, his real complaint is that Mr. MacNulty as Secretary of the Commission of Human Rights refused to present to the commission the plaintiff's claim against the Government of the German Federal Republic in the terms in which the plaintiff had drafted it, but presented instead a bowdlerised or edited version. The plaintiff's claim against Sir Humphrey Waldock appears to be that as president of the commission he is vicariously liable for the acts or omissions of Mr. MacNulty.

So far as Mr. MacNulty is concerned, once it is established that he is a member of the staff of the Council of Europe and that he was a member of the secretariat of the commission provided by the Secretary-General of the Council of Europe pursuant to article 37 of the Convention for the Protection of Human Rights and Fundamental Freedoms, the plaintiff's case against **[690]** him seems to me to be unarguable. The immunity from legal process conferred upon him by paragraph 11 of the Order in Council of 1960 is clearly intra vires the powers conferred by section 1 (2) (*c*) and paragraph 10 of the Schedule to the Act of 1950 and the proviso to section 1 (2), since it does not exceed the privileges agreed to be conferred on officers of the council by article 18 (*a*) of the General Agreement on Privileges and Immunities of the Council of Europe. Mr. MacNulty's immunity is in my view independent of whether or not the commission is an "organ" of the Council of Europe, for he was acting as secretary of the commission in his capacity as an officer of the Council of Europe provided by the Secretary-General of the Council of Europe to perform such secretarial duties and was thus acting in his official capacity.

So far as Sir Humphrey Waldock is concerned, there are two points which seem to me to merit consideration. The first is whether the commission is an organ of the Council of Europe: for it is conceded that if it is not, paragraph 12 of the Order in Council, on which Sir Humphrey Waldock relies for his immunity is ultra vires. The second is whether Sir Humphrey Waldock's immunity for acts done in his official capacity continues after he has ceased to be a member of the commission.

As regards the first question, I have little to add to the judgments which have already been delivered. In the context in which the expression is used in the Act of 1950 it is plain that "organ" means a body of persons; and "organ" of an "organisation" means, in my view, a body of persons whose function is to do acts for the purpose of carrying out the aims or objects of the organisation. The only argument against the commission being an organ of the Council of Europe is that it was constituted by a separate agreement providing for common action in the maintenance and further realisation of human rights and fundamental freedoms. But this is a method of achieving the aim of the Council of Europe which is expressly contemplated by article 1 of the Statute of the Council of Europe. The achievement of this aim of the Council of Europe is expressed to be the purpose of the Convention for the Protection of Human Rights and Fundamental Freedoms, by which the commission was established, and participation in the convention is limited to members of the Council of Europe. The members of the commission are elected not by the signatories of the convention, but by the Committee of Ministers of the Council of Europe. They report not to the signatories of the convention but to the Committee of Ministers who prescribe the action to be taken unless the question is referred to the court. The expenses of the commission are borne by the Council of Europe and its secretariat provided by the Council of Europe. I am clearly of opinion that the commission is an "organ" of the Council of Europe in the sense in which that expression is used in the Act of 1950. **[691]**

The second question is in my view concluded by section 2 (2) of the Act to which my Lords have referred. But I should be reluctant to decide the appeal on this ground if I were of opinion that the Secretary of State had wrongly retained the name of Sir Humphrey Waldock on the list of persons entitled to privileges after he had ceased to be entitled to them; for, it is the statutory duty of the Secretary of State under section 2 (1) (*c*) to amend the list when any person ceases to be entitled to the immunities and privileges to which the list relates, and that duty he could, in my view, by appropriate proceedings be compelled to perform. But I agree with my Lords that Sir Humphrey Waldock continues to be entitled to the immunity conferred upon him by paragraph 12 of the Order in Council of 1960, notwithstanding that he has ceased to be a member of the commission.

The acts done by Sir Humphrey Waldock in respect of which the plaintiff claims relief by his writ clearly fall within the terms of article 12 of the Order in Council of 1960 in their ordinary meaning. The plaintiff's contention, however, is (1) that section 1 (2) (*b*) and paragraph 7 of the Schedule to the Act of 1950 only authorised the conferment on Sir Humphrey Waldock of "the like immunity from suit and legal process as is accorded to an envoy of a foreign sovereign power accredited to Her Majesty"; (2) that the immunity from suit and legal process accorded to a foreign envoy ceases upon his ceasing to be accredited to Her Majesty; and (3) that if and so far as upon its true construction the Order in Council of 1960 purports to confer upon Sir Humphrey Waldock any immunity which continues after he ceased to be a member of the commission, it is ultra vires.

The fallacy in this argument lies in its failure to distinguish between the immunity from suit and legal process enjoyed by a foreign envoy in respect of acts done in his private capacity and the immunity enjoyed by him in respect of acts done in his official capacity on behalf of his government. This distinction has recently received statutory recognition in the Diplomatic Immunities Restriction Act, 1955, where the former type of immunity is referred to as "personal immunities."

Mr. Bathurst has addressed to us a helpful and erudite argument as to the international law on this topic, which he contends, I think correctly, forms part of the law of England administered by the courts. But if the matter required any fine distinctions or detailed examination of English authorities or of sources of international law, I myself should not have thought it appropriate to dispose of it under the summary procedure for setting aside a writ. For my part, however, I think the point is a simple one depending upon elementary well-recognised principles.

The immunity of an envoy from suit or legal process arises from the duties owed by states to one another in international law. In respect of acts done by an envoy in his private capacity the purpose of his immunity from suit or legal process is so that **[692]** he may perform his duties to his government without harassment while "en poste." The immunity is from legal process, not from liability, and its purpose is fulfilled when he has ceased to be "en poste" and has had a reasonable time to wind up his affairs in the country to which he is accredited. The English cases show that in English law an envoy's immunity from suit and legal process in respect of acts done in his private capacity only endures so long as he is "en poste" and for a sufficient time thereafter to enable him to wind up his affairs: *Magdalena Steam Navigation Co.* v. *Martin*[14]*; *Musurus Bey* v. *Gadban*.[15]* But quite different considerations apply to acts done by him in his official capacity. Such acts are done on behalf of his government. His government being a foreign sovereign government, under principles of English law which are so well known that I refrain from citing authority, is immune from the jurisdiction of the English courts. The propriety of its acts

[14] (1859) 2 E. & E. 494.
[15] [1894] 2 Q.B. 352; 10 T.L.R. 493, C.A.

cannot be examined in a municipal court unless it consents to waive its immunity. A foreign sovereign government, apart from personal sovereigns, can only act through agents, and the immunity to which it is entitled in respect of its acts would be illusory unless it extended also to its agents in respect of acts done by them on its behalf. To sue an envoy in respect of acts done in his official capacity would be, in effect, to sue his government irrespective of whether the envoy had ceased to be "en poste" at the date of the suit.

Even if there were no previous authority upon the subject, I should have no hesitation in holding that an envoy's immunity from suit and legal process in respect of acts done in his official capacity was permanent, unless waived by his government, and did not cease with his ceasing to be "en poste." But I think that there is already authority for this proposition in *Rahimtoola* v. *Nizam of Hyderabad*.[16]* The claim there was made against the former High Commissioner for Pakistan personally for money had and received. He succeeded in showing that he had received the money in England in his official capacity as High Commissioner. In these circumstances it was held, in accordance with the principles which I have stated, that an English court had no jurisdiction to entertain the claim.

Applying these principles to the present case the Order in Council of 1960 does not purport to confer upon Sir Humphrey Waldock any immunity in respect of acts done in his private capacity. It confers immunity from suit and legal process in respect of acts done in his official capacity as a member of the commission. This, under the proviso to section 1 (2) of the Act of 1950 was all that could be conferred, since it was the extent of the relevant immunity agreed to be granted to members of the commission under article 1 (*a*) to the Second Protocol to the **[693]** General Agreement on Privileges and Immunities of the Council of Europe. The Order in Council confers immunity from suit and legal process in respect of acts done by members of the commission without any limit to the duration of the immunity and it would indeed have been a breach of article 3 of the second protocol if the Order in Council had not done so too. In my view the Secretary of State was right in retaining Sir Humphrey Waldock's name on the list of persons entitled under section 2 (1) of the Act of 1950 to immunities notwithstanding that he had ceased to be a member of the commission.

That being so, this appeal fails as against Sir Humphrey Waldock also.

Appeal dismissed with costs.
Leave to appeal to the House of Lords refused.

Solicitors: *Herbert & Gowers & Co.; Treasury Solicitor.*

[16] [1958] A.C. 379.

6

TREATIES

3

OPERATION AND IMPLEMENTATION OF TREATIES

IN THE MATTER OF AN APPLICATION OF GEAROID O' LAIGHLÉIS AND IN THE MATTER OF THE CONSTITUTION AND IN THE MATTER OF THE COURTS OF JUSTICE ACTS

([1960] I.R. 93)

Republic of Ireland—

October 8, 9, 10, 11, 1957: High Court, Davitt P., Dixon, Teevan JJ.

October 21, 22, 23, 24, 25, 28, 29, 30, November 6, December 3, 1957: Supreme Court: Maguire C.J., Lavery, Kingsmill Moore, O'Daly, Maguire JJ.

Constitution—Arrest—Detention of person under Minister's warrant—Validity —Person suspected of illegal and subversive activities—Ground for detention—Appointment of commission by Government to inquire into the continuation of the detention—Powers of commission—Procedure of commission—Evidence—Information furnished to commission by Government—Information not disclosed at any time to detained person or his advisors—Documents marked "Secret and confidential"—Commission sitting in camera—Convention of Human Rights—Applicability of Convention within the State—Supremacy of Constitution—The Constitution of Ireland, Articles 15, 28, 29, 34, 40—*Offences Against the State Act,* 1939 (*No.* 13 *of* 1939), *ss.* 30, 35—*Offences Against the State* (*Amendment*) *Act,* 1940 (*No.* 2 *of* 1940), *ss.* 4, 8.

The applicant was arrested on the 11th July, 1957, in pursuance of a warrant issued under s. 30 of the Offences Against the State Act, 1939, and taken to, and detained in, the Bridewell. The said section authorised the detention for twenty-four hours of a person arrested under its provisions, but provided that he could be detained for a further twenty-four hours if an officer of the Gárda Síochána not below the rank of Chief Superintendent so directed. On the 12th July, 1957, a Chief Superintendent directed the applicant's detention for a further period of twenty-four hours expiring at 7.45 p.m. on the 13th July, 1957. Early on the morning of the 13th July, 1957, the applicant was taken to Mountjoy Prison, outside which a lorry was waiting and into which he was transferred and driven to the Military Detention Barracks at the Curragh, Co. Kildare. At about 11.00 a.m. he was handed the warrant of the Minister for Justice, dated the 12th July, 1957, made under s. 4 of the Offences Against the State (Amendment) Act, 1940, and in the warrant the Minister gave his opinion that the applicant was engaged in activities which, in his opinion, were prejudicial to the security of the State and ordered the arrest and detention of the applicant under s. 4 of the Act of 1940. The applicant, at the same time, was also given a copy of s. 8 of the Act of 1940, which informed him of his right to have the continuation of his detention inquired into by a commission appointed by the Government. The applicant, by his solicitor, on the 8th September, 1957, applied in writing to the Secretary to the Government to have his detention inquired into by the commission. The commission sat on the 17th September, 1957, and ruled that they had a discretion whether to sit *in camera* or in public and that they were not satisfied that they had power to take evidence on oath. They ruled that the proceedings should be held *in camera*. The commission further ruled that they were not bound by the rules of evidence; that they were not a judicial body; that they would not divest themselves of a file of papers marked "Secret and confidential" furnished to them and would, in all probability, read the file; that the commission reserved the right to receive evidence and documents without disclosing such evidence or the contents of such documents to the applicant or his legal advisers, and, also, to act on evidence which was undisclosed to the applicant or his legal advisers.

The commission stated that there was no covering letter to explain the origin of the file marked "Secret and confidential"; that the file contained, *inter alia*, carbon copies of certain documents, the originals of which were not attached; unsigned and anonymous reports from unspecified persons or undefined bodies, and at least one report or letter from the "Special Branch" of the Gárda Síochána, Dublin Castle, which was unsigned.

The applicant obtained in the High Court a conditional order of *habeas corpus* on the 18th September, 1957. On the 30th September, 1957, he served a notice of motion to have the said conditional order made absolute **[94]** notwithstanding cause shown, in which he contended, *inter alia*, that his detention was unlawful as it contravened the provisions of the Convention for the Protection of Human Rights and Fundamental Freedoms, to which the State was a party, and by which the State, it was claimed, was bound.

Held by the Supreme Court (Maguire C.J., Lavery, Kingsmill Moore, O'Daly and Maguire JJ.) affirming the High Court:—

1. The Convention of Human Rights and Fundamental Freedoms was not part of the domestic law of the State and, under Article 29 of the Constitution, it could not be so.

2. The Court could not accept that the primacy of domestic legislation was displaced by the State becoming a party to the Convention for the Protection of Human Rights and Fundamental Freedoms, nor was the executive in the domestic forum in any way estopped from relying on the domestic law.

3. Sect. 3 of the Offences Against the State (Amendment) Act, 1940, clearly authorised the making of a proclamation if and when the Government considered such a course necessary, and the proclamation made by the Government was, therefore, in accordance with law.

4. The applicant was not entitled to be released from custody after the expiration of the forty-eight hours authorised by s. 30 of the Offences Against the State Act, 1939, as before that forty-eight hours had expired he was lawfully detained in pursuance of the Minister's warrant under s. 4 of the Offences Against the State (Amendment) Act, 1940.

Accordingly, the applicant's appeal failed; the cause shown was allowed and the conditional order of *habeas corpus* was discharged.

MOTION ON NOTICE.

On the 11th July, 1957, the applicant Gearóid O' Laighléis, was arrested at Dun Laoghaire as he was boarding the mail boat about 8.00 p.m. to travel to England. He alleged that he was so travelling to England to obtain employment. Having obtained in the High Court a conditional order of *habeas corpus*, he moved the Court to have the said conditional order made absolute. In his affidavit in support of the motion he stated that he was taken to the Bridewell and lodged in a cell there; that after about one and a half hours he was interviewed in the cell by a number of Gárdaí officers; that on the following day, the 12th July, 1957, he was visited in the cell by a member of the Gárdaí shortly after 5.00 p.m., and that the Gárda read from a paper informing him that he would be detained in custody for a further period of twenty-four hours under the provisions of s. 30 of the Offences Against the State Act, 1939; that on the following day, the 13th July, 1957, he was taken, first, to Mountjoy Prison and thence by lorry to the Military Detention Barracks at the Curragh Camp, Co. Kildare, and that about 11.00 a.m. on that day he was handed a copy of a warrant signed by the Minister for Justice in which the Minister ordered his arrest and detention by virtue of the powers conferred upon him by s. 4 of the Offences Against the State (Amendment) Act, 1940, and that the warrant was dated the 12th July, 1957; that on the 17th July, **[95]** 1957, he was transferred to the Curragh Internment Camp. The applicant stated further that he was not, at the time of his arrest, engaged in any illegal activities nor was he a member of any illegal organisation.

Certain of the matters set out above were not accepted as accurate by the respondent, Commandant Carl O'Sullivan, the Officer Commanding the Curragh Internment Camp. On the hearing of the application to make absolute the said conditional order it was stated on behalf of the respondent that at the time the applicant was arrested one of the detective officers making the arrest informed the applicant that he was detaining him pursuant to the provisions of s. 30 of the Offences Against the State Act, 1939, on the grounds that he, the detective officer, believed him to be a member of an illegal organisation. The Minister's warrant was in the following terms:—

"OFFENCES AGAINST THE STATE (AMENDMENT) ACT, 1940.

"Section 4.

"In exercise of the powers conferred on me by section 4 of the Offences Against the State (Amendment) Act, 1940 (No. 2 of 1940) I, Oscar Traynor, Minister of Justice being of opinion that Gearóid Richard Lawless, of No. 2 Larkin Flats, Ballybough, Dublin, is engaged in activities which, in my opinion, are prejudicial to the security of the State, do by this warrant order the arrest and detention of the said Gearóid Richard Lawless under the said section 4.

"Given under my Official Seal this 12th day of July, 1957.

"OSCAR TRAYNOR,
"Minister for Justice."

On the 8th September, 1957, the applicant wrote to the Secretary of the Government applying to the Government under s. 8 of the Act of 1940 to have his detention considered by the commission set up by the Government under s. 8 of the Act. He also asked that on such hearing he should be represented by his solicitor and by such counsel as his solicitor might instruct in the matter.

Applications made by the applicant's solicitor to the Government for a summary of the evidence which they proposed to adduce at the hearing before the commission were refused.

The commission sat on the 17th September, 1957, in the Courts Martial Room, Connolly Barracks, Curragh Camp. The applicant was represented by solicitor and by senior and **[96]** junior counsel, as was also the Attorney General. At the hearing, His Honour Judge O'Briain stated on behalf of the commission that it had no chairman and no president and that the members of the commission were in doubt as to (*a*) their power to administer an oath, and (*b*) their right to sit *in camera*.

Counsel on both sides then addressed the commission on these points and, following an adjournment, the commission announced that they had come to the conclusion that they had discretion to sit in public or *in camera* or partly in public and partly *in camera* as they thought fit. Following further argument and another adjournment the commission announced that they were not satisfied that they had power to administer an oath. The commission then ruled that the remainder of the proceedings should be held *in camera*. His Honour Judge O'Briain then announced that the commission were unanimously of the opinion that the obligation to furnish evidence to the commission rested in the first instance on the Minister for Justice under the provisions of s. 8, sub-s. 3 of the Offences Against the State (Amendment) Act, 1940. He further stated that the registrar of the commission had requested the Minister for Justice by letter to furnish the information and documents relevant to the application under s. 8 sub-s. 3 (*c*), aforesaid and that the commission had received no reply in writing to that request, but had received on the morning on the 17th September, 1957, a file marked "Secret and confidential" which contained, *inter alia*, the following documents:—(*a*) carbon copies of certain documents, the originals of which were not attached; (*b*) unsigned and anonymous reports from unspecified persons or undefined bodies; (*c*) at least one report or letter purporting to emanate from the "Special Branch" of the Garda Siochána, Dublin Castle, which was unsigned.

After further legal argument, the commission adjourned to the 20th September, 1957.

On the 18th September, 1957, application was made to the High Court (Teevan J.) for a conditional order of *habeas corpus* directed to Commandant Carl O'Sullivan, to have before the Court the body of Gearóid O'Laighléis. Mr. Justice Teevan granted the order and directed that it be served on Commandant Carl O'Sullivan and on the registrar of the commission.

Affidavits by way of cause shown were filed on the 24th September, 1957, and the prosecutor then moved, by notice of motion dated the 30th September, 1957, to make absolute the conditional order notwithstanding the cause shown. **[97]**

Seán MacBride, Senior Counsel, T. J. Conolly, Senior Counsel and *S. Sorohan* for the applicant.

Brian Walsh, Senior Counsel, and *A. Hederman* for Commandant Carl O'Sullivan and the Attorney General.

The arguments were similar to those in the Supreme Court, reported *post.*

The judgment of the Court was read by Davitt P.

Cur. adv. vult.

Davitt P.

Gearóid O'Laighléis, who describes himself as a builder's labourer by occupation, and resides at 2, Teach Lorcain, North Strand, Dublin, makes this application for an order of *habeas corpus* on the ground that he is being unlawfully detained in custody in the Curragh Internment Camp by Commandant Carl O'Sullivan, the officer commanding the camp. We shall refer to him as the applicant.

Commandant O'Sullivan seeks to justify the detention of the applicant, relying on a warrant under the hand and seal of the Minister for Justice ordering the applicant's arrest and detention, and issued in exercise of the powers conferred upon him by s. 4, sub-s. 1, of the Offences Against the State (Amendment) Act, 1940. We shall refer to him as the respondent.

The essential facts of the matter are, in brief outline, as follows:

On the evening of the 11th July last the applicant was arrested as he was about to board the Holyhead boat at Dun Laoghaire. The arrest was effected by Detective Officer Daniel Connor of the Gárda Síochána who acted in pursuance of the powers conferred by s. 30 of the Offences Against the State Act, 1939. He was conveyed in custody by car to the Bridewell Gárda Station where he was handed over to Sergeant Clifford, who was then the acting station sergeant and responsible for the safe custody of all prisoners detained there. Sergeant Clifford received him into custody as a person arrested under the provisions of s. 30 of the Act and detained him at the Bridewell overnight and the following day.

On the 12th July, Chief Superintendent Michael Farrell of the Gárda Síochána directed that the applicant be detained in custody for a further period of twenty-four hours expiring at 7.45 p.m. on the 13th July. This direction was given in exercise of the power conferred by s. 30, sub-s. 3, of the Act of 1939. On the same day the Minister for Justice in exercise of his powers under s. 4, sub-s. 1, of the Act of 1940 issued his warrant ordering the arrest and detention of the applicant **[98]** under the said section. The warrant was duly conveyed for execution to Inspector McMahon.

The applicant was detained in custody at the Bridewell until the early morning of the 13th July. On that morning Detective Sergeant Connolly, acting on Inspector McMahon's instructions, received the custody of the applicant from the sergeant in charge of the Bridewell and conveyed him by car to the entrance to Mountjoy Prison. A number of other persons, whose detention had also been ordered by the Minister for Justice, were there awaiting transfer to the Curragh Internment Camp; and the applicant was placed along with them in a lorry and driven to the Curragh escorted by Inspector McMahon. On arrival he was delivered into the custody of Commandant O'Leary, the officer in charge of the military detention barracks to whom the Minister's warrant was handed by Inspector McMahon. In accordance with the provisions of s. 4, sub-s. 3, of the Act of 1940 the applicant was furnished with a copy. He was kept in the detention barracks for a few days, and on the 17th July was delivered into the custody of the respondent, Commandant O'Sullivan, to whom the Minister's warrant was duly delivered. He has been detained in the Curragh Internment Camp since that date.

On the 8th September the applicant wrote to the Secretary to the Government applying to have the matter of his detention considered by the commission set up by the Government under the provisions of s. 8 of the Act of 1940. The matter was, presumably, referred to the commission by the Government in accordance with the section, and on the 17th September the commission sat to consider the matter. The applicant was represented by solicitor and counsel. The Minister for Justice was not represented, but the Attorney General appeared by counsel instructed by the Chief State Solicitor. After hearing counsel upon the points involved the commission ruled on certain preliminary matters. They ruled that the onus lay upon the Minister to show that the continued detention of the applicant was justified; that they had no power to administer an oath; that they could sit in public or in private as they thought fit; and that they could, in their discretion, consider without necessarily making full disclosure of the same to the applicant, certain information supplied to them by the Minister in accordance with the provisions of s. 8 of the Act; such, for instance, as the contents of a secret and confidential file. Having ruled upon these matters the commission adjourned until the 20th September.

On the 18th September the applicant obtained from this **[99]** Court a conditional order of *habeas corpus ad subjicendum* directed to the respondent. One of the grounds upon which the order was sought was that Part II of the Act of 1940 was not legally in force. When the commission sat again on the 20th September it would seem that they took the view that, if Part II was not in force, they had no legal right to function or power to act; and that, pending the determination of this issue by this Court, they should not proceed further with the inquiry into the matter of the applicant's detention.

Affidavits have been filed on behalf of the respondent showing cause why the conditional order should not be made absolute, and the applicant now moves to have it made absolute notwithstanding the cause shown.

Several grounds were advanced on behalf of the applicant on any or all of which, it was contended, his continued detenton is unlawful and he should be set at liberty. It is convenient to deal with these contentions in the order in which they were made, while bearing in mind and accepting that, as stated by counsel for the applicant, they were not necessarily advanced in the order of their importance.

The first ground is that Part II of the Offences Against the State (Amendment) Act, 1940, under the provisions of which the Minister's warrant was issued and the applicant's detention is sought to be justified, is not legally in force.

Sect. 3, which is the first section of Part II, provides, in sub-s. 1, that Part II shall not come into or be in force save as and when and for so long as is provided in the other sub-sections of the section. Sub-sect. 2 provides as follows:—

"If and when and so often as the Government makes and publishes a proclamation declaring that the powers conferred by this Part of this Act are necessary to secure the preservation of public peace and order and that it is expedient that this Part of this Act should come into force immediately, this Part of this Act shall come into force forthwith."

A proclamation in the terms of this sub-section was made by the Government on the 5th July last, and published in *Iris Oifigiúil* on the 8th July. It was pointed out by counsel for the applicant that, while sub-s. 2 prescribes the effect which such a proclamation is to have, neither in that sub-section nor anywhere else in the Act is there any provision which empowers the Government to make such a proclamation. It was argued that the Act gave the Government no express power to make the proclamation, that no such power could be implied, and that therefore the Government **[100]** had no such power. Both the Act of 1939 and the Act of 1940 are to be read together; and Part II of the later enactment replaces with some few, but significant, alterations, Part VI of the earlier one which has been held to be unconstitutional. Sect. 3, sub-s. 2, of the Act of 1940 was contrasted with s. 35, sub-s. 2, of the Act of 1939 which does provide expressly that the Government may make the proclamation necessary to bring Part V of that Act into force.

We are of opinion that this first ground is not a good ground. In the first place it seems to us that while s. 35, sub-s. 2, does contain this express enabling provision it does not follow that such a provision is or was necessary in that or any other case. A proclamation is merely a method of making a public and official announcement and its legal effect or consequence, if any, is merely what the existing law gives to it. Authority is not required from the Legislature to do an act which is already perfectly lawful and in no way prohibited; and the Government requires no statutory authority or power, express or implied, to enable them to issue the necessary proclamation. In the second place it seems to us that if statutory authority is necessary it can be, and is, implied in the provisions of s. 3, sub-s. 2. To hold otherwise would be to make nonsense of the enactment. The Legislature clearly contemplated that in certain circumstances the Government would require certain special powers, and provided that, by issuing a certain proclamation, they could acquire those powers. No one reading the section can, it seems to us, be in any doubt that the Legislature intended them to have power to make the necessary proclamation, and by implication to give them the power to do so if such were necessary. In our opinion this first ground has not been made good.

The second ground was not pressed in argument and may be dealt with briefly. As has been mentioned, s. 3, which is contained in Part II of the Act, provides in sub-s. 1, that Part II is not to come into force until the Government make the necessary proclamation; while sub-s. 2 provides that when they do make the proclamation Part II shall come into force. It was pointed out that on a strictly literal construction of these provisions Part II of the Act could never come into force, since the provision which gives to the proclamation the effect of bringing it into force is itself contained in Part II. Until, therefore, Part II is in force there is no way of bringing it into force. This constructon would, of course, make nonsense of the enactment. The absurdity does not, however, end there. The prohibition **[101]** against Part II coming into force (until the proclamation is made) is itself contained in Part II, so that it cannot operate until Part II is already in force; in other words it cannot operate at all. This somewhat metaphysical approach to the interpretation of the section would defeat and stultify the clear intention of the legislature not only in the present instance but also in the case of the numerous statutes which have depended for their coming into operation or effect on the making of an order or proclamation. It involves no straining of the principles of interpretation of statutes to hold that s. 3 is, and was always, in operation and operable as the machinery for bringing into force the other, substantive, provisions of Part II.

The next two grounds are concerned with the *Convention for the Protection of Human Rights and Fundamental Freedoms* and may be considered together. This Convention was adopted by thirteen European states, including our own, at Rome on the 4th November, 1950. It is stated to have come into force on the 3rd September, 1953, by which date, presumably, the ten instruments of ratification contemplated by Article 66 of the Convention as necessary to bring it into force had been deposited with the Secretary-General of the Council of Europe. The Irish instrument of ratification was deposited on the 25th February, 1953. Printed Stationery Office copies, containing some typescript additions pasted in, of the version of the Convention in the English language were put in evidence without objection to their admissibility or authenticity.

The Convention is in form an agreement by the High Contracting Parties with one another. Article 1 provides that they shall secure to everyone within their jurisdiction the rights and freedoms defined in Section I. Section II provides for the setting up of a European Commission of Human Rights to ensure the observance of the engagements of the parties to the Convention. Provision is made for the reception by the Commission of a complaint by one of the parties as to an alleged breach of the Convention by another party, and also for the reception of a petition from any individual claiming to be the victim of a violation by one of the parties of the rights set forth in the Convention. Provision is also made for the inquiry by the Commission into such complaints and petitions; and, in the event of failure to reach a solution, for reference of the matter to the European Court of Human Rights to be set up under Section IV of the Convention. Article 50 provides that if the Court finds that a decision or measure taken by a legal authority, or any other authority, of one of the parties is **[102]** completely or partially in conflict with the obligations arising from the Convention, and if the internal law of the said party allows only partial reparation to be made for the consequences of the decision or measure, the decision of the Court shall, if necessary, afford just satisfaction to the injured party. Article 15 provides that in time of war or other public emergency threatening the life of the nation any party may take measures derogating from its obligations under the Convention to the extent strictly required by the exigencies of the situation, provided that such measures are not inconsistent with its other obligations under international law. It also provides that any party availing itself of this right of derogation shall keep the Secretary-General of the Council of Europe fully informed of the measures taken and the reasons therefor.

The third and fourth grounds relied on by counsel for the applicant, taken together, may be summarised as follows. This Convention is an effective agreement and statement of international law; and any Court construing any enactment, including Part II of the Act of 1940, should do so in such a way as to avoid any conflict with the principles of international law including the provisions of the Convention. If the enactment cannot be so construed then, since the State has become a party to the Convention, the Government, or any person acting under its authority, should not be permitted to rely upon the enactment.

Counsel for the applicant submitted that the rights and freedoms defined in Section I of the Convention, so far as they deal with the liberty of the person, do not sanction preventive detention or allow it as a legitimate modification of the right to liberty; and that, to that extent, there is, *prima facie*, a conflict between the Convention and Part II of the Act of 1940. It was submitted, however, that it was possible to construe Part II in such a way as to avoid this conflict.

We accept the principle, as enunciated by Maxwell, that "every statute is to be so interpreted and applied, as far as its language admits, as not to be inconsistent with the comity of nations, or with the established rules of international law." It seems to us, however, that, accepting the submission that the Convention does not sanction preventive detention, the language of Part II of the Act of 1940 does not admit of an interpretation that would prevent a conflict with its provisions, and that the matter must be dealt with on the basis that such a conflict does exist. We should, at the same time, make it clear that we have not heard counsel for the respondent on the question whether **[103]** such conflict does exist, or whether the statute and the Convention are irreconcilable.

Counsel for the applicant expressly stated that he was not contending that the Convention had become part of our domestic law. We think he was right in this. Apart from any provision of the Constitution the position would appear to be that the rules of international law are not part of the domestic law, except in so far as they have been made so by legislation, judicial decision, or established usage. To that extent its rules may be applied by the Courts so long as they are not in conflict with an enactment of the Legislature or a rule of the common law (Halsbury's Laws of England, Simonds ed., vol. 7, art. 567, at p. 264; and see *R.* v. *Keyn*[1]*; *West Rand Central Gold Mining Co.* v. *Rex*[2]*). Article 29, clause 6, of the Constitution provides that no international agreement shall be part of the domestic law of the State save as may be determined by the Oireachtas; and Article 15, clause 2, provides that the sole and exclusive power of making laws for the State is vested in the Oireachtas, and no other legislative authority has power to make laws for the State. It is quite clear that the Convention, though the State be a party to it, cannot of itself in any way qualify or affect our domestic legislation. Where there is an irreconcilable conflict between a domestic statute and the principles of international law or the provisions of an international convention, the Courts administering the domestic law must give effect to the statute (*Cail* v. *Papayanni. The "Amalia"*[3]; *Niboyet* v. *Niboyet*[4];). If this principle were not to be observed it would follow that the Executive Government by means of an international agreement might, in certain circumstances, be able to exercise powers of legislation contrary to the letter and the spirit of the Constitution. The right of the citizens of this State to be bound by no other laws than those enacted by their elected representatives in the Oireachtas assembled is one to be carefully preserved and jealously guarded.

Before the Act of 1940 was finally enacted its provisions, as contained in the Bill passed by both houses of the Oireachtas, were by the President, under the provisions of Article 26 of the Constitution, referred to the Supreme Court for a decision whether or not they were repugnant to the Constitution; and were by that Court declared to be constitutional. If the Government, or anyone acting under its authority, is not to be permitted to rely on the provisions of Part II then those provisions are a nullity. **[104]**

It is to be noted that the effect and scope of the Convention's provisions as to the liberty of the person are not absolute or unqualified. Article 15 recognises as possible the existence of conditions and circumstances in which temporary and exceptional restrictions on personal liberty may be legitimate. It may not be impossible to equate the condition, contemplated by the Article, of public emergency threatening the life of the State, with the necessity to secure the preservation of public peace and order and the security of the State, contemplated by Part II of the Act of 1940. The Court did not pursue any inquiry whether, in accordance with the provisions of Article 15 (3) the Government had informed the Secretary-General of the Council of Europe of their action in bringing into operation Part II of the Act of 1940, as the matter would appear to be irrelevant and immaterial. Failure to furnish such information could give the applicant no enforceable right or claim in the domestic Courts.

In our opinion the Government, and anyone acting under its authority, is entitled to rely on the provisions of Part II of the Act of 1940 as part of the domestic law which has been expressly declared to be constitutional. The two grounds based upon the Convention have not, in our opinion, been established.

Counsel for the applicant on a fifth ground sought to impugn the validity of the warrant itself. In the first place, it was submitted that the applicant could not possibly have been engaged in subversive activities at the time when the Minister issued his warrant, as he was then in custody under s. 30 of the Act of 1939. To justify the issue of a warrant the Minister must, it was argued, be of opinion that the person concerned "is engaged" in the activities specified. In this case, it was submitted, the Minister could not have genuinely held the requisite opinion in respect of the applicant because he was already in custody. We would not like to commit ourselves to the view that it is impossible for a person in custody to be engaged in activities of the nature specified; but quite apart from such a consideration it seems to us that s. 4 of the Act of 1940 contemplates not merely actions which are contemporaneous with the issue of the

[1] (1876), 2 Ex. D. 63, at p. 202.
[2] [1905] 2 K.B. 391, at pp. 406-8.
[3] (1863), 1 Moo. P. C. (N.S.) 471.
[4] (1878), 4 P. D. 1.

Minister's warrant but also a previous course of conduct which, but for arrest and detention under the section, would, in all probability have been continued or renewed. Such a course of conduct may be intermittent, or may be interrupted by an arrest, as in this case, under s. 30 of the Act of 1939. We do not think such an intermission or interruption makes it impossible for the Minister to be genuinely of the requisite opinon. **[105]**

In the second place, it was contended that the Minister should, in order to justify the applicant's detention, have made an affidavit that he was of the requisite opinion; and, furthermore, that he should have shown that he had reasonable grounds on which to found it. The first branch of this submission was based upon para. 10 of the applicant's affidavit in which he states that he was not *at the time of his arrest* engaged in any illegal activities, and that he is not a member of any illegal organisation. These averments, it was submitted, put the respondent upon proof that the Minister was in fact of the requisite opinion.

The determining factor is not the question whether the applicant was engaged in illegal activities but whether the Minister was of opinion that he was so engaged. It might be quite true that the applicant was not at any time engaged in such activities, and at the same time true that the Minister was, wrongly, of opinion that he was. The mere denial by the applicant of such activities does not therefore suffice to put the respondent upon proof of the Minister's opinion, already stated in a warrant in the statutory form and good on its face.

The second branch of the submission is that the respondent, by reason of the applicant's averment, was put on proof that the Minister's opinion was genuine and well-founded. It is to be noted that the applicant's denial of illegal activities is confined to the time of his arrest. It may be that he had been, prior to his arrest, engaged in a course of subversive conduct, and that the Minister could not merely genuinely, but also correctly, have held the requisite opinion, in the sense which we have already indicated, that he was engaged in illegal activities. We cannot see therefore that the applicant's averment has the effect of casting upon the respondent any onus of the kind suggested.

In any event we are of opinion that the question whether the Minister's opinion was well founded is not one which this Court can consider. The matter is covered by authority. We have already made reference to the fact that the provisions of Part II of the Act of 1940 have been held by the Supreme Court to be constitutional (*In re Article* 26 *of the Constitution and the Offences Against the State* (*Amendment*) *Bill,* 1940.[5] The judgment of the Court was delivered by Sullivan C.J. At p. 479 he said:—"The only essential preliminary to the exercise by a Minister of the powers contained in s. 4 is that he should have formed opinions on the matters specifically mentioned in the section. The validity of such opinions is not a matter which should be questioned in any Court." **[106]**

In our opinion the fifth ground relied on by counsel for the applicant is not a good ground.

Points of, perhaps, more substance but technical in nature were founded on the provisions of s. 30 of the Act of 1939 and s. 4 of the Act of 1940. While put as separate propositions the points are essentially related and depend upon the combined effect of these two sections. Under s. 30, sub-s. 4, a person detained under the section may, at any time during such detention, be charged before the District Court, or a Special Criminal Court, with an offence, or be released by direction of an officer of the Gárda Síochána and shall, if not so charged or released, be released at the expiration of the detention authorised by the section. The section authorises a maximum period of detention of only forty-eight hours at the end of which, unless previously charged or released, a right to release arises. It was contended that, as the applicant had been neither charged nor released within the forty-eight hours, this right to release accrued to him at the end of this period; and that his continued detention was an invasion of this right and unlawfully deprived him of his liberty. While s. 30 is apparently absolute in its terms, it cannot be read wholly independently of s. 4. The Acts of 1939 and 1940 are to be construed as one, with the result that the sections must be

[5] **[1940] I. R. 470.**

read and construed as if they were both contained in the same statute and, so far as possible, read consistently with each other and not so as to give one an undue effect relative to the other. If there had been no preliminary detention under s. 30, there is no doubt that the Minister's warrant could have been a valid authority under s. 4 for the arrest and detention of the applicant, and would be a sufficient answer to his present application. Equally, if the applicant had, during his detention under s. 30, been set at liberty, or had obtained his liberty (whether in the manner contemplated by the section or not) there seems to us to be no doubt that the Minister's warrant would have been a valid justification for his arrest and detention under s. 4. This leads to the conclusion that, if the determination of the detention under s. 30 is a condition precedent to the execution of a warrant under s. 4, it is immaterial, for the purpose of the validity of the action taken under s. 4, how that detention was terminated. In our view the handing over of the applicant by the sergeant in charge of the Bridewell Station, Dublin, on the morning of the 13th July last to Detective Sergeant Connolly, who had come on the instructions of Inspector McMahon to remove him for the purpose of detention in the Internment Camp at the Curragh, Co. Kildare, under the **[107]** Minister's warrant, did in fact put an end to the previously existing detention under s. 30.

It was, however, contended on behalf of the applicant that, even on this view, his continued detention at the Curragh is illegal. This proposition depends on the circumstance that the authority conferred by s. 4, sub-s. 3, to detain a person in a prescribed place of detention is limited in terms to persons arrested under the warrant of a Minister of State; and that the applicant was not such a person because he was not in fact arrested but merely transferred from the custody of one member of the Gárda Síochána to that of another member and that, in any event, he could not have been arrested at all while he was already deprived of his liberty and held in a detention which, for this purpose, should be assumed to be legal.

It is possibly correct, as contended by counsel for the respondent, that, while detention would normally cover arrest, the detention contemplated by s. 4 is restraint at a particular place, and that the "arrest" contemplated and provided for by the section is the restraint during the period from the moment of apprehension until the time of lodgment in the place of detention; and he referred to the circumstance that, under the section, the person detained is entitled to a copy of the warrant only after he arrives at the place of detention. We propose, however, to deal with the matter on the basis that there must be an arrest, in the ordinary sense of the term, before detention under s. 4 can be justified. The contention, then, is that there can be no arrest, in this sense, of a person already in a lawful and unexpired custody. It is at first impression a plausible proposition but, on consideration, it is not in our view a sound one.

A dictionary definition of "arrest" in the legal sense is "to lay hold upon or apprehend by legal authority" (Shorter Oxford English Dictionary, 3rd edition). According to *Termes de la Ley* "an arrest is when one is taken and restrained from his liberty." Whichever definition is regarded, it is clear that the essential element is the taking into legal custody for the purpose of depriving the person arrested of his liberty or of restraining him; and this is, in our opinion, the sense in which the term is ordinarily used. In this sense it seems to us clear that there was an arrest of the applicant on the morning of the 13th July when he was taken into the custody of Detective Sergeant Connolly pursuant to the warrant of the Minister. The custody of Detective Sergeant Connolly, acting under the warrant, then commenced and became effective to restrain the applicant from his liberty and to deprive him of the right, which he **[108]** would otherwise have had, of being released at the end of his detention under s. 30. Does it make any difference to this view that the applicant was then in another lawful and subsisting custody? The fallacy in contending that it does lies in regarding an arrest as essentially the determination of a pre-existing liberty. This is not, in our view, an essential or necessary feature of an arrest. The essence is the restraint from liberty as from the moment of arrest, that is, the subsequent or future restraint. It is irrelevant, therefore, to the true nature of an arrest whether the person arrested was then at liberty or not. It is true that an attempted arrest of this nature may not be successful if the existing custodian insists on continuing his own custody. This did not, however, happen in the present case. The applicant was handed over by the sergeant in charge of the Bridewell to the custody of Detective Sergeant Connolly, and the sergeant in charge thereby relinquished his custody of the applicant. In our view it would have made no difference to the occurrence of an arrest or to its validity even if the transfer of custody had taken place against the wishes, or in face of the opposition, of the sergeant in charge. Whatever complaint or remedy the first custodian might have, the person arrested cannot complain of the premature termination of the prior custody or insist on it being continued for the purpose of avoiding the transfer to another custody. He can, of course, question its legality and, if he does so successfully, he has the advantage and benefit also of the prior custody having come to an end.

In the result we do not think that there is any legal principle which prevents a person already in one custody from being arrested and taken into another custody. To put the matter another way, the transfer from one custody to another can be regarded as an arrest, in the ordinary sense of the term, by the new custodian. In ordinary language a person can be properly said to be arrested when he is taken into custody whether he is taken from a state of freedom or of previous restraint. On this view, it does not avail the applicant here that, but for the intervening arrest and detention under the warrant, he would have been due to be released at the end of the period of detention under s. 30. The sole question is whether the arrest and detention were lawful. In our view the applicant *was* arrested under the warrant of the Minister within the meaning of s. 4. As a person so arrested he was a person who could be detained under the warrant. The warrant itself is a sufficient justification for the arrest and detention when, as here, its existence and authenticity are established **[109]** and there is in reality nothing adduced by the applicant to show or suggest that it was not made regularly and in good faith.

In our view the applicant's custody in the Bridewell under s. 30 of the Act of 1939 gave him no immunity from arrest under the Minister's warrant; and we are of opinion that he was lawfully arrested under the warrant in accordance with the provisions of s. 4 of the Act of 1940. We hold that grounds 6 and 7 relied on by counsel for the applicant have not been established.

Finally, counsel for the applicant submitted that certain rulings of the commission, to which we have already made reference, amounted in effect to a refusal to discharge its duty under s. 8 of the Act of 1940, and deprived the applicant of his only safeguard against the consequences of a wrong decision by the Minister. It seems to us that the rulings of the commission, as far as the present application is concerned, are *nihil ad rem* and are irrelevant and immaterial. Once the applicant has been properly arrested and detained under a valid warrant of the Minister nothing that the commission can do or leave undone can suffice to render the warrant invalid. The commission can, in effect by their report secure the applicant's release; but such a report cannot legally impugn the warrant which, until his release consequent upon the report, continues as a sufficient justification for his detention. The terms of s. 8 leave the commission at large as to how they are to conduct their inquiry. This, we think, was done designedly as much in the interest of internees as in the public interest; and it is no part of our function to lay down rules for the commission's procedure, or to confine them in the discharge of their duties by imposing restrictions which the Legislature refrained from imposing.

If the commission did refuse to discharge their duties under the Statute there is, no doubt, an appropriate way of compelling them to discharge them. We are far, indeed, from suggesting that they have failed in their duty in any respect; we merely consider that, whether they fail or not, their action or inaction can have no effect on the validity of the Minister's warrant as a justification for the applicant's detention. In our opinion this final ground has not been made good.

For the reasons which we have thus briefly stated we have seen fit to order that the cause shown by the respondent be allowed and the conditional order discharged.

From the above judgment the prosecutor appealed to the Supreme Court. **[110]**

The grounds of appeal were as follows:—

(1) That the High Court misdirected itself in law, and upon the facts, in making the said order dated the 11th October, 1957.

(2) That the High Court in particular misdirected itself in law in not holding (*i*) that the Offences Against the State (Amendment) Act, 1940 (No. 2 of 1940), Part II, contains no power enabling the Government to make the Proclamation referred to in s. 3, sub-s. 2, of the said Act, and that accordingly Part II of the said Act at no time came into force and is not in force.

(*ii*) That the State, through the Government, having become a party to, and having confirmed and ratified, the Convention for the Protection of Human Rights and Fundamental Freedoms, and having undertaken faithfully to perform and carry out all the stipulations therein contained (subject to a reservation contained in the Instrument of Ratification), it was not open to the Government to rely on powers which are in violation of that Convention.

(*iii*) In the alternative, that since the 3rd September, 1953, the Offences Against the State Acts, 1939 and 1940, and decisions relating thereto, must be construed so as to avoid violating the said Convention solemnly entered into and ratified by the State.

(*iv*) That there was no evidence or proof that (*a*) the Minister for Justice, when signing the warrant dated the 12th July, 1957, ordering the arrest and detention of the applicant under s. 4 of the said Act of 1940 or at any material time, was of opinion that the applicant was then engaged in any such activities as are referred to in s. 4, sub-s. 1, of the said Act of 1940; or (*b*) that such activities (if any) were in the opinion of the said Minister prejudicial to the security of the State; or (*c*) that the Minister had applied his mind to the facts of this particular case.

(*v*) That on the uncontradicted evidence before the High Court, the applicant was not, when the said warrant was signed, or at any material time, engaged in any such activities as are referred to in s. 4, sub-s. 1, of the said Act of 1940.

(*vi*) That the applicant, having been arrested under the provisions of s. 30 of the Offences Against the State Act, 1939, and not charged with any offence, was entitled by virtue of the provisions of the said s. 30 to be released and was not in fact so released.

(*vii*) That the powers of detention contained in s. 4, sub-s. 3, of the Offences Against the State (Amendment) **[111]** Act, 1940, are limited to persons arrested under s. 4, sub-s. 2, of the said Act of 1940 and that the applicant was not such a person.

(*viii*) That the said warrant was invalid, unenforceable and bad in law.

(*ix*) That the commission set up under s. 8 of the said Act of 1940 having failed and neglected properly to discharge its functions in a number of matters materially affecting the applicant's rights, the applicant was now deprived of his only safeguard against indeterminate imprisonment and accordingly was not detained in accordance with law and was entitled to his liberty.

Seán MacBride, Senior Counsel, and *S. Sorahan* (with them *T. J. Connolly, Senior Counsel*), for the appellant:—

It is submitted that the State having become a party to, and having solemnly ratified, the European Convention of Human Rights and Fundamental Freedoms, it is not open to the Government to rely on powers which violate the Convention. In the alternative, it is submitted that the domestic law of the State must be construed in a manner which will avoid violating the Convention. It is further submitted that, in any case of doubt as to the true construction of domestic law, such doubt must be resolved in the light of the Convention.

It is submitted that the powers of arrest and imprisonment for an indefinite period without charge or trial exercisable by the Executive under the provisions of the Offences Against the State Act, 1939, and the amending Act of 1940 are a clear violation of Articles 9, 10 and 11 of the United Nations Declaration of Human Rights. The Declaration, being a codification of the human rights which civilised States are expected to grant and observe in regard to individuals, forms part of the law of nations or of international law. International law itself forms part of the common law, and, as such, it is incorporated in the domestic law without legislative intervention: *Zarine* v. *Owners of S.S. "Ramava"*[6]*; *The Parlement Belge*[7]*; *Reg.* v. *Keyn*[8]*; *West Rand Central Gold Mining Co.* v. *Rex*[9]*; *Chung Chi Cheung* v. *The King*[10]*; *Compania Naviera Vascongado* v. *SS. Cristina.*[11]*

Accordingly it is submitted that if any act of the Legislature conflicts with the provisions of the said Declaration the Declaration should prevail, the State having accepted it by ratifying it. **[112]**

The Convention of Human Rights and Fundamental Freedoms, which was signed on behalf of the State on the 4th November, 1950, creates common international obligations. It also, it is submitted, confers enforceable rights on individuals in the member nations and places a limitation on the executve action which the Governments of member nations may take. The actions complained of in this case are not the actions of the Legislature, but executive actions of the Government. It is submitted that the combined effect of Article 1 of the Convention and Article 3 of the Statute of the Council of Europe is (1) to incorporate the rules of international law or safeguarding of personal liberty, and (2) to confer rights on individuals which are enforceable against Governments. It is quite clear that arbitrary arrest and indeterminate imprisonment without charge or trial conflict with the provisions of Articles 5 and 6 of the Convention.

Paragraphs (1) and (3) of Article 29 of the Constitution provide that the State in its external relations accepts (*a*) international justice and morality and (*b*) the generally recognised principles of international law. It is submitted that a breach by the Government of an international convention such as the Convention of Human Rights and Fundamental Freedoms would constitute a breach of both of those provisions.

It is submitted that the applicant is not being detained in accordance with the law. The Minister for Justice, before invoking the aid of the provisions of s. 4 of the Offences Against the State (Amendment) Act, 1940, must be of opinion 1, that some definite person is engaged in activities, and 2, that such activities are prejudicial to the public peace and good order. It is submitted that the power of detention provided for in sub-s. 3 is limited to the category of persons set forth in sub-s. 2, that is, persons arrested by the Gárda Síochána in pursuance of a warrant, and the sub-section does not extend to any other persons; it is submitted that it could not apply to a person arrested by a military officer or by a civilian. The applicant, it is submitted, is not one of the persons to whom sub-s. 3 applies as he was arrested without a warrant; therefore his detention in purported pursuance of this Act is unlawful.

It is submitted that as the applicant was arrested in pursuance of the provisions of s. 30 of the Offences Against the State Act, 1939, he was, by that section, entitled to be released, at the latest, in not more than forty-eight hours after his arrest. The provisions for release after forty-eight hours of the person arrested thereunder if not charged in the District Court before that time are mandatory. It is **[113]** submitted that it is no answer to this contention to show that it was within the forty-eight hours that he was ordered to be detained under the Minister's warrant. It is submitted that that warrant has no force or effect to detain the applicant. Such a warrant, made under s. 4 of the Offences Against the State (Amendment) Act, 1940, only applies to persons arrested under s. 4 of the Act of 1940. The applicant was not arrested under that Act, but under the Act of 1939. Therefore the Minister's warrant is not a lawful authority for his detention and he is, it is submitted, accordingly entitled to be released as the period of forty-eight hours from his arrest has long since expired.

It is submitted that the Offences Against the State (Amendment) Act, 1940,

[6] [1942] I.R. 148.
[7] L. R. 5 P. D. 197.
[8] (1876), 2 Ex. D. 63.
[9] [1905] 2 K.B. 391.
[10] [1939] A. C. 160.
[11] [1938] A. C. 485.

contains no enabling power which would empower the Government to make the necessary proclamation to bring the Act into force. It is obviously an omission in the drafting of the Act, as in Part V of the Offences Against the State Act, 1939, which is comparable with the Act of 1940, there is a perfectly good enabling section, namely, s. 35, sub-s. 2: *In re Art.* 26 *of the Constitution and the Offences Against the State* (*Amendment*) *Bill,* 1940.[12]

It is submitted that the opinion of the Minister ordering the arrest and detention is reviewable by the Court after the arrest of the person concerned. Once the opinion of the Minister is challenged it is for him to justify his opinion in Court and also the grounds of this opinion. If the Minister's opinion is not so reviewable, grave injustice might be done because the Minister might order arrest and imprisonment out of mere caprice and without any proper opinion at all.

It is submitted that the commission, as set up by the Government under s. 8 of the Act of 1940, by the rules it made precluded itself from affording the applicant the protection to which he was entitled under the Act, the Constitution and the Convention of Human Rights. The commission held that although it desired to do so, it had no power to take sworn evidence. It also held that it could sit *in camera,* and it did so. Furthermore, it held that it was not bound to disclose the information and documents which were adduced to justify the imprisonment to the person imprisoned or to his legal advisers. It did in fact receive such documents, which were not disclosed to the applicant or to his legal advisers. It is submitted that these rules were wrong and, accordingly, that the applicant is not being detained in accordance with law.

The standard of natural justice which tribunals or other bodies entrusted with the power to determine a right or to **[114]** impose a liability should follow has been clearly laid down in numerous Irish and English decisions: see *R.* v. *Corporation of Dublin*[13]; *R.* (*Wexford County Council*) v. *Local Government Board*[14]; *The State* (*Horgan*) v. *Exporters' Livestock Insurance Board*[15]; *The State* (*Murphy*) v. *Cork County Council*[16]; *The State* (*Crowley*) v. *The Irish Land Commission*[17]; *Foley* v. *The Irish Land Commission*[18]; *In re Estate of Roscrea Meat Products Ltd.*[19]; *General Medical Council* v. *Spackman*[20]; *R.* (*Ex parte Jagger*) v. *Arctitects Registration Tribunal.*[21]

It is submitted that the commission comes within the provisions of Article 37 of the Constitution and is exercising powers of a judicial nature: *General Medical Council* v. *Spackman.*[20] [They also cited *Liversidge* v. *Anderson*[22]; *Green* v. *Secretary of State for Home Affairs*[23]; *Nakkuda Ali* v. *Jayaratne*[24]; *Jencks* v. *U.S.* (decided in June, 1957); *Murray* v. *The Charming Betsy*[25]; *Board of Education* v. *Rice*[26]; *Ex parte Lees*[27]; Convention of Human Rights and Fundamental Freedoms, Articles 1, 5, 6, 15; The Constitution of Ireland, Articles 28, 29.]

Brian Walsh, Senior Counsel (with him *A. Hederman*), for Commandant Carl O'Sullivan and the Attorney General:—

It is submitted that the domestic law of the State is, in all respects, paramount in the internal matters of the State. It is the law of the land, and no rule of international law can, or can be allowed to, derogate therefrom. If there is a conflict between a rule of international law and the domestic law of the State, then the domestic law must prevail in internal matters. The Commandant of the internment camp is entitled to rely on the law of the land. If he can show what he did was provided for by statute, he cannot be forced out of that position by any rule of international law.

It is contended on behalf of the applicant that the Courts should have regard

12 [1940] I. R. 470.
13 2 L. R. Ir. 371.
14 [1902] 2 I. R. 349.
15 [1943] I. R. 581.
16 [1946] I. R. 171.
17 [1951] I. R. 250.
18 [1952] I. R. 118.
19 [1958] I. R. 47.
20 [1943] A. C. 627.
21 [1945] 2 All E. R. 131.
22 [1942] A. C. 206.
23 [1942] A. C. 284.
24 [1951] A. C. 66.
25 2 Cr. 64.
26 [1911] A. C. 179.
27 [1941] 1 K. B. 72.

to the principles of international law. It is submitted that as regards customary international law that contention is only partly correct, while as regards treaty-made law it is not correct at all. Customary international law forms no part of domestic law save in so far as it is adopted into it; so far as it does not conflict with **[115]** domestic law it may be enforced with it: *Chung Chi Cheung* v. *The King*[28]*; *Compania Naviera Vascongado* v. *SS. Cristina*[29]*; *R.* v. *Keyn*[30]*; *Attorney-General for Canada* v. *Attorney-General for Ontario.*[31]*

It is submitted therefore that the Convention of Human Rights has no effect on the domestic law of the State and the Court should not have any regard thereto in deciding the case before it. Article 15, 2, 1° of the Constitution provides that the only body which can make laws for the State is the Oireachtas; it provides also that no other legislative authority has power to make laws for the State. That clearly covers the arguments based on international law on behalf of the applicant. The matter is, however, carried further and made even more clear and definite by Article 29, 6, which provides that, unless so determined by the Oireachtas, no international agreement shall be part of the domestic law of the State. The Oireachtas, by the ratification of the Convention of Human Rights, clearly did not and, it is submitted, did not intend to, make that Convention part of the domestic law of the State or give to it any supreme position in the State. It is merely an international agreement to which the State has given its approval through the Oireachtas.

In s. 4 of the Offences Against the State (Amendment) Act, 1940, arrest is spoken of as a condition which precedes detention, as the word, "detention," is there used. It is submitted that in the Act the word, "detention," refers to the period of time spent by a person in the scheduled place of detention. It is submitted that even if the arrest for some technicality were not carried out correctly, that is not a matter which should now be considered. It is the detention of the prosecutor which the Court has to consider. If the preliminary steps were not carried out accurately but yet the detention is lawful, then it is submitted that any technical flaws in the procedure followed in arresting the applicant are now irrelevant and should not be considered by the Court. It is not, however, conceded that there was any flaw in the arrest of the applicant.

It is submitted that although the applicant was originally arrested under s. 30 of the Offences Against the State Act, 1939, that did not prevent his being detained in accordance with the Minister's warrant issued under s. 4 of the Act of 1940. There is a power of arrest contained in sub-s. 1 of s. 4 of the Act of 1940. It is submitted that the applicant was quite clearly arrested in accordance with that power when **[116]** he was taken from the Bridewell to Mountjoy Prison in pursuance of the Minister's warrant for transfer to the Curragh. While arrest when a person is already in custody is a mere formality, it is submitted that, nevertheless, the power to arrest in such circumstances still exists. Furthermore, it is submitted that the important matter is not the power to arrest, which is only a means of apprehension, but the power of detention. When the applicant was given the Minister's warrant he was lawfully detained.

It is submitted that the commission is not a judicial body and never was intended to be such. It is not, and never was intended, to be bound by the ordinary laws of evidence. The members of the commission have to consider merely whether the Minister has grounds for making the order of detention and whether that detention should be continued or discontinued. In order to arrive at that decision they must consider matters which the Minister considered. It may not be in the public interest to make such matters known to the person detained or his advisers. The commission is not administering penalties or punishment, but only deciding whether the detention of the person should be continued or terminated. The commission has never been permitted to discharge its functions properly as these proceedings were started and the hearing before the commission had to be suspended pending their outcome. Its duties and functions are merely to inquire into the continuation of the detention of the

28 [1939] A. C. 160.
29 [1938] A. C. 485.
30 (1876) 2 Ex. D. 63.
31 [1937] A. C. 326.

applicant and this, it is submitted, the commission should be allowed to do as the applicant has requested it.

Seán MacBride, Senior Counsel, in reply.

MAGUIRE C.J.:—

We are unanimously of opinion that the appeal fails and that the order of the High Court should be affirmed. We shall give our reasons later.

On the 3rd December, 1957, the judgment of the Court was delivered by Maguire C.J.

MAGUIRE C.J.:—

This is an appeal from an order of the High Court dated the 14th October, 1957, allowing the cause shown against a conditional order of *habeas corpus ad subjiciendum* dated the 18th September, 1957, and discharging the order. The applicant, Gearóid O'Laighléis, is at present detained in the Curragh Internment Camp by virtue of a warrant dated the 12th July, 1957, signed by the Minister for Justice **[117]** in exercise of the powers conferred on him by s. 4 of the Offences Against the State (Amendment) Act, 1940, and made in the form set out in the Schedule to that Act. In the warrant the Minister affirms his opinion that the applicant is engaged in activities which, in his opinion, are prejudicial to the security of the State and orders the arrest and detention of the applicant under s. 4.

Article 40, 4, 1°, of the Constitution provides that "no citizen shall be deprived of his personal liberty save in accordance with law."

Section 4, 2° provides:—"Upon complaint being made by or on behalf of any person to the High Court or any judge thereof alleging that such person is being unlawfully detained, the High Court and any and every judge thereof to whom such complaint is made shall forthwith enquire into the said complaint and may order the person in whose custody such person is detained to produce the body of such person before the High Court on a named day and to certify in writing the grounds of his detention, and the High Court shall, upon the body of such person being produced before that Court and after giving the person in whose custody he is detained an opportunity of justifying the detention, order the release of such person from such detention unless satisfied that he is being detained in accordance with the law."

The applicant having complained that he is being unlawfully detained it is the duty of the Court to enquire into this. The High Court and this Court have no more important and onerous function.

The Offences Against the State (Amendment) Act, 1940, under which the detention is sought to be justified was, before being signed as a law, referred by the President in the form of a Bill under the powers conferred on him by Article 26 of the Constitution for a decision on the question whether it was repugnant to the Constitution or any provision thereof. The Court decided that there was no repugnancy. The President accordingly signed the Bill and the Act was thereupon promulgated as law.

Article 34, 3, 3°, of the Constitution declares:—"No Court whatever shall have jurisdiction to question the validity of a law, or any provision of a law, the Bill for which shall have been referred to the Supreme Court by the President under Article 26 of this Constitution . . ."

The Court is therefore bound to approach the consideration of this appeal on the basis that the Act is valid and incapable of being challenged as repugnant to the Constitution in these or any other proceedings. This is accepted by Mr. MacBride.

The conditional order was served on Commandant Carl **[118]** O'Sullivan, in charge of the Curragh Internment Camp, and on the registrar of the commission set up under s. 8 of the Offences Against the State (Amendment) Act, 1940 (which is referred to hereafter as the Act of 1940). On cause being shown by the said Commandant O'Sullivan, the notice of motion to make absolute the conditional order was served on the State Solicitor who appeared for the Commandant, on the registrar of the commission and on the Minister for Justice. In the course of the hearing before us the Court intimated a view that the Attorney General should be represented and subsequently Mr. Walsh, Senior Counsel, and Mr. Hederman, counsel for the Commandant, informed the Court that they were instructed also to appear for and represent the Attorney General. It will be necessary subsequently to refer to some of the affidavits in detail but the story set out in them may be broadly summarised as follows.

The applicant, a builder's labourer and unmarried, on the 11th July, last, was about to board the Mail Boat at Dun Laoghaire pier to go to England for the purpose, as he says, of obtaining employment. He had purchased a single third class ticket to London. Detective Sergeant Connor with two other Guards prevented the applicant from going on board and took him in a car to the Bridewell. The applicant says that no warrant was produced and no reason given for the arrest, but Detective Sergeant Connor has sworn that he informed the applicant that he was being detained pursuant to the provisions of s. 30 of the Offences Against the State Act, 1939, on the grounds that he believed him to be a member of an illegal organisation. At the Bridewell the applicant was handed over to the custody of Sergeant Clifford who was informed in the presence of the applicant that he was being detained pursuant to s. 30. The Occurrence Book of the Bridewell contains a note dated the 11th July to this effect. The evidence of Sergeant Connor is corroborated by Sergeant Clifford.

On the 12th July, Chief Superintendent Michael Farrell, acting under s. 30 of the Act of 1939, made an order that the applicant be detained for a further period of twenty-four hours expiring at 7.45 p.m. on the 13th July.

The applicant deposes that early on the morning of the 13th July he was awakened in his cell in the Bridewell, told to dress, and, when dressed, was taken in a car to Mountjoy Prison outside which a lorry was waiting. Together with fifteen men who had been discharged from Mountjoy Prison that morning and re-arrested, he was driven to the military detention barracks at the Curragh and at about 11 a.m. **[119]** was visited there by Captain Kevin Barry who handed him a copy of the warrant to which we have referred and a copy of s. 8 of the Act of 1940. This was done pursuant to s. 4, sub-s. 4, of that Act. The applicant is still detained at the Curragh Detention Camp under and by virtue of that warrant.

The applicant, acting by his solicitor, Mr. P. C. Moore, on the 8th September applied in writing to have his detention considered by the commission set up under s. 8 of the Act of 1940. A correspondence ensued which it is not at this stage necessary to detail. On the 17th September the commission sat, the applicant and his counsel, Mr. Seán MacBride and Mr. Sorahan, being present. Mr. Walsh and Mr. Hederman were also present representing the Attorney General, instructed by the Chief State Solicitor, for the purpose of assisting the commission on certain questions which they had raised as to their powers and procedure. After argument the commission determined that they had power to sit in public or *in camera* and that they were not satisfied that they had power to administer an oath. They announced their decision that the remainder of the proceeding should take place *in camera.* When the proceedings were resumed *in camera* the commission made certain rulings on procedure.

Mr. MacBride took exception to these rulings. The commission adjourned to Friday the 20th September. On the 19th September the conditional order was obtained and was served on Commandant O'Sullivan. On Friday, the 20th September, the commission further adjourned the hearing *sine die.*

Before us Mr. MacBride maintained that his client was illegally interned on a number of grounds. The respondent relied upon the Act of 1940, the proclamation made thereunder and the warrant of the Minister for Justice as justifying the detention. It will be convenient to set out ss. 3, 4 and 8 of that Act on which the arguments chiefly centred.

"3.—(1) This Part of this Act shall not come into or be in force save as and when and for so long as is provided by the subsequent sub-sections of this section.

"(2) If and whenever and so often as the Government makes and publishes a proclamation declaring that the powers conferred by this Part of this Act are necessary to secure the preservation of public peace and order and that it is expedient that this Part of this Act should come into force immediately, this Part of this Act shall come into force forthwith. **[120]**

"(3) If at any time while this Part of this Act is in force the Government makes and publishes a proclamation declaring that this Part of this Act shall cease to be in force, this Part of this Act shall forthwith cease to be in force.

"(4) Whenever the Government has made and published a proclamation under the second sub-section of this section, it shall be lawful for Dáil Eireann, at any time while this Part of this Act is in force by virtue of such proclamation, to pass a resolution annulling such proclamation, and thereupon such proclamation shall be annulled and this Part of this Act shall cease to be in force, but without prejudice to the validity of anything done under this Part of this Act after the making of such proclamation and before the passing of such resolution.

"(5) A proclamation made by the Government under this section shall be published by publishing a copy thereof in the *Iris Oifigiúil* and may also be published in any other manner which the Government shall think proper."

"4.—(1) Whenever a Minister of State is of opinion that any particular person is engaged in activities which, in his opinion, are prejudicial to the preservation of public peace and order or to the security of the State, such Minister may by warrant under his hand and sealed with his official seal order the arrest and detention of such person under this section.

"(2) Any member of the Gárda Síochána may arrest without warrant any person in respect of whom a warrant has been issued by a Minister of State under the foregoing sub-section of this section.

"(3) Every person arrested under the next preceding sub-section of this section shall be detained in a prison or other place prescribed in that behalf by regulations made under this Part of this Act until this Part of this Act ceases to be in force or until he is released under the subsequent provisions of this Part of this Act, whichever first happens.

"(4) Whenever a person is detained under this section, there shall be furnished to such person, as soon as may be after he arrives at a prison or other place of detention prescribed in that behalf by regulations made under this Part of this Act, a copy of the warrant issued under this section in relation to such person and of the provisions of section 8 of this Act.

"(5) Every warrant issued by a Minister of State under this section shall be in the form set out in the Schedule to this Act or in a form to the like effect." **[121]**

"8.—(1) As soon as conveniently may be after this Part of the Act comes into force, the Government shall set up a Commission (in this section referred to as the Commission) to perform the functions imposed upon the Commission by this section.

"(2) The following provisions shall apply and have effect in relation to the Commission, that is to say:—

"(*a*) the members of the Commission shall be appointed and be removable by the Government;

"(*b*) the Commission shall consist of three persons of whom one shall be a commissioned officer of the Defence Forces with not less than seven years' service and each of the others shall be a barrister or solicitor of not less than seven years' standing or be or have been a judge of the Supreme Court, the High Court, or the Circuit Court or a justice of the District Court;

"(*c*) there may be paid out of moneys provided by the Oireachtas to any member of the Commission such (if any) fees or remuneration as the Minister for Finance shall determine.

"(3) Any person who is detained under this Part of this Act may apply in writing to the Government to have the continuation of his said detention considered by the Commission, and upon such application being so made the following provisions shall have effect, that is to say:—

"(*a*) The Government shall, with all convenient speed, refer the matter of the continuation of such person's detention to the Commission;

"(*b*) The Commission shall inquire into the grounds of such person's detention and shall, with all convenient speed, report thereon to the Government;

"(*c*) The Minister for Justice shall furnish to the Commission such information and documents (relevant to the subject-matter of such inquiry) in the possession or procurement of the Government or of any Minister of State as shall be called for by the Commission;

"(*d*) If the Commission reports that no reasonable grounds exist for the continued detention of such person, such person shall, with all convenient speed, be released."

Mr. MacBride's first series of arguments was based upon the Convention for the Protection of Human Rights and Fundamental Freedoms adopted by the Council of Europe which was signed at Rome on the 4th November, 1950, by the Minister for External Affairs, confirmed and ratified **[122]** by the Government of Ireland on the 18th February, 1953, and laid before Dáil Eireann on the 29th March, 1954. In the Instrument of Ratification the Government of Ireland undertook faithfully to perform and carry out all the stipulations of the Convention. Mr. MacBride contended (*a*) that the State, through the Government, having become a party to, and having confirmed and ratified, the Convention and having undertaken faithfully to perform and carry out all the stipulations therein contained (subject to a reservation not now material contained in the Instrument of Ratification), it was not open to the Government to rely on powers which are in violation of that Convention; and (*b*) in the alternative, that since the 3rd September, 1953, the date upon which the Convention entered into force, the Offences Against the State Acts, 1939 and 1940, and decisions relating thereto, must be construed so as to avoid violating the said Convention solemnly entered into and ratified by the State.

The provisions of the Convention on which Mr. MacBride relied are as follows:—

"Article 1.

"The High Contracting Parties shall secure to everyone within their jurisdiction the rights and freedoms defined in Section I of this Convention.

Section I includes the following Articles:—

"Article 5.

"(1) Everyone has the right to liberty and security of person.

"No one shall be deprived of his liberty save in the following cases and in accordance with a procedure prescribed by law:

"(*c*) the lawful arrest or detention of a person effected for the purpose of bringing him before the competent legal authority on reasonable suspicion of having committed an offence or when it is reasonably considered necessary to prevent his committing an offence or fleeing after having done so;

"(2) Everyone who is arrested shall be informed promptly, in a language which he understands, of the reasons for his arrest and of any charge against him.

"(3) Everyone arrested or detained in accordance with the provisions of paragraph 1 (*c*) of this Article shall be brought promptly before a judge or other officer authorised by law to exercise judicial power and shall be entitled to trial within a reasonable time or to release pending trial. **[123]** Release may be conditioned by guarantees to appear for trial.

"(4) Everyone who is deprived of his liberty by arrest or detention shall be entitled to take proceedings by which the lawfulness of his detention shall be decided speedily by a court and his release ordered if the detention is not lawful.

"Article 6.

"(1) In the determination of his civil rights and obligations or of any criminal charge against him, everyone is entitled to a fair and public hearing within a reasonable time by an independent and impartial tribunal established by law. Judgment shall be pronounced publicly but the press and public may be excluded from all or part of the trial in the interests of morals, public order or national security in a democratic society, where the interests of juveniles or the protection of the private life of the parties so require, or to the extent strictly necessary in the opinion of the court in special circumstances where publicity would prejudice the interests of justice."

Mr. MacBride submitted that Article 5 of the Convention had been violated, for two reasons, firstly, because s. 4 of the Act of 1940 authorises detention of a kind not provided for in Section I of the Article and secondly, because the Commission established under s. 8 of the Act of 1940 is not a tribunal of the character specified in s. 3 of the Article. Mr. MacBride submitted, in the alternative, that detention under s. 4 of the Act of 1940 was not a violation of Article 5 of the Convention if it could be regarded as falling within the middle limb of Section 1, (*c*) of the Article, viz., detention reasonably considered necessary to prevent the commission of an offence. He also submitted that the functions of the commission established under s. 8 of the Act of 1940 could likewise be regarded as not being in violation of Section 3 of Article 5 of the Convention if s. 8 be construed as entitling the person detained to a judicial trial.

Ireland has a written, rigid Constitution which came into force on the 29th December, 1937, having been enacted by the People on the 1st July, 1937. Article 29 of the Constitution deals with "International Relations." Mr. MacBride relied upon ss. 1 and 3 of Article 29, which are as follows:—

"1. Ireland affirms its devotion to the ideal of peace and friendly co-operation amongst nations founded on international justice and morality."

"3. Ireland accepts the generally recognised principles of international law as its rule of conduct in its relations with other States." **[124]**

These provisions, Mr. MacBride submitted, reproduce the pre-existing common law, and by the common law, he said, those principles which were commonly accepted as binding by civilised nations became part of the domestic law unless they could be shown to be contrary to it. He referred to the English authorities, *West Rand Central Gold Mining Co.* v. *Rex*[32]*; *Chung Chi Cheung* v. *The King.*[33]* From the latter case he cited in particular this passage from the speech of Lord Atkin (at p. 167):—". . . so far, at any rate, as the Courts of this country are concerned, international law has no validity save in so far as its principles are accepted and adopted by our own domestic law. There is no external power that imposes its rules upon our own code of substantive law or procedure. The Courts acknowledge the existence of a body of rules which nations accept amongst themselves. On any judicial issue they seek to ascertain what the relevant rule is, and, having found it, they will treat it as incorporated into the domestic law, so far as it is not inconsistent with rules enacted by statutes or finally declared by their tribunals."

Clauses 1 and 3 of Article 29 of the Constitution clearly refer only to relations between states and confer no rights on individuals; they can in no way assist Mr. MacBride's argument.

Nor is Mr. MacBride's submission aided by what he says is the position at common law, as set out in Lord Atkin's speech. Inconsistency with municipal law is there stated to be a ground upon which the common law rejects the principles of international law. Mr. MacBride submits that the Act of 1940 is inconsistent with the provisions of the Convention. If it is, then clearly by the common law principles relied upon the Act prevails over the Convention. When the domestic law makes its own provisions it cannot be controlled by any inconsistent provisions in international law: *Mortensen* v. *Peters.*[34]* The principle of incorporation upon which Mr. MacBride relies applies to such parts of international law as are based on universally recognised custom and not to such parts as depend upon convention.

The insuperable obstacle to importing the provisions of the Convention for the Protection of Human Rights and Fundamental Freedoms into the domestic law of Ireland—if they be at variance with that law—is, however, the terms of the Constitution of Ireland. By Article 15, 2, 1°, of the Constitution it is provided that "the sole and exclusive power of making laws for the State is hereby vested in the **[125]** Oireachtas: no other legislative authority has power to make

[32] [1905] 2 K.B. 391, at pp. 406, 407.

[33] [1939] A. C. 160.

[34] (1906) 8 F. 93.

laws for the State." Moreover, Article 29, the Article dealing with international relations, provides at section 6 that "no international agreement shall be part of the domestic law of the State save as may be determined by the Oireachtas."

The Oireachtas has not determined that the Convention of Human Rights and Fundamental Freedoms is to be part of the domestic law of the State, and accordingly this Court cannot give effect to the Convention if it be contrary to domestic law or purports to grant rights or impose obligations additional to those of domestic law.

No argument can prevail against the express command of section 6 of Article 29 of the Constitution before judges whose declared duty it is to uphold the Constitution and the laws.

The Court accordingly cannot accept the idea that the primacy of domestic legislation is displaced by the State becoming a party to the Convention for the Protection of Human Rights and Fundamental Freedoms. Nor can the Court accede to the view that in the domestic forum the Executive is in any way estopped from relying on the domestic law. It may be that such estoppel might operate as between the High Contracting Parties to the Convention, or in the Court contemplated by Section IV of the Convention if it comes into existence, but it cannot operate in a domestic Court administering domestic law. Nor can the Court accept the contention that the Act of 1940 is to be construed in the light of, and so as to produce conformity with, a convention entered into ten years afterwards. The intention of the Oireachtas must be sought in the conditions which existed when it became law.

The Court must therefore reject Mr. MacBride's first series of arguments.

In the course of the argument reference was made to the provisions in Article 15 of the Convention for a high contracting party derogating from its obligations under the Convention in certain circumstances, viz., "time of war or other public emergency threatening the life of the nation." Mr. MacBride said these circumstances were to be equated with the circumstances specified in Article 28, 3, 3°, of the Constitution as warranting legislation in derogation of Constitutional rights, viz., "time of war or armed rebellion" or "national emergency . . . affecting the vital interests of the State" arising out of an armed conflict in which the State was not a participant. The circumstances under which Part II of the Act of 1940 may be brought **[126]** into force (Part II was not in operation at the time of the signing of the Convention for the Protection of Human Rights and Fundamental Freedoms) are a declaration by the Government, by proclamation, that the powers conferred by Part II are necessary to secure "the preservation of public peace and order." The latter circumstances Mr. MacBride submitted were not such as would justify notice of derogation under Article 15 being given.

In the view which the Court takes of the status of the Convention of Human Rights and Fundamental Freedoms under our municipal law it has not been necessary for the Court to enter into this question, and the Court does not express any opinion upon it. For the same reason, the Court does not find it necessary to express any opinion on the question whether the provisions of the Act of 1940 are in violation of the Convention. The Court has not examined nor has it been invited to examine whether in fact circumstances exist which would justify notice of derogation under Article 15.

There remain for consideration the six other grounds which Mr. MacBride put forward in support of the applicant's appeal.

The first of these grounds is that Part II of the Act of 1940 (under which the applicant is detained) is not in operation and cannot be brought into operation because of defect of form in the Act.

Part II of the Act of 1940 commences at s. 3. Sub-sects. 1, 2 and 5 have already been quoted but it is convenient to quote them again:—

"(1) This Part of this Act shall not come into or be in force save as and when and for so long as is provided by the subsequent sub-sections of this section.

"(2) If and whenever and so often as the Government makes and publishes a proclamation declaring that the powers conferred by this Part of this Act are necessary to secure the preservation of public peace and order and that it is expedient that this Part of this Act should come into force immediately, this Part of this Act shall come into force forthwith."

"(5) A proclamation made by the Government under this section shall be published by publishing a copy thereof in the *Iris Oifigiúil* and may also be published in any other manner which the Government shall think proper."

Mr. MacBride submitted that because of the omission of an express power to make a proclamation in the terms of sub-s. 2 it was not possible to bring Part II of the Act into **[127]** force. He gave as examples of an enabling provision s. 35, sub-s. 2, of the Offences Against the State Act, 1939 (No. 13 of 1939), since repealed, and s. 1, sub-s. 1, of the Public Safety Emergency Powers Act, 1926 (No. 42 of 1926).

In the opinion of the Court s. 3 of the Act of 1940 clearly authorises the making of a proclamation if and when the Government consider the situation exists requiring it. When a statute provides that certain consequences follow if and when an act is done, power to do that act is given. Many parallels could be quoted. One is the provisions of Article 28, 3, 3°, of the Constitution. Article 28 does not provide that each House of the Oireachtas may pass the resolution referred to in the Article, but merely enacts that certain consequences shall follow when they do so. No one can doubt that the Houses of the Oireachtas are given power to bring the provisions of the Article into effect by passing the resolutions. This submission is wholly unsustainable.

The next ground of appeal is that the applicant was entitled to be released at the expiration of forty-eight hours from his arrest. Sect. 30 of the Offences Against the State Act, 1939, is relied upon. The applicant was first arrested under this section. The section authorises detention for a period of twenty-four hours and, if an officer of the Gárda Síochána not below the rank of Chief Superintendent so directs, for a further period of twenty-four hours. A direction was given extending the applicant's detention. Sub-sect. 4 then provides that a person so detained "may at any time during such detention be charged before the District Court or a Special Criminal Court with an offence and shall if not so charged be released at the expiration of the detention authorised. . . ." The applicant was not at any time during such detention charged with an offence. Mr. MacBride submitted that the provision in sub-s. 4 for release was in the circumstances mandatory.

The period of forty-eight hours' detention authorised under s. 30 of the Act of 1939, was due to expire at 7.45 o'clock on the afternoon of the 13th July, 1957. At six o'clock on the morning of the same day Detective Sergeant Connolly attended at the Bridewell Gárda Station where the applicant was being detained and took the applicant into his custody. The detective sergeant's instructions were to remove the applicant from the Bridewell Gárda Station in order to have him conveyed to the Military Detention Camp at the Curragh for detention there.

The applicant's detention under s. 30 then ceased. He was thereafter detained under the authority of the Minister's warrant. Whether or not the detention under s. 30 continued **[128]** until 7.45 o'clock on the 13th July, 1957, is immaterial. At that moment he was already detained under another and continuing authority, viz., the Minister's warrant; and it is that warrant which is relied upon as justifying the applicant's detention. It frequently happens that a convicted person is imprisoned under two warrants for different terms of imprisonment. When the warrant for the shorter term of imprisonment expires the convicted person is not entitled to be released but his imprisonment is properly continued under the second warrant.

The applicant's next ground of appeal is a challenge to the validity of the Minister's warrant. It is submitted on the applicant's behalf that s. 4 of the Act of 1940 authorises only the detention of persons who had been arrested under the section. The submission is rested upon s. 4, sub-s. 3, which is in these terms:—"Every person arrested under the next preceding sub-section of this section shall be detained in a prison or other place prescribed in that behalf by regulations made under this Part of this Act until this Part of this Act ceases to be in force or until he is released under the subsequent provisions of this

Part of this Act, whichever first happens." The preceding sub-section sub-s. 2, permits of an arrest without warrant by any member of the Gárda Síochána of any person in respect of whom a warrant has been issued by a Minister of State under sub-s. 1.

In our opinion the applicant's submission is based upon a misconstruction of s. 4. Sub-sect. 3 has for its subject-matter the place and duration of detention. The power to arrest and detain is conferred by s. 4, sub-s. 1, cited earlier. This power is to be read distributively. There is a power to arrest and a power to detain. Where a person is already in custody under a conviction or other authority an arrest—save in a formal sense—may not be possible. But the power to detain is not therefore done away with. On the contrary, the power to detain is the substantive power; the power to arrest is ancillary.

Moreover, a transfer of custody of a person by an authority holding under one order or warrant to an authority claiming to receive and hold that person under another order or warrant is, in the opinion of the Court, an arrest by that latter authority.

The applicant's next ground of appeal is that his arrest at the Bridewell Gárda Station under the Minister's warrant was unlawful because he was not told the reason for it. The arrest was made without a warrant being produced. Sect. 4, sub-s. 2, authorises such arrest provided the Minister's **[129]** warrant has been issued. Sect. 4, sub-s. 4, however requires that a copy of the warrant shall be furnished to a person detained under the section as soon as may be after he arrives at the prescribed place of detention. Counsel for the respondent submitted that it was sufficient to comply with the requirement of sub-s. 4 and that this requirement was of itself an indication that no more was necessary for a lawful arrest under s. 4. We accept it as settled law that in the case of an arrest without the production of a warrant the arrest will not be lawful unless the person being arrested is told why he is being arrested or unless he otherwise knows: see *Christie* v. *Leachinsky*.[35] The reason for the rule is not far to seek. Arrest must be for a lawful purpose; and since no one is obliged to submit to an unlawful arrest the citizen has a right before acquiescing in his arrest to know why he is being arrested. The Court sees nothing in s. 4 of the Act of 1940 which manifests an intention on the part of the Oireachtas to modify this wholesome rule of law; and accordingly the Court is of opinion that a person arrested under a Minister's warrant must be told that such a warrant exists and that he is being arrested and will be detained under it.

But can this avail the applicant? Firstly, he has not established that he did not know why he was being arrested at the Bridewell Gárda Station. Secondly, a *prima facie* case is not made out that he was not told why he was being arrested. The point he makes in his affidavit about his arrest at the Bridewell Gárda Station is that he was not told where he was being taken and not that he was not told and did not know why he was taken in custody by the detective sergeant. In contrast with this the applicant in his account of his arrest at Dún Laoghaire two days earlier, on the 11th July, says forthrightly that no reason was given to him for the arrest. In the case of that arrest the respondent was in a position to file an affidavit in reply and he did so. It is enough, however, to say that the applicant has not laid the ground for challenging the lawfulness of the arrest at the Bridewell Gárda Station. Moreover, an invalidity in the arrest would not render the subsequent detention under the Minister's warrant unlawful though it might give the applicant other rights in respect of the period from the arrest until the warrant was produced and shown to him.

The applicant's next ground of appeal was that the High Court misdirected itself in law in not holding that the Minister should have made an affidavit to prove that he did in fact entertain the opinion set out in his warrant, viz., **[130]** that the applicant was engaged in activities which in the Minister's opinion were prejudicial to the security of the State.

Mr. MacBride said that he did not question the Minister's bona fides; but, he went on, the applicant's affidavit had so challenged the basis for the Minister's

35 [1947] A. C. 573, at p. 587.

opinion that an enquiry into the truth of the respondent's return was called for under s. 3 of the Habeas Corpus Act, 1816.

Counsel for the respondent accepted for the purpose of his argument that the Act of 1816 applies. But s. 3 of the Act is an enabling, not a mandatory, provision. As an enabling provision s. 3 would permit, if the Court thought fit, an enquiry as to whether the Minister did in fact entertain the opinion he states in his warrant. But Mr. MacBride, since he has said he does not question the Minister's bona fides, makes no point about the existence of the Minister's opinion. His real purpose, it appears, is to seek in these proceedings to question the validity of the Minister's opinion. The applicant swore in his affidavit that he was not engaged in illegal activities at the time of his arrest. The applicant's assertion, Mr. MacBride submitted, puts the Minister on proof that the applicant was a person to whom s. 4 of the Act of 1940 applied.

What Mr. MacBride seeks to do cannot be done. In the course of its consideration of the Offences Against the State (Amendment) Bill, 1940, before it became law[36] this Court had occasion to consider the meaning of s. 4. Chief Justice Sullivan, delivering the judgment of the Court, said (at p. 479):—"The only essential preliminary to the exercise by the Minister of the powers contained in s. 4 is that he should have formed opinions on the matters specifically mentioned in the section. The validity of such opinions cannot be questioned in any Court."

Mr. MacBride wishes to do precisely what in 1940 the Court said cannot be done.

Moreover, attention has been called by counsel for the respondent to the form of the applicant's assertion. The applicant did not say he was not engaged in activities of the kind specified in the Minister's warrant, but merely that he was not engaged in such activities when he was arrested. Even if the validity of the Minister's opinion were examinable, the applicant, it may be said, has not laid the ground for such an examination.

On this branch of his argument Mr. MacBride cited from the speech of Lord Atkin in the English cases of *Liversidge* v. *Sir John Anderson*[37] and *Greene* v. *Secretary of State for* **[131]** *Home Affairs.*[38] *Liversidge's Case,*[39], it will be recalled, was an action for false imprisonment, and *Green's Case*[38] was a *habeas corpus* application. Liversidge had been detained under Regulation 18B of the Defence (General) Regulations, 1939, and the question was whether the Home Secretary should be ordered to furnish particulars of the grounds upon which he made an order for Liversidge's detention. Regulation 18B authorised the Home Secretary to order detention *if he had reasonable cause to believe* any person to be of hostile associations and that by reason thereof it was necessary to exercise control over him. Lord Atkin, contrary to the view of the majority of the House, was of opinion that particulars should be ordered.

In *Greene's Case*[38] the Home Secretary had sworn an affidavit showing cause, and, as Lord Atkin said (at p. 246) he appeared to be ready to meet the allegation of absence of reasonable cause. Lord Atkin's colleagues, however, were of opinion that it was unnecessary for the Home Secretary to make an affidavit, because the question whether or not the cause which moved the Home Secretary to order detention was reasonable could not be examined by the Courts.

Lord Atkin's view, on the other hand, was that "reasonable cause" for a belief had always been treated as an objective fact to be proved by one or other party and to be determined by the appropriate tribunal (p. 288).

Mr. MacBride says Lord Atkin's reasoning supports his submission that the Minister must make an affidavit. Mr. MacBride's submission, however, ignores the reason why Lord Atkin thought an affidavit was necessary in *Greene's Case*[38] and that particulars should be delivered in *Liversidge's Case.*[39] Lord Atkin regarded "reasonable cause" for a belief as an objective fact, examinable and triable like any other fact. The contrast he drew was between "reasonable cause" for a belief and "mere belief" that a fact exists. His difference with his brethren was as to the construction of Regulation 18B. The Act of 1940 does not require

[36] [1940] I. R. 470.
[37] [1942] A. C. 206.
[38] [1942] A. C. 284.
[39] [1942] A. C. 206.

a Minister of State to have "reasonable cause" for his belief: he is authorised to act on his opinion. "Mere belief" is enough. Lord Atkin clearly regarded "mere belief" as a subjective state which was not examinable or triable by a Court.

It remains to consider the applicant's last ground of appeal, namely, that the commission set up under s. 8 of the Act of 1940 having failed and neglected properly to discharge its functions in a number of matters materially affecting the applicant's rights, the applicant is now deprived of his only **[132]** safeguard against indeterminate imprisonment and accordingly is not detained in accordance with law and is entitled to his liberty.

Having regard to our decision that the appellant is lawfully detained under the warrant of the Minister, and that this warrant is lawful and valid, it is difficult to see how the matters relied upon in support of this ground of appeal can be raised on an application for an order of *habeas corpus*. However, as a considerable part of the argument of counsel for the appellant was directed to this ground of appeal it is necessary that it should be examined in detail.

As has been stated earlier, the applicant, acting by his solicitor, Mr. P. C. Moore, on the 8th September, 1957, applied by letter to the Secretary of the Government to have his detention inquired into by the commission set up by the Government under s. 8 of the Act of 1940. The third and fourth paragraphs of Mr. Moore's letter were as follows:—"I would like to make it clear that my client's application is put forward on the condition that he be legally represented at the proposed inquiry by his solicitor and counsel and that his legal representatives be accorded the usual rights regarding the production of documents, the right to cross-examine State witnesses, the right to *sub-poena* witnesses and all the usual rights and privileges enjoyed by legal representatives in a Court of law.

"I consequently would be obliged if you would inform me at your earliest convenience of the date of the proposed inquiry and the venue where same will be held, and I also require before the hearing a summary of the evidence which it is proposed to produce against my client on behalf of the State."

The assistant secretary to the Government, by letter dated the 11th September, 1957, replied that the Government had referred the matter of the *continuation of the detention* of Mr. O'Laighléis (the phraseology of s. 8, sub-s. 3, of the Act) to the commission. The letter then continued:—"I am to point out that, in the Act, there is no provision for entertaining such applications subject to conditions imposed by the applicant. While the manner of conducting the inquiry is for the commission to settle, I am to say that the third and fourth paragraphs of your letter appear to be based on a mistaken view of the statutory position. Copies of your letter and the application have been forwarded to the commission."

As stated earlier the commission when it sat on the 17th September, after argument, announced certain rulings on procedure. **[133]**

Mr. MacBride thereupon on behalf of the applicant submitted that his client's interests had already been gravely prejudiced by the transmission to members of the commission of some anonymous documents marked "Secret and confidential" the origin of which was undisclosed and the authenticity of which was unsubstantiated and said that unless the applicant's legal advisers were made aware of all the evidence tendered to the commission to justify the detention of the applicant that it would be impossible for them to discharge their duty to the applicant. He requested the commission to divest itself of the documents forthwith and to refuse to read them or act upon them unless and until they had been duly proved and made available to the applicant's legal advisers. The commission then adjourned to Friday, the 20th September.

On the day following the adjournment, the 18th September, Mr. MacBride moved for, and obtained in the High Court, a conditional order of *habeas corpus* on, among other grounds, the ground that Part II of the Act of 1940 was not in force and accordingly that the commission had not been lawfully constituted. In these circumstances the commission when it sat on the 20th September thought fit to adjourn its sittings until the legality of its constitution had been ruled upon in the High Court proceedings although Mr. MacBride requested them to proceed with the inquiry.

The application is still before the commission. The commission has not yet inquired into the grounds of his detention. So far the commission has concerned itself only with procedural matters, and even if it were to be shown that the commission's rulings on those questions were wrong that would not render the applicant's detention unlawful. The applicant is not detained by virtue of anything the commission has done but under the Minister's warrant and the applicant's challenge to the validity of the warrant has not been sustained.

While a case is at hearing in a Court erroneous rulings on procedural matters cannot ground an application for *habeas corpus*. An examination of s. 8 of the Act of 1940 shows that the commission set up under the section is not a court, and an application to the commission is not a court proceeding. It is what the section says it is and no more—an inquiry. The commission's only duty is to enquire into the grounds of detention and to report thereon to the Government

The commission is entitled to have before it such information and documents (relevant to the subject-matter of its inquiry) in the possession or procurement of the Government [**134**] or of any Minister of State as it shall call for. The requirement of the statute is that such information and documents shall be furnished to the commission for the purpose of its inquiry. The statute does not require the commission to disclose to the applicant such information or documents.

It having been determined that the provisions of the Act are not repugnant to the Constitution the only matter with which this Court is concerned is the meaning and intendment of s. 8. The section contemplates an inquiry which is entirely of an administrative character and the applicant's submissions have proceeded on the wrong basis that the commission is a court.

This ground of appeal, together with the applicant's other grounds of appeal, fails. Accordingly his appeal must be refused and the order of the High Court allowing the cause shown affirmed.

Solicitor for the appellant: *P. C. Moore.*

Solicitor for the respondents: *The Chief State Solicitor.*

[On the 9th November, 1957, an application and statement of claim was lodged on behalf of Mr. Ó Laighléis with the European Commission of Human Rights at Strasbourg, claiming his release and damages for wrongful imprisonment. The applicant complained that his imprisonment constituted a breach of the European Convention of Human Rights, in particular of Articles 5 and 6 thereof which guarantee the rights to liberty, to security of person and to the proper administration of justice.

On the 11th December, 1967, the applicant was released by order of the Minister for Justice made on the same date. The application was then treated by the Commission of Human Rights as a claim for damages for wrongful imprisonment in breach of the Convention. After an exchange of written pleadings, the Commission requested the parties to appear before it for oral argument as to the admissibility of the application. The Commission heard the arguments of counsel for Mr. Ó Laighléis and counsel for the Irish Government at Strasbourg on the 19th and 20th June, 1958, and reserved its decision.

On the 2nd September, 1958, the Commission declared the application to be "admissible." A sub-Commission consisting of seven members was then appointed, pusuant to Articles 28 and 29, for the purpose of establishing the facts and of seeking to arrange a friendly settlement. After a further exchange of written pleadings the sub-Commission, sitting at Strasbourg, heard the oral evidence of the applicant and of Inspector McMahon and the submissions of counsel.

At the hearings before the Commission and the sub-Commission the applicant was represented by S. MacBride, Senior Counsel, T. J. Conolly, Senior Counsel, and S. Sorahan, instructed by P. C. Moore, Solicitor. The Irish Government was represented by the Attorney General, Andreas O'Keeffe, Senior Counsel, B. Walsh, Senior Counsel, and A. Hederman, instructed by the Chief State Solicitor, and were assisted by Mr. S. Morrissey and Mr. T. Woods of the Department of External Affairs and by Mr. T. J. Coyne and Mr. Berry of the Department of Justice. The proceedings before the Commission and sub-Commission were heard *in camera.* [**135**]

The report of the Commission, which is confidential, was transmitted to the Committee of Ministers and to the Irish Government on the 1st February, 1960.

On the 4th April, 1960, the Commission announced that, although it had expressed the opinion by a majority that the applicant's detention did not constitute a violation of the Convention, it had nevertheless decided, in view of the fundamental legal issues involved, to refer the case to the European Court of Human Rights.

The European Court of Human Rights sat in Strasbourg on the 3rd and 4th days of October, 1960, to hear preliminary objections lodged by the Irish Government and gave its judgment on the 14th November, 1960. Most of the objections lodged by the Irish Government were either withdrawn or overruled by the Court and the hearing of the case was fixed for the 7th April, 1961.

The applicant was not represented before the Court, as under the Convention, there is no provision for the representation of an individual applicant save by direction of the Court or in an advisory role to the Commission. The objections of the Irish Government were opposed by the President of the Commission, Professor Sir C. H. M. Waldock. The Irish Government was represented before the Court by the Attorney General, Andreas O'Keeffe, Senior Counsel, and S. Morrissey and A. Hederman, instructed by the Chief State Solicitor, who were assisted by Professor Paul Reuter, a French lawyer—ED.]

ANISMINIC LTD. v. FOREIGN COMPENSATION COMMISSION AND ANOTHER

((1964) 108 Sol. Jo. 541)

June 24, 1964: Court of Appeal: Lord Denning M.R., Harman, Diplock L.JJ.

Practice—Preliminary Point of Law—Jurisdiction of Court—Triable as Preliminary Issue—R.S.C., Ord. 34, *r.* 2.

Interlocutory appeal from John Stephenson, J.

The plaintiffs, a mining company, applied to the defendant commission in respect of property belonging to the plaintiffs in Egypt, pursuant to the Foreign Compensation (Egypt) (Determination and Registration of Claims) Order, 1962, the commission subsequently informing the plaintiffs that they had failed to establish a claim. The plaintiffs claimed declarations in the Queen's Bench Division against the commission and their legal officer seeking to establish that their determination was wrong in law and invalid. By their defence, the commission relied upon the provisions of s. 4 (4) of the Foreign Compensation Act, 1950, that the determination by the commission of any application to them under the Act should not be called in question in any court of law. John Stephenson J., dismissed the plaintiffs' appeal from the order of Master Ritchie that the question of the court's jurisdiction to entertain the plaintiffs' claim should be dealt with as a preliminary point of law. The plaintiffs appealed.

LORD DENNING, M.R., said that the authorities showed that as a rule it was undesirable that a point of law should be ordered to be decided as a preliminary point unless it was reasonably clear that the issues would be determined and costs saved: *David* v. *Abdul Cader* [1963] 1 W.L.R. 834. The general principle applied that the determination of a point of law should not be ordered unless the court was satisfied that it would dispose of all the issues in the case. Here points of jurisdiction were much mixed up with points of interpretation; this was one of those cases where it would be better to allow one judge to deal with the whole case: *Barraclough* v. *Brown* [1897] A.C. 615; his lordship would allow the appeal.

HARMAN, L.J., concurred.

DIPLOCK, L.J. dissenting, said that under R.S.C., Ord. 34, r. 2, it was a matter for the discretion of the judge and not of the Court of Appeal. A distinction should be drawn between preliminary points of law which went to the jurisdiction and those that did not.

Appeal allowed.

APPEARANCES: *Roger Parker, Q.C.*, and *F. P. Neill* (*Linklater & Paines*); *Nigel Bridge* (*Treasury Solicitor*).

ANISMINIC LTD. v. FOREIGN COMPENSATION COMMISSION

((1964) 108 Sol. Jo. 638)

July 29, 1964: House of Lords: Lords Radcliffe, Cohen, Upjohn.

Practice—Preliminary Point of Law—Jurisdiction of Court—Petition for Leave to Appeal Dismissed.

Petition for leave to appeal from the Court of Appeal* (Lord Denning, M.R. and Harman, L.J., Diplock, L.J., dissenting).

The plaintiffs, a mining company, applied to the defendants, the Foreign Compensation Commission, for compensation in respect of property in Egypt. The commission found that they had failed to establish their claim. The plaintiffs claimed a declaration that that determination was wrong in law or invalid. By their defence the commission relied on s. 4 (4) of the Foreign Compensation Act, 1950, which provided that the determination by the commission of any application to them should not be called in question in any court of law. The Court of Appeal allowed an appeal from an order of John Stephenson, J., who had dismissed the plaintiffs' appeal from the order of Master Ritchie, that the question of the court's jurisdiction to entertain the plaintiff's claim should be dealt with as a preliminary point of law. The commission appealed. The Attorney-General said that although the matter was one of practice, the Court of Appeal's decision would almost preclude the use of R.S.C., Ord. 34, r. 2, for deciding preliminary points of law. The first question was whether the matter was one of complete discretion or whether the Court of Appeal could only exercise discretion if satisfied that the judge had acted on wrong principles. The second question was whether the warnings about the inconvenience of trying preliminary points of law were inapplicable to a preliminary point going to the jurisdiction. The matter turned on the 1950 Act, and could be tried without any investigation of the facts. The third question was whether a preliminary issue should only be allowed if it was likely to dispose of the whole issue. Counsel for the plaintiffs said that it was a purely procedural matter and an appeal would not normally lie. The Court of Appeal had laid down no principle of law in their decision. The matters in question depended not only on the 1950 Act but on Orders in Council as well.

LORD RADCLIFFE said that the commission had not made out a case for an appeal to the House of Lords and the petition could not be granted. But in saying that they were not to be understood as indorsing all that could be found or read into the judgments of the Court of Appeal. Petition dismissed.

APPEARANCES: *Sir John Hobson, Q.C., A.-G.*, and *Nigel Bridge* (*Treasury Solicitor*); *Roger Parker, Q.C.*, and *F. P. Neill* (*Linklaters & Paines*).

ANISMINIC LTD. v. FOREIGN COMPENSATION COMMISSION AND ANOTHER

([1968] 2 Q.B. 862)

January 16, 17, 18, 19, 20, 23, 24, 25, 26, 27, 30, 31, February 1, March 22, 1967: Court of Appeal: Sellers, Diplock, Russell L.JJ.

Crown Practice—Certiorari—Inferior tribunal—Statutory—Foreign Compensation Commission—Determination—Construction of Order in Council—Whether error going to jurisdiction—"No certiorari clause"—Whether certiorari lies—Foreign Compensation Act, 1950 (14 *Geo.* 6, *c.* 12), *s.* 4 (4).
Practice—Declaratory judgment—Certiorari, relation to—Inferior tribunal—Foreign Compensation Commission—Determination—"No certiorari clause"—Construction of Order in Council—Whether error within jurisdiction—Tribunal's power to determine but not to enforce the liability—Whether tribunal party to action for declaration that determination a nullity—Foreign Compensation Act, 1950, *s.* 4 (4).
Tribunal—Statutory—Control by courts—Declaration—Foreign Compensation Commission—Determination—Construction of Order in **[863]** *Council—Whether error within jurisdiction—Tribunal's power to determine but not to enforce—Whether party to action for declaration—Whether jurisdiction in court to entertain proceedings—Foreign Compensation Act,* 1950, *s.* 4 (4).
Ouster of Jurisdiction of Court—Statute—Determination by statutory commission—Not to "be called in question in any court of law"—Effect—Foreign Compensation Act, 1950, *s.* 4 (4).

Before the Suez Incident and on October 31, 1956, the plaintiffs, an English company, owned property in Egypt which was sequestrated, under the provisions of Proclamation No. 5 of 1956, by the Egyptian authorities. In 1957, the plaintiffs sold the sequestrated property to an Egyptian organisation, T.E.D.O. In 1959, the plaintiffs, who were named in Annex E within the meaning of article 1 (2) of the Foreign Compensation (Egypt) (Determination and Registration of Claims) Order, 1962,[1] made an application to the

[1] Foreign Compensation (Egypt) (Determination and Registration of Claims) Order, 1962, art. 1: ". . . (2) 'Annex E' means the revised text of Annex E to the Agreement substituted by an Exchange of Notes between Her Majesty's Government and the Government of the United Arab Republic on August 7, 1962."

Part III, art. 4: "(1) The commission shall treat a claim under this Part of the Order as established if the applicant satisfies them of the following matters:—(*a*) that his application relates to property in Egypt which is referred to in Annex E; (*b*) if the property is referred to in para. 1 (*a*) or para. 2 of Annex E—(i) that the applicant is the person referred to in para. (1) (*a*) or in para. 2 as the case may be, as the owner of the property or is the successor in title of such person; and (ii) that the person referred to as aforesaid and any person who became successor in title of such person on or before February 28, 1959, were British nationals on October 31, 1956, and February 28, 1959; (*c*) if the property is referred to in para. (1) (*b*) of Annex E—(i) that the applicant was the owner on October 31, 1956, or, at the option of the applicant, on the date of the sale of the property at any time before February 28, 1959, by the Government of the United Arab Republic under the provisions of Egyptian Proclamation No. 5 of November 1, 1956, or is the successor in title of such owner; and (ii) that the owner on October 31, 1956, or on the date of such sale, as the case may be, and any person who became successor in title of such owner on or before February 28, 1959, were British nationals on October 31, 1956, and February 28, 1959. . . ."

Pt. IV, art. 6: "(1) The commission shall treat a claim under this Part of the Order as established if the applicant satisfies them of the following matters:—(*a*) that his application relates to property in Egypt in respect of which no claim can be established under Part III of this Order and which has been lost, injured or damaged after October 30, 1956, and before February 28, 1959, as a result of Egyptian measures; (*b*) that he

Foreign Compensation Commission claiming that they were persons entitled to participate in the Egyptian **[864]** Compensation Fund in respect of their sequestrated property. The commission's provisional determination was that they had failed to establish a claim under the Order. The plaintiffs brought this action against the commission for declarations to the effect that the provisional determination was a nullity and that they were entitled to participate in the compensation fund. They contended that the commission had misconstrued the Order in finding that T.E.D.O. was their successor in title. The commission contended that, under section 4 (4) of the Foreign Compensation Act, 1950,[2] the court had no jurisdiction to entertain the proceedings. Browne J. found for the plaintiffs and granted them declarations. The commission appealed on the grounds, inter alia, that the judge erred in law in holding that he had jurisdiction to entertain the plaintiffs' claim in the action; that the commission's provisional determination was a nullity and that the commission had no jurisdiction to construe the provisions of the Order:—

Held, that the commission alone was empowered to determine whether the plaintiffs were persons entitled to participate in the compensation fund, and section 4 (4) of the Foreign Compensation Act, 1950, clearly stated that their determination could not be questioned in any court of law. The commission had made a determination and it was a necessary incident to that determination that the commission had to construe the Foreign Compensation (Egypt) (Determination and Registration of Claims) Order, 1962, which included consideration of the question whether T.E.D.O. was the plaintiffs' successor in title, and no court could question the determination by substituting its views on the construction of the Order for those of the commission. Accordingly, the court had no jurisdiction to entertain the plaintiffs' action.

Per Diplock L.J. The jurisdiction of the High Court to give declaratory judgments is limited to deciding the existence of legally enforceable rights or liabilities and it will in many cases afford an alternative procedure to certiorari for questioning the determination of an inferior tribunal. The defendant to such an action is not the tribunal as such but the person who is entitled to enforce the liability if the determination is valid. Where the only function of the tribunal is to make a determination, it is doubtful whether an action for a declaration lies against the inferior tribunal (post, pp. 910-911).

APPEAL from Browne J.

The plaintiffs, Anisminic Ltd., were an English company incorporated in 1913, and from that date until 1958 their registered name was The Sinai Mining Co. Ltd. Before and on October 31, 1956, they carried on the business of mining manganese in the Sinai **[865]** Peninsula under mining leases or concessions granted by the Egyptian Government. Their valuation of their property and assets in that area was about £4.5 million. The events known as the Suez Incident began on October 31, 1956.

On November 1, 1956, the Egyptian Government issued a proclamation, Proclamation No. 5 of 1956, by which two general sequestrators and special sequestrators were appointed to take over and manage the assets of British and French nationals. The plaintiffs' property was sequestrated and, after sequestration, the Israeli armed forces destroyed, damaged or removed about £500,000 worth of that property.

---

was the owner at the time of such loss, injury or damage or is the successor in title of such owner; and (*c*) that the owner at the time of the loss, injury or damage and any person who became successor in title of such owner on or before February 28, 1959, were British nationals on October 31, 1956, and February 28, 1959. . . ."

Art 8: "If the applicant satisfies the commission of all the matters specified in art. 6 of this Order other than that the loss, injury or damage was the result of Egyptian measures, the commission shall register the claim and report thereon to Her Majesty's Principal Secretary of State for Foreign Affairs in such manner as he shall direct."

[2] Foreign Compensation Act, 1950, s. 4 (4): "The determination by the commission of any application made to them under this Act shall not be called in question in any court of law."

In April, 1957, the Israeli forces withdrew and, on April 29, 1957, the Egyptian Government, by Decree No. 387 of 1957, granted the Custodian General of property of British, French and Australian nationals authority to sell and to liquidate the establishments and other property subject to sequestration. On that date, the Custodian General and the Chairman of the Economic Board, who was also the representative of a company under formation and to be known as the Sinai Manganese Co. S.A.E., entered into a contract of sale by which the plaintiffs' sequestrated property was sold to the Economic Board. The Economic Board was the same body as The Economic Development Organisation ("T.E.D.O.").

On June 11, 1957, the plaintiffs registered with the Foreign Office in London a claim setting out details of the assets and goodwill of their undertakings in Egypt as at October 31, 1956. The plaintiffs then decided to enter into negotiations with the Egyptian authorities and, on November 23, 1957, they agreed to sell to T.E.D.O. the whole of their business carried on and situated in Egypt for the sum of £500,000 sterling. The agreement specifically provided that the plaintiffs' assets should not include any claim which they had against any government authority other than the Egyptian Government. The plaintiffs also agreed to take measures to change their name and did so on January 30, 1958.

By an agreement dated February 28, 1959, between the United Kingdom Government and the Government of the United Arab Republic, the Government of the United Arab Republic agreed to pay to the British Government the sum of £27,500,000 in full and final settlement of claims by United Kingdom nationals for certain property in Egypt, including property subject to the provisions of Proclamation No. 5 and referred to in Annex E to that agreement and in Annex E to the Exchange of Notes dated August 7, 1962, which was supplementary to the agreement of February 28, 1959. The sum of £27,500,000 and other moneys provided by the **[866]** British Government formed the Egyptian Compensation Fund and, pursuant to the Foreign Compensation Act, 1950, and Orders in Council, the Foreign Compensation Commission (referred to as the commission) were empowered to make provisional determinations as to whether applicants had made out their claims to be entitled to participate in the compensation fund. The plaintiffs' name appeared in Annex E "(subject to a special arrangement)."

On September 15, 1959, the plaintiffs made an application to the commission claiming that they were entitled to participate in the compensation fund and, on May 8, 1963, the commission provisionally determined that the plaintiffs had failed to establish a claim under the Foreign Compensation (Egypt) (Determination and Registration of Claims) Order, 1962, in respect of their sequestrated property but their claim for certain property damaged by the Israeli armed forces was fit for registration. On June 21, 1963, by a further provisional determination, the commission ordered that their claim for damage should be registered, under article 8 of the Order, in the sum of £532,773. The commission released to the plaintiffs their minutes of adjudication which disclosed, inter alia, that the commission considered that T.E.D.O., who were not British nationals, were the plaintiffs' successors in title.

The plaintiffs brought this action against the defendants, the commission and the legal advisor appointed by them to represent the interests of the compensation fund, for declarations to the effect that the commission's provisional determination was wrong in law and was either invalid or a nullity. The plaintiffs contended, inter alia, that T.E.D.O. was not their successor in title and that they had proved that they were persons entitled to participate in the compensation fund. By their amended defence, the defendants contended, inter alia, that the High Court had no jurisdiction to entertain the proceedings.

On July 29, 1966, Browne J. found for the plaintiffs and made the declarations that the commission's provisional determination of May 8, 1963, was made without or in excess of jurisdiction and was a nullity; and the commission's further provisional determination of June 21, 1963, was a nullity and that the commission were under a statutory duty to treat as established under Part III (art. 4) of the Foreign Compensation (Egypt) (Determination and Registration of Claims) Order, 1962, the plaintiffs' claim in respect of their property in Egypt.

The defendants appealed against the judgment of Browne J. on the grounds, inter alia, that the judge erred in law in holding that he had jurisdiction to entertain the plaintiffs' claim in the **[867]** action and to make all or any of the declarations; that he erred in law in holding that the commission's provisional determinations were a nullity and in holding that the commission had no jurisdiction to construe the provisions of the Foreign Compensation (Egypt) (Determination and Registration of Claims) Order, 1962, and that the judge erred in law in holding that T.E.D.O. had not become the successor in title of the plaintiffs.

Sydney Templeman Q.C., Nigel Bridge and *C. D. Cochrane* for the defendants.

[SELLERS L.J. We desire to hear argument first on whether the court had jurisdiction to entertain the plaintiffs' action.]

The plaintiffs were a mining company whose assets were sequestrated and whose mining leases were cancelled by the Egyptian Government. They entered into an agreement with the Egyptian Government to sell their business and assets in Egypt to T.E.D.O. for £500,000. When the plaintiffs made that agreement with the Egyptian Government, they thereby lost their right to claim compensation against the fund set aside for the payment of claims of British nationals. When the plaintiffs' property was seized, they had a spes restitutionis, a claim for the return of their property or for adequate compensation. That claim was assignable or saleable, and, if it was assigned for value, the assignment would have been upheld. The agreement which the plaintiffs made with the Egyptian Government operated as a sale of their property to T.E.D.O., to make T.E.D.O. the successor in title to their property in Egypt and also to release any claims which they had against the Egyptian Government. True, it is claimed that £500,000 was only one-ninth of the value of their business, but the agreement which they made has to be judged by what it says. By that agreement there was an assignment of the claim which they had against the Egyptian Government. No doubt the plaintiffs thought that a bird in the hand was worth two in the bush. The plaintiffs had registered their claim with the British Government. Even after they had made their agreement with the Egyptian Government, they merely asked by letter that their claim be reduced by £500,000. But the Egyptian Government had no claim to pay so far as the plaintiffs were concerned because by their own separate agreement with the Egyptian Government they had assigned it, and so far as the British Government was concerned they had no claim to press, so far as the plaintiffs were concerned, because there was none.

On the true construction of the Foreign Compensation (Egypt) **[868]** (Determination and Registration of Claims) Order, 1962, the plaintiffs were unable to establish any claim to compensation because another person, who was not a British national, became their successor in title on February 28, 1959. The provisional determination of the commission was that the claim failed because there cannot be a claim by an owner of property unless he himself has an existing claim against the Egyptian Government, which the plaintiffs had not, nor can there be a claim by a successor in title unless he is or was on February 28, 1959, a British national.

It is always open to an applicant who is aggrieved by a decision of the commission to approach the Foreign Office. But it is not possible to appeal against a determination of the commission in respect of a claim for compensation to the courts. That is because by section 4 (4) of the Foreign Compensation Act, 1950, the determination by the commission of any application made to them under the Act cannot be called in question in any court of law. Prior to the Act of 1950 compensation was dealt with by the Crown in the exercise of its prerogative, and the Crown would deal with the fund received from a foreign government for the purposes of compensation as a matter of prerogative. The Foreign Compensation Commission is merely machinery by which that prerogative is exercised. If it should transpire as a result of the commission's determinations that a worthy applicant had been excluded from compensation, the Crown can remedy the situation by making an appropriate Order in Council. Although the commission in a sense exercise a judicial function, they really exercise an administrative function on behalf of the Crown by determining which of the applicants for compensation should be paid out of a special fund which has been set aside for that purpose.

The courts will only consider a finding of a tribunal where there is no statutory enactment precluding the jurisdiction of the court to hear an application for an order of certiorari and will only interfere with such a finding if the tribunal has acted outside its jurisdiction or there is an error of law on the face of the record: *Rex* v. *Northumberland Compensation Appeal Tribunal, Ex parte Shaw.*[3] By the Tribunals Act, 1958, all tribunals are ordered to give their reasons for their decisions and, with certain exceptions, there is a prohibition on a no cetiorari clause. Those exceptions are where a speedy decision is essential because a speedy decision, even if there has only been rough justice, is more important to the parties than a delayed decision given after **[869]** long and protracted hearings of the matter. The Insurance Acts provide for an appeal only to a single judge for the same reason that speed is of the essence of justice being done to the parties. Here, money to be paid out of a limited fund to third parties is held up until this matter is resolved. Parliament intended to leave the whole matter of compensation to the commission and their determination should be final and conclusive. Parliament plainly intended to exclude the jurisdiction of the courts: see section 4 (4) of the Act of 1950. Browne J. accepted that construction of the section and the following authorities support such a construction: *Rex* v. *Northumberland Compensation Appeal Tribunal, Ex parte Shaw*[4]; *Brittain* v. *Kinnaird*[5]; *Reg.* v. *St. Olave's District Board*[6]; *Rex* v. *Minister of Health*[7]; *Smith* v. *East Elloe Rural District Council*[8]; *Reg.* v. *Foreign Compensation Commission, Ex parte Oak and Timber Co. Ltd.*[9]

The Tribunals and Inquiries Act, 1958, shows that the commission are in a different category from other administrative tribunals because by section 11 (3) of the Act of 1958 the provisions of that Act were not to apply to them. That shows that Parliament thought that the commission should be treated in a different category from other administrative tribunals and that their decisions should not even have to be subject to reasons as provided by the Tribunals and Inquiries Act, 1958.

On the true construction of section 4 (4) of the Foreign Compensation Act, 1950, it was not open to the plaintiffs to appeal because the courts have no jurisdiction to consider whether the commission erred in their determination. They made a determination on an application made to them by the plaintiffs which the commission had jurisdiction to determine, and that determination cannot be called into question. A person making an application to the commission brings himself within their jurisdiction. They have jurisdiction to determine any claim which he makes to share in a fund provided by the Egyptian Government for compensation. The commission gives reasons why they are not satisfied that the claim should be upheld. The reasons given show that they have exercised their jurisdiction. It might be that they have made a mistake in the sense that someone else might decide the matter differently. It might even be that, if the matter had been taken **[870]** to a court of law, the matter might have been decided differently on some legal principle. Even so, if there be a mistake, it was an error within the jurisdiction and on the wording of the Act of 1950 there was a "determination," which cannot be questioned. Parliament could not have used stronger words to have excluded the jurisdiction of the courts, and short of compelling authorities to the contrary the words of section 4 (4) could not be stronger.

One should also have regard to the intent of the Act of 1950, which was to

[3] [1951] 1 K.B. 711; [1951] 1 T.L.R. 270; [1951] 1 All E.R. 268, D.C.; [1952] 1 K.B. 338; [1952] 1 T.L.R. 61; [1952] 1 All E.R. 122, C.A.

[4] [1951] 1 K.B. 711.

[5] (1819) 1 Brod. & B. 432.

[6] (1857) 8 E. & B. 529.

[7] [1939] 1 K.B. 232; 55 T.L.R. 4; [1938] 4 All E.R. 32, C.A.

[8] [1956] A.C. 736; [1956] 2 W.L.R. 888; [1956] 1 All E.R. 855, H.L.(E.).

[9] Unreported, November 11, 1955.

provide for an administrative arrangement to deal as equitably as possible with compensation in unusual circumstances, which might give rise to many difficult questions of fact and law. In many respects it is an odd Act because it applies only if the government does certain things, for its operation is conditional upon the acts of the government; even if the government obtains a fund from a foreign government, the Act of 1950 operates only if the government hands over the fund to the commission.

Here something is being called in question, the "determination" of the commission which is the very thing that Parliament said should not be called into question. The judge said that the commission had erred in their construction of the terms of the Order of 1962 and that made their determination a nullity. But Parliament did not consider that an error in the construction of a document, albeit the Order was no more than a document, should suffice to make the determination of the commission a nullity. The commission in their determination said that they were not satisfied of the conditions specified in article 4 (1) of the Order of 1962. Any issue which depends upon whether the commission were satisfied of certain conditions must be an issue within the jurisdiction of the commission, be it an issue of law or of fact, because, in all these cases, issues of fact and of law are inextricably bound up.

If the commission are faced with a question which they have to decide in the course of exercising their primary jurisdiction and they fall into error, that is nevertheless an error within their jurisdiction. Article 4 is conferring jurisdiction, and at the same time telling the commission how to exercise the jurisdiction; in the course of exercising it, innumerable questions of fact and law will arise. Whatever error the commission made, provided it was bona fide made in the exercise of jurisdiction to determine the plaintiffs' claim, was an error made within jurisdiction.

The judge divided the authorities on jurisdiction and the court's power to entertain appeals from inferior tribunals operating under an exclusion of jurisdiction clause in a statute into four categories: **[871]** (1) cases where the tribunal had no jurisdiction to embark upon an inquiry, which is not this case; (2) cases where an inferior tribunal had jurisdiction to embark on an inquiry, but made an order outside its jurisdiction; here the commission made an order debarring the plaintiffs from compensation payable out of the fund—which is an order which they were entitled to make; (3) cases where an inferior tribunal made an error of fact or law while exercising its jurisdiction; (4) cases where the inferior tribunal had no jurisdiction to consider the issue presented to it.

The judge relied mainly on *Rex* v. *Shoreditch Assessment Committee,*[10] but that was a class 1 case and has nothing to do with the present case. There it was held that the jurisdiction of the assessment committee did not arise until the valuer had made a provisional list, which he had not done. But it is plain that here the commission on any view were entitled to embark upon the inquiry which they entertained. The judge also relied on *Ex parte Bradlaugh,*[11] but that again is distinguishable because there the order for the destruction of the obscene books did not state the existence of a matter which was a condition precedent to its validity, namely, that the books were of such character as to make them a misdemeanour. It was a class 2 case, which on any view the present case is not. The plaintiffs also relied upon *Estate and Trust Agencies* (*1927*) *Ltd.* v. *Singapore Improvement Trust,*[12] but that case is distinguishable for there was no provision of the colonial ordinance excluding the jurisdiction of the High Court. The judge relied also on *Reg.* v. *Fulham, Hammersmith and Kensington Rent Tribunal, Ex parte Hierowski,*[13] but that again was a class 1 case because there the rent tribunal, which had power to reconsider its previous decision only on the ground of change in circumstances, purported to reconsider the whole matter again de novo.

In none of the cases on which the judge relied was the error of the inferior

[10] [1910] 2 K.B. 859; 26 T.L.R. 663, C.A.
[11] (1878) 3 Q.B.D. 509, D.C.
[12] [1937] A.C. 898; 53 T.L.R. 829; [1937] 3 All E.R. 324, P.C.
[13] [1953] 2 Q.B. 147; [1953] 2 W.L.R. 1028; [1953] 2 All E.R. 4, D.C.

tribunal an error within its jurisdiction. *Board of Trustees of the Maradana Mosque* v. *Badiuddin Mahmud*[14] is distinguishable because the decision turned on the fact that there had been a denial of natural justice in the inquiry which preceded the order of the inferior tribunal. *Rex* v. *Northumberland Compensation Appeal Tribunal, Ex parte Shaw*[15] shows the difference **[872]** in law between errors within the jurisdiction and errors outside the jurisdiction. The error in that case as to the amount of the award for compensation was held to be an error within the jurisdiction. All the cases relied upon by the judge were cases of error outside the jurisdiction. The present case, if there be an error at all, is one of error within the jurisdiction. *Reg.* v. *Foreign Compensation Commission, Ex parte Oak and Timber Co. Ltd.*[16] is an illustration of the difficult questions of fact and of law which can be raised before the commission upon a determination of an application for compensation.

An error by an inferior tribunal in construing a statute does not go to want of jurisdiction, but only to the wrong exercise of jurisdiction which the tribunal undoubtedly had: see *per* Parker L.J. in *Davies* v. *Price*.[17] As to what is needed to prove the ingredients of satisfaction where something is left to be determined to the satisfaction of an independent third person, see the statement of Lord Tomlin in *Cammell Laird & Co. Ltd.* v. *Manganese Bronze and Brass Co. Ltd.*[18] [Reference was also made to *In re Gale, decd.*[19]]

Roger Parker Q.C. and *F. P. Neill Q.C.* for the plaintiffs. The question of jurisdiction and of the true construction of the orders are inextricably bound up together. It was so decided by the Court of Appeal in the interlocutory proceedings in this case: see *Anisminic Ltd.* v. *Foreign Compensation Commission*.[20]*

The judge was right for neither of the two questions raised in this case, the question as to jurisdiction or as to construction, can be decided unless the facts, relevant statute and orders are properly analysed. If an inferior tribunal makes an error within the jurisdiction, the courts might be unable to act if there is no speaking order. The making of a speaking order, giving reasons for the decision, is regarded as praiseworthy: see *Estate and Trust Agencies (1927) Ltd.* v. *Singapore Improvement Trust*.[21] Parliament has considered that it is not only praiseworthy, but has required a large number of administrative tribunals to give reasons for their decisions: see the Tribunals and Inquiries Act, 1958. It does not follow that because the commission are excluded from the Act of 1958 that it is not praiseworthy that they give reasons for their decisions. **[873]**

If the Crown had not attempted to secure a fund for compensation to people who had property in Egypt at the material time then there would be no ground for applying for relief. If the Crown does obtain money by treaty with Egypt, there is no obligation on the Crown, but for the Foreign Compensation Act, 1950, to distribute that money and, if the Crown does distribute the money, it may do so in any manner and for any purpose, but the Crown has surrendered its prerogative and substituted an Act of Parliament and, as long as the Act applies, there is a temporary surrender of the prerogative and the money must be distributed in accordance with the Act and Order in Council applying the Act to the fund. In respect of this fund the Orders in Council incorporate the terms of the treaty on several points but for the purposes of distribution it is the Order of 1962 which is relevant and not the terms of the treaty. The Order of 1962 informs the commission of its jurisdiction in the matter and the commission can neither by its own decision confer on itself any other jurisdiction nor decide not to carry out its obligations to consider a valid claim.

[14] [1967] 1 A.C. 13; [1966] 2 W.L.R. 921; [1966] 1 All E.R. 545, P.C.
[15] [1952] 1 K.B. 338.
[16] Unreported, November 11, 1955.
[17] [1958] 1 W.L.R. 434, 441; [1958] 1 All E.R. 671, C.A.
[18] [1934] A.C. 402, 412; 50 T.L.R. 550, H.L.(E.).
[19] [1966] Ch. 236; [1966] 2 W.L.R. 571; [1966] 1 All E.R. 945, C.A.
[20] (1964) 108 S.J. 541, C.A.; affd. *The Times*, July 29, 1964, H.L.(E.).
[21] [1937] A.C. 898.

It might appear at first sight that the court is acting contrary to the expressed intention of Parliament by considering this case but, in fact and in law, the court, far from defeating the Act, is giving it its true effect because the court is refusing to impute to Parliament the intention of creating a tribunal with power to act only in certain circumstances and at the same time stating that if the tribunal chooses to act in any other circumstances it would be in order. Section 4 (4) of the Foreign Compensation Act, 1950, does not specifically exclude the jurisdiction of the court to exercise its supervisory powers of certiorari over an inferior tribunal and the section is no wider than past sections which have prohibited an appeal to a court of law from the findings of an inferior tribunal. There being no specific prohibition, the court has a supervisory jurisdiction: see Lord Sumner in *Rex* v. *Nat Bell Liquors Ltd.*[22] Parliament never intended that the commission should have unlimited power to distribute the fund in any way it pleased. Parliament has stated that provided the commission acts within its powers granted by the Act and the Orders then its decisions will not be questioned in a court of law.

The courts, under section 4 (4) of the Act of 1960, cannot question an error of law within the jurisdiction of the tribunal. The question is whether the error of law is within the jurisdiction or goes to the jurisdiction: *Rex* v. *Bradford.*[23] If the commission **[874]** thought that this was not a claim then they should have considered that they had no power to proceed and, if they did proceed, they could not thereby confer jurisdiction on themselves. If the commission misconstrues the claim then there is an error of law going to the jurisdiction and section 4 (4) of the Act of 1950 does not apply: see *Reg.* v. *Medical Appeal Tribunal, Ex parte Gilmore*[24]; *Reg.* v. *Hurst, Ex parte Smith*[25]; *Evans* v. *McLoughlan*[26]; *Board of Education* v. *Rice*[27]; *Board of Trustees of the Maradana Mosque* v. *Badiuddin Mahmud.*[28]

It is a fallacy to say that an error in the construction of matters committed to the determination of the commission can never go to want of jurisdiction. If a claim is put forward under article 4 of the Order of 1962, and the commission are satisfied that all the ingredients for a proper claim are established except for the fact of British nationality on the relevant date, then on its face that is a good decision beyond the purview of the courts. But if it appeared that the commission found as facts that at both relevant dates the applicant was a British protected person belonging to a territory for which Britain was responsible in international law, that would show the commission were satisfied on all relevant matters necessary to establish a claim and it would be wrong to say that their determination did not go to jurisdiction because they had erred in their view of who was a British national. The reason why they would have erred is because they would not have directed themselves to the question which had been asked of them. Whether an error of law goes to jurisdiction or not is often a fine question: see Denning L.J. in *Rex* v. *Northumberland Compensation Appeal Tribunal, Ex parte Shaw.*[29] Reliance is placed on his view that an error of law could go to jurisdiction.

Section 4 (4) of the Act of 1950 protects all errors of fact within the jurisdiction from review by the courts, and also all errors of law truly regarded as errors exercised in the course of the jurisdiction of the commission. It is a mistake to suppose, however, that a document which says that the claim is not established is necessarily a determination, because the actual result of the commission's findings is a matter of pure machinery. Once they have found certain facts, or not found certain facts, their determination follows automatically because there is no discretion which **[875]** has been entrusted to them. If they are satisfied of certain matters, they are bound to treat the claim

[22] [1922] 2 A.C. 128, 159; 38 T.L.R. 541, P.C.
[23] [1908] 1 K.B. 365; 24 T.L.R. 195, D.C.
[24] [1957] 1 Q.B. 574; [1957] 2 W.L.R. 498; [1957] 1 All E.R. 796, C.A.
[25] [1960] 2 Q.B. 133; [1960] 2 W.L.R. 961; [1960] 2 All E.R. 385, D.C.
[26] (1861) 4 L.T. 31, H.L.
[27] [1911] A.C. 179; 27 T.L.R. 378, H.L.(E.).
[28] [1967] 1 A.C. 13.
[29] [1952] 1 K.B. 338, 353.

as established for they have only to decide the specified matters. The establishment or non-establishment of a claim is not of itself a determination: it is the automatic outcome of the previous findings of the commission. Suppose that the commission said that nobody who was not a member of the Church of England could qualify for compensation. It would be horrifying to think that in such a case their "determination" could not be questioned in the courts. It was conceded by the defendants that, if the commission were to award costs, the courts could upset their decision. The commission cannot by an error of construction, or by misconstruction, give themselves a jurisdiction which they do not possess.

The commission cannot require an applicant to satisfy them of matters which are additional to the conditions set out in the articles of the Order for the establishment of a claim to compensation. If they seek to impose additional requirements upon applicants, and but for those additional requirements they would have been satisfied that the claim had been established, the commission are failing in their statutory duty if they do not treat the claim as established. In this case the commission said that no person could qualify for compensation unless he had a claim against the United Arab Republic at the date of the treaty, but that is nowhere to be found in the Order of 1962.

The commission did not treat the claim of the plaintiffs, which was established, as established. Having been satisfied of the necessary ingredients for the establishment of the claim, the commission should have treated the claim as established and by not doing so they have ignored the injunction in the Act of 1950 to treat the claim as established; and that goes to jurisdiction. If a jurisdiction of an inferior tribunal does not end with a discretion, and it has in fact been satisfied of all the relevant matters on which it has to be satisfied the tribunal is not wrong in respect of the matters committed to it, but it exceeds its jurisdiction, alternatively it does not carry out its statutory duty, if it does not record its satisfaction. The view of Parker L.J. in *Davies* v. *Price*,[30] which was obiter, that an error in the construction of a statute could not be an error of jurisdiction was based upon *Reg.* v. *Agricultural Land Tribunal, East of England, Ex parte Grant*,[31] where the decision of the inferior tribunal was quashed because it had made a wrong approach to the case. But that case provides [**876**] a good contrast to the present case because there the tribunal had a discretion once it was satisfied upon certain matters, whereas in the present case the commission, once they were satisfied of certain matters, had no discretion, but were required to treat as established the claim for compensation. In an earlier case on the Agricultural Holdings Act, 1948, *Reg.* v. *Agricultural Land Tribunal, Wales and Monmouth, Ex parte Davies*,[32] the Divisional Court took the approach which the court is invited to take in this case, namely, it looked at what the order setting up the tribunal said.

It was a condition precedent to the jurisdiction which the commission asserted to refuse the claim for them to say that the relevant successor in title was not British, but on the true construction of the Order of 1962 there was no relevant successor in title and, therefore, their error goes to jurisdiction. In deciding that "claim" meant what they said it meant they were making an error of construction, which it was not for them to make, and were imposing upon all applicants for compensation an additional requirement which was not provided for in the Act of 1950 and the rules made thereunder. As to the point about "successor in title," first, there was on the true construction of the Order no successor in title, and the commission could not make that a condition precedent to the carrying out of their statutory duty to assess the loss, and secondly, even if the "successor in title" was relevant, they made an error whereby they produced a result which would defeat the manifest intention of the Order of 1962 and such an error goes to jurisdiction.

30 [1958] 1 W.L.R. 434, 441.
31 [1956] 1 W.L.R. 1240; [1956] 3 All E.R. 321, C.A.
32 [1953] 1 W.L.R. 722; [1953] 1 All E.R. 1182, D.C.

The term "jurisdiction" is used in different senses in different cases. There are two cases where what a person has done can be a nullity for want of jurisdiction. Either where the tribunal has no entitlement to embark on the inquiry which it did, or where it has no entitlement to make the order which it did. The present case is an example of the latter category. A more difficult case arises where there has been an error of construction of a statute. If the construction, which an inferior tribunal puts upon a statute or regulation made under it, would lead to the manifest intention of the statute or order being defeated, or if the construction results in the tribunal asking themselves the wrong question, the error goes to want of jurisdiction.

Incidental misconstruction of an Act of Parliament in pursuance of the commission's primary duty would not affect jurisdiction and would not be subject to review by the courts. But if they misconstrue the sections of the Act of 1950 or of the rules made **[877]** under it, giving them jurisdiction, so as to adopt a wrong approach to the question which they have to determine and so as to pose a wrong test for the establishment of a claim, that is a matter going to jurisdiction and such as to make their decision a nullity if they adopt the wrong approach. If they err in construing the section giving them the jurisdiction in such a way that they ask themselves questions not committed to them, that goes to jurisdiction. Here the commission asked themselves the wrong questions and because of that they posed the wrong test for the establishment of the plaintiff's claim.

The wrong questions posed by the commission were: (1) whether the plaintiffs had on February 28, 1959, an existing claim against the United Arab Republic; (2) whether the plaintiffs had satisfied the commission either that they had no successor in title prior to February 28, 1959, or that any or all possible successors in title before that date were British nationals both on that date and on October 30, 1956. By requiring an affirmative answer to question (1) the commission were imposing upon the plaintiffs an additional burden not found in the Order of 1962. The commission raised a hurdle which the plaintiffs were not required to surmount, and by so doing they were in breach of their statutory duty. By requiring an affirmative answer to question (2), the commission were imposing two additional burdens upon the plaintiffs which were not imposed by the Order of 1962 and, therefore, again were failing in their statutory duty. If a statute requires a tribunal to decide a particular question and by a misconstruction of the statute an inferior tribunal embarks on an inquiry into a totally different question, that is a matter going to jurisdiction. In such circumstances the courts can intervene even where there is a section in a statute excluding their jurisdiction: see *Estate and Trust Agencies (1927) Ltd.* v. *Singapore Improvement Trust*,[33] and the *Board of Trustees of the Maradana Mosque* v. *Badiuddin Mahmud*.[34]

The defendants relied upon *Brittain* v. *Kinnaird*[35] but it does not help for it was an action against a magistrate's decision and the question there was how far his finding of fact was conclusive. *Reg.* v. *St. Olave's District Board*,[36] like *Reg.* v. *Foreign Compensation Commission, Ex parte Oak and Timber Co. Ltd.*,[37] was a case where it was held that the error did not go to jurisdiction and it should be compared with cases where the opposite was **[878]** held; c.f., *Rex* v. *Minister of Health*.[38] *Smith* v. *East Elloe Rural District Council*[39] does not really help as it was not concerned with the question of a tribunal's jurisdiction [Reference was also made to *Ex parte Bradlaugh*.[40]]

F. P. Niell Q.C. following. For about 300 years statutes have been enacted with provisions to oust the jurisdiction of the courts and those provisions have increased in severity and have been as wide as section 4 (4) of the Foreign Compensation Act, 1950. The courts approach has been that, where the provisions are ambiguous, then they should be construed as not to oust the court's jurisdiction and, where unambiguous, as not applicable when an inferior tribunal

33 [1937] A.C. 898.
34 [1967] 1 A.C. 13.
35 1 Brod. & B. 432.
36 8 E. & B. 529.
37 Unreported, November 11, 1955.
38 [1939] 1 K.B. 232.
39 [1956] A.C. 736.
40 3 Q.B.D. 509.

has exceeded or acted without jurisdiction. It is now accepted that there is an absence of jurisdiction if the inferior tribunal refuses to ask the right question or asks the wrong question. That approach by the court was well known and recognised in 1950 and it might properly be considered that Parliament intended the courts to construe section 4 (4) of the Act of 1950 in the recognised manner. It is also now well established that there is a distinction between the jurisdiction of an inferior tribunal to entertain a matter and their jurisdiction in arriving at a decision and thus it is not possible to construe a determination by considering simply the matters presented to it and the determination. The authorities support these propositions: *Reg.* v. *St. Albans Justices*[41]; *Reg.* v. *Grosse*[42]; *Reg.* v. *Warwickshire Justices*[43]; *Reg.* v. *Cridland*[44]; *Ex parte Bradlaugh*[45]; *Rex* v. *Bradford*[46]; *Murphy* v. *The King*[47]; *Estate and Trust Agencies (1927) Ltd.* v. *Singapore Improvement Trust*[48]; *The State* v. *O'Donnell*[49]; *Reg.* v. *Medical Appeal Tribunal, Ex parte Gilmore*[50]; *Reg.* v. *Hurst, Ex parte Smith*[51]; *Essex County Council* v. *Essex Incorporated Congregational Church Union*[52]; *Seereelall Jhuggroo* v. *Central Arbritation & Control Board*[53] and *Board of Trustees of the Maradana Mosque* v. *Badiuddin Mahmud.*[54] **[879]**

Templeman Q.C. replied contending that neither the authorities cited nor *Reg.* v. *Bolton*[55] *and Andrews* v. *Mitchell,*[56] were contrary to the defendants' submissions.

[The appeal continued on the ground that the judge had erred in law in holding that T.E.D.O. had not become the successors in title to the plaintiffs.]

Sydney W. Templeman Q.C. for the defendants on construction. "Successor in title" in the Order of 1962 means anyone who becomes entitled to the property or anyone who assigns the claim. The judge erred in thinking that "successor in title" referred only to universal succession. He held that the words must refer to the personal representatives in the case of a deceased owner or to the assignees of a living owner and in the case of a company he held there could be no successor except possibly on nationalisation or merger.

The question is whether "successor in title" has the narrow meaning attributed to it by the judge or whether it has its normal meaning of assignee to a claim or interest in property. If it be asked "successor in title to what?" the defendants maintain successor in title to a claim, and the normal method of succession to a claim is by assignment. The claim of the plaintiffs against the government of the United Arab Republic for compensation was a claim capable of assignment and can be equated with a spes successionis. *In re Lind*[57] is authority for the proposition that a spes successionis takes effect not only in contract, but also on the property on which the spes operates. It was there held that an assignment for value of future property binds the property and does not rest merely in contract. Assuming that the plaintiffs had a spes successionis, the right to claim back their property which had been sequestrated or compensation in lieu, they assigned such claim or spes for value to the government of the United Arab Republic. In the same way as it was held in *In re Lind*[57] that an assignment has some effect on the property, so in the present case the assignment had the effect

41 (1853) 22 L.J.M.C. 142.
42 (1860) 3 E. & E. 277.
43 (1856) 6 E. & B. 837.
44 (1857) 7 E. & B. 853.
45 3 Q.B.D. 509.
46 [1908] 1 K.B. 365.
47 [1911] A.C. 401; 27 T.L.R. 453, H.L.(I.).
48 [1937] A.C. 898.
49 [1945] I.R. 126.
50 [1957] 1 Q.B. 574.
51 [1960] 2 Q.B. 133.
52 [1963] A.C. 808; [1963] 2 W.L.R. 802; [1963] 1 All E.R. 326, H.L.(E.).
53 [1953] A.C. 151, P.C.
54 [1967] 1 A.C. 13.
55 (1841) 1 Q.B. 66.
56 [1905] A.C. 78, H.L.(E.).
57 [1915] 2 Ch. 345, C.A.

of a transfer of the claim to a successor in title. To give "successor in title" a meaning which includes the personal representatives of a beneficary under a will, but excludes an assignee for value is illogical. There is no reason why an equitable assignee cannot claim or be included in the meaning of the term "successor in title." Where there is a successor in title, the applicant for compensation has to show that the successor in title was a British national on the **[880]** relevant date. The commission reach a logical conclusion: namely, that if one has given up a claim against the government of the United Arab Republic, one is not entitled to share in the fund for compensation meant for claimants who have not surrendered their claims against that government. When the plaintiffs made their agreement with the government of the United Arab Republic, they meant to go it alone. The conclusion of the commission is both logical as regards construction of the Order of 1962 and just as regards the practical results of its decision.

Roger Parker Q.C. for the plaintiffs on construction. The wording of article 4 and of article 6 of the Order of 1962 is not successor in title *to* anything. The words are successor in title *of* such person or *of such owner.* Both article 4 and article 6 clearly contemplated someone who was not born on February 26, 1956, having a claim by February 28, 1959. It was most unlikely that anyone contemplated an assignment to a baby who was not more than three years old; on the other hand, a three year old baby could stand in the shoes of a father whose property had been taken away by the government of the United Arab Republic. That was the sort of situation which was contemplated and is a much easier one to fit in with the language of the articles than any of the other alternatives which have been presented to the court.

The plaintiffs contend (1) that "successor in title" in the Order of 1962 cannot mean successor in title to a claim because successors were not contemplated before the first claim was made. (2) It cannot mean successors to a claim against the United Arab Republic because it contemplated that persons could become successors at any time after February 28, 1959, and, indeed, up to the date when an individual claimant set out to satisfy the commission that he was a successor in title and, therefore, long after the time when all claims against the United Arab Republic would have been extinguished. (3) "Successor in title" cannot mean successor in title to the property because the Order of 1962 contemplated persons becoming successors after the property had been destroyed or sold. (4) The Order of 1962 contemplated that the successor in title could claim in his own right before the commission. Any question of what was meant by successorship to a claim would be a matter of English law because the claim was made in England under an English Order in Council in respect of an English chose of action situate in England. Reliance is placed on the use of the words "successor *of*" in the Order of 1962 which shows some form of succession, not "successor *to*" which **[881]** includes assignment and would involve terribly difficult problems. The judge was right in construing "successor in title" in the Order of 1962 as meaning a form of universal succession.

A claim under the Order of 1962, albeit Part III or IV, is a claim in respect of British property in Egypt which is made on a form approved or issued by the commission and it is nothing more. An applicant has to establish the matters, which under that Order he must establish in order that his claim should be treated as an established claim or, alternatively, as a registered claim. In establishing that claim there are no conditions precedent, the government has stated what has to be established and nobody has any power to require other matters to be established. However it may be disguised, the plaintiffs' claim cannot be rejected without introducing an overriding condition precedent and any discussion about the meaning of successor in title or property referred to in Annex E is irrelevant. The agreement itself is in reality irrelevant because nobody has suggested that it dealt with either the plaintiffs' right to ask assistance of the British Government or the British Government's own claim under international law, for the reduction in the value of the property by sequestration, sale or cancellation of the mining leases. For the plaintiffs did not purport to assign the British Government's claim and that claim was included in the treaty negotiations. There is nothing in the treaty or the Order of 1962 to exclude the plaintiffs' claim for compensation and the commission's duty was to treat the plaintiffs' claim as established.

Templeman Q.C. replied.

Cur. adv. vult.

March 22. The following judgments were read.

SELLERS L.J., whose judgment was read by Russell L.J. The extensive judgments of Browne J. in the Queen's Bench and of Diplock L.J. in this court, which I have already had an opportunity of reading, permit me to turn almost at once to my conclusions on this appeal, in so doing adopting as widely as possible the surveys in the judgments of these two judges, including their statements of the facts and the issues.

The plaintiffs have appealed from a decision, unfavourable to them, of the Foreign Compensation Commission. Browne J. entertained the action and made a declaration favourable to the plaintiffs notwithstanding that section 4 (4) of the Foreign Compensation Act, 1950, provides that "The determination by the commission of **[882]** any application made to them under this Act shall not be called in question in any court of law."

Further, the Tribunals and Inquiries Act, 1958, constituted a Council on Tribunals and provided for appeals to the courts from decisions of, or on appeal from, certain tribunals: required the giving of reasons for certain decisions of tribunals and ministries, and extended the supervisory powers of the High Court. Section 11 (1) enacts:

> "As respects England and Wales or Northern Ireland, any provision in an Act passed before the commencement of this Act that any order or determination shall not be called into question in any court, or any provision in such an Act which by similar words excludes any of the powers of the High Court, shall not have effect so as to prevent the removal of the proceedings into the High Court by order of certiorari or to prejudice the powers of the High Court to make orders of mandamus . . ."

But, it is to be noted, section 11 (3) expressly stipulates that subsection (1) shall not apply to any order or determination of the Foreign Compensation Commission. Those are clear and emphatic statutory provisions, and the question in this case is whether the courts can disregard them and, if so, in what circumstances and to what extent.

This action seeks declarations which undoubtedly call in question the determination by the Foreign Compensation Commission of an application made to the tribunal under the Act of 1950. Nothing relevant to the appeal turns on the fact that the determination was provisional. The application was in proper form, the proceedings were regularly conducted, and the tribunal, properly constituted, reached a reasoned decision which it made available to the parties, as I am inclined to think, unnecessarily and perhaps undesirably.

On what, then, is this action at law based? It is alleged that the commission have misconstrued the terms of the Order in Council stipulating the matters to be proved by an applicant in order to establish a claim. They have, it is said, required more to be proved than the Order warrants or considered matters which do not arise on a true construction of the Order and have failed to make the proper order when the requirements of the Order in Council had been fulfilled by the applicants. The plaintiffs did not shrink from submitting that whether the commission had so erred or not could not be ascertained until the facts, the relevant statutes and Orders in Council had been fully analysed and considered. Consequently both courts, here and below, have been **[883]** subjected to a complete consideration of all the matters which arose before the commission, as well as the ample authorities dealing with the circumstances in which the courts have interfered with the decisions of inferior tribunals where there has been a statutory clause similar, or with the like effect, to section 4 (4) of the Act of 1950.

I am of opinion that the courts cannot substitute their views on the construction of the Order in Council for that of the commission, who alone have to be satisfied that a claim has been established. A determination may in the view of some be wrong either in fact or in law, but it may nonetheless be a determination. The Foreign Compensation Commission is not an inferior court administering the general law of the land. It is a special commission of selected commissioners called upon in its present relevant jurisdiction to adjudicate upon claims made by applicants to participate in a sum of £27,500,000 (supplemented by moneys provided by Parliament) which the British Government have received from the Egyptian Government following the events at Suez in 1956. War and confiscation and their aftermaths had brought about confusion, complications and uncertainties with regard to property and rights. The Government had negotiated this sum in the interests generally of British nationals who had suffered loss, and any distribution of that sum was at the Government's discretion and decision. By Orders in Council provisions were made as to the qualifications of claimants and the entitlement to participate in the funds. This involves the commission in ascertaining what are the requirements to substantiate a claim. It is an inherent and indeed the initial part of their adjudication to construe the relevant Order in Council and then to review an applicant's claim and to reach their determination upon it.

The commission have been entrusted under the Act of 1950 with this special and defined task and, having regard to the nature and the purpose of their adjudication, Parliament has decreed that their decision shall be final. The wisdom of this is established, rather than defeated, by the nature and the extent of these proceedings and the inevitable delay so far involved.

What the commission had to do was to determine the application made to them. I think it would be a travesty to say that they have not done so. I am in general agreement with what Diplock L.J. has so fully said in the judgment he is about to read, and like him I do not find any satisfactory reason or authority to support the plaintiffs' endeavour to reopen this matter before the courts. **[884]**

The submission for the plaintiffs has been that the commission acted without jurisdiction in that its decision refusing the claim was wrong in law and invalid and therefore a nullity.

The question of jurisdiction is determinable at the commencement, not at the conclusion, of the inquiry. The test on jurisdiction, in the only sense in which it is relevant here, is whether the commission had power to enter upon the inquiry and make a determination; not whether their determination was right or wrong in fact or in law.

> "The question of jurisdiction does not depend on the truth or falsehood of the charge, but upon its nature: it is determinable on the commencement, not at the conclusion, of the inquiry: and affidavits, to be receivable, must be directed to what appears at the former stage, and not to the facts disclosed in the progress of the inquiry": *per* Lord Denman C.J. in *Reg.* v. *Bolton*.[58]

Diplock L.J. has enumerated four respects in which the authority or "jurisdiction" of a tribunal to determine matters submitted to it is limited. With these I agree. It was not suggested that any of these conditions has been infringed. The commission was properly constituted. It held an inquiry in accordance with the statutory requirements and in a judicial manner. The plaintiffs' claim related to the subject-matter of the commission's authority to determine. The commission reached a conclusion and determined the claim. They did not fail in regard to any condition precedent to their adjudication.

I do not question the classification of Browne J. in his detailed and helpful review of the many authorities cited to him and to us. I apprehend that such a citation will rarely be necessary in the future as the Tribunal and Inquiries Act, 1958, will readily enable the appropriate court to exercise an appellate or at least a supervisory control over a wide field.

[58] (1841) 1 Q.B. 66, 74.

It is when the judge concluded by saying, as he did, that, if he were right in his view that the commission's decision was wrong, section 4 (4) did not oust the jurisdiction of the court that I would with respect disagree. His view was formed, as he said, after much hesitation. Unless established authority clearly requires such a conclusion, this does not seem to me to be a case where the courts should strive to disregard the statutory provision that the determination should not be called in question in any court of law, which prohibition received further emphasis by the Tribunals and Inquiries Act, 1958. The courts, it is true, **[885]** have not looked with favour on legislative provisions for ousting the jurisdiction of the court, but if the words of prohibition in this Act are to be given the meaning which they clearly express, as I read them, they do not admit of any qualification or distinguish one part of the commission's task from another. In the performance of its duties the commission may have to construe innumerable statutes, orders, contracts and documents of many kinds, some English, some foreign, and I see no reason for excepting from their adjudication the Order in Council whose terms, as they understand them, direct their administration.

The argument for the plaintiffs in both courts has somewhat remarkably been based fundamentally on *Ex parte Bradlaugh.*[59]. It was submitted that the commission had gone outside their jurisdiction because they had asked themselves the wrong questions or had required one too many questions or had answered the relevant questions correctly and failed to give proper effect to their answers. The *Bradlaugh* case[59] has been referred to in some later cases, and the general observations of Mellor J.[60] that "It is well established that the provision taking away the certiorari does not apply where there was absence of jurisdiction" have been quoted and accepted, but in my view the case and the decision provide no secure foundation for a case such as the present. It concerned a hearing in a magistrates' court in a matter penal in nature. The form of the order did not reveal that the magistrate had been satisfied of all the matters the relevant statute required. It seems to have been the form of the order rather than the substance of the matter which was involved.

I agree with the observations of Diplock L.J. on the other three cases on which Browne J. mainly relied: *Rex* v. *Shoreditch Assessment Committee*[61]; *Reg.* v. *Fulham, Hammersmith and Kensington Rent Tribunal, Ex parte Hierowski*[62]; and *Board of Trustees of the Maradana Mosque* v. *Badiuddin Mahmud.*[63] In my view they fall short of establishing a principle, applicable here.

In the present case, in my judgment, it fell to the commission and to them alone to construe the Order in Council which directed the matters which had to be established to their satisfaction by applicants claiming to share in the fund. I do not **[886]** think that Browne J. had any jurisdiction to consider whether the commission was right or wrong in its conclusion, nor has this court.

I feel no temptation to express a view on the reasoning of the minute of adjudication which I think was unnecessarily revealed to the plaintiffs and which alone has given rise to these sustained submissions.

The plaintiffs seized an early opportunity and made a bargain direct with the Egyptian authorities which they thought at the time would preclude them from any further relief such as they now claim. They may not therefore command much sympathetic consideration, but I apprehend that the machinery of government could operate, if thought fit by the Government, to rectify any decision of the commission which proved unjust in the administration and distribution of the funds available.

I would allow the appeal and would dismiss the action.

DIPLOCK L.J. As has been foreshadowed in the judgment of Sellers L.J.

[59] (1878) 3 Q.B.D. 509, D.C.
[60] Ibid. 513.
[61] [1910] 2 K.B. 859; 26 T.L.R. 663, C.A.
[62] [1953] 2 Q.B. 147; [1953] 2 W.L.R. 1028; [1953] 2 All E.R. 4, D.C.
[63] [1967] 1 A.C. 13; [1966] 2 W.L.R. 921; [1966] 1 All E.R. 545, P.C.

which has just been read, the judgment which I am about to read is very long and very tedious, and it is perhaps unfortunate that it could not be handed down but must be read viva voce. However, I will undertake that lengthy task.

Section 4 (4) of the Foreign Compensation Act, 1950, provides that "The determination of the commission of any application made to them under this Act shall not be called in question in any court of law." In this action, the plaintiffs sought to call in question in the High Court what purports to be a determination by the commission of an application by the plaintiffs to establish certain claims to participate in compensation paid by the Government of the United Arab Republic to the Government of the United Kingdom. If the decision of the commission to which the action relates was "a determination by the Commission of an application made to them under the Act" within the meaning of the subsection, a simple man could be forgiven for thinking that Browne J. had no right to make any declaration about it. I think so too; and since it is conceded that proceedings before the commission in which their decision was made were "an application made to them under the Act," the only ground upon which it can be called in question in any court of law is that it was not a "determination" of that application. That is what this appeal is about.

Stated thus, the answer to the only question in this appeal **[887]** depends upon the true construction of the Foreign Compensation Act, 1950, and the Orders in Council made under it, and I venture to think that a similar question of construction of a statute has been involved in each of the relevant cases in which the High Court has been invited to intermeddle with decisions of "inferior tribunals"—an expression in which I include not only all courts of law other than the Supreme Court of Judicature and the House of Lords but also all other tribunals and persons upon whom authority has been conferred by statute to decide disputes between two or more parties or claims by a subject to a right against or exemption from a liability or duty to the Crown. There are many such cases. In its 113 foolscap pages the judgment under appeal cites and summarises a representative selection of them which have been decided in the last century-and-a-quarter. Although the reports contain many other cases on this topic the judge's survey is sufficiently complete and thorough to save me the necessity of any general citation of authority.

These cases abound with references to "error" and to "jurisdiction," to "error of fact" and to "error of law," to error "going to jurisdiction" and to "error within jurisdiction"; and these expressions are not always used in the same sense in one case as in another. We must, I think, go back to first principles and start by analysing and defining our terms.

Lawyers are concerned with facts only in so far as those facts may have legal consequences, that is, give rise directly or indirectly to a right or liability in any individual which the executive branch of Government will or may enforce.

There must be some person to decide in a case affecting any individual: first, what are the facts that exist, and, secondly, what are the legal consequences of those facts? It is not necessarily the same person who decides both those matters, even in the first instance (for example, trial by jury), but for the purposes of the present appeal we may confine our attention to cases where it is. That person must state what his decision is. Since it is the legal consequences that matter, his statement of his decision will always disclose his view as to the legal consequences of the facts which he thinks exist, but it will not necessarily disclose what those facts are.

Lawyers, when they talk of "error," whether of "fact" or of "law," in such a statement, are dealing not with absolutes but with the opinions of human beings. A statement that there **[888]** exist particular facts which give rise to specified legal consequences is "right" if it is made by a person to whose opinion as to the existence or non-existence of those facts, and as to their legal consequences, effect will be given by the executive branch of Government. But such a statement from being "right" may become "wrong" if subsequently a contrary statement is made by some other person to whose opinion as to the legal consequences of those facts effect will be given by the executive branch of Government in substitution for that of the person who made the first statement. It is then the latter statement that is "right." But it may be that effect will be given to the substituted opinion of such other person as to the legal consequences of facts only, and not as to the existence or non-existence of the particular facts which give rise to those legal consequences. In that event the original statement that particular facts exist remains "right" and must be so treated by the person to whose substituted opinion as to the legal consequences of facts effect will be given.

Legal consequences of facts depend upon whether the particular facts which exist are of a kind which conforms with a description which expresses a general idea of "universal" in the Aristotelian sense. To state that there exists particular facts which fall within that description is to make a statement about the legal consequences of those particular facts. Thus, to state of an individual, John Bull, that he is a "British national" is to state a legal consequence of the existence of other facts particular to John Bull which bring him within the description "British national," such as that he was born in the United Kingdom, or that he was born elsewhere but was granted a certificate of naturalisation by the Secretary of State. Those other facts particular to John Bull may or may not be set out in the statement. If the statement is made by a person to whose opinion as to the existence or non-existence of the facts particular to John Bull, and as to the legal consequences of those facts as respects his British nationality, effect will be given by the executive branch of the Government, and there is another person to whose substituted opinion as to the legal consequences of those particular facts effect will be given, but no effect will be given to his substituted opinion as to the existence or non-existence of the facts particular to John Bull, the question whether the statement can ever be said to be "wrong" depends upon whether the particular facts are set out in the original statement. If they are, it is possible to say **[889]** that the maker of the statement has made a mistake in stating the legal consequences of the particular facts, and this is called an "error of law." But if the particular facts are not set out it is impossible to say this. The bare statement that "John Bull is a British national" is a statement that there exist facts particular to John Bull of which the legal consequence is that he is a British national. It can only be said to be wrong if there is some person to whose substituted opinion as to the existence or non-existence of facts particular to John Bull as well as to their legal consequences effect will be given.

Where, as in the present appeal, the description of the kind of facts which give rise to legal rights or liabilities is contained in legislation, a statement by a person to whose opinion effect will be given that facts particular to an individual fall within that description is, perhaps anomalously, treated in English law as a statement of the legal consequences of those particular facts, even though the description itself does not appear to involve what would, in any other context, be regarded as legal concepts. This is what is meant by the rule that the construction of a statute is always a question of law. And so, if there is some person to whose substituted opinion as to the legal consequences of the particular facts effect will be given, and he states his opinion that the particular facts stated to exist do not fall within the description contained in the legislation, the original statement is "wrong" and the error is an "error of law."

"Jurisdiction" is an expression which is used in a variety of senses and takes its colour from its context. In the present appeal, as in most of the authorities which have been cited, we are concerned only with statutory jurisdiction in the sense of an authority conferred by statute upon a person to determine, after inquiry into a case of a kind described in the statute conferring that authority and submitted to him for decision, whether or not there exists a situation, of a kind described in the statute, the existence of which is a condition precedent to a right or liability of an individual who is party to the inquiry, to which effect will or may be given by the executive branch of Government. A determination made pursuant to such statutory authority is thus a statement made by a person to whose opinion effect will be given by the executive branch of Government that a situation of the kind described in the statute exists. I have used the word "situation" to cover **[890]** both facts and the legal consequences of facts, for the description in the statute of the situation may be a description of the kind of facts the existence or non-existence of which is to be determined, or a description of legal consequences to which facts give rise, or a combination of both types of description. But because of the rule that the construction of a statute is always a matter of law, whatever type of description is used in the statute, the determination will always be or include a statement of the legal consequences of particular facts which in the opinion of the maker of the statement exist, whether the particular facts are set out in the statement or not. Authority to make such a determination thus always includes authority to decide some questions of law.

The authority to determine whether a described situation exists is to be distinguished from an additional authority which is often conferred upon the same person to make an order, of a kind described in the statute, requiring the executive branch of Government to give effect to the right or liability to which the determination that such situation exists is a condition precedent. This additional authority where it exists is also included in the expression "jurisdiction," and some of the cases cited deal with it under that name. But we are not concerned with that kind of authority in the present appeal.

The authority or "jurisdiction" to determine whether a situation of a kind described in a statute exists is limited in a number of respects:

(1) The person or persons by whom it is exercised must possess the qualifications laid down in the statute. In addition, unless it is otherwise provided in the statute either expressly or by necessary implication, the presumed intention of Parliament is that one of the qualifications is absence of bias.

(2) The determination must be preceded by inquiry. The nature of the inquiry, any conditions precedent to the inquiry, and the procedure to be adopted in the inquiry, may be laid down expressly in the statute. In the absence of express provision to the contrary, the presumed intention of Parliament is that the inquiry shall be conducted in accordance with the rules of natural justice. A convenient summary of the relevant rules is to be found in the speech of Lord Loreburn L.C. in *Board of Education* v. *Rice*.[64]

(3) The case in which the determination is made must be **[891]** one of the kind described in the statute. The statute may define the kind of cases which it confers authority upon a person to determine in a number of different ways. The description will necessarily include words identifying the person or class of persons who are entitled to initiate the inquiry leading to the determination, and probably the other person or class of persons (if any) who are entitled to be parties to the inquiry. It will also necessarily contain a description of the subject-matter of the determination, that is, of the kind of dispute or claim to be determined.

(4) The determination must state whether a situation of the kind described in the Act exists or not in the case of the individual to whom the determination relates.

If any of these conditions is not complied with, the statement is not a "determination" within the authority conferred by the statute, and effect will not be given to it by the executive branch of Government.

The person authorised to make the determination must necessarily form an opinion as to whether each of those conditions is complied with, in order to embark upon and to proceed with the inquiry and to make the determination; but his opinion as to whether they are or not is not one to which effect will be given by the executive branch of Government. If it is "wrong" in the opinion of a person to whose opinion as to whether or not any of the conditions are complied with effect will be given by the executive branch of Government, the error is an "error going to the jurisdiction" of the inferior tribunal, and the purported determination is a nullity. This is not the substitution of the opinion of one person to whose opinion effect will be given for that of another to whose opinion effect would have been given but for such substitution. It is the first statement of any opinion to which effect will be given by the executive branch of

[64] [1911] A.C. 179, 180; 27 T.L.R. 378, H.L.(E.).

Government. This is what distinguishes it from the case of a determination made where all these conditions are complied with, and to which effect would be given by the executive branch of Government but for the fact that the determination contains a statement as to the legal consequences of particular facts which in the opinion of the maker exist, and such statement is "wrong" in the opinion of some other person to whose substituted opinion as to the legal consequences of particular facts effect will be given by the executive branch of Government. The error is then an "error within jurisdiction." **[892]**

In the present appeal we are concerned with the "jurisdiction," not only of a particular inferior tribunal, the Foreign Compensation Commission, but also with that of the High Court itself. The High Court, too, is the creation of statute and its "jurisdiction" is statutory, although the principal statute, the Judicature Act, 1925, confers that jurisdiction in part by reference to the jurisdiction formerly exercised by the courts of common law before 1875, when the original Judicature Act of 1873 took effect. In relation to determinations of inferior tribunals the former Court of Queen's Bench exercised jurisdiction of two kinds. It was the person whose opinion as to whether the conditions limiting the authority of the inferior tribunal to make a statement which purported to be a determination were fulfilled would be given effect to: that is to say, it corrected "errors going to the jurisdiction" of the inferior tribunal. It was also the person to whose opinion about the legal consequences of particular facts found to exist by the inferior tribunal effect would be given in substitution for that of the inferior tribunal; that is to say, it corrected "errors within jurisdiction." In exercising its own jurisdiction to correct "errors going to jurisdiction" of an inferior tribunal, the Court of Queen's Bench was making the first effective statement as to whether or not particular facts existed which had the legal consequences of fulfilling the conditions limiting the authority of the inferior tribunal. It could therefore make its own inquiry into the existence or non-existence of the particular facts. It could correct "errors of fact" as well as "errors of law" in the opinion formed by the inferior tribunal as to whether or not the conditions limiting its authority to make a determination were fulfilled. But in exercising its own jurisdiction to correct "errors within jurisdiction" of the inferior tribunal, the Court of Queen's Bench could only correct "errors of law," because it was not the person to whose opinion about the existence or non-existence of particular facts effect would be given in substitution for that of the inferior tribunal. Consequently, where the particular facts which in the opinion of the inferior tribunal existed were not set out in the statement of their determination, but only the legal consequences of those facts, the "errors of law," if any, could not be detected by the Court of Queen's Bench. It was only where the particular facts were set out in the statement that that court could form an opinion as to the correctness of the statement of the inferior tribunal about the **[893]** legal consequences of those facts. It could correct only "errors of law on the face of the record."

The procedure by which the Court of Queen's Bench exercised its own jurisdiction to correct "errors within jurisdiction" of an inferior tribunal was by certiorari. This was also the commonest procedure by which it exercised its own jurisdiction to correct "errors going to jurisdiction" of an inferior tribunal. Although the present appeal is in an action for a declaratory judgment it has been treated for the purposes of argument as if it were brought in proceedings for certiorari, and I, too, shall deal with it on this basis.

We are concerned with a statute passed after the jurisdiction of the former Court of Queen's Bench had been transferred to the High Court of Justice. Where a statute passed after 1875 confers or imposes on any individual, when a situation described in the statute exists, a new right or a new liability which the executive branch of Government will enforce, it is a question of construction of that statute (a) whether jurisdiction to determine whether or not that situation exists in the case of a particular individual is conferred upon the High Court or upon some inferior tribunal, and, if upon the latter, (b) whether or not jurisdiction is conferred upon the High Court to correct the determination of the inferior tribunal for "errors within jurisdiction." If the statute contains no express provision as to (a), the intention of Parliament is presumed to be that the High Court shall have jurisdiction to determine whether the described situation exists or not. The statute thus confers upon the High Court a new jurisdiction which it would not otherwise have. But if the statute does contain express provision conferring jurisdiction upon some inferior tribunal to determine whether or not the described situation exists, there is no room for this presumption, and the High Court has no concomitant jurisdiction to make such a determination itself. But even where this is the case, the intention of Parliament as to (b) is presumed to be that the High Court shall have jurisdiction to correct the determinations of the inferior tribunal for "errors within jurisdiction" unless the statute contains provisions which expressly deprive the High Court of jurisdiction of this kind. Provision of this type, of which section 4 (4) of the Foreign Compensation Act, 1950, is an example, I shall call "no certiorari clauses." But since a determination of an inferior tribunal that the described situation exists or does not exist, if made in compliance with the conditions laid down in the statute, will affect legally enforceable **[894]** rights or liabilities of an individual, whereas if it is not made in compliance with such conditions it will be a nullity and have no such effect, neither an express provision conferring jurisdiction upon an inferior tribunal to make such a determination nor a "no certiorari clause" will deprive the High Court of its jurisdiction to correct a purported determination of the inferior tribunal for "error going to the jurisdiction" of the inferior tribunal and to decide whether the statement of the inferior tribunal, which purports to be a determination, is a nullity or not.

It is common ground in the present appeal that section 4 (4) of the Foreign Compensation Act, 1950, has the effect of a "no certiorari clause" and deprives the High Court of any jurisdiction to correct any determination of the Foreign Compensation Commission for "errors within jurisdiction," even though they are "errors of law on the face of the record." We must therefore look at the legislation, that is to say, the Act itself and any statutory instruments made in pursuance of the Act, to see what are the conditions limiting the jurisdiction of the commission to make determinations.

The Act provides in section 1 for the constitution of the Foreign Compensation Commission, but does not itself confer any jurisdiction upon the commission. This is done by Orders in Council made under the Act. Such Orders in Council may be made, inter alia, "If Her Majesty's Government in the United Kingdom enter into . . . an agreement with the government of any foreign country providing for the payment of compensation by the latter government." The agreement of February 28, 1959 (which I will call "the Egyptian Compensation Agreement"), did provide for the payment of £27,500,000 compensation by the Government of the United Arab Republic to the United Kingdom Government, which thereupon became entitled to make Orders in Council providing (inter alia):

(1) "for the registration by the commission of claims to participate in such compensation, and for the making of reports by the commission with respect to such claims" (s. 3 (*a*));

(2) "for the determination of such claims by the commission" (s. 3 (*b*));

(3) "for defining the persons who are to be qualified, in respect of nationality or status, to make applications to the commission for the purpose of establishing such claims as aforesaid, and for imposing any other conditions to be fulfilled before such claims can be entertained" (s. 3 (*c*) and s. 2 (2) (*a*)); **[895]**

(4) "for prescribing the matters which have to be established to the satisfaction of the commission by persons making such applications" (s. 3 (*c*) and s. 2 (2) (*b*)); and

(5) "for any supplementary and incidental matters for which provision appears to His Majesty to be necessary or expedient" (s. 3 (*e*)).

Although under the Egyptian Compensation Agreement the £27,500,000 was expressed to be paid to the United Kingdom in full and final settlement of claims by United Kingdom nationals against the Government of the United Arab Republic and its nationals, no United Kingdom national would have had at common law any legally enforceable right against the United Kingdom

Government to recover any part of the compensation fund received by the United Kingdom Government: *Rustomjee* v. *The Queen.*[65]* Any right to participate in the compensation would therefore be a new right created by the Act and Orders in Council made under it, and the High Court would have no jurisdiction to determine whether a situation existed in the case of a particular individual which gave rise to a right in him to participate in the compensation, if the Act or Orders in Council made under it expressly confer such jurisdiction upon some inferior tribunal.

By the provisions which I have quoted the Act does authorise the making of Orders in Council conferring this jurisdiction on the commission. In those provisions "claims" means claims by a person to participate in the compensation fund. These are the claims which, if an Order in Council so provides, are to be "determined" by the commission. "Applications" made to the Commission under the Act are applications made by a person for the purpose of establishing his claim to participate in the compensation fund. A "determination" by the commission of any application made to them under this Act, which by section 4 (4) of the Act "shall not be called in question in any court of law," therefore includes a statement by the commission of their opinion that an applicant's claim to be entitled to participate in the compensation fund has or has not been established. The kind of situation, the existence or non-existence of which is to be determined by the commission, is thus described in the Act in terms of legal consequences only. It is for the commission to decide whether in the case of any applicant they are of opinion that facts exist which give rise to those legal consequences, **[896]** but, whether they state such facts or not, it is their opinion that the applicant's claim to participate in the compensation fund is established or is not established to which effect will be given by the executive branch of Government, and the High Court has no jurisdiction to substitute its own contrary opinion for it.

A determination by the commission that an applicant's claim to participate in the compensation fund is established or is not established must, of course, comply with the conditions with respect to such determinations laid down in the Act and Orders in Council. The Act makes provision for imposing by Orders in Council or by rules of procedure made by the Lord Chancellor, under section 4 (2) of the Act, limitations of the four types listed earlier in this judgment, upon the jurisdiction of the commission to make determinations.

First: the determinations must be made by the appropriate number (laid down in the rules) of members of the commission duly appointed under section 1 of the Act. It is not suggested that this condition was not fulfilled in the present case.

Secondly: it must have been preceded by an inquiry conducted by the commission in accordance with the rules. It is common ground that this condition too was fulfilled. The Act does provide for Orders in Council to be made imposing conditions to be fulfilled before a claim can be entertained by the commission. But the only condition imposed in the relevant Order in Council under this power is that the application shall be made in accordance with the rules (see art. 9 of the Foreign Compensation (Egypt) (Determination and Registration of Claims) Order, 1962), and this condition was fulfilled.

Thirdly: the application must be one of the kind described in the Act or Order in Council; and fourthly: the determination must state whether a situation of the kind described in the Act or Order in Council exists or not in the case of the applicant.

The Act itself requires that the application must be an application made by an applicant "for the purpose of establishing [a claim]" to participate in the compensation fund, but for a more detailed description of the application one must look at the Order in Council itself. For the description of the kind of situation which the determination must state exists or does not exist in the case of the applicant one must also look at the Order in Council. But it is important to bear in mind that any provision in the Order in Council "prescribing the

[65] (1876) 1 Q.B.D. 487.

matters which **[897]** have to be established to the satisfaction of the commission by persons making such applications" is not a description of the kind of applications in which the commission have jurisdiction to make determinations, but a more detailed description of the kind of situation the existence or non-existence of which in the case of the applicant they have jurisdiction to determine.

I turn then to the Order in Council; but, in order to construe it, it is necessary first to say something about the Egyptian Compensation Agreement which is referred to in the recitals to the Foreign Compensation (Egypt) (Determination and Registration of Claims) Order, 1962.

The Egyptian Compensation Agreement was originally made on February 28, 1959. Its terms were revised on August 7, 1962, by an Exchange of Notes. It was made in the following circumstances:

During the Suez Incident the Egyptian Government took measures against the property in Egypt of British nationals. These measures included the sequestration of such property and its management by sequestrators, who were empowered in some cases to sell the property, and did so. The proclamation, No. 5 of 1956, under which these measures were taken did not purport to deal with the ultimate disposal of the property or of the income derived from it during sequestration or of the proceeds of sale of properties sold by the sequestrators. So far as the proclamation was concerned, the property and the income and proceeds of sale thereof were to remain in the possession of the sequestrators, whose duties were described as being to represent the British nationals concerned. Legal proceedings, if brought by them, were in the name of and on behalf of the British national for whom they were acting. The proclamation appears to have been made by the Military Governor-General under powers vested in him during the existence of a "state of emergency." Whether under Egyptian law the British owners would in the absence of further legislation have been entitled to the return of the property or its income or any proceeds of its sale at the end of the state of emergency we do not know, nor do we know whether subsequent legislation purporting to deprive the British owners of any title to such property, income or proceeds of sale without adequate compensation would have been valid under the Egyptian Constitution. At any rate no such legislation appears to have been passed by February 28, 1959. The proclamation suspended the right of access of British nationals to Egyptian courts, but I see no reason for assuming that the proclamation deprived **[898]** the owners permanently of all title in Egyptian law to the property, income or proceeds of sale in the possession of the sequestrators or of a right to recover compensation from the sequestrators for any loss sustained as a result of their mismanagement of the property during the period of sequestration. Thus it does not seem to me that any misuse of language is involved, while the proclamation remained in force, in describing the owner of the sequestrated property as having "claims" against the Egyptian Government for the return of the property and the income thereof or any proceeds of sale at the end of the emergency, or for compensation for its mismanagement by the sequestrators, although such claims could not be pursued in the Egyptian courts during the emergency. At any rate, they were subsequently described as "claims" in the Egyptian Compensation Agreement.

I also see no reason for supposing that the owner's title to the property, and any claims which he might have against the sequestrators for mismanagement, were in Egyptian law rights of a kind which were incapable of being assigned to third parties. An assignment made in Egypt, and probably one made to an Egyptian national anywhere, without the consent of the Minister of Finance or the sequestrators, would be void under articles 3 and 12 of the proclamation, but one made with such consent would appear clearly to be valid. Whether consent was needed to an assignment made outside Egypt to a person who was not an Egyptian national may be doubtful. It depends upon the view which Egyptian courts would take of the ambit of article 3.

It follows that I see no reason for holding that a British national who was the owner of property in Egypt under sequestration was not entitled under

Egyptian municipal law to rights against the Egyptian Government and the sequestrators which were capable of being assigned, and to which the assignee might, without abuse of language, be called a "successor in title" of the original owner.

It is, to say the least, debatable whether these measures taken by the Egyptian Government were contrary to international law. So far as they relate to property they were based upon what are broadly the same principles as those applied in our own Trading with the Enemy Acts and regulations in the First and Second World Wars, though they were less Draconian, if I am right in construing them as leaving the beneficial title in the owner instead of converting it into a mere "spes successionis" as the majority of the House of Lords held our own legislation did: **[899]** *Bank voor Handel en Scheepvaart N.V.* v. *Administrator of Hungarian Property.*[66]* If the Suez Incident can be equiparated to a state of war between Egypt and Great Britain (which publicists may debate) there would seem to be an arguable case that the Egyptian Government was entitled in international law to adopt the measures provided for in the proclamation.

Measures of this kind taken by one belligerent against the property in its own territory of enemy nationals may well cease to be justifiable when a state of war between the belligerents comes to an end. The normal practice, where there has been a formal declaration of war, is for provision to be made in the treaty of peace for what is to be done by each government about the enemy property which has been subjected to such measures. And this, despite the absence of any formal declaration of war, is what was done in the present case by the Egyptian Compensation Agreement. In making agreements of this kind a government is exercising its right in international law to adopt and to settle claims by persons who are its nationals at the date of the agreement against the government of another state which is party to the agreement. Such claims may be claims to rights recognised by the municipal law of the other state but which the person entitled to the right is prevented from enforcing, as, for instance, by a procedural disability precluding him from access to the courts (deni de justice); or they may be claims to rights not recognised by the municipal law of the other state, if failure to recognise such rights is contrary to international law. Failure to recognise a right to adequate compensation for property confiscated by the government is often asserted as constituting grounds for a claim of the latter kind.

So far as is relevant to the present appeal the Egyptian Compensation Agreement adopted and settled two types of claims on the part of British nationals against the Egyptian Government, that is to say, claims to the return of property under sequestration and claims for damage to property sustained as a result of sequestration. In general, measures of sequestration were to be terminated at the date of the agreement and the property or its proceeds of sale were to be returned. But there were excluded from the obligation to return them certain properties of named British nationals which had been sold under the proclamation and which were referred to in Annex E to the agreement. Claims in respect of these properties were to be settled and all liability **[900]** of the Egyptian Government or Egyptian nationals in respect of them discharged upon payment by the Egyptian Government to the British Government of the compensation fund of £27,500,000. Claims for damage to property sustained as a result of sequestration were also to be settled and all liability for them discharged upon payment of the compensation fund. These were the only two type of claims in settlement of which the £27,500,000 was paid. In the original agreement of February 28, 1959, the claims in respect of property referred to in Annex E which were to be settled by the payment of the compensation fund were limited to claims in respect of such property as was sold under the proclamation. But by the Exchange of Notes of August 7, 1962, the definition of these claims was altered so as to cover any claims in respect of properties in Egypt of British nationals named in Annex E, without any express reference to whether or not the properties had been sold under the proclamation.

[66] [1954] A.C. 584; [1954] 2 W.L.R. 867; [1954] 1 All E.R. 969, H.L.(E.).

The provisions of the Order in Council which are most germane to this appeal are known by heart by everyone in this court and I will not bother to read them out.

The words in article 4 (1) (*a*) and (*b*), in article 6 (1) (*a*) (*b*) and (*c*) and the words in article 8, "all the matters specified in article 6 of this Order other than that the loss, injury or damage was the result of Egyptian measures," describe the various situations which the commissioners must be of opinion exist in the case of a particular applicant if they are to determine that his claim, under Part III or Part IV of the Order, to participate in the compensation fund is established and the loss with respect to it assessed, or is to be registered and reported to the Secretary of State, as the case may be.

They bristle with expressions which are descriptive of legal consequences and thus involve "questions of law," quite apart from the anomalous rule referred to earlier in this judgment that the question whether particular facts fall within the description contained in legislation of the kind of facts which give rise to legal rights and liabilities is treated as a statement of the legal consequences of those particular facts and is itself a "question of law." Thus, to take article 4 (1) (*a*) and (*b*) alone, "property in Egypt" and "successor in title" are examples of expressions which in any context are descriptive of legal consequences of the existence of particular facts, and the words "which is referred to in Annex E" qualifying the expression "property in Egypt" contain an additional description of the kind of facts to which the particular **[901]** facts whose existence has the legal consequences described by the expression "property in Egypt" must also conform in order that the claim may be established.

These are but illustrations of the many "questions of law" about which the commission must form an opinion as to the answer, in order to arrive at a decision whether the applicant has satisfied them that a situation described in paragraphs (*a*) and (*b*) of article 4 (1), or paragraphs (*a*), (*b*) and (*c*) of article 6 (1), or the words I have quoted in article 8, exists in the case of that applicant. To answer such "questions of law" is a necessary incident of their jurisdiction to determine whether a claim made in an application is established or not. The High Court has no jurisdiction to substitute its own opinion as to the answer to any of these "questions of law" for the opinion of the commission, so as to lead to a different determination as to whether the claim is established or not. Even if the High Court thought that the commissioners' answers were erroneous the error would be an "error within jurisdiction."

The relevant facts about the property to which the plaintiffs' application related are set out in detail in the judgment of Browne J. For the purposes of this appeal it is sufficient to say that the property comprised a mining business in Egypt owned by the plaintiffs on October 31, 1956, which was sequestrated under the provisions of Proclamation No. 5 of 1956. While under sequestration it sustained war damage inflicted by the armed forces of Israel, which I will call "Israeli war damage." After sustaining such damage, it was purportedly sold on April 29, 1957, by the sequestrator to an Egyptian organisation, T.E.D.O., under the powers of sale conferred by the proclamation. Subsequently the Egyptian Government as lessor purported to terminate the plaintiffs' mineral leases. The plaintiff company refused to recognise this purported sale as effective to divest it of its property in the assets of its mining business and threatened legal action to recover the products of its mines exported from Egypt. These threats were not without effect, and on November 23, 1957, the plaintiff company entered into an agreement with T.E.D.O. and the sequestrator whereby it purported to sell to T.E.D.O. the whole of its business as carried on and situate in Egypt for the sum of £500,000 to be paid to the company. In the opinion of the commission the effect of this agreement was also to transfer to T.E.D.O. any claims which the plaintiffs might have under Egyptian municipal **[902]** law against the Egyptian Government or the sequestrator arising out of the sequestration or any acts or omissions of the sequestrator.

By their provisional determination of May 8, 1963, the commission determined that the plaintiffs had failed to establish any claim under article 4 or article 6 of the Order in Council, but that its claim in respect of the war damage inflicted by the Israeli armed forces was fit for registration under article 8 of the Order. On the face of it this provisional determination, for which no reasons were given, was a "determination" which the commission had jurisdiction under the Act to make. But the plaintiffs, despite the provisions of section 4 (4) of the Act, attempted to call it in question in the High Court by bringing the present action against the commission for declarations. In that action there was disclosed another document, a "Minute of Adjudication," in which the commission had recorded for their own use the reasons which had lead them to form the opinion stated in their provisional determination.

Broadly speaking, the plaintiffs' case was, and still is, that the particular facts about the property to which their application related that were found by the commission to exist were of the kind described in article 4 (1) (*a*) and (*b*), and that accordingly the commission were under a statutory duty to treat the claim as established. But to state the proposition so baldly exposes it to the immediate answer that under the provisions of the Act and Order in Council it is the commission who have to be satisfied that the particular facts are of the kind described, and that it is to their opinion on this matter and not to any substituted opinion of the High Court that effect will be given by the executive branch of the Government. In attempting to escape from this answer the plaintiffs' contentions have in the course of the argument been put in three different ways. First: that in the inquiry which preceded their determination the commission considered matters which they had no jurisdiction to consider—they asked themselves the wrong question. Secondly: that they treated as conditions precedent to a claim under the Order in Council matters which were not conditions precedent. Thirdly: that the provisional determination either by itself or read with the minute of adjudication shows that the commission were satisfied of all the matters set out in Article 4 (1) (*a*) and (*b*).

But on analysis all these arguments are three different ways of saying the same thing. It is apparent from their minute of adjudication that the commission were of opinion that T.E.D.O. **[903]** which was never a British national, became the "successor in title" to the plaintiffs before February 28, 1959, and that accordingly the requirement of article 4 (1) (*b*) (ii) was not satisfied in the case of Anisminic's claim under Part III of the Order. It is less apparent, but said to be discernible upon a close analysis of the minute of adjudication, that the commission were of opinion that no applicant could establish a claim under article 4 or article 6 unless he had a claim against the Egyptian Government on February 28, 1959. These are the two "errors" which it is contended the commission made. The judge was of opinion that upon a true construction of the Order in Council "successor in title" meant universal successor only, so that there could never be a "successor in title" of a person referred to in paragraph 1 (*a*) or paragraph 2 of Annex E so long as the person so referred to was in existence. He was also of opinion that upon the true construction of the Order the commission were in error in thinking that no applicant could establish a claim under article 4 or article 6 unless he had a claim against the Egyptian Government on February 28, 1959. As a result of these two errors in the construction of the Order he considered that the commission had asked themselves two questions, neither of which had they jurisdiction to consider, videlicet: (1) "Had the plaintiffs a successor in title?"; and (2) "Had the plaintiffs a claim against the Egyptian Government on February 28, 1959?" This is the way of putting the plaintiffs' argument that the judge accepted.

But as respects the second of these questions which it is alleged the commission asked themselves, the argument in this court has also been presented in the alternative way, videlicet, the commission had treated the existence of a "claim" by the applicant against the Egyptian Government on February 28, 1959, as a condition precedent to the existence of a "claim" to participate in the compensation fund.

The third way in which the argument has been put is more devious: namely, the minute of adjudication discloses that the commission were satisfied that the plaintiffs were the person referred to in paragraph 1 (*a*) of Annex E so that, as the plaintiffs were the applicants, the requirements of article 4 (1) (*b*) (i) were also satisfied. Their provisional determination that the plaintiffs' claim in respect of the Israeli war damage was fit for registration under article 8 shows that they were satisfied of all the matters specified in article 6, except that the damage was the result of Egyptian measures. They were therefore satisfied that the **[904]** property to which the plaintiffs' claim related was "property in Egypt" (see art. 6 (1) (*a*)) of which the plaintiffs were the owners at the time of the damage (see art. 6 (1) (*b*)) and that there was no non-British national who became "successor in title" of the plaintiffs on or before February 28, 1959, that is, that the requirements of article 4 (1) (*b*) (ii) were also satisfied. This leaves only the requirements of article 4 (1) (*a*) to be satisfied: and since the only identification contained in Annex E of the property referred to therein was by the name of its owner and the plaintiffs were the person referred to in Annex E the "property in Egypt" to which the plaintiffs' claim related must have been "property in Egypt" which is referred to in Annex E within the meaning of article 4 (1) (*a*). The commission must therefore have been of opinion that all the requirements of article 4 (1) (*a*) and (*b*) (i) and (ii) were satisfied; and their statutory duty was to treat the plaintiffs' claim as established. A determination which accepts the claim in respect of the Israeli war damage as fit for registration under article 8 while rejecting the claim under article 4 cannot, it is argued, be arrived at by any construction put upon the words "claim," "property in Egypt" or "successor in title," for all these expressions are common to articles 4 and 6 and incorporated by reference in article 8 itself. The commission, even if they had jurisdiction to decide matters of construction, cannot have reached their determination as a result of construing the Order in Council, but must have asked themselves some quite different question which they had no jurisdiction to consider.

The fallacy in the first and second ways of putting the plaintiffs' argument lies, I think, in a confusion between the description in the statute of the kind of case into which an inferior tribunal has jurisdiction to inquire, and the description in the same statute of the kind of situation the existence or non-existence of which that tribunal has jurisdiction to determine. If the inferior tribunal, as a result of its misconstruing the statutory description of the kind of case into which it has jurisdiction to inquire, makes a purported determination in a case of a kind into which it has no jurisdiction to inquire, its purported determination is a nullity. The question which it has to put itself before entering on the inquiry and to which, for the reasons already explained, its answer is *not* conclusive is: "Is this a case of the kind described in the statute?" If the tribunal's opinion is that it is, and the High Court's opinion is that it is not, the tribunal's "error going to jurisdiction" in giving the wrong answer to the right question may equally well be **[905]** accounted for by saying that the tribunal's answer shows that they must have asked themselves the wrong question. To say this does not advance the matter or change the character of the "error."

But it is not suggested that the plaintiffs' application was not a case of the kind into which the commission had jurisdiction to inquire. They accordingly were bound to ask themselves the questions: (1) "What are the particular facts relating to the plaintiffs that exist?" and (2) "Do those particular facts conform to the description of a situation which is contained in article 4 (1) (*a*) and (*b*) (i) and (ii) of the Order in Council?" and to both these questions the commission's answer is conclusive. Any "error" which the High Court thinks they made in the answer is an "error within jurisdiction."

In order to answer the second question they have to form an opinion of the meaning of the words used in the description of the situation, for their opinion as to whether the particular facts conform to that description must depend upon the meaning which in their opinion is borne by the words by which the situation is described. If they have formed the opinion that an expression used in the description such as "successor in title" of a particular person includes an assignee of that person, and the High Court is of opinion that it does not, the error is nevertheless as "error of law within the jurisdiction" of the inferior tribunal. Such an error must always have the consequence that in considering whether the particular facts conform to the description, the tribunal will ask itself the question: "Is there an assignee of that particular person?"; so that it may be said that in coming to its determination the tribunal has asked itself the wrong question. But this can be said of any error of construction of the statutory description of the situation the existence of which the inferior tribunal has jurisdiction to determine, and to say it does not advance the matter or change the character of the "error."

I think that it can be inferred from what is said in the minute of adjudication that the commission was of opinion that upon the true construction of the Order in Council an applicant, in order to establish a claim to participate in the compensation, must have had a claim against the Egyptian Government on February 28, 1959, either in his own right or as assignee of a person previously entitled to a claim; although this opinion would seem to be either part of the reasoning which supported the construction which it adopted of the expression "successor in title," or a statement of a consequence of adopting that construction of "successor in title," rather than an independent ground of their determination. But **[906]** assuming that this was the opinion of the commission and that it was erroneous in the opinion of the High Court, it was an "error of law within jurisdiction," and its character is not altered by describing its consequence as the commission asking itself the wrong question: "Did the applicant have a claim against the Egyptian Government on February 28, 1959?" or by saying, as one equally well could, that by requiring a negative answer to that question the commission wrongly treated the existence of a claim vested in the applicant against the Egyptian Government on February 28, 1959, as a condition precedent to the establishment of a claim to participate in the compensation fund.

The third way in which the plaintiffs' argument has been put is intended to evade the conclusion that, if the commission were in "error," their error was an error of construction of expressions in the Order in Council which they had jurisdiction to construe. The argument is founded upon the alleged inconsistency in determining that there was no claim established under article 4 or 6 of the Order in Council but that there was a claim fit for registration under article 8. This inconsistency, if there be one, cannot be deduced from the provisional determination itself. There is nothing which is inconsistent per se in determining that a claim is not established under article 4 or article 6 but is fit for registration under article 8. The plaintiffs are thus driven to rely upon the minute of adjudication to show that there was an inconsistency. But they must take the minute of adjudication as they find it. It is clear that what the commission were applying their mind to was the true construction of articles 4, 6 and 8 of the Order in Council, and that in their opinion fell to be construed in the light of the Egyptian Compensation Agreement referred to in the recitals to the Order and by the specific reference to Annex E in article 4 (1) (*a*) itself. But the minute of adjudication does not dissect those articles into their component words and phrases, nor does it explicitly disclose what meaning the commission thought should be attached to any individual words or phrases other than the expression "successor in title." The alleged inconsistency is based upon two premises, one of fact, videlicet, that the commissioners construed "claim," "property in Egypt" and "successor in title" in the same sense in articles 4 and 6, and one of logic, videlicet, that if they did so, this necessarily led to the conclusion that if the claim in respect of Israeli war damage was registrable under article 8, the remainder of the claim was established under article 4. But neither premise can be shown to be true. The commission may **[907]** have construed these words and phrases differently in articles 4 and 6, respectively. If they did, and in the opinion of the High Court were wrong in doing so, this would be an "error within jurisdiction." And even if the commission construed these words and phrases in the same sense in articles 4 and 6 the alleged conclusion does not necessarily follow as a matter of logic. If the commission were of opinion that "successor in title" included a person to whom there had been assigned before February 28, 1959, the original claim of the former owner of the property, whether the claim so assigned was one against the Egyptian Government in respect of which a claim to participate in the compensation fund was sought to be established under article 4 or article 6, or was one against some other government or person in respect of which registration under article 8 was claimed, there would be no inconsistency in their determination. One claim might be assigned and the other not. And this, so far as it is possible to discover the detailed reasoning of the commission from their minute of adjudication (which was never intended for publication), is the opinion which the commission held. It is an opinion as to the true construction of the Order in Council and if erroneous is an "error within the jurisdiction."

The judge, as I have said, took the view that the minute of adjudication disclosed that the commission had misconstrued the Order in Council both as to the meaning of "successor in title" and as to the necessity for an applicant to be a person who had a claim against the Egyptian Government on February 28, 1959, or a "successor in title" of such person; and that these were "errors going to the jurisdiction." His ratio decidendi is summarised in two sentences of his judgment:

> "In my judgment the commission has no jurisdiction to consider under article 4 (1) any other question than those which sub-paragraphs (*a*) and (*b*) of that article, on their true construction require them to consider, and if satisfied of those matters they are under a statutory duty to treat the claim as established and have no jurisdiction to do anything else. . . . It follows, in my view, that if the commission wrongly construed article 4 (1) (*a*) and (*b*) as requiring them to consider something which on their true construction those sub-paragraphs do not require to be considered before the claim is established, they act without jurisdiction or in excess of jurisdiction."

In reaching his conclusion that, despite section 4 (4) of the Act the High Court was entitled to substitute its opinion as to the meaning of paragraphs (*a*) and (*b*) of the **[908]** Order in Council for that of the commission, the judge relied particularly on four cases on which I must briefly comment. *Rex* v. *Shoreditch Assessment Committee*[67]; *Ex parte Bradlaugh*[68]; *Reg.* v. *Fulham, Hammersmith and Kensington Rent Tribunal*[69]; and *Board of Trustees of the Maradana Mosque* v. *Badiuddin Mahmud.*[70] *The Shoreditch case*[71] seems to me to be a simple example of a case in which a condition precedent to the inferior tribunal's entering upon an inquiry (namely, the making of a provisional valuation list by a valuer) was not fulfilled. *Bradlaugh's* case[72] contains a wholly unexceptionable statement by Cockburn C.J.[73] that a "no certiorari clause" does not apply where the inferior tribunal has exceeded the limits of its jurisdiction; but with great respect to that strong-minded Lord Chief Justice I am unable to follow his process of reasoning from that principle to the actual decision of the court in *Bradlaugh's* case.[74] The real objection was to the form of the order made by the magistrate, in that he omitted to recite that he was satisfied of one of the matters of which he was required by the statute to be satisfied before making the order which he made. The *Fulham Rent Tribunal* case[75] was a case in which the inferior tribunal had already fixed a rent for premises. The only kind of application which the statute gave them jurisdiction to entertain in relation to premises for which a rent had been already fixed was an application to alter the rent so fixed owing to subsequent change of circumstances. The tenant made an application to the tribunal, not to alter the rent already fixed, but to fix it ab initio, and this the tribunal purported to do. The matter was complicated by the fact that the landlord by his answer asked the tribunal to alter the rent already fixed owing to subsequent change of circumstances, and this the tribunal did have jurisdiction to do. But it was apparent from the facts that the tribunal had purported to determine the tenant's application and to fix the rent ab initio.

67 [1910] 2 K.B. 859.
68 3 Q.B.D. 509.
69 [1953] 2 Q.B. 147.
70 [1967] 1 A.C. 13.
71 [1910] 2 K.B. 859.
72 3 Q.B.D. 509.
73 Ibid. 512.
74 3 Q.B.D. 509.
75 [1953] 2 Q.B. 147.

The *Maradana Mosque* case,[76] a decision of the Privy Council in which none of the English cases were cited, was mainly decided on the ground that the inferior tribunal, the Minister of Education, had not observed the rules of natural justice in the inquiry which preceded his order; but the Judicial Committee did deal briefly with an alternative contention that the Minister had acted in excess of jurisdiction "in that he failed to consider the right questions and **[909]** failed to make decisions which were the requisite foundations for the order."[77] I must confess that I find difficulty in reconciling this part of the judgment of the Privy Council with previous authorities. They appear to have considered that if in their opinion there was no evidence upon which the Minister could properly come to the decision which he reached, this was an "error going to jurisdiction." But so to hold is contrary to the statement of Lord Sumner in another decision of the Privy Council in *Rex* v. *Nat Bell Liquors Ltd.*[78] which has hitherto been regarded as an authoritative pronouncement upon the history and scope of the jurisdiction of the High Court in proceedings to certiorari. They appear also to have regarded the Ceylon statute as one which did not give the Minister any jurisdiction to construe the words in the statute which described the matters of which he was to be satisfied. That may have been the effect of that particular statute, but as a general proposition it is contrary to decisions of English courts which are binding upon us. The two most recent of these decisions, both in the Court of Appeal, to which Browne J. was not referred, are *Rex* v. *Minister of Health*[79] and more particularly *Davies* v. *Price.*[80] The ratio decidendi of the of the latter case, as stated in the judgment of Parker L.J., with which the two other members expressed their agreement, was that an error by the inferior tribunal in construing the statutory description of the matters on which it was to be satisfied was an "error within jurisdiction" and could not be corrected by the High Court if it disagreed with that construction.

In my judgment, therefore, Browne J. had no jurisdiction to consider whether or not the commission has misconstrued that part of the Order in Council which prescribed the matters which have to be established to the satisfaction of the commission by persons making applications for the purpose of establishing claims to participate in the compensation fund.

For my part I find nothing in the subject-matter of the kind of claims which the commission were authorised to determine which makes it unlikely that Parliament should have intended to entrust to the commission exclusive authority to decide what that part of the Order in Council meant. The expressions used in that part of the Order do not relate to any rights previously enjoyed by applicants under English law, but to events in Egypt which give **[910]** rise to a newly created statutory right of a different character, namely, to participate in the compensation fund. To determine their meaning may involve, as the argument in this appeal has demonstrated, considering questions of Egyptian municipal law, of the private international law of England and of Egypt, of public international law and the interpretation of an international agreement—matters on which it may well be thought that judges of the High Court are not the sole depositaries of wisdom and learning, and on which in the interests of the timeous distribution of the fund among the numerous persons entitled to participate the decision of the commission might well be final. In this particular instance I have, as I think, no jurisdiction to question the decision of the commission or to examine the construction which they placed on article 4 (1) (*a*) and (*b*), article 6 (1) (*a*) (*b*) and (*c*) and article 8 of the Order in Council; but as we have heard full argument on the matter, and as Browne J. has expressed his view that the commission erred in the construction they placed on these articles, I think it only fair to say by way of obiter dictum that for the reasons indicated at various points in the earlier part of this judgment I am far from satisfied that the commission did misapply these articles in determining the plaintiffs'

[76] [1967] 1 A.C. 13.
[77] [1967] 1 A.C. 13, 22.
[78] [1922] 2 A.C. 128, 131; 38 T.L.R. 541, P.C.
[79] [1939] 1 K.B. 232, 245; 55 T.L.R. 4; [1938] 4 All E.R. 32, C.A.
[80] [1958] 1 W.L.R. 434, 441; [1958] 1 All E.R. 671, C.A.

application, although their minute of adjudication may not express their reasons in precisely the same terms as those which I should myself have chosen.

I have dealt with this appeal as if it were brought in proceedings for an order for certiorari. It is in fact brought in an action for a declaratory judgment, and if we were not prepared to allow it upon the ground already discussed I should have wished to hear argument on the question whether the High Court has any jurisdiction to make declarations in an action brought against an inferior tribunal in a case of this kind.

The jurisdiction of the High Court to give declaratory judgments is limited to declaring the existence of legally enforceable rights or liabilities. This will in many cases afford an alternative procedure for questioning a determination of an inferior tribunal on the grounds that it was made without jurisdiction and is therefore a nullity. Thus if it purports to impose upon a person a liability enforceable by the executive branch of Government, its enforcement will inevitably interfere with that person's common law rights. In such a case, instead of waiting for his common law rights to be infringed he may take the initiative by bringing an action in the High Court against the person who would be entitled to enforce, **[911]** or to order or authorise the enforcement of, that liability if the determination were valid, for a declaration that the purported determination is a nullity. The defendant to such an action is not the inferior tribunal as such, but the person by whom the purported liability is enforceable, that is, the person against whom an action for tort would lie if the purported liability were enforced. It may well be that the inferior tribunal has in addition to its quasi-judicial function of making determinations the administrative function of enforcing them or ordering or authorising their enforcement, and where this is so the administrative tribunal may be an appropriate defendant in its administrative capacity to an action for a declaration. But where its only function is to make a determination, and the right to enforce or to order the enforcement of the liability to which the determination is a condition precedent is conferred upon other persons, I doubt whether any action for a declaration lies against the inferior tribunal itself. If the liability to which the determination is a condition precedent were enforced, there would be no right of action against the inferior tribunal on the part of the person against whom the liability was enforced; and I find difficulty in seeing how the High Court has jurisdiction to make a declaration against a defendant in respect of conduct by him which could never give rise to a cause of action against him by the plaintiff or by him against the defendant. The only remedy against the inferior tribunal itself in such a case would, I think, be by certiorari.

Similar difficulties would seem to me to lie in the way of any action for a declaration brought by a claimant to a right created by statute in respect of a purported determination by an inferior tribunal that he is not entitled to such right, when the tribunal's determination that he is entitled to the right is a condition to the enforcement of it by him. So long as there has been no determination that the claimant is entitled to the right, there is nothing capable of giving rise to any cause of action against the person against whom the right would be enforceable; and if the inferior tribunal's purported determination of non-entitlement is a nullity, this still leaves nothing capable of giving rise to any cause of action against the person against whom the right would be enforceable, and thus capable of being the subject-matter of a declaration against him. The conduct of the inferior tribunal itself in making the purported determination, whether it is a nullity or not, is not capable of giving rise to any cause of action against it on the part of the claimant. His only remedy against it would be by certiorari and mandamus. **[912]**

However, this objection has not been taken on behalf of the commission, and as I would allow the appeal it is unnecessary to decide it. But equally it must not be thought that this judgment is any authority for the proposition that the High Court has jurisdiction to make a declaration in an action against an inferior tribunal that its determination is a nullity in all cases where proceedings for an order of certiorari or mandamus would lie.

RUSSELL L.J. When is a determination not a determination? That is the question. Or rather, when is a determination which a court of law would consider to be erroneous not a determination at all? If it be a determination by the commission of a claim, its correctness cannot be questioned in any court of law; the statute says so: the commission is ex hypothesi "right" for the purposes for which it is established, and the fact that a judge or judges would come to a different conclusion simply means that for those purposes they would be "wrong." Judicial views would have no more relevance than those of the clientele of Carnaby Street. To speak in general terms of an "error of law" by the commission is but a convenient misnomer. The only ground upon which the courts may be approached is an assertion that for some reason the purported determination of a claim by the commission was not such a determination at all.

I have studied the close analysis in the judgment of Diplock L.J. of this branch of the law in general, and its application to this case in particular, and I do not feel that I can usefully say much more than that I am entirely in agreement with that judgment. I also think that a crucial passage in the judgment of Browne J. is where he says:

"In my judgment, the commission has no jurisdiction to consider under article 4 (1) any other question than those which sub-paragraphs (*a*) and (*b*) of that article on their true construction require them to consider, and if satisfied of those matters they are under a statutory duty to treat the claim as established and have no jurisdiction to do anything else."

But in the course of determination of a claim it is for the commission to decide upon "their true construction" and not a court.

From my general agreement with the judgment of Diplock L.J. I exclude his references to jurisdiction to give declaratory judgments: not because I disagree, but because I have not addressed my mind to the matter.

I add this. To some it may seem strange or even obnoxious that prospects of compensation for damage suffered should be **[913]** subjected to infallible error by the commission: or indeed that any tribunal (excepting always the House of Lords) should be infallible in error (I am not asserting that the commission did err in this case.) But in all mundane matters requiring decision or adjudication there must as a practical matter be an apropriate level at which a question must be finally resolved. In the particular field now under review it does not seem to me in any way inappropriate that the commission should be at that level: and that was the view of the legislature when the Tribunals and Inquiries Act, 1958, was enacted. In substance the executive is dealing broadly with matters not strictly matters of right, and the time-consuming precision of the ordinary judicial processes may well be out of place. In terms (now no doubt outdated) of field artillery, a quadrant elevation to the nearest 25 yards is a work of supererogation if you are working off a one-inch map. Morever, if it were to appear to the executive that in a particular case injustice had been done, correction by Order in Council is available, subject only to approval by Parliament.

Lastly, it is to be observed that the plaintiffs, when they entered into agreement with the sequestrator and T.E.D.O., assumed (as was frankly admitted) that they would get nothing more as a result of any treaty, having decided to "go it alone." This fact makes no contribution whatever to my opinion on this case: but I think it should be known by the man in the street—Carnaby or other.

Appeal allowed with costs.
Judgment of Browne J. set aside.
Leave to appeal to the House of Lords granted.

Solicitors: *Treasury Solicitor; Linklaters & Paines.*

ANISMINIC LTD. v. FOREIGN COMPENSATION COMMISSION AND ANOTHER

([1969] 2 A.C. 147)

2, 3, 7, 8, 10, 14, 15, 16, 17, 21, 22, 23 October, 17 December, 1968: House of Lords, Lords Reid, Morris of Borth-y-Gest, Pearce, Wilberforce, Pearson.

29 July, 1966: Queen's Bench Division, Browne J.

Crown Practice—Certiorari—Inferior tribunal—Statutory—Foreign Compensation Commission—Determination—Construction of Order in Council—Whether error going to jurisdiction—"No certiorari clause"—Whether certiorari lies—Foreign Compensation Act, 1950 (14 *Geo.* 6, *c.* 12), *s.* 4 (4).
Practice—Declaratory judgment—Certiorari, relation to—Inferior tribunal—Foreign Compensation Commission—Determination—"No Certiorari clause"—Construction of Order in Council—Whether error within jurisdiction—Tribunal's power to determine but not to enforce the liability—Whether tribunal party to action for declaration that determination a nullity—Foreign Compensation Act, 1950, *s.* 4 (4).
Tribunal—Statutory—Control by courts—Declaration—Foreign Compensation Commission—Determination—Construction of Order in Council—Whether error within jurisdiction—Tribunal's power to determine but not to enforce—Whether party to action for declaration—Whether jurisdiction in court to entertain proceedings—Foreign Compensation Act, 1950, *s.* 4 (4).
Ouster of Jurisdiction of Court—Statute—Determination by statutory commission—Not to "be called in question in any court of law"—Effect—Foreign Compensation Act, 1950, *s.* 4 (4). **[148]**

By section 4 (4) of the Foreign Compensation Act, 1950:

> "The determination by the commission of any application made to them under this Act shall not be called in question in any court of law."

By article 4 (1) in Part III of the Foreign Compensation (Egypt) (Determination and Registration of Claims) Order, 1962:

> "The commission shall treat a claim under this Part of the Order as established if the applicant satisfies them of the following matters:—(*a*) that his application relates to property in Egypt which is referred to in Annex E; (*b*) if the property is referred to in paragraph (1) (*a*) or paragraph (2) of Annex E—(i) that the applicant is the person referred to in paragraph (1) (*a*) or in paragraph (2), as the case may be, as the owner of the property or is the successor in title of such person; and (ii) that the person referred to as aforesaid and any person who became successor in title of such person on or before February 28, 1959, were British nationals on October 31, 1956, and February 28, 1959; (*c*) if the property is referred to in paragraph 1 (*b*) of Annex E—(i) that the applicant was the owner on October 31, 1956, or, at the option of the applicant, on the date of the sale of the property at any time before February 28, 1959, by the Government of the United Arab Republic under the provisions of Egyptian Proclamation No. 5 of November 1, 1956, or is the successor in title of such owner; and (ii) that the owner on October 31, 1956, or on the date of such sale, as the case may be, and any person who became successor in title of such owner on or before February 28, 1959, were British nationals on October 31, 1956 and February 28, 1959."

Before the Suez Incident and on October 31, 1956, the plaintiffs, an

English company, owned property in Egypt which was sequestrated, under the provisions of Proclamation No. 5 of 1956, by the Egyptian authorities. In 1957, the plaintiffs sold the sequestrated property to an Egyptian organisation, T.E.D.O. In 1959, the plaintiffs, who were named in Annex E within the meaning of article 1 (2) of the Foreign Compensation (Egypt) (Determination and Registration of Claims) Order, 1962, made an application to the Foreign Compensation Commission claiming that they were persons entitled to participate in the Egyptian Compensation Fund in respect of their sequestrated property. The commission's provisional determination was that they had failed to establish a claim under the Order. The plaintiffs brought this action against the commission for declarations to the effect that the provisional determination was a nullity and that they were entitled to participate in the compensation fund. They contended that the commission had misconstrued the Order in finding that T.E.D.O. was their successor in title. The commission contended that, under section 4 (4) of the Foreign Compensation Act, 1950, the court had no jurisdiction to entertain the proceedings.

Held (Lord Morris of Borth-y-Gest dissenting) that the word "determination" in section 4 (4) of the Act of 1950 should not be construed as including everything which purported to be a determination but was not in fact a determination because the commission had misconstrued the provision of the Order defining their jurisdiction. Accordingly, the court was not precluded from inquiring whether or not the order of the commission was a nullity. [149]

Per Lord Wilberforce. Just as it is the duty of the court to attribute autonomy of decision to the tribunal within the designated area, so the counterpart of this autonomy is that the court must ensure that the limits of the area laid down are observed (post, p. 208).

Smith v. *East Elloe Rural District Council* [1956] A.C. 736; [1956] 2 W.L.R. 888; [1956] 1 All E.R. 855, H.L.(E.) distinguished.

Davies v. *Price* [1958] 1 W.L.R. 434; [1958] 1 All E.R. 671, C.A. disapproved.

Per Lord Morris of Borth-y-Gest. The commission were acting within their jurisdiction when they entertained the application. They did not fail to obey any mandatory injunction of the Order and if in reaching an honest conclusion in regard to a question of construction, they made an error, such an error would be one made while acting within the jurisdiction and in the discharge of their function within it (post, p. 194).

Held further (Lord Pearson dissenting) that the applicant having satisfied the listed requirements of the Order, it was outside the jurisdiction of the commission to consider whether or not the applicant had a successor in title and in this the commission misconstrued article 4. The expression "successor in title" was inappropriate to denote any person while the original owner was still in existence.

Per Lord Pearce. A successor in title to a person is different from a successor in title to a part of his property (post, p. 203).

Held, further, that the appellants were entitled to the declarations sought.

Decision of the Court of Appeal* [1968] 2 Q.B. 862; [1967] 3 W.L.R. 382; [1967] 2 All E.R. 986, C.A. reversed

The following cases were referred to in their Lordships' opinions:

Board of Education v. *Rice* [1911] A.C. 179, H.L.(E.) on appeal from *Rex* v. *Board of Education* [1910] 2 K.B. 165, C.A. affirming [1909] 2 K.B. 1045, D.C.

Bradlaugh, Ex parte (1878) 3 Q.B.D. 509, D.C.

Bunbury v. *Fuller* (1853) 9 Ex. 111.

Campbell v. *Brown* (1829) 3 Wils & S. 441, H.L.(Sc.).

Davies v. *Price* [1958] 1 W.L.R. 434; [1958] 1 All E.R. 671, C.A.

Estate and Trust Agencies (1927) Ltd. v *Singapore Improvement Trust* [1937] A.C. 898; [1937] 3 All E.R. 324, P.C.

Maradana Mosque Trustees v. *Mahmud* [1967] 1 A.C. 13; [1966] 2 W.L.R. 921; [1966] 1 All E.R. 545, P.C.
Reg. v. *Bolton* (1841) 1 Q.B. 66.
Reg. v. *Cotham* [1898] 1 Q.B. 802, D.C.
Reg. v. *Fulham, Hammersmith and Kensington Rent Tribunal, Ex parte Hierowski* [1953] 2 Q.B. 147; [1953] 2 W.L.R. 1028; [1953] 2 All E.R. 4, D.C.
Reg. v. *Governor of Brixton Prison, Ex parte Armah** [1968] A.C. 192; [1966] 3 W.L.R. 828; [1966] 3 All E.R. 177, H.L.(E.).
Reg. v. *Hurst, Ex parte Smith* [1960] 2 Q.B. 133; [1960] 2 W.L.R. 961; [1960] 2 All E.R. 385, D.C.
Reg. v. *Income Tax Special Purposes Commissioners* (1888) 21 Q.B.D. 313, C.A.
Reg. v. *Medical Appeal Tribunal, Ex parte Gilmore* [1957] 1 Q.B. 574; [1957] 2 W.L.R. 498; [1957] 1 All E.R. 796, C.A.
Reg. v. *St. Olave's District Board* (1857) 8 E. & B. 529. **[150]**
Rex v. *Cheshire Justices, Ex parte Heaver* (1912) 108 L.T. 374; 29 T.L.R. 23, D.C.
Rex v. *Minister of Health* [1939] 1 K.B. 232; [1938] 4 All E.R. 32, C.A.
Rex v. *Nat Bell Liquors Ltd.* [1922] 2 A.C. 128, P.C.
Rex v. *Northumberland Compensation Appeal Tribunal, Ex parte Shaw* [1951] 1 K.B. 711; [1951] 1 All E.R. 268; [1952] 1 K.B. 338; [1952] 1 All E.R. 122, C.A.
Rex v. *Shoreditch Assessment Committee, Ex parte Morgan* [1910] 2 K.B. 859, C.A.
Ridge v. *Baldwin* [1964] A.C. 40; [1963] 2 W.L.R. 935; [1963] 2 All E.R. 66, H.L.(E.)
Rustomjee v. *The Queen** (1876) 1 Q.B.D. 487, D.C.; (1876) 2 Q.B.D. 69, C.A.
Seereelall Jhuggroo v. *Central Arbitration and Control Board* [1953] A.C. 151, P.C.
Smith v. *East Elloe Rural District Council* [1956] A.C. 736; [1956] 2 W.L.R. 888; [1956] 1 All E.R. 855, H.L.(E.).

The following additional cases were cited in argument:
Barnard v. *National Dock Labour Board* [1953] 2 Q.B. 18; [1953] 2 W.L.R. 995; [1953] 1 All E.R. 1113, C.A.
Brittain v. *Kinnaird* (1819) 1 Brod. & B. 432.
Dever, Ex parte (1887) 18 Q.B.D. 660, C.A.
Durayappah v. *Fernando* [1967] 2 A.C. 337; [1967] 3 W.L.R. 289; [1967] 2 All E.R. 152, P.C.
Lind, In re [1915] 2 Ch. 345, C.A.
Padfield v. *Minister of Agriculture, Fisheries and Food* [1968] A.C. 997; [1968] 2 W.L.R. 924; [1968] 1 All E.R. 694, H.L.(E.).
Pyx Granite Co. Ltd. v. *Ministry of Housing and Local Government* [1960] A.C. 260; [1959] 3 W.L.R. 346; [1959] 3 All E.R. 1, H.L.(E.).
Reg. v. *City of London Licensing Justices, Ex parte Stewart* [1954] 1 W.L.R. 1325; [1954] 3 All E.R. 270, D.C.
Reg. v. *Farmer* [1892] 1 Q.B. 637, C.A.
Rex v. *Ludlow, Ex parte Barnsley Corporation* [1947] K.B. 634; [1947] 1 All E.R. 880, D.C.

APPEAL from the Court of Appeal* (Sellers, Diplock and Russell L.JJ.).

This was an appeal by leave of the Court of Appeal from a decision of that court dated March 22, 1967, allowing an appeal of the respondents, (the defendants in the action), the Foreign Compensation Commission and Cecil Frank Cooper, against a judgment of Browne J.† given in the Queen's Bench Division of the High Court of Justice. By that judgment it was adjudged and declared by Browne J. against the respondents: (i) that the first respondents'

† A note of the judgment of Browne J. appears at p. 223, at the end of this report.

provisional determination of May 8, 1963, as explained in the first respondents' provisional letter dated June 12, 1963, in answer to a letter of the solicitors of the appellant company (the plaintiffs in the action), Anisminic Ltd., dated May 16, 1963, and of which the minute of adjudication formed part, was made without or in excess of jurisdiction and was a nullity. (ii) That the first respondents' further provisional determination of June 21, 1963, was a nullity. (iii) That the first respondents were under a statutory duty to treat as established under part III (article 4) of the **[151]** Foreign Compensation (Egypt) (Determination and Registration of Claims) Order, 1962 (S.I. 1962 No. 2187), the appellant company's claim referred to in paragraph 7 of their statement of claim. By his judgment Browne J. ordered that the first respondents should pay the costs of the plaintiffs. By its order the Court of Appeal reversed that order and gave the present respondents their costs in the Court of Appeal and before Browne J.

The Foreign Compensation (Egypt) (Determination and Registration of Claims) Order, 1959 (S.I. 1959 No. 625) was made on April 6, 1959. The Order of 1962 was made on October 2, 1962.

The appellants were an English company incorporated in 1913, and from that date until 1958 their registered name was the Sinai Mining Co. Ltd. Before and on October 31, 1956, they carried on the business of mining manganese ore in the Sinai Peninsula under mining leases or concessions granted by the Egyptian Government. Their valuation of their property and assets in that area was about £4.5 million. The events and hostilities known as the Suez Incident began on October 31, 1956.

On November 1, 1956, the Egyptian Government issued a proclamation, Proclamation No. 5 of 1956, by which two general sequestrators and special sequestrators were appointed to take over and manage the assets of British and French nationals. The appellants' property was sequestrated and, after sequestration, the Israeli armed forces destroyed, damaged or removed £532,773 worth of that property.

In April, 1957, the Israeli forces withdrew and, on April 29, 1957, the Egyptian Government, by Decree No. 387 of 1957, granted the Custodian General of property of British, French and Australian nationals authority to sell and to liquidate the establishments and other property subject to sequestration. On that date, the Custodian General and the Chairman of the Economic Board, who was also the representative of a company under formation and to be known as the Sinai Manganese Co. S.A.E., entered into a contract of sale by which the appellants' sequestrated property was sold to the Economic Board, a department of the Egyptian Government. The Economic Board was the same body as the Economic Development Organisation ("T.E.D.O."). As a result of a Presidential decision of May 18, 1957, the proposed new company was brought into existence.

On June 11, 1957, the appellants registered with the Foreign Office in London a claim setting out details of the assets and goodwill of their undertakings in Egypt as at October 31, 1956. The appellants' property included a large quantity of manganese ore and they took steps to dissuade their customers from buying ore from T.E.D.O., thereby embarrassing the Egyptian authorities, with whom they entered into negotiations and, on November 23, 1957, they agreed with T.E.D.O. and the Sequestrator General to sell to T.E.D.O. the whole of their business carried on and situated in Egypt for the sum of £500,000 sterling. The agreement specifically provided that the appellants' assets should not include any claim to which they "might be entitled to assert against any Government authority other than the Egyptian Government, as a result of loss suffered by, or damage to or reduction in the value of" their business or assets during the events of October and November, 1956. The appellants also **[152]** agreed to take measures to change their name and did so on January 30, 1958.

By an agreement dated February 28, 1959, between the United Kingdom Government and the Government of the United Arab Republic, the Government of the United Arab Republic agreed to pay to the British Government the sum of £27,500,000 in full and final settlement of claims by United Kingdom nationals for certain property in Egypt, including property subject to the provisions of Proclamation No. 5 and referred to in Annex E to that agreement and in Annex E to the Exchange of Notes dated August 7, 1962, which was supplementary to the agreement of February 28, 1959. The treaty provides for the return to British subjects of their sequestrated property except properties sold between October 30, 1956, and August 2, 1958, listed in Annex E. The sum of £27,500,000 and other moneys provided by the British Government formed the Egyptian Compensation Fund and, pursuant to the Foreign Compensation Act, 1950, and Orders in Council, the Foreign Compensation Commission (referred to as the commission) were empowered to make provisional determinations as to whether applicants had made out their claims to be entitled to participate in the compensation fund. The appellants' name appeared in Annex E "(Subject to a special arrangement)."

On September 15, 1959, the appellants made an application to the commission claiming that they were entitled to participate in the compensation fund and, on May 8, 1963, the commission provisionally determined that the appellants had failed to establish a claim under the Foreign Compensation (Egypt) (Determination and Registration of Claims) Order, 1962, in respect of their sequestrated property but their claim for certain property damaged by the Israeli armed forces was fit for registration. On June 21, 1963, by a further provisional determination, the commission ordered that their claim for damage should be registered, under article 8 of the Order, in the sum of £532,773. The commission released to the appellants their minutes of adjudication which disclosed, inter alia, that the commission considered that T.E.D.O., who were not British nationals, were the appellants' successors in title.

The appellants brought this action against the respondents, the commission, and the legal adviser appointed by them to represent the interests of the compensation fund, for declarations to the effect that the commission's provisional determination was wrong in law and was either invalid or a nullity. The appellants contended, inter alia, that T.E.D.O. was not their successor in title and that they had proved that they were persons entitled to participate in the compensation fund. By their amended defence, the respondents contended, inter alia, that the High Court had no jurisdiction to entertain the proceedings.

R. J. Parker Q.C. and *F. P. Neill Q.C.* for the appellant company. Some decisions are good while they stand; others are void ab initio. The decision of the commission is a complete nullity. If it is not a nullity the appellants must fail.

Ridge v. *Baldwin* [1964] A. C. 40 demonstrates that for a period the courts had forgotten the old rules. There the judge and all the members **[153]** of the Court of Appeal declined to hold the decision of the watch committee bad but Ridge appealed successfully to the House of Lords. But there have been other cases when a wrong decision of the Court of Appeal has stood uncorrected for long periods.

As to the effect when a tribunal has made an order under the Fugitive Offenders Act, 1881, and the alleged offender appeals, see *Armah's* case* [1968] A.C. 192.

When a tribunal misconstrues the very statute which confers jurisdiction on it, the question arises whether that renders the decision a nullity in all cases or only in some and what cases.

The word jurisdiction has been and is used in several different senses. There may be "jurisdiction" to embark on an enquiry or the "jurisdiction" may be exceeded in the course of the inquiry, so that there is no "jurisdiction" to make the order.

The cases are confusing. Sometimes a case has been conceded to be authority for a proposition for which it is not an authority. Sometimes there are parallel lines of authority which never meet. There are decisions on certiorari which ignore decisions on mandamus. There has also been a tendency to treat decisions on one topic as being applicable to other topics within the same subject.

The respondents rely on section 4 (4) of the Foreign Compensation Act, 1950, but such enactments do not bite on nullities, where there is no determination and therefore nothing on which the subsection can operate. Section 4 (4) refers to a real and not to a purported determination which in law has no existence. In such a case there is nothing to be questioned.

Take a case where a tribunal is not properly constituted or where the application is not in accordance with the Act, so that the tribunal has no jurisdiction from the outset, or where the inquiry is not conducted in accordance with statutory form or natural justice, or where the so-called determination was of a kind not authorised by the Act, e.g., sending to prison a defendant who was under age, or where a tribunal, by a miscontruction of a relevant section, has assumed a wider jurisdiction than the law has committed to it. In all such cases the purported determination is a nullity and the section does not then confer a bite.

This section admittedly bites if the tribunal has merely made an error of law or fact, but it cannot misconstrue the very section on which its jurisdiction arises: see *Rex* v. *Board of Education* [1910] 2 K.B. 165, 178 and *Rex* v. *Shoreditch Assessment Committee* [1910] 2 K.B. 859, 880.

It is a wrong approach to say that, if there has been a mistake, the executive can correct it, for that would be an abrogation of the court's function. The construction of a statute conferring jurisdiction is always a matter for the court, and misconstruction of it by the relevant tribunal will result in the decision being a nullity, not least when the error is such that the tribunal asked itself a question the determination of which was not committed to it.

In this case the appellants are entitled to succeed in respect of the property as it stood before the Suez incident, ignoring the war damage; or alternatively, at least in respect of the war-damaged part of it. Browne J. was right in holding that the commission was under a manda-[**154**]tory duty to treat the whole of the claim as established. The commission were satisfied of everything of which they had to be satisfied in respect of the property which afterwards suffered war damage.

It is accepted that the commission might find difficult subsidiary questions of law and fact arising and that, if they erred in respect of them, they would be protected by section 4 (4) of the Act. But it is otherwise as regards the questions they asked themselves as to their jurisdiction. In respect of them one is entitled to ask whether they have directed their minds to the right statutory questions. They might have said simply: "We reject the claim." But that rejection might have been for any of several reasons, and one must go into their reasons to see whether they were within their jurisdiction.

The commission were concerned, not with the policy of the treaty, but only with seeing whether the persons before it had established the listed matters which gave them a right to have their claim allowed. One is entitled to see whether they were satisfied on the necessary points. Here, because they went outside the questions submitted to them, their decision was a nullity.

In *Reg.* v. *City of London Licensing Justices* [1954] 1 W.L.R. 1325 a similar point arose. Mandamus was granted there, but, if there is an existing decision which is a real decision, mandamus will not issue. It is accepted that in that case the word "nullity" was not used and there was no ouster clause, but the justices had no power to adjudicate on the question whether the condition was a condition within the meaning of the relevant section; it was for the court to say what the section meant. So, in the present case, the commission have jurisdiction to deal with the matters committed to them by Parliament, but it is not for them to construe the sections conferring jurisdiction on them. When Parliament gave the executive power to prescribe the matters on which the commission must be satisfied, it did not intend to commit to the commission the power to determine what the prescribed matters were. The court must determine the extent of their jurisdiction. It would not be justifiable to construe the Act and the Order as conferring on the commission a power which would cover even a complete "howler" on their part. Thus, article 4 (1) (*a*) of the Order of 1962 relates to "property in Egypt, which is referred to in Annex E" and the commission would go wholly outside their jurisdiction if they allowed a claim relating to property not referred to in Annex E. There is no indication that Parliament intended to confer on the commission a jurisdiction to interpret the Order generally. That would confer on them unlimited power to determine the limits of their own jurisdiction. The Order has, however, narrow and specific confines. Numerous provisions would have been unnecessary if the commission had had power to adjudicate on the limits of the section which gives them their jurisdiction.

The commission wrongly required the appellants to establish that T.E.D.O. was not their successor in title. Where the owner is claiming, that question is not relevant. All claimants must satisfy article 4 (1) (*a*). If a person is claiming as a successor in title he must satisfy the commission that he is a successor in title. But if he is an original owner that question does not come into the matter at all. It was never contemplated that there might be both an original owner and a successor in title at the same time. **[155]** Article 4 (1) (*b*) (ii), relating to successors in title, cannot apply to an original claimant because that would be putting on him the burden of proving that he had no successor in title before the relevant date or that any person whom he cannot establish was not a successor in title was British on the relevant dates. If the original owner proves that he was British at the relevant dates, it cannot be made part of his duty to satisfy the commission on anything that relates to a successor in title. Article 4 (5) of the original Foreign Compensation (Egypt) (Determination and Registration of Claims) Order, 1959, shows that Parliament was only contemplating the straightforward and obvious case of a British national who had died and had a successor.

As to the jurisdiction of the High Court to substitute its opinion for that of the commission, see *Ex parte Bradlaugh* (1878) 3 Q.B.D. 509; *Rex* v. *Shoreditch Assessment Committee* [1910] 2 K.B. 859; *Reg.* v. *Fulham, Hammersmith and Kensington Rent Tribunal* [1953] 2 Q.B. 147; and *Maradana Mosque Trustees* v. *Mahmud* [1967] 1 A.C. 13, 24. The stream of authority on which the appellants rely goes far back. *Seereelall Jhuggroo* v. *Central Arbitration and Control Board* [1953] A.C. 151 is not a departure from it.

If a decision is a nullity there is, strictly speaking, nothing for certiorari to operate on, whereas by mandamus a tribunal can be ordered to get on with its job. Certiorari has always been the classic way of enabling the superior tribunal to decide whether an inferior tribunal has kept within its jurisdiction, but a declaration does just as well. Thus, if a tribunal was required to take something into consideration and neglected to do so, that would go to jurisdiction. So, too, would the case of a tribunal taking something into consideration which it should not have taken into consideration; that, too, would make the decision a nullity. Here the commission took into consideration matters which they should not have taken into consideration, see *Reg.* v. *Cotham* [1898] 1 Q.B. 802, 805, 807-808 (mandamus); *Rex* v. *Board of Education* [1909] 2 K.B. 1045; [1910] 2 K.B. 165, 173, 179, 188; *Board of Education* v. *Rice* [1911] A.C. 179, 182 (mandamus); and *Estate and Trust Agencies (1927) Ltd.* v. *Singapore Improvement Trust* [1937] A.C. 898, 902, 904, 906, 908.

What the court must do is to give the statute its proper interpretation and then see whether what was done was within it. It does not matter whether the reason for the inferior tribunal's action was misconstruction, mistake, bad faith or fraud, whether it asked itself the wrong question or whether it took into account something which was extraneous, the result is a nullity. If the tribunal has misconstrued the statute giving it jurisdiction and has acted on the misconstruction, it follows that it is not within its jurisdiction: see *Ridge* v. *Baldwin* [1964] A.C. 40, 71, 80; *Armah's* case* [1968] A.C. 192, 212, 225, 230, 233, 237-238, 241, 250, 253, 257, 260-61, 263-264; and *Padfield* v. *Minister of Agriculture, Fisheries and Food* [1968] A.C. 997.

Reg. v. *Bolton* (1841) 1 Q.B. 66 on which the respondents relied is the start of an unfortunate line of authority. In that case isolated observations can be cited against the appellants, but the whole must be considered in the light of what was before the court. No question of want of jurisdiction or excess of jurisdiction relevant to the present case **[156]** arose there. Nothing of the sort now being discussed was present in the problem. The subject under discussion was weight of evidence.

So, too, in *Rex* v. *Nat Bell Liquors Ltd.* [1922] 2 A.C. 128, 132, 141, 159, though good law is only relevant to the question of introducing new evidence or dealing with the evidence before the court. The case does not purport to touch the question of acting wrongly in the course of a case which is rightly entertained.

The reasoning in *Rex* v. *Minister of Health* [1939] 1 K.B. 232 is not satisfactory. It would appear to be a case where the Minister was given a wide scope of policy making.

Davies v. *Price* [1958] 1 W.L.R. 434 was wrongly decided and is outside the main current of authority. It goes too far and does not fit into the pattern of the authorities. The applicant should have succeeded because the tribunal had directed its mind to the wrong question. Parker L.J. misconstrued the *Nat Bell* case [1922] 2 A.C. 128 and gave it far too wide an ambit: see *Nat Bell* case at pp. 158, 159, and *Rex* v. *Northumberland Compensation Appeal Tribunal* [1951] 1 K.B. 711, 720, and *Reg.* v. *Income Tax Special Purposes Commissions* (1888) 21 Q.B.D. 313, 315-316, 318, from which it appears that it is for the courts to construe a statute giving jurisdiction to an inferior tribunal.

In *Rex* v. *Cheshire Justices* (1912) 108 L.T. 374, 376, 377, 378 the justices might have to consider the legal effect of their decision between the three claimants for compensation, and, if they went wrong on that, it was held that mandamus would not lie. But if they had taken into account extraneous matters or had not taken into account relevant matters or had asked themselves the wrong question, the position would have been different.

Bunbury v. *Fuller* (1853) 9 Ex. 111 is an example of want of jurisdiction. *Brittain* v. *Kinnaird* (1819) 1 Brod. & B. 432, 437 was distinguished in *Reg.* v. *Farmer* [1892] 1 Q.B. 637, 638-639, 640-641. When it can be shown affirmatively that magistrates have not asked themselves the right questions mandamus will lie. But in *Brittain*'s case (1819) 1 Brod. & B. 432 there was no suggestion that the magistrates had applied the wrong test and, on the face of it, that is a perfectly good case.

When Parliament gives an inferior tribunal jurisdiction to see whether they are satisfied that a particular thing is established, that allows them to inquire into facts and see whether they fit in with what the Act says. But, when the Act may have one of two possible meanings, both cannot apply and it is for the court to say which meaning is right. In the present case "successor in title" in article 4 (1) (*b*) may mean several things and if several different claimants claimed to be a "successor in title," mandamus would issue to obtain the court's ruling as to its proper meaning in the Order. The commission only has jurisdiction to inquire into the facts.

The question for the House of Lords is whether the inquiry which the commission has conducted is the one which Parliament meant it to conduct. The earliest date when anybody could have any claim, legal or moral, against anybody else was February 28, 1959, the date of the agreement between the United Kingdom and the United Arab Republic, because until then nobody knew whether or not the property was going to be **[157]** returned. The agreement created a situation in which the individual knew for the first time that he was not going to get his property back. Before that date there was the hope of a claim against the United Arab Republic. From that date until the date of the first Order, on April 6, 1959, there was a hope of legislation by the British Government or of an exercise of the prerogative, but there were no rights. From then onwards "successor in title" would have to be read, according to the commission, as successor to a claim under the Order. If the commission is right the expression would mean different things in each of the three periods.

But "successor in title" must mean successor to a person and not to a claim. Parliament was looking to a personal successor. The other view would be too complicated for one to suppose that Parliament intended it. One cannot be a successor to property which is not in existence. Successor in title to a claim would be a possible meaning, were it not for the three different periods. The whole thing is hooked onto Annex E which contains a list of people who, if they die, will have successors. If the original owner listed in Annex E is alive, there is no question of a successor in title and the situation is very simple. It is unlikely that Parliament anticipated that persons would assign claims against the United Arab Republic where there was an obvious hope that the British Government would do something for them, producing a situation where two persons were entitled to make a claim.

As to the jurisdiction point, a very wide form of words could confer an absolute power on a tribunal, for example, the National Service Mobilization Regulations, 1942, of Canada. By regulation 9 (1) the board thereunder is given power to adjudicate on every application for a postponement order and

"shall undertake and carry out any other duties which may be imposed upon it by these regulations or by the Governor in Council."

By regulation 9 (5):

"... no decision of a board shall, by means of an injunction, prohibition, mandamus, certiorari, habeas corpus or other process, issuing out of court, be enjoined, restrained, staged, removed, or subjected to review or consideration on any ground, whether arising out of alleged absence of jurisdiction in the board, nullity, defect, or irregularity of the proceedings or any other cause whatsoever, nor shall any such proceedings or decision be questioned, reviewed or reconsidered in any court."

That was a wartime regulation and that is the way the intention, when it exists, should be achieved.

On this point the appellants submit: (1) The commission in making their determination misconstrued the Order of 1962. (2) The misconstruction resulted in the commission asking themselves the wrong questions. (3) Alternatively, it resulted in the commission requiring the appellants to satisfy a condition which they ought not to have been required to satisfy. (4) If the commission had not misconstrued the Order of 1962 they would have treated the appellants' claim as established. (5) Therefore the determination was made without jurisdiction **[158]**.

To allow the appeal does not involve disregarding section 4 (4) of the Act. The duty of the commission is not to determine claims but to say whether they are satisfied of certain matters.

As to the history of certiorari, see *Judicial Review of Administrative Action* by Professor S. A. de Smith, 2nd ed. (1968), pp. 386 et seq. It was used for many purposes, the court requiring the inferior tribunal to show what it had done, so that it might be examined and, if necessary, quashed after examination.

In exercising its jurisdiction to review, the Court of Session in Scotland adopted the same approach as the English courts: see *Campbell* v. *Brown* (1829) 3 Wils. & S. 441, 442-448.

The commission were wrong: (1) in going into the question of a successor in title at all, when they had before them a person named in Annex E, (2) in inquiring whether the appellants' claim was one which existed at February 28, 1959, and was settled by the treaty, and (3) in looking for an assignee of a claim against the Egyptian Government, which was not what the Act directed them to look for.

If it is found that the commission have done things which they ought not to have done or have omitted things which they should have done, their decision is a nullity.

Sydney Templeman Q.C. and *Gordon Slynn* for the respondents. The questions in this appeal are: (1) What determination did the commission have the jurisdiction to make? (2) What, if anything, did it purport to determine? (3) What is the true meaning and effect of section 4 (4) of the Act? The answers lie within the Act, the Orders and the minute of adjudication.

The following propositions are submitted: (1) The commission had jurisdiction to determine whether or not a claim to participate in the Egyptian Compensation Fund must be treated as established.

(2) It had jurisdiction to determine whether the claim to participate in the fund must be registered.

(3) It determined that a claim by the appellants to participate in the fund in respect of their sequestrated property was not established but that their claim in respect of certain property damaged by the Israeli forces was fit for registration.

(4) The commission had jurisdiction to determine and assess the loss in respect of the registered claim and they assessed it at £532,773.

(5) The determination by the commission of the appellants' application to the commission to participate in the fund cannot be called in question in any court of law.

As to proposition (1), section 3 of the Act of 1950 enables an Order in Council to provide for the determination by the commission of claims to participate in the Egyptian fund. Articles 4 and 6 of the Order of 1962 gave the commission jurisdiction to determine such claims. A claim is determined when the commission decide what to do about it, when the commission adjudicate upon it and come to a decision. Articles 4 and 6 gave the commission jurisdiction to determine that a claim had been established; that jurisdiction must include jurisdiction to determine that a claim had not been established. Articles 4 and 6 as well as conferring jurisdiction, also gave directions to the commission as to how **[159]** that jurisdiction was to be exercised. If the commission failed to carry out those instructions by misconstruing the articles or by asking the wrong questions or for some other reason, the commission committed an error within jurisdiction and their determination that the claim had not been established was not a nullity. The commission had jurisdiction to make a wrong determination as well as a right determination. Different considerations might apply if the commission infringed the rules of natural justice or did not act bona fide.

As to proposition (2), article 8 of the Order of 1960 conferred jurisdiction on the commission to determine whether a claim to participate in the Egyptian compensation fund must be registered or not.

As to proposition (3) the provisional determination and the minute of adjudication make it plain that the commission determined that the claim by Anisminic to participate in the Egyptian compensation fund must not be treated as established. The provisional determination and the minute of adjudication equally make it plain that the commission determined that the claim must be registered so far as that claim arose out of certain specific damage. The commission may have been wrong but they had jurisdiction to make those determinations. In order to arrive at their determination, the commission had to construe the April 1957 agreement, the November 1957 agreement and the Order of 1962. If they committed any error of construction it was an error within jurisdiction.

As to proposition (4) it is common ground that the commission had jurisdiction to assess the amount of loss with respect to the registered claim and that they did in fact do so.

As to proposition (5), section 2 (2) (*a*) of the Act of 1950 defines applications as applications to the commission for the purpose of establishing claims. By section (3) (*a*) a claim is a claim to participate in compensation. As a result of the Act of 1950 and the 1962 Order an application under the Act includes an application to the commission for the purpose of establishing a claim to participate in the Egyptian compensation. An application made to the commission for the purpose of establishing a claim to participate in the compensation can be determined by treating the claim as established by registering the claim or by dismissing the application. Section 4 (4) of the Act provides that the determination by the commission of any application made to them under the Act shall not be called in question in any court of law. The commission have determined the application in the present instance by registering part of the claim and dismissing the remainder of the application. The application has been determined and that application cannot be called in question. The appeal fails as a matter of construction of the Act of 1950. The authorities do not deal with an Act which is worded in the same way as the Act of 1950 but on the authorities also the appeal fails.

Normally the court can interfere with the decision of an inferior tribunal (1) when it exceeds or fails to exercise its jurisdiction or when the tribunal has done something which it has no power to do at all and there is a nullity, or (2) when the inferior tribunal has done something which it has power to do, but in the course of exercising its jurisdiction has made an error in law. Whether it is a case of nullity or error in law the court can interfere either by certiorari or mandamus. In a case of nullity the **[160]** court can interfere in any event. In the case of error of law it can interfere, provided there is no ouster clause in the Act conferring jurisdiction and in some cases provided the error of law was on the record. In the case of most tribunals the court can order production of the record: see sections 11 and 12 of the Tribunals and Inquiries Act, 1958.

The appellants' main proposition is that misconstruction by a tribunal of the statute conferring jurisdiction will result in the determination of the tribunal being a nullity. This proposition would abolish the distinction between excess of jurisdiction and error of law within jurisdiction and abolish section 4 (4) of the Act of 1950 and similar ouster sections.

The Order of 1962 bristles with words which must be construed, for example, "British nationals" in article 4 and "successors in title." Every application involves a construction of the statute conferring jurisdiction. There are no pure questions of fact. It is a question of the facts in the light of the words used. It is impossible to make a determination without construing the order. Therefore the main proposition of the appellants means that the court can interfere whether there was excess of jurisdiction or error of law or error of fact.

The appellants' subsidiary propositions are that a determination is a nullity where it is based on an error which led to the tribunal asking a question not permitted to it or led to the tribunal seeking to impose additional burdens on an applicant. But every error of law results in the tribunal asking a question which it ought not to ask or imposing additional burdens on an applicant whose application is dismissed as a result of an error of law.

When Anisminic made its application, the tribunal was obliged to construe the whole of article 4. It was obliged to construe article 4 in the light of all the facts including the April 1957 agreement and the November 1957 agreement. The commission was exercising its jurisdiction when in the light of the facts before the commission and for the purpose of reaching its determination with regard to the application, the commission construed "successor in title" and "property in Egypt" and every other expression used by the Order of 1962.

When the appellants made their application the commission had jurisdiction and were directed by article 4 (1) (*b*) (i) to make an inquiry whether they were persons referred to in paragraph (1) (*a*) or paragraph (*b*) of Annex E and by article 4 (1) (*b*) (ii) whether any successors in title of the appellants were British nationals on the relevant dates. If nothing had happened to the appellants since the damage occurred the question of a successor in title might not have arisen, but in view of the agreement of November 23, 1957, it did arise, so that the commission were obliged to construe the article in the light of the facts appearing on the application. It is not clear from the article that an original owner never has to prove anything with regard to a successor in title. Thus the question of the "successor in title" arose as part of the inquiry and the commission were not put outside their jurisdiction by construing it. It cannot be the duty of the commission to construe part of the article but not the whole. One cannot divide the jurisdiction to construe it into little bits. The commission are not outside their jurisdiction if they construe the article and **[161]** get it wrong, since it is either within their jurisdiction or it is not to construe the article in the light of all the facts which they know.

The authorities as to limitations on the jurisdiction of tribunals fall into several categories:

Category (1). Cases where the tribunal has no jurisdiction to embark on an inquiry and make a determination unless a condition precedent was satisfied. If in the view of the court the condition was not satisfied, then the so-called determination is a nullity: *Reg.* v. *Income Tax Special Purposes Commissioners*

(1888) 21 Q.B.D. 313; *Reg.* v. *Farmer* [1892] 1 Q.B. 637 and *Rex* v. *Shoreditch Assessment Committee* [1910] 2 K.B. 859.

Category (2). Where the statute expressly forbids the tribunal to exercise jurisdiction over the subject-matter of the inquiry and determination, e.g., where a tribunal has jurisdiction to fix the rent of a residential tenancy, but not a business tenancy: *Bunbury* v. *Fuller* (1853) 9 Ex. 111; *Reg.* v. *Cotham* [1898] 1 Q.B. 802; *Rex* v. *Fulham, Hammersmith and Kensington Rent Tribunal* [1951] 2 K.B. 1; [1953] 2 Q.B. 147.

Category (3). Where the tribunal had no jurisdiction to make the order it in fact made.

Category (4). Cases in which there have been different reasons for the decisions and in which the distinction between nullity and error in law may not have been considered: *Campbell* v. *Brown* (1829) 3 Wils. & S. 441; *Ex parte Bradlaugh* (1878) 3 Q.B.D. 509; *Rex* v. *Cheshire Justices* (1912) 108 L.T. 374; *Estate and Trust Agencies (1927) Ltd.* v. *Singapore Improvement Trust* [1937] A.C. 898; *Seereelall Jhuggroo* v. *Central Arbitration and Control Board* [1953] A.C. 151; *Ridge* v. *Baldwin* [1964] A.C. 40; *Maradana Mosque Trustees* v. *Mahmud* [1967] 1 A.C. 13. These are difficult cases in that it is sometimes hard to see what the precise point was but it may be possible to build up from them a proposition of general validity that a tribunal has no jurisdiction to make a determination if it has acted in complete disregard of its duties.

Category (5). The tribunal has jurisdiction, so long as it has not disregarded its duties, even if it wrongly determines a question of construction in the course of the inquiry, committing an error in law. This determination is not a nullity. The court cannot intervene on grounds of error of law if there is an ouster clause or its equivalent. In the present case the commission did not wholly disregard its instructions. If it made an error in law, that did not produce a nullity. The cases are all in the respondents' favour: *Brittain* v. *Kinnaird* (1819) 1 Brod. & B. 432; *Reg.* v. *Bolton* (1841) 1 Q.B. 66, 71 et seq.; *Reg.* v. *St. Olave's District Board* (1857) 8 E. & B. 529; *Rex* v. *Minister of Health* [1939] 1 K.B. 232; *Rex* v. *Ludlow* [1947] K.B. 634; *Davies* v. *Price* [1958] 1 W.L.R. 434, 441; *Rex* v. *Nat Bell Liquors Ltd.* [1922] 2 A.C. 128; *Rex* v. *Northumberland Compensation Appeal Tribunal* [1951] 1 K.B. 711; [1952] I K.B. 338; *Smith* v. *East Elloe Rural District Council* [1956] A.C. 736, 764-765; *Armah's* case* [1968] A.C. 192, 201, 218, 233-234, 237-238. If there was any error in the present case it was of a type covered by these authorities. The present case is distinguishable from the first four categories, and, since it fits into the fifth category, the appeal must fail.

Bunbury v. *Fuller* (1853) 9 Ex. 111, 140, is distinguishable from the present case. *Ex parte Bradlaugh* (1878) 3 Q.B.D. 509, 511, stands very **[162]** much on its own but its central feature is that the magistrate had not made an order of the type which he was entitled to make. In *Reg.* v. *Income Tax Special Purposes Commissioners* (1888) 21 Q.B.D. 313 one must distinguish a condition precedent to entering onto the inquiry at all from an error made by the tribunal in conducting the inquiry. What was said at pp. 318-319 is acceptable if it refers to a condition precedent, but not if it would take away the jurisdiction. *Reg.* v. *Farmer* [1892] 1 Q.B. 637 is a case of a condition precedent to the exercise of the jurisdiction. In *Reg.* v. *Cotham* [1898] 1 Q.B. 802, the magistrates acted in a case where they had no jurisdiction at all. In *Board of Education* v. *Rice* [1911] A.C. 179, 180, 182, 184, 185 the Minister was purporting to act in a field in which the legislation had not given jurisdiction. One must distinguish between the inquiry on which the Minister should have embarked and that on which he in fact embarked: see *Rex* v. *Board of Education* [1910] 2 K.B. 165, 168. That case does not impinge on the present problem, since the government department completely disregarded their directions. *Rex* v. *Shoreditch Assessment Committee* [1910] 2 K.B. 859 is not helpful in the present type of case. *Rex* v. *Cheshire Justices* (1912) 108 L.T. 374 is a difficult case, which is not helpful in jurisdiction or error in law.

In the normal case it does not matter whether the fact that the tribunal has disregarded its duties appears on the record or not. The decision can be quashed for error of law or disregard of duty. But a decision cannot be quashed on either ground if Parliament has said that it cannot be questioned. The ouster clause in section 4 (4) of the Act which says that "the determination ... shall not be called in question" prevents the court from intervening. One cannot even issue a writ, because that would amount to calling the determination in question. It is different from a provision that the determination shall be final. *Smith* v. *East Elloe Rural District Council* [1956] A.C. 736 turned on a similar form of words. Such a phrase does not appear in the category (4) cases. When there is an ouster clause the tribunal cannot be interfered with once it has entered into the inquiry entrusted to it, however much it may abuse its power en route: see the *Nat Bell* case [1922] 2 A.C. 128, 151. A court may wrongly convict by perversity, by misunderstanding the evidence or by misunderstanding a statute, but, if Parliament has said that the conviction cannot be questioned in any court of law, it must stand nevertheless, whether or not the reason appears on the record.

Estate and Trust Agencies (1927) Ltd. v. *Singapore Improvement Trust* [1937] A.C. 898 is distinguishable from category (5) because there the courts were not prohibited from interfering and there was no ouster clause of the type present in this case. It was not wrongly decided on category (4).

Rex v. *Minister of Health* [1939] 1 K.B. 232 is indistinguishable from the present case.

In *Rex* v. *Northumberland Compensation Appeal Tribunal* [1951] 1 K.B. 711, 712-713, 716, 722; [1952] 1 K.B. 338, 344, 346-347, 348, 353-354 the court did not treat the case as one of want of jurisdiction but one of mere error of law. If the contentions of the present appellants were right, the whole argument in that case would have been unnecessary.

In *Seereelall Jhuggroo's* case [1953] A.C. 151 there was an ouster **[163]** clause in a limited form. *Reg.* v. *Fulham, Hammersmith & Kensington Rent Tribunal* [1953] 2 Q.B. 147, 152 is a category (2) case. *Reg.* v. *City of London Licensing Justices* [1954] 1 W.L.R. 1325, 1328 is of no great assistance and does not carry the matter much further. It was an example of the use of mandamus instead of certiorari in licensing cases: see *Wade on Administrative Law,* 2nd ed. (1967), p. 148. In the *Maradana Mosque* case [1967] 1 A.C. 13 there was no ouster clause and it does not provide support for the wider proposition of the appellants.

Section 4 (4) of the Act extends to any dismissal of an application based on a bona fide misconstruction of article 4 of the Order, whether on analysis the misconstruction proves to be an error of law within the jurisdiction or in excess of the jurisdiction. Parliament did not intend the commission to be at risk as regarded some errors of construction and not others. The present case is a fortiori *Smith* v. *East Elloe Rural District Council* [1956] A.C. 737, 747, 750, 754, 756, 764-765, 767, 770, 772.

As to the distinction between void and voidable, a nullity and a non-nullity, see *Ridge* v. *Baldwin* [1964] A.C. 51, 80, 81, 90-91, 125, 141-142, 155, and *Durayappah* v. *Fernando* [1967] 2 A.C. 337.

On the assumption that there was an error of construction by the commission, it is submitted: (1) Any misconstruction of article 4 of the Order is an error of law. (2) Section 4 (4) of the Act covers any dismissal of an application based on a bona fide misconstruction of article 4 (3) because that is what the Act plainly says, and it can only have one meaning. (3) Section 4 (4) covers any error based on a bona fide misconstruction of article 4 because the determination, which is on the face of it valid, stands until it is set aside, and the subsection forbids any attempt to set it aside. It could only be shown to be a nullity by bringing proceedings.

As to the construction of article 4, it is submitted: (1) "successor in title" there means successor to a claim for the return of property or for compensation or for damages. (2) In articles 4 and 6 the claim to which a successor in title succeeds is a claim against the Egyptian Government, and in article 8 it is a claim against any other government. (3) A successor in title to a claim against the Egyptian Government in articles 4 and 6 takes the place of the original owner for the purpose of establishing a claim to the fund. So here the appellants started with a claim against the Egyptian Government for the return of their property or for damages, if it has been damaged. The appellants, by the assignment to T.E.D.O., ceased to be entitled to claim against the Egyptian Government. The successor in title to the claim was T.E.D.O. which, not being a British national, cannot itself put forward the claim.

A claim may be assigned, as can a spes successionis: *In re Lind* [1915] 2 Ch. 345. Once a claim is assigned it ceases to be enforceable by the assignor for his own benefit, though perhaps he can enforce it on behalf of the assignee.

Before the date of the treaty there was no spes against the British Government. The source of the claim is the money paid by the Egyptian Government to the British Government. Before the treaty there was a spes that the Egyptian Government would pay for the property. After the treaty there was a spes that the British Government would pay. After **[164]** the Order there was a right to make a claim. The original claim against the Egyptian Government had turned into a claim against the British Government, but if, meanwhile, a possible claimant had assigned his right against the Egyptian Government, he could not claim.

R. J. Parker Q.C. in reply. The word "and" in article 4 (1) (*b*) (ii) does not mean that the original owner need say anything about a successor in title. If the original owner is before the commission, the nationality of a successor in title does not concern it. Only when the successor in title is before the commission need his nationality be proved.

The treaty extinguished all rights against Egypt. Article 6 of the Order of 1962 deals with the making of claims in respect of property lost or damaged, and the claimant under it must prove that the loss or injury was the result of Egyptian measures. "Egyptian measures," as defined by article 1 (2), does not include war damage. Article 8 relates to all claims other than Annex E claims. The claimant who is in Annex E is unconcerned with the fate of the property and will be compensated whoever caused the damage.

In re Lind [1915] 2 Ch. 345, 355, 359, 360, 365-366, 373, relied on by the respondents, only shows that a spes cannot operate until there is property in existence on which it can operate. So here until the treaty no one knew whether or not he would get his property back or whether or not he would get compensation. After the treaty he had a spes of compensation from the British Government. At the date of the assignment there was no such spes, because no fund existed, nor was there an Egyptian spes. The notion that there was a spes at all is not acceptable in this case.

The agreement between the British Government and the United Arab Republic was entered into on its own behalf and on behalf of British nationals. Only the British Government can release its claims. So far as the claimants were concerned, a claim against the United Arab Republic until the treaty was just as remote as a claim against the fund after it.

The question to be considered now is whether Parliament intended that anyone who had accepted compensation from the Egyptian Government should automatically bar themselves from participation in the fund or that they should participate but should account for the compensation they had obtained, as provided by article 10.

Mandamus, prohibition, certiorari and habeas corpus are all writs which will be granted where what the inferior tribunal has done is a nullity. In the absence of an ouster clause, certiorari will also go for an error in law on the face of the record, even if the error is not of such a character as to render the decision a nullity. There has been a tendency to present the problem in the form: (a) Was there an error in law at all? (b) If so, was it a mere error going to the jurisdiction? Mandamus cannot go for a mere error of law, but goes only where the purported decision is a nullity.

The correct approach is to ask: (1) What is the proper construction of the Act? (2) Has the tribunal done or omitted to do anything which on that construction it should not have done or should have done, as the case may be? (3) If so, did the act or omission affect the result, or might it have done so?

(4) When the unauthorised act or omission is excluded from consideration, was the tribunal left with only one course open to it? **[165]** (5) If the answers to (2) and (3) are in the affirmative, the decision will be a nullity and one simply goes back to the beginning with, if necessary, an order to hear and determine. (6) If, in addition, the answer to (4) is also in the affirmative, not only will the decision be a nullity, but there will be an order to do, or refrain from doing, the thing in question, as the case may be, or a declaration that the tribunal must do or refrain from doing it.

As to natural justice, what is the basis on which a duty to comply with it rests on the courts? On what basis does non-compliance with the rules of natural justice enable the court to interfere, even if there is an ouster clause? It is because otherwise the decision is not a decision: see *Ridge* v. *Baldwin* [1964] A.C. 40, 123. The obligation rests on an implied instruction.

If a breach of an implied instruction creates a nullity, it cannot be said that a breach of an express instruction would be less serious. The fact (if it were a fact) that on the wording of the Act it is hard to ascertain whether, and to what extent, the rules of natural justice are excluded and the tribunal had made an honest effort to reach a right result, would not affect the matter. The fact (if it were a fact) that the tribunal, while recognising that the rules were incorporated, wrongly intepreted their requirements, would make no difference. If the misconstruction of an implied instruction would result in a nullity, it cannot be that a misinterpretation of an express instruction would lead to a less serious result: see *Board of Education* v. *Rice* [1911] A.C. 179, 182. Not every wrong act or omission will lead to the final conclusion being a nullity.

The argument for the respondents involves that section 3 (*b*) of the Act of 1950 would read that provision may be made "for the determination of claims, which excludes all power of control by the court" and that section 4 (4) must be read to refer to "the purported determination by the commission, even if it is not a determination at all...." But words and phrases must prima facie be given their natural meaning and read in the context of the Act.

But the words of the Order on their plain and ordinary meaning are a straightforward instruction. It is an abuse of language to say that the words "shall treat a claim ... as established" is equivalent to "may." The Order gives the commission power to assess the loss and to say whether they are satisfied of certain matters; they can go no further.

The root principle is that if the order, decision or determination is not a determination at all, it is not within the Act and there is nothing on which the ouster clause can bite. One must consider what is a determination and not what is said to be a determination. For example, if one is charged with taking £5 notes out of the country, contrary to law, one is not guilty if they were forged notes. One may be guilty of another offence, but not of the one charged.

Smith v. *East Elloe Rural District Council* [1956] A.C. 738, 740, 742, 769, 770 was a case where there was an ouster clause, but paragraph 15 (1) of Part IV of Schedule I to the Acquisition of Land (Authorisation Procedure) Act, 1946, gave the subject a special right to resort to the court. That was of importance. None of the authorities cited relate to the court's attitude to ouster clauses. Lord Simonds in his opinion cites no authorities at all. Because no authorities as to ouster clauses were **[166]** cited in that case, it is no authority on the effect of such a section as section 4 (4) in an Act which contains no alternative mode of access to the courts. It may be authority for the proposition that, when one is dealing with ministerial process and there is alternative mode of access to the courts, even bad faith by the tribunal may not create a nullity. If it went further than that it could be impliedly overruling a long line of authorities, including House of Lords authorities. The effect of that case is limited as suggested and, even so, is doubtful. If it is not so limited, it was wrongly decided. It would, on the respondents' contentions, involve reading the words of section 4 (4) as "determination or purported determination." There is no principle which enables one to read words into a statute by implication, thereby depriving the subject of access to the courts.

Assuming that the appellant is not driven from the courts by section 4 (4), how does the commission's action fit into the authorities? When a person is claiming in respect of property referred to in Annex E the only matters which he must establish are: (1) that the claim relates to property in Egypt referred to in Annex E, which includes all property sequestrated; (2) that he is the person referred to in Annex E; and (3) that he was a British national at the relevant dates.

The commission have done something they should not have done in asking additional questions and imposing additional requirements over and above those imposed by the articles on their true interpretation. The asking of those additional questions affected the result and, if all those matters wrongly considered are excluded, the only course left is to treat the claim as established.

If, contrary to the appellants' contentions, the original owner is obliged, on the true construction of the Act, to prove that he has no successor in title or that any successor in title is a British national, then a successor in title within the article does not include the assignee of a moral claim against the United Arab Republic. In asking themselves whether the appellants had shown that there was no such assignee, the commission asked themselves a question which they should not have done. That affected the result and, but for that, there would have been only one course open to them, to find the claim established.

As to the question of the existence of a spes, see *Halsbury's Laws of England*, 3rd ed., vol. 2 (1953), p. 410, para. 825, and also *Ex parte Dever* (1887) 18 Q.B.D. 660, 665, 670, decided under the Bankruptcy Act, 1884, in which the definition of "property" in section 168 (1) was the same as that in section 167 of the Bankruptcy Act, 1914.

What is the nature of the assignment of a spes? A legatee under a will has only a spes, but he can enter into a contract dealing with it, the effect of which is that the person with whom he has contracts will get an equitable charge, or hope that the assignor will live long enough to take, that the testator will not change his will and that there will be enough money in the estate to pay the legacy. But the hope is the entirely personal hope of the person mentioned in the will, who cannot pass it to a trustee. The assignee has only a hope upon a hope.

In the present case, between 1956 and 1959 no one could have anything more than a hope of compensation for damage suffered in the Suez Incident. That remained a personal hope, so long as the original owner was in existence. Parliament dealt with the situation which would arise if the person died or the company went out of existence. The claim must be either by the original owner or, if there was a successor in title, then by him—not by both. As long as the original owner was there, there was no room for a successor. No beneficial interest of any kind vests in an assignee until the property comes into existence: *In re Lind* [1915] 2 Ch. 345. [**167**]

The House of Lords here has the opportunity to say (1) that no ouster clause will protect a nullity without specific words to that effect, because a nullity is not a determination and (2) that it is for the courts to interpret the statute, by which an inferior tribunal is given jurisdiction, to see whether it acted within it.

Not every error in law can be corrected, but what can be done is to see whether the tribunal asked itself the questions which the statute, truly interpreted, says it should ask.

Sydney Templeman Q.C. Ex parte Dever (1887) 18 Q.B.D. 660 only shows that in bankruptcy a spes does not vest in the trustee in bankruptcy. It was otherwise in the case of an assignee for value: *In re Lind* [1915] 2 Ch. 345.

As to the declaration sought by the appellants on the assumption that the House decides in their favour, they have asked for the wrong remedy. The court had no jurisdiction to grant a declaration, though it may order certiorari. In the Court of Appeal it appeared that Diplock L.J. did not consider a declaration appropriate: [1968] 2 Q.B. 862, 910. See also R.S.C., Ord. 15, r. 16, and Ord. 53. On the view opposite to mine there is no reason why declarations should not take the place of certiorari and mandamus. If a declaration can be granted here, it is hard to see why certiorari and mandamus should even be used at all. There is no reported case where proceedings have been taken against a tribunal for a declaration.

The jurisdiction to determine belongs to the commission and not to the High Court, and that would be trenched upon if it were held proper to go for a declaration.

R. J. Parker Q.C. The appellants have established all they had to prove, and there was a statutory duty on the commission to treat the claim as established. The appellants are only asking for what they would have got by mandamus if they had gone for that: see *Pyx Granite Co. Ltd.* v. *Ministry of Housing and Local Government* [1960] A.C. 260, 290 and *Barnard* v. *National Dock Labour Board* [1953] 2 Q.B. 18, 41.

Their Lordships took time for consideration.

Dec. 17, 1968. LORD REID. My Lords, in 1956 the appellants owned a mining property in Egypt which they claim was worth over £4,000,000. On the outbreak of hostilities in the autumn of that year it was occupied by Israeli forces and damaged to the extent of some £500,000. On November 1, 1956, property in Egypt belonging to British subjects was sequestrated by the Egyptian Government and on April 29, 1957, after the Israeli forces had withdrawn, the Egyptian Government authorised a sale **[168]** of the appellants' property and it was sold to an Egyptian organisation referred to in this case as T.E.D.O.

The appellants' property had included a large quantity of manganese ore and steps were taken by them to dissuade their customers from buying ore from T.E.D.O. This seems to have embarrassed the Egyptian authorities, and on November 23, 1957, an agreement was made between the appellants, T.E.D.O. and the Sequestrator General whereby the appellants purported to sell to T.E.D.O. for a price of £500,000 their whole business in Egypt, but this was not to include any claim which the appellants might

> "be entitled to assert against any government authority other than the Egyptian government, as a result of loss suffered by, or of damage to or reduction in the value of"

their business or assets during the events of October and November, 1956.

Beyond the fact that the appellants received the sum of £500,000 the effect of the agreement is not very clear; for their property had already been sold to T.E.D.O. by the sequestrator. Before the agreement was made the appellants had no legal right to sue in Egypt either for the return of their property or for compensation for its loss. But they had some hope or prospect of getting something after relations between the United Kingdom and the United Arab Republic returned to normal. This could have been a direct payment to them by the Egyptian Government: or, if the method was followed which the British Government had adopted in earlier cases, the Egyptian Government might pay a lump sum of compensation to the British Government to cover all claims by British subjects, and then it would be in the discretion of the British Government to determine how any such sum should be distributed among claimants. And similarly with regard to damage done by the Israeli forces there might have been some payment made by the Israeli Government. It is not disputed that by this agreement the appellants gave up or assigned to T.E.D.O. any claim they might have to receive compensation directly from the Egyptian Government: but I think that they did not give up or assign any claim, hope or prospect they might have to receive something from the British or Israeli Governments.

The next material event was the making of a treaty between the Governments of the United Kingdom and the United Arab Republic on February 28, 1959. That treaty provided for the return to British subjects of their sequestrated property excepting properties sold between October 30, 1956, and August 2, 1958: those excepted properties were listed in Annex E which included the property of "Sinai Mining (subject to a special arrangement)." Sinai

Mining was the name of the appellant company before its name was changed to Anisminic. It is not clear what was meant by "subject to a special arrangement." Under the treaty the United Arab Republic paid to the British Government the sum of £27,500,000 in full and final settlement of claims of a kind mentioned in article IV. It is not disputed that at that stage the appellants had no legal right to claim to participate in that sum. The disposal of that sum was in the discretion of the British Government. The most the appellants had was a hope that they would receive some part of it.

This case arises out of the making of an Order in Council: The [169] Foreign Compensation (Egypt) (Determination and Registration of Claims) Order 1959 (S.I. 1959 No. 625). That Order has now been superseded by a similar Order, S.I. 1962 No. 2187 and I shall refer throughout to this later Order. These Orders were made under powers contained in the Foreign Compensation Act, 1950. That Act set up the respondents, the Foreign Compensation Commission, to deal with compensation payments made by the Governments of Yugoslavia and Czechoslovakia but it also provides for the commission acting should there be future compensation agreements with foreign governments.

The appellants duly submitted a claim under this Order to the respondent commissioner. They also submitted a separate claim in respect of damage done by the Israeli forces. These claims were opposed by the legal officer of the commission and after sundry procedure including a long oral hearing the commission on May 8, 1963, made a provisional determination that:

> "... the above-named applicants, Anisminic Ltd. fail to establish a claim under the Egypt Order aforesaid in respect of the matters referred to in paragraph 2 (*a*) of the amended answer and that the application in respect of such claims be and is hereby dismissed. But that the claim in respect of damage referred to in paragraph 2 (*b*) of the amended answer is fit for registration under article 8 of the said Order in a sum to be hereafter determined."

The claim which was dismissed was the main claim with which this case is concerned, and the claim which was held fit for registration was a claim in respect of the damage done by the Israeli forces.

Browne J. on July 29, 1966, made a declaration that the respondent's provisional determination was a nullity and that the respondents are under a statutory duty to treat the appellants' first claim as established. The Court of Appeal on April 5, 1967, set aside the judgment of Browne J. (post, p. 223) and the appellants now seek to have his judgment restored.

The respondent's first argument was that in any event such a declaration could not competently be made. I agree with your Lordships in rejecting that argument. If the appellants succeed on the merits the declarations made by Browne J. should be restored.

The next argument was that, by reason of the provisions of section 4 (4) of the 1950 Act, the courts are precluded from considering whether the respondent's determination was a nullity, and therefore it must be treated as valid whether or not inquiry would disclose that it was a nullity. Section 4 (4) is in these terms:

> 'The determination by the commission of any application made to them under this Act shall not be called in question in any court of law.'

The respondent maintains that these are plain words only capable of having one meaning. Here is a determination which is apparently valid: there is nothing on the face of the document to cast any doubt on its validity. If it is a nullity, that could only be established by raising some kind of proceedings in court. But that would be calling the determination in question, and that is expressly prohibited by the statute. The appellants **[170]** maintain that that is not the meaning of the words of this provision. They say that "determination" means a real determination and does not include an apparent or purported determination which in the eyes of the law has no existence because it is a nullity. Or, putting it in another way, if you seek to show that a determination is a nullity you are not questioning the purported determination—you are maintaining that it does not exist as a determination. It is one thing to question a determination which does exist: it is quite another thing to say that there is nothing to be questioned.

Let me illustrate the matter by supposing a simple case. A statute provides that a certain order may be made by a person who holds a specified qualification or appointment, and it contains a provision, similar to section 4 (4), that such an order made by such a person shall not be called in question in any court of law. A person aggrieved by an order alleges that it is a forgery or that the person who made the order did not hold that qualification or appointment. Does such a provision require the court to treat that order as a valid order? It is a well established principle that a provision ousting the ordinary jurisdiction of the court must be construed strictly—meaning, I think, that, if such a provision is reasonably capable of having two meanings, that meaning shall be taken which preserves the ordinary jurisdiction of the court.

Statutory provisions which seek to limit the ordinary jurisdiction of the court have a long history. No case has been cited in which any other form of words limiting the jurisdiction of the court had been held to protect a nullity. If the draftsman or Parliament had intended to introduce a new kind of ouster clause so as to prevent any inquiry even as to whether the document relied on was a forgery, I would have expected to find something much more specific than the bald statement that a determination shall not be called in question in any court of law. Undoubtedly such a provision protects every determination which is not a nullity. But I do not think that it is necessary or even reasonable to construe the word "determination" as including everything which purports to be a determination but which is in fact no determination at all. And there are no degrees of nullity. There are a number of reasons why the law will hold a purported decision to be a nullity. I do not see how it could be said that such a provision protects some kinds of nullity but not others: if that were intended it would be easy to say so.

The case which gives most difficulty is *Smith* v. *East Elloe Rural District Council* [1956] A.C. 736 where the form of ouster clause was similar to that in the present case. But I cannot regard it as a very satisfactory case. The plaintiff was aggrieved by a compulsory purchase order. After two unsuccessful actions she tried again after six years. As this case never reached the stage of a statement of claim we do not know whether her case was that the clerk of the council had fraudulently misled the council and the Ministry, or whether it was that the council and the Ministry were parties to the fraud. The result would be quite different, in my view, for it is only if the authority which made the order had itself acted in mala fide that the order would be a nullity. I think that the case which it was intended to present must have been that the fraud was only the fraud of the clerk because almost the whole of the argument was on the question **[171]** whether a time limit in the Act applied where fraud was alleged; there was no citation of the authorities on the question whether a clause ousting the jurisdiction of the court applied when nullity was in question, and there was little about this matter in the speeches. I do not therefore regard this case as a binding authority on this question. The other authorities are dealt with in the speeches of my noble and learned friends, and it is unnecessary for me to deal with them in detail. I have come without hesitation to the conclusion that in this case we are not prevented from inquiring whether the order of the commission was a nullity.

It has sometimes been said that it is only where a tribunal acts without jurisdiction that its decision is a nullity. But in such cases the word "jurisdiction" has been used in a very wide sense, and I have come to the conclusion that it is better not to use the term except in the narrow and original sense of the tribunal being entitled to enter on the inquiry in question. But there are many cases where, although the tribunal has jurisdiction to enter on the inquiry, it has done or failed to do something in the course of the inquiry which is of such a nature that its decision is a nullity. It may have given its decision in bad faith. It may have made a decision which it had no power to make. It may have failed in the course of the inquiry to comply with the requirements of natural justice. It may in perfect good faith have misconstrued the provisions giving it power to act so that it failed to deal with the question remitted to it and decided some question which was not remitted to it. It may have refused to take into account something which it was required to take into account. Or it may have based its decision on some matter which, under the provisions setting it up, it had no right to take into account. I do not intend this list to be exhaustive. But if it decides a question remitted to it for decision without committing any of these errors it is as much entitled to decide that question wrongly as it is to decide it rightly. I understand that some confusion has been caused by my having said in *Reg.* v. *Governor of Brixton Prison, Ex parte Armah** [1968] A.C. 192, 234 that if a tribunal has jurisdiction to go right it has jurisdiction to go wrong. So it has, if one uses "jurisdiction" in the narrow original sense. If it is entitled to enter on the inquiry and does not do any of those things which I have mentioned in the course of the proceedings, then its decision is equally valid whether it is right or wrong subject only to the power of the court in certain circumstances to correct an error of law. I think that, if these views are correct, the only case cited which was plainly wrongly decided is *Davies* v. *Price* [1958] 1 W.L.R. 434. But in a number of other cases some of the grounds of judgment are questionable.

I can now turn to the provisions of the Order under which the commission acted, and to the way in which the commission reached their decision. It was said in the Court of Appeal that publication of their reasons was unnecessary and perhaps undesirable. Whether or not they could have been required to publish their reasons, I dissent emphatically from the view that publication may have been undesirable. In my view, the commission acted with complete propriety, as one would expect looking to its membership.

The meaning of the important parts of this Order is extremely difficult to discover, and, in my view, a main cause of this is the deplorable modern drafting practice of compressing to the point of obscurity provisions which would not be difficult to understand if written out at rather greater length.

[172]

The effect of the Order was to confer legal rights on persons who might previously have hoped or expected that in allocating any sums available discretion would be exercised in their favour. We are concerned in this case with article 4 of the Order and more particularly with paragraph (1) (*b*) (ii) of that article. Article 4 is as follows:

"(1) The Commission shall treat a claim under this Part of the Order as established if the applicant satisfies them of the following matters:— (*a*) that his application relates to property in Egypt which is referred to in Annex E; (*b*) if the property is referred to in paragraph (1) (*a*) or paragraph (2) of Annex E—(i) that the applicant is the person referred to in paragraph (1) (*a*) or in paragraph (2), as the case may be, as the owner of the property or is the successor in title of such person; and (ii) that the person referred to as aforesaid and any person who became successor in title of such person on or before February 28, 1959, were British nationals on October 31, 1956, and February 28, 1959; (*c*) if the property is referred to in paragraph (1) (*b*) of Annex E—(i) that the applicant was the owner on October 31, 1956, or, at the option of the applicant, on the date of the sale of the property at any time before February 28, 1959, by the Government of the United Arab Republic under the provisions of Egyptian Proclamation No. 5 of November 1, 1956, or is the successor in title of such owner; and (ii) that the owner on October 31, 1956, or on the date of such sale, as the case may be, and any person who became successor in title of such owner on or before February 28, 1959, were British nationals on October 31, 1956, and February 28, 1959. (2) For the purposes of sub-paragraph (*b*) (i) of paragraph (1) this article, any reference in paragraph (2) of Annex E to the estate of a deceased person shall be interpreted as a reference to the persons entitled to such estate under the testamentary dispositions or intestacy of such deceased person. (3) For the purposes of sub-paragraphs (*b*) (ii) and (*c*) (ii) of paragraph (1) of this article, a British national who died, or in the case of a corporation or association ceased to exist, between October 31, 1956, and on February 28, 1959, shall be deemed to have been a British national on the latter date and a person who had not been born, or in the case of a corporation or association had not been constituted, on October 31, 1956, shall be deemed to have been a British national on that date if such person became a British national at birth or when constituted, as the case may be; provided that a converted company shall for the purposes of sub-paragraphs (*b*) (ii) and (*c*) (ii) of paragraph (1) of this article be deemed not to have been a British national. (4) If it shall appear to the commission in relation to any Egyptian controlled company referred to in paragraph (1) (*a*) or paragraph (2) of Annex E that under the provisions of any Egyptian measure the shares of any British national in such company have at any time between October 30, 1956, and February 28, 1959, been sold, or purported to be sold, by a sequestrator or by any person acting under his authority without the consent of the holder thereof, the commission may, if they think it just and equitable so to do, and shall if the company is a converted company, hold that such shares **[173]** were property in Egypt referred to in paragraph (1) (*b*) of Annex E and determine any application in relation to the company or to such shares as if the said company had been incorporated in Egypt and named in the said paragraph."

The task of the commission was to receive claims and to determine the rights of each applicant. It is enacted that they shall treat a claim as established if the applicant satisfies them of certain matters. About the first there is no difficulty: the appellants' application does relate to property in Egypt referred to in Annex E. But then the difficulty begins.

Annex E originally only included properties which had been sold during the sequestration, so the person mentioned in Annex E as the owner is the person who owned the property before that sale, and his claim is a claim for compensation for having been deprived of that property. Normally he will be the applicant. But there is also provision for an application by a "successor in title." The first difficulty is to determine what is meant by "successor in title." Before the Order was made the position was that former owners whose property had been sold during the sequestration had no title to anything. They had no title to the property because it had been sold. And they had no title to compensation. All they had was a hope or expectation that they might receive some compensation. They had no legal rights at all. It is now common ground that "successor in title" cannot mean the person who obtained a title to the property which formerly belonged to the applicant. The person who acquired the property from the sequestrator was generally an Egyptian and he could have no ground for claiming compensation. So "successor in title" must refer to some person who somehow succeeded to the original owner as the person now having the original owner's hope or expectation of receiving compensation. The obvious case would be where the original owner had died. But for the moment I shall leave that problem.

The main difficulty in this case springs from the fact that the draftsman did not state separately what conditions have to be satisfied (1) where the applicant is the original owner and (2) where the applicant claims as the successor in title of the original owner. It is clear that where the applicant is the original owner he must prove that he was a British national on the dates stated. And it is equally clear that where the applicant claims as being the original owner's successor in title he must prove that both he and the original owner were British nationals on those dates, subject to later provisions in the article about persons who had died or had been born within the relevant period. What is left in obscurity is whether the provisions with regard to successors in title have any application at all in cases where the applicant is himself the original owner. If this provision had been split up as it should have been, and the conditions, to be satisfied where the original owner is the applicant had been set out, there could have been no such obscurity.

This is the crucial question in this case. It appears from the commission's reasons that they construed this provision as requiring them to inquire, when the applicant is himself the original owner, whether he had a successor in title. So they made that inquiry in this case and held that T.E.D.O. was the applicant's successor in title. As T.E.D.O. was not **[174]** a British national they rejected the appellants' claim. But if, on a true construction of the Order, a claimant who is an original owner does not have to prove anything about successors in title, then the commission made an inquiry which the Order did not empower them to make, and they based their decision on a matter which they had no right to take into account. If one uses the word "jurisdiction" in its wider sense, they went beyond their jurisdiction in considering this matter. It was argued that the whole matter of construing the Order was something remitted to the commission for their decision. I cannot accept that argument. I find nothing in the Order to support it. The Order requires the commission to consider whether they are satisfied with regard to the prescribed matters. That is all they have to do. It cannot be for the commission to determine the limits of its powers. Of course if one party submits to a tribunal that its powers are wider than in fact they are, then the tribunal must deal with that submission. But if they reach a wrong conclusion as to the width of their powers, the court must be able to correct that—not because the tribunal has made an error of law, but because as a result of making an error of law they have dealt with and based their decision on a matter with which, on a true construction of their powers, they had no right to deal. If they base their decision on some matter which is not prescribed for their adjudication, they are doing something which they have no right to do and, if the view which I expressed earlier is right, their decision is a nullity. So the question is whether on a true construction of the Order the applicants did or did not have to prove anything with regard to successors in title. If the commission were entitled to enter on the inquiry whether the applicants had a successor in title, then their decision as to whether T.E.D.O. was their successor in title would I think be unassailable whether it was right or wrong: it would be a decision on a matter remitted to them for their decision. The question I have to consider is not whether they made a wrong decision but whether they inquired into and decided a matter which they had no right to consider.

I have great difficulty in seeing how in the circumstances there could be a successor in title of a person who is still in existence. This provision is dealing with the period before the Order was made when the original owner had no title to anything: he had nothing but a hope that some day somehow he might get some compensation. The rest of the article makes it clear that the phrase (though inaccurate) must apply to a person who can be regarded as having inherited in some way the hope which a deceased original owner had that he would get some compensation. But "successor in title" must I think mean some person who could come forward and make a claim in his own right. There can only be a successor in title where the title of its original possessor has passed to another person, his successor, so that the original possessor of the title can no longer make a claim, but his successor can make the claim which the original possessor of the title could have made if his title had not passed to his successor. The "successor" of a deceased person can do that. But how could any "successor" do that while the original owner is still in existence? One can imagine the improbable case of the original owner agreeing with someone that, for a consideration immediately paid to him, he would pay over to the other party **[175]** any compensation which he might ultimately receive. But that would not create a "successor in title" in any true sense. And I can think of no other way in which the original owner could transfer inter vivos his expectation of receiving compensation. If there were anything in the rest of the Order to indicate that such a case was intended to be covered, we might have to attribute to the phrase "successor in title" some unusual and inaccurate meaning which would cover it. But there is nothing of that kind. In themselves the words "successor in title" are, in my opinion, inappropriate in the circumstances of this Order to denote any person while the original owner is still in existence, and I think it most improbable that they were ever intended to denote any such person. There is no necessity to stretch them to cover any such person. I would therefore hold that the words "and any person who became successor in title to such person" in article 4 (1) (*b*) (ii) have no application to a case where the applicant is the original owner. It follows that the commission rejected the appellants' claim on a ground which they had no right to take into account and that their decision was a nullity. I would allow this appeal.

LORD MORRIS OF BORTH-Y-GEST. My Lords, the appellants made claims to participate in the compensation received from the United Arab Republic. Pursuant to the authority given by the Foreign Compensation Act, 1950, Orders in Council were made providing for the determination of such claims by the Foreign Compensation Commission. The application of the appellants was the subject of an oral hearing which took four days. At the hearing the applicants were represented by counsel. In due course the commission, in provisional determinations, gave their decision. The applicants thereupon brought an action claiming that the determinations of the commission were wrong in law or invalid. But the Act provides that the determination by the commission of any application made to them "shall not be called in question in any court of law." For many days in successive stages of these proceedings the applicants have done nothing else. They have presented the arguments which they unsuccessfully advanced before the commission. The commission had been properly constituted and had been presided over by its appointed chairman—an eminent Queen's Counsel. How, then, have the appellants justified this somewhat startling procedure?

As the facts which comprise the background to this litigation are so carefully narrated in the judgment of the learned judge I need only refer to them in summary form. At the time of the events at Suez, in October, 1956, the appellants (then called the Sinai Mining Co. Ltd.) were carrying out operations for the extraction of manganese ore in the Sinai Peninsula. They had mining leases or concessions granted to them by the Egyptian Government. Their undertaking was valued at about £4,400,000. A proclamation was passed (Proclamation No. 5) which resulted in the undertaking being placed under sequestration. That was on November 1, 1956. The company lost possession and control of their undertaking and it became illegal under Egyptian law for them to dispose of or deal with their undertaking in the absence of ministerial consent. There followed a period within which Israeli forces caused serious damage (to the extent of £532,773) to the property. Those forces withdrew in or about April, 1957. **[176]** In that month (on April 29) the United Arab Republic passed Decree No. 387. By that decree authority was given to the Custodian General of the property of British, French and Australian subjects to sell and liquidate the property of certain persons including the appellant company who were subject to Proclamation No. 5. On April 29, 1957, an agreement was made (called a contract of sale) between the Custodian General of British Property and the chairman of the Economic Board, which organisation was a department of the Egyptian Government. It has been referred to as T.E.D.O. What the agreement purported to do was to sell all the assets of the appellant company to the chairman, who acted both as chairman of T.E.D.O. and also as the representative of a company which was being formed and which was called the Sinai Manganese Co. S.A.E. As a result of a Presidential decision of May 18, 1957, the proposed new company was brought into existence.

It was hardly to be expected that the appellants would accept or acquiesce in the expropriation of their property. Nor was it likely that they would be inactive in the protection of their rights and in the assertion of any claims that they could advance. Though they may have been without remedy in the

Egyptian courts they took various steps to assert their rights. On June 11, 1957, they registered with the Foreign Office in London a claim setting out details of the assets and goodwill of their undertaking in Egypt as at October 31, 1956. In the further endeavour to protect their interests they instructed their agents to write to all their former customers. That was done by means of a circular letter dated July 9, 1957. The letter made it very plain that the appellants in no way recognised the assumption of control by the sequestrator of their assets. The letter recorded that the appellants were advised that

> "the action of the Egyptian Government must be regarded as a breach of international law which is incapable of giving rise to any valid legal effects."

There was an emphatic warning that the appellants disputed the right of any person or any company to deal in any way with their ores and would regard "as a violation of its legal rights any transaction of any kind whatsoever involving the said ores" and would take in any country any steps that it might consider necessary to assert or protect their rights. No more resolute and complete assertion of their claims and their rights could be imagined. Nor were their efforts unproductive of result. Though on September 4, 1957, the Minister of Industry in Egypt issued an Order, (Order 426 of 1957) purporting to cancel the appellants' 16 mining leases and though the newly formed company, the Sinai Manganese Co. S.A.E., issued in Egypt a writ in respect of the circular letter of July 9, when the appellants decided, as they did, that they would negotiate with the Egyptian authorities, they found them ready to come to terms. The result was that an agreement was concluded on November 23, 1957. The parties to it were the appellants, the new company (the Sinai Manganese Co. S.A.A.), T.E.D.O. and the Sequestrator General. The appellants agreed to sell and T.E.D.O. agreed to buy "the whole business" of the appellants "as carried on and situate in Egypt." The sequestrator consented to and acquiesced in the sale. The business was deemed to include all the assets **[177]** of the appellants situate in Egypt and all their liabilities in Egypt, arising out of or in connection with the conduct of its business in Egypt including any sums payable to employees. From the assets there was, however, excluded any claim which the appellants could assert against any government other than the Egyptian Government as a result of loss or reduction in value of their business consequent on the events of October and November, 1956. "The price of the said sale" was £500,000. There were terms of payment. The appellants did in due course receive the whole of the purchase price. The appellants agreed that they would change their name. They did so and became Anisminic Ltd.

At the date of that agreement negotiations were in progress between Her Majesty's Government and the United Arab Republic. Though this cannot be a matter affecting the legal issues in this litigation, it may be said as a matter of history that when the appellants made their agreement they believed, as the learned judge found,

> "that they were doing better for themselves than Her Majesty's Government was likely to do for them, and that they did not expect to get any additional compensation out of any future international governmental agreement."

It must, however, be clear that if they could qualify to establish a claim under any later Order in Council they would not be debarred by the fact that it was their firm calculation that their best policy would be to fend for themselves. By way of anticipation in the narrative, it may be said that when the agreement was in due course considered by the commission, they held that the terms of the agreement made it quite clear that the subject-matter of the sale was the whole business of the appellants in Egypt and that included in it was "any claim of the applicant against the Egyptian Government" resulting from the events of October-November, 1956. It was "an assignment of all claims for compensation" that the appellants might have against the United Arab Republic in respect of "the business and its assets including cancellation of the mining concessions." The commission held that the appellants, being fully aware of the cancellation of their leases and of the damage to their business and of the purported sale of it,

> "sold and intended to sell to T.E.D.O. all claims arising thereout together with the goodwill of the company."

They held, as was, of course, undeniable, that T.E.D.O. was not at any time a British national.

Some 15 months after the appellants made their agreement of November 23, 1957, an agreement was made between H.M. Government and the Government of the United Arab Republic. It was an agreement in relation to financial and commercial relations and British property in Egypt. It was made on February 28, 1959. The agreement or treaty cannot easily be summarised, but one part of it provided for the return of British property by the United Arab Republic. From that provision there was, however, an exclusion of property which had been sold between October 30, 1956, and August 2, 1958, under the provisions of Proclamation No. 5: such property was referred to in what was called Annex E. (The **[178]** terms of Annex E were altered (by agreement) in August, 1962.) An important provision of the treaty was that the Government of the United Arab Republic would pay a sum of £27,500,000 to the United Kingdom Government in full and final settlement of certain "claims" which included "all claims in respect of the property" which had been excluded from the requirement to return property. The exclusion, as above stated, was of the property sold under Proclamation No. 5 and referred to in Annex E. In Annex E the name of the appellants appeared. In its amended form Annex E referred to the properties in the United Arab Republic "of any United Kingdom nationals appearing on the following list": in the list was the entry "The Sinai Mining Co. Ltd., 1 Sh. El Bustan, Cairo (subject to a special arrangement)." In the treaty there were various definitions of "property," "British property," "United Kingdom nationals" and "owners."

It is clear that merely because of the conclusion of the treaty and the receipt of £27,500,000 by H.M. Government the appellants could not assert any rights against H.M. Government. (*Rustomjee* v. *The Queen** (1876) 1 Q.B.D. 487; (1876) 2 Q.B.D. 69.) What H.M. Government did was to have recourse to the provisions of the Foreign Compensation Act, 1950. Accordingly, an Order in Council was made on April 6, 1959 (S.I. 1959 No. 625). It recited the authority given by the Act to make provision for the "determination" by the Foreign Compensation Commission of "claims to participate in compensation received under agreements with foreign governments." It recited the treaty of February 28, 1959, and recited that it was

> "expedient that provision should be made with regard to sums received from the Government of the United Arab Republic and for the registration, assessment and determination of claims in respect of British property in Egypt."

The Order proceeded to give directions to the commission. The appellants made claims (on September 15, 1959). They were willing to accept that if they established their claim and if their loss was being assessed, the commission should regard the £500,000 as being "compensation or recoupment" which the appellants had received. The legal officer (on July 14, 1961) filed an answer and an oral hearing began in March, 1962. I need not refer to any pleading matters, because a new Order in Council (S.I. 1962 No. 2187) was made on October 2, 1962, under which certain important changes were made. After pleading amendments the oral hearing of the appellants' claim was begun again on April 1, 1963. Part III of the new Order in Council was in particular relevant and applicable as regards the appellants' claim. All of its provisions as well as the other Parts of the Order demanded consideration by the commission. Here I set out merely the opening paragraphs:

"PART III

"CLAIMS IN RESPECT OF PROPERTY REFERRED TO IN ANNEX E

"4. (1) The commission shall treat a claim under this Part of the Order as established if the applicant satisfies them of the following **[179]** matters:—(*a*) that his application relates to property in Egypt which is referred to in Annex E; (*b*) if the property is referred to in paragraph (1) (*a*) or paragraph (2) of Annex E—(i) that the applicant is the person referred to in paragraph (1) (*a*) or in paragraph (2), as the case may be, as the owner of the property or is the successor in title of such person; and (ii) that the person referred to as aforesaid and any person who became successor in title of such person on or before February 28, 1959, were British nationals on October 31, 1956, and February 28, 1959; (*c*) if the property is referred to in paragraph (1) (*b*) of Annex E—(i) that the applicant was the owner on October 31, 1956, or, at the option of the applicant, on the date of the sale of the property at any time before February 28, 1959, by the Government of the United Arab Republic under the provisions of Egyptian Proclamation No. 5 of November 1, 1956, or is the successor in title of such owner; and (ii) that the owner on October 31, 1956, or on the date of such sale, as the case may be, and any person who became successor in title of such owner on or before February 28, 1959, were British nationals on October 31, 1956, and February 28, 1959. (2) For the purposes of sub-paragraph (*b*) (i) of paragraph (1) of this article, any reference in paragraph (2) of Annex E to the estate of a deceased person shall be interpreted as a reference to the persons entitled to such estate under the testamentary dispositions or intestacy of such deceased person."

The decision of the commission (on May 8, 1963) was that the appellants had failed to establish their main claim (which was dismissed) but that their claim in reference to damage done to their property arising out of the military action of Israeli armed forces was fit for registration under article 8 of the Order in Council in the sum (which they assessed) of £532,773.

In the reasoned document (called minutes of adjudication) which was later made available the reasons of the commission were amply recorded. If this were an appeal from their decision much argument might result. As, however, the document is being looked at for the limited purpose of ascertaining whether the commission exceeded the bounds of their jurisdiction, it must suffice to see what it was that they decided. Very shortly stated it is, I think, clear that what was decided was that as the appellants had sold their property to T.E.D.O. and as T.E.D.O. was not a British national and as T.E.D.O. was the "successor in title" or assignee of the appellants the commission had not been satisfied of the matters referred to in article 4, with the result that they could not treat the main claim as established. As, however, there had been no successor in title of the appellants in regard to their claim concerning loss which was not the result of Egyptian measures (that is, the loss caused by Israeli forces) that claim should be registered under article 8 of the Order in Council.

The commission recorded the nature of what was contended before them namely:

"Mr. Parker stated that the present hearing was in fact limited to the question of entitlement, as it might appear at first sight that the sole question for determination was whether, by virtue of the agreement of **[180]** November, 1957, the Economic Development Organisation, which was one of the other parties to that agreement, became the applicant company's successor in title within the meaning of the Orders; as, if it did, it was not a British national, and it would have become successor in title between the two vital dates, which would defeat the claim. In a sense, he stated, that was the only question, but he submitted that it involved the consideration of basically four issues: First, as the applicant company claim as original owner and not by succession, is the question of successor in title relevant? Secondly, if it is relevant, did the agreement of November 23, 1957, constitute T.E.D.O. the applicant company's successor in title within the meaning of the Order, to anything in respect of which a claim would otherwise lie? Thirdly, if it did, did it so constitute T.E.D.O. the applicant company's successor in title to the whole of that which otherwise would have been the subject of a good claim? And, finally, if not, in respect of what can the applicant company still claim?"

Numerous questions arose in regard to the construction and effect of the November, 1957, agreement as well as questions of construction in regard to the Order in Council and as to the matters of which the commission had to be satisfied. The commission held that the expression "successor in title" throughout the Order in Council referred not to the property which had been "Egyptianised, lost, injured or damaged but to the claim." They held that the recitals to the Order in Council showed that the "claims" which they had to consider were claims to participate in the fund which, as the treaty of February, 1959, showed, was a fund which was in settlement (*inter alia*) of all "claims" in respect of (shortly stated) the properties which did not have to be returned and which were denoted in Annex E. On a construction of the November, 1957, agreement (and the appellants have accepted that its construction was entirely the function of the commission and is not to be challenged) the commission were satisfied that it

> "operated as an assignment of all claims for compensation that the applicant might have against the U.A.R. in respect of the business and its assets, including cancellation of the mining concessions."

The applicants, they held, being fully aware of such cancellation and of the damage to and purported sale of their business had "sold and intended to sell to T.E.D.O. all claims arising thereout together with the goodwill of the company." As T.E.D.O. was not a British national but

> "as it became in the view of the commission the successor in title of the applicant to the claim against the U.A.R. and any consequent claim to participate in compensation provided to meet that claim the applicant was unable to succeed under article 4 or article 6 in establishing any claim arising out of a claim against the U.A.R."

That was the decision of the commission whose determination of any application made to them "shall not be called in question in any court of law."

This is not a case in which there has been any sort of suggestion of irregularity either of conduct or procedure on the part of the commission. **[181]** It has not been said that anything took place which disqualified the commission from making a determination. No occasion arises, therefore, to refer to decisions which have pointed to the consequences of failing to obey or of defying the rules of natural justice: nor to decisions relating to bias in a tribunal: nor to decisions in cases where bad faith has been alleged: nor to decisions in cases where a tribunal has not been properly constituted. If a case arose where bad faith was alleged the difficult case of *Smith* v. *East Elloe Rural District Council* [1956] A.C. 736 would need consideration: but the present case can, in my view, be approached without any examination of or reliance upon that case.

The provisions of section 4 (4) of the Act do not, in my view, operate to debar any inquiry that may be necessary to decide whether the commission has acted within its authority or jurisdiction. The provisions do operate to debar contentions that the commission while acting within its jurisdiction has come to wrong or erroneous conclusions. There would be no difficulty in pursuing, and in adducing evidence in support of, an allegation such as an allegation that those who heard a claim had never been appointed or that those who had been appointed had by some irregular conduct disqualified themselves from adjudicating or continuing to adjudicate. There would be no difficulty in raising any matter that goes to the right or power of the commission to adjudicate (see *Reg.* v. *Bolton* (1841) 1 Q.B. 66). What is forbidden is to question the correctness of a decision or determination which it was within the area of their jurisdiction to make.

It is, of course, clear that no appeal is given from a determination of the commission. When Parliament sets up a tribunal and refers matters to it, it becomes a question of policy as to whether to provide for an appeal. Sometimes that is thought to be appropriate. Thus, where (by the Indemnity Act, 1920), provision was made for the assessment by the War Compensation Court of certain claims for compensation for acts done in pursuance of prerogative powers it was enacted that though the decision of the tribunal (presided over by a judge) was to be final there could be an appeal by a party aggrieved by a direction or determination of the tribunal on any point of law. Sometimes, on the other hand, it is not thought appropriate to provide for an appeal. In reference to the Foreign Compensation Tribunal it was presumably thought that the advantages of securing finality of decision outweighed any disadvantages that might possibly result from having no appeal procedure. It was presumably thought that there was every prospect that right determinations would be reached if those appointed to reach them were persons in whom there could be every confidence.

I return, then, to the question as to how the appellants can justify the calling in question by them of the determination of the commission. The answer is that they boldly say that what looks like a determination was in fact no determination but was a mere nullity. That which, they say, should be disregarded as being null and void, is a determination explained in a carefully reasoned document nearly ten pages in length which is signed by the chairman of the commission. There is no question here of a sham or spurious or merely purported determination. Why, then, is it said to be null and void? The answer given is that it contains errors in law which **[182]** have caused the commission to exceed their jurisdiction. When analysed this really means that it is contended that when the commission considered the meaning of certain words in article 4 of the Order in Council they gave them a wrong construction with the consequence that they had no jurisdiction to disallow the claim of the applicants.

It is not suggested that the commission were not acting within their jurisdiction when they entertained the application of the appellants and gave it their consideration nor when they heard argument and submissions for four days in regard to it. The moment when it is said that they strayed outside their allotted jurisdiction must, therefore, have been at the moment when they gave their "determination."

The control which is exercised by the High Court over inferior tribunals (a categorising but not a derogatory description) is of a supervisory but not of an appellate nature. It enables the High Court to correct errors of law if they are revealed on the face of the record. The control cannot, however, be exercised if there is some provision (such as a "no certiorari" clause) which prohibits removal to the High Court. But it is well settled that even such a clause is of no avail if the inferior tribunal acts without jurisdiction or exceeds the limit of its jurisdiction.

In all cases similar to the present one it becomes necessary, therefore, to ascertain what was the question submitted for the determination of a tribunal. What were its terms of reference? What was its remit? What were the questions left to it or sent to it for its decision? What were the limits of its duties and powers? Were there any conditions precedent which had to be satisfied before its functions began? If there were, was it or was it not left to the tribunal itself to decide whether or not the conditions precedent were satisfied? If Parliament has enacted that provided a certain situation exists then a tribunal may have certain powers, it is clear that the tribunal will not have those powers unless the situation exists. The decided cases illustrate the infinite variety of the situations which may exist and the variations of statutory wording which have called for consideration. Most of the cases depend, therefore, upon an examination of their own particular facts and of particular sets of words. It is, however, abundantly clear that questions of law as well as of fact can be remitted for the determination of a tribunal.

If a tribunal while acting within its jurisdiction makes an error of law which it reveals on the face of its recorded determination, then the court, in the exercise of its supervisory function, may correct the error unless there is some provision preventing a review by a court of law. If a particular issue is left to a tribunal to decide, then even where it is shown (in cases where it is possible to show) that in deciding the issue left to it the tribunal has come to a wrong conclusion, that does not involve that the tribunal has gone outside its jurisdiction. It follows that if any errors of law are made in deciding matters which are left to a tribunal for its decision such errors will be errors within jurisdiction. If issues of law as well as of fact are referred to a tribunal for its determination, then its determination cannot be asserted to be wrong if Parliament has enacted that the determination is not to be called in question in any court of law.

In a passage in his speech in *Reg.* v. *Governor of Brixton Prison, Ex* **[183]**
*parte Armah** [1968] A.C. 192, 234, my noble and learned friend, Lord Reid, thus stated the matter:

> "If a magistrate or any other tribunal has jurisdiction to enter on the inquiry and to decide a particular issue, and there is no irregularity in the procedure, he does not destroy his jurisdiction by reaching a wrong decision. If he has jurisdiction to go right he has jurisdiction to go wrong. Neither an error in fact nor an error in law will destroy his jurisdiction."

To the same effect were words spoken by Denning L.J. (as my noble and learned friend then was) in *Rex* v. *Northumberland Compensation Appeal Tribunal, Ex parte Shaw* [1952] 1 K.B. 338, 346:

> "No one has ever doubted that the Court of King's Bench can intervene to prevent a statutory tribunal from exceeding the jurisdiction which Parliament has conferred on it: but it is quite another thing to say that the King's Bench can intervene when a tribunal makes a mistake of law. A tribunal may often decide a point of law wrongly whilst keeping well within its jurisdiction."

In the *Northumberland* case the whole argument proceeded on the basis that the error or errors of law were within jurisdiction. The judgments would have been unnecessary if it could have been asserted that error of construction was tantamount to excess of jurisdiction.

In speaking of the supervisory jurisdiction of the superior court Lord Sumner in his speech in *Rex* v. *Nat Bell Liquors Ltd.* [1922] 2 A.C. 128, 156 said:

> "Its jurisdiction is to see that the inferior court has not exceeded its own, and for that very reason it is bound to interfere in what has been done within that jurisdiction, for in so doing it would itself, in turn, transgress the limits within which its own jurisdiction of supervision, not of review, is confined. That supervision goes on two points: one is the area of the inferior jurisdiction and the qualifications and conditions of its exercise; the other is the observance of the law in the course of its exercise."

If, therefore, a tribunal while within the area of its jurisdiction committed some error of law and if such error was made apparent in the determination itself (or, as it is often expressed, on the face of the record) then the superior court could correct that error unless it was forbidden to do so. It would be so forbidden if the determination was "not to be called in question in any court of law." If so forbidden it could not then even hear argument which suggested that error of law had been made. It could, however, still consider whether the determination was within "the area of the inferior jurisdiction."

So the question is raised whether in the present case the commission went out of bounds. Did it wander outside its designated area? Did it outstep the confines of the territory of its inquiry? Did it digress away from its allotted task? Was there some preliminary inquiry upon the correct determination of which its later jurisdiction was dependent?

For the reasons which I will endeavour to explain it seems to me that at **[184]** no time did the commission stray from the direct path which it was required to tread. Under article 4 of the Order in Council the commission was under a positive duty to treat a claim under Part III as established if the applicant satisfied them of certain matters. If they had stated that they were satisfied of those matters but had then declined to treat a claim as established, there would have been a situation very different from that now under consideration and one in which the court could clearly act. So also if they had stated that they were not satisfied of the matters but had nevertheless treated the claim as established. They would have had no right to treat the claim as established unless they were satisfied of the matters. The present is a case in which, faithfully following the wording of article 4, they stated that they were not satisfied of the matters and, therefore, did not treat the claim as established. In stating why they were not satisfied of the matters they have set out the processes of their reasoning. The more that reasoning is examined the more apparent does it, in my view, become that the members of the commission applied their minds very carefully to a consideration of the matters about which the applicant had to satisfy "them." To no one else were the matters remitted but to "them." It was for them to be satisfied and not for anyone else. The words of article 4 state their terms of reference. In those terms were certain words and certain phrases. The commission could not possibly discharge their duty without considering those words and phrases and without reaching a decision as to their meaning. The commission could not burk that task. It seems to me that the words which stated that it was for the commission to be satisfied of certain matters, and defined those matters, inevitably involved that any necessary interpretation of words within the compass of those matters was for the commission. They could not come to a conclusion as to whether they were satisfied as to the specified matters unless and until they gave meaning to the words which they had to follow. Unless such a phrase as "successor in title" was defined in the Order—and it was not—it was an inescapable duty of the commission to consider and to decide what the phrase signified. Doubtless they heard ample argument before forming a view. The same applies in regard to many other words and sequences of words in article 4. But the forming of views as to these matters lay in the direct path of the commission's duties. They were duties that could not be shirked. They were central to the exercise of their jurisdiction. When their fully reasoned statement of their conclusions (which in this case can be regarded as a part of their "determination") is studied it becomes possible for someone to contend that an alternative construction of article 4 should be preferred to that which was thought correct by the commission. But this calling in question cannot, in my view, take place in any court of law. Parliament has forbidden it.

The most careful and valuable judgment of the learned judge contained detailed references to most of the decided cases and acknowledgment was made in the Court of Appeal of the help derived from considering his survey. The learned judge said that the commission had no jurisdiction to consider under article 4 (1) any other question than those which subparagraphs (*a*) and (*b*) of that article on their true construction required them to consider and that if satisfied of those matters they were under a statutory duty to treat the claim as established and had no jurisdiction to do anything else. That is entirely correct. Nor have the commission **[185]** done anything else. They were obliged to consider what was the true construction of sub-paragraphs (*a*) and (*b*): they came to conclusions: they followed those conclusions. All that was inevitably left to them for them to decide.

Before returning to this aspect of the matter I must refer to some of the decisions relied upon by the appellants. I do so only because a comprehensive and careful argument was addressed to your Lordships directed to the submission that the decided cases support the view that the determination of the commission can in this case be challenged. In my view, they point to exactly the contrary view. When examined the cases seem to me to reveal a consistent line of authority to the effect that provisions such as the provision in section 4 (4) of the Act of 1950 will not avail to bar recourse to the courts if a tribunal has acted without or in excess of jurisdiction, but will bar such recourse if the tribunal has kept within and travelled within its jurisdiction, even if in so doing it has erred in law and even if such error of law is revealed on "the face" of the tribunal's determination.

In *Reg.* v. *St. Olave's District Board* (1857) 8 E. & B. 529 a question arose whether someone had been an officer of certain commissioners (whose functions by statute came to an end) and so had become entitled to compensation. He applied for it to the district board. They rejected his claim. He appealed to the Metropolitan Board of Works who allowed it. In respect of their decision there was a "no certiorari" clause. A rule was obtained to quash the order of the metropolitan board and affidavits were filed in support of a contention that the person concerned had ceased to be an officer before the Act came into operation which determined the commissioners' functions. In showing cause against the rule it was submitted that the question whether the person was an officer was the very point that the metropolitan board had on appeal to decide. In support of the rule it was submitted that the facts were not disputed on the appeal and that the decision "was entirely on a mistake of law." To that submission Lord Campbell C.J. replied, ibid., 533: "Supposing it to be so the court of appeal were to decide both on law and fact." The Court held that the certiorari ought not to have been granted and the rule to quash the order of the metropolitan board was discharged. Lord Campbell C.J. said that it was not a case in which the jurisdiction of the board depended on a preliminary point and that if they thought that the person was de jure an officer and entitled to compensation their order was not removable.

In his judgment in *Reg.* v. *Cotham* [1898] 1 Q.B. 802, 808, Kennedy J. noted the distinction between, on the one hand, disregarding the provisions of a statute and considering matters which ought not to be considered and, on the other hand, what he called "a mere misconstruction of an Act of Parliament." This perhaps illustrates the clear distinction which exists between an error when in the exercise of jurisdiction and an error in deciding whether jurisdiction can be assumed: in the latter case an error may have the consequence that jurisdiction was lacking and was wrongly assumed and the result would be that any purported decision would have no validity. **[186]**

In *Rex* v. *Cheshire Justices, Ex parte Heaver* (1912) 108 L.T. 374 the compensation authority, after the renewal of a licence of a public-house had been refused, had to decide how compensation was to be divided amongst the persons interested in the licensed premises. The lessees of the premises had been held (by the High Court after a case stated) to be entitled to be treated as persons interested in the premises. There was a proviso in the lease that if the renewal of the licence was refused the lease should cease and determine. By reason of the refusal of renewal the lease came to an end seven years before what would have been its ordinary expiration. The lessees claimed to participate by reference to the loss they sustained in consequence of not having the lease for its full term. The compensation authority awarded them a sum which was so small that there were strong grounds for thinking that the authority had proceeded upon a wrong basis. Upon applications by the lessees for certiorari and mandamus it was held that certiorari would not be granted because the order made was good on its face and that mandamus would not be granted because the authority had not declined jurisdiction and because, whether they were right or wrong in their decision upon any question of law arising on the construction of a proviso in the lease or on the facts, the court could not interfere by mandamus as there would at most be an erroneous decision on matters within their jurisdiction. Channel J. said, ibid., 379:

"If there was an error in deciding a point of law which came before them for their decision in the course of their duty, we cannot set it right."

In *Rex* v. *Minister of Health* [1939] 1 K.B. 232 there was a question whether a claimant was entitled to a pension (a superannuation allowance). It was said that under the relevant legislation he could only get a pension if he had served for a certain number of years. That he had not done. It was said, however, that under one section of the legislation he would be entitled to receive a pension although he had not served for the stated period. There was a provision that in the case of any dispute as to the right of an officer to receive a pension (or as to its amount) such dispute was to be determined by the Secretary of State whose decision was to be final. The dispute was referred by the claimant to the Secretary of State. He decided that the claimant was entitled. One view was that if on a correct interpretation of the law no one *could* be granted a pension who lacked the requisite years of service, then there could be no dispute which the Minister had jurisdiction to entertain and that consequently the provision as to the finality of his decision would be no bar to an application for certiorari. A rule nisi for a writ of certiorari was discharged by the Divisional Court and an appeal from their decision was dismissed. The Court of Appeal held that the construction of the sections of the legislation came within the jurisdiction of the Minister with the result that even if he made a mistake of law in construing the sections his decision could not be challenged. Certiorari would not lie because if there were any mistakes of law (which the court doubted but as to which the court did not have to pronounce) they were mistakes of law within jurisdiction. Greer L.J. said, ibid., 245: **[187]**

"... if the Minister has wrongly construed the section, still he has not acted without jurisdiction, because a mere misconstruction of this section would not entitle the committee to say that the order was made without jurisdiction."

Greer L.J. referred with approval to the following passage in paragraph 1493 in volume 9 of *Halsbury's Laws of England*, 2nd ed. (1933).

"Where the proceedings are regular upon their face and the magistrates had jurisdiction, the superior court will not grant the writ of certiorari on the ground that the court below has misconceived a point of law. When the court below has jurisdiction to decide a matter, it cannot be deemed to exceed or abuse its jurisdiction, merely because it incidentally misconstrues a statute, or admits illegal evidence, or rejects legal evidence, or misdirects itself as to the weight of the evidence, or convicts without evidence." (See now 3rd ed., (1955), vol. 11, p. 62).

Slesser L.J. said that at the highest it could not be said that the Minister had done anything more than to arrive at an erroneous decision.

The reasoning of that case is very much applicable in the present one. The Minister in that case could not determine the dispute which arose without coming to a conclusion as to the construction of the sections of the Act which were the subject of rival contentions. So here the commission had to be satisfied by an applicant that his application related to "property." Property included all rights or interests of any kind in property. The commission might have to decide whether someone had an "interest" in property. Questions of law might arise. The commission had to decide whether an application related to property "in Egypt." Questions of law might arise—apart from questions of geography—as to whether rights or interests were in Egypt. The commission had to decide if an application related to property in Egypt whether such property was referred to in Annex E. What were referred to in Annex E were "the properties in the United Arab Republic of any United Kingdom nationals appearing on" the list which followed. For the meaning of "United Kingdom nationals" the commission would presumably have to look to Annex A of the Treaty of February 28, 1959. The commission then had to decide whether an applicant was one of the United Kingdom nationals referred to in the appropriate part of Annex E "as the owner of the property." Stated more fully the duty of the commission was a duty to decide whether an applicant satisfied them (inter alia) that he "is the person referred to in paragraph (1) (*a*) or in paragraph (2), as the case may be, as the owner of the property or is the successor in title of such person." In this case there has been much concentration on the question whether the commission correctly decided that the phrase "successor in title" included an assignee. But this was but one of very many matters which might receive determination by the commission. A perusal of the Orders in Council shows that they bristle with words and phrases needing construction. For my part I cannot accept that if, in regard to any one of the many points in respect of which interpretation and construction became necessary a view can be formed that the commission made an error, the **[188]** consequence follows that their determination became a nullity as being made in excess of jurisdiction.

If the commission decided that an assignee was a "successor in title" they would have to be satisfied

> "that the person referred to as aforesaid and any person who became successor in title of such person on or before February 28, 1959, were British nationals on October 31, 1956, and February 28, 1959."

If the commission decided that the word "and" meant "and" (which I would not be disposed to regard as being very irrational) they might have to decide some question as to whether an assignment made someone a successor in title on or before the stated date and they might have to decide as to whether the "person referred to" and the "successor in title" were British nationals on each one of two dates. The term "British nationals" is elaborately defined. Is it to be said if the commission decided that someone was not a British national and refused to treat a claim as established that it could be sought to show that the person was a British national after all and that the commission exceeded their jurisdiction in refusing the claim? The first part of the definition of "British nationals" has only to be recited to illustrate how varied and perplexing might be the points of construction as well as of law and of fact that might have to be decided, namely:

> "(*a*) citizens of the United Kingdom and Colonies, citizens of Rhodesia and Nyasaland, citizens of Southern Rhodesia, British subjects without citizenship, and British protected persons belonging to any of the territories for whose international relations the Government of the United Kingdom were on February 28, 1959, responsible."

Problems far more elusive and perplexing could arise in regard to these words than those relating to the meaning of the phrase "successor in title." Many of the United Kingdom nationals referred to in Annex E were, however, corporations. One part of the definition of "British nationals" which they would have to satisfy reads:

> "corporations and unincorporated associations constituted under the laws in force in the United Kingdom of Great Britain and Northern Ireland or in any territory for whose international relations the government of the United Kingdom were on February 28, 1959, responsible."

In an application of these words many difficult points both of law and of construction and of fact could arise. All these points are comparable in character with the particular points relating to successor in title which have been the focus of attention in this particular case. Many other illustrations could be given in regard to issues of law as well as of fact which might inescapably present themselves for the determination of the commission. Thus paragraph 4 of article 4 begins with the words:

> "If it shall appear to the commission in relation to any Egyptian controlled company ...":

"Egyptian controlled company" is defined: the definition picks up the definition of a British national: the paragraph proceeds to lay down how **[189]** the commission may hold if the shares of a British national in such a company had been sold by a sequestrator and how the commission must hold if the Egyptian controlled company was a "converted company" within the definition of those words. Shortly stated, a converted company is an Egyptian controlled company which at certain times was authorised under the laws of the Republic of Egypt or of the United Arab Republic to continue its activities as an Egyptian or United Arab Republic corporation limited by shares. If the commission in steering a course through the elaborations of these and many other complicated provisions made some error of construction or of law which caused the result that they were not satisfied of certain matters and consequently did not treat a claim as established—which they would have done but for some error—I cannot think that it would be right to say that they exceeded their jurisdiction or acted without jurisdiction so that their determination was a nullity. The argument for the appellants involves that if in various cases that may arise before the commission there is some misconstruction of some words in the Order in Council then any resultant decision is a mere nullity.

The claim of the applicants had to be determined by the commission and the applicants were under the obligation of satisfying the commission as to certain stated matters. They could not decide whether or not they were satisfied until they had construed the relevant parts of the Order in Council. When they were hearing argument as to the meaning of those relevant parts they were not acting without jurisdiction. They were at the very heart of their duty, their task and their jurisdiction. It cannot be that their necessary duty of deciding as to the meaning would be or could be followed by the result that if they took one view they would be within jurisdiction and if they took another view that they would be without. If at the moment of decision they were inevitably within their jurisdiction because they were doing what they had to do, I cannot think that a later view of someone else, if it differed from theirs, could involve that they trespassed from within their jurisdiction at the moment of decision.

It is sometimes the case that the jurisdiction of a tribunal is made dependent upon or subject to some condition. Parliament may enact that if a certain state of affairs exists then there will be jurisdiction. If in such case it appears that the state of affairs did not exist, then it follows that there would be no jurisdiction. Sometimes, however, a tribunal might undertake the task of considering whether the state of affairs existed. If it made error in that task such error would be in regard to a matter preliminary to the existence of jurisdiction. It would not be an error within the limited jurisdiction intended to be conferred. An illustration of this appeared in 1853 in *Bunbury* v. *Fuller* (1853) 9 Ex. 111. A section of an Act of Parliament imposed a restraint on the jurisdiction of tithe commissioners in the case of lands in respect of which the tithes had already been perpetually commuted or statutorily extinguished. The tithe commissioners had, therefore, no jurisdiction over such lands. Coleridge J. said (ibid., 140):

> "Now it is a general rule, that no court of limited jurisdiction can give itself jurisdiction by a wrong decision on a point collateral to the merits of the case upon which the limit to its jurisdiction depends; and however its decision may be final on all particulars, making up **[190]** together that subject-matter which, if true, is within its jurisdiction, and, however necessary in many cases it may be for it to make a preliminary inquiry, whether some collateral matter be or be not within the limits, yet upon this preliminary question, its decision must always be open to inquiry in the superior court."

The learned judge instanced the case of a judge having a jurisdiction limited to a particular hundred before whom a matter was brought as having arisen within it: if the party charged contended that it arose in another hundred, then there would be a collateral matter which was independent of the merits of the claim:

"... on its being presented, the judge must not immediately forbear to proceed, but must inquire into its truth or falsehood, and for the time decide it, and either proceed or not with the principal subject-matter according as he finds on that point; but this decision must be open to question, and if he has improperly either forborne or proceeded on the main matter in consequence of an error, on this the Court of Queen's Bench will issue its mandamus or prohibition to correct his mistake."

In his judgment in *Reg.* v. *Commissioners for Special Purposes of the Income Tax* (1888) 21 Q.B.D. 313, 319, Lord Esher M.R. pointed out that while it is generally correct to say that a tribunal cannot give itself jurisdiction by a wrong decision on the facts, there may be cases in which the legislature endows a tribunal with jurisdiction, provided that a certain state of facts exists and further endows it with jurisdiction to decide, without any appeal from their decision, whether or not that state of affairs does or did exist, that is, to decide whether a condition precedent was satisfied for the further exercise of jurisdiction:

"The legislature may intrust the tribunal or body with a jurisdiction, which includes the jurisdiction to determine whether the preliminary state of affairs exists as well as the jurisdiction, on finding that it does exist, to proceed further or do something more."

In the present case there was no question of the commission being endowed with jurisdiction only conditionally. The Order in Council made it mandatory that a certain result should follow after the commission came to certain conclusions as to matters remitted to them for their decision. Their jurisdiction and the area and range of it is clear and specific. No condition precedent has to be satisfied before their jurisdiction in regard to a claim begins. An obligation results if in the exercise of their jurisdiction they come to certain conclusions. If a claimant satisfied "them" of certain matters then they were obliged to treat a claim as established. The clear directive to them (which defined the area of their jurisdiction) was that they should address themselves to the question: Has the applicant satisfied us that his application relates to property in Egypt which is referred to in Annex E and (taking the case of property referred to in paragraph (1) (*a*) or paragraph (2) of Annex E) that the applicant is the person referred to as the owner of the property or is the successor in title of such person and that the person referred to as aforesaid and any person who became successor in title of such person on or before February 28, 1959, were British **[191]** nationals on October 31, 1956, and February 28, 1959? There was no condition to be satisfied before their jurisdiction to deal with that question arose. The tribunal decided that the applicant had not satisfied them. The circumstances that the commission have helpfully and quite voluntarily (see sections 11 and 12 of the Tribunals and Inquiries Act, 1958) made available the careful processes of reasoning which guided them to decision has but served to emphasise that they were within their allotted area. That availability may have made criticism of their reasoning possible but it has not made it lawful.

Some of the cases reviewed by the learned judge were those in which it was manifest that a condition precedent for the exercise of a jurisdiction had not been satisfied. Such a case was *Ex parte Bradlaugh* (1878) 3 Q.B.D. 509. A statutory provision gave jurisdiction to a magistrate to order the destruction of books subject to two conditions, namely, first that the publication must be obscene and, secondly, that it must in the magistrate's judgment be such as was a misdemeanour and proper to be prosecuted as such. An order for the destruction of books on the stated ground that the magistrate was satisfied that they were obscene was, therefore, manifestly made without or in excess of jurisdiction. As Cockburn C.J. said (ibid., 512):

"The order, therefore, does not state the existence of matter that is essential to the jurisdiction."

Even on the assumption that a "no certiorari" section was applicable a rule for certiorari was made absolute.

> "This is an objection founded upon an absence of jurisdiction appearing on the face of the order; and I am clearly of opinion that the section does not apply when the application for the certiorari is on the ground that the inferior tribunal has exceeded the limits of its jurisdiction" (*per* Cockburn C.J., ibid., 512-513).

The statutory provision was definite. The relevant part read:

> "... and if ... the magistrate or justices shall be satisfied that such articles, or any of them, are of the character stated in the warrant and that such or any of them have been kept for any of the purposes aforesaid, it shall be lawful for the said magistrate or justices, and he or they are hereby required to order the articles so seized, ... to be destroyed ..."

The reference to being kept for the purposes aforesaid was a reference to keeping articles for the purpose of sale or distribution or being otherwise published for the purposes of gain, which articles were of such a character and description that their publication would be a misdemeanour and proper to be prosecuted as such. Mellor J. said (ibid., 513), that it was well established that a provision "taking away the certiorari" does not apply where there is an absence of jurisdiction. He said that the order for destruction omitted to state:

> "that the magistrate who made it was satisfied that the books ordered to be destroyed were the proper subject of a prosecution, and therefore the order on the face of it shows an absence of jurisdiction."

The case was really a very plain one and it refers to the undisputed **[192]** and well-recognised proposition that a "no certiorari" provision will not apply where there is an absence of jurisdiction. The decision has, however, no other bearing upon the present case for there is here no room for any suggestion that the commission failed to satisfy any condition precedent or failed to state the existence of any matter essential to their jurisdiction.

In *Rex* v. *Shoreditch Assessment Committee, Ex parte Morgan* [1910] 2 K.B. 859 a ratepayer claimed that the value of his hereditament had been reduced in value. Pursuant to section 47 of the Valuation (Metropolis) Act, 1869, he addressed a written requisition to the overseers. The section provided that:

> "If in the course of any year the value of any hereditament is increased by the addition of ... any building, or is from any cause increased or reduced in value ... (1) The overseers of the parish ... on the written requisition of ... any ratepayer ... shall, send to the assessment committee a provisional list containing the gross and rateable value as so increased or reduced of such hereditament."

The section further provided that a person sending a requisition had to send a copy of it to the clerk to the assessment committee. The section further provided that if within fourteen days after the service of the requisition on the overseers they made default in sending the provisional list, then the clerk to the assessment committee was required forthwith to summon the assessment committee.

> "and the assessment committee shall appoint a person to make such provisional list, in the same manner as is in this Act provided in the case of the overseers failing to transmit a valuation list."

After the ratepayer had addressed his written requisition to the overseers they failed, as required, to send a provisional list to the assessment committee. Because of the default of the overseers the assessment committee was summoned. The assessment committee instead of appointing a person to make a provisional list proceeded to consider the matter themselves and after hearing the ratepayer's representative passed a resolution that they found as a question of fact that the premises had not been reduced in value during the year so as to warrant the committee appointing a person to make a provisional list. It was held that the ratepayer was entitled to a mandamus commanding the assessment committee to appoint a person to make a provisional list. Provided that there was prima facie evidence of a reduction in value, as it was held that there was, then it seemed plain on the wording of the section that the assessment committee were under obligation to "appoint a person to make such provisional list." As Cozens-Hardy M.R. put it (ibid., 875):

> "The ascertainment of the fact of reduction cannot be a condition precedent to the putting in force of the machinery by which it may be ascertained whether in truth there has been any reduction in value."

The consideration of statutory wording in that case seems to me to have little relation to the problems arising in the present case.

Nor do I find anything in *Reg.* v. *Fulham, Hammersmith and Kensington Rent Tribunal, Ex parte Hierowski* [1953] 2 Q.B. 147 (on which the appellants relied) which runs counter to the stream of authority. A rent **[193]** had been determined and registered by a rent tribunal. A statutory provision gave power to reconsider the rent "on the ground of change of circumstances." Where no change of circumstances was alleged it was not unnaturally held that there was no jurisdiction to inquire whether a proper rent had been determined on the previous occasion.

In the submissions on behalf of the appellants a phrase much used was that the commission had asked themselves wrong questions. The phrase can be employed when consideration is being given to a question whether a tribunal has correctly decided some point of construction. If, however, the point of construction is fairly and squarely within the jurisdiction of the tribunal for them to decide, then a suggestion that a wrong question has been posed is no more than a means of deploying an argument: and if construction has been left to the tribunal the argument is unavailing. The phrase is, however, valuable and relevant in cases where it can be suggested that some condition precedent has not been satisfied or where jurisdiction is related to the existence of some state of affairs. Thus in the *Bradlaugh* case (1878) 3 Q.B.D. 509, it could properly be said that a wrong question had been asked. In the *Fulham* case [1953] 2 Q.B. 147, the basis for the start of an inquiry did not exist. So in some cases a tribunal may reveal that by asking some wrong question it fails to bring itself within the area of the demarcation of its jurisdiction. In *Maradana Mosque Trustees* v. *Mahmud* [1967] 1 A.C. 13, P.C., one part of the decision was that the rules of natural justice had been violated. The other part of the decision, relevant for present purposes was that where statutory authority was given to a Minister to act if he was satisfied that a school *is* being administered in a certain way he was not given authority to act because he was satisfied that the school *had been* administered in that way. It could be said that the Minister had asked himself the wrong question: so he had, but the relevant result was that he never brought himself within the area of his jurisdiction.

I do not find it necessary to deal fully with *Davies* v. *Price* [1958] 1 W.L.R. 434 or with the actual decision in that case, but I see no reason for thinking that what was expressed by Parker L.J. (with the concurrence of Lord Evershed M.R. and Sellers L.J.) was out of line with the current of authority: it was there held that even if the Agricultural Land Tribunal had misconstrued a statute that did not mean that they had exceeded their jurisdiction—

> "they clearly had jurisdiction to decide whether to give or withhold consent, and if they misconstrued the statute or acted on no evidence, they merely erred in law" (ibid., 441).

If affidavits "showed that they must have misconstrued the statute, that is not a question of want of jurisdiction ..." (ibid., 442).

Without further elaborate citation it is sufficient to refer again to the speech of Lord Sumner in *Rex* v. *Nat Bell Liquors Ltd.* [1922] 2 A.C. 128, in which he distinguished between a usurpation of a jurisdiction which someone has not got and the wrong exercise of a jurisdiction which someone has got. He used the illustration of a justice who convicted without evidence. He would be doing something that he ought not to do but he would be doing it as a judge: **[194]**

> "To say that there is no jurisdiction to convict without evidence is the same thing as saying that there is jurisdiction if the decision is right, and none if it is wrong; or that jurisdiction at the outset of a case continues so long as the decision stands, but that, if it is set aside, the real conclusion is that there never was any jurisdiction at all" (ibid., 152).

In the present case the commission could be controlled if being "satisfied" of the matters referred to "them" they failed to obey the mandatory direction of the Order in Council. But in deciding whether or not they were satisfied of the matters they were working within the confines of their denoted delegated and remitted jurisdiction. In the exercise of it very many questions of construction were inevitably bound to arise. At no time was the commission more centrally within their jurisdiction than when they were grappling with those problems. If anyone could assert that in reaching honest conclusions in regard to the questions of construction they made any error, such error would, in my view, be an error while acting within their jurisdiction and while acting in the discharge of their function within it.

In agreement with Sellers, Diplock and Russell L.JJ. I consider that the commission acted entirely within their designated area of jurisdiction. I do not think that their decision or determination is to be jettisoned as being a nullity.

I would dismiss the appeal.

LORD PEARCE. My Lords, the courts have a general jurisdiction over the administration of justice in this country. From time to time Parliament sets up special tribunals to deal with special matters and gives them jurisdiction to decide these matters without any appeal to the courts. When this happens the courts cannot hear appeals from such a tribunal or substitute their own views on any matters which have been specifically committed by Parliament to the tribunal.

Such tribunals must, however, confine themselves within the powers specially committed to them on a true construction of the relevant Acts of Parliament. It would lead to an absurd situation if a tribunal, having been given a circumscribed area of inquiry, carved out from the general jurisdiction of the courts, were entitled of its own motion to extend that area by misconstruing the limits of its mandate to inquire and decide as set out in the Act of Parliament.

If, for instance, Parliament were to carve out an area of inquiry within which an inferior domestic tribunal could give certain relief to wives against their husbands, it would not lie within the power of that tribunal to extend the area of inquiry and decision, that is, jurisdiction, thus committed to it by construing "wives" as including all women who have, without marriage, cohabitated with a man for a substantial period, or by misconstruing the limits of that into which they were to inquire. It would equally not be within the power of that tribunal to reduce the area committed to it by construing "wives" as excluding all those who, though married, have not been recently co-habiting with their husbands. Again, if it is instructed to give relief wherever on inquiry it finds that two stated conditions are satisfied, it cannot alter or restrict its jurisdiction by adding a **[195]** third condition which has to be satisfied before it will give relief. It is, therefore, for the courts to decide the true construction of the statute which defines the area of a tribunal's jurisdiction. This is the only logical way of dealing with the situation and it is the way in which the courts have acted in a supervisory capacity.

Lack of jurisdiction may arise in various ways. There may be an absence of those formalities or things which are conditions precedent to the tribunal having any jurisdiction to embark on an inquiry. Or the tribunal may at the end make an order that it has no jurisdiction to make. Or in the intervening stage, while engaged on a proper inquiry, the tribunal may depart from the rules of natural justice; or it may ask itself the wrong questions; or it may take into account matters which it was not directed to take into account. Thereby it would step outside its jurisdiction. It would turn its inquiry into something not directed by Parliament and fail to make the inquiry whch Parliament did direct. Any of these things would cause its purported decision to be a nullity.

Further, it is assumed, unless special provisions provide otherwise, that the tribunal will make its inquiry and decision according to the law of the land. For that reason the courts will intervene when it is manifest from the record that the tribunal, though keeping within its mandated area of jurisdiction, comes to an erroneous decision through an error of law. In such a case the courts have intervened to correct the error.

The courts have, however, always been careful to distinguish their intervention whether on excess of jurisdiction or error of law from an appellate function. Their jurisdiction over inferior tribunals is supervision, not review.

> "That supervision goes to two points: one is the area of the inferior jurisdiction and the qualification and conditions of its exercise; the other is the observance of the law in the course of its exercise" (*Rex* v. *Nat Bell Liquors Ltd.* [1922] 2 A.C. 128, 156).

It is simply an enforcement of Parliament's mandate to the tribunal. If the tribunal is intended on a true construction of the Act to inquire into and finally decide questions within a certain area, the courts' supervisory duty is to see that it makes the authorised inquiry according to natural justice and arrives at a decision whether right or wrong. They will intervene if the tribunal asks itself the wrong questions (that is, questions other than those which Parliament directed it to ask itself). But if it directs itself to the right inquiry, asking the right questions, they will not intervene merely because it has or may have come to the wrong answer, provided that this is an answer that lies within its jurisdiction.

It is convenient to set out the matter in broad outline because there has been evolution over the centuries and there have been many technicalities. There have also been many border-line cases. And the courts have at times taken a more robust line to see that the law is carried out and justice administered by inferior tribunals, and at times taken a more cautious and reluctant line in their anxiety not to seem to encroach or to assume an appellate function which they have not got.

Thus an historical survey of the ancient remedies by which the courts have exercised their supervisory jurisdiction by prerogative writs is not very **[196]** helpful. By writ of certiorari they have called the decision of an inferior tribunal into the court of the King's Bench Division and examined it and quashed it if it is due to an error of law which can be seen on the face of the record. And, having quashed, the courts can by writ of mandamus direct the tribunal to do its duty according to law, or by writ of prohibition forbid the tribunal to do that which is not in accordance with the law. Where a decision is found to be in excess of or without jurisdiction, there is strictly no need to quash it, since it is a nullity, before issuing a writ of prohibition or mandamus. But on these technical matters the courts have not always been wholly consistent. And it has been argued that certain decisions may have a temporary validity until quashed and only then become a true nullity. These technical matters are not of importance until one comes to consider the effect of what have been referred to as "ouster" or "no certiorari" clauses in Acts of Parliament and in particular the article to that effect in the present case.

In 1883 the courts were given wide discretionary powers to make declarations. In recent years, partly owing to the technical difficulties which have formerly beset the procedure with regard to prerogative writs, there has been an increasing tendency for the courts simply to make declarations without issuing prerogative writs. Pursuant to that practice a declaration was claimed and given in the present case.

There is no need to deal with all the many cases on this subject which have been referred to by counsel and have been carefully, and in my opinion, correctly, analysed in the judgment of Browne J. with which I agree. The principles set out above are established by the following cases.

In *Bunbury* v. *Fuller* (1853) 9 Exch. 111, 140 Coleridge J. in holding that the decision of an assistant tithe commissioner was not in the circumstances "final and conclusive" within the relevant Act said:

"Now it is a general rule, that no court of limited jurisdiction can give itself jurisdiction by a wrong decision on a point collateral to the merits of the case upon which the limit to its jurisdiction depends; and however its decision may be final on all particulars, making up together the subject matter which, if true, is within its jurisdiction, and however necessary in many cases it may be for it to make a preliminary inquiry, whether some collateral matter be or be not within the limits, yet upon this preliminary question, its decision must always be open to inquiry in the superior court."

In *Reg.* v. *Commissioners for Special Purposes of the Income Tax* (1888) 21 Q.B.D. 313 Lord Esher M.R. made it clear that it was for the courts to construe the statute which gave jurisdiction to the inferior tribunal. He construed the section in respect of which the commissioners were inquiring and left the facts to them. He said (ibid., 319):

"This view of the section involves the result that the question, whether the party claiming has so satisfied the terms of the section, must be the subject of inquiry with reference to the particular circumstances in each case.... They have to determine the question, and they must determine it ... according to the rule I have laid down."
And later: **[197]**

"When an inferior court or tribunal or body, which has to exercise the power of deciding facts, is first established by Act of Parliament, the legislature has to consider what powers it will give that tribunal or body. It may in effect say that, if a certain state of facts exists and is shown to such tribunal or body before it proceeds to do certain things, it shall have jurisdiction to do such things, but not otherwise. There it is not for them conclusively to decide whether that state of facts exists, and, if they exercise the jurisdiction without its existence, what they do may be questioned, and it will be held that they have acted without jurisdiction. But there is another state of things which may exist. The legislature may intrust the tribunal or body with a jurisdiction, which includes the jurisdiction to determine whether the preliminary state of facts exists as well as the jurisdiction, on finding that it does exist, to proceed further or do something more."

In *Rex* v. *Board of Education* [1909] 2 K.B. 1045 the Divisional Court quashed a decision of the board on the ground that they

"... have not only not decided the question submitted to them, but have raised and made an order upon a matter never submitted to them, ... or, in other words, they have given themselves jurisdiction to determine the question in favour of the local authority by changing the question submitted to them into the one which we have quoted...." (Lord Alverstone C.J., ibid., 1061.)

In *Rex* v. *Shoreditch Assessment Committee, Ex parte Morgan* [1910] 2 K.B. 859 the Court of Appeal issued a mandamus because the committee had misconceived its duties. Farwell L.J. there said (ibid., 880):

"No tribunal of inferior jurisdiction can by its own decision finally decide on the question of the existence or extent of such jurisdiction: such question is always subject to review by the High Court, which does not permit the inferior tribunal either to usurp a jurisdiction which it does not possess, whether at all or to the extent claimed, or to refuse to exercise a jurisdiction which it has and ought to exercise. Subjection in this respect to the High

Court is a necessary and inseparable incident to all tribunals of limited jurisdiction; for the existence of the limit necessitates an authority to determine and enforce it: it is a contradiction in terms to create a tribunal with limited jurisdiction and unlimited power to determine such limit at its own will and pleasure—such a tribunal would be autocratic, not limited—and it is immaterial whether the decision of the inferior tribunal on the question of the existence or non-existence of its own jurisdiction is founded on law or fact."

Again in *Board of Education* v. *Rice* [1911] A.C. 179, H.L.(E.) this House quashed the board's decision and issued a mandamus on the ground that it had not determined the question committed to it by Parliament. Lord Loreburn L.C. there said (ibid., 182):

> "The board is in the nature of the arbitral tribunal, and a court of law has no jurisdiction to hear appeals from the determination either upon law or upon fact. But if the court is satisfied either that the board have not acted judicially in the way I have described, or have **[198]** not determined the question which they are required by the Act to determine, then there is a remedy by mandamus and certiorari."

In *Estate and Trust Agencies (1927) Ltd.* v. *Singapore Improvement Trust* [1937] A.C. 898 the Privy Council issued a writ of prohibition, holding that a housing authority had made a declaration beyond its statutory powers because it had in effect asked itself the wrong question:

> "In other words, the respondents were applying a wrong and an inadmissible test in making the declaration and in deciding to submit it to the Governor in Council. They were therefore acting beyond their powers, and the declaration is not enforceable" (ibid., 917).

In *Seereelall Jhuggroo* v. *Central Arbitration and Control Board* [1953] A.C. 151, P.C., the Privy Council declined to interfere. The arbitration board had a discretion to decide the amount of payment to planters of sugar cane in Mauritius but there was a statutory fetter that they

> "shall be guided by the principle that the average amount of sugar which planters might expect to receive for their canes would be not less than two-thirds of the amount of sugar canes which a ton of such delivered at the factory may normally be expected to yield."

Lord Porter, giving the judgment there, said (ibid., 162-163):

> "If, then, the board, in coming to its determination, had neglected or rejected that consideration," (that is, the guidance by the principle) "it might well have been held to have exceeded its jurisdiction in taking it to be unfettered, whereas it was subject to a limitation of outlook but not confined to a particular proportion. Whether they used a correct discretion or not is, of course, irrelevant in a case where certiorari is claimed. As long as they take into consideration only matters within their jurisdiction, the resultant decision, right or wrong, is for them and for them only."

He concluded (ibid., 163) that

> ". . . the board was not precluded from taking the matters complained of into consideration, and it follows that the board did not exceed its powers and that the Supreme Court were right in refusing to grant certiorari or mandamus."

The judgment makes it clear that an inferior tribunal which properly embarks on an inquiry may go outside its jurisdiction if, in the course of that inquiry, it rejects a consideration which it was told to have in mind. It would then in effect be directing itself to an inquiry other than that which was laid on it by Parliament. *Reg.* v. *Fulham, Hammersmith and Kensington Rent Tribunal, Ex parte Hierowski* [1953] 2 Q.B. 147 is another case where a tribunal embarked properly on an inquiry within its jurisdiction, but at the end of it made an order in excess of jurisdiction which was held to be a nullity though it was an order of the kind which it was entitled to make in a proper case.

In the case of the *Maradana Mosque* [1967] 1 A.C. 13 the Privy Council held that the Minister of Education in Ceylon acted without or in excess of jurisdiction in that he asked himself the wrong question in deciding whether to make an order. **[199]**

All these cases give firm support for the principles outlined above.

The case of *Rex* v. *Minister of Health* [1939] 1 K.B. 232 might seem to give difficulty. The Minister had been given the duty to decide the right to superannuation of a servant and he decided that the servant had such a right. The court thought that probably the Minister construed the relevant section right, but it held that in any event it had not been shown that he acted outside his jurisdiction. It may be that the court was saying rightly that when it appears more probable that a Minister has not misconstrued anything, there is no ground for certiorari. But it seems possible that the court was saying (which I found difficult) that on the construction of the particular words giving jurisdiction to the Minister, he was given power to construe the regulations as well as investigate the facts. I do not find the reasoning in the case very satisfactory.

The case of *Davies* v. *Price* [1958] 1 W.L.R. 434 seems to be out of accord with the main line of authority. The inquiry under review was in effect directed to the wrong question and therefore the applicant should have succeeded. In my opinion, the case was wrongly decided.

Many of the cases cited turn on the difficult question of how far, if at all, the court should take cognisance of an error that was not manifest on the record. That problem did not arise in cases of excess or lack of jurisdiction since there the court for obvious reasons did not confine itself to the record. It looked into all relevant circumstances to see whether jurisdiction did or did not exist. Therefore the problem does not occur here. Indeed, it has to a great extent been eliminated by the Tribunals and Inquiries Act, 1958, under which so many tribunals now have to give reasons. Although the defendant commission is not compelled to do so, it very properly disclosed its reasons in a thoughtful minute of adjudication which has in fact been relied on in the particulars of the defence.

The above principles may, however, be affected by the existence (as here) of an ouster or no certiorari clause. The words of section 4 (4) of the Foreign Compensation Act, 1950, are:

> "The determination by the commission of any application made to them under this Act shall not be called in question in any court of law."

It has been argued that your Lordships should construe "determination" as meaning anything which is on its face a determination of the commission including even a purported determination which has no jurisdiction. It would seem that on such an argument the court must accept and could not even inquire whether a purported determination was a forged or inaccurate order which did not represent that which the commission had really decided. Moreover, it would mean that however far the commission ranged outside its jurisdiction or that which it was required to do, or however far it departed from natural justice its determination could not be questioned. A more reasonable and logical construction is that by "determination" Parliament meant a real determination, not a purported determination. On the assumption, however, that either meaning is a possible construction and that therefore the word "determination" is ambiguous, the latter meaning would accord with a long-established line of cases which adopted that con-**[200]**-struction. One must assume that Parliament in 1950 had cognisance of these in adopting the words used in section 4 (4).

In 1829 in *Campbell* v. *Brown* (1829) 3 Wils. & S. 441 this House upheld a decision of the Lord Ordinary that although by the statute 43 Geo. III, c. 54, s. 21, the judgment of the Presbytery is declared to be final without appeal or review by the court, civil or ecclesiastical, yet if the proceedings upon which judgment was pronounced were contrary to law or if that court exceeded the powers committed to it by statute, they may be reversed and set aside by the court. Lord Lyndhurst L.C., in dealing with the argument that the court's power was ousted by the statute, said (ibid., 445):

> "But I apprehend, that (particularly from the circumstance of the appeal being taken away) a jurisdiction is given in this case to the Court of Session, not to review the judgment on the merits, but to take care that the Court of Presbytery shall keep within the line of its duty, and conform to the provisions of the Act of Parliament. There is in the Court of Session in Scotland, that superintending authority over inferior jurisdictions, which is requisite in all countries, for the purpose of confining those inferior jurisdictions within the bounds of their duty; and the only question here is, whether this case is of such a nature and description as to justify the calling into action that authority of the superior court? Cases were cited at the Bar, and mentioned in the printed papers now on your Lordships' table, in which the Court of Session has exercised a superintending authority over inferior jurisdictions, when they have been guilty of excess of their jurisdiction, or have acted inconsistently with the authority with which they were invested."

In *Bradlaugh's* case (1878) 3 Q.B.D. 509 there was an ouster clause, but Cockburn C.J. said at p. 513:

> "I am clearly of the opinion that the section does not apply when the application for the certiorari is on the ground that the inferior tribunal has exceeded the limits of its jurisdiction."

Mellor J. said:

> "It is well established that the provision taking away the certiorari does not apply where there was an absence of jurisdiction. The consequence of holding otherwise would be that a metropolitan magistrate could make any order he pleased without question."

This case has been treated as a leading authority that "no certiorari" clauses do not oust the courts where there is an absence of jurisdiction (Lord Parker C.J. in *Reg.* v. *Hurst, Ex parte Smith* [1960] 2 Q.B. 133, 142) or an excess of jurisdiction (Denning L.J. in *Reg.* v. *Medical Appeal Tribunal, Ex parte Gilmore* [1957] 1 Q.B. 574, 586). Had Parliament intended to make a departure in 1950 from the more reasonable construction previously given for so many decades to no certiorari clauses, it must have made the matter more clear.

In my opinion, the subsequent case of *Smith* v. *East Elloe Rural District Council* [1956] A.C. 736 does not compel your Lordships to decide otherwise. If it seemed to do so, I would think it necessary to reconsider the **[201]** case in the light of the powerful dissenting opinions of my noble and learned friends, Lord Reid and Lord Somervell. It might possibly be said that it related to an administrative or executive decision, not a judicial decision, and somewhat different considerations might have applied; certainly none of the authorities relating to absence or excess of jurisdiction were cited to the House. I agree with Browne J. that it is not a compelling authority in the present case. Again, the fact that this commission was expressly exempted from the provisions of section 11 of the Tribunals and Inquiries Act passed in 1958, though no doubt a tribute to the high standard of the commission and the fact that its chairman was a lawyer of distinction, cannot have any bearing on the construction of the Foreign Compensation Act, 1950.

If, therefore, the commission by misconstruing the Order in Council which gave them their jurisdiction and laid down the precise limit of their duty to inquire and determine, exceeded or departed from their mandate, their determination was without jurisdiction and Browne J. was right in making the order appealed from.

The Foreign Compensation Act, 1950, gave wide powers to provide by

Orders in Council for the determination by the commission of claims to compensation payable by foreign governments under future agreements (see section 3 (*a*), (*b*) and (*c*)). Subsection (*c*) embodied the powers under section 2 (2) (*a*) for defining the persons who are to be qualified to make claims and the powers under 2 (2) (*b*) for prescribing the matters which have to be established to the satisfaction of the commission. Thus it provided for the giving of wide or narrow powers. Pursuant to that Act the Order in Council which deals with the present claim gave a wide power to determine the amount of compensation. But with regard to the establishment of the claims under article 4 it gave narrow powers. It gave no general discretion at all. If the applicant satisfies them of certain listed matters, the commission shall treat the claim as established. The only listed matters so far as relevant to the present claim were, the appellants argue, (1) the fact that the property referred to in Annex E was in Egypt; (2) the identity of the claimant as referred to in Annex E; and (3) the nationality of the claimant on certain dates. There is no dispute that on these matters they satisfied the commission. Therefore, on the appellants' argument, the commission had a mandatory duty to treat their claim as established. If their construction of article 4 is correct, the appellants are right in this contention. There was no discretion in the commission, no jurisdiction to put further hurdles, other than those listed, in the path of the appellants' claim or to embark on inquiries other than those which the Order in Council directed. The commission, on the other hand, construed the Order as giving them jurisdiction to inquire and be satisfied on two further points; since they were not satisfied on these they rejected the claim. If *their* construction is correct, they were entitled to do so and have not exceeded their jurisdiction.

The substance of the point is this. Once the claimants proved their identity as persons mentioned in Annex E of the Anglo-Egyptian Treaty and their nationality, did they also have to prove on a true construction of the Order that they had no successor in title, successor in title meaning for this purpose successor to the claim against Egypt (later transmuted **[202]** by the treaty into a claim to participate in the compensation)? If so, did they have to prove further that any such successor also fulfilled the nationality qualifications? If the claimants had to prove those additional things, admittedly their claim fails. If they did not, then the inquiry made was not the limited inquiry directed by Parliament.

Substantially the whole of the Order is concerned with the treaty between the British and Egyptian Governments of 1959 and the whole of article 4 is concerned with Annex E of the treaty.

After Suez the Egyptians had sequestrated the properties of British subjects, including the appellants, and barred their access to Egyptian courts of law. Later, certain of those properties, including the appellants' mines and property, had been sold by the sequestrator to an Egyptian authority, T.E.D.O. Finally a treaty was made between the British and Egyptian Governments whereby, inter alia, the property of certain persons listed in Annex E of the treaty was retained by the Egyptians on payment of £27,500,000 compensation. Other property was returned. The negotiation of compensation for Annex E property was not directly based on a calculation of separate amounts for each property but on a general consideration of all the claims. But it is obvious that in the bargaining which preceded the agreement the argument must have ranged over many of the particular items of which the global arrangement was composed.

Before the treaty was signed the appellants had managed to secure some compensation (amounting to about one-eighth of the value of their property) from the Egyptians. They achieved this by establishing a nuisance value. They wrote round to American and European customers pointing out that the Egyptians had unlawfully supplanted them in their mining business. From the Egyptian point of view this was bad for business. The appellants' mining leases were cancelled and threats of legal action were made against them by the Egyptians. The appellants persisted, however, until an agreement was made whereby, in effect, they received £500,000 for their nuisance value (the mines had been worth about £4,000,000 or upwards). They agreed to abandon their name of Sinai Mining Co. Ltd. The form of the agreement was a sale by them to T.E.D.O. of their assets in Egypt, but by Egyptian law the property had already been validly sold to T.E.D.O. by the sequestrator and, therefore, the appellants had no property to sell. The Foreign Office was kept informed of these matters contemporaneously. One may presume that in the bargaining over Annex E the Egyptian representatives tried to claim that the appellants' property had been sold to them by the appellants and, therefore, did not call for any compensation. One may also presume that the British representatives rejected this purported sale at one-eighth of the value of the property seized while accepting, of course, that credit must be given for the £500,000. I accept the learned judge's view that by extracting the £500,000 from the Egyptians by their own efforts the appellants did "nothing but good to the other claimants for compensation," since the appellants would of course have to give credit for it in their present claim.

Be that as it may, the appellants (under their former name) were included in Annex E and there were added the words "(special arrangement)." I read these words as an indication that there were special con-**[203]**-siderations in respect of this company, *i.e.*, the fact that credit must be given by them for £500,000 already received.

It is to be noted that Annex E refers to:

> "The properties in the United Arab Republic of any United Kingdom nationals appearing on the following list."

It is a list of *persons* not properties. And by Annex A (4) "'owners' shall include any successor of the owner." It would be necessary to provide for a successor in case one of the named persons had died or in case one of the undertakings had been dissolved. If assignments of property as opposed to universal successions had been contemplated, I would expect the words "in respect of such property" to be inserted. In my opinion, the mind of the draftsman was addressed to the normal neccessity of providing for universal successors and not to the unlikely event of assignment of some rights (if any) to the sequestrated property by the owners after the sequestration.

When one comes to the Order, article 4 is headed: "Claims in respect of property referred to in Annex E." It sets out to distribute the compensation to the persons there listed. The applicant must first prove (4 (1) (*a*)) that his application relates to property in Egypt which is referred to in Annex E. Next he must prove (4 (1) (*b*)) that he is the person referred to in Annex E or is the successor in title of such person and (4 (1) (*b*) (ii)) that he

> "and any person who became successor in title of such owner on or before February 28, 1959, were British nationals on October 31, 1956, and February 28, 1959."

Article 4 (3) reads:

> "For the purposes of sub-paragraphs (*b*) (ii) and (*c*) (ii) of paragraph (1) of this article, a British national who died, or in the case of a corporation or association ceased to exist" between the relevant dates "shall be deemed to have been a British national on the latter date and a person who had not been born, or in the case of a corporation or association had not been constituted," on the earlier date "shall be deemed to have been a British national on that date if such person became a British national at birth or when constituted, as the case may be."

The tenor of the article and in particular the reference to unborn children shows that the draftsman is directing his mind, primarily at least, to universal successors.

In my view, therefore, the treaty was originally concerned to obtain compensation for listed persons in respect of their property in Egypt, provided they were British nationals. In case any human persons had died or corporations had ceased their universal successors were included as alternatives to the listed persons, provided the successor was also a British national. Later the Order in Council was concerned likewise to give compensation to the listed persons or, if they had ceased to exist, to their successors. As long, therefore, as the listed persons survived, their successors would not be relevant, since there would not be any. A successor in title of a person is different from a successor in title to a part of his property. **[204]** T.E.D.O. were never strictly a successor in title of the appellants who, no doubt, being a British company, had some assets other than those in Egypt; and these did not pass to T.E.D.O. Successor in title in the context means universal successor. There are difficulties that might arise under such a construction in certain unlikely circumstances, but I do not think that these were in the contemplation of the draftsman, since he did not envisage that a successor in title would exist while the original person or corporation on the list existed. Such a construction would enable one to give a clear, simple meaning to the words. I appreciate that one would not expect the "and" in 4 (1) (*b*) (ii). But this is due to the unfortunate compression of the subsection. Since the unattractive composite and/or was denied to him, the draftsman had to choose between the two words, neither of which alone would import the right meaning for both situations, namely, where the original claimant was claiming and where the successor was doing so. In the latter case only must two things be proved, namely, that both the successor and the person in Annex E were British. The mere presence of the word "and" in this highly compressed subsection would not justify turning the section from an otherwise clear meaning in accordance with the apparent general intention into a devious and complicated meaning out of accord with it.

The other construction which reads a successor in title as an assignee of or successor to some particular thing creates various difficulties. First, one must write in words that show to what he was successor in title. This is not a straightforward matter of implication. There might be some justification for writing in the words "to the said property" since "property" is the matter with which 4 (1) (*a*) and 4 (1) (*b*) are concerned and almost immediately precedes the words "successor in title." If one does that, however, one reduces the article to absurdity, since the assignee of the property of nearly all the listed persons was T.E.D.O. which was not a British national. Therefore, almost every claimant who was intended to benefit must fail. To avoid this obvious absurdity, therefore, one must write in further words to the effect that "successor in title to the property does not include any person taking by virtue of the sequestration." In my view, such a rewriting of the article is not permissible if any reasonable meaning can be given to the words as they stand.

Alternatively one must write in the words "to such claim" taking the word (rather dubiously) from the heading and first line of article 4 (1). But there was no such claim in existence when the appellants made the purported sale to T.E.D.O. The matters upon which the appellants made a claim, viz., Annex E and the payment under it, did not exist. Moreover, any claim (which then could only be a moral claim) against the British government was expressly excluded from the purported sale to T.E.D.O., and there was never any successor in title in respect of such a claim. Then, is one to write further into the article "any claim against the Egyptian government"? I see no reason to do so. That would lead to great complication since such claims were not enforceable, and there is no clear indication what happened to such claims when the British government accepted compensation. Thus, there is no relevance in claims against the Egyptian government, as opposed to the moral claims against both governments. And the claim had vanished by the time of the Order. **[205]**

Nor do I think that the purported sale to T.E.D.O. can be read as an assignment of claims in respect of confiscation. There cannot surely be implied the assignment of a claim against the Egyptian government in respect of the confiscation of the business, since the whole agreement was a denial that it had been confiscated. The agreement of "sale" was a document based on the seller still owning the business. It was made on the assumption that there had been no expropriation of the business and there could be no claim in respect of it. It would be absurd for T.E.D.O. to acquire as owners a claim in respect of that which had made them owners. As one would expect, therefore, the only claims referred to in the "sale" agreement were claims in respect to "damage to or reduction in value of" the business. This is quite different from a claim for total expropriation; it refers presumably to war damage. By Egyptian law (which applied to the "sale" agreement) there was no claim for the expropriation. In my view, it is impossible to torture the "sale" agreement into some implication that thereby the appellants impliedly assigned a claim against Egypt (inconsistent with the basis of the document) for expropriation of the business. This, however, would be an error within the jurisdiction and would not create a nullity. Therefore, in view of the ouster clause it would not be a ground for interference in this case.

I do not accede to any argument that a spes or moral claim came into this matter; nor do I see why, if so, it should be a spes against the Egyptian government rather than a spes against the British government. The appellants had a moral claim against both the Egyptian and British governments, the effect of whose policies had brought this loss upon them. Additionally the British government had a duty to protect the interests of the appellants. But assignments of moral claims or hopes were not within the contemplation of the purported sale or of article 4. Moreover, if the appellants *had* assigned any claims, it would be an equitable assignment. The appellants would still have their legal right to pursue any claim, but a court of equity would compel them to pay the fruits to an assignee.

In my opinion, the respondents' construction of article 4 necessitates an unjustifiable writing in of words and leads to quite needless complexity and difficulty. The appellants' construction, however, gives a more direct interpretation which is in accordance with the general intention shown by the treaty and the Order in Council. These did not envisage the extraordinarily unlikely events of persons in Annex E selling tenuous claims against either or both of the governments concerned. A fortiori I do not think that the British government was concerning itself with subtle and complicated preventions of a benefit to a non-British person who might conceivably have bought up such a claim, or with defeating both a sufferer and his mortgagee if the sufferer should mortgage the fruits of his claim to a non-British person or the sufferer if he should sell part of it.

The purported sale of the appellants' property only arose from their ingenious use of their nuisance value. That was known to the British government and was adequately covered by article 10 which directed the commission when assessing the loss to have regard to and record separately any compensation or recoupment in respect of that loss. It is not impossible that the article was originally inspired by the knowledge of the appellants' bargain with T.E.D.O. And if it had been intended to exclude the appel-[**206**]-lants, though listed in Annex E, from compensation, it would have been easy to say so.

I therefore prefer the learned judge's construction of article 4 as being simpler, more literal and more in accordance with the general intention of the Order in Council and the treaty with which it is concerned.

It has been suggested that the appellants have no merits. I do not think that merits come into this matter. The appellants have just so much merits as a person has when, through no fault of his own, he has been deprived of property worth £4,000,000 and has received by his own efforts £500,000 in compensation. True, the appellants thought at one time they would get no more. And if they now share in the compensation they will get in toto (after giving credit for the half million pounds) somewhat more than they would have done had they brought in nothing by their own efforts, since the larger claims are scaled down to make the money go round. Whether this is unfair as against another claimant who lost four million pounds and brought nothing into the contra account by his own efforts is a matter of opinion. So, too, is the fairness of those with smaller losses getting a larger proportion than the appellants with their larger loss. All these are part of a sensible rough and ready attempt to ration the compensation when there is not enough to go round. No doubt in many cases it works rather unfairly. It would certainly seem a little hard if the appellants were wholly debarred from the fund merely because they secured £500,000 by their own efforts.

It was argued that the declaration should not have been made, because this was not an apt form of relief. I do not accept that argument. It was also argued that the form of the declaration went too far. But these are matters in which the learned judge has a wide experience and it appears that Mr. Bridge (as he then was) who then appeared for the respondents and also has a wide experience did not argue about the form of the declaration (while of course resisting the making of any such order at all). I think it would be wrong for your Lordships to embark now on such an argument.

I would therefore allow the appeal and restore the order of Browne J.

Lord Wilberforce. My Lords, the appellant, Anisminic Ltd. (an English company) claims the right to participate in the Egyptian compensation fund composed of £27·5 million made available to Her Majesty's government under a treaty with the United Arab Republic of February 28, 1959, and any money added to this sum by subsequent Parliamentary authority. The Foreign Compensation Commission has by "provisional determination" rejected this claim, and we have to decide whether, in doing so, it has made a determination which, in the words of section 4 (4) of the Foreign Compensation Act, cannot be called in question in the courts. The commission has also admitted to registration a claim by the appellants in respect of war damage but it is agreed that this claim does not arise if the first claim is established.

I must first say something as to the legal framework of this appeal: for though, in my opinion, the solution of this case is to be looked for in the thickets of subsidiary legislation, it is useful to be clear as to the general character of the argument. I do not think that it is difficult to **[207]** describe this and I shall endeavour to do so, initially at least, in non-technical terms, avoiding for the moment such words as "jurisdiction," "error" and "nullity" which create many problems.

The Foreign Compensation Commission is one of many tribunals set up to deal with matters of a specialised character, in the interest of economy, speed, and expertise. It has acquired a unique status, since it alone has been excepted from the provisions of section 11 of the Tribunals and Inquiries Act, 1958. It is now well established that specialised tribunals may, depending on their nature and on the subject-matter, have the power to decide questions of law, and the position may be reached, as the result of statutory provision, that even if they make what the courts might regard as decisions wrong in law, these are to stand. The Foreign Compensation Commission is certainly within this category; its functions are predominantly judicial; it is a permanent body, composed of lawyers, with a learned chairman, and there is every ground, having regard to the number and the complexity of the cases with which it must deal, for giving a wide measure of finality to its decisions. There is no reason for giving a restrictive interpretation to section 4 (4) which provides that its "determinations" are not to be "called in question" in courts of law.

In every case, whatever the character of a tribunal, however wide the range of questions remitted to it, however great the permissible margin of mistake, the essential point remains that the tribunal has a derived authority, derived, that is, from statute: at some point, and to be found from a consideration of the legislation, the field within which it operates is marked out and limited. There is always an area, narrow or wide, which is the tribunal's area; a residual area, wide or narrow, in which the legislature has previously expressed its will and into which the tribunal may not enter. Equally, though this is not something that arises in the present case, there are certain fundamental assumptions, which without explicit restatement in every case, necessarily underlie the remission of power to decide such as (I do not attempt more than a general reference, since the strength and shade of these matters will depend upon the nature of the tribunal and the kind of question it has to decide) the requirement that a decision must be made in accordance with principles of natural justice and good faith. The principle that failure to fulfil these assumptions may be equivalent to a departure from the remitted area must be taken to follow from the decision of this House in *Ridge* v. *Baldwin* [1964] A.C. 40. Although, in theory perhaps, it may be possible for Parliament to set up a tribunal which has full and autonomous powers to fix its own area of operation, that has, so far, not been done in this country. The question, what is the tribunal's proper area, is one which it has always been permissible to ask and to answer, and it must follow that examination of its extent is not precluded by a clause conferring conclusiveness, finality, or unquestionability upon its decisions. These clauses in their nature can only relate to decisions given within the field of operation entrusted to the tribunal. They may, according to the width and emphasis of their formulation, help to ascertain the extent of that field, to narrow it or to enlarge it, but unless one is to deny the statutory origin of the tribunal and of its powers, they cannot preclude examination of that extent.

It is sometimes said, the argument was presented in these terms, that the **[208]** preclusive clause does not operate on decisions outside the permitted field because they are a nullity. There are dangers in the use of this word if it draws with it the difficult distinction between what is void and what is voidable, and I certainly do not wish to be taken to recognise that this distinction exists or to analyse it if it does. But it may be convenient so long as it is used to describe a decision made outside the permitted field, in other words, as a word of description rather than as in itself a touchstone.

The courts, when they decide that a "decision" is a "nullity," are not disregarding the preclusive clause. For, just as it is their duty to attribute autonomy of decision of action to the tribunal within the designated area, so, as the counterpart of this autonomy, they must ensure that the limits of that area which have been laid down are observed (see the formulation of Lord Sumner in *Rex* v. *Nat Bell Liquors Ltd.* [1922] 2 A.C. 128, 156). In each task they are carrying out the intention of the legislature, and it would be misdescription to state it in terms of a struggle between the courts and the executive. What would be the purpose of defining by statute the limit of a tribunal's powers if, by means of a clause inserted in the instrument of definition, those limits could safely be passed?

After the admirable analysis of the authorities made by Browne J. in his judgment (available in the record in this House) no elaborate discussion of authority is needed in order to support this view of the courts' powers. I extract some well-known pronouncements which have stood the test of time. One may find difficulty in some of the cases in following the reasoning by which the conclusion has been reached that a particular area of decision was or was not remitted to the tribunal concerned. Some of these are complicated by the procedural refinements of the prerogative writs: in others perhaps the apparent merits or demerits of the decision may have led the courts into strained distinctions between facts which the tribunal might legitimately find and others (called "jurisdictional") which it might not. But the principle is now becoming reasonably clear.

The separate but complementary responsibilities of court and tribunal were very clearly stated by Lord Esher M.R. in *Reg.* v. *Commissioner for Special Purposes of the Income Tax* (1888) 21 Q.B.D. 313, 319, in these words:

> "When an inferior court or tribunal or body, which has to exercise the power of deciding facts, is first established by Act of Parliament, the legislature has to consider what powers it will give that tribunal or body. It may in effect say that, if a certain state of facts exists and is shown to such tribunal or body before it proceeds to do certain things, it shall have jurisdiction to do such things, but not otherwise. There it is not for them conclusively to decide whether that state of facts exists, and, if they exercise the jurisdiction without its existence, what they do may be questioned, and it will be held that they have acted without jurisdiction."

That the ascertainment of the proper limits of the tribunal's power of decision is a task for the court was stated by Farwell L.J. in *Rex* v. *Shoreditch Assessment Committee, Ex parte Morgan* [1910] 2 K.B. 859, 880 in language which, though perhaps vulnerable to logical analysis, has proved its value as guidance to the courts: **[209]**

> "Subjection in this respect to the High Court is a necessary and inseparable incident for all tribunals of limited jurisdiction; for the existence of the limit necessitates an authority to determine and enforce it: it is a contradiction in terms to create a tribunal with limited jurisdiction and unlimited power to determine such limit at its own will and pleasure—such a tribunal would be autocratic, not limited—and it is immaterial whether the decision of the inferior tribunal on the question of the existence or non-existence of its own jurisdictions is founded on law or fact."

Denning L.J. added his authority to this in *Rex* v. *Northumberland Compensation Appeal Tribunal, Ex parte Shaw* [1952] 1 K.B. 338, 346 in the words:

> "No one has ever doubted that the Court of King's Bench can intervene to prevent a statutory tribunal from exceeding the jurisdiction which Parliament has conferred on it, but it is quite another thing to say that the King's Bench can intervene when a tribunal makes a mistake of law. A tribunal may often decide a point of law wrongly whilst keeping well within its jurisdiction."

These passages at least answer one of the respondents' main arguments, to some extent accepted by the members of the Court of Appeal, which is that *because* the commission has (admittedly) been given power, indeed required, to decide some questions of law, arising out of the construction of the relevant Order in Council, it must necessarily have power to decide those questions which relate to the delimitation of its powers; or conversely that if the court has power to review the latter, it must also have power to review the former. But the one does not follow from the other: there is no reason why the Order in Council should not (as a matter of construction to be decided by the court) limit the tribunal's powers and at the same time (by the same process of construction) confer upon the tribunal power, in the exercise of its permitted task, to decide other questions of law, including questions of construction of the Order. I shall endeavour to show that this is what the Order has done.

The extent of the interpretatory power conferred upon the tribunal may sometimes be difficult to ascertain and argument may be possible whether this or that question of construction has been left to the tribunal, that is, is within the tribunal's field, or whether, because it pertains to the delimitation of the tribunal's area by the legislature, it is reserved for decision by the courts. Sometimes it will be possible to form a conclusion from the form and subject matter of the legislation. In one case it may be seen that the legislature, while stating general objectives, is prepared to concede a wide area to the authority it establishes: this will often be the case where the decision involves a degree of policy-making rather than fact-finding, especially if the authority is a department of government or the Minister at its head. I think that we have reached a stage in our administrative law when we can view this question quite objectively, without any necessary predisposition towards one that questions of law, or questions of construction, are necessarily for the courts. In the kind of case I have mentioned there is no need to make this assumption. In another type of case it may be apparent that Parliament is itself directly **[210]** and closely concerned with the definition and delimitation of certain matters of comparative detail and has marked by its language the intention that these shall accurately be observed. If *Rex* v. *Minister of Health* [1939] 1 K.B. 232 was rightly decided, it must be because it was a case of the former type. The dispute related to a superannuation allowance and the statute provided that "any dispute" should be determined by the Minister. The basis of the decision is not very clearly expressed but can, I think, be taken to be that, as the context and subject-matter showed, the Minister had a field of decision extending to the construction of the superannuation provisions of the Act. The present case, by contrast, as examination of the relevant Order in Council will show, is clearly of the latter category.

I do not think it desirable to discuss further in detail the many decisions in the reports in this field. But two points may perhaps be made. First, the cases in which a tribunal has been held to have passed outside its proper limits are not limited to those in which it had no power to enter upon its inquiry or its jurisdiction, or has not satisfied a condition precedent. Certainly such cases exist (for example *Ex parte Bradlaugh* (1873) 3 Q.B.D. 509) but they do not exhaust the principle. A tribunal may quite properly validly enter upon its task and in the course of carrying it out may make a decision which is invalid—not merely erroneous. This may be described as "asking the wrong question" or "applying the wrong test"—expressions not wholly satisfactory since they do not, in themselves, distinguish between doing something which is not in the tribunal's area and doing something wrong within that area—a crucial distinction which the court has to make. Cases held to be of the former kind (whether, on their facts, correctly or not does not affect the principles) are *Estate and Trust Agencies (1927) Ltd.* v. *Singapore Improvement Trust* [1937] A.C. 898, 915-917; *Seereelall Jhuggroo* v. *Central Arbitration and Control Board* [1953] A.C. 151, 161.

("whether [the board] took into consideration matters outside the ambit of its jurisdiction and beyond the matters which it was entitled to consider");

Reg. v. *Fulham, Hammersmith and Kensington Rent Tribunal, Ex parte Hierowski* [1953] 2 Q.B. 147. The present case, in my opinion, and it is at this point that I respectfully differ from the Court of Appeal, is of this kind. Secondly, I find myself obliged to state that I cannot regard *Smith* v. *East Elloe Rural District Council* [1956] A.C. 736 as a reliable solvent of this appeal, or of any case where similar questions arise. The preclusive clause was indeed very similar to the present but, however inevitable the particular decision may have been, it was given on too narrow a basis to assist us here. I agree with my noble and learned friends, Lord Reid and Lord Pearce, on this matter. I am also unable to accept the correctness of *Davies* v. *Price* [1958] 1 W.L.R. 434, if relied on as a decision that, in giving consent on a ground which was not one of those stated by the statute, the tribunal was acting (though wrongly) within its powers.

I proceed now to consider the relevant statutory provisions. The Foreign Compensation Act, 1950, was passed in order to provide, immediately, for the constitution of the commission and for the distribu- **[211]** -tion by it of compensation under agreements entered into with Yugoslavia and Czechoslovakia. It also provided a framework for the eventual distribution of any compensation which might be received from other governments. This was done by section 3, which was as follows:

"If His Majesty's Government in the United Kingdom enter into or contemplate an agreement with the government of any foreign country providing for the payment of compensation by the latter government, His Majesty may by Order in Council make provision for all or any of the following matters, that is to say:—(*a*) for the registration by the commission of claims to participate in such compensation, and for the making of reports by the commission with respect to such claims; (*b*) for the determination of such claims by the commission; (*c*) for any matters arising in relation to such claims for which, in relation to the claims mentioned in the last preceding section, provision may be made under that section; (*d*) for the distribution by the commission of any sums paid to them by His Majesty's Government in the United Kingdom, being sums received under the agreement; (*e*) for any supplementary and incidental matters for which provision appears to His Majesty to be necessary or expedient."

The reference in paragraph (*c*) to section 2 enabled the Order in Council to make provision

"(*a*) for defining the persons who are to be qualified, in respect of nationality or status, to make applications to the commission for the purpose of establishing such claims as aforesaid, and for imposing any other conditions to be fulfilled before such claims can be entertained; (*b*) for prescribing the matters which have to be established to the satisfaction of the commission by persons making such applications;"

This shows very clearly that as and when machinery should be set up enabling the commission to deal with compensation under future agreements, this should be within fixed and determined limits which the legislature itself would lay down: thus Parliament might (under section 2 (2) (*a*)) define qualified persons and impose conditions, and (under section 2 (2) (*b*)) prescribe matters to be established to the commission's satisfaction. There could be no doubt that if, so far as such power was exercised and such definitions, conditions and prescribed matters were laid down, these would be architectural directions binding the commission, so that if it departed from them, it would be acting beyond its powers, Moreover, when one compares the terminology of section 4 (4) "the determination by the commission of any application made to them under this Act ..." with that of section 3 (*b*) "the determination of claims ..." and appreciates that the power to determine claims is to be subject to such limits (as to definitions, conditions or prescribed matters) as might be approved by Parliament, the conclusion must follow that the preclusive clause can have no application except to a determination made within the limits, whatever they turn out to be, fixed by Parliament. The respondents' argument that the commission has only to make a self-styled **[212]** "determination" in order to enjoy automatic protection is thus at once seen to be unsustainable.

Equally open to objection is another argument of the respondents which I mention because it obtained some approval in the Court of Appeal. That is that this fund was derived from a foreign power under a treaty, so that, in accordance with well-known principles (see *Rustomjee* v. *The Queen** (1876) 1 Q.B.D. 487; (1876) 2 Q.B.D. 69) no subject had any legal claim to any part of it. The distribution of the fund was solely a matter for the executive and it would be inconsistent with this situation to recognise any right of an aggrieved person to bring any claim before the court. I cannot follow this argument. Of course it would have been open to Parliament, or the executive, to provide that the distribution of this fund should be carried out entirely according to the unreviewable discretion of the commission or any other person, and if they had done so it would have been futile for any claimant to try to bring the court into the matter. The question is whether this is what has been done, or whether, on the contrary, Parliament, while leaving it to the commission to decide whether specified qualifications have been satisfied in individual cases, has itself laid down those qualifications, or some of them, in terms which admit of no departure. It is at least certain that Parliament was concerned that the fund should, in principle, go to British nationals only and the whole question is whether it has also decided, or left to the commission, an incidental question connected with that of nationality.

I turn now to the Order in Council in order to see to what extent the circumscribing power has been exercised. This, up to a point is extremely clear. Article 4 opens with the words: "The commission shall treat a claim ... as established if the applicant satisfies them of the following matters." More imperative words could not be devised. The word "shall" serves, and no word could serve better, to indicate those matters which have been decided and laid down by the legislature, as part of its policy and within which the commission is to make its determination. The commission's own sphere of operaton (ample enough) is conveyed by the words "satisfies them," by subsequent references such as "the commission may" by their duty to "assess ... as seems just and equitable," by "if it shall appear to the commission" and similar words. So, whatever difficulties there may in some cases be in ascertaining what is left to the tribunal, on the one hand, and what is reserved from them, on the other, do not exist here: the demarcation is plainly made.

The next step, and the really difficult one, is to ascertain exactly where the limits of the commission's powers have been set. These must be found from an examination and construction of (relevantly) article 4 (1) (*a*) and (*b*). The historical antecedents of this article, including the relevant provisions of the agreement of February 28, 1959, have been fully set out in your Lordships' opinions, and provisions of the Order in Council have been analysed both there and by Browne J. in his judgment. I forbear from repeating this analysis, as to which I am in agreement with my noble and learned friends, Lord Reid and Lord Pearce, as well as with the learned judge.

I would summarise the considerations which persuade me that the learned judge's conclusions were correct as follows: **[213]**

1. The use of words. Throughout article 4 the words are "successor in title of such person"; never is there any reference to the property or any property. The first reference, in Annex A of the treaty of February 28, 1959, was to "successors of such person." If a particular successor, by assignment, to a particular property had been meant, one would have expected a clearer reference. I recognise that there are difficulties in the way of an interpretation which refers to successorship on death and it may well be that these references are not accurately thought out. But the Order is dealing with property abroad, in which some foreign nationals may be interested, and I do not think that such inaccuracy as there is should determine the broader question which concerns us. We must accept that the Order uses "successors" as *including* successors on death and the question is whether in addition the word includes assignees.

2. The difficulty of working out any conception of assignment. It is clear that, if any assignments are included, those particular assignments which took place when Annex E properties were sold by Egyptian sequestrators under Proclamation No. 5 cannot be included: to include them would stultify the whole article. But neither is there any warrant for treating such assignments as non-existent, nor, if they are not so treated, is it easy to give any meaning to assignment. It was at one time thought that the article contemplated assignments which would have taken effect if no sale by sequestration had occurred; in the end this was, rightly in my view, given up. But if these sales are not disregarded, the difficulty of stating what kind of assignment is meant becomes very great. It becomes necessary to wrestle with the concept of a spes restitutionis against the United Arab Republic, converted, after February 28, 1959, into a spes of compensation against the United Kingdom government, transmuted again after April, 1959 (the first Order in Council), into a hope of sharing in the fund. Perhaps this, with all its difficulties, can be worked out, but the difficulties add to the objections against this interpretation.

3. As a matter of policy, one starts with Her Majesty's Government's claim under the treaty, which was to recover British property, and with the receipt of money to compensate for the retention of Annex E property; then, on the one hand, it is perfectly comprehensible that the requirement should be imposed that either the claimant, being an original owner, should be a British national, or that, if he is dead and someone else claims in his place, that person should also be a British national. It can be seen from Annex E that many, if not most, of the claimants were resident if not domiciled in Egypt. On the other hand, there seems no obvious reason why a British national who has disposed of, or charged, any rights he might have in respect of his property should recover if he has done so in favour of a British subject, but should not do so if he has done so in favour of a non-British subject. As between such a person and the other claimants on the fund, that person has just as good a claim, provided that he does not recover twice. And, in order to prevent this, there is article 10.

4. Article 10 provides that in assessing any loss the commission shall have regard to any compensation or recoupment in respect of that loss which the applicant has received from any other source. This was accepted by Browne J. as a strong argument in favour of the "successor on death" **[214]** argument. I think this was right. It seems very appropriately to fit such a case as the applicant's where, whether by "assignment" or not, the original owner has succeeded in obtaining some "recoupment" for loss of his property. Compensa-

tion or recoupment is hardly likely to be made without some assignment of rights; and, in the conditions prevailing before 1959, it does not seem probable that any assignment would be possible to a British national, or indeed otherwise than to a national of the United Arab Republic.

These considerations, cumulatively, are, in my opinion, compelling. There remains, of course, the drafting of article 4 (1) (*b*) (ii) "that the person referred to *and* any person who became successor in title," which does appear to suggest that a situation may exist where a successor in title is relevant even if the claim is made by the original owner. But I think that this is not decisive: it is merely the result of unfortunate telescopic drafting. The draftsman ought to have dealt separately with the two cases saying (i) if a claim is made by the person referred to as aforesaid that he was a British national.... (ii) if a claim is made by the successor in title of such person and such person succeeded before February 28, 1959, that both he and the person referred to as aforesaid were British nationals. We are well used to doing, by interpretation, this kind of work on the draftsman's behalf, and I think we can do so here.

In my opinion, therefore, article 4 should be read as if it imposed three conditions only on satisfaction of which the applicant was entitled, under statutory direction, to have his claim admitted, namely—(*a*) that his application relates to property in Egypt referred to in Annex E; (*b*) that he was the person referred to in Annex E paragraph (1) (*a*) as the owner of the property; (*c*) that he was a British national at the specified dates. As, ex concessis, all these conditions were fulfilled to the satisfaction of the commission, the appellants' claim was in law established; the commission by seeking to impose another condition, not warranted by the Order, was acting outside its remitted powers and made no determination of that which alone it could determine. Indeed one might almost say, conversely, that having been satisfied of the three conditions, the commission has, in law, however it described its actions, determined the claim to have been established.

I should mention, in justice to the respondents' argument, that a contention was put forward to the effect that, even if the commission had acted outside its power in the respect suggested, its decision could be upheld on other grounds. I need only say of this that it too involved introducing considerations not laid down in the Order in Council and for the same reasons could not be accepted. Finally there is the question of remedy. Once it is established that the commission, basing its decision on an interpretation of the Order in Council which cannot be maintained, has made a determination beyond its powers, it appears to me to be clear that the court has power to declare this and the correct interpretation of the Order in Council by declaration. Indeed this remedy is in every respect the most suitable in the circumstances of the case. No objection to the actual form of the declaration was taken before Browne J. In my opinion, the appeal should be allowed and the order of Browne J. restored. **[215]**

Lord Pearson. My Lords, I have had the advantage of reading in advance the opinions of my noble and learned friends, Lord Reid, Lord Pearce and Lord Wilberforce. As to the general nature of the court's supervisory function (as distinct from any appellate function) in relation to decisions of tribunals I agree with what they have said and have nothing to add. I agree with them also that what has been called the "ouster provision" in section 3 (4) of the Foreign Compensation Act, 1950, does not exclude the court's intervention in a case where there is a merely purported determination given in excess of jurisdiction. Also in relation to the present case I would join with my noble and learned friends to this extent, that if the appellants' contentions as to the true construction of the relevant Order in Council are upheld, it must follow that the commission have acted in excess of jurisdiction and the court should intervene in the exercise of its supervisory function. According to the appellants' contentions, the commission were satisfied of the only matters of which on the true construction of the Order in Council the appellants as applicants had to satisfy them, and so the appellants were entitled to a determination in their favour; but the commission, misconstruing the Order in Council, erroneously thought that there were further matters of which the appellants had to satisfy them, and so the commission embarked upon an irrelevant inquiry and (in the familiar phrase) asked themselves the wrong question and gave a purported determination which was outside the area of their jurisdiction. If that is the right view of what the commission have done, there has been excess of jurisdiction.

I am, however, not able to agree that the commission misunderstood the Order in Council, or made any error affecting their jurisdiction. The questions of construction arise with regard to the provisions of article 4 (1) (*b*) of the relevant Order in Council, which is the Foreign Compensation (Egypt) (Determination and Registration of Claims) Order, 1962. In order to supply the necessary background to these provisions it is necessary to make some reference to the outline of the history and to certain provisions of previous instruments.

On November 1, 1956, soon after the commencement of the "Suez Incident" the Egyptian Government issued Proclamation No. 5 of 1956, and thereby they sequestrated the assets in Egypt of British and French subjects, including the appellants' manganese mine in the Sinai Peninsula. The mine was in the territory which came to be occupied by Israeli forces. In April, 1957, after the Israeli forces had withdrawn, the Egyptian Minister of Finance and Economy, acting under article 9 of the proclamation, authorised the Custodian General of the property of British, French and Australian subjects to sell and liquidate the establishments and other property of persons set out in a list, in which the appellants were included. On April 29, 1957, there was a contract of sale, to which the first party was the Custodian General and the second party was Alsayed Hassan Ibrahim "in his capacity as the Chairman of the Economic Board and representative of the Sinai Manganese Co. S.A.E. (under formation)." The appellants were not a party. By the contract, all assets belonging to the appellants were sold by the first party to the second party at a price to be determined by a committee, and it was provided by clause 5 that **[216]**

> "all title to the assets sold hereunder shall be assigned to and taken over by the purchaser immediately this contract is signed by the parties hereto."

Presumably the sale by that contract was valid under Egyptian law, but in July, 1957, the appellants through agents wrote letters to customers of the manganese mine stating that the sequestrator had no authority whatever to act on behalf of the company or to deal in any way with its assets, whether in Egypt or elsewhere, and that the company regarded as a violation of its legal rights any transaction involving ores from the mine and would take in any country any steps which it might consider necessary to assert or protect these rights. On the other side the Egyptian Minister of Industry in September, 1957, promulgated an order whereby the mining leases previously granted to the appellants were cancelled.

> "as from the date the said company's property was liquidated and the assets thereof were sold to the Economic Board on April 29, 1957."

Also the newly-formed Egyptian company, the Sinai Manganese Co S.A.E., issued a writ against the appellants' agents and others. Then there were discussions and an agreement was made on November 23, 1957. The parties to this November agreement were (1) the appellants, (2) the Egyptian company, Sinai Manganese Co. S.A.E., (3) the Economic Development Organisation, called T.E.D.O., which, I think, is the same as the "Economic Board" represented by Mr. Ibrahim in the April agreement, (4) the Sequestrator General of British property in Egypt, who may be the same as the Custodian General referred to in the April agreement. By clause 1A the appellants agreed to sell and T.E.D.O. agreed to buy the whole business of the first party as carried on and situate in Egypt, and the Sequestrator General consented to and acquiesced in the sale. By clause 1B (i) (*a*) the business was deemed to include all the assets of the appellants situate in Egypt. By clause 1B (ii):

> "The said assets of the first party shall not include any claim which the first party may be entitled to assert against any governmental authority other than the Egyptian Government, as a result of loss suffered by, or of damage to or reduction in the value of the business or assets of the first party during or following on the events of October and November, 1956."

The price was £500,000 sterling, payable out of the proceeds of sales of ore other than local sales in Egypt. Clause 12B included a provision that:

> "This agreement ... shall in no respect be deemed a waiver of the claims or rights of the first party save to the extent that it expressly so provides."

This November agreement is in some respects a puzzling document. The appellants' property had already been sold by the April agreement to a person representing T.E.D.O. and the Egyptian company, Sinai Manganese Company S.A.E. How then could the appellants now sell it and how could T.E.D.O. buy it? I think this November agreement can only be explained by reference to the assertions which the appellants' agents had been making to customers of the manganese mine The possible weakness of the April **[217]** agreement (though it would be a weakness in international law or politics or morals rather than in Egyptian law) was that the appellants were not a party to it and refused to accept the authority of the sequestrator to act on their behalf. The object of the November agreement was to clarify the position. The appellants were a party to the November agreement and by it they sold or purported to sell their property to T.E.D.O. at an agreed price. After that they would be precluded (whether legally or politically or morally) from asserting any right or title to the property. Also clause 1 of the November agreement can be construed as involving a sale by the appellants to T.E.D.O. of any claims which the appellants might have against the Egyptian Government in respect of the sequestration and expropriation of their property. By this clause the appellants sold to T.E.D.O. their whole business as carried on and situate in Egypt, and the business was deemed to include all their assets situate in Egypt, and paragraph B (ii) of the clause can be regarded as showing that any such claims of the appellants against the Egyptian Government would constitute assets of the business situate in Egypt and would pass under this contract of sale in T.E.D.O. That is a possible view.

On February 28, 1959, a treaty or agreement was made between the Government of the United Kingdom and the Government of the United Arab Republic concerning financial and commercial relations and British property in Egypt. The first three paragraphs of article III provided that:

> "The Government of the United Arab Republic shall: (*a*) on the date of the signature of the present agreement terminate the application of all measures of sequestration taken by the government of the United Arab Republic against British property between October 30, 1956, and the date of signature of the present agreement.... (*b*) return all British property (or the proceeds of any such property sold between October 30, 1956, and the date of the signature of the present agreement) to the owners thereof in accordance with the provisions of Annex B to the present agreement.... (*c*) be entitled to exclude from the provisions of paragraph (*b*) of this article property sold between October 30, 1956, and August 2, 1958, under the provisions of Proclamation No. 5 of November 1, 1956, and referred to in Annex E to the present agreement...."

Paragraph 1 of Article IV provided that:

> "The Government of the United Arab Republic shall pay to the United Kingdom Government the sum of £27,500,000 sterling in full and final settlement of the following: (*a*) all claims in respect of the property referred to in paragraph (*c*) of article III of the present agreement; (*b*) all claims in

respect of injury or damage to property suffered prior to the date of the signature of the present agreement as a result of the measures referred to in paragraph (*a*) of article III of the present agreement."

Article I and Annex A provided certain definitions:

> "(2) 'British property' shall mean the property in Egypt of United Kingdom nationals.... (3) 'United Kingdom nationals' are (i) physical persons who at the date of the signature of the present agreement are **[218]** citizens of the United Kingdom and Colonies ... (ii) corporations and associations incorporated or constituted under the laws in force in the United Kingdom ... or in any territory for whose international relations the United Kingdom Government are, at the date of the signature of the present agreement, responsible provided that the persons, corporations and associations concerned were equally United Kingdom nationals on October 31, 1956. (4) 'Owners' shall mean United Kingdom nationals who on any date between October 30, 1956, and the date of the signature of the present agreement, were entitled to the property, rights or interests in question, to the extent to which they were so entitled, and shall include any successors of the owners provided such successors are United Kingdom nationals as defined in paragraph (3) of this annex."

Paragraph (1) of Annex E had a heading which included the words

> "The properties in the United Arab Republic of any United Kingdom nationals ... appearing on the following list: ..."

and the list included "Sinai Mining (subject to a special arrangement)."

It is important to note that the requirements in respect of nationality were stringent. To qualify as an "owner" an individual had to be a United Kingdom national, and he was not a United Kingdom national unless he was a citizen both on October 20, 1956, and on February 28, 1959. A person who was a successor of an owner qualified as an owner, but to be a successor he must have been a citizen both on October 30, 1956, and on February 28, 1959. There were similar requirements for corporations.

In April, 1959, the Foreign Compensation (Egypt) (Determination and Registration of Claims) Order, 1959, was made. The first recital referred to the Foreign Compensation Act, 1950, and the second recital referred to the provision in the treaty of February 28, 1959, for payment by the Government of the United Arab Republic to the United Kingdom Government of the sum of £27,500,000 "in full and final settlement of the claims referred to in paragraph (1) of article IV of the agreement." The third recital was:

> "And whereas it is expedient that provision should be made with regard to sums received from the Government of the United Arab Republic and for the registration, assessment and determination of claims in respect of British property in Egypt."

There was in article 1 a definition of "British nationals." Article 4 was as follows:

> "The commission shall treat a claim under this Part of the Order as established if the applicant satisfies them of the following matters:—(1) that his application relates to property in Egypt which was sold between October 30, 1956, and August 2, 1958, under the provisions of Egyptian Proclamation No. 5 of November 1, 1956; (2) that the property at the time of such sale was owned by a British national; (3) that the property is referred to in Annex E to the agreement; (4) that he was the owner at the time of such sale or is the successor in title of such owner; and (5) that the owner at the time of such sale and his successor in title, if any, were British nationals on **[219]** October 31, 1956, and February 28, 1959. For the purposes of this paragraph, a British national who died, or in the case of a corporation or

association ceased to exist, between October 31, 1956, and February 28, 1959, shall be deemed to have been a British national on the latter date."

This Order in Council of 1959 is only a predecessor of the Order in Council of 1962, under which the appellants applied, but it has interesting features. First, as to the meaning of the word "claim." The claims referred to were until the treaty was made outstanding claims against the Egyptian Government (the Government of the United Arab Republic) for restitution or compensation. Under the treaty the Egyptian Government paid to the United Kingdom Government a sum in full and final settlement of these claims. That was an international transaction between governments. The claims probably had no validity by the law of Egypt, the country in which the expropriated or damaged property was situate. They were claims of a political character, presented by the United Kingdom Government in diplomatic negotiations and settled by the payment made by the Egyptian Government to the United Kingdom Government. When the payment had been made there was a fund available for compensating the claimants, and the Order in Council was providing for the registration, assessment and determination of "claims." The claims would now be claims to participate in the distribution of the fund, but they would be derived from, rooted in and identifiable with the previous claims against the Egyptian Government.

Secondly, the nationality requirements of this Order in Council of 1959 were stringent and evidently based largely on the nationality requirements of the treaty. The property must have been owned by a British national at the time of the sale which took place between October 30, 1956 and February 28, 1959, under the proclamation. The claimant must be the person who was the owner at the time of such sale or his successor in title. Both the owner and the successor in title, if any, must have been British nationals both on October 31, 1956, and on February 28, 1959. I see no reason for doubting that this last-mentioned requirement, contained in paragraph 5 of article 4, is to be read literally as requiring that both of them must have been British nationals on both of the specified dates. It was because of this requirement that the deeming provision in the second sentence of paragraph 5 had to be inserted. Suppose the person who was the owner at the time of the sale had (being an individual) died or (being a corporation) ceased to exist before February 28, 1959, and his successor in title was the claimant. The owner still had to have British nationality on February 28, 1959, and it had to be fictitiously conferred on him by the deeming provision.

Thirdly, there is not in the language of paragraph (5) any indication that if the owner is making the claim and has a successor in title the owner is relieved from the need to prove that both he and the successor in title were British nationals on the two specified dates.

Fourthly, it is noted that the property referred to in this article was property in Egypt which was sold between October 30, 1956, and August 2, 1958. This is evidently a reference to the sales by the **[220]** Sequestrator General (Custodian General) under the proclamation, and one of these sales was the April agreement. The successor in title could not be a successor in title to the ownership of the property. He could only be a successor in title to the former owner's claim for restitution or compensation.

The Order in Council of 1959 was amended by an Order in Council of 1960, one of the objects of which (as appears from the explanatory note) was to facilitate the establishment of claims under article 4 of the Order of 1959 in cases in which the applicants had been unable to obtain formal evidence of the sale or of the date of sale of their properties under the proclamation. It would be sufficient to show a sale or a deprivation of possession and enjoyment of the property. But the stringent nationality requirements were continued in a slightly different form. The applicant had to show:

"(*b*) that the property at the time of such sale or deprivation was owned by a British national . . . ; (*d*) that the applicant was the owner at the time of such sale or deprivation or is the successor in title of such owner; and (*e*) that the owner at the time of such sale or deprivation and any person who became successor in title of such owner on or before February, 28, 1959, were British nationals on October 31, 1956, and February 28, 1959."

Again there seems to be no reason for reading the nationality requirements otherwise than literally. Both of them had to have British nationality on both of the dates. There is another point of interest in sub-paragraph (*e*). A person could have become successor in title on or before February 28, 1959, and therefore at a time when the property had been sold, so that the owner had lost his ownership and had nothing left but a claim against the Egyptian Government for restitution or compensation. If the claim had no validity in Egyptian law, and was merely political and not legal in character and could be described as only a "spes," nevertheless a person could within the meaning of the Order in Council become a successor in title to the claim. It was something the title to which could pass from one person to another.

In August, 1962, by an exchange of notes between the United Kingdom Government and the Egyptian Government (the Government of the United Arab Republic) a new and partly different Annex E was substituted for the Annex E which was originally incorporated in the treaty: The heading now omitted any reference to a sale under the proclamation, but referred to "the properties of any United Kingdom nationals appearing on the following list...." The appellants were still included in the list and after their name there were still the words "(subject to a special arrangement)." This must have been a reference to the November agreement, but there was nothing to show what the effect of the special arrangement was intended to be.

Then in October 1962 the Order in Council of 1962, which is the crucial Order in Council under which the appellants made their application, was made in substitution for the Order in Council of 1959 as amended. I think it is sufficient to set out the following portions of article 4:

"(1) The commission shall treat a claim under this Part of the Order **[221]** as established if the applicant satisfies them of the following matters:— (*a*) that his application relates to property in Egypt which is referred to in Annex E; (*b*) if the property is referred to in paragraph (1) (*a*) or paragraph (2) of Annex E—(i) that the applicant is the person referred to in paragraph (1) (*a*) or in paragraph (2), as the case may be, as the owner of the property or is the successor in title of such person; and (ii) that the person referred to as aforesaid and any person who became successor in title of such person on or before February 28, 1959, were British nationals on October 31, 1956, and February 28, 1959 ... (2) For the purposes of sub-paragraph (*b*) (i) of paragraph (1) of this article, any reference in paragraph (2) of Annex E to the estate of a deceased person shall be interpreted as a reference to the persons entitled to such estate under the testamentary dispositions or intestacy of such deceased person. (3) For the purpose of sub-paragraphs (*b*) (ii) and (*c*) (ii) of paragraph (1) of this article, a British national who died, or in the case of a corporation or association ceased to exist, between October 31, 1956, and February 28, 1959, shall be deemed to have been a British national on the latter date, and a person who had not been born, or in the case of a corporation or association had not been constituted on October 31, 1956, shall be deemed to have been a British national on that date if such person became a British national at birth or when constituted, as the case may be...."

It seems to me that the provisions of sub-paragraph (*b*) can and should be read quite literally as meaning what they appear to say. "Successor in title" means a person, whether an individual or a corporation, to whom the claim for restitution or compensation (being all that was left of the owner's interest in the property) has passed by any mode, whether by testamentary disposition or by devolution or intestacy or by assignment or otherwise. By "assignment"

I mean a transfer of the beneficial interest. The applicant may be the initial owner claiming on his own behalf, or the initial owner claiming for the benefit of a successor in title, or he may be the successor in title. The applicant, whoever he may be, has to prove that both the initial owner and any person who became successor in title on or before February 28, 1959, were British nationals on October 31, 1956, and February 28, 1959. It was natural to require that the claim should have been British held on October 31, 1956, just before the Egyptian measures of sequestration began, and on February 28, 1959, the date of the treaty. The stringent requirement that each of them must have been a British national on both of the dates (so that an initial owner would have to remain a British national after he had parted with the beneficial interest in the claim and a successor in title would need to have been a British national before he acquired any interest in the claim), though prima facie surprising, was entirely natural because it was following the requirements of the treaty under which the compensation money for meeting such claims had been paid.

Paragraph (2) of the article shows that in a case where there has been a passing of the property on death the successor in title is the holder of the beneficial interest and not the executor or administrator.

Paragraph (3) contains the "deeming" provisions which are necessitated **[222]** by the stringent nationality requirements. If the owner (being an individual) has died or (being a corporation) has gone out of existence in the period between the two dates, he or it can be *deemed* to have been a British national on the latter date. And, conversely, if he or it had been born or come into existence between the two dates, he or it can only be *deemed* to have been a British national on the earlier date.

As the provisions of sub-paragraph (*b*) can be understood literally, without any artificial limitation or distortion of the grammatical sense of the words, and the resulting effects are not unreasonable or unnatural, I think the provision should be so understood.

The rival theory is beset with difficulties. It involves reading "successor in title" as meaning only a universal successor. There is no warrant for this limitation in the provisions of the article, and the words "in title" naturally refer to the title to some property, in this case at the material times a claim. The phrase "successor in title" is not apt in relation to a universal successor, and indeed the concept of a universal successor is unfamiliar in English law and would need to be specially indicated in some way, if it was intended. Moreover it seems to me that theory breaks down in the case of testamentary dispositions, which are expressly contemplated by paragraph (2). It is not only possible but usual for testamentary dispositions to divide the testator's estate into several portions allotted to different beneficiaries. In that case there is no universal successor, and, if the theory is right, there is nobody qualified to claim under the article: the testator cannot claim because he is dead, and the beneficiary to whom the claim is given by the will cannot claim because he is not a successor in title in the sense of universal successor. Similarly in the case of a corporation going into liquidation and being dissolved, the concept of a universal successor is inappropriate and unworkable. The liquidator sells the assets and conveys or delivers or assigns them to the purchaser or purchasers. The succession must be effected by means of the sale and conveyance or delivery or assignment—by act of parties and not by operation of law. If there are several purchasers, none of them is a universal successor, and again nobody can claim under the article if the theory is right.

Moreover, the theory requires a departure from the natural meaning of sub-paragraph (*b*) (ii). It has to be regarded as a compressed or telescoped provision. As the learned judge Browne J., said:

> "At any given moment there can only be in existence either the original owner or his successor in title but not both."

If there is a successor in title, he is the only possible claimant, having wholly displaced the original owner. He has to prove both his own British nationality and the British nationality of the initial owner, but can only do this under the deeming provisions as the initial owner must have died or ceased to exist in order to let in the universal successor. If the initial owner still exists, he is the only possible claimant and he has to prove only his own British nationality on the two dates. If he has sold his beneficial interest in the claim to X, he does not have to say anything about that, because that is only a transfer of a particular interest and not a universal succession. Thus a claim which is beneficially a foreign-held claim at the date of the treaty is admitted to participation in the fund. All these results **[223]** seem to me inconsistent with the probable intention appearing from the provisions of the article.

I would say therefore that the commission construed the article correctly and did not ask themselves any wrong question, or exceed their jurisdiction in any way.

Having so construed the article, the commission had to make a decision as to the effect of the November agreement. They decided that by that agreement the claim passed to T.E.D.O., and so was at the date of the treaty foreign-held and therefore it was excluded by the provisions of article 4 (*b*) (ii) from participation in the fund. The decision as to the effect of the November agreement, whether right or wrong, was plainly within their jurisdiction, and therefore by virtue of section 4 (4) of the Foreign Compensation Act, 1950, it cannot be called in question in any court.

I would dismiss the appeal.

Appeal allowed.

Solicitors: *Linklaters & Paines; Treasury Solicitor.*

NOTE

[QUEEN'S BENCH DIVISION]

ANISMINIC LTD. *v.* FOREIGN COMPENSATION COMMISSION AND ANOTHER

Judgment delivered July 29, 1966 Browne J.

R. J. Parker Q.C. and *F. P. Neill Q.C.* for the plaintiffs.
Nigel Bridge for the defendants.

July 29, 1966. BROWNE J. read the following judgment.

In this case the plaintiffs claim a number of declarations relating to claims which they have made for compensation arising out of events in Egypt and the Sinai Peninsula from October 31, 1956, onwards.

The plaintiffs are an English limited liability company incorporated in 1913. From its incorporation until 1958 the company was known as The Sinai Mining Company Ltd., but its name was then changed to Anisminic Ltd. The first defendant, the Foreign Compensation Commission ("the commission") is a body corporate set up by the Foreign Compensation Act, 1950. ... The commission consists of a chairman and such number of other members as the Secretary of State with the approval of the Treasury may determine. The chairman and members are appointed by the Lord Chancellor, and I was told by Mr. Bridge that the commission now consists of ten members, all of whom are lawyers. The Act empowered His Majesty to provide by Order in Council for the distribution by the commission of sums received by H.M. Government under agreements with the governments of Yugoslavia and **[224]** Czechoslovakia for the payment of compensation in respect of British property, rights and interests affected by certain measures of those governments; it also empowered His Majesty to provide by Order in Council that the commission should deal with the distribution of compensation received under any future agreement with a foreign government. Section 4 (4) of the Act provides that "The determination by the commission of any application made to them under this Act shall not be called in question in any court of law" and most of the 40 or 50 authorities cited to me related to the effect of this provision. [His Lordship referred to the substitution of the new legal officer as a defendant and continued:]

In April, 1959, Her Majesty exercised by Order in Council Her powers under the Act of 1950 relating to future agreements with foreign governments in respect of £27,500,000 compensation payable by the Government of the United Arab Republic under an agreement with Her Majesty's Government made on February 28, 1959, and the claims referred to in that Order in Council were thereafter dealt with by the commission. This Order was the Foreign Compensation (Egypt) (Determination and Registration of Claims) Order, 1959, (S.I. 1959 No. 625). The Foreign Compensation Act, 1962, empowered the Secretary of State to supplement the compensation received from the United Arab Republic under the 1959 agreement out of moneys provided by Parliament and also enlarged the potential basis of claims on the Fund as so supplemented. Before this Act had been passed, the 1959 Order had been revoked and replaced by the Foreign Compensation (Egypt) (Determination and Registration of Claims) Order 1962 (S.I. 1962 No. 2187), which is the relevant Order for the purposes of the present litigation. On March 4, 1963 there came into operation the Foreign Compensation (Egypt) (Final Distribution) Order, 1963 (S.I. 1963 No. 365). [His Lordship referred to the Foreign Compensation (Egyptian Claims) Rules, 1959, as set out in the Schedule to S.I. 1959 No. 640 subsequently amended and continued:] No oral evidence was called before me, but a considerable mass of documents was put in evidence and there was some dispute as to the inferences which should be drawn from them.

Before October 30, 1956, the plaintiffs carried on the business of mining manganese in the Sinai Peninsula under mining leases or concessions granted by the Egyptian Government. In the claim which they afterwards made to the commission they valued their property in Egypt at that date at about £4½ million, though this figure has not yet been investigated and is not admitted by the defendants; all this property has been absorbed into the economy of the United Arab Republic or destroyed or removed by the Israeli armed forces. Under an agreement which the plaintiffs made with the Egyptian authorities on November 23, 1957 they have received £500,000 out of the proceeds of ore produced from their former mines, but as matters now stand they will not receive anything out of the £27½ million paid by the government of the U.A.R. or the additional moneys provided by Parliament.

On November 1, 1956, the Egyptian Government issued Proclamation No. 5 of 1956. It prohibited the conclusion, either directly or through an intermediary, of any contract, or the effecting of any act of disposition or of any other nature with or in favour of British or French subjects: article 3. It prohibited the fulfilment of any financial or non-financial obligation arising out of a contract or an act of disposition or transaction made in favour of British or French subjects either before or after the date on which the Proclamation came into force: article 4. It prohibited any British or French subject from instituting or pursuing any legal proceedings in Egypt: article 5. Subject to certain exceptions, it placed under sequestration every British or French subject possessing **[225]** assets in Egypt: article 6. British or French subjects were required to hand over to the sequestrator all assets owned by them: article 17. The Minister of Finance and Economy was to appoint two general sequestrators who were to be entrusted with the management of the assets of British and French subjects: article 8. The duties of the sequestrators were to represent the British or French subjects and the prohibitions in articles 3, 4 and 5 were not to be applicable to them; they were to take over and manage the assets placed under sequestration and draw up an inventory thereof and they were entitled with the permission of the Minister of Finance and Economy to proceed with the sale of the property and liquidate the business placed under sequestration and in particular to apply for or agree to the dissolution of any company: article 9. The Minister of Finance and Economy was entitled to decide either generally or progressively the liquidation of certain categories of assets or of all the assets owned by British or French subjects placed under sequestration and could entrust such liquidations to such bodies or persons as he might appoint: article 11. Article 12 provided that "Unless authorised by the Minister of Finance and Economy or the sequestrator concerned every transaction or contract or act of disposition made or carried out contrary to the provisions of this Proclamation shall be regarded as being legally null and void."

Between this sequestration and some time early in 1957 the war damage to which I have already referred was done by the Israeli forces; this damage included both physical destruction of and damage to the mines and their equipment, and also the removal of some of the plaintiffs' assets. In April 1957, the Israeli forces withdrew and on April 29 the Egyptian Government made its Decree No. 387 of 1957 which came into force on its publication on May 23, 1957. By this Decree authority was granted to the Custodian General of the property of British, French and Australian subjects to sell and liquidate the establishments and other property belonging to certain persons subject to Proclamation No. 5 of 1956 who were specified in a list attached to the Decree and included the plaintiff company; the assessment of the assets and liabilities of these bodies was referred to an arbitral tribunal. On April 29 a "contract of sale" was entered into between the custodian general of British property (described as "the first party") and the chairman of the Economic Board, acting in that capacity and also as representative of a company known as Sinai Manganese Company S.A.E. which was then under formation (described as "the second party"); it was common ground that the Economic Board was the same as a body described as The Economic Development Organisation or T.E.D.O., which was a department or emanation of the Egyptian Government. By this contract it was agreed that "the first party hereby sells to the second party all assets belonging to the Sinai Mining Company Ltd. by shares having its principal office in Egypt" at a price to be determined by a committee made up as specified in the agreement. On May 18, 1957 a presidential decision was made authorising the incorporation of an Egyptian Joint Stock Company under the name of "Société Sinai pour la Manganese" and by a Presidential Order No. 560 of 1957 issued on June 27 a chairman and managing director of the Sinai Manganese Company were appointed. It appears from the quarterly economic review of the Banque Belge et Internationale pour Egypte for July 1957, that the capital of this new company was £E400,000 and its object was mining business of any kind, the extraction, purification, reduction, industrialisation of raw ore, trade in metals, etc.

A list of undertakings purchased by the Economic Organisation from the custodian general was published in the Journal du Commerce et de la Marine of Alexandria on July 26-27, 1957, which included the plaintiffs, and on July 29, the Foreign Office sent to Mr. Denham, the chairman of the [**226**] presidium board of the plaintiff company which had been appointed in February 1957, a translation of the Presidential decision of May 18, saying that "it is clear from this that your company has been sold to 'The Société Sinai pour la Manganese'." On February 8, 1961, an Egyptian Decree No. 14 of 1961 was published in the official gazette of the United Arab Republic; this decree provided that the sequestrator or the Minister of Finance should deposit with the Economic Organisation "the amounts paid by the latter or by their companies as advances or as instalments in respect of the property of British subjects which has been acquired"; and contained a list of "British companies and undertakings of which the assets, the liabilities and the stock had been acquired for the account of the companies of the Economic Organisation," which included the Sinai Mining Co. at a "purchase price" of £E487,500. It was common ground that this referred to the sale under the April 1957 agreement, and I think it is clear that under Egyptian law there was in April, 1957, a sale of all the assets in Egypt of the plaintiffs to the Economic Board.

Meanwhile, on June 11, 1957, the plaintiffs had registered with the Foreign Office in London a claim setting out details of the assets and goodwill of their undertaking in Egypt as at October 31, 1956, and on July 9 they took further action in an attempt to protect their interests. On that day their agents, Messrs. Fergusson Wild & Co. Ltd., sent out a circular letter to all the plaintiffs' former customers saying that the plaintiffs had been advised that the appointment of the sequestrator was a breach of international law which was incapable of giving rise to any legal effects; that the sequestrator had no authority whatsoever to act on behalf of the plaintiffs or to deal with their assets; and that the plaintiffs regarded as a violation of their legal rights any transaction involving ores derived from their former area of operations in the Sinai Peninsula and would take in any country any steps which they might consider necessary to assert or protect their rights.

On September 4, 1957, the Minister of Industry in Egypt issued an Order No. 426 of 1957 cancelling mining leases previously granted to the plaintiffs "as from the date the said company's property was liquidated and the assets thereof were sold to the Economic Board on April 29, 1957." Soon afterwards, the exact date is not clear but it appears to have been about September 28, the Sinai Manganese Company S.A.E. issued a writ against the plaintiffs and Messrs. Fergusson Wild & Co. complaining of the circular letter of July 9. This writ stated that the Egyptian government had cancelled all the leases previously granted to the plaintiffs, and authorised Egyptian companies, including the Sinai Manganese Company to undertake mining activities in the Sinai Peninsula. It also stated that the newly formed Sinai Manganese Company had purchased from the sequestrator general all the assets belonging to the plaintiffs and had since April 29, 1957, acquired an absolute right to practise "mining operations which were previously carried on by" the plaintiffs. This writ was withdrawn on February 5, 1958, as a result of the agreement reached in November, 1957.

Some time about October, 1957, the presidium board of the plaintiffs decided to open negotiations with the Egyptian authorities. On November 4 General Ghaleb, the managing director of the Sinai Manganese Company, was appointed deputy sequestrator general "for settling the assessment of assets of" the plaintiffs, and on November 23 an agreement was signed between the plaintiffs, the Sinai Manganese Company S.A.E., T.E.D.O. and the sequestrator general; General Ghaleb signed on behalf of all three Egyptian parties. [His Lordship referred to details of the agreement for sale between the plaintiffs and T.E.D.O. of the plaintiffs' "whole business ... as carried on and situate in Egypt," and continued:] **[227]**

The price of "the said sale" was to be £500,000 sterling, payable out of the proceeds of sales of ore made by the Sinai Manganese Company; I was told that the whole of this sum has now been paid. The agreement also provided that the plaintiffs would change their name, and it was as a result of this provision that the change of name took place in 1958.... It will be seen that the parties to this agreement (except of course the plaintiffs) were the same as the parties to the contract of April 29, 1957. Whatever may be the legal effect of this agreement, I agree with Mr. Parker's description of it as purporting to sell something the plaintiffs had not got to someone who had bought it already (in April) with the consent of the person who had sold it before. I also agree with him that in substance this agreement was a device by which the plaintiffs successfully used their nuisance value to extract from the Egyptian Government some measure of compensation for the loss of their business and assets in Egypt, and this seems to have been common ground between Mr. Parker and the legal officer at the hearing before the commission ... ; on the figures claimed by the plaintiffs which, however, as I have said, are not admitted by the defendants, the £500,000 received by the plaintiffs under this agreement was only about one-ninth of the value of that business before October 30, 1956.

If the November agreement can be regarded as a sale of any business or assets of the plaintiffs, those assets were very different from what they had owned on October 30, 1956. Over £500,000 worth of assets had been destroyed, damaged or removed by the Israeli forces, all the plaintiffs' mining leases had been cancelled and their title to what was left was non-existent under Egyptian law.

On February 28, 1959, an agreement was reached between H.M. Government and the Government of the United Arab Republic "concerning financial and commercial relations and British property in Egypt" (Treaty Series No. 35 of 1959). The negotiations which led to this treaty had already opened in Rome before the plaintiffs made their agreement in November, 1957. I am satisfied that when the plaintiffs made that agreement they believed that they were doing better for themselves than Her Majesty's Government was likely to do for them, and that they did not expect to get any additional compensation out of any possible future [international] governmental agreement. Their claim was not expressly excluded from the treaty, but Mr. Bridge asks me to infer that it must have been the belief and intention of the Government of the United Arab Republic that it should be excluded from the inter-governmental negotiations and the compensation agreed to be paid, though General Ghaleb's letter to Mr. Denham of October 28, 1957, seems to imply the contrary. But even if it is legitimate in considering an international treaty to inquire what the subjective intentions of the parties were, I find it impossible to say that H.M. Government intended to exclude the plaintiffs' claims; on balance I think it more probable that they did not. The plaintiffs had reported to the Foreign Office in November, 1957, that they were negotiating with the Egyptians and later informed H.M. Government of their agreement. Their claim remained registered with the Foreign Office throughout. In July, 1962, the plaintiffs' solicitors wrote to the Foreign Office asking for information about the way in which the November agreement had been dealt with in the negotiations which led up to the inter-governmental agreement. [His Lordship referred to the correspondence with the Foreign Office.]

There is in my view no evidence that the sum of £27½ million compensation paid under the treaty would have been any larger if the plaintiffs had not made the November 1957 agreement. If it would not, the plaintiffs (even though it might be said that they do not deserve any share of this money because they intended or believed that their private agreement was to be in **[228]** substitution for any future governmental compensation) have done nothing but good to other claimants for compensation and to H.M. Treasury by making that agreement. If they had not made it, they would have had an unanswerable claim on the Fund for their whole loss (subject of course to the same scaling-down as other claimants) and they have always been willing to give credit for the £500,000 received under the November agreement, thereby increasing the amount available for other claimants before the Act of 1962 and thereafter reducing the additional calls on the Treasury. [His Lordship then referred to the inter-governmental agreement of February 28, 1959, and continued.]

As a result of this agreement, the 1959 Order was made on April 6, 1959, laid before Parliament on April 7, and came into operation on April 9. I need not refer to this Order in detail because it was afterwards superseded by the 1962 Order. I think, however, that it should be noted that it deals with four classes of claims:—

(1) Claims in respect of property sold under Proclamation No. 5 between October 30, 1956, and August 2, 1958, and referred to in Annex E of the treaty, i.e., property not returned to its owners and covered by articles III (c) and IV (1) (a) of the treaty. The commission was put under a duty to treat this class of claims as established if the applicant satisfied them of the matters specified in article 4 (1) to (5) of the Order and then to assess the amount of loss with respect to each established claim; ... (2) Claims in respect of properties sold between the same dates and otherwise satisfying the requirements of article 4 except that they were not referred to in Annex E, in respect of which

the commission's duty was to register the claim and report thereon to the Foreign Secretary in such manner as he should direct.... (3) Claims in respect of property which do not fall within either class 1 or class 2, presumably because the property had not been sold, but which had been lost, injured or damaged as a result of the Egyptian measures of sequestration or restriction between September 30, 1956, and February 28, 1959. In respect of such property, the commission's duty was to treat the claim as established if the applicant satisfied them of the matters specified in article 8 (1)-(3) and then to assess the amount of the loss with respect to each established claim.... (4) Claims in respect of property which was not within class 1 or class 2 but which fulfilled all the requirements of class 3 except that its loss, injury or damage was caused otherwise than by the Egyptian measures of sequestration. In respect of such property the commission's duty was to register the claim and report thereon to the Foreign Secretary.... The Order contains in article 12 provisions relating to compensation received from other sources, corresponding to article 10 of the 1962 Order, on which Mr. Parker strongly relied.

On September 15, 1959, the plaintiffs made an application to the commission in accordance with rule 6 of the commission's rules of procedure, 1959. ... The plaintiffs stated that they were incorporated in England in the name of the Sinai Mining Company Ltd. on April 3, 1913, and that their name had been changed to its present name on January 13, 1958.... In answer to question 6 as to the categories into which their claim fell the plaintiffs claimed in respect of property (a) sold under Proclamation No. 5 and referred to in Annex E; (b) loss, injury or damage to property suffered as a result of the Egyptian measures of sequestration; (c) other loss arising directly or indirectly from the sale; category (d) in this question was "any loss injury or damage to property in Egypt not due to Egyptian measures" and in answer to this the plaintiffs said "as to part of the claim (the exact figure is still the subject of investigation) the amount of loss arising is attributable **[229]** to non-Egyptian measures consequent upon military and other action by the Israelis. The present estimate will be in the region of £500,000." ...

On July 14, 1961, the legal officer delivered an answer under rule 12 of the commission's rules. The legal officer seems to have misunderstood the position as to the claim for war damage by Israeli forces and to have thought that it was additional to the plaintiffs' main claim for the value of their assets sequestrated by the Egyptian Government, whereas it is clear from the plaintiffs' application that it was part of that claim. So far as the main claim was concerned, the only point raised by the answer was that the plaintiffs' property was not sold *under the provisions of Proclamation No. 5,* apparently because it was said that it was sold under the November 1957 agreement and not under the Proclamation. The answer also submitted that if the plaintiffs could establish a claim in respect of the sale of their assets they must give credit for the £500,000 received under the November 1957 agreement, which they had made it clear in their application that they were willing to do.

In March, 1962, the hearing of the plaintiffs' application before the commission began but it was adjourned after the opening because it became clear that considerable further discovery of documents was required.

On July 25, 1962, the chairman of the commission sent a minute to the registrar and the legal officer in which he said "I think it would be desirable that the answer should be amended so as to raise expressly the 'successor in title' point which was the foundation of the decision in Cory Brothers' application. Leave is accordingly given to do so." The applicant was also given leave to serve a reply to the amended answer. I shall return later to the decision in the Cory Brothers' case. The "successor in title" point was based on what was article 4 (5) of the 1959 Order and is now article 4 (1) (*b*) (ii) of the 1962 Order and on the effect of the November 1957 Agreement.

On August 7, 1962, Her Majesty's Government and the Government of the United Arab Republic agreed to an amendment of the 1959 Treaty. The relevant parts of this amendment are set out at pp. 22-23 of Command Paper 1820 (Treaty Series No. 56 of 1962). The effect of this amendment was to delete from article III (*c*) of the treaty the requirement that the property should have been sold between October 30, 1956, and August 2, 1958, under the provisions of the Proclamation. On August 9, the legal officer served an amended answer pursuant to the leave given by the commission....

On October 9, 1962, the 1959 Order was revoked and replaced by the 1962 Order. [His Lordship read the recitals in the Foreign Compensation (Egypt) (Determination of Claims) Order, 1962, S.I. 1962, No. 2187, and referred to provisions therein including the interpretation article 1 (2) and Parts III and IV.]

The four classes of claim covered by the 1959 Order are reduced by the 1962 Order to three. The requirement of the 1959 Order that the commission must be satisfied that the property was sold under the Proclamation between October 30, 1956, and August 2, 1958, disappears as the result of the amendment made to the treaty in 1962, and the second class of property included in the 1959 Order, i.e., property sold between those dates but not specified in Annex E, also disappears. The other two points on which the 1959 Order seems to me to go beyond the treaty reappear in the 1962 Order. The Order does not appear to cover the obligation of the Government of the United Arab Republic under article III (b) of the treaty to return the proceeds of any property sold between the relevant dates but not referred to in Annex E.

On October 12, 1962, the plaintiffs delivered their reply ... On December 20, 1962, the Foreign Compensation Act, 1962, came into force. On March 4, 1963, the Foreign Compensation (Egypt) (Final Distribution) Order 1963 (S.I. 1963 No. 365) came into force ... The general effect of this Order was as **[230]** follows. So far as established claims were concerned (i.e., claims established under article 4 or 6 of the 1962 Order), the amount of the loss assessed by the commission was to be scaled down and paid in accordance with a sliding scale set out in the schedule to the distribution order; for example, if the claim did not exceed £10,000 it was to be paid in full, while if it exceeded £2,000,000 the payment was to be £665,000 and 20 per cent. of the balance of the amount assessed over £2,000,000. So far as registered claims were concerned (i.e., claims registered under article 8 of the 1962 Order), the commission was to treat all claims so registered on or before December 31, 1962, as established claims. [His Lordship read article 7 (*b*) of the distribution order.]

The hearing of the plaintiffs' claim before the commission took place on April 1, 2, 3, 4, 1963. On May 8, the commission made its provisional determination. This document is headed "Provisional Determination" and includes the following words: "It is hereby provisionally determined that the applicants Anisminic Ltd. failed to establish a claim under the Egypt Order aforesaid in respect of the matters referred to in paragraph 2 (*a*) of the amended answer. And that the application in respect of such claims be and is hereby dismissed. But that the claim in respect of damage referred to in para. 2 (*b*) of the amended answer is fit for registration under article 8 of the said Order in a sum to be hereafter determined."

The matters "referred to in paragraph 2 (a) of the amended answer" were the claim for £4,500,000 in respect of the total assets of the plaintiffs' Egyptian business as at October 31, 1956, and the "matters referred to in paragraph 2 (b) of the amended answer" were the property destroyed, removed or damaged by the Israeli forces. This document was not published or sent to the plaintiffs, but on May 9, 1963, the secretary of the commission wrote to the plaintiffs' solicitors informing them of its effect. [His Lordship referred to correspondence between the plaintiffs' solicitors, the commission and the Foreign Office and continued.] The commission on June 21, 1963 made a "Further Provisional Determination" ordering that this claim should be registered "in the sum of £532,773"—which was the full amount claimed under this head.

Although the face of the provisional determination of May 8, was entirely "sphinx-like" and although the commission's letter of June 12, only "spoke" with considerable reticence, there emerged in the course of this action a "minute of adjudication" which is in effect a full and formal judgment by the commission setting out the facts and arguments and their reasons for rejecting the plaintiffs' main claim and allowing registration of the war damage claim. This document first became available to the plaintiffs when it was pleaded on October 30, 1964, by way of further and better particulars of a plea of estoppel by res judicata raised by paragraph 6 of the defence.... It seems to be the practice of the commission to put such judgments on record, because I had before me similar documents in two other cases, the claim of Cory Brothers already referred to and the claim of the Oak and Timber Co. Ltd. which came before the Divisional Court on Nov. 11, 1955. I shall of course have to return later to consider in detail the grounds of the commission's decision as set out in the minute of adjudication. In substance, they decided against the plaintiffs' claim on the "successor in title" point, but giving "successor in title" a meaning different from that pleaded by the legal officer on the commission's invitation and also, as I think, on another ground which was not pleaded at all. Both points were based on the agreement made by the plaintiffs with the Egyptian authorities in November, 1957. The only point originally pleaded by the legal officer in his answer—namely that the plaintiffs' property was not sold under the Proclamation—had dis-[**231**]-appeared as a result of the amendment of the treaty made in 1962 and the resulting amendment of the 1959 Order by the 1962 Order.

On July 30, 1963, the writ in this action was issued. [His Lordship read the statement of claim endorsed on the writ.]

By their defence delivered on November 18, 1963, the defendants pleaded that the High Court had no jurisdiction to entertain these proceedings, and the master and the judge in chambers subsequently ordered that the question of jurisdiction should be tried as a preliminary point of law. The plaintiffs appealed to the Court of Appeal, and on June 25, 1964, that court by a majority (Lord Denning, M.R., and Harman L.J., Diplock L.J. dissenting) allowed the appeal and set aside the Order for the trial of the preliminary point of law. The defendants applied to the House of Lords for leave to appeal from this decision, but on July 29, 1964, the House refused leave, though Lord Radcliffe said that the Committee "were not to be understood as endorsing all that could be found in or read into the judgments of the Court of Appeal." [His Lordship referred to sections 2, 3, 4, 5 and 8 of the Act of 1950 and to section 11 of the Tribunals and Inquiries Act, 1958, and continued.]

I should record at this point that Mr. Bridge made no formal concessions. He was not being unhelpful—on the contrary he was extremely helpful—but he naturally wished to keep open all points for the appeal which seems to be inevitable in this case. Perhaps he had in mind the experience of his predecessor in *Rex* v. *Northumberland Compensation Appeal Tribunal, Ex parte Shaw* [1951] 1 K.B. 711 and [1952] 1 K.B., 338. If I say in the course of this judgment that Mr. Bridge "agreed" to anything or "accepted" anything or that anything was "common ground," these phrases must always be read subject to this reservation.

I think the first question in this case is whether there is anything which is capable of being a "determination by the commission" within the meaning of section 4 (4) of the Act of 1950 and if so in what document or documents is it to be found. Mr. Parker says that "determination" means only a final determination and does not include a provisional determination, and further that it does not include an order for registration under article 8 of the 1962 Order. If one reads section 4 (4) with sections 2 (1), 2 (2) (*a*) and (*b*), and 3 (*a*) and (*b*), the phrase "any application made to them under this Act" in section 4 (4) means any application for the purpose of establishing a claim in respect of losses suffered in such circumstances as may be prescribed by Order in Council under the Act or a claim to participate in compensation which is in course of being distributed by the commission. Mr. Parker accepts, and indeed submits, that the determination of applications under the Act includes the determination of applications under the Order, and this is clearly right. No applications or determinations are made directly under the Act and in the unreported case of *Reg.* v. *The Foreign Compensation Commission, Ex parte*

Oak and Timber Co., Nov. 11, 1955, Donovan J. said "[Counsel] says the application was made under the Order in Council and not under the Act of Parliament; but for this purpose the two are really one." On this point Mr. Parker relied largely on amendments to rule 38 of the commission rules of procedure, 1959, and on a new rule 39, which were made or added in 1961, 1962 and 1964, which appear to draw distinctions between "determinations" and "provisional determinations," and between "determinations" and "orders for registration." In my view the construction of the Act of 1950 cannot be affected by rules of procedure made by the commission more than ten years later, even though laid before Parliament, and even if any weight should be given to the rules they cannot override what I think is the natural meaning of the words in the Act itself. In my judgment, **[232]** "determination" is wide enough to include any decision of the commission as to the disposal of a claim for compensation, whether provisional or final and whether as to the establishment of a claim, the registration of a claim (which necessarily involves a decision that the claim is not established) or the assessment of loss. It seems to me almost absurd to suppose that the vital decision—the final decision whether or not a claim is established—could not be challenged but that the subsidiary decisions could be.

Where then is the determination in this case to be found? ... I am not concerned here with the technical problems of what is or is not part of the "record." In my judgment the minute of adjudication clearly is, or is part of, the commission's decision as to the disposal of the plaintiffs' claim. Further, the defendants pleaded in paragraph 6 of their defence that

> "the questions whether the plaintiffs have established their claims or any of them and all questions of fact and law relevant thereto are res judicata and the plaintiffs are estopped from ... seeking any relief inconsistent with any of the said determinations of the [commission]."

By way of further and better particulars of this allegation, they delivered a copy of the minute of adjudication and said "the questions of fact and law which are alleged to be res judicata and the decisions of the commission upon such questions are those set forth in the paragraphs numbered (1) to (9) expressing the commission's conclusions. In face of this plea, I do not see how the defendants can say that the minute of adjudication is not part of the determination.

As a result of the decision of the Court of Appeal on the plaintiffs' interlocutory appeal in this case, I heard full argument both on the question whether I had jurisdiction to make the declarations claimed by the plaintiffs or any of them and on the question whether the reasoning and conclusions of the commission as set out in their minute of adjudication were right or wrong, and if they were wrong as to the nature of the error. As the case went on it became more and more clear that as Lord Denning M.R. and Harman L.J. thought in the Court of Appeal the two questions were very closely bound up together.

[His Lordship stated the main submissions of counsel.]

Barraclough v. *Brown* [1897] A.C. 615 was decided by the House of Lords on the familiar principle that where a statute creates a new right and also prescribes the method by which that right is to be enforced, that method is normally the exclusive remedy of a person seeking to enforce the right. [His Lordship referred to Lord Herschell at p. 620, and Lord Watson, at p. 622.] Mr. Bridge was, I think, disposed to submit at first that, quite apart from section 4 (4) this authority would prevent a claimant from coming to the High Court until after the commission had given its final determination, but in the end he agreed that, if there was no section 4 (4), the principle of *Barraclough* v. *Brown* [1897] A.C. 615 would not prevent certiorari lying in respect of a provisional determination, at any rate if it was a nullity. But he said there was another difficulty in the way of the plaintiff in this case, because his proceedings are for a declaration and not by way of certiorari. When a decision of an inferior tribunal is brought up on certiorari it can, if found to contain error of law, be quashed, but if a declaration is made that a decision of the inferior tribunal is wrong in law it still stands, unless the error is such as to make the decision a complete nullity. The result of making a declaration in a case where the inferior decision was not a nullity would be to leave standing two inconsistent decisions, of which the effective one would be the decision of the inferior court. [His Lordship referred to **[233]** *Punton* v. *Ministry of Pensions and National Insurance* (No. 2) [1964] 1 W.L.R. 226, *per* Sellers L.J., at pp. 236, 237.]

On this part of his argument Mr. Bridge also relied on *Pyx Granite Co. Ltd.* v. *Ministry of Housing and Local Government* [1960] A.C. 260, especially the speech of Lord Jenkins, at pp. 299-300. If section 4 (4) did not exist, I am not satisfied that my jurisdiction to make the declarations claimed would be excluded on the grounds suggested by Mr. Bridge in this part of his argument, though I express no final opinion. Sellers L.J. in *Punton's* case [1964] 1 W.L.R. 226 seems to have attached importance to the fact that there was no machinery for amending or reviewing the decision of the National Insurance Commissioner if the court granted a declaration that it was wrong (see pp. 235 and 238). In the present case, the provisional determination of the commission must in due course be reviewed, and the views expressed by the High Court and by any appellate tribunal before which the case may go could, and presumably would, be taken into account by the commission at that stage, but I think the point is academic, because I am satisfied that section 4 (4) must at least exclude the jurisdiction of the High Court in any case where the determination of the commission is not a complete nullity.

It is beyond question that the High Court has inherent jurisdiction to supervise and control all inferior tribunals. The phrase "inferior tribunal" is not used in any offensive sense, but merely means that the tribunal has a limited jurisdiction, usually in modern times defined by the statute which sets up the tribunal.

[His Lordship referred to *Rex* v. *Shoreditch Assessment Committee, Ex parte Morgan* [1910] 2 K.B. 859, *per* Farwell L.J., at p. 880.] I am much indebted for this authority and for other help to an article by Professor H. W. R. Wade on "Anglo-American Administrative Law" in (1966) 82 L.Q.R., p. 226.

[His Lordship referred to *Rex* v. *Northumberland Compensation Appeal Tribunal, Ex parte Shaw* [1952] 1 K.B. 338, per Denning L.J. at pp. 346, 347 and also *per* Morris L.J. at p. 357.]

The supervision by certiorari "goes to two points; one is the area of the inferior jurisdiction and the qualifications and conditions of its exercise; the other is the observance of the law in the course of its exercise": *Rex* v. *Nat Bell Liquors Ltd.* [1922] 2 A.C. 128, 156.

This jurisdiction of the High Court is normally exercised by means of the prerogative writs of certiorari, mandamus or prohibition, but it has been established in late years that it can also be exercised by means of declarations in suitable cases. When the High Court quashes a decision of an inferior tribunal on certiorari, it may be doing either of two things; if the decision of the inferior tribunal was given without jurisdiction or in excess of jurisdiction, the quashing is merely a formal recording of what is already the position, namely, that the decision is a nullity, but where a decision is quashed for error of law within jurisdiction it remains a good decision until it is quashed: for example, *Reg.* v. *Medical Appeal Tribunal, Ex parte Gilmore* [1957] 1 Q.B. 574, *per* Parker L.J., at p. 588. I have already referred to the difficulties which may arise over the granting of declarations in the latter type of case: see *Punton's* case [1964] 1 W.L.R. 226.

Parliament can, of course, by statute wholly or partly exclude the supervisory powers of the High Court and many different forms of excluding sections are to be found in the books. The general principle is that the powers of the High Court to supervise inferior tribunals by means of certiorari will not be taken away except by clear and express words and I think that the same must apply to the exercise of these supervisory powers by way of declaration;

see *Reg.* v. *Medical Appeal Tribunal, Ex parte Gilmore* [1957] 1 Q.B. 574, especially *per* Denning L.J. at p. 585; but Mr. Bridge submits that **[234]** I should approach this case in a different way and ask myself whether Parliament intended by the Act of 1950 to *confer* jurisdiction on the courts, not whether it intended to take it away. He says that before the Act of 1950 the distribution of compensation received under agreements with foreign governments was a matter entirely for the Crown in the exercise of its discretion under its prerogative powers and that the courts of this country never had any concern with such matters. This is undoubtedly correct: see *Rustomjee* v. *The Queen** (1876) 1 Q.B.D. 487; 2 Q.B.D. 69; *Civilian War Claimants Association* v. *The King** [1932] A.C. 14. He also says that it is unlikely that Parliament would have intended the courts to have power to intervene in decisions of the commission, because of the importance of reaching finality in the matter of the distribution of this compensation. Compensation being distributed by the commission is usually (though not in the case of Egypt) a limited fund, so that no final distribution can be made until the rights of all claimants have been finally determined. In spite of these arguments I think that I must approach the construction of section 4 (4) on the general principle stated above. In my view, whenever Parliament creates a new inferior tribunal the High Court has an inherent jurisdiction to supervise and control it, and any person aggrieved by a decision of the tribunal has an inherent right to ask the court to exercise those powers.

The effect of sections excluding the supervisory powers of the High Court depends, or at least may depend, on the nature of the error or defect which is said to vitiate the decision of the inferior tribunal. Where an order or decision of an inferior tribunal has been made without jurisdiction, so that it is a nullity, a section excluding the jurisdiction of the High Court to interfere with orders or decisions of that tribunal does not normally apply, because there is in truth no order or decision of the tribunal at all.

[His Lordship referred to the *Northumberland* case [1951] 1 K.B. 711, 716, *per* Lord Goddard C.J.].

In *Reg.* v. *Hurst, Ex parte Smith* [1960] 2 Q.B. 133, the Divisional Court quashed by certiorari an order of a county court judge in spite of the provision of section 107 of the County Courts Act, 1959, that "no judgment or order of any judge of county courts, nor any proceedings brought before him or pending in his court, shall be removed by appeal, motion, certiorari or otherwise into any other court whatever ...," with certain exceptions specifically provided in the Act. [His Lordship referred to the words of Lord Parker C.J., with whom Gorman and Ashworth JJ. agreed, at pp. 142, 143.]

Other authorities to the same effect are *Evans* v. *McLoughlan* (1861) 4 L.T. 31, 33, 34, 35, though the House of Lords held in that case that the magistrate in fact had jurisdiction; *Rex* (*Martin*) v. *Mahony* [1910] 2 I.R. 695, 738, 743, 750; the *Nat Bell* case [1922] 2 A.C. 128, 152; *Reg.* v. *Medical Appeal Tribunal, Ex parte Gilmore* [1957] 1 Q.B. 574, 586, 588; and *The State* v. *O'Donnell* [1945] I.R. 126, 161. One of the most difficult of the many difficult questions which have arisen in this case is the precise meaning of "jurisdiction" in this context. It should be noted that while the cases in which the court will interfere by certiorari are often classified as being *either* those going to jurisdiction *or* those in which there is an error of law on the face of the record: see the *Northumberland* case [1951] 1 K.B. 711 and *Ex parte Bradlaugh*, 3 Q.B.D. 509.

I was referred to a number of authorities as to the principles on which the courts act when supervising by certiorari the decisions of administrative or executive persons or bodies. It is common ground between Mr. Parker and Mr. Bridge that somewhat different considerations apply to such cases from those which apply to decisions of persons or bodies exercising judicial or quasi-judicial functions. The differences are illustrated if one compares the **[235]** authorities on judicial or quasi-judicial decisions cited below with (for example) the principles applicable to administrative or executive decisions as stated by Lord Greene M.R. in *Associated Provincial Picture Houses Ltd.* v. *Wednesbury Corporation* [1948] 1 K.B. 223, 228-229, 233-234 and by Lord Reid in *Smith* v.

East Elloe Rural District Council [1956] A.C. 736, 761-763. The commission is plainly a body exercising judicial functions. I have looked again at the authorities on executive or administrative decisions, but I do not think I need still further lengthen this judgment by referring to them and I shall confine myself to authorities relating to judicial or quasi-judicial bodies, with the exception of the decision of the House of Lords in *Smith* v. *East Elloe Rural District Council* [1956] A.C. 736, on which Mr. Bridge placed great reliance.

I think that the cases in which the High Court exercises its supervisory powers over inferior tribunals can be divided into four classes, and that the effect of sections excluding the supervisory powers of the court varies between these classes.

Class 1. Cases where the inferior tribunal has no jurisdiction to embark on an inquiry at all—what Mr. Bridge called "want of jurisdiction." Any purported decision of this class is a nullity and the ordinary "no certiorari" clause will not exclude the jurisdiction of the High Court, because the purported order or decision is no order or decision at all. In *Andrews* v. *Mitchell* [1905] A.C. 78, the respondent was a member of a friendly society of which the appellants were the trustees. The respondent was summoned before the arbitration committee of the society to answer a charge that in breach of a rule he had been out after 9 p.m. when in receipt of sick allowance, an offence which carried a penalty of a fine of 2s. 6d. At the end of the hearing, in the course of which it appeared that the respondent had given an untrue account, the committee asked the respondent to withdraw and in his absence passed a resolution expelling him from the society on the ground of fraud and disgraceful conduct. The rules of the society provided that "any member proved guilty of fraud, or any conduct or offence calculated to bring disgrace upon the order, before any recognised arbitration committee, provided a charge has been preferred against him as required by the general laws with regard to arbitrations, may be expelled ..." and that "no case shall be adjudicated upon unless ... seven clear days' notice of the time of hearing has been served in writing ... upon the parties...." Section 68 (1) of the Friendly Societies Act, 1896, provides that "Every dispute between ... a member or any person aggrieved who has for not more than six months ceased to be a member of a registered society or branch ... and the society or branch ... shall be decided in manner directed by the rules of the society or branch, and the decision so given shall be binding and conclusive on all parties without appeal, and shall not be removable into any court of law or restrainable by injunction; and application for the enforcement thereof may be made to the county court." The respondent sued the appellants in a county court claiming damages for the wrongful expulsion and an injunction; the county court judge held that he had jurisdiction to hear the action and adjourned the hearing. The appellants then applied to the High Court for a writ of prohibition to the county court; this application was refused by the judge of first instance and the appellants' appeals were dismissed by the Divisional Court, the Court of Appeal and the House of Lords. Lord Halsbury L.C., said at pp. 81-82:

> "When one looks to see what the course of procedure must necessarily be in order to justify an expulsion, counsel points out that there is a rule which certainly does justify expulsion, but it justifies expulsion upon the express proviso that the charge has been made as provided by the rules. In this case the charge never was made as provided by the rules; and if you **[236]** have no power given under the rules to expel a member except upon a charge made and tried according to the rules, you have no power to expel in a case like this ... to my mind this most important principle ought to be brought home to the minds of these courts, presided over as they are by comparatively uneducated men, that some of these forms are matters of substance, and that you must summon a man, and you must give him time to consider what he has got to do, and you must give him the charge against him in writing. Those are all matters of substance, and not mere matters of form. They are the foundation of the subsequent litigation arising between

the parties, and if they were neglected in this case, it appears to me that there was no jurisdiction to entertain that charge at the time .... My Lords, the result to my mind is that the arbitration committee had no jurisdiction to entertain this question, and under those circumstances I think the county court had jurisdiction to do what it did; and therefore this appeal must be dismissed, and I move your Lordships accordingly."

Lord Davey, at pp. 82-83, said that the failure to make the charge in accordance with the rules was

" an informality which went to the root of the jurisdiction, and the omission to follow the directions of the rules for preferring charges has had the unfortunate effect of making the resolution which was come to for the expulsion of the respondent, in my opinion, altogether null and void."

Lord Robertson, at p. 83, said:

"the Act of 1896 has not given carte-blanche to the tribunals of these societies to pronounce decisions which shall be exempt from examination in courts of law. The decisions protected from review are constitutional decisions—decisions pronounced according to the rules ...,"

and the decision pronounced against the respondent in that case had not been pronounced according to the rules because they required written notice of the charge, which had not been given. I am inclined to think that Lord Halsbury and Lord Davey took the view that section 68 did not apply because there was no "decision" at all and Lord Robertson that the section only applied where the decision had been given "in manner directed by the rules" and this decision had not been so given. *Andrews* v. *Mitchell* [1905] A.C. 78 was applied in *Wayman* v. *Perseverance Lodge of Cambridgeshire Order of United Brethren Friendly Society* [1917] 1 K.B. 677, another case dealing with the same section of the Friendly Societies Act, 1896. Another example of a case in which an inferior tribunal had no jurisdiction to embark on a case at all because the procedural steps necessary to give it jurisdiction had not been taken is *Reg.* v. *Hurst, Ex parte Smith* [1960] 2 Q.B. 133; in effect, what had happened there was that an order had been made against the applicant in proceedings to which he had never been a party at all. Want of jurisdiction in this sense may also arise when some condition precedent to jurisdiction, other than a procedural one, has not been fulfilled. For example, a rent tribunal under the Furnished Houses (Rent Control) Act, 1946, has no jurisdiction to entertain a reference unless there is at the date of the reference a subsisting contract for a furnished letting. I think that *Reg.* v. *Gosse* (1860) 3 El. & El. 277, was a case of this type. In that case the court quashed by certiorari an order of justices made under the Nuisances Removal Act, 1855, for the payment by the surveyors of highways of money spent on improving a sewer. It was argued for the applicant that the justices had no "jurisdiction" to make an order for the payment of these expenses out of the Highway Funds **[237]** until they had first exhausted the possibility of raising the money under section 22 of the Act from the persons using the sewer, which had not been done. The Act of 1855 contained in section 39 a "no certiorari" clause.... Cockburn C.J. said, at p. 281:

"The affidavits show clearly that the works which have been executed fall within the provisions of s. 22 of the Act; and it follows that the fund pointed out by that section is the fund primarily chargeable with the expense of them. It is unnecessary to determine whether, if that fund failed, the nuisances removal committee could, under s. 7, resort to the highway rate to make up the deficit; for there is nothing to show us that recourse has been had in the first instance to the proper fund. It is further said that s. 39 takes away the jurisdiction of this Court to issue the certiorari; but that section can apply only to cases in which the justices have jurisdiction. It cannot be said that they have jurisdiction to make an order clearly contrary to the provisions of the Act; or that s. 39 protects such an order when made."

Mr. Bridge says that Cockburn C.J. is there using the word "jurisdiction" in too wide a sense, because an order might be "clearly contrary to the provisions of the Act" but still be an error of law within jurisdiction and not an error of law going to jurisdiction. As I have said, I am inclined to think that the explanation of this case is that the court construed the Act as making the exhaustion of the right of recovery under section 22 a condition precedent to the jurisdiction of the justices to consider an application for payment by the surveyors of highways under section 7.

I think that *Rex* v. *Shoreditch Assessment Committee, Ex parte Morgan* [1910] 2 K.B. 859, is in a sense the converse of the "condition precedent" cases. The Valuation (Metropolis) Act, 1869, provides by section 47 that in certain circumstances (which the Divisional Court and the Court of Appeal held to exist in that case) an assessment committee "shall" appoint a valuer to make a provisional valuation list. The Act also provided for the making of objections to the provisional valuation list and for the hearing and determination of such objections by the assessment committee. The applicant required the assessment committee under section 47 to appoint the valuer, but instead of doing so the committee proceeded at once to make a valuation itself. The Divisional Court and the Court of Appeal held that if the applicant showed a prima facie case for a reduction in value the committee was bound to appoint a valuer, and that the only possible conclusion in that case was that a prima facie case was established, and made an order for the issue of a writ of mandamus requiring the assessment committee to appoint a valuer. I think the decision can be put either on the basis that (all the relevant statutory conditions being fulfilled) the assessment committee was under an absolute statutory duty to appoint the valuer and had no jurisdiction to do anything else, or on the basis that the committee had itself no jurisdiction to determine the value because the necessary conditions precedent to that jurisdiction (the making of the provisional list and of an objection thereto) had not been fulfilled: see for example the argument at p. 873 and the judgment of Farwell L.J. at pp. 879, 880. On either view, the courts must, I think, have regarded the committee's purported decision of the value as a nullity, because they made the order for mandamus to appoint the valuer but without also making an order of certiorari to quash the purported valuation.

Class 2. Cases where the inferior tribunal has jurisdiction to embark on the inquiry, but ultimately makes an order which it has no jurisdiction to make. Mr. Bridge described this class of case as "excess of jurisdiction." In this class of case also any purported order is a nullity, for the same **[238]** reasons as those applicable to class 1, and the ordinary "no certiorari" clause does not exclude the jurisdiction of the High Court. Mr. Bridge submitted that this class only included cases where the inferior tribunal has made an order of a "kind" which it has no power to make. He gave as examples a case where justices having convicted a motorist of a first offence of speeding then proceeded to disqualify him, or a case where the commission made an order for the payment of costs, which it has no power to do. Mr. Parker submitted, in reliance on a number of authorities, that this class is considerably wider than Mr. Bridge submits. He said that it was not necessary in this case to define the precise limits of the class, but submitted that the errors which he said appeared on the face of the commission's minute of adjudication were well within the area of this class of "excess of jurisdiction." I think it is extremely difficult to define the limits of this class and the point at which error of law ceases to be excess of jurisdiction and becomes error within jurisdiction (with which I am going to deal under my class 3). In principle, I find it difficult to see the distinction between Mr. Bridge's example of justices imposing disqualification for a first offence of speeding (which is an order of a "kind" which they have power to make in certain cases) and a case in which for example a sentence of 12 months' imprisonment is imposed for an offence which carries a maximum of six months' imprisonment, and on the authorities I am satisfied that this class is wider than Mr. Bridge submits.

One of the main pillars of Mr. Parker's argument on this part of the case was *Ex parte Bradlaugh*, 3 Q.B.D. 509. In that case, a metropolitan magistrate had made an order for the destruction of certain books under the Obscene Publications Act 1857 (20 & 21 Vict. c. 83), s. 1, which provides that such an order can be made if the magistrate is satisfied (a) that the books are obscene and (b) that they are "of such a character and description that the publication of them would be misdemeanour, and proper to be prosecuted as such." The magistrate's order stated that he was satisfied that the books were obscene but did not state that he was satisfied that they were of such a character and description ... etc. Section 49 of the Metropolitan Police Courts Act, 1839 (2 & 3 Vict. c. 71) enacted that no information, conviction, or other proceeding before or by any of the said magistrates, shall be quashed or set aside, or adjudged void or insufficient for want of form, or be removed by certiorari into Her Majesty's Court of Queen's Bench. The Divisional Court nevertheless granted a rule absolute to bring up the order of the metropolitan magistrate (it appears from this and other cases that at that time the procedure for certiorari was in two stages, first a rule nisi and a rule absolute to bring up the order of the inferior tribunal and later a rule nisi and a rule absolute to quash the order). Cockburn C.J. said, at pp. 511-513:

> "The Act of Parliament makes the magistrate's jurisdiction dependent, upon two conditions, first, that the publication must be obscene, and secondly, that it must in the magistrate's judgment be such as is a misdemeanour and proper to be prosecuted as such. It is not enough that it should be obscene.... When the matter comes before the magistrate ... he must ... be satisfied, on the production before him of the publication ... not only that it is obscene, but also that it amounts to a misdemeanour proper to be prosecuted. It is, therefore, essential to his jurisdiction that he should be so satisfied ... when we come to the order for their destruction, that omits to state that they were the proper subject of a prosecution for misdemeanour, but finds merely that they were obscene. The order, therefore, does not state the existence of a matter that is essential to the jurisdiction. It was contended that the certiorari is taken away by 2 & 3 Vict. c. 71, s. 49.... This is an objection founded upon an absence of jurisdiction appearing on the face of the **[239]** order; and I am clearly of the opinion that the section does not apply when the application for the certiorari is on the ground that the inferior tribunal has exceeded the limits of its jurisdiction. It may possibly be that when this order is brought before us on certiorari, section 7 of 12 & 13 Vict. c. 45, may enable us, if satisfied that the necessary ingredients of jurisdiction existed, to cure the defect; but it is unnecessary to pronounce any opinion on that now. At present the only question is whether the writ is to issue. I am of the opinion for the reasons I have stated that the rule should be absolute for a certiorari."
>
> Mellor J. at p. 513, "I am of the same opinion. It is well established that the provision taking away the certiorari does not apply where there was an absence of jurisdiction. The consequence of holding otherwise would be that a metropolitan magistrate could make any order he pleased without question. ... The order omits to state that the magistrate who made it was satisfied that the books ordered to be destroyed were the proper subject of a prosecution, and therefore the order on the face of it shows an absence of jurisdiction."

Mr. Bridge says that in this case Cockburn C.J. and Mellor J. were using "jurisdiction" in a loose and wide sense, and that this was not really a case of excess of jurisdiction at all but of "abuse of jurisdiction," in the sense of error within jurisdiction. He also submitted that the "no-certiorari" clause in that case only took away certiorari for defects of form and did not therefore apply there because the defect appeared to be one of substance. I cannot accept this latter argument in view of the generality of the last few words of section 49. I was at first impressed by Mr. Bridge's argument that the court could not have regarded the decision of the magistrate as a nullity, because they contemplated that the defect might be "cured" at the later stage of certiorari to quash if the defect turned out to be merely one of form and not of substance. Mr. Parker satisfied me, however, that even if the order was a nullity it could have been "cured" under the special statutory powers given by section 7 of the Quarter Sessions Act of 1849 [12 & 13 Vict. c. 45] which is referred to by Cockburn C.J. at p. 513.

Mr. Bridge's argument that *Ex parte Bradlaugh*, 3 Q.B.D. 509 was not a case of want or excess of jurisdiction at all seems to me to involve the conclusion that not only Cockburn C.J. and Mellor J., but also Denning L.J. in *Reg.* v. *Medical Appeal Tribunal, Ex parte Gilmore* [1957] 1 Q.B. 574, 586 (who treated *Ex parte Bradlaugh* as an authority that "no certiorari" clauses do not apply where the inferior tribunal has "exceeded its jurisdiction") and Lord Parker in the passage which I have already quoted from *Reg.* v. *Hurst, Ex parte Smith* [1960] 2 Q.B. 133, 142 (where he treated *Ex parte Bradlaugh* as the "leading case" establishing that a "no certiorari" clause does not apply when the inferior tribunal has acted without jurisdiction) were guilty of confusion of thought or at least of confusion of expression.

I cannot take so robust a view. In my judgment, *Ex parte Bradlaugh*, 3 Q.B.D. 509 is authority that the order made by the magistrate in that case was made in excess of jurisdiction, that it was therefore a nullity and that the "no certiorari" section did not therefore oust the jurisdiction of the High Court.

The next authority relied upon by Mr. Parker on this part of his argument was *Estate and Trust Agencies (1927) Ltd.* v. *Singapore Improvement Trust*, [1937] A.C. 898 ("*The Singapore Case*"). That case was an appeal to the Privy Council from an order of the Court of Appeal of the Straits Settlements. The respondents were constituted by the Singapore Improvement Ordinance, 1927, and entrusted with the duty of carrying out the provisions of that ordinance, which included a provision, section 57, that: "Whenever it appears **[240]** to the Board that within its administrative area any building which is used or is intended or is likely to be used as a dwelling place is of such a construction or is in such a condition as to be unfit for human habitation, the Board may by resolution declare such building insanitary." The ordinance provided for the making by owners of objections to any such declaration, and for the consideration of such objections by the respondents. After considering any objections, the respondents had power to submit their declaration to the Governor in Council for his approval, and the governor, after a further hearing, if the objection was still maintained, had power to approve or revoke the declaration: the various stages of the procedure appear from pp. 906-907, 913.

In that case the procedure had reached the end of the second stage, the respondents having considered the appellants' objections and submitted their declaration to the Governor for his consideration. The appellants applied for a writ of prohibition, prohibiting the respondents from proceeding further in respect of the declaration in question. The Board had before it a report on the appellants' house by the acting health officer and also an affidavit by the chairman of the respondents, and the Board took the view that this affidavit made it clear that in deciding that the appellants' house was unfit for human habitation the respondents had applied standards laid down in a manual issued by the Ministry of Health in England for different purposes.

[His Lordship referred to pp. 915-917, 919.]

Mr. Bridge submits that that case did not really relate to the control of judicial or quasi-judicial proceedings but only to administrative or executive proceedings. The courts of the Straits Settlements had held that the respondents were exercising functions of a judicial or quasi-judicial character; before the Board it was conceded that at the relevant stage of the proceedings the respondents were exercising quasi-judicial functions, but the Board expressed the view that the courts in Singapore had been right in their conclusion: see pp. 913-914.

It should be noted that there was in that case no provision of the ordinance excluding the jurisdiction of the High Court, and therefore the distinction between errors going to jurisdiction and errors within jurisdiction did not have to be considered in that context. But the admission of affidavit evidence implies that the case was treated as one going to jurisdiction, although I suppose that it may have been admitted by consent. I confess that I find it very difficult to see the distinction in principle between the error of construction of the phrase "unfit for human habitation" of which the respondents were guilty in that case, and the error of construction in question in the *Northumberland* case [1951] 1 K.B. 711; [1952] 1 K.B. 338, which everybody treated as an error of law within jurisdiction; further, although the Board treated it as a "judicial" case, the language used ("beyond powers" and "ultra vires") is more appropriate to an administrative case. I do not find I can get much help from this authority.

The next case relied upon by Mr. Parker was also in the Privy Council, on appeal from the Supreme Court of Mauritius: *Seereelall Jhuggroo* v. *Central Arbitration and Control Board* [1953] A.C. 151.

The appellant contended that on the true construction of section 6 (2) of the Sale of Canes (Control) Ordinance, 1941, of Mauritius the respondents had no power to assess the amount of sugar according to the planters for their canes at less than two-thirds of the extraction. The Board contended that it merely gave general guidance as to the way in which they should approach the problem but did not prevent them from looking at all the circumstances of the case (as they had done in this case) and giving more or less than two-thirds if they thought it right to do so. The appellant applied to the Supreme **[241]** Court of Mauritius for certiorari to quash the respondents' decision arrived at on this basis.

[His Lordship referred to the judgment of the Supreme Court of Mauritius [1953] A.C. 151, read by Lord Porter at p. 161, and to the opinion delivered by Lord Porter at pp. 161, 162, 163.]

Section 6 (1) of the Ordinance provided that the decision of the respondent on any dispute referred to it for settlement should be conclusive and binding on the parties, but neither in argument nor in the opinion of the Board does this subsection seem to be referred to. The conclusion in that case was, of course, that the respondents had not exceeded their jurisdiction, but I think the case is authority that if an inferior tribunal which has jurisdiction to embark on an inquiry thereafter "neglects" or "rejects" a consideration which it is required to bear in mind, this may amount to excess of jurisdiction.

I think that *Reg.* v. *Fulham, Hammersmith & Kensington Rent Tribunal, Ex parte Hierowski* [1953] 2 Q.B. 147, is important. The tenant had referred his rent to the tribunal, but unknown to him the rent had already been determined on a previous reference. The landlord, in answer, relied on an increase in outgoings. On the hearing of the reference the tribunal reduced the rent which had previously been fixed, on the ground that the change of circumstances resulting from the increase of outgoings enabled them to reconsider the whole matter. The Divisional Court quashed this decision by certiorari, on the ground that, while the change of circumstances gave the tribunal jurisdiction to embark on the inquiry, they had no jurisdiction to reopen the whole matter but could only give effect to the results of the change of circumstances. [His Lordship referred to pp. 150-151, 152.]

I think that case is authority that a tribunal which has full jurisdiction to embark on an inquiry may yet act in excess of jurisdiction if it makes an order at the end of the case which it has no power to make in that particular case, even though the order is of the type which it would be entitled to make in other cases.

Finally, Mr. Parker relied strongly on the decision of the Privy Council, on appeal from the Supreme Court of Ceylon in *Maradana Mosque Trustees* v. *Mahmud* [1967] 1 A.C. 13. [His Lordship referred to pp. 14, 23, 25, 26.]

There was in that case no section purporting to exclude the jurisdiction of the courts, but it is in my view strong authority that on grounds (ii) and (iii) the Commission in this case acted without or in excess of jurisdiction if they did fall into the error which Mr. Parker imputes to them. I find it difficult to reconcile ground (i) with what was said in the *Nat Bell* case [1922] 2 A.C. 128 (which does not appear to have been cited) about absence of evidence not going to jurisdiction.

Class 3. Cases in which the inferior tribunal has made an error of fact or law within its jurisdiction. Mr. Bridge called this class "abuse of jurisdiction," and said that in some of the authorities cited by Mr. Parker the words "absence" or "excess" of jurisdiction are used when what is really meant is "abuse" of jurisdiction. When there is an error of this class, the decision of the inferior tribunal is not a nullity, though it may be quashed by a certiorari if—but not unless—the error is an error of law and appears on the face of the "record." It may be very difficult in a particular case to distinguish between an error going to jurisdiction and an error within jurisdiction (see Denning L.J. in the *Northumberland* case [1952] 1 K.B. 338, 353), but the distinction is well established in principle. As illustrations of this class of case, Mr. Bridge relied on *Reg.* v. *Bolton* (1841) 1 Q.B. 66; *Rex* (*Martin*) v. *Mahony* [1910] 2 I.R. 695; the *Nat Bell* case [1922] 2 A.C. 128 and the *Northumberland* case [1951] 1 K.B. 711; [1952] 1 K.B. **[242]** 338; he also referred to the famous "Bum-boat" case, *Brittain* v. *Kinnaird* (1819) I Brod. & B. 432.

The problem before the courts in the first three and the last of these cases has no direct relevance to the present case, although they relate to an analogous problem. The question in those cases was whether the High Court was entitled to look at material outside what appeared on the face of the order or decision itself as to matters of fact. The rule is that the court may look at materials outside the "record" to see whether the inferior tribunal has rightly decided a question of fact going to the question of whether the tribunal has jurisdiction or not (sometimes called "collateral fact" or "jurisdictional fact"), but may not look at anything outside the "record" as to facts which it is within the jurisdiction of the inferior tribunal to decide.

In *Reg.* v. *Bolton* (1841) 1 Q.B. 66, the justices had made an order for possession of a "parish house." [His Lordship referred to the affidavit which the court held to be inadmissible (p. 68) and to the judgment of the court delivered by Lord Denman C.J., at pp. 71-75, citing two authorities, including *Brittain* v. *Kinnaird* (1819) 1 Brod. & B. 432, and continued.] The court then examined the relevant documents and held that by this test the justices had jurisdiction. As I understand it, there was no question in that case of "want of jurisdiction" or "excess of jurisdiction" in the sense in which I have used these phrases in my class 1 and class 2. Such a question might well have arisen if it had been disputed that the house in question was a "parish house," in view of the provisions of sections 24 and 25 of 59 Geo. 3, c. 12, under which the justices had made their order, but this was not disputed: see p. 76; and the argument at p. 71 was that there was not "even a scintilla of evidence in favour of the order." The statement of Lord Denman at p. 74 that "The question of jurisdiction ... is determinable on the commencement, not at the conclusion, of the inquiry ..." must, I think, be read in relation to the question which arose in that particular case; in my judgment it is clear from the authorities to which I have referred under class 2 that a tribunal may have jurisdiction to commence an inquiry but may act without or in excess of jurisdiction at a later stage.

In *Rex* (*Martin*) v. *Mahony* [1910] 2 I.R. 695, the applicant had been convicted by a Dublin divisional magistrate of an offence under the Betting Act, 1853. It was admitted that this conviction was erroneous because the magistrate had failed to apply, or had mis-applied, the decision of the House of Lords in *Powell* v. *Kempton Park Racecourse Co. Ltd.* [1899] A.C. 143: *per* Palles C.B., at pp. 719-720 and Gibson J., at 728. The conviction however, was in a statutory short form which did not set out or incorporate the evidence and the court held that the conviction being regular on its face and following the statutory form the evidence could not be examined and certiorari would not lie. The conviction in that case had been under the Dublin Summary Procedure Acts, and much of the judgments are devoted to the question whether, if the prosecution had been instead under the Petty Sessions (Ireland) Act, 1851, which contained certain requirements as to the taking of depositions, it would have been legitimate to examine the evidence; on this point Palles C.B. dissented from the rest of the court. The majority of the court thought that absence or insufficiency of evidence to warrant a conviction did not establish want of jurisdiction, but was merely error within jurisdiction, while Palles C.B. thought that if there was no evidence to support a conviction it was made without jurisdiction, but that the applicant in that case could not establish this want of jurisdiction because he could not go behind the face of the order. [His Lordship referred to the judgment of Lord O'Brien C.J., at pp. 705, 706, to pp. 710, 711, 714, 715, 716, to Palles **[243]** C.B.'s judgment, at pp. 721, 722, 726, to Gibson J., at pp. 749, 750, to Maddon J. and Wright J., at p. 750, and to Kenny and Boyd JJ., at p. 718.]

The Opinion of the Privy Council delivered by Lord Sumner in the *Nat Bell* case [1922] 2 A.C. 128, is of course one of the classic statements of the law relating to certiorari.... The Courts of Alberta had quashed a conviction by a magistrate on grounds which are stated in the opinion of the Board at p. 143. Reasons (5) and (6) related to suggested differences between the law of Alberta and English law which the Board held not to exist. The Board ... went on to hold that absence of evidence does not affect the *jurisdiction* of the inferior tribunal. [His Lordship referred to pp. 151-153.]

The Board said at p. 154 that "The law laid down in *Reg.* v. *Bolton* (1841) 1 Q.B. 66 has never since been seriously disputed in England"; and dealt, at pp. 159, 160, with the effect of the English Summary Jurisdiction Act of 1848, ... and to what the Board had previously said at pp. 155, 156.

I have dealt with these authorities at some length because Mr. Bridge strongly relied on them, but they seem to me to have no direct relevance to this case, beyond, of course, emphasising the distinction between errors going to jurisdiction and errors within jurisdiction. In all of them, the question was whether evidence of facts was admissible beyond what appeared on the face of the record. In *Reg.* v. *Bolton* (1841) 1 Q.B. 66 the applicant seems to have been asking the court to retry the case on the merits, which can never be done on certiorari (see *Nat Bell* [1922] 2 A.C. 128, 160), while in *Mahony* [1910] 2 I.R. 695 and *Nat Bell* the error or alleged error was in my view plainly an error within jurisdiction. In the present case the error, if any, is one of law, and appears on the face of the record if I am right in my finding that the minute of adjudication is part of the record; as I have already said, it is clear that an error of law going to jurisdiction may appear on the face of the record.

The *Northumberland* case [1951] 1 K.B. 711; [1952] 1 K.B. 338, seems to me more nearly in point. It is clear that everyone in that case thought that the error was an error within jurisdiction; the whole point of the case was whether the jurisdiction of the High Court to control inferior tribunals by certiorari extends to error of law within jurisdiction appearing on the face of the record or whether it is limited to errors going to jurisdiction. The error in that case was a misconstruction of regulations providing for compensation for loss of office. The tribunal had construed the word "service" in the regulations as including only the applicant's service with a hospital board, while it was conceded in the Divisional Court that on its true construction the word included the whole of his local government service. I confess I find it very difficult to distinguish the error of construction of the regulations in that case (which is binding on me) from the error of construction of the phrase "unfit for human habitation" in the *Singapore* case [1937] A.C. 898 (which is not binding on me). I think, however, that it may well be distinguishable from the error suggested in the *Seereelall* [1953] A.C. 151 case and found to exist in the *Maradana Mosque* [1967] 1 A.C. 13 case; in my view there is a distinction between a case where the inferior tribunal asks itself the right question and gives the wrong answer ("Was this house unfit for human habitation?" "What was the length of this man's service?") and a case where the inferior tribunal asks itself entirely the wrong question. In the end, I think the question whether error is error within jurisdiction or amounts to acting without or in excess of jurisdiction will usually depend on the construction of the particular statutory provision in question. "No certiorari" clauses would normally exclude the power of the court to inquire into or control errors within jurisdiction, and I am satisfied that section 4 (4) would do so—as indeed Mr. Parker conceded. In my judgment, the general **[244]** principle is that provisions limiting the power of the High Court to interfere with an order or decision of an inferior tribunal do not apply to cases falling within my class 1 or class 2 because there is in such cases no "order" or "decision" at all, but would normally preclude the power of the court to interfere in cases falling within class 3. In the end, however, I think that this also must usually depend on the construction of the particular section excluding the jurisdiction of the courts which is in question. The industry of Mr. Parker's research team discovered a provision in the Canadian National Selective Service Mobilisation Regulations, 1942, which excluded the jurisdiction of the High Court even if a decision of the mobilisation board was made without jurisdiction or was a nullity.

Class 4. Cases in which the inferior tribunal has been guilty of bias, or has acted in bad faith, or has disregarded the principles of natural justice. Mr. Bridge put this class of case in class 1, but I am not satisfied that this is right. It is not necessary to decide it for the purposes of this case, but I am inclined to think that such decisions are not nullities but are good until quashed (cf. the decision of the majority of the House of Lords in *Smith* v. *East Elloe Rural District Council* [1956] A.C. 736, that a decision made in bad faith cannot be challenged on the ground that it was made beyond powers and Lord Radcliffe's dissenting speech on this point, at pp. 769-770). Of course no question of this type of defect arises in this case; if it did, I should feel bound by the decision in the *East Elloe* case [1956] A.C. 736 to hold that section 4 (4) debarred me from inquiring into it. Mr. Bridge said it would be odd if Parliament had excluded the power of the courts to control bad faith, bias or disregard of natural justice by the commission while leaving them free to control some errors of law, but I do not think so. Parliament might well have thought that there was not the slightest risk of the commission's falling into the former type of error, but that, as we all know only too well, any court can go wrong in law; if I may say so without disrespect, even the House of Lords, like the Supreme Court of the United States, is "infallible because it is final, not final because it is infallible."

To complete my review of the authorities, I must refer to the decision of the House of Lords in *Smith* v. *East Elloe Rural District Council* [1956] A.C. 736, and the unreported decision of the Divisional Court in *Reg.* v. *Foreign Compensation Commission, Ex parte Oak and Timber Co. Ltd.*, Nov. 11, 1955, D.C. on both of which Mr. Bridge strongly relied. In the *East Elloe* case the plaintiff (appellant) had brought an action against the council and the Ministry for amongst other things a declaration that a compulsory purchase order made by the council and confirmed by the Ministry of Health had been made and confirmed in bad faith.

The order had been made under the Acquisition of Land (Authorisation Procedure) Act, 1946, Sch. I, which contained paragraph 15 (1): "If any person aggrieved by a compulsory purchase order desires to question the validity thereof ... on the ground that the authorisation of a compulsory purchase thereby granted is not empowered to be granted under this Act ... he may, within six weeks from the date on which notice of the confirmation or making of the order ... is first published ... make an application to the High Court ..." and paragraph 16: "Subject to the provisions of the last foregoing paragraph, a compulsory purchase order ... shall not ... be questioned in any legal proceedings whatsoever...."

The appellant had not taken any steps to challenge the order under paragraph 15. The House of Lords held by a majority (Lord Simonds, Lord Morton of Henryton and Lord Radcliffe) that the action against the council and the Ministry could not proceed by reason of the plain prohibition in paragraph 16, which ousted the jurisdiction of the courts; Lord Reid and **[245]** Lord Somervell of Harrow dissented, on the ground that the general words of paragraph 16 must be limited so as not to apply to deliberate fraud: see pp. 764-766, 772-773. As to paragraph 15, the House held, again by a majority (Lord Morton of Henryton, Lord Reid and Lord Somervell of Harrow, Lord Radcliffe dissenting) that the validity of an order could not be challenged under that paragraph on the ground that it was made in bad faith; Lord Simonds, without expressing a final opinion, was inclined to agree on this point with Lord Radcliffe: see p. 752.

[His Lordship referred to the judgments of Lord Simonds, at pp. 750, 751, Lord Morton of Henryton, at pp. 756, 757 and 758, and Lord Radcliffe, at pp. 768-770.]

None of the members of the majority regarded the question whether or not the appellant could have challenged the order under paragraph 15 as affecting the construction of paragraph 16 (and indeed they differed among themselves on the question whether or not the appellant could have challenged the order under paragraph 15).

That case, decided on a clause very like section 4 (4), is, of course, a compelling authority, especially the speech of Lord Simonds, at p. 751, (though the Canadian Regulations produced by Mr. Parker show that even wider words can be used). But in my judgment that decision does not directly bind me to hold that section 4 (4) excludes my jurisdiction in the present case. It related to an administrative or executive decision, not a judicial decison, to which Mr. Bridge and Mr. Parker agreed that rather different considerations apply and none of the authorities as to want or excess or abuse of jurisdiction by judicial tribunals appear to have been cited to the House. The appellant's contention there was that words should be read into paragraph 16 but this never seems to have been the approach when the High Court was asked, in spite of a "no certiorari" clause, to quash by certiorari a judicial decision by an inferior tribunal for an error going to jurisdiction. The words "a compulsory purchase order ... shall not ... be questioned in any legal proceedings whatsoever ..." (or "The determination by the commission ... shall not be called in question in any court of law"), do not really seem to me any wider than the words of the "no certiorari" clauses which have been held to oust the jurisdiction of the High Court when a decision of an inferior tribunal is a nullity because given without jurisdiction (for example, section 107 of the County Courts Act, 1959, the section in question in *Reg.* v. *Hurst, Ex parte Smith* [1960] 2 Q.B. 133 ... and also the section which was before the House of Lords in *Evans* v. *McLoughlan* (1861) 4 L.T. 31, 32). Perhaps more important, Lord Simonds, at p. 751, Lord Radcliffe, at pp. 769-770, Lord Somervell, at p. 772, and I think Lord Morton of Henryton, at p. 757, all drew the distinction between an order bad on its face, and an order good on its face which it was sought to go behind and challenge on the ground of bad faith; I think the decision might have been different if the order had been a nullity, in the sense of being manifestly bad on its face (which is what Mr. Parker alleges here), or at least that the point was left open. I think that Lord Morton's statement, at p. 758, as to "jurisdiction" which I have already quoted was obiter, since he had already in effect held that the council had "jurisdiction" to make the compulsory purchase order by holding that it could have been challenged under paragraph 15.

The only later case cited to me in which the *East Elloe* [1956] A.C. 736 case has been referred to was *Director of Public Prosecutions* v. *Head* [1959] A.C. 83. One of the questions which arose in that case was whether a detention order under the Mental Deficiency Act, 1913, was void because bad on its face or because made without evidence, or whether it was merely voidable. **[246]** Lord Denning drew the distinction established by the authorities on judicial decisions between an order made outside jurisdiction, which is automatically null and void and needs no order to quash it, and erroneous decisions within jurisdiction, which are good until quashed (see pp. 111-112), and held that the order in that case was voidable only. The majority of the House, however, (three of whom had been parties to the *East Elloe* decision), made express reservations on this point. [His Lordship referred to Lord Somervell, at p. 104, Lord Simonds, at p. 98, Lord Reid, at p. 98, and Lord Tucker, at pp. 103, 104.] I think this tends to support the view that if the order in the *East Elloe* case had been bad and a nullity on its face the decision might well have been different.

In *Reg.* v. *Foreign Compensation Commission, Ex parte Oak and Timber Co. Ltd.* (unreported, Nov. 11, 1955) the applicants applied to the Divisional Court for an order of certiorari to bring up and quash a confirmed decision of the commission under the Foreign Compensation Commission (Czechoslovakia)

Order in Council, 1950 (S.I. 1950 No. 9911). The Divisional Court (Lord Goddard C.J., Cassels and Donovan JJ.) refused the application, Lord Goddard saying:

> "I entirely fail to understand how this court can be asked to make an order bringing up the determination of the tribunal for the purpose of having it quashed, and how it is said that that would not be calling the determination of the commission in question. If we were to entertain this application, we should be flying in the face of the clear words of the Act of Parliament. In my opinion there is no ground whatever for saying that this court has jurisdiction to entertain this application because it is forbidden to do so by the Act of Parliament. Therefore this application fails and is dismissed...."

Donovan J. made the statement, which I have already quoted, that the Act and the Order in Council are for the purposes of section 4 (4) really one.

Mr. Parker told me that he had consulted Mr. Andrew Martin, counsel for the applicants in that case, who had told him that, according to his memory, no question as to the jurisdiction of the commission was raised in that case, and that, in answer to an inquiry from Lord Goddard C.J., he had told the Divisional Court that no such question arose. This is confirmed by the papers which were before the Divisional Court including the Commission's "Statement of Decision," which Mr. Bridge was good enough to make available for me.

The applicants had claimed as the owner of certain shares, and in order to succeed in their claim for compensation they had to establish that they were the owners of the shares at the date when the companies in question were nationalised by the Czechoslovak Government after the war. For this purpose, they relied on certain alleged contracts of purchase entered into during the war.

The commission considered the question whether these transactions of purchase

> "were invalid by reason of the fact (a) that at the respective dates when they were entered into, Slovakia, in which territory the [companies concerned] were registered and carrying on business, was enemy territory, and the said companies were working, willingly or otherwise, for the benefit of the enemy, or (b) that subsequently, namely on December 7, 1941, a state of war arose between the United Kingdom and Hungary."

As to point (a) the commission held that "the transaction seems to be forbidden by section 1 (2) (*a*) of the Trading with the Enemy Act, 1939 ..." **[247]** and as to point (b), that the contracts were abrogated by Hungary becoming enemy territory on April 12, 1941, or by that country entering the war on December 7, 1941. The grounds of the application, as set out in the "Statement" for the Divisional Court, were

> "that (a) the Commission has wrongly applied section 1 (2) (*a*) of the Trading with the Enemy Act, 1939, to the contracts by which the applicant acquired its title to the said shares, (b) the commission has wrongly treated the said contract as abrogated in toto by operation of law on either or both of the following dates (i) the date when the Trading with the Enemy Act, 1939, became applicable to Hungary, (ii) the date when a state of war came into existence between the United Kingdom and Hungary, (c) the commission has failed to apply to the said contracts the relevant provisions of the treaty of peace with Hungary."

In my judgment, the error complained of in that case, if it was an error, was an error within jurisdiction, not an error going to jurisdiction, and that case also is therefore not an authority directly binding in this case, though I must of course give full weight to the forceful words of Lord Goddard.

I come now to the vital questions in this case. Does the minute of adjudication disclose any error of law? If so, is it an error of a nature falling within what I have called class 1 or class 2, or merely an error falling within class 3?

If it is an error falling within class 1 or class 2, does section 4 (4) nevertheless oust the jurisdiction of the High Court? [His Lordship then set out the conclusions of the commission.]

As I understand it, the commission's decision was based on the following grounds: (a) Even when a claimant claims as the original owner, he must establish that not only he himself but also any person who became his successor in title on or before February 28, 1959, were British nationals on October 31, 1956, and February 28, 1959; (b) "Successor in title" means a successor in title to a claim against the Egyptian or U.A.R. Government; (c) T.E.D.O. which of course was not a British national, became successor in title to the plaintiffs' claim against the Egyptian Government by assignment by virtue of the November, 1957, agreement; (d) A person cannot establish a claim under article 4 or article 6 of the Order unless he can establish that he had a claim against the Government of the United Arab Republic immediately before the inter-governmental agreement of February 28, 1959, and the plaintiffs had no such claim because of the 1957 Agreement.

I will deal first with a new point raised by Mr. Bridge before me, namely what is the meaning of the phrase "property ... which is referred to Annex E" in article 4 (1) (*a*) of the 1962 Order. Before the commission, it appears to have been common ground that so far as the plaintiffs were concerned the "property referred to in Annex E" meant the whole of their property in Egypt as it stood on October 31, 1956, including the property afterwards destroyed or removed by the Israeli forces, and the commission so held in paragraph (5) of their adjudication. By an amendment to paragraph 7 of the defence made on the first day of the hearing before me (though the defendants had given notice of their intention to apply for leave to make this amendment long before) the defendants denied that "property referred to in Annex E" included what has been called the "war damage" claim for £500,000. It may be convenient to call it that, but I think it is important to remember that this is not an additional and separate claim in respect of war damage as such, but a claim for the loss of part of the plaintiffs' whole property as it existed in Egypt on October 31, 1956. I think that the legal officer and the commission may have been under some misunderstanding on this point. Mr. Bridge submitted that the phrase did not mean the **[248]** property as it stood at October 31, 1956, but the property as it stood on the date it was sold by the Egyptian sequestrators or the date when it was included in the new Annex E contained in the amendment to the treaty made in 1962, whichever was the earlier (all the properties included in the original Annex E had been sold); for the purposes of this case, the importance of the argument was, of course, that if Mr. Bridge is right any claim under Part III of the order would only relate to the property as it stood after the war damage. In my judgment it is not open to the defendants to raise this point. It was pleaded in paragraph 6 of the defence and the further and better particulars thereunder that the decisions of the commission, including paragraph (5), were res judicata and in face of that plea I do not see how the defendants can now say that the decision of the commission on this point was wrong. Further, if the commission were in error on this point, it seems to me that this would clearly be an error within jurisdiction and that I am therefore precluded by section 4 (4) from calling it in question; it is clear that *some* property of the plaintiffs is referred to in Annex E and in my view it must be within the jurisdiction of the commission to decide what property. Anyhow, I agree with the commission's decision on this point. Mr. Parker asked me in his reply to recant something I said in the course of Mr. Bridge's argument as to the possible effect of the Israeli war damage on the assessment of loss under article 5 of the order. I confess that by the time Mr. Parker raised the point I had forgotten exactly what I did say, but whatever it was I was merely trying to test Mr. Bridge's argument on the meaning of "property referred to in Annex E" and not intending to express any concluded opinion whatever as to the effect of article 5; I have quite enough other problems in this case.

The question of the meaning of "successor in title" is much more difficult. It seems fairly clear that the general purpose of limiting the persons entitled to claim to those who were British nationals between October 31, 1956, and February 28, 1959, was that Her Majesty's Government, in negotiating the agreement of the latter date with the Government of the U.A.R., would only have been concerned—and indeed only entitled—to protect the interests of British nationals. Her Majesty's Government was negotiating in its own right, and not as agent or trustee for the British nationals who had suffered loss, but its right to negotiate with a foreign government for compensation is limited to the protection of its own nationals: see *Mavrommatis Palestine Concessions* (1924) Permanent Court of International Justice, series A, judgment No. 2 at pp. 12-13; *Railway Line Panevezys-Saldutiskis* (1939) Permanent Court of International Justice, series A-B No. 76 at p. 16; *Rustomjee* v. *The Queen** (1876) 1 Q.B.D. 487; 2 Q.B.D. 69; *Civilian War Claimants Association Ltd.* v. *The King** [1932] A.C. 14

In the case of *Cory Bros. & Co. Ltd.*, where there had been successive "sales" of shares on the same lines as the April and November, 1957, agreements in the present case, the commission rejected the submission that successor in title meant successor to the claim, though it might well include such a person. They held that successor in title meant the person who would have succeeded to the title of the owner if the sale under Proclamation No. 5 had never taken place. (The hypothesis being part of the definition of "successor in title," no difficulty was caused by the words "who became"). (See page 9 (d) of the commission's minute of adjudication in the *Cory Bros.* case.) This was the meaning of "successor in title" pleaded by the legal officer on the invitation of the commission. In the present case the commission rejected its own previous decision (though it said that the construction which it now thought right would have led to the same result in the *Cory Bros.* case—see paragraph (3) of the minute of adjudication) and held that "the **[249]** expression 'successor in title' throughout the order referred not to the property which had been Egyptianised, lost, injured or damaged but to the claim." It further held that "successor in title" to a claim meant or at any rate included an assignee of a claim. Mr. Bridge submitted that "successor in title" includes any successor to the beneficial interest in the property or the claim, including a successor by assignment. Mr. Parker said that whatever "successor in title" does mean it does not include T.E.D.O. as assignee under either the April or the November agreement. He submitted that it meant a successor of the original *owner* (the context in which the word "successor" appears in the inter-governmental agreement of February 28, 1959: see Annex A paragraph (4)); that is, in the case of an individual, a person who had succeeded as a result of death or perhaps bankruptcy; he had some difficulty in suggesting how there could in this sense be a "successor" of a corporation, but he said that here also there could only be a successor when the corporation had ceased to exist, and gave as posssible examples a merger and a vesting under some types of nationalised legislation (though no nationalisation statutes were passed in the United Kingdom during the relevant period).

Mr. Parker relied on two general considerations: (a) He said that if it had been intended to exclude the plaintiff's claim, it would have been easy to say so in the Order; Her Majesty's Government knew all about the November agreement before the 1959 Order was made and its attention was specifically called to the agreement shortly before the 1962 Order was made, in the correspondence with the plaintiffs' solicitors to which I have already referred. It is not usually a very strong argument to say that the draftsman could have used clearer words, but Mr. Parker was able to give it some additional force in this case by pointing to examples in earlier orders under the 1950 Act (not relating to Egypt) in which there had been specific exclusions of named claimants.

(b) He strongly relied on article 10 of the 1962 Order. He said that Parliament having specifically provided that compensation from other sources should be taken into account in assessing the loss, they cannot have intended it to have any relevance at the earlier stage of deciding entitlement; and that the

November agreement was in substance simply a device by which the plaintiffs successfully used their nuisance value to extract some measure of compensation. Mr. Bridge submitted that "compensation" in article 10 should be limited to compensation received ex gratia or in circumstances not involving any assignment or release of the claim. I think it is difficult to limit the meaning of the words as Mr. Bridge suggests, and that there is great force in Mr. Parker's argument on this point.

I have to consider two questions: (1) are successors in title relevant at all when the claimant is the original owner? (2) if so, what does "successor in title" mean? I shall try to answer question (2) first, because I think it also answers question (1).

I was at first impressed by the apparent difficulty that if the commission's view was right there would be double claims, since the commission would apparently have held that the plaintiffs were entitled to succeed in their claim if the assignee under the November agreement had been a British national; it seemed to me that, the plaintiffs having succeeded in their claim, the assignee could then come along and make a claim too. But I think the commission must have regarded the November agreement as an equitable and not a legal assignment (as they would otherwise have dismissed the claim on the ground that the plaintiffs had no title to claim, and need not have considered the "successor in title" point at all); if so, the claim would **[250]** have to be brought by the plaintiffs as assignor on behalf of the assignee, and there could not be a claim by the assignee himself.

"Successor in title" must have the same meaning in article 4 (1) (*b*) (i) and (ii), and in article 4 (1) (*c*) (i) and (ii) (where it includes a person who became successor after the sale of the shares) and in article 6 (1) (*b*) and (*c*) (where it includes a person who became successor after the loss of the property).

I think the phrase "successor in title" in articles 4 (1) (*b*) (i), (*c*) (i) and 6 (1) (*b*) would in its ordinary meaning be wide enough to include anyone who has succeeded to the property or the claim by any of the ordinary methods, including death or assignment, but not, I think, a merely equitable assignee.

But I think there are great difficulties in construing "successor in title" in articles 4 (1) (*b*) (ii), (*c*) (ii) and 6 (1) (*c*) as meaning or including an assignee of sequestrated property or of a claim against the Egyptian Government in respect of such property:

(a) Everyone agrees that "successor in title" cannot include the Egyptian organisations or companies to whom British properties had been sold by the sequestrator under the Proclamation; if it did, no one (or very few people) would have a claim under Part III of the Order at all, since all the properties originally included in Annex E had been so sold (I suppose some properties which had not been sold may have been added in the new Annex E as revised in 1962, though there was no evidence of this). I was never able to understand why, if the April agreement did not constitute T.E.D.O. "the successor in title" of the plaintiffs, the November agreement did. The subject-matter of the sale under the April agreement was "all assets belonging to" the plaintiffs, and of the sale under the November agreement "the whole business of (the plaintiffs) as carried on and situated in Egypt," which was "deemed to include all those assets of the (plaintiffs) situated in Egypt." The commission said in paragraph (3) of its decision that "prima facie an assignment of expropriated property would carry the right to receive compensation in respect of that property," though I am not sure that this is right. The commission was not right in saying (paragraph (6) of the minute of adjudication) that the plaintiffs' claim against the Egyptian Government was *expressly* included in the November agreement (though claims against other Governments were expressly excluded from the assets); if it was assigned, it was assigned as part of the assets, which had already been assigned by the April agreement. The fact that the plaintiffs were parties to the November agreement but not to the April agreement does not seem to me to be a relevant difference for this purpose. The April agreement was plainly a good sale under Egyptian law, and is so treated in the various later documents to which I referred earlier in this judgment—ending with the Egyptian Decree No. 14 of 1961, long after the November agreement. Of course, the fact that the plaintiffs were parties to the November agreement means that it is capable of being a release or waiver of their claim, which the April agreement is not, and at one point Mr. Bridge sought to support the decision of the commission on this ground. I shall return to this point later.

(b) The only relevant "successor in title" for the purposes of articles 4 (1) (*b*) (ii), (*c*) (ii) and 6 (*c*) is one who became successor between October 31, 1956, and February 28, 1959. The phrase cannot, therefore, there mean or include a successor in title to a claim on the fund, which did not come into existence until it was created by the 1959 Order on April 9, 1959. Throughout the relevant period, all British property in Egypt was under sequestration and access by British nationals to the Egyptian courts was forbidden. No assignment of property or claims to a British national was **[251]** possible under Egyptian law, except in the unlikely event of the sequestrator giving his consent under article 12 of the Proclamation, and any purported assignment without such consent would have been null and void by virtue of articles 3 and 12. On the evidence before me, the sequestrator only gave his consent during that period in two cases to assignments *by* a British national—the plaintiffs and Cory Bros. and some other shareholders in the same company—and there is no evidence that he ever gave consent to an assignment *to* a British national. Further, throughout that period no individual British national had any claim against the Egyptian Government in any legal sense under Egyptian law, International law or English law. Nor had he any claim against Her Majesty's Government. The first time anything came into existence which was in any legal sense a "claim" was when the fund was set up, after the end of the relevant period. The property being in Egypt, and any claim against the Egyptian Government—regarded as a chose in action—being also in Egypt, the English courts would regard any question as to the validity of an assignment as being governed by Egyptian law. In my judgment, throughout the relevant period, the possibility of a valid assignment of sequestrated property to a British national was so remote that it cannot be contemplated by the Order and there was nothing capable of legal or equitable assignment under English law in respect of claims relating to such property.

Mr. Bridge relied on two passages in *Halsbury's Laws of England*, 3rd ed., Vol. 11, p. 459, and Vol. 14, pp. 532 to 533—as to assignments of after-acquired property, and in particular this passage: "Neither in equity nor at law can there be an assignment of what has no existence. The assignment operates as a contract, and if it is for value, then when the property comes into existence equity, treating that as done which ought to be done, fastens upon the property, and the contract to assign becomes in equity a complete assignment." Mr. Bridge submitted that on this principle a contract to assign property or claims made between October 31, 1956, and February 28, 1959, would become a complete and good equitable assignment when the property was returned to its owner or the former owner became entitled to claim compensation. But, as Mr. Parker pointed out, article 4 (1) (*b*) (ii) of the Order cannot have been contemplating this type of assignment. The Order contemplates that a person may have become "successor in title" at any time between October 31, 1956, and February 28, 1959; the obligation of the Egyptian Government to return sequestrated property first arose when the Treaty was signed on February 28, 1959 (and it had three months after that within which to do so—see Annex B, paragraph (4) (i)) and no legal right to claim compensation arose until the fund was set up on April 9, 1959. It follows that no assignment of this type could have taken effect within the relevant period (or at earliest not before February 28, 1959). The commission seems to have taken the view (in paragraph (5) of the adjudication) that the obligation of the U.A.R. to return British property, and the co-relative right to claim compensation against the U.A.R. in respect of property not returned, arose for the first time when the Treaty was signed on February 28, 1959; if so, no one could have become successor in title to such a claim before that date.

Mr. Bridge fell back on the argument that dispossessed British nationals had a "moral" claim against the Egyptian Government which was capable of assignment—though it seems to me that such an assignment could have no legal effect, except perhaps as a contract to assign after-acquired property. Mr. Bridge relied on article 4 (2) as supporting the view that the Order was not concerned with strict legal rights, since some at least of the persons referred to in that paragraph were probably only beneficial owners and not **[252]** full legal owners. In my view, that paragraph has only the limited purpose of enabling certain claimants whose names were not then known to be identified and does not affect the general construction of the Order; even if it has any wider effect it cannot, I think, go so far as to establish that moral claims were within the contemplation of the Order. I cannot accept that Parliament intended "successor in title" to include anything so vague and insubstantial as an assignee of a moral claim.

Mr. Parker also had his difficulties. All the persons referred to in paragraph (1) (*a*) of Annex E are corporations, and I think the Order must contemplate that there could be a "successor in title" to such corporations. Further, I think that the provisions of article 4 (3) that a corporation coming into existence after October 31, 1956, shall be deemed to have been a British national on that date must contemplate that such a corporation could become successor to a person who had been the owner before its formation; it hardly seems likely that this provision was put in only to cover the possibility of a newly formed corporation becoming an executor of a former owner. I have already referred to Mr. Parker's difficulty in suggesting circumstances in which a corporation could become successor in title in his sense.

Both Mr. Bridge and Mr. Parker relied on the anomalies which they said would be produced by the other's suggested construction of the Order as between a person who became successor immediately before February 28, 1959, and a person who became successor immediately after that date, but so far as I can see, this sort of anomaly could arise whatever construction was given to the phrase "successor in title."

Because of the difficulties to which I have referred, which seem to me insuperable, and of the argument based on article 10, I have come to the conclusion that the phrase "person who became successor in title of such owner on or before February 28, 1959 ..." in article 4 (1) (*b*) (ii) does not mean or include a purported assignee between that date and October 31, 1956 of a claim against the Egyptian Government; the same applies to articles 4 (1) (*c*) (ii) and 6 (1) (*c*). In view of the plea of res judicata, I doubt whether Mr Bridge is really entitled to support the commission's decision on the ground that "successor in title" in those articles means or includes an assignee of the property, but I think, that this construction is also unacceptable for substantially the same reasons, even though the difficulty about moral claims does not arise. A further difficulty in making "successor in title" mean an assignee of the property is that article 4 (1) (*c*) (i) and article 6 (1) (*b*) contemplate that a person may become successor in title after the property has been sold or lost. I feel bound to accept Mr. Parker's construction, in spite of the difficulty of finding examples of a successor in that sense to a corporation, which seems to me much less than those involved in the commission's or Mr. Bridge's construction. Since "successor in title" must bear the same meaning throughout the Order, and since (in my judgment) it does not include an assignee of property or claims in articles 4 (1) (*b*) (ii) and (*c*) (ii) and 6 (*c*) its meaning must be similarly limited in articles 4 (1) (*b*) (i) and (*c*) (i) and 6 (1) (*b*).

In view of my conclusion on this point, the question whether "successors in title" are relevant when the claimant is the original owner has answered itself; they are not. At any given moment there can only be in existence either the original owner or his successor in title but not both. This view is perfectly consistent with article 4 (1) (*b*) (i) which refers to the owner *or* the successor in title. The commission's view that even where the claimant is the original owner he has to prove either that he has no successor in title or that any successor in title was at the relevant time a British national seems to **[253]** have been based entirely on the use of the word "and" in article 4 (1) (*b*) (ii) (see paragraph

(1) of the minute of adjudication). I do not think the word will carry that weight. Reading article 4 (1) (*b*) (i) and (ii) together, I think they mean that when the applicant claims as the original owner he must prove that he was a British national on the relevant dates and that when he claims as successor in title he must prove this and also that he himself was then a British national. The construction of the Order cannot, of course, be affected by the form of application issued or approved by the commission, but it is interesting to note from the wording of question 4 that the commission did not then think that successors were relevant when the claim was by the original owner.

In my view, the construction which I think right would not prevent the assignment of claims on the fund after it was set up or the enforcement of such claims for the benefit of the assignee; such an assignment would be of an unascertained share in the fund, and would operate as an equitable assignment only and the claim could and would be enforced by the original owner as assignor on behalf of the assignee. A contract to assign, operating as an assignment of after-acquired property, would also be only an equitable assignment, and a claim on the fund would be similarly enforced. I am not satisfied that a sale of the property by the original owner after it was returned would pass a claim on the fund to a purchaser unless the claim was expressly assigned, in which case again the assignment would be equitable.

I must now deal with the commission's findings that an applicant cannot establish a claim under the Order unless he can establish that immediately before the treaty was signed on February 28, 1959, he had a claim against the U.A.R. which was among the claims in respect of which £27½ million compensation was expressed to be paid in article IV of the Treaty—"Claims [under the Order] to participate (in the compensation) and claims against the U.A.R. were thus identical, and were the claims referred to in articles 4 and 6 of the Order" (see paragraphs (4), (5), (7) and (8) of the minute of adjudication). The commission held that the plaintiffs had no such claim because they had assigned it by the November agreement, but if the commission's view is right, the plaintiffs' claim would be equally excluded if the November agreement was a release or waiver of that claim (which seems to me a more plausible view of its effect, in spite of the provisions of paragraph 12 B and the absence of any express waiver). The commission seems to have treated this point as a matter of construction of the words "shall treat a claim ... as established" in articles 4 and 6 of the Order and, as Mr. Parker points out, it was on this basis inconsistent to allow registration of the "war damage claim" under article 8, while disallowing it under articles 4 and 6, because article 8 requires all the conditions laid down by article 6 to be satisfied other than that the loss was the result of Egyptian measures. The commission seems to have relied in support of its views largely or entirely on the recitals to the 1959 and 1962 Orders, but these do not seem to me to be conclusive. It is true that the first recital of the 1962 Order refers to "claims to participate in compensation received under agreements with foreign Governments" and the third to the agreement of February 28, 1959, but the last recital refers to the "registration, assessment and determination of claims in respect of British property in Egypt"; the British property in Egypt to which such claims were to relate was not limited, at any rate expressly, to the property in respect of which the £27½ million was paid under the 1959 agreement. I have already said that, as a matter of fact, I am not satisfied that the plaintiffs' claim was excluded from the inter-governmental negotiations, and that on balance I think it more probable that it was not. **[254]**

The plaintiffs, as an individual, had no legal claim against the U.A.R. (nor indeed had any other claimant on the fund), and the only possible claim was a claim under international law by Her Majesty's Government in its own right, which the plaintiffs had no power to assign or release. It might be said (on the authority of the cases in the Permanent Court of International Justice to which I have referred) that if the plaintiffs had assigned or released their claim, they no longer had any interest which Her Majesty's Government was entitled to protect, but if the plaintiffs' valuation of their business is anywhere nearly right their loss was far greater than the amount they received under the

November agreement, and I think there still remained an "injury" in respect of which Her Majesty's Government was entitled to negotiate.

As a matter of construction, I cannot read "claim" in article 4 or article 6 of the Order as requiring a claimant to establish that he had a claim against the Government of the U.A.R. If the commission's decision on this point was not based on the construction of the Order, but on their view of what was just and right and in accordance with the intentions of Her Majesty's Government and the Government of the U.A.R. when they signed the 1959 Treaty, this is in my judgment something which the commission was not entitled to take into account. The question who is entitled to "establish" claims under the order to "participate in compensation" must in my view be solely a question of the construction of the Order, and the intentions of the governments when they signed the treaty are irrelevant.

It is true that there are statements in *Rustomjee* v. *The Queen** (1876) 1 Q.B.D. 487; 2 Q.B.D. 69 that it is the "duty" of the Crown to distribute the money received from the foreign government among persons having "claims" against that government, or among "the persons towards whose losses it was paid" or "according to the stipulations of the Treaty" or that there was a "moral claim that it be given to the right person," though this "duty" could not be enforced or its exercise questioned in the courts: see (1876) 1 Q.B.D. 487 Cockburn C.J., at p. 492, Blackburn J., at p. 496, Lush J., at p. 497; 2 Q.B.D. 69, 74. In this case, the Crown and Parliament have exercised their discretion as to the distribution of the compensation by the Order in Council and in my view one cannot go behind the Order; I have pointed out earlier in this judgment some respects in which it seems to me that the effect of the 1959 and 1962 Orders differs from the provisions of the Treaty In any event, it would have been impossible in this case to distribute the compensation to individual claimants and claims in respect of whom and which it had been paid by the Government of the U.A.R., because the £27½ million was not based on the consideration of individual claims but upon "a lump sum payment by Egypt against which claims would be assessed and paid by the U.K. authorities and not the Egyptian authorities."

If I am right in my view that the commission's decision was wrong, both on the "successor in title" point and on the "claim against the U.A.R." point, does section 4 (4) oust my jurisdiction to make declarations giving effect to my view? After much hesitation I have come to the conclusion that it does not. Articles 4 (1) and 6 (1) of the 1962 Order provide that "the commission shall treat a claim ... as established if the applicant satisfies them of the" matters specified in those paragraphs; if they are satisfied of those matters, they are bound to treat the claim as established. In my judgment, the commission has no jurisdiction to consider under article 4 (1) any other question than those which sub-paragraphs (a) and (b) of that paragraph on their true construction require them to consider, and if satisfied of those matters they are under a statutory duty to treat the claim as **[255]** established and have no jurisdiction to do anything else. The structure of articles 4 and 6 of the 1962 Order seems to me closely analogous to that of the provisions which were in question in *Rex* v. *Shoreditch Assessment Committee, Ex parte Morgan* [1910] 2 K.B. 859, where it was held that the conditions precedent to the operation of a statutory duty having been fulfilled the assessment committee had no jurisdiction to do anything except perform their duty.

It follows, in my view, that if the commission wrongly construes paragraph 4 (1) (*a*) or (*b*) as requiring them to consider something which on their true construction those sub-paragraphs do not require to be considered before the claim is established, they act without jurisdiction or in excess of jurisdiction. In my judgment, that is what the commission has done, as to the "successor in title" point by misconstruing article 4 (1) (*b*) (i) and (ii) and as to the "claim against the U.A.R." point either by misconstruing "claim" in article 4 (1) or by adding a condition precedent to the establishment of a claim which is not to be found in the Order itself.

It is alleged in paragraph 9 of the statement of claim that

> "at the said hearing [before the commission] it was proved by the plaintiffs, admitted by the second defendant, and established to the satisfaction of the first defendant; (a) that the plaintiffs' application in respect of the aforesaid property related to property in Egypt referred to in the said Annex E; (b) (i) that the plaintiffs were the persons referred to in paragraph 1 (a) of the said Annex E as the owner of the said property; and (ii) that the plaintiffs were British nationals on October 31, 1956, and February 28, 1959."

This paragraph was admitted by paragraph 7 of the defence, subject to the amendment as to the "war damage claim." If my view as to the construction of article 4 (1) is right, these were all the matters of which they had to satisfy the commission, and the commission was under a statutory duty to treat their claim as established.

Besides the *Shoreditch* case [1910] 2 K.B. 859, I regard this case as being in principle within *Ex parte Bradlaugh*, 3 Q.B.D. 509, *Reg.* v. *Fulham, Hammersmith & Kensington Rent Tribunal, Ex parte Hierowski* [1953] 2 Q.B. 147, and the case of the *Maradana Mosque* [1967] 1 A.C. 13. In my judgment, the general principles relied upon by Mr. Parker apply here; a decision of an inferior tribunal given without jurisdiction or in excess of jurisdiction is a nullity, and clauses ousting the power of the High Court to interfere with decisions of the tribunal do not exclude the jurisdiction of the High Court when the decision is a nullity. Section 4 (4) of the 1950 Act excludes the jurisdiction of the High Court to question a determination, but it does not exclude the jurisdiction of the High Court to question whether there has in truth been a determination at all. Mr. Bridge says that if this view of the effect of section 4 (4) is right, there would be nothing left on which that subsection could effectively operate. I do not agree. If I had thought that the commission were right in their view that article 4 (1) required them to consider whether the plaintiffs had a "successor in title" and that "successor in title" meant an assignee of the claim, I should have thought that section 4 (4) debarred me from questioning whether the November agreement was an assignment of the plaintiffs' claim, though I have perhaps made my view on this point clearer than I should have; other examples are the point in this case as to "property referred to in Annex E" and the alleged error in the *Oak and Timber Company's* case (unreported), Nov. 11, 1955, D.C. which was clearly an error within jurisdiction. **[256]**

[His Lordship dealt with the form of the declarations and continued:] I propose to make declaration [1] in the form

> "that the first defendant's provisional determination of May 8, 1963, as explained in the first defendant's letter dated June 12, 1963, in answer to the plaintiffs' solicitors' letter of May 16, 1963, and of which the minute of adjudication formed part, was made without or in excess of jurisdiction and is a nullity."

If the provisional determination of May 8, 1963, was a nullity, it must I think follow that the further provisional determination of June 21, 1963, was also a nullity, because it was based on the first determination. I propose to make this declaration simply in the form "that the first defendant's further provisional determination of June 21, 1963, was a nullity." Mr. Parker agreed that I could not make declaration 3 in the form claimed because again it would cover errors within jurisdiction as well as errors going to jurisdiction. He suggested that I should amend the wording from "the Economic Development Organisation was not the plaintiffs' successor ..." to "the Economic Development Organisation could not be the plaintiffs' successor." At present I do not feel disposed to make this declaration at all; it seems to me unnecessary, and I am not prepared to commit myself to the view that in no concievable circumstances could the Economic Development Organisation become the successor of the plaintiffs.

Declaration 4 I propose to make as claimed. Declarations 5 and 6 seem to me unnecessary. If I had thought that the commission were right on the "successor in title" point, I should not have felt able to accept Mr. Parker's argument that I should still make declaration 5. If "successor in title" meant an assignee of the claim and the plaintiffs had assigned their claim to T.E.D.O., this assignment would have covered the whole claim, including the claim in respect of the property destroyed or removed by the Israeli forces and the cancellation of the mining leases. [Judgment was given for the plaintiffs for the declarations indicated.]

Solicitors: *Linklaters & Paines; Treasury Solicitor.*